LAND USE PLANNING AND THE ENVIRONMENT: A CASEBOOK

by

Charles M. Haar

Harvard Law School

and

Michael Allan Wolf

University of Florida Levin College of Law

ENVIRONMENTAL LAW INSTITUTE

Washington, D.C.

Published January 2010.

Printed in the United States of America
ISBN 978-158576-128-9

About the Authors

Charles M. Haar joined the Harvard Law School faculty in 1952, serving as the Louis D. Brandeis Professor of Law. In addition to his landmark work in the fields of land use planning and property law, Professor Haar has taught and written in the areas of corporate mergers, housing policy, poverty, international law, and third world development. He served as assistant secretary in the U.S. Department of Housing and Urban Development, where he played a key role in formulating Great Society programs, and has chaired presidential task forces on urban and suburban issues. Among Professor Haar's recent publications is Mastering Boston Harbor: Courts, Dolphins, and Imperiled Waters (Harvard University Press 2005). Professor Haar received his LL.B. degree from Harvard Law School, an M.A. degree from the University of Wisconsin, and an A.B. degree from New York University. Professor Haar can be reached by e-mail at: haar@law.harvard.edu.

Michael Allan Wolf is the Richard E. Nelson Chair in Local Government Law at the University of Florida Levin College of Law. His teaching and scholarly areas of interest include land use planning, environmental law, property law, local government, urban revitalization, constitutional law, and legal and constitutional history. Professor Wolf is the General Editor of Powell on Real Property (the leading treatise in the field) and Powell on Real Property: Michael Allan Wolf Desk Edition (Matthew Bender LexisNexis 2009), and the author of The Zoning of America: *Euclid v. Ambler* (University Press of Kansas 2008). Professor Wolf received his Ph.D. (History of American Civilization) and A.M. degrees from Harvard University, a J.D. degree from Georgetown University Law Center, and a B.A. degree from Emory University. Professor Wolf can be reached by e-mail at: wolfm@law.ufl.edu.

To our children:

Jeremy and Susan
and
Daniel and Rachel

"Fortunate is the man who has his quiver full of them."

—Psalm 127:5

Table of Contents

Table of Cases

Acknowledgments

We would like to thank Wade Berryhill, Joel Eisen, and Jerold Kayden, who with sage counsel have long served as sounding boards for our ideas. Hundreds of law students at the University of Florida, the University of Miami, and the University of Richmond have used manuscript versions of this casebook over the past few years, and we appreciate their insightful feedback. Andrea Becker, Tara Nelson, and Steve Wernick took the lead among the many students who provided excellent research assistance. We are pleased to single out Tom Potter for his careful attention to essential details—grand and minute. The University of Florida Levin College of Law provided generous research support, for which Michael Allan Wolf is most grateful. Professor Haar would like to thank the Institute for Advanced Study in Princeton, New Jersey, for generously making their facilities available. Suzanne Keller and Betty Morganstern Wolf contributed to this and other efforts in ways too numerous to mention, so a simple, heartfelt "thank you" will have to suffice. Finally, we wish to thank Scott Schang, Vice President, Publications and Associates, at the Environmental Law Institute (ELI), for his help in publishing this casebook; Carolyn Fischer, former ELI Books Editor, for her editorial expertise; and Rachel Jean-Baptiste, Managing Editor, *Environmental Law Reporter*, for seeing clearly the forest and the trees.

Preface

As our subtitle states—simply and directly—this is a casebook. While other authors choose to provide students with ample excerpts from law review articles and treatises, along with generous explanatory passages that are commonly found in hornbooks, we move the cases—and judicial analysis—back to center stage. The basic reason for this choice is that even in an area largely delineated by local ordinances and state statutes, judges remain key makers and interpreters of land use planning law. The central inquiries of this discipline are disputed in legal briefs and oral arguments, and are addressed in judicial opinions: What is the nature of the comprehensive plan? How close a fit is required between zoning decisions and the plan? When does regulation go so far that it amounts to a taking requiring invalidation or compensation? When do constitutional rights such as free speech and the free exercise of religion trump the police power? What kinds of behavior amount to unreasonable interference with one's neighbor's use and enjoyment of real property? How do we know if a zoning or planning decision constitutes unlawful, invidious discrimination? How do we decide which local regulatory decisions are legislative and which are quasi-judicial, and what are the legal and practical implications of that definitional choice? When does local innovation fall beyond the bounds established by state-enabling legislation?

We have spent several decades engaged in land use planning and environmental law not only as teachers and scholars, but as partners to private- and public-sector participants involved in acts and decisionmaking at the cutting edge of these fields—from urban renewal and Model Cities, through enterprise zones and inclusionary zoning, to New Urbanism and green building. The bulk of our writing—separately and as a team—has been intended for instructors, practitioners, and students who are fascinated by the issues at the core of land use planning law: (1) zoning; (2) comprehensive planning; and (3) eminent domain. To us, a casebook is not an extended advocacy piece designed to advance one legal, jurisprudential, or political strategy regarding the regulation of land use and development. We have one overriding obligation—to consider in an evenhanded and thorough manner the chief challenges facing lawyers and planners who, on a regular basis, are tasked with finding the correct balance between the needs and rights of private landowners and the protection and advancement of the public interest, between the urgencies of the present and the anticipated impacts on future generations. Given this orientation, it is not surprising that cases, not commentary, remain the central teaching and learning tool of Land Use Planning and the Environment.

While other casebook authors identify one case to represent each issue in the casebook, we are uncomfortable with this practice. Therefore, throughout the book, we include cases and selections from cases that illustrate competing or complementary approaches. In this way, we have tried to craft a casebook with jurisdictional and analytical depth, making it a better match for the complex world of land use planning law "on the ground." We provide guidance to our readers (teachers and students) through informative introductions that ask provocative questions about the materials that follow and, when appropriate, we offer insights from leading commentators in law and planning. However, we envision that these materials will play a supportive role.

The separation between traditional land use planning law and environmental regulation, while never exactly a "bright-line" distinction, has become more cloudy over the past few decades. Increasingly state and federal officials find themselves engaged in legislative, regulatory, and bureaucratic activities regarding the use of private land. Moreover, local and state governments have shared environmental regulatory responsibilities with their federal counterparts to a much greater extent in the early 21st century than ever before. For this and many other reasons, it no longer makes sense either to ignore environmental law topics or to segregate them into an "autonomous" chapter. Land Use Planning and the Environment offers a pervasive approach by addressing overlapping and, at times, conflicting administrative regimes. Throughout the casebook, we identify and explore intersections between land use planning law and environmental laws such as the National Environmental Policy Act, the Clean Water Act, and the Endangered Species Act. While some of the connections are obvious—for example in the areas of nuisance law and wetlands regulation— we also identify more subtle interconnections, such as the hidden environmental "agenda" behind exclusionary zoning. Moreover, our discrete regulatory takings chapter (Chapter Five) is organized chronologically and by the nature of the environmental regulation of land that is under attack. One of the important lessons taught by environmental law—that is not yet fully heeded by local land use regulators—is that some of the most serious problems cross artificial political boundaries, necessitating regional and metropolitan strategies. The rapidly growing numbers of professors and students with strong backgrounds and exposure to "traditional" environmental law courses will find these intersections a wonderful opportunity to examine familiar topics from a different, though intimately related, perspective. For other classroom users, this casebook will serve as a valuable introduction to the world of federal, state, and local environmental controls.

Traditional height, area, and use regulation—that is, Euclidean zoning—has of late fallen out of favor among a growing number of planners, architects, and lawyers who gravitate toward Smart Growth or form-based paradigms. Moreover, the national debate over the nature and implications of urban and suburban sprawl is attracting page-one media coverage and the attention of national policymakers and candidates for America's highest political offices. The planning law reflections of these social and political shifts appear not only in our collection of cases and notes on growth management in Chapter Seven, but also throughout most of the previous chapters, often in contrast to the Euclidean tools that still dominate the decisional law.

This casebook, like many of the works that appear in our bibliographies, reflects a deep regard for planning as an art and a science, with theories, vocabulary, and tools worthy of respect by co-professionals. More than 50 years ago, in the preface to his first casebook, Professor Haar expressed the hope "that this volume will be of interest to the planner as well as the lawyer" and the belief that "the case method is a vivid way of introducing the planner to the legal and institutional implications of a conscious fashioning of the physical environment." Today, we are pleased to highlight the deep historical and contemporary connections between these two complementary disciplines, and we hope to eliminate the unfortunate message that is often conveyed to budding lawyers that attorneys are the key, if not sole, players in the decisionmaking and implementation process.

The organization of the seven chapters that follow is fairly straightforward. The opening chapter introduces the reader to the structure and ideas of American planning and to the central concept of the comprehensive plan. Chapter Two explores the major private law methods for reconciling incompatible land uses, chiefly private and public nuisance. The mechanics of Euclidean and post-Euclidean zoning are addressed in Chapter Three; while Chapter Four contains a collection of cases regarding departures from and within the zoning ordinance, such as nonconforming uses, zoning amendments, and variances. Chapter Five, with its heavy component of constitutional law, closely examines the brooding omnipresence of land use planning and environmental regulation—regulatory takings. The constitutional law focus continues into Chapter Six, which studies the legal constraints on the exclusion of people and of specially protected uses. The closing chapter reviews various growth management tools and the potential pitfalls their proponents may encounter.

Editorial Notice: Throughout this volume, we have routinely omitted most of the citations, footnotes, and headings from quoted materials, in order not to disturb the flow of the material. In those instances in which we have decided to include the original footnotes, we have maintained the footnote numbers contained in quoted materials. We have numbered our own footnotes, beginning with 1 at the start of each chapter. Whenever our footnotes are appended to quoted material, we have indicated such by beginning the footnote with "Authors' note."

Internet Links: Throughout this volume, we have provided links to Internet web pages that contain illustrations, photographs, charts, monographs, and other documents of interest to the reader. Because, unfortunately, it is common practice to move, shift, or replace material on the web, we anticipate that some of the links that we have provided in this printed book will become unusable. Therefore, we have made the following web page available to users of this book, not only to keep web addresses updated, but also to provide our readers with information regarding new developments in the area of land use and the environment: http://www.landuseplanningcasebook.com/.

Chapter One

Planning and Law: Shaping the Legal Environment of Land Development and Preservation

I. Figures and Lies: Appreciating the Demographic Landscape of Our Increasingly Urbanized Society

Although quantitative analysis is an essential part of the curriculum and practice for professional planners, this is not the case for many members of the bar. In order to serve their clients successfully, land use attorneys who represent clients on the public and private side should be at ease with people and with statistics. While admittedly these skills do not always go hand in hand, experience shows that the measure of success in the field of land use law is in the outcome of the many meetings lawyers hold with concerned parties, not a won-loss record in the courtroom. Indeed, when a land use dispute ends up in court that is often the surest sign of failure.

Land use planning law practitioners should feel comfortable working with a wide range of people whose interests often *appear* to be directly in opposition—for example, representatives of neighborhoods whose residents are concerned about the impact of commercial growth and shopping mall developers that have purchased at great cost options on land in the vicinity, landowners who are frustrated by regulatory requirements that stand in the way of plans for enhancing the use and value of their property and professional planners who are employed by local and state governments and charged with overseeing the implementation of the master plan, grass-roots environmental and conservation groups who are concerned about the pace of growth and government transportation officials who provide the corridors for residential, commercial, and residential expansion. Often the major challenges faced by the land use attorney are enabling these potential foes to appreciate the common ground that they occupy and in the process to minimize the friction and delay that mark the most acrimonious examples of process failure. This is what the "people" side entails.

On the "statistics" side, the most skillful land use law practitioners are well aware that as the old chestnut states, "figures lie and liars figure." Nevertheless, often the most compelling evidence at a planning commission hearing or the most convincing argument at a gathering of disgruntled neighbors is expressed in cold, hard, numbers—numbers that appear in floor area ratios, vehicle miles traveled, school body size, densities per acre, or parts per million of pollutants. We are not suggesting that the land use attorney should be able to generate this kind of statistical information on her own. Rather, not unlike the medical malpractice attorney who works closely with skilled professionals in the health care fields, the top practitioners in land use planning law benefit from active and mutually respectful partnerships with planners, transportation engineers, architects, and others whose work helps shape, and in turn is shaped by, planning, zoning, and environmental law.

Time, technology, and the changing needs and aspirations of human beings produce stresses upon existing legal institutions and doctrines. Thanks to the Internet, we have nearly instant access to valuable quantitative displays that suggest many salient facts about the conditions of land interdependence in the United States that have intensified ancient conflicts or spawned new problems. Many of these data collections teach the central lesson of change in the scale and pattern of growth found in America's urban, suburban, and rural communities. These numbers, charts, and tables convey some startling transformations in our social composition, in our settlement and work patterns, and in the state of our unbuilt environment over the past several decades. It is the impact of these and related forces that underlies and sometimes frustrates those efforts to arrive at a new synthesis of framework and function commonly subsumed under the title of planning law.

A major challenge for the lawyer is gathering the data necessary for an effective presentation of the client's side in discussions and disputes over the use or conservation of land. In Dolan v. City of Tigard (discussed in Chapter Five), the U.S. Supreme Court, in articulating a "rough-proportionality" standard for exaction cases, criticized local officials for their failure to link their regulatory activities closely enough to specific, local floodplain, and traffic realities. While allowing that "[n]o precise mathematical calculation is required," the Court instructed that "the city must make some effort to quantify its findings in support of the dedication for the pedestrian/bicycle pathway beyond the conclusory statement that it could offset some of the traffic demand generated."[1] Compare the way in which attorneys for local homebuilders and organizations representing senior citizens and tenants mounted a successful attack on minimum floor area requirements imposed by Berlin Township, New Jersey,[2] with the failed attempt by a similarly situated developer challenging Wayne Township's ordinance 27 years before.[3] Or consider a Florida county's reliance on the report of a nationally recognized consultant in devising a school impact fee ordinance that gained the approval of the state supreme court.[4] And of equal importance is an acquaintance with the limitations of such information: some figures require as much reading between the lines as down the columns. It is on these same raw statistics—although with a different orientation and purpose—that the judge, legislator, administrator, planner, real estate speculator, builder, and all others concerned with land development often base their decisions.

Statistics can be revealing (or misleading) on the macro (that is, national) level as well. For example, search through the diverse set of data included in the *Statistical Abstract of the United States*[5] for the answers to the following inquiries, all of which are related to the important issues of urban and suburban sprawl, the aging of America, and the disappearance of important natural resources:

1. What was the percentage of developed land in the United States in the early 1980s as compared with the two subsequent decades?[6]

2. What percentage of developed land in the United States was found in "large urban and built-up areas" in the early 1980s as compared with the two subsequent decades?[7]

3. By what percentage did the population of Americans aged 75 and older increase in the 25 years since 1980?[8]

---

1. Dolan v. City of Tigard, 512 U.S. 374, 391, 395-96 (1994).
2. Home Builders League of S. Jersey v. Berlin Twp., 81 N.J. 127, 405 A.2d 381 (1979).
3. Lionshead Lake, Inc. v. Wayne Twp., 10 N.J. 165, 89 A.2d 693 (1952). For one law professor's reaction to the problematic reasoning in this case, and to the exclusionary potential of zoning, see Charles M. Haar, *Zoning for Minimum Standards: The* Wayne Township Case, 66 Harv. L. Rev. 1051 (1953), Charles M. Haar, Wayne Township: *Zoning for Whom?—In Brief Reply*, 67 Harv. L. Rev. 986 (1954).
4. St. Johns County v. Northeast Fla. Builders Ass'n, 583 So. 2d 635 (Fla. 1991) (the expert was Dr. James Nicholas).
5. The abstract is available on the Internet at http://www.census.gov/compendia/statab/.
6. Hint: Search for a table containing information on Land Cover/Use by Type.
7. Hint: Search for a table containing information on Developed Land by Type.
8. Hint: Search for a table containing information on Resident Population by Age and Sex.

4. What percentage of Americans lived in the Atlantic, Gulf, and Pacific coastal regions in 2000?[9]

5. How much wetlands loss has the nation experienced in the last several years?[10]

6. In 2006, what percentage of new American single-family homes were 2,400 square feet and larger?[11]

7. According to the latest figures, workers in which state had the longest mean commute time to work, what percentage of Americans took public transportation to work, and what percentage of Americans worked at home?[12]

When you find the numerical answers, consider how these "disembodied" figures have significance for the practice and theory of real property, land use, and environmental law, and for the existing institutions of private and public ordering of development. Consider, too, what kind of statistical and nonstatistical information would be most relevant to the following questions: How can the organization of land uses maximize the satisfaction of "valid" human wants? Are there still land use patterns and problems peculiar to the central city in a metropolitan area that are not shared by older suburbs or "edge cities"?[13] What are the effects of innovations in transportation such as light rail or ridesharing (also known as "slugging" in the northern Virginia suburbs of Washington, D.C.)?[14] What is the significance of the growing minority presence in suburbia and of gentrification in the inner city?[15] How do efforts to preserve endangered and threat-

---

9. Hint: Search for a table containing information on Population in Coastal Counties.
10. Hint: Search for a table containing information on Wetland Resources and Deepwater Habitats.
11. Hint: Search for a table containing information on Characteristics of New Privately Owned One-Family Houses.
12. Hint: Search for a table containing information on Commuting to Work.
13. The term was coined by Joel Garreau in EDGE CITY: LIFE ON THE NEW FRONTIER (1991). On page 4, he writes:

      I have come to call these new urban centers Edge Cities. Cities, because they contain all the functions a city ever has, albeit in a spread-out form that few have come to recognize for what it is. Edge, because they are a vigorous world of pioneers and immigrants, raising far from the old downtowns, where little save villages or farmland lay only thirty years before.

    Prominent examples include Tyson's Corner in northern Virginia, the Route 128 Corridor outside Boston, and metropolitan Atlanta's Perimeter Center.
14. See A Unique Commuter Solution, http://www.slug-lines.com (last visited Apr. 2, 2009).
15. See, e.g., Center on Urban & Metropolitan Policy, Melting Pot Suburbs: A Census 2000 Study of Suburban Diversity 2 (2001) (Brookings Institution study prepared by William H. Frey), available at http://www.brookings.edu/~/media/Files/rc/reports/2001/06demographics_frey/frey.pdf:

      This study of Census 2000 data reveals that racial and ethnic diversity is rising substantially in America's suburbs. Among the nation's 102 largest metropolitan areas, with populations exceeding half a million, minorities comprised more than a quarter (27.3 percent) of the suburban populations in 2000, up from 19.3 percent in 1990. Almost half (47 percent) of the minorities in the large metropolitan areas in this study lived in the suburbs in 2000, compared to just over 40 percent a decade ago.

      Of course, these overall statistics mask variations across metropolitan areas and variations in the residential patterns of different racial and ethnic groups. The 1990-2000 surge in minority suburbanization at the national level reflects disproportionate gains in the suburbs of 35 metropolitan areas, which we describe below as "melting pot metros." These areas have experienced large, immigrant-driven Hispanic and Asian population growth in their cities and suburbs in recent decades. The national numbers also are influenced, although to a lesser extent, by metropolitan areas in the South and West that have seen increases in their black suburban populations. In metros located in the slow-growing North, the pace of minority suburbanization lags far behind that of the nation as a whole.

ened wildlife and their critical habitats affect development practices and land planning policies?[16] What effects will the aging of the population have on the provision of metropolitan services?[17] Have the shift to a service economy and the increased popularity of telecommuting made the traditional segregation of residential and nonresidential uses obsolete and unworkable?[18] What are the advantages (beyond the preservation of agricultural and environmentally sensitive land) and drawbacks (in addition to increased air pollution) of growing up in the central city as opposed to growing out into the exurbs?

On the micro (or local) level, imagine that you are an attorney representing a developer of a new planned community that will include within its boundaries a range of housing, some commercial uses and offices, and a public park and school. What kind of information regarding the topics addressed in the national statistical charts, tables, and graphs—such as age, race, income, wetlands, transportation, and housing stock—would be relevant and appropriate in your presentations to potential neighbors and local officials? What would be the most effective methods of presenting that statistical information?

II.   Meanings and Means of Planning

A. The Plan: An "Impermanent Constitution"

You may be surprised to hear that Herbert Hoover, whose infamous presidential administration was cursed by the stock market crash of 1929 and the ensuing Great Depression, was an important player in the predominantly local and state planning and zoning movement during its crucial growing stage. As Secretary of Commerce during the pro-business Calvin Coolidge administration, Hoover appointed the Advisory Committee on City Planning and Zoning, which produced two important model acts: the Standard State Zoning Enabling Act (SZEA)[19] (published in 1924 and revised two years later) and the Standard City Planning Enabling Act (SCPEA) (published

---

16. The inevitable, and sometimes, awkward, overlay of land-use planning and environmental control has inspired its own set of commentators. *See* Daniel R. Mandelker, Environment and Equity: A Regulatory Challenge (1981); Linda A. Malone, Environmental Regulation of Land Use (1995); John R. Nolan, New Ground: The Advent of Local Environmental Law (2003); A. Dan Tarlock, *Local Government Protection of Biodiversity*, 60 U. Chi. L. Rev. 555 (1993); Michael Allan Wolf, *Fruits of the Impenetrable Jungle: Navigating the Boundary Between Land-Use Planning and Environmental Law*, 50 Wash. U. Urb. & Contemp. L. 5 (1996).

17. *See, e.g.*, Center on Urban & Metropolitan Policy, *Boomers and Seniors in the Suburbs: Aging Patterns in Census 2000*, at 2 (2003) (Brookings Institution study prepared by William H. Frey), *available at* www.brookings.edu/~/media/Files/rc/reports/2003/01demographics_frey/freyboomers.pdf:

   The aging of the Baby Boomers has also produced tectonic shifts in the age profile of the nation's population. For example, Census 2000 found that, for the first time, more than half of the U.S. population (50.5 percent) was age 35 or older. This represented a large shift from ten years prior, when 54 percent of the population was under the age of 35. The shift owed to the fact that in the 1990s, the nation's largest population cohorts—representing younger Boomers born between 1956 and 1965—transitioned into the 35-and-over age category.

18. An October 20, 2004, press release from the Census Bureau reported:

   Nearly 4.2 million people worked at home in 2000, according to Census 2000 tabulations, up from 3.4 million in 1990, the Census Bureau reported today. This 23 percent increase in home-based workers age 16 and older was double the growth in the overall work force during the decade.

   The data released today include information on home-based workers by age, sex, educational attainment, race and Hispanic origin, industry, occupation, disability status and earnings at the national and state levels. More recent estimates from the American Community Survey (ACS) <www.census.gov/acs/www/> show 4.5 million people worked at home in 2003.

   U.S. Census Bureau, Press Release, Census Bureau Releases Information on Home Workers (Oct. 20, 2004).

19. The actual title was "A Standard State Zoning Enabling Act Under Which Municipalities May Adopt Zoning Regulations."

in 1928). Committee members came from business, law, planning, real estate, and industry, and included such important figures as Edward Bassett (law), Alfred Bettman (law), Frederick Law Olmsted Jr. (landscape architecture), and Lawrence Veiller (housing). While the SCPEA was not as popular as its predecessor (by 1930, the zoning act was relied upon by 35 states, whereas the planning act was used by 10), it nonetheless was and remains influential among those responsible for shaping planning laws and policies throughout the nation.[20]

Section 6 of the SCPEA ("General Powers and Duties") provided: "It shall be the function and duty of the [planning] commission to make and adopt a master plan for the physical development of the municipality, including any areas outside of its boundaries which, in the commission's judgment, bear relation to the planning of such municipality." A footnote at this point explains that, by "a master plan" the drafters "meant a comprehensive scheme of development of the general fundamentals of a municipal plan. An express definition has not been thought desirable or necessary." Instead the model act provided illustrations, noting that the plan, supplemented by "maps, plats, charts, and descriptive matter" would reveal

> the commission's recommendations for the development of said territory, including, among other things, the general location, character, and extent of streets, viaducts, subways, bridges, waterways, water fronts, boulevards, parkways, playgrounds, squares, parks, aviation fields, and other public ways, grounds and open spaces, the general location of public buildings and other public property, and the general location and extent of public utilities and terminals, whether publicly or privately owned or operated, for water, light, sanitation, transportation, communication, power, and other purposes; also the removal, relocation, widening, narrowing, vacating, abandonment, change of use or extension of any of the foregoing ways, grounds, open spaces, buildings, property, utilities, or terminals; as well as a zoning plan for the control of the height, area, bulk, location, and use of buildings and premises. . . .

Section 7 ("Purposes in View") established a very ambitious goal for the master plan, such as

> guiding and accomplishing a coordinated, adjusted, and harmonious development of the municipality and its environs which will, in accordance with present and future needs, best promote health, safety, morals, order, convenience, prosperity, and general welfare, as well as efficiency and economy in the process of development; including, among other things, adequate provision for traffic, the promotion of safety from fire and other dangers, adequate provision for light and air, the promotion of the healthful and convenient distribution of population, the promotion of good civic design and arrangement, wise and efficient expenditure of public funds, and the adequate provision of public utilities and other public requirements.

Note that the drafters were evidently mindful that courts then, as now, envisioned that the state's police power was designed to protect the public health, safety, morals, and general welfare.

A few decades later, when many American local governments had enacted or were in the process of developing master or comprehensive plans, the serious question arose as to the *legal* status of this

---

20. For more details on both model acts, see Ruth Knack, Stuart Meck & Israel Stollman, *The Real Story Behind the Standard Planning and Zoning Acts of the 1920s*, LAND USE L. & ZONING DIG., Feb. 1996, at 3.

unique document. Professor Haar, in *The Master Plan: An Impermanent Constitution*, 20 Law & Contemp. Probs. 353, 375-76 (1955), has conceptualized the problem in this fashion:

> If the plan is regarded not as the vest-pocket tool of the planning commission, but as a broad statement to be adopted by the most representative municipal body—the local legislature—then the plan becomes a law through such adoption. A unique type of law, it should be noted, in that it purports to bind future legislatures when they enact implementary materials. So far as impact is concerned, the law purports to control the enactment of other laws (the so-called implementary legislation) solely. It thus has the cardinal characteristic of a constitution. But unlike that legal form it is subject to amendatory procedures not significantly different from the course followed in enacting ordinary legislation. To enact a nonconforming measure amounts merely to passing the law twice. . . .
>
> [T]his seems the limited function to which the master plan can withdraw in order to perform most effectively in the grand effort to improve American cities: a reminder of the myriad of activities affecting land, their inter-relation, their long-run effects which the day-to-day administrator is too busy to consider. The implementing legislation, on pain of being outside the statute, must conform to its generalized propositions. . . .

For the remainder of the 20th century (and even beyond), courts and commentators have continued to wrestle with the nature of the relationship between this "quasi-constitution" and its conforming and implementing "legislation."

Two studies dating from the turbulent 1960s and 1970s do a good job of introducing the very broad scope and aspirational nature of the comprehensive plan. Although it is a common practice to include "planning and zoning" in the same breath, in theory and practice the former term encompasses much more than the latter.

William I. Goldman & Jerome L. Kaufman, in City Planning in the Sixties 4-7 (1965), noted that "[c]omprehensive planning is generally considered to be divided into four working processes," which they identified as:

1. *Survey and analysis*, or collection of basic data related to physical, economic, and social conditions.

2. *Goal formulation*, or identification of and agreement upon social and economic objectives.

3. *Plan making*, or determination of suitable uses and densities for specific areas and for the circulation system and public facilities.

4. *Plan effectuation*, or legal and administrative tools to carry out the plan and to coordinate decisions.

A "well-drawn" comprehensive plan will in turn serve:

1. To provide information about the present status and resources of the community; to make citizens aware of how the community is constituted.

2. To chart the future growth of the municipality and to outline the goals and objectives publicly agreed upon to provide a clue to the character and quality of the area that might be anticipated at some later date.

3. To serve as a rallying point for worthy proposals and as a test of the validity of development schemes.

4. To act as a framework of the kinds of tools required to carry out the plan.

5. To stimulate understanding and support among the citizenry, and so to elicit the necessary fiscal resources and legal tools.

6. To put property interests on notice as to the intent of the city to take action in various locations and in regard to specific projects.

Thus, the process of preparing this ambitious, forward-looking document would not only join government officials and members of community in important fact-gathering and goal-setting activities, but also provide important information for landowners and investors interested in local land development.

On May 21, 1975, after more than a decade of study, the American Law Institute released its official draft of *A Model Land Development Code (MLDC)*, a document designed "to coordinate and integrate all legislation of a state that attempts to control or influence development of land."[21] This creative effort, unlike its predecessors from the 1920s, failed to stimulate a significant amount of legislative imitation (with the important exception of the state of Florida). Nevertheless, the *MLDC*'s concept of a Local Land Development Plan remains an important starting point for the discussion of the role of planning in the early 21st century. According to §3-101 of the *MLDC*, this development plan would "be a statement (in words, maps, illustrations or other media of communication) setting forth its objectives, policies and standards to guide public and private development of land within its planning jurisdiction and including a short-term program of public actions. . . ." In the following section, the drafters identified the purposes of preparing this plan:

1. to initiate comprehensive studies of factors relevant to development;

2. to recognize and state major problems and opportunities concerning development and the social and economic effects of development;

3. to set forth the desired sequence, patterns, and characteristics of future development and its probable environmental, economic, and social consequences;

4. to provide a statement of programs to obtain the desired sequence, patterns, and characteristics of development; and

5. to determine the probable environmental, economic and social consequences of the desired development and the proposed programs.

As the fifth purpose makes clear, as with the National Environmental Policy Act (NEPA) of 1969 that became federal law a few years before, under the *MLDC* the consideration of the wisdom of

---

21. AMERICAN LAW INSTITUTE, A MODEL LAND DEVELOPMENT CODE xv (1976) (Chief Reporter's Preface).

land development would not take place in a vacuum devoid of social, economic, and environmental impacts.[22]

While the *MLDC*'s efforts did not attract widespread legislative attention, two decades later state capitals were abuzz with planning and zoning reform bills. As reported by Professor Patricia E. Salkin in *From* Euclid *to Growing Smart: The Transformation of the American Local Land Use Ethic Into Local Land Use and Environmental Controls*, 20 Pace Envtl. L. Rev. 109, 119-20 (2002),

> by the end of the 1990s, there was so much activity in the business of land use law reform that it was a challenge to keep current on trends. By 1999, more than one thousand land use related bills were introduced in state legislatures across the country in one year alone. By the beginning of 2002, more than two thousand land use planning and land use control bills had been introduced by state legislatures; seventeen governors had issued nineteen executive orders; eighteen states had created legislative task forces or study commissions to evaluate smart growth ideas and opportunities; and 553 ballot initiatives in thirty-eight states focused on issues of planning and/or smart growth.

Many of these initiatives fit within the wide umbrella of the "smart growth movement." Professor Salkin has explained:

> Armed with statistics about the costs of sprawl (such as unplanned leap frog development), the loss of the prime agricultural lands, and degradation of significant environmental and natural resources, the smart growth movement continues to promote statutory reforms to the state planning and zoning enabling acts. Advocates have also encouraged states to provide localities with more flexible zoning tools to best meet local and regional challenges. The smart growth legislation advocates local flexibility and promotes mixed-use development, in contrast to Euclidean zoning that promotes a more rigid separation of uses. Different from the environmental reforms of the 1970s and 1980s, the smart growth movement attracts notable private sector support as it broadens the message to include economic vitality and quality of life as two of the key platforms for necessitating change. Urban renewal, traffic congestion and infrastructure issues have also been part of the smart growth debate.

---

22. *See* Stuart Meck, *Model Planning and Zoning Enabling Legislation: A Short History, in* MODERNIZING STATE PLANNING STATUTES: THE GROWING SMART WORKING PAPERS (PAS Report Nos. 462/463, 1996). He notes that the *MLDC* "was not intended as a unified document to be adopted in its entirety by states to replace the Standard Acts, but instead as a source of various statutory models to address specific development concerns. Each state could select the provisions it needed from the 12 articles in the code." *See also* James H. Wickersham, *The Quiet Revolution Continues: The Emerging New Model for State Growth Management Statutes*, 18 HARV. ENVTL. L. REV. 489, 512 (1994) (internal footnotes omitted):

> Both the Vermont and Florida growth management statutes require regional or state level approval for major development projects, thus shifting final authority away from municipalities. The Florida statute also enables state and regional agencies to identify certain natural areas of critical concern, in which local regulations can be superseded. The American Law Institute's Model Land Development Code ("MLDC") was strongly influenced by the Vermont statute, and it served in turn as the model for both provisions of the Florida statute.

Two difficulties facing contemporary observers and advocates are, on the one hand, distinguishing truly innovative "smart growth" tools[23] from the simple repackaging of zoning devices, and, on the other hand, making sure that the new agenda isn't in actuality an anti-regulation Trojan Horse.

How do the excerpts from actual plans and proposals found in the following paragraphs reflect the sociopolitical realities of a specific time and place? Not only does one size not fit all (communities); it doesn't even fit one place for a significant period of time. You should pay special attention to the different meanings of "environment" in these documents.

The Chicago Department of Development and Planning's 1966 Comprehensive Plan identified six "strategic objectives" related to "quality of life":

1. Family Life and the Environment

2. Expanded Opportunities for the Disadvantaged

3. Economic Developments and Job Opportunities

4. Moving People and Goods

5. The Proper Allocation of Land

6. Unified City Development

The drafters explained that "the first three strategic objectives represent the 'ends' of the plan, while the second three represent 'means.'"

Moving from the general to the specific, the "Improvement Plan" provided details on future initiatives. For example, to meet its *"Business"* target, the city would

Support Central Business District growth, especially with transportation and environmental improvements.

Rehabilitate regional and other centers.

Develop special districts for offices and other special business functions.

Rebuild strip business in conjunction with residential and street improvements.

Similarly, the city would *"[e]xpand the housing supply"* by

Rebuilding 2500 acres of severely blighted housing with 100,000 new homes.

Developing four central opportunity areas with new housing for 200,000 people.

---

23. The Smart Growth Network website is available on the Internet at http://www.smartgrowth.org/about/principles. It has identified the following 10 Principles of Smart Growth:

1. Create Range of Housing Opportunities and Choices

2. Create Walkable Neighborhoods

3. Encourage Community and Stakeholder Collaboration

4. Foster Distinctive, Attractive Communities with a Strong Sense of Place

5. Make Development Decisions Predictable, Fair, and Cost Effective;

6. Mix Land Uses

7. Preserve Open Space, Farmland, Natural Beauty, and Critical Environmental Areas

8. Provide a Variety of Transportation Choices

9. Strengthen and Direct Development Toward Existing Communities

10. Take Advantage of Compact Building Design.

Increasing the supply of public housing by 35,000 units through leasing, rehabilitation, and new construction.

The New York City Planning Commission's 1969 Plan for New York City included such wide-ranging headings including "National Center" ("Battery Park City and the other waterfront communities . . . will mix office towers with housing for every income range, a wide variety of commercial activities, museums, parks and marinas."), "Job Development" ("As a major purchaser of goods and services, the City can stimulate business enterprise in the ghetto."), "Welfare" ("For the long term the nation must seek a form of guaranteed minimum income. One way to achieve this would be a negative income tax."), "Environment" ("We reject the concept of wholesale demolition and barrack-like projects. Instead of clearing away neighborhoods, we must work with the fabric of them and put as much emphasis on maintenance and rehabilitation as on new construction."), "Crime" ("Pretrial detention, which helps overcrowd our jails, could be sharply reduced. Bail procedures which unfairly discriminate against the poor should be liberalized."), and "Government" ("The relationship between the City and the State and Federal government must be changed. The City is not allowed to be master in its own house."). This was certainly a plan that reached far beyond a local zoning map, indeed far beyond any parochial concerns.[24]

In the late 1970s and early 1980s, as the legal tools for managing growth worked their way into judicial acceptability, more and more governments—even at the regional level—embarked on an ambitious attempt to meet the private sector's demand for more development with the financial burdens placed on the public providers of essential health, safety, and educational services. A good early attempt to strike that delicate balance issued from a highly urbanized Washington, D.C., suburb with very high land values. In 1979, Montgomery County, Maryland, presented its *Growth Policy Report*, which noted that while "[p]rior to 1970, urban planning was based largely on the implicit concept of growth 'accommodation,'" since that time, "planning has been shifted to a growth 'management' approach, in response to public demand." In keeping with this shift, the report employed the concept of "carrying capacity":

> By dividing total growth into its private sector and public sector components, it is possible to portray the capacity of the public sector, to carry the weight of the private sector, in terms of an equation:
>
> $$\frac{\text{Public}}{\text{Private}} = \text{Level of Public Service}$$

---

24. The broad approach for New York's plan was short-lived. *See* N.Y. Times, June 26, 1974:

A new concept in neighborhood planning, epitomized by a series of "miniplans" tailored to the needs of individual communities, is being inaugurated by the City Planning Commission.

The approach is in marked contrast to the master plan for New York City, drawn up with much fanfare six years ago but shelved by the commission last year as little more than a handy reference tool.

"This, we think, is planning for the seventies," said John E. Zuccotti, the commission"s chairman, in making public the first three miniplans - for the Kingsbridge, Soundview and Hunts Point sections of the Bronx.

"The glossy-covered brochures may have had their place," Mr. Zuccotti said, referring to the expensively produced volumes of the citywide master plan, complete with elaborate graphics. "But times have changed. With a city the size of New York, in a democratic society that is as diverse as ours, there is clearly a need for more attention to local needs and desires."

Mr. Zuccotti, who became a member of the commission in 1971 and took over as chairman a year ago last February, has fostered the neighborhood approach in planning. He has sought greater involvement by the 62 community boards and local civic organizations in the planning process.

By developing a level-of-public-service measuring technique, it is possible to translate this general equation into a specific tool for growth management.

The county in turn developed an "Adequate Public Facilities" Ordinance, which mandated "that no subdivision be approved, if the total public facilities available under the adopted Capital Improvements Program (CIP) are not adequate to the task." Moreover, as an amendment to its general plan, the county adopted a "Comprehensive Staging Plan," establishing "interim thresholds of private-sector growth, that are keyed to incremental additions of public facility projects in the Capital Improvements Program." In this way, by requiring essential services to be in place beforehand, Montgomery County sought to avoid the premature subdivision phenomenon that plagued many American communities in the go-go growth decades following World War II.

As more and more cities and urban counties instituted controls on growth, not all communities were in favor of putting the brakes on development, even those located in regions known for their natural beauty. For example, *A Master Plan for Salt Lake County*, prepared by Salt Lake County's Planning Commission in 1986, was "designed to serve as a base of reference to which both public and private groups can refer and on which they can rely in making future plans." Accordingly, the plan identified several "major policies and proposals," such as:

- Residential uses are considered in three density categories: high density residence, close to major business districts; medium density residence, adjacent to and surrounding high density residence; and low density residence, filling in the balance of the proposed living areas.

- Central Business Districts are encouraged to grow and develop to provide a range and depth of services. Regional shopping centers are proposed for each urban planning area. Commercial districts providing general commercial and service activities are encouraged to expand in areas with adequate transportation facilities and in locations convenient to their needs.

- Dispersal of industrial activity is a key recommendation of the Plan. Existing industrial districts are enlarged to fill in presently vacant land and to encourage the transition of nonindustrial uses to industry. . . .

- Recreation areas are greatly expanded. The Jordan River complex is proposed to be the major focus of park and lake development in the Valley. The Wasatch and Oquirrh Mountains are proposed for continued recreational development.

- An integrated transportation system is proposed. The interstate freeways would be linked by a belt route freeway and comprehensive network of expressways and major arterials. . . .

For decades, the American Northwest has been identified in the national psyche with conservation and environmental protection. We should not be surprised, therefore, that comprehensive planning in the metropolitan regions of northern California, Oregon, and Washington has a strong "green" tint. As the 20th century gave way to its successor, a new reconception of the master plan arose. A Plan for Managing Growth 2004–2015, produced by Seattle's Department of Planning and Development, illustrates how environmental concerns have moved from the periphery to the center in some communities. A major impetus for the Seattle plan was the state legislature's adoption of the Growth Management Act of 1990, Rev. Code Wash. §36.70A.010, in which the lawmakers found that uncoordinated and unplanned growth, together with a lack of common goals expressing the public's interest in the conservation and the wise use of our lands, pose a threat to the environment, sustainable economic development, and the health, safety, and high quality of life enjoyed by residents of this state. It is in the public interest that citizens, communities, local governments, and the private sector cooperate and coordinate with one another in comprehensive land use planning. Further, the legislature finds that it is in the public interest that economic development programs be shared with communities experiencing insufficient economic growth.

The Plan for Managing Growth noted that the city's comprehensive plan, titled Toward a Sustainable Seattle, was "a 20-year policy plan (1994-2014) designed to articulate a vision of how Seattle will grow in ways that sustain its citizens' values. . . . The ideas in the plan were developed over five years through discussion and debate and the creative thinking of thousands of Seattle citizens working with City staff and elected officials."[25] These citizens and officials identified four "core values": (1) Community; (2) Environmental Stewardship; (3) Economic Opportunity and Security; and (4) Social Equity. The plan provided the following details regarding the Environmental Stewardship core value:

> This Comprehensive Plan tries to address some of the Seattle area's broad environmental problems. For example, the Plan's urban villages concept addresses a number of environmental concerns. The urban village concept promotes compact, more pedestrian-oriented development and alternative (non-auto) transportation choices such as transit, as well as incentive and disincentive programs to encourage getting around without a car. The emphasis on compact development is intended to mitigate air and stormwater discharge pollution from automobiles, loss of green space, and increases in impervious surfaces that results from non-compact development. . . .
>
> A Native American proverb reminds us that "Every decision must take into account its effect on the next seven generations." Sustainability refers to the long-term social, economic and environmental health of our community. A sustainable culture thrives without compromising the ability of future generations to meet their needs.

Notes

1. The term "urban villages" is a favorite of the New Urbanist movement. For an earlier usage, see Herbert J. Gans, The Urban Villagers: Group and Class in the Life of Italian Americans (1962), a classic study of the socioeconomic effects of urban renewal. For a much less inhibited "ecotopian" manifesto, see Ernest Callenbach, The Fate of Our Cities Is the Fate of the Earth, in Sustainable Cities: Concepts and Strategies for Eco-City Development 10, 14 (Bob Walter et al. eds. 1992):

> [A]t this crucial juncture in our history, if salvation has to come through greed, and it probably does, let's work on Congress to replace its subsidies to military contractors with subsidies to city rebuilders. Let's end protectionism of American gas-guzzlers, and start protecting streetcar builders for a change, so that we don't have to buy German trolleys. Let's turn Bechtel around from building airports and nuclear plants, to building inexpensive but delightful dense mixed-use structures for dwellings, stores, and offices, such as great cities have always relied on. Let's put Boeing to work building a decent long-

---

25. The current online version of the plan can be found on the Internet at http://www.seattle.gov/DPD/Planning/Seattle_s_Comprehensive_Plan/ComprehensivePlan/default.asp.

distance train network, so we can recapture some of the land wasted in vast airports, and get people from center-city to center-city, the way every other advanced country does. We need a new America that will work ecologically and economically, and it's within our grasp. If we can continue working to dramatize the vision, the legislators will come around. As the old saying says: If the people will lead, the leaders will follow. It's time.

2. In the early years of the 21st century, two of America's greatest cities faced the profound challenges of rebuilding after widespread disasters—one the result of terrorism, the other caused by nature's vast power. For samples of the debate over the nature and extent of rebuilding, see David W. Dunlap, *Amid Plans for the Trade Center, a Revived Call for Housing*, N.Y. Times, Oct. 27, 2005:

> Housing in the World Trade Center project? Who ever heard of such an idea? Actually, anyone who paid attention to the planning concepts presented in 2002 by the Lower Manhattan Development Corporation and the Port Authority of New York and New Jersey. Five of the six plans identified 130 Liberty Street, where the badly damaged former Deutsche Bank building stands, as the location of "potential residential development." Though all six concepts were later rejected, the notion of residential development at 130 Liberty Street endured through 2003 in Daniel Libeskind's master site plan. In other words, despite the surprise that greeted Mayor Michael R. Bloomberg's recent call for housing at ground zero, he was simply reviving one of the longest-standing ideas about creating a community around the trade center's commercial, memorial and cultural core.

See also Jeffrey Mietrodt et al., *Plan Shrinks City Footprint; Nagin Panel May Call for 3-Year Test*, New Orleans Times-Picayune, Dec. 14, 2005:

> Key members of Mayor Ray Nagin's rebuilding commission have endorsed a controversial proposal to shrink the city's footprint, but they want to modify the idea in ways they said would make it more palatable to homeowners who want to rebuild in the lowest-lying parts of New Orleans.
>
> Local developer Joe Canizaro on Tuesday said he and other appointees to the Bring New Orleans Back commission agree that some floodprone parts of the city should be returned to wetland, a key recommendation from the Urban Land Institute that has drawn protests from many residents and the politicians who represent them. Canizaro is co-chairman of the commission's city planning subcommittee.

On March 29, 2007, the city announced that it was establishing seventeen Target Recovery Zones, each roughly one-half mile in diameter. According to a New Orleans press release, the zones "will be built around public assets in key business corridors in an effort to generate further private investment from developers. . . . Target areas are consistent with the development approaches citizens suggested in earlier redevelopment plans, such as the Unified New Orleans Plan, the Lambert Plan and the Bring New Orleans Back Commission plan." There are three "formats" for the zones:

> Rebuild areas have experienced severe destruction of physical structures and social networks. These areas will require major rebuilding, or significant public and private investment in order to recover.
>
> Redevelop areas are places where some recovery components and resources are already present. They have a high potential for attracting investment and acting as a catalyst for further redevelopment and recovery of the affected community.

Renew areas include specific projects that require relatively modest public intervention in order to supplement work already underway by the private and nonprofit sector.

B. The Structure of Local Government Planning

Typically, the members of the first formal body to hear a land use change proposal—known most
often as the planning commission—are not elected by the voters of the community. The same is
also almost always true of the body that decides on variances, which is usually known as the Board
of Adjustment or Board of Zoning Appeals. Consider whether the functions of these bodies makes
them more like the local legislature (the city council, county commission, and the like), a court,
or an administrative agency. What qualifications would you deem most important for the persons
serving on these commissions or boards? Which of the following professions would be the best
match for membership of the planning commission or board of adjustment: real estate developers,
building contractors, real estate agents, lawyers, land use planners, bankers, environmental engineers, architects, real estate appraisers? Or, does it make more sense to populate these bodies with
local citizens regardless of their day jobs? Would your answer differ depending on the size of the
jurisdiction?

An Internet search will yield examples of varying planning structures and approaches, some of
which can be quite complex. The Development Process for Austin, Texas, for example,[26] includes
headings for Zoning, Subdivision, Site Plan, Building Plan, and Inspection. The approval authority switches from the Austin City Council (for zoning) to the Zoning and Platting Commission
(for subdivision and site plan) to the Neighborhood Planning and Zoning Department (for inspection). In addition, Watershed Protection and Development Review comes into play for all but
zoning decisions.

The flow chart depicting the Permit Process for South San Francisco, California,[27] includes
three separate processes: Design Review Board, Environmental Review (required by the California
Environmental Review Act (CEQA), and City Council. Along the way, the city planning staff,
technical advisory group, planning commission, and chief planner also play a role. Do your own
Internet search to see if you can find out how these organizational structures compare with the
ones found in your hometown, the community in which you are attending school, and the place
in which you plan to work after graduation. Does the local plan you found combine functions in
a different fashion than the city of Austin? Does your local planning process include the heavy
environmental review component found in South San Francisco? Which of these plans is the most
complex? Do you think that complexity is warranted? If so, what legitimate factors would justify
the complexity? If not, what steps or decisionmakers would you eliminate?

C. The Structure of Active Statewide Planning

Dissatisfied with the performance of local government planning and zoning bodies, particularly
in their decisions affecting environmentally sensitive lands and water bodies, some states have
attempted to "recapture" some significant supervisory responsibilities by instituting state layers of

---

26. The plan is available on the Internet at http:///www.ci.austin.tx.us/development/downloads/development_description.
doc.

27. The flow chart is available on the Internet at http://www.ci.ssf.ca.us/DocumentView.aspx?DID=259.

planning controls.[28] This is the case with Florida, a state that has been tinkering with statewide review since the 1970s. The current incarnation is found in Florida Statutes §163.3184. Key components include:

- Coordination: "The state land planning agency shall have responsibility for plan review, coordination, and the preparation and transmission of comments, pursuant to this section, to the local governing body responsible for the comprehensive plan."

- Transmittal: "Each local governing body shall transmit the complete proposed comprehensive plan or plan amendment to the state land planning agency, the appropriate regional planning council and water management district, the Department of Environmental Protection, the Department of State, and the Department of Transportation, and, in the case of municipal plans, to the appropriate county, and, in the case of county plans, to the Fish and Wildlife Conservation Commission and the Department of Agriculture and Consumer Services, immediately following a public hearing . . . ."

- Intergovernmental Review: "The governmental agencies . . . shall provide comments to the state land planning agency within 30 days after receipt by the state land planning agency of the complete proposed plan amendment."

- Regional, County, and Municipal Review: "The review of the regional planning council . . . shall be limited to effects on regional resources or facilities identified in the strategic regional policy plan and extrajurisdictional impacts which would be inconsistent with the comprehensive plan of the affected local government."

---

28. *See, e.g.*, Patricia E. Salkin, *From* Euclid *to Growing Smart: The Transformation of the American Local Land Use Ethic Into Local Land Use and Environmental Controls*, 20 Pace Envtl. L. Rev. 109, 116 (2002):

> As a result of the growing interest in addressing environmental concerns, some states began to adopt major land use reform in the 1970s. The result was a "quiet revolution" in land use law wherein states, including Vermont (1970 and 1988), Florida (1972 and 1985), Oregon (1973) and Hawaii (1978), made significant modifications to their systems of land use control, giving more power to the regional and state governments to deal with environmental protection through land use controls. Four more states made reforms in the 1980s, New Jersey (1985), Maine (1988), Rhode Island (1988), and Georgia (1988).

The term "quiet revolution" derives from an influential early study of the statewide zoning phenomenon: Fred Bosselman & David Callies, The Quiet Revolution in Land Use Control (1971).

The 1970s also witnessed keen interest in federal land use legislation. Only a few weeks after President Richard Nixon signed the National Environmental Policy Act (NEPA) in January 1970, the chair of the U.S. Senate Committee on the Interior, Sen. Henry (Scoop) Jackson (D - Wash.)

> introduced the first National Land Use Policy Bill, a bill which he called "the next logical step (to NEPA) in our national effort to provide a quality life in a quality environment. . . . " Jackson's bill would have provided money to develop state land use plans. Plans drawn up by each state would identify where to put projects like airports, powerplants, housing developments and parks. In Jackson's view, this was the way to avoid—or at least reduce—the increasingly bitter clashes between environmentalists and the developers; the way to assure economic growth and, at the same time, protect the environment.

Noreen Lyday, The Law of the Land: Debating National Land Use Legislation 1970-1975, at 1 (Urban Inst. 1976).

By the middle of the decade, federal land use planning was an idea that no longer carried significant political weight. According to Lyday: "The combination of grassroots opposition on an issue as volatile and complex as property rights, heavy lobbying among the mining, timber, farm interests and construction trades, and the Chamber [of Commerce], coupled with the confusion engendered by the [Nixon] Administration's defection, were sufficient to defeat the bill." *Id.* at 48.

- State Land Planning Agency Review: "The state land planning agency shall review a proposed plan amendment upon request of a regional planning council, affected person, or local government transmitting the plan amendment."

- Local Government Review of Comments: "The local government, upon receipt of written comments from the state land planning agency, shall have 120 days to adopt or adopt with changes the proposed comprehensive plan or . . . plan amendments."

- State Review of Plan Amendments: "[T]he state land planning agency, upon receipt of a local government's complete adopted comprehensive plan or plan amendment, shall have 45 days for review and to determine if the plan or plan amendment is in compliance with this act."[29]

A state level of review would seem to have two major advantages: First, officials who make the tough decisions are physically removed from any undue pressures exerted by developers or those in opposition to the plan change. Second, the central government typically has more funding available for sophisticated environmental, economic, and community development analysis. What would you say are the major drawbacks to this super-imposed level of review by the state?

Critics of this statewide approval process in Florida, asserting that comprehensive plan amendments are still too easy for developers to secure, have proposed a state constitutional amendment that would require a positive vote in a local referendum before a local government can adopt a new comprehensive plan or a plan amendment. In June 2009, the Florida Division of Elections certified the proposed "Hometown Democracy" amendment for inclusion in the November 2010 ballot. Supporters submitted more than 700,000 signatures so that "Amendment 4" would be presented to the voters.

III.   The Evolution of Planning Theory, Tools, and Techniques

A. Urban Design

The long and storied history of city planning has taken many interesting turns over the last few thousand years. The complex relationship between humans and their built environment, and the effects each has on the other, has captured the attention of philosophers, architects, planners, social scientists, and politicians. Several examples of their thoughts on the subject appear on the pages that follow.

Chapter 35, verses 1-5 of the Book of Numbers (*Bamidmar*, 35: 2-5), contains the following biblical version of urban design:

> Command the Children of Israel that they shall give to the Levites, from the heritage of their possession, cities for dwelling, and open space[30] for the cities all around them shall you give to the Levites. The cities shall be theirs for dwelling, and their open space shall be for their animals, for their wealth, and for all of their needs. The open spaces of the cities that you shall give to the Levites, from the wall of the city outward: a thousand cubits all around. You shall measure from outside the city on the eastern side two thousand cubits; on the southern side two thousand cubits; on the western side two thousand

---

29. A graphic representation of Florida's Comprehensive Plan Amendment Process can be found on the Internet at http://www.dca.state.fl.us/fdcp/dcp/Procedures/Files/PlanAdmb&w85x14.PDF.

30. Authors' note: The King James version translates this phrase as "suburbs."

cubits; and on the northern side two thousand cubits, with the city in the middle; this shall be for them the open spaces of the cities.[31]

René Descartes, in his Discourse on the Method of Rightly Conducting the Reason (1637), observed

> that there is very often less perfection in works composed of several portions, and carried out by the hands of various masters, than in those on which one individual alone has worked. Thus we see that buildings planned and carried out by one architect alone are usually more beautiful and better proportioned than those which many have tried to put in order and improve, making use of old walls which are built with other ends in view.[32] In the same way also, those ancient cities which, originally mere villages, have become in the process of time great towns, are usually badly constructed in comparison with those which are regularly laid out on a plain by a surveyor who is free to follow his own ideas. Even though, considering their buildings each one apart, there is often as much or more display of skill in the one case than in the other, the former having large buildings and small buildings indiscriminately placed together, thus rendering the streets crooked and irregular, so that it might be said that it was chance rather than the will of men guided by reason that led to such an arrangement. And if we consider that this happens despite the fact that from all time there have been certain officials who have had the special duty of looking after the buildings of private individuals in order that they may be public ornaments, we shall understand how difficult it is to bring about much that is satisfactory in operating only upon the works of others.[33]

This metaphor of interdependency recurs in urban design, looked at from the outside. Thus, Arthur Cecil Pigou, in The Economics of Welfare 195 (4th ed. 1932), stated:

> It is as idle to expect a well-planned town to result from the independent activities of isolated speculators as it would be to expect a satisfactory picture to result if each separate square inch were painted by an independent artist. No "invisible hand" can be relied on to produce a good arrangement of the whole from a combination of separate treatments of the parts. It is, therefore, necessary that an authority of wider reach should intervene and should tackle the collective problems of beauty, of air and of light, as those other collective problems of gas and water have been tackled. Hence, shortly before the war, there came into being, on the pattern of long previous German practice, Mr. Burns's extremely important town-planning Act. In this Act, for the first time, control over individual buildings, from the standpoint, not of individual structure, but of the structure of

---

31. Authors' note: This translation is from The Chumash: The Stone Edition 927 (Rabbi Nosson Scherman ed., 1993).

32. Authors' note: For an opposing view, consider the opinion of Sergeant Francis Troy, one of British literature's most famous cads:

> "A philosopher once said in my hearing that the old builders, who worked when art was a living thing, had no respect for the work of builders who went before them, but pulled down and altered as they thought fit; and why shouldn't we? 'Creation and preservation don't do well together,' says he, 'and a million of antiquarians can't invent a style.' My mind exactly. I am for making this place more modern, that we may be cheerful whilst we can."

Thomas Hardy, Far From the Madding Crowd 235 (Signet Classic ed. 2002). Hardy was an architect by profession.

33. Authors' note: This translation comes from Philosophical Works 87-88 (Elizabeth Haldane & G.R.T. Ross trans., 1931).

the town as a whole, was definitely conferred upon those town councils that are willing to accept the powers offered to them.

Pigou, at 183, 185-86, also offered these observations concerning what we would today label positive and negative externalities:

> [T]he essence of the matter is that one person A, in the course of rendering some service, for which payment is made, to a second person B, incidentally also renders services or disservices to other persons (not producers of like services), of such a sort that payment cannot be exacted from the benefited parties or compensation enforced on behalf of the injured parties. . . .

> Thus, incidental uncharged disservices are rendered to third parties . . . when the owner of a site in a residential quarter of a city builds a factory there and so destroys a great part of the amenities of the neighbouring sites; or, in a less degree, when he uses his site in such a way as to spoil the lighting of the houses opposite; or when he invests resources in erecting buildings in a crowded centre, which, by contracting the air space and the playing-room of the neighbourhood, tend to injure the health and efficiency of the families living there. . . .

The most famous critique of Pigou is found in the highly influential article, R.H. Coase, *The Problem of Social Cost*, 3 J.L. & Econ. 1 (1960). In a late 20th-century reconsideration of the Pigou/Coase dispute, Professor A.W.B. Simpson, in *Coase v. Pigou Reexamined*, 25 J. Legal Stud. 53, 58-59 (1996), wrote:

> The first idea, which runs through all Coase's writings, is deep skepticism as to the desirability of government intervention. Various expressions are used, but the thought is the same. In "The Problem of Social Cost" this skepticism is very mildly expressed; he argues that action against a smoke-emitting factory will lead to results which "are not necessarily, or even usually, desirable." In *The Firm, the Market and the Law* Coase hardens his position, arguing that whether government intervention is desirable or not is a "factual question" and that economic theory does not support any presumption in its favor. He goes on: "The ubiquitous nature of 'externalities' suggests to me that there is a prima facie case against intervention, and the studies of the effects of regulation which have been made in recent years in the United States, ranging from agriculture to zoning, which indicate that regulation has commonly made matters worse, lend support to this view." . . .

> The second idea is the corollary of the first; since government intervention is suspect, the alternatives to government intervention are viewed sympathetically. The drift of the argument favors leaving matters to the market. This possibility is dramatized by the thesis which has come to be called the Coase theorem: that in the absence of transaction costs the allocation of resources reached by negotiation and bargain, assuming economic rationality, would be unaffected by the rule as to legal liability. . . . This of course is a purely theoretical view as to what would happen in a world which does not exist. . . .[34]

---

34. Authors' note: A.W.B. Simpson, *Coase v. Pigou Reexamined*, 25 J. LEGAL STUD. 53, 75 (1996), asserted that Coase used Pigou as a strawman, portraying the latter as an unabashed defender of government interference with the market:

> Coase, in the tradition of the political economists, adopts a rhetorical device, which is first of all to attribute a commitment to the merits of government intervention to Pigou and then to present Pigou as a deeply confused thinker. The form of the argument then is this: if you believe X, then you are in bad company, for you believe something particularly associated with the thinking of Y, a deeply confused economist. The very fact that Y believed X becomes itself a reason for skepticism.

The legendary architect, Le Corbusier, in Concerning Town Planning 67-68 (Clive Entwistle trans., 1948), condemned the phrase "family house" as touching and admirable, but one which no longer applied in reality, since the family "melts" in the course of twenty years and the family house has no duration. While the stability on which it is founded has been upset, "[a] society seeking to defend an equilibrium which it has already lost, looks for means of tying down the nomadic elements of a society which is in need of a new and harmonious organization of its life." The result, to paraphrase him, would be a universal wasteland of garden cities. The solution he advanced was the vertical garden city.

Pictures of planned cities tell thousands of words and emotions. Using your favorite search engine, find on the Internet images of Le Corbusier's Ville Radieuse, Frank Lloyd Wright's Broadacre City, and Paolo Soleri's Babel series. These illustrations present in diagram form the visions of some famous (and infamous) physical planners. In examining the plans with a view to their implementation in the real world, consider the new and broader planning controls, the reevaluation of the social role of land, and the realignment of property rights that each of them may entail.

As the 20th century progressed, "planning" expanded far beyond the technical issue of physical interfaces between uses and into the very quality of urban life. Professor Suzanne Keller, in The Urban Neighborhood 9 (1968), offered a sparkling effort to reduce the gap "between analytic social science and practical planning."[35] In recent years, some visionaries have looked backwards in an attempt to re-create at least the physical trappings of a simpler past. The best example is Seaside, Florida, whose origins are described on the community's website (http://www.seasidefl.com/communityHistory3.asp):

> The idea of Seaside started with the notion of reviving Northwest Florida's building tradition, which had produced wood-frame cottages so well adapted to the climate that they enhanced the sensual pleasure of life by the sea, while accommodating generations of family members; kids, if they were good, got to sleep on the porch . . . .
>
> These cottages had deep roof overhangs, ample windows and cross ventilation in all rooms. They were built of wood and other time-tested materials and with reasonable maintenance, could last several generations. . . .

Seaside has been called "a template for a kind of community planning called New Urbanism: anti-sprawl, pedestrian-friendly villages symbolized by bustling town squares and houses with inviting front porches and hidden garages."[36] But what do you make of the fact that Seaside was selected as the setting for *The Truman Show*, a 1998 motion picture in which Jim Carrey's character discovers that his life and surroundings are artificial and that the town he lives in is actually a giant movie studio?

B. Planning for People

In the midst of the devastation wrought by World War II, one of the planning giants of the previous century offered a stark assessment of the crucial role place played in shaping not just community, but character. Lewis Mumford, in The Social Foundations of Post-War Building 9-13 (1943), observed:

---

35. Professor Keller has continued to explore the meanings of community, and the way in which relationships are affected by the physical forms selected by developers and planners. *See* SUZANNE KELLER, COMMUNITY: PURSUING THE DREAM, LIVING THE REALITY (2003), a compelling study focusing on three decades of life in Twin Rivers—New Jersey's first planned unit development.

36. *Inside Seaside*, WASH. POST, Jan. 29, 2004, at H3.

In our anticipations of post-war planning, perhaps the most important thing to remember is that our task is not the simple one of rebuilding demolished houses and ruined cities. If only the material shell of our society needed repair, our designs might follow familiar patterns. But the fact is our task is a far heavier one; it is that of replacing an outworn civilization. The question is not how much of the superstructure should be replaced, but how much of the foundations can be used for a new set of purposes and for a radically different mode of life.

About the "great industrial towns of the last two centuries . . . ," Mumford instructed that "[n]o money income could make amends for a life-confinement in these dreary infernos: counterirritants, narcotics, aphrodisiacs, mechanized fantasies only increase the debasement they seek to alleviate." Not surprisingly, "those who wish better conditions find a temporary surcease, if not an effective permanent solution, on the outskirts." This is far from a solution, however:

> Where the automobile has been most freely used, the disorganization and disruption of our urban centers is most marked; Los Angeles and Detroit, both largely the creations of this new machine, are also its most conspicuous victims. But in one degree or another, the tendency to planless dispersion is world-wide; in a hundred futile ways people seek an individual solution for their social problem, and so ultimately create a second social problem.

The post-war challenge for planners, indeed for society, amounted to much more that the rebuilding of physical structures:

> The task for our age is to decentralize power in all its manifestations and to build up balanced personalities, capable of utilizing all our immense resources of energy, knowledge, and wealth without being demoralized by them. Our job is to repair the mistakes of a one-sided specialization that has disintegrated the human personality, and of a pursuit of power and material wealth that has crippled Western man's capacity for life-fulfillment. We must provide an environment and a routine in which the inner life can flourish, no less than the outer life . . . .

> In short, the balanced personality needs a balanced environment to support it, to encourage it, to give it the variety of stimuli and interests it needs in order to grow steadily and to maintain its equilibrium during this process. In purely urban terms—hence unbalanced in terms of man's fuller life-needs—the great metropolis provided this essential variety for man's occupational, professional, and political interests; and because of that fact the metropolis has played an indispensable part in the human economy since the seventeenth century. Now that the metropolis can no longer serve the new economy, except by helping to direct in the decentralization of its own power and authority, we must utilize the organizing and planning ability of the metropolis to achieve a much more comprehensive balance.

Do you think that the planners, planning lawyers, and judges engaged in contemporary zoning disputes dare share anything approaching this daunting vision? If not, is it because Mumford and his ilk were unrealistic about planning's potential, because the actors in land use disputes are focused on narrower issues, or for some other reason?

In response to criticisms that elitist intellectuals in the planning and other professions were too far removed from those affected most directly by their theories, Paul Davidoff (in *Advocacy and Pluralism and Planning*, 34 J. Am. Inst. Planners 331 (1965), among other works) and others countered with advocacy planning. Lisa R. Peattie, in *Reflections on Advocacy Planning*, 34 J. Am. Inst. Planners 80 (1968), noted that "we have developed a set of bureaucratic management institutions which often seem impersonal and alien to human feelings." As a result,

> it can well be argued that those most disadvantaged will be the people at the bottom of the system—those who are, through lack of education and of technical sophistication, particularly ill-prepared to deal with the presentation of issues in a technical framework. Such groups tend to be disadvantaged in the traditional political framework, and still more so when it comes to dealing with those who speak the language of maps, diagrams, and statistical tables. Advocacy planning has its origins initially in the perception that such groups need planners to make their case, to express their interests. Therefore, it represents a search by planners for new kinds of clientele.
>
> Advocate planners take the view that any plan is the embodiment of particular group interests, and therefore they see it as important that any group which has interests at stake in the planning process should have those interests articulated. In effect, they reject both the notion of a single "best" solution and the notion of a general welfare which such a solution might serve. Planning in this view becomes pluralistic and partisan—in a word, overtly political.

Do you think that "public interest" planners faced some of the same challenges and frustrations as the public interest lawyers of the 1960s who played important roles in the revolution in landlord-tenant law and in the environmental movement?[37]

Advocacy eventually gave way to empowerment, as many planners emphasized their role as facilitator rather than mouthpiece. This seems to be the equivalent of the modern lawyer who is trained to provide clients with the legal information that will enable them to make wise decisions for themselves. In Planning With Neighborhoods 3-5 (1985), William M. Rohe and Lauren B. Gates identified three types of neighborhood planning:

---

37. For a radical critique of this movement in law and planning, see Donald F. Mazziotti, *The Underlying Assumptions of Advocacy Planning: Pluralism and Reform*, 40 J. Am. Inst. Planners 38, 45 (1974):

> The argument made here with respect to the analogy between the advocate lawyer and planner is that the uncritical acceptance of such a comparison assumes that the adoption of the legal-advocate model will somehow establish an effective urban democracy, one in which citizens may be able to play an active role in the process of deciding public policy. The analogy is an extension of the pluralist faith that given the opportunity to be heard, the demands of competing groups will go through an adversary process through which the best decisions concerning planned community change will result. . . .
>
> As the socioeconomic organization of American society is based upon property rights and the balancing of public and private relations, so the law serves the most powerful property interests; as argued in the section dealing with the myth of pluralism, the masses of people and interest groups who have no direct connection to the bases of power are governed by rules intended to maintain and fortify existing power relationships. To the assertion that the adversary process establishes equality before the law, a radical critique of such a sweeping statement can be placed with a well-constructed and documented syllogism: law serves power, the law is made by those holding power, it perpetuates those in power, it decides what the tolerable limits of justice are—law is made by the power elite to protect and enshrine its own interests.
>
> From a conceptual and theoretical standpoint, the great majority of commentators on advocacy planning either explicitly or implicitly make inaccurate, misleading, and incongruent assumptions regarding the political economy within which advocacy must be made operational. Acceptance of the assumptions discussed here requires an endorsement of the political myth of pluralism, a posture which must ultimately embrace the status quo or the liberal-reformist approach to solving complex social problems, and the adoption of a set of tactical strategies which emulate existing professions so as to preserve centers of power and frustrate the notion of participatory democracy. . . .

The first involves independently organized efforts sponsored by indigenous neighbor-hood organizations. Although these organizations may receive grants from public agen-cies or private foundations, they are not sanctioned or controlled by them. These efforts typically aim to address a perceived problem or set of problems in the neighborhood through self-help or advocacy efforts.

The second form of contemporary neighborhood planning consists of federally spon-sored community development programs. Planners employed by local municipalities are charged with identifying problem areas, called neighborhood strategy areas (NSAs), developing a comprehensive rehabilitation program, and administering the implementa-tion of that program. Although citizens have opportunities to comment at several public hearings required by federal regulations, their involvement in designing and implement-ing improvements is often limited. Furthermore, program activities are typically limited to a relatively small number of neighborhoods compared to the total number in any city.

The third form comprises locally sponsored, city-wide neighborhood planning programs. These programs seek to involve all neighborhoods in public planning and municipal affairs. They are sponsored by municipal government, although federal funds are often used to subsidize their operation. Participating neighborhood groups become involved in a wide variety of issues, including zoning changes, evaluation of local service delivery, comprehensive planning, and local problem solving. . . .

Does this planner/lawyer analogue stand a better or worse chance of succeeding than advocacy planning? Do you think plans truly percolate from the bottom up, or is there any way to avoid top-down guidance from planning and legal "experts"?[38]

In a provocative essay entitled *The Two Cultures of Planning: Toward the New Pragmatism*, Land Use L. & Zoning Dig., July 1991, at 3, Stuart Meck, former president of the American Planning Association, identified four qualities of the "old culture of planning . . . derived from the govern-mental reform tradition of the late 19th and early 20th centuries, which also included the civil service movement and the city manager form of government":

First, the old culture believed that elected officials could not be trusted to plan, that planning was above politics; it removed the institutions of planning from their direct control. . . .

Second, the old culture believed in environmental or physical determinism—that one's physical surroundings affected behavior. . . .

Third, the old culture, reflecting the values of the dominant groups, believed in a middle-class lifestyle for all. . . .

---

38. The city of Plano, Texas, describes various phases of the neighborhood planning process—"the cycle we follow to cre-ate a new neighborhood action plan." The "research/analysis phase" leads to the "planning phase" (including a "vision-ing process" in which "residents develop a set of goals for the neighborhood"), followed by the "adoption" (by the city council) and "implementation phases" (in which "the plan is implemented by a collaborative group of organizations and individuals to enhance the neighborhood's quality of life"). The "evaluation phase" is described as "an ongoing part of the planning process, which consists of continuous monitoring and oversight of the programs past and present." *See* http://www.plano.gov/Departments/Planning/Long%20Range%20Planning/Neighborhood%20Planning/Pages/Plan-ning%20Process.aspx.

Fourth, the old culture, the result of a relatively stable environment, took the long view—20 to 30 years—because events weren't changing fast enough to cause it to alter its time span.

In contrast, the "New Pragmatism" "embraces politics, rather than rejects it"; "values the small scale and the intimate in the everyday environment over the monumental and imposing"; "recognizes that the city and the suburbs may no longer be middle class in the purist sense"; and "is less concerned about the long-term."

Meck identifies four causes for these definite shifts: (1) decisions from the courts imposing damages for regulatory takings; (2) a new perspective of land "as a resource as well as a commodity"; (3) pressure from citizen groups that are "smarter and tougher and more tenacious and who eye everything [planners] do with suspicion," leading to zoning by initiative and referendum; and (4) a greater state presence in the land use planning process. Many of the cases and materials included in this book are representative of the trends that Meck discusses.

C. New Urbanism: Restoration and Sustainability

Disturbed with the socioeconomic, aesthetic, and ecological problems plaguing our sprawling megalopolises, the Congress of New Urbanism (founded by a group of architects in 1993 and now also including members of the planning, development, law, and environmental communities among its leadership) offers an alternative vision. The Charter of the New Urbanism (found on the group's website—http://www.cnu.org/charter) is quite ambitious:

The Congress for the New Urbanism views disinvestment in central cities, the spread of placeless sprawl, increasing separation by race and income, environmental deterioration, loss of agricultural lands and wilderness, and the erosion of society's built heritage as one interrelated community-building challenge.

We stand for the restoration of existing urban centers and towns within coherent metropolitan regions, the reconfiguration of sprawling suburbs into communities of real neighborhoods and diverse districts, the conservation of natural environments, and the preservation of our built legacy.

We recognize that physical solutions by themselves will not solve social and economic problems, but neither can economic vitality, community stability, and environmental health be sustained without a coherent and supportive physical framework.

We advocate the restructuring of public policy and development practices to support the following principles: neighborhoods should be diverse in use and population; communities should be designed for the pedestrian and transit as well as the car; cities and towns should be shaped by physically defined and universally accessible public spaces and community institutions; urban places should be framed by architecture and landscape design that celebrate local history, climate, ecology, and building practice.

We represent a broad-based citizenry, composed of public and private sector leaders, community activists, and multidisciplinary professionals. We are committed to reestablishing the relationship between the art of building and the making of community, through citizen-based participatory planning and design.

We dedicate ourselves to reclaiming our homes, blocks, streets, parks, neighborhoods, districts, towns, cities, regions, and environment.

Some of the leading figures of the New Urbanist movement call for a reconnection between the design of human built communities and nature. Peter Calthorpe, in The Next American Metropolis: Ecology, Community, and the American Dream 25-26 (1993), presented this provocative perspective on the role of nature in the planning process:

> Nature should provide the order and underlying structure of the metropolis. Ridgelands, bays, rivers, ocean, agriculture, and mountains form the inherent boundaries of our regions. They set the natural edge and can become the internal connectors, the larger common ground of place. They should provide the identity and character that unifies the multiplicity of neighborhoods, communities, towns, and cities which now make up our metropolitan regions. Preservation and care for a region's natural ecologies is the fundamental prerequisite of a sustainable and humane urbanism. . . .
>
> At the regional scale, the man-made environment should fit into and along natural systems. Urban limit lines or growth boundaries should be set to preserve major natural resources at the edge of metropolis. This line should be large enough to accommodate growth for the next generation but small enough to encourage infill, redevelopment, and density at the core. Within this regional boundary major natural features and streams should form an internal structure of park-like linkages, trails, and bikeways throughout the metropolis. Such open space elements should link and limit individual communities. In these areas the natural systems should be preserved and repaired.
>
> At the scale of the neighborhood, parks and open space should stop occupying residual space or "buffer" zones between segregated uses. They should be used as formative elements, providing the focus and order of the neighborhood. Neighborhood parks could be smaller and more accessible, and have a strong civic character. Every child should be able to walk safely to a neighborhood park, a park that need not be "naturalist" but should be of the place, socially and ecologically. Such parks can become the foundation of a memorable unique public domain for each neighborhood, community, or town.

For more on Calthorpe's vision, including details on his firm's projects including Regional Plans, Urban Revitalization, Community Design, and International Masterplans, see http://www.calthorpe.com/projects.

Andres Duany et al., in Suburban Nation: The Rise of Sprawl and the Decline of the American Dream 258-60 (2000), used the term "neotraditionalism" to describe New Urbanism,

> because the New Urbanism's intention is to advocate what works best: what pattern of development is the most environmentally sensitive, socially responsible, and economically sustainable. As is often the case, what seems to work best is a historic model—the traditional neighborhood—adapted as necessary to serve the needs of modern man.
>
> The commonsense nature of the New Urbanism bodes well for its future. The fact that it was not invented, but selected and adapted from existing models, dramatically distinguishes it from the concepts of total replacement that preceded it. It took many years and many failures for planners and architects to reach this point, but so many new inventions have fared so badly that designers have been forced to put some faith

in human experience. Further experience will no doubt modify the precepts and techniques of the New Urbanism, but that is as it should be.[39]

Do you think it is possible to preserve nature and to have human-designed communities, or is sustainable development an oxymoron? Consider the role that lawyers play in making the transition to this "neotraditionalist" vision possible. In many instances, attorneys will be called upon to help dismantle existing comprehensive plans and zoning ordinances that may have contributed to the problems of sprawl targeted by New Urbanists. But how does the lawyer distinguish those general principles and specific provisions worth saving from those that are dispensable? Where do individual, as opposed to community, rights and protections fit into this equation, and can we count on non-lawyers to protect those interests adequately? Finally, should it be up to consumer law practitioners to blow the whistle on the many exurban developments that today are labeled "New Urbanist" by their developers, although these developments will lead to the same problems of congestion and aesthetic clutter that plague older suburban communities?

D. Updating the Planning Toolbox

The course of planning practice has long been tied to developing technologies. In the early years of the profession according to The Practice of Local Government Planning 41, 42 (Charles J. Hoch et al. eds., 3d ed. 2000),

> [p]lanners depended on printed national census reports that were soon out of date. Local information on land ownership, land use, and land use controls had to be gathered from paper maps, and from voluminous printed volumes that were often incomplete, inconsistent, and outdated. Planning analysis and communication required laborious (and error-prone) computations, hand copying of information, and manual typing of maps and graphs.

From the 1960s to the 1970s, the move was made from data processing to management information systems (MIS) and geographic information systems (GIS). As the 20th century closed, planners were employing computer models, the Internet, and other decision support systems (DSS) and planning support systems (PSS). Not all attempts to integrate computer technology have been successful, particularly when the goals were too ambitious and the equipment too meager. GIS has proved to be one of the most promising technologies, not only in planning but also in many planning-related fields such as transportation, ecology, geology, taxation, and sociology. According to Elliot Allen and Randy Goers, in *Beyond Maps: The Next Generation of GIS*, Planning, Sept. 2002, at 26-27:

> The new generation of GIS tools can empower planners and citizens in three ways:
>
> *Accessibility*: GIS technology is increasingly accessible, both to professional planners using distributed desktop systems and to citizens doing community mapping via the Internet. In some cases, tools are showing up at public meetings for real-time use during deliberations.

---

39. Authors' note: *See* Beth Dunlop, *The New Urbanists: The Second Generation*, ARCHITECTURAL REC., Jan. 1997, at 132:

    A new generation of New Urbanists is coming of age. No less fervent or idealistic than their mentors, these latter-day New Urbanists carry the movement's banner but are unafraid to diverge a bit. Responding in part to criticism that the first wave of New Urbanist projects were mostly middle-class, suburban developments comfortably buffeted from the hard realities of urban America, the second generation of New Urbanists (as well as many of the first generation) are now applying the principles of traditional town planning to a wider range of projects—including ones in the inner city and third-world countries.

Analysis: The new tools produce much more than colorful maps because GIS technology can now create complex models. Community data can be turned into insightful evaluations of alternative plans and development impacts.

Action: Perhaps most exciting about these GIS tools is their interactivity and relevance to real world decision making. Non-technical users can create scenarios "on-the-fly," get immediate feedback on the implications of their choices, and reach consensus on outcomes much more quickly. [40]

Does the website for your hometown, the community in which you are attending school, or the place in which you plan to work after graduation have on-line GIS? If so, what kind of data other than zoning and land use are available for display and analysis?[41] With the availability of GIS maps and other data on the Internet, is it too much to expect that the future will see a lot more do-it-yourself planning and less reliance on experts?

IV. Putting Theory and Practice Together: The Legal Effect of the Plan

There is probably no phrase that has caused more consternation in all of land use planning law than "in accordance with a comprehensive plan." The meaning and legal import of these six words, included in the standard act circulated by Secretary Herbert Hoover's Department of Commerce and then adopted by more than 40 state legislatures in the early decades of the 20th century, have generated mounds of expert commentary[42] and reams of case pleadings and court opinions. Section 1 of the SZEA, titled "Purposes in View," reads as follows:

---

40. Authors' note: For further reading on the use of GIS by planners, community organizations, and citizens, see Emily Talen, *Bottom-Up GIS: A New Tool for Individual and Group Expression in Participatory Planning*, 66 J. Am. Planning Ass'n 279 (2000): ("[I]n addition to using GIS to inform and analyze in a conventional sense, planners should consider using it as a cognitive tool. In this alternative approach, residents learn to manipulate GIS data to express their views about planning issues, neighborhood meaning, and future preferences."); Robert B. Kent & Richard E. Klosterman, *GIS and Mapping: Pitfalls for Planners*, 66 J. Am. Planning Ass'n 189 (2000) (some of the mistakes noted in the article are "Failing to Understand the Purpose of the Map," "Trying to Improve Accuracy by 'Zooming In,'" "Neglecting Map Projections and Coordinate Systems," and "Failing to Evaluate and Document Map Sources").

41. The data downloads available on the Gainesville, Florida, GIS page include the official city limits, future land use, zoning, historic districts and buildings, redevelopment areas, special area plans, and wellfield protection zones. The GIS Map Library features two dozen maps on subjects ranging from zoning and future land use to enterprise zones, neighborhood groups and organizations, creeks, annexation history, and park and recreation sites. *See* http://www.cityofgainesville.org/ GOVERNMENT/CityDepartmentsNZ/PlanningDepartment/DataDownloads/tabid/257/Default.aspx *and* http://www. cityofgainesville.org/GOVERNMENT/CityDepartmentsNZ/PlanningDepartment/MapLibrary/tabid/259/Default.aspx.

42. Representative articles include Charles M. Haar, *In Accordance with a Comprehensive Plan*, 68 Harv. L. Rev. 1154 (1955); Carol M. Rose, *Planning and Dealing: Piecemeal Land Controls as a Problem of Local Legitimacy*, 71 Cal. L. Rev. 839 (1983); and Charles L. Siemon, *The Paradox of "In Accordance With a Comprehensive Plan" and Post Hoc Rationalizations: The Need for Efficient and Effective Judicial Review of Land Use Regulations*, 16 Stetson L. Rev. 603 (1987).

In his 1955 article, Professor Haar, at 1174, articulated the fundamental problem of zoning without planning, which was a reality in most of the states that had passed an enabling act authorizing local governments to engage in zoning but had not passed planning enabling legislation:

It is difficult to see why zoning should not be required, legislatively and judicially, to justify itself by consonance with a master plan . . . . It might even be argued that any zoning done before a formal master plan has been considered and promulgated is per se unreasonable, because of failure to consider as a whole the complex relationships between the various controls which a municipality may seek to exercise over its inhabitants in furtherance of the general welfare. Granted that this argument would have small chance of success because of judicial precedent, there is still strong reason for legislative action on the state level to make accordance with a master plan a statutory requirement for zoning regulation. Such a requirement will mean that the municipal legislature has an ever-present reminder of long-term goals which it has been forced to articulate, and will give lesser play to the pressures by individuals for special treatment which tend over a period of years to turn the once uniformly regulated district into a patchwork. Further it will give courts a standard for review more sharply defined than the reasonable *in vacuo* test upon which they are now forced so largely to rely.

By the end of the century, several jurisdictions, by statutes, court decisions, or both, had moved in the direction urged by this article, with mixed results.

Such regulations shall be made in accordance with a comprehensive plan[43]and designed to lessen congestion in the streets; to secure safety from fire, panic, and other dangers; to promote health and the general welfare; to provide adequate light and air; to prevent the overcrowding of land; to facilitate the adequate provision of transportation, water, sewerage, schools, parks, and other public requirements. Such regulations shall be made with reasonable consideration, among other things, to the character of the district and its peculiar suitability for particular uses, and with a view to conserving the value of buildings and encouraging the most appropriate use of land throughout the municipality.[44]

Were the drafters of the SZEA acting naively or with the utmost (or, should we say, "valorous") discretion when they failed to provide further elaboration?

The two cases that follow illustrate two extreme judicial (and legislative) positions related to the "in accordance" requirement. Do you think that the members of the Missouri Legislature, when they originally voted in favor of a version of the SZEA, anticipated that, even several decades later, some municipalities would still not have a plan that was distinct from a zoning ordinance or map? If so, how could they have made that intent more clear? If not, why do you think they chose to authorize planning without requiring the development of a separate comprehensive plan?

STATE *EX REL.* CHIAVOLA v. VILLAGE OF OAKWOOD
886 S.W.2d 74 (Mo. Ct. App. 1994),
cert. denied, 514 U.S. 1078 (1995)

Lowenstein, Presiding Judge.

This appeal stems from a trial court determination that the single zoning ordinance (Ordinance No. 10) of the Village of Oakwood (Oakwood), which allows only single family residential usage in Oakwood: (1) is unconstitutional on due process grounds; and (2) [*sic*] as being infirm because Oakwood failed to develop a comprehensive plan under § 89.040, RSMo 1986. The Appellant, Oakwood, is a small bedroom community located in Clay County, and is a suburb of Kansas City. Oakwood consists of 80 single family dwellings on 80 platted lots.

The Plaintiffs/Respondents (Landowners) filed a multi-count petition. The trial court granted summary judgment on Count I which prayed for a declaration that Ordinance No. 10, and "all zoning ordinances" of Oakwood, were unconstitutional both facially, and as applied to Landowners and for the municipality's failure to have a separate comprehensive plan. The remaining counts, which prayed for damages under several theories, were not reached since they hinged on the ruling of Count I. . . .

At the very heart of this appeal lies the issue of whether a Missouri municipality may enact valid zoning ordinances without having first formally adopted a "comprehensive plan," under §

---

43. Authors' note: The drafters inserted the following footnote here—"With a comprehensive plan: This will prevent haphazard or piecemeal zoning. No zoning should be done without such a comprehensive study."

44. Authors' note: Even more than 80 years after the SZEA was first circulated, many states still have identical or nearly identical versions of §3 in their statute books. The diverse list of states includes, among several others, Alabama, Connecticut, Delaware, Iowa, Louisiana, New York, North Dakota, Oklahoma, and Wisconsin. In a few instances, state lawmakers made minor adjustments to incorporate special needs. *See, e.g.,* Colo. Rev. Stat. §31-23-303 ("to promote energy conservation"); Conn. Gen. Stat. §8-2: ("Such regulations may, to the extent consistent with soil types, terrain, infrastructure capacity and the plan of conservation and development for the community, provide for cluster development . . . in residential zones."); and Wyo. Stat. §15-1-601: ("With consideration given to the historic integrity of certain neighborhoods or districts and a view to preserving, rehabilitating and maintaining historic properties and encouraging compatible uses within the neighborhoods or districts, but no regulation made to carry out the purposes of this paragraph is valid to the extent it constitutes an unconstitutional taking without compensation.").

89.040, which provides that regulations on zoning and districts ". . . shall be made in accordance with a comprehensive plan . . . ."

Summary judgment was granted on the portion of Landowners' petition which sought declaratory relief from Oakwood's only ordinance, Ordinance No. 10, relating to zoning and land use. Ordinance No. 10 was adopted in 1955, shortly after residents of a housing subdivision were incorporated as a village under § 80.020 RSMo 1986. The ordinance limited the use of the 80 lots comprising Oakwood to single-family residential use with a lot size of 30,000 square feet.

Oakwood is now bordered by a major thoroughfare, North Oak Trafficway (North Oak), as well as a portion of Kansas City and other villages in Clay County. North Oak carries approximately 25,000 cars per day and contains many commercial properties in the other municipalities it passes through.

In 1981 the Landowners, Chiavola and Flott purchased a house in Oakwood located on a six acre lot. They sought to rezone the portion of their land which abuts North Oak, approximately 4.7 acres, for commercial use. Oakwood's zoning commission, and later its trustees, denied the rezoning petition. The circuit court reversed, holding among other reasons; Ordinance No. 10 was invalid because Oakwood had not previously adopted a "comprehensive plan" pursuant to chapter 89, and the ordinance would not suffice as both the zoning "plan" and the zoning ordinance. As a result of the demise of Ordinance No. 10 Oakwood presently has no zoning ordinance on any land within its boundaries.

Ordinance No. 10 was the product of an Oakwood Zoning Commission hearing held in February, 1955, which recommended to the Trustees that the boundaries of Oakwood be zoned as "one residential district." Attached to the Commission's report was a description of the 80 lot plats of Oakwood. The report and subsequent ordinances provided for streets and parks but no commercial areas. This ordinance was passed in March, 1955. Although amendments were made to Ordinance No. 10 in 1966 and 1967, Oakwood has limited the land use to single-family dwellings. . . .

Standard of Review

Since zoning and refusal to rezone are legislative acts, this court reviews de novo any challenges to their validity. This court is to first determine whether or not the legislative judgement was fairly debatable, and if it is, then the decision must stand. Euclid v. Ambler Realty Co., 272 U.S. 365, 71 L. Ed. 303, 47 S. Ct. 114 (1926); Binger v. Independence, 588 S.W.2d 481 (Mo. banc 1979). There is a presumption of validity for zoning ordinances; the presumption is rebuttable, but Landowners bear the burden of proving Ordinance No. 10 is unreasonable in order to successfully rebut the presumption. Where there is uncertainty regarding the reasonableness of a zoning regulation, it is to be resolved in the government's favor.

I. Constitutional Attack

A. Reasonableness . . .

Here the zoning regulation, calling for singe-family residential use, is facially reasonable. The general plan, as it can be inferred from Ordinance No. 10, its amendments via subsequent ordinances, and the development of Oakwood, was to establish a small bedroom community consisting of 80 homes. The ordinance provided for the single-family homes, churches and community buildings, public parks, and accessory uses customarily incident to the other allowable uses not involving the conduct of business or industry. This court can not say the zoning ordinance does not bear a substantial relationship to public health, safety, morals or general welfare and, therefore, is unreasonable or, that the detriment to Landowners outweighs the public benefits.

B. Comprehensive Single Use Zoning

The judgment also infers the ordinance is facially unconstitutional because it provides for only one type of zoning . . . single-family residential. . . .
The Village of Oakwood is a bedroom community which has been divided into 80 lots and borders the neighboring city of Gladstone near North Oak Trafficway, Barry Road and Vivion Road (all heavily traveled thoroughfares). There are numerous commercial facilities located a short distance from Oakwood. Given the nature of the community, it was appropriate for Oakwood to zone all of the land in its boundaries as single-family residential.

C. Comprehensive Plan

Contrary to the assertion by Landowners, there is no requirement for the existence of a separate comprehensive plan in order for a zoning regulation to be constitutional. While the existence of a separate well-delineated plan may make it easier to establish an appropriate use of Oakwood's police power, and the reasonableness of the regulation or ordinance, it is not a constitutional requirement. If it were a constitutional requirement, all zoning prior to the enactment of § 89.040 which requires all zoning to be done "in accordance with the comprehensive plan," would have been unconstitutional. Furthermore, even if it were a constitutional requirement, a plan may be inferred from Ordinance No. 10, and Oakwood's subsequent zoning ordinances (specifically ordinances 33, 46, 48, and 66), that Oakwood planned on being a small residential bedroom community.

II. Statutory Attack

The second part of the appeal is that Ordinance No. 10 is invalid due to Oakwood's failure to provide a comprehensive plan pursuant to § 89.040 RSMo 1986. § 89.040 provides:
> Such regulations *shall be made in accordance with a comprehensive plan* and designed to lessen congestion in the streets; to secure safety from fire, panic and other dangers; to promote health and the general welfare; to provide adequate light and air . . . . Such regulations shall be made with reasonable consideration, among other things, to the character of the district and its peculiar suitability for particular uses, and with a view to conserving the values of buildings and encouraging the most appropriate use of land throughout such municipality. (emphasis added).

In their petition, Landowners assert in their petition, since there is not a separate document or documents designated as the "comprehensive plan," Oakwood did not comply with the statute. Remember that the requirement of a plan is based on the premise that zoning regulations are not an end in and of themselves, but are the means to the end to sound planning for the public good. Zoning "does no more than apply the rules of good housekeeping to public affairs. It keeps the kitchen stove out of the parlor, the bookcase out of the pantry, and the dinner table out of the bedroom." Lebanon v. Woods, 153 Conn. 182, 215 A.2d 112, 121 (Conn. 1965) (Murphy, J., dissenting) (citing Metzenbaum, Law of Zoning (1930) p.6) (Judge Murphy dissents because the zoning provision in *Woods* did not regulate use in addition to the area). The requirement of a comprehensive plan is not a "mere technicality which serves only as an obstacle for public officials to overcome in carrying out their duties" but, rather, is the essence of zoning. Udell v. Haas, 21 N.Y.2d 463, 235 N.E.2d 897, 900-901, 288 N.Y.S.2d 888 (N.Y. 1968). Without a plan there can be no rational allocation of land use. The crux of this appeal is the question: what form must a comprehensive plan take in order to comply with § 89.040?

There is no definition of a comprehensive plan in chapter 89, governing zoning and planning of municipalities in Missouri. The language used in the Missouri statute mirrors that used in the Standard State Zoning Enabling Act, which has acted as the model for a majority of the states— i.e., all regulations must be "in accordance with the comprehensive plan." While there is not an exact definition, it can be said that a:

> "plan" connotes an integrated product of a rational process and "comprehensive" requires something beyond a piecemeal approach, both to be revealed by the ordinance in relation to the physical facts and the purposes authorized by [statute]. Kozesnik v. Montgomery, Twp., 24 N.J. 154, 131 A.2d 1 (N.J. 1957). . . .

No additional guidance is provided for the 89.040 language "comprehensive plan" in the statutes. This court therefore, looks to other jurisdictions for guidance. The notes accompanying the 1926 version of the Standard State Zoning Enabling Act indicate:

> ". . . the draftsman intended to require some planning as an integral part of the zoning process. It is equally clear that no provision for the preparation or adoption of a written plan beyond the text of the zoning ordinance was spelled out in the act or referred in the notes. It remained for the courts to give dimension to the requirement that zoning regulations be made in accordance with a comprehensive plan." Dawson Enterprises Inc v. Blaine County, 98 Idaho 506, 567 P.2d 1257, 1260 (Idaho 1977) (citing 1 Anderson, American Law of Zoning § 5.03, p. 265 (2nd Ed. 1976)).

This court finds the better reasoned cases, as they apply to the fact pattern at hand, are those which do not require a comprehensive plan separate and apart from the zoning ordinance itself. This court holds a comprehensive plan may be validly enacted in an ordinance itself without existing in some form separate from the ordinance. *See* Furtney v. Simsbury Zoning Com., 159 Conn. 585, 271 A.2d 319 (Conn. 1970); Lebanon v. Woods, 153 Conn. 182, 215 A.2d 112 (Conn. 1965); Dawson Enterprises, Inc. v. Blaine County, 98 Idaho 506, 567 P.2d 1257 (Idaho 1977) (superseded by legislative act requiring passage of a comprehensive plan prior to zoning ordinances); Drake v. Craven, 105 Idaho 734, 672 P.2d 1064 (Idaho App. 1983); Nottingham Village Inc. v. Baltimore County, 266 Md. 339, 292 A.2d 680 (Md. 1972); Allred v. Raleigh, 7 N.C. App. 602, 173 S.E.2d 533 (N.C. App. 1970); Kozesnik v. Montgomery, 24 N.J. 154, 131 A.2d 1 (N.J. 1957); Asian Americans for Equality v. Koch, 72 N.Y.2d 121, 527 N.E.2d 265, 531 N.Y.S.2d 782 (N.Y. 1987); Osiecki v. Huntington, 170 A.D.2d 490, 565 N.Y.S.2d 564 (A.D. 2 Dept. 1991). See Bousquet v. Transportation Ins. Co., 354 Mass. 152, 235 N.E.2d 807 (N.Y. 1968); Columbia Oldsmobile Inc. v. City of Montgomery, 56 Ohio St. 3d 60, 564 N.E.2d 455 (Ohio 1990); Tulsa Rock Co. v. Board of County Comm'rs, 531 P.2d 351, 357 (Okla. App. 1974); Bruno v. Brown, 414 Pa. 361, 200 A.2d 405 (Pa. 1964); Bell v. Elkhorn, 122 Wis. 2d 558, 364 N.W.2d 144 (Wisc. 1985). Comprehensiveness may be found in the fact the ordinance zones all, or substantially all, of a political subdivision; that it regulates all uses; or that it covers all of the usual factors of land utilization, height area and use. Haar, In Accordance with a Comprehensive Plan, 68 Harv.L.Rev. 1154, 1158-1167 (1955).

First, in looking at the statutes themselves, there is no mandate requiring Oakwood to adopt a separate plan as a condition precedent to the enactment of the ordinance. Furthermore, "the general rule has become . . . that, absent specific requirements in enabling legislation, the comprehensive plan need not have a separate physical existence apart for the zoning ordinances, and it need not be in writing, but its design may be found in the scheme apparent in the zoning regulations themselves." Dawson, 567 P.2d at 1261 (cites omitted). Where the enabling statute expressly requires the adoption of a comprehensive plan as a condition precedent to the passage of zoning regulations and ordinances, then a different result must occur. *Id.* at 1262; Baker v. Milwaukie, 17 Ore. App. 89, 520 P.2d 479 (Ore. App. 1974); Pro-Eco v. Board of Comm'rs, 956 F.2d 635 (7th Cir. 1992).

There are a number of cases from other jurisdictions which have been faced with the issue now before this court.

Kozesnik v. Montgomery Twp., 24 N.J. 154, 131 A.2d 1 (N.J. 1957), an oft-cited case, is one of the earlier cases to attack this question. In *Kozesnik*, the plaintiff landowners challenged the validity of amendments to zoning ordinances of two townships, Hillsborough and Montgomery, proposed by a rock mining company (Minnesota Mining and Manufacturing Co.). The amendments permitted the mining company to quarry and process rock in Hillsborough and establish a plant to color the rock for roofing granules in Montgomery. At the time of the application for amendment the relevant areas were zoned for agricultural or residential uses. Both townships had few people living in them; most of the land in the townships was used for farming, a few businesses were also there.

Plaintiffs contended the amendments were not in accordance with the comprehensive plan. Their first argument was that there could not be a comprehensive plan unless it was evidenced in writing separate from the regulation itself. The court said a "plan" connoted an integrated product of a rational process and "comprehensive" requires something beyond a "piecemeal approach," which was evidenced by the ordinance considered in relation to the physical facts and purposes as authorized by the New Jersey statute. *Id.* at 7. The court held the plan did not have to have a separate physical form . . . the "plan may readily be revealed in an end-product—here the zoning ordinance—and no more is required by statute." *Id.* at 8. . . .

In Osiecki v. Huntington, 170 A.D.2d 490, 565 N.Y.S.2d 564 (A.D. 2 Dept. 1991) the court held there need not be a separate plan where the plaintiffs challenged the zoning of its land, (approximately five and one-half acres) for residential use. The neighboring properties were not of the same zoning or use. Two parcels to the west were zoned for commercial office buildings and have been used as such; the property to the south and east are zoned residential, but were used for farm and water district purposes by the Town.

Similarly, this court finds that Oakwood acted in conformance with its comprehensive plan because the preamble to the ordinance indicated an intent to create a single residential district with the same boundaries as the incorporated Oakwood; because there was a meeting by the trustees of the village which appointed a zoning commission to meet and make recommendations regarding regulations. The board met and the notice for a public hearing was given. The commission made its final record at the meeting and recommended the ordinance be enacted. The ordinance was subsequently enacted. The ordinance was comprehensive in scope; setting out both the area, height, and use requirements. Since there is evidence that planning was done, and there is no specific requirement that the village pass a separate comprehensive plan as a condition precedent to the passage of zoning ordinances. This court finds that Ordinance No. 10 was both constitutionally and statutorily valid.

This opinion does not stand for the proposition that a municipality, no matter what its size, does not have to adopt a comprehensive plan separate from the zoning ordinance. What was sufficient for Oakwood in this case, an ordinance which provided comprehensive zoning for a single land use, and which evidenced future plans for the community, will not necessarily suffice for all larger towns or cities. . . .

As the following case indicates, many Florida voters took a strong pro-planning stance, providing the impetus for state lawmakers to respond with a mandate that comprehensive plans be passed and followed. Do you think the appellate court took that popular and legislative support too far in granting standing to the neighbor and in affirming a most extreme remedy? Is there a one-size-fits-all happy medium between the approaches of the Show Me and Sunshine States, or are there differences (political, demographic, ecological, or historical) that justify such divergent approaches?

PINECREST LAKES, INC. v. SHIDEL
795 So. 2d 191 (Fla. Ct. App. 2001), *rev. denied*, 821 So. 2d 300 (2002)

FARMER, J.

The ultimate issue raised in this case is unprecedented in Florida. The question is whether a trial court has the authority to order the complete demolition and removal of several multi-story buildings because the buildings are inconsistent with the County's comprehensive land use plan. We conclude that the court is so empowered and affirm the decision under review.

Some twenty years ago, a developer purchased a 500-acre parcel of land in Martin County and set out to develop it in phases. Development there is governed by the Martin County Comprehensive Plan (the Comprehensive Plan).[1] Phase One of the property was designated under the Comprehensive Plan as "Residential Estate," meaning single-family homes on individual lots with a maximum density of 2 units per acre (UPA). The Comprehensive Plan provides that

> "[w]here single family structures comprise the dominant structure type within these areas, new development of undeveloped abutting lands *shall be required* to include compatible structure types of land immediately adjacent to existing single family development."

Phases One through Nine were developed as single-family homes on individual lots in very low densities.

The subject of this litigation, Phase Ten, is a 21-acre parcel between Phase One and Jensen Beach Boulevard, a divided highway designated both as "major" and "arterial." Phase Ten was designated by the Comprehensive Plan as "Medium Density Residential" with a maximum of 8 UPA. The developer sought approval of three different site plans before finally erecting the buildings that are the subject of this litigation. In 1988, the developer first sought approval for an initial scheme of 3-story apartment buildings with a density of just under 8 UPA. Karen Shidel, since 1986 an owner of a single-family residence in the adjoining area of Phase One, along with other residents, opposed the project proposed by the developer. This initial site plan for Phase Ten was approved by the County but never acted upon.

Five years later the developer changed the proposed scheme to single family residences, and the County Commission approved a revised site plan for 29 single-family homes with a density of 1.37 UPA. Two years after that, however, the developer again changed its mind and returned to its original concept of multi-family structures. This time, the developer sought to develop 136 units in two-story buildings, with a density of 6.5 UPA. The County's growth management staff recommended that the County Commission approve this second revised site plan for Phase Ten. Following a hearing at which a number of people objected to the proposal, including Shidel, the County

---

1. *See* §163.3167(2), Fla. Stat. (2000) ("Each local government shall prepare a comprehensive plan of the type and in the manner set out in this act or shall prepare amendments to its existing comprehensive plan to conform it to the requirements of this part in the manner set out in this part.")

Commission approved the revision and issued a Development Order[2] for Phase Ten permitting the construction of 19 two-story buildings.

Claiming statutory authority, Shidel and another Phase One homeowner, one Charles Brooks, along with the Homeowners Associations for Phases One through Nine, then filed a verified complaint with the Martin County Commission challenging the consistency of the Development Order with the Comprehensive Plan, requesting rescission of the Development Order. In response to the verified complaint, after a hearing the County Commission confirmed its previous decision to issue the Development Order.

Shidel and Brooks then filed a civil action in the Circuit Court against Martin County under the same statutory authority. They alleged that the Development Order was inconsistent with the Comprehensive Plan. The developer intervened. Shidel and Brooks argued that their statutory challenge was a de novo proceeding in which the court should decide in the first instance whether the Development Order was consistent with the Comprehensive Plan. Martin County and the developer argued that the proceeding was in the nature of appellate review in which the County's determination was entitled to deference and the court should consider only whether there was substantial competent evidence supporting the Development Order. Basing its decision solely on a review of the record created before the County Commission, the trial court found that the Development Order was consistent with the Comprehensive Plan and entered final judgment in favor of the developer.

At that point, the developer took stock of its position. It had prevailed before the County Commission and—at least initially—in the trial court. Technically, however, its approval for the project was not final. Developer considered whether to proceed to construct the buildings or instead await appellate review of the trial court's decision. Ultimately the developer decided to commence construction, notwithstanding the pendency of an appeal. Accordingly, it applied for and received building permits for construction of Buildings 8, 9, 10, 11 and 12, and started on each of those buildings while the case was under consideration in court. When construction was just beginning, Shidel and Brooks sent written notice to the developer of their intention, should they prove successful in court, to seek demolition and removal of any construction undertaken while judicial consideration of the consistency issue was pending.

Appellate review did not produce the outcome for which the developer had hoped. In 1997 we reversed the trial court's decision that the County's consistency determination complied with the Comprehensive Plan. Poulos v. Martin County, 700 So. 2d 163 (Fla. 4th DCA 1997). Specifically, we concluded that section 163.3215 required de novo consideration in the trial court on the consistency issue. . . . We remanded the case for a trial de novo and for any appropriate relief.

On remand, the trial judge proceeded in two stages: the first stage involved a determination whether the Development Order was consistent with the Comprehensive Plan; and the second stage, which became necessary, addressed the remedy. While the case was pending on remand, developer continued with construction. The County conducted final inspections of Building 11 and 12, issuing certificates of occupancy (CO), and residents moved into the buildings. At the end of the consistency phase, the trial court entered a partial judgment finding that the Development Order was not consistent with the Comprehensive Plan. The trial de novo then proceeded to the remedy.

At the conclusion of the remedy phase, the trial court entered a Final Judgment. The court found that the Comprehensive Plan established a hierarchy of land uses, paying deference to lower

---

2. *See* §163.3164(7) and (8), Fla. Stat. (2000) ("'Development permit' includes any building permit, zoning permit, sub-division approval, rezoning, certification, special exception, variance, or any other official action of local government having the effect of permitting the development of land. . . . 'Development order' means any order granting, denying, or granting with conditions an application for a development permit.").

density residential uses and providing protection to those areas. The "tiering policy" required that, for structures immediately adjacent to each other, any new structures to be added to the area must be both comparable and compatible to those already built and occupied. The court then found significant differences between the northern tier of Phase One and the adjacent southern tier of Phase Ten. The structures in Phase One were single level, single family residences, while the structures in Phase Ten were two-story apartment buildings with eight residential units. Therefore, the court found, the 8-residential unit, two-story, apartment buildings in Phase Ten were not compatible or comparable types of dwelling units with the single family, single level residences in Phase One; nor were they of comparable density. Consequently, the court determined, the Development Order was inconsistent with the Comprehensive Plan.

As regards the remedy, the Final Judgment found no evidence indicating that either Brooks or the Homeowners Association were damaged by any diminution in value. The court found that the Homeowners Association was not a person within the meaning of section 163.3215(2) and therefore had no standing to seek relief under section 163.3215. Accordingly, only plaintiff Shidel was entitled to seek injunctive relief under section 163.3215. In granting such relief, the court found that the developer had acted in bad faith. Specifically, the court found that the developer continued construction during the pendency of the prior appeal and continued to build and lease during the trial—even after losing on the consistency issue. The court found that the developer "acted at [its] own peril in doing precisely what this lawsuit sought to prevent and now [is] subject to the power of the court to compel restoration of the status prior to construction." The relief awarded was:

(1)   the Court permanently enjoined Martin County from taking any further action on the subject Development Order for Phase Ten, other than to rescind it;

(2)   the Court permanently enjoined developer and its successors in interest from any further development of Phase Ten under the subject Development Order; and

(3)   the Court ordered developer to remove all apartment buildings from Phase Ten either through demolition or physical relocation by a date certain.

When the Final Judgment was entered, five of the eight-unit buildings had been constructed in Phase Ten (Buildings 8-12). Buildings 11 and 12 had already received their CO's, and fifteen of their sixteen units were actually occupied. Building 10 was fully completed and was awaiting final inspection as of the date the remedies stage of trial began. Buildings 8 and 9 were 50% and 66% completed, respectively, also as of that date.

Following the entry of Final Judgment, the developer filed this timely appeal and moved for a stay pending review. The trial court granted a stay only as to the demolition order, allowing lessees to continue in possession of those apartments in Buildings 9-12 under actual lease when the trial court entered final judgment, as well as to those leases in Building 8 in existence as of the date of filing of the notice of appeal. The developer was prohibited, however, from entering into any renewals of existing leases upon expiration of the original term or any new leases of any apartments. Upon review, we affirmed the stay order. We now explain our decision on the merits.

I. The Consistency Issue

Initially the developer argues that the trial court erred in the consistency phase by failing to accord any deference to the County Commission's interpretation of its own Comprehensive Plan when the County approved the second revised site plan and its multi-story, multi-family buildings. Conceding that the proceedings are de novo and that the Development Order is subject to "strict scrutiny" under the Comprehensive Plan as to the consistency issue, the developer nevertheless argues that the court must bow to the County's interpretation of its own Comprehensive Plan and the application of its many elements to the site plan. Developer argues that the statutes and cases accord such deference to a local government's interpretation of its own Comprehensive Plan and that it was reversible error for the trial court in this case to fail to do so. In particular, developer relies on Southwest Ranches Homeowners Ass'n v. Broward County, 502 So. 2d 931 (Fla. 4th DCA 1987), and B.B. McCormick & Sons, Inc. v. City of Jacksonville, 559 So. 2d 252 (Fla. 1st DCA 1990). According to developer, these cases authorize the use of the highly deferential "fairly debatable" standard of review—customary with zoning decisions—to land use determination such as the issue of consistency in this case. We disagree. . . .

[T]he applicable statute provides that:

> "any aggrieved or adversely affected party may maintain an action for injunctive or other relief against any local government to prevent such local government from taking any action on a development order . . . which materially alters the use or density or intensity of use on a particular piece of property that is not consistent with the comprehensive plan . . . ."

§ 163.3215(1), Fla. Stat. (2000). This statute obviously creates an action for an injunction against the enforcement of a development order, rather than to carry out such an order. The statute is aimed at development orders—which, by their very nature, must have been approved by a local government—so it is clear that the Legislature did not mean that local governments or developers would be the parties seeking injunctive relief under this provision.

Moreover there is but one basis for issuing the injunction: that the development order is not consistent with the Comprehensive Plan to the detriment of adjoining property owners. Hence the issuance of an injunction under section 163.3215(1) necessarily requires the judge to determine in the first instance whether a development order is consistent with the Comprehensive Plan. When a statute authorizes a citizen to bring an action to enjoin official conduct that is made improper by the statute, and that same statute necessitates a determination by the judge in the action as to whether the official's conduct was improper under the statute, as a general matter the requirement for a determination of the propriety of the official action should not be understood as requiring the court to defer to the official whose conduct is being judged. While the Legislature could nevertheless possibly have some reason to require some deference to the officials whose conduct was thus put in issue, we would certainly expect to see such a requirement of deference spelled out in the statute with unmistakable clarity. Here it is not a question of any lack of clarity; the statute is utterly silent on the notion of deference. It is thus apparent that the structure and text of the statute do not impliedly involve any deference to the decision of the county officials. So we necessarily presume none was intended.

Section 163.3194 requires that all development conform to the approved Comprehensive Plan, and that development orders be consistent with that Plan.[11] The statute is framed as a rule, a command to cities and counties that they must comply with their own Comprehensive Plans after they have been approved by the State. The statute does not say that local governments shall have some discretion as to whether a proposed development should be consistent with the Comprehensive Plan. Consistency with a Comprehensive Plan is therefore not a discretionary matter. When the Legislature wants to give an agency discretion and then for the courts to defer to such discretion,

---

11. See §163.3194(1)(a), Fla. Stat. (2000) ("After a comprehensive plan . . . has been adopted in conformity with this act, *all development* undertaken by, and all actions taken in regard to development orders by, governmental agencies in regard to land covered by such plan or element *shall be consistent with such plan* or element as adopted.").

it knows how to say that. Here it has not. We thus reject the developer's contention that the trial court erred in failing to defer to the County's interpretation of its own comprehensive plan.

Before we proceed to assess the trial court's determination on the consistency issue, we pause to consider the history of the land development statutes. The State of Florida did not assert meaningful formal control over the explosive and unplanned development of land in this state until the passage of the first growth management statute, the Local Government Comprehensive Planning Act of 1975. Chapter 75-257, Laws of Fla. (the 1975 Act). The 1975 Act forced counties and cities to adopt comprehensive plans, but they were left to interpret such plans for themselves, largely free from effective oversight by the state. The requirement of a adopting a Comprehensive Plan was, therefore, only a small step. Moreover nothing in the legislation required local governments to comply with their own Comprehensive Plans or that all development be consistent with the Plan.

By the early 1980's it was widely recognized that the 1975 Act was proving ineffectual in regulating Florida's development. The lack of state control over interpretation of the Comprehensive Plan was often cited as a serious deficiency. As one such criticism described the situation:

> "[f]rustration grew at the state level as well. Lacking the actual power to approve or disapprove local planning decisions, state and regional planners could not effectively coordinate and oversee local planning and regulation. Local governments changed their plans 'willy-nilly virtually every time a city council or county commission met . . .'"

John M. DeGrove, *State and Regional Planning and Regulatory Activity: The Florida Experience and Lessons for Other Jurisdictions*, C390 ALI-ABA 397, 428 (1994).

For another thing, the 1975 Act was criticized for failing to give affected property owners and citizen groups standing to challenge the land development decisions of local governments on the grounds that they were inconsistent with the Comprehensive Plan. . . .

Again, to return to the criticism, this limitation on standing to enforce local planning laws resulted in:

> "a failure to conform development decisions to the plan based upon the fact that citizens lacked standing to challenge development orders for lack of consistency with the comprehensive plan."

James C. Nicholas & Ruth L. Steiner, *Growth Management and Smart Growth in Florida*, 35 Wake Forest L. Rev. 645, 657 (2000) (quoting Daniel W. O'Connell, *Growth Management in Florida: Will State and Local Governments Get Their Acts Together?*, Florida Envt'l & Urban Issues, 1-5 (June 1984)). If affected property owners in the area of newly permitted development could not challenge a project on the grounds that it would be inconsistent with the Comprehensive Plan, that eliminated the only real check on local government compliance—a challenge by those most directly affected by a proposed development.

The growing pressure for a fundamental change in the growth management law is reflected in the following statement made just prior to the Legislature's adoption of the current law in 1985:

> "In response to this lack of citizen standing, a citizen initiative began last year and thousands of signatures were collected around the state to bring the standing issue to a referendum vote. The petition specifically calls for a referendum on the issues of giving citizens a right in the state constitution to environmental health and welfare and providing them with legal standing to sue if government at the local, regional, or state level is not doing its job.

> "That initiative fell just a few thousand signatures short of the required number for qualifying for a referendum in 1984. However, the initiative is continuing, and I feel

confident that the issue will be brought to the voters of the state in 1985 unless the legislature addresses the issue more effectively than it did last year."

Kathleen Shea Abrams, *An Environmental Word*, 1 J.Land Use & Envt'l Law 155, 159 (1985).
Clearly the pressure from a "civically militant electorate" was growing, and the elected representa-
tive took notice of it. The result was the Growth Management Act of 1985. Chap. 8555, Laws of
Fla. . . . Its most important provision for our purposes was section 163.3215, the provision used by
Shidel to bring this action into court. . . .

[T]he criticism described above certainly was of great influence in the 1985 Legislature's formulation of the new standing provision. Affected citizens have been given a significantly enhanced
standing to challenge the consistency of development decisions with the Comprehensive Plan. . . .

The Growth Management Act of 1985 was discussed in what is now recognized as the most
significant land use decision by the supreme court in the past decade, namely Board of County
Commissioners of Brevard County v. Snyder, 627 So. 2d 469 (Fla. 1993). Snyder involved a parcel
then zoned only for single family homes and a proposed development of 5-6 units. The proposal
also necessarily required a change of zoning. After substantial opposition, and in spite of a favorable staff recommendation, the County voted to deny the request without giving any reasons.
Certiorari was denied in the circuit court, one judge dissenting. The Fifth District held that rezoning actions entailing the application of a general rule or policy to specific individuals, interests,
or activities are quasi-judicial in nature and should be subjected to a stricter standard of judicial
review. The court found that the proposed site plan was consistent with the Comprehensive Plan,
that there was no evidence supporting the denial of any necessary rezoning, and that the denial of
the request without giving any reasons was arbitrary and unreasonable.

After granting review, the supreme court was first concerned with the level of review given by
the courts to such proceedings. . . .

The court explained that in Florida the 1975 Act "was substantially strengthened by the
Growth Management Act [of 1985]." 627 So. 2d at 473. After analyzing various provisions of the
Growth Management Act of 1985, the court stated:

> "We also agree with the court below that the review is subject to strict scrutiny. In prac-
> tical effect, the review by strict scrutiny in zoning cases appears to be the same as that
> given in the review of other quasi-judicial decisions. *See* Lee County v. Sunbelt Equities,
> II, Ltd. Partnership, 619 So. 2d 996 (Fla. 2d DCA 1993) (The term 'strict scrutiny' arises
> from the necessity of strict compliance with comprehensive plan.). This term as used in
> the review of land use decisions must be distinguished from the type of strict scrutiny
> review afforded in some constitutional cases."

627 So. 2d at 475. . . .

In light of this history, deferential review of the kind advocated by developer here is no longer
the rule after *Snyder*.

Under section 163.3215 citizen enforcement is the primary tool for insuring consistency of
development decisions with the Comprehensive Plan. Deference by the courts—especially of the
kind argued by the developer in this case—would not only be inconsistent with the text and
structure of the statute, but it would ignore the very reasons for adopting the legislation in the
first place. When an affected property owner in the area of a newly allowed development brings a
consistency challenge to a development order, a cause of action—as it were—for compliance with
the Comprehensive Plan is presented to the court, in which the judge is required to pay deference
only to the facts in the case and the applicable law. In light of the text of section 163.3215 and the

foregoing history, we reject the developer's contention that the trial court erred in failing to defer to the County's interpretation of its own Comprehensive Plan.

Having thus decided that the trial court was correct in failing to accord any particular deference to the Martin County Commission in its interpretation of the Comprehensive Plan, we now proceed to consider the court's determination on the consistency issue. . . .

We have carefully reviewed the record of the trial and the evidence presented. It is apparent that there is substantial competent evidence to support these findings. Developer argues that the court erred in its interpretation of the "tiering policy," in deeming it a mandatory requirement rather than a discretionary guide. We conclude that the trial court's construction is consistent with the plain meaning of the text of the Comprehensive Plan. *See* Comprehensive Plan, § 4-5(A)(2)(b) ("a density transition zone of comparable density and compatible dwelling unit types shall be established in the new project for a depth from the shared property line that is equivalent to the depth of the first tier of the adjoining development's lower density (i.e. the depth of the first block of single-family lots)."). Moreover, given the evidence as to Martin County's adoption of the tiering policy, the record clearly supports the finding that the policy was intended to be applied in all instances of projects abutting single-family residential areas. We therefore affirm the finding of inconsistency and proceed to explain our decision on the remedy.

II. Remedy of Demolition

Developer challenges what it terms the "enormity and extremity of the injunctive remedy imposed by the trial court." It argues that the trial court's order requiring the demolition of 5 multi-family residential buildings is the most radical remedy ever mandated by a Florida court because of an inconsistency with a Comprehensive Plan. Specifically, the contention is that the trial judge failed to balance the equities between the parties and thus ignored the evidence of a $3.3 million dollar loss the developer will suffer from the demolition of the buildings. The court failed to consider alternative remedies in damages, it argues, that would have adequately remedied any harm resulting from the construction of structures inconsistent with the Comprehensive Plan. Developer maintains that the trial court erroneously failed to give meaningful consideration to the traditional elements for the imposition of injunctive relief. It contends that the trial court proceeded on an erroneous conclusion that where an injunction is sought on the basis of a statutory violation, no proof is required as to the traditional elements for an injunction.

Traditionally, as the trial judge noted, it is true that injunctions are usually denied where the party seeking such relief fails to demonstrate a clear legal right, a particular harm for which there is no adequate remedy at law, and that considerations of the public interest would support the injunction. These are, of course, the necessary ingredients for equitable relief when we labor in the interplay of common law and equity, where ordinary legal remedies are unavailing.

Nonetheless, as between the State legislature and the several counties, the Legislature is the dominant creator of public duties and citizen rights. Recognizing that the Legislature has the sole power to create such public duties and citizens rights, it logically follows that the Legislature is necessarily endowed with the authority to specify precisely what remedies shall be used by judges to enforce a statutory duty—regardless of whether in general usage such a remedy usually requires additional factors before it is traditionally employed.

When the Legislature creates a public duty and a corresponding right in its citizens to enforce the duty it has created, and provides explicitly that the remedy of vindication shall be an injunction, the Legislature has not thereby encroached on judicial powers . . . .

In our view when the Legislature provides for an injunction in these circumstances, it has deliberately made the new public duty and its corresponding right of enforcement an integrated statutory prescription. By specifying that the public interest requires that a certain duty be vindicated in the courts and not primarily within other branches of government, the Legislature is well within its powers. Surely the Legislature's primary role in defining public policy under the constitution is broad enough to enable it to specify a legal remedy in an enactment, regardless of whether the traditional judicial restrictions on that remedy in other, non-statutory contexts would limit its usage. As the author of the primary duty, the Legislature alone shapes the form of its effectuating mechanism.

In section 163.3215, we think the Legislature has constructed such a statute. The statute leads off with a declaration that:

> "Any aggrieved or adversely affected party may maintain an action for injunctive or other relief against any local government to prevent such local government from taking any action on a development order, as defined in s. 163.3164, which materially alters the use or density or intensity of use on a particular piece of property that is not consistent with the comprehensive plan adopted under this part."

From the plain and obvious meaning of this text we discern only two elements to the granting of an injunction against the enforcement of a development order: (a) the party is affected or aggrieved by (b) an approved project that is inconsistent with the Comprehensive Plan. In short, the existence of an affected neighbor is all that is necessary for the issuance of an injunction against a proposed land use that is inconsistent with the Comprehensive Plan. . . .

Developer lays great stress on the size of the monetary loss that it claims it will suffer from demolition, as opposed to the much smaller diminution in value that the affected property owner bringing this action may have suffered. It contends that a $3.3 million loss far outweighs the evidence of diminution in the value of Shidel's property, less than $26,000. Its primary contention here is that the trial judge erred in failing to weigh these equities in its favor and deny any remedy of demolition. Instead, as developer sees it, the court should have awarded money damages to eliminate the objector's diminution in value. Developer also argued that instead of demolition it should be allowed to build environmental barriers, green areas of trees and shrubbery, between the apartment buildings and the adjoining area of single family homes.

Developer emphasizes that we deal here with an expensive development: "a high quality, upscale project;" "forty units of high-quality, upscale apartments;" "five upscale multi-family dwellings, housing 40 garden apartments, as a value of approximately $3 million." Developer concedes that there is evidence showing that plaintiff Shidel's property is diminished by $26,000. It also concedes that the total diminution for all the homes bordering its project is just under $300,000. Developer contends, however, that the real countervailing harm to all these affected property owners in the vicinity is not any diminution in the value of their homes, but instead is merely "knowing that there is an upscale apartment building approximately a football field away, partially visible through some trees behind the house."

Section 163.3215 says nothing about weighing these specific equities before granting an injunction. If the legislature had intended that injunctive enforcement of comprehensive plans in the courts be limited to cases where such imbalances of equities were not present, we assume that it would have said so. As important, such balancing if applied generally would lead to substantial non-compliance with comprehensive plans. We doubt that there will be many instances where the cost of the newly allowed construction will be less than any diminution resulting from an inconsistency. Entire projects of the kind permitted here will frequently far exceed the monetary harms caused to individual neighbors affected by the inconsistency. In other words, if balancing the equities—that is, weighing the loss suffered by the developer against the diminution in value of the objecting party—were required before demolition could be ordered, then demolition will never be ordered.

Moreover it is an argument that would allow those with financial resources to buy their way out of compliance with comprehensive plans. In all cases where the proposed use is for multiple acres and multiple buildings, the expenditures will be great. The greater will be its cost, and so will be a resulting loss from an after-the-fact demolition order. The more costly and elaborate the project, the greater will be the "imbalance in the equities." The more a developer is able to gild an inconsistency with nature's ornaments—trees, plants, flowers and their symbiotic fauna—the more certain under this argument will be the result that no court will enjoin an inconsistency and require its removal if already built.

In this case the alleged inequity could have been entirely avoided if developer had simply awaited the exhaustion of all legal remedies before undertaking construction. It is therefore difficult to perceive from the record any great inequity in requiring demolition. Shidel let the developer know when it was beginning construction of the first building that she would seek demolition if the court found the project inconsistent. . . .

It also seems quite inappropriate, if balancing of equities were truly required by this statute, to focus on the relatively small financial impacts suffered by those adjoining an inconsistent land use. The real countervailing equity to any monetary loss of the developer is in the flouting of the legal requirements of the Comprehensive Plan. Every citizen in the community is intangibly harmed by a failure to comply with the Comprehensive Plan, even those whose properties may not have been directly diminished in value.

We claim to be a society of laws, not of individual eccentricities in attempting to evade the rule of law. A society of law must respect law, not its evasion. If the rule of law requires land uses to meet specific standards, then allowing those who develop land to escape its requirements by spending a project out of compliance would make the standards of growth management of little real consequence. It would allow developers such as this one to build in defiance of the limits and then escape compliance by making the cost of correction too high. That would render section 163.3215 meaningless and ineffectual. . . .

The statute says that an affected or aggrieved party may bring an action to enjoin an inconsistent development allowed by the County under its Comprehensive Plan. The statutory rule is that if you build it, and in court it later proves inconsistent, it will have to come down. The court's injunction enforces the statutory scheme as written. The County has been ordered to comply with its own Comprehensive Plan and restrained from allowing inconsistent development; and the developer has been found to have built an inconsistent land use and has been ordered to remove it. The rule of law has prevailed.

We therefore affirm the final judgment of the trial court in all respects.

Notes

1. Is *Pinecrest Lakes* a fact pattern just begging for a Coasean solution? Given the value to the developer of the "illegal" units ($3 million) and the financial harm suffered collectively by the neighbors ($300,000), in the absence of transaction costs, would a negotiated settlement between the directly affected parties have resulted in the destruction of those units? Does the court offer a solid, independent reason for granting the injunction other than the judges' interpretation of the relevant statutes?

2. In Board of County Comm'rs v. Crow, 170 P.3d 117, 118 (Wyo. 2007), the state supreme court affirmed the trial court's decision not to order "abatement of the 3,000 square feet of habitable

space that the Crows added to the house in violation of the LDRs [Land Development Regulations]." The court explained that "[i]mmediately following the issuance of a certificate of occupancy for the 8,000 square foot home, the Crows enlarged the home to 11,000 square feet by converting porches to habitable space, and by flooring in rooms with cathedral ceilings so as to provide more habitable space." The supreme court noted the remedy in *Pinecrest Lakes*, but concluded that the lower "court's balancing of the equities was supported by the evidence and within the court's sound discretion." The Crows did receive an alternative punishment for their violation of the zoning ordinance; they were assessed fines totaling over $700,000, which neither side appealed.

V.   Environmental Regulation and Land Use Planning: Common Ground and Important Distinctions

Land use planning and environmental regulation are often confused in practice and in legal analysis. Local governments are becoming increasingly active in the regulation and control of the environmental impact of activities that occur within their borders.[45] Typically, this local regulation is in compliance with or complementary to federal and state standards and mandates. Indeed, many federal environmental laws encourage state and local experimentation, as long as minimal safety standards are not violated.

Even Supreme Court Justices have split over the distinction between these two sets of controls. In California Coastal Commission v. Granite Rock Co., 480 U.S. 572, 587-88 (1987), a decision involving the validity of a permit imposed by a state agency on mining activities in a national forest, Justice Sandra Day O'Connor wrote for the majority, which held that the federal Mining Act of 1872 did not preempt the permit requirement under the California Coastal Act. She explained:

> The line between environmental regulation and land use planning will not always be bright; for example, one may hypothesize a state environmental regulation so severe that a particular land use would become commercially impracticable. However, the core activity described by each phrase is undoubtedly different. Land use planning in essence chooses particular uses for the land; environmental regulation, at its core, does not mandate particular uses of the land but requires only that, however the land is used, damage to the environment is kept within prescribed limits. Congress has indicated its understanding of land use planning and environmental regulation as distinct activities. . . . 43 U. S. C. § 1712(c)(9) [part of the Federal Land Policy and Management Act of 1976] requires that the Secretary of the Interior's land use plans be consistent with state plans only "to the extent he finds practical." The immediately preceding subsection, however, requires that the Secretary's land use plans "provide for compliance with applicable pollution control laws, including State and Federal air, water, noise, or other pollution standards or implementation plans." § 1712(c)(8). Congress has also illustrated its understanding of land use planning and environmental regulation as distinct activities by delegating the authority to regulate these activities to different agencies. The stated purpose of part 228, subpart A of the Forest Service regulations, 36 CFR § 228.1 (1986), is to "set forth rules and procedures" through which mining on unpatented claims in national forests "shall be conducted so as to minimize adverse environmental impacts on National Forest System surface resources." The next sentence of the subsection, however, declares that "[i]t is not the purpose of these regulations to provide for the

---

45. For two provocative collection of essays on this topic, see JOHN R. NOLON, NEW GROUND: THE ADVENT OF LOCAL ENVIRONMENTAL LAW (Envtl. L. Inst. 2002); and CRAIG ANTHONY (TONY) ARNOLD, WET GROWTH: SHOULD WATER LAW CONTROL LAND USE? (Envtl. L. Inst. 2005).

management of mineral resources; the responsibility for managing such resources is in the Secretary of the Interior." Congress clearly envisioned that although environmental regulation and land use planning may hypothetically overlap in some instances, these two types of activity would in most cases be capable of differentiation. Considering the legislative understanding of environmental regulation and land use planning as distinct activities, it would be anomalous to maintain that Congress intended any state environmental regulation of unpatented mining claims in national forests to be per se preempted as an impermissible exercise of state land use planning. Congress' treatment of environmental regulation and land use planning as generally distinguishable calls for this Court to treat them as distinct, until an actual overlap between the two is demonstrated in a particular case.

Justice Lewis Powell, joined by Justice John Paul Stevens, begged to differ, at 601, 603 n.5:

[T]he Court nevertheless holds that the Coastal Commission can require Granite Rock to secure a state permit before conducting mining operations in a national forest. This conclusion rests on a distinction between "land use planning" and "environmental regulation." In the Court's view, the [federal statutes] indicate a congressional intent to pre-empt state land use regulations, but not state environmental regulations. I find this analysis unsupportable, either as an interpretation of the governing statutes or as a matter of logic. . . .

The lack of statutory support for the Court's distinction is not surprising, because—with all respect—it seems to me that the distinction is one without a rational difference. As the Court puts it: "Land use planning in essence chooses particular uses for the land; environmental regulation, at its core, does not mandate particular uses of the land but requires only that, however the land is used, damage to the environment is kept within prescribed limits." This explanation separates one of the reasons for Forest Service decisions from the decisions themselves. In considering a proposed use of a parcel of land in the national forest, the Forest Service regulations consider the damage the use will cause to the environment as well as the federal interest in making resources on public lands accessible to development. The Forest Service may decide that the proposed use is appropriate, that it is inappropriate, or that it would be appropriate only if further steps are taken to protect the environment. The Court divides this decision into two distinct types of regulation and holds that Congress intended to pre-empt duplicative state regulation of one part but not the other. Common sense suggests that it would be best for one expert federal agency, the Forest Service, to consider all these factors and decide what use best furthers the relevant federal policies.

In the years since the *Granite Rock* decision, the "environmentalization" of land use controls has accelerated at a significant pace.

Many local governments are striking out on their own without federal and state mandates. They place heavy emphasis on ecological criteria in making their zoning and planning decisions, provide for conservation and preservation through their growth management programs, restrict development that has a negative impact on visual access, and outlaw real estate development activities that are deemed dangerous to human and nonhuman life.

Similarly, federal and state lawmakers over the last few decades have entered the land use planning arena with increasing frequency. Congress requires bureaucrats who manage federal lands to produce and follow detailed land use plans. The federal government has provided seed money to states and localities through the Coastal Zone Management Act so that well-balanced and effective land use plans can be developed for coastal areas. Additionally, federal controls on criteria air pollutants have had a direct impact on the commuting patterns to and from central cities and an indirect impact on local planning decisions. Since the "quiet revolution" that began in the 1970s, even more states have taken up planning approval functions either statewide or in areas deemed environmentally sensitive. Some states, feeling the pressure from federal waste treatment and disposal legislation, have intervened in local planning decisions that concern the siting of treatment and disposal sites. Other states have brought local zoning and planning decisions under the umbrella of state environmental policy acts.

Some major problems exist with the "environmentalization" phenomenon. First, because there is no barrier separating land use planning from environmental regulation, local officials often operate in a realm in which they have little expertise and even less control over negative externalities. The spillover effects are greater, the public health and private property stakes are higher, and the opportunities for abuse (for example, cloaking discrimination or outright confiscation of private lands for public use) are greater in the absence of administrative law protections, interest group give and take, and technical expertise.

Second, activist judges can use the corruption, haphazardness, and prejudice frequently associated with local land use planning and zoning to rationalize greater activism in the area of environmental regulation—at local, state, and federal levels. It is very tempting for judges who believe strongly in the protection of private property rights to jump on the anti-environmental bandwagon. In other words, confusing the two realms of regulation of the use and abuse of land invites judicial interference with elected officials by some judges.

Third, decisionmaking in private real estate markets is frustrated because of the ambiguities of decisional law on the boundary between private property rights and public protection and because of the merging of land use planning and environmental law tools and analysis. Developers put a premium on predictability when it comes to regulatory schemes, and multiple layers of environmental regulation can prolong the already protracted period between land assembly and construction.

It is much too late to call for the segregation of land use planning and environmental regulation, in theory and in practice. It may be noncontroversial to assert that planning and zoning are designed to function as preemptive tools to separate discordant land uses, to enhance and maintain real property values for the community as a whole, and to accommodate growth and change when and where they are needed. Similarly, we can appreciate that lawmakers often intend modern, federal environmental statutes to serve as reactive controls designed to ensure that human life and health are protected from a wide range of harms. However, the proliferation of hybrid and duplicative regulations and the discomfort with the kind of hairsplitting found in *Granite Rock* illustrate the difficulty involved in drawing meaningful distinctions in practice.[46]

VI. The Role of the Land Use Attorney

The objectives of a legal system may complement or conflict with those of a land use planning system. On the one hand, in 1953, a most distinguished planner, Dennis O'Harrow, wrote in an editorial in the official newsletter of the American Society of Planning Officials:

> It is my belief, based on bitter experience, that (a) with few exceptions, attorneys have not the faintest knowledge of zoning theory; and (b) with the exception of those cities that have had the foresight to assign a special assistant corporation counsel to the plan-

---

46. Much of the discussion in these paragraphs derives from Michael Allan Wolf, *Fruits of the "Impenetrable Jungle": Navigating the Boundary Between Land-Use Planning and Environmental Law*, 50 Wash. U. J. Urb. & Contemp. L. 5 (1996).

ning and zoning department, the chief planner in a city is much more familiar with zoning law than the corporation counsel's office. So don't let yourself be pushed around.

On the other hand, in Planning Problems of Town, City, and Region 201 (1925), Harlan Bartholomew (for many years the head of one of the largest planning firms), could opine:

> Most of the favorable decisions on zoning appear to me to be the result of a clear expression of ideas and the principles in the minds of city planners by competent lawyers. I should like to cite two illustrations. Two years ago the Ware case in Wichita, Kansas, was decided by the Supreme Court in favor of the constitutionality of zoning. More recently Mr. Ware brought a whole series of cases involving practically every phase of zoning. When these cases came before the court, the city was represented by an exceedingly able city attorney who presented to the courts the broader aspects of zoning and only ten days ago one of the most cleancut and remarkable decisions in favor of zoning was handed down. . . .

Success in the practice of land use planning law is not marked by courtroom victories. Indeed, the existence of a lawsuit is, in nearly all instances, an indication that the lawyering on all sides has failed. The best land use attorneys work closely, comfortably, and respectfully with professional planners, especially those who advise municipal planning commissions and local legislators, with representatives of neighborhood organizations, and with developers and builders. Negotiation and compromise, not deposition and interrogatory, are their specialities. Perhaps most importantly, they are skilled in explaining to nonlawyers the legal import of the database of demographic, socio-economic, financial, ecological, architectural, and historical information that comprises a real-life zoning, planning, or eminent domain situation. A great deal of listening and questioning precedes articulation. Undoubtedly the interdisciplinary and intractable nature of land use problems will necessitate the perseverance of this close but uneasy alliance between planning and law.

Chapter Two

The Limitations of *"Sic Utere Tuo . . ."*: Planning by Private Law Devices

I. Identifying Problems With Judicial Reconciliation of Discordant Uses of Land

As suggested in Chapter One, and demonstrated in the chapters that follow, since the 1920s, zoning and planning have comprised the primary system of land use regulation in America. Zoning ordinances are local enactments, and the adoption of large-scale zoning changes is typically viewed as a legislative act. There is a large dose of administrative law in local land use law as well, especially when landowners seeking variances ask boards of adjustment or zoning appeals to resolve their plight. In fact, laissez-faire mythmaking to the contrary, statutes and ordinances regulating the use of real property date back to early American history. In *Colonial Land Use Law and Its Significance for Modern Takings Doctrine*, 109 Harv. L. Rev. 1252, 1257 (1996), John F. Hart has shown us that

> [c]ontrary to the conventional image of minimal land use regulation, government in the colonial period often exerted extensive authority over private land for purposes unrelated to avoiding nuisance. Colonial lawmakers often regulated private landowners' usage of their land in order to secure public benefits, not merely to prevent harm to health and safety. Indeed, the public benefits pursued by such legislative action included some that consisted essentially of benefits for other private landowners. Legislatures often attempted to influence or control the development of land for particular productive purposes thought to be in the public good. Legislatures compelled owners of undeveloped land to develop it, beyond what was required by the original grants, and compelled owners of wetlands to participate in drainage projects. Owners risked losing preexisting mineral rights if they failed to conduct their mining with sufficient promptness. Owners of land suitable for iron forges risked losing their land if they declined to erect such forges themselves. In towns and cities, landowners were constrained by measures intended to channel the spatial pattern of development, to optimize the density of habitation, to promote development of certain kinds of land, and to implement aesthetic goals.[1]

Despite this proto-regulation, the predominant form of land use regulation until the early decades of the 20th century was common, that is, judge-made, law.

By the end of the 19th century, American judges and lawyers had developed five common-law tools to address or avoid conflicts between competing property owners over the use and abuse of land: (1) private nuisance; (2) trespass to land; (3) public nuisance; (4) defeasible fees; and (5)

---

1. Authors' note: See also John F. Hart, *Land Use Law in the Early Republic and the Original Meaning of the Takings Clause*, 94 Nw. Univ. L. Rev. 1099 (2000).

restrictive covenants. While these legal doctrines are often conceptually related, each is technically a discrete area of Anglo-American property or tort law for which judges and commentators, over the course of decades (even centuries), have developed a separate set of doctrines, operating rules, and exceptions. It became clear by the early decades of the 20th century that no one method or even any combination of these five methods could perform the important task of protecting landowners from the negative impacts of their neighbors' use of land while respecting all property owners' important constitutional, statutory, and common-law rights.

Private nuisance law—a tort action typically brought by one landowner against a neighboring or nearby owner who unreasonably and substantially interferes with the first owner's use and enjoyment of real property—has in many instances provided neighbors with some protections against actual or impending injuries and disturbances. Another tort action—trespass to land—is often confused with private nuisance. The key to recovering under a trespass theory is the physical invasion of another's property without the owner's consent. The slightest invasion *in theory* can lead a successful trespass action. Still, courts have long struggled to decide whether landowners whose homes, stores, and other structures crack, break, and suffer other physical damage because of the activities of others should prevail in trespass in the absence of a demonstration of an actual physical intrusion. Chiefly for this reason, trespass to land has not proved to be an effective device for regulating competing land uses located in the same general vicinity.

Even before the existence of residential zoning, many new neighborhoods throughout America were created as havens for single-family homes, and these enclaves were often protected by covenants and equitable servitudes. Dolores Hayden, in Building Suburbia: Green Fields and Urban Growth, 1820-2000, at 61-62 (2003), has noted:

> When landscape designer Frederick Law Olmsted and his partner, Calvert Vaux, were asked to design Riverside, Illinois, in 1869, they were already well known for their work on New York's Central Park. Olmsted held a critical view of many of the subdivisions going up on the outskirts of cities after the Civil War. . . .
>
> [A]t Riverside, Olmsted designed a small business district around the railroad station. . . . Lots were fairly regular and boosting the price of the lots was his job. He was sure some owners would build ugly or unsuitable houses, but "they shall not be allowed to force them disagreeably upon our attention." He wrote a covenant requiring that houses be set back thirty feet from the road and that each owner have one or two trees in the planting strip between the house and the street. This was the first of many restrictive covenants for suburban communities drafted by the Olmsted office over the next decades.[2]

Even after the triumph of zoning, these neighborhood restrictions have remained important complementary tools.

Sometimes developers employed defeasible fees, with much less success in the long run.[3] And, in instances where an activity posed harms to the community at large, not just to an isolated set of neighboring landowners, local and state governments resorted to public nuisance laws, which threatened offenders with fines, abatement, or even imprisonment.

---

2. Authors' note: *See also* Robert Fishman, Bourgeois Utopias: The Rise and Fall of Suburbia (1987); Evan McKenzie, Privatopia: Homeowner Associations and the Rise of Residential Private Government (1994), Marc A. Weiss, The Rise of the Community Builders: The American Real Estate Industry and Urban Land Planning (1987); Robert M. Fogelson, Bourgeois Nightmares: Suburbia, 1870-1930 (2005); and Gerald Korngold, *The Emergence of Private Land Use Controls in Large-Scale Subdivisions: The Companion Story to* Village of Euclid v. Ambler Realty Co., 51 Case W. Res. L. Rev. 617 (2001).

3. *See* Timothy Stoltzfus Jost, *The Defeasible Fee and the Birth of the Modern Residential Subdivision*, 49 Mo. L. Rev. 695 (1984).

In reality, zoning and planning never replaced private nuisance, servitudes, and public nuisance. Sometimes these common-law alternatives fill in the gaps of an improperly drawn zoning map or of an unworkable comprehensive plan. At other times, neighbors choose to impose greater restrictions on themselves than are deemed wise or permissible by government officials. The relationship between zoning and its precursors is a complex one, rendered even more perplexing by technological changes such as solar energy devices and by ideological shifts on courts charged with balancing regulatory needs with private rights.

The primary concern of this chapter, then, is to illustrate the judicial treatment of conflicts that date from a time of unplanned urban life, when an increasing population pressed on diminishing quantities of land. Where competing land interests vie to dominate, the court is the traditional forum for decision. Realistically evaluated within the framework of the conventional syntax in which the courts operate, such decisions may be regarded as planning and zoning by the judiciary. The history of this process affords insight into the attempt by society to develop a coherent and efficient ordering of land uses. In this field of sharp human conflict arising out of the interdependence of land, we can appreciate the contributions, as well as the limitations, of the judicial process.

It is apparent that protection of the environment can be enhanced by updating the common law, but there are limits to such tinkering. The doctrines and remedies of private and public nuisance remain relevant to the contemporary lawyer who must pay careful attention to how common-law devices dovetail with the "administrative" techniques of land use planning that are widely available and with today's extensive body of federal and state administrative law mandating protection of the environment and preservation of scenic beauty.

The cases and materials included in this chapter raise some intriguing questions: How does a court evaluate the pertinent factors in land use disputes? How does it ascertain the value placed by the community on a particular land use in comparison with other uses? Is there a generally accepted scale of social values relating to land uses to which courts can refer? Can some land use activities be said to produce a direct public benefit, while others are to be carried on primarily for the benefit of the individual? Does judicial resolution of conflicts here reflect, in its results, the social, economic, and political convictions of the dominant class? How does a court become informed of the bases of competing claims? How can it ascertain the existing land use pattern, or likely future development, or the ideal development? How can it determine the suitability of a particular activity to a locality, or the size of the neighborhood with which a use should be compatible? How often, in fact, have judges' decisions coincided with what we would today label "good land use planning"? How does the process of judicial decisionmaking differ from that of the urban or suburban planner? Granting the difficulties, in our society, where courts are traditionally the first-line institutions for adjusting disputes, are there real alternatives? Should the vagaries and ambiguities of the common law yield to the relative certainty of administrative rules and regulations? Are the problems instead attributable to the adversarial mode of resolution?

II. Private Nuisance: Protecting the Use and Enjoyment of Private Land

No plot of land, to borrow John Donne's phrase, is "intire of itselfe." Its value depends upon its physical location with respect to other land, and upon the line drawn by society between the privilege of use and the interest of surrounding owners in the untrammeled use of their land. Private nuisance doctrines, which have evolved case by case over the centuries, reveal those limitations on a landowner's freedom that the equal (and potentially competitive) rights of his or her neighbors impose. Or, as the distinguished philosopher Morris R. Cohen, in *Property and Sovereignty*, 13 Cornell L.Q. 8, 21 (1927), phrased the converse:

To permit anyone to do absolutely what he likes with his property in creating noise, smells, or danger of fire, would be to make property in general valueless. To be really effective, therefore, the right of property must be supported by restrictions or positive duties on the part of the owners, enforced by the state as much as the right to exclude others which is the essence of property.

The "law" of private nuisance is a property-tort hybrid. The tort concept stresses the wrongfulness of conduct and the relation of nuisance to intentional, negligent, or ultrahazardous behavior. The property concept emphasizes the private interest—the use and enjoyment of land to which the courts have accorded legal protection. From either viewpoint courts may be seen to be teasing out the scope and extent of interests in land, delimiting at the same time both the owner's power of free use and the neighbor's power to veto such use.

What is now called "public" or "common" nuisance—where control by the sovereign for a public purpose is involved[4]—is also considered in this chapter. True, the law here has developed along different lines from private nuisance, and the two are far apart conceptually. Yet historically there has been an overlap between the class of crimes known as purprestures and cases covered by the 13th-century assize of nuisance. The interplay is often crucial in the relations of landowners. Courts still weave the terms together. An action may exist for both a public and private nuisance at one and the same time. Elements of modern litigation, such as the recovery of special damages in a "private" public nuisance suit, the availability of citizen suits under environmental statutes, and the bringing of mass tort suits that join dozens or more plaintiffs in one action, cause even further blurring.[5]

A. Distant Origins

The roots of private nuisance reach back several centuries, as illustrated by this report of an early 14th-century decision, Raising a Covert to the Nuisance, Y.B. 33-35 Edw. 1 (R.S.) 258 (C.P. 1306):

> A. has complained to us that B. has raised a certain covert to the nuisance &c. And tortiously for this that whereas the said A. has his land adjoining to B.'s land on the north, B. has planted in his soil trees so that by reason of the shade &c. the corn of A. can not ripen.—
>
> *Toudeby.* Any one can make a covert except for birds, judgment of the writ.

No judgment appears in the report of this case; what should the judgment be? Why should the result differ if the covert were for birds? Apparently, Serjeant Toudeby's argument is somewhat incorrect: a lord of the manor, by customary law, could erect such a covert on his parcel of land. See Viner's Abridgment, Nuisance §F.2 (2d ed. 1793). Tenants also could purchase a license from their lord to keep a covert for birds.

---

4. 8 W.S. HOLDSWORTH, HISTORY OF ENGLISH LAW 424, 425 (2d ed. 1937).

5. According to Dean Prosser, judges, practitioners, and students who confuse concepts and terms are in good company:

    There is perhaps no more impenetrable jungle in the entire law than that which surrounds the word "nuisance." It has meant all things to all men, and has been applied indiscriminately to everything from an alarming advertisement to a cockroach baked in a pie. There is general agreement that it is incapable of any exact or comprehensive definition. Few terms have afforded so excellent an illustration of the familiar tendency of the courts to seize upon a catchword as a substitute for any analysis of a problem; the defendant's interference with the plaintiff's interests is characterized as a "nuisance," and there is nothing more to be said.

    W. Prosser, Law of Torts 571 (4th ed. 1971).

When do we cross the line between disputes that can be settled by market transactions and those that require resort to the courts or agencies? The guidance provided by the commentators only gets us so far. In The Logic of Liberty 148 (1951), Michael Polanyi wrote that "money-making organizes those aspects of economic life which are atomistic, localizable and additive, and leaves uncontrolled its 'diffuse' or 'social' aspects. Wherever these repercussions become prominent, there is a case for action by the public authorities, who are ultimately responsible for social welfare." But Friedrich A. Hayek, in Individualism and Economic Order 113 (1948) contributed this perspective:

> Where the law of property is concerned, it is not difficult to see that the simple rules which are adequate to ordinary mobile "things" or "chattel" are not suitable for indefinite extension. We need only turn to the problems in connection with land, particularly with regard to urban land in modern large towns, in order to realize that a conception of property which is based on the assumption that the use of a particular item of property affects only the interests of its owner breaks down. There can be no doubt that a good many, at least, of the problems with which the modern town planner is concerned are genuine problems with which governments or local authorities are bound to concern themselves. Unless we can provide some guidance in fields like this about what are legitimate or necessary government activities and what are its limits, we must not complain if our views are not taken seriously when we oppose other kinds of less justified "planning."

As you read the private nuisance cases that follow, consider whether the private market could have more efficiently and fairly settled the disputes that ended up in the winner-take-all world of litigation.

B. The Puzzle of Reasonableness

By the middle of the 20th century, the period of the ascendancy of zoning and planning, private nuisance law was encrusted with many principles and ancient maxims, but relatively few hard-and-fast rules. The result was that judges at the trial and appellate level were left with great freedom to craft holdings that they deemed equitable and logical, but not necessarily predictable for those investing large sums in the development of real property. The following case is a good introduction to the nuances of private nuisance law. How helpful are the Latin phrases that appear throughout the opinion? Does the court do a good job of explaining why trespass law does not govern this dispute? Given the importance of the terms "unreasonable" and "substantial," should (or could) the court provide further clarification of their specific meanings?

AMPHITHEATERS, INC. v. PORTLAND MEADOWS
184 Ore. 336, 198 P.2d 847 (1948)

BRAND, Justice. . . .

During the summer of 1945 the defendant commenced arrangements for the purchase of land and the construction thereon of a one-mile race track. On 25 August, 1945, an option for the purchase of 21 acres of the required land was secured from H. M. Seivert who is one of the promoters of the theater project and is the owner of the land on which the theater is situated. On 15 October, 1945, defendant applied for a license to operate a race meet to be held in May, 1946, and the license was issued. In October and early November, 1945, extensive newspaper publicity was given to the race track project, featuring the fact that the property would be lighted for night racing. On 15 October, 1945, a contractor was employed to plan and construct the race track and the facilities incidental thereto. Grading was commenced in November and the work was continued until the project was completed on 14 September, 1946.

During the fall of 1945 the land on which the plaintiff's theater is located was being prepared and equipped for night auto racing by Northwest Sports, Inc., an activity which, like that of defendant, would have involved the use of flood lights. On 29 November, 1945, a lease agreement was executed between Northwest Sports, Inc. and the promoters of the plaintiff corporation, entitling the lessees and their assignee, Amphitheaters, Inc., to construct and operate a drive-in outdoor motion picture theater upon the property adjoining the race track of defendants. But the lease provided that the operation of the theater must not interfere with the operations of the same property for auto racing. Plans for the construction of the theater were turned over in March, 1946, and construction was commenced in May or June of that year. At least some of the promoters of the theater project knew that the race track was to be lighted for night racing, though they may not have known the volume or extent of the proposed lighting.

The outdoor theater was completed and commenced operating on 31 August, 1946. The race track was completed and the first races held fifteen days later. The plaintiff invested $135,000 in the construction of the outdoor theater and sums greatly in excess of that amount were expended by the defendant in the development of the race track and facilities. The lighting facilities alone involved an investment by the defendant of $100,000. The two tracts operated by plaintiff and defendant respectively are located just north of the city limits of Portland, Oregon. They adjoin and lie between two arterial highways, Denver Avenue and Union Avenue. The defendant's track consists of a mile-long oval extending in a general northerly and southerly direction. The auto race track which encloses the plaintiff's moving picture amphitheater lies between Union Avenue and the Northeast curve of the defendant's oval track. Union Avenue runs in a northwesterly direction along and parallel to the plaintiff's property of which it forms the northeasterly boundary. The theater screen, approximately 40 feet high and 50 feet wide, is backed up against the westerly line of Union Avenue and faces slightly south of west and directly toward the defendant's race track. . . .[6]

In installing outdoor moving picture theaters, it is necessary to protect the premises from outside light interference. For that purpose the plaintiff constructed wing fences for a considerable distance on each side of the screen and along the westerly line of Union Avenue for the purpose of shutting off the light from the cars traveling on that arterial highway. It was also necessary to construct a shadow box extending on both sides and above the screen for the purpose of excluding the light from the moon and stars. The testimony indicates that the construction of the shadow box was necessary if a good picture was to be presented on the screen. The extreme delicacy of plaintiff's operation and the susceptibility of outdoor moving pictures to light in any form was conclusively established by the evidence.

In order to illuminate the defendant's track for night horse racing, approximately 350 1500-watt lights are mounted in clusters on 80-foot poles placed at intervals of approximately 250 feet around the track. The flood lights are in general, directed at the track, but there is substantial evidence to the effect that reflected light "spills" over onto the plaintiff's premises and has a serious effect on the quality of pictures shown on the screen. The nearest cluster of lights on the defendant's track is 832 feet distant from the plaintiff's screen. The light from the defendant's track not only impairs the quality of the pictures exhibited by the plaintiff, but there is also substantial evidence that plaintiffs have suffered financial loss as the result of the illumination of which they complain. On one occasion at least, plaintiffs felt themselves required to refund admission fees to their patrons on account of the poor quality of the picture exhibited. The evidence discloses that

---

6. Authors' note: The printed version of the case (which can be viewed on Westlaw) features a photograph of the two properties that was offered into evidence at the trial.

the light from the defendant's race track when measured at plaintiff's screen is approximately that of full moonlight.

Upon the opening of the racing season in September, 1946, the plaintiff immediately complained to the defendant concerning the detrimental effect of defendant's lights, and shortly thereafter suit was filed. In the fall of 1946 the defendant, while denying liability, nevertheless made substantial efforts to protect the plaintiff from the effect of defendant's lights. One hundred hoods were installed on the lights, and particular attention was given to those nearest to the plaintiff's property. In 1947, and prior to the spring racing season, which was to last 25 days, thirty louvers were also installed for the purpose of further confining the light to the defendant's property. These efforts materially reduced, but did not eliminate the conditions of which plaintiff complains.

Plaintiff contends that the defendant, by casting light equivalent to that of a full moon upon plaintiff's screen has committed a trespass upon real property and error is assigned by reason of the failure of the court to submit to the jury the question of trespass. While the dividing line between trespass and nuisance is not always a sharp one, we think it clear that the case at bar is governed by the law of nuisance and not by the law of trespass. Under our decisions every unauthorized entry upon land of another, although without damage, constitutes actionable trespass. The mere suggestion that the casting of light upon the premises of a plaintiff would render a defendant liable without proof of any actual damage, carries its own refutation. Actions for damages on account of smoke, noxious odors and the like have been universally classified as falling within the law of nuisance. In fact, cases of this type are described in the Restatement of the Law as "non trespassory" invasions. Restatement of the Law of Torts, Vol. 4, Ch. 40, p. 214, et seq.

Many of the cases on which plaintiff relies in support of its theory of trespass involve the flight of airplanes at low level over plaintiffs' land. The modern law with reference to trespass by airplanes has developed under the influence of ancient rules concerning the nature of property. Ownership of lands, it has been said, "includes, not only the face of the earth, but everything under it or over it, and has in its legal signification an indefinite extent upward and downward, giving rise to the maxim, Cujus est solum ejus est usque ad coelum".[7] 50 C. J. 752, Property, § 24. Harmonizing the ancient rule with the necessities of modern life, the Restatement of the Law declares that one who intentionally and without a privilege enters land, is a trespasser. Restatement of the Law of Torts, Vol. 1, § 158, p. 359. Air travel over a plaintiff's land is still recognized as trespass prima facie imposing liability but the rights of airplane travel are established or recognized by the doctrine of privilege. Restatement of the Law of Torts, § § 158, 159, 194. . . .

We have considered the other cases cited in support of the theory of trespass and find them not in point.

As its second assignment, the plaintiff asserts that the trial court erred in failing to submit the case to the jury on the theory of nuisance.

This is a case of first impression. It differs in essential particulars from any case which has received consideration by this court. The nuisance cases appearing in our reports fall into four easily recognizable classes: (1) Cases involving harm to human comfort, safety or health by reason of the maintenance by a defendant upon his land of noxious or dangerous instrumentalities causing damage to the plaintiff in respect to legally protected interests of the plaintiff in his land. (2) Cases involving illegal or immoral practices, most of them being public as distinct from private nuisances. They relate to bawdy houses, gambling, abortions, lotteries, illegal possession of liquor, and acts outraging public decency. (3) Cases involving obstructions to streets, public ways, com-

---

7. Authors' note: "The person who owns the soil owns up to the sky." Black's Law Dictionary (8th ed. 2004). For a recent examination of the origins, implications, and shortcoming of this maxim, see John G. Sprankling, *Owning the Center of the Earth*, 55 UCLA L. Rev. 979 (2008).

mon rights, access to property and the like. (4) Cases involving damage to the land itself, as by flooding. The cases, with the exception of those falling in the first class, bear no resemblance to the one at bar, and require no further comment. . . .

The cases listed in the first class are the only ones which bear any faint resemblance to the case at bar. Examination of those cases will disclose that no Oregon decision has ever held that the casting of light in any quantity or form upon the land of another gives rise to a cause of action upon any legal theory. If the cases involving smoke, noxious odors, flies and disease germs are claimed to be analogous to the case at bar, it must be answered that in every case the activity or thing which has been held to be a nuisance has been something which was, 1, inherently harmful, and 2, an unreasonable and substantial interference with the ordinary use or enjoyment of property. No one can contend that light is inherently harmful to persons in the ordinary enjoyment of property.

Since there is no Oregon precedent to support plaintiff's contention, we must go back to fundamental principles. Plaintiff relies upon the general definition of a nuisance as set forth in Adams v. City of Toledo, [163 Or. 185, 96 P.2d 1078 (1939)] and State ex rel Rudd v. Ringold, 102 Or. 401, 202 P. 734. A private nuisance is defined as "anything done to the hurt, annoyance or detriment of the lands or hereditaments of another, and not amounting to a trespass." Definitions in such general terms are of no practical assistance to the court. "It has been said that the term 'nuisance' is incapable of an exact and exhaustive definition which will fit all cases, because the controlling facts are seldom alike, and each case stands on its own footing. * * *" 39 Am. Jur., § 2, p. 281.

This court has repeatedly quoted the ancient maxim, Sic utere tuo ut alienum non laedas.[8] In this connection we quote the words of Lord Esher in Yarmouth v. France, 19 Q. B. 647, 653, 17 E. R. C. 217, as follows: "I need hardly repeat that I detest the attempt to fetter the law by maxims. They are almost invariably misleading; they are for the most part so large and general in their language that they always include something which really is not intended to be included in them."

And to this we add the crisp comment of Justice Holmes: "Decisions * * * often are presented as hollow deductions from empty general propositions like sic utere tuo ut alienum non laedas, which teaches nothing but a benevolent yearning." [Oliver Wendell Holmes Jr., *Privilege, Malice, and Intent,*] 8 Harv. L. Rev. [1,] 3 [(1894)].

The statement of Addison, Torts, 8th Ed. 66, that "The due regulation and subordination of conflicting rights constitute the chief part of the science of law" is peculiarly applicable in the field of private nuisance, for the rights of neither party in the use and enjoyment of their respective properties are absolute. . . .

Notwithstanding the fact that the existence vel non of a nuisance is generally a question of fact, there have arisen several rules of law which guide and sometimes control decision. It is established law that an intentional interference with the use and enjoyment of land is not actionable unless that interference be both substantial and unreasonable.

Again it is held that whether a particular annoyance or inconvenience is sufficient to constitute a nuisance depends upon its effect upon an ordinarily reasonable man, that is, a normal person of ordinary habits and sensibilities. The doctrine . . . appears to have had its origin in Aldred's Case, (1601) 9 Coke 57b, 77 Eng. Reprint 816. The rule announced in that case, "Lex non favet delicatorum votis,"[9] was quoted with approval by this court in Kramer v. Sweet, [179 Or. 324, 169 P.2d 892 (1946)]. This doctrine has been applied in many cases involving smoke, dust, noxious odors,

---

8. Authors' note: For those of you whose Latin is rusty, here is a workable translation of this seemingly ubiquitous maxim: "Individuals must use their own so as not to injure others." United States v. New Bedford Bridge, 27 F. Cas. 91, 98 (D. Mass. 1847).

9. Authors' note: "The law favors not the wishes of the fastidious." BLACK'S LAW DICTIONARY, *supra* Authors' note 7.

vibration and the like, in which the injury was not to the land itself but to the personal comfort of dwellers on the land.

It is highly significant that an identical principle has been applied where the uses to which a plaintiff puts his land are abnormally sensitive to the type of interference caused by the defendant.

> "No action will lie for a nuisance in respect of damage which, even though substantial, is due solely to the fact that the plaintiff is abnormally sensitive to deleterious influences, or uses his land for some purpose which requires exceptional freedom from any such influences * * *

> "So if I carry on a manufacture or other business which is so sensitive to adverse influences that it suffers damage from smoke, fumes, vibrations, or heat, which would in no way interfere with the ordinary occupation of land, the law of nuisance will not confer upon me any such special and extraordinary protection. I must acquire immunity from damage of this sort by special contract with my neighbours. . . ." Salmond on the Law of Torts, 9th Ed., pp. 238, 239.

The same rule has been laid down by another author: "It has been shown that the interference with property or personal comfort must be substantial. But even if the interference is substantial, no action will lie where it can be shown that, but for the infirmity of the person or property, there would have been no substantial interference * * * Nor again can damage to sensitive property be complained of if the act causing the damage would not have harmed more ordinary things * * *." Pearce and Meston, Ch. 1, p. 19.

The same doctrine is followed by Joyce, Law of Nuisances, § 26: "* * * But the doing of something not in itself noxious does not become a nuisance merely because it does harm to some particular trade of a delicate nature in the adjoining property where it does not affect any ordinary trade carried on there nor interfere with the ordinary enjoyment of life. A man who carries on an exceptionally delicate trade cannot complain because it is injured by his neighbor doing something lawful on his property, if it is something which would not injure an ordinary trade or anything but an exceptionally delicate trade." . . .

The plaintiff is not the owner of the real property on which its outdoor theater is located. Its only right in the property which has any bearing on this case is the right to operate a moving picture theater thereon. We adopt the following rule as stated in Restatement of Torts, § 822, p. 229: "* * * One having 'property rights and privileges' in land can maintain an action under the rule here stated, only when the conduct of the actor interferes with the exercise of the particular rights and privileges which he owns. * * *"

It follows from the application of this rule that the plaintiff's only basis of complaint is the fact that it is attempting to show upon the screen moving pictures, and that the operation is such a delicate one that it has been necessary for the plaintiff to build high fences to prevent the light of automobiles upon the public highway from invading the property and to build a shadow box over the screen to protect it from the ordinary light of moon and stars, and that it now claims damage because the lights from the defendant's property, which it has not excluded by high fences, shine with the approximate intensity of full moonlight upon the screen and interfere thereby with the showing of the pictures. We think that this is a clear case coming within the doctrine of the English and American cases, and that a man cannot increase the liabilities of his neighbor by applying his own property to special and delicate uses, whether for business or pleasure.

Finding no case in this jurisdiction in which the casting of light upon the premises of another has been judged as a nuisance, we turn to the cases from other jurisdictions in which that question has been discussed. We call attention first to the fundamental distinction between cases involving light and those involving smoke, gas, noxious odors and the like. The fact that the plaintiff in this case loves darkness rather than light does not mean that light can be classed as a noxious or generally injurious instrumentality.

In Shepler v. Kansas Milling Co., 128 Kan. 554, 278 P. 757, the plaintiff sued the defendant milling company for damages because it had erected a number of grain tanks 60 feet high across the street from plaintiff's residence. He alleged that the tanks were painted white and reflected the afternoon sun on his front porch "to his great annoyance and discomfort, and that his house was thereby rendered unsalable and no longer fit for residential purposes whereby its value was reduced some $1800." The court quoted the ancient maxim, Sic utere tuo, but stated that it has its limitations.

> "The law does not in every instance provide directly for compensation or financial redress
> for every damnum a man may sustain as a member of an organized community. . . ." . . .

The only case which has been brought to our attention, and in which it has been held that light unaccompanied by any other element of an offensive character constitutes a nuisance, is the case of The Shelburne, Inc. v. Crossan Corporation, [95 N.J. Eq. 188, 122 A. 749 (1923)]. The plaintiff was the owner of a large hotel on the board walk in Atlantic City which had been operated in the same location for many years. Sixty of its bedrooms had a southerly or southwesterly exposure. The defendant corporation was the owner of property immediately to the southwest, upon which was erected an apartment house. On the roof of the apartment house defendants had erected a sign 66 feet in height and 72 feet in length on which there were 1084 15-watt lights and 6 100-watt lights and 28 75-watt lights. The sign was parallel to the wing of the hotel and about 110 feet distant therefrom. The evidence disclosed that the sign "lights up 40 or 45 rooms in the new wing of the hotel," disturbs the guests and lowers the value of the rooms. The court held that light "may become a nuisance if it materially interferes with the ordinary comfort physically of human existence." The trial judge held that the complainant was entitled to a decree restricting the operation of the electric lights during each night after the hour of 12 o'clock midnight. The plaintiff's hotel was located on the famous board walk at Atlantic City, where the primary activity appears to be the entertainment of luxury-loving people. We suspect that the court was moved by a comparison of the utility of plaintiff's hotel in that district with the utility of an advertising sign. In any event, the interference was with the normal and ordinary sensibilities of dwellers in the hotel, and with the ordinary use of property. . . .

By way of summary, we have found no case in which it has been held that light alone constitutes a nuisance merely because it damaged one who was abnormally sensitive or whose use of his land was of a peculiarly delicate and sensitive character. . . .

We do not say that the shedding of light upon another's property may never under any conditions become a nuisance, but we do say that extreme caution must be employed in applying any such legal theory. The conditions of modern city life impose upon the city dweller and his property many burdens more severe than that of light reflected upon him or it. . . .

We limit our decision to the specific facts of this case and hold as a matter of law that the loss sustained by the plaintiff by the spilled light which has been reflected onto the highly sensitized moving picture screen from the defendant's property 832 feet distant, and which light in intensity is approximately that of a full moon, is damnum absque injuria.

The trial court did not err in directing a verdict. The judgment is affirmed.

Notes

1. An Oregon appellate court wrestled with the question of whether landowners who were offended by nudity and sexual acts occurring on adjacent public lands could bring a private nuisance action against a state agency for failing to prevent the offending activities. Citing *Amphitheaters*, the court concluded: "Although the question is the effect of the challenged activity on an ordinary person, and although the law does not protect the delicate, plaintiff's allegations would allow finding that the nudity constituted a nuisance." Mark v. State Dep't of Fish & Wildlife, 158 Ore. App. 355, 361, P.2d 716, 720 (Or. Ct. App. 1999).

Professor John Copeland Nagle, in *Moral Nuisances*, 50 Emory L.J. 265, 266-68 (2001), has observed:

> The deployment of nuisance law to combat immoral activities evokes images of nine-teenth century cases involving brothels, saloons, gambling parlors, and other unsavory venues. The leading nineteenth century treatise on nuisances is filled with descriptions of such cases. To be sure, the standard definition of a nuisance still refers to moral harms. But commentators have assumed that immoral conduct can no longer serve as the basis for a nuisance claim. The prostitutes, saloon keepers, and other bad actors who starred in the moral nuisance cases seem like they belong to a bygone era. . . .

> Mark v. Oregon State Department of Fish and Wildlife is one of a number of recent moral nuisance cases. Crack houses have been targeted as nuisances because of their impact on the moral fiber of urban communities. A St. Louis hotel has been targeted as a nuisance because of its relationship to prostitution in the neighborhood. The Arkansas Supreme Court has enjoined a church bingo game as a nuisance. Adult entertainment facilities have been challenged in a variety of cases. Many of these cases involve gov-ernmental actions to abate public nuisances, but the reasoning would support nuisance actions brought by neighbors affected by such immoral conduct as well. The nineteenth century cases could reappear just as we enter the twenty-first century. . . .

> Today, a cause of action that enables a landowner to seek relief from the unwanted effects of a neighbor's purportedly immoral activities rests on several controversial prem-ises. It presumes that the conduct of one's neighbor can be judged immoral, that such conduct causes real harms, and that those harms can be remedied by the law. It pre-sumes that what one does on one's own land can be limited by the moral sensibilities of one's neighbor. It presumes that the courts are properly positioned to render such judg-ments rather than relying on zoning laws and other land use regulations.

2. Can the fear of harm from electromagnetic fields (EMFs) give rise to a successful private nui-sance action? The Supreme Court of California thought not, in San Diego Gas & Elec. Co. v. Superior Court, 13 Cal. 4th 893, 920 P.2d 669, 55 Cal. Rptr. 2d 724 (1996), a challenge brought by landowners against a public utility that ran electric currents through the power lines located on the company's easement located adjacent to the plaintiffs' property:

> Plaintiffs have abandoned their claim that the electric and magnetic fields arising from SDG&E's powerlines impaired their use and enjoyment of their property by causing them to suffer actual physical harm. Instead, plaintiffs now contend the fields impaired their use and enjoyment of the property simply because they assertedly feared that the fields would cause them physical harm. We need not and do not decide here whether a fear of future harm will support a cause of action for private nuisance, or, if so, whether

the fear must be reasonable, i.e., grounded in scientific fact. Even if we assume arguendo that plaintiffs could amend their complaint to allege such a fear, an award of damages on that basis would interfere with the policy of the commission on powerline electric and magnetic fields. As we have seen, in order to award such damages on a nuisance theory the trier of fact would be required to find that reasonable persons viewing the matter objectively (1) would experience a substantial fear that the fields cause physical harm and (2) would deem the invasion so serious that it outweighs the social utility of SDG&E's conduct. Such findings, however, would be inconsistent with the commission's conclusion, reached after consulting with DHS [state Department of Health Services], studying the reports of advisory groups and experts, and holding evidentiary hearings, that the available evidence does not support a reasonable belief that 60 Hz electric and magnetic fields present a substantial risk of physical harm, and that unless and until the evidence supports such a belief regulated utilities need take no action to reduce field levels from existing powerlines.

3. In a Massachusetts case, Westchester Assocs. v. Boston Edison Co., 47 Mass. App. Ct. 133, 137-38, 712 N.E.2d 1145, 1149 (1999), the owner of a six-story office building brought a nuisance action against the Boston Edison Company because the magnetic fields produced by the company's nearby power lines interfered with the images displayed on tenants' computer monitors. The appellate court was not persuaded by the complaint:

> A significant difficulty with Westchester's attempt to characterize the magnetic fields as a nuisance is that their adverse effects would be experienced only by particular users of equipment sensitive to the fields. There is no contention that the fields are directly detectable by human senses. Thus, they do not constitute an annoyance to a plaintiff of "ordinary sensibility." Malm v. Dubrey, 325 Mass. 63, 65, 88 N.E.2d 900 (1949), and cases cited. The inquiry to determine whether such fields constitute a nuisance will likely vary as computers and other electronic equipment may become more sophisticated and sensitive. There may come a time when increasing knowledge or changing uses may require, as [a] matter of public policy, the modification of the use of electric power line easements, but this case does not call for such remediation. We conclude that Westchester's nuisance claim, unsupported in the law, fails, and that because Edison reasonably is exercising its easement rights, it is entitled to summary judgment.

C. A Delicate Social and Economic Balance

The following case explores whether traditional private nuisance, trespass, and underground water law doctrines were up to the task of resolving disputes between agricultural and industrial interests. The court considered whether capital investment and employment trumped benefits such as crop production and healthy livestock. Is there something special about the long and continued use of one's real property that outweighs more recent, but potentially more lucrative, economic pursuits? If so, what are those special qualities? If not, is it time to abandon the special protection private nuisance affords landowners?

ROSE v. SOCONY-VACUUM CORP.
54 R.I. 411, 173 A. 627 (1934)

MURDOCK, Justice. These cases, described in the writs as trespass on the case for causing a nuisance, were heard together for the reason that the same questions of law are involved in each case. They are here on plaintiffs' exceptions to a ruling of the superior court sustaining demurrers to the declarations which are summarized in plaintiffs' brief as follows:

The plaintiff (Manuel Rose) for thirty years prior to and in June 1930, owned a farm in East Providence, bounding southerly on the state highway known as the Wampanoag Trail, comprising fifty-seven acres with a dwelling house, large barn and other out buildings thereon, and occupied by him and his family. On the farm was a well of pure water used for drinking purposes, and on the westerly part of the farm was a stream in part fed by percolations of water in and under the land of the defendant and said highway and into said stream. On the farm was a large piggery and a hennery, the hens supplied by water from the well, and the pigs supplied by water of the stream. On the southerly side of and bounding northerly on said highway and opposite said farm the defendant had a large tract of land at a higher elevation than the farm.

Years before 1930, the defendant acquired said tract of land and built upon it a large oil refinery and a large number of tanks for storing petroleum, gasoline and other petroleum products, and operated the same and from time to time suffered and permitted to be discharged on its land and into settling basins, bodies of water and natural ponds and ways thereon large quantities of petroleum, gasoline, petroleum products and waste substances from its refinery and tanks with the result that large parts of its said land, basins, bodies of water and natural water ponds and ways became impregnated, and polluted by the same, and that it was the duty of the defendant to confine to its said land said polluting matters and substances and said waters in their polluted condition and not suffer or permit the same to be discharged or escape from its land to, in, under and on any adjoining or neighboring land, and thereby create a nuisance thereon to its injury, but the defendant disregarding its duty wrongfully and injuriously suffered and permitted large quantites of said polluting matters and substances and said waters in their polluted condition to escape from time to time from its land by means of percolations thereof in, under and through its land to, in, under and through said highway and to, in, under, on and through said farm and parts thereof and to and into said well and said stream, with the direct result that in said June, 1930, said well became polluted by the same and especially by gasoline and rendered unfit as drinking water for use by man or beast, and also said stream theretofore fit for use then became polluted and unfit for use by man or beast with the direct result the plaintiff in June, 1930, and until the present time was deprived of the use of said well and stream and obliged since to obtain water from other sources off his farm for the supply of his house for drinking and domestic uses and watering his hens and for watering his hogs and pigs and other uses for which the stream was available.

Further the declaration sets forth that because of the pollution of the stream 136 of his hogs and pigs died from drinking the waters, including 75 breeding sows, and because of the pollution of the well about 700 of his hens died from drinking the well waters, and that because of a lack of a wholesome water supply the plaintiff has been deprived of raising on his farm as large a number of pigs and hens as theretofore and his business in raising and selling the same interfered with and greatly reduced in amount to his monetary damage and loss. The declaration concludes with a general allegation as to other damages from said nuisance caused by the defendant.

The declarations allege no negligent act, and recovery is sought principally on the ground that the acts set forth in the declarations have resulted in a nuisance for which defendant is liable even though not negligent. The assertion that the acts of the defendant complained of have resulted in a nuisance is petitio principii.

There is no wholly satisfactory definition of what constitutes a nuisance, but it is generally agreed that a nuisance has its origin in the invasion of a legal right. In Cooley on Torts, vol. 3 (4th Ed.) §398, it is said that "An actionable nuisance may, therefore, be said to be anything wrongfully done or permitted which injures or annoys another in the enjoyment of his legal rights," and in Joyce on Nuisances, §29, that "a nuisance does not necessarily exist even though one may by the use of his property cause an injury or damage to another." The plaintiffs must therefore go further to establish liability than the mere assertion that a nuisance exists on their land by reason of the acts of the defendant.

The plaintiffs' cases rest on the proposition that they have a cause of action from the fact that contaminating and deleterious substances have escaped from the land of the defendant through the medium of percolating waters to their land. The plaintiffs rely on the much-discussed case of Rylands v. Fletcher, L.R. 3 H.L. 330, where the following rule laid down by Mr. Justice Blackburn in Fletcher vs. Rylands, L.R. 1 Ex. 265, was approved:

> We think that the true rule of law is, that the person who, for his own purposes, brings on his land and collects and keeps there anything likely to do mischief if it escapes, must keep it in at his peril, and if he does not do so, is prima facie answerable for all the damage which is the natural consequence of its escape. He can excuse himself by showing that the escape was owing to the plaintiffs default; or, perhaps that it was the consequence of vis major, or the act of God; but as nothing of this sort exists here, it is unnecessary to inquire what excuse would be sufficient. The general rule, as above stated, seems on principle just . . . and it seems but reasonable and just that the neighbour who has brought something on his own property (which was not naturally there), harmless to others so long as it is confined to his own property, but which he knows will be mischievous if it gets on his neighbour's, should be obliged to make good the damage which ensues if he does not succeed in confining it to his own property.

This rule is a radical departure from the commonly accepted doctrine of the law of torts that liability is predicated on fault. It has not found general acceptance in this country, and in England it has been greatly modified by later decisions.

A profound criticism of the rule is found in the opinion of Mr. Justice Doe in Brown v. Collins, 53 N.H. 442, at page 448, 16 Am. Rep. 372, where it is said:

> Everything that a man can bring on his land is capable of escaping,—against his will, and without his fault, with or without assistance, in some form, solid, liquid, or gaseous, changed or unchanged by the transforming processes of nature or art,—and of doing damage after its escape. Moreover, if there is a legal principle that makes a man liable for the natural consequences of the escape of things which he brings on his land, the application of such a principle cannot be limited to those things; it must be applied to all his acts that disturb the original order of creation; or, at least, to all things which he undertakes to possess or control anywhere, and which were not used and enjoyed in what is called the natural or primitive condition of mankind, whatever that may have been. This is going back a long way for a standard of legal rights, and adopting an arbitrary test of responsibility that confounds all degrees of danger, pays no heed to the essential elements of actual fault, puts a clog upon natural and reasonably necessary uses of matter, and tends to embarrass and obstruct much of the work which it seems to be man's duty carefully to do.

Losee v. Buchanan, 51 N.Y. 476, 10 Am. Rep. 623; Burdick, Law of Torts (4th Ed.) §12: "The rule in Rylands v. Fletcher, even with the recognized limitations, finds no favor even in England, and American courts have generally refused to follow it." See also, Bohlen, Studies in the Law of Torts, p. 421.

We think, therefore, that reason and the great weight of authority in this country sustain us in refusing to adopt the rule of absolute liability as stated in Rylands v. Fletcher, *supra*.

The plaintiffs lean heavily on the maxim sic utere tuo ut alienum non laedas. This maxim, so often cited as the governing principle of decisions, affords little, if any, aid in the determination of the rights of parties in litigation. If it be taken to mean any injury to another by the use of one's own, it is not true, and, if it means legal injury, it is simply a restatement of what has already been determined.

> The maxim, sic utere tuo ut alienum non laedas, is mere verbiage. A party may damage the property of another where the law permits; and he may not where the law prohibits: so that the maxim can never be applied till the law is ascertained; and, when it is, the maxim is superfluous.

Erle, J., in Bonomi v. Backhouse, El. Bl. & El. 622, 643; 2 Austin, Jur. (3d) 795, 829. The maxim is undoubtedly a sound moral precept expressing an ideal never fully attained in the social state.

We must therefore look for some fault on the part of the defendant. It is well-settled law that one who accumulates filth or other deleterious matter on his land must confine it there and not allow it to spread over the surface of his land to the surface of the land of another. "Where one has filth deposited on his premises, he whose dirt it is must keep it that it may not trespass." Tenant v. Goldwin, 1 Salk. 360. And this rule will apply where the objectional [*sic*] matter permeates the soil superficially and by the action of the elements reaches the soil of another. Liability in this class of cases sounds in trespass.

The owner of land bounding on a surface stream may not pollute the same to the impairment of the use and enjoyment of the stream by other riparian owners; and this rule applies to subterranean streams following a known or readily ascertainable and well-defined course. 27 R.C.L. p. 1170. Liability for the pollution of a surface stream or subterranean stream following a well-defined course is predicated on the invasion of a correlative right of the injured party in such waters. This leads to an inquiry into the nature and extent of the right of a landowner in the waters beneath the soil which pass from his land, not in a well-defined stream, but by percolation or seepage.

The leading case on this question is Acton v. Blundell, 12 Mees. & Wels. Rep. 324, decided in 1843. In that case it was held that the right to the waters in the soil was not governed by the rule applicable to surface streams. . . .

In England this right to underground waters has been held to be absolute, and the motive of the owner in appropriating or diverting the same is immaterial. In this country the authorities are in conflict as to the nature of the right in underground waters. Some jurisdictions follow the English rule and others modify the rule to the extent that the owner of land may not through malice or negligence deprive the adjoining owner of percolating waters. To this extent in the latter jurisdictions the right is not absolute but relative.

In this state the right to subterranean waters appears to be relative to the extent that they may not be purposely or negligently diverted. . . .

While the defendant could appropriate to its own use the percolating waters under its soil, providing that in so doing it was not actuated by an improper motive and was not negligent, can it, by the use to which it puts its land, deprive the plaintiffs of such waters by rendering them unfit for plaintiffs' use by contamination? Authorities, few in number, which bear directly on this question, are in conflict. . . .

Dillon v. Acme Oil Co., 49 Hun 565, 2 N.Y.S. 289, 291, is strikingly similar in many particulars to the instant case. In that case the plaintiff owned land on which there were two wells; twenty rods away, and separated therefrom by a public street and a railroad with several tracks, defendant conducted an oil refinery. Plaintiff's wells were polluted by oil from this refinery which had percolated through the earth and was carried by some subterranean stream to plaintiff's wells. It was held that the law controlling the rights of the parties to surface streams had no application to subterranean waters running through unknown channels and that, "In the absence of negligence and of knowledge as to the existence of such subterranean water-courses, when the business is legitimate, and conducted with care and skill, there can be no liability if such subterranean courses become contaminated."

In Upjohn v. Richland Board of Health, 46 Mich. 542, 9 N.W. 845, 848, relief, by way of injunction to restrain the board of health in said township from extending its cemetery so as to bring it closer to complainant's premises was denied. The opinion in this case is of particular interest for the reason that it was written by that distinguished commentator on the law, Mr. Justice Cooley. While relief appears to have been denied in part on other grounds, the opinion discusses at length the law pertaining to percolating waters. After stating the distinction between surface streams and percolating waters, the opinion proceeds:

> But if withdrawing the water from one's well by an excavation on adjoining lands will give no right of action, it is difficult to understand how corrupting its waters by a proper use of the adjoining premises can be actionable, when there was no actual intent to injure, and no negligence. The one act destroys the well, and the other does no more; the injury is the same in kind and degree in the two cases.

The rationale of these opinions is that the courses of subterranean waters are as a rule indefinite and obscure, and therefore the rights relating to them cannot well be defined as in the case of surface streams. To give to others a right in such waters may subject a landowner to liability for consequences, arising from a legitimate use of his land, which he did not intend and which he could not foresee. . . .

A query arises as to whether the divergence of views expressed in these cases is not due to the influence of the predominating economic interests of the jurisdictions to which these apply; in other words, whether these opinions do not rest on public policy rather than legal theory. On the question of public policy as a ground of judicial decision, see an article by Mr. Justice Holmes in 8 Harvard Law Review, 1.[10]

It will be observed that in jurisdictions holding that, even though there is no negligence, there is liability for the pollution of subterranean waters, the predominating economic interest is agricultural.

Defendant's refinery is located at the head of Narragansett Bay, a natural waterway for commerce. This plant is situated in the heart of a region highly developed industrially. Here it prepares for use and distributes a product which has become one of the prime necessities of modern life.

---

10. Authors' note: The article is Oliver Wendell Holmes Jr., Privilege, Malice, and Intent, 8 Harv. L. Rev. 1 (1894). In this piece, Justice Holmes wrote:

> [W]hether, and how far, a privilege shall be allowed is a question of policy. Questions of policy are legislative questions, and judges are shy of reasoning from such grounds. Therefore, decisions for or against the privilege, which can really stand only upon such grounds, often are presented as hollow deductions from empty general propositions like *sic utere tuo ut alienum non laedas*, which teaches nothing but a benevolent yearning, or else are put as if they themselves embodied a postulate of the law and admitted of no further deduction, as when it is said that, although there is temporal damage, there is no wrong; whereas the very thing to be found out is whether there is a wrong or not, and if not, why not.

Id. at 3.

It is an unavoidable incident of the growth of population and its segregation in restricted areas that individual rights recognized in a sparsely settled state have to be surrendered for the benefit of the community, as it develops and expands. If, in the process of refining petroleum, injury is occasioned to those in the vicinity, not through negligence or lack of skill or the invasion of a recognized legal right, but by the contamination of percolating waters whose courses are not known, we think that public policy justifies a determination that such harm is damnum absque injuria.

The plaintiff's exceptions in each case are overruled, and each case is remitted to the superior court for further proceedings.

Notes

1. The plaintiff took up the court's suggestion to pursue a claim in negligent (as opposed to intentional) nuisance. Rose v. Socony-Vacuum Corp., 56 R.I. 272, 185 A. 251 (1936). The court explained:

> In the instant case, the proposed amendment would be entirely consistent with the description of the cause of action in the writ as one in "trespass on the case for causing a nuisance," and the only substantial change which it would make would be to change a declaration sounding in nuisance, which this court has held to be insufficient, into a sufficient one, still sounding in nuisance, by adding an allegation of negligence by the defendant as the cause of the escape of the deleterious substances into the defendant's land and thence into the plaintiff's.

2. Section 822 of the *Restatement (Second) of Torts* notes that liability for a private nuisance will occur

> if, but only if, his conduct is a legal cause of an invasion of another's interest in the private use and enjoyment of land, and the invasion is either
>
> (a) intentional and unreasonable, or
>
> (b) unintentional and otherwise actionable under the rules controlling liability for negligent or reckless conduct, or for abnormally dangerous conditions or activities.

> Comment b explains:

> Failure to recognize that private nuisance has reference to the interest invaded and not to the type of conduct that subjects the actor to liability has led to confusion. Thus, in respect to an interference with the use and enjoyment of land, attempts are made to distinguish between private nuisance and negligence, overlooking the fact that private nuisance has reference to the interest invaded and negligence to the conduct that subjects the actor to liability for the invasion. Similar distinctions are attempted between private nuisance and abnormally dangerous activities for the same reason.

3. In much the same way that the *Rose* court considered the contributions to the economy made by the refinery, §828 of the *Restatement (Second) of Torts* includes "the social value that the law attaches to the primary purpose of the conduct" as one of three important factors used to determine "the utility of conduct that causes" the invasion. The other two factors are "the suitability of the conduct to the character of the locality" and "the impracticability of preventing or avoiding the invasion."

4. Why not let the state legislature define this difficult term? The early 21st-century version of Cal. Civ. Code §3479, combining traditional notions of private and public nuisance, provides:

> Anything which is injurious to health, including, but not limited to, the illegal sale of controlled substances,[11] or is indecent or offensive to the senses, or an obstruction to the free use of property, so as to interfere with the comfortable enjoyment of life or property, or unlawfully obstructs the free passage or use, in the customary manner, of any navigable lake, or river, bay, stream, canal, or basin, or any public park, square, street, or highway, is a nuisance.

Consider whether this statute is an improvement over judicial interpretation or over the version replaced in the 1870s, which read:

> A nuisance consists in unlawfully doing an act, or omitting to perform a duty, which act or omission either:
>
> 1. Annoys, injures, or endangers the comfort, repose, health, or safety of others; or,
>
> 2. Offends decency; or,
>
> 3. Unlawfully interferes with, obstructs, or tends to obstruct, or renders dangerous for passage, any lake, or navigable river, bay, stream, canal, or basin, or any public park, square, street, or highway; or,
>
> 4. In any way renders other persons insecure in life, or in the use of property.

5. The inadequacies of common-law doctrines are accentuated when the number of actual or potential defendants is increased, which was, unfortunately, often the case when early 20th-century courts employed nuisance law in the battle against harmful air and water pollution. See, for example, Slater v. Pacific American Oil Co., 212 Cal. 648, 655, 300 P. 31, 34 (1931), a case involving multiple contributors causing harm to the plaintiff's land: "While fully appreciating the difficulty surrounding the production of evidence tending to establish the defendant's contribution to the wrong suffered by plaintiff, we are not prepared to conclude that it is utterly impossible to offer some evidence upon which defendant's proportionate liability might fairly be determined." In Ingram v. City of Gridley, 100 Cal. App. 2d 815, 819-20, 224 P.2d 798, 801 (1950), the court refused to allow one defendant to escape liability: "It is true that the district itself, as claimed by it, contributed no material that would add to the nuisance-creating sewage, but the effect of its acts as related was to make it a joint tort feasor with the other appellants in the creation and the continuance of the nuisance."

D. But Is It Substantial?

Private nuisance typically pits neighboring landowners against each other. In some cases, such as *Rose*, the negative externalities are very serious. In others, it is a much closer call. Given the flexibility granted to judges in the common-law regime, it is not easy to predict when a neighbor crosses the line between simple rudeness and actionable conduct. Would you commend the court in the following case for its analysis, or should this dispute have been handled by some other means (legal or extralegal)?

---

11. Authors' note: The phrase preceding the comma was added in 1996.

RODRIGUE v. COPELAND
475 So. 2d 1071 (La. 1985), *cert. denied*, 475 U.S. 1046 (1986)

DIXON, Chief Justice.

Plaintiffs, three residents of the Pontchartrain Shores Subdivision in Jefferson Parish, instituted this action to enjoin defendant, Alvin C. Copeland, from erecting and operating his annual Christmas display. The plaintiffs sought injunctive relief under C.C. 667-669 due to problems associated with an enormous influx of visitors to their limited access, residential neighborhood. . . .

Since 1977 defendant has annually maintained a Christmas display on his premises at 5001 Folse Drive. The display has grown in size and popularity since the year of its inception. The display consists of an extravagant array of lights and lighted figures accompanied by traditional Christmas music.[12]

The neighborhood is a limited access area which is zoned solely for single family residences. Defendant's premises, which front on Folse Drive, are bounded to the north by the Lake Pontchartrain levee, to the east by a public right-of-way and to the west by the residence of plaintiff Mary Borrell. . . .

Since 1982 defendant's exhibition has drawn numerous spectators to the neighborhood during the hours while the display is in operation. The spectators view the display either from their automobiles or on foot after parking their vehicles in the surrounding neighborhood. The increased congestion in the neighborhood has created numerous problems for some of the defendant's neighbors such as restricted access to their homes, noise, public urination, property damage and a lack of on-street parking. . . .

Owners of immovable property are restrained in the use of their property by certain obligations. These obligations include the responsibilities imposed by articles 667-669 of the Civil Code:

> Although a proprietor may do with his estate whatever he pleases, still he can not make any work on it, which may deprive his neighbor of the liberty of enjoying his own, or which may be the cause of any damage to him. C.C. 667.

> Although one be not at liberty to make any work by which his neighbor's buildings may be damaged, yet every one has the liberty of doing on his own ground whatsoever he pleases, although it should occasion some inconvenience to his neighbor.

> Thus he who is not subject to any servitude originating from a particular agreement in that respect, may raise his house as high as he pleases, although by such elevation he should darken the lights of his neighbor's house, because this act occasions only an inconvenience, but not a real damage. C.C. 668.

> If the works or materials for any manufactory or other operation, cause an inconvenience to those in the same or in the neighboring houses, by diffusing smoke or nauseous smell, and there be no servitude established by which they are regulated, their sufferance must be determined by the rules of the police, or the customs of the place. C.C. 669.

These obligations of vicinage are legal servitudes imposed on the owner of property. These provisions embody a balancing of rights and obligations associated with the ownership of immovables.

---

12. Authors' note: Copeland testified "that the cost of the display, $30,000-$50,000, has been borne by his business, A. Copeland Enterprises, Inc., since 1980. Defendant owns 100% of the stock in A. Copeland Enterprises, Inc. This corporation is the parent company of Popeye's Famous Fried Chicken, Inc." *Copeland*, 475 So. 2d at 1076.

As a general rule, the landowner is free to exercise his rights of ownership in any manner he sees fit. He may even use his property in ways which ". . . occasion some inconvenience to his neighbor." However, his extensive rights do not allow him to do "real damage" to his neighbor.

At issue in this case is whether Copeland's light and sound display has caused a mere inconvenience or real damage to his neighbors and their right to enjoy their own premises.

In determining whether an activity or work occasions real damage or mere inconvenience, a court is required to determine the reasonableness of the conduct in light of the circumstances. This analysis requires consideration of factors such as the character of the neighborhood, the degree of the intrusion and the effect of the activity on the health and safety of the neighbors.

In the past, this court has borrowed from the common law of nuisance in describing the type of conduct which violates the pronouncements embodied in C.C. 667-669. . . .

Defendant's exhibition constitutes an unreasonable intrusion into the lives of his neighbors when considered in light of the character of the neighborhood, the degree of the intrusion and its effect on the use and enjoyment of their properties by his neighbors. . . .

The damage suffered by plaintiffs during the operation of defendant's display is extensive, both in terms of its duration and its size. Defendant's display becomes operative in early December and remains in operation until January 5. During this period, plaintiffs are forced to contend with a flow of bumper to bumper traffic through their limited access neighborhood. In addition, they must endure the noise and property abuse associated with the crowd of visitors who congregate near the display.

The display begins operation at dusk each evening and continues until 11:00 p.m. on weekdays and 12:00 midnight on weekends. The display is occasionally operational beyond midnight. While in operation, it features an extravagant display of lights which are located across the front of defendant's residence, on the roof and in the enclosed yard to the west of the residence. Some of the lights comprising the display are shaped into figures such as a star, a reindeer, a snowman, three angels and a depiction of Santa and his reindeer. Lights are also located in the trees and shrubs. In addition to the lights, the display features a tapestry proclaiming "Glory to God in the Highest" and a creche.

Noise emanates from the display and from the visitors. The display is accompanied by traditional Christmas music which is amplified through loudspeakers located on the second floor of defendant's residence. The music is audible inside the home of Mary Borrell. The plaintiffs also complain of noise emanating from car engines, car horns, the slamming of car doors and police whistles. . . .

The increased traffic attracted to the display has some impact on the health and safety of the residents. The response time for emergency services is increased due to the traffic congestion. However, the record indicates that this danger was minimized under the sheriff's plan through the creation of an emergency lane on Transcontinental and the presence of two motor scooters to be used in medical emergencies. If the physical health and safety of the plaintiffs had been the only factor to consider, we would not have deemed it necessary to restrain defendant's display. However, in consideration of all the factors, the district court committed clear error in failing to find that plaintiffs suffered damage under C.C. 667-669 and irreparable injury. Likewise, the court of appeal erred in affirming the district court.

Plaintiffs' injury stems from the nature and size of the display which render it incompatible with the restricted access, residential neighborhood. Defendant is enjoined from erecting and operating a Christmas exhibition which is calculated to and does attract an unusually large number of visitors to the neighborhood.

In complying with our order, defendant is specifically enjoined from placing oversized lighted figures, such as the reindeer and snowman, in his yards or upon the roof of his residence. The proper place for these "commercial size" decorations is not within a quiet, residential neighborhood. Defendant is also specifically ordered to reduce the volume of any sound accompanying the display so that it is not audible from within the closest homes of his neighbors.

In limiting his display, the burden is placed on defendant to reduce substantially the size and extravagance of his display to a level at which it will not attract the large crowds that have been drawn to the neighborhood in the past.

Of course, defendant is free to maintain his display unrestricted, at a location which is appropriate. The injunction granted herein is limited to activity at defendant's premises on Folse Drive.
. . .

In consideration of defendant's right of religious expression, he is free to retain the religious symbols which are included in his display, that is, the Star of Bethlehem, nativity scene, religious tapestry and oversized lighted angels. The limitations on defendant's activity do not extend to the content of the display. . . .

Notes

1. Alvin Copeland's legal battle did not end here. *See* Klein v. Copeland, 482 So. 2d 613, 616-17 (La. 1986):

> We find that defendant wilfully disobeyed this court's ruling of September 10, 1985; hence, he was in contempt of court. We ordered defendant to reduce the size and extravagance of his display to a level which would not draw large crowds to the neighborhood and which would not create bumper to bumper traffic. Almost all of the witnesses called at the trial of the rule to show cause testified that the crowds and traffic were "the same as last year," and defendant himself admitted that the traffic was "bumper to bumper" since the display was activated on December 6, 1985. We ordered defendant to reduce the volume of any sound accompanying the display so that it would not be audible from within the closest homes of his neighbors. Yet, the testimony of plaintiff and another witness who lives across the street from Copeland revealed that the sound from this year's display was still audible inside their homes, that is, when the noise of the bumper to bumper traffic did not exceed the sound emanating from the display. Contrary to our order to reduce substantially the size and extravagance of his display, defendant added new figures to the creche and added neon lights to the overall display. Last, we enjoined defendant from placing oversized lighted figures in his yards or upon his roof, noting that "the proper place for those 'commercial size' decorations is not within a quiet residential neighborhood." In circumvention of this directive, he permitted some of his neighbors to erect the figures on their lawns at his expense. It was not the religious display on defendant's property that caused the bumper to bumper traffic but rather the enlargement of his existing display and the transfer of the oversized lighted figures to the various lawns in his neighborhood. Defendant knew or should have known that the present displays would create the intolerable traffic situation of previous years. Contrary to our September 10, 1985 decree, defendant's actions have resulted in a display that has

continued to attract bumper to bumper traffic and extremely large numbers of visitors to his neighborhood.[13]

2. How can you distinguish a temporary from a permanent nuisance? The court in Kentucky-Ohio Gas Co. v. Bowling, 264 Ky. 470, 477-79, 95 S.W.2d 1, 4-5 (1936) employed the following analysis:

> If it be permanent, usually it is necessary that it be created by the inherent character of the structure or business, and that its lawful and necessary operation creates a permanent injury; but where the structure or the business when properly conducted and operated does not constitute a nuisance and only becomes such through negligence, it is temporary. If the structure is in character relatively enduring and not likely to be abated, either voluntarily or by an order of court, it is generally held that the nuisance is a permanent one; and if the prospective damages resulting therefrom can be estimated with reasonable certainty, the diminution of the value of the property is immediately recoverable as damages.

> It is ruled that a nuisance may be regarded as permanent, where the damages recoverable would obviously be small as compared with the cause of its removal or installing another or an auxiliary plant. Also, if the owner of the property damaged by the nuisance would be obliged to bring from time to time actions for his damages in rental, [it] would be so onerous as to deny him adequate relief.

> And permanent damages are allowable where the nuisance, although arising from a continuing cause, cannot be abated because of public interest. . . .

> Where the structure or business is permanent within the purview of the principles herein reiterated, but the structure is negligently constructed, or if either is negligently operated, recurring damages are recoverable. In either case, however, the duty rests upon the person damaged to minimize his damages if it is in his power to do so.

> It is very plain that the facts bring the Kentucky-Ohio Gas Company's business and power plant and pumping station within the term permanent, as it is herein defined, and establish that it was not negligently constructed nor negligently operated. Therefore, the measure of Bowling's damages is the diminution of the market value of his property, proximately resulting from its invasion with the nuisance complained of.

---

13. Authors' note: After a hiatus, the display regained its prominence:

[Copeland] moved it to his former corporate headquarters in Elmwood for four years. It made a one-time appearance at the grave of former Gov. Huey P. Long near the state Capitol in Baton Rouge. Finally in 1991, under a court order to rein in the show so it doesn't cause bumper-to-bumper traffic, he was allowed to return it to Folse Drive.

Copeland admitted the display has gradually gotten bigger since then. It now runs on two generators because it demands more electricity than the power grid can handle. But the tensions with neighbors have eased, and the show has won over some of its previous opponents.

New Orleans Times-Picayune, Dec. 23, 2004, at 1.

The 34th Christmas lights spectacular—at Copeland's lakefront home in Metarie—took place in 2007. It would be Copeland's last, as he died the following spring. The April 1, 2008, story on the front page of the *Times-Picayune* reported that "[t]he path leading to the mausoleum's door had been strewn with white rose petals, and tiny beads resembling Christmas lights—a reminder of Copeland's over-the-top yuletide displays—had been threaded through some of the white flowers that banked the stand where the coffin rested."

E. Right Use, Wrong Place

Another source of confusion in this area concerns the distinction between private nuisances *per se* and *per accidens*. According to treatise law:

> Private nuisances are often classified as either *per accidens* (that is, in fact) or *per se* (that is, at law). A private nuisance *per accidens* is a nuisance by reason of its location or the manner in which it is constructed, maintained or operated. A private nuisance *per se*, typically an activity or pursuit made illegal by local or state law, is an act, occupation, or structure that is deemed a nuisance at all times and under all circumstances, regardless of location or surroundings.

Powell on Real Property §64.04[1] (Michael Allan Wolf gen. ed. 2009).

Do the majority and dissenting judges in the following decision follow these blackletter distinctions? Is this simply another case of an abnormally sensitive plaintiff? Or is the fear of the dead, though irrational, widespread enough to be "normal"?

POWELL v. TAYLOR
222 Ark. 896, 263 S.W.2d 906 (1954)

GEORGE ROSE SMITH, Justice. This is a suit brought by six residents of Gurdon to enjoin the appellees from establishing a funeral home in a residential district within the city. The defendants intend to remodel a dwelling known as the Taylor place and to use it as a combined residence and undertaking parlor. The plaintiffs, who own homes nearby, objected to the proposal and offered to reimburse the defendants for the preliminary expenses already incurred. This effort to dissuade the defendants having failed, the present suit was filed. The chancellor denied relief upon the ground that the neighborhood is not exclusively residential.

On this particular subject the law has undergone a marked change in the past fifty years. Until about the end of the nineteenth century the only limitation upon one's right to use his property as he pleased was the prohibition against inflicting upon his neighbors injury affecting the physical senses. Hence the older cases went no farther than to exclude as nuisances, in residential districts, such offensive businesses as slaughterhouses, livery stables, blasting operations, and the like.

Today this narrow view prevails, if at all, in a few jurisdictions only. It is now generally recognized that the inhabitants of a residential neighborhood may, by taking prompt action before a funeral home has been established therein, prevent its intrusion. In 1952 the Supreme Court of Louisiana reviewed the more recent decisions in twenty-two States and found that nineteen prohibit the entry of a mortuary into a residential area, while only three courts adhered to the older view. Frederick v. Brown Funeral Homes, Inc., 222 La. 57, 62 So. 2d 100. In a casenote the matter is summed up in these words: "The modern tendency to expand equity's protection of aesthetics and mental health has led the majority of jurisdictions to bar funeral homes or cemeteries from the residential sanctuaries of ordinarily sensitive people." 4 Ark. L. Rev. 483. These decisions rest not upon a finding that an undertaking parlor is physically offensive but rather upon the premise that its continuous suggestion of death and dead bodies tends to destroy the comfort and repose sought in home ownership. . . .

It is our conclusion in the case at bar that the neighborhood in question is so essentially residential in character as to entitle the appellants to the relief asked. The Taylor place is situated at the corner of Eighth and East Main Streets, and the testimony is largely directed to the area extending for two blocks in each direction, or a total of sixteen city blocks. In a relatively small city an area of this size may well be treated as a district in itself, else there might be no residential districts in the whole community. Gurdon is a city of the second class, having had a population of 2,390 in the year 1950. It is not shown to have adopted a zoning ordinance.

This square of sixteen blocks is bounded on the west by a public highway which is bordered by commercial establishments, their exact nature not being shown in detail. Otherwise the neighborhood is exclusively residential in appearance and almost so in its actual use. A seamstress living two doors east of the Taylor place earns some income by sewing at home. The couple in the house just south of the Taylor place rent rooms to elderly people and take care of them when they are ill. J.T. McAllister lives diagonally across the intersection from the Taylor place. He is in the wholesale lumber business and uses one room as an office, keeping books there and transacting business by telephone and with persons who call. A photograph of this home shows that there is no sign or anything else to indicate that business is carried on there. Farther up the street an eighty-year-old dentist has a small office in his yard and occasionally treats patients. The testimony discloses no other commercial activity within the area.

On the other hand, the residential quality of the neighborhood is convincingly shown. A real estate dealer describes it as the best residential section in Gurdon. Estimates as to the value of various homes range from $15,000 to $35,000. Many inhabitants of the area confirm its residential character and earnestly protest the entry of the mortuary. One, whose wife suffered a mental illness some years ago, says that he will be forced to move away if the funeral home is established. Another testifies that he will not build a home on his vacant lots across the street from the Taylor place if it is converted to a funeral parlor. A third testifies that she lost interest in buying the house next to the Taylor place when she learned of the defendants' plans. It is true that other witnesses state that they have no objection to the proposal, and the chancellor found that property values will not be adversely affected. But we regard the residential character of the vicinity as the controlling issue, and the evidence upon that question preponderates in favor of the appellants.

Reversed.

MILLWEE, Justice (dissenting). As I read the opinion of the majority, it is now the law in Arkansas that the operation of a modest undertaking parlor in a mixed residential and business area of a city of the second class constitutes a nuisance per se and may be abated as such by injunction. This holding is so foreign to the traditional attitude of this court and the general legislative policy of this state that I must respectfully dissent. . . .

About the only businesses or operations which this court has seen fit to enjoin as nuisances per se are: a gaming house, Vandeworker v. State, 13 Ark. 700; a bawdy house, State v. Porter, 38 Ark. 637; and the standing of a stallion or jackass within the limits of a municipality, Ex parte Foote, 70 Ark. 12, 65 S.W. 706. To this select group must now be added the operation of a modest undertaking parlor, where no funerals are to be held, in an area of a city of the second class which is "essentially" but not "actually" or "exclusively" residential. . . .[14]

---

14. Authors' note: Contrary to Justice Minor Milwee's dissent, in Arkansas, funeral homes are not nuisances per se. *See* Mitchell v. Bearden, 255 Ark. 888, 889, 503 S.W.2d 904, 905 (1974):

The intrusion of a funeral home into an exclusively residential district would ordinarily constitute a nuisance. It may be a nuisance in an area essentially residential in character. If, however, transition of the district from residential to business has so far progressed that the value of surrounding property would be enhanced as business property, rather than depreciated as residential property, the establishment of a funeral home would not constitute a nuisance.

In *Mitchell*, because the neighborhood had maintained its residential character, the trial court's finding of a nuisance was affirmed. In Potter v. Bryan Funeral Home, 307 Ark. 142, 817 S.W.2d 882 (1991), however, the court found that the proposed site for the funeral home was in a mixed residential and commercial area and affirmed the trial court's denial of injunctive relief.

Notes

1. Cemeteries, which also remind neighbors of death, pose similar challenges to courts. In McCaw v. Harrison, 259 S.W.2d 457, 458 (Ky. 1953), a dairy farmer sought to enjoin the use of adjoining land as a cemetery site. The land was underlaid with cavernous limestone and the topsoil was shallow; therefore, it was alleged, wells in the area would be contaminated by the bacteria from dead human bodies. The court, affirming the trial court's dismissal of the action, concluded:

> A cemetery does not constitute a nuisance merely because it is a constant reminder of death and has a depressing influence on the minds of persons who observe it, or because it tends to depreciate the value of property in the neighborhood, or is offensive to the aesthetic sense of an adjoining proprietor. On the other hand, if the location or maintenance of a cemetery endangers the public health, either by corrupting the surrounding atmosphere, or water of wells or springs, it constitutes a nuisance.

2. In cases of environmental contamination, plaintiffs have sought to recover damages for the diminution in property values attributable to the stigma of living in the impacted area. In Wilson v. Amoco Corp., 33 F. Supp. 2d 981, 986 (D. Wyo. 1998), an action brought by property owners and others against the Amoco Corporation, the Burlington Northern Railroad Company, and the owner of a dry cleaning facility, a federal district court summarized judicial treatment of stigma claims:

> It is apparent from the maps submitted by Plaintiffs' damages experts that some Plaintiffs whose properties arguably have not been physically impacted or physically injured may nonetheless be seeking damages for the diminution in value of their properties allegedly caused by the stigma associated with living on or owning property that is in close proximity to property that has in fact been physically impacted or affected by contamination. Few courts, if any, have permitted recovery on the basis of stigmatization alone. In Berry v. Armstrong Rubber Co., the Fifth Circuit Court of Appeals, applying Mississippi law, responded to plaintiffs' claim for stigma damages by noting that plaintiffs had "cited no case, and the court has found none, holding that Mississippi common law allows recovery for a decrease in property value caused by a public perception without accompanying physical harm to the property." 989 F.2d 822, 829 (1993). The Fifth Circuit reaffirmed this rule only recently in Bradley v. Armstrong Rubber Co., 130 F.3d 168, 175-76 (1997) (allowing recovery for stigma damages where permanent and physical injury to plaintiff's property has occurred). The Third Circuit adopted a similar rule in the case of In re Paoli R.R. Yard PCB Litig., holding there that stigma damages were recoverable only when a physical impact on the particular plaintiff's property had occurred. 35 F.3d 717, 797 (1994). Finally, both Michigan and California have rejected claims for stigma damages absent some proof of permanent physical injury. See Adkins v. Thomas Solvent Co., 440 Mich. 293, 487 N.W.2d 715, 721 (Mich. 1992); Santa Fe Partnership v. Arco Prods. Co., 46 Cal. App. 4th 967, 983-84 (Cal. App. 1996). The Court agrees with the rationale expressed in these and other cases that claims of stigma damages absent some other definable physical harm to the property are simply too speculative to warrant serious consideration. See Adams v. Star Enter., 851 F. Supp. 770, 773 (E.D. Va. 1994); Chance v. BP Chems., Inc., 77 Ohio St. 3d 17, 670 N.E.2d 985, 993 (Ohio 1996). Consequently, Plaintiffs in the instant matter may not recover damages based solely on stigma absent proof of some physical injury or harm to the

specific Plaintiff's property (i.e., separate establishment of a claim for trespass, nuisance, or negligence).

3. Should courts grant relief solely on the grounds that an activity offends aesthetic sensibilities? While the traditional rule says "no," some courts in dictum and some commentators have advocated a shift. *See* Powell on Real Property §64.04[4] (Michael Allan Wolf gen. ed. 2009). Raymond Robert Coletta, in *The Case for Aesthetic Nuisance: Rethinking Traditional Judicial Attitudes*, 48 Ohio St. L.J. 141, 141-42 (1987), has observed:

> This judicial reluctance to recognize an action in nuisance based on aesthetic considerations is . . . based on a fundamental error. By equating aesthetics with beauty, courts have predetermined their rejection of aesthetic nuisance actions. Certainly, if individuals were allowed injunctive or monetary relief merely because their concept of beauty was not reflected in their neighbor's house, courts would become embroiled in innumerable, unresolvable lawsuits. Property rights are not, and should not be, subject to the vagaries of individual taste. But in allowing nuisance actions based on aesthetics, courts need not become judicial arbiters of beauty. Aesthetics, rather than a synonym for visual beauty, properly refers to the symbolic and emotional meanings conveyed by the visual environment, meanings which arise, in large part, from the cultural identity of the particular neighborhood. Nuisance actions should not be based on whether a particular land use is "inherently ugly," but rather on whether the land use is visually consonant with established community values. Giving recognition to aesthetic interests would simply reflect the significant effect that visual harmony has on an individual's relation to his or her environment. Thus, judicial inquiry should focus not on an archetypal concept of beauty but simply on visual harmony within the social neighborhood setting. In this context, nuisance actions based on aesthetics would merely lead to judicial recognition of, and protection of, community values and preferences, without falling into the abyss of ontological subjectivity.

Do you share Professor Raymond Coletta's faith that judges can objectively gauge a community's aesthetic "values and preferences"?

4. How effective is private nuisance as a land use planning device? In American Smelting & Refining Co. v. Godfrey, 158 F. 225, 229 (8th Cir. 1907), the court stated: "The rights of habitation are superior to the rights of trade, and whenever they conflict, the rights of trade must yield to the primary or natural right."

The court in Stevens v. Rockport Granite Co., 216 Mass. 486, 489, 104 N.E. 371, 374 (1914), observed:

> The neighborhood in question is of a mixed character. It is adjacent to the sea, with inlets upon a somewhat bold and rocky shore. On this account it has become increasingly attractive for summer residence. The plaintiffs and others nearby, and more at a greater distance, have estates for this purpose. Nature also has planted valuable stone quarries in the vicinity, which have been opened and worked, and are useful not only to their owners but also in centers of population where they give beauty and strength to public buildings. This circumstance renders apposite the words of James, L.J., in Salvin v. North Brancepeth, L.R. 9 Ch. App. 705, at 709: "If some picturesque haven opens its arms to invite the commerce of the world, it is not for this court to forbid the embrace, although the fruit of it should be the sights and sounds and smells of a common seaport and shipbuilding town, which would drive the Dryads and their masters from

their ancient solitudes." Both these uses, commencing about the same time, have grown together in the same village. It cannot be said upon the evidence or upon the findings of the master that either has become so dominant as to impress its special character upon the community. The village is not given over exclusively to the granite industry, nor has the summer resident so overwhelmed it as to have become its distinctive feature. Therefore, each must yield something to the presence of the other. The plaintiffs cannot demand the quiet of a remote cove far distant from any industry. The defendant cannot insist upon conducting its business in disregard of those who seek some degree of rest and refreshment by the ocean side. The standard of comfort for the one is affected by the reasonable business needs of the other, and the same is true conversely.

Compare *Stevens* with Adams v. Snouffer, 88 Ohio App. 79, 85, 87 N.E.2d 484, 488 (Ct. App. 1949):

The plaintiffs proceed upon the theory that their homes are in a residential section and therefore the relief sought is peculiarly applicable. It is the contention of the appellants that the section involved is not residential but open country. They point to the fact that the residences are widely separated, some are of little value; that the terrain in the vicinity of the properties involved is rough and rocky, and, in all, the presence of the quarry, because of these physical conditions, and particularly because of its distance from the homes of the plaintiffs, is not a nuisance. It is true that the district in which plaintiffs' homes are located is not closely built up but the parcels of land in which they live have been and are used exclusively for residential purposes. The section involved may be designated as the highest type of exclusive residential territory. Manifestly, it is a modern development where those who can afford it and care for that manner of living move where they may have spacious grounds upon which their homes are built and the opportunity for rustic environment where in part, at least, natural beauty is found in a somewhat wild and uncultivated state.

5. Should existing uses be protected from plaintiffs who "come to the nuisance"? In Bove v. Donner-Hanna Coke Corp., 236 App. Div. 37, 41, 258 N.Y.S. 229, 233 (Sup. Ct. 1932), the court stated:

With all the dirt, smoke and gas which necessarily come from factory chimneys, trains and boats, and with full knowledge that this region was especially adapted for industrial rather than residential purposes, and that factories would increase in the future, plaintiff selected this locality as the site of her future home. She voluntarily moved into this district, fully aware of the fact that the atmosphere would constantly be contaminated by dirt, gas and foul odors; and she could not hope to find in this locality the pure air of a strictly residential zone. She evidently saw certain advantages in living in this congested center. This is not the case of an industry, with its attendant noise and dirt, invading a quiet, residential district. It is just the opposite. Here a residence is built in an area naturally adapted for industrial purposes and already dedicated to that use. Plaintiff can hardly be heard to complain at this late date that her peace and comfort have been disturbed by a situation which existed, to some extent at least, at the very time she bought her property, and which condition she must have known would grow worse rather than better as the years went by.

See also Note, 41 Cal. L. Rev. 148, 148-49 (1953): "Although a few courts apparently still follow Rex v. Cross [2C. & P. 483, 172 Eng. Rep. 219 (1826)], the overwhelming majority of American and English courts have rejected the doctrine. A host of cases emphatically declare that 'coming to the nuisance' is not a defense either in an action for damages or in a suit for an injunction."

6. Can nature untended cause a private nuisance? In Giles v. Walker, 24 Q.B.D. 656, 657 (1890), in reversing a finding that the defendant had been negligent in failing to mow land on which thistles had sprung up after cultivation had ceased, the court, in a two-sentence opinion, stated: "I never heard of such an action as this. There can be no duty as between adjoining occupiers to cut the thistles, which are the natural growth of the soil."

Roots of a black Italian poplar growing on the defendant's land extended under the plaintiffs land, causing the subsidence of the plaintiff's house by undermining the foundation. The defendant's house had been built in 1904 and the plaintiff's in 1912. In 1950, the plaintiff brought an action for damages "for trespass and nuisance" and for an injunction. In McCombe v. Read, [1955] 2 Q.B. 429, the court granted an injunction to restrain the continuing nuisance, but ordered an inquiry as to the amount of damages that could be recovered. For a more recent decision also granting relief to the plaintiff, see Delaware Mansions Ltd v. Westminster City Council [2001] 4 All E.R. 737 (House of Lords).

Consider the findings of James T.R. Jones, *Trains, Trucks, Trees, and Shrubs: Vision-Blocking Natural Vegetation and a Landowner's Duty to Those Off the Premises*, 39 Vill. L. Rev. 1263 (1994):

> Thus, British and related courts long declined to award damages in negligence/nuisance cases involving harm caused by natural conditions to those off the land. The English Court of Common Pleas may have been the first tribunal to deny recovery for an off-premises injury caused by a "natural" condition when it issued the late sixteenth century decision in *Boulston's Case* [77 Eng. Rep. 216 (C.P. 1597)]. The court held that a landowner was not responsible for damage wild rabbits living on his land caused to the property of his neighbor.

> A number of subsequent courts cited *Boulston's Case* as precedent that one has no duty to control natural conditions on his or her property. Many courts found for landowners and against those situated nearby when, for example, large numbers of pheasants invaded the neighbors' property and consumed their crops; hordes of fecund rats ate the neighbor's grain; or, as in *Boulston's Case* itself, overly prolific rabbits damaged the neighbor's fields. Tribunals also extended the no liability principle to vegetable or inanimate natural conditions, exculpating defendants whose land contained large rocks which overhung and threatened their neighbors, an excess of thistles whose seeds blew to germination and abundant destructive growth next door, or many noxious prickly pears which broke down a protective fence and permitted wild native dogs to ravage an adjoining herd of sheep. . . .

> American courts early on adopted the British "no duty" approach to suits for damage natural conditions caused to adjoining property. They denied recovery, for example, in cases involving untrimmed vegetation that contributed to collisions and injurious weeds which invaded a neighbor's acreage. American courts further held a landowner has no duty to manage sand naturally on his or her premises or to remove dead leaves and similar combustible natural materials which are lying on a forest floor. Additionally, the courts ruled that a landowner is not responsible when the stench from a naturally occurring, putrid and stagnant pond bothers those in the vicinity or the natural flow or drainage of water from a landowner's property harms a neighbor. All concurred that "a man does not become a wrongdoer by leaving his property in a state of nature." . . .

While many American jurisdictions no longer adopt this position, or at least not when the issue is overgrown vegetation that obstructs the view of drivers on public highways, a number of jurisdictions still follow the traditional rule or at least the rule as it is set forth in the non-proviso portion of the Restatement.[15]

See also Dix W. Noel, *Nuisances From Land in Its Natural Condition*, 56 Harv. L. Rev. 722 (1943).

F.   Covenants That Outlaw Nuisances: Mere Surplusage?

Millions of Americans live in neighborhoods that are "governed" by Covenants, Conditions, and Restrictions (CC&Rs). From a private land use regulation perspective, the most important feature of this package of controls is the set of restrictive covenants that address a wide range of activities by local homeowners. The descendants of the running covenants and equitable servitudes that puzzled English and American law and equity courts during the 19th and early 20th centuries, these modern restrictions often contain anti-nuisance provisions. As the following case indicates, however, mentioning "nuisance" in the CC&Rs does not in and of itself provide landowners with very much additional protection from their offensive neighbors.

TURNER v. CAPLAN
268 Va. 122, 596 S.E.2d 525 (2004)

OPINION BY JUSTICE DONALD W. LEMONS . . .

In 1975, Robert E. Turner, III ("Turner") acquired a 101.4 acre tract of land in Pittsylvania County, Virginia, and thereafter established a subdivision known as Windermere. This dispute concerns the use of Lots 4B, 5, 6, and 7 in Section D of the subdivision which will be referred to herein as the "pasture."

In 1979, Turner recorded a declaration of protective covenants, restrictions, and conditions (the "Agreement") of which relevant portions provide:

1. All of the lots above described shall be used exclusively for residential purposes. . . . .

3. Only one single family dwelling may be erected on any lot, but in addition thereto, there may be erected a car garage and other structures incidental to the use of such property for residential purposes. . . . .

5. No nuisance shall be maintained or permitted on any of said lots.

6. There shall be no raising or harboring of pigs, goats, sheep, cows, or any other livestock or poultry on said lots, with the exception of a usual domestic pet. This restriction shall not be applicable to Lots Nos. 1-7, inclusive, Section D.

Covenant 10 further specifies that should a court invalidate any one of the Agreement's Covenants, all others remain in full force and effect.

---

15. Authors' note: RESTATEMENT (SECOND) OF TORTS §363 (1965) provides:

(1) Except as stated in Subsection (2), neither a possessor of land, nor a vendor, lessor, or other transferor, is liable for physical harm caused to others outside of the land by a natural condition of the land.

(2) A possessor of land in an urban area is subject to liability to persons using a public highway for physical harm resulting from his failure to exercise reasonable care to prevent an unreasonable risk of harm arising from the condition of trees on the land near the highway.

The ALI included the following "caveat": "The Institute expresses no opinion as to whether the rule stated in Subsection (2) may not apply to the possessor of land in a rural area."

Turner sold most of Windermere's lots; however, he retained ownership of the pasture. Michael and Carol Caplan ("the Caplans") and Grady and Martha Carrigan ("the Carrigans") reside on lots adjoining the pasture.

At some time in the early 1980's, Turner kept a horse on the pasture for approximately six months. Again, in the late 1990's a horse was periodically kept on the pasture. Finally, since 2002 a horse has been kept periodically on the pasture depending upon the time of year and the weather.

In 2002, the Caplans filed a bill of complaint for injunctive relief with the Circuit Court of Pittsylvania County asking the court to permanently enjoin Turner from placing a horse on the pasture. Thereafter, the trial court granted the Carrigans' motion to intervene in the lawsuit.

The trial court held that the maintenance of a horse on the pasture violated the Agreement because it was inconsistent with the intent to create a residential subdivision and because the trial court held that keeping a horse at that location constituted a nuisance. The trial court entered a permanent injunction forbidding Turner from keeping a horse on the pasture. Turner appeals the adverse judgment of the trial court and alleges that the trial court erred in its judgment that maintaining a horse on the pasture was inconsistent with the intent of the Agreement, that the specific exception from the ban upon livestock for the pasture was unreasonable, and that keeping a horse on the pasture was a nuisance. . . .

The trial court found that Turner intended to create an exclusively residential neighborhood when he formed the Windermere subdivision. The trial court further concluded that placing livestock on any of Windermere's lots is inconsistent with this intent.

Covenant 1 of the Agreement is clear and unambiguous in restricting Windermere's lots exclusively for residential purposes; however, Covenant 1 is subject to an equally clear and unambiguous exception in Covenant 6. Covenant 1 states that all of the lots "shall be used exclusively for residential purposes." Covenant 6 prohibits raising or harboring of livestock or poultry on the lots but further states that, "this Restriction shall not be applicable to Lots Nos. 1 -7, inclusive, Section D," which includes the pasture. We must construe the Agreement as a whole and, if possible, interpret its provisions consistently with one another. First American Title Ins. Co. v. Seaboard Sav. & Loan Ass'n, 227 Va. 379, 386, 315 S.E.2d 842, 846 (1984); Tate v. Tate, 75 Va. 522, 527 (1881). In *First American Title*, we said:

> it is the, duty of the court to construe the [Agreement] as a whole, and *in the performance of this duty it will not treat as meaningless any word thereof, if any meaning, reasonably consistent with other parts of the [Agreement], can be given.*

Id. at 386, 315 S.E.2d at 846 (quoting Pilot Life Ins. Co. v. Crosswhite, 206 Va. 558, 561, 145 S.E.2d 143, 146 (1965)).

Adhering to this principle, we hold that Covenant 1's residential purpose, when read in context with Covenant 6, does not exclude raising or harboring livestock or poultry. Such activity is prohibited under Covenant 6 for all lots except Lots 1 through 7 of Section D, which includes the lots comprising the pasture. Turner's reservation of this right is clearly expressed.

Further, Turner states that the trial court erred in holding that exempting the pasture from the covenant forbidding raising or harboring livestock or poultry is unreasonable. While we are aware of case law holding that use of property may not be unreasonably restricted, counsel and the trial court cite no cases applying the concept of "unreasonability" to the exemptions specifically allowing the use of restricted land for particular purposes.

In holding the exemption unreasonable, the trial court apparently relied on the fact that Turner, as the original grantor/owner, is the only Windermere landowner exempted from Covenant 6's restriction. This assumption is incorrect because the exception to restrictions in Covenant 6 applies to Lots 1 through 7 of Section D. The Carrigans, who are appellees herein, own Lots 1 and 2B.

Additionally, the property owners knew at the time they purchased the lots, and assented to Windermere's covenants, that Lots 1 through 7 had been exempted from the livestock restriction. Presumably, they considered the restriction and its exemptions reasonable or they would not have purchased their lots. On this record, we hold that the trial court plainly erred in concluding that the exemption here was void for unreasonableness.

Finally, Turner asserts that the trial court erred in holding that "to allow the placement of livestock on lots in the subdivision would also create a nuisance in violation of Restriction No. 5." Of course, the law of nuisance exists independently of restrictive covenants. The fact that a prohibition upon maintaining a nuisance is found in a covenant adds nothing to analysis of whether the facts presented constitute a nuisance.

The case of Bragg v. Ives, 149 Va. 482, 140 S.E. 656 (1927), involved the proposed intrusion of a funeral home into a residential neighborhood. In the course of determining whether the trial court erred by dismissing the bill for injunctive relief upon demurrer, we considered what is necessary to sustain a cause of action for nuisance. Quoting decisions from other jurisdictions and secondary authorities with approval, we stated:

> "In all such cases the question is whether the nuisance complained of will or does produce such a condition of things as, in the judgment of reasonable [persons], is naturally productive of actual physical discomfort to persons of ordinary sensibilities and of ordinary tastes and habits, and as, in view of the circumstances of the case, is reasonable and in derogation of the rights of the complainant." . . . .
>
> "The decisions establish that the term nuisance, in legal parlance, extends to everything that endangers life or health, gives offense to the senses, violates the laws of decency, or obstructs the reasonable and comfortable use of property."

Id. at 496-497, 140 S.E. at 660 (citations omitted).

Although the trial court does not expressly use the term "nuisance *per se*," the language of its order embraces the concept. As we have previously noted, "while there is some confusion in the books as to the meaning of the term nuisance *per se*, the tendency of modern times is to restrict its use to such things as are nuisances at all times and under all circumstances." Price v. Travis, 149 Va. 536, 547, 140 S.E. 644, 647 (1927).

The trial court's order is too broad and improperly expresses its judgment in terms that can only be interpreted as a holding of nuisance *per se*. First, the order refers to "livestock" when the pasturing of a horse is the issue. Second, the order refers to "lots in the subdivision" when the only lots in question constitute the "pasture." Finally, the trial court erred in its entry of a judgment that effectively holds that the mere "placement" of livestock, including a horse, on the lots at issue constitutes a nuisance at all times and under all circumstances.

We hold that the trial court erred in its interpretation of the legal effect of the covenants in the agreement. Further, we hold that the trial court erred in its entry of a judgment that is too broad in its application and, in effect, holds that the mere placement of a horse on the pasture constitutes a nuisance *per se*. We will reverse the judgment of the trial court and enter final judgment for Turner.

Notes

1. The Douglases complained that their three neighbors—the only neighbors they had—in the Satinwood subdivision "operated motorized all-terrain vehicles, played loud music, and fired loaded weapons on property located within the subdivision." The Douglases appealed to the Supreme Court of Georgia a lower court ruling denying them injunctive relief. The restrictive covenants for

the subdivision allowed only residential uses and stated that "no noxious or offensive activity shall be erected, maintained or conducted upon any lot or any party thereof, nor shall anything be done thereon which may be or may become an annoyance or nuisance in the neighborhood." In Douglas v. Wages, 271 Ga. 616, 616-18, 523 S.E.2d 330, 331 (1999), the high court affirmed the holding of the lower court, noting that "[n]on-commercial recreational activities . . . are within the purpose of a residence," and that "the evidence did not demand a finding that the activities complained of constituted a statutorily-defined nuisance." The Georgia statute cited by the court (O.G.C.A. §41-1-1) defined nuisance "as anything, lawful or unlawful, 'that causes hurt, inconvenience, or damage to another.'"

2. In another covenant/nuisance challenge to the objectionable activities of a neighbor, the Supreme Court of Idaho, in Gabriel v. Cazier, 130 Idaho 171, 172-74, 938 P.2d 1209, 1210-12 (1997), affirmed the lower court's denial of a permanent injunction that would have prohibited the defendants from allowing their children to continue to conduct swimming lessons in the family's backyard pool in a residential subdivision. Under the heading "NUISANCES," the "declaration of protective restrictions" for the subdivision provided:

> No business or trade or offensive or noxious activity shall be carried on upon any lot in the Subdivision, nor shall anything be done thereon which may become an annoyance or a nuisance to the neighborhood by unreasonably interfering with the use and enjoyment of other property within the Subdivision, nor shall any residence be utilized for public purposes or services including public worship or church services. Weeds shall be kept cut and portions of any lot not in use for lawn or otherwise shall be kept trimmed and in a neat and orderly condition.

Because the state supreme court found that the word "business" was ambiguous, the justices sought evidence regarding the intent of the parties who drafted the language, concluding "that the term 'business' as used in the declaration was not intended nor interpreted by the owners of lots in the subdivision to prohibit swimming lessons conducted by a homeowner's children in their own back-yard during a limited time in the summer." Nor did the lessons constitute a nuisance (although the defendants were ordered not to use the portable chemical toilet they had maintained outside their home), as, according to the trial court, "the lessons do not create an undue amount of noise, they are conducted in the Caziers' backyard, they are during reasonable hours of the day, the parking is confined to the Caziers' own frontage, and the increased traffic is within the capacity of the subdivision's streets."

G. Remedying the Wrong: From Chancellors to Coase (and Beyond)

The next case is a classic, not only because of the innovative (and controversial) remedy devised by the majority, but also because the decision appeared on the eve of the dramatic revolution in American environmental law. With the benefit of hindsight, the state high court's skepticism about the ability of industry to develop technologies for retarding or eliminating their pollution seems naive. Nevertheless, it is fair to ask if we would have witnessed these new technologies in the absence of comprehensive federal (as opposed to patchwork state and local) legislation and regulation.

BOOMER v. ATLANTIC CEMENT CO.
26 N.Y.2d 219, 257 N.E.2d 870, 309 N.Y.S.2d 312 (1970)

[This was an action for injunction and damages for injury to property from dirt, smoke, and vibration emanating from the defendant's cement plant. The trial court determined that defendant maintained a nuisance, awarded temporary damages, but denied an injunction. The appellate division affirmed. The court of appeals affirmed the denial of a permanent injunction expressly because of the "large disparity in economic consequences of the nuisance and the injunction,"[16] but reversed and remitted the case to the trial court "to grant an injunction which shall be vacated upon payment . . . of amounts of permanent damage to respective plaintiffs." Portions of the majority opinion, per Justice BERGAN, follow.]

A court performs its essential function when it decides the rights of parties before it. Its decision of private controversies may sometimes greatly affect public issues. Large questions of law are often resolved by the manner in which private litigation is decided. But this is normally an incident to the court's main function to settle controversy. It is a rare exercise of judicial power to use a decision in private litigation as a purposeful mechanism to achieve direct public objectives greatly beyond the rights and interests before the court.

Effective control of air pollution is a problem presently far from solution even with the full public and financial powers of government. In large measure adequate technical procedures are yet to be developed and some that appear possible may be economically impracticable.

It seems apparent that the amelioration of air pollution will depend on technical research in great depth; on a carefully balanced consideration of the economic impact of close regulation; and on the actual effect on public health. It is likely to require massive public expenditure and to demand more than any local community can accomplish and to depend on regional and interstate controls.

A court should not try to do this on its own as a by-product of private litigation and it seems manifest that the judicial establishment is neither equipped in the limited nature of any judgment it can pronounce nor prepared to lay down and implement an effective policy for the elimination of air pollution. This is an area beyond the circumference of one private lawsuit. It is a direct responsibility for government and should not thus be undertaken as an incident to solving a dispute between property owners and a single cement plant—one of many—in the Hudson River valley. . . .

If the injunction were to be granted unless within a short period—e.g., 18 months—the nuisance be abated by improved methods, there would be no assurance that any significant technical improvement would occur.

The parties could settle this private litigation at any time if defendant paid enough money and the imminent threat of closing the plant would build up the pressure on defendant. If there were no improved techniques found, there would inevitably be applications to the court at Special Term for extensions of time to perform on showing of good faith efforts to find such techniques.

Moreover, techniques to eliminate dust and other annoying byproducts of cement making are unlikely to be developed by any research the defendant can undertake within any short period, but will depend on the total resources of the cement industry nationwide and throughout the world. The problem is universal wherever cement is made.

For obvious reasons the rate of the research is beyond control of defendant. . . .

JASEN, Judge (dissenting). I agree with the majority that a reversal is required here, but I do not subscribe to the newly enunciated doctrine of assessment of permanent damages, in lieu of an injunction, where substantial property rights have been impaired by the creation of a nuisance.

It has long been the rule in this State, as the majority acknowledges, that a nuisance which results in substantial continuing damage to neighbors must be enjoined. (Whalen v. Union Bag & Paper Co., 208 N.Y. 1, 101 N.E. 805; Campbell v. Seaman, 63 N.Y. 568; see, also, Kennedy

---

16. Authors' note: Investment in the plant was in excess of $45 million, and it employed over 300 people; the trial court found plaintiffs had suffered permanent damages of $185,000.

v. Moog Servocontrols, 21 N.Y.2d 966, 290 N.Y.S.2d 193, 237 N.E.2d 356.) To now change the rule to permit the cement company to continue polluting the air indefinitely upon the payment of permanent damages is, in my opinion, compounding the magnitude of a very serious problem in our State and Nation today.

In recognition of this problem, the Legislature of this State has enacted the Air Pollution Control Act (Public Health Law, Consol. Laws, c. 45, §§1264 to 1299-m) declaring that it is the State policy to require the use of all available and reasonable methods to prevent and control air pollution (Public Health Law §1265).

The harmful nature and widespread occurrence of air pollution have been extensively documented. Congressional hearings have revealed that air pollution causes substantial property damage, as well as being a contributing factor to a rising incidence of lung cancer, emphysema, bronchitis and asthma.

The specific problem faced here is known as particulate contamination because of the fine dust particles emanating from defendant's cement plant. The particular type of nuisance is not new, having appeared in many cases for at least the past 60 years. (See Hulbert v. California Portland Cement Co., 161 Cal. 239, 118 P. 928 [1911].) It is interesting to note that cement production has recently been identified as a significant source of particulate contamination in the Hudson Valley. This type of pollution, wherein very small particles escape and stay in the atmosphere, has been denominated as the type of air pollution which produces the greatest hazard to human health. We have thus a nuisance which not only is damaging to the plaintiffs, but also is decidedly harmful to the general public.

I see grave dangers in overruling our long-established rule of granting an injunction where a nuisance results in substantial continuing damage. In permitting the injunction to become inoperative upon the payment of permanent damages, the majority is, in effect, licensing a continuing wrong. It is the same as saying to the cement company, you may continue to do harm to your neighbors so long as you pay a fee for it. Furthermore, once such permanent damages are assessed and paid, the incentive to alleviate the wrong would be eliminated, thereby continuing air pollution of an area without abatement.

It is true that some courts have sanctioned the remedy here proposed by the majority in a number of cases, but none of the authorities relied upon by the majority are analogous to the situations before us. In those cases, the courts, in denying an injunction and awarding money damages, grounded their decision on a showing that the use to which the property was intended to be put was primarily for the public benefit. Here, on the other hand, it is clearly established that the cement company is creating a continuing air pollution nuisance primarily for its own private interest with no public benefit.

This kind of inverse condemnation may not be invoked by a private person or corporation for private gain or advantage. Inverse condemnation should only be permitted when the public is primarily served in the taking or impairment of property.

The promotion of the interests of the polluting cement company has, in my opinion, no public use or benefit.

Nor is it constitutionally permissible to impose servitude on land, without consent of the owner, by payment of permanent damages where the continuing impairment of the land is for a private use. This is made clear by the State Constitution (art. I, §7, subd. [a]) which provides that "[p]rivate property shall not be taken for *public use* without just compensation" (emphasis added). It is, of course, significant that the section makes no mention of taking for a *private use*. . . .

It is not my intention to cause the removal of the cement plant from the Albany area, but to recognize the urgency of the problem stemming from this stationary source of air pollution, and to allow the company a specified period of time to develop a means to alleviate this nuisance.

I am aware that the trial court found that the most modern dust control devices available have been installed in defendant's plant, but, I submit, this does not mean that *better* and more effective dust control devices could not be developed within the time allowed to abate the pollution.

Moreover, I believe it is incumbent upon the defendant to develop such devices, since the cement company, at the time the plant commenced production (1962), was well aware of the plaintiffs' presence in the area, as well as the probable consequences of its contemplated operation. Yet, it still chose to build and operate the plant at this site.

In a day when there is growing concern for clean air, highly developed industry should not expect acquiescence by the courts, but should, instead, plan its operations to eliminate contamination of our air and damage to its neighbors. . . .

Notes

1. The paper plant involved in the *Whalen* case (decided in 1913), cited by New York Court of Appeals Judge Matthew J. Jasen, cost $1 million and employed over 400 people; plaintiff's operation of a 255-acre farm was damaged $100 a year by water pollution. The plant involved in the *Hulbert* case had a monthly payroll of $35,000 but emitted a contaminant which coated the oranges of a small grower with a cement-like crust. Against the wishes of the cement plant owner, the Supreme Court of California dismissed a temporary order that had stayed, pending the disposition of two appeals, an injunction secured by the grower.

The result reached in *Boomer* bears the imprimatur of two of America's leading jurists. When defendant's stone-crushing mill, worth $1 million, damaged plaintiff's summer residence, variously valued from $10,000 to $40,000, by air pollution and blasting vibrations, Judge Learned Hand, while stating that there was a violation of a legal right, found the situation required "a quantitative compromise between two conflicting interests" to be settled by balancing the conveniences. Smith v. Staso Milling Co., 18 F.2d 736 (2d Cir. 1927). See also the opinion of Justice Louis Brandeis in City of Harrisonville v. W.S. Dickey Clay Manufacturing Co., 289 U.S. 334, 337-38 (1933):

> For an injunction is not a remedy which issues as of course. Where substantial redress can be afforded by the payment of money and issuance of an injunction would subject the defendant to grossly disproportionate hardship, equitable relief may be denied although the nuisance is indisputable. This is true even if the conflict is between interests which are primarily private. Where an important public interest would be prejudiced, the reasons for denying the injunction may be compelling.

Should employment of the most approved and skilled methods in the construction and operation of defendant's plant, or other facts, such as the relative utility and social value of the conflicting uses, relieve defendant of damage liability as well? *Compare* Jost v. Dairyland Power Coop., 45 Wis. 2d 164, 172 N.W.2d 647 (1970) (the defendant's social utility was not relevant), *with* Watts v. Parma Manufacturing Co., 256 N.C. 611, 124 S.E.2d 809 (1962) (utility and social value were relevant). For an early reaction to the muddle in *Boomer*, see E.F. Roberts, *The Right to a Decent Environment; E = MC²: Environment Equals Men Times Courts Redoubling Their Efforts*, 55 Cornell L. Rev. 674 (1970).

2. Debate surrounding injunctive relief in nuisance actions is rooted in part in the entwined, yet distinct, histories of nuisance adjudication and equity jurisprudence. The remedy of the medieval

assize of nuisance was judicial abatement, but this action had fallen into disuse by William Blackstone's time. Blackstone reports that Action on the Case for Nuisance, for which damages were granted, was considered sufficient to compel voluntary abatement, for a neighbor would need to be "illnatured" to continue a nuisance knowing he would be liable for further injury. William Blackstone, 3 Commentaries *221. Bush v. Western, Prec. in Ch. 530 (1720) is the first reported case to enjoin a nuisance; exercise of this power remained infrequent until Lord Eldon sat on the woolsack from 1801 to 1827.

Concerns over the power of the injunctive remedy resulted in two doctrines, evolved in both England and America, limiting its use. First, but not relevant since the merger of law and equity, was the doctrine that the plaintiff could appeal to the chancellor only after his or her "right" had been determined in a law court. See Zechariah Chaffee Jr., Cases on Equitable Relief Against Tort 55-60 (1924).

Second was an attempt to limit the discretionary power of the chancellor—the doctrine that when a suitor brings his cause within the rules of equity jurisprudence the relief asked for is "demandable ex debito justitiae, and needs not be implored ex gratia." Walters v. McElroy, 151 Pa. 549, 25 A. 125, 127 (1892). Consider the differing approaches one court, the Supreme Court of Pennsylvania, used in attempting to settle this issue. In Richards's Appeal, 57 Pa. 105, 113, 98 Am. Dec. 202, 205 (1868), the court wrote:

> It seems to be supposed that, as at law, whenever a case is made out of wrongful acts on the one side and consequent injury on the other, a decree to restrain the act complained of, must as certainly follow, as a judgment would follow a verdict at common law. This is a mistake. It is elementary law, that in Equity a decree is never of right, as a judgment at law is, but of grace. Hence the chancellor will consider whether he would not do a greater injury by enjoining than would result from refusing, and leaving the party to his redress at the hands of a court and a jury. If in conscience the former should appear, he will refuse to enjoin.

Twenty-four years later, in *Walters*, 151 Pa. 549, 557, 25 A. 125, 127 (1892), the same court reasoned:

> The phrase "of grace," predicated of a decree in equity, had its origin in an age when kings dispensed their royal favors by the hands of their chancellors, but, although it continues to be repeated occasionally, it has no rightful place in the jurisprudence of a free commonwealth, and ought to be relegated to the age in which it was appropriate. It has been somewhere said that equity has its laws, as law has its equity. This is but another form of saying that equitable remedies are administered in accordance with rules as certain as human wisdom can devise, leaving their application only in doubtful cases to the discretion, not the unmerited favor or grace, of the chancellor. . . . And as to the principle invoked, that a chancellor will refuse to enjoin when greater injury will result from granting than from refusing an injunction, it is enough to observe that it has no application where the act complained of is in itself, as well as in its incidents, tortious. In such case it cannot be said that injury would result from an injunction, for no man can complain that he is injured by being prevented from doing, to the hurt of another, that which he has no right to do.

3. Sullivan v. Jones & Laughlin Steel Co., 208 Pa. 540, 554, 57 A. 1065, 1071 (1904), involved the operations of the Eliza Blast Furnaces, then the largest in the United States. One of the plaintiffs removed three barrels of dust weighing 1,200 pounds from his porch roof, and there was testimony that the corrosive effect of the dust would rot cloth on contact. In granting an injunction, the court said:

> A chancellor does act as of grace, but that grace sometimes becomes a matter of right to the suitor in his court, and, when it is clear that the law cannot give protection and relief—to which the complainant in equity is admittedly entitled the chancellor can no more withhold his grace than the law can deny protection and relief, if able to give them.

Four years later the plaintiff asked the court to find the defendant in contempt of the prior order. The defendant had spent $285,000 in alterations of the furnaces. See Sullivan v. Jones & Laughlin Steel Co., 222 Pa. 72, 70 A. 775 (1908).

4. Is the injunction, in the context of private nuisance, an effective way to prevent pollution? Some of the most intriguing early law and economics scholarship focused on this issue. See, for example, Ronald H. Coase, *The Problem of Social Cost*, 3 J.L. & Econ. 1 (1960); Guido Calabresi, *Transaction Costs, Resource Allocation, and Liability Rules—A Comment*, 11 J.L. & Econ. 67 (1968); James R. Atwood, Note, *An Economic Analysis of Land Use Conflicts*, 21 Stan. L. Rev. 293 (1969); and Richard Posner, Economic Analysis of Law 42-48, 56-57 (3d ed. 1986).

In his 1968 piece, Professor (now Judge) Guido Calabresi wrote, at 67-68:

> [I]f we assume that the cost of factory smoke which destroys neighboring farmers' wheat can be avoided more cheaply by a smoke control device than by growing a smoke resistant wheat, then, even if the loss is left on the farmers they will, under the assumptions made, pay the factory to install the smoke control device. This would . . . result in more factories relative to farmers and lower relative farm output than if the liability rule had been reversed. But if, as a result of this liability rule, farm output is too low relative to factory output those who lose from this "misallocation" would have every reason to bribe farmers to produce more and factories to produce less. This process would continue until no bargain could improve the allocation of resources. . . . We can, therefore, state as an axiom the proposition that all externalities can be internalized and all misallocations, even those created by legal structures, can be remedied by the market, except to the extent that transactions cost money or the structure itself creates some impediments to bargaining.

What values, other than optimum resource allocation, is nuisance doctrine designed to foster? If some of these values are regarded as dearer than resource allocation, can you suggest how the legal system should impede the bargaining process?

5. Nuisance doctrine, remedy, and economic analysis reached a pinnacle of sorts in a highly influential article: Guido Calabresi & A. Douglas Melamed, *Property Rules, Liability Rules, and Inalienability: One View of the Cathedral*, 85 Harv. L. Rev. 1089, 1115-16 (1972). Consider this provocative passage:

> Nuisance or pollution is one of the most interesting areas where the question of who will be given an entitlement, and how it will be protected, is in frequent issue. Traditionally, . . . the nuisance-pollution problem is viewed in terms of three rules. First, Taney may not pollute unless his neighbor (his only neighbor let us assume), Marshall, allows it (Marshall may enjoin Taney's nuisance). Second, Taney may pollute but must compensate Marshall for damages caused (nuisance is found but the remedy is limited to damages). Third, Taney may pollute at will and can only be stopped by Marshall if Marshall pays him off (Taney's pollution is not held to be a nuisance to Marshall). The first is an entitlement to be free from pollution and is protected by a property rule; the second is also an entitlement to be free from pollution but is protected only by a liability rule. Rule

three (no nuisance) is instead an entitlement to Taney protected by a property rule, for only by buying Taney out at Taney's price can Marshall end the pollution.

The very statement of these rules in the context of our framework suggests that something is missing. Missing is a fourth rule representing an entitlement in Taney to pollute, but an entitlement which is protected only by a liability rule. The fourth rule, really a kind of partial eminent domain coupled with a benefits tax, can be stated as follows: Marshall may stop Taney from polluting, but if he does he must compensate Taney.

6. At the same time this highly influential article was moving through the editorial process, a controversy was making its way to the Arizona Supreme Court. Farming started in an area some 15 miles west of Phoenix in 1911. By 1950, the only urban areas were agriculturally related communities. In 1954, the retirement community of Youngstown was begun. In 1956, Spur Industries' predecessor developed feedlots, and by 1959, there were 25 cattle feeding pens within a 7-mile radius.

In May 1959, Del E. Webb Development Co. began to plan the development of Sun City. For this purpose, some 20,000 acres of farmland were purchased for $15,000,000, or $750 per acre, a price considerably less than the price of land located near Phoenix. By September 1959, it started construction of a golf course south of Grand Avenue, and Spur's predecessor started to level ground for more feedlots. In 1960, Spur began a rebuilding and expansion program extending both to the north and south of the original facilities; by 1962, its expansion program was completed and occupied 114 acres.

Originally, Webb did not consider odors from the Spur feed pens a problem and it continued to develop in a southerly direction, until sales resistance became so great that the parcels became impossible to sell. At the time of the suit by Del Webb, Spur was feeding between 20,000 and 30,000 head of cattle; testimony indicated that cattle in a commercial feedlot will produce 35 to 40 pounds of wet manure per day, per head, or over one million pounds per day for 30,000 head of cattle, and that despite the admittedly good feedlot management and housekeeping practices by Spur, the resulting odor and flies produced an annoying if not unhealthy situation so far as the senior citizens of southern Sun City were concerned.

For the state supreme court's creative resolution, see Spur Indus., Inc., v. Del E. Webb Dev. Co., 108 Ariz. 178, 494 P.2d 700 (1972):

> It is clear that as to the citizens of Sun City, the operation of Spur's feedlot was both a public and a private nuisance. They could have successfully maintained an action to abate the nuisance. Del Webb, having shown a special injury in the loss of sales, had a standing to bring suit to enjoin the nuisance. The judgment of the trial court permanently enjoining the operation of the feedlot is affirmed. . . .

> Having brought people to the nuisance to the foreseeable detriment of Spur, Webb must indemnify Spur for a reasonable amount of the cost of moving or shutting down. It should be noted that this relief to Spur is limited to a case wherein a developer has, with foreseeability, brought into a previously agricultural or industrial area the population which makes necessary the granting of an injunction against a lawful business and for which the business has no adequate relief.

> It is therefore the decision of this court that the matter be remanded to the trial court for a hearing upon the damages sustained by the defendant Spur as a reasonable and direct result of the granting of the permanent injunction.

We hope that you paid careful attention to the paragraphs quoted above, because what you have read is a court order that requires a plaintiff to pay damages to a defendant in the absence of a counterclaim for those damages. This remedy may be unique in American law. See also Spur Feeding Co. v. Superior Court of Maricopa County, 109 Ariz. 105, 505 P.2d 1377 (1973) (holding that the *Spur Industries* decision was not res judicata as to the issue presented by a feedlot operator in a third-party claim seeking indemnity against Webb for the developer's liability to property owners).

7. For more on the timing of Calabresi and Melamed, see James E. Krier & Stewart J. Schwab, *The Cathedral at Twenty-Five: Citations and Impressions*, 106 Yale L.J. 2121, 2131 (1997):

> [A] little luck helps, and sometimes more than marginally. For example, the celebrity of a work is promoted by its originality, but originality itself can be a matter of chance. One obvious instance is where we get an idea before you, but you are lucky enough to publish it before us. Another and more troubling instance is where we get an idea before you and publish it before you, but you are lucky enough to get the kudos anyway. Calabresi and Melamed have enjoyed a few such happy twists of fate. They are generally credited for identifying the relevance of high versus low transaction costs in connection with the merits of injunctive relief, yet their discussion was anticipated in a book review published prior to *The Cathedral*. Furthermore, the so-called Rule 4 (reverse damages), widely regarded as Calabresi and Melamed's signature contribution, was simultaneously and independently discovered by the Supreme Court of Arizona. This itself is well-known, so the *Spur Industries* court has gotten its share of the limelight. Much less well-known is the fact that Rule 4 was plainly suggested in a law student note that appeared three years prior to *The Cathedral* and the decision in *Spur Industries*.[33]

8. Problems with modern land use regulations have caused some leading thinkers to revisit and retool private nuisance. The most prominent example can be found in Robert C. Ellickson, *Alternatives to Zoning: Covenants, Nuisance Rules, and Fines as Land Use Controls*, 40 U. Chi. L. Rev. 681, 748, 761-64, 772 (1973), in which the distinguished Yale law professor proposed

> that private nuisance remedies become the exclusive remedy for "localized" spillovers— that is, those that concern no more than several dozen parties. Private nuisance remedies, however, are not the optimal internalization system for all types of harmful spillovers from land use activity; in particular private remedies are likely to be an inefficient means of handling insubstantial injuries from "pervasive" nuisances that affect many outsiders. More centralized systems for internalizing pervasive harms may be capable of achieving savings in administrative costs that outweigh the inevitable allocative inefficiencies of collective regulation. This article will suggest that fines be assessed by a public authority to internalize insubstantial injuries from those pervasive nuisances that present a reasonably objective index of noxiousness. These fines would complement the nuisance remedies that would remain available to persons able to show substantial injury from the pervasive problem. Lack of an objective index of noxiousness may justify imposition of mandatory standards on pervasive nuisance activity, but such an approach is usually justified only when the public authority is willing to impose standards retroactively. To develop and administer these systems, this article proposes creation of a specialized metropolitan body. . . .

---

33. *See* James R. Atwood, Note, *An Economic Analysis of Land Use Conflicts*, 21 Stan. L. Rev. 293, 315 (1969). We learned about Atwood's contribution only recently, thanks to Jeff L. Lewin, Boomer *and the American Law of Nuisance: Past, Present, and Future*, 54 Alb. L. Rev. 189, 246-47 n.295 (1990). Doug Melamed, co-author of *The Cathedral*, has told us that he and Atwood were near-classmates at Yale College, and that both of them took a course there that touched generally on the matters later developed by Atwood and Calabresi and Melamed. Interview by Stewart J. Schwab with A. Douglas Melamed, Attorney, Washington, D.C. (Jan. 5, 1996).

The body Professor Robert Ellickson had in mind was a metropolitan "Nuisance Board" which would be given "primary jurisdiction over nuisance cases and exclusive rule making power over land use problems in [its] metropolitan area." Each board would specify through regulations those activities deemed "unneighborly," "identify hypersensitive uses with similar specificity," "establish threshold levels of 'substantial harm,' and create "schedules of bonus payments for losses of common nonfungible consumer surplus." Though conceding that the boards "would not be wholly immune from the evils of ineptness, corruption, and discrimination often characteristic of zoning administration," Ellickson asserted that this system had several advantages of the kind of zoning that dominates modern land use regulation.

Note that Professor Ellickson's recipe for relief from centralized regulation has a definite Coasean flavor. For a reevaluation of transaction costs and liability rules in the light of actual disputes between landowners, see Robert C. Ellickson, *Of Coase and Cattle: Dispute Resolution Among Neighbors in Shasta County*, 38 Stan. L. Rev. 623 (1986).[17]

H.   New Technologies at the Boundaries of the Common Law

In the closing decades of the 20th century, the new frontier for nuisance law was the accommodation of alternative forms of providing energy in the wake of (real and threatened) fossil fuel shortages. In the case that follows, consider whether the common-law principles are being stretched too far beyond their intended uses. Do statutes and ordinances do a better job of reflecting modern norms and expectations? Consider how relevant Chief Justice Shaw's famous observation from Norway Plains Co. v. Boston & Maine R.R., 67 Mass. (1 Gray) 263, 267 (1854), remains:

> It is one of the great merits and advantages of the common law, that . . . when the practice and course of business . . . should cease or change, the common law consists of a few broad and comprehensive principles, founded on reason, natural justice, and enlightened public policy, modified and adapted to the circumstances of all particular cases which fall within it.

PRAH v. MARETTI
108 Wis. 2d 223, 321 N.W.2d 182 (1982)

SHIRLEY S. ABRAHAMSON, J. . . . This case . . . involves a conflict between one landowner (Glenn Prah, the plaintiff) interested in unobstructed access to sunlight across adjoining property as a natural source of energy and an adjoining landowner (Richard D. Maretti, the defendant) interested in the development of his land. . . .

According to the complaint, the plaintiff is the owner of a residence which was constructed during the years 1978-1979. The complaint alleges that the residence has a solar system which includes collectors on the roof to supply energy for heat and hot water and that after the plaintiff built his solar-heated house, the defendant purchased the lot adjacent to and immediately to the

---

17. In the 1986 article, at 686, Ellickson observed:

> The Shasta County evidence suggests that law and economics scholars need to pay more heed to how transaction costs influence the resolution of disputes. Because it is costly to carry out legal research and to engage in legal proceedings, a rational actor often has good reason to apply informal norms, not law, to evaluate the propriety of human behavior. Contracts scholars have long known that norms are likely to be especially influential when disputants share a continuing relationship. A farmer and a rancher who own adjoining lands are enduringly intertwined, and therefore readily able to employ nonlegal methods of dispute resolution. Law-and-economics scholars misdirect their readers and students when they invoke examples—such as the Parable of the Farmer and the Rancher—that greatly exaggerate the domain of human activity upon which the law casts a shadow.

south of the plaintiffs lot and commenced planning construction of a home. The complaint further states that when the plaintiff learned of defendant's plans to build the house he advised the defendant that if the house were built at the proposed location, defendant's house would substantially and adversely affect the integrity of plaintiffs solar system and could cause plaintiff other damage. Nevertheless, the defendant began construction. The complaint further alleges that the plaintiff is entitled to "unrestricted use of the sun and its solar power" and demands judgment for injunctive relief and damages. . . .

Plaintiff's home was the first residence built in the subdivision, and although plaintiff did not build his house in the center of the lot it was built in accordance with applicable restrictions. Plaintiff advised defendant that if the defendant's home were built at the proposed site it would cause a shadowing effect on the solar collectors which would reduce the efficiency of the system and possibly damage the system. To avoid these adverse effects, plaintiff requested defendant to locate his home an additional several feet away from the plaintiff's lot line, the exact number being disputed. Plaintiff and defendant failed to reach an agreement on the location of defendant's home before defendant started construction. The Architectural Control Committee of the subdivision and the Planning Commission of the City of Muskego approved the defendant's plans for his home, including its location on the lot. After such approval, the defendant apparently changed the grade of the property without prior notice to the Architectural Control Committee. The problem with defendant's proposed construction, as far as the plaintiff's interests are concerned, arises from a combination of the grade and the distance of defendant's home from the defendant's lot line. . . .

The private nuisance doctrine has traditionally been employed in this state to balance the conflicting rights of landowners, and this court has recently adopted the analysis of private nuisance set forth in the Restatement (Second) of Torts. The Restatement defines private nuisance as "a nontrespassory invasion of another's interest in the private use and enjoyment of land." Restatement (Second) of Torts Sec. 821D (1977). The phrase "interest in the private use and enjoyment of land" as used in sec. 821D is broadly defined to include any disturbance of the enjoyment of property. . . .

Although the defendant's obstruction of the plaintiff's access to sunlight appears to fall within the Restatement's broad concept of a private nuisance as a nontrespassory invasion of another's interest in the private use and enjoyment of land, the defendant asserts that he has a right to develop his property in compliance with statutes, ordinances and private covenants without regard to the effect of such development upon the plaintiff's access to sunlight. In essence, the defendant is asking this court to hold that the private nuisance doctrine is not applicable in the instant case and that his right to develop his land is a right which is per se superior to his neighbor's interest in access to sunlight. This position is expressed in the maxim "cujus est solum, ejus est usque ad coelum et ad infernos," that is, the owner of land owns up to the sky and down to the center of the earth. The rights of the surface owner are, however, not unlimited. U.S. v. Causby, 328 U.S. 256, 260-1 (1946).

The defendant is not completely correct in asserting that the common law did not protect a landowner's access to sunlight across adjoining property. At English common law a landowner could acquire a right to receive sunlight across adjoining land by both express agreement and under the judge-made doctrine of "ancient lights." Under the doctrine of ancient lights if the landowner had received sunlight across adjoining property for a specified period of time, the landowner was entitled to continue to receive unobstructed access to sunlight across the adjoining property. Under the doctrine the landowner acquired a negative prescriptive easement and could prevent the adjoining landowner from obstructing access to light.

Although American courts have not been as receptive to protecting a landowner's access to sunlight as the English courts, American courts have afforded some protection to a landowner's interest in access to sunlight. American courts honor express easements to sunlight. American courts initially enforced the English common law doctrine of ancient lights, but later every state which considered the doctrine repudiated it as inconsistent with the needs of a developing country. Indeed, for just that reason this court concluded that an easement to light and air over adjacent property could not be created or acquired by prescription and has been unwilling to recognize such an easement by implication.

Many jurisdictions in this country have protected a landowner from malicious obstruction of access to light (the spite fence cases) under the common law private nuisance doctrine. If an activity is motivated by malice it lacks utility and the harm it causes others outweighs any social values. . . . This court's reluctance in the nineteenth and early part of the twentieth century to provide broader protection for a landowner's access to sunlight was premised on three policy considerations. First, the right of landowners to use their property as they wished, as long as they did not cause physical damage to a neighbor, was jealously guarded.

Second, sunlight was valued only for aesthetic enjoyment or as illumination. Since artificial light could be used for illumination, loss of sunlight was at most a personal annoyance which was given little, if any, weight by society.

Third, society had a significant interest in not restricting or impeding land

development . . . . These three policies are no longer fully accepted or applicable. They reflect factual circumstances and social priorities that are now obsolete.

First, society has increasingly regulated the use of land by the landowner for the general welfare. Euclid v. Ambler Realty Co., 272 U.S. 365 (1926); Just v. Marinette, 56 Wis. 2d 7, 201 N.W.2d 761 (1972).

Second, access to sunlight has taken on a new significance in recent years. In this case the plaintiff seeks to protect access to sunlight, not for aesthetic reasons or as a source of illumination but as a source of energy. Access to sunlight as an energy source is of significance both to the landowner who invests in solar collectors and to a society which has an interest in developing alternative sources of energy.

Third, the policy of favoring unhindered private development in an expanding economy is no longer in harmony with the realities of our society. The need for easy and rapid development is not as great today as it once was, while our perception of the value of sunlight as a source of energy has increased significantly.

Courts should not implement obsolete policies that have lost their vigor over the course of the years. The law of private nuisance is better suited to resolve landowners' disputes about property development in the 1980's than is a rigid rule which does not recognize a landowner's interest in access to sunlight. . . .

Yet the defendant would have us ignore the flexible private nuisance law as a means of resolving the dispute between the landowners in this case and would have us adopt an approach . . . of favoring the unrestricted development of land and of applying a rigid and inflexible rule protecting his right to build on his land and disregarding any interest of the plaintiff in the use and enjoyment of his land. This we refuse to do.[13]

Private nuisance law, the law traditionally used to adjudicate conflicts between private land-owners, has the flexibility to protect both the landowner's right of access to sunlight and another landowner's right to develop land. Private nuisance law is better suited to regulate access to sunlight in modern society and is more in harmony with legislative policy and the prior decisions of this court than is an inflexible doctrine of non-recognition of any interest in access to sunlight across adjoining land.

We therefore hold that private nuisance law, that is, the reasonable use doctrine as set forth in the Restatement, is applicable to the instant case. Recognition of a nuisance claim for unreasonable obstruction of access to sunlight will not prevent land development or unduly hinder the use of adjoining land. It will promote the reasonable use and enjoyment of land in a manner suitable to the 1980's. That obstruction of access to light might be found to constitute a nuisance in certain circumstances does not mean that it will be or must be found to constitute a nuisance under all circumstances. The result in each case depends on whether the conduct complained of is unreasonable.

Accordingly we hold that the plaintiff in this case has stated a claim under which relief can be granted. Nonetheless we do not determine whether the plaintiff in this case is entitled to relief. In order to be entitled to relief the plaintiff must prove the elements required to establish actionable nuisance, and the conduct of the defendant herein must be judged by the reasonable use doctrine. . . .

For the reasons set forth, we reverse the judgment of the circuit court dismissing the complaint and remand the matter to circuit court for further proceedings not inconsistent with this opinion. . . .

WILLIAM G. CALLOW, J. (dissenting). . . .

I firmly believe that a landowner's right to use his property within the limits of ordinances, statutes, and restrictions of record where such use is necessary to serve his legitimate needs is a fundamental precept of a free society which this court should strive to uphold. . . .

Regarding the third policy the majority apparently believes is obsolete (that society has a significant interest in not restricting land development) . . . I concede the law may be tending to recognize the value of aesthetics over increased volume development and that an individual may not use his land in such a way as to harm the public. The instant case, however, deals with a private benefit. . . . It is clear that community planners are acutely aware of the present housing shortages,

---

13. Defendant's position that a landowner's interest in access to sunlight across adjoining land is not "legally enforceable" and is therefore excluded per se from private nuisance law was adopted in Fontainebleau Hotel Corp. v. Forty-five Twenty-five, Inc., 114 So. 2d 357 (Fla. Ct. App. 1959), *cert. denied*, 117 So. 2d 842 (Fla. 1960). The Florida district court of appeals permitted construction of a building which cast a shadow on a neighboring hotel's swimming pool. The court asserted that nuisance law protects only those interests "which [are] recognized and protected by law," and that there is no legally recognized or protected right to access to sunlight. A property owner does not, said the Florida court, in the absence of a contract or statute, acquire a presumptive or implied right to the free flow of light and air across adjoining land. The Florida court then concluded that a lawful structure which causes injury to another by cutting off light and air—whether or not erected partly for spite—does not give rise to a cause of action for damages or for an injunction.

We do not find the reasoning of *Fontainebleau* persuasive. The court leaped from rejecting an easement by prescription (the doctrine of ancient lights) and an easement by implication to the conclusion that there is no right to protection from obstruction of access to sunlight. The court's statement that a landowner has no right to light should be the conclusion, not its initial premise. The court did not explain why an owner's interest in unobstructed light should not be protected or in what manner an owner's interest in unobstructed sunlight differs from an owner's interest in being free from obtrusive noises or smells or differs from an owner's interest in unobstructed use of water. The recognition of a per se exception to private nuisance law may invite unreasonable behavior.

particularly among those two groups with limited financial resources, the young and the elderly. While the majority's policy arguments may be directed to a cause of action for public nuisance, we are presented with a private nuisance case which I believe is distinguishable in this regard. . . .

I conclude that plaintiff's solar heating system is an unusually sensitive use. In other words, the defendant's proposed construction of his home, under ordinary circumstances, would not interfere with the use and enjoyment of the usual person's property. . . .

I believe the facts of the instant controversy present the classic case of the owner of a solar collector who fails to take any action to protect his investment. There is nothing in the record to indicate that Mr. Prah disclosed his situation to Mr. Maretti prior to Maretti's purchase of the lot or attempted to secure protection for his solar collector prior to Maretti's submission of his building plans to the architectural committee. Such inaction should be considered a significant factor in determining whether a cause of action exists.

The majority's failure to recognize the need for notice may perpetuate a vicious cycle. Maretti may feel compelled to sell his lot because of Prah's solar collector's interference with his plans to build his family home. If so, Maretti will not be obliged to inform prospective purchasers of the problem. Certainly, such information will reduce the value of his land. If the presence of collectors is sufficient notice, it cannot be said that the seller of the lot has a duty to disclose information peculiarly within his knowledge. I do not believe that an adjacent lot owner should be obliged to experience the substantial economic loss resulting from the lot being rendered unbuildable by the contour of the land as it relates to the location and design of the adjoining home using solar collectors.

Notes

1. The Supreme Court of New Hampshire, in Tenn v. 889 Assocs., 500 A.2d 366, 370 (N.H. 1985), cited *Prah* with approval and stated that "there is no reason in principle why the law of nuisance should not be applied to claims for the protection of a property owner's interests in light and air." Still, the court, in an opinion written by Justice David Souter (before his appointment to the U.S. Supreme Court), upheld the superior court's dismissal of plaintiffs bill in equity, for she failed to demonstrate that the defendant company's planned six-story building would unreasonably interfere with the use and enjoyment of property by blocking the windows and the walls of the light shaft in plaintiff's neighboring structure. Justice Souter, at 327, articulated a flexible approach, rejecting the rigidity prevailing in most jurisdictions:

> The present defendant urges us to adopt the *Fontainebleau* rule and thereby to refuse any common law recognition to interests in light and air, but we decline to do so. If we were so to limit the ability of the common law to grow, we would in effect be rejecting one of the wise assumptions underlying the traditional law of nuisance: that we cannot anticipate at any one time the variety of predicaments in which protection of property interests or redress for their violation will be justifiable. For it is just this recognition that has led the courts to avoid rigid formulations for determining when an interference with the use of property will be actionable, and to rest instead on the flexible rule that actionable, private nuisance consists of an unreasonable as well as a substantial interference with another person's use and enjoyment of his property. That is, because we have to anticipate that the uses of property will change over time, we have developed a law of nuisance that protects the use and enjoyment of property when a threatened harm to the plaintiff owner can be said to outweigh the utility of the defendant owner's conduct to himself and to the community.

2. Perhaps this is an area that begs for a legislative solution, such as the California Solar Shade Control Act. Cal. Pub. Res. Code §25980, originally passed in 1978, articulating the following legislative purpose:

> It is the policy of the state to promote all feasible means of energy conservation and all feasible uses of alternative energy supply sources. In particular, the state encourages the planting and maintenance of trees and shrubs to create shading, moderate outdoor temperatures, and provide various economic and aesthetic benefits. However, there are certain situations in which the need for widespread use of alternative energy devices, such as solar collectors, requires specific and limited controls on trees and shrubs.

Sections 25982 and 25983 (as enacted in 2008) further provide:

> After the installation of a solar collector, a person owning or in control of another property shall not allow a tree or shrub to be placed or, if placed, to grow on that property so as to cast a shadow greater than 10 percent of the collector absorption area upon that solar collector surface at any one time between the hours of 10 a.m. and 2 p.m., local standard time.

> A tree or shrub that is maintained in violation of Section 25982 is a private nuisance, as defined in Section 3481 of the Civil Code, if the person who maintains or permits the tree or shrub to be maintained fails to remove or alter the tree or shrub after receiving a written notice from the owner or agent of the affected solar collector requesting compliance with the requirements of Section 25982.

In Sher v. Leiderman, 181 Cal. App. 3d 867, 226 Cal. Rptr. 698 (Cal. Ct. App. 1986), the state appellate court found that the Solar Shade Control Act did not apply to a "passive solar" home:

> The design features and structures [south-facing windows and concrete patio, skylights, insulation, and more] . . . form a system intended to transform solar into thermal energy. The court also found that a concomitant design goal was to create a bright and cheerful living environment. Though the home includes many passive solar features, it does not make use of any "active" solar collectors or panels. Nor does it employ any "thermal mass" for heat storage and distribution. Building materials used throughout were typical and conventional for the time; the house does not contain any special materials primarily selected for effective thermal retention.

Id. at 873-74. The court also concluded that state private nuisance law did not cover blockage of sunlight.

The direct impetus for the 2008 changes came from a couple who were forced to prune their redwood trees following a neighbor's complaint under the original legislation.

3. Some states shield solar energy devices from neighborhood restrictions as well. Ariz. Rev. Stat. §33-439 makes "void and unenforceable" "[a]ny covenant, restriction or condition contained in any deed, contract, security agreement or other instrument affecting the transfer or sale of, or any interest in, real property which effectively prohibits the installation or use of a solar energy device." In Garden Lakes Community Ass'n v. Madigan, 204 Ariz. 238, 62 P.3d 983 (Ct. App. 2003), the court found that a neighborhood association's "architectural restrictions governing the construction and appearance of solar energy devices on homes within the subdivision" were in violation of the statute and therefore unenforceable. In 2007, state lawmakers enacted Ariz. Rev. Stat. §33-1816, which permitted community and homeowner associations to "adopt reasonable rules regard-

ing the placement of a solar energy device if those rules do not prevent the installation, impair the functioning of the device or restrict its use or adversely affect the cost or efficiency of the device."

4. Other alternative energy sources have pushed the private nuisance envelope as well. In Rose v. Chaikin, 187 N.J. Super. 210, 218-20, 453 A.2d 1378, 1382-83 (Super. Ct. Ch. Div. 1982), neighbors sought to enjoin the operation of a windmill (atop a 60-foot tower) on residential property as a private nuisance and a zoning violation. On the former claim, the court held:

> [D]efendants' windmill constitutes an actionable nuisance. As indicated, the noise produced is offensive because of its character, volume and duration. It is a sound which is not only distinctive, but one which is louder than others and is more or less constant. Its intrusive quality is heightened because of the locality. The neighborhood is quiet and residential. It is well separated, not only from commercial sounds, but from the heavier residential traffic as well. Plaintiffs specifically chose the area because of these qualities and the proximity to the ocean. Sounds which are natural to this area—the sea, the shore birds, the ocean breeze—are soothing and welcome. The noise of the windmill, which would be unwelcome in most neighborhoods, is particularly alien here. . . .
>
> When consideration is given to the social utility of the windmill and the availability of reasonable alternatives, the conclusion supporting an injunction is the same. Defendants' purpose in installing the windmill was to conserve energy and save on electric bills. Speaking to the latter goal first, clearly the court can take judicial notice that alternative devices are available which are significantly less intrusive. As to its social utility, a more careful analysis is required. Defendants argue that the windmill furthers the national need to conserve energy by the use of an alternate renewable source of power. See, generally, Wind Energy Systems Act of 1980, 42 U.S.C.A., §§9201-13, and Public Utility Regulatory Policies Act of 1978, 16 U.S.C.A., §824a-3. The social utility of alternate energy sources cannot be denied; nor should the court ignore the proposition that scientific and social progress sometimes reasonably require a reduction in personal comfort. On the other hand, the fact that a device represents a scientific advance and has social utility does not mean that it is permissible at any cost. Such factors must be weighed against the quantum of harm the device brings to others.
>
> In this case the activity in question substantially interferes with the health and comfort of plaintiffs. In addition to the negative effect on their health, their ability to enjoy the sanctity of their homes has been significantly reduced. The ability to look to one's home as a refuge from the noise and stress associated with the outside world is a right to be jealously guarded. Before that right can be eroded in the name of social progress, the benefit to society must be clear and the intrusion must be warranted under all of the circumstances. Here, the benefits are relatively small and the irritation is substantial. On balance, therefore, the social utility of this windmill is outweighed by the quantum of harm that it creates.

Similarly, in 2007, the Supreme Court of West Virginia, in Burch v. NedPower Mount Storm, Ltd. Liab. Co., 220 W. Va. 443, 647 S.E.2d 879 (2007), reversed a lower court's dismissal on the pleadings of a private nuisance suit brought by landowners seeking to enjoin the construction and operation of a wind power facility. The supreme court refused to find that the state Public Service Commission's grant of a siting certificate for the project preempted the common-law action, instead holding that the right of a person under the common law to bring in circuit court a nuisance claim to enjoin the construction and/or operation of an electric generating facility that is designated under federal law as an exempt wholesale generator is not precluded by the fact that the Public Service Commission of West Virginia has granted a siting certificate to the owner or operator of the facility pursuant to W.Va. Code § 24-2-1(c)(1) (2006) and related statutes.

In Rassier v. Houim, 488 N.W.2d 635, 638 (N.D. 1992), a North Dakota landowner was more successful when his neighbor attempted to abate his wind generator as a private nuisance, defined by a state statute as "one which affects a single individual or a determinate number of persons in the enjoyment of some private right not common to the public." Citing common-law principles such as "coming to the nuisance," the state supreme court observed:

> Rassier points to evidence supporting a finding of unreasonable interference, including the fact that the wind generator is located approximately 40 feet from her house and created noise measured by an environmental scientist from the North Dakota State Department of Health and Consolidated Laboratories, and a mechanical engineer who worked in the area of psychoacoustics, in the range from 50 to 69 decibels. Those North Dakota communities which have enacted noise ordinances prohibit noise exceeding 55 decibels in residential areas; Mandan has not enacted such an ordinance. Both witnesses indicated that noise at the measured levels could be irritating, stressful, and interfere with sleep. Rassier stated that her family's use of the yard was interfered with because the noise disrupted conversations. Rassier also indicated a concern with the safety of locating the generator and its tower near her house; she described one instance when she found a large ice chunk in her yard, an ice chunk she suspected was thrown from the wind generator.

> Houim points to evidence that under these circumstances the wind generator does not unreasonably interfere with Rassier's use of her property. The wind generator was put up in 1986; Rassiers moved onto the adjoining lot in 1988. Rassier brought this action two years after her family moved into their house, after conflicts arose between Mr. Rassier and Houim. Several neighbors testified for Houim; no neighbor, other than Rassier, complained of noise from the wind generator. Houim offered to teach the Rassiers to turn the wind generator off when the noise bothered them, but they did not attempt this accommodation. Finally, Houim said that the tower supporting the generator was engineered for a larger model than his, and that safety features eliminated the danger of blades, or ice, being thrown from the wind generator.

5. A confrontation between alternative energy sources and the preservation of environmentally sensitive lands and waters frequented by the nation's chic and elite slowly worked its way through the National Environmental Policy Act's (NEPA's) environmental impact statement process as the 21st century began. See the Notice of Availability of the Draft Environmental Impact Statement for the Cape Wind Energy Project, Nantucket Sound and Yarmouth, MA, Application for Corps Section 10 Individual Permit, 69 Fed. Reg. 64919 (Nov. 9, 2004):

> Cape Wind Associates, LLC (the applicant) has requested a permit under Section 10 of the Rivers and Harbors Act of 1899 to install 130 wind turbine generators, an electric service platform, and associated cable in an area of Nantucket Sound, Massachusetts known as Horseshoe Shoals. The applicant's intended purpose is to provide wind-generated energy that will be transmitted to the regional power grid. The wind turbine

generators would be spaced one-third to one-half mile apart over a 24 square mile area, producing up to 454 megawatts of wind generated energy to be transmitted from a centrally located electric service platform via a submarine cable to a landfall location in Yarmouth, MA. The proposed wind turbines would be up to 420 feet high with the hub height approximately 260 feet above the water surface. The northernmost turbines would be approximately 4 miles from Yarmouth, MA, the southeastern most turbines would be approximately 11 miles from Nantucket, and the westernmost turbines would be approximately 5.5 miles from Martha's Vineyard. The proposed submarine cable system, consisting of two 115 kV solid dielectric cable circuits, would be jet-plow embedded into the seabed to a depth of approximately 6 feet below the present bottom. The overland cable system would be installed underground within existing public right-of-ways and roadways in the town of Yarmouth, MA to NSTAR's existing electric system in Barnstable, MA. The approximate construction start date for the proposed project is November 2005, with commercial operation starting in November 2006.

The DEIS is intended to provide the information needed for the Corps to perform a public interest review for the Section 10 permit decision. Significant issues analyzed in the DEIS included geology and sediment conditions; physical oceanographic conditions; benthic and shellfish resources; finfish resources and commercial and recreational fisheries; protected marine species; terrestrial ecology, wildlife, and protected species; avian resources; coastal and freshwater wetland resources; water quality; cultural and recreational resources; visual resources; noise; transportation; electrical and magnetic fields, telecommunications systems; air quality; and socioeconomic resources. Several alternatives were evaluated for comparative purposes, including the No Action Alternative under which the new facility will not be built. In addition to the applicant's proposed location, which is Nantucket Sound, the potential impacts and benefits of locating a wind energy project at the Massachusetts Military Reservation, a site south of Tuckernuck Island, and a combination site comprised of two areas south of New Bedford with a reduced footprint in Nantucket Sound were evaluated for comparison purposes. Public comment on any or all of the alternatives is encouraged.

The *Boston Globe* provided this update on January 17, 2009:

A benchmark was reached yesterday in efforts to expand clean energy as a key federal agency concluded that the nation's first proposed offshore wind farm would have no major adverse effect on the environment of Nantucket Sound. But Cape Wind's seven-year quest to win final approval is not over, and the incoming Obama administration will face a dilemma with the 130-turbine wind farm, which is tied to the president-elect's energy agenda and his political allegiances.

The project's supporters, including major environmental groups, celebrated the release of the final environmental impact report by the Minerals Management Service, but they acknowledged that the project will continue to face challenges. Cape Wind's opponents, concerned about navigational hazards, property values, and the view of the turbines from beaches and historical sites, have promised lawsuits. And an Interior Department inspector general's investigation of the minerals agency's handling of the process is underway.

Calling his agency's report "a milestone," culminating years of review by government agencies, Randall Luthi, Minerals Management Service director, said in an interview that Cape Wind could become "a bellwether for many offshore wind projects to come." The next step is for the new secretary of the interior to decide whether to award Cape Wind a lease for the project, and federal officials expect he will be strongly influenced by the favorable review. The decision cannot be made for at least 30 days, which will push the pending approval of Cape Wind into the Obama administration, at which point US Senator Ken Salazar will have taken the helm at the Interior Department.

The article—Bina Venkataraman & Stephanie Ebbert, *Agency Report Helps Bolster Cape Wind Finds Project Would Not Harm Local Environment*, Boston Globe, Jan. 17, 2009, at B1—noted that there were many more hurdles for the project over the regulatory horizon: "Several pending federal, state, and local permits also remain. But the project's supporters say they expect final approval of all permits could come this spring if the department's decision is favorable."

III. Public Nuisance: Invoking the Police Power to Protect the Community From Harm

We have seen that in the judge's common-law arsenal, private nuisance is something of a blunder-buss, striking out in many directions at the same time. If we follow Professor Ellickson's advice, perhaps we can make it into a more precise weapon for protecting landowners from neighbors who interfere with the use and enjoyment of land. Or maybe there is some advantage to the ambiguity that Dean Prosser noted, in that judges can massage the facts and craft remedies to resolve property disputes more equitably.

The criminal courts had their own means of protecting the general community from activities that posed harm to the public, not just to those privileged enough to own real property. Unfortunately, the crime—public nuisance—shared the same name as its tort "cousin." As you read the following 18th-century English indictment for air pollution and the notes that follow, consider how skillfully and successfully local and state governments have turned public nuisance into an all-purpose tool for fighting a wide variety of real and perceived evils. State and local governments feel secure in outlawing activities as public (or common) nuisances, because of judicial respect for the wide-ranging police power in accordance with which government officials seek to protect the public health, safety, morals, and general welfare. Does the Constitution—with its First Amendment Free Speech, and Fourteenth Amendment Due Process and Equal Protection Clauses—provide adequate checks on government abuse in the name of the police power? Is public nuisance more effective than its private counterpart in the continuing battle to protect the fragile environment and to conserve natural resources? And is the combination of the two, while necessary, still insufficient?

REX v. WHITE AND WARD
1 Burr. Rep. 333, 97 Eng. Rep. 338 (K.B. 1757)

The defendants had been convicted of a nuisance in erecting and continuing their works at Twickenham, for making acid spirit of sulphur, oil of vitriol, and oil of aqua fords. The indictment runs thus, viz. that

> at the parish of Twickenham, &c. near the King's common highway there, and near the dwelling-houses of several of the inhabitants, the defendants erected twenty buildings for making noisome, stinking and offensive liquors; and then and there made fires of sea-coal and other things, which sent forth abundance of noisome, offensive and stinking smoke, and made, &c. great quantities of noisome, offensive, stinking liquors,

called, &c.; whereby and by reason of which noisome, offensive and stinking, &c. the air was impregnated with noisome and offensive stinks and smells; to the common nuisance of all the King's liege subjects inhabiting, &c. and travelling and passing the said King's common highway; and against the peace, &c. . . .

Mr. Just. DENISON reported the evidence; which was of great length he said, there being about seventy-five witnesses on each side: however, he collected the substance of it together in his report. It appeared to be very strong on the part of the prosecution and he declared himself satisfied with the verdict. And it appeared upon his report, that the smell was not only intolerably offensive, but also noxious and hurtful, and made many persons sick, and gave them head-achs . . . .

Lord MANSFIELD thought there was nothing in the objections, which, he said, are reducible to three heads; viz.

1st. That there is no sufficient charge of the hurtfulness;

2dly. That it is not precisely charged, "to whom" the hurt is done;

3dly. That it only laid generally, "in the parish of Twickenham."

First—The jury have found "that it is to the common nuisance of the King's subjects dwelling, &c. and travelling, &c."

And the word "noxious" not only means "hurtful and offensive to the smell;" but it is also the translation of the very technical term "nocivus;" and has been always used for it, ever since the Act, for the proceedings being in English.

But it is not necessary that the smell should be unwholesome: it is enough, if it renders the enjoyment of life and property uncomfortable.

Secondly—The persons incommoded are sufficiently described: and the offence is charged to be to the common nuisance of persons inhabiting and travelling near, &c. And unless they had been so near as to be hurt by it, the indictment could not have been proved. Whereas in the case of Wilkes and Broadbent, it was quite uncertain how near the rubbish might be laid.

Thirdly—It is sufficiently laid, and in the accustomed manner. The very existence of the nuisance depends upon the number of houses and concourse of people: and this is a matter of fact, to be judged of by the jury. And in the very cases in Tremaine 195, of a glasshouse, and 298, of a soap-boiler's furnace,—they are laid in parishes "apud paroch' &c." Therefore there is no foundation for the objections. . . .

On Thursday 5th May 1757, on a motion for the judgment (or rather sentence) of the Court upon the defendants, for the offence whereof they stood convicted,—it appearing that the nuisance was absolutely removed; (the works being demolished, and the materials, utensils and instruments, all sold and parted with;) they were, upon entering (each for himself only, and for such as acted for or under him) into a rule "not to renew them," only fined 6s. 8d. each. But on a dispute afterwards arising, how the rule should be drawn up, it was on Friday 20th May settled by the Court to be thus—

By consent of counsel on both sides, it is ordered that, upon the defendant Ward's undertaking that neither he nor any other person by his consent or direction or for his use or benefit, shall for the future make or cause to be made in the works lately carried on by the defendant White at Twickenham, mentioned in the indictment in this cause, any acid spirit of sulphur, or preparations of vitriol, or oil of aqua fords; a fine of 6s. 8d. be set upon the said defendant Ward, for the nuisance of which he has been convicted.

And

The defendant White entered into a like rule, *mutatis mutandis*.

Notes

1. An early American utilization of public nuisance power can be seen in Acts and Resolves of the Province of Massachusetts Bay (Province Laws, 1692-1693), ch. 23:

> An Act for Prevention of Common Nusances [sic] Arising By SlaughterHouses, Still-Houses, &c., Tallow Chandlers, and Curriers . . . .
>
> Sec. 1. That the selectmen of the towns of Boston, Salem and Charlestown respectively, or other market towns in the province, with two or more justices of the peace dwelling in the town, or two of the next justices in the county, shall at or before the last day of March, one thousand six hundred ninety-three, assign some certain places in each of said towns (where it may be least offensive) for the erecting or setting up of slaughter-houses for the killing of all meat, still-houses, and houses for trying of tallow and currying of leather (which houses may be erected of timber, the law referring to building with brick or stone notwithstanding), and shall cause an entry to be made in the townbook of what places shall be by them so assigned, and make known the same by posting it up in some publick places of the town; at which houses and places respectively, and no other, all butchers and slaughtermen, distillers, chandlers and curriers shall exercise and practice their respective trades and mysteries; on pain that any butcher or slaughterman transgressing of this act by killing of meat in any other place, for every conviction thereof before one or more justices of the peace, shall forfeit and pay the sum of twenty shillings; and any distiller, chandler or currier offending against this act, for every conviction thereof before their majesties' justices at the general sessions of the peace for the county, shall forfeit and pay the sum of five pounds; one-third part of said forfeitures to be the use of their majesties for the support of the government of the province and the incident charges thereof, one-third to the poor of the town where such offence shall be committed, and the other third to him or them that shall inform and sue for the same.

2. Lawton v. Steele, 152 U.S. 133, 135-37, 141 (1894), is a classic police power case in which a state used the threat of a public prosecution as a way of eliminating not a health risk but an economic harm. The case involved the constitutionality of a New York statute providing that

> [a]ny net, pound, or other means or device for taking or capturing fish, or whereby they may be taken or captured, set, put, floated, had, found, or maintained, in or upon any of the waters of this State, or upon the shores of or islands in any of the waters of this State, in violation of any existing or hereafter enacted statutes or laws for the protection of fish, is hereby declared to be, and is, a public nuisance, and may be abated and summarily destroyed by any person, and it shall be the duty of each and every protector aforesaid and of every game constable to seize and remove and forthwith destroy the same . . . and no action for damages shall lie or be maintained against any person for or on account of any such seizure or destruction.

In upholding the legislation, the Court presented an expansive version of the police power that the U.S. Constitution reserved to the states (and, in turn, to their political subdivisions such as cities, towns, and villages):

> The extent and limits of what is known as the police power have been a fruitful subject of discussion in the appellate courts of nearly every State in the Union. It is universally conceded to include everything essential to the public safety, health, and morals, and

to justify the destruction or abatement, by summary proceedings, of whatever may be regarded as a public nuisance. Under this power it has been held that the State may order the destruction of a house falling to decay or otherwise endangering the lives of passers-by; the demolition of such as are in the path of a conflagration; the slaughter of diseased cattle; the destruction of decayed or unwholesome food; the prohibition of wooden buildings in cities; the regulation of railways and other means of public convey-ance, and of interments in burial grounds; the restriction of objectionable trades to cer-tain localities; the compulsory vaccination of children; the confinement of the insane or those afflicted with contagious diseases; the restraint of vagrants, beggars, and habitual drunkards; the suppression of obscene publications and houses of ill fame; and the pro-hibition of gambling houses and places where intoxicating liquors are sold. Beyond this, however, the State may interfere wherever the public interests demand it, and in this particular a large discretion is necessarily vested in the legislature to determine, not only what the interests of the public require, but what measures are necessary for the protec-tion of such interests. To justify the state in thus interposing its authority in behalf of the public, it must appear, first, that the interests of the public generally, as distinguished from those of a particular class, require such interference; and, second, that the means are reasonably necessary for the accomplishment of the purpose, and not unduly oppres-sive upon individuals. The legislature may not, under the guise of protecting the public interests, arbitrarily interfere with private business, or impose unusual and unnecessary restrictions upon lawful occupations. In other words, its determination as to what is a proper exercise of its police powers is not final or conclusive, but is subject to the supervi-sion of the courts. . . .

Keeping the legitimate goals of the police power in mind, and cognizant of the need for limited judicial review, the majority concluded:

It is evident that the efficacy of this statute would be very seriously impaired by requir-ing every net illegally used to be carefully taken from the water, carried before a court or magistrate, notice of the seizure to be given by publication, and regular judicial proceed-ings to be instituted for its condemnation.

Three Justices disagreed with that part of the statute that "authorize[d] the summary destruc-tion of fishing nets and prohibit[ed] any action for damages on account of such destruction," reasoning that "[t]he police power rests upon necessity and the right of self-protection, but private property cannot be arbitrarily invaded under the mere guise of police regulation, nor forfeited for the alleged violation of law by its owner, nor destroyed by way of penalty inflicted upon him, with-out opportunity to be heard." *Id.* at 144 (Fuller, C.J., dissenting).

The police power/private-property pendulum can swing both ways, however, as evidenced four years later by the opinion of the Court of Appeals of the State of New York in Colon v. Lisk, 153 N.Y. 188, 197-98, 47 N.E. 302, 305 (1897). The state high court, exercising the (minimal, but effective) judicial supervision presented by *Lawton*, invalidated a statute authorizing the seizure and sale of boats used in disturbing oyster beds:

It is to be observed that the statute does not relate to the health, morals, safety or welfare of the public, but only to the private interests of a particular class of individuals. Nor can it be fairly said that the means provided for the protection of those interests are reasonably necessary to accomplish that purpose. But, on the contrary, they are plainly oppressive and amount to an unauthorized confiscation of private property for the mere protection of private rights. It is in no manner attempted by this statute to protect any public interest, or defend any public right. Nor is it calculated to accomplish that end, but, under the guise of a pretended police regulation, it arbitrarily invades personal rights and private property.

3. Disasters often breed new environmental law. For example, it is not hard to trace the origins of several federal statutory schemes to specific calamities. While it would be an exaggeration to isolate one incident and identify it as the sole cause for a statute, we can legitimately ask whether the United States Code would have contained the Air Pollution Control Act of 1955 without the Donora, Pennsylvania, disaster[18] and Los Angeles' poisonous smog; the Coastal Zone Management Act of 1972 without the Santa Barbara oil spill; the Oil Pollution Act of 1990 without the *Exxon Valdez* debacle; or the Comprehensive Environmental Response, Compensation, and Liability Act (CERCLA) without the horrors of Love Canal. (And, indeed, a correlation can be made between such events and the contents of law reviews: Note, *Smog—Can Legislation Clear the Air?*, 1 Stan. L. Rev. 452 (1949), followed the Donora disaster, while *Smog and the Law—Legal Aspects of Air Pollution*, 27 S. Cal. L. Rev. 347 (1954) manifested the interest of the legal profession in the situation in Los Angeles.)

4. Pollution of the atmosphere by people is an ancient problem. Early English smoke abatement laws date back to the late 13th century. In 1307, a Royal Proclamation prohibited the use of coal in furnaces; the following year a person was executed for this offense. See W.R. Hornby Steer, *The Law of Smoke Nuisances* (2d ed. 1945). And, reinverting the proverb, in 1648 Londoners petitioned Parliament to prohibit the importation of coal from Newcastle.

Before the advent of modern, regulation-based federal and state environmental controls, a typical "primitive type" ordinance seeking to control air pollution read as follows:

> The emission of dense smoke from the smokestack of any locomotive or engine, or from the smokestack of any stationary engine, or from the smokestack, chimney or fireplace of any building or plant anywhere within the corporate limits of the City of Lorain, Ohio, shall be deemed, and is hereby declared to be a public nuisance and is hereby prohibited except as hereafter provided.

Ord. No. 4991, §1 (1941).

The Sacramento ordinance that survived a judicial test in In re Junqua, 10 Cal. App. 602, 604, 103 P. 159, 160 (1909) read: "it shall be unlawful for any person . . . to permit any soot to escape from the smokestack or from the chimney of any furnace . . . in which distillate or crude oil is consumed as fuel." As to the question of constitutionality for early, local controls on smoke and dust, see Penn-Dixie Cement Corp. v. Kingsport, 189 Tenn. 450, 460, 225 S.W.2d 270, 275 (1949):

> We can conceive of no higher duty to be performed by a municipality than that of conserving the health of its inhabitants. The public welfare requires that conditions which are detrimental to health should be abated, or speedily regulated, without waiting for the legislature to declare by special act that such regulation is directly authorized. The

---

18. *See Steel Company Pays $235,000 to Settle $4,636,000 in Donora Smog Death Suits*, N.Y. Times, Apr. 18, 1951, at 33:

> The American Steel and Wire Company made an out-of-court settlement of about 130 damage suits that asked $4,643,000 as a result of the 1948 Donora smog disaster in which 22 persons died and 5,190 were made ill. . . .

> Donora, a steel town of 13,000 persons, lies in a deep valley of the Monongahela River about twenty miles from [Pittsburgh]. A fog blanket covered the valley beginning about Oct. 27, 1948, and remained immovable for five days. Most of the deaths occurred on Oct. 30.

> Within a year after the disaster, the market value of Donora property, principally residential, had declined 9 1/2 percent . . . .

health of the community, menaced by that which is commonly known to everyone as injurious, cannot always be made to wait upon the slow process of legislation. The law has never been so inconsiderate of the public welfare as to impose upon a municipality the necessity of obtaining specific legislative authority before it can cope with every condition which may be detrimental to the health of its people. If a municipality must have specific authority, either by a charter provision or under some general law, to enable it to deal with every cause or condition that is detrimental to public health the legislature would be compelled to adopt as many enabling acts as there are conditions thought to be dangerous to the community.

After efforts on the local and state levels proved not up to the task of addressing the severe health problems posed by air pollution by industry and vehicles, on the last day of 1970, Congress replaced relatively toothless federal provisions with the modern Clean Air Act (codified beginning at 42 U.S.C. §7401). The act set up primary (to protect public health) and secondary (to protect general welfare) national ambient air quality standards and emission standards by new sources.

5. As explained by Professor John H. Norwich, in *Environmental Planning: Lessons From New South Wales, Australia in the Integration of Land-Use Planning and Environmental Protection*, 17 Va. Envtl. L.J. 267, 318-19 (1998), at first, but not for long, federal lawmakers tied their pollution-fighting measures to local planning efforts:

> The history of the Clean Air Act provides the clearest example of the futility of tackling land-use dependent environmental issues without explicitly regulating land use. The connections among land use, transportation patterns, and urban air quality were well known when the modern Clean Air Act was adopted in 1970. Indeed, the Act contained several provisions tying land-use planning to air quality management, including requiring state implementation plans to address land-use planning and even identifying traffic-generating land uses such as shopping centers and sports stadiums as "indirect sources" of pollution subject to regulation. These provisions were criticized for infringing on the traditional local domain of land-use planning and they were excised from the law when it was amended in 1977. Since that time, federal legislation and state implementation plans have struggled to find methods to reduce transportation-related and land-use related air pollution.

> Transportation-related air pollution, for instance, is a function of two primary factors: emissions per vehicle mile traveled and the number of vehicle miles traveled. Land-use planning has nothing to do with the former, but it has everything to do with the latter. To the extent federal and state air quality programs are unable to regulate land use directly, they are severely constrained in battling urban smog. As a result, federal and state programs dealing with transportation-related pollution focus on reducing the emissions per vehicle mile traveled by imposing standards on the emission of air pollutants from new motor vehicles, reformulating gasoline, and requiring that vehicles be inspected and maintained to operate with the least emissions possible. These federal and state programs do little to reduce vehicle miles traveled. Sadly, while such programs have achieved a dramatic decrease in emissions per vehicle mile traveled, these reductions have been accompanied by an equally dramatic increase in vehicle miles traveled.

6. Under some circumstances, the lines between the crime of public nuisance and the tort of private nuisance become quite blurred, particularly when plaintiffs in a civil action are allowed to recover damages when they have suffered the effects of a public nuisance. This prospect often arises

in cases addressing serious environmental harms. For example, in Thompson v. Kimball, 165 F.2d 677, 681 (8th Cir. 1948), the U.S. Court of Appeals for the Eighth Circuit explained that

> [t]he [trial] court found special damages because the smoke, soot, etc. thrown upon plaintiffs' property were in excess of that thrown upon other property in the vicinity of plaintiffs' home and premises. That excess was due to two elements present in the situation: first, the proximity of plaintiffs' house to the railroad tracks; and, second, the use of the track nearest the house, that is, the scale track, by the defendant as a convenient place to spot its engines for necessary purposes, when, as claimed by plaintiffs and found by the court, they might have been spotted elsewhere.

On appeal, the trial court decision was reversed:

> No citation of authority is necessary to demonstrate that in so far as the smoke, soot, etc. thrown upon plaintiffs' property are due to the proximity of their property to the railroad tracks there can be no recovery of damages. Such injury as results from that fact is "common to the public at large." Any difference in amount is one of degree only. All homes constructed near a railroad or acquired after the railroad has been located and put in use are subject to the inconveniences necessarily incident to the reasonable operation of the railroad as a public utility.

Four decades later, in a legal milieu much more accepting of environmental controls on regulated industries, a much more plaintiff-friendly opinion was rendered in a state appellate court decision concerning pollution of the Hudson River. In Leo v. General Elec. Co., 145 A.D.2d 291, 292-94, 538 N.Y.S.2d 844, 845-47 (App. Div. 1989), the court reasoned:

> It is not disputed that over a 30-year period the defendant discharged a total of at least 500,000 pounds of polychlorinated biphenyls (hereinafter PCBs) from two of its manufacturing plants into the Hudson River. The PCBs collected on the river floor and were absorbed by the marine life, including the striped bass, a species which returns to the Hudson River each year to spawn. . . .
>
> The individual plaintiffs, each a member of one of the plaintiff associations, are commercial fishermen who, as a means of earning a livelihood, fish the Hudson River or the waters of Long Island. The plaintiffs allege in their complaint that the defendant intentionally discharged PCBs into the river in spite of its awareness of their toxicity and in reckless disregard of the consequences. They also allege that the defendant negligently allowed PCBs to enter the river through percolation and runoff from contaminated earth used by the defendant as a dumping ground, and that the defendant intentionally or recklessly failed to adopt effective means for the removal of PCBs from the river. The plaintiffs claim that the sale of striped bass accounted for a substantial part of a commercial fisherman's income, that as commercial fishermen they have a special interest in use of public waters, that this special interest was invaded by the defendant's pollution of the water and contamination of the fish and, in effect, that the defendant's creation of a public nuisance had and will continue to have a devastating effect upon the individual plaintiffs' ability to earn a living. As indicated, they seek damages and injunctive relief.
>
> Pollution of navigable public waters which causes death to or contamination of fish constitutes a public nuisance. It is settled law in this State that, in the absence of special damage, a public nuisance is subject to correction only by a public authority. "It is equally clear, however, that one who suffers damage or injury, beyond that of the general

inconvenience to the public at large, may recover for such nuisance in damages or obtain [an] injunction to prevent its continuance. This is old law" (Graceland Corp. v Consolidated Laundries Corp., [7 A.D. 2d 89,] at 91 [1958]). If there is some injury peculiar to a plaintiff, a private action premised on a public nuisance may be maintained. Allegations of pecuniary injury may be sufficient to satisfy the peculiar injury test so long as the injuries involved are not common to the entire community exercising the same public right.

It cannot be gainsaid that profound damage common to the entire community has been caused by the pollution of our waters. However, assuming the allegations of the complaint to be true, as we must on a motion to dismiss, the breadth and depth of the tragedy do not preclude a determination that a peculiar or special harm has also been done to these plaintiffs: diminution or loss of livelihood is not suffered by every person who fishes in the Hudson River or waters of Long Island; the harm alleged is peculiar to the individual plaintiffs in their capacity as commercial fishermen and goes beyond the harm done them as members of the community at large.

7. Public nuisance and First Amendment protections for free speech often come into conflict. For example, the city of New York responded to complaints about loud rock concerts in Central Park's Naumberg Acoustic Bandshell by instituting a Use Guideline for the Bandshell, under which the city furnished sound equipment and a sound technician for all performances. Rock Against Racism, an unincorporated association "dedicated to the espousal and promotion of antiracist views" that had sponsored concerts from 1979-1986, challenged the sound-amplification guideline as an invalid restriction of protected speech. Five Justices, in an opinion written by Justice Anthony Kennedy, upheld the city's solution in Ward v. Rock Against Racism, 491 U.S. 781, 791 (1989), in the process reviewing the special (and often confusing) standards that the Court has created for evaluating certain public restrictions on speech and expression:

> Our cases make clear . . . that even in a public forum the government may impose reasonable restrictions on the time, place, or manner of protected speech, provided the restrictions "are justified without reference to the content of the regulated speech, that they are narrowly tailored to serve a significant governmental interest, and that they leave open ample alternative channels for communication of the information." Clark v. Community for Creative Non-Violence, 468 U.S. 288, 293 (1984). . . .

> The city's regulation is . . . "narrowly tailored to serve a significant governmental interest." Despite respondent's protestations to the contrary, it can no longer be doubted that government "ha[s] a substantial interest in protecting its citizens from unwelcome noise." City Council of Los Angeles v. Taxpayers for Vincent, 466 U.S. 789, 806 (1984). . . .

> The Court of Appeals erred in sifting through all the available or imagined alternative means of regulating sound volume in order to determine whether the city's solution was "the least intrusive means" of achieving the desired end. This "less-restrictive-alternative analysis . . . has never been a part of the inquiry into the validity of a time, place, and manner regulation." Regan v. Time, Inc., 468 U.S. 641 (1984) (opinion of White, J.). Instead our cases quite clearly hold that restrictions on the time, place, or manner of protected speech are not invalid "simply because there is some imaginable alternative that might be less burdensome on speech." United States v. Albertini, 472 U.S. 675, 689 (1985). . . .

Lest any confusion on the point remain, we reaffirm today that a regulation of the time, place, or manner of protected speech must be narrowly tailored to serve the government's legitimate content-neutral interests but that it need not be the least-restrictive or least-intrusive means of doing so. Rather, the requirement of narrow tailoring is satisfied "so long as the . . . regulation promotes a substantial government interest that would be achieved less effectively absent the regulation." United States v. Albertini, 472 U.S. 675, 689 (1985).

Justices Thurgood Marshall, William Brennan, and John Paul Stevens disagreed with the finding that the guidelines were narrowly tailored and insisted that the regulatory scheme constituted an unconstitutional prior restraint.

8. Local efforts to use public nuisance to outlaw pornography have met with limited success in the High Court. Before being found invalid, §330.313 of the Jacksonville, Florida, city ordinances read:

It shall be unlawful and it is hereby declared a public nuisance for any ticket seller, ticket taker, usher, motion picture projection machine operator, manager, owner, or any other person, connected with or employed by any drive-in theater in the City to exhibit, aid or assist in exhibiting, any motion picture, slide, or other exhibit in which a human male or female bare buttocks, human female bare breasts, or human bare pubic areas are shown, if such motion picture, slide, or other exhibit is visible from any public street or public place.

The manager of the University Drive-In Theatre was charged with violating the ordinance, because of his showing of the R-rated movie "Class of '74," featuring female buttocks and bare breasts. On appeal, in Erznoznik v. City of Jacksonville, 422 U.S. 205, 209 (1975), Justice Lewis Powell, for six members of the Court, found that the statute was facially invalid:

A State or municipality may protect individual privacy by enacting reasonable time, place, and manner regulations applicable to all speech irrespective of content. But when the government, acting as censor, undertakes selectively to shield the public from some kinds of speech on the ground that they are more offensive than others, the First Amendment strictly limits its power.

The majority rejected the city's proffered reasons for the ordinance—to protect children (overbroad) and to regulate traffic (underinclusive)—and concluded that "the deterrent effect of this ordinance is both real and substantial." *Id.* at 217.

Chief Justice Warren Burger, joined by then-Associate Justice William H. Rehnquist, dissented, noting that the public nuisance law, "although no model of draftsmanship, is narrowly drawn to regulate only certain unique public exhibitions of nudity; it would be absurd to suggest that it operates to suppress expression of ideas." *Id.* at 205 (Burger, C.J., dissenting). Justice Byron White also dissented.

Eleven years later, in Arcara v. Cloud Books, Inc., 478 U.S. 697 (1986), one of the final opinions penned by Chief Justice Burger, the Court upheld against a First Amendment challenge the use of a state nuisance statute to close an adult bookstore in which prostitution and other illicit sexual activity were occurring. Section 2320 of the New York Public Health Law stated: "1. Whoever shall erect, establish, continue, maintain, use, own, or lease any building, erection, or place used for the purpose of lewdness, assignation, or prostitution is guilty of maintaining a nuisance."

Justice Harry Blackmun, joined by Justices Brennan and Marshall, took exception, reasoning that "[t]he State's purpose in stopping public lewdness cannot justify such a substantial infringement on First Amendment rights. First Amendment interests require the use of more 'sensitive tools.'" *Id.* at 711 (Blackmun, J., dissenting).

Is the apparent inconsistency of these two cases explainable on grounds other than a shift in Court membership? In Chapter Six, we will explore whether courts do a better job of reconciling the protections of the First Amendment with the demands of (non-nuisance) land use regulations.

9. Recently, American cities and other concerned parties, following a long history of employing public nuisance to attack the popularly perceived harm du jour, have brought public nuisance suits against firearms manufacturers. While a case brought by the city of New York against the "Gun Industry" was pending in federal district court, Congress passed and President George W. Bush signed the Protection of Lawful Commerce in Arms Act (PLCAA) (Pub. L. No. 109-92, 119 Stat. 2095). The PLCAA required that any pending "qualified civil liability action" be dismissed. In City of New York v. Baretta U.S.A. Corp., 401 F. Supp. 2d 244 (E.D.N.Y. 2005), the court, while refusing to find the PLCAA unconstitutional, held that the lawsuit could proceed because it fit within one of the exceptions to the dismissal provision: "[A]n action in which a manufacturer or seller of a qualified product knowingly violated a State or Federal statute applicable to the sale or marketing of the product, and the violation was a proximate cause of the harm for which relief is sought." (PLCAA §4(5)(A)(iii).) A New York statute (New York Penal Law §240.45) stated that a person who "knowingly or recklessly creates or maintains a condition which endangers the safety or health of a considerable number of persons" is guilty of criminal nuisance. Because the city contended that it could demonstrate that the "Gun Industry" had knowingly violated this state statute and that the violation was the proximate cause of the public nuisance suit, the court decided that the case fit within the PLCAA exception.

IV. Complement or Confusion?: The Relationship Between Traditional Common-Law Causes of Action and Modern Land Use and Environmental Regulation

By the closing decades of the 20th century, comprehensive federal and state statutory and regulatory schemes governed the manufacture, transport, control, and disposal of a wide range of dangerous air, water, and soil pollutants. Moreover, many local governments were using their planning and zoning tools to attack pollution and protect precious natural resources. Naturally, the question would arise in the courts whether nuisance, trespass, and other state common-law tools were and should continue to be part of the anti-pollution arsenal. The following federal district court case illustrates the fascinating interplay of judge-made and statutory controls on the use and abuse of land.

GILL v. LDI
19 F. Supp. 2d 1188 (W.D. Wash. 1998)

OPINION BY: THOMAS S. ZILLY . . .

This suit arises from a long-standing dispute between adjacent property owners in rural Snohomish County. Plaintiff Doris Hall and her husband purchased a home on a multiple acre lot with a pristine pond of several acres in 1968. With the property came a water right in the springs feeding the pond, granted to the Hall's predecessor by the State of Washington. The other two plaintiffs are Ms. Hall's daughter and son-in-law, Dianne and Stephen Gill, who now live with her on the property.

Wayne Schuett purchased property next to the Hall property in 1988 and established a quarry operation. He, his company, LDI, and his wife are the defendants in the case. Plaintiffs contend that the quarry operation discharges plumes of silt into their pond through a spring that lies under and next to the quarry and feeds their pond. The silt is blamed for their sudden inability to continue raising fish in the pond and allegedly makes it impossible to use the water for domestic or recreational purposes. Plaintiffs also contend that the operation pollutes a beaver pond that straddles the properties and feeds the Stillaguamish River, causes unbearable noise, and occasionally deposits rocks and other debris on their property.

Repeated complaints from the plaintiffs and their neighbors have led to some action by Snohomish County and the state Department of Ecology ("DOE"). In 1991, Snohomish County issued an order requiring Mr. Schuett to obtain a conditional use permit prior to continuing his operations. A hearing examiner upheld the order but opined that Mr. Schuett could operate without a license if he provided rock only for "forest practices" such as building roads. Claiming that he limits his sales to such activities, Mr. Schuett has not gotten a conditional use permit, and the county has not brought an enforcement action. In 1996, the DOE found that Mr. Schuett required a pollutant discharge permit under the Clean Water Act ("CWA"). Later, Mr. Schuett obtained a permit and belatedly fulfilled the planning and best management practices requirements in the permit. Plaintiffs brought suit in this Court in March of 1997. Mr. Schuett claims to have "cleaned up his act" in March of 1998. . . .

Plaintiffs move for summary judgment on three claims: (1) LDI has violated the Clean Water Act, (2) LDI has trespassed on their property, and (3) LDI's operations are a nuisance per se. LDI opposes all three motions and argues that the case should be dismissed because plaintiffs have failed to join an indispensable party, North Central Construction, Inc., co-owner of the property on which LDI's quarrying activities take place. . . .

> The CWA authorizes citizen suits brought by "any citizen" on his own behalf against any person . . . who is alleged to be in violation of (A) an effluent standard or limitation under this chapter or (B) an order issued by the Administrator [of the EPA] or a State with respect to such standard or limitation.

33 U.S.C. § 1365(a)(1). For the purposes of this citizen suit provision, the term "effluent standard or limitation under this chapter" includes "a permit or condition thereof." 33 U.S.C. § 1365(f).

Persons bringing a citizen's suit against an alleged CWA violator must clear three hurdles. They must prove that (1) they have standing to bring a complaint, (2) they have provided the alleged violator with a notice listing the alleged violations of the CWA at least sixty days prior to filing their suit, and (3) the defendant was engaged in ongoing violations at the time the complaint was filed. LDI challenges plaintiffs' ability to meet the last two requirements for a citizens suit. . . .

[The court found no standing or notice problems.]

Plaintiffs must show that violations are ongoing at the time the complaint is filed. Chesapeake Bay Foundation, Inc. v. Gwaltney of Smithfield, Ltd., 484 U.S. 49 (1987). Plaintiffs argue that LDI has engaged in ongoing violations of at least eight conditions of its permit, including conditions (1) S2.A.1 (quarterly water quality monitoring), (2) S4.B (timely implementation of Storm Water Pollution Prevention Plan ("SWPPP")), (3) S4.C (timely implementation of Storm Water Pollution Prevention Plan for Erosion and Sediment Control ("SWPPP/ESC")), (4) S6 (SWPPP contents and requirements), (5) S7 (SWPPP/ESC contents and requirements), (6) S9.A (Storm Water Inspections and Monitoring), (7) S9B. (Storm Water Reports and Recordkeeping), and (8) S12 (Compliance with Washington State Water Quality Standards). . . .

All of these violations are ongoing because they have continued after the date that the Complaint was filed, March 24, 1997, as well as beyond the date on which the First Amended Complaint was filed, May 28, 1997. Based on these allegations, the plaintiffs contend that LDI has engaged in a total of 5,101 violations of the CWA. Their calculations appear to be correct. . . .

LDI makes five arguments opposing plaintiffs' contention that it was engaging in ongoing violations at the time this case was filed. LDI argues that (1) the only instance on which they exceeded the effluent limitations in their permit occurred prior to this suit, (2) broader or more restrictive state standards cannot be the subject of a citizen's suit, (3) effluent discharge violations are the only violations that count, (4) this suit has been rendered moot by changes LDI has made in its operations since March 16, 1998, and (5) LDI's operation is not required to have a permit because it produce[d] contaminated storm water and it is not a point source. . . .

[The court found the first four defenses unconvincing.]

LDI argues that NPDES permits are not required for discharges of storm water from mining operations "which are not contaminated by contact with, or do not come into contact with, any overburden, raw material, intermediate products, finished product, byproduct, or waste products located on the site of such operations." 33 U.S.C. §1342(1). LDI argues that the alleged pollution "is simply rainwater coming into contact with natural silt and clay, which is not a product of the mining operation, but is a naturally occurrence [sic] under the surface of the mining operations." This argument is belied by the fact that the Washington Department of Ecology, to which the Environmental Protection Agency has delegated authority to enforce the CWA, determined that LDI required an NPDES permit under the CWA. In any case, this exemption would not apply because the discharge from LDI's property into plaintiffs' pond is the result of precipitation contacting raw material, i.e. the talus deposit in and below the quarry.

LDI also argues that it is not required to carry a permit to discharge storm water because it is not a "point source." The CWA prohibits all discharges of pollutants from identifiable "point sources" to waters of the United States absent an NPDES permit. 33 U.S.C. §§1311(a) and 1342. A "point source" is:

> any discernible, confined and discrete conveyance, including but not limited to any pipe, ditch, channel, tunnel, conduit, well, [or] discrete fissure . . . from which pollutants are or may be discharged.

33 U.S.C. §1362(14) (1986 & Supp.1995). As above, the fact that Washington's Department of Ecology determined that LDI requires a permit weighs heavily against this contention. . . .

The defendant was not exempt from the CWA's permit requirements. The plaintiffs have proved that the defendant engaged in numerous violations of the CWA and are entitled to summary judgment on that claim. . . .

Plaintiffs argue that LDI has trespassed against them by interfering with their exclusive possession of the pond on their property and water to which they hold a water right. They move for summary judgment on this claim. Plaintiffs rely on a four-part test for trespass established by the Washington State Supreme Court in Bradley v. American Smelting and Refining Co., 104 Wash. 2d 677, 691, 709 P.2d 782 (1985). In *Bradley*, the Washington court held that plaintiffs wishing to sue a company for the intangible and indirect trespass of microscopic airborne particles deposited on their property must show (1) an invasion affecting an interest in the exclusive possession of plaintiffs' property, (2) an intentional doing of the act which results in the invasion, (3) reasonable foreseeability that the act done could result in an invasion of plaintiffs' possessory interest, and (4) substantial damage to the *res*. Plaintiffs argue that the silt discharged by LDI's operations is a physical invasion of their property, that Mr. Schuett has intentionally carried on his rock quarry operation despite obviously foreseeable impacts on their property, and that it creates substantial damage to their property.

Defendants argue it is a question of fact whether they intended to cause a release of silt and clay. This argument misconstrues the law of trespass. The law does not require that the invasion or trespass itself be intentional—it is sufficient that the act resulting in the trespass is intentional. Defendants clearly intended to engage in quarrying activity.

Defendants also argue that it is a question of fact whether it was reasonably foreseeable that their activities would result in pollution of the plaintiffs' pond. Intent to trespass may include "an act that the actor undertakes realizing that there is a high probability of injury to others and yet the actor behaves with disregard of those likely consequences." *Bradley*, 104 Wash. 2d at 684. LDI's quarry originally lay about fifteen feet away from the edge of plaintiffs' pond and about 100 feet from their house. According to the Department of Ecology, the original quarry area was on top of the springs supplying plaintiffs' pond with water. Declaration of Wayne Schuett, CR 68, Exhibit M. Under the circumstances, Schuett must have realized that his activity was the likely cause of the silt discharges in plaintiffs' pond and he worked the quarry anyway. He did not move his activity further away from the Gill's property until they sued him and his consultant recommended that he take such action.

LDI finally argues that plaintiffs cannot satisfy their burden to prove substantial damage to their property. While this may be true, it is not fatal to the plaintiffs' cause of action, because the substantial damages requirement of Bradley does not apply to this case. "Historically, an invasion must constitute an interference with possession in order to be actionable as a trespass." Mock v. Potlatch Corporation, 786 F. Supp. 1545, 1548 (D. Idaho 1992). "The requirement of damages to the res limits 'trespass by airborne [or other intangible] pollutants' to cases in which there has occurred an injury that actually interferes with the right to possession." Bradley v. American Smelting & Refining Co., 635 F. Supp. 1154, 1157 (W.D. Wash. 1986). Where there is an actual entry on the land, however, either by the defendant or by some tangible thing intruding on the land because of the defendant's actions, interference with the exclusive right of possession is assumed. *Mock*, 786 F. Supp. at 1548 (citing Restatement (Second) of Torts §158(a) (1965), Keeton, Prosser and Keeton on the Law of Torts, § 13, at 67 (5th ed. 1984)); see also, Hedlund v. White, 67 Wash. App. 409, 418, 836 P.2d 250 (1992) (acknowledging trespass and imposing an injunction even though trespass caused only *de minimis* damages to plaintiff's property). The distinction between the traditional trespass remedy and the modern remedy for intangible trespasses has been summarized as follows:

> If there is a direct and tangible invasion of another's property, there is an infringement of the right of exclusive possession, and the law will presume damages. On the other hand, if the invasion is indirect and intangible (such as noise, odors, light, smoke, etc.), the proper remedy lies in an action for nuisance, based on interference with the right of use and enjoyment of the land. However, if the intangible invasion causes substantial damage to the plaintiff's property, this damage will be considered to be an infringement on the plaintiff's right to exclusive possession, and an action for trespass may be brought.

Mock, 786 F. Supp. at 1550-51. Plaintiffs have provided a great deal of evidence of tangible invasions of their property, including silt plumes in their pond and rocks deposited on their lawn. Defendants have not provided any evidence to rebut the plaintiffs' evidence. There is no genuine issue of material fact to be determined by a jury and plaintiffs are entitled to judgment as a matter of law. . . .

Plaintiffs claim that LDI's quarry is a nuisance because it interferes with their use and enjoyment of their property, both because of the pollution of their pond and because of the loud noises produced by LDI's activities. Under Washington law, a business activity that interferes with a person's use and enjoyment of their property may constitute a nuisance. If the activity is conducted lawfully, it only becomes a nuisance if it *unreasonably* interferes with a person's use or enjoyment of property. If it is conducted unlawfully, that is in violation of statutes, regulations, or permits, and it interferes with someone's use and enjoyment of their property, it is a nuisance per se.

Plaintiffs argue that LDI's operations are a nuisance per se in three respects: (1) they violate the requirements of their NPDES permit, (2) they violate noise regulations in the Snohomish County Code, and (3) they violate conditional use permit requirements of the Snohomish County Code. They have moved for summary judgment on all three points.

LDI contests each of plaintiffs' grounds for finding a nuisance per se. In addition, LDI argues that it is protected from nuisance actions by the Washington "Right to Farm" law, RCW 7.48.300. Its arguments are unavailing on all issues except the conditional use permit issue. . . .

There is no genuine issue of material fact as to whether LDI violated the provisions of its NPDES permit. Mr. Schuett admitted several violations of the permit's planning and monitoring requirements in his deposition. Mr. Schuett has not stated specific facts to contradict plaintiffs' allegations that the silt plumes invading their pond violate Washington state laws prohibiting water pollution rendering waterways unfit for their characteristic uses. WAC 173-201A-070(1). The Washington State Supreme Court has explicitly stated that "discharges in violation of permit requirements constitute a nuisance which subjects violators to damages." It is also clear from the averments of the plaintiffs that these violations have interfered with the plaintiffs' use and enjoyment of their property, preventing them from swimming in and growing fish stocks in their pond.
. . .

Plaintiffs argue that LDI's operations are a nuisance per se because they violate the relevant noise limits in Washington State regulations and the Snohomish County Code. Plaintiffs argue that because both their property and the defendant's property are zoned rural, the most restrictive noise standards apply. SCC 10.01.020(7)(a); WAC 173-060-030(2). Plaintiffs rely on the declaration of the sound expert, who concluded that noise from defendant's activities violated both the Washington state and Snohomish County noise limits.

LDI begins its assault on plaintiffs' claim by noting correctly that the Snohomish County standards in place at the time that plaintiffs' expert took his measurements in August of 1996 were identical to, not more strict than, the standards in the relevant state regulation. LDI concludes correctly that the base sound level for the combination of plaintiffs' property, a Class A property, and defendant's property, a Class C property, was 60 dBA. Finally, LDI notes that both the state regulation and the county code contain deviation provisions, which allow increases of 5 dBA for 15 minutes, 10dBA for 5 minutes, and 15 dBA for 1.5 minutes in every hour.

Plaintiff's expert used the new county code standards in preparing his declaration, which makes it difficult to determine if his declaration proves that defendant violated the noise laws. Exhibits 7A, 7B and 7C of his declaration appear to correlate with the 15, 5 and 1.5 minute deviation provisions and suggest that there was no violation in any context since the 15 minute limit is 65 dBA, the 5 minute limit is 70 dBA, and the 1.5 minute limit is 75 dBA. On the other hand, Exhibit 7D shows numerous instances over several days in which the loudest noise in a given hour was well over 75 dBA, which suggests that there may have been violations of the noise laws. Defendants note correctly, however, that in the more closely calibrated test illustrated in Exhibit 9, the noise level from the quarry did not go much over 70 dBA and appeared to hover closer to 60 dBA. This presents a material issue of fact which precludes summary judgment on this issue. . . .

LDI argues that it is protected from nuisance suits under Washington's "Right to Farm" law, RCW 7.48.300, which provides that:

> The legislature finds that agricultural activities conducted on farmland and forest practices in urbanizing areas are often subjected to nuisance lawsuits, and that such suits encourage and even force the premature removal of the lands from agricultural uses and timber productions. It is therefore the purpose of RCW 7.48.300 through 7.48.310 and

7.48.905 to provide the agricultural activities conducted on farmland and forest practices be protected from nuisance lawsuits.

RCW 7.48.305 states that such activities, "if consistent with good . . . practices and established prior to surrounding nonagricultural and nonforestry activities, are presumed to be reasonable and shall not be found to constitute a nuisance unless the activity has a substantial adverse effect on the public health and safety."

The defendant can find no solace in this statute because plaintiffs were there first. RCW 7.48.305 states explicitly that forest practices are only exempt when they are established prior to non-forest practices activities. The Washington Supreme Court has recently confirmed that the *raison d'etre* of the statute is to protect certain activities from encroachment by residential land uses. Buchanan v. Simplot Feeders Limited Partnership, 134 Wash. 2d 673, 952 P.2d 610 (1998). In this case, the residence was there before defendants. While Mr. Schuett argues that the area was used for a quarry prior to the 1950s and prior to settlement by the plaintiffs' predecessors, the Snohomish County Hearing Examiner already concluded that the defendants could not get prior nonconforming use status under the county code based on activities that were so separated in scope and time from the defendant's activities in the 1980s and 1990s. In any case, LDI cannot benefit from the statute because it has not engaged in "good forestry practices" as demonstrated by the fact that it violated several water quality laws. *Buchanan*, 134 Wash. 2d at 680. . . .

Plaintiffs have shown that there are no issues of material fact whether the defendant has violated the CWA, whether the defendant has trespassed on their property, and whether the defendant has caused a nuisance through violations of the CWA. The plaintiffs' motions for summary judgment on those three claims are GRANTED. . . .

Notes

1. The defendants in *Gill* failed in their attempt to raise an affirmative defense under the state of Washington's right to farm law. Can you see how the properly positioned agricultural user can use such a law to, in effect, reinstate "coming to the nuisance" as a formidable defense? The application of Iowa's statute was at issue in Weinhold v. Wolff, 555 N.W.2d 454, 457-58, 461-62 (Iowa 1996). The relevant facts included the following:

> In 1977 Dennis and Ruth Weinhold purchased about four acres of real property in Buena Vista County for $ 8000. They have lived on this acreage since the purchase. They raise various breeds of alternative livestock such as deer, emu, rhea, antelope, and occasionally elk.

> In February 1974 Norman and Pam Wolff purchased an eighty-acre tract of land approximately one-half mile directly south of the Weinholds' land. The Wolffs originally planted all the land with grain. Since November 1990 the Wolffs have operated a commercial hog feeding and confinement facility on part of this land, which they commute to from their home located about two and one-half miles away. . . .

> In the fall of 1991, the Wolffs and several farmers neighboring the facility applied for an "agricultural area" designation for the land on which the facility sits. The Wolffs filed the application with the Buena Vista County Board of Supervisors pursuant to what is now Iowa Code section 352.6. The board approved the application on October 8. This was about a year after the Wolffs began the hog feeding and confinement operation.

This chronology proved important to the Weinholds' nuisance action against the Wolffs, as the court found the protections of the act inapplicable to the defendants:

> The Weinholds agree section 352.11(1) is clear on its face, but they argue the statute plainly favors their claim. The Weinholds contend their nuisance action arose out of "injury created and damage sustained" before the county approved the Wolffs' property as an agricultural area. In short, the Weinholds rely on the following language in section 352.11(1): "This subsection does not apply to actions or proceedings arising from injury or damage to person or property caused by the farm or farm operation before the creation of the agricultural area."
>
> Section 352.11(1) is a "right to farm" law designed to protect agricultural operations by giving those operations meeting the statutory requirements a defense to nuisance actions. All fifty states have enacted right to farm laws in various forms.
>
> Negligent operation of the farm resulting in the nuisance defeats the defense. Additionally, the defense does not apply to actions or proceedings arising from injury or damage to property caused by the farm operation *before* the agricultural area is established.

Because the plaintiffs' permanent nuisance cause of action accrued before the county approved the Wolffs' property as an agricultural area under the statute, the statutory defense was unavailing.

2. Trickett v. Ochs, 176 Vt. 89, 91, 95, 98-99, 838 A.2d 66, 68, 71-72, 74 (2003) is another unsuccessful attempt by defendants to employ a state right to farm statute. The Tricketts brought nuisance and trespass claims against the Ochses, from whom the Tricketts bought their house:

> Plaintiffs purchased their home from defendants in 1992. At the time of the purchase, the residence was the homestead for an apple orchard and was directly across the road from the barn that served as the main collecting point for the apples. Defendants continued to operate the apple orchard after the sale of the farmhouse, though the business initially had little impact on plaintiffs because most of the apples were immediately transported following harvest to the Shoreham Food Co-op, where they were stored for sale.
>
> During the mid-1990s, defendants expanded their operation in response to changes in market demands. They began waxing their apples and storing them on-site in refrigerated tractor trailer trucks. Tractor trailer trucks also came to the barn to take apples to market. During the winter months, these trucks began arriving in the predawn hours and continued throughout the day. Because the barn is very close to plaintiffs' home, additional noise and light glare entered the home and disturbed plaintiffs.

In determining whether the right-to-farm law allowed a defense, the Supreme Court of Vermont focused its attention on the intensification of use by the Ochses:

> The origin of this conflict was the act of selling the farmhouse to persons who have no involvement in farm activities. Buildings built to function together for one economic and social unit must now function separately. As a result, land use conflicts once worked out over the dinner table now end up in court. The conflict sown by the sale of the house took root and grew when business conditions in the apple industry required a significant change in defendants' methods of operation. As defendants' evidence disclosed, they could no longer rely upon the local co-op to store and market their apples. Rather, they had to wax the apples at the farm. They also had to store, pack and ship the apples from

the farm. They purchased and used refrigerated tractor-trailer trucks to extend the life of the apples so they could ship them year-round. According to plaintiffs' evidence, although the new methods of operation did not increase the number of apples sold, they increased the truck traffic and noise at the farm and extended both the hours of operation and the season in which those operations occurred.

The court concluded:

> Unless we define the prior protected activities to include the expanded orchard operations engaged in by defendants after plaintiffs bought their home, the statute does not apply. We decline to do so.

The high court also found that collateral estoppel did not prevent the Tricketts from litigating their common-law claims against their neighbors. Notice the interaction between zoning laws and private nuisance:

> [T]he issues adjudicated in the two actions were not the same. The issue before the zoning board was whether defendants fully complied with the zoning ordinance. In contrast, the issue in the superior court was whether defendants' conduct, particularly the noise generation, was a private nuisance causing damage to plaintiffs. Compliance with the zoning ordinance may be a factor in determining whether defendants' conduct was a nuisance, but it is not determinative.
>
> In this case in particular, compliance with the zoning ordinance is of little consequence to the main nuisance issue—whether defendants generated excessive noise. The Orwell zoning ordinance contains a noise standard, but it is inapplicable to agricultural and forestry uses. Orwell Zoning Bylaws § 1140. Thus, zoning imposes no restriction on the noise generated by defendants' orchard operation. Because the issues in the two actions were not the same, defendants have failed to satisfy the second element of collateral estoppel.

3. In the early decades of zoning, state courts ensured that private nuisance would survive the new regulatory onslaught. See, for example, Weltshe v. Graf, 323 Mass. 498, 500, 82 N.E.2d 795, 796 (1948), in which the court concluded:

> The hotel and the freight terminal are located at the boundaries of a district zoned for business and adjoin a district zoned for residences in which all the plaintiffs have their homes. The fact that the operation of certain kinds of commercial enterprises is permitted under a zoning ordinance is an important factor in determining whether the use being made of the land in conducting a particular enterprise goes beyond what is reasonable in view of the nature and character of the locality, the effect of the use upon those who live in the neighborhood, and the strength and force appropriately due to the various conflicting interests usually involved in the subject matter. But a zoning ordinance affords no protection to one who uses his land in such a manner as to constitute a private nuisance.

4. An exploration of the intersection between public nuisance and local land use regulation can be found in Robinson v. Indianola Mun. Separate Sch. Dist., 467 So. 2d 911, 913, 917-18 (Miss. 1985):

> Appellants Robinson and Gardner requested the Chancery Court of Sunflower County to enjoin the Indianola Municipal Separate School District from constructing a high

school gymnasium across the street from their homes on the ground that it would constitute a public nuisance. . . .

The question becomes whether this non-compliance with the offstreet parking ordinance is a public nuisance which the appellants, as abutting landowners, are entitled to enjoin. While it is generally acknowledged that the violation of a municipal ordinance does not constitute a public nuisance, the continuing violation of a valid ordinance may constitute a nuisance. A private individual cannot ordinarily maintain an action with respect to the enforcement of a zoning regulation, except where the use constitutes a nuisance per se or the individual has suffered or is threatened with special damage, i.e., injury or threat of injury of a special or peculiar nature amounting to a private wrong affecting his personal or property rights. . . .

[A]ppellants have alleged the existence of a public nuisance in the form of obstruction of Battle Street by traffic. This condition is directly traceable to the school district's non-compliance with the Indianola off-street parking ordinance. While it is true that ordinarily a private individual may not maintain a suit to enforce a zoning ordinance, nor may he enjoin what is in essence a public nuisance, where, as here, the condition obstructs an abutting landowner's right of ingress and egress, an injunction will lie. Under the established law, we are required to reverse the chancellor and issue an injunction barring the school district from proceeding with the construction of the Gentry High School gymnatorium unless and until it complies with the Indianola off-street parking ordinance.

5. In Town of Hull v. Massachusetts Port Auth., 441 Mass. 508, 519, 806 N.E.2d 901, 909 (2004), the Supreme Judicial Court of Massachusetts concluded that the town could not bring a public nuisance action against the Massachusetts Port Authority for the operation of Logan International Airport. The court concluded:

Here the town makes no allegation that Massport has exceeded its statutory authority or violated any of the extensive FAA regulations that govern the operation of Logan. Given the fact that the Legislature established Massport to operate the airport and that the FAA has jurisdiction over flight paths and noise, we see no need to disturb the principles set forth in [earlier cases], particularly concerning the Legislature's right to determine what is in the public interest. We conclude that the town may not maintain an action against Massport for public nuisance.

6. *Gill* indicates that state common-law doctrines can still be used to fight environmental harm, despite statutory and regulatory initiatives by the federal and state "supreme sovereigns." While, in Milwaukee v. Illinois, 451 U.S. 304, 317 (1981), the Court held that in enacting the enforcement mechanisms of the Clean Water Act (also known as the Federal Water Pollution Control Act), Congress intended to preempt *federal* common law ("Congress has not left the formulation of appropriate federal standards to the courts through application of often vague and indeterminate nuisance concepts and maxims of equity jurisprudence, but rather has occupied the field through the establishment of a comprehensive regulatory program supervised by an expert administrative agency"), *state* common law is alive and kicking in this area. For example, a North Carolina appellate court endorsed a complementary approach in Biddix v. Henredon Furniture Indus., Inc., 76 N.C. App. 30, 33, 40, 331 S.E.2d 717, 720, 724 (Ct. App. 1985):

Notwithstanding the trial court's order which states that federal law has abrogated the common law actions asserted by plaintiff, defendant concedes on appeal that nothing in the Federal Water Pollution Control Act (hereinafter FWPCA), as amended, 33 U.S.C. §§1251-1376 (1982), preempts the common law of this state concerning private actions in nuisance and trespass to land for industrial pollution. Defendant correctly recognizes that state statutory and common law rights survive enactment of a federal statute unless the federal enactment specifically preempts or conflicts with the state law. Nothing in the FWPCA abrogates the common law of any state. The remaining question is whether the [North Carolina] Clean Water Act abrogates the common law civil actions asserted by plaintiff. Defendant's argument before this court recognizes that nothing in the General Assembly's specific statutory language abrogates these common law civil actions; defendant relies on interpretation of the nature and scope of the Clean Water Act to support the trial court's order. . . .

We conclude that the Clean Water Act does not abrogate the common law civil actions for private nuisance and trespass to land for pollution of waters resulting from violation of [an] NPDES [national pollutant discharge elimination system] permit. First, the Clean Water Act, as amended, does not specifically abrogate these common law civil actions. Assuming for the purposes of this appeal that industrial discharges made under [an] NPDES permit would constitute a "reasonable use" of water in accordance with the common law, thereby effectively preventing a civil action founded in nuisance or trespass to land, plaintiff's allegations in the case before us allege waste discharges in violation of defendant's NPDES permit.

Second, to adopt the holding of the trial court would lead to absurd results. By holding that the common law actions of common law nuisance and trespass to land were abrogated by the Clean Water Act, plaintiff would be left in the untenable position of having suffered damage to real property without an effective remedy under the Act. While the Clean Water Act provides for criminal and civil penalties, the Act does not provide a mechanism for compensation of private landowners for damage to their property or personal injury. Based on the trial court's order, plaintiff's only remedy would be to report any NPDES violation by defendant to NRCD [the state Department of Natural Resources and Community Development] without legal recourse for the alleged damages to his property. We cannot conceive that the General Assembly intended any such result in adopting the Clean Water Act. We agree with defendant that the General Assembly has provided a comprehensive statutory scheme for remedial correction of water pollution as well as other forms of industrial and private pollution. Preservation of the common law actions of nuisance and trespass to land for industrial discharges in violation of the laws of this state is consistent with the General Assembly's enactments rather than inconsistent with them as argued by defendant. By retaining the common law civil actions of nuisance and trespass to land, the legislative intent to maintain the waters of this state in a clean and wholesome state for present and future generations is strengthened.

V. Constitutional Protections Against Police Power Regulations That Go "Too Far"

Just saying that a public nuisance statute—or, for that matter, any other police power regulation—is designed to protect the public health, safety, morals, or general welfare does not necessarily insulate the law from judicial scrutiny. In 1922, Justice Oliver Wendell Holmes Jr., the "Yankee from Olympus" (at least, according to at least one biographer),[19] wrote an opinion for the High Court in a dispute concerning the legitimacy of a Pennsylvania coal mining statute that sought to place meaningful limits on the state's regulatory reach. In the process, Holmes deposited a legal chestnut—his "goes too far" test—that has grown into the tall, jurisprudential tree known as regulatory takings law. As you read Holmes' highly influential (if not necessarily seminal)[20] opinion, consider whether the facts called for the majority to deviate from one of the Justices' long-standing prudential practices—"never to formulate a rule of constitutional law broader than is required by the precise facts to which it is to be applied."[21]

PENNSYLVANIA COAL CO. v. MAHON
260 U.S. 393 (1922)

MR. JUSTICE HOLMES delivered the opinion of the Court.

This is a bill in equity brought by the defendants in error to prevent the Pennsylvania Coal Company from mining under their property in such way as to remove the supports and cause a subsidence of the surface and of their house. The bill sets out a deed executed by the Coal Company in 1878, under which the plaintiffs claim. The deed conveys the surface, but in express terms reserves the right to remove all the coal under the same, and the grantee takes the premises with the risk, and waives all claim for damages that may arise from mining out the coal. But the plaintiffs say that whatever may have been the Coal Company's rights, they were taken away by an Act of Pennsylvania, approved May 27, 1921, P.L. 1198, commonly known there as the Kohler Act. The Court of Common Pleas found that if not restrained the defendant would cause the damage to prevent which the bill was brought, but denied an injunction, holding that the statute if applied to this case would be unconstitutional. On appeal the Supreme Court of the State agreed that the defendant had contract and property rights protected by the Constitution of the United States, but held that the statute was a legitimate exercise of the police power and directed a decree for the plaintiffs. A writ of error was granted bringing the case to this Court.

The statute forbids the mining of anthracite coal in such way as to cause the subsidence of, among other things, any structure used as a human habitation, with certain exceptions, including among them land where the surface is owned by the owner of the underlying coal and is distant more than one hundred and fifty feet from any improved property belonging to any other person. As applied to this case the statute is admitted to destroy previously existing rights of property and contract. The question is whether the police power can be stretched so far.

---

19. CATHERINE DRINKER BOWEN, YANKEE FROM OLYMPUS: JUSTICE HOLMES AND HIS FAMILY (1944). Much more useful than Bowen's hero study is G. EDWARD WHITE, JUSTICE OLIVER WENDELL HOLMES: LAW AND THE INNER SELF (1993).

20. *See* Robert Brauneis, *"The Foundation of Our 'Regulatory Takings' Jurisprudence": The Myth and Meaning of Justice Holmes's Opinion in* Pennsylvania Coal Co. v. Mahon, 106 YALE L.J. 613, 701 (1996):

Justice Holmes's opinion in *Pennsylvania Coal Co. v. Mahon* has been simultaneously acclaimed as the seminal case in the law of "regulatory takings" and blamed for the doctrinal confusion in that area. Both the commendations and the accusations, however, have been largely misplaced. *Mahon* was not the "first regulatory takings case." It was not decided under the Takings Clause. It was not the first case to hold that the Constitution protected nonphysical property or property as value. And it was not the first case to hold that a use restriction might be constitutional if and only if accompanied by just compensation. Its supposed status as the progenitor of all regulatory takings cases is the result of erroneous genealogy.

21. Liverpool, New York & Philadelphia Steamship Co. v. Commissioners of Emigration, 113 U.S. 33, 39 (1885). Justice Louis Brandeis, in one of his most memorable and enduring opinions, included the quoted language as one of "a series of rules under which [the Supreme Court] has avoided passing upon a large part of all the constitutional questions pressed upon it for decision." Ashwander v. Tennessee Valley Auth., 297 U.S. 288, 346-48 (1936) (Brandeis, J., concurring).

Government hardly could go on if to some extent values incident to property could not be diminished without paying for every such change in the general law. As long recognized, some values are enjoyed under an implied limitation and must yield to the police power. But obviously the implied limitation must have its limits, or the contract and due process clauses are gone. One fact for consideration in determining such limits is the extent of the diminution. When it reaches a certain magnitude, in most if not in all cases there must be an exercise of eminent domain and compensation to sustain the act. So the question depends upon the particular facts. The greatest weight is given to the judgment of the legislature, but it always is open to interested parties to contend that the legislature has gone beyond its constitutional power.

This is the case of a single private house. No doubt there is a public interest even in this, as there is in every purchase and sale and in all that happens within the commonwealth. Some existing rights may be modified even in such a case. But usually in ordinary private affairs the public interest does not warrant much of this kind of interference. A source of damage to such a house is not a public nuisance even if similar damage is inflicted on others in different places. The damage is not common or public. The extent of the public interest is shown by the statute to be limited, since the statute ordinarily does not apply to land when the surface is owned by the owner of the coal. Furthermore, it is not justified as a protection of personal safety. That could be provided for by notice. Indeed the very foundation of this bill is that the defendant gave timely notice of its intent to mine under the house. On the other hand the extent of the taking is great. It purports to abolish what is recognized in Pennsylvania as an estate in land—a very valuable estate—and what is declared by the Court below to be a contract hitherto binding the plaintiffs. If we were called upon to deal with the plaintiffs' position alone, we should think it clear that the statute does not disclose a public interest sufficient to warrant so extensive a destruction of the defendant's constitutionally protected rights.

But the case has been treated as one in which the general validity of the act should be discussed. The Attorney General of the State, the City of Scranton, and the representatives of other extensive interests were allowed to take part in the argument below and have submitted their contentions here. It seems, therefore, to be our duty to go farther in the statement of our opinion, in order that it may be known at once, and that further suits should not be brought in vain.

It is our opinion that the act cannot be sustained as an exercise of the police power, so far as it affects the mining of coal under streets or cities in places where the right to mine such coal has been reserved. As said in a Pennsylvania case, "For practical purposes, the right to coal consists in the right to mine it." Commonwealth v. Clearview Coal Co., 256 Pa. St. 328, 331. What makes the right to mine coal valuable is that it can be exercised with profit. To make it commercially impracticable to mine certain coal has very nearly the same effect for constitutional purposes as appropriating or destroying it. This we think that we are warranted in assuming that the statute does.

It is true that in Plymouth Coal Co. v. Pennsylvania, 232 U.S. 531, it was held competent for the legislature to require a pillar of coal to be left along the line of adjoining property, that, with the pillar on the other side of the line, would be a barrier sufficient for the safety of the employees of either mine in case the other should be abandoned and allowed to fill with water. But that was a requirement for the safety of employees invited into the mine, and secured an average reciprocity of advantage that has been recognized as a justification of various laws. . . .

The protection of private property in the Fifth Amendment presupposes that it is wanted for public use, but provides that it shall not be taken for such use without compensation. . . . When this seemingly absolute protection is found to be qualified by the police power, the natural tendency of human nature is to extend the qualification more and more until at last private property disappears. But that cannot be accomplished in this way under the Constitution of the United States.

The general rule at least is, that while property may be regulated to a certain extent, if regulation goes too far it will be recognized as a taking. It may be doubted how far exceptional cases, like the blowing up of a house to stop a conflagration, go—and if they go beyond the general rule, whether they do not stand as much upon tradition as upon principle. Bowditch v. Boston, 101 U.S. 16. In general it is not plain that a man's misfortunes or necessities will justify his shifting the damages to his neighbor's shoulders. Spade v. Lynn & Boston R.R. Co., 172 Mass. 488, 489. We are in danger of forgetting that a strong public desire to improve the public condition is not enough to warrant achieving the desire by a shorter cut than the constitutional way of paying for the change. As we already have said, this is a question of degree—and therefore cannot be disposed of by general propositions. But we regard this as going beyond any of the cases decided by this Court. The late decisions upon laws dealing with the congestion of Washington and New York, caused by the war, dealt with laws intended to meet a temporary emergency and providing for compensation determined to be reasonable by an impartial board. They went to the verge of the law but fell far short of the present act. Block v. Hirsh, 256 U.S. 135. Marcus Brown Holding Co. v. Feldman, 256 U.S. 170. Levy Leasing Co. v. Siegel, 258 U.S. 242.

We assume, of course, that the statute was passed upon the conviction that an exigency existed that would warrant it, and we assume that an exigency exists that would warrant the exercise of eminent domain. But the question at bottom is upon whom the loss of the changes desired should fall. So far as private persons or communities have seen fit to take the risk of acquiring only surface rights, we cannot see that the fact that their risk has become a danger warrants the giving to them greater rights than they bought.

Decree reversed.

MR. JUSTICE BRANDEIS, dissenting.

The Kohler Act prohibits, under certain conditions, the mining of anthracite coal within the limits of a city in such a manner or to such an extent "as to cause the . . . subsidence of any dwelling or other structure used as a human habitation, or any factory, store, or other industrial or mercantile establishment in which human labor is employed." Coal in place is land; and the right of the owner to use his land is not absolute. He may not so use it as to create a public nuisance; and uses, once harmless, may, owing to changed conditions, seriously threaten the public welfare. Whenever they do, the legislature has power to prohibit such uses without paying compensation; and the power to prohibit extends alike to the manner, the character and the purpose of the use. Are we justified in declaring that the Legislature of Pennsylvania has, in restricting the right to mine anthracite, exercised this power so arbitrarily as to violate the Fourteenth Amendment?

Every restriction upon the use of property imposed in the exercise of the police power deprives the owner of some right theretofore enjoyed, and is, in that sense, an abridgment by the State of rights in property without making compensation. But restriction imposed to protect the public health, safety or morals from dangers threatened is not a taking. The restriction here in question is merely the prohibition of a noxious use. The property so restricted remains in the possession of its owner. The State does not appropriate it or make any use of it. The State merely prevents the owner from making a use which interferes with paramount rights of the public. Whenever the use prohibited ceases to be noxious,—as it may because of further change in local or social conditions,—the restriction will have to be removed and the owner will again be free to enjoy his property as heretofore.

The restriction upon the use of this property can not, of course, be lawfully imposed, unless its purpose is to protect the public. But the purpose of a restriction does not cease to be public, because incidentally some private persons may thereby receive gratuitously valuable special benefits. Thus, owners of low buildings may obtain, through statutory restrictions upon the height of neighboring structures, benefits equivalent to an easement of light and air. Furthermore, a restriction, though imposed for a public purpose, will not be lawful, unless the restriction is an appropriate means to the public end. But to keep coal in place is surely an appropriate means of preventing subsidence of the surface; and ordinarily it is the only available means. Restriction upon use does not become inappropriate as a means, merely because it deprives the owner of the only use to which the property can then be profitably put. . . . Nor is a restriction imposed through exercise of the police power inappropriate as a means, merely because the same end might be effected through exercise of the power of eminent domain, or otherwise at public expense. Every restriction upon the height of buildings might be secured through acquiring by eminent domain the right of each owner to build above the limiting height; but it is settled that the State need not resort to that power. If by mining anthracite coal the owner would necessarily unloose poisonous gasses, I suppose no one would doubt the power of the State to prevent the mining, without buying his coal fields. And why may not the State, likewise, without paying compensation, prohibit one from digging so deep or excavating so near the surface, as to expose the community to like dangers? In the latter case, as in the former, carrying on the business would be a public nuisance.

It is said that one fact for consideration in determining whether the limits of the police power have been exceeded is the extent of the resulting diminution in value; and that here the restriction destroys existing rights of property and contract. But values are relative. If we are to consider the value of the coal kept in place by the restriction, we should compare it with the value of all other parts of the land. That is, with the value not of the coal alone, but with the value of the whole property. The rights of an owner as against the public are not increased by dividing the interests in his property into surface and subsoil. The sum of the rights in the parts can not be greater than the rights in the whole. . . . And why should a sale of underground rights bar the State's power? For aught that appears the value of the coal kept in place by the restriction may be negligible as compared with the value of the whole property, or even as compared with that part of it which is represented by the coal remaining in place and which may be extracted despite the statute. Ordinarily a police regulation, general in operation, will not be held void as to a particular property, although proof is offered that owing to conditions peculiar to it the restriction could not reasonably be applied. But even if the particular facts are to govern, the statute should, in my opinion, be upheld in this case. For the defendant has failed to adduce any evidence from which it appears that to restrict its mining operations was an unreasonable exercise of the police power. Where the surface and the coal belong to the same person, self-interest would ordinarily prevent mining to such an extent as to cause a subsidence. It was, doubtless, for this reason that the legislature, estimating the degrees of danger, deemed statutory restriction unnecessary for the public safety under such conditions. . . .

Reciprocity of advantage is an important consideration, and may even be an essential, where the State's power is exercised for the purpose of conferring benefits upon the property of a neighborhood, as in drainage projects; or upon adjoining owners, as by party wall provisions. But where the police power is exercised, not to confer benefits upon property owners, but to protect the public from detriment and danger, there is, in my opinion, no room for considering reciprocity of advantage. There was no reciprocal advantage to the owner prohibited from using his oil tanks in 248 U.S. 498; his brickyard, in 239 U.S. 394; his livery stable, in 237 U.S. 171; his billiard hall, in 225 U.S. 623; his oleomargarine factory, in 127 U.S. 678; his brewery, in 123 U.S. 623; unless it be the advantage of living and doing business in a civilized community. That reciprocal advantage is given by the act to the coal operators.

Notes

1. Sometimes a judicial opinion raises many more questions than it resolves. This seems to be the case with *Pennsylvania Coal* and its supposed "general rule." From where did the majority derive this "rule," and just how "general" is its applicability? How can a "rule" be so indeterminate? Exactly how far is "*too* far"? By "taking," does Justice Holmes mean a violation of the Fifth Amendment's Takings Clause[22] that requires compensation if requested by the property owner, or instead a deprivation that violates the Due Process Clause?[23] By 1922, there was ample precedent in support of a finding in favor of the Pennsylvania Coal Company, meaning that the Justices did not have to rely, even indirectly or metaphorically, on the Takings Clause.

2. It is somewhat surprising that Justice Holmes penned the majority opinion in *Pennsylvania Coal*, an opinion which seemed to open the door to the kind of judicial second-guessing of legislative schemes that the same jurist so eloquently condemned in his dissent in the still-notorious[24] case of Lochner v. New York, 198 U.S. 45 (1905). Seventeen years before *Pennsylvania Coal*, Holmes had claimed:

> This case is decided upon an economic theory which a large part of the country does not entertain. If it were a question whether I agreed with that theory, I should desire to study it further and long before making up my mind. But I do not conceive that to be my duty . . . . [A] constitution is not intended to embody a particular economic theory, whether of paternalism and the organic relation of the citizen to the State or of laissez faire. It is made for people of fundamentally differing views, and the accident of our finding certain opinions natural and familiar or novel and even shocking ought not to conclude our judgment upon the question whether statutes embodying them conflict with the Constitution of the United States.

Id. at 75-76 (Holmes, J., dissenting).

The author of this impassioned defense of judicial deference should not have been surprised that Justice Brandeis, Holmes' decidedly Progressive colleague, not only dissented from Holmes' apparent about-face in *Pennsylvania Coal*, but also voiced ex parte concern with the majority opinion, telling Justice Felix Frankfurter that "heightened respect for property has been part of Holmes' growing old."[25]

3. While Shepard's instructs us that citations to *Pennsylvania Coal* run into the thousands, in the years immediately following its release, the majority opinion apparently had little impact on how the Court analyzed the legitimacy of regulations affecting the use and development of land. *Penn-*

---

22. The Takings Clause of the Fifth Amendment, made applicable to the states (and localities) through the Due Process Clause of the Fourteenth Amendment, reads: "[N]or shall private property be taken for public use, without just compensation."

23. The Due Process Clause of the Fourteenth Amendment reads: "[N]or shall any state deprive any person of life, liberty, or property, without due process of law."

24. *See* Gary D. Rowe, Lochner *Revisionism Revisited*, 24 Law & Soc. Inquiry 221, 222 (1999):

    Although simply the name of the 1905 case in which the United States Supreme Court ruled unconstitutional a New York statute limiting bakers to a 10 hour work day and a 60 hour work week, the word *Lochner* has for some three generations of lawyers, jurists, and historians taken on an additional resonance, summing up in two syllables everything wrong with a constitutional jurisprudence that could do no right.

    Lochner does have its modern groupies, however. *See, e.g.*, Michael J. Phillips, The *Lochner* Court, Myth and Reality: Substantive Due Process From the 1890s to the 1930s (2001); David E. Bernstein, Lochner *Era Revisionism, Revised*: Lochner *and the Origins of Fundamental Rights Constitutionalism*, 92 Geo. L.J. 1 (2003).

25. Melvin I. Urofsky, *The Brandeis-Frankfurter Conversations*, 1985 Sup. Ct. Rev. 299, 321 (quoting Frankfurter's written recollections of conversations with Brandeis, The Louis Brandeis Papers) (internal quotation marks omitted).

sylvania Coal did not earn even a mention in the four zoning cases decided between 1926 and 1928 in which landowners claimed that government officials were passing and enforcing arbitrary and confiscatory regulations: Nectow v. City of Cambridge, 277 U.S. 183 (1928); Gorieb v. Fox, 274 U.S. 603 (1927); Zahn v. Board of Pub. Works, 274 U.S. 325 (1927); Village of Euclid v. Ambler Realty Co., 272 U.S. 365 (1926).[26] Nevertheless, as many of the succeeding decisions from state and federal trial and appellate courts included in the subsequent chapters of this volume so strongly indicate, the notion that a regulation can amount to an illegal taking is a brooding omnipresence that informs litigation and settlement strategies as well as the judicial decisionmaking process.

---

26. However, in the 1920s and early 1930s, during the apex of conservative judicial activism, Justice Holmes' opinion was cited with approval by his conservative brethren in several majority and dissenting opinions in non-land use cases that we today associate with the apex of conservative judicial activism. These opinions include Nebbia v. New York, 291 U.S. 502, 552 (1934) (McReynolds, J., dissenting) (disagreeing with the majority's refusal to invalidate price controls for milk under the Equal Protection Clause); Home Bldg. & Loan Ass'n v. Blaisdell, 290 U.S. 398, 478-79 (1934) (Sutherland, J., dissenting) (objecting to the majority's holding that Minnesota's Mortgage Moratorium Law did not violate the Contracts Clause); Charles Wolff Packing Co. v. Court of Indus. Relations, 262 U.S. 522, 544 (1923) (holding that a Kansas act that vested in an industrial court the power to decide disputes arising in certain industries deprived a packing house of property and liberty of contract without due process of law); and Adkins v. Children's Hosp., 261 U.S. 525, 554-59 (1923) (holding that a minimum wage law for women violated freedom of contract).

Chapter Three

The "Euclidean" Strategy: Authorizing and Implementing the Legislative Districting of Permissible Land Uses

I.   A National Movement

Since the early decades of the 20th century, the most widely employed land use control has been zoning; it is in fact the workhorse of the planning and, locally, the environmental movement in this country. That it has gained acceptance as an indispensable tool of planning may be seen from the figures: "According to a 1981 report, zoning codes had been adopted not only by 98% of all cities with a population over 10,000 but also by nearly 90% of all suburban municipalities with a population of at least 5,000 and by nearly half of suburban municipalities with less than 5,000 residents."[1] Because zoning has achieved such general application, it is clearly the legislative process most worthy of detailed consideration in this field.

To formulate a practical system of zoning for American municipalities and to present a legal theory to sustain such an exercise of power was a major creative achievement of the American bar. This was no easy task. And, as with all social engineering, considerable ingenuity was required to convert philosophy into legislation and implementation. An illuminating insight into the strategy of litigation is provided by the annual discussions at the National Conference on City Planning.[2] Given the popularity of zoning it is hard to conceive of an alternative system of land use control that could have been devised and so widely accepted. It is equally challenging to formulate a set of alternative rationales that might have been woven from existing legal doctrines and precedents.

During the decade preceding 1926, the advocates of zoning fought a vigorous battle for its judicial recognition. At first, some courts were loath to sustain any legislative attempt to restrict or regulate the free exercise of what were then deemed the rights of property. Indeed, many states considered, and a few adopted,[3] constitutional amendments to permit zoning. But there always remained the very real possibility that the U.S. Supreme Court would interpret the innovation as an unconstitutional use of state power under the Fourteenth Amendment.

---

1.   Rathkopf's The Law of Zoning and Planning §1:3 (4th ed. 2009) (citing Peter Wolf, Land in America 140 (1981)).

2.   *See* Alfred Bettman, *Discussion, in* National Conference on City Planning 111 (1914); Edward M. Bassett, *Legal Aspects of Zoning, id.* at 193 (1919); Ernst Freund, *Discussion, id.* at 62 (1913); Ernst Freund, *Discussion, id.* at 73 (1926). For more on some of the early giants of planning and zoning, see William M. Randle, *Professors, Reformers, Bureaucrats, and Cronies: The Players in* Euclid v. Ambler, *in* Zoning and the American Dream 31-70 (Charles M. Haar & Jerold S. Kayden eds., 1989). A valuable online resource for those interested in reading early planning materials is Urban Planning, 1794-1918: An International Anthology of Articles, Conference Papers, and Reports (John W. Reps ed., 1999), *available at* http://www.library.cornell.edu/Reps/DOCS/.

3.   *See, e.g.,* Ga. Const. art. 3, §2-1923 (1945); La. Const. art. 14, §29 (1921); Mass. Const. art. 60, §190 (1918); N.J. Const. art. 4. §6, ¶ 2 (1928).

Zoning received only passing attention at the first City Planning Conference in 1909.[4] Although in 1911 the Committee on Legislative and Administrative Methods presented model acts for other aspects of city planning, it suggested no comprehensive zoning act; the reason given for this omission was that the views of conference members were as yet too undecided on the subject.[5] However, a paper the following year, *The Control of Municipal Development by the "Zoning System" and Its Application in the United States*,[6] was followed up, in 1913, by the report, *Districting*, by the Height of Buildings Commission.[7]

New York City is generally credited with enacting the first comprehensive zoning ordinance, in 1916. Prior to this time, California's high court had upheld use restrictions (at least, those enforced against Chinese-Americans),[8] and the U.S. Supreme Court had approved height restrictions in Boston.[9] The movement in favor of this new form of comprehensive zoning took on the aspects of a fervid crusade.[10] Whereas, in 1916, Lawrence Veiller had announced that zoning "sounds like a beautiful dream,"[11] by the following year George Ford was able to state that as a result of the success in New York, zoning was being organized, actively promoted, or actually carried on in 20 municipalities.[12] In 1922, Frank B. Williams published The Law of City Planning and Zoning, the first comprehensive American work in the field. The same year Theodora Kimball could write that "[z]oning has taken the country by storm"; she reported 20 enabling acts, nearly 50 ordinances, and about 100 zone plans in progress.[13]

---

4. *See* George B. Ford, *The Scope of City Planning in the United States*, S. Doc. No. 422, Hearing on City Planning, 61st Cong., 2d Sess. 70 (1910); Henry Morgenthau, A National Constructive Programme for City Planning, *id*. at 59. A news article covering the event carried the following headlines: "Cities Must Guard Health of Workers; Henry Morgenthau Outlines in Washington a Plan to Obtain Model Homes for Poor; Better Transit Needed; Present Conditions a Crime, He Declares—Cabinet Officers to Preside at Conference To-day," N.Y. TIMES, May 22, 1909, at 3.

5. *See* Andrew Wright Crawford, *Certain Principles of a Uniform City Planning Code, in* NATIONAL CONFERENCE ON CITY PLANNING 231, 239 (1911). And see the comments by Ernst Freund, and the reactions thereto, *id*. at 241, 258.

6. *Id*. at 173 (1912).

7. Reprinted in Commission on Building Districts and Restrictions, Final Report, app. III, at 51 (1916).

8. In the case of In re Hang Kie, 69 Cal. 149, 10 P. 327 (1886), the court turned down a habeas corpus challenge to an ordinance that read:

   It shall be unlawful for any person to establish, maintain, or carry on the business of a public laundry or washhouse where articles are washed and cleansed for hire, within the city of Modesto, except within that part of the city which lies west of the railroad track and south of G Street.

9. Welch v. Swasey, 214 U.S. 91 (1909) (rejecting a taking and equal protection challenge to "a discrimination or classification between sections of the city, one of which, the business or commercial part, has a limitation of one hundred and twenty-five feet, and the other, used for residential purposes, has a permitted height of buildings from eighty to one hundred feet"). Thirteen years before the *Pennsylvania Coal* decision, Justice Rufus Peckham, the author of the anti-regulation, majority opinion in *Lochner*, wrote for a unanimous Court:

   We are not prepared to hold that this limitation of eighty to one hundred feet, while in fact a discrimination or classification, is so unreasonable that it deprives the owner of the property of its profitable use without justification, and that he is therefore entitled under the Constitution to compensation for such invasion of his rights. The discrimination thus made is, as we think, reasonable, and is justified by the police power.

   Id. at 107.

   On October 17, 1791, President George Washington issued a regulation "that the wall of no House shall be higher than forty feet to the Roof, in any part of the City, nor shall any be lower than thirty-five feet on any of the avenues." In order to attract the settlement of "Mechanics and others whose Circumstances did not admit of erecting Houses authorized by the said Regulations," they were suspended in 1796. *See* THOMAS JEFFERSON AND THE NATIONAL CAPITAL 197 (Saul K. Padover ed., 1946).

10. James Metzenbaum, the successful attorney for the Village of Euclid in the case establishing the constitutional validity of zoning, expounded on "the great sacrifice and efforts on the part of many noble men who consecrated themselves." 1 LAW OF ZONING 52 (2d ed. 1955).

11. *Districting by Municipal Regulation, in* NATIONAL CONFERENCE ON CITY PLANNING 147 (1916).

12. *What Has Been Accomplished in City Planning During the Past Year*, 6 NAT'L MUN. REV. 346 (1917).

13. *Review of Planning in the United States, 1920-1921*, 11 NAT'L MUN. REV. 27, 32 (1922).

Perhaps the most noteworthy advance in zoning in the pre-*Euclid v. Ambler* period was the appointment, by Secretary of Commerce Herbert Hoover, of an Advisory Committee on Building Codes and Zoning. The committee published much valuable material designed to acquaint interested parties with sound zoning techniques and related legal issues. It drafted a Standard State Zoning Enabling Act which was adopted, in whole or in part, by 19 states in 1925, and which is still the model for much state enabling legislation.[14]

The readings in this chapter are concerned with the legislative and administrative structure of Euclidean zoning and of some of the alternative land use regulatory structures proffered by planners and lawmakers. While the primary emphasis in the preceding chapter was on the active formulation and adaptation of common-law rules and principles by members of the judiciary, the cases and materials that follow reflect a more discrete, interpretive mode of decisionmaking, as judges subject the work of the co-equal branches to a mild degree of judicial scrutiny, in harmony with the deferential tone set by the Supreme Court's landmark holding in *Euclid v. Ambler*.

Before one can evaluate in a meaningful way the criticisms of zoning–raised not only by those who would have us return to something approaching a free market in land values, but also by those who propose stricter state and federal oversight of permissive local authorities—we must first understand the structure of height, bulk, and use regulation and the relationship of zoning to comprehensive planning. Morever, in the chapter following this one, we will study the mechanisms for modifying or avoiding the initial assignment of categories and the avenues of judicial relief should local decisionmakers fail to perform their tasks satisfactorily. Likewise, before we study in subsequent chapters the increasingly active role recent courts have taken in the area of planning and zoning, we need to understand the statutes and ordinances by which significant public control of land development was attempted and, despite some pockets of resistance, achieved.

The major cases in this chapter have comprised the introduction to the mechanics of zoning for thousands of law students in all regions of the nation (and, in turn, thousands of land use attorneys and planners) over the past 50 years. Despite the passage of time and changes in public attitudes toward government regulation, judicial consideration of local zoning ordinances, on their face and as applied, strays very little from the approaches of these classic cases. The major inquiries remain important: Is the local government authorized to engage in this regulatory activity? How deferential should the judiciary be to elected officials and to the experts who advise them? When does a regulation move from being legitimate to being confiscatory? What do we mean by "comprehensive" zoning and planning? What is the optimum amount of flexibility that benefits developers, neighbors, and the public good? How far from the comfortable and traditional Euclidean paradigm should courts allow localities to stray?

II.   From Where Does the Power to Zone Derive?

Often lost sight of in academic and jurisprudential discussions of the nature and import of the American brand of federalism—that is, the role of sovereign states in our national system—are the

---

14. *See* Ruth Knack, Stuart Meck & Israel Stollman, *The Real Story Behind the Standard Planning and Zoning Acts of the 1920s*, Land Use L. & Zoning Dig., Feb. 1996, at 3.

status and function of local governments. Though mere creatures and possessions of the state,[15] cities, towns, villages, and boroughs have been delegated far-reaching authority to regulate the most important and meaningful asset Americans own—real property and the improvements thereon. Notwithstanding this delegation, however, counsel representing land developers should be aware that localities that stray too far from state enabling laws run the risk of a judicial finding that they have acted in an ultra vires manner. Consider the following pair of cases from the Keystone State, which illustrate the long and enduring, though often overlooked, requirement that local governments be able to demonstrate that they have been granted authority by the state.

RESPUBLICA v. PHILIP URBIN DUQUET
2 Yeates 493 (Pa. 1799)

SHIPPEN, C.J., pronounced the opinion of the court.

The questions in this case are principally two: 1st, Whether the corporation of the city of Philadelphia have passed such an ordinance under the powers vested in them by act of assembly, as by law they might do, both with respect to the mode of punishment, and the court in which the offender is to be tried. And 2d, If they have passed a valid ordinance according to the act,, is that act a constitutional one?

The material objection to the ordinance is, that they have directed a prosecution by indictment, whereas it is contended, that a corporation has only power to inflict pecuniary penalties to be levied by distress, or recovered by action of debt. This is undoubtedly true, with regard to ordinances founded on no authority but their own; but in this case they are vested with extraordinary powers by the acknowledged legislature of the state. By the act of assembly of 11th March 1789, § 20, the corporation have power to make bye laws, &c. for the well governing and welfare of the city, and to try and determine certain specified offences named, as larcenies, forgeries, &c. and likewise all offences which shall be committed within the said city, against the laws, ordinances, regulations or constitutions, that shall be made, ordained or established in pursuance of that act, and to punish the offenders as by the said laws or ordinances shall be prescribed. 2dly, By the act of 18th April 1795, the legislature enacts, that the mayor, aldermen and common council shall be empowered to pass ordinances to prevent any person or persons, from erecting or causing to be erected, any wooden mansion house, shop, ware house, store, carriage house, or stable, within such part of the city of Philadelphia, as lies to the eastward of Tenth street from the river Delaware, "as they may

---

15. The classic and enduring characterization appears in Hunter v. City of Pittsburgh, 207 U.S. 161, 178-79 (1907):

> Municipal corporations are political subdivisions of the state, created as convenient agencies for exercising such of the governmental powers of the state as may be intrusted to them. For the purpose of executing these powers properly and efficiently they usually are given the power to acquire, hold, and manage personal and real property. The number, nature, and duration of the powers conferred upon these corporations and the territory over which they shall be exercised rests in the absolute discretion of the state. Neither their charters, nor any law conferring governmental powers, or vesting in them property to be used for governmental purposes, or authorizing them to hold or manage such property, or exempting them from taxation upon it, constitutes a contract with the state within the meaning of the Federal Constitution. The state, therefore, at its pleasure, may modify or withdraw all such powers, may take without compensation such property, hold it itself, or vest it in other agencies, expand or contract the territorial area, unite the whole or a part of it with another municipality, repeal the charter and destroy the corporation. All this may be done, conditionally or unconditionally, with or without the consent of the citizens, or even against their protest. In all these respects the state is supreme, and its legislative body, conforming its action to the state Constitution, may do as it will, unrestrained by any provision of the Constitution of the United States. Although the inhabitants and property owners may, by such changes, suffer inconvenience, and their property may be lessened in value by the burden of increased taxation, or for any other reason, they have no right, by contract or otherwise, in the unaltered or continued existence of the corporation or its powers, and there is nothing in the Federal Constitution which protects them from these injurious consequences. The power is in the state, and those who legislate for the state are alone responsible for any unjust or oppressive exercise of it.

judge proper." So that the state legislature have exercised their judgment upon the subject matter, and directed by law, that every person should be prevented from erecting wooden buildings within certain populous parts of the city; and the mode of preventing such an evil is left to the mayor, aldermen and common council, by very general words, "as they may judge proper."

This act, connected with the former act, giving the Mayor's Court power to try all offences against the laws and ordinances which the said corporation shall make in pursuance of the former act, and to punish the offences as by the said laws and ordinances shall be prescribed, appears to us decisive, that they may punish offenders against the ordinance, by indictment in the Mayor's Court.

It is not sufficient to say, that the corporation could not of their own authority pass ordinances to punish by indictment or imprisonment, because they are expressly authorized to try and punish offenders against their ordinances in the same court and in the same manner as larcenies, forgeries, and other such offences as are directed to be punished. And although corporations cannot of themselves make ordinances to punish offenders by imprisonment, yet the law cases are express, that if such a power is founded on the custom, they may; and surely an act of the legislature is as effectual as any custom can be.

As to the constitutionality of these laws, a breach of the constitution by the legislature, and the clashing of the law with the constitution, must be evident indeed, before we should think ourselves at liberty to declare a law void and a nullity on that account; yet if a violation of the constitution should in any case be made by an act of the legislature, and that violation should unequivocally appear to us, we shall think it our duty not to shrink from the task of saying such law is void. We however see no such violation in the present case, and therefore give judgment for the commonwealth.

Notes

1. Not all ordinances regulating wooden structures passed judicial scrutiny, nor were all motivated solely by public safety concerns. In Yick Wo v. Hopkins, 118 U.S. 356 (1886), the Supreme Court, having granted writs of habeas corpus, ordered the release from custody of two Chinese immigrants who had been imprisoned for violating an 1880 San Francisco ordinance that outlawed wooden laundries, unless permission had first been obtained from the board of supervisors. Despite the apparently legitimate exercise of the police power in a city with a history of devastating fires, the Court held that the officials' race-based selective enforcement of the ordinance (200 Chinese applicants were denied permission, while 8 non-Chinese were allowed "to carry on their business under similar conditions") amounted to a constitutional violation.

2. Philadelphia's land use regulation history is a long and storied one. For example, in May 1985, ground was broken in Philadelphia for One Liberty Place, featuring "a 60-story skyscraper that is shattering Philadelphia tradition. The post-modern shaft of blue-and-gray granite, designed by Chicago architect Helmut Jahn, will be the first Philadelphia building to rise higher than the Quaker hat on the statue of William Penn atop City Hall's bell tower." William K. Stevens, *Downtown Developer: Willard G. Rouse 3d; Reshaping Philadelphia's Skyline*, N.Y. Times, May 4, 1986, at 3-6. Thus was the "gentlemen's agreement" regarding the height of buildings in the City of Brotherly Love dissolved:

> The height limit wasn't a city ordinance or a zoning law; the only place it appeared was in the code of the city's redevelopment authority. But generations of Philadelphians accepted it as a "moral consensus, more powerful than the law," says Edmund N. Bacon, director of the city planning commission in the 1950s and 1960s.

Eileen White, *Putting William Penn in the Shade*, Wall St. J., May 15, 1985, at 28.

3. Did you notice that the Pennsylvania high court in evaluating the constitutionality of the statute was engaged in judicial review a few years before that practice was supposedly "invented" by Chief Justice John Marshall in Marbury v. Madison, 5 U.S. 137 (1803)?

KLINE v. CITY OF HARRISBURG
362 Pa. 438, 68 A.2d 182 (1949)

The following is the opinion of Judge WOODSIDE in the court below:

The plaintiffs here are seeking to restrain the City of Harrisburg and certain of its officials from enforcing the provisions of what is sometimes called an "interim" zoning ordinance, and to direct the proper city officials to issue a building permit to the plaintiffs authorizing the construction of five apartment buildings in the city.

It is admitted by the defendants that the application, drawing and specifications and statement on the basis of which the building permit was requested conform in all respects to the requirements of the Building Code of the City of Harrisburg, and that the permit was refused by the defendants because of the aforesaid ordinance. . . .

One of the plaintiffs who owns a four acre tract of land in the City of Harrisburg entered into an agreement with the other two plaintiffs whereby a business corporation is to be formed and five garden-type apartment buildings are to be erected on said tract and financed in the manner provided by the National Housing Act, 12 U.S.C.A. § 1701 et seq. . . .

On April 25, the plaintiffs applied to the Building Inspector of the City of Harrisburg, requesting the issuance of a building permit authorizing the construction of the apartment building, and as required by the Building Code a fee of $1300 was tendered.

On May 6, 1949, Ordinance No. 153 Session of 1948-49 was read and placed before the Council of the City of Harrisburg and was passed finally on May 10 and, if valid, became effective May 20.

The following preamble is in the Ordinance:

> Whereas, the City Planning Commission of the City of Harrisburg, has for several years been studying the details of a comprehensive zoning ordinance for the City, and

> Whereas, the various zoning districts together with the regulations and restrictions to be imposed therein, have in a large part been reduced to writing, but the work has not matured to the point where public hearings can be had, and

> Whereas, in the opinion of City Council it will take additional time to work out the details of a zoning plan, and, further, that it will be destructive of the plan if before the date of its final completion the status quo of the residential districts as contemplated by the plan should not be preserved, and

> Whereas, it is the desire of City Council in order to promote the general welfare of the community to preserve the status quo of the residential districts of the City until the final zoning ordinance can be completed and adopted.

The Ordinance then provides: "that the erection or construction within the residential districts of the City of Harrisburg as hereinafter defined, of any building or premises which shall be used for, or designed for other than a single family detached dwelling, together with its usual accessories, or the alteration within the said residential districts of any existing single family detached dwelling for any other purpose be and the same is hereby prohibited." . . .

The land on which the plaintiffs propose to erect the apartment lies wholly within one of the two residential areas described in Ordinance No. 153.

The City Planning Commission, which has been in existence since 1923, recommended the employment of a zoning specialist, who was employed by the City on about May 15, 1945.

On July 12, 1945 the City Planning Commission directed the office of the City Engineer to which the zoning specialist was assigned, to make a complete study of the problems arising in the preparation of a zoning ordinance and to present a zoning plan. Such plan was submitted to the City Planning Commission in 1946 and contained two residential areas known as "R-1" areas, which are the same areas as set forth in Ordinance No. 153. These areas accommodate in the main, single family detached dwellings. The final details of the comprehensive zoning plan and the regulations and restrictions to be imposed in the various districts have not as yet been approved by the said City Planning Commission. . . .

The only question argued and submitted to us is whether Ordinance No. 153 is ultra vires and invalid in that:

"(a) its enactment was contrary to the express provisions of subheading '(b) Zoning' of Article XLI of the Third Class City Law [53 P.S. § 12198-4101 et seq.];

"(b) its enactment was not within any power, implied or inherent, under the provisions of said sub-heading "(b) Zoning" of Article XLI of the Third Class City Law;

"(c) its enactment was contrary to the provisions of said sub-heading '(b) Zoning' of Article XLI of the Third Class City Law, since no comprehensive zoning plan was adopted by said Ordinance; and

"(d) its enactment was not within any general police power, or any other power, either express, implied or inherent, other than that expressly provided for by said sub-heading "(b) Zoning" of Article XLI of the Third Class City Law?"

Municipalities are not sovereigns. Their powers are limited. It has been said that: "Nothing is better settled than that a municipal corporation does not possess and cannot exercise any other than the following powers: (1) those granted in express words; (2) those necessarily or fairly implied in or incident to the powers expressly granted; (3) those essential to the declared objects and purposes of the corporation, not simply convenient but indispensable. Any fair, reasonable doubt as to the existence of power is resolved by the courts against its existence in the corporation, and therefore denied. Dillon on Municipal Corporations, sec. 89."

Express authority is given to Third Class Cities to enact zoning ordinance[s] under Sections 4110-4113 of The Third Class City Law of June 23, 1931, P.L. 932, 53 P.S. §§ 12198-4110 to 4113, inclusive.

The Act provides as follows: . . .

"Section 4110. . . . Cities may, by ordinance, regulate and restrict the height, number of stories, bulk, and size of buildings and other structures, the percentage of lots that may be occupied, the size, depth, and width of yards, courts, and other open spaces, the density of population, and the location and use of buildings, structures, and land for trade, industry, residents, or other purposes, and may make different regulations for different districts thereof, and may alter the same; but no alteration of such regulations may be made, except by the affirmative vote of not less than four of the members of council. Such regulations shall provide that a board of appeals may determine and vary their application in harmony with their general purpose and intent, and in accordance with general or specific rules therein contained. . . .

It is to be noted that Section 4111 provides that:

> (1) The City Planning Commission shall recommend to Council the boundaries and appropriate regulations and restrictions to be imposed therein; (2) shall make a tentative report and hold public meetings thereon before submitting its final report; (3) Council shall specify in a notice to be published for ten consecutive days in a daily newspaper a time and place of hearing; (4) Council shall afford persons affected an opportunity to be heard after the aforesaid final report.

Council is specifically prohibited from imposing any regulation or restriction until after the final report and after said hearing.

It is agreed that none of these things was done prior to the passage of the Ordinance in question. Furthermore, no Board of Appeals has been appointed as required by Sec. 4113.

The defendants admit that they did not comply with the above provisions of the statute, and cannot rely upon the expressed authority to zone contained therein, but contend

that such provisions "carry with them the implied or inherent power to pass an interim ordinance to give effect to the power expressly granted in said sub-heading in order to prevent the defeat of the legislative intent of the expressed powers thus granted. And, furthermore, it is contended that the said Ordinance No. 153 was within the express grant of the police power as provided in Section 2403 of The Third Class City Law, 53 P.S. § 12198-2403."

Section 2403 of The Third Class City Law, *supra*, provides as follows:

> "Specific powers. In addition to other powers granted by this act, the council of each city shall have power, by ordinance:

(then after 53 paragraphs)

> "54. Local Self-Government. In addition to the powers and authority vested in each city by the provisions of this act, to make and adopt all such ordinances, by-laws, rules and regulations, not inconsistent with or restrained by the Constitution and laws of this Commonwealth, as may be expedient or necessary for the proper management, care and control of the city and its finances, and the maintenance of the peace, good government, safety and welfare of the city, and its trade, commerce and manufactures; and also all such ordinances, by-laws, rules and regulations as may be necessary in and to the exercise of the powers and authority of local self-government in all municipal affairs; . . ."

We cannot agree that the above provision authorizes a city to enact a zoning ordinance without following the provisions of Article XLI of the same act which relate to zoning, nor that said zoning provisions carry with them the implied or inherent power to pass an interim zoning ordinance.

It is settled in Pennsylvania that in the absence of the granting of specific power from the Legislature municipalities do not have the authority to pass zoning ordinances.

Pennsylvania has had what today would be called "zoning" since the days of George Washington. The City of Philadelphia adopted an Ordinance on June 6, 1796, prohibiting the erection of wooden buildings in a specifically described area of the city. The Ordinance however was adopted under authority given to the City by the Act of April 18, 1795, 3 Dall. St. Laws 771, which empowered it to pass ordinances to prevent persons from erecting wooden mansion houses, etc., within such part of the city "as lies to the eastward of Tenth Street from the River Delaware as they may judge proper." In Respublica v. Duquet, 1799, 2 Yeates 493, the Supreme Court declared the Act and the Ordinance constitutional.

Nearly a century later when the Borough of Norristown attempted to limit the construction of frame buildings without express legislative authority the Supreme Court pointed out that the above Philadelphia Ordinance rested upon specific legislative authority and said: "The Charter of the Borough of Norristown contains no authority to the Council to enact ordinances prohibiting the erection of wooden buildings. Nor is there anything in the grant of general powers conferred upon the borough from which such an authority can be necessarily inferred or to which it is indispensable. Lacking these requirements the qualities necessary to create the power in question are not present." Kneedler v. Borough of Norristown, 1882, 100 Pa. 368, 371, 45 Am. Rep. 384.

In Junge's Appeal (No. 2), 1926, 89 Pa. Super. 548, 556, judge Keller said: "It may be admitted that such zoning ordinance without a statute authorizing it would be void in this state. Whatever may be the law in other states the decisions of our Supreme Court make it clear that in the absence of a grant of power from the Legislature the municipalities of this Commonwealth do not possess the authority to pass such Ordinance." . . .

The legislature was clear and explicit in its language. Note the "may's and the shall's." Cities "may" regulate and restrict, and "may" make different regulations for different districts, and "may" alter them. But the regulation "shall" provide that a board of appeals "may" vary their application. Note that the legislature says the planning commission (or other body) "shall" recommend to council, "shall" make a tentative report and hold public hearings, council "shall" afford persons an opportunity to be heard. And then to make doubly sure that the procedure outlined in the section would be followed the legislature provided that *"Council shall not determine the boundaries of any district, nor impose any regulations or restrictions, until after the final report and after said hearing."*

It is contended by the defendants that without the power to enact such an interim ordinance as is here in question it would be possible for an owner of land to proceed with the erection of an undesirable building in a residential section immediately before the enactment of a zoning ordinance which would prohibit such building, and thus defeat what the city was attempting to establish after years of deliberation and study. There are two answers to this. In the first place, although the argument is not entirely without merit, it is one which must be directed to the legislature and not to the courts. If the legislature wishes to authorize the enactment of a "temporary" or "interim" ordinance to maintain the status quo it can so provide by legislation with proper safeguards. In the second place, apparently experience has not indicated that the failure to pass a "temporary" or "interim" ordinance has been any substantial menace to zoning. . . . Although there are scores and possibly hundreds of municipalities in Pennyslvania which have enacted zoning ordinances in accordance with the expressed provisions of the relevant statutes, all of which are similar in nature, there is no indication that we could find either by proposed legislation or by cases in any of the courts of this state that these municipalities have suffered from inability to maintain the status quo during the enactment of zoning ordinances. . . .

A few states have approved temporary zoning ordinances. Cases of each jurisdiction, of course, rest upon the constitution, statutes and decisions of the particular state, as well as the peculiar facts of the particular case, and are not satisfactory authority for our determination of the matter before us. . . .

McCurley v. City of El Reno, 1929, 138 Okla. 92, 280 P. 467 is in our opinion the only case which supports the contention of the defendants. The Oklahoma Court relied upon [two of the cases] . . . which . . . are not authority for the proposition here advanced. As pointed out in State ex rel. Kramer v. Schwartz, 1935, 336 Mo. 932, 82 S.W.2d 63 these cases although relied upon by the Oklahoma Court did not lend support to the views expressed by that court.

The *Oklahoma* case is not in accord with the prevailing views as reference to the cases of many other jurisdictions will show.

We think it is not necessary to demonstrate that the Ordinance before us is a zoning ordinance. It may be intended to be a temporary or interim one but a zoning ordinance nevertheless.

The defendants admit that the Ordinance before us could not "permanently" restrict the use or erection of the forbidden buildings in the described areas. Yet the Ordinance is drafted to do just that. There is nothing in it limiting the time when it shall be effective. In this respect it differs from the temporary ordinances referred to in the . . . *Oklahoma* case[ ] where the time the ordinance was to be effective was limited by the ordinance itself.

It is contended by the defendants that the Ordinance will remain in effect until the passage of another zoning ordinance, or for a "reasonable time." If there have been ordinances or statutes, which have been adopted without any provisions limiting their effective time, and which are admittedly illegal except for a "reasonable time," we have no recollection of ever having heard of such.

We have here the anomalous situation of an Ordinance providing an absolute prohibition without limit of time which the defendants admit cannot be valid for an unlimited time.

The record of the case indicates that the City has been in the process of preparing a zoning ordinance since May 15, 1945, a period of over four years, and that "the work has not matured to the point where public hearings can be had" before the City Planning Commission. As a matter of fact a "final" zoning ordinance may never be enacted. There is no duty upon the Council to enact any zoning Ordinance. There is nothing contained in the so-called interim Ordinance by which the present Council even pledges itself to the enactment of a "final" Ordinance. . . .

In summarizing we point out that we start in this case with the proposition that before specific legislative authority to zone was given municipalities, they did not have the authority under their general powers to enact zoning ordinances; that the legislature then gave them power to enact zoning ordinances but specifically set forth what they shall do before they impose any regulations or restrictions. It is our opinion that the municipalities must comply with the provisions of the statute relating to zoning before they can enact any restrictions. The Ordinance before us containing restrictions was not enacted in accordance with the provisions of the statute relating to zoning and is therefore void, and the defendants must be restrained from enforcing it. As the building permit would be issued except for the Ordinance the building inspector must be directed to issue it. . . .

MAXEY, Chief Justice. . . . [I]t is Ordered that the decree of the court below in the above entitled case be affirmed on the opinion of Judge Robert E. Woodside. . . .

Notes

1. More than 50 years later, the Pennsylvania Supreme Court considered whether a township had the power to "enact a temporary moratorium on certain types of subdivision and land development while the municipality revises its zoning and subdivision land development ordinances." The court, in Naylor v. Township of Hellam, 565 Pa. 397, 400, 408, 773 A.2d 770, 772, 777 (2001), cited *Kline* in support of its holding "that the Municipalities Planning Code (MPC), Act of July 31, 1968, P.L. 805, as reenacted and amended, 53 P.S. §§ 10101-11202, does not grant a municipality such power . . . ." Although *Kline* and other early decisions were decided before passage of the MPC, the court observed that they

> clearly demonstrate that the power to "halt" development is not an extension of or incidental to any power to regulate land use or development. Despite our Court's previous pronouncements rejecting the existence of an implicit power of imposing a moratorium, the legislature has not acted to authorize municipalities to meet their planning objectives through the suspension, temporary or otherwise, of the process for reviewing land use proposals. As we stated in *Kline* over fifty years ago, "if the legislature wishes to authorize the enactment of a 'temporary' or 'interim' ordinance to maintain the status quo it can so provide by legislation with proper safeguards." 68 A.2d at 189. The Gen-

eral Assembly is better suited to examine the significant policy issues at stake and to determine the appropriate legal standards to govern the application of such a powerful planning tool.

2. In State ex rel. Randall v. Snohomish County, 79 Wash. 2d 619, 620-21, 625, 488 P.2d 511, 512, 514-15 (1971), a case involving the authority of a local government to employ "holding zones," the Supreme Court of Washington was more understanding:

> Prior to 1957, plaintiffs acquired about 37 acres in what later became the "Marysville Planning Area" of Snohomish County. Although it is asserted that the land was intended for commercial usage, the property has not been used for any business purpose. Since 1957, the property has been zoned "rural use," a broad classification which originally allowed commercial usages and which is considered an intermediate or "holding" zone. In 1962, Snohomish County elected to proceed with future zoning under the terms of RCW 36.70. In 1964, the Marysville Comprehensive Plan (one of nine in the county) was adopted and promulgated. Meanwhile, the property in question remained under the "rural use" classification. In 1966, the "rural use" zoning resolution was changed to substantially reduce the number and kinds of uses permitted within that classification. The resolution was again amended in 1967, after planning commission hearings, to remove all business and commercial uses from the list of those permitted in "rural use" zones. . . .

> The evil inferred by plaintiffs is the abuse of "holding zone" techniques to effect a chronic and unreckonable grip upon each citizen's future use of his property. Courts are and should be well cognizant of that potential species of arbitrary and capricious action. But the record before us does not demonstrate such unreasonableness. In this case, there is a fatal hiatus of proof between the inference and plaintiffs' desired conclusion.

> This court has noticed an increasing volume of litigation pertaining to zoning legislation and administration. It therefore seems appropriate to emphasize that the role of the judiciary in reviewing such enactments and decisions is limited to the determination of whether they satisfy constitutional requirements and to the determination of whether administrative decisions are arbitrary and capricious or ultra vires. Beyond those limits there are serious questions of wisdom and practicality. But, by long tradition, built upon the principle of separation of powers, such latter matters are beyond the purview of the courts. Such questions are to be resolved by the political, not the judicial, process.

3. Some states have legislated permission for limited interim zoning. See, for example, Colo. Rev. Stat. §30-28-121:

> **Temporary Regulations.** The board of county commissioners of any county, after appointment of a county or district planning commission and pending the adoption by such commission of a zoning plan, where in the opinion of the board conditions require such action, may promulgate, by resolution without a public hearing, regulations of a temporary nature, to be effective for a limited period only and in any event not to exceed six months, prohibiting or regulating in any part or all of the unincorporated territory of the county or district the erection, construction, reconstruction, or alteration of any building or structure used or to be used for any business, residential, industrial, or commercial purpose.

In Dollaghan v. County of Boulder, 749 P.2d 444 (Colo. Ct. App. 1987), the court ruled that "the statute allows a county to adopt temporary regulations only prior to the first or original zoning plan," and was therefore inapplicable to a rezoning situation.

4. How long can regulators keep landowners waiting before violating constitutional standards? As we will see in Chapter Five, the Supreme Court, in Tahoe-Sierra Pres. Council v. Tahoe Reg'l Planning Agency, 535 U.S. 302 (2002), rejected the landowners' argument that a set of moratoria totaling 32 months imposed on development in the Lake Tahoe Basin amounted to a regulatory taking.

5. Professor Hendrik Hartog, in Public Property and Private Power: The Corporation of the City of New York in American Law, 1730-1870, at 1 (1983), has provided this helpful introduction to the important 19th-century legal principle upon which the *Kline* court, like so many tribunals before and since, relied:

> For the past 150 years American lawyers and judges have used the term "municipal corporation" to characterize the legal existence of a city. In doing so they have pictured urban government in ways that might surprise those not fully acculturated into legal ways of thinking. American courts do not usually regard a municipal corporation as the embodiment of a local political community. To the contrary, a municipal corporation is said to be a public corporation created by a state legislature solely for the purpose of providing subordinate administration. In legal theory, cities, towns, counties, and villages exist only because they serve as useful agencies of state power. No local government has any natural or inherent rights or constitutional authority. A municipal corporation is whatever the state legislature says it is, and it does whatever the state legislature and the state courts say it can do. As John Dillon insisted in the famous "Rule" proclaimed in his treatise of 1872 (which remained for many years the definitive legal source in all matters local governmental), unless municipal authority was expressly granted, necessarily implied, or crucial to the accomplishment of a legislatively defined goal, its legitimacy would not be recognized by an American court. "Any fair, reasonable (substantial) doubt concerning the existence of power is resolved by the courts against the municipal corporation, and the power is denied.

6. Gerald E. Frug and Richard Briffault are articulate representatives of two dramatically different schools of thought regarding local versus state power. In *The City as a Legal Concept*, 93 Harv. L. Rev. 1057, 1105-08 (1980), Professor Frug has asserted that at the time of the American Revolution, "the proper relationship of city to state was instead a hotly contested political issue. Some argued that the sovereignty of the people required control at the local level, but others feared the power of democratic cities over the allocation of property in America." One important factor that helps explain the loss of influence by local governments is "the fear of democratic power," a fear that

> plainly existed . . . even in the minds of such champions of local power as Jefferson and de Tocqueville. While Jefferson saw towns as the "elementary republics" of the nation that must be preserved so that "the voice of the whole people would be fairly, fully, and peaceably expressed . . . by the common reason" of all citizens, he also saw them as objects to be feared: "The mobs of great cities add just so much to the support of pure government, as sores do to the strength of the human body.". . . Indeed, the vision of cities as being the home of "mobs," the working class, immigrants, and, finally, racial minorities, is a theme that runs throughout much of nineteenth and twentieth century thought.

To Frug, the key legal measure encompassing municipal powerlessness was "the classification of American cities as corporations," which

> can be understood as helping to repress the notion that associational rights were being affected in defining the laws governing city rights. No rights of association needed to be articulated when discussing the rights of "private" corporations, since property rights were sufficient to protect them against state power, and there was nothing that required rights of association to be imagined in discussing the subordination of "public" corporations. Yet, if no rights of association were recognized, cities, increasingly deprived of their economic character—the basis of their power for hundreds of years—had little defense against the reallocation of their power to the individual and to the state. There was nothing left that seemed to demand protection; therefore, nothing could prevent the control of the cities by the state.

While Professor Frug's somewhat controversial findings have been quite influential, not all commentators were convinced.

A decade later Professor Briffault, in *Our Localism: Part I, the Structure of Local Government Law*, 90 Colum. L. Rev. 1, 6-14 (1990), observed:

> According to Professor Frug, the limited nature of local power derives from, first, the principles of nineteenth-century legal theory that established cities as decidedly inferior political institutions and, second, the failure of state constitutional reforms, most notably home rule, to change that. Although this critique captures some of the black-letter principles of local government law, it ignores much of the formal legal power local governments possess as well as all of their legally significant informal authority.

Briffault calls "unwarranted" the "wholesale dismissal" by Frug and others "of the state constitutional protections of local government." Painting with a narrower brush, he envisions a more subtle legal landscape:

> State-local relations do not consist simply of "unremitting" raids by hostile antiurban or centralizing state legislatures on vulnerable local governments. Moreover, treating state court decisions upholding state laws affecting local governments as manifestations of an obdurate hostility to localism ignores the serious conceptual difficulties state courts have faced in defining and enforcing the notion of local autonomy.

7. Today, the debate between proponents and opponents of local rule takes place in the context of the nagging issue of urban and suburban sprawl. Is sprawl evidence of parochial self-government or does this multi-faceted phenomenon occur in spite of local powerlessness? David J. Barron, in *Reclaiming Home Rule*, 116 Harv. L. Rev. 2255, 2261, 2263 (2003), has noted:

> [W]hile law once treated local governments as mere creatures of the state, all but two states now have express constitutional or statutory home rule provisions. These measures self-consciously reject the notion that cities and suburbs have no independent powers of their own, and they overturn the rule of strict construction of local governmental powers (known as Dillon's Rule) that accompanied the once-dominant state creature idea.

In a 21st-century synthesis to Frug's thesis and Briffault's antithesis, Professor Barron has explained that

> anti-sprawl reformers—as well as their opponents—err in presenting the critical choice as one between preserving home rule and accepting an alternative that seems to be its

opposite. There is a broad, if overlooked, middle space within which one can challenge the substance of the particular mix of grants of, and limits on, local power that now constitute what reformers and defenders of the legal status quo both generally describe as "home rule." Meaningful change need not, therefore, consolidate local governments into enormous regional ones, nor need it strictly limit local powers to a narrow sphere. Instead, it could alter the current mix of state law grants and limits that gives substance to local legal power. In this way, anti-sprawl reform could actually expand the ability of cities and suburbs to promote a different pattern of development themselves.

Of what significance to this ongoing debate is the fact that, since the 1920s, the nearly universal pattern in America is that states delegate to their local government creations the critical power to zone and plan, without any significant interference from state lawmakers?

III. Judicial Acceptance by a Conservative High Court

The written judicial opinion, the lifeblood of the Anglo-American system of common law, on occasion is imbued by jurists, teachers, and scholars with the trappings and influence of symbol. There lies within the body of cases studied in nearly each American legal discipline one opinion from which the careful reader may perceive the dominant themes, the pervasive pattern of decisionmaking, the extralegal underpinnings, or the operative vocabulary of the pertinent area of the law.

So, for example, the torts student struggles with Benjamin Cardozo's daedal text in *Palsgraf*,[16] hoping to be rewarded with a fundamental appreciation of foreseeability. Every exercise of judicial review, the essential tool of constitutional litigation, is justified or criticized in Chief Justice Marshall's terms, derived from his jurisprudential and political coup in Marbury v. Madison.[17]

Land use law has its central opinion as well. That 19-page majority opinion by Justice George Sutherland was rendered in a case known by a geographical name, Euclid, that suggests to the layperson the lines, points, and planes of elementary geometry. The importance of the words and holding in *Euclid v. Ambler* is undisputed. Even more than 80 years after the High Court gave its approval to comprehensive zoning, *Euclid v. Ambler* endures as substance and symbol, despite waves of demographic, economic, and political change.

The tools of the land use lawyer and planner have certainly changed since the 1920s, as professionals have sought to match the socioeconomic intricacy and technological sophistication of urban and suburban life in the 2000s and beyond. Given this profound temporal and developmental gap, it is easy to dismiss *Euclid v. Ambler* as relevant only to a Model-T, Lochnerian universe. Such a dismissal, however, would ignore the important fact that even eight decades later, the letter and spirit of *Euclid v. Ambler* and its companion case—Nectow v. City of Cambridge—continue to inform the judicial interpretation of modern state and local planning and environmental regulation.

VILLAGE OF EUCLID v. AMBLER REALTY CO.
272 U.S. 365 (1926)

Mr. Justice SUTHERLAND delivered the opinion of the Court.

The Village of Euclid is an Ohio municipal corporation. It adjoins and practically is a suburb of the City of Cleveland. Its estimated population is between 5,000 and 10,000, and its area from twelve to fourteen square miles, the greater part of which is farm lands or unimproved acreage. It lies, roughly, in the form of a parallelogram measuring approximately three and-one-half

---

16. Palsgraf v. Long Island R.R., 248 N.Y. 339, 162 N.E. 99 (1928).
17. 5 U.S. (1 Cranch) 137 (1803).

miles each way. East and west it is traversed by three principal highways: Euclid Avenue, through the southerly border, St. Clair Avenue, through the central portion, and Lake Shore Boulevard, through the northerly border in close proximity to the shore of Lake Erie. The Nickel Plate railroad lies from 1,500 to 1,800 feet north of Euclid Avenue, and the Lake Shore railroad 1,600 feet farther to the north. The three highways and the two railroads are substantially parallel.

Appellee is the owner of a tract of land containing 68 acres, situated in the westerly end of the village, abutting on Euclid Avenue to the south and the Nickel Plate railroad to the north. Adjoining this tract, both on the east and on the west, there have been laid out restricted residential plats upon which residences have been erected.

On November 13, 1922, an ordinance was adopted by the Village Council, establishing a comprehensive zoning plan for regulating and restricting the location of trades, industries, apartment houses, two-family houses, single family houses, etc., the lot area to be built upon, the size and height of buildings, etc.

The entire area of the village is divided by the ordinance into six classes of use districts, denominated U-1 to U-6, inclusive; three classes of height districts, denominated H-1 to H-3, inclusive; and four classes of area districts, denominated A-1 to A-4, inclusive. The use districts are classified in respect of the buildings which may be erected within their respective limits, as follows: U-1 is restricted to single family dwellings, public parks, water towers and reservoirs, suburban and interurban electric railway passenger stations and rights of way, and farming, noncommercial greenhouse nurseries and truck gardening; U-2 is extended to include two-family dwellings; U-3 is further extended to include apartment houses, hotels, churches, schools, public libraries, museums, private clubs, community center buildings, hospitals, sanitariums, public playgrounds and recreation buildings, and a city hall and courthouse; U-4 is further extended 'to include banks, offices, studios, telephone exchanges, fire and police stations, restaurants, theatres and moving picture shows, retail stores and shops, sales offices, sample rooms, wholesale stores for hardware, drugs and groceries, stations for gasoline and oil (not exceeding 1,000 gallons storage) and for ice delivery, skating rinks and dance halls, electric substations, job and newspaper printing, public garages for motor vehicles, stables and wagon sheds (not exceeding five horses, wagons or motor trucks) and distributing stations for central store and commercial enterprises; U-5 is further extended to include billboards and advertising signs (if permitted), warehouses, ice and ice cream manufacturing and cold storage plants, bottling works, milk bottling and central distribution stations, laundries, carpet cleaning, dry cleaning and dyeing establishments, blacksmith, horseshoeing, wagon and motor vehicle repair shops, freight stations, street car barns, stables and wagon sheds (for more than five horses, wagons or motor trucks), and wholesale produce markets and salesrooms; U-6 is further extended to include plants for sewage disposal and for producing gas, garbage and refuse incineration, scrap iron, junk, scrap paper and rag storage, aviation fields, cemeteries, crematories, penal and correctional institutions, insane and feeble minded institutions, storage of oil and gasoline (not to exceed 25,000 gallons), and manufacturing and industrial operations of any kind other than, and any public utility not included in, a class U-1, U-2, U-3, U-4, or U-5 use. There is a seventh class of uses which is prohibited altogether.

Class U-1 is the only district in which buildings are restricted to those enumerated. In the other classes the uses are cumulative; that is to say, uses in class U-2 include those enumerated in the preceding class, U-1; class U-3 includes uses enumerated in the preceding classes, U-2 and U-1; and so on. In addition to the enumerated uses, the ordinance provides for accessory uses, that is, for uses customarily incident to the principal use, such as private garages. Many regulations are provided in respect of such accessory uses.

The height districts are classified as follows: In class H-1, buildings are limited to a height of two and one-half stories or thirty-five feet; in class H-2, to four stories or fifty feet; in class H-3, to eighty feet. To all of these, certain exceptions are made, as in the case of church spires, water tanks, etc.

The classification of area districts is: In A-1 districts, dwellings or apartment houses to accommodate more than one family must have at least 5,000 square feet for interior lots and at least 4,000 square feet for corner lots; in A-2 districts, the area must be at least 2,500 square feet for interior lots, and 2,000 square feet for corner lots; in A-3 districts, the limits are 1,250 and 1,000 square feet, respectively; in A-4 districts, the limits are 900 and 700 square feet, respectively. The ordinance contains, in great variety and detail, provisions in respect of width of lots, front, side and rear yards, and other matters, including restrictions and regulations as to the use of bill boards, sign boards and advertising signs.

A single family dwelling consists of a basement and not less than three rooms and a bathroom. A two-family dwelling consists of a basement and not less than four living rooms and a bathroom for each family; and is further described as a detached dwelling for the occupation of two families, one having its principal living rooms on the first floor and the other on the second floor.

Appellee's tract of land comes under U-2, U-3 and U-6. The first strip of 620 feet immediately north of Euclid Avenue falls in class U-2, the next 130 feet to the north, in U-3, and the remainder in U-6. The uses of the first 620 feet, therefore, do not include apartment houses, hotels, churches, schools, or other public and semi-public buildings, or other uses enumerated in respect of U-3 to U-6, inclusive. The uses of the next 130 feet include all of these, but exclude industries, theatres, banks, shops, and the various other uses set forth in respect of U-4 to U-6, inclusive.*

Annexed to the ordinance, and made a part of it, is a zone map, showing the location and limits of the various use, height and area districts, from which it appears that the three classes overlap one another; that is to say, for example, both U-5 and U-6 use districts are in A-4 area districts, but the former is in H-2 and the latter in H-3 height districts. The plan is a complicated one and can be better understood by an inspection of the map, though it does not seem necessary to reproduce it for present purposes.

The lands lying between the two railroads for the entire length of the village area and extending some distance on either side to the north and south, having an average width of about 1,600 feet, are left open, with slight exceptions, for industrial and all other uses. This includes the larger part of appellee's tract. Approximately one-sixth of the area of the entire village is included in U-5 and U-6 use districts. That part of the village lying south of Euclid Avenue is principally in U-1 districts. The lands lying north of Euclid Avenue and bordering on the long strip just described are included in U-1, U-2, U-3 and U-4 districts, principally in U-2.

The enforcement of the ordinance is entrusted to the inspector of buildings, under rules and regulations of the board of zoning appeals. Meetings of the board are public, and minutes of its proceedings are kept. It is authorized to adopt rules and regulations to carry into effect provisions of the ordinance. Decisions of the inspector of buildings may be appealed to the board by any person claiming to be adversely affected by any such decision. The board is given power in specific cases of practical difficulty or unnecessary hardship to interpret the ordinance in harmony with its general purpose and intent, so that the public health, safety and general welfare may be secure and substantial justice done. Penalties are prescribed for violations, and it is provided that the various

---

* Appellee's tract of land comes under U-2, U-3 and U-6. The first strip of 620 feet immediately north of Euclid Avenue falls in class U-2, the next 130 feet to the north, in U-3, and the remainder in U-6. The uses of the first 620 feet, therefore, do not include apartment houses, hotels, churches, schools, or other public and semi-public buildings, or other uses enumerated in respect of U-3 to U-6, inclusive. The uses of the next 130 feet include all of these, but exclude industries, theatres, banks, shops, and the various other uses set forth in respect of U-4 to U-6, inclusive.

provisions are to be regarded as independent and the holding of any provision to be unconstitutional, void or ineffective shall not affect any of the others.

The ordinance is assailed on the grounds that it is in derogation of § 1 of the Fourteenth Amendment to the Federal Constitution in that it deprives appellee of liberty and property without due process of law and denies it the equal protection of the law, and that it offends against certain provisions of the Constitution of the State of Ohio. The prayer of the bill is for an injunction restraining the enforcement of the ordinance and all attempts to impose or maintain as to appellee's property any of the restrictions, limitations or conditions. The court below held the ordinance to be unconstitutional and void, and enjoined its enforcement. 297 Fed. 307.

Before proceeding to a consideration of the case, it is necessary to determine the scope of the inquiry. The bill alleges that the tract of land in question is vacant and has been held for years for the purpose of selling and developing it for industrial uses, for which it is especially adapted, being immediately in the path of progressive industrial development; that for such uses it has a market value of about $10,000 per acre, but if the use be limited to residential purposes the market value is not in excess of $2,500 per acre; that the first 200 feet of the parcel back from Euclid Avenue, if unrestricted in respect of use, has a value of $150 per front foot, but if limited to residential uses, and ordinary mercantile business be excluded therefrom, its value is not in excess of $50 per front foot.

It is specifically averred that the ordinance attempts to restrict and control the lawful uses of appellee's land so as to confiscate and destroy a great part of its value; that it is being enforced in accordance with its terms; that prospective buyers of land for industrial, commercial and residential uses in the metropolitan district of Cleveland are deterred from buying any part of this land because of the existence of the ordinance and the necessity thereby entailed of conducting burdensome and expensive litigation in order to vindicate the right to use the land for lawful and legitimate purposes; that the ordinance constitutes a cloud upon the land, reduces and destroys its value, and has the effect of diverting the normal industrial, commercial and residential development thereof to other and less favorable locations.

The record goes no farther than to show, as the lower court found, that the normal, and reasonably to be expected, use and development of that part of appellee's land adjoining Euclid Avenue is for general trade and commercial purposes, particularly retail stores and like establishments, and that the normal, and reasonably to be expected, use and development of the residue of the land is for industrial and trade purposes. Whatever injury is inflicted by the mere existence and threatened enforcement of the ordinance is due to restrictions in respect of these and similar uses; to which perhaps should be added—if not included in the foregoing—restrictions in respect of apartment houses. Specifically, there is nothing in the record to suggest that any damage results from the presence in the ordinance of those restrictions relating to churches, schools, libraries and other public and semi-public buildings. It is neither alleged nor proved that there is, or may be, a demand for any part of appellee's land for any of the last named uses; and we cannot assume the existence of facts which would justify an injunction upon this record in respect of this class of restrictions. For present purposes the provisions of the ordinance in respect of these uses may, therefore, be put aside as unnecessary to be considered. It is also unnecessary to consider the effect of the restrictions in respect of U-1 districts, since none of appellee's land falls within that class.

We proceed, then, to a consideration of those provisions of the ordinance to which the case as it is made relates, first disposing of a preliminary matter.

A motion was made in the court below to dismiss the bill on the ground that, because complainant [appellee] had made no effort to obtain a building permit or apply to the zoning board of appeals for relief as it might have done under the terms of the ordinance, the suit was premature. The motion was properly overruled. The effect of the allegations of the bill is that the ordinance of its own force operates greatly to reduce the value of appellee's lands and destroy their marketability for industrial, commercial and residential uses; and the attack is directed, not against any specific provision or provisions, but against the ordinance as an entirety. Assuming the premises, the existence and maintenance of the ordinance, in effect, constitutes a present invasion of appellee's property rights and a threat to continue it. Under these circumstances, the equitable jurisdiction is clear. See Terrace v. Thompson, 263 U.S. 197, 215; Pierce v. Society of Sisters, 268 U.S. 510, 535.

It is not necessary to set forth the provisions of the Ohio Constitution which are thought to be infringed. The question is the same under both Constitutions, namely, as stated by appellee: Is the ordinance invalid in that it violates the constitutional protection "to the right of property in the appellee by attempted regulations under the guise of the police power, which are unreasonable and confiscatory?"

Building zone laws are of modern origin. They began in this country about twenty-five years ago. Until recent years, urban life was comparatively simple; but with the great increase and concentration of population, problems have developed, and constantly are developing, which require, and will continue to require, additional restrictions in respect of the use and occupation of private lands in urban communities. Regulations, the wisdom, necessity and validity of which, as applied to existing conditions, are so apparent that they are now uniformly sustained, a century ago, or even half a century ago, probably would have been rejected as arbitrary and oppressive. Such regulations are sustained, under the complex conditions of our day, for reasons analogous to those which justify traffic regulations, which, before the advent of automobiles and rapid transit street railways, would have been condemned as fatally arbitrary and unreasonable. And in this there is no inconsistency, for while the meaning of constitutional guaranties never varies, the scope of their application must expand or contract to meet the new and different conditions which are constantly coming within the field of their operation. In a changing world, it is impossible that it should be otherwise. But although a degree of elasticity is thus imparted, not to the meaning, but to the application of constitutional principles, statutes and ordinances, which, after giving due weight to the new conditions, are found clearly not to conform to the Constitution, of course, must fall.

The ordinance now under review, and all similar laws and regulations, must find their justification in some aspect of the police power, asserted for the public welfare. The line which in this field separates the legitimate from the illegitimate assumption of power is not capable of precise delimitation. It varies with circumstances and conditions. A regulatory zoning ordinance, which would be clearly valid as applied to the great cities, might be clearly invalid as applied to rural communities. In solving doubts, the maxim sic utere tuo ut alienum non laedas, which lies at the foundation of so much of the common law of nuisances, ordinarily will furnish a fairly helpful clew. And the law of nuisances, likewise, may be consulted, not for the purpose of controlling, but for the helpful aid of its analogies in the process of ascertaining the scope of, the power. Thus the question whether the power exists to forbid the erection of a building of a particular kind or for a particular use, like the question whether a particular thing is a nuisance, is to be determined, not by an abstract consideration of the building or of the thing considered apart, but by considering it in connection with the circumstances and the locality. Sturgis v. Bridgeman, L.R. 11 Ch. 852, 865. A nuisance may be merely a right thing in the wrong place, — like a pig in the parlor instead of the barnyard. If the validity of the legislative classification for zoning purposes be fairly debatable, the legislative judgment must be allowed to control. Radice v. New York, 264 U.S. 292, 294.

There is no serious difference of opinion in respect of the validity of laws and regulations fixing the height of buildings within reasonable limits, the character of materials and methods of construction, and the adjoining area which must be left open, in order to minimize the danger of fire or collapse, the evils of overcrowding, and the like, and excluding from residential sections offensive trades, industries and structures likely to create nuisances. See Welch v. Swasey, 214 U.S. 91; Hadacheck v. Los Angeles, 239 U.S. 394; Reinman v. Little Rock, 237 U.S. 171; Cusack Co. v. City of Chicago, 242 U.S. 526, 529-530.

Here, however, the exclusion is in general terms of all industrial establishments, and it may thereby happen that not only offensive or dangerous industries will be excluded, but those which are neither offensive nor dangerous will share the same fate. But this is no more than happens in respect of many practice-forbidding laws which this Court has upheld although drawn in general terms so as to include individual cases that may turn out to be innocuous in themselves. Hebe Co. v. Shaw, 248 U.S. 297, 303; Pierce Oil Corp. v. City of Hope, 248 U.S. 498, 500. The inclusion of a reasonable margin to insure effective enforcement, will not put upon a law, otherwise valid, the stamp of invalidity. Such laws may also find their justification in the fact that, in some fields, the bad fades into the good by such insensible degrees that the two are not capable of being readily distinguished and separated in terms of legislation. In the light of these considerations, we are not prepared to say that the end in view was not sufficient to justify the general rule of the ordinance, although some industries of an innocent character might fall within the proscribed class. It can not be said that the ordinance in this respect "passes the bounds of reason and assumes the character of a merely arbitrary fiat." Purity Extract Co. v. Lynch, 226 U.S. 192, 204. Moreover, the restrictive provisions of the ordinance in this particular may be sustained upon the principles applicable to the broader exclusion from residential districts of all business and trade structures, presently to be discussed.

It is said that the Village of Euclid is a mere suburb of the City of Cleveland; that the industrial development of that city has now reached and in some degree extended into the village and, in the obvious course of things, will soon absorb the entire area for industrial enterprises; that the effect of the ordinance is to divert this natural development elsewhere with the consequent loss of increased values to the owners of the lands within the village borders. But the village, though physically a suburb of Cleveland, is politically a separate municipality, with powers of its own and authority to govern itself as it sees fit within the limits of the organic law of its creation and the State and Federal Constitutions. Its governing authorities, presumably representing a majority of its inhabitants and voicing their will, have determined, not that industrial development shall cease at its boundaries, but that the course of such development shall proceed within definitely fixed lines. If it be a proper exercise of the police power to relegate industrial establishments to localities separated from residential sections, it is not easy to find a sufficient reason for denying the power because the effect of its exercise is to divert an industrial flow from the course which it would follow, to the injury of the residential public if left alone, to another course where such injury will be obviated. It is not meant by this, however, to exclude the possibility of cases where the general public interest would so far outweigh the interest of the municipality that the municipality would not be allowed to stand in the way.

We find no difficulty in sustaining restrictions of the kind thus far reviewed. The serious question in the case arises over the provisions of the ordinance excluding from residential districts, apartment houses, business houses, retail stores and shops, and other like establishments. This question involves the validity of what is really the crux of the more recent zoning legislation, namely, the creation and maintenance of residential districts, from which business and trade of every sort, including hotels and apartment houses, are excluded. Upon that question this Court has not thus far spoken. The decisions of the state courts are numerous and conflicting; but those which broadly sustain the power greatly outnumber those which deny altogether or narrowly limit it; and it is very apparent that there is a constantly increasing tendency in the direction of the broader view. We shall not attempt to review these decisions at length, but content ourselves with citing a few as illustrative of all. . . .

The matter of zoning has received much attention at the hands of commissions and experts, and the results of their investigations have been set forth in comprehensive reports. These reports, which bear every evidence of painstaking consideration, concur in the view that the segregation of residential, business, and industrial buildings will make it easier to provide fire apparatus suitable for the character and intensity of the development in each section; that it will increase the safety and security of home life; greatly tend to prevent street accidents, especially to children, by reducing the traffic and resulting confusion in residential sections; decrease noise and other conditions which produce or intensify nervous disorders; preserve a more favorable environment in which to rear children, etc. With particular reference to apartment houses, it is pointed out that the development of detached house sections is greatly retarded by the coming of apartment houses, which has sometimes resulted in destroying the entire section for private house purposes; that in such sections very often the apartment house is a mere parasite, constructed in order to take advantage of the open spaces and attractive surroundings created by the residential character of the district. Moreover, the coming of one apartment house is followed by others, interfering by their height and bulk with the free circulation of air and monopolizing the rays of the sun which otherwise would fall upon the smaller homes, and bringing, as their necessary accompaniments, the disturbing noises incident to increased traffic and business, and the occupation, by means of moving and parked automobiles, of larger portions of the streets, thus detracting from their safety and depriving children of the privilege of quiet and open spaces for play, enjoyed by those in more favored localities,—until, finally, the residential character of the neighborhood and its desirability as a place of detached residences are utterly destroyed. Under these circumstances, apartment houses, which in a different environment would be not only entirely unobjectionable but highly desirable, come very near to being nuisances.

If these reasons, thus summarized, do not demonstrate the wisdom or sound policy in all respects of those restrictions which we have indicated as pertinent to the inquiry, at least, the reasons are sufficiently cogent to preclude us from saying, as it must be said before the ordinance can be declared unconstitutional, that such provisions are clearly arbitrary and unreasonable, having no substantial relation to the public health, safety, morals, or general welfare.

It is true that when, if ever, the provisions set forth in the ordinance in tedious and minute detail, come to be concretely applied to particular premises, including those of the appellee, or to particular conditions, or to be considered in connection with specific complaints, some of them, or even many of them, may be found to be clearly arbitrary and unreasonable. But where the equitable remedy of injunction is sought, as it is here, not upon the ground of a present infringement or denial of a specific right, or of a particular injury in process of actual execution, but upon the broad ground that the mere existence and threatened enforcement of the ordinance, by materially and adversely affecting values and curtailing the opportunities of the market, constitute a present and irreparable injury, the court will not scrutinize its provisions, sentence by sentence, to ascertain by a process of piecemeal dissection whether there may be, here and there, provisions of a minor character, or relating to matters of administration, or not shown to contribute to the injury complained of, which, if attacked separately, might not withstand the test of constitutionality. In respect of such provisions, of which specific complaint is not made, it cannot be said that the land owner has suffered or is threatened with an injury which entitles him to challenge their constitutionality. . . .

The relief sought here is of the same character, namely, an injunction against the enforcement of any of the restrictions, limitations or conditions of the ordinance. And the gravamen of the complaint is that a portion of the land of the appellee cannot be sold for certain enumerated uses because of the general and broad restraints of the ordinance. What would be the effect of a restraint imposed by one or more of the innumerable provisions of the ordinance, considered apart, upon the value or marketability of the lands is neither disclosed by the bill nor by the evidence, and we are afforded no basis, apart from mere speculation, upon which to rest a conclusion that it or they would have any appreciable effect upon those matters. Under these circumstances, therefore, it is enough for us to determine, as we do, that the ordinance in its general scope and dominant features, so far as its provisions are here involved, is a valid exercise of authority, leaving other provisions to be dealt with as cases arise directly involving them.

And this is in accordance with the traditional policy of this Court. In the realm of constitutional law, especially, this Court has perceived the embarrassment which is likely to result from an attempt to formulate rules or decide questions beyond the necessities of the immediate issue. It has preferred to follow the method of a gradual approach to the general by a systematically guarded application and extension of constitutional principles to particular cases as they arise, rather than by out of hand attempts to establish general rules to which future cases must be fitted. This process applies with peculiar force to the solution of questions arising under the due process clause of the Constitution as applied to the exercise of the flexible powers of police, with which we are here concerned.

Decree reversed.

Mr. Justice VAN DEVANTER, Mr. Justice McREYNOLDS and Mr. Justice BUTLER, dissent.

Notes

1. Federal district court judge D.C. Westenhaver, in Ambler Realty Co. v. Village of Euclid, 297 F. 307, 313, 316 (N.D. Ohio 1924), upheld the landowner's challenge, reasoning:

> The argument supporting this ordinance proceeds, it seems to me, both on a mistaken view of what is property and of what is police power. Property, generally speaking, defendant's counsel concede, is protected against a taking without compensation, by the guaranties of the Ohio and United States Constitutions. But their view seems to be that so long as the owner remains clothed with the legal title thereto and is not ousted from the physical possession thereof, his property is not taken, no matter to what extent his right to use it is invaded or destroyed or its present or prospective value is depreciated. This is an erroneous view. The right to property, as used in the Constitution, has no such limited meaning. As has often been said is substance by the Supreme Court: "There can be no conception of property aside from its control and use, and upon its use depends its value." . . .

> The plain truth is that the true object of the ordinance in question is to place all the property in an undeveloped area of 16 square miles in a strait jacket. The purpose to be accomplished is really to regulate the mode of living of persons who may hereafter inhabit it. In the last analysis, the result to be accomplished is to classify the population and segregate them according to their income or situation in life. The true reason why some persons live in a mansion and others in a shack, why some live in a single-family dwelling and others in a double-family dwelling, why some live in a two-family dwelling and others in an apartment, or why some live in a well-kept apartment and others in a tenement, is primarily economic. It is a matter of income and wealth, plus the labor and difficulty of procuring adequate domestic service. Aside from contributing to these results and furthering such class tendencies, the ordinance has also an esthetic purpose;

that is to say, to make this village develop into a city along lines now conceived by the village council to be attractive and beautiful.

Judge Westenhaver, whose disapproval of Euclid's zoning ordinance was reversed by the Supreme Court, was a long-time personal friend and professional associate of Ambler counsel Newton D. Baker, former Cleveland mayor and Secretary of War in the Wilson Administration. In 1917, Westenhaver had replaced Judge John H. Clarke on the district court bench after Clarke was elevated to the Supreme Court to replace Justice Charles Evans Hughes. A headline in the *Cleveland Plain Dealer* announced: "Westenhaver, Baker's Choice, Named U.S. District Judge." When Justice Clarke resigned, he was replaced by none other than George Sutherland. These details can be found in William M. Randle, *Professors, Reformers, Bureaucrats, and Cronies: The Players in* Euclid v. Ambler, in Zoning and the American Dream: Promises Still to Keep 31 33-35 (Charles M. Haar & Jerold S. Kayden eds., 1989).

Euclid's zealous counsel, James Metzenbaum, had helped draft the village's ordinance and would later gain a national reputation as a zoning expert. For more on Metzenbaum's devotion to the cause, see Michael Allan Wolf, *"Compelled by Conscientious Duty"*: Village of Euclid v. Ambler Realty Co. *as Romance*, 2 J. Sup. Ct. Hist. 88, 90 (1997).

2. The history of Ambler Realty's first federal court challenge to zoning, as chronicled in Michael Allan Wolf, The Zoning of America: *Euclid v. Ambler* (2008), and in numerous articles and book chapters, is the story of the adoption of zoning in this country. Two opposing lines of decision in the state courts were presented to the Supreme Court. The cases, as well as many of the arguments that apparently swayed the Court, can be found in the amici curiae brief filed by Alfred Bettman on behalf of the National Conference on City Planning, the Ohio State Conference on City Planning, the National Housing Association, and the Massachusetts Federation of Town Planning Boards. In a student note regarding *The Constitutionality of Zoning Laws*, 72 U. Pa. L. Rev. 421 (1924), the author explained that "[t]he great number of zoning ordinances, enacted by many American cities, in pursuance of state enabling statutes, since the war period, are now coming before the [s]upreme [c]ourts of the various states, it seems almost simultaneously."

3. Thanks to the perhaps faulty or exaggerated remembrances of a former law clerk in Alfred McCormack, *A Law Clerk's Recollections*, 46 Colum. L. Rev. 710 (1946), legend has it that following the first set of oral arguments in January 1926, a majority of the Court had concluded that zoning was an unconstitutional interference with property. What we do know is that Justice Sutherland was not on the bench to hear those arguments and that the Court did ask for a reargument in October 1926. For a dramatic, though far from objective, account of the rehearing and the events that preceded it, the reader can consult the winning counsel's treatise—James Metzenbaum, The Law of Zoning 108-22 (1930). Professor Garrett Power, in *Advocates at Cross-Purposes: The Briefs on Behalf of Zoning in the Supreme Court*, 2 J. Sup. Ct. Hist. 79 (1997), echoed the views of many planners and lawyers when he noted that Bettman's brief "made a significant tactical departure from the Metzenbaum brief [for the village]. Rather than expansively defining zoning as a promoter of the general welfare, Bettman narrowly justified it as a nuisance suppressant."

4. With the Court's blessing, zoning took off swiftly—and nationally. By the end of the year following the decision, zoning laws had been enacted by some 45 states, according to the U.S. Department of Commerce, Survey of Zoning Laws and Ordinances 2 (1928). At the close of 1930, authority for the adoption of zoning ordinances had been extended to municipalities in 47 states, and in the 48th, the general home-rule provisions of the U.S. Constitution had been judicially construed to grant authority for the adoption of zoning ordinances by cities of the first class. U.S. Department of Commerce, Survey of Zoning Laws and Ordinances Adopted During 1930, at 2-3

(1931). At the close of 1930, zoning ordinances were in effect in 981 municipalities throughout the United States, representing a population of more than 46 million, some 67% of the urban population. U.S. Department of Commerce, Zoned Municipalities in the United States 1 (1931).

5. Appropriately enough the subject of a biography subtitled *A Man Against the State*,[18] Justice George Sutherland is unfortunately more famous (or even infamous) for the ultra-conservative views he espoused on the Court during the heyday of judicial activism in the early 20th century. In Adkins v. Children's Hosp., 261 U.S. 525, 560, 561 (1923), he wrote the opinion invalidating a minimum wage law for women. While acknowledging the "mass of reports, opinions of special observers and students of the subject," the Court found the data "interesting but only mildly persuasive" and overruled the legislature. "To sustain the individual freedom of action contemplated by the Constitution," wrote Justice Sutherland, "is not to strike down the common good, but to exalt it; for surely the good of society as a whole cannot be better served than by the preservation against arbitrary restraint of the liberties of its constituent members." To view this talented and thoughtful jurist in a one-dimensional fashion is a mistake, however, as evidenced by Sutherland's majority opinion in Powell v. Alabama, 287 U.S. 45 (1932). The Court reversed the capital convictions in the notorious "Scottsboro Boys" case in *Powell*, because the African-American defendants wrongly accused of raping "two white girls" were denied access to counsel. For more on Justice Sutherland and his years before and on the Court, see Michael Allan Wolf, The Zoning of America: *Euclid v. Ambler* 112-20 (2008).

6. The Village of Euclid's successful counsel was not hesitant to stress the importance of the decision and of zoning on the life of the community. See 1 James Metzenbaum, The Law of Zoning 60 (2d ed. 1955):

> Euclid has not been hampered, as was predicted by those opposed to the zoning.
>
> On the contrary, it has enjoyed what is said to have been one of the most singular ratios of growth, among all municipalities in this land, from 1940 to 1950; then numbering more than 42,000 population. It has become the third largest of the municipalities in its county. . . .
>
> It is believed that its Zoning Ordinance—early enacted—has played no inconspicuous part in this almost unmatched development, for homes have felt safe against intrusion of factories and business; great industrial plants have abundant acreage for their fine buildings; retail business is advantageously situated.

Is this valid evidence of the efficacy of zoning? From 1926 on, industrial growth in Cleveland extended largely along the railroad lines, and the area between the Nickel Plate and New York Central tracks became almost wholly industrialized. The Ambler Realty Company property was eventually rezoned for industry. (Letter from Regional Planning Commission to Charles Haar, Nov. 22, 1954.) For more recent developments, see Michael Allan Wolf, *"Compelled by Conscientious Duty": Village of Euclid v. Ambler Realty Co. as Romance*, 2 J. Sup. Ct. Hist. 88, 89 (1977) (quoting Stan Bullard, *Fisher Guide Plant to Be Converted for Multi-Use*, Crain's Cleveland Bus., May 13, 1996, at 3, and Ruth Eckdish Knack, *Return to Euclid*, Planning, Nov. 1, 1996, at 4):

---

18. JOEL FRANCIS PASCHAL, MR. JUSTICE SUTHERLAND: A MAN AGAINST THE STATE (1951). A more recent biography enshrines Justice Sutherland as a true believer in natural rights: HADLEY ARKES, THE RETURN OF GEORGE SUTHERLAND: RESTORING A JURISPRUDENCE OF NATURAL RIGHTS (1994). Arkes responds to conservative opponents of regulation who are puzzled by Sutherland's 1926 opinion by pointing out the opinion was based on the "moral inclination, even among conservative judges, to presume in favor of local regulations that are rooted in the genuine concerns of the police power," one of which (in *Euclid v. Ambler*) was the "obvious connection to the public health." ARKES, *supra* at 71.

During World War II, General Motors opened a one-million square-foot plant to produce aircraft engines and landing gear. When peace arrived, GM produced automobile bodies until 1970, when the company turned out seats and trim in what was then called the Inland Fisher Guide Plant. In December 1992, GM officials announced that the plant would be mothballed in 1994 . . . .

In March 1996, the GM parcel was purchased for $2.5 million by a St. Louis investment company, which plans "to redevelop the property as a multitenant industrial complex." These plans should fit in well with the neighborhood—"a potpourri of residential, commercial, and industrial uses. Modest bungalows and high-rise apartments, including some subsidized developments, are intermingled on the streets that stretch north from Euclid Avenue to the railroads that bisect the city."

For information on 2009 occupants of the site (20001 Euclid Avenue), see http://www.euclidsportsplant.com ("The Euclid Sports Plant is a 60,000 square foot sports complex that was previously owned by General Motors and was known as the Fisher Body Plant. The Euclid Sports Plant is dedicated to providing local athletic and recreational organizations with a facility for practice, game, league and tournament play."); http://www.hgrindustrialsurplus.com ("HGR Industrial Surplus is the largest stocking buyer and re-seller of used industrial surplus in the Midwest. Our motto is we Sell everything and Anything you'll ever want.").

As you read the zoning cases that take up much of the remainder of this volume, it should strike you that the nature of the typical land use case differs very little from *Euclid*. Disgruntled property owners (sometimes developers, at other times their neighbors) seek access to the courts to redress the negative economic and social consequences of local decisionmakers' acts or omissions. Litigants and their advocates call on courts to draw useful lines between the valid exercise of the police power and confiscatory or arbitrary regulations that amount to due process violations, if not compensable takings. Members of the judiciary still wrestle with the appropriate level of deference to state and local legislators and administrators.

Within two years after November 22, 1926, the day on which the Court announced its decision in *Euclid v. Ambler*, the Justices offered three other opinions in cases involving challenges to zoning.[19] In Zahn v. Board of Public Works, 274 U.S. 325, 327-28 (1927), Justice Sutherland, relying on the rationale of *Euclid v. Ambler* for a unanimous Court, affirmed a decision of the California Supreme Court, which denied mandamus relief in a challenge brought to a zoning ordinance that limited the landowners' use:

The property of plaintiffs in error adjoins Wilshire Avenue, a main artery of travel through and beyond the city; and if such property were available for business purposes its market value would be greatly enhanced. The lands within the district were, when the ordinance was adopted, sparsely occupied by buildings, those in which business was carried on being limited to a few real estate offices, a grocery store, a market, a fruit stand, and a two-story business block. Much of the land adjoining the boulevard within the restricted district had already been sold with restrictions against buildings for business purposes, although the property of plaintiffs in error and the adjacent property had not been so restricted. The effect of the evidence is to show that the entire neighborhood, at

---

19. In a fourth case, Beery v. Houghton, 273 U.S. 671 (1927), the Court, per curium and on the authority of *Euclid v. Ambler*, affirmed a decision of the Minnesota Supreme Court that upheld comprehensive zoning: State *ex rel.* Beery v. Houghton, 164 Minn. 146, 204 N.W. 569 (1925).

the time of the passage of the zoning ordinance, was largely unimproved, but in course of rapid development. The Common Council of the city, upon these and other facts, concluded that the public welfare would be promoted by constituting the area, including the property of plaintiffs in error, a zone "B" district; and it is impossible for us to say that their conclusion in that respect was clearly arbitrary and unreasonable. The most that can be said is that whether that determination was an unreasonable, arbitrary or unequal exercise of power is fairly debatable. In such circumstances, the settled rule of this court is that it will not substitute its judgment for that of the legislative body charged with the primary duty and responsibility of determining the question.

Similarly, in Gorieb v. Fox, 274 U.S. 603, 608 (1927), a case from Virginia, Justice Sutherland, this time writing for a unanimous Court, upheld a local set-back regulation, again relying on *Euclid v. Ambler*:

It is hard to see any controlling difference between regulations which require the lot-owner to leave open areas at the sides and rear of his house and limit the extent of his use of the space above his lot and a regulation which requires him to set his building a reasonable distance back from the street. Each interferes in the same way, if not to the same extent, with the owner's general right of dominion over his property. All rest for their justification upon the same reasons which have arisen in recent times as a result of the great increase and concentration of population in urban communities and the vast changes in the extent and complexity of the problems of modern city life. Euclid v. Ambler Co., *supra*, p. 386. State legislatures and city councils, who deal with the situation from a practical standpoint, are better qualified than the courts to determine the necessity, character and degree of regulation which these new and perplexing conditions require; and their conclusions should not be disturbed by the courts unless clearly arbitrary and unreasonable.

The final case in the set, which follows, proved a winner for the landowner. As you read Justice Sutherland's fourth zoning opinion, notice how seriously the Court takes its reviewing function, despite the generous amount of discretion accorded local regulators in the previous three decisions and in the state court below.

NECTOW v. CITY OF CAMBRIDGE
277 U.S. 183 (1928)

Mr. Justice SUTHERLAND delivered the opinion of the Court.

A zoning ordinance of the City of Cambridge divides the city into three kinds of districts: residential, business and unrestricted. Each of these districts is subclassified in respect of the kind of buildings which may be erected. The ordinance is an elaborate one, and of the same general character as that considered by this Court in Euclid v. Ambler Co., 272 U.S. 365. In its general scope it is conceded to be constitutional within that decision. The land of plaintiff in error was put in district R-3, in which are permitted only dwellings, hotels, clubs, churches, schools, philanthropic institutions, greenhouses and gardening, with customary incidental accessories. The attack upon the ordinance is that, as specifically applied to plaintiff in error, it deprived him of his property without due process of law in contravention of the Fourteenth Amendment.

The suit was for a mandatory injunction directing the city and its inspector of buildings to pass upon an application of the plaintiff in error for a permit to erect any lawful buildings upon a tract of land without regard to the provisions of the ordinance including such tract within a residential district. The case was referred to a master to make and report findings of fact. After a view of the premises and the surrounding territory, and a hearing, the master made and reported his findings. The case came on to be heard by a justice of the court, who, after confirming the master's report, reported the case for the determination of the full court. Upon consideration, that court sustained the ordinance as applied to plaintiff in error, and dismissed the bill. 260 Mass. 441.

A condensed statement of facts, taken from the master's report, is all that is necessary. When the zoning ordinance was enacted, plaintiff in error was and still is the owner of a tract of land containing 140,000 square feet, of which the locus here in question is a part. The locus contains about 29,000 square feet, with a frontage on Brookline street, lying west, of 304.75 feet, on Henry street, lying north, of 100 feet, on the other land of the plaintiff in error, lying east, of 264 feet, and on land of the Ford Motor Company, lying southerly, of 75 feet. The territory lying east-and south is unrestricted. The lands beyond Henry street to the north and beyond Brookline street to the west are within a restricted residential district. The effect of the zoning is to separate from the west end of plaintiff in error's tract a strip 100 feet in width. The Ford Motor Company has a large auto assembling factory south of the locus; and a soap factory and the tracks of the Boston & Albany Railroad lie near. Opposite the locus, on Brookline street, and included in the same district, there are some residences; and opposite the locus, on Henry street, and in the same district, are other residences. The locus is now vacant, although it was once occupied by a mansion house. Before the passage of the ordinance in question, plaintiff in error had outstanding a contract for the sale of the greater part of his entire tract of land for the sum of $63,000. Because of the zoning restrictions, the purchaser refused to comply with the contract. Under the ordinance, business and industry of all sorts are excluded from the locus, while the remainder of the tract is unrestricted. It further appears that provision has been made for widening Brookline street, the effect of which, if carried out, will be to reduce the depth of the locus to 65 feet. After a statement at length of further facts, the master finds "that no practical use can be made of the land in question for residential purposes, because among other reasons herein related, there would not be adequate return on the amount of any investment for the development of the property." The last finding of the master is:

> I am satisfied that the districting of the plaintiff's land in a residence district would not promote the health, safety, convenience and general welfare of the inhabitants of that part of the defendant City, taking into account the natural development thereof and the character of the district and the resulting benefit to accrue to the whole City and I so find.

It is made pretty clear that because of the industrial and railroad purposes to which the immediately adjoining lands to the south and east have been devoted and for which they are zoned, the locus is of comparatively little value for the limited uses permitted by the ordinance.

We quite agree with the opinion expressed below that a court should not set aside the determination of public officers in such a matter unless it is clear that their action "has no foundation in reason and is a mere arbitrary or irrational exercise of power having no substantial relation to the public health, the public morals, the public safety or the public welfare in its proper sense." Euclid v. Ambler Co., *supra*, p. 395.

An inspection of a plat of the city upon which the zoning districts are outlined, taken in connection with the master's findings, shows with reasonable certainty that the inclusion of the locus in question is not indispensable to the general plan. The boundary line of the residential district before reaching the locus runs for some distance along the streets, and to exclude the locus from the residential district requires only that such line shall be continued 100 feet further along Henry street and thence south along Brookline street. There does not appear to be any reason why this should not be done. Nevertheless, if that were all, we should not be warranted in substituting our judgment for that of the zoning authorities primarily charged with the duty and responsibility of determining the question. Zahn v. Bd. of Public Works, 274 U.S. 325, 328, and cases cited. But that is not all. The governmental power to interfere by zoning regulations with the general rights of the land owner by restricting the character of his use, is not unlimited, and other questions aside, such restriction cannot be imposed if it does not bear a substantial relation to the public health, safety, morals, or general welfare. Euclid v. Ambler Co., *supra*, p. 395. Here, the express finding of the master, already quoted, confirmed by the court below, is that the health, safety, convenience and general welfare of the inhabitants of the part of the city affected will not be promoted by the disposition made by the ordinance of the locus in question. This finding of the master, after a hearing and an inspection of the entire area affected, supported, as we think it is, by other findings of fact, is determinative of the case. That the invasion of the property of plaintiff in error was serious and highly injurious is clearly established; and, since a necessary basis for the support of that invasion is wanting, the action of the zoning authorities comes within the ban of the Fourteenth Amendment and cannot be sustained.

Judgment reversed.

Notes

1. In the *Nectow* decision, the Supreme Court seems to enunciate what had been foreshadowed in *Euclid v. Ambler*—a close supervision of the recently validated zoning power. Yet you will note in the subsequent cases that the Court has consistently refused to pass judgment in zoning cases. For example, during the six terms of the Court from 1949-1950 to 1954-1955, appeals were dismissed or petitions for certiorari denied in 21 cases involving zoning and local planning matters, according to Corwin J. Johnson, *Constitutional Law and Community Planning*, 20 Law & Contemp. Probs. 199, 208 (1955). As we will see later, the Burger and Rehnquist Courts, despite some failures to resolve such nagging questions as the remedy for regulatory takings, put an end to the period of nonintervention.

2. Compare the approach of the Supreme Court with that taken by the state high court in Nectow v. City of Cambridge, 260 Mass. 441, 446-48, 157 N.E. 618, 619-20 (1927):

> After the passage of the ordinance, the plaintiff applied to the city government for an amendment to the zoning ordinance so as to reclassify the locus as business or unrestricted land. This application was denied. Thereafter, he applied to the superintendent of buildings of the defendant city for a permit to construct a building essentially different from any allowed by the ordinance but otherwise lawful. He declined to issue such permit and thereupon the plaintiff, pursuant to G.L. c. 40, § 27, and St. 1924, c. 133, petitioned the board of appeals to vary the application of the ordinance so as to permit the plaintiff to erect a business building on the locus. This was refused. Thereupon the present suit was brought. . . .

> If there is to be zoning at all, the dividing line must be drawn somewhere. There cannot be a twilight zone. If residence districts are to exist, they must be bounded. In the nature of things, the location of the precise limits of the several districts demands the exercise of judgment and sagacity. There can be no standard susceptible of mathematical exactness in its application. Opinions of the wise and good well may differ as to the place to put the separation between different districts. . . . Courts cannot set aside the decisions of public officers in such a matter unless compelled to the conclusion that it has no foundation in reason and is a mere arbitrary or irrational exercise of power having

no substantial relation to the public health, the public morals, the public safety or the public welfare in its proper sense. These considerations cannot be weighed with exactness. That they demand the placing of the boundary of a zone 100 feet one way or the other in land having similar material features would be hard to say as matter of law. . . . The case at bar is close to the line. But we do not feel justified in holding that the zoning line established is whimsical and without foundation in reason.

Is there a meaningful and useful difference between the wisdom of a decision that is not even "fairly debatable" and one that is "whimsical and without foundation in reason"? Which test is more favorable to the regulator?

3. *Euclid v. Ambler* and *Nectow* are good representations of what the authors have called "Progressive Jurisprudence" in Charles M. Haar & Michael Allan Wolf, Euclid *Lives: The Survival of Progressive Jurisprudence*, 115 Harv. L. Rev. 2158, 2174-75 (2002). The authors of this casebook argued in those pages that

> *Euclid*, imbued as it is with Progressive jurisprudence, still serves as a useful paradigm of the judicial craft, for today the Court is once again sharply divided in its efforts to articulate a meaningful distinction between valid regulations and illegal confiscations. For more than three-quarters of a century, *Euclid*'s logic and text, and the approach to judicial decisionmaking the majority opinion represents, have weathered profound societal, political, and ideological shifts on the Court and in the American polity. *Euclid*'s strength over the years, however, should not be taken to mean that our courts have mined all of its value. Regardless of how well-known Euclid is to certain courts and scholars, it has much more to offer in the basic principles it expounds.
>
> The attributes of Progressive jurisprudence to which we can attribute Euclid's "staying power" are represented by the five questions that appear within and between the lines of Sutherland's opinion for the Court:
>
> (1) Does the challenged regulation reflect the elasticity and adaptability of traditional common law methodology?
>
> (2) Was the challenged regulation crafted with important input by experts from non-legal fields, thus leaving the property owner with the heavy burden of demonstrating unreasonableness?
>
> (3) Does the challenged regulation hold the capacity to reduce and, at the same time, enhance individual wealth and personal rights?
>
> (4) Is the Court being asked to affirm judicial and popular acceptance in the "laboratory" of the states?
>
> (5) Is the regulatory scheme fundamentally flexible, in that it furthers a wide range of public interests and features exemption provisions for property owners who would otherwise be asked to shoulder heavy burdens?
>
> These questions, and some of the aspects of Progressiveness they reflect, are not expressly articulated by the Court. These inquiries must be distilled from the text, as read in its historical and ideological context. . . .
>
> Progressive jurisprudence presents to the current Court: (1) a respectful understanding of the contextual nature of modern regulatory law, which is tied to a notion of the

common law that meaningfully responds and adapts even to profound societal changes; (2) a model of temperate judicial lawmaking that, when appropriate, translates into deference to the findings of qualified experts; (3) an accurate perspective of the nature and impact of regulations affecting private property; (4) a prudential approach that awaits and, barring serious error, endorses the work product of state judges; and (5) a consideration of the devices that are included in regulatory schemes to provide relief to those property owners suffering special hardships.[20]

IV. Zoning in the State Judicial Laboratory

In the decades following the 1920s, state and lower federal court judges evaluating early zoning and planning schemes who were looking for guidance from the Supreme Court were left with two messages: (1) deference to local regulators employing comprehensive zoning schemes was appropriate (*Euclid v. Ambler*), (2) but not if the landowner was subjected to confiscation (*Nectow*). For the most part, Justice Sutherland's initial word on the subject has been heeded and in the great majority of cases judges have given planners and local legislators a great amount of leeway. Nevertheless, as the four cases that follow illustrate, there is a limit to any court's patience with a zoning scheme that proves confiscatory or arbitrary, and thus violates federal and state constitutional notions of due process. Even without a detailed Supreme Court blueprint, notice how judges—inspired and instructed by the legal commentators—moved from a visceral reaction to local regulatory abuse toward a studious inquiry as to the existence of a meaningful nexus between a single zoning act and the demands of comprehensive planning.

ARVERNE BAY CONSTRUCTION CO. v. THATCHER
278 N.Y. 222, 15 N.E.2d 587 (1938)

LEHMAN, Judge. The plaintiff is the owner of a plot of vacant land on the northerly side of Linden boulevard in the borough of Brooklyn. Until 1928 the district in which the property is situated was classified as an "unrestricted zone, under the Building Zone Resolution of the city of New York (New York Code of Ordinances, Appendix B). Then, by amendment of the ordinance and the "Use District Map," the district was placed in a residence zone. The plaintiff, claiming that its property could not be used properly or profitably for any purpose permitted in a residence zone and that, in consequence, the zoning ordinance imposed unnecessary hardship upon it, applied to the Board of Standards and Appeals, under section 21 of the Building Zone Resolution, for a variance which would permit the use of the premises for a gasoline service station. The application was denied, and, upon review in certiorari proceedings, the courts sustained the determination of the board. People ex rel. Arverne Bay Construction Co. v. Murdock, 247 App. Div. 889, 286 N.Y.S. 785; affirmed, 271 N.Y. 631, 3 N.E.2d 457.

Defeated in its attempt to obtain permission to put its property to a profitable use, the plaintiff has brought this action to secure an adjudication that the restrictions placed upon the use of its property by the zoning ordinance result in deprivation of its property without due process of law and that, in so far as the ordinance affects its property, the ordinance violates the provisions of the Constitution of the United States and the Constitution of the State of New York. U.S.C.A. Const. Amend. 14; Const. N.Y. art. 1, § 6. In this action it demands as a right what has been refused to it as a favor. . . .

---

20. Authors' note: For a subsequent exchange regarding the Progressive origins of zoning, see Eric R. Claeys, Euclid *Lives?: The Uneasy Legacy of Progressivism in Zoning*, 73 FORDHAM L. REV. 731 (2004); and Charles M. Haar & Michael Allan Wolf, *Yes, Thankfully,* Euclid *Lives*, 73 FORDHAM L. REV. 771 (2004).

The amendment to the zoning ordinance, about which complaint is made, changed from an unrestricted zone to a residential district the property abutting on Linden boulevard for a distance of four miles, with the exception of a small section at a railroad crossing. The district is almost undeveloped. There had been no building construction in that area for many years prior to the amendment. The chairman of the building zone commission which drafted the zoning ordinance, testifying as an expert witness for the defendant, described the district as in a "transition state from the farms as I knew them thirty and forty years ago south of this location." There are some old buildings used for non-conforming purposes, left from the days when the district was used for farming. There are only three buildings in Linden boulevard in a distance of about a mile. One of these buildings is a cow stable and a second building is used as an office in connection with the dairy business conducted there. A gasoline station erected on that boulevard would, it is plain, not adversely affect the health, morals, safety or general welfare of the people who now live in that neighborhood. Justification, if any, for the ordinance restricting the use of the property on Linden boulevard to residential purposes must be found in the control over future development which will result from such restrictions.

Without zoning restrictions, the self-interest of the individual property owners will almost inevitably dictate the form of the development of the district. The plaintiff claims, and has conclusively shown at the trial, that at no time since the amendment of the zoning resolution could its property be profitably used for residential purposes. The expert witness for the city, to whose testimony we have already referred and whose qualifications are universally recognized, admits that such a residential improvement would, even now after the lapse of ten years, be "premature." The property, then, must for the present remain unimproved and unproductive, a source of expense to the owner, or must be put to some non-conforming use. In a district otherwise well adapted for residences a gasoline station or other non-conforming use of property may render neighboring property less desirable for use as a private residence. The development of a district for residential purposes might best serve the interests of the city as a whole and, in the end, might perhaps prove the most profitable use of the property within such district. A majority of the property owners might conceivably be content to bear the burden of taxes and other carrying charges upon unimproved land in order to reap profit in the future from the development of the land for residential purposes. They could not safely do so without reasonable assurance that the district will remain adapted for residence use and will not be spoilt for such purpose by the intrusion of structures used for less desirable purposes. The zoning ordinance is calculated to provide such assurance to property owners in the district and to constrain the property owners to develop their land in manner which in the future will prove of benefit to the city. Such considerations have induced the Appellate Division to hold that the ordinance is valid.

There is little room for disagreement with the general rules and tests set forth in the opinion of the Appellate Division. The difficulty arises in the application of such rules and tests to the particular facts in this case. We are not disposed to define the police power of the State so narrowly that it would exclude reasonable restrictions placed upon the use of property in order to aid the development of new districts in accordance with plans calculated to advance the public welfare of the city in the future. We have said that "the need for vision of the future in the governance of cities has not lessened with the years. The dweller within the gates, even more than the stranger from afar, will pay the price of blindness." Hesse v. Rath, 249 N.Y. 436, 438, 164 N.E. 342. We have, indeed, recognized that long-time planning for zoning purposes may be a valid exercise of the police power, but at the same time we have pointed out that the power is not unlimited. "We are not required to say that a merely temporary restraint of beneficial enjoyment is unlawful where the interference is necessary to promote the ultimate good either of the municipality as a whole or of the immediate neighborhood. Such problems will have to be solved when they arise. If we assume that the restraint may be permitted, the interference must be not unreasonable, but on the contrary must be kept within the limits of necessity." (People ex rel. St. Albans-Springfield Corporation v. Connell, 257 N.Y. 73, 83, 177 N.E. 313, 316.)[21] The problem presented upon this appeal is whether or not the zoning ordinance as applied to the plaintiff's property is unreasonable.

Findings of the trial judge, sustained by evidence presented by the plaintiff, establish that, in the vicinity of the plaintiff's premises, the city operates an incinerator which "gives off offensive fumes and odors which permeate plaintiff's premises." About 1,200 or 1,500 feet from the plaintiff's land, "a trunk sewer carrying both storm and sanitary sewage empties into an open creek. . . . The said creek runs to the south of plaintiff's premises and gives off nauseating odors which permeate the said property." The trial judge further found that other conditions exist which, it is plain, render the property entirely unfit, at present, for any conforming use. Though the defendant urges that the conditions are not as bad as the plaintiff's witnesses have pictured, yet as the Appellate Division has said: "It must be conceded, upon the undisputed facts in this case, that this property cannot, presently or in the immediate future, be profitably used for residential purposes." 253 App. Div. 285, 286, 2 N.Y.S.2d 112, 114.

We may assume that the zoning ordinance is the product of farsighted planning calculated to promote the general welfare of the city at some future time. . . .

The warning of Mr. Justice Holmes [in Pennsylvania Coal Co. v. Mahon, 260 U.S. 393, 415 (1922)] should perhaps be directed rather to Legislatures than to courts; for the courts have not hesitated to declare statutes invalid wherever regulation has gone so far that it is clearly unreasonable and must be "recognized as [a] taking"; and unless regulation does clearly go so far the courts may not deny force to the regulation. We have already pointed out that in the case which we are reviewing, the plaintiff's land cannot at present or in the immediate future be profitably or reasonably used without violation of the restriction. An ordinance which permanently so restricts the use of property that it cannot be used for any reasonable purpose goes, it is plain, beyond regulation, and must be recognized as a taking of the property. The only substantial difference, in such case, between restriction and actual taking, is that the restriction leaves the owner subject to the burden of payment of taxation, while outright confiscation would relieve him of that burden.

The situation, of course, might be quite different where it appears that within a reasonable time the property can be put to a profitable use. The temporary inconvenience or even hardship of holding unproductive property might then be compensated by ultimate benefit to the owner

---

21. Authors' note: In this case, the plaintiff owned a vacant lot in a rural section of Queens, New York:

> While some of the property has been laid out in building lots, almost the entire section consists of vacant land, there being only six buildings in the entire area extending 400 feet from the premises in each direction. Four of these are brick buildings, with stores in the ground floor and apartments for dwelling purposes overhead, which cannot be rented for enough to bring in a reasonable return upon the investment. As transit facilities do not reach this territory, it has been slow in development; the few families who do live in the neighborhood being transported by bus or in their own automobiles.

The plaintiff's property was placed in a business district. Finding that it could not profitably dispose of the property either for residential or business purposes, it applied to the Board of Standards and Appeals to permit the construction of a gasoline station. The application was denied. On appeal, the special referee found "that the site in question is not suitable for the erection of a business building of any character whatever, and that a gasoline-selling station is the only available use to which the property in question can be put." The lower court then directed the Board of Appeals to grant the relief. On appeal it was held:

> The order, therefore, of the court below, which authorizes and permits the erection and use of this gasoline station, must be modified by a direction that when the circumstances so change by the development of the city that the property is reasonably susceptible of being applied to business uses, then, upon the application of the authorities or any one interested, the gasoline station must be removed.

257 N.Y. at 76, 83, 177 N.E. at 313, 316.

or, perhaps, even without such compensation, the individual owners might be compelled to bear a temporary burden in order to promote the public good. We do not pass upon such problems now, for here no inference is permissible that within a reasonable time the property can be put to a profitable use or that the present inconvenience or hardship imposed upon the plaintiff is temporary. True, there is evidence that the neighborhood is improving and that some or all of the conditions which now render the district entirely unsuitable for residence purposes will in time be removed. Even so, it is conceded that prognostication that the district will in time become suited for residences rests upon hope and not upon certainty, and no estimate can be made of the time which must elapse before the hope becomes fact.

During the nine years from 1928 to 1936, when concededly the property was unsuitable for any conforming use, the property was assessed at $18,000, and taxes amounting to $4,566 were levied upon it, in addition to assessments of several thousand dollars; yet, so far as appears, the district was no better suited for residence purposes at the time of the trial in 1936 than it was when the zoning ordinance was amended in 1928. In such case the ordinance is clearly more than a temporary and reasonable restriction placed upon the land to promote the general welfare. It is in substance a taking of the land prohibited by the Constitution of the United States and by the Constitution of the State.

We repeat here what under similar circumstances the court said in People ex rel. St. Albans-Springfield Corporation v. Connell, *supra*, page 83, 177 N.E. page 316: "we are not required to say that a merely temporary restraint of beneficial enjoyment is unlawful where the interference is necessary to promote the ultimate good either of the municipality as a whole or of the immediate neighborhood." There the court held that the "ultimate good" could be attained and a "productive use" allowed by a variation of the zoning ordinance that "will be temporary and provisional and readily terminable." Here the application of the plaintiff for any variation was properly refused, for the conditions which render the plaintiff's property unsuitable for residential use are general and not confined to plaintiff's property. In such case, we have held that the general hardship should be remedied by revision of the general regulation, not by granting the special privilege of a variation to single owners. Levy v. Board of Standards and Appeals of City of New York, 267 N.Y. 347, 196 N.E. 284. Perhaps a new ordinance might be evolved by which the "ultimate good" may be attained without depriving owners of the productive use of their property. That is a problem for the legislative authority, not for the courts. Now we hold only that the present regulation as applied to plaintiff's property is not valid.

The judgment of the Appellate Division should be reversed and that of the Special Term affirmed, with costs in this court and in the Appellate Division.

Notes

1. The court was skeptical about conditions in the area improving in the "immediate future" or "within a reasonable time." Consider the following extract from the report of the New York City Board of Standards and Appeals, No. 740-38-BZ (Feb. 11, 1939):

> It is apparent that the question of the then existing nuisances played a large part in the consideration of the Courts in both Arverne Bay Construction Co. v. Thatcher and Arverne Bay Construction Co. v. Murdock. The applicant in this present application, two blocks away to the east on the same side of Linden boulevard, claims that his hardship consists of the same nuisance conditions which persuaded the Court of Appeals in their decision on the question of constitutionality. He mentioned the incinerator and garbage disposal plant, the trunk and open sewer, the dumping ground for deposit-

ing and burning garbage, the cow shed, as among the nuisances still existing. That he is incorrect in these statements is evident from the testimony of nearby owners at the hearing and from the exhaustive inspection made by the Committee of the Board of the extensive area between Linden boulevard and Jamaica Bay and from reports requested by the Board from the Borough President of Brooklyn, the Department of Public Works, the Department of Parks and the Department of Sanitation. By these reports, confirming the inspection by a Committee of the Board, it is shown that the main nuisances referred to have been entirely abated by the construction and extension of a large sewer for 2500 feet southerly and the filling in of the meadow lands adjoining Fresh Creek Basin, by the filling in and grading by a W.P.A. project of vacant plots formerly used for dumping and burning garbage, by chlorination, and by discontinuance of the incinerator formerly used by the Sanitation Department. . . . The Committee found that no nonconforming uses existed in the area of notification, other than the gasoline station on the northerly side of Linden boulevard diagonally opposite and the pocket book factory at 818 Pennsylvania avenue. . . . While the immediate area adjacent to the plot under appeal and to the south of Linden boulevard, is not greatly developed, west thereof and across Linden boulevard, is largely developed. This photograph does not show. . . . the new public school now being erected on Pennsylvania avenue, approximately three hundred feet distant from the plot under appeal. Air-view Exhibit A-1 does not correctly show present conditions or the street and sewer development that has since taken place. Pennsylvania avenue southerly from Linden boulevard is a wide paved avenue to Fairfield avenue, which is an extension of Flatlands avenue and is used largely as a short cut for traffic from South Brooklyn. When the Circumferential Highway is completed, the entire area between it and Linden boulevard should be immediately available for development. . . .

2. In cases such as *Arverne Bay*, state courts were contending with the challenge of setting aside undeveloped or underdeveloped land for future uses. In Acker v. Baldwin, 18 Cal. 2d 341, 344-45, 115 P.2d 455, 457 (1941), the court observed:

In earlier times, zoning regulations were, in the main, enacted to restrict the use of property in districts already partially, or somewhat completely, built up. With the growth of the large cities as the result of motor transportation, governmental authorities have endeavored to set aside areas for residential purposes in advance of their use. Certainly, it is more in the interest of the general welfare that certain districts be set aside to residential uses before there has been any large investment for improvements than to apply restrictions after business has become established. This is wise city planning in the public interest. It has been made possible by general judicial approval of the doctrine that zoning may properly take into consideration those factors which, although they may not be exactly defined as relating to public health, safety or morals, come under the broad term of general welfare.

3. In early zoning cases, courts had to be vigilant that this new police power tool was not being abused by local regulators. See, for example, Frederick v. Jackson County, 197 Miss. 293, 300, 20 So. 2d 92, 95 (1944):

We can perceive from this record that the real object which was sought to be served by this ordinance was to prevent the erection and operation by appellant of a large dance pavilion and public clubhouse, the construction of which appellant had begun, and which it was believed would be detrimental to the efficiency and output of an immense shipbuilding plant, employing more than ten thousand workers located in the adjoining municipality. However worthy the object, it must be obvious that if the entire area here in question cannot be brought at this time within the operation of a zoning ordinance, such as here proposed, then for the stronger reason it cannot be made to apply to a particular piece of property, no larger than that owned by appellant, within that area. In fact, we think it is safe to say that a particular object, of the particular character mentioned, directed towards a particular piece of small property, owned by a particular person, is not within the province of the zoning laws.

VERNON PARK REALTY, INC. v. CITY OF MOUNT VERNON
307 N.Y. 493, 121 N.E.2d 517 (1954)

DYE, Judge. The City of Mount Vernon appeals as of right on constitutional grounds from a judgment declaring invalid and void insofar as they affected the plaintiff's property, the City Zoning Ordinance and Zoning Map of the City of Mount Vernon, enacted and adopted March 22, 1927, as amended March 9, 1949, and the amendment thereto, chapter 4A, enacted and adopted January 16, 1952.

The subject premises are known locally as the "Plaza," consisting of an open area containing approximately 86,000 square feet adjacent to the New York, New Haven & Hartford Railroad station. It is in the middle of a highly developed Business "B" district (Zoning Ordinance, 1927, ch. 12) and as such constitutes an island completely surrounded by business buildings. It has always been used by the patrons of the railroad and others for the parking of private automobiles. When the city first enacted a zoning ordinance, the Plaza was placed in a Business "B" district (Zoning Ordinance adopted 1922), later being changed without objection to a Resident "B" district (Zoning Ordinance adopted 1927), following which the parking of automobiles was continued as a valid nonconforming use. In 1932, upon the application of the railroad and its then tenant, the city granted a variance to permit the installation of a gasoline filling station. Later and in 1951 the railroad sold the premises to the plaintiff, the title being closed June 21, 1951. The purchaser applied without success for a variance to permit the erection of a retail shopping center, a prohibited use as the zoning ordinance then read (Zoning Ordinance adopted 1927, chs. 9-10).

The plaintiff then commenced this action for a judgment declaring the 1927 ordinance unconstitutional, unreasonable, and void and not binding on the plaintiff insofar as the same pertains to the use of plaintiff's premises, and for injunctive relief. After joinder of issue and on January 16, 1952, the common council amended the zoning ordinance by adding thereto a new district to be known as "D.P.D." (Designed Parking District). In substance, the effect of this amendment was to prohibit the use of the property for any purpose except the parking and storage of automobiles, a service station within the parking area and the continuance of prior non-conforming uses (Zoning Ordinance as amended January 16, 1952, ch. 4A). Faced with this change in classification, the plaintiff amended its complaint so as to include an attack on both the zoning ordinance and the 1952 amendment. The amended complaint alleges that the ordinance and its 1952 amendment, as pertaining to the plaintiff's property, work an undue hardship as to use, destroy the greater part of its value, are discriminatory as a denial of the equal protection of the law, and amount to a taking of private property without just compensation contrary to due process and, as such, are constitutionally invalid and void. The city justifies the ordinance and its amendment by reason of the congested traffic and parking conditions now existing in Mount Vernon which, it says, have become so acute as to reach a strangulation point. However compelling and acute the community traffic problem may be, its solution does not lie in placing an undue and uncompensated burden on the individual owner of a single parcel of land in the guise of regulation, even for a public purpose. True it is that for a long time the land has been devoted to parking, a non-conforming use, but it does not follow that an ordinance prohibiting any other use is a reasonable exercise of the police power. While the common council has the unquestioned right to enact zoning laws respecting the use of property in accordance with a well-considered and comprehensive plan designed to promote public health, safety and general welfare, General City Law, Consol. Laws, c. 21, § 83, such power is subject to the constitutional limitation that it may not be exerted arbitrarily or unreasonably, and this is so whenever the zoning ordinance precludes the use of the property for any purpose for which it is reasonably adapted (Arverne Bay Construction Co. v. Thatcher, 278 N.Y. 222, 15 N.E.2d 587). By the same token, an ordinance valid when adopted will nevertheless be stricken down as invalid when, at a later time, its operation under changed conditions proves confiscatory, such, for instance, as when the greater part of its value is destroyed, for which the courts will afford relief in an appropriate case.

On this record, the plaintiff, having asserted an invasion of his property rights, has met the burden of proof by establishing that the property is so situated that it has no possibilities for residential use and that the use added by the 1952 amendment does not improve the situation but, in fact, will operate to destroy the greater part of the value of the property since, in authorizing its use for parking and incidental services, it necessarily permanently precludes the use for which it is most readily adapted, i.e., a business use such as permitted and actually carried on by the owners of all the surrounding property. Under such circumstances, the 1927 zoning ordinance and zoning map and the 1952 amendment, as they pertain to the plaintiff's property, are so unreasonable and arbitrary as to constitute an invasion of property rights, contrary to constitutional due process and, as such, are invalid, illegal and void enactments.

Mention should be made of appellant's contention that plaintiff has no right to bring this action because it has not shown good faith in that the contract of purchase provided for a reconveyance of the premises to the seller, at the option of the purchaser, in the event that, within one year from the date of closing title, the purchaser was unable to obtain from the city or through court action a change of zoning so as to permit use of the premises for a business purpose, and, in that it purchased the property with knowledge of the zoning restrictions. There is no merit to this claim of lack of good faith. The plaintiff took title to the property by deed prior to the enactment of the 1952 amendment and could not very well have known or anticipated that the city, under the guise of regulating traffic, would permanently limit the use of the property to the parking of automobiles and incidental services, such as we have said constituted an illegal invasion of the plaintiff's property rights. Under such circumstances, the validity of the zoning ordinance and its zoning map may be attacked at any time and at any stage of the proceedings. . . .

Purchase of property with knowledge of the restriction does not bar the purchaser from testing the validity of the zoning ordinance since the zoning ordinance in the very nature of things has reference to land rather than to owner (Bassett on Zoning, p. 177). Knowledge of the owner cannot validate an otherwise invalid ordinance. The owner's right to attack the validity of a zoning ordinance is not waived by the circumstance that he has on a previous occasion applied for a variance. Such an application is, primarily, an appeal to the discretion of the board and, for that purpose, the validity of the ordinance is assumed[;] but that does not operate to confer validity if, in fact, as here, the zoning ordinance is clearly confiscatory (cf. Arverne Bay Construction Co. v. Thatcher, *supra*). Conversely, an attack on the legality of a zoning ordinance prior to any request for a variance has long been accepted as proper procedure. . . .

The judgment appealed from should be affirmed, with costs.

FULD, Judge (dissenting). I cannot agree that the zoning ordinance of the City of Mount Vernon here under attack is unconstitutional.

A zoning ordinance is confiscatory and, hence, unconstitutional only when it "so restricts the use of property that it cannot be used for any reasonable purpose" (Arverne Bay Construction Co. v. Thatcher, 278 N.Y. 222, 232), or when it restricts it "to a use for which the property is not adapted". (Dowsey v. Village of Kensington, 257 N.Y. 221, 231). But, if "the validity of the legislative classification for zoning purposes be fairly debatable, the legislative judgment must be allowed to control." (Euclid, Ohio v. Ambler Co., 272 U.S. 365, 388.) It seems to me that neither the 1927 ordinance nor its 1952 amendment is so unreasonable as to permit us to interfere with the judgment of Mount Vernon's Common Council.

In the present case, although the 1927 ordinance placed the property in a residential zone, all of the area was in fact employed for parking purposes since 1922. That being so we may not ignore realities and say that the ordinance was invalid because it singled out a small area in the midst of a large business zone for residential use. For all practical purposes, the district continued, as it had been, zoned for parking. Adjacent to the New York, New Haven & Hartford Railroad, the area served the community's obvious need for parking facilities. Accordingly, the continuance—indeed, even the creation—of a special parking zone was more than warranted. Serving, as it did, the parking needs of railroad passengers, permitting easier access to the trains and reducing congestion in the crowded business section, the ordinance not only afforded the owner an entirely reasonable use for his property, but advanced the public good and well-being.

Nor may the ordinance be condemned because it affected but a small area. It has long been recognized that, if it is done for the general welfare of the community as a whole, a municipality may, as part of a comprehensive zoning plan, set aside even a single plot in the center of a large zone devoted to a different use. And land adjacent to a railroad station has been regarded as a particularly appropriate subject for such treatment.

The ordinance being valid in 1927, it is valid today unless conditions have changed. Not even respondent claims that they have, and the fact is that, except for the erection of a gas station on part of the space involved, neither the area nor the surrounding business district has undergone any alteration. There has, of course, been an increase in population and in the number of automobiles, but that—a general and widespread change affecting all of Mount Vernon—only serves to render the long-continued parking use still more suitable and necessary. It is, perhaps, true, that a parking lot may not afford a purchaser as great a return on his money as a shopping center, but that circumstance, standing alone, does not justify invalidation of the ordinance. . . .

There is at least one other reason for upholding the 1927 ordinance. While mere acquiescence in an unconstitutional ordinance cannot serve to validate it, the fact that for over twenty-five years the owner railroad actually occupied the property satisfactorily as a parking space without objection or the slightest claim that it effected a confiscation cannot be overlooked. Since an ordinance is unconstitutional only if it bars "any reasonable" use of property, it is difficult to see how it may be attacked successfully as confiscatory or invalid where it appears that the land was put to a "reasonable" use for a quarter of a century under conditions which have up to the present remained unchanged. And, that being so, a vendee, such as respondent, who buys with full knowledge of the applicable zoning regulations, certainly stands in no better or stronger position than his predecessor in title.

The 1927 law, being, as I believe, constitutional, no fault may be found with the 1952 amendment. That merely brought about by enactment what had previously been accomplished by a nonconforming use and is no more subject to attack than the 1927 ordinance. . . .

I would reverse the judgment rendered below.

Notes

1. The *Vernon Park* majority cited *Arverne Bay* for the notion that a local government acts in an arbitrary or unreasonable fashion "whenever the zoning ordinance precludes the use of the property for any purpose for which it is reasonably adapted." Look back at the previous case and determine on your own whether that is an accurate restatement of the rule from *Arverne Bay*.

2. Some localities have been more successful in implementing "creative" zoning districts. For example, in McCarthy v. City of Manhattan Beach, 41 Cal. 2d 879, 884-85, 890-91, 895, 264 P.2d 932, 935, 938-39, 941 (1953), the plaintiffs owned three-fifths of a mile of sandy beach frontage, varying in width from 174 to 186 feet. In 1924, the city brought a quiet-title action, claiming that the land had been dedicated for public use. Judgment went against the city. Thereafter the plaintiffs and the city cooperated in various unsuccessful efforts to persuade the county or the state to acquire the land for a public beach.

In 1940, the plaintiffs began to construct a fence in the hope of charging admission for the property's use. It was never fully completed, as parts of it were destroyed by the public. The plaintiffs demanded police protection, and stated their intention of holding the city responsible for all damage suffered. Later the plaintiffs requested rezoning of the property, which had been classified single-family residential under a 1929 ordinance, for business purposes. This was denied.

In 1941, the city council adopted a zoning ordinance providing for 10 zoning districts. The plaintiffs' property was placed in a "beach recreation district" and could be used only for the operation of beach facilities for an admission fee; the only structures permitted were lifeguard towers, open smooth wire fences, and small signs. The plaintiffs made no use of their property as permitted by the 1941 zoning ordinance. In 1950, they applied to the city for a zoning amendment to reclassify the property to a single-family residence district. This being denied they brought an action for declaratory relief. At the time of the action, the plaintiffs' land was the only privately owned property falling within the beach recreation zone.

The trial court had concluded

> that plaintiffs' property is, from time to time, subject to erosion and replacement by reason of storms and wave action of the Pacific Ocean; that any residences which could be constructed upon the property would necessarily be erected on pilings, and reasonable minds might differ as to the safety of residence properties so constructed; that such construction might also create police problems by reason of possible uses of the areas underneath the residences for immoral purposes; that one of the principal characteristics of the city is its beach advantage bordering upon the Pacific Ocean; that at all times since adoption of the 1941 ordinance, plaintiffs' property has been suitable for use and has been used by the city and visitors thereto for beach recreational purposes; that it is not true that the city, through its mayor and councilmen, or otherwise, conceived any scheme designed to accomplish the keeping of the property unimproved so it could be used as a public beach recreational area or to depreciate the value of the property so as to enable the public authorities to acquire it at the lowest possible price. The court also found that "reasonable minds might reasonably differ and might have in the year 1941 reasonably differed" as to the following matters: whether the property is or was suitable for residential or commercial development; whether the city would be subjected to liability by reason of the necessity of employing lifeguards, wrecking crews and salvage employees to protect the property and installations thereon from the ravages of high tides and frequent storms; the propriety of the enactment of the zoning restriction declared in section 10 of the 1941 ordinance; and the proper classification

of the property as being within a beach recreational district. Upon such findings the court concluded that the zoning restriction is a valid enactment within the city's police power; that it does not deprive plaintiffs of their property without due process of law or deny them the equal protection of the laws; that it has a foundation in reason and is not a mere arbitrary or irrational exercise of power; and that the scheme of classification and districting followed in the ordinance "has been applied fairly and impartially in the instance of plaintiffs' property."

The state supreme court affirmed, rejecting the landowners' reliance on *Pennsylvania Coal*:

The fact that plaintiffs may suffer some financial detriment does not require invalidation of the zoning restriction, for "every exercise of the police power is apt to affect adversely the property interest of somebody." (Zahn v. Board of Public Works, 195 Cal. 497, 512.) As was said in Wilkins v. City of San Bernardino, *supra*, 29 Cal.2d 332, at page 338: "It is implicit in the theory of police power that an individual cannot complain of incidental injury, if the power is exercised for proper purposes of public health, safety, morals and general welfare, and if there is no arbitrary and unreasonable application in the particular case." While plaintiffs recognize that some value incident to property must yield to the police power, they argue that the zoning restriction as applied to their beach land goes beyond mere regulation and constitutes an unwarranted interference with the use of their property so as to exceed the scope of permissible zoning. They cite in particular the case of Pennsylvania Coal Co. v. Mahon, 260 U.S. 393, 413. But as there stated, "the question depends upon the particular facts." That was an action between two private parties, the statute involved admittedly destroyed previously existing rights of property and contract as reserved between the parties, and the propriety of the statute's prohibition upon the single valuable use of the property for coal-mining operations was considered in relation to special benefits to be gained by an individual rather than by the whole community. In those circumstances application of the statute to the property was held to effect such diminution in its value as to be unconstitutional and beyond the legitimate scope of the police power. . . .

As the record has been reviewed, the zoning restriction of the 1941 ordinance (§10) on the use of plaintiffs' property appears to be a fair, just and reasonable regulation for the general welfare of the city as a whole, and not so burdensome that it contravenes the constitutional guarantees in protection of property rights.

For a holding much more sympathetic to beachfront owners, see King v. Incorporated Village of Ocean Beach, 207 Misc. 100, 136 N.Y.S.2d 690 (Sup. Ct. 1954):

The ordinance in question provides in substance, (1) that no structure of any kind shall be constructed or maintained on any land lying within the affected area, (2) that no structure of any kind, now existing on land within that area, shall be enlarged by structural alteration or otherwise, and (3) that in the event any existing structure now located within that area shall be destroyed, demolished or removed by the action of the elements, by the owner or otherwise, or so substantially destroyed that the structure, in the sole judgment of the board of trustees of the village, amounts to a total loss, then it may not be replaced with any other kind of structure. In short, the owners of the property affected can neither build, enlarge nor replace a structure thereon. All they can do, in the words of counsel for the defendants, is: "They can still walk on it." . . .

This court is therefore of the opinion that the ordinance is confiscatory and an attempt to accomplish without compensation what may only be done legally through the exercise of the power of eminent domain. The purposes which led to the enactment of the ordinance, though laudable, are not sufficient to warrant the taking of private property without paying for it. "While property may be regulated to a certain extent, if regulation goes too far it will be recognized as a taking." (Pennsylvania Coal Co. v. Mahon, 260 U.S. 393.) As Mr. Justice Holmes warned in that case, at page 416: "We are in danger of forgetting that a strong public desire to improve the public condition is not enough to warrant achieving the desire by a shorter cut than the constitutional way of paying for the change."

The Supreme Court's use of an "essential nexus" test in Nollan v. California Coastal Comm'n and the requirement of "rough proportionality" in Dolan v. City of Tigard (both discussed in Chapter Five), will have an impact for years to come on judicial scrutiny not only of such creative coastal zoning, but also of the popular practice of conditioning development approval on certain concessions extracted by the permitting agency.

ROCKHILL v. CHESTERFIELD TOWNSHIP
23 N.J. 117, 128 A.2d 473 (1956)

HEHER, J. The issue here concerns the legal sufficiency of an ordinance of the defendant Township of Chesterfield adopted October 1, 1955, entitled "An ordinance regulating and restricting the location, the size and use of buildings and structures and the use of land in the Township of Chesterfield in the County of Burlington, providing for [its] administration and enforcement . . . fixing penalties for the violation thereof and establishing a zoning board of adjustment."

The regulation is denominated a "zoning ordinance"; and its "purpose" is declared to be: ". . . lessening congestion in the streets; securing safety from fire, panic and other dangers; promoting health, morals or the general welfare; providing adequate light, air and sanitation; preventing the overcrowding of land or buildings; and avoiding undue concentration of population . . .," the statutorily-enumerated consideration of policy involved in use zoning. R.S. 40:55-32, N J.S.A.

But the zoning scheme laid down in the ordinance is not in the conventional pattern; and the inquiry is whether it conforms to the constitutional and statutory principle and policy.

Land and building uses, Article III, shall be "in conformance with the provisions" of the ordinance and the attached "schedule of regulations" entitled "Schedule of Permitted Uses and General Regulations"; and "In addition, certain uses may be permitted and certain modification of requirements may be made in accordance with the special provisions" of the ordinance. "Normal agricultural uses shall be permitted in accordance with the general standards set forth in the schedule." . . .

"Residential uses shall be permitted in accordance with the general standards set forth in the schedule, Article V, including certain "Accessory uses on the same lot and customarily incidental to the permitted dwelling unit," provided that (a) "No dwelling unit shall be located within 250 feet of, or between buildings of an existing or permitted light industrial activity"; (b) where a dwelling unit is located on a corner lot, there shall be a side yard as therein prescribed; and (c) there shall be "off-street parking for all residences," as set down in the schedule.

Provision is then made, Article VI, for "Special Uses"; and this is the declared "Purpose": "In view of the rural characteristics of the Township, it is deemed desirable to permit certain structures and uses but only after investigation has shown that such structures and uses will be beneficial to the general development"; and "In order to assure that such structures and uses meet all requirements and standards, all applications for zoning permits shall be referred to the Planning Board for review in accordance with Revised Statutes 40:55-1.13 [N.J.S.A.]." The planning board is directed to "investigate the matter in accordance with the standards herein provided and submit its recommendations in writing to the Governing Body within 45 days after the filing of the application with the Zoning Officer.". . . And the governing body "shall, no later than the second regularly scheduled meeting after the receipt" of the board's report, "either approve or disapprove the application by resolution based on the standards as set forth" in the ordinance; and "if approved, the necessary zoning permit shall then be issued."

These are the stated "special structures and uses which may be permitted only in keeping with the special standards herein listed," Article VI: (a) an "existing one-family dwelling may be converted into multi-family dwelling units," subject to certain conditions and specifications and the submission of the plans to the planning board "prior to approval or disapproval"; (b) "Neighborhood business" may be permitted subject to prescribed physical conditions . . . ; (c) "Designed shopping center units may be permitted" subject to specified conditions, and "Any business use that is not specifically prohibited within the Township and not included in Section 3, paragraph b, of Article VI may be considered to be a permitted business use if the Planning Board deems such business use to be desirable and to the best interests of the Township," provided that "An area at least five feet in width and following the lot lines of the business property if adjacent to residential properties shall be properly landscaped to form a buffer screen between residential and business uses," and the required illumination during evening business periods "shall be shielded from adjacent residential properties and public roads or streets"; (d) "Gasoline and Filling stations may be permitted" if certain requirements are met . . .; (e) "Restaurants and roadside refreshment uses may be permitted," at the same distances from other land uses prescribed in (d) *supra*, and provided, inter alia, that parking space "shall be available to adequately meet maximum capacity conditions," and parking areas shall be illuminated during evening business operations and "shielded from adjacent residential properties and public roads or streets"; (f) "Light industrial uses and other similar facilities having no adverse effect on surrounding property and deemed desirable to the general economic well-being of the Township may be permitted," and "Included among such uses may be administrative offices, laboratories, research offices and light manufacturing or processing," provided that the "industrial activity shall not by its own inherent characteristics or industrial processes be noxious or injurious to the adjacent properties by reason of the production or emission of dust, smoke, refuse matter, odor, gas, fumes, noise, vibration, unsightly conditions, or other similar conditions," also that certain sanitation requirements shall be met, and that no "building or structure" shall be located within 1,000 feet of an "existing or proposed school or public facility" or 250 feet from the "adjoining lot line of any existing dwelling unit" or 200 feet from the "adjoining lot line of any business use"; and (g) "Public utility uses such as distribution lines, towers, substations and telephone exchanges but no service or storage yards may be permitted," provided the planning board finds that the "design of any structure in connection with [the] facility conforms to the general character of the surrounding area and will in no way adversely affect the safe and comfortable enjoyment of property rights of the Township," and there is provision for "adequate and attractive fences and other safety devices" and "sufficient landscaping . . . periodically maintained.". . .

Certain uses are prohibited altogether, Article IX . . . these among others: "Commercial or periodic auction sales"; "Used car lots or used car sales"; "Tourist cabins, motels and trailer camps"; "Manufacture or sale of pottery and cast stone decorations"; "Drive-in theatres"; "Slaughter houses and abattoirs"; "Junk yards and scrap reclamation"; "Garbage-fed piggeries"; "Billboards and advertising of products not for sale on the premises"; "Salvage and wrecking activities"; and "Multi-family dwelling units, other than permitted conversions; and similar types of uses of land, structures and buildings so adjudged by the Zoning Board of Adjustment.". . .

The Law Division of the Superior Court set aside Article VI, section 3(c) iv, of the ordinance providing that "any business use . . . not specifically prohibited" within the township, and not included in section 3, paragraph B of that Article, "may be considered to be a permitted business use," if the planning board deems such use "to be desirable and to the best interest of the township," as a regulation wanting in "proper constitutional standards to guide the administrative action" of the board and the township committee, but sustained the ordinance otherwise; and we certified here plaintiff's appeal from so much of the judgment as affirms the ordinance in part. There was no cross-appeal. . . .

The constitutional and statutory zoning principle is territorial division according to the character of the lands and structures and their peculiar suitability for particular uses, and uniformity of use within the division. And the legislative grant of authority has the selfsame delineation. R.S. 40:55-30, as amended by L. 1948, c. 305, p. 1221, N J.S.A.

The local governing body is empowered, R.S. 40:55-3 1, as amended by L. 1948, c. 305, N J.S.A., to divide the municipality into districts of such number, shape, and area as may be deemed best suited to carry out the statutory policy, and to regulate and restrict the construction and use of buildings and other structures and the use of land within such districts, provided that "All such regulations shall be uniform for each class or kind of buildings or other structures or uses of land throughout each district, but the regulations in one district may be different from those in other districts." And such regulations shall be, R.S. 40:55-32, N.J.S.A., in accordance with a "comprehensive plan and designed" to subserve the public welfare in one or more of the enumerated particulars involving the public health, safety, morals, or the general welfare, and "shall be made with reasonable consideration, among other things, to the character of the district and its peculiar suitability for particular uses, and with a view of conserving the value of property and encouraging the most appropriate use of land throughout such municipality." And thus it is basic to the local exercise of the power that the use restrictions be general and uniform in the particular district, delimited in keeping with the constitutional and statutory considerations; otherwise, there would be the arbitrary discrimination at war with the substance of due process and the equal protection of the laws.

The scheme of the ordinance is the negation of zoning. It overrides the basic concept of use zoning by districts, that is to say, territorial division according to the character of the lands and structures and their peculiar use suitability and a comprehensive regulatory plan to advance the general good within the prescribed range of the police power. The local design is "normal agricultural" and residence uses and the specified "special uses" by the authority of the planning board and the local governing body, generally where "investigation has shown that such structures and uses will be beneficial to the general development," and "light industrial uses and other similar facilities having no adverse effect on surrounding property and deemed desirable to the general economic well-being of the Township," terms hardly adequate to channel local administrative discretion but, at all events, making for the "piecemeal" and "spot" zoning alien to the constitutional and statutory principle of land use zoning by districts and comprehensive planning for the fulfillment of the declared policy. The fault is elementary and vital; the rule of the ordinance is ultra vires and void. See Raskin v. Town of Morristown, 21 NJ. 180, 121 A.2d 378 (1956).

Reserving the use of the whole of the municipal area for "normal agricultural" and residence uses, and then providing for all manner of "special uses," "neighborhood" and other businesses, even "light industrial" uses and "other similar facilities," placed according to local discretion without regard to districts, ruled by vague and illusive criteria, is indeed the antithesis of zoning. It makes for arbitrary and discriminatory interference with the basic right of private property, in no real sense concerned with the essential common welfare. The statute, N.J.S.A. 40:55-39, provides for regulation by districts and for exceptions and variances from the prescribed land uses under given conditions. The course taken here would flout this essential concept of district zoning according to a comprehensive plan designed to fulfill the declared statutory policy. Comprehensive zoning means an orderly and coordinate system of community development according to socio-economic needs. See Professor Haar's exposition of the relation between planning principles and the exercise of the zoning power, "In Accordance With a Comprehensive Plan," 68 Harv. L. Rev. 1154, and the comment, p. 1170, that the phrase "in accordance with a comprehensive plan" apparently had its origin in section 3 of the Standard State Zoning Enabling Act, accompanied by this explanatory note: "This will prevent haphazard or piecemeal zoning.". . .

Zoning and planning are not identical in concept. Mansfield & Swett, Inc., v. Town of West Orange, 120 N.J.L. 145, 198 A. 225 (Sup. Ct. 1938). Zoning is a separation of the municipality into districts for the most appropriate use of the land, by general rules according to a comprehensive plan for the common good in matters within the domain of the police power. And, though the landowner does not have a vested right to a particular zone classification, one of the essential purposes of zoning regulation is the stabilization of property uses. Investments are made in lands and structures on the faith of district use control having some degree of permanency, a well considered plan that will stand until changing conditions dictate otherwise. Such is the nature of use zoning by districts according to a comprehensive plan. The regulations here are in contravention of the principle.

The ordinance is vacated as ultra vires the enabling statute; and the cause is remanded for judicial action accordingly. . . .

Notes

1. Consider an ordinance that defines a "residence district" as

> a territory or district within 1000 feet in a direct line in every direction from the nearest part of a building proposed or intended to be located, built, constructed or used for the purpose of a factory or manufacturing plant, in which territory or district more than half of the existing buildings are used wholly or partly for residential purposes.

Do you see any problems with this language? See Matter of Kensington-Davis Corp. v. Schwab, 239 N.Y. 54, 145 N.E. 738 (1924) ("This is not a division into districts, within the meaning of the [state] statute.").

2. In 1984, the Hardin County (Kentucky) Fiscal Court adopted a Development Guidance System, which, according to the trial court opinion adopted by the state supreme court in Hardin County v. Jost, 897 S.W.2d 592, 593-95, 597 (Ky. 1995),

> is said to be unique in the Commonwealth of Kentucky and, perhaps, in the United States. It admittedly does not follow the traditional approach of establishing separate zones for particular types of development with identifiable permitted and conditional uses. Instead, it designates the entire unincorporated area of the county as one zone, and designates three types of uses for that zone. Agricultural and single family residential uses are designated as "uses-by-right." Uses having a negative impact on the quality and supply of water, or which endanger public health, or historic sites, are designated as "prohibited uses" (as are certain flashing signs). Everything else is designated as a "conditional use." Conditional use is defined as "a use of land or activity permitted

only after fulfillment of all local regulations." Thus, anyone desiring to use his property for any purpose other than agricultural or single family residential use must obtain a conditional use permit. The Development Guidance System contains no provision for a board of adjustment, but vests the traditional functions of that board in the planning commission. Thus, the commission's functions include not only preparation of the comprehensive plan and any amendments, but also the functions of a traditional board of adjustment, including hearing and deciding applications for conditional use permits.

A landowner seeking a permit to operate an Animal Refuge Center challenged the validity of the ordinance when she was denied a conditional use permit. The trial court reasoned:

> It is clear that in enacting KRS chapter 100, the legislature considered careful planning as a prerequisite of good zoning. A comprehensive plan must have general application throughout the community, so that the facts to be considered do not relate as such to a particular individual or the status of his property. Zoning must conform to planning, so as to prohibit indiscriminate, ad hoc zoning. Thus, in Kindred Homes, Inc. v. Dean, Ky. App., 605 S.W.2d 15 (1979), a comprehensive plan which relegated the entire unincorporated areas of Jessamine County to an agricultural zone, so that modifications could only be made piecemeal, was struck down as contrary to the very theory of zoning. And in Rockhill v. Township of Chesterfield, 23 N.J. 117, 128 A.2d 473 (1956), the supreme court of New Jersey struck down an ordinance almost identical to Hardin County's ordinance, holding that reserving the use of the whole of the area to agricultural and residential use, then providing for all manner of "special uses" was the antithesis of zoning. "It makes for arbitrary and discriminatory interference with the basic right of private property, in no real sense concerned with the essential common welfare." Id., 128 A.2d at 479.

The supreme court concluded: "The naked labeling of all uses other than agricultural or residential uses as "conditional uses" leaves land use to the subjective whim and caprice of the zoning authority."

3. Not all state courts are averse to some departures from the zoning norm. In a recent Wyoming case, Laughter v. Board of County Comm'rs, 110 P.3d 875, 878, 887 (Wyo. 2005), landowners attempted to convince the court that the Sweetwater County Growth Area Management Plan contained the same fatal flaw as Chesterfield Township's scheme. They had purchased land in the Urban Reserve Study Area, governed by the following regulation:

> The purpose of the urban reserve study area is to allow established commercial agriculture, grazing, livestock trailing and animal migration uses to continue on agriculturally-zoned areas within the urbanizing area that have long-term potential for urban growth, while Sweetwater County studies the most appropriate zoning and regulations for the area. These Urban Reserve Areas are zoned agriculture on Exhibit "B." This area shall be under study for a three-year period of time with the option to extend the length of the study period if it becomes necessary. The study period will begin upon the adoption of the agreement.

> During this time frame existing commercial[,] agriculture, grazing, livestock trailing, animal migration and oil/gas/mineral extraction are all considered permitted uses within this area. All other proposed uses, including residential accessory use, will require a Conditional Use Permit or a zone change depending on the nature of the application.

Each application will be reviewed on a case-by-case basis. The availability of public water will be a consideration/condition [for] each Conditional Use Permit and/or zone change.

The Supreme Court of Wyoming was unimpressed with the landowners' reliance on *Rockhill*:

The gist of the landowners' illegal restraint argument is that the county's extensive conditional use permit system is the antithesis of zoning. In other words, instead of a conditional use permit system designed to consider land uses not specifically allowed in a particular zoning district, the county uses the special permit process to control all land uses, whether or not consistent with underlying zoning. . . . This is not sufficient analysis from which we can conclude that the county's dissimilar conditional use permit structure violates Wyoming's statutes or constitution. There is simply no showing in this case that a temporary work program containing special study areas designed to deal with urbanization, superimposed on an existing zoning scheme, is an illegal restraint on land use.

4. If a municipality chooses not to adopt cumulative zoning, is that too drastic a departure to merit judicial approval? In Grubel v. MacLaughlin, 286 F. Supp. 24, 27-29 (D.V.I. 1968), here's what one federal district court judge found when surveying the decisional law concerning the legitimacy of what is known as "noncumulative zoning":

The type of zoning regulation with which we are here concerned—a regulation which does not include residential use of property within its permitted uses—is a rather recent innovation. The presence of homes in industrial and commercial areas has been a matter of every-day experience. But under the modern view, as we shall see, a comprehensive plan for the development of separate districts for residential and commercial purposes may be appropriate, and, indeed, under some circumstances, necessary.

It is settled that the exclusion of all industrial and commercial establishments from residential districts may bear a rational relation to the health and safety of the community. Euclid v. Ambler Realty Co., 1926, 272 U.S. 365. And, it has likewise been held that an ordinance excluding residences from an area zoned for industrial and commercial purposes may, under particular circumstances, be a valid exercise of the police power. Lamb v. City of Monroe, 1959, 358 Mich. 136, 99 N.W.2d 566; People v. Village of Morton Grove, 1959, 16 Ill. 2d 183, 157 N.E.2d 33, 35-36; Roney v. Board of Supervisors of Contra Costa County, 1956, 138 Cal. App. 2d 740, 292 P.2d 529; Corthouts v. Town of Newington, 1953, 140 Conn. 284, 99 A.2d 112, 114, 38 A.L.R.2d 1136, 1139-1140.

Whether such a zoning regulation is valid depends, of course, upon the facts of the particular case. Thus an ordinance has been held valid which excluded residences from an industrial zone where there was no showing that the land thus restricted was not usable for industrial purposes within a reasonable time. Roney v. Board of Supervisors of Contra Costa County, 1956, 138 Cal. App. 2d 740, 292 P.2d 529. On the other hand an amendment to a zoning regulation was held unreasonable and confiscatory which rezoned property from residential to solely industrial use where it was shown that the land was adaptable to and in demand for residential purposes but was not needed, and would not in the near future be needed, for industrial development. Corthouts v. Town of Newington, 1953, 140 Conn. 284, 99 A.2d 112, 38 A.L.R.2d 1136.

The basic rationale underlying the separation of residential from commercial areas—whether the particular case involves the exclusion of businesses from a residential area or the converse, the exclusion of dwellings from a business area—is the same. It is recognized that sound social, economic and governmental policy may dictate a separation of residential areas from commercial and industrial areas. Duffcon Concrete Products v. Borough of Cresskill, 1949, 1 N.J. 509, 64 A.2d 347, 351, 9 A.L.R.2d 678. The growing complexity of our civilization, the multiplying forms of industry, the dangers of heavy traffic in mixed residential and commercial districts, the noise, the fumes—are all factors which may well justify the allocation of industries, commercial businesses and dwellings to separate districts in order to promote and preserve the general welfare of the community.

Nor is it valid any longer to consider the problem in terms of a "higher" use or a "lower" use. The Supreme Court of Illinois has rejected the assertion that a zoning ordinance excluding residential development in commercial and industrial districts conflicted with the generally acknowledged principle that zoning was intended to preserve rather than to restrict dwellings, saying: "the only constitutional limitation upon a municipality's power to exclude future residences from commercial and industrial districts is that the exclusion bear a substantial relationship to the preservation of the public health, safety, morals, or general welfare." People ex rel. Skokie Town House Builders Inc., v. Village of Morton Grove, 1959, 16 Ill. 2d 183, 157 N.E.2d 33, 35-36. And in Lamb v. City of Monroe, 1959, 358 Mich. 136, 99 N.W.2d 566, 570-571, the court observed that the statement of the problem in terms of higher use versus lower use, or more desirable versus less desirable use, was misleading; the question of such zoning being one of reasonableness under the circumstances of the case. See, also, Roney v. Board of Supervisors of Contra Costa County, 1956, 138 Cal. App. 2d 740, 292 P.2d 529, 532, where the court stated:

> * * * it cannot be held that there is anything arbitrary or unreasonable per se in the plan of zoning to prevent the so-called 'higher' uses from invading a "lower" use area, a plan described by respondent as "exclusive industrial zoning." In fact, the term "higher" as applied to residential uses, or to uses closer than others to domestic purposes, is not an accurate one; for, although the use of property for homes is "higher" in the sense that commercial and industrial uses exist for the purpose of serving family life, the better these secondary uses can accomplish their purpose, the better is the primary use of property served. Moreover, the early decline of new residential districts into blighted areas by their being surrounded by heavy industry is prevented. These considerations, added to those of public health and safety by removing residences from fumes, as set forth above, and viewed in the light of the law that regards the police power as capable of expansion to meet existing conditions of modern life, * * * place the ordinance with its exclusive industrial feature and the decision of the governing authorities well within the limits of those legislative and administrative acts which are acts where reasonable minds might differ, and therefore, not subject to judicial interference.

It is thus clear that there is no rule of law, statutory or constitutional, which ordains that any particular use has an exalted position in a zoning scheme entitling it to move everywhere as of right. Kozesnik v. Montgomery Twp., 1957, 24 N.J. 154, 131 A.2d 1, 9.

Today, many "traditional" zoning ordinances create exclusive commercial and industrial zones. In this one aspect, those New Urbanists who strongly advocate mixed uses as a reaction to strict segregation of homes find themselves closer in theory to the early zoners.

EVES v. ZONING BOARD OF ADJUSTMENT OF LOWER GWYNEDD TOWNSHIP
401 Pa. 211, 164 A.2d 7 (1960)

COHEN, Justice. These appeals, involving specifically the validity of two ordinances which amend respectively the general zoning ordinance and the zoning map of Lower Gwynedd Township, present the problem of the validity of a method of zoning aptly termed by the appellants as "flexible selective zoning."

On April 28, 1958 the Board of Supervisors of Lower Gwynedd Township adopted Ordinance 28 which officially amended the General Zoning Ordinance of the township to provide for the new zoning district known as "F-1" Limited Industrial District. This ordinance sets forth in detail the requirements, conditions and restrictive uses for an "F-1" classification, including the requirements that any proposed development be constructed in accordance with an overall plan; that any plan shall be designed as a single architectural scheme with appropriate common landscaping and shall provide a minimum size of 25 acres; that adequate parking space shall be provided for all employees and visitors' vehicles; that parking, loading or service areas used by motor vehicles shall be located within the lot lines of the Limited Industrial District, and shall be physically separated from the public streets by a buffer strip; that no building or other permanent structure, nor parking lot, shall be located within 200 feet of a public street, right-of-way, or property line; and that the area of land occupied by the buildings shall not exceed 10% of each site within the Limited Industrial District. The ordinance reserves the right in the board of supervisors to prescribe particular requirements or any further reasonable conditions deemed appropriate with respect to the suitability of the Limited Industrial District in the neighborhood.

Ordinance 28, however, does not itself delineate the boundaries of those specific areas which are to be classified as "F-1" districts. Instead, the ordinance outlines a procedure whereby anyone may submit to the board an application requesting that his land be rezoned to "F-1" limited industrial, together with plans showing the nature of the industry the applicant wishes to establish and the conformity of any proposed construction with the requirements of the district as enumerated in the ordinance. The supervisors must in turn refer the application and plans to the Planning Commission of Lower Gwynedd Township, which is to review them and then return them to the supervisors accompanied by its recommendations within 45 days. The board of supervisors must then hold public hearings and finally decide whether or not to reject or approve the application and accordingly amend the zoning map. The ordinance finally provides that should any successful applicant fail to undertake substantial construction of any proposed building within 18 months after the rezoning, or after the issuance of a permit for an area previously zoned "F-1" Limited Industrial District, the area is to revert to its former zoning classification.

Pursuant to the terms of Ordinance 28, on September 11, 1958, the Moore Construction Company, a Pennsylvania corporation desiring to construct an industrial plant and a sewage treatment plant in Lower Gwynedd Township, applied for a rezoning of a 103 acre tract of land known as the "Hardwick Tract" from "A residential to "F-1" Limited Industrial. A public hearing was held by the supervisors to consider the rezoning on September 20, 1958, at which time a petition signed by 300 residents, all property owners, who opposed the change, was filed. On January 5, 1959, the supervisors adopted Ordinance 34 which rezoned the area in question to the requested "F-1" classification (although it reduced the area rezoned from 103 acres to 86 acres). On January 14, 1959, a certificate of conformity (building permit) was issued to the Moore Products Company.

Schuyler Eves, a resident of the township, and the Sisters of Mercy appealed to the zoning board, challenging the validity of the two ordinances on the grounds that they were unconstitutional and that they failed to conform to the enabling legislation. Sustaining the validity of the ordinances, the board dismissed the appeal. The Court of Common Pleas of Montgomery County affirmed and these appeals followed.

The authority of a municipality to enact zoning legislation must be strictly construed. "Any fair, reasonable doubt as to the existence of power is resolved by the courts against its existence in the corporation, and therefore denied." Kline v. City of Harrisburg, 1949, 362 Pa. 438, 443, 68 A.2d 182, 185. Appellants' principal contention is that the zoning scheme as contemplated by ordinances 28 and 34 fails to comport with the same enabling legislation from which the township derives its power to zone. After having thoroughly examined the relevant portions of that statute, we are in complete accord.

"Zoning is the legislative division of a community into areas in each of which only certain designated uses of land are permitted so that the community may develop in an orderly manner in accordance with a comprehensive plan." Best v. Zoning Board of Adjustment, 1958, 393 Pa. 106, 110, 141 A.2d 606, 609. The zoning regulations of a second class township, by legislative edict, must be the implementation of such a comprehensive plan. Just what the precise attributes of a comprehensive plan must be, or the extent to which the plan must approach a development plan for the township formulated by a planning commission should one exist is not now before us. See Haar, In Accordance With a Comprehensive Plan, 68 Harv. L. Rev. 1154 (1955), Kozesnik v. Township of Montgomery, 1957, 24 NJ. 154, 131 A.2d 1. For present purposes, it is only important to point out that the focus of any plan is land use, and the considerations in the formulation of a plan for the orderly development of a community must be made with regard thereto. This positive focus is thrust upon the township supervisors by the enabling legislation itself, for their "purpose in view" in fulfilling their zoning functions must be to enact regulations

> designed to lessen congestion in the roads and highways; to secure safety from fire, panic and other dangers; to promote health and the general welfare; to provide adequate light and air; to prevent the overcrowding of land; to avoid undue congestion of the population; to facilitate the adequate provision of transportation, water, sewerage, schools, parks and other public requirements. Such regulations shall be made with reasonable consideration, among other things, to the character of the district and its peculiar suitability for particular uses, and with a view to conserving the value of buildings and encouraging the most appropriate use of land throughout such municipality.

Second Class Township Code, § 2003, 53 P.S. § 67003. And since any zoning ordinance must be enacted in accordance with the comprehensive plan, the plan itself, embodying resolutions of land use and restrictions, must have been at the point of enactment a final formulation.

The role of the township supervisors in the field of zoning, as contemplated by the enabling legislation, emerges quite clearly upon consideration of the powers granted the supervisors and the duties they are bound to perform. Their duty is to implement the comprehensive plan by enacting zoning regulations in accordance therewith. Section 2003, 53 P.S. § 67003. They are to shape the land uses "into districts of such number, shape and area as may be deemed best suited to carry out the purpose of this article. . . ," Section 2002, 53 P.S. § 67002, which "purpose in view" is set out above in Section 2003. They may regulate or restrict "the erection, construction, reconstruction, alteration, repair or use of buildings, structures or land" within any district, and may regulate one district differently from the next, but all "such regulations shall be uniform for each class or kind of buildings throughout each district. . . ." Section 2002, 53 P.S. § 67002. All such regulations are to be embodied initially in a general zoning ordinance for the township, which may be subsequently amended, supplemented or repealed by the supervisors as conditions require, Section 2004,53 P.S. § 67004, although again such alterations must be "in accordance with a comprehensive plan."

The zoning scheme as outlined by Ordinances 28 and 34 is at variance with these legislative directives for second class townships in two objectionable ways: (1) The ordinances were not enacted "in accordance with a comprehensive plan" and (2) they devolve upon the township supervisors duties quite beyond those duties outlined for them in the enabling legislation. Accordingly, the ordinances are invalid and the certificates of conformity (building permits) were improperly issued.

The adoption of a procedure whereby it is decided which areas of land will eventually be zoned "F-1" Limited Industrial Districts on a case by case basis patently admits that at the point of enactment of Ordinance 28 there was no orderly plan of particular land use for the community. Final determination under such a scheme would expressly await solicitation by individual landowners, thus making the planned land use of the community dependent upon its development. In other words, the development itself would become the plan, which is manifestly the antithesis of zoning "in accordance with a comprehensive plan."

Several secondary evils of such a scheme are cogently advanced by counsel for the appellants. It would produce situations in which the personal predilections of the supervisors or the affluence or political power of the applicant would have a greater part in determining rezoning applications than the suitability of the land for a particular use from an overall community point of view. Further, while it may not be readily apparent with a minimum acreage requirement of 25 acres, "flexible selective zoning" carries evils akin to "spot zoning," for in theory it allows piecemeal placement of relatively small acreage areas in differently zoned districts. Finally, because of the absence of a simultaneous delineation of the boundaries of the new "F-1" district, no notice of the true nature of his vicinity or its limitations is afforded the property owner or the prospective property owner. While it is undoubtedly true that a property owner has no vested interest in an existing zoning map and, accordingly, is always subject to the possibility of a rezoning without notice, the zoning ordinance and its accompanying zoning maps should nevertheless at any given time reflect the current planned use of the community's land so as to afford as much notice as possible.

Appellees vigorously contend that a comprehensive plan does exist for the Township of Lower Gwynedd and is set forth in the record. Essentially, appellees argue, the plan contemplates a "greenbelt" township predominately residential in character with a certain amount of compatible non-residential occupancy consisting of shopping centers, research and engineering centers and limited industrial uses. It also contemplates that these non-residential uses shall be strictly controlled as to setback, building area, noise, smoke, sewage disposal, etc., and that the means of such control shall be vested in the supervisors through strict ordinances of general application such as Ordinance 28, *supra*, setting up the requirements and limitations on limited industrial uses. In turn, these tools of control and minimum standards are to be the polestars (along with other factors, such as the proximity of through highways, availability of adequate streams for effluent disposal, etc.), in any further consideration to be given by the planning commission and the supervisors to applications for specific locations or areas. By adopting this approach, the appellees have confused comprehensive planning with a comprehensive plan. The foregoing are certainly the rudiments and fundamentals which enter into the promulgation of a planned zoning scheme for the township. They are, however, only the most preliminary and basic considerations from which the ultimate decision[s] of selective land uses are to be made. Until such time, no final formulation exists which satisfies the "comprehensive plan" requirement within the meaning of the enabling legislation.

As to the second objection, the township supervisors have gone beyond their function of implementing a comprehensive plan with zoning regulations: they are to analyze on a case by case basis for rezoning purposes individual applications and accompanying technical plans for structure and development to determine their suitability and compliance with the standards they themselves established in the ordinance.

In the enabling legislation, only the specialized township board of adjustment was empowered to permit deviations from the prevailing zoning regulations on a case by case basis, and then only by means of two detailed procedures — variances and special exceptions. § 2007, 53 P.S. § 67007. To obtain either, a petitioner must follow a system specifically devised to give certain protection to any affected property owners. To obtain a variance, a petitioner must convince the board of adjustment that "owing to special conditions a literal enforcement of the provisions of the ordinance will result in unnecessary hardship, and . . . that the spirit of the ordinance shall be observed and substantial justice done." Section 2007, 53 P.S. § 67007. The board's determination is then subject to careful review by our courts to assure that in exercising its discretion in these matters the board of adjustment has adhered to the statutory standards. And in reviewing such matters, this Court has been quite demanding. See, e.g., Luciany v. Zoning Board of Adjustment, 1960, 399 Pa. 176, 159 A.2d 701; Springfield Township Zoning Case, 1960, 399 Pa. 53, 159 A.2d 684. Those who protest against the variance are allowed to resist any change both before the board and in the courts. Section 2007, 53 P.S. § 67007.

Special exceptions are handled somewhat differently, but similar safeguards are still provided. In planning the original comprehensive ordinance, the supervisors may anticipate that certain special uses for particular districts may become desirable, even though, to some extent, they should be in derogation of the character of the district. The ordinance will then provide that an exceptional use may exist within a particular district if the board of adjustment determines its availability. Such uses are thus made available as a privilege, assuming that the requisite facts and conditions detailed in the ordinance are found to exist. Again, there is scrutinizing court review to assure that the board has not overstepped its boundaries of prudent discretion. Importantly, all property owners are put on notice of the possibility of an exceptional use within their district because such use is set out originally as part of the district's scheme in the ordinance.

Under the "flexible selective zoning" scheme here under attack, changes in the prevailing zoning regulations are to be made on a case by case basis, not, however, by a specialized body such as the zoning board of adjustment, but by the legislative body, without rigid statutory standards and without any scintilla of notice of potential change as in the case of special exceptions. The standard review by the courts, as indeed the appellees argue we should adopt herein, would be nothing more than to assure ourselves that each legislative act of amending the zoning map by the township supervisors was not "arbitrary, capricious, or unreasonable." If the legislature contemplated such a novel scheme of zoning, withdrawing as it does a close standard of court review in the very delicate area of protecting property rights, and shifting as it does the focus from planned use to individual solicitation, we are convinced it would have said so in more clear and exact terms than are found anywhere in the enabling legislation.

Order reversed.

Notes

1. Three years earlier, in Huff v. Board of Zoning Appeals, 214 Md. 48, 133 A.2d 83 (1957), Maryland's high court, in upholding the use of floating zones, stated: "A zoning plan does not cease to be a comprehensive plan because it looks to reasonably foreseeable potential uses of land which cannot be precisely determined when the zoning is passed."

In response to the Pennsylvania decision, Charles M. Haar & Barbara Hering, in *The Lower Gwynedd Township Case: Too Flexible Zoning or an Inflexible Judiciary?*, 74 Harv. L. Rev. 1552, 1574-75 (1961), offered the following observation:

> [T]he *Gwynedd Township* case has usefully, albeit hesitantly, launched an examination of the relations between planning, zoning, and the regulatory ordinances of implementation. If the court is indicating approval of alignment of zoning principles with planning principles advocated by professional planners, the decision represents a significant advance in judicial thinking on land-use problems. The progress of the courts would be simplified by rethinking by the legislative branch. The legislature should define clearly what it means by its requirement of a "comprehensive plan." . . .
>
> New conditions in metropolitan areas require new approaches to zoning, outlooks which stress flexibility and individualization for the large, integrated undertaking. What the *Gwynedd Township* court may be doing is to leave these definitions to statutory directive. Herein lies the creative challenge to the state legislature—to participate in remolding land-use controls in attaining realistic policies for guiding land development.

Eventually lawmakers and judges responded to this call for flexibility, as illustrated by the many post-Euclidean devices that typify the modern zoning ordinance.

2. For a more recent Maryland case comparing floating zones with special exceptions, conditional zoning, and other concepts, see Mayor & Council of Rockville v. Rylyns Enters., 372 Md. 514, 814 A.2d 469 (2002). For other jurisdictions approving the use of floating zones, see Rodgers v. Tarrytown, 302 N.Y. 115, 96 N.E.2d 731 (1951); Sheridan v. Planning Bd. of Stamford, 159 Conn. 1, 266 A.2d 396 (1969); and Bellemeade Co. v. Priddle, 503 S.W.2d 734, 738 (Ky. 1973), in which the court explained:

> "The phrase 'floating zone' has been coined to designate a method of zoning whereby selected uses of property are authorized in districts devoted to other uses under terms and conditions laid down in the ordinance themselves." Zoning Law and Practice, Yokley, 3d Ed., p. 133, Sec. 3.7. A floating zone is differentiated from a fixed ("Euclidean") zone in that the latter is a specifically defined area under the zoning ordinance, while the boundaries of the former are undefined and it "floats" over the entire district until by appropriate action the boundaries are fixed and it is anchored. Furthermore, it is the landowner who instigates the procedure which results in the settling of the floating zone.

Fasano v. Board of County Comm'rs, an important decision included in Chapter Four, involved a floating zone as well.

3. Professor Craig Anthony (Tony) Arnold, in *Planning Milagros: Environmental Justice and Land Use Regulation*, 76 Denv. U. L. Rev. 1, 120-21 (1998), has warned environmental justice advocates that this technique, in the wrong regulator's hands, could place special burdens on vulnerable populations:

> Floating zones are flexible zoning techniques that require particular scrutiny and monitoring by environmental justice groups to ensure that low-income communities and neighborhoods of color are not assigned harmful or burdensome floating uses. . . .
>
> Floating zones pose an uncertain threat to local residents and landowners, who do not know whether a neighboring property will be chosen for a floating zone use. If it is chosen for this designation, they may face (in some cases, literally!) an unexpected new

use. Furthermore, floating zones appear to be used most often for either industrial uses or high-density residential uses. For example, in McQuail v. Shell Oil Co., [183 A.2d 572, 574 (1962),] New Castle County, Delaware, applied an industrial floating zone to an undeveloped parcel previously zoned residential, so that Shell Oil Co. could build a refinery. Residents of low-income and minority neighborhoods may find that property zoned for nonintensive uses, for example residential, may be rezoned for industrial uses through the application of a floating zone at the request of the landowner. In fact, parcels in these neighborhoods might be particularly attractive to industrial companies wanting to take advantage of floating zones for their activities: the land may be cheaper; local residents might not have the political power, information, or resources to oppose the rezoning; there would likely be other nearby industrial uses or industrially zoned property; and there might be proximity to transportation facilities like railroads, interstate freeways, waterways, and airports. In addition, the decision about whether or not to apply a floating zone to a particular parcel or tract will be made on the basis of criteria already established at the creation of the use initially. Therefore, grassroots environmental groups should pay particular attention to the existence of unmapped floating zones in local zoning codes and any possible requests to apply those zones in their neighborhoods. They will need to be politically active in opposing any unwanted floating zones, both in the text (the existence of the unmapped district altogether) and on the map (the application of the zone to land in their neighborhoods). Opposition to particular applications of floating zones will be most successful when based on the articulated criteria, as well as political activity.

V. The Euclidean Zoning Trio of Height, Bulk, and Use: Seeking Judicial Checks on Arbitrary Application of Zoning Tools

Imagine that you are commissioned to render the visual richness of a golden sunset from the perspective of an ocean beach on a cloudy day—and that you are given just three crayons and a clean, white canvas. While a few gifted artists might be up to the challenge, for the vast majority of us this would be an impossible task. Now imagine that you are a planner or local elected official who is seeking to accomplish a highly nuanced and detailed urban design—and that you are given just three basic land use tools: the Euclidean trio of height, bulk, and use controls. While you would have no trouble excluding from the design those structures that are too tall, that have a footprint that is too massive, or that house undesirable or incompatible functions, you will also find that you will often be (1) outlawing buildings and uses that do not fit into traditional categories, (2) encouraging uniformity from builders and landowners who seek to take full advantage of the development envelope, and (3) conveying the message that zoning is a very inflexible system that stifles creativity and experimentation. Sometimes judges will back up local zoning authorities who are not only striving to realize an urban design but also engaging in the practice of social engineering. At other times, as several of the cases that follow illustrate, judges will rely on federal and state constitutional principles to outlaw zoning practices that stray from the Euclidean mold.

A. Is Zoning About Use, Ownership, or Both?

Should the form of ownership—fee simple, leasehold, condominium or cooperative—be irrelevant to land use regulators? The debate between the majority and dissenting opinions in the following case illustrates a sharp difference of opinion regarding the negative effects of owning rather than renting a small house. In your opinion whose position is more convincing, and why? By way of background for the case, you should know that bungalow courts were a popular form of residential development in southern California in the years before World War II. James R. Curtis & Larry Ford, in *Bungalow Courts in San Diego: Monitoring a Sense of Place*, J. San Diego Hist., Spring 1998 (available at http://www.sandiegohistory.org/journal/88spring/bungalow.htm), have provided this useful historical account:

> In the years immediately following World War I, revolutionary social changes were occurring in American cities. Many of these changes would soon affect the housing market as new types of people located so as to do new types of things. For example, large numbers of young, single women entered the labor force as office workers in the new downtown skyscrapers. Large numbers of young men returned from service in the military and, having been uprooted from family and tradition, sought new opportunities in the cities. Mass transit lines sprang up everywhere enabling people to move en masse to the edges of the metropolis. The old housing stock, consisting largely of single family homes and subdivided (tenement-ized) buildings was ill-suited to this new demand. Boarding houses were out and the apartment was in.

> In Southern California, a utopian new type of housing evolved to provide dwellings for those who dreamed of a house and garden but who could either not afford one or were too busy to be bothered with the upkeep—a new type of housing for those who longed for an independent lifestyle but one with a strong sense of community and security. This type of housing was the bungalow court. . . .

> It was in 1909 that the first bungalow court appeared, reportedly an innovation of architect Sylvanus Marston who built eleven full-sized bungalows in a court arrangement in Pasadena. Derived in all likelihood from Eastern resort communities, the typical bungalow court came to feature a group of six to ten small, individual houses placed around a communal garden. Usually two standard lots were enough.

> Bungalow courts were seen as a compromise between expensive and demanding single-family homes on the one hand, and the "indecent propinquities" of apartment life on the other. They could offer settings with sufficient density for a sense of community and shared responsibility while still allowing the space for greenery and even private gardens. Much of the early literature on courts suggested that in them, a great deal of daily living could be communal with people taking turns cooking, washing, gardening, etc. with social life centered in a sort of dining hall/social center. Although these Utopian ideals did not work out, in part because self-contained household appliances came on the market at the same time such as small stoves, refrigerators, vacuum cleaners, electric irons, and radios, courts continued to be seen as an ideal setting for community involvement. In fact, some were referred to as "community courts." Thus, bungalow courts featured the aesthetics of the bungalow in the garden coupled with the ideology of semi-communal living in a friendly place.

CLEMONS v. CITY OF LOS ANGELES
36 Cal. 2d 95, 222 P.2d 439 (1950)

SPENCE, Justice. . . .

It appears from the agreed statement of facts that within two years prior to the commencement of this action on December 12, 1946, plaintiff purchased the property in question, a bungalow court of nine units which had been built some twenty years previously and had been used continuously for residential purposes. Located in zone C-2 on Beverly Boulevard, the property was subject to section 12.21-C of the Los Angeles Municipal Code (Ordinance No. 77,000 adopted September 28, 1936, as amended by Ordinance No. 90,500, adopted March 7, 1946) providing that no lot "held under separate ownership" at the law's effective date and "used . . . for dwelling purposes" shall be "reduced in any manner below the minimum lot area, size or dimensions" prescribed— "a minimum average width of fifty (50) feet and a minimum area of five thousand (5000) square feet."

Following his purchase, plaintiff subdivided the property into nine separate parcels, each averaging 925 square feet (25' x 37') and having a bungalow thereon. Through sale or 99-year lease arrangements plaintiff conveyed eight of these parcels to various individuals—transactions contrary to the minimum lot area and width requirements of the ordinance as a zoning regulation. Each parcel was conveyed with an easement to Beverly Boulevard over the walkways within the bungalow court. Two of the parcels had no frontage on any street or alley. The entire property was serviced by only one incinerator and two sewer connections.

Threatened with arrest and prosecution for violation of the ordinance, plaintiff instituted this action for declaratory and injunctive relief from the enforcement of such municipal regulation against him as a property owner, charging that it transcended the legitimate scope of the exercise of the police power and constituted "an unwarranted and arbitrary interference with [his] constitutional rights." . . .

Zoning is an essential part of a city's overall master plan for community development, Planning Act of 1929, Stats. 1929, p. 1805, as amended, 2 Deering's Gen. Laws, Act 5211b; later superseded by Conservation and Planning Act, Stats. 1947, ch. 807, p. 1909, as amended, 2 Deering's Gen. Laws, Act 5211c, and a city is vested with control of "the design and improvement of subdivisions," subject to judicial review as to reasonableness. Subdivision Map Act, Stats. 1937, p. 1864, as amended, now Bus. & Prof. Code, sec. 11500 et seq.; sec. 11525. The word "design" is defined in the latter Act to include, among other things, provision for "minimum lot area and width," Bus. & Prof. Code sec. 11510, by "local ordinance." *Ibid.* secs. 11506, 11526. Consistent with this state recognition of municipal functions and in line with its autonomous character, the city of Los Angeles adopted the zoning ordinance prohibiting the reduction of residential lots below the specified minimum of 5,000 square feet in area and 50-foot frontage. The city's charter expressly contemplates the adoption of regulations pursuant to the authority granted by the Subdivision Map Act, charter, sec. 95(g), and on this point the trial court found that the ordinance " . . . constitutes an essential part of the master plan for the comprehensive development of the City of Los Angeles in that it is designed to prevent the cutting up of lots into unduly small areas and into parcels of economically unusable widths; that the ordinance . . . supplements the California Subdivision Map Act in that it prevents lots sold pursuant to said Act from being further subdivided, and in so doing, the ordinance prevents or diminishes the possibility of circumvention of [said] Act." In support of its view that the "ordinance is an important factor in the orderly development of the city," the trial court found that the "attempted cutting up" of such property as plaintiff's bungalow court would "tend to create and accelerate the creation of slum conditions" and "overcrowd[ing]," thus "militating against orderly, quiet and peaceful living"; that "health and sanitary regulations and laws would be more difficult to enforce" if the bungalow units "were sold to various separate owners"; and that therefore "said ordinance has a reasonable relation to the public health, safety and general welfare, and was enacted for the public good."

Where from a consideration of the evidence the trial court has found certain physical facts and conditions to exist in relation to the particular property restriction involved as would justify regulation by the city through the exercise of its police power, all intendments must be indulged to sustain such findings and resulting judgment. Ayres v. City Council of Los Angeles, 34 Cal. 2d 31, 39, 207 P.2d 1. So significant are these factors in accord with the objectives found by the trial court to be within the design of the ordinance. The benefits of the Subdivision Map Act would be of little practical value in aid of desirable community planning if following the subdivider's compliance for the terms of the initial sale, the purchasers of the lots could erect multiple dwellings thereon according to authorized specifications and then "cut up" the units for separate sale. In this regard the ordinance clearly appears to supplement the state act and to operate in avoidance of its circumvention as the trial court found. Likewise appropriate for consideration here is the memorandum opinion filed by the trial judge and included in the record . . . as bearing on the interpretation of the findings. The comment is there made that according to the view of experts in the field of community development, the subdivision of "bungalow courts into separate parcels" tends "to create slum conditions" because it would be unlikely that a uniform state of repair would be maintained by the various owners and a "hodge-podge appearance" would result, with a consequent depreciation in value of the entire property; "overcrowding" develops because where it is "a common practice for landlords to limit the number of people who may occupy a bungalow in a court," such restriction would not apply under separate ownership of the various units, and the probable increase and concentration of people within the limited area would "add to the noise and other irritations that militate against orderly, quiet and peaceful living"; "health and sanitary regulations" become "more difficult to provide for and enforce," and particularly where such "close living" in separately owned bungalow units contemplates "each person . . . constantly making use of easements over the others' property, and where there is no one to make or enforce any rules touching items of common necessity to all, such as, for example, use of incinerators or other disposal of trash, and keeping clean the common walkways," the situation could create disturbing tensions. As is further there said, the "City Council may well have had all these matters in mind in passing the ordinance here under attack and may have concluded that it was necessary in furtherance of the general welfare of the city and its orderly development." . . .

Plaintiff argues that the zoning ordinance prohibiting his conveyance of the bungalow units in separate parcels to individuals as he chooses encroaches upon constitutional guarantees attaching to the ownership of property and securing him in his right to contract concerning the use, enjoyment, and disposition of his property. U.S. Const., Fourteenth Amend., sec. 1; Cal. Const., art. I, secs. 1, 13, and 14. But the fact that the ordinance so restricts plaintiff in his right to dispose of his property is not determinative of its invalidity, for in innumerable situations the sale of various types of property has been subject to regulation by public authority. . . . A property owner may not divide his tract of land into lots to sell before developing or improving them without complying with the Subdivision Map Act. . . . Likewise here the zoning ordinance as above considered in relation to the city's accomplishment of a comprehensive and systematic plan of community development shows the challenged regulation to have been reasonably adopted in furtherance of the "general welfare," and plaintiff's individual liberty in the disposition of his property may be curtailed to that extent in the public interest. Moreover, it should be noted that plaintiff still has the right to sell the property as he bought it—the bungalow court as a single entity—and he has only been deprived of his right to "cut it up" into individual units for conveyance to separate individuals, to what reasonably appears would be to the public detriment and at variance with the dictates of the city's overall plan of community design.

Plaintiff further argues that the zoning ordinance is unreasonable and arbitrary in its application to his property because his subdivision and separate conveyance of the bungalow units to various individuals would effect only a change in ownership, and not a change in their use for dwelling purposes. In this connection reliance is placed on these factors: that the bungalow units were constructed on plaintiff's property some twenty years before the adoption of the ordinance in question; that the city laws do not purport to require the removal of these improvements nor cessation of the present use thereof; that the property would remain exactly as it has been in the past, without a change in its improvements, its use or its existing yard areas, and the sole difference would be the circumstance of single ownership of the bungalow units through the respective conveyances; and that the city manifestly does not consider such bungalow courts a nuisance, for the very ordinance here considered permits the present construction of just such improvements on 5,000-square-foot lots held under single ownership in the C-2 zone (where plaintiff's property is situated), with a requirement of only 800 square feet of lot area per dwelling unit—while each of the parcels into which plaintiff has subdivided his property contains approximately 925 square feet. But the mere fact that the property in its existing condition is not deemed a nuisance *per se* nor objectionable as a "near-nuisance" in constituting a menace to health, safety or morals in the strict sense of the phrase does not strengthen plaintiff's position. The "police power as evidenced in zoning ordinances has a much wider scope than the mere suppression of the offensive uses of property . . . it acts not only negatively but constructively and affirmatively for the promotion of the public welfare." Miller v. Board of Public Works, 195 Cal. 477, 487-488, 234 P. 381, 384 [1925)]. . . .

The various factors above reviewed as found by the trial court to be possible motivating forces in the city's adoption of the ordinance show it to have a reasonable relation to the interests of the community as a whole in establishing a recommended residential pattern through regulation of minimum lot areas under single ownership. . . .

The purported appeal from the court denying a new trial is dismissed. The judgment is affirmed.
GIBSON, C. J., and SHENK, EDMONDS, and TRAYNOR, J. J., concur.
CARTER, Justice. I dissent. . . .

It would seem that the ordinance here involved is not the usual type of zoning ordinance, nor does it fall within the definitions given above insofar as it applied to the *ownership* of lots of certain size. By it a restriction is placed on the ownership, *not the use*, of parcels of land below a certain specified area.

I concede that the objectives of zoning are within the police power—that the public health, safety, morals and general welfare must be safeguarded. *But* there must be a rational connection between the means used and the end result to be attained. The majority opinion sets forth the reasons why this ordinance providing for single ownership of the units, rather than individual ownership, is a rational basis for the ordinance enacted under the police power of the municipalities. These reasons would have validity if, and only if, the ordinance prohibited more than a single dwelling or two on each 5000 square foot parcel of land (which was heretofore used by the occupants of the nine bungalows). These reasons are: (1) Avoidance of congestion in the streets. The absurdity of this is apparent—because a man owns his own home, does he tend to make for greater congestion in the streets? (2) Prevention of overcrowding the land—because a man owns his land, does he tend to have more children, more guests, more relatives? (3) Facilitation in furnishing transportation, water, light, sewer and other public necessities—I may be obtuse, but it appears that this reason is less than valid. In bungalow courts, unfurnished apartments, and the like, each tenant usually pays for his own water, light, and public utilities these facilities are furnished to him as an individual tenant, and have nothing whatsoever to do with his ownership of the property. The transportation argument seems so ridiculous as to require no answer. (4) Provision of recreational space for children to play—how can individual ownership of the various units have the slightest bearing on such space? (5) Encouragement of the cultivation of flowers, shrubs, vegetables—it has been my experience that individual ownership tends toward the encouragement of interest in the land, rather than tending to diminish it, and the same argument applies so far as the upkeep of property is concerned. Tenants are only too willing to let the landlord take care of any repairs, and if the landlord fails to do so, the tenant is not willing to expend his funds on someone else's property. (6) As another reason we are told that a "probable increase in occupancy" would add to the noise and other irritations which militate against orderly, quiet and peaceful living. As I have pointed out previously, this is a valid argument if we are to prohibit absolutely such bungalow courts, but, in the very nature of things, can have no validity when we take into consideration the fact that these units will be occupied in the same manner whether or not they are individually owned. (7) Health and Sanitary regulations—this argument is equally delusive. There is one incinerator and two sewer connections servicing the nine units and it would seem that individual ownership would not make these services less adequate. There are common walkways which will need to be cleaned, we are told, and there are easements over other property which will need to be regulated. And on these very speculative and improbable future neighborhood squabbles, we are asked to say that the ordinance has a reasonable basis in that it will tend to promote the public health, welfare, safety and general well-being! A corollary of finding this ordinance a sound and rational exercise of the police power of the municipality is to restrain the free alienation of property. . . .

When the Constitution is disregarded we reach the perimeter of the police state. True, city councilmen are elected, but what chance has a property owner who may be in the minority to protect himself against arbitrary and unreasonable action by a city council who may see fit to zone his property for a use for which it is wholly unsuited? This Court has said it will not interfere with such action. Of what value to him is the inalienable right guaranteed by the Constitution to acquire, possess and protect property when a city council or board of supervisors tells him he can only use his property for a purpose dictated by whim or caprice and the courts refuse to grant him relief? The instant case is a shining example of such arbitrary action. The bungalow units were legally constructed and have been legally occupied, but they cannot be legally sold in separate units. Does this really make sense? Is there a scintilla of reason or logic behind such a rule? If there is, it is not apparent to me, and I doubt that it would be to any unprejudiced mind. . . .

Notes

1. In Morris v. City of Los Angeles, 116 Cal. App. 2d 856, 856-61, 254 P.2d 935, 936-39 (Ct. App. 1953), the plaintiffs owned a corner lot with a frontage of 45 feet on Pennsylvania Avenue and a depth of 120.9 feet on Fickett Street. There were two houses and a double garage on the lot, one facing the street and the other the avenue. The location was zoned for multiple dwellings, within which "every lot shall have a minimum width of fifty (50) feet and a minimum area of five thousand (5,000) square feet." Although the lot was nonconforming as to minimum area, this did not constitute a violation, since the construction of the houses antedated passage of the ordinance. However, the zoning ordinance further provided: "No lot or parcel of land held under separate ownership at the time this Article became effective shall be separated in ownership or reduced in size below the minimum lot width or lot area required by this Article." The plaintiffs sold the northerly 40 feet and the house fronting on Fickett Street. After the sale, a criminal prosecution was commenced against them.

The plaintiffs brought an action seeking to enjoin prosecution of the municipal court action and for a declaratory judgment that the zoning was invalid. The trial court found that both residences had been on the property for more than 25 years, as was true of most of the buildings in the neighborhood, and that practically all of the corner lots in the area had more than one dwelling unit. The court further found that each of the dwelling units had separate utility connections and that

[c]orner lots having thereon two or more separate and unconnected dwelling units, when such lots are divided and sold, together with a residence, to separate owners who occupy the same, are better kept, maintained or occupied by a better type of occupant and have fewer occupants than those which are tenant occupied, and neither public health or sanitary regulations are adversely affected where such corner lots are sold and the residences thereon are occupied by separate owners.

The court then concluded that the relevant provisions of the ordinance, "as applied under the evidence in this case to the subject property, are invalid, arbitrary, discriminatory and unconstitutional and [is] not a reasonable use of the police power," and permanently enjoined the city from prosecuting or bringing any civil or criminal action against the plaintiffs by reason of the accomplished sale of the northerly 40 feet or by reason of the maintenance or future sale of the southerly 80 feet.

The city appealed, asserting "that all the issues of this case were settled adversely to the plaintiffs by Clemons v. City of Los Angeles," and that "the trial court erroneously refused to follow that decision." The district court of appeals disagreed, noting that "[t]he conditions considered in the Clemons case were novel and they were extreme conditions."

2. The Clemons court makes several references to the California Subdivision Map Act, an important statute governing local regulation of the process of dividing and selling existing parcels to multiple owners. The current statutory definition of a subdivision can be found in Cal. Gov. Code §66424:

"Subdivision" means the division, by any subdivider, of any unit or units of improved or unimproved land, or any portion thereof, shown on the latest equalized county assessment roll as a unit or as contiguous units, for the purpose of sale, lease or financing, whether immediate or future. Property shall be considered as contiguous units, even if it is separated by roads, streets, utility easement or railroad rights-of-way. "Subdivision" includes a condominium project, as defined in subdivision (f) of Section 1351 of the Civil Code, a community apartment project, as defined in subdivision (d) of Section 1351 of the Civil Code, or the conversion of five or more existing dwelling units to a stock cooperative, as defined in subdivision (m) of Section 1351 of the Civil Code.

The authority for local regulation of the subdivision process is located in Cal. Gov. Code §66411:

Regulation and control of the design and improvement of subdivisions are vested in the legislative bodies of local agencies. Each local agency shall, by ordinance, regulate and control the initial design and improvement of common interest developments as defined in Section 1351 of the Civil Code and subdivisions for which this division requires a tentative and final or parcel map. In the development, adoption, revision, and application of such ordinance, the local agency shall comply with the provisions of Section 65913.2. The ordinance shall specifically provide for proper grading and erosion control, including the prevention of sedimentation or damage to offsite property. Each local agency may by ordinance regulate and control other subdivisions, provided that the regulations are not more restrictive than the regulations for those subdivisions for which a tentative and final or parcel map are required by this division . . . .

While the basic structure is similar, as with zoning enabling acts, there are many variations in subdivision statutes from state to state and within localities in one state.

3. How are potential purchasers supposed to know whether the property they are considering is in compliance with zoning ordinances and other regulations? Pennsylvania lawmakers, concerned that

> many owners of properties are using such properties in violation of the zoning ordinances and regulations of such municipalities, and are maintaining such properties in violation of housing, building, safety, and fire ordinances and regulations, and are offering such properties for sale without revealing such illegal use or the receipt of notice of the existence of housing, building, safety and fire violations,

mandated in 21 Pa. Stat. §611 the following disclosure for sellers in many of the state's municipalities: "[A]ll sellers of property shall be required to advise the purchaser of the legal use of such property, and to deliver to the purchaser not later than at the settlement held for such property a use registration permit showing the legal use and zoning classification for such property."

4. How would the *Clemons* facts be affected by Cal. Civ. Code §1372 (first added in 1963 and later amended): "Unless a contrary intent is clearly expressed, local zoning ordinances shall be construed to treat like structures, lots, parcels, areas, or spaces in like manner regardless of whether the common interest development is a community apartment project, condominium project, planned development, or stock cooperative"?

5. For a more recent review of judicial answers to the question of whether zoning is about ownership as well as use, see Gangemi v. Zoning Bd. of Appeals, 255 Conn. 143, 164-68, 763 A.2d 1011, 1022-24 (2001) (Sullivan, J., dissenting):

> We have recognized . . . "the basic zoning principle that zoning regulations must directly affect land, not the owners of land . . . ." Reid v. Zoning Board of Appeals, 235 Conn. [850,] 857, 670 A.2d 1271 [(1996)]; see also Dinan v. Board of Zoning Appeals, 220 Conn. 61, 66-67 n.4, 595 A.2d 864 (1991) ("the identity of the user is irrelevant to zoning"); Builders Service Corp. v. Planning & Zoning Commission, 208 Conn. [267,] 285, 545 A.2d 530 [(1988)] ("zoning is concerned with the use of property and not primarily with its ownership" [internal quotation marks omitted]). This principle derives from the more general principle that "zoning power may only be used to regulate the use, not the user of the land." (Internal quotation marks omitted.) Reid v. Zoning Board of Appeals, *supra*, 857, quoting T. Tondro, Connecticut Land Use Regulation (2d Ed. 1992) p. 88. These principles suggest that a regulation that limits occupancy of a property to owners of the property is not within the zoning power. This, in turn, suggests that a variance condition that operates to achieve the same end does not advance a legitimate zoning purpose.
>
> The general trend, both in this state and in other jurisdictions, however, has been toward a less strict application of the principle that the zoning power must be used to regulate the use and not the user of the land. See Dinan v. Board of Zoning Appeals, *supra*, 220 Conn. 67 (considering validity of ordinance restricting "the term family to persons related by blood, marriage or adoption" and concluding that "if there is a reasonable basis to support the separate treatment for zoning purposes of families of related individuals as compared to groups of unrelated individuals, the broad grant of authority conferred by [General Statutes] § 8-2 to adopt regulations designed . . . to promote . . . the general welfare must be deemed to sanction a zoning regulation reflecting that distinction in the uses permitted in different zoning districts" [internal quotation marks omitted]); *id.*, 66-67 n.4 ("the identity of the user is irrelevant to zoning, but user ter-

minology may be employed to describe particular uses"); Taxpayers Assn. of Weymouth Township, Inc. v. Weymouth Township, 80 N.J. 6, 71 N.J. 249, 259, 275, 364 A.2d 1016 (1976), *cert. denied sub nom.* Feldman v. Weymouth Township, 430 U.S. 977 (1977) (zoning ordinance limiting mobile home units to trailer parks and their use to families in which head of household is at least fifty-two years old is within zoning power as promoting general welfare); *id.*, 277 (observing that "regulation of *land use* cannot be precisely dissociated from regulation of *land users*" [emphasis in original]); Bonner Properties, Inc. v. Franklin Township Planning Board, 185 N.J. Super. 553, 572, 449 A.2d 1350 (1982) (zoning ordinance prohibiting certain form of land ownership was within power delegated to municipality under enabling statute); *id.*, 567 (principle that "the zoning power . . . cannot be employed to regulate ownership of land or the identity of its occupants" implicitly overruled); see also 5 A. Rathkopf & D. Rathkopf, The Law of Zoning and Planning (4th Ed. Ziegler 2000) § 56A.02 [1] [c], p. 56A-5 ("this ultra vires principle that zoning regulates the use of land and not the status or identity of the owner or person who occupies the land has not always been strictly applied"). These authorities suggest that regulations that restrict forms of ownership and that affect the occupants, rather than the particular use, of a property, may be valid if they are reasonably related to a legitimate zoning purpose. But see FGL & L Property Corp. v. Rye, 66 N.Y.2d 111, 114, 116, 485 N.E.2d 986, 495 N.Y.S.2d 321 (1985) (recognizing that "it is a 'fundamental rule that zoning deals basically with land use and not with the person who owns or occupies it'" and holding that planning board does not have power to require certain form of ownership).

Although this court previously has not considered the issue, other jurisdictions have considered the application of the principle that the zoning power must be exercised to regulate the use, not the user, to restrictions on the rental of property. A number of courts have upheld such restrictions. See, e.g., Ewing v. Carmel-by-the-Sea, 234 Cal. App. 3d 1579, 1584, 1598, 286 Cal. Rptr. 382 (1991), *cert. denied*, 504 U.S. 914 (1992) (upholding constitutionality of ordinance prohibiting rental of residential property for fewer than thirty days as protecting residential character of neighborhood and having "substantial relation to the public health, safety, morals or general welfare" [internal quotation marks omitted]); Kasper v. Brookhaven, 142 A.D.2d 213, 215-19, 535 N.Y.S.2d 621 (1988) (upholding ordinance limiting availability of permits for accessory rental apartments to those homeowners who occupy home in which accessory rental apartment is to be maintained); *id.*, 222 (recognizing that "many zoning laws extend beyond the mere regulation of property to affect the owners and users thereof").

Several courts, however, have invalidated zoning actions restricting the rental of property. See Kirsch Holding Co. v. Manasquan, 59 N.J. 241, 251-52, 281 A.2d 513 (1971) (holding that zoning ordinances prohibiting rental to groups of individuals not qualifying as families under statutory definition violates substantive due process); United Property Owners Assn. of Belmar v. Belmar, 185 N.J. Super. 163, 167, 170, 171, 447 A.2d 933, *cert. denied*, 91 N.J. 568, 453 A.2d 880 (1982) (invalidating portion of ordinance prohibiting temporary or seasonal rentals except when occupant intends to reside permanently in dwelling as "an extreme limitation on rights of ownership of private property" and arbitrary); Kulak v. Zoning Hearing Board, 128 Pa. Commw. 457, 462, 563 A.2d 978 (1989) (concluding that condition to special exception to zoning regulations requiring owner of apartment building to reside in one apartment did not serve zoning purpose because "the . . . identity of an apartment occupant obviously has no relationship to public health, safety or general welfare," but holding that, because original owner had not appealed imposition of condition, he nevertheless was bound by it); see also 5 A. Rathkopf & D. Rathkopf, *supra*, § 56A.02, p. 56A-8 ("the principle that zoning enabling acts authorize local regulation of land use and not regulation of the identity or status of owners or persons who occupy the land would likely be held to apply to invalidate zoning provisions distinguishing between owner-occupied and rental housing" [internal quotation marks omitted]).

The intended target of planners in the next case was the rowhouse (or row house), once a very popular form of housing in the working class neighborhoods of Baltimore and Philadelphia, as explained by Mary Ellen Hayward & Charles Belfoure in, The Baltimore Rowhouse 1-2 (2001):

> For more than one hundred fifty years [the rowhouse] symbolized homeownership and stability for Baltimore's working and middle class. After World War II, the rowhouse was spurned in favor of the single-family suburban home and the apartment. Derided in the 1940s and 1950s as an outmoded housing type, it was not the choice of postwar planners to cure the country's urban housing crisis.
>
> In fact, older rowhouses were seen as the enemy: overcrowded, dilapidated, and neglected by absentee landlords. Even worse, many rowhouses in the inner city had become the homes of the poor, those Baltimoreans who could not escape to the suburbs.

NORWOOD HEIGHTS IMPROVEMENT ASS'N v. MAYOR AND CITY COUNCIL OF BALTIMORE
191 Md. 155, 60 A.2d 192 (1948)

COLLINS, Judge. This is an appeal by Norwood Heights Improvement Association, Inc., appellant, from a decision of the Baltimore City Court affirming a resolution of the Board of Municipal and Zoning Appeals approving an application for a permit by the Stulman Building Company, Inc., one of the appellees, (hereinafter known as appellee), to erect on a 15 acre tract, 10 apartment buildings made up of 34 units containing 168 suites and open parking spaces for 168 cars thereon. . . .

The plan of the development in this case shows a tract of land, after the area for streets is deducted, of 9.3 acres located partly in E-area and partly in C-area districts, where row houses are prohibited. 80 familes are to be housed on the 5.2 acres which constitute the E-area, which is within the limit under the zoning law. 88 families are to be housed on the 4.1 acres which comprise the C-area, which is well within the limit provided by the zoning ordinance. The project calls for a garden apartment development. There are 168 open-air off-street parking spaces for the use of tenants. The apartment houses are comprised of groups of two-story units containing varying numbers of apartments. The apartments are of four and five rooms. 34 such units are grouped into the 10 apartment buildings. These units are planned to over-lap and connect at the corners, leaving them separate fronts, sides and backs, except for the corner connections, where the foundation walls and roofs are to be continuous, as in the case of Akers v. City of Baltimore, 179 Md. 448, 20 A.2d 181. Each apartment building is heated by a common heating plant from a central boiler. Each group has its own water and sewage pipes and playground facilities. Each unit is to be encompassed by a firewall. There is a continuous foundation for each group and each group constitutes one building under one roof. The appellee claims that none of the apartment buildings are to be sold separately, nor can any of the units be separated from the apartment group of which they are a part. It claims that no basements are to be put under most of the units, no places for separate heating and other facilities are provided, and the cost of excavating basements would be costly and difficult. It is contended that the project is to remain as an entity under the ownership and control of the appellee which will manage it, rent out individual apartments, and collect the rents. The open-air parking spaces and playground are for the common use of all tenants and are not to be rented to anyone. There is only one gas meter, one water meter and one electric meter for the entire project. It is all financed by one mortgage on the entire development. The appellee strenuously contends that the project is designed and will always remain as one unit. It is admitted, however, by the appellee, that there are no "lot lines" laid out on the project for each building.

The primary question for us in this case is whether the present application violates the area and yard provisions of Paragraphs 21 and 24 of Ordinance No. 1247. . . . Paragraph 44(b) provides: "Lot. A lot is a parcel of land now or hereafter laid out and occupied by one building and the accessory buildings or uses customarily or necessarily incident to it, including such open spaces as are required by this ordinance."

Paragraph 44(1) defines a yard as: "The clear, unoccupied space on the same lot with a building required by the provisions of this ordinance."

Paragraph 44(m) defines a front yard as: "A clear, unoccupied space on the same lot with a building, extending across the entire width of the lot and situated between the front line of the building and the front line of the lot."

Paragraph 44(n) defines a rear yard as: "A clear, unoccupied space on the same lot with a building, extending across the entire width of the lot and situated between the rear line of the building and the rear line of the lot."

Paragraph 44(o) defines a side yard as: "A clear, unoccupied space on the same lot with a building and extending for the full length of the building between the building and the side lot line."

Paragraph 44(u) defines a group house as: "Not less than three and not more than six single family habitations, designed and erected as a unit on a lot."

Appellee relies strongly on the case of Akers v. City of Baltimore, 179 Md. 448, 20 A.2d 181, which involved a permit for a more or less similar type of garden apartments. However, the six separated buildings or groups containing 27 units and housing 108 families in that case, were on separate lots. It was said there, 179 Md. at page 451, 20 A.2d 182: "The six separated buildings or groups, on separated lots, are to contain twenty-seven units in all, housing one hundred and eight families." The zoning ordinance #1247, *supra*, in Paragraphs 21 and 24, sets up the percentage of area of lot, rear yards, side yards and population density. The definitions in Paragraph 44, *supra*, seem to make it clear that "lots" and "buildings" are the units of zoning. The opinion in *Akers v. City of Baltimore* emphasizes the fact that there are lots for each building in that case. Chief Judge Bond, who wrote that opinion, carefully considered whether an aggregation of garden type apartments constituted six buildings, "on separate lots," or 27 buildings. Nothing in that opinion remotely suggested that the whole "development" could be regarded as one building.

Perhaps a surveyor or an advanced mathematician might keep the score of percentages of the whole, though this would be difficult and not worth doing. A wilderness at the rear of the whole might furnish percentages for row houses where row houses are prohibited. Unless lots are defined in advance, sales of parts might leave a crazy-quilt of remnants and force the zoning authorities either (a) to rezone and thereby remove restrictions or else (b) to block further sales—or even use of the property—by maintaining restrictions that have become unworkable. "Yard" requirements, however, expressed not in percentages but in feet, mean nothing at all except with reference to defined "lots" and "buildings."

To disregard "lot lines" and treat an entire development as a unit would seem to disregard the plain words of the zoning ordinance. It is, of course, true that it is undoubtedly the intention of the present owners to keep this whole project as a single unit and under one ownership and, if that is done, compliance with the zoning laws as to "lot lines" will not embarrass the owner. However, if because of voluntary, or even forced sale by reason of financial difficulties, the buildings in the project hereafter become separately owned and changes in lines then become necessary, that will be the owner's problem, as it should be. This possibility, however, does not seem to justify the ignoring of the plain requirements in the zoning laws requiring division into lots. It is, of course, possible that the plans for this project might be revised to provide for "lot lines" for each building.

The order affirming the decision and resolution of the Board of Municipal and Zoning Appeals in this case must therefore be reversed.

Notes

1. Subsequently an ordinance was passed by the city of Baltimore to the effect that garden-type apartments are permitted "without providing a separate lot for each structure . . . provided the area of such project shall cover at least five acres of land." Thereafter, an application to erect 3 apartment houses, to contain 9 houses in all, to house 45 families on less than 5 acres was approved by the Board of Municipal and Zoning Appeals. A neighboring homeowners association objected, pointing out that the units "are connected—and separated—at the sides by a solid wall, and that the roof lines are, for sake of appearance broken." The Maryland Court of Appeals, in Windsor Hills Improvement Ass'n v. Mayor & City Council of Baltimore, 195 Md. 383, 390-91, 73 A.2d 531, 533 (1950), upheld the permit, observing, "By the latter test presumably the House of the Seven Gables would not be one house but several."

2. A few decades later, in Baltimore and many other American cities, apartment units were converted from rental to condominium or cooperative ownership. Fearful of the negative effects of gentrification, which would shut out senior citizens, students, and others from this essential housing stock, many localities placed restrictions on these conversions. Not surprisingly, these ordinances were challenged in court. See, for example, Flynn v. City of Cambridge, 383 Mass. 152, 153 418 N.E.2d 335 (1981):

> The plaintiffs contest the legal power and authority of the Cambridge city council to enact c. 23 of the Code of the City of Cambridge, Ordinance 926 (ordinance), an ordinance regulating eviction from and condominium conversion of housing subject to rent control (controlled rental units). They contend that, even if the ordinance was properly enacted, it so restricts the uses for which their units may be utilized as to amount to an unconstitutional taking of their property. We uphold the validity of the ordinance.

3. Baltimore's rowhouse story has "come full circle" in recent years, according to Mary Ellen Hayward & Charles Belfoure in, The Baltimore Rowhouse 1 (2001):

> On a winter's morning in 1955, a bulldozer started up and plowed into a group of brick rowhouses at the corner of Lexington and Asquith Streets. When it was through, every rowhouse in the area bounded by Aisquith, Colvin, Fayette, and Orleans Street was gone. In its place came a high rise housing project called Lafayette Courts.
>
> Forty years later, on a summer's morning in 1995, an electronic signal ignited 995 pounds of dynamite and the six, eleven-story high-rise towers of Lafayette Courts came crashing down. In its place came 228 rowhouses.

4. The traditional technique of controlling intensity of use by means of height limitation and yard and setback requirements has largely been a geometric control, or, as many consultants complain, a "zoning envelope" that dictates the shape of the building by prescribing its outer measurements. More modern zoning ordinances have tried to break through this rigid dictation of size in order to permit the greatest possible flexibility in protecting neighborhood character and in satisfying individual needs and architectural design. Chad Emerson, writing about *The SmartCode* in, A Legal Guide to Urban and Sustainable Development for Planners, Developers, and Architects 136 (Daniel K. Slone & Doris S. Goldstein eds., 2008), has explained that

> the SmartCode [developed by the New Urbanist architects and planners at the Duany Plater-Zyberk firm] regulates areas such as setbacks by setting ranges or parameters. A conventional setback of 10 feet, for example, would allow a building to be no closer than 10 feet, but would permit it to be 20 feet back, or more, even if other buildings were only 10 feet back. If parameters are used instead, the permitted front setbacks on the main street . . . may range from 5 to 12 feet in the model code instead of mandating a specific distance throughout the transect zone. While still providing flexibility, this approach will result in a more predictable urban form than the minimum or maximum measurements typical of Euclidean codes.

Local ordinances for many American municipalities are available online at http://municode. com. You should examine the zoning ordinance for your hometown, the community in which you are attending school, or the place in which you plan to work after graduation, through the Internet or in hard copy. What are the purposes of bulk controls, and which techniques can most readily foster them? For whose guidance are the various regulations framed? In what way do they stimulate the construction of certain types of buildings? In general, what are the relative advantages of regulations based on requirements regarding height, setback, yard, court, coverage, lot area per family, dwelling unit or room, cubage, or floor area ratio? Note, to take one instance, that the minimum dimension for a yard could be set according to different principles: an absolute dimension, one that is related to the height of the nearest outside wall of the building, or one that increases with the height of the wall above the ground. For what purpose should any be used, and what combinations might be most effective?

5. The use of a floor area ratio (FAR) relating the floor area of a structure to the lot area has long been a popular zoning device. FAR gives the multiple by which the maximum permitted floor area may be calculated.[22] While this formula can be applied to all types of buildings, regardless of the shape of the lot, and does not restrict the building to a specific shape or location, it is nevertheless

---

22. Some illustrations from Manhattan may be helpful: the Empire State Building has a FAR of 25:1; Radio City and Stuyvesant Town, 3.13:1 each. The definition found in section 12-10 of the Zoning Resolution of the City of New York (first enacted in 1961) reads:

"Floor area ratio" is the total *floor area* on a *zoning lot*, divided by the *lot area* of that *zoning lot*. (For example, a *building* containing 20,000 square feet of *floor area* on a *zoning lot* of 10,000 square feet has a *floor area ratio* of 2.0.)

Each of the italicized words in the quoted paragraph is separately defined in the ordinance.

subject to certain defects.[23] Consider, for example, its efficiency in retaining a balance between bulk and open space; one illustration, which may suggest others, is the case in which the first story covers 100% of the site, and the remaining permitted bulk goes into a tower set upon this "pedestal." For an example of the use of FAR with a helpful illustration, see Pasadena, California's online zoning code: http://www.ci.pasadena.ca.us/zoning/P-8.html#f.

6. To fill the gap caused by rejection of the English "ancient lights" doctrine (as discussed in Prah v. Maretti in Chapter Two), and to supplement other bulk controls, municipalities often employ "daylighting" techniques. A common device is a regulation based on the "angle of light" of a structure, as, for example, in the following excerpt from Denver's zoning ordinance:

Bulk of structures in the B-A-2 and B-A-4 districts. No part of any structure (except church spires, church towers, flagpoles, antennas, chimneys, flues, vents or accessory water tanks) shall project up through bulk limits which are defined by planes extending up over the zone lot at an angle of forty-five (45) degrees with respect to the horizontal (a pitch of one (1) foot additional rise for each foot additional setback) and which planes start:

(1) At horizontal lines which are co-directional to the side line or lines of the zone lot and pass through points ten (10) feet above the midpoint of each such side line; and

(2) At horizontal lines which are co-directional to the center lines of all streets abutting the zone lot and pass through points ten (10) feet above the midpoint of such center lines between the boundary lines of the zone lot extended; and

(3) At, if no alley abuts the zone lot, a horizontal line which is co-directional to the rear line of the zone lot and passes through a point ten (10) feet above the midpoint of such rear line of the zone lot; and if the rear line or lines of the zone lot are established by an abutting alley or alleys such planes shall start at horizontal lines which are co-directional to the center lines of such abutting alley or alleys and pass through points ten (10) feet above the midpoint of such center lines between the boundary lines of the zone lot extended.

---

23. For example, the definitions of key terms can be quite complicated. Consider the New York City ordinance's (section 12-10) definition of "floor area":

"Floor area" is the sum of the gross areas of the several floors of a building or buildings, measured from the exterior faces of exterior walls or from the center lines of walls separating two buildings. In particular, floor area includes:

(a) basement space, except as specifically excluded in this definition;

(b) elevator shafts or stairwells at each floor;

(c) floor space in penthouses;

(d) attic space (whether or not a floor has been laid) providing structural headroom of five feet or more in R2A, R2X, R3, R4 or R5 Districts and eight feet or more in other districts;

(e) floor space in gallerias, interior balconies, mezzanines or bridges;

(f) floor space in open or roofed terraces, bridges, breeze ways or porches, if more than 50 percent of the perimeter of such terrace, breeze way, or porch is enclosed, and provided that a parapet not higher than 3 feet, 8 inches, or a railing not less than 50 percent open and not higher than 4 feet, 6 inches, shall not constitute an enclosure;

(g) any other floor space used for dwelling purposes, no matter where located within a building,   when not specifically excluded;

(h) floor space in accessory buildings, except for floor space used for accessory off-street parking; . . .

You get the idea.

Revised Municipal Code City and County of Denver, Colorado §59-266(d).[24]

7. British experience has shown that in some cases controls that are flexible in concept nevertheless produce uniformity of construction because of the dictates of building costs that rule out alternative shapes and sizes allowed by the law. For example, a FAR of 3.0 permits a three-story building to cover all of the lot, or a six-story building to cover 50% of the lot (or endless permutations of coverages and stories). The economics of building, however, may overwhelmingly favor a three-story structure. In this case, a FAR may produce a spate of buildings of uniform height, and the net effect will not differ from a rigid three-story height "envelope," the very result that the FAR was designed to prevent.

The idea has therefore evolved of introducing "situations of choice" into the investment decision. If, for example, high-rise building (to follow the illustration) is more costly than low-rise, why not permit an additional floor area where the developer chooses a "50% coverage—six story" as opposed to "100% coverage—three story" construction? The additional rentable floor area will thus offset, to some degree, the additional cost. The FAR itself can thus be put on a sliding scale, increasing as the amount of usable open space is increased. Once this basic incentive principle is brought into play, all sorts of modifications suggest themselves: rewards for front rather than rear open space (if such is desired); for ground open space; for space on the first- or second-story roof; for arcaded space (for example, Lever House: http://www.greatbuildings.com/buildings/Lever_House.html); and for experiments which introduce amenities judged to be socially desirable. Can such incentives be calculated with sufficient finesse to offset the market pressures toward a given type of structure under given regulations? Are there any abuses inherent in such devices? How far can judicial review go in assessing the reasonableness of such mechanisms?

B. Reading Between the Lines of the Zoning Code: Which Accessory Uses and Home Occupations Are Permissible?

Drafters of zoning codes are well aware that they cannot anticipate every possible use of property, particularly in a nation that prides itself on technological innovation. Courts are often called upon to determine whether a professional who works out of the home or whether the newest telecommunication gadget is compatible with the letter and spirit of the use classification for the district. As the following case and notes illustrate, this area of zoning law promises to be a growth area as telecommuting becomes even more popular and is often further complicated by legal directives (statutes and regulations) issued from the higher levels of government.

MARCHAND v. TOWN OF HUDSON
47 N.H. 380, 788 A.2d 250 (2001)

BROCK, C.J. . . .
Muller resides in a section of Hudson zoned Residential-Two (R-2), and is an amateur or "ham" radio operator. In December 1998, when Muller applied for a building permit, the town had no regulations restricting the number or height of amateur radio towers. The town zoning administrator granted Muller a building permit to erect three ninety-foot amateur radio towers with antennae to be added at a later date that would bring the total height of each tower to one hundred feet.

---

24. "To insure enough light and air," wrote Lewis Mumford, "the distance between buildings should increase with their length. Our municipal setback regulations make a hypocritical acknowledgment of this principle, but since they were framed to keep land values high rather than buildings low or widely spaced, they have never come within shooting distance of achieving an ideal." LEWIS MUMFORD, FROM THE GROUND UP 117 (1956).

Shortly thereafter the plaintiffs, Suzanne Marchand, Joanne Radziewicz and Peter Radziewicz, Muller's neighbors, appealed the grant of the building permit to Hudson's zoning board of adjustment (ZBA), arguing that radio communications towers were not permitted in the R-2 zone. Following a hearing on the merits, the ZBA upheld the grant of the building permit. . . .

Following a rehearing at the plaintiffs' request, the ZBA upheld its decision. The plaintiffs appealed to the superior court.

The superior court did not hold a hearing, but relied on the ZBA's certified record to evaluate the ZBA's decision. The court ruled that while the ZBA heard sufficient evidence to establish ham radio as an accessory use in residential districts in the town, "there was no evidence of ham radio operations in residential neighborhoods which included anything reasonably close to the scale of the three antennae proposed in this case." The court also addressed whether the federal government had preempted local regulation in this area, see Amateur Radio Preemption, 101 F.C.C. 2d 952 (1985), and concluded that the size and height of the towers "would upset the balance between the federal interest in promoting amateur operations and the legitimate interest of local governments in regulating local zoning matters." The court therefore reversed the ZBA decision, rescinded the building permit and ordered the towers removed. . . .

We first address the town's argument that the superior court erred when it failed to uphold the ZBA's conclusion that the building permit was properly issued as an accessory use under the town zoning ordinance.

The interpretation of a zoning ordinance and the determination of whether a particular use is an accessory use are ultimately questions of law for this court to decide. KSC Realty Trust v. Town of Freedom, 146 N.H. 271, 772 A.2d 321, 322-23 (2001) (quotations omitted). The town's zoning ordinance expressly permits, as an accessory use, "traditional secondary accessory uses and structures, including garages, toolsheds, parking areas, recreational facilities, outdoor in-ground swimming pools and other customary uses and structures." Town of Hudson Zoning Ordinance Table of Permitted Accessory Uses (1996). The ordinance defines accessory use as "any use which is customary, incidental, and subordinate to the principal use of a structure or lot." Town of Hudson Zoning Ordinance § 334-6 (1996).

We have generally held that the language "customary, incidental and subordinate" requires that the accessory use be minor in relation to the permitted use, bear a reasonable relationship to the primary use, and have been habitually established as reasonably associated with the primary use. An aggregation of incidental uses, however, may result in the loss of "accessory" status. If the scope and significance of the proposed use is at least equal to the permitted residential use, the proposed use may no longer be subordinate or incidental and thus not permitted as an accessory use.

The plaintiffs have not challenged the ZBA's finding that historically, ham radio antennae have been permitted as an accessory use in the town. Rather, they argued to the superior court, and now argue on appeal, that there was no evidence presented to the ZBA to support the position that three 100-foot towers are a customary, accessory use in the R-2 zone. The superior court found that, given the scale of the proposed towers, they no longer qualified as accessory uses under the Hudson Zoning Ordinance. We agree.

The ZBA minutes reflect that a number of town residents stated that they had amateur radio towers. One resident stated that he had a seventy-foot tower attached to his house, and another stated that her neighbors had a 100-foot tower at their house. There was no evidence presented, however, that there exist in Hudson three, or even two 100-foot radio towers which are accessory to a residence. Indeed, as the superior court noted, "There was no evidence of ham radio operations in [any] residential neighborhoods which included anything reasonably close to the scale of the three antennae proposed in this case." We therefore agree with the superior court that, to the extent the ZBA decision rested upon the conclusion that the construction of three 100-foot amateur radio towers qualified as an "accessory use" under the ordinance, it is unreasonable.

We turn now to the town's argument that the superior court erred as a matter of law when it ordered relief that conflicted with federal objectives to allow and promote amateur ham radio facilities. According to the town, the superior court's order to remove all three radio towers, thereby preventing all ham radio operation by Muller, fails to preserve the FCC's legitimate interest in promoting amateur radio operations. We agree.

Because a municipality's power to zone property to promote the health, safety and general welfare of the community is delegated to it by the State, the municipality must exercise this power in conformance with the enabling legislation. See Britton v. Town of Chester, 134 N.H. 434, 441, 595 A.2d 492 (1991). RSA 674:16 grants municipalities the power to enact zoning ordinances, but expressly prohibits any such ordinance that fails to conform "to the limited federal preemption entitled Amateur Radio Preemption, 101 FCC 2nd 952 (1985) issued by the Federal Communications Commission." RSA 674:16, IV (Supp. 2000). The limited preemption to which the statute refers is a limited preemption of state and local regulations governing amateur radio station facilities, including antennae and support structures designed to protect the "strong federal interest in promoting amateur communications." Amateur Radio Preemption, 101 F.C.C. 2d 952, 959-60 (1985). The FCC codified the central holding of *Amateur Radio Preemption*, the FCC Memorandum Opinion referred to in RSA 674:16, IV, when it revised its amateur radio rules to provide as follows:

> Except as otherwise provided [by the regulations], a station antenna structure may be erected at heights and dimensions sufficient to accommodate amateur service communications (State and local regulation of a station antenna structure must not preclude amateur service communications. Rather, it must reasonably accommodate such communications and must constitute the minimum practicable regulation to accomplish the state or local authority's legitimate purpose).

47 C.F.R. § 97.15(b) (2000).

In light of the FCC's clear directive that "state and local regulations that operate to preclude amateur communications in their communities are in direct conflict with federal objectives and must be preempted," Amateur Radio Preemption, 101 F.C.C. 2d at 960, we agree with the town that the superior court erred when it ordered the towers removed. Regarding the federal preemption issue, the superior court held that the size and height of the towers "would upset the balance between the federal interest in promoting amateur operations and the legitimate interest of local governments in regulating local zoning matters." While some courts have focused on whether the municipality properly balanced its interest against the federal government's interests in promoting amateur communications, see, e.g., Howard v. City of Burlingame, 937 F.2d 1376, 1380 (9th Cir. 1991); Williams v. City of Columbia, 906 F.2d 994, 998 (4th Cir. 1990), we agree with the United States Court of Appeals for the Eighth Circuit that the federal directive requires municipalities to do more:

> PRB-1 specifically requires the city to accommodate reasonably amateur communications. This distinction is important, because a standard that requires a city to accommodate amateur communications in a reasonable fashion is certainly more rigorous than one that simply requires a city to balance local and federal interests when deciding whether to permit a radio antenna.

Pentel v. City of Mendota Heights, 13 F.3d 1261, 1264 (8th Cir. 1994) (citation omitted). Thus, we conclude that the manner in which the superior court applied the zoning ordinance violates PRB-1.

We note, however, that while New Hampshire and federal law require municipalities to accommodate amateur communications, they do not require the town to allow an amateur operator to erect any antenna he or she desires. *See Pentel*, 13 F.3d at 1264. Instead, they require only that the town "consider the application, make factual findings, and attempt to negotiate a satisfactory compromise with the applicant." *Id.* (quotations, citation and brackets omitted).

In light of the FCC's requirement, a zoning board's fact-finding and analysis should focus, first, on whether the three towers are permitted under local zoning regulations. If, as we have determined here, they are not, the zoning board should then consider what steps must be taken to "reasonably accommodate" amateur radio communications. In making this determination, the ZBA may consider whether the particular height and number of towers are necessary to accommodate the particular ham operator's communication objectives.

There was some evidence presented to the ZBA that the tower and antenna operation "was not the typical installation, but rather was something that every ham who was interested in reliable international communication on a regular basis aspired to own." The ZBA, however, did not make any factual findings regarding whether Muller even requires the proposed three radio towers to facilitate his international ham radio operations. Therefore, we vacate the superior court's decision and remand with instructions to remand to the ZBA for proceedings consistent with this opinion.

Affirmed in part; reversed in part; vacated and remanded.

Notes

1. When it comes to the location of seemingly ubiquitous mobile phone towers, 42 U.S.C. §332(7), part of the Telecommunications Act of 1996, seeks to strike a balance between federal and non-federal authority:

> (A) General authority. Except as provided in this paragraph, nothing in this Act shall limit or affect the authority of a State or local government or instrumentality thereof over decisions regarding the placement, construction, and modification of personal wireless service facilities.
>
> (B) Limitations.
>
> > (i) The regulation of the placement, construction, and modification of personal wireless service facilities by any State or local government or instrumentality thereof—
> >
> > > (I) shall not unreasonably discriminate among providers of functionally equivalent services; and
> > >
> > > (II) shall not prohibit or have the effect of prohibiting the provision of personal wireless services.
> >
> > (ii) A State or local government or instrumentality thereof shall act on any request for authorization to place, construct, or modify personal wireless service facilities within a reasonable period of time after the request is duly filed with such government or instrumentality, taking into account the nature and scope of such request.

(iii) Any decision by a State or local government or instrumentality thereof to deny a request to place, construct, or modify personal wireless service facilities shall be in writing and supported by substantial evidence contained in a written record.

(iv) No State or local government or instrumentality thereof may regulate the placement, construction, and modification of personal wireless service facilities on the basis of the environmental effects of radio frequency emissions to the extent that such facilities comply with the Commission's regulations concerning such emissions.

(v) Any person adversely affected by any final action or failure to act by a State or local government or any instrumentality thereof that is inconsistent with this subparagraph may, within 30 days after such action or failure to act, commence an action in any court of competent jurisdiction. The court shall hear and decide such action on an expedited basis. Any person adversely affected by an act or failure to act by a State or local government or any instrumentality thereof that is inconsistent with clause (iv) may petition the Commission for relief.

In two recent cases, a very small sampling of the reported cases in this litigation growth area, panels from the U.S. Court of Appeals for the Third Circuit sided first with a local government, then with a telecommunications service provider. In Omnipoint Communication Enters., Ltd. Partnership v. Zoning Hearing Bd. of Easttown Twp., 331 F.3d 386, 390-91 (3d Cir. 2003), the appellate court agreed with the magistrate judge below who had "upheld the Zoning Board's rejection of Omnipoint's application for a variance to locate its telecommunications tower in a residential district." The lower court had reasoned "that Omnipoint had failed to establish a 'significant gap' [in wireless service] or unreasonable discrimination under the TCA, or unconstitutional exclusion under Pennsylvania [zoning] law."

The local government came up short in Ogden Fire Co. No. 1 v. Upper Chichester Twp., 504 F.3d 370, 374, 376, 387-88 (3d Cir. 2007), as the appellate panel affirmed the lower court's finding that the township Zoning Hearing Board's "denial of requested zoning approvals and a building permit violated the Telecommunications Act of 1996." The fire department along with Sprint Spectrum had "filed a joint application with the Zoning Board on August 31, 2004, for approval of the erection of a steel monopole 130 feet high for mounting emergency service and wireless telecommunications antennas." The board, however, determined that Sprint was the sole applicant and that the application violated the zoning ordinance:

According to that interpretation, Sprint was requesting Zoning Board approval to construct its own WCF [wireless telecommunications facility] tower, and Ogden would thereafter attach its radio antenna to the tower to enhance Ogden's communication systems. The Zoning Board concluded that Sprint had not established the propriety of erecting a stand-alone WCF tower in an R-2 Residential District. The Board concluded that the WCF was not an accessory structure to the firehouse because it was not a use "customarily incidental and subordinate to the principal use of the land or building and located on the same lot with such principal use." The Board also refused to grant the special exception required to build a tower taller than 15 feet because the WCF is not an accessory use or structure to the firehouse. The Board refused to grant a special exception to build the WCF because stand-alone WCF towers are not permitted in R-2 Residential Districts. Finally, the Board also rejected the alternate request for a variance because a 133 foot stand-alone WCF tower is not a structure permitted in an R-2

Residential District and because Sprint had not satisfied the requirements for a variance under the Pennsylvania Municipal Planning Code.

The Third Circuit disagreed and offered this resolution of the accessory use issue:

> [T]he Zoning Ordinance defines an "accessory use" as "[a] use of land or of a building or portion thereof customarily incidental and subordinate to the principal use of the land or building and located on the same lot with such principal use." Zoning Ordinance, Appendix (i). "Once something is defined as an accessory use, it is allowed by right." AWACS, Inc. v. Zoning Hearing Bd. of Newtown Twp., 702 A.2d 604, 607 (Pa. Commw. Ct. 1997) (citation omitted). "In order to establish that right, an applicant must prove that the use sought is secondary to a principal use and that the use is usually found with that principal use." *Id.* (citation omitted). The Zoning Ordinance also provides for, and allows, an "accessory structure." An "accessory structure" is defined as one that is "detached from a principal building on the same lot and incidental and subordinate to the principal use of the building or use." Zoning Ordinance, Appendix I.B.
>
> Here, it is clear that the tower is an accessory use/structure to Ogden's firehouse. Robinson, Ogden's Vice-President, explained the relationship of the proposed tower to the firehouse:
>
>> Communications are necessary so, essentially, this is an accessory use. If you look at communications, without it we are nowhere. We look upon redundancy in this age, particularly this age after 9/11, as critical to emergency operations. As a result we have taken action with regard to further alerting people through our cell phones, regular pagers in addition to fire pagers which we found to be inadequate in certain areas. So communication is definitely associated with any emergency service.
>
> App. 288. Accordingly, the district court quite correctly concluded that Ogden's use of "a radio tower to enhance its existing radio-communications system would be an accessory use. . . ."

2. Advances in telecommunications are having another significant impact on local zoning regulations, as more and more Americans are able to work without leaving their residences. As Professor Patricia E. Salkin notes in her timely piece, *Zoning for Home Occupations: Modernizing Zoning Codes to Accommodate Growth in Home-Based Businesses*, 35 Real Est. L.J. 181, 181-82 (2006): "According to the U.S. Census report for the year 2000, over four million people work from home, a total of 3.3% of the nation's population. That number can rise between 18.8 million to 20.3 million depending on how one defines working from home." While the typical 20th-century zoning ordinance included a provision allowing home occupations in residential zones, the current list goes far beyond piano teachers, dance instructors, barbers and beauticians, and dressmaking. Professor Salkin, commenting on the rapidly changing employment and regulatory landscape, has observed:

> Zoning codes have traditionally been designed to separate incompatible land uses, leading to the establishment of separate zoning districts for businesses and for residential areas. However, with the growth in home-based businesses and home occupations, municipalities must be more creative in balancing the public health, safety, and welfare in residential districts and the pressures necessitating the accommodation of appropriate home-based businesses.

Professor Nicolle Stelle Garnett, in *On Castles and Commerce: Zoning Law and the Home-Business Dilemma*, 42 Wm. & Mary L. Rev. 1191 (2001), has provided this valuable historical perspective:

> Drafters of early zoning codes had to contend with the fact that home occupations remained quite prevalent well into the twentieth century. As a result, most early codes did not prohibit working from home altogether, but rather permitted either "accessory uses" of residential property, "customary" home occupations, or both. Many modern codes still contain these types of provisions. Whether a given use of a home is permitted under these exceptions to municipal zoning codes has been the subject of a great deal of litigation, with courts tending to construe accessory use provisions quite narrowly. The resolution of these disputes often turns on seemingly silly distinctions. For example, the New Hampshire Supreme Court held that a roofing contractor could not use his residence as a business headquarters where he maintained business records and conducted business by mail and telephone.[78] The Massachusetts Supreme Judicial Court, however, held that a homeowner could use the sunroom in his house to make telephone calls and pay bills related to his masonry business, in part because he did not maintain a filing cabinet in the sunroom.[79]

> Perhaps in an effort to reduce the uncertainty caused by these vague restrictions, most municipalities have enacted zoning restrictions that more specifically address home-based businesses. Some cities simply prohibit all home occupations in residential zones. Zoning codes in jurisdictions that do not prohibit all home occupations often list permitted occupations, prohibited occupations, or both. Many allow "professionals" to ply their trade in residential areas, at least if the home office is not their primary one.

3. Two recent cases demonstrate the challenges the growing variety of home occupations pose to local regulators and to judicial interpreters of relevant statutes and ordinances. In City of Minot v. Boger, 744 N.W.2d 277, 279, 280-81 (N.D. 2008), the state supreme court interpreted the following provision from the city's zoning ordinance:

Home Occupation: Any occupation or activity which meets all of the following tests:

a. The occupation is managed and owned by a person residing on the premises and not more than one other person is employed by the owner/manager on the premises except members of the immediate family of the owner/manager who also live on the premises.

b. The exterior of the premises used for the home occupation is indistinguishable from any other residential dwelling of like design and character, in that no commercial displays, show windows, exterior storage areas, parking areas, are evident except that a name plate or business sign not more than 2 feet square may be exhibited, which is attached flush to the side of the building.

c. The home occupation does not generate pedestrian traffic substantially greater, or vehicular traffic or vehicular parking substantially greater or substantially different in kind or character, than that ordinarily associated with a similar dwelling which is used solely for residential purposes.

---

78. *See* Perron v. City of Concord, 150 A.2d 403 (N.H. 1959).
79. *See* Wellesley v. Brossi, 164 N.E.2d 883, 886 (Mass. 1960).

d. The home occupation is no more dangerous to life, personal safety, or property than any other activity ordinarily carried on with respect to premises used solely for residential purposes.

e. No loud or unpleasant noises, bright, or glaring lights, offensive or noxious fumes, or odors, or perceptible vibrations attributable to the home occupation are emitted from the premises.

The Bogers, who operated street-sweeping and lawn care businesses in a single-family residential zone,

have used their property to store business equipment when it is not in use. The equipment includes street sweepers, front-end loaders, dump trucks, and other machinery. Employees of the businesses reported to work at the Boger residence, picked up the equipment they needed, and left their personal vehicles at the residence until their work days were completed.

The trial court granted an injunction against the Bogers that was sought by the city and dismissed the Bogers' counterclaim that the city had taken their property by enforcing the zoning ordinance. The justices agreed, concluding that "the district court's finding that the Bogers did not have a permissible "home occupation" under the Minot zoning ordinance is not clearly erroneous."

A state statute provided an extra (and determinative) complication in Hawthorne v. Village of Olympia Fields, 204 Ill. 2d 243, 246-47, 254-55, 790 N.E.2d 832, 835-36, 840 (2003). After the Hawthornes acquired their home, located in a residential zone, they successfully applied to the Illinois Department of Children and Family Services for a license to operate a day care home on the premises. When the Hawthornes sought a building permit to remodel the house, village officials informed them that they were in violation of the zoning ordinance, Olympia Fields Municipal Code §22-3 (Ord. No. 17, *as revised* May 11, 1981), which defined "home occupation" as

any gainful occupation or profession engaged in by an occupant of a dwelling unit as a use which is clearly incidental to the use of the dwelling unit for residential purposes. The "home occupation" shall be carried on wholly within the principal building or within a building accessory thereto, and only by members of the family occupying the premises * * *. There shall be no exterior display, no exterior sign except as allowed by the sign regulations for the district in which such "home occupation" is located, no exterior storage of materials, no other exterior indication of the "home occupation," or variation from the residential character of the principal building, and no offensive noise, vibration, smoke, dust, odors, heat or glare shall be produced. Offices, clinics, doctors' offices, hospitals, barbershops, beauty parlors, dress shops, millinery shops, tearooms, restaurants, tourist homes, animal hospitals and kennels, among other things, shall not be deemed to be home occupations.

The state supreme court noted that "[a]t issue is the construction of and interplay between Olympia Fields' zoning ordinance, on the one hand, and the Child Care Act and related DCFS regulations, on the other." Because the village was "a non-home rule unit of government," it had no "inherent powers" and "may exercise only those powers that the state legislature confers upon them, either expressly or impliedly, by statute."

The intermediate appellate court had found that the city had in effect totally excluded day-care homes, thereby exceeding its delegated zoning powers. The state supreme court felt no need to address that argument, however, for it based its holding on preemption grounds:

Because it is a non-home-rule unit, Olympia Fields cannot adopt ordinances under a general grant of power that infringe upon the spirit of state law or are repugnant to the general policy of the state. Although the village possesses zoning powers by virtue of article 11, division 13, of the Illinois Municipal Code (65 ILCS 5/11-13-1 et seq.), ordinances enacted under those powers that conflict with the spirit and purpose of a state statute are preempted by the statute. . . .

[T]he operation of child-care facilities in Illinois is regulated by the state. The governing statute is the Child Care Act of 1969 (225 ILCS 10/1 et seq. (West 2000)), which requires "any person, group of persons or corporation who or which receives children or arranges for care or placement of one or more children unrelated to the operator" to apply for and obtain a license from the Department of Children and Family Services (DCFS). Under the Act, responsibility for prescribing and publishing "minimum standards for licensing that apply to the various types of facilities for child care defined in [the] Act," including day-care homes, rests with DCFS.

The court concluded that "the municipality's ordinance stands as a complete bar to the operation of a state-licensed day-care home. Under Olympia Fields' zoning ordinance, the licensing system for day-care homes is rendered a nullity."

C. Do the Equal Protection, Due Process, and Takings Clauses Provide Adequate Protection From the Alleged Government Misuse of Land Use Powers?

While claims that zoning ordinances and other forms of land use regulation effect confiscation in violation of the Takings Clause are commonplace today, landowners and their counsel should be mindful that there are other constitutional provisions (federal and state) that may well afford protection as well. In the first case that follows, the Illinois Supreme Court interpreted its own state constitution in favor of those asserting that a local zoning ordinance contained an unfair classification. In the second case, two of the Supreme Court's most liberal members disagreed over the legality of a controversial definition employed by a New York community to "zone out" groups of student tenants. In the third case, the majority arrived at a "Euclidean" conclusion, though the Justices took a *Pennsylvania Coal* detour. Sometimes the language of a constitutional clause does not sufficiently explain seemingly inconsistent outcomes. It is at that point that speculation turns to such factors as the makeup of the judicial panel, the specific language of the challenged ordinance, and the prevailing ideological ethos at the time of the decision. The final decision in this grouping, a 2005 case involving the meaning of the phrase "public use" in the Takings Clause, has turned out to be one of the most controversial High Court decisions in recent memory.

RONDA REALTY CORP. v. LAWTON
414 Ill. 313, 111 N.E.2d 310 (1953)

DAILY, Justice. This is an appeal from a judgment of the circuit court of Cook County which found subparagraph (2) of section 8 of the Chicago zoning ordinance (Municipal Code of Chicago, sec. 194A8(2)), to be unconstitutional and void. The trial court has certified that the validity of a municipal ordinance is involved and, that in its opinion, the public interest requires a direct appeal to this court.

The leading facts show that appellee, which is the Ronda Realty Corporation, applied to the commissioner of buildings in the city of Chicago, for a permit to remodel appellee's apartment building at 420115 North Sheridan Road, from twenty-one to fifty-three apartments. Accompanying the application was a certificate, by the secretary of the appellee, to the effect that on the premises there would be off-street facilities for parking eighteen automobiles. The commissioner issued the permit, whereupon thirteen tenants of the building, who are some of the appellants here, appealed to the zoning board of appeals seeking to reverse the action of the commissioner. The ground of the appeal was that the remodeling would result in the creation of fifty-three apartments; that section 194A-8(2) of the Municipal Code of Chicago requires an apartment building to provide off-street automobile parking facilities on the lot where the apartment building is maintained at the ratio of one automobile for each three apartments, that there is only space on appellee's lot for parking eight automobiles; that fifty-three apartments would require eighteen parking spaces and therefore the commissioner should not have issued the permit.

A hearing was held before the zoning board of appeals, which body, after hearing evidence and viewing the premises, concluded that there were not enough off-street parking facilities on appellee's property to comply with the ordinance and entered an order reversing the action of the commissioner and revoking the permit. Appellee then filed a complaint in the circuit court for review under the provisions of the Administrative Review Act (Ill. Rev. Stat. 1951, chap. 110, pars. 264279) setting forth the facts and pleading the invalidity of the ordinance relied upon by the board. On the hearing for review, the court stated that it was deciding the case purely on a question of law and not on questions of fact, and entered its judgment that the section of the ordinance relied upon was unconstitutional and void in that it discriminated against appellee and deprived it of equal protection of the law. The order of the zoning board of appeals was reversed and the issuance of the building permit sustained. The tenants, the commissioner of buildings, the zoning board of appeals and the city of Chicago have perfected the appeal to this court.

The errors assigned in this court present but one decisive issue, namely, whether subparagraph (2) of section 8 of the zoning ordinance is invalid because it creates an unlawful classification, discriminatory in its nature. The complete provisions of section 8 of the ordinance are as follows:

> 194A-8. (Section 8.) Apartment House Districts. Permitted uses in Apartment House districts are:
>
> (1) Any use permitted in a Family Residence district without restrictions except such as are applicable to auxiliary uses and any other use permitted in a Duplex Residence or Group House district;
>
> (2) Apartment house, provided that where there are more than two apartments in the building a private garage or automobile compound for the storage of one passenger automobile for each of 33 per cent of the number of apartments shall be erected or established and maintained on the lot used for the apartment house;
>
> (3) Boarding or lodging house, hotel, hospital, home for dependents or nursing home;
>
> (4) Boarding school, vocational school, college or university, when not operated for pecuniary profit;
>
> (5) Club, fraternity or sorority house, when not operated for pecuniary profit;
>
> (6) Public art gallery, library or museum;
>
> (7) Auxiliary uses . . .

Laws will not be regarded as special or class legislation merely because they affect one class and not another, provided they affect all members of the same class alike. A classification which is not purely arbitrary and is reasonably adapted to secure the purpose for which it was intended will not be disturbed by the courts unless it can be clearly seen that there is no fair reason for the distinction made. Stearns v. City of Chicago, 368 Ill. 112, 13 N.E.2d 63. Also, in this regard, we have held that even though a zoning ordinance be based upon proper statutory authority and is reasonably designed to protect the public health or safety, it cannot, in such guise, under the rights guaranteed by the Illinois and Federal constitutions, effect an arbitrary discrimination against the class on which it operates by omitting from its coverage persons and objects similarly situated. Statutory classifications can only be sustained where there are real differences between the classes, and where the selection of the particular class, as distinguished from others, is reasonably related to the evils to be remedied by the statute or ordinance.

Tested in the light of these established rules of law, we believe it is manifest that subparagraph (2) of section 8 creates an unlawful classification, both arbitrary and discriminatory in its nature. Of all the different types of structures upon which the section is made to operate, it is only apartment buildings that are required to furnish off-street parking facilities. The evils to be remedied on crowded city streets are well known, but we do not see that the singling out of apartment buildings from the other types of buildings embraced by the ordinance is reasonably related to the elimination of those evils. Appellants urge that the classification is not discriminatory because it applies to all apartment buildings equally and because it is apartment buildings, more than any other type structure permitted, which contribute the most to street congestion caused by parked automobiles. We see neither a fair nor reasonable basis for such classification nor its reasonable relation to the object and purpose of the ordinance. The street congestion problems created by boarding or rooming houses, hotels, and the like, are not essentially different from those caused by apartment buildings. All are similarly situated in their relation to the problems of congestion that are caused by parking cars in the street, and all contribute proportionately to the evil sought to be remedied. Indeed, we think it not unreasonable to say that the scope and nature of the congestion may be greater in the case of large rooming houses and hotels than in the case of apartment houses. First, due to the comparative number of persons accommodated and, second, because the apartment dweller suggests a resident of some permanency who would seek to alleviate the problem of parking on the street, whereas the hotel or rooming house guest suggests a transient who makes no effort to solve his parking problem. It is our conclusion that the differences in kind between apartment buildings and numerous of the other structures upon which the section is made to operate are not such as to warrant the distinction made by subparagraph (2). Relieving congestion in the streets is no doubt a proper legislative purpose, but imposing the burden on one kind of property, while excepting other kinds not significantly different, is not a valid means for its accomplishment. A statute or ordinance cannot be sustained which applies to some cases and does not apply to other cases not essentially different in kind. Josma v. Western Steel Car & Foundry Co., 249 Ill. 508, 94 N.E. 945. . . .

Judgment affirmed.[25]

Notes

1. *Ronda Realty* reminds us that state high courts are the ultimate interpreters of the language and import of state constitutional provisions. Even if the language of the state and federal equal protec-

---

25. Authors' note: In August 1953, the Chicago City Council adopted an amendment to the zoning ordinance, listing 26 property uses for which off-street parking facilities are required. *See also* Peoria v. Heim, 229 Ill. App. 3d 1016, 1018, 594 N.E.2d 778, 780 (App. Ct. 1992), in which the appellate court did not allow the city to enforce parking requirements enacted in 1979 against the owner of multi-family buildings who acquired the properties in 1975: "We further hold that the zoning ordinance cannot be retroactively applied. The ordinance does not evidence intent for any retroactive application. Any intent that an ordinance operate retroactively must be evident, as where the pertinent language specifically requires compliance by pre-existing buildings."

tion clauses (or due process or takings clauses for that matter) are a close or even perfect match, state judges can choose to be *more protective* of the rights of private property owners. Of course, litigants who found state judges to be *less protective* of their individual liberties would (and have) naturally explore the federal option. A recent example of a state court providing extra protection for property owners is Community Resources for Justice v. City of Manchester, 154 N.H. 748, 756, 758, 762, 917 A.2d 707, 716, 717, 721 (2007), in which the court reversed and remanded a trial court decision that had upheld a citywide ban on correctional facilities. The successful appeal was brought by a landowner seeking to operate a halfway house under a contract with the Federal Bureau of Prisons. After applying the rational basis test, the Supreme Court of New Hampshire rejected the landowner's claim "that the ban on correctional facilities violates its substantive due process rights under the New Hampshire Constitution." In a surprising move, however, the court ratcheted up the intensity of its review when considering the landowner's as-applied equal protection challenge: "As the right to use and enjoy property is an important substantive right, we use our intermediate scrutiny test to review equal protection challenges to zoning ordinances that infringe upon this right." Moreover, the court took the case as an "opportunity to clarify our middle tier scrutiny test" by adopting the federal approach: "To eliminate the confusion in our intermediate level of review and to make our test more consistent with the federal test, we now hold that intermediate scrutiny under the State Constitution requires that the challenged legislation be substantially related to an important governmental objective." What this means is that, while the intermediate scrutiny tests are identical, New Hampshire now applies that more demanding test to a wider range of cases, a range that arguably encompasses even the most routine zoning challenge. Only time will tell whether the state supreme court decides to reconsider the impact of its finding that "the right to use and enjoy property is an important substantive right."

2. Ever since *Euclid v. Ambler*, Fourteenth Amendment Equal Protection Clause challenges to run-of-the-mill zoning have typically been unsuccessful. Unless the private property owner can convince the court to employ more than minimal (rational basis) scrutiny—by demonstrating discrimination against a suspect or quasi-suspect classification or the violation of a judicially recognized federal fundamental right (the right to own and use private property not being in that category)—such challenges almost always will prove frustrating. There are exceptions to the prevailing pattern, however, most notably the per curium decision in Village of Willowbrook v. Olech, 528 U.S. 562, 564-65 (2000). The Olechs, who had successfully sued the village over another matter, brought an equal protection challenge when the village conditioned their agreement to connect the Olechs' property to the municipal water supply on the grant of a 33-foot easement, while other property owners had only been asked for a 15-foot easement. When the U.S. Court of Appeals for the Seventh Circuit, noting "that a plaintiff can allege an equal protection violation by asserting that state action was motivated solely by a 'spiteful effort to "get" him for reasons wholly unrelated to any legitimate state objective,'" reversed the district court's dismissal of the lawsuit, the Supreme Court "granted certiorari to determine whether the Equal Protection Clause gives rise to a cause of action on behalf of a 'class of one' where the plaintiff did not allege membership in a class or group." The Court's rationale for affirmance was pithy:

> Our cases have recognized successful equal protection claims brought by a "class of one," where the plaintiff alleges that she has been intentionally treated differently from others similarly situated and that there is no rational basis for the difference in treatment. In so doing, we have explained that "'the purpose of the equal protection clause of the Fourteenth Amendment is to secure every person within the State's jurisdiction against intentional and arbitrary discrimination, whether occasioned by express terms of a statute or by its improper execution through duly constituted agents.'" Sioux City

Bridge Co., [260 U.S. 441,] at 445 [(1923)] (quoting Sunday Lake Iron Co. v. Township of Wakefield, 247 U.S. 350, 352 (1918)).

That reasoning is applicable to this case. Olech's complaint can fairly be construed as alleging that the Village intentionally demanded a 33-foot easement as a condition of connecting her property to the municipal water supply where the Village required only a 15-foot easement from other similarly situated property owners. The complaint also alleged that the Village's demand was "irrational and wholly arbitrary" and that the Village ultimately connected her property after receiving a clearly adequate 15-foot easement. These allegations, quite apart from the Village's subjective motivation, are sufficient to state a claim for relief under traditional equal protection analysis. We therefore affirm the judgment of the Court of Appeals, but do not reach the alternative theory of "subjective ill will" relied on by that court.

In a concurring opinion, Justice Stephen Breyer, 528 U.S. at 565-66, noted that the case

does not directly raise the question whether the simple and common instance of a faulty zoning decision would violate the Equal Protection Clause. That is because the Court of Appeals found that in this case respondent had alleged an extra factor as well—a factor that the Court of Appeals called "vindictive action," "illegitimate animus," or "ill will."
. . .

In my view, the presence of that added factor in this case is sufficient to minimize any concern about transforming run-of-the-mill zoning cases into cases of constitutional right.

While *Olech* quickly became part of the disgruntled property owner's litigation arsenal, so far Euclidean deference rules in the absence of such highly unusual facts. Professor William D. Araiza, in *Irrationality and Animus in Class-of-One Equal Protection Cases*, 34 Ecology L.Q. 493, 494 (2007), has provided this summary of *Olech*'s early legacy:

Initially, *Olech* caused a great deal of concern among government officials, as it held the potential to expand their federal liability for disputes growing out of everyday local issues ranging from land use to police protection. For the most part, experience has not borne out this fear. Continued application of traditional deferential rational basis analysis dooms most of these claims. In the land use context in particular, the uniqueness of each property parcel makes it even less likely that a court would find both that two parties were relevantly similarly situated and that the differential treatment lacked any conceivable rational basis. *Olech*'s most noticeable practical effect may well turn out to be the increased litigation leverage enjoyed by plaintiffs, as Olech allows a plaintiff to survive a motion to dismiss without having to plead anything more than irrational government action.

As a more theoretical matter, though, *Olech* raises fundamental issues about equal protection law: does equal protection protect only against class-based discrimination or does it also guard against government singling out of individuals without reference to their possession of a class characteristic such as race or gender? *Olech* clearly and unanimously extended the equal protection guarantee to situations of such individual singling-out, or "classes of one." But the Court, and especially post-*Olech* lower courts, have split on a second issue: whether such class-of-one claims can be based purely on claims of irrational government action, or whether government animus is an essential part of the claim.

3. Given the centrality of the automobile to American urban and suburban life, it is not surprising to find that parking often occupies a prominent place in local zoning ordinances. In parts of Pasadena, California, certain landowners can voluntarily enter into a contract with the city by which the owner can meet the parking requirements included in the zoning code. The code specifications will thereby be met not by the provision of on-site parking, but by the purchase of a Zoning Parking Credit that for a fee, entitles the owner to apply a parking space in an available public parking facility toward the owner's parking requirement. See Pasadena Zoning Code §17.46.030 (Alternative Means for Providing Required Parking).

Minimum parking requirements and the location of parking spaces mandated by traditional zoning ordinances are specially targeted by New Urbanist critics. According to Brian Ohm & Mark White, *Changing the Rules: New Approaches to Zoning*, in A Legal Guide to Urban and Sustainable Development for Planners, Developers, and Architects 105 (Daniel K. Slone & Doris S. Goldstein eds. 2008):

> One of the most important objectives of an urban code is to tame parking. Conventional zoning ordinances permit parking lots to line suburban corridors in front of stores and parking garages to dominate the front facade of residential dwellings. In addition, minimum parking ratios may require more parking than is needed, resulting in barriers to pedestrian movement and a loss of enclosure and a corresponding sense of placelessness along the corridor. Moreover, excess on-site parking sometimes means that no one parks along the street, and this aspect of traffic calming disappears. Accordingly many urban codes [that is, New Urbanist or "Smart Codes"] feature maximum parking standards and require parking to be screened by buildings, many times in the center of blocks.

4. Today, zoning ordinances contain special provisions on the number of spaces per use, the dimensions and designs of spaces, and, as an environmental protection measure, the surface treatment and drainage for the spaces. See for example, the following excerpt from the City of Alexandria, Virginia Zoning Digest, Parking and Loading Requirements (http://alexandriava.gov/index_quicklinks.aspx?id=7622):

KING STREET METRO PARKING DISTRICT

Office Uses—1 space/530 sq. ft. by right 1 space/665 sq.ft. with parking study Single-Family, Two-Family, Townhouse and Multi-Family Dwellings—1 space/unit Retail and Service (freestanding)—1space/500 sq.ft.

Restaurants (freestanding) required for carryout—1 space/10 seats; none Auto Service Stations—1 space/service bay; 1 space/employee for self service Hotels—0.7 space/guest room . . .

DESIGN OF PARKING SPACES AND FACILITIES

(1) DIMENSIONS

Minimum dimensions for off-street parking spaces and off-street parking aisles shall be as shown in the table below. Such requirement shall not apply to specially approved attendant-operated parking facilities, including those used for valet parking.

Parking Angle	Stall Width (Feet)	Depth of Stalls Perpendicular to Aisle (Feet)	One-Way Aisle Width (Feet)	Two-Way Aisle Width (Feet)
45°	8.5	19.0	16.0	20.0
60°	8.5	20.0	16.0	20.0
90°	9.0	18.5	22.0	22.0
	8.0 (compact)	16.0 (compact)	20.0 (compact)	20.0 (compact)
Parallel	8.0	22.0	12.0	20.0
	7.0 (compact)	18.0 (compact)	16.0 (where adjacent to building)	

(2) COMPACT CAR SPACES

Non-retail uses requiring ten or more off-street parking spaces may provide up to 75 percent of such parking as compact car parking spaces.

Retail uses requiring two or more off-street parking spaces may provide up to 30 percent of such parking as compact car parking spaces. . . .

(3) SURFACE TREATMENT, DRAINAGE AND MAINTENANCE

Driveways and parking spaces shall be smoothly graded, adequately drained and constructed with suitable subgrade, base and surfacing to be durable under the use and maintenance contemplated.

Any grade transitions shall be designed and constructed to prevent undercarriage and bumper guards from scraping the pavement surface.

Such parking facilities shall be property maintained and aisles shall remain open and free for traffic flow.

5. At least as early as the settlement of "streetcar suburbs" in the 19th century, American planning and land development has been inextricably tied to modes of transportation, from horse drawn trolleys to cable cars, subways, elevated trains, automobiles, buses, high-speed rail, monorails, and people movers. An important component of New Urbanism is a group of planning practices that share the moniker transit-oriented development (TOD). Peter Calthorpe, in *The Urban Network: A Radical Proposal*, Planning, May 2002, at 11-15, has explained:

The old paradigm is simple: a grid of arterials spaced at one-mile increments with major retail located at the intersections and commercial strips lining its inhospitable but very visible edges. Overlaying the grid in rings and radials is the freeway system. The intersection of the grid and freeway is fertile ground for malls and office parks. This system is rational, coherent, and true to itself, even if increasingly dysfunctional. . . .

We must develop a new circulation pattern that will accommodate cars as well as transit and will reinforce walkable places rather than isolating them. Bringing daily destinations closer to home is a fundamental aspect of urbanism, but it is not the complete solution to our access needs. . . .

The alternative transportation network proposed here is diverse and complex. It calls for a new hierarchy of arterials and boulevards that allow for through-traffic without always bypassing commercial centers—a road network that reinforces access to walkable neighborhoods and urban town centers without cutting them off from local pedestrian movement.

This new network must incorporate transit in a way that is affordable, appropriately placed, and integral to the system. It should reserve freeway capacity for long trips and provide alternate means for daily work commutes and shopping trips. . . .

This urban network would replace the old system of functional street types, where streets serve a single function in a linear hierarchy of capacities. The new street types combine uses, capacities, and scales.

The transit boulevards combine the capacity of a major arterial with the intimacy of local frontage roads and the pedestrian orientation that comes with the transit system. Local arterials are multi-lane facilities that transition into a couplet of "main streets" at the village centers. This approach is fundamental to the more complex mixed land-use patterns of the New Urbanism. Streets, like land uses, can no longer afford to be single-purpose.

The urban network integrates new and old forms of urban development in appropriate and accessible locations. Walkable town and village centers are placed at the crossroads of the transit boulevards and local arterials. Residential neighborhoods are directly accessible to these centers by way of local connector streets as well as the arterials. Industrial, warehouse, and other auto-oriented uses are close to the throughways.

Each urban land-use type has the appropriate scale and type of access. The town center is both pedestrian friendly and accessible to the boulevard's through-traffic and transit line. The villages are directly accessible by foot, bus, car, or bicycle from their surrounding neighborhoods, while the couplet streets bring the auto access needed for retail. Auto- and truck-oriented uses can locate at the intersections of the throughways away from the transit and mixed-use centers.

VILLAGE OF BELLE TERRE v. BORAAS
416 U.S. 1 (1974)

Mr. Justice DOUGLAS delivered the opinion of the Court.

Belle Terre is a village on Long Island's north shore of about 220 homes inhabited by 700 people. Its total land area is less than one square mile. It has restricted land use to one-family dwellings excluding lodging houses, boarding houses, fraternity houses, or multiple dwelling houses. The word "family" as used in the ordinance means, "one or more persons related by blood, adoption, or marriage, living and cooking together as a single housekeeping unit, exclusive of household servants. A number of persons but not exceeding two (2) living and cooking together as a single housekeeping unit though not related by blood, adoption, or marriage shall be deemed to constitute a family."

Appellees the Dickmans are owners of a house in the village and leased it in December, 1971 for a term of 18 months to Michael Truman. Later Bruce Boraas became a colessee. Then Anne Parish moved into the house along with three others. These six are students at nearby State University at Stony Brook and none is related to the other by blood, adoption, or marriage. When the village served the Dickmans with an "Order to Remedy Violations" of the ordinance, the owners plus three tenants thereupon brought this action under 42 U.S.C. § 1983 for an injunction declaring the ordinance unconstitutional. The District Court held the ordinance constitutional and the Court of Appeals reversed, one judge dissenting. . . .

This case brings to this Court a different phase of local zoning regulations than we have previously reviewed. Village of Euclid v. Ambler Realty Co., 272 U.S. 365, involved a zoning ordinance classifying land use in a given area into six categories. . . .

line "which in this field separates the legitimate from the illegitimate assumption of power is not capable of precise delimitation. It varies with circumstances and conditions." 272 U.S., at 387. . . . The ordinance was sanctioned because the validity of the legislative classification was "fairly debatable" and therefore could not be said to be wholly arbitrary. . . .

The present ordinance is challenged on several grounds: that it interferes with a person's right to travel; that it interferes with the right to migrate to and settle within a State; that it bars people who are uncongenial to the present residents; that the ordinance expresses the social preferences of the residents for groups that will be congenial to them; that social homogeneity is not a legitimate interest of government; that the restriction of those whom the neighbors do not like trenches on the newcomers' rights of privacy; that it is of no rightful concern to villagers whether the residents are married or unmarried; that the ordinance is antithetical to the Nation's experience, ideology and selfperception as an open, egalitarian, and integrated society.

We find none of these reasons in the record before us. It is not aimed at transients. Cf. Shapiro v. Thompson, 394 U.S. 618. It involves no procedural disparity inflicted on some but not on others such as was presented by Griffin v. Illinois, 351 U.S. 12. It involves no "fundamental" right guaranteed by the Constitution, such as voting, the right of association, the right of access to the courts, or any rights of privacy. We deal with economic and social legislation where legislatures have historically drawn lines which we respect against the charge of violation of the Equal Protection Clause if the law be "reasonable, not arbitrary" (quoting F. S. Royster Guano Co. v. Virginia, 253 U.S. 412, 415) and bears "a rational relationship to a [permissible] state objective." Reed v. Reed, 404 U.S. 71, 76.

It is said, however, that if two unmarried people can constitute a "family," there is no reason why three or four may not. But every line drawn by a legislature leaves some out that might well have been included[5] That exercise of discretion, however, is a legislative not a judicial function.

It is said that the Belle Terre ordinance reeks with an animosity to unmarried couples who live together.[6] There is no evidence to support it; and the provision of the ordinance bringing within the definition of a "family" two unmarried people belies the charge.

The ordinance places no ban on other forms of association, for a "family" may, so far as the ordinance is concerned, entertain whomever they like.

The regimes of boarding houses, fraternity houses, and the like present urban problems. More people occupy a given space; more cars rather continuously pass by; more cars are parked; noise travels with crowds.

---

5. Mr. Justice Holmes made the point a half century ago.

   When a legal distinction is determined, as no one doubts that it may be, between night and day, childhood and maturity, or any other extremes, a point has to be fixed or a line has to be drawn, or gradually picked out by successive decisions, to mark where the change takes place. Looked at by itself without regard to the necessity behind it the line or point seems arbitrary. It might as well or nearly as well be a little more to one side or the other. But when it is seen that a line or point there must be, and that there is no mathematical or logical way of fixing it precisely, the decision of the legislature must be accepted unless we can say that it is very wide of any reasonable mark.

   Louisville Gas & Electric Co. v. Coleman, 277 U.S. 32, 41 (dissenting).

6. U.S. Dept. of Agriculture v. Moreno, 413 U.S. 528 (1973), is therefore inapt as there a household containing anyone unrelated to the rest was denied food stamps.

A quiet place where yards are wide, people few, and motor vehicles restricted are legitimate guidelines in a land use project addressed to family needs. This goal is a permissible one within Berman v. Parker [348 U.S. 26 (1954)]. The police power is not confined to elimination of filth, stench, and unhealthy places. It is ample to lay out zones where family values, youth values, and the blessings of quiet seclusion, and clean air make the area a sanctuary for people.

The suggestion that the case may be moot need not detain us. A zoning ordinance usually has an impact on the value of the property which it regulates. But in spite of the fact that the precise impact of the ordinance sustained in *Euclid* on a given piece of property was not known, 272 U.S., at 397, the Court, considering the matter a controversy in the realm of city planning, sustained the ordinance. Here we are a step closer to the impact of the ordinance on the value of the lessor's property. He has not only lost six tenants and acquired only two in their place; it is obvious that the scale of rental values rides on what we decide today. When *Berman* reached us it was not certain whether an entire tract would be taken or only the buildings on it and a scenic easement. 348 U.S., at 36. But that did not make the case any the less a controversy in the constitutional sense. When Mr. Justice Holmes said for the Court in Block v. Hirsh, 256 U.S. 135, 155, "property rights may be cut down, and to that extent taken, without pay," he stated the issue here. As is true in most zoning cases, the precise impact on value may, at the threshold of litigation over validity, not yet be known.

Reversed.

Mr. Justice BRENNAN, dissenting.

The constitutional challenge to the village ordinance is premised solely on alleged infringement of associational and other constitutional rights of tenants. But the named tenant appellees have quit the house, thus raising a serious question whether there now exists a cognizable "case or controversy" that satisfies that indispensable requisite of Art. III of the Constitution. Existence of a case or controversy must of course appear at every stage of review. . . . In my view it does not appear at this stage of this case.

Mr. Justice MARSHALL, dissenting. . . .

Appellees, the two owners of a Belle Terre residence, and three unrelated student tenants challenged the ordinance on the grounds that it establishes a classification between households of related and unrelated individuals, which deprives them of equal protection of the laws. In my view, the disputed classification burdens the students' fundamental rights of association and privacy guaranteed by the First and Fourteenth Amendments. Because the application of strict equal protection scrutiny is therefore required, I am at odds with my brethren's conclusion that the ordinance may be sustained on a showing that it bears a rational relationship to the accomplishment of legitimate governmental objectives.

I am in full agreement with the majority that zoning is a complex and important function of the State. It may indeed be the most essential function performed by local government, for it is one of the primary means by which we protect that sometimes difficult to define concept of quality of life. I therefore continue to adhere to the principle of Village of Euclid v. Ambler Realty Co., 272 U.S. 365 (1926), that deference should be given to governmental judgments concerning proper land use allocation. That deference is a principle which has served this Court well and which is necessary for the continued development of effective zoning and land use control mechanisms. Had the owners alone brought this suit alleging that the restrictive ordinance deprived them of their property or was an irrational legislative classification, I would agree that the ordinance would have to be sustained. Our role is not and should not be to sit as a zoning board of appeals. . . .

My disagreement with the Court today is based upon my view that the ordinance in this case unnecessarily burdens appellees' First Amendment freedom of association and their constitutionally guaranteed right to privacy. Our decisions establish that the First and Fourteenth Amendments protect the freedom to choose one's associates. NAACP v. Button, 371 U.S. 415, 430 (1963). Constitutional protection is extended not only to modes of association that are political in the usual sense, but also to those that pertain to the social and economic benefit of the members. . . . The selection of one's living companions involves similar choices as to the emotional, social, or economic benefits to be derived from alternative living arrangements. . . .

This is not a case where the Court is being asked to nullify a township's sincere efforts to maintain its residential character by preventing the operation of rooming houses, fraternity houses or other commercial or high-density residential uses. Unquestionably, a town is free to restrict such uses. Moreover, as a general proposition, I see no constitutional infirmity in a town limiting the density of use in residential areas by zoning regulations which do not discriminate on the basis of constitutionally suspect criteria. This ordinance, however, limits the density of occupancy of only those homes occupied by unrelated persons. It thus reaches beyond control of the use of land or the density of population, and undertakes to regulate the way people choose to associate with each other within the privacy of their own homes.

It is no answer to say, as does the majority that associational interests are not infringed because Belle Terre residents may entertain whomever they choose. Only last Term Mr. Justice Douglas indicated in concurrence that he saw the right of association protected by the First Amendment as involving far more than the right to entertain visitors. He found that right infringed by a restriction on food stamp assistance, penalizing households of "unrelated persons." As Mr. Justice Douglas there said, freedom of association encompasses the "right to invite a stranger into one's home" not only for "entertainment" but to join the household as well. Moreno v. Department of Agriculture, 413 U.S. 528, 538–545 (1973, Douglas, J., concurring). I am still persuaded that the choice of those who will form one's household implicates constitutionally protected rights.

Because I believe that this zoning ordinance creates a classification which impinges upon fundamental personal rights, it can withstand constitutional scrutiny only upon a clear showing that the burden imposed is necessary to protect a compelling and substantial governmental interest, Shapiro v. Thompson, 394 U.S. 618 (1969). And, once it be determined that a burden has been placed upon a constitutional right, the onus of demonstrating that no less intrusive means will adequately protect the compelling state interest and that the challenged statute is sufficiently narrowly drawn, is upon the party seeking to justify the burden. . . .

By limiting unrelated households to two persons while placing no limitation on households of related individuals, the village has embarked upon its commendable course in a constitutionally faulty vessel. I would find the challenged ordinance unconstitutional. But I would not ask the village to abandon its goal of providing quiet streets, little traffic, and a pleasant and reasonably priced environment in which families might raise their children. Rather, I would commend the town to continue to pursue those purposes but by means of more carefully drawn and even-handed legislation.

I respectfully dissent.

Notes

1. *Belle Terre* has received a less-than-warm reception in many state courts, which, as in *Ronda Realty* (above) and the *Mt. Laurel* litigation (see Chapter Six), are charged with interpreting their *own* state constitutions in the way they deem most appropriate. For example, a New York case decided two months after *Belle Terre* was announced involved "Abbott House, a private agency licensed by the State to care for neglected and abandoned children, [which] leases the house in an 'R-2' single-family zone." Inside the group home lived a married couple, their 2 children, and 10

foster children. The local zoning ordinance defined "family" as "one or more persons limited to the spouse, parents, grandparents, grandchildren, sons, daughters, brothers or sisters of the owner or the tenant or of the owner's spouse or tenant's spouse living together as a single housekeeping unit with kitchen facilities." In City of White Plains v. Ferrailoli, 34 N.Y.2d 300, 303-05, 313 N.E.2d 756, 757-58 (1974), the New York Court of Appeals granted summary judgment to the defendants, noting that "[z]oning is intended to control types of housing and living and not the genetic or intimate internal family relations of human beings." The state jurists attempted to distinguish *Belle Terre*:

> The group home is not, for purposes of a zoning ordinance, a temporary living arrangement as would be a group of college students sharing a house and commuting to a nearby school (cf. Village of Belle Terre v. Boraas, 416 U.S. 1). Every year or so, different college students would come to take the place of those before them. There would be none of the permanency of community that characterizes a residential neighborhood of private homes. Nor is it like the so-called "commune" style of living. The group home is a permanent arrangement and akin to a traditional family, which also may be sundered by death, divorce, or emancipation of the young. Neither the foster parents nor the children are to be shifted about; the intention is that they remain and develop ties in the community. The purpose is to emulate the traditional family and not to introduce a different "life style."

> Of course, the Supreme Court of the United States, in the recent *Belle Terre* case, has held that it is a proper purpose of zoning to lay out districts devoted to "family values" and "youth values." Hence, toward that end those uses which conflict with a stable, uncongested single family environment may be restricted. High density uses, for example, may be restricted; so too those uses which are associated with occupancy by numbers of transient persons may be limited. By requiring single family use of a house, the ordinance emphasizes and ensures the character of the neighborhood to promote the family environment. The group home does not conflict with that character and, indeed, is deliberately designed to conform with it.

In State v. Baker, 81 N.J. 99, 405 A.2d 368 (1979), in a 5-2 holding, New Jersey's high court struck down a zoning ordinance that prohibited more than four persons who were "not related by blood, marriage or adoption" from occupying a single-family unit. As long as a group bore the "generic character of a family unit as a relatively permanent household," it should be treated similarly to "its biologically related neighbors." Can this be squared with the Supreme Court's holding? The New Jersey Supreme Court thought not:

> In any event, *Belle Terre* is at most dispositive of any federal constitutional question here involved. We, of course, remain free to interpret our constitution and statutes more stringently. *See generally* Brennan, "State Constitutions and the Protection of Individual Rights," 90 *Harv. L. Rev.* 489 (1977).[8] We find the reasoning of *Belle Terre* to be both unpersuasive and inconsistent with the results reached by this Court in [previous opinions]. Hence we do not choose to follow it.

---

8. As Justice Brennan aptly remarked, "state courts cannot rest when they have afforded their citizens the full protections of the federal Constitution. State Constitutions, too, are a font of individual liberties, their protections often extending beyond those required by the [United States] Supreme Court's interpretation of federal law." *Id.* at 491. Constitutional decisions by federal courts, he declared, should only be considered as "guideposts" in interpreting state constitutional provisions "if they are found to be logically persuasive and well-reasoned, paying due regard to precedent and the policies underlying specific constitutional guarantees * * *." *Id.* at 502.

See also Borough of Glassboro v. Vallorosi, 117 N.J. 421 422, 568 A.2d 888, 889 (1990):

> The narrow issue presented in this case is whether a group of ten unrelated college students living in defendants' home constitutes a "family" within the definition of a restrictive zoning ordinance. The Borough of Glassboro concedes that a primary purpose of the ordinance was to prevent groups of unrelated college students from living together in the Borough's residential districts. The ordinance limits residence in such districts to stable and permanent "single housekeeping units" that constitute either a "traditional family unit" or its functional equivalent. The Chancery Division concluded that the relationship among this group of students and their living arrangements within the home demonstrated the "generic character" of a family, and denied the Borough injunctive relief. The Appellate Division affirmed. We now affirm the judgment of the Appellate Division.

2. Courts have also been called upon to interpret the term "family" as used in neighborhood restrictive covenants. In Jackson v. Williams, 714 P.2d 1017 (Okla. 1985), the court held that use of a residence as a group home for five mentally handicapped women and their housekeeper did not violate a covenant restricting use to a "single-family dwelling." *See also* Double D Manor, Inc. v. Evergreen Meadows Homeowners' Ass'n, 773 P.2d 1046, 1049 (Colo. 1989), in which the Colorado Supreme Court joined several other "jurisdictions which have addressed similar questions [and] have concluded that the phrase 'single-family dwelling' is merely a structural restriction."

3. Section 1341.08 of the Codified Ordinances of the City of East Cleveland, Ohio, read:

> "Family" means a number of individuals related to the nominal head of the household or to the spouse of the nominal head of the household living as a single housekeeping unit in a single dwelling unit, but limited to the following:
>
> > (a) Husband or wife of the nominal head of the household.
> >
> > (b) Unmarried children of the nominal head of the household or of the spouse of the nominal head of the household, provided, however, that such unmarried children have no children residing with them.
> >
> > (c) Father or mother of the nominal head of the household or of the spouse of the nominal head of the household.
> >
> > (d) Notwithstanding the provisions of subsection (b) hereof, a family may include not more than one dependent married or unmarried child of the nominal head of the household or of the spouse of the nominal head of the household and the spouse and dependent children of such dependent child. For the purpose of this subsection, a dependent person is one who has more than fifty percent of his total support furnished for him by the nominal head of the household and the spouse of the nominal head of the household.
> >
> > (e) A family may consist of one individual.

In Moore v. City of East Cleveland, 431 U.S. 494, 496-99 (1977), the Court considered the following facts:

> Appellant, Mrs. Inez Moore, lives in her East Cleveland home together with her son, Dale Moore Sr., and her two grandsons, Dale, Jr., and John Moore, Jr. The two boys

are first cousins rather than brothers; we are told that John came to live with his grandmother and with the elder and younger Dale Moores after his mother's death.

In early 1973, Mrs. Moore received a notice of violation from the city, stating that John was an "illegal occupant" and directing her to comply with the ordinance. When she failed to remove him from her home, the city filed a criminal charge. Mrs. Moore moved to dismiss, claiming that the ordinance was constitutionally invalid on its face. Her motion was overruled, and upon conviction she was sentenced to five days in jail and a $25 fine. The Ohio Court of Appeals affirmed after giving full consideration to her constitutional claims, and the Ohio Supreme Court denied review.

Justice Lewis Powell, writing for a plurality, reluctantly unsheathed the sword of substantive due process in order to rescue Mrs. Moore from her criminal predicament. The "one overriding factor" distinguishing this case from *Belle Terre* was that the

ordinance there affected only unrelated individuals. It expressly allowed all who were related by "blood, adoption, or marriage" to live together, and in sustaining the ordinance we were careful to note that it promoted "family needs" and "family values." East Cleveland, in contrast, has chosen to regulate the occupancy of its housing by slicing deeply into the family itself. . . .

When a city undertakes such intrusive regulation of the family, neither *Belle Terre* nor *Euclid* governs; the usual judicial deference to the legislature is inappropriate. "This Court has long recognized that freedom of personal choice in matters of marriage and family life is one of the liberties protected by the Due Process Clause of the Fourteenth Amendment." . . .

Justice Stevens, concurring in the judgment and noting state decisions in this troublesome area, found that the ordinance failed even the limited standard of review articulated in *Euclid*. Four Justices dissented.

4. In McMinn v. Town of Oyster Bay, 105 A.D. 2d 46, 482 N.Y.S.2d 773, 775, 782 (App. Div. 1984), the challenged ordinance

define[d] "family" as "any number of persons related by blood, marriage or legal adoption, living and cooking on the premises together as a single nonprofit housekeeping unit" or any two persons not so related who are 62 years of age or over and live and cook together on the premises as a single nonprofit housekeeping unit.

The ordinance did not survive the court's scrutiny, for its arbitrariness amounted to a denial of due process under the state constitution:

The fact that restrictions in the Oyster Bay ordinance are arbitrary and unreasonable does not imply that single-family zoning is an unsound concept. What it does indicate, however, is something that other states and many municipalities in New York recognize the viability of single-family zoning restrictions no longer depends on biological or legal relationships but on the single housekeeping unit which reflects a certain level of stability.

5. Through 42 U.S.C. §3607(b)(1), Congress provided the following exemption from the strictures of the federal Fair Housing Acts: "Nothing in this title limits the applicability of any reasonable local, State, or Federal restrictions regarding the maximum number of occupants permitted to occupy a dwelling." A provision of the zoning code for Edmonds, Washington, defined "family" as

"an individual or two or more persons related by genetics, adoption, or marriage, or a group of five or fewer persons who are not related by genetics, adoption, or marriage." The relationship between the statute and the ordinance was the focus of the Supreme Court's attention in City of Edmunds v. Oxford House, 514 U.S. 725, 729-30, 732, 733-35, 737 (1995). When the city received word that Oxford House had opened a group home for 10 to 12 adults who were recovering alcoholics and drug addicts in a single-family residential zone, the owner and a resident of the house received criminal citations for violating the zoning code. Oxford House pointed to another provision of the Fair Housing Act, 42 U.S.C. §3604(f)(1)(a), making it unlawful "[t]o discriminate in the sale or rental, or to otherwise make unavailable or deny, a dwelling to any buyer or renter because of a handicap of . . . that buyer or renter." The city refused Oxford House's request "to make a 'reasonable accommodation' [under the Act] by allowing it to remain in the single-family dwelling it had leased," choosing instead to enact "an ordinance listing group homes as permitted uses in multifamily and general commercial zones."

The federal district court and court of appeals disagreed as to the relevance of the exemption in §3607(b)(1). While the trial court found that the city's ordinance was exempt under the Act, the appellate court deemed the provision inapplicable and reversed the lower court's grant of summary judgment in favor of the city. The Supreme Court affirmed in a majority decision written by Justice Ruth Bader Ginsburg, who noted that the Fair Housing Act was enacted "against the backdrop of an evident distinction between municipal land-use restrictions and maximum occupancy restrictions." The difference between the two types of restrictions was crucial to evaluating the language of the exemption provision:

> To limit land use to single-family residences, a municipality must define the term "family"; thus family composition rules are an essential component of single-family residential use restrictions.
>
> Maximum occupancy restrictions, in contradistinction, cap the number of occupants per dwelling, typically in relation to available floor space or the number and type of rooms. See, e. g., International Conference of Building Officials, Uniform Housing Code § 503(b) (1988); Building Officials and Code Administrators International, Inc., BOCA National Property Maintenance Code §§PM-405.3, PM-405.5 (1993) (hereinafter BOCA Code); Southern Building Code Congress, International, Inc., Standard Housing Code §§ 306.1, 306.2 (1991); E. Mood, APHA-CDC Recommended Minimum Housing Standards § 9.02, p. 37 (1986) (hereinafter APHA-CDC Standards). These restrictions ordinarily apply uniformly to all residents of all dwelling units. Their purpose is to protect health and safety by preventing dwelling overcrowding. . . .
>
> Section 3607(b)(1)'s language—"restrictions regarding the maximum number of occupants permitted to occupy a dwelling"—surely encompasses maximum occupancy restrictions. But the formulation does not fit family composition rules typically tied to land-use restrictions. In sum, rules that cap the total number of occupants in order to prevent overcrowding of a dwelling "plainly and unmistakably," see A. H. Phillips, Inc. v. Walling, 324 U.S. 490, 493 (1945), fall within § 3607(b)(1)'s absolute exemption from the FHA's governance; rules designed to preserve the family character of a neighborhood, fastening on the composition of households rather than on the total number of occupants living quarters can contain, do not.

Because the "use restriction and complementing family composition rule" found in the city code, "do not cap the number of people who may live in a dwelling," and because the code provision describes "[f]amily living, not living space per occupant," the Court concluded that the definition of "family" under the zoning code was not a maximum occupancy restriction that was exempt under 42 U.S.C. §3607(b)(1).

Justice Clarence Thomas, joined by Justices Antonin Scalia and Anthony Kennedy, dissented, illustrating disagreement with the logic of the majority with two scenarios (514 U.S. at 740, 748 (Thomas, J., dissenting)):

> Consider a real estate agent who is assigned responsibility for the city of Edmonds. Desiring to learn all he can about his new territory, the agent inquires: "Does the city have any restrictions regarding the maximum number of occupants permitted to occupy a dwelling?" The accurate answer must surely be in the affirmative—yes, the maximum number of unrelated persons permitted to occupy a dwelling in a single-family neighborhood is five. Or consider a different example. Assume that the Federal Republic of Germany imposes no restrictions on the speed of "cars" that drive on the Autobahn but does cap the speed of "trucks" (which are defined as all other vehicles). If a conscientious visitor to Germany asks whether there are "any restrictions regarding the maximum speed of motor vehicles permitted to drive on the Autobahn," the accurate answer again is surely the affirmative one—yes, there is a restriction regarding the maximum speed of trucks on the Autobahn.

In closing, Justice Thomas opined that

> it is immaterial under § 3607(b)(1) whether § 21.030.010 constitutes a "family composition rule" but not a "maximum occupancy restriction." The sole relevant question is whether petitioner's zoning code imposes "any . . . restrictions regarding the maximum number of occupants permitted to occupy a dwelling." Because I believe it does, I respectfully dissent.

Further discussion of the Fair Housing Act can be found in Chapter Six.

6. *Belle Terre* is not the only important opinion in which Justice William O. Douglas invoked environmental values in support of governments seeking to improve the quality of life through land use regulation and other tools ("It is ample to lay out zones where family values, youth values, and the blessings of quiet seclusion, and clean air make the area a sanctuary for people."). One should also read Douglas' stirring language in the 1954 eminent domain decision, Berman v. Parker, 348 U.S. 26, 32-33 (1954):

> Miserable and disreputable housing conditions may do more than spread disease and crime and immorality. They may also suffocate the spirit by reducing the people who live there to the status of cattle. They may indeed make living an almost insufferable burden. They may also be an ugly sore, a blight on the community which robs it of charm, which makes it a place from which men turn. The misery of housing may despoil a community as an open sewer may ruin a river.

For more on Justice Douglas' unique brand of environmentalism on the High Court, see Richard J. Lazarus, *Restoring What's Environmental About Environmental Law in the Supreme Court*, 47 UCLA L. Rev. 703, 764-65 (2000):

> His [Douglas'] personal experiences with the natural environment made him value more highly governmental efforts designed to protect environmental amenities. They also apparently made him far more willing to accommodate other competing values, reflected in legal principles and doctrines intersecting those advanced by environmental protection

laws. His near-unanimous support of environmental ends profoundly influenced both his initial framing of the issues presented and ultimately his votes on those issues.

For more than five decades, Justice Holmes' dictum asserting that "[w]hile property may be regulated to a certain extent, if regulation goes too far it will be recognized as a taking," virtually disappeared from Supreme Court jurisprudence. The notion was kept alive by state and lower federal court judges who were asked to distinguish legitimate from confiscatory land use regulations, and by a number of talented commentators searching for a usable and internally consistent theory that would insulate regulatory regimes—traditional ones, such as zoning, and emerging ones, such as comprehensive environmental protection laws—while protecting the rights of property owners who were especially burdened by government programs. The two most important commentators during this regulatory takings interregnum on the High Court were Professors Joseph Sax and Frank Michelman, whose works are cited in the decision that followed, which opened the regulatory takings litigation floodgates.

The historic preservation movement, and particularly the effort to protect New York City's Grand Central Terminal, attracted the attention of celebrities (most notably Jacqueline Kennedy Onassis) and ultimately of the Supreme Court Justices. With the benefit of hindsight, we can see that the majority and dissenting opinions in the landmark (pun intended) case that follows produced the vocabulary and presaged the sharp ideological debate that would dominate a large segment of land use jurisprudence over the succeeding three decades. As you read these opinions, pay careful attention to the meaning of the following terms and to the context in which these phrases appear: "parcel as a whole," "investment-backed expectations," "economically viable," "reasonable beneficial use," "temporary taking," "reasonable return," "ad hoc, factual inquiries," "physical invasion," "diminution in value," "group of rights," and "nuisance exception." With the ascendancy of the Takings Clause star in the constitutional constellation, the land use attorney's mastery of this special nomenclature (and, of course, of the underlying concepts) will often spell the difference between victory and defeat for a public or private client.

PENN CENTRAL TRANSPORTATION CO. v. NEW YORK CITY
438 U.S. 104 (1978)

MR. JUSTICE BRENNAN delivered the opinion of the Court.

The question presented is whether a city may, as part of a comprehensive program to preserve historic landmarks and historic districts, place restrictions on the development of individual historic landmarks—in addition to those imposed by applicable zoning ordinances—without effecting a "taking" requiring the payment of "just compensation." Specifically, we must decide whether the application of New York City's Landmarks Preservation Law to the parcel of land occupied by Grand Central Terminal has "taken" its owners' property in violation of the Fifth and Fourteenth Amendments.

I

A

Over the past 50 years, all 50 States and over 500 municipalities have enacted laws to encourage or require the preservation of buildings and areas with historic or aesthetic importance. . . .

New York City, responding to similar concerns and acting pursuant to a New York State enabling Act, adopted its Landmarks Preservation Law in 1965. See N. Y. C. Admin. Code, ch. 8-A, § 205-1.0 et seq. (1976). The city acted from the conviction that "the standing of [New York City] as a world-wide tourist center and world capital of business, culture and government" would be threatened if legislation were not enacted to protect historic landmarks and neighborhoods from precipitate decisions to destroy or fundamentally alter their character. § 205-1.0 (a). . . .

The New York City law is typical of many urban landmark laws in that its primary method of achieving its goals is not by acquisitions of historic properties, but rather by involving public entities in land-use decisions affecting these properties and providing services, standards, controls, and incentives that will encourage preservation by private owners and users. While the law does place special restrictions on landmark properties as a necessary feature to the attainment of its larger objectives, the major theme of the law is to ensure the owners of any such properties both a "reasonable return" on their investments and maximum latitude to use their parcels for purposes not inconsistent with the preservation goals.

The operation of the law can be briefly summarized. The primary responsibility for administering the law is vested in the Landmarks Preservation Commission (Commission), a broad based, 11-member agency assisted by a technical staff. The Commission first performs the function, critical to any landmark preservation effort, of identifying properties and areas that have "a special character or special historical or aesthetic interest or value as part of the development, heritage or cultural characteristics of the city, state or nation." § 207-1.0 (n); see § 207-1.0 (h). If the Commission determines, after giving all interested parties an opportunity to be heard, that a building or area satisfies the ordinance's criteria, it will designate a building to be a "landmark," § 207-1.0 (n), situated on a particular "landmark site," § 207-1.0 (o), or will designate an area to be a "historic district," § 207-1.0 (h). After the Commission makes a designation, New York City's Board of Estimate, after considering the relationship of the designated property "to the master plan, the zoning resolution, projected public improvements and any plans for the renewal of the area involved," § 207-2.0 (g)(1), may modify or disapprove the designation, and the owner may seek judicial review of the final designation decision. Thus far, 31 historic districts and over 400 individual landmarks have been finally designated, and the process is a continuing one.

Final designation as a landmark results in restrictions upon the property owner's options concerning use of the landmark site. First, the law imposes a duty upon the owner to keep the exterior features of the building "in good repair" to assure that the law's objectives not be defeated by the landmark's falling into a state of irremediable disrepair. Second, the Commission must approve in advance any proposal to alter the exterior architectural features of the landmark or to construct any exterior improvement on the landmark site, thus ensuring that decisions concerning construction on the landmark site are made with due consideration of both the public interest in the maintenance of the structure and the landowner's interest in use of the property.

In the event an owner wishes to alter a landmark site, three separate procedures are available through which administrative approval may be obtained. First, the owner may apply to the Commission for a "certificate of no effect on protected architectural features": that is, for an order approving the improvement or alteration on the ground that it will not change or affect any architectural feature of the landmark and will be in harmony therewith. Denial of the certificate is subject to judicial review.

Second, the owner may apply to the Commission for a certificate of "appropriateness." Such certificates will be granted if the Commission concludes—focusing upon aesthetic, historical, and architectural values—that the proposed construction on the landmark site would not unduly hinder the protection, enhancement, perpetuation, and use of the landmark. Again, denial of the certificate is subject to judicial review. Moreover, the owner who is denied either a certificate of no exterior effect or a certificate of appropriateness may submit an alternative or modified plan for approval. The final procedure—seeking a certificate of appropriateness on the ground of "insufficient return," see § 207-8.0—provides special mechanisms, which vary depending on whether or not the landmark enjoys a tax exemption, to ensure that designation does not cause economic hardship.

Although the designation of a landmark and landmark site restricts the owner's control over the parcel, designation also enhances the economic position of the landmark owner in one significant respect. Under New York City's zoning laws, owners of real property who have not developed their property to the full extent permitted by the applicable zoning laws are allowed to transfer development rights to contiguous parcels on the same city block. A 1968 ordinance gave the owners of landmark sites additional opportunities to transfer development rights to other parcels. Subject to a restriction that the floor area of the transferee lot may not be increased by more than 20% above its authorized level, the ordinance permitted transfers from a landmark parcel to property across the street or across a street intersection. In 1969, the law governing the conditions under which transfers from landmark parcels could occur was liberalized, apparently to ensure that the Landmarks Law would not unduly restrict the development options of the owners of Grand Central Terminal. The class of recipient lots was expanded to include lots "across a street and opposite to another lot or lots which except for the intervention of streets or street intersections [form] a series extending to the lot occupied by the landmark [building, provided that] all lots [are] in the same ownership." New York City Zoning Resolution 74-79 (emphasis deleted). In addition, the 1969 amendment permits, in highly commercialized areas like midtown Manhattan, the transfer of all unused development rights to a single parcel.

B

This case involves the application of New York City's Landmarks Preservation Law to Grand Central Terminal (Terminal). The Terminal, which is owned by the Penn Central Transportation Co. and its affiliates (Penn Central), is one of New York City's most famous buildings. Opened in 1913, it is regarded not only as providing an ingenious engineering solution to the problems presented by urban railroad stations, but also as a magnificent example of the French beaux-arts style.

The Terminal is located in midtown Manhattan. Its south facade faces 42d Street and that street's intersection with Park Avenue. At street level, the Terminal is bounded on the west by Vanderbilt Avenue, on the east by the Commodore Hotel, and on the north by the Pan-American Building. Although a 20-story office tower, to have been located above the Terminal, was part of the original design, the planned tower was never constructed. The Terminal itself is an eight-story structure which Penn Central uses as a railroad station and in which it rents space not needed for railroad purposes to a variety of commercial interests. The Terminal is one of a number of properties owned by appellant Penn Central in this area of midtown Manhattan. The others include the Barclay, Biltmore, Commodore, Roosevelt, and Waldorf-Astoria Hotels, the Pan-American Building and other office buildings along Park Avenue, and the Yale Club. At least eight of these are eligible to be recipients of development rights afforded the Terminal by virtue of landmark designation.

On August 2, 1967, following a public hearing, the Commission designated the Terminal a "landmark" and designated the "city tax block" it occupies a "landmark site."[16] The Board of Estimate confirmed this action on September 21, 1967. Although appellant Penn Central had

---

16. The Commission's report stated:

"Grand Central Station, one of the great buildings of America, evokes a spirit that is unique in this City. It combines distinguished architecture with a brilliant engineering solution, wedded to one of the most fabulous railroad terminals of our time. Monumental in scale, this great building functions as well today as it did when built. In style, it represents the best of the French Beaux Arts." Record 2240.

opposed the designation before the Commission, it did not seek judicial review of the final designation decision.

On January 22, 1968, appellant Penn Central, to increase its income, entered into a renewable 50-year lease and sublease agreement with appellant UGP Properties, Inc. (UGP), a wholly owned subsidiary of Union General Properties, Ltd., a United Kingdom corporation. Under the terms of the agreement, UGP was to construct a multistory office building above the Terminal. UGP promised to pay Penn Central $1 million annually during construction and at least $3 million annually thereafter. The rentals would be offset in part by a loss of some $700,000 to $1 million in net rentals presently received from concessionaires displaced by the new building.

Appellants UGP and Penn Central then applied to the Commission for permission to construct an office building atop the Terminal. Two separate plans, both designed by architect Marcel Breuer and both apparently satisfying the terms of the applicable zoning ordinance, were submitted to the Commission for approval. The first, Breuer I, provided for the construction of a 55-story office building, to be cantilevered above the existing facade and to rest on the roof of the Terminal. The second, Breuer II Revised,[17] called for tearing down a portion of the Terminal that included the 42d Street facade, stripping off some of the remaining features of the Terminal's facade, and constructing a 53-story office building. The Commission denied a certificate of no exterior effect on September 20, 1968. Appellants then applied for a certificate of "appropriateness" as to both proposals. After four days of hearings at which over 80 witnesses testified, the Commission denied this application as to both proposals. . . .

Appellants did not seek judicial review of the denial of either certificate. Because the Terminal site enjoyed a tax exemption, remained suitable for its present and future uses, and was not the subject of a contract of sale, there were no further administrative remedies available to appellants as to the Breuer I and Breuer II Revised plans. Further, appellants did not avail themselves of the opportunity to develop and submit other plans for the Commission's consideration and approval. Instead, appellants filed suit in New York Supreme Court, Trial Term, claiming, *inter alia*, that the application of the Landmarks Preservation Law had "taken" their property without just compensation in violation of the Fifth and Fourteenth Amendments and arbitrarily deprived them of their property without due process of law in violation of the Fourteenth Amendment. Appellants sought a declaratory judgment, injunctive relief barring the city from using the Landmarks Law to impede the construction of any structure that might otherwise lawfully be constructed on the Terminal site, and damages for the "temporary taking" that occurred between August 2, 1967, the designation date, and the date when the restrictions arising from the Landmarks Law would be lifted. The trial court granted the injunctive and declaratory relief, but severed the question of damages for a "temporary taking."

Appellees appealed, and the New York Supreme Court, Appellate Division, reversed. The Appellate Division held that the restrictions on the development of the Terminal site were necessary to promote the legitimate public purpose of protecting landmarks and therefore that appellants could sustain their constitutional claims only by proof that the regulation deprived them of all reasonable beneficial use of the property. . . . The Appellate Division concluded that all appellants had succeeded in showing was that they had been deprived of the property's most profitable use, and that this showing did not establish that appellants had been unconstitutionally deprived of their property.

The New York Court of Appeals affirmed. 42 N. Y. 2d 324, 366 N. E. 2d 1271 (1977). That court summarily rejected any claim that the Landmarks Law had "taken" property without "just

---

17. Appellants also submitted a plan, denominated Breuer II, to the Commission. However, because appellants learned that Breuer II would have violated existing easements, they substituted Breuer II Revised for Breuer II, and the Commission evaluated the appropriateness only of Breuer II Revised.

compensation," indicating that there could be no "taking" since the law had not transferred control of the property to the city, but only restricted appellants' exploitation of it. In that circumstance, the Court of Appeals held that appellants' attack on the law could prevail only if the law deprived appellants of their property in violation of the Due Process Clause of the Fourteenth Amendment. Whether or not there was a denial of substantive due process turned on whether the restrictions deprived Penn Central of a "reasonable return" on the "privately created and privately managed ingredient" of the Terminal. *Id.*, at 328, 366 N. E. 2d, at 1273.[23] The Court of Appeals concluded that the Landmarks Law had not effected a denial of due process because: (1) the landmark regulation permitted the same use as had been made of the Terminal for more than half a century; (2) the appellants had failed to show that they could not earn a reasonable return on their investment in the Terminal itself; (3) even if the Terminal proper could never operate at a reasonable profit, some of the income from Penn Central's extensive real estate holdings in the area, which include hotels and office buildings, must realistically be imputed to the Terminal; and (4) the development rights above the Terminal, which had been made transferable to numerous sites in the vicinity of the Terminal, one or two of which were suitable for the construction of office buildings, were valuable to appellants and provided "significant, perhaps 'fair,' compensation for the loss of rights above the terminal itself." *Id.*, at 333-336, 366 N. E. 2d, at 1276-1278. . . .

II

The issues presented by appellants are (1) whether the restrictions imposed by New York City's law upon appellants' exploitation of the Terminal site effect a "taking" of appellants' property for a public use within the meaning of the Fifth Amendment, which of course is made applicable to the States through the Fourteenth Amendment, see Chicago, B. & Q. R. Co. v. Chicago, 166 U.S. 226, 239 (1897), and, (2), if so, whether the transferable development rights afforded appellants constitute "just compensation" within the meaning of the Fifth Amendment. We need only address the question whether a "taking" has occurred.

A

Before considering appellants' specific contentions, it will be useful to review the factors that have shaped the jurisprudence of the Fifth Amendment injunction "nor shall private property be taken for public use, without just compensation." The question of what constitutes a "taking" for purposes of the Fifth Amendment has proved to be a problem of considerable difficulty. While this Court has recognized that the "Fifth Amendment's guarantee . . . [is] designed to bar Government from forcing some people alone to bear public burdens which, in all fairness and justice, should be borne by the public as a whole," Armstrong v. United States, 364 U.S. 40, 49 (1960), this Court, quite simply, has been unable to develop any "set formula" for determining when "justice and fairness" require that economic injuries caused by public action be compensated by the government, rather than remain disproportionately concentrated on a few persons. See Goldblatt v. Hempstead, 369 U.S. 590, 594 (1962). Indeed, we have frequently observed that whether a particular restriction will be rendered invalid by the government's failure to pay for any losses proximately caused

---

23. The Court of Appeals suggested that in calculating the value of the property upon which appellants were entitled to earn a reasonable return, the "publicly created" components of the value of the property—*i.e.*, those elements of its value attributable to the "efforts of organized society" or to the "social complex" in which the Terminal is located—had to be excluded. However, since the record upon which the Court of Appeals decided the case did not, as that court recognized, contain a basis for segregating the privately created from the publicly created elements of the value of the Terminal site and since the judgment of the Court of Appeals in any event rests upon bases that support our affirmance, we have no occasion to address the question whether it is permissible or feasible to separate out the "social increments" of the value of property. See Costonis, The Disparity Issue: A Context for the Grand Central Terminal Decision, 91 Harv. L. Rev. 402, 416-417 (1977).

by it depends largely "upon the particular circumstances [in that] case." United States v. Central Eureka Mining Co., 357 U.S. 155, 168 (1958); see United States v. Caltex, Inc., 344 U.S. 149, 156 (1952).

In engaging in these essentially ad hoc, factual inquiries, the Court's decisions have identified several factors that have particular significance. The economic impact of the regulation on the claimant and, particularly, the extent to which the regulation has interfered with distinct invest-ment-backed expectations are, of course, relevant considerations. So, too, is the character of the governmental action. A "taking" may more readily be found when the interference with property can be characterized as a physical invasion by government, see, e. g., United States v. Causby, 328 U.S. 256 (1946), than when interference arises from some public program adjusting the benefits and burdens of economic life to promote the common good.

"Government hardly could go on if to some extent values incident to property could not be diminished without paying for every such change in the general law," Pennsylvania Coal Co. v. Mahon, 260 U.S. 393, 413 (1922), and this Court has accordingly recognized, in a wide variety of contexts, that government may execute laws or programs that adversely affect recognized economic values. Exercises of the taxing power are one obvious example. A second are the decisions in which this Court has dismissed "taking" challenges on the ground that, while the challenged government action caused economic harm, it did not interfere with interests that were sufficiently bound up with the reasonable expectations of the claimant to constitute "property" for Fifth Amendment purposes. Sax, Takings and the Police Power, 74 Yale L. J. 36, 61-62 (1964).

More importantly for the present case, in instances in which a state tribunal reasonably con-cluded that "the health, safety, morals, or general welfare" would be promoted by prohibiting particular contemplated uses of land, this Court has upheld land-use regulations that destroyed or adversely affected recognized real property interests. See Nectow v. Cambridge, 277 U.S. 183, 188 (1928). Zoning laws are, of course, the classic example, see Euclid v. Ambler Realty Co., 272 U.S. 365 (1926) (prohibition of industrial use); Gorieb v. Fox, 274 U.S. 603, 608 (1927) (requirement that portions of parcels be left unbuilt); Welch v. Swasey, 214 U.S. 91 (1909) (height restriction), which have been viewed as permissible governmental action even when prohibiting the most ben-eficial use of the property.

Zoning laws generally do not affect existing uses of real property, but "taking" challenges have also been held to be without merit in a wide variety of situations when the challenged governmen-tal actions prohibited a beneficial use to which individual parcels had previously been devoted and thus caused substantial individualized harm. . . .

Again, Hadacheck v. Sebastian, 239 U.S. 394 (1915), upheld a law prohibiting the claimant from continuing his otherwise lawful business of operating a brickyard in a particular physical community on the ground that the legislature had reasonably concluded that the presence of the brickyard was inconsistent with neighboring uses.

Goldblatt v. Hempstead, *supra*, is a recent example. There, a 1958 city safety ordinance banned any excavations below the water table and effectively prohibited the claimant from continuing a sand and gravel mining business that had been operated on the particular parcel since 1927. The Court upheld the ordinance against a "taking" challenge, although the ordinance prohibited the present and presumably most beneficial use of the property and had . . . severely affected a particu-lar owner. The Court assumed that the ordinance did not prevent the owner's reasonable use of the property since the owner made no showing of an adverse effect on the value of the land. Because the restriction served a substantial public purpose, the Court thus held no taking had occurred. It is, of course, implicit in *Goldblatt* that a use restriction on real property may constitute a "taking" if not reasonably necessary to the effectuation of a substantial public purpose, or perhaps if it has an unduly harsh impact upon the owner's use of the property.

Pennsylvania Coal Co. v. Mahon, 260 U.S. 393 (1922), is the leading case for the proposition that a state statute that substantially furthers important public policies may so frustrate distinct investment-backed expectations as to amount to a "taking." . . . Because the statute made it commercially impracticable to mine the coal, and thus had nearly the same effect as the complete destruction of rights claimant had reserved from the owners of the surface land, the Court held that the statute was invalid as effecting a "taking" without just compensation. See also Armstrong v. United States, 364 U.S. 40 (1960) (Government's complete destruction of a materialman's lien in certain property held a "taking"); Hudson Water Co. v. McCarter, 209 U.S. 349, 355 (1908) (if height restriction makes property wholly useless "the rights of property . . . prevail over the other public interest" and compensation is required). See generally Michelman, Property, Utility, and Fairness: Comments on the Ethical Foundations of "Just Compensation" Law, 80 Harv. L. Rev. 1165, 1229-1234 (1967).

Finally, government actions that may be characterized as acquisitions of resources to permit or facilitate uniquely public functions have often been held to constitute "takings." United States v. Causby, 328 U.S. 256 (1946), is illustrative. In holding that direct overflights above the claimant's land, that destroyed the present use of the land as a chicken farm, constituted a "taking," Causby emphasized that Government had not "merely destroyed property [but was] using a part of it for the flight of its planes." *Id.*, at 262-263, n.7. See generally Michelman, *supra*, at 1226-1229; Sax, Takings and the Police Power, 74 Yale L. J. 36 (1964).

B

In contending that the New York City law has "taken" their property in violation of the Fifth and Fourteenth Amendments, appellants make a series of arguments, which, while tailored to the facts of this case, essentially urge that any substantial restriction imposed pursuant to a landmark law must be accompanied by just compensation if it is to be constitutional. . . . They accept for present purposes both that the parcel of land occupied by Grand Central Terminal must, in its present state, be regarded as capable of earning a reasonable return, and that the transferable development rights afforded appellants by virtue of the Terminal's designation as a landmark are valuable, even if not as valuable as the rights to construct above the Terminal. In appellants' view none of these factors derogate from their claim that New York City's law has effected a "taking."

Apart from our own disagreement with appellants' characterization of the effect of the New York City law, the submission that appellants may establish a "taking" simply by showing that they have been denied the ability to exploit a property interest that they heretofore had believed was available for development is quite simply untenable. Were this the rule, this Court would have erred not only in upholding laws restricting the development of air rights, see Welch v. Swasey, *supra*, but also in approving those prohibiting both the subjacent, see Goldblatt v. Hempstead, 369 U.S. 590 (1962), and the lateral, see Gorieb v. Fox, 274 U.S. 603 (1927), development of particular parcels.[27] "Taking" jurisprudence does not divide a single parcel into discrete segments and attempt to determine whether rights in a particular segment have been entirely abrogated. In deciding whether a particular governmental action has effected a taking, this Court focuses rather both on

---

27. These cases dispose of any contention that might be based on Pennsylvania Coal Co. v. Mahon, 260 U.S. 393 (1922), that full use of air rights is so bound up with the investment-backed expectations of appellants that governmental deprivation of these rights invariably—*i.e.*, irrespective of the impact of the restriction on the value of the parcel as a whole—constitutes a "taking." Similarly, *Welch*, *Goldblatt*, and *Gorieb* illustrate the fallacy of appellants' related contention that a "taking" must be found to have occurred whenever the land-use restriction may be characterized as imposing a "servitude" on the claimant's parcel.

the character of the action and on the nature and extent of the interference with rights in the parcel as a whole—here, the city tax block designated as the "landmark site."

Secondly, appellants, focusing on the character and impact of the New York City law, argue that it effects a "taking" because its operation has significantly diminished the value of the Terminal site. Appellants concede that the decisions sustaining other land-use regulations, which, like the New York City law, are reasonably related to the promotion of the general welfare, uniformly reject the proposition that diminution in property value, standing alone, can establish a "taking," see Euclid v. Ambler Realty Co., 272 U.S. 365 (1926) (75% diminution in value caused by zoning law); Hadacheck v. Sebastian, 239 U.S. 394 (1915) (87 1/2% diminution in value); and that the "taking" issue in these contexts is resolved by focusing on the uses the regulations permit. Appellants, moreover, also do not dispute that a showing of diminution in property value would not establish a "taking" if the restriction had been imposed as a result of historic-district legislation, see generally Maher v. New Orleans, 516 F.2d 1051 (CA5 1975), but appellants argue that New York City's regulation of individual landmarks is fundamentally different from zoning or from historic-district legislation because the controls imposed by New York City's law apply only to individuals who own selected properties.

Stated baldly, appellants' position appears to be that the only means of ensuring that selected owners are not singled out to endure financial hardship for no reason is to hold that any restriction imposed on individual landmarks pursuant to the New York City scheme is a "taking" requiring the payment of "just compensation." Agreement with this argument would, of course, invalidate not just New York City's law, but all comparable landmark legislation in the Nation. We find no merit in it.

It is true, as appellants emphasize, that both historic-district legislation and zoning laws regulate all properties within given physical communities whereas landmark laws apply only to selected parcels. But, contrary to appellants' suggestions, landmark laws are not like discriminatory, or "reverse spot," zoning: that is, a land-use decision which arbitrarily singles out a particular parcel for different, less favorable treatment than the neighboring ones. In contrast to discriminatory zoning, which is the antithesis of land-use control as part of some comprehensive plan, the New York City law embodies a comprehensive plan to preserve structures of historic or aesthetic interest wherever they might be found in the city, and as noted, over 400 landmarks and 31 historic districts have been designated pursuant to this plan. . . .

Next, appellants observe that New York City's law differs from zoning laws and historic-district ordinances in that the Landmarks Law does not impose identical or similar restrictions on all structures located in particular physical communities. It follows, they argue, that New York City's law is inherently incapable of producing the fair and equitable distribution of benefits and burdens of governmental action which is characteristic of zoning laws and historic-district legislation and which they maintain is a constitutional requirement if "just compensation" is not to be afforded. It is, of course, true that the Landmarks Law has a more severe impact on some landowners than on others, but that in itself does not mean that the law effects a "taking." Legislation designed to promote the general welfare commonly burdens some more than others. . . .[Z]oning laws often affect some property owners more severely than others but have not been held to be invalid on that account. For example, the property owner in *Euclid* who wished to use its property for industrial purposes was affected far more severely by the ordinance than its neighbors who wished to use their land for residences.

In any event, appellants' repeated suggestions that they are solely burdened and unbenefited is factually inaccurate. This contention overlooks the fact that the New York City law applies to vast numbers of structures in the city in addition to the Terminal—all the structures contained in the

31 historic districts and over 400 individual landmarks, many of which are close to the Terminal. Unless we are to reject the judgment of the New York City Council that the preservation of landmarks benefits all New York citizens and all structures, both economically and by improving the quality of life in the city as a whole—which we are unwilling to do—we cannot conclude that the owners of the Terminal have in no sense been benefited by the Landmarks Law. . . .

C

Rejection of appellants' broad arguments is not, however, the end of our inquiry, for all we thus far have established is that the New York City law is not rendered invalid by its failure to provide "just compensation" whenever a landmark owner is restricted in the exploitation of property interests, such as air rights, to a greater extent than provided for under applicable zoning laws. We now must consider whether the interference with appellants' property is of such a magnitude that "there must be an exercise of eminent domain and compensation to sustain [it]." Pennsylvania Coal Co. v. Mahon, 260 U.S., at 413. That inquiry may be narrowed to the question of the severity of the impact of the law on appellants' parcel, and its resolution in turn requires a careful assessment of the impact of the regulation on the Terminal site. . . .

[T]he New York City law does not interfere in any way with the present uses of the Terminal. Its designation as a landmark not only permits but contemplates that appellants may continue to use the property precisely as it has been used for the past 65 years: as a railroad terminal containing office space and concessions. So the law does not interfere with what must be regarded as Penn Central's primary expectation concerning the use of the parcel. More importantly, on this record, we must regard the New York City law as permitting Penn Central not only to profit from the Terminal but also to obtain a "reasonable return" on its investment. . . .

[T]o the extent appellants have been denied the right to build above the Terminal, it is not literally accurate to say that they have been denied all use of even those pre-existing air rights. Their ability to use these rights has not been abrogated; they are made transferable to at least eight parcels in the vicinity of the Terminal, one or two of which have been found suitable for the construction of new office buildings. Although appellants and others have argued that New York City's transferable development-rights program is far from ideal, the New York courts here supportably found that, at least in the case of the Terminal, the rights afforded are valuable. While these rights may well not have constituted "just compensation" if a "taking" had occurred, the rights nevertheless undoubtedly mitigate whatever financial burdens the law has imposed on appellants and, for that reason, are to be taken into account in considering the impact of regulation.

On this record, we conclude that the application of New York City's Landmarks Law has not effected a "taking" of appellants' property. The restrictions imposed are substantially related to the promotion of the general welfare and not only permit reasonable beneficial use of the landmark site but also afford appellants opportunities further to enhance not only the Terminal site proper but also other properties.[36]

Affirmed.

MR. JUSTICE REHNQUIST, with whom THE CHIEF JUSTICE and MR. JUSTICE STEVENS join, dissenting.

Of the over one million buildings and structures in the city of New York, appellees have singled out 400 for designation as official landmarks. . . . The question in this case is whether the cost associated with the city of New York's desire to preserve a limited number of "landmarks" within

---

36. We emphasize that our holding today is on the present record, which in turn is based on Penn Central's present ability to use the Terminal for its intended purposes and in a gainful fashion. The city conceded at oral argument that if appellants can demonstrate at some point in the future that circumstances have so changed that the Terminal ceases to be "economically viable," appellants may obtain relief. See Tr. of Oral Arg. 42-43.

its borders must be borne by all of its taxpayers or whether it can instead be imposed entirely on the owners of the individual properties.

Only in the most superficial sense of the word can this case be said to involve "zoning." Typical zoning restrictions may, it is true, so limit the prospective uses of a piece of property as to diminish the value of that property in the abstract because it may not be used for the forbidden purposes. But any such abstract decrease in value will more than likely be at least partially offset by an increase in value which flows from similar restrictions as to use on neighboring properties. All property owners in a designated area are placed under the same restrictions, not only for the benefit of the municipality as a whole but also for the common benefit of one another. In the words of Mr. Justice Holmes, speaking for the Court in Pennsylvania Coal Co. v. Mahon, 260 U.S. 393, 415 (1922), there is "an average reciprocity of advantage."

Where a relatively few individual buildings, all separated from one another, are singled out and treated differently from surrounding buildings, no such reciprocity exists. The cost to the property owner which results from the imposition of restrictions applicable only to his property and not that of his neighbors may be substantial—in this case, several million dollars—with no comparable reciprocal benefits. And the cost associated with landmark legislation is likely to be of a completely different order of magnitude than that which results from the imposition of normal zoning restrictions. Unlike the regime affected by the latter, the landowner is not simply prohibited from using his property for certain purposes, while allowed to use it for all other purposes. Under the historic-landmark preservation scheme adopted by New York, the property owner is under an affirmative duty to preserve his property as a landmark at his own expense. To suggest that because traditional zoning results in some limitation of use of the property zoned, the New York City landmark preservation scheme should likewise be upheld, represents the ultimate in treating as alike things which are different. The rubric of "zoning" has not yet sufficed to avoid the well-established proposition that the Fifth Amendment bars the "Government from forcing some people alone to bear public burdens which, in all fairness and justice, should be borne by the public as a whole." Armstrong v. United States, 364 U.S. 40, 49 (1960). . . .

I

The Fifth Amendment provides in part: "nor shall private property be taken for public use, without just compensation." In a very literal sense, the actions of appellees violated this constitutional prohibition. Before the city of New York declared Grand Central Terminal to be a landmark, Penn Central could have used its "air rights" over the Terminal to build a multistory office building, at an apparent value of several million dollars per year. Today, the Terminal cannot be modified in any form, including the erection of additional stories, without the permission of the Landmark Preservation Commission, a permission which appellants, despite good-faith attempts, have so far been unable to obtain. Because the Taking Clause of the Fifth Amendment has not always been read literally, however, the constitutionality of appellees' actions requires a closer scrutiny of this Court's interpretation of the three key words in the Taking Clause—"property," "taken," and "just compensation."

A

Appellees do not dispute that valuable property rights have been destroyed. And the Court has frequently emphasized that the term "property" as used in the Taking Clause includes the entire "group of rights inhering in the citizen's [ownership]." United States v. General Motors Corp., 323 U.S. 373 (1945). The term is not used in the "vulgar and untechnical sense of the physical thing with respect to which the citizen exercises rights recognized by law. [Instead, it] . . . [denotes] the *group of rights* inhering in the citizen's relation to the physical thing, *as the right to possess, use and dispose of it.* . . . The constitutional provision is addressed to *every sort of interest* the citizen may possess." *Id.*, at 377-378 (emphasis added).

While neighboring landowners are free to use their land and "air rights" in any way consistent with the broad boundaries of New York zoning, Penn Central, absent the permission of appellees, must forever maintain its property in its present state.[5] The property has been thus subjected to a nonconsensual servitude not borne by any neighboring or similar properties.

B

Appellees have thus destroyed—in a literal sense, "taken"—substantial property rights of Penn Central. While the term "taken" might have been narrowly interpreted to include only physical seizures of property rights, "the construction of the phrase has not been so narrow. The courts have held that the deprivation of the former owner rather than the accretion of a right or interest to the sovereign constitutes the taking." *Id.*, at 378. Because "not every destruction or injury to property by governmental action has been held to be a 'taking' in the constitutional sense," Armstrong v. United States, 364 U.S., at 48, however, this does not end our inquiry. But an examination of the two exceptions where the destruction of property does not constitute a taking demonstrates that a compensable taking has occurred here.

1

As early as 1887, the Court recognized that the government can prevent a property owner from using his property to injure others without having to compensate the owner for the value of the forbidden use.

"A prohibition simply upon the use of property for purposes that are declared, by valid legislation, to be *injurious to the health, morals, or safety of the community*, cannot, in any just sense, be deemed a taking or an appropriation of property for the public benefit. Such legislation does not disturb the owner in the control or use of his property for lawful purposes, nor restrict his right to dispose of it, but is only a declaration by the State that its use by any one, for certain forbidden purposes, is prejudicial to the public interests. . . . The power which the States have of prohibiting such use by individuals of their property as will be prejudicial to the health, the morals, or the safety of the public, is not—and, consistently with the existence and safety of organized society, cannot be—burdened with the condition that the State must compensate such individual owners for pecuniary losses they may sustain, *by reason of their not being permitted, by a noxious use of their property, to inflict injury upon the community.*" Mugler v. Kansas, 123 U.S. 623, 668-669.

Thus, there is no "taking" where a city prohibits the operation of a brickyard within a residential area, see Hadacheck v. Sebastian, 239 U.S. 394 (1915), or forbids excavation for sand and gravel below the water line, see Goldblatt v. Hempstead, 369 U.S. 590 (1962). Nor is it relevant, where

---

5. In particular, Penn Central cannot increase the height of the Terminal. This Court has previously held that the "air rights" over an area of land are "property" for purposes of the Fifth Amendment. See United States v. Causby, 328 U.S. 256 (1946) ("air rights" taken by low-flying airplanes); Griggs v. Allegheny County, 369 U.S. 84 (1962) (same); Portsmouth Harbor Land & Hotel Co. v. United States, 260 U.S. 327 (1922) (firing of projectiles over summer resort can constitute taking).

the government is merely prohibiting a noxious use of property, that the government would seem to be singling out a particular property owner. Hadacheck, *supra*, at 413.

The nuisance exception to the taking guarantee is not coterminous with the police power itself. The question is whether the forbidden use is dangerous to the safety, health, or welfare of others. . . .

Appellees are not prohibiting a nuisance. The record is clear that the proposed addition to the Grand Central Terminal would be in full compliance with zoning, height limitations, and other health and safety requirements. Instead, appellees are seeking to preserve what they believe to be an outstanding example of beaux arts architecture. Penn Central is prevented from further developing its property basically because too good a job was done in designing and building it. The city of New York, because of its unadorned admiration for the design, has decided that the owners of the building must preserve it unchanged for the benefit of sightseeing New Yorkers and tourists.

Unlike land-use regulations, appellees' actions do not merely prohibit Penn Central from using its property in a narrow set of noxious ways. Instead, appellees have placed an affirmative duty on Penn Central to maintain the Terminal in its present state and in "good repair." Appellants are not free to use their property as they see fit within broad outer boundaries but must strictly adhere to their past use except where appellees conclude that alternative uses would not detract from the landmark. . . .

2

Even where the government prohibits a noninjurious use, the Court has ruled that a taking does not take place if the prohibition applies over a broad cross section of land and thereby "[secures] an average reciprocity of advantage." Pennsylvania Coal Co. v. Mahon, 260 U.S., at 415. It is for this reason that zoning does not constitute a "taking." While zoning at times reduces individual property values, the burden is shared relatively evenly and it is reasonable to conclude that on the whole an individual who is harmed by one aspect of the zoning will be benefited by another.

Here, however, a multimillion dollar loss has been imposed on appellants; it is uniquely felt and is not offset by any benefits flowing from the preservation of some 400 other "landmarks" in New York City. Appellees have imposed a substantial cost on less than one one-tenth of one percent of the buildings in New York City for the general benefit of all its people. It is exactly this imposition of general costs on a few individuals at which the "taking" protection is directed. . . .

Less than 20 years ago, this Court reiterated that the

> "Fifth Amendment's guarantee that private property shall not be taken for a public use without just compensation was designed to bar Government from forcing some people alone to bear public burdens which, in all fairness and justice, should be borne by the public as a whole." Armstrong v. United States, 364 U.S., at 49.

As Mr. Justice Holmes pointed out in Pennsylvania Coal Co. v. Mahon, "the question at bottom" in an eminent domain case "is upon whom the loss of the changes desired should fall." 260 U.S., at 416. The benefits that appellees believe will flow from preservation of the Grand Central Terminal will accrue to all the citizens of New York City. There is no reason to believe that appellants will enjoy a substantially greater share of these benefits. If the cost of preserving Grand Central Terminal were spread evenly across the entire population of the city of New York, the burden per person would be in cents per year—a minor cost appellees would surely concede for the benefit accrued. Instead, however, appellees would impose the entire cost of several million dollars per year on Penn Central. But it is precisely this sort of discrimination that the Fifth Amendment prohibits. . . .

C

Appellees, apparently recognizing that the constraints imposed on a landmark site constitute a taking for Fifth Amendment purposes, do not leave the property owner emptyhanded. As the Court notes, the property owner may theoretically "transfer" his previous right to develop the landmark property to adjacent properties if they are under his control. Appellees have coined this system "Transfer Development Rights," or TDR's.

Of all the terms used in the Taking Clause, "just compensation" has the strictest meaning. The Fifth Amendment does not allow simply an approximate compensation but requires "a full and perfect equivalent for the property taken." Monongahela Navigation Co. v. United States, 148 U.S., at 326. . . .

Appellees contend that, even if they have "taken" appellants' property, TDR's constitute "just compensation." Appellants, of course, argue that TDR's are highly imperfect compensation. Because the lower courts held that there was no "taking," they did not have to reach the question of whether or not just compensation has already been awarded. The New York Court of Appeals' discussion of TDR's gives some support to appellants:

> "The many defects in New York City's program for development rights transfers have been detailed elsewhere . . . . The area to which transfer is permitted is severely limited [and] complex procedures are required to obtain a transfer permit." 42 N. Y. 2d 324, 334-335, 366 N. E. 2d 1271, 1277 (1977).

And in other cases the Court of Appeals has noted that TDR's have an "uncertain and contingent market value" and do "not adequately preserve" the value lost when a building is declared to be a landmark. French Investing Co. v. City of New York, 39 N. Y. 2d 587, 591, 350 N. E. 2d 381, 383, appeal dismissed, 429 U.S. 990 (1976). On the other hand, there is evidence in the record that Penn Central has been offered substantial amounts for its TDR's. Because the record on appeal is relatively slim, I would remand to the Court of Appeals for a determination of whether TDR's constitute a "full and perfect equivalent for the property taken."

II . . .

The city of New York is in a precarious financial state, and some may believe that the costs of landmark preservation will be more easily borne by corporations such as Penn Central than the overburdened individual taxpayers of New York. But these concerns do not allow us to ignore past precedents construing the Eminent Domain Clause to the end that the desire to improve the public condition is, indeed, achieved by a shorter cut than the constitutional way of paying for the change.

Notes

1. The source of the phrase "investment-backed expectations" appears to be Professor Frank Michelman's influential article, *Property, Utility, and Fairness: Comments on the Ethical Foundations of "Just Compensation" Law*, 80 Harv. L. Rev. 1165, 1213, 1233 (1967):

> The problem, then, is to show that utilitarian property theory, applied with utmost consistency, does *not* require payment of compensation in every case of social action which is disappointing to justified, investment-backed expectations. . . .

> [T]he [diminution of value] test poses not nearly so loose a question of degree; it does not ask "how much," but rather (like the physical-occupation test) it asks "whether or not": whether or not the measure in question can easily be seen to have practically

deprived the claimant of some distinctly perceived, sharply crystallized, investment-backed expectation.

Professor Barton "Buzz" Thompson, in *The Allure of Consequential Fit*, 51 Ala. L. Rev. 1261, 291 and n.160 (2000), has noted that "[t]he Supreme Court's current preoccupation in the takings arena with 'investment-backed expectations' . . . actually stems from a misreading," of the article, as "Michelman coined the term to explain why the taking of a mere subset of property might require compensation, not as a general explanation for when a governmental regulation should be found to be a taking."

2. Then-Associate Justice Rehnquist's discussion of property as "the group of rights inhering in the citizen's relation to the physical thing, as the right to possess, use and dispose of it," deriving from United States v. General Motors Corp., 323 U.S. 373, 377-78 (1945), presages his opinion for the majority in a case decided one year after *Penn Central*. In Kaiser Aetna v. United States, 444 U.S. 164, 169, 176, 179-80 (1979), a divided Court answered affirmatively the question of

> whether the Court of Appeals erred in holding that petitioners' improvements to Kuapa Pond caused its original character to be so altered that it became subject to an overriding federal navigational servitude, thus converting into a public aquatic park that which petitioners had invested millions of dollars in improving on the assumption that it was a privately owned pond leased to Kaiser Aetna.

Writing for the six-member majority, Rehnquist rejected the government's assertion "that as a result of . . . the pond's connection to the navigable water in a manner approved by the Corps of Engineers, the owner has somehow lost one of the most essential sticks in the bundle of rights that are commonly characterized as property—the right to exclude others." Again focusing on property as a collection of rights and not as a corporeal "thing," Rehnquist concluded: "In this case, we hold that the "right to exclude," so universally held to be a fundamental element of the property right, falls within this category of interests that the Government cannot take without compensation."

The sticks and bundle metaphor, which is usually traced to Wesley Hohfeld and Benjamin Cardozo,[26] appeared in five subsequent cases in which the Court granted relief to parties who claimed that the government had, by regulatory means, taken their private property without compensation: Dolan v. City of Tigard, 512 U.S. 374, 384 (1994) ("right to exclude others"); Nollan v. California Coastal Comm'n, 483 U.S. 825, 831 (1987) ("right to exclude others"); Hodel v. Irving, 481 U.S. 704, 716 (1987) ("right to pass on a certain type of property . . . to one's heirs"); Ruckelshaus v. Monsanto Co., 467 U.S. 986, 1011 (1984) ("right to exclude others"); Loretto v. Teleprompter Manhattan CATV Corp., 458 U.S. 419, 436 (1982) ("power to exclude"). The bundle argument is not a sure-fire winner, however. Only one week before *Kaiser Aetna* was published, the Court rejected a regulatory takings claim in Andrus v. Allard, 444 U.S. 51, 65-66 (1979) ("But the denial of one traditional property right does not always amount to a taking. At least where an owner possesses a full 'bundle' of property rights, the destruction of one 'strand' in the bundle is not a taking, because the aggregate must be viewed in its entirety.").

---

26. *See* Henneford v. Silas Mason Co., 300 U.S. 577, 582 (1937) (Cardozo, J.) ("The privilege of use is only one attribute, among many, of the bundle of privileges that make up property or ownership."); Robert J. Goldstein, *Green Wood in the Bundle of Sticks: Fitting Environmental Ethics and Ecology Into Real Property Law*, 25 B.C. Envtl. Aff. L. Rev. 347, 367 n.122 (1998) ("'Legal interest' or 'property' relating to the tangible object that we call land consists of a complex aggregate of rights (or claims), privileges, powers, and immunities." (quoting Wesley Newcomb Hohfeld, Fundamental Legal Conceptions as Applied in Judicial Reasoning and Other Legal Essays 96 (Walter Wheeler Cook ed., 1923)).

3. While most courts and commentators view *Penn Central* as "*Pennsylvania Coal* revisted," in reality, the majority opinion takes as much, perhaps even more, from *Euclid v. Ambler* and its deferential posture toward local, comprehensive zoning. Because the multi-factor test presented in the Court's *Penn Central* opinion has become the predominant regulatory takings test, as we shall study in more detail in Chapter Five, it is easy to overlook those parts of the decision that seek to place New York City's landmark ordinance in the zoning mainstream.

There is a third precedent, cited by the majority and dissenting opinions, that casts a broader shadow over *Penn Central* and its ample and growing progeny—Armstrong v. United States, 364 U.S. 40, 41, 48-49 (1960), a dispute in which the "petitioners assert[ed] materialmen's liens under state law for materials furnished to a prime contractor building boats for the United States, and [sought] just compensation under the Fifth Amendment for the value of their liens on accumulated materials and uncompleted work which have been conveyed to the United States." The Supreme Court, in an opinion by Justice Hugo Black (for five Justices), reversed the Court of Claims decision that had denied the existence of valid liens and remanded the case for a determination of the value of the property taken by the federal government. The majority reasoned:

> The total destruction by the Government of all value of these liens, which constitute compensable property, has every possible element of a Fifth Amendment "taking" and is not a mere "consequential incidence" of a valid regulatory measure. Before the liens were destroyed, the lienholders admittedly had compensable property. Immediately afterwards, they had none. This was not because their property vanished into thin air. It was because the Government for its own advantage destroyed the value of the liens, something that the Government could do because its property was not subject to suit, but which no private purchaser could have done. Since this acquisition was for a public use, however accomplished, whether with an intent and purpose of extinguishing the liens or not, the Government's action did destroy them and in the circumstances of this case did thereby take the property value of those liens within the meaning of the Fifth Amendment. . . .

> The Fifth Amendment's guarantee that private property shall not be taken for a public use without just compensation was designed to bar Government from forcing some people alone to bear public burdens which, in all fairness and justice, should be borne by the public as a whole. A fair interpretation of this constitutional protection entitles these lienholders to just compensation here.

Notice how Justice Black ties the Takings Clause to two important goals, justice and fairness, that are more readily identified with complementary (though distinct) constitutional provisions: the notion of equal justice embedded in the Equal Protection Clause and the guarantee of fair proceedings found in the Due Process Clause.

4. *Penn Central* provided legal "cover" for what has become a nationwide movement to protect historically and architecturally significant structures and districts. Not all judges have been as supportive as Justice Brennan and his colleagues in the majority. The Supreme Court of Pennsylvania took two bites of this regulatory takings apple in United Artists Theater Circuit v. City of Philadelphia, 528 Pa. 12, 14, 595 A.2d 6, 7 (1991), *rev'd*, 535 Pa. 370, 383, 389, 635 A.2d 612, 619, 622 (1993). In its first decision, the court determined "that by designating the theater building as historic, over the objections of the owner, the City of Philadelphia through its Historical Commission has 'taken' the appellee's property for public use without just compensation in violation of Article 1, Section 10 of the Pennsylvania Constitution." At the city's request, the case was reargued twice, and the justices reversed their decision that a taking had occurred, noting that "in

fifteen years since *Penn Central*, no other state has rejected the notion that no taking occurs when a state designates a building as historic. The decade and a half in which the *Penn Central* decision has enjoyed widespread acceptance weighs against our rejecting the *Penn Central* analysis." However, the court also held "that the Commission exceeded its statutory authority by designating the interior of the Boyd Theater," because the "Historical Commission is not explicitly authorized by statute to designate the interior of the building as historically or aesthetically significant."

5. Local officials have used their landmarking powers to punish certain landowners, at least according to some disgruntled landowners. In Rector, Wardens, & Members of Vestry of St. Bartholomew's Church v. City of New York, 914 F.2d 348, 350, 354 (2d Cir. 1990), the court affirmed the trial court's holding "that the New York City Landmarks Law, as applied to an auxiliary structure next to the Church's main house of worship, did not impose an unconstitutional burden on the free exercise of religion or effect a taking of property without just compensation." In its brief, the church "cite[d] commentators, including a former chair of the [Landmarks Preservation] Commission, who are highly critical of the Landmarks Law on grounds that it accords great discretion to the Commission and that persons who have interests other than the preservation of historic sites or aesthetic structures may influence Commission decisions." At this point, the panel of the U.S. Court of Appeals for the Second Circuit dropped the following literary footnote:

> The Landmarks Law made a cameo appearance in a recent best-selling novel as a vehicle for political retaliation against a clerical official seeking to develop Church property. *See* T. Wolfe, Bonfire of the Vanities 569 (1987) ("Mort? You know that church, St. Timothy's? . . . Right . . . LANDMARK THE SON OF A BITCH!").

In a similar vein, in Northwestern Univ. v. City of Evanston, 2002 U.S. Dist. LEXIS 17104 (N.D. Ill.), at *2, the university accused city officials of abusing their historic preservation authority:

> Northwestern claims that its exemption from property taxation has fueled a long-running dispute with Evanston—Evanston believes Northwestern should make voluntary financial contributions to offset the cost of services provided by the City, but the University has refused to make such contributions. Northwestern alleges this dispute led the City to include two large parcels of land containing numerous University properties in an historic preservation district in an effort to pressure the University to make such contributions.

As reported by Lisa Black in *Dispute Between Evanston, NU Ends; Judge OKs Deal on Historic Area*, Chicago Tribune, Feb. 18, 2004, at 3, a few weeks before the case was scheduled for trial, the federal district judge approved a settlement in which the city redrew the borders of the Northwestern Evanson Historic District to exclude nearly a quarter of Northwestern's buildings, and the university picked up the city's $700,000 in legal fees.

6. Today, critics of zoning often focus their negative attention on the standard set of controls contained in the 1920s version that the Supreme Court majority approved in *Euclid*. New York City's use of landmark designation and transferable development rights (TDRs) are two of many examples of post-Euclidean devices that local and state land use regulators have devised over the past few decades to add flexibility and responsiveness to the land use regulation. In other words, zoning practices have not remained static during the eight decades following the Court's initial review.

As part of the ongoing process of state and local experimentation with regulation generally, and in response specifically to the critics of "traditional" zoning and to the demands and needs of each separate locality, lawmakers and planners have crafted variations from the Euclidean pattern, while retaining the heart of comprehensive, governmental land use planning: the recognition that the public holds the development rights for each separate parcel in excess of the reasonable limitations set by a properly promulgated land use plan. The new planning and zoning tools, many of which are championed by the Smart Growth movement, have been consciously designed to make the applicable regulations more responsive to the desires of private and public actors. These approaches often involve landowners and regulators in a bargaining process that results in permission to develop above and beyond established limits (such as development agreements, TDRs, and conditional zoning), the provision of public amenities (such as incentive zoning and density bonuses), the elimination of harmful spillovers and unimaginative rigidity (such as performance zoning), and the integration of traditionally segregated uses (such as mixed use development, planned unit development (PUD), and traditional neighborhood development (TND)). Examples of each of these devices can be found in the following paragraphs.

As you review these post-Euclidean approaches in the notes that follow, consider whether a "modern" zoning ordinance with one or more of these features would have passed judicial muster in 1926. Does the more flexible nature of 21st-century zoning make it more or less appealing to judges concerned about private-property rights and abuses of local government powers? In their article on one increasingly popular strategy, Elizabeth Garvin & Dawn Jourdan, in *Through the Looking Glass: Analyzing the Potential Legal Challenges to Form-Based Codes*, 23 J. Land Use & Envtl. L. 395, 410 (2008), have noted that "there is very little case law addressing the many regulatory aspects of form-based codes. Yet, from the vast source of case law on zoning, it is possible to anticipate the types of legal issues which may generate challenges to the ways in which form-based codes are currently written." Included among the potential legal issues are adherence to the state zoning enabling act, substantive and procedural due process issues raised by aesthetic controls, regulatory takings, spot zoning, and consistency with the comprehensive plan.

7. Hawaii's lawmakers, in Haw. Rev. Stat. §46-121, provided this explanation of and justifications for **development agreements**:

> The legislature finds that with land use laws taking on refinements that make the development of land complex, time consuming, and requiring advance financial commitments, the development approval process involves the expenditure of considerable sums of money. Generally speaking, the larger the project contemplated, the greater the expenses and the more time involved in complying with the conditions precedent to filing for a building permit.

> The lack of certainty in the development approval process can result in a waste of resources, escalate the cost of housing and other development to the consumer, and discourage investment in and commitment to comprehensive planning. Predictability would encourage maximum efficient utilization of resources at the least economic cost to the public.

> Public benefits derived from development agreements may include, but are not limited to, affordable housing, design standards, and on- and off-site infrastructure and other improvements. Such benefits may be negotiated for in return for the vesting of development rights for a specific period.

> Under appropriate circumstances, development agreements could strengthen the public planning process, encourage private and public participation in the comprehensive planning process, reduce the economic cost of development, allow for the orderly planning of public facilities and services and the allocation of cost. As an administrative act, development agreements will provide assurances to the applicant for a particular

development project, that upon approval of the project, the applicant may proceed with the project in accordance with all applicable statutes, ordinances, resolutions, rules, and policies in existence at the time the development agreement is executed and that the project will not be restricted or prohibited by the county's subsequent enactment or adoption of laws, ordinances, resolutions, rules, or policies.

Development agreements will encourage the vesting of property rights by protecting such rights from the effect of subsequently enacted county legislation which may conflict with any term or provision of the development agreement or in any way hinder, restrict, or prevent the development of the project. Development agreements are intended to provide a reasonable certainty as to the lawful requirements that must be met in protecting vested property rights, while maintaining the authority and duty of government to enact and enforce laws which promote the public safety, health, and general welfare of the citizens of our State. The purpose of this part is to provide a means by which an individual may be assured at a specific point in time that having met or having agreed to meet all of the terms and conditions of the development agreement, the individual's rights to develop a property in a certain manner shall be vested.

8. For Arizona's authorization of **TDRs**, see Ariz. Rev. Stat. §11-821.03:

The [county] board of supervisors may establish procedures, methods and standards for the transfer of development rights within its jurisdiction. Any proposed transfer of all or any portion of the development rights of a sending property to a receiving property is subject to the written approval and consent of the property owners of both the sending property and the receiving property. A county may not condition a change of zone on a property owner's consent to or other participation in a proposed transfer of development rights, except that a change of zone may be required to implement a development agreement if it is voluntarily entered into by a property owner or owners with a county for the transfer of development rights concurrently with the county's approval of the change of zone.

TDRs have been promoted as effective means for preserving farmland and sensitive environmental parcels, as well as historically and architecturally significant sites. Maryland's Rural Legal Program, for example, in Md. Nat. Res. Code Ann. §5-9A-01(a)(3), explains:

A grant program that leverages available funding, focuses on preservation of strategic resources, including those resources threatened by sprawl development, streamlines real property acquisition procedures to expedite land preservation, takes advantage of innovative preservation techniques such as transferable development rights and the purchase of development rights, and promotes a greater level of natural and environmental resources protection than is provided by existing efforts, will establish a rural legacy for future generations.

Similarly, the New York Legislature, in N.Y. Town §261-a(2) (Consol.), has noted:

The purpose of providing for transfer of development rights shall be to protect the natural, scenic or agricultural qualities of open lands, to enhance sites and areas of special character or special historical, cultural, aesthetic or economic interest or value and to enable and encourage flexibility of design and careful management of land in recognition of land as a basic and valuable natural resource.

9. Two of Virginia's key **conditional zoning** statutes read in part:

> Frequently, where competing and incompatible uses conflict, traditional zoning methods and procedures are inadequate. In these cases, more flexible and adaptable zoning methods are needed to permit differing land uses and the same time to recognize effects of change. It is the purpose of §§ 15.2-2296 through 15.2-2300 to provide a more flexible and adaptable zoning method to cope with situations found in such zones through conditional zoning, whereby a zoning reclassification may be allowed subject to certain conditions proffered by the zoning applicant for the protection of the community that are not generally applicable to land similarly zoned. . . . (Va. Code Ann. § 15.2-2296.)

> In ["certain high-growth localities"] . . . a zoning ordinance may include and provide for the voluntary proffering in writing, by the owner, of reasonable conditions, prior to a public hearing before the governing body, in addition to the regulations provided for the zoning district or zone by the ordinance, as a part of a rezoning or amendment to a zoning map, provided that (i) the rezoning itself gives rise to the need for the conditions; (ii) the conditions have a reasonable relation to the rezoning; and (iii) all conditions are in conformity with the comprehensive plan as defined in § 15.2-2223. (Va. Code Ann. § 15.2-2298(A).)[27]

10. The New York Legislature has authorized **incentive zoning** in N.Y. Gen. City §81-d (Consol):

> 1. Definitions. As used in this section:

> (a) "Incentives or bonuses" shall mean adjustments to the permissible population density, area, height, open space, use, or other provisions of a zoning ordinance, local law, or regulation for a specific purpose authorized by the legislative body of a city.

---

27. Authors' note: Defenders of conditional zoning have long sought to distinguish this innovative tool from the long-reviled practice of "contract zoning." Professor Susan French, in *Moving Toward the Bargaining Table: Contract Zoning, Development Agreements, and the Theoretical Foundations of Government Land Use Deals*, 65 N.C. L. Rev. 957, 979-80, 981-82 (1987), has explained why the attempt to create distance between the two concepts is problematic:

> A number of courts have referred to rezoning decisions tied to explicit or implied government-private agreements as "contract zoning." Others have used the phrase "conditional zoning" as a means of characterizing decisions of this sort, commonly, but not universally, when no express agreement is present. Some courts and commentators have avoided these two basic catch phrases; in an effort to recast a troublesome doctrinal mold, they have adopted modified descriptors by, for example, focusing on the use of "unilateral contracts" or "concomitant" agreements.

> Care must be taken in evaluating this body of precedent to determine whether the terminology adopted was intended to characterize the land use control mechanisms in question for purposes of defining the applicable theoretical framework, or whether instead, it was adopted for purposes of describing the ultimate disposition of the case. An examination of the cases supports the latter view. Early cases adopting the "contract zoning" terminology seemed intent to condemn the proposed arrangements on reserved powers as well as other grounds. By characterizing such cases as ones that involve "contract zoning," later courts could use this broad phrase as a convenient epithet; alternatively, they could give it a much narrower, literal application, to distinguish earlier precedent that involved express bilateral contract and to allow other types of arrangements . . . . Courts deliberately chose the "conditional zoning" terminology, on the other hand, in contravention of the earlier designation as a means of describing rezoning arrangements perceived as legitimate. In some instances, cases adopting this terminology included more fully developed explanations of the view that the imposition of conditions on rezoning approvals constituted an appropriate exercise of the police power, but they said little regarding the role or effect of related agreements on this theoretical universe. In short, judicial precedent characterizing novel rezoning arrangements has tended to adopt labels that (1) suggest a relevant theoretical framework but serve primarily to describe ultimate outcomes, and (2) create an apparent dichotomy of classification, without adequately considering potential interrelationship or overlap. . . .

> [T]his Article adopts the neutral term "contingent zoning" to describe all types of individualized rezoning arrangements, instead of the more traditional dichotomy "contract" and "conditional zoning" . . . .

(b) "Community benefits or amenities" shall mean open space, housing for persons of low or moderate income, parks, elder care, day care, or other specific physical, social, or cultural amenities, or cash in lieu thereof, of benefit to the residents of the community authorized by the legislative body of a city.

(c) "Incentive zoning" shall mean the system by which specific incentives or bonuses are granted, pursuant to this section, on condition that specific physical, social, or cultural benefits or amenities would inure to the community.

2. Authority and purposes. In addition to existing powers and authorities to regulate by planning or zoning, including authorization to provide for the granting of incentives, or bonuses pursuant to other enabling law, a legislative body of a city is hereby empowered, as part of a zoning ordinance, local law or regulation, to provide for a system of zoning incentives, or bonuses, as the legislative body deems necessary and appropriate, consistent with the purposes and conditions set forth in this section. The purpose of the system of incentive or bonus zoning shall be to advance the city's specific physical, cultural and social policies in accordance with the city's comprehensive plan and in coordination with other community planning mechanisms or land use techniques. The system of zoning incentives or bonuses shall be in accordance with a locally-adopted comprehensive plan.[28]

Nev. Rev. Stat. Ann. §278.250(5)(a) provides the following definition of "**density bonus**" as

an incentive granted by a governing body to a developer of real property that authorizes the developer to build at a greater density than would otherwise be allowed under the master plan, in exchange for an agreement by the developer to perform certain functions that the governing body determines to be socially desirable, including, without limitation, developing an area to include a certain proportion of affordable housing.

11. South Carolina lawmakers, in S.C. Code Ann. §6-29-720(C)(3) have defined "**performance zoning**" as

---

28. Authors' note: Professor Jerold S. Kayden has written an insightful and critical study of how the idea of employing incentives to increase the supply of public amenities can easily go awry. *See* JEROLD S. KAYDEN, PRIVATELY OWNED PUBLIC SPACE: THE NEW YORK CITY EXPERIENCE (2000).

zoning which specifies a minimum requirement or maximum limit on the effects of a land use rather than, or in addition to, specifying the use itself, simultaneously assuring compatibility with surrounding development and increasing a developer's flexibility."[29]

12. In Massachusetts, a "smart growth zoning district" may allow "**mixed-use development**," which is defined in ALM GL ch. 40R, §2 as "a development containing a mix of some or all of multi-family residential, single-family residential, commercial, institutional, industrial and other uses, all conceived, planned and integrated to create vibrant, workable, livable and attractive neighborhoods." Similarly, R.I. Gen. Laws §45-24-47(a) provides:

> A zoning ordinance may provide for land development projects which are projects in which one or more lots, tracts, or parcels of land are to be developed or redeveloped as a coordinated site for a complex of uses, units, or structures, including, but not limited to, planned development and/or cluster development for residential, commercial, institutional, industrial, recreational, open space, and/or mixed uses as may be provided for in the zoning ordinance.

13. Michigan's lawmakers, in Mich. Comp. Laws Serv. §125.3503, provided this definition in their **PUD** enabling legislation:

> (1) As used in this section, "planned unit development" includes such terms as cluster zoning, planned development, community unit plan, and planned residential development and other terminology denoting zoning requirements designed to accomplish the objectives of the zoning ordinance through a land development project review process based on the application of site planning criteria to achieve integration of the proposed land development project with the characteristics of the project area.

> (2) The legislative body may establish planned unit development requirements in a zoning ordinance that permit flexibility in the regulation of land development, encourage innovation in land use and variety in design, layout, and type of structures constructed, achieve economy and efficiency in the use of land, natural resources, energy, and the

---

29. Authors' note: You can review the Bucks County, Pennsylvania, Performance Zoning Model Ordinance, originally drafted by the pioneer in this field—Lane Kendig—at http://www.smartcommunities.ncat.org/codes/bucks.shtml. *See also* LANE KENDIG, PERFORMANCE ZONING (1980); Frederick W. Acker, *Performance Zoning*, 67 Notre Dame L. Rev. 363 (1991).

Professor Tony Arnold, in *Planning Milagros: Environmental Justice and Land Use Regulation*, 76 DENV. U. L. REV. 1, 117-18 (1998) explains the concept in this manner:

Performance zoning does not regulate land uses, but instead regulates the impacts of activities that occur on land. A performance zoning ordinance establishes certain performance standards for possible negative impacts on neighboring property, such as dust, smoke, noise, odor, vibration, toxic pollutants, runoff, glare, heat, and other nuisances (negative externalities). It prohibits any land use with impacts that exceed levels predetermined to be tolerable. Two ways of classifying performance standards exist. One is to distinguish between standards related to development density, design, and preservation of natural resources—often associated with areas of new development—and standards related to the nuisance-like impacts of industrial activity, such as air, water, and soil pollution; noise; vibration; and odors—often in established industrial areas. Another classification distinguishes between what are known as "primitive" standards, which have only general definitions stemming from common law nuisance concepts (e.g., prohibitions on emission of "any offensive odor, dust, noxious gas, noise, vibration, smoke, heat or glare beyond the boundaries of the lot") and "precision" standards, which are developed from scientific data and reflected in quantifiable measurements (e.g., limits on permissible decibel levels in designated ocave bands per second or designated center frequency-cycles per second). Nevertheless, all types of performance zoning ordinances supplement, as opposed to replace, traditional, use-based Euclidean zoning. And courts have largely upheld the validity of performance zoning standards both as reasonable means of protecting the public from nuisances and as sufficiently measurable according to a "reasonable person" nuisance standard.

Can you see why Professor Arnold observes that "[p]erformance zoning is essentially local environmental law"?

provision of public services and utilities, encourage useful open space, and provide better housing, employment, and shopping opportunities particularly suited to the needs of the residents of this state. The review and approval of planned unit developments shall be by the zoning commission, an individual charged with administration of the zoning ordinance, or the legislative body, as specified in the zoning ordinance.

(3) Within a land development project designated as a planned unit development, regulations relating to the use of land, including, but not limited to, permitted uses, lot sizes, setbacks, height limits, required facilities, buffers, open space areas, and land use density, shall be determined in accordance with the planned unit development regulations specified in the zoning ordinance. The planned unit development regulations need not be uniform with regard to each type of land use if equitable procedures recognizing due process principles and avoiding arbitrary decisions are followed in making regulatory decisions. Unless explicitly prohibited by the planned unit development regulations, if requested by the landowner, a local unit of government may approve a planned unit development with open space that is not contiguous with the rest of the planned unit development.

14. The Pennsylvania Legislature, as evidenced by 53 Pa. Stat. §§10107 and 10702-A below, has encouraged the commonwealth's municipalities to experiment with **TND**,[30] a variation on a theme known as "form-based codes"[31]:

> "TRADITIONAL NEIGHBORHOOD DEVELOPMENT," an area of land developed for a compatible mixture of residential units for various income levels and non-residential commercial and workplace uses, including some structures that provide for a mix of uses within the same building. Residences, shops, offices, workplaces, public buildings and parks are interwoven within the neighborhood so that all are within relatively close proximity to each other. Traditional neighborhood development is relatively compact, limited in size and oriented toward pedestrian activity. It has an identifiable center and a discernible edge. The center of the neighborhood is in the form of a public park, commons, plaza, square or prominent intersection of two or more major streets.

---

30. Wisconsin lawmakers have gone even further in Wis. Stat. § 66.1027 (passed in 1999), mandating the development of "a model ordinance for a traditional neighborhood development [defined as "a compact, mixed-use neighborhood where residential, commercial and civic buildings are within close proximity to each other"] and an ordinance for a conservation subdivision." Moreover, state law requires that, "[n]ot later than January 1, 2002, every city and village with a population of at least 12,500 shall enact an ordinance that is similar to the model traditional neighborhood development ordinance . . . "The legislature duly approved "A Model Ordinance for a Traditional Neighborhood Development" in July 2001, which can be found at http://www.urpl.wisc.edu/people/ohm/tndord.pdf.

31. *See* Patricia E. Salkin, *Squaring the Circle on Sprawl: What More Can We Do? Progress Toward Sustainable Land Use in the States*, 16 WIDENER L.J. 787, 833-34 (2007) (quoting FORM-BASED CODES INST., DEFINITION OF A FORM-BASED CODE (2006), *available at* http:///www.formbasedcodes.org/definition.html).

  Although still a relatively new concept, another new urbanist technique, form-based zoning, seems to be gaining popularity among city planners. Form-based zoning has been defined as:

    A method of regulating development to achieve a specific urban form. Form-based codes create a predictable public realm by controlling physical form primarily, with a lesser focus on land use . . . . The regulations and standards in form-based codes . . . designate[ ] the appropriate form and scale (and therefore, character) of development rather than only distinctions in land use types. This is in contrast to conventional zoning's focus on the control of development intensity through simple numerical parameters. . . .

  A form-based code may apply to just one area of a city, such as a downtown neighborhood. In more complex form-based codes, the municipality is divided into transects depending on the character of the land and appropriate forms are prescribed for each transect in order to preserve and enhance its particular characteristics. Form-based zoning can also be adopted as a parallel development regulation, leaving the traditional zoning scheme in place and allowing developers to choose between the two.

Generally, there is a hierarchy of streets laid out in a rectilinear or grid pattern of interconnecting streets and blocks that provides multiple routes from origins to destinations and are appropriately designed to serve the needs of pedestrians and vehicles equally. . . .

The governing body of each municipality may enact, amend and repeal provisions of a zoning ordinance in order to fix standards and conditions for traditional neighborhood development. The provisions for standards and conditions for traditional neighborhood development shall be included within the zoning ordinance, and the enactment of the traditional neighborhood development provisions shall be in accordance with the procedures required for the enactment of an amendment of a zoning ordinance . . . .[32]

Many of the cases in the chapters that follow involve these and other post-Euclidean devices. As long as property owners are not treated arbitrarily and as long as they maintain what has been variously labeled "reasonable return," "reasonable use," "reasonably beneficial use," and "economically viable use," courts generally will defer to today's local regulators in the fashion they deferred to the first generation of zoners.

KELO v. CITY OF NEW LONDON
545 U.S. 469 (2005)

JUSTICE STEVENS delivered the opinion of the Court.

In 2000, the city of New London approved a development plan that, in the words of the Supreme Court of Connecticut, was "projected to create in excess of 1,000 jobs, to increase tax and other revenues, and to revitalize an economically distressed city, including its downtown and waterfront areas." 268 Conn. 1, 5, 843 A.2d 500, 507 (2004). In assembling the land needed for this project, the city's development agent has purchased property from willing sellers and proposes to use the power of eminent domain to acquire the remainder of the property from unwilling owners in exchange for just compensation. The question presented is whether the city's proposed disposition of this property qualifies as a "public use" within the meaning of the Takings Clause of the Fifth Amendment to the Constitution.

The city of New London (hereinafter City) sits at the junction of the Thames River and the Long Island Sound in southeastern Connecticut. Decades of economic decline led a state agency in

---

32. Authors' note: According to one account of the genesis of this legislation, "Rep. [Robert] Freeman based his legislation on the "TND Checklist" contained in Andres Duany's book *Suburban Nation*. He intended to not only bring more attention to the form of TND, but to ensure that development was actually executed in this form." Robert J. Sitkowski et al., *Enabling Legislation for Traditional Neighborhood Development Regulations*, in PLANNING & ENVIRONMENTAL LAW COMMENTARY (2001), *available at http://myapa.planning.org/PEL/commentary/oct01comm.htm* . For more on Duany's "Smart Code" alternative to Euclidean zoning, derived from the private "codes" he used in his New Urbanist communities, see Andres Duany & Emily Talen, *Making the Good Easy: The Smart Code Alternative*, 29 FORDHAM URB. L.J. 1445, 1453 (2002):

> The Smart Code differs from other approaches to smart growth implementation in that it is explicitly based on the concept of the Transect. As a Transect-based code, the Smart Code offers an alternative to Euclidean-based zoning by proposing a system of classification that arranges the elements of urbanism according to the principles of a Transect-based distribution. . . .

> Transect is a geographic cross-section of a region used to reveal a sequence of environments. For human environments, this cross-section can be used to identify a set of habitats that vary by their level and intensity of urban character—a continuum that ranges from rural to urban. This range of environments is the basis for organizing the components of the built world: building, lot, land use, street, and all of the other physical elements of the human habitat. In each human habitat along the rural to urban Transect, "immersive" environments are created—places that have an integrity and coherence about them because of their particular combinations of elements.

We would assume that a deep understanding of the "transect" is not a prerequisite to adoption and implementation of this new kind of post-zoning code.

1990 to designate the City a "distressed municipality." In 1996, the Federal Government closed the Naval Undersea Warfare Center, which had been located in the Fort Trumbull area of the City and had employed over 1,500 people. In 1998, the City's unemployment rate was nearly double that of the State, and its population of just under 24,000 residents was at its lowest since 1920.

These conditions prompted state and local officials to target New London, and particularly its Fort Trumbull area, for economic revitalization. To this end, respondent New London Development Corporation (NLDC), a private nonprofit entity established some years earlier to assist the City in planning economic development, was reactivated. In January 1998, the State authorized a $5.35 million bond issue to support the NLDC's planning activities and a $10 million bond issue toward the creation of a Fort Trumbull State Park. In February, the pharmaceutical company Pfizer Inc. announced that it would build a $300 million research facility on a site immediately adjacent to Fort Trumbull; local planners hoped that Pfizer would draw new business to the area, thereby serving as a catalyst to the area's rejuvenation. After receiving initial approval from the city council, the NLDC continued its planning activities and held a series of neighborhood meetings to educate the public about the process. In May, the city council authorized the NLDC to formally submit its plans to the relevant state agencies for review. Upon obtaining state-level approval, the NLDC finalized an integrated development plan focused on 90 acres of the Fort Trumbull area.

The Fort Trumbull area is situated on a peninsula that juts into the Thames River. The area comprises approximately 115 privately owned properties, as well as the 32 acres of land formerly occupied by the naval facility (Trumbull State Park now occupies 18 of those 32 acres). The development plan encompasses seven parcels. Parcel 1 is designated for a waterfront conference hotel at the center of a "small urban village" that will include restaurants and shopping. This parcel will also have marinas for both recreational and commercial uses. A pedestrian "riverwalk" will originate here and continue down the coast, connecting the waterfront areas of the development. Parcel 2 will be the site of approximately 80 new residences organized into an urban neighborhood and linked by public walkway to the remainder of the development, including the state park. This parcel also includes space reserved for a new U. S. Coast Guard Museum. Parcel 3, which is located immediately north of the Pfizer facility, will contain at least 90,000 square feet of research and development office space. Parcel 4A is a 2.4-acre site that will be used either to support the adjacent state park, by providing parking or retail services for visitors, or to support the nearby marina. Parcel 4B will include a renovated marina, as well as the final stretch of the riverwalk. Parcels 5, 6, and 7 will provide land for office and retail space, parking, and water-dependent commercial uses. App. 109-113.

The NLDC intended the development plan to capitalize on the arrival of the Pfizer facility and the new commerce it was expected to attract. In addition to creating jobs, generating tax revenue, and helping to "build momentum for the revitalization of downtown New London," id., at 92, the plan was also designed to make the City more attractive and to create leisure and recreational opportunities on the waterfront and in the park.

The city council approved the plan in January 2000, and designated the NLDC as its development agent in charge of implementation. The city council also authorized the NLDC to purchase property or to acquire property by exercising eminent domain in the City's name. The NLDC successfully negotiated the purchase of most of the real estate in the 90-acre area, but its negotiations with petitioners failed. As a consequence, in November 2000, the NLDC initiated the condemnation proceedings that gave rise to this case.

Petitioner Susette Kelo has lived in the Fort Trumbull area since 1997. She has made extensive improvements to her house, which she prizes for its water view. Petitioner Wilhelmina Dery was born in her Fort Trumbull house in 1918 and has lived there her entire life. Her husband Charles (also a petitioner) has lived in the house since they married some 60 years ago. In all, the nine petitioners own 15 properties in Fort Trumbull—4 in parcel 3 of the development plan and 11 in parcel 4A. Ten of the parcels are occupied by the owner or a family member; the other five are held as investment properties. There is no allegation that any of these properties is blighted or otherwise in poor condition; rather, they were condemned only because they happen to be located in the development area.

In December 2000, petitioners brought this action in the New London Superior Court. They claimed, among other things, that the taking of their properties would violate the "public use" restriction in the Fifth Amendment. After a 7-day bench trial, the Superior Court granted a permanent restraining order prohibiting the taking of the properties located in parcel 4A (park or marina support). It, however, denied petitioners relief as to the properties located in parcel 3 (office space).[4]

After the Superior Court ruled, both sides took appeals to the Supreme Court of Connecticut. That court held, over a dissent, that all of the City's proposed takings were valid. It began by upholding the lower court's determination that the takings were authorized by chapter 132, the State's municipal development statute. See Conn. Gen. Stat. § 8-186 et seq (2005). That statute expresses a legislative determination that the taking of land, even developed land, as part of an economic development project is a "public use" and in the "public interest." 268 Conn., at 18-28, 843 A. 2d, at 515-521. Next, relying on cases such as Hawaii Housing Authority v. Midkiff, 467 U.S. 229 (1984), and Berman v. Parker, 348 U.S. 26 (1954), the court held that such economic development qualified as a valid public use under both the Federal and State Constitutions.

Finally, adhering to its precedents, the court went on to determine, first, whether the takings of the particular properties at issue were "reasonably necessary" to achieving the City's intended public use, and, second, whether the takings were for "reasonably foreseeable needs," [268 Conn.], at 93-94, 843 A. 2d, at 558-559. The court upheld the trial court's factual findings as to parcel 3, but reversed the trial court as to parcel 4A, agreeing with the City that the intended use of this land was sufficiently definite and had been given "reasonable attention" during the planning process. Id., at 120-121, 843 A. 2d, at 574.

The three dissenting justices would have imposed a "heightened" standard of judicial review for takings justified by economic development. Although they agreed that the plan was intended to serve a valid public use, they would have found all the takings unconstitutional because the City had failed to adduce "clear and convincing evidence" that the economic benefits of the plan would in fact come to pass. Id., at 144, 146, 843 A. 2d, at 587, 588 (Zarella, J., joined by Sullivan, C. J., and Katz, J., concurring in part and dissenting in part).

We granted certiorari to determine whether a city's decision to take property for the purpose of economic development satisfies the "public use" requirement of the Fifth Amendment.

Two polar propositions are perfectly clear. On the one hand, it has long been accepted that the sovereign may not take the property of A for the sole purpose of transferring it to another private party B, even though A is paid just compensation. On the other hand, it is equally clear that a State may transfer property from one private party to another if future "use by the public" is the purpose of the taking; the condemnation of land for a railroad with common-carrier duties is a familiar example. Neither of these propositions, however, determines the disposition of this case.

As for the first proposition, the City would no doubt be forbidden from taking petitioners' land for the purpose of conferring a private benefit on a particular private party. See Midkiff, 467 U.S.,

---

4. While this litigation was pending before the Superior Court, the NLDC announced that it would lease some of the parcels to private developers in exchange for their agreement to develop the land according to the terms of the development plan. Specifically, the NLDC was negotiating a 99-year ground lease with Corcoran Jennison, a developer selected from a group of applicants. The negotiations contemplated a nominal rent of $1 per year, but no agreement had yet been signed.

at 245 ("A purely private taking could not withstand the scrutiny of the public use requirement; it would serve no legitimate purpose of government and would thus be void"); Missouri Pacific R. Co. v. Nebraska, 164 U.S. 403 (1896).[5] Nor would the City be allowed to take property under the mere pretext of a public purpose, when its actual purpose was to bestow a private benefit. The takings before us, however, would be executed pursuant to a "carefully considered" development plan. 268 Conn., at 54, 843 A. 2d, at 536. The trial judge and all the members of the Supreme Court of Connecticut agreed that there was no evidence of an illegitimate purpose in this case.[6] Therefore, as was true of the statute challenged in *Midkiff*, 467 U.S., at 245, the City's development plan was not adopted "to benefit a particular class of identifiable individuals."

On the other hand, this is not a case in which the City is planning to open the condemned land—at least not in its entirety—to use by the general public. Nor will the private lessees of the land in any sense be required to operate like common carriers, making their services available to all comers. But although such a projected use would be sufficient to satisfy the public use requirement, this "Court long ago rejected any literal requirement that condemned property be put into use for the general public." *Id.*, at 244. Indeed, while many state courts in the mid-19th century endorsed "use by the public" as the proper definition of public use, that narrow view steadily eroded over time. Not only was the "use by the public" test difficult to administer (*e.g.*, what proportion of the public need have access to the property? at what price?), but it proved to be impractical given the diverse and always evolving needs of society. Accordingly, when this Court began applying the Fifth Amendment to the States at the close of the 19th century, it embraced the broader and more natural interpretation of public use as "public purpose." See, *e.g.*, Fallbrook Irrigation Dist. v. Bradley, 164 U.S. 112, 158-164 (1896). Thus, in a case upholding a mining company's use of an aerial bucket line to transport ore over property it did not own, Justice Holmes' opinion for the Court stressed "the inadequacy of use by the general public as a universal test." Strickley v. Highland Boy Gold Mining Co., 200 U.S. 527, 531 (1906). We have repeatedly and consistently rejected that narrow test ever since.

The disposition of this case therefore turns on the question whether the City's development plan serves a "public purpose." Without exception, our cases have defined that concept broadly, reflecting our longstanding policy of deference to legislative judgments in this field.

In Berman v. Parker, 348 U.S. 26 (1954), this Court upheld a redevelopment plan targeting a blighted area of Washington, D. C., in which most of the housing for the area's 5,000 inhabitants was beyond repair. Under the plan, the area would be condemned and part of it utilized for the construction of streets, schools, and other public facilities. The remainder of the land would be leased or sold to private parties for the purpose of redevelopment, including the construction of low-cost housing.

---

5. *See also* Calder v. Bull, 3 U.S. 386 (1798) ("An act of the Legislature (for I cannot call it a law) contrary to the great first principles of the social compact, cannot be considered a rightful exercise of legislative authority.... A few instances will suffice to explain what I mean... [A] law that takes property from A and gives it to B: It is against all reason and justice, for a people to entrust a Legislature with such powers; and, therefore, it cannot be presumed that they have done it. The genius, the nature, and the spirit, of our State Governments, amount to a prohibition of such acts of legislation; and the general principles of law and reason forbid them" (emphasis deleted)).

6. *See* 268 Conn., at 159, 843 A. 2d, at 595 (Zarella, J., concurring in part and dissenting in part) ("The record clearly demonstrates that the development plan was not intended to serve the interests of Pfizer, Inc., or any other private entity, but rather, to revitalize the local economy by creating temporary and permanent jobs, generating a significant increase in tax revenue, encouraging spin-off economic activities and maximizing public access to the waterfront"). And while the City intends to transfer certain of the parcels to a private developer in a long-term lease—which developer, in turn, is expected to lease the office space and so forth to other private tenants—the identities of those private parties were not known when the plan was adopted. It is, of course, difficult to accuse the government of having taken A's property to benefit the private interests of B when the identity of B was unknown.

The owner of a department store located in the area challenged the condemnation, pointing out that his store was not itself blighted and arguing that the creation of a "better balanced, more attractive community" was not a valid public use. *Id.*, at 31. Writing for a unanimous Court, Justice Douglas refused to evaluate this claim in isolation, deferring instead to the legislative and agency judgment that the area "must be planned as a whole" for the plan to be successful. *Id.*, at 34. The Court explained that "community redevelopment programs need not, by force of the Constitution, be on a piecemeal basis—lot by lot, building by building." *Id.*, at 35. The public use underlying the taking was unequivocally affirmed:

> "We do not sit to determine whether a particular housing project is or is not desirable. The concept of the public welfare is broad and inclusive. . . . The values it represents are spiritual as well as physical, aesthetic as well as monetary. It is within the power of the legislature to determine that the community should be beautiful as well as healthy, spacious as well as clean, well-balanced as well as carefully patrolled. In the present case, the Congress and its authorized agencies have made determinations that take into account a wide variety of values. It is not for us to reappraise them. If those who govern the District of Columbia decide that the Nation's Capital should be beautiful as well as sanitary, there is nothing in the Fifth Amendment that stands in the way." *Id.*, at 33.

In Hawaii Housing Authority v. Midkiff, 467 U.S. 229 (1984), the Court considered a Hawaii statute whereby fee title was taken from lessors and transferred to lessees (for just compensation) in order to reduce the concentration of land ownership. We unanimously upheld the statute and rejected the Ninth Circuit's view that it was "a naked attempt on the part of the state of Hawaii to take the property of A and transfer it to B solely for B's private use and benefit." *Id.*, at 235 (internal quotation marks omitted). Reaffirming *Berman*'s deferential approach to legislative judgments in this field, we concluded that the State's purpose of eliminating the "social and economic evils of a land oligopoly" qualified as a valid public use. 467 U.S., at 241–242. Our opinion also rejected the contention that the mere fact that the State immediately transferred the properties to private individuals upon condemnation somehow diminished the public character of the taking. "[I]t is only the taking's purpose, and not its mechanics," we explained, that matters in determining public use. *Id.*, at 244. . . .

Viewed as a whole, our jurisprudence has recognized that the needs of society have varied between different parts of the Nation, just as they have evolved over time in response to changed circumstances. . . .

Those who govern the City were not confronted with the need to remove blight in the Fort Trumbull area, but their determination that the area was sufficiently distressed to justify a program of economic rejuvenation is entitled to our deference. The City has carefully formulated an economic development plan that it believes will provide appreciable benefits to the community, including—but by no means limited to—new jobs and increased tax revenue. As with other exercises in urban planning and development,[12] the City is endeavoring to coordinate a variety of commercial, residential, and recreational uses of land, with the hope that they will form a whole greater than the sum of its parts. To effectuate this plan, the City has invoked a state statute that specifically authorizes the use of eminent domain to promote economic development. Given the comprehensive character of the plan, the thorough deliberation that preceded its adoption, and the limited scope of our review, it is appropriate for us, as it was in *Berman*, to resolve the challenges of the individual owners, not on a piecemeal basis, but rather in light of the entire plan. Because

---

12. *Cf.* Village of Euclid v. Ambler Realty Co., 272 U.S. 365 (1926).

that plan unquestionably serves a public purpose, the takings challenged here satisfy the public use requirement of the Fifth Amendment.

To avoid this result, petitioners urge us to adopt a new bright-line rule that economic development does not qualify as a public use. Putting aside the unpersuasive suggestion that the City's plan will provide only purely economic benefits, neither precedent nor logic supports petitioners' proposal. Promoting economic development is a traditional and long-accepted function of government. There is, moreover, no principled way of distinguishing economic development from the other public purposes that we have recognized. In our cases upholding takings that facilitated agriculture and mining, for example, we emphasized the importance of those industries to the welfare of the States in question; in *Berman*, we endorsed the purpose of transforming a blighted area into a "well-balanced" community through redevelopment, 348 U.S., at 33;[13] in *Midkiff*, we upheld the interest in breaking up a land oligopoly that "created artificial deterrents to the normal functioning of the State's residential land market," 467 U.S., at 242 . . . . It would be incongruous to hold that the City's interest in the economic benefits to be derived from the development of the Fort Trumbull area has less of a public character than any of those other interests. Clearly, there is no basis for exempting economic development from our traditionally broad understanding of public purpose.

Petitioners contend that using eminent domain for economic development impermissibly blurs the boundary between public and private takings. Again, our cases foreclose this objection. Quite simply, the government's pursuit of a public purpose will often benefit individual private parties. For example, in *Midkiff*, the forced transfer of property conferred a direct and significant benefit on those lessees who were previously unable to purchase their homes. . . . The owner of the department store in *Berman* objected to "taking from one businessman for the benefit of another businessman," 348 U.S., at 32, referring to the fact that under the redevelopment plan land would be leased or sold to private developers for redevelopment. Our rejection of that contention has particular relevance to the instant case: "The public end may be as well or better served through an agency of private enterprise than through a department of government—or so the Congress might conclude. We cannot say that public ownership is the sole method of promoting the public purposes of community redevelopment projects." *Id.*, at 34.

It is further argued that without a bright-line rule nothing would stop a city from transferring citizen *A*'s property to citizen *B* for the sole reason that citizen *B* will put the property to a more productive use and thus pay more taxes. Such a one-to-one transfer of property, executed outside the confines of an integrated development plan, is not presented in this case. While such an unusual exercise of government power would certainly raise a suspicion that a private purpose was afoot,[17] the hypothetical cases posited by petitioners can be confronted if and when they arise. They do not warrant the crafting of an artificial restriction on the concept of public use.

Alternatively, petitioners maintain that for takings of this kind we should require a "reasonable certainty" that the expected public benefits will actually accrue. Such a rule, however, would rep-

---

13. It is a misreading of *Berman* to suggest that the only public use upheld in that case was the initial removal of blight. The public use described in *Berman* extended beyond that to encompass the purpose of developing that area to create conditions that would prevent a reversion to blight in the future. *See* 348 U.S., at 34-35 ("It was not enough, [the experts] believed, to remove existing buildings that were insanitary or unsightly. It was important to redesign the whole area so as to eliminate the conditions that cause slums . . . . The entire area needed redesigning so that a balanced, integrated plan could be developed for the region, including not only new homes, but also schools, churches, parks, streets, and shopping centers. In this way it was hoped that the cycle of decay of the area could be controlled and the birth of future slums prevented"). Had the public use in *Berman* been defined more narrowly, it would have been difficult to justify the taking of the plaintiff's nonblighted department store

17. Courts have viewed such aberrations with a skeptical eye. *See, e.g.*, 99 Cents Only Stores v. Lancaster Redevelopment Agency, 237 F. Supp. 2d 1123 (CD Cal. 2001); cf. Cincinnati v. Vester, 281 U.S. 439, 448 (1930) (taking invalid under state eminent domain statute for lack of a reasoned explanation). These types of takings may also implicate other constitutional guarantees. See Village of Willowbrook v. Olech, 528 U.S. 562 (2000) (*per curiam*).

resent an even greater departure from our precedent. "When the legislature's purpose is legitimate and its means are not irrational, our cases make clear that empirical debates over the wisdom of takings—no less than debates over the wisdom of other kinds of socioeconomic legislation—are not to be carried out in the federal courts." *Midkiff*, 467 U.S., at 242. Indeed, earlier this Term we explained why similar practical concerns (among others) undermined the use of the "substantially advances" formula in our regulatory takings doctrine. See Lingle v. Chevron U.S.A. Inc., 544 U.S. 528 (2005) (noting that this formula "would empower—and might often require—courts to substitute their predictive judgments for those of elected legislatures and expert agencies"). The disadvantages of a heightened form of review are especially pronounced in this type of case. Orderly implementation of a comprehensive redevelopment plan obviously requires that the legal rights of all interested parties be established before new construction can be commenced. A constitutional rule that required postponement of the judicial approval of every condemnation until the likelihood of success of the plan had been assured would unquestionably impose a significant impediment to the successful consummation of many such plans.

Just as we decline to second-guess the City's considered judgments about the efficacy of its development plan, we also decline to second-guess the City's determinations as to what lands it needs to acquire in order to effectuate the project. "It is not for the courts to oversee the choice of the boundary line nor to sit in review on the size of a particular project area. Once the question of the public purpose has been decided, the amount and character of land to be taken for the project and the need for a particular tract to complete the integrated plan rests in the discretion of the legislative branch." *Berman*, 348 U.S., at 35-36.

In affirming the City's authority to take petitioners' properties, we do not minimize the hardship that condemnations may entail, notwithstanding the payment of just compensation. We emphasize that nothing in our opinion precludes any State from placing further restrictions on its exercise of the takings power. Indeed, many States already impose "public use" requirements that are stricter than the federal baseline. Some of these requirements have been established as a matter of state constitutional law,[22] while others are expressed in state eminent domain statutes that carefully limit the grounds upon which takings may be exercised.[23] As the submissions of the parties and their *amici* make clear, the necessity and wisdom of using eminent domain to promote economic development are certainly matters of legitimate public debate. This Court's authority, however, extends only to determining whether the City's proposed condemnations are for a "public use" within the meaning of the Fifth Amendment to the Federal Constitution. Because over a century of our case law interpreting that provision dictates an affirmative answer to that question, we may not grant petitioners the relief that they seek.

The judgment of the Supreme Court of Connecticut is affirmed.

It is so ordered.

JUSTICE KENNEDY, concurring.

I join the opinion for the Court and add these further observations.

This Court has declared that a taking should be upheld as consistent with the Public Use Clause, U.S. Const., Amdt. 5, as long as it is "rationally related to a conceivable public purpose." Hawaii Housing Authority v. Midkiff, 467 U.S. 229, 241(1984); see also Berman v. Parker, 348 U.S. 26 (1954). This deferential standard of review echoes the rational-basis test used to review economic regulation under the Due Process and Equal Protection Clauses. The determination that

---

22. *See, e.g.*, County of Wayne v. Hathcock, 471 Mich. 445, 684 N.W.2d 765 (2004).

23. Under California law, for instance, a city may only take land for economic development purposes in blighted areas. Cal. Health & Safety Code Ann. §§ 33030-33037 (West 1999). *See, e.g.*, Redevelopment Agency of Chula Vista v. Rados Bros., 95 Cal. App. 4th 309, 115 Cal. Rptr. 2d 234 (2002).

a rational-basis standard of review is appropriate does not, however, alter the fact that transfers intended to confer benefits on particular, favored private entities, and with only incidental or pretextual public benefits, are forbidden by the Public Use Clause.

A court applying rational-basis review under the Public Use Clause should strike down a taking that, by a clear showing, is intended to favor a particular private party, with only incidental or pretextual public benefits, just as a court applying rational-basis review under the Equal Protection Clause must strike down a government classification that is clearly intended to injure a particular class of private parties, with only incidental or pretextual public justifications. See Cleburne v. Cleburne Living Center, Inc., 473 U.S. 432, 446-447, 450 (1985); Department of Agriculture v. Moreno, 413 U.S. 528, 533-536 (1973). As the trial court in this case was correct to observe: "Where the purpose [of a taking] is economic development and that development is to be carried out by private parties or private parties will be benefited, the court must decide if the stated public purpose—economic advantage to a city sorely in need of it—is only incidental to the benefits that will be confined on private parties of a development plan." App. to Pet. for Cert. 263.

A court confronted with a plausible accusation of impermissible favoritism to private parties should treat the objection as a serious one and review the record to see if it has merit, though with the presumption that the government's actions were reasonable and intended to serve a public purpose. . . .

The trial court concluded . . . that benefiting Pfizer was not "the primary motivation or effect of this development plan"; instead, "the primary motivation for [respondents] was to take advantage of Pfizer 's presence." Id., at 276. Likewise, the trial court concluded that "[t]here is nothing in the record to indicate that . . . [respondents] were motivated by a desire to aid [other] particular private entities." *Id.*, at 278. Even the dissenting justices on the Connecticut Supreme Court agreed that respondents' development plan was intended to revitalize the local economy, not to serve the interests of Pfizer, Corcoran Jennison, or any other private party. This case, then, survives the meaningful rational basis review that in my view is required under the Public Use Clause. . . .

My agreement with the Court that a presumption of invalidity is not warranted for economic development takings in general, or for the particular takings at issue in this case, does not foreclose the possibility that a more stringent standard of review than that announced in *Berman* and *Midkiff* might be appropriate for a more narrowly drawn category of takings. There may be private transfers in which the risk of undetected impermissible favoritism of private parties is so acute that a presumption (rebuttable or otherwise) of invalidity is warranted under the Public Use Clause. This demanding level of scrutiny, however, is not required simply because the purpose of the taking is economic development.

This is not the occasion for conjecture as to what sort of cases might justify a more demanding standard, but it is appropriate to underscore aspects of the instant case that convince me no departure from *Berman* and *Midkiff* is appropriate here. This taking occurred in the context of a comprehensive development plan meant to address a serious city wide depression, and the projected economic benefits of the project cannot be characterized as *de minimis*. The identities of most of the private beneficiaries were unknown at the time the city formulated its plans. The city complied with elaborate procedural requirements that facilitate review of the record and inquiry into the city's purposes. In sum, while there may be categories of cases in which the transfers are so suspicious, or the procedures employed so prone to abuse, or the purported benefits are so trivial or implausible, that courts should presume an impermissible private purpose, no such circumstances are present in this case.

* * *

For the foregoing reasons, I join in the Court's opinion.

JUSTICE O'CONNOR, with whom the CHIEF JUSTICE, JUSTICE SCALIA, and JUSTICE THOMAS join, dissenting. . . .

Under the banner of economic development, all private property is now vulnerable to being taken and transferred to another private owner, so long as it might be upgraded—*i.e.*, given to an owner who will use it in a way that the legislature deems more beneficial to the public—iin the process. To reason, as the Court does, that the incidental public benefits resulting from the subsequent ordinary use of private property render economic development takings "for public use" is to wash out any distinction between private and public use of property--and thereby effectively to delete the words "for public use" from the Takings Clause of the Fifth Amendment. Accordingly I respectfully dissent. . . .

Our cases have generally identified three categories of takings that comply with the public use requirement, though it is in the nature of things that the boundaries between these categories are not always firm. Two are relatively straightforward and uncontroversial. First, the sovereign may transfer private property to public ownership—such as for a road, a hospital, or a military base. Second, the sovereign may transfer private property to private parties, often common carriers, who make the property available for the public's use—such as with a railroad, a public utility, or a stadium. But "public ownership" and "use-by-the-public" are sometimes too constricting and impractical ways to define the scope of the Public Use Clause. Thus we have allowed that, in certain circumstances and to meet certain exigencies, takings that serve a public purpose also satisfy the Constitution even if the property is destined for subsequent private use. *See, e.g.*, Berman v. Parker, 348 U.S. 26 (1954); Hawaii Housing Authority v. Midkiff, 467 U.S. 229 (1984).

This case returns us for the first time in over 20 years to the hard question of when a purportedly "public purpose" taking meets the public use requirement. It presents an issue of first impression: Are economic development takings constitutional? I would hold that they are not. We are guided by two precedents about the taking of real property by eminent domain. In *Berman*, we upheld takings within a blighted neighborhood of Washington, D. C. The neighborhood had so deteriorated that, for example, 64.3% of its dwellings were beyond repair. 348 U.S., at 30. It had become burdened with "overcrowding of dwellings," "lack of adequate streets and alleys," and "lack of light and air." *Id.*, at 34. Congress had determined that the neighborhood had become "injurious to the public health, safety, morals, and welfare" and that it was necessary to "eliminat[e] all such injurious conditions by employing all means necessary and appropriate for the purpose," including eminent domain. *Id.*, at 28. Mr. Berman's department store was not itself blighted. Having approved of Congress' decision to eliminate the harm to the public emanating from the blighted neighborhood, however, we did not second-guess its decision to treat the neighborhood as a whole rather than lot-by-lot. *Id.*, at 34-35 ("It is only the taking's purpose, and not its mechanics, that must pass scrutiny").

In *Midkiff*, we upheld a land condemnation scheme in Hawaii whereby title in real property was taken from lessors and transferred to lessees. At that time, the State and Federal Governments owned nearly 49% of the State's land, and another 47% was in the hands of only 72 private landowners. Concentration of land ownership was so dramatic that on the State's most urbanized island, Oahu, 22 landowners owned 72.5% of the fee simple titles. *Id.* at 232. The Hawaii Legislature had concluded that the oligopoly in land ownership was "skewing the State's residential fee simple market, inflating land prices, and injuring the public tranquility and welfare," and therefore enacted a condemnation scheme for redistributing title. *Ibid.* . . .

The Court's holdings in *Berman* and *Midkiff* were true to the principle underlying the Public Use Clause. In both those cases, the extraordinary, precondemnation use of the targeted property inflicted affirmative harm on society—in *Berman* through blight resulting from extreme poverty and in *Midkiff* through oligopoly resulting from extreme wealth. And in both cases, the relevant legislative body had found that eliminating the existing property use was necessary to remedy the harm. Thus a public purpose was realized when the harmful use was eliminated. Because each taking directly achieved a public benefit, it did not matter that the property was turned over to private use. Here, in contrast, New London does not claim that Susette Kelo's and Wilhelmina Dery's well-maintained homes are the source of any social harm. Indeed, it could not so claim without adopting the absurd argument that any single-family home that might be razed to make way for an apartment building, or any church that might be replaced with a retail store, or any small business that might be more lucrative if it were instead part of a national franchise, is inherently harmful to society and thus within the government's power to condemn.

In moving away from our decisions sanctioning the condemnation of harmful property use, the Court today significantly expands the meaning of public use. It holds that the sovereign may take private property currently put to ordinary private use, and give it over for new, ordinary private use, so long as the new use is predicted to generate some secondary benefit for the public—such as increased tax revenue, more jobs, maybe even esthetic pleasure. But nearly any lawful use of real private property can be said to generate some incidental benefit to the public. Thus, if predicted (or even guaranteed) positive side effects are enough to render transfer from one private party to another constitutional, then the words "for public use" do not realistically exclude any takings, and thus do not exert any constraint on the eminent domain power.

There is a sense in which this troubling result follows from errant language in *Berman* and *Midkiff.* In discussing whether takings within a blighted neighborhood were for a public use, Berman began by observing: "We deal, in other words, with what traditionally has been known as the police power." 348 U.S., at 32. From there it declared that "[o]nce the object is within the authority of Congress, the right to realize it through the exercise of eminent domain is clear." *Id.,* at 33. Following up, we said in *Midkiff* that "[t]he 'public use' requirement is coterminous with the scope of a sovereign's police powers." 467 U.S., at 240. This language was unnecessary to the specific holdings of those decisions. *Berman* and *Midkiff* simply did not put such language to the constitutional test, because the takings in those cases were within the police power but also for "public use" for the reasons I have described. The case before us now demonstrates why, when deciding if a taking's purpose is constitutional, the police power and "public use" cannot always be equated. . . .

The logic of today's decision is that eminent domain may only be used to upgrade—not downgrade—property. At best this makes the Public Use Clause redundant with the Due Process Clause, which already prohibits irrational government action. The Court rightfully admits, however, that the judiciary cannot get bogged down in predictive judgments about whether the public will actually be better off after a property transfer. In any event, this constraint has no realistic import. For who among us can say she already makes the most productive or attractive possible use of her property? The specter of condemnation hangs over all property. Nothing is to prevent the State from replacing any Motel 6 with a Ritz-Carlton, any home with a shopping mall, or any farm with a factory. Cf. Bugryn v. Bristol, 63 Conn. App. 98, 774 A.2d 1042 (2001) (taking the homes and farm of four owners in their 70's and 80's and giving it to an "industrial park"); 99 Cents Only Stores v. Lancaster Redevelopment Agency, 237 F. Supp. 2d 1123 (CD Cal. 2001) (attempted taking of 99 Cents store to replace with a Costco); Poletown Neighborhood Council v. Detroit, 410 Mich. 616, 304 N.W.2d 455 (1981) (taking a working-class, immigrant community in Detroit and giving it to a General Motors assembly plant), overruled by County of Wayne v. Hathcock, 471 Mich. 445, 684 N.W.2d 765 (2004); Brief for Becket Fund for Religious Liberty as Amicus Curiae 4-11 (describing takings of religious institutions' properties); Institute for Justice, D. Berliner,

Public Power, Private Gain: A Five-Year, State-by-State Report Examining the Abuse of Eminent Domain (2003) (collecting accounts of economic development takings). . . .

Any property may now be taken for the benefit of another private party, but the fallout from this decision will not be random. The beneficiaries are likely to be those citizens with disproportionate influence and power in the political process, including large corporations and development firms. As for the victims, the government now has license to transfer property from those with fewer resources to those with more. The Founders cannot have intended this perverse result. "[T] hat alone is a just government," wrote James Madison, "which impartially secures to every man, whatever is his own." For the National Gazette, Property, (Mar. 27, 1792), reprinted in 14 Papers of James Madison 266 (R. Rutland et al. eds. 1983).

I would hold that the takings in both Parcel 3 and Parcel 4A are unconstitutional, reverse the judgment of the Supreme Court of Connecticut, and remand for further proceedings.

JUSTICE THOMAS, dissenting. . . .

Today's decision is simply the latest in a string of our cases construing the Public Use Clause to be a virtual nullity, without the slightest nod to its original meaning. In my view, the Public Use Clause, originally understood, is a meaningful limit on the government's eminent domain power. Our cases have strayed from the Clause's original meaning, and I would reconsider them. . . .

In my view, it is "imperative that the Court maintain absolute fidelity to" the Clause's express limit on the power of the government over the individual, no less than with every other liberty expressly enumerated in the Fifth Amendment or the Bill of Rights more generally. . . .

[T]he Court in *Berman* and *Midkiff* upheld condemnations for the purposes of slum clearance and land redistribution, respectively. "Subject to specific constitutional limitations," *Berman* proclaimed, "when the legislature has spoken, the public interest has been declared in terms well-nigh conclusive. In such cases the legislature, not the judiciary, is the main guardian of the public needs to be served by social legislation." 348 U.S., at 32. That reasoning was question begging, since the question to be decided was whether the "specific constitutional limitation" of the Public Use Clause prevented the taking of the appellant's (concededly "nonblighted") department store. *Berman* also appeared to reason that any exercise by Congress of an enumerated power (in this case, its plenary power over the District of Columbia) was *per se* a "public use" under the Fifth Amendment. But the very point of the Public Use Clause is to limit that power.

More fundamentally, *Berman* and *Midkiff* erred by equating the eminent domain power with the police power of States. Traditional uses of that regulatory power, such as the power to abate a nuisance, required no compensation whatsoever, in sharp contrast to the takings power, which has always required compensation. The question whether the State can take property using the power of eminent domain is therefore distinct from the question whether it can regulate property pursuant to the police power. In *Berman*, for example, if the slums at issue were truly "blighted," then state nuisance law, not the power of eminent domain, would provide the appropriate remedy. To construe the Public Use Clause to overlap with the States' police power conflates these two categories. . . .

For all these reasons, I would revisit our Public Use Clause cases and consider returning to the original meaning of the Public Use Clause: that the government may take property only if it actually uses or gives the public a legal right to use the property.

The consequences of today's decision are not difficult to predict, and promise to be harmful. So-called "urban renewal" programs provide some compensation for the properties they take, but no compensation is possible for the subjective value of these lands to the individuals displaced and the indignity inflicted by uprooting them from their homes. Allowing the government to take property solely for public purposes is bad enough, but extending the concept of public purpose to encompass any economically beneficial goal guarantees that these losses will fall disproportionately on poor communities. Those communities are not only systematically less likely to put their lands to the highest and best social use, but are also the least politically powerful. If ever there were justification for intrusive judicial review of constitutional provisions that protect "discrete and insular minorities," United States v. Carolene Products Co., 304 U.S. 144, 152, n. 4 (1938), surely that principle would apply with great force to the powerless groups and individuals the Public Use Clause protects. The deferential standard this Court has adopted for the Public Use Clause is therefore deeply perverse. It encourages "those citizens with disproportionate influence and power in the political process, including large corporations and development firms," to victimize the weak. *Ante*, at 505 (O'Connor, J., dissenting).

Those incentives have made the legacy of this Court's "public purpose" test an unhappy one. In the 1950's, no doubt emboldened in part by the expansive understanding of "public use" this Court adopted in *Berman*, cities "rushed to draw plans" for downtown development. B. Frieden & L. Sagalyn, Downtown, Inc. How America Rebuilds Cities 17 (1989). "Of all the families displaced by urban renewal from 1949 through 1963, 63 percent of those whose race was known were nonwhite, and of these families, 56 percent of nonwhites and 38 percent of whites had incomes low enough to qualify for public housing, which, however, was seldom available to them." *Id.*, at 28. Public works projects in the 1950's and 1960's destroyed predominantly minority communities in St. Paul, Minnesota, and Baltimore, Maryland. *Id.*, at 28-29. In 1981, urban planners in Detroit, Michigan, uprooted the largely "lower-income and elderly" Poletown neighborhood for the benefit of the General Motors Corporation. J. Wylie, Poletown: Community Betrayed 58 (1989). Urban renewal projects have long been associated with the displacement of blacks; "[i]n cities across the country, urban renewal came to be known as 'Negro removal.'" Pritchett, The "Public Menace" of Blight: Urban Renewal and the Private Uses of Eminent Domain, 21 Yale L. & Pol'y Rev. 1, 47 (2003). Over 97 percent of the individuals forcibly removed from their homes by the "slum-clearance" project upheld by this Court in Berman were black. 348 U.S., at 30. Regrettably, the predictable consequence of the Court's decision will be to exacerbate these effects. . . .

Notes

1. A victory for New London was not unexpected by those familiar with *Berman* and *Midkiff.* What was surprising was that Justice Sandra Day O'Connor and Chief Justice William H. Rehnquist, both of whom approved the taking in the latter case, were dissenting voices 21 years later. In fact, Justice O'Connor wrote the unanimous opinion upholding Hawaii's anti-oligopoly scheme. Even more surprising was the decidedly negative reaction to the majority opinion in national and local media that helped fuel widespread state statutory and constitutional eminent domain reforms.[33]

State lawmakers in every region of the country were eager to clarify that unlike in Connecticut, the phrase "public use" was not elastic enough to include the benefits gained from private economic development projects. By the end of 2006 (one and one-half years after the *Kelo* decision was announced), the following states, in chronological order, had made procedural or substantive changes in their takings laws: Delaware, Alabama, Texas, Ohio, South Dakota, Utah, Idaho, Indiana, Kentucky, Wisconsin, Georgia, West Virginia, Maine, Nebraska, Vermont, Pennsylvania, Florida, Kansas, Minnesota, Tennessee, Colorado, New Hampshire, Alaska, Missouri, Iowa, Illinois, North Carolina, Michigan, and California. Wyoming, New Mexico, Virginia, North

---

33. For details on coverage on the Internet, in newspapers, and on network news, and for a comparison with the media response to *Berman* and *Midkiff,* see Michael Allan Wolf, *Hysteria v. History: Public Use in the Public Eye, in* PRIVATE PROPERTY, COMMUNITY DEVELOPMENT, AND EMINENT DOMAIN 15 (Robin Paul Malloy ed., 2008).

Dakota, Washington, Maryland, Montana, Nevada, and Connecticut joined the fold the following year.[34]

After taking the opportunity to revisit often outdated eminent domain provisions, many state legislators tweaked existing law in areas beyond public use. Some of the more common changes involved enhanced public notice requirements, increased attorneys fees, additional compensation for targeted landowners, and stiffer requirements for the taking of property in blighted areas. Florida lawmakers in Fla. Stat. §73.014(2) even eliminated the taking of "private property for the purpose of preventing or eliminating slum or blight conditions" as a public purpose, in effect nullifying the holding of *Berman* under state law.

In September 2006, Louisiana became the first of several states to amend their state constitution's takings provisions when voters passed a ballot measure that limited the definition of "public purpose" and made clear that "[n]either economic development, enhancement of tax revenue, or any incidental benefit to the public shall be considered in determining whether the taking or damaging of property is for a public purpose." In November 2006, voters in Florida, Georgia, Michigan, New Hampshire, and South Carolina approved similar constitutional changes to eminent domain law that were placed on the ballot by state lawmakers, while eminent domain ballot measures originating in citizen petitions were successful in a few other states.

There was even a bit of "bait-and-switch" by private property rights activists. Arizona voters approved statutory changes that not only narrowed the definition of "public use," but also included a "regulatory takings" provision that puts at risk land use regulations that reduce property values.[35] Voters in California, Idaho, and Washington struck down similar ballot measures that would have added this anti-regulatory measure.

2. While *Kelo* is the latest in a continuous line of Supreme Court decisions indicating that the Fifth Amendment mandates generous deference to the other branches' determination of "public use," there has been some wavering on the state level. Both dissents in *Kelo* cited the highly controversial split decision of the Supreme Court of Michigan in Poletown Neighborhood Council v. City of Detroit, 410 Mich. 616, 629, 304 N.W.2d 455, 457 (1981), in which the court answered the following question affirmatively: "Can a municipality use the power of eminent domain granted to it by the Economic Development Corporations Act to condemn property for transfer to a private corporation to build a plant to promote industry and commerce, thereby adding jobs and taxes to the economic base of the municipality and state?"

Twenty-three years later, in County of Wayne v. Hathcock, 471 Mich. 445, 450, 483, 684 N.W.2d 765, 769, 787 (2004), the same court overturned *Poletown*. The court noted:

> We are presented again with a clash of two bedrock principles of our legal tradition: the sacrosanct right of individuals to dominion over their private property, on the one hand and, on the other, the state's authority to condemn private property for the commonweal. In this case, Wayne County would use the power of eminent domain to condemn defendants' real properties for the construction of a 1,300-acre business and technology park. This proposed commercial center is intended to reinvigorate the strug-

---

34. For more details on these state reforms, see *Powell on Real Property* §79F.03[3][b][iv] (Michael Allan Wolf gen. ed. 2009) and http://www.castlecoalition.org (a website for the "nationwide grassroots property rights activism project" of the Institute for Justice, the public interest law firm that represented Susette Kelo).

35. *See* Ariz. Rev. Stat. §12-1134(A):

> If the existing rights to use, divide, sell or possess private real property are reduced by the enactment or applicability of any land use law enacted after the date the property is transferred to the owner and such action reduces the fair market value of the property the owner is entitled to just compensation from this state or the political subdivision of the state that enacted the land use law.

gling economy of southeastern Michigan by attracting businesses, particularly those involved in developing new technologies, to the area.

This time the "sacrosanct right" won over the "state's authority," as the justices in the majority corrected the error of their predecessors:

> Because *Poletown*'s conception of a public use—that of "alleviating unemployment and revitalizing the economic base of the community"—has no support in the Court's eminent domain jurisprudence before the [Michigan] Constitution's ratification, its interpretation of "public use" in art 10, § 2 cannot reflect the common understanding of that phrase among those sophisticated in the law at ratification. Consequently, the *Poletown* analysis provides no legitimate support for the condemnations proposed in this case and, for the reasons stated above, is overruled.

3. Not surprisingly, state courts in other jurisdictions have responded negatively to the failure of the *Kelo* majority to show the proper respect for landowners' rights. In City of Norwood v. Horney, 110 Ohio St. 3d 353, 361-62, 376-77, 853 N.E.2d 1115, 1128, 1140-41 (2006), a unanimous court cited Justice O'Connor's *Kelo* dissent favorably in its invalidation of the city's use of eminent domain to take homes located in, to use a phrase from the city code, a "deteriorating area." This state high court opinion, based on the interpretation of the Ohio Constitution, emphasized the importance, even fundamentality, of private-property rights: "The rights related to property, i.e., to acquire, use, enjoy, and dispose of property, are among the most revered in our law and traditions. Indeed, property rights are integral aspects of our theory of democracy and notions of liberty." The opinion then reviewed the long and winding history of public use and judicial review in public use cases on the state and federal levels, including this important observation and conclusion:

> Given the individual's fundamental property rights in Ohio, the courts' role in reviewing eminent-domain appropriations, though limited, is important in all cases. Judicial review is even more imperative in cases in which the taking involves an ensuing transfer of the property to a private entity, where a novel theory of public use is asserted, and in cases in which there is a showing of discrimination, bad faith, impermissible financial gain, or other improper purpose. With our proper role as arbiters of the scope of eminent domain clarified, we turn to the public use at issue in these cases.
>
> Although we have permitted economic concerns to be considered in addition to other factors, such as slum clearance, when determining whether the public-use requirement is sufficient, we have never found economic benefits alone to be a sufficient public use for a valid taking. We decline to do so now.

Similarly, in Board of County Comm'rs v. Lowery, 136 P.3d 639, 653-54 (2006), the court accepted the *Kelo* majority's invitation to interpret its own state constitution independently. The *Lowery* court rejected a county's use of eminent domain in support of a privately owned electric generation plant, which required two pipelines between its plant site and the Arkansas River:

> We hold the takings in the four instant cases are unlawful takings of Landowners' private property to confer a private benefit on a private party, Energetix, in violation of Article 2, §§ 23 & 24 of the Oklahoma Constitution. We further hold that takings for the purpose of economic development alone (not in connection with the removal of blighted property) do not constitute a public use or public purpose to support the exercise of eminent domain as a matter of Oklahoma constitutional law, nor does it satisfy the public purpose requirement of 27 O.S. 2001 § 5.

Given these judicial (and legislative and constitutional) shifts, the "public use" question promises to be a hot topic in takings law for the foreseeable future.

4. The affinity between the judicial deference in *Kelo* and in *Euclid v. Ambler* is important and purposeful. Note that the majority grouped New London's ambitious economic development plan with "other exercises in urban planning and development" (dropping a footnote to the 1926 case). Can a carefully conceived comprehensive plan that has received popular and political approval meet the constitutional mandate for a public use, or do the words and framework of the Constitution require something more?

Chapter Four

Accommodating Change: Departures From (and Within) the Zoning Ordinance

No zoning scheme, Euclidean, post-Euclidean, or even non-Euclidean can anticipate every change in technology, demographics, and economics; nor can its drafters be error-free in evaluating past trends, present capabilities, and future needs. These inevitable shortcomings have given rise to the doctrine of nonconforming use to allow for past development, and have led to amendments, special use permits, exceptions, variances, and the other "zoning forms of action," to use Professor Donald Hagman's coinage in Urban Planning and Land Development Control Law 190 (1975):

> As with common law forms of action, the choice of a form may or will dictate the allegations to be made, decision makers involved, subject matter jurisdiction of the decision makers, evidence to be presented, parties who have standing to be proponents or opponents, scope of relief and routes of appeal.

As you evaluate the complaints of frustrated developers and disgruntled neighbors in the following cases, compare the methods the courts employ to resolve these disputes to the common-law forms you confronted in your first year of law study, and to the quasi-judicial mode of resolution found in the realm of "public law." Do the private property protections afforded by American law require that current uses, even if they fail to comply with new regulations, continue potentially forever, or should there be a reasonable time period after which the landowner has to comply like everyone else in the neighborhood? Does the fairly debatable standard give too much license to local officials who are easily influenced by powerful development interests? If the court chooses instead to require the finding of a significant mistake or change in circumstances before allowing a zoning change, does this unnecessarily restrict local innovation and creativity? Does the difference between implementing a general program for land use and deciding what is appropriate for a particular parcel justify varying levels of scrutiny? Is deference to lawmakers, particularly local decisionmakers who are too easily tempted by the promise of political and financial rewards, an outmoded and stultifying concept, or a wise strategy for avoiding domination by the so-called least dangerous (judicial) branch? If there is no meaningful way to distinguish a use variance from a zoning amendment, should the former be permitted? Why are the variance and the special use permit so easily confused?[1]

As you study each of the devices for departing from "normal" zoning classifications, keep these four questions in mind: (1) What procedures must be followed by the landowner? (2) Which

---

1. For a typical case distinguishing between a special exception and a variance, see Carson v. Board of Appeals of Lexington, 321 Mass. 649, 75 N.E.2d 116 (1947). *See also* Mitchell Land Co. v. Planning & Zoning Bd. of Appeals, 140 Conn. 527, 532, 102 A.2d 316, 319 n.1 (1953) (listing several "[c]ases in which a variance has been sought, although in certain instances the owner was actually, though unwittingly, seeking an exception"), and Grasso v. Zoning Bd. of Appeals, 69 Conn. App. 230, 794 A.2d 1016 (App. Ct. 2002).

government bodies (boards, local legislatures, courts) are involved in the decisionmaking process? (3) What is the legal standard for allowing or disallowing the departure? (4) Who has standing to object to the departure?

I.   Nonconforming Uses: Preexisting Uses That Won't Fade Away

The corner grocery store in the midst of a neighborhood about to be zoned residential attracted relatively little attention from the advocates of zoning in 1913. The spirit of the times is typified by the following statement by one of the early greats of the zoning movement, Edward M. Bassett, in Zoning: The Laws, Administration, and Court Decisions During the First Twenty Years 105 (1936): "Zoning has sought to safeguard the future, in the expectation that time will repair the mistakes of the past." But in 2013 the store building may still be there—and even joined by other nonresidential uses whose existence it encourages. Nonconforming uses seldom die—nor do they fade away. Consider the testimony of a well-known planner, Harland Bartholomew, in *Non-Conforming Uses Destroy the Neighborhood*, 15 J. Land & Pub. Util. Econ. 96 (1939):

> The thesis of this paper is that in the now familiar "non-conforming use" is found one of the most potent factors — if not the principal factor — which cause prospective home builders and buyers to seek newly developing suburban areas.
>
> At a public hearing called to consider the adoption of a zoning ordinance one citizen stated that during his lifetime his family had built six homes, each successive home being farther removed from the city's center than the last, that each home had been well built but had to be abandoned because the environment of the neighborhood became objectionable as the result of the intrusion of non-residential uses. Each of the old homes was sold at a small sum compared with its original cost, and all but one were still standing.
>
> This story caused the city plan commission to make an exhaustive study of non-conforming uses throughout the city's area. The study revealed a definite pattern. The older the neighborhood the higher the percentage of non-conforming uses. The oldest centrally located neighborhoods contained non-residential uses occupying approximately 15% of net block area. Midtown districts contained about 5% of net block area. As outlying districts were approached, non-conforming uses occupied less than 1 % of net block area, while the newest subdivisions usually contained no non-conforming uses.
>
> The history of property development and of trends in property values in American cities is thus illustrated. It is a record of gradual abandonment and loss caused by inadequate protection of home environment. . . .

Not long after Euclidean zoning spread from municipality to municipality across the country, local governments began to experiment with ways of restricting and eliminating these pesky and persistent nonconformities.

The following two cases, representing the majority and minority positions, respectively, demonstrate the difficulties courts face in evaluating the fairness and efficacy of one popular strategy— amortization. Is there a middle ground between the two positions articulated in these decisions?

CITY OF LOS ANGELES v. GAGE
127 Cal. App. 2d 442, 274 P.2d 34 (1954)

VALLEE, Justice. . . .

In 1930 Gage acquired adjoining lots 220 and 221 located on Cochran Avenue in Los Angeles. He constructed a two-family residential building on lot 221 and rented the upper half solely for residential purposes. He established a wholesale and retail plumbing supply business on the property. He used a room in the lower half of the residential building on lot 221 as the office for the conduct of the business, and the rest of the lower half for residential purposes for himself and his family; he used a garage on lot 221 for the storage of plumbing supplies and materials; and he constructed and used racks, bins, and stalls for the storage of such supplies and materials on lot 220. Later Gage incorporated defendant company. . . .

In 1930 the two lots and other property facing on Cochran Avenue in their vicinity were classified in "C" zone by the zoning ordinance then in effect. Under this classification the use to which Gage put the property was permitted. Shortly after Gage acquired lots 220 and 221, they were classified "C-3" zone and the use to which he put the property was expressly permitted. In 1936 the city council of the city passed Ordinance 77,000 which contained a comprehensive zoning plan for the city. Ordinance 77,000 re-enacted the prior ordinances with respect to the use of lots 220 and 221. In 1941 the city council passed' Ordinance 85,015 by the terms of which the use of a residential building for the conduct of an office in connection with the plumbing supply business was permitted. Ordinance 85,015 prohibited the open storage of materials in zone "C-3" but permitted such uses as had been established to continue as nonconforming uses. The use to which lots 220 and 221 was put by defendants was a nonconforming use that might be continued. In 1946 the city council passed Ordinance 90,500. This ordinance reclassified lots 220 and 221 and other property fronting on Cochran Avenue in their vicinity from zone "C-3" to zone "R-4" (Multiple dwelling zone). Use of lots 220 and 221 for the conduct of a plumbing business was not permitted in zone "R-4." At the time Ordinance 90,500 was passed, and at all times since, the Los Angeles Municipal Code (§ 12.23 B & C) provided:

> (a) The nonconforming use of a conforming building or structure may be continued, except that in the "R" Zones any nonconforming commercial or industrial use of a residential building or residential accessory building shall be discontinued within five (5)' years from June 1, 1946, or five (5) years from the date the use becomes nonconforming, whichever date is later. . . .

> (b) The nonconforming use of land shall be discontinued within five (5) years from June 1, 1946, or within five (5) years from the date the use became nonconforming, in each of the following cases: (1) where no buildings are employed in connection with such use; (2) where the only buildings employed are accessory or incidental to such use; (3) where such use is maintained in connection with a conforming building.

Prior to the passage of Ordinance 90,500 about 50% of the city had been zoned. It was the first ordinance which "attempted to zone the entire corporate limits of the city." Prior to its passage, several thousand exceptions and variances were granted from restrictive provisions of prior ordinances, some of which permitted commercial use of property zoned for residential use, "and in some cases permitted the use of land for particular purposes like or similar to use of subject property which otherwise would have been prohibited." Under Ordinance 90,500, the uses permitted by these exceptions and variances that did not carry a time limit maybe continued indefinitely.

The business conducted by Gage on the property has produced a gross revenue varying between $125,000 and $350,000 a year. If he is required to abandon the use of the property for his business, he will be put to the following expenses:

> (1) The value of a suitable site for the conduct of its business would be about $10,000; which would be offset by the value of $7,500 of the lot now used. (2) The cost incident to

removing of supplies to another location and construction of the necessary racks, sheds, bins and stalls which would be about $2,500. (3) The cost necessary to expend to advertise a new location. (4) The risk of a gain or a loss of business while moving, and the cost necessary to reestablish the business at a new location, the amount of which is uncertain.

The noise and disturbance caused by the loading and unloading of supplies, trucking, and the going and coming of workmen in connection with the operation of a plumbing business with an open storage yard is greater than the noise and disturbance that is normal in a district used solely for residential purposes. . . .

The fact that various exceptions and variances were granted under zoning ordinances prior to Ordinance 90,500, and that some of them permitted the use of land for particular purposes like or similar to the use of defendants' property which otherwise would have been prohibited, presents a question for the zoning authorities of the city. They are the persons charged with the duty of deciding whether the conditions in other parts of the city require like prohibition. The mere fact that a prior ordinance excepts a parcel of land in a residential district does not give the owner thereof a vested right to have the exception continued so as to entitle him, on that ground, to attack the validity of a later ordinance repealing the former. . . .

The right of a city council, in the exercise of the police power, to regulate or, in proper cases, to prohibit the conduct of a given business, is not limited by the fact that the value of investments made in the business prior to any legislative actions will be greatly diminished. A business which, when established, was entirely unobjectionable, may, by the growth or change in the character of the neighborhood, become a source of danger to the public health, morals, safety, or general welfare of those who have come to be occupants of the surrounding territory. . . .

No case seems to have been decided in this state squarely involving the precise question presented in the case at bar. Until recently zoning ordinances have made no provision for any systematic and comprehensive elimination of the nonconforming use. The expectation seems to have been that existing nonconforming uses would be of little consequence and that they would eventually disappear. The contrary appears to be the case. It is said that the fundamental problem facing zoning is the inability to eliminate the nonconforming use. The general purpose of present-day zoning ordinances is to eventually end all nonconforming uses. There is a growing tendency to guard against the indefinite continuance of nonconforming uses by providing for their liquidation within a prescribed period. It is said, "The only positive method of getting rid of nonconforming uses yet devised is to amortize a nonconforming building. That is, to determine the normal useful remaining life of the building and prohibit the owner from maintaining it after the expiration of that time." Crolly and Norton, Termination of Nonconforming Uses, 62 Zoning Bulletin 1, Regional Plan Assn., June 1952.

Amortization of nonconforming uses has been expressly authorized by recent amendments to zoning enabling laws in a number of states. Ordinances providing for amortization of nonconforming uses have been passed in a number of large cities. The length of time given the owner to eliminate his nonconforming use or building varies with the city and with the type of structure. . . .

In State ex rel. Dema Realty Co. v. McDonald, 168 La. 172, 121 So. 613, the defendants had used their property as a retail grocery store for a great many years prior to 1927. In 1927 the city passed a zoning ordinance which established the area in which the property was located as a residential district and provided that all businesses then in operation within that area should be liquidated within one year from the passage of the ordinance. It was contended that this provision was unconstitutional as being arbitrary and unreasonable, and that it amounted to a taking of the defendants' property without due process of law. . . . [T]he court stated, 121 So. 617:

It is to be observed, too, that the ordinance there under consideration provided for the establishment and maintenance of residential districts from which every kind of business was excluded. The ordinance did not deal specially with any already established business in the zoned district. But, if the village had the authority to create and to maintain a purely residential district, which the court held it did have, and if such an ordinance was not arbitrary and unreasonable, it follows necessarily that the village was vested with the authority to remove any business or trade from the district and to fix a limit of time in which the same shall be done.

The Supreme Court of the United States denied certiorari. 280 U.S. 556. . . .

In Standard Oil Co. v. City of Tallahassee, 5 Cir., 183 F.2d 410 the plaintiff was operating a motor vehicle service station at the time the area in which it was located was, by a zoning ordinance, made a residence district. The ordinance, adopted in April 1948, provided that all locations then used for motor vehicle service stations should be discontinued as such on and after January 1, 1949. In upholding the validity of the ordinance the court stated, 183 F.2d at page 413:

> The power of a municipality to require by ordinance the discontinuance of an existing property use also appears to be well established law in Florida. Here, plaintiffs service station is near the State Capitol and the State Supreme Court Building, as well as several other state office buildings and a public school. It therefore becomes manifest that its discontinuance under the ordinance cannot be viewed as arbitrary and unreasonable, or as having no relation to the safety and general welfare of the community affected. We find no merit in appellant's contention that enforcement of this ordinance would entail any unjust discrimination, or would be tantamount to depriving it of its property without due process merely because the site was acquired and improved at considerable expense before the zoning ordinance was enacted. The general rule here applicable is that considerations of financial loss or of so-called "vested rights" in private property are insufficient to outweigh the necessity for legitimate exercise of the police power of a municipality.

The Supreme Court of the United States denied certiorari. 340 U.S. 892. . . .

The theory in zoning is that each district is an appropriate area for the location of the uses which the zone plan permits in that area, and that the existence or entrance of other uses will tend to impair the development and stability of the area for the appropriate uses. . . . The presence of any nonconforming use endangers the benefits to be derived from a comprehensive zoning plan. Having the undoubted power to establish residential districts, the legislative body has the power to make such classification really effective by adopting such reasonable regulations as would be conducive to the welfare, health, and safety of those desiring to live in such district and enjoy the benefits thereof. There would be no object in creating a residential district unless there were to be secured to those dwelling therein the advantages which are ordinarily considered the benefits of such residence. It would seem to be the logical and reasonable method of approach to place a time limit upon the continuance of existing nonconforming uses, commensurate with the investment involved and based on the nature of the use; and in cases of nonconforming structures, on their character, age, and other relevant factors. . . .

The distinction between an ordinance restricting future uses and one requiring the termination of present uses within a reasonable period of time is merely one of degree, and constitutionality depends on the relative importance to be given to the public gain and to the private loss. Zoning as it affects every piece of property is to some extent retroactive in that it applies to property already owned at the time of the effective date of the ordinance. The elimination of existing uses within a reasonable time does not amount to a taking of property nor does it necessarily restrict the use of property so that it cannot be used for any reasonable purpose. Use of a reasonable amortization scheme provides an equitable means of reconciliation of the conflicting interests in satisfaction of due process requirements. As a method of eliminating existing nonconforming uses it allows the owner of the nonconforming use, by affording an opportunity to make new plans, at least partially to offset any loss he might suffer. The loss he suffers, if any, is spread out over a period of years, and he enjoys a monopolistic position by virtue of the zoning ordinance as long as he remains. If the amortization period is reasonable the loss to the owner may be small when compared with the benefit to the public. Nonconforming uses will eventually be eliminated. A legislative body may well conclude that the beneficial effect on the community of the eventual elimination of all non-conforming uses by a reasonable amortization plan more than offsets individual losses.

The ordinance in question provides, according to a graduated periodic schedule, for the gradual and ultimate elimination of all commercial and industrial uses in residential zones. These provisions require the discontinuance of nonconforming uses of land within a five-year period, and the discontinuance of nonconforming commercial and industrial uses of residential buildings in the "R" zones within the same five-year period. These provisions are the only ones pertinent to the decision in this case. However, it may be noted that other provisions of the ordinance require the discontinuance of nonconforming billboards and, in residential zones, the discontinuance of nonconforming buildings and of nonconforming uses of nonconforming buildings, within specified periods running from 20 to 40 years according to the type of building construction.

We have no doubt that Ordinance 90,500, in compelling the discontinuance of the use of defendants' property for a wholesale and retail plumbing and plumbing supply business, and for the open storage of plumbing supplies within five years after its passage, is a valid exercise of the police power. Lots 220 and 221 are several blocks from a business center and it appears that they are not within any reasonable or logical extension of such a center. The ordinance does not prevent the operation of defendants' business; it merely restricts its location. Discontinuance of the non-conforming use requires only that Gage move his plumbing business to property that is zoned for it. Such property can be found within a half mile of Gage's property. The cost of moving is $5,000, or less than 1 % of Gage's minimum gross business for five years, or less than half of 1 % of the mean of his gross business for five years. He has had eight years within which to move. The property is usable for residential purpose. Since 1930 lot 221 has been used for residential purposes. All of the land within 500 feet of Gage's property is now improved and used for such purposes. Lot 220, now unimproved, can be improved for the same purposes.

We think it apparent that none of the agreed facts and none of the ultimate facts found by the court justify the conclusion that Ordinance 90,500, as applied to Gage's property, is clearly arbitrary or unreasonable, or has no substantial relation to the public's health, safety, morals, or general welfare, or that it is an unconstitutional impairment of his property rights. . . .

Notes

1. Just two years later, in City of La Mesa v. Tweed & Gambrell Planing Mill, 146 Cal. App. 2d 762, 770-71, 304 P.2d 803, 808 (1956), the court held a five-year period for amortization of a non-conforming use unconstitutional ("unreasonable and arbitrary") as applied to a planing mill that had 21 years of economic life remaining. How well was the Gage case distinguished?

> In [Gage] . . . , the individual's loss was limited to that involved in moving his business. He was given five years within which to accomplish this change. The building on his property was of a type approved for use in the zone where situated; it would not have to be moved or altered. In the case at bar, not only are the defendants required to move

their business within five years, but also to terminate the use of their buildings, which are not capable of being converted into residences, and cannot be moved without a total loss. Moreover, in this case not only is the private loss greater than in the *Gage* case, but the public gain is less. It is contemplated that the block in which the defendants' property is located, the balance of which already has been acquired by the city, eventually will become part of a civic center. In the interim, it is proposed, under zoning ordinance Number 618, to restrict the use of this block to single family dwellings. However, shortly before the adoption of that ordinance negotiations were under way to transfer a part of the city's property to the defendants, in exchange for the right of way which is the subject of this action, and to zone the block in question for industrial uses.

In order to effect its change of plans, which would permit only a residential use of defendants' land during the interim period awaiting the creation of a civic center, the city, by its ordinance, requires the defendants, within five years, to liquidate their investment which has an estimated remaining 21 years of economic life, although shortly before the adoption of that ordinance, the land in question was considered a proper subject for classification as an industrial site; was recommended by the planning consultants for inclusion within a professional zone; is bordered on the east by a railroad track; and surrounded on three sides by industrial and commercial businesses. This is unreasonable and arbitrary.

2. A table accompanying Article 4 of the Model Land Development Code (commentary at 148) includes amortization cases from a number of jurisdictions, evidencing the lack of uniformity from locality to locality even within the same state. From example, the amortization period for junkyards, salvage yards, and automobile wrecking yards ranges from one year up to five years. One Texas case involved a one-year period for a self-service gasoline station, while another locality in the same state amortized a gasoline station over 25 years.

3. One popular way to restrict existing uses that are inconsistent with subsequent zoning provisions is to provide that discontinuance or abandonment will result in a loss of the right to continue the nonconformity. For example, in an Alaska case, Cizek v. Concerned Citizens of Eagle River Valley, Inc., 49 P.3d 228, 231-32 (Alaska 2002), there was evidence that the nonconforming use of land as an airstrip had lapsed between 1985 and 1995. Still, the landowners insisted that they still had the right to use the airstrip:

> The Cizeks argue that the fact that the airstrip was usable as an airstrip throughout the relevant time period should suffice to continue an existing nonconforming use. They reason that the "use" contemplated by the Municipal Code is the "use of the land as an airstrip, not use of the airstrip by planes."

The state supreme court was unconvinced:

> But the Cizeks' interpretation of what satisfies the Municipal Code to continue a nonconforming use is illogical. If we were to adopt the Cizeks' interpretation, local governments could almost never terminate a nonconformity because it would legally continue as long as the land's physical suitability for actual nonconforming use remained. In effect, then, the Cizeks propose to define cessation of use under AMC 21.55.030(C) as cessation of all potential for use. We doubt that the Anchorage Assembly had this result in mind when it provided for the termination of nonconformities after more than one year of the cessation of the prior use of the land. . . .

Moreover, we have noted a policy that "nonconforming uses are to be restricted and terminated as quickly as possible" because those uses frustrate a local government's implementation of consistent and logical land use planning. The Anchorage Municipal Code [21.55.010] echoes this policy stating an intent to "permit . . . nonconformities to continue until they are removed, but not to encourage their perpetuation." We will not frustrate that intent by defining use to include usability.

4. A nearly universal method for eliminating nonconforming uses over time is to restrict their expansion, enlargement, or alteration. This short and sweet opinion from the New York Court of Appeals in 550 Halstead Corp. v. Zoning Bd. of Appeals, 1 N.Y.3d 561, 562-63, 804 N.E.2d 413, 414 (2003), is instructive:

Because nonconforming uses are viewed as detrimental to zoning schemes, public policy favors their reasonable restriction and eventual elimination. Accordingly, municipalities may adopt measures regulating nonconforming uses and may, in a reasonable fashion, eliminate them. Here, one of the purposes of the Town of Harrison's Comprehensive Zoning Plan is to promote the "gradual elimination of nonconforming uses" (Town of Harrison Code § 235-2 [F]). To carry out this purpose, the Code prohibits the expansion, enlargement, extension, reconstruction, or structural alteration of any nonconforming use "by any means or in any respect whatsoever" (Town of Harrison Code § 235-52).

The Zoning Board of Appeals of the Town/Village of Harrison (ZBA) determined that when petitioner replaced its wooden pallet storage system with steel-frame storage racks, it impermissibly expanded or extended its nonconforming lumberyard. Substantial record evidence supports this determination: the new racks were significantly higher than the wooden pallets and could store three times the lumber; petitioner installed four additional racks; unlike the wooden pallets, the racks have roofs. Further, the ZBA's denial of petitioner's application for use and area variances was rational; the ZBA properly balanced benefits to the applicant with the detriment to the health, safety and welfare of the surrounding neighborhood.

Compare Nettleton v. Zoning Bd. of Adjustment, 574 Pa. 45, 55, 828 A.2d 1033, 1039 (2003), in which the Pennsylvania Supreme Court found that a vertical addition to a building that did not conform with subsequent yard and setback requirements did not amount to invalid expansion of a nonconforming use:

The vertical addition here proposed would have no effect on the existing building's footprint and, therefore, would not increase the encroachment of the building within the required front or side yard setback. Since the proposal would not have the effect of increasing the degree of nonconformity, the zoning authorities correctly determined that the addition was permitted by right pursuant to Code § 921.03.D.1.

See also City of Marion v. Rapp, 655 N.W.2d 88, 91 (S.D. 2002) ("Replacing the old 14 by 70 foot trailer with a 16 by 76 foot trailer is an enlargement of a pre-existing nonconforming structure.").

5. In 2008, Virginia lawmakers added the following additional protection to Va. Code Ann. §15.2-2307 for certain established landowners:

Notwithstanding any local ordinance to the contrary, if (i) the local government has issued a building permit, the building or structure was thereafter constructed in accordance with the building permit, and upon completion of construction, the local government issued a certificate of occupancy or a use permit therefor, or (ii) the owner of the building or structure has paid taxes to the locality for such building or structure for a period in excess of 15 years, a zoning ordinance may provide that the building or structure is nonconforming, but shall not provide that such building or structure is illegal and shall be removed solely due to such nonconformity. Further, a zoning ordinance may provide that such building or structure be brought in compliance with the Uniform Statewide Building Code.

Do you think that this bill unnecessarily ties the hands of local officials or is a measured response to overregulation?

6. New and increasing billboard restrictions often place outdoor advertisers in a bind. In *Ex parte Lamar Adver. Co.*, 849 So.2d 928, 929-31 (Ala. 2002), the Alabama Supreme Court, with dictionary in hand, held that the use of new technology did not result in the "expansion" of a nonconforming billboard:

> After Ordinance No. IV was adopted, Lamar replaced the existing face on the sign with a "trivision sign face."[1] In June 1999, the Land Use Department sent Lamar a notice directing Lamar either to remove the sign or to get a variance for it. In the notice, the Department told Lamar that the trivision sign face constituted an improper "expansion" under Ordinance No. IV.G.3.b. The expansion complained of by the Department was either (1) that the trivision aspect of the sign resulted in the sign's having more than the 672 square feet of display space that had been grandfathered in when the ordinance took effect, or (2) that the turning motor itself expanded the size of the sign. . . .

> Merriam-Webster's Collegiate Dictionary (10th ed. 1997) includes among its definitions of "expand" the following: "to increase the extent, number, volume, or scope of: enlarge." The sign at issue here was not "enlarged." The Board argues that the trivision sign is an expansion either because a motor connected to the sign constitutes an expansion or because the ability to display three different advertisements constitutes an expansion. We disagree.

> The motor connected to the sign does not enlarge the sign; it does not increase the extent, number, volume, or scope of the sign. Lamar's vice president and general manager, Troy Tatum, testified at trial that the trivision sign, including the motor, occupied the same physical space as the original sign occupied.

> Finally, the fact that the new technology embodied in the trivision sign allows the sign to be changed to display three different advertisements in a short period does not make the trivision sign an expansion of the original nonconforming sign. The speed with which advertisements can be changed does not increase the extent—the sign face remains 672 square feet; the number—it is a single sign; the volume—it occupies the same amount of physical space as the original sign; or the scope of the sign. The fact that the number of different advertisements that can be displayed during a certain period has increased does not mean that the sign itself has been expanded.

---

1. The advertisement on a traditional sign face has to be changed manually; therefore, it takes a crew half an hour to change the sign face. As a practical matter, that meant that a single sign face was presented to the public, usually for several weeks or months, depending on the lease period. A trivision sign face allows automatic changing of the sign face, thus making it possible to present up to three advertisements during a relatively short period by automatically changing the sign face, for example, every 20 seconds on a rotating basis. The square footage of the original sign face was 672 square feet of display; the new sign face remained at 672 square feet displayed. However, the new sign face contained three advertisements and changed periodically to reveal each advertisement.

The Outdoor Advertising Association of America has offered this position on the question of amortization: "Regarding billboards, amortization is the forced government removal of private property over time without payment of just compensation to the owner. Therefore, amortization is slow-motion taking." http://www.oaaa.org/legislativeandregulatory/issues/amortization.aspx. The industry has responded to local efforts to amortize billboards by lobbying for state legislative restrictions. See, for example, Fla. Stat. §70.20:

> It is a policy of this state to encourage municipalities, counties, and other governmental entities and sign owners to enter into relocation and reconstruction agreements that allow governmental entities to undertake public projects and accomplish public goals without the expenditure of public funds while allowing the continued maintenance of private investment in signage as a medium of commercial and noncommercial communication.

> (1) Municipalities, counties, and all other governmental entities are specifically empowered to enter into relocation and reconstruction agreements on whatever terms are agreeable to the sign owner and the municipality, county, or other governmental entity involved and to provide for relocation and reconstruction of signs by agreement, ordinance, or resolution. As used in this section, a "relocation and reconstruction agreement" means a consensual, contractual agreement between a sign owner and a municipality, county, or other governmental entity for either the reconstruction of an existing sign or the removal of a sign and construction of a new sign to substitute for the sign removed.

> (2) Except as otherwise provided in this section, no municipality, county, or other governmental entity may remove, or cause to be removed, any lawfully erected sign located along any portion of the interstate, federal-aid primary or other highway system, or any other road without first paying just compensation for such removal as determined by agreement between the parties or through eminent domain proceedings. Except as otherwise provided in this section, no municipality, county, or other governmental entity may cause in any way the alteration of any lawfully erected sign located along any portion of the interstate, federal-aid primary or other highway system, or any other road without first paying just compensation for such alteration as determined by agreement between the parties or through eminent domain proceedings. The provisions of this section shall not apply to any ordinance the validity, constitutionality, and enforceability of which the owner has by written agreement waived all right to challenge.

7. In State ex rel. Morehouse v. Hunt, 235 Wis. 358, 373, 291 N.W. 745, 752 (1940), a zoning ordinance passed in 1928 contained this common provision: "Whenever a nonconforming use of a building has been changed to a more restricted use or to a conforming use, such use shall not thereafter be changed to a less restricted use." A building constructed and especially adapted for use as a fraternity house was so used before the ordinance zoned its district for single-family residences. The building was occupied as a fraternity house up to 1932, when the defendant took possession under a mortgage. From 1932 to 1934, the building was operated as a rooming house. From 1934 to 1938, it was leased and used as a single-family residence; the lease provided that the premises were to be "used for the purpose of residence only." No major structural changes in the house have been made. In 1938, a college fraternity wanted to purchase it, if a ruling could be obtained allowing the building to revert to its earlier use. The court reasoned:

> It is true that certain acts of the owner are indicative of abandonment of the nonconforming use. The original leasing for two years tends to support such inference. But the reservation of right to cancel the lease on sale of the premises is indicative of intent to

sell for a fraternity house if opportunity arose. Putting in the lease for "residence only" indicates that the lessee should not turn the house into a tearoom or restaurant or a boardinghouse, but it does not preclude the idea of making it a two-family residence, as later was done, to the knowledge and with the implied assent of the owner, and as might have been done forthwith without violation of the ordinance. Whether under all the circumstances the owner's acts constituted a "voluntary relinquishment or abandonment" of the right to devote the premises to a Class B use depends on whether the use of the building as a single-family residence for a year was a reasonable time under all the circumstances, to allow the owner to devote the premises to the Class B use of a two-family residence. The appeal board thought it was. This was a question for the board to decide and its decision should be sustained.

8. The city of Moscow, Idaho, adopted an ordinance making it unlawful to open or operate on First Street any new or additional place of business in which any pool, billiard, card, or dice game was played, or in which draft beer or liquor by the drink was sold. The ordinance stated: "Any change of ownership of an existing business of the type herein defined shall be deemed a new or additional business." For the past 10 years, the plaintiff operated a combined pool hall, card room, and retail beer parlor. He brought suit for a declaratory judgment to void the ordinance. In O'Connor v. City of Moscow, 69 Idaho 37, 43, 202 P.2d 401, 404 (1949), the court voided the provision, noting: "Use, not ownership, is the concern of this type of zoning. There is no reasonable relation between a provision in an ordinance which, as here, makes a change in ownership a new business, and the objects to be accomplished by the ordinance, when existing non-conforming uses of property are necessarily permitted to continue."

PENNSYLVANIA NORTHWESTERN DISTRIBUTORS, INC. v. ZONING HEARING BOARD OF TOWNSHIP OF MOON
584 A.2d 1372 (Pa. 1991)

LARSEN, Justice

This appeal presents an issue of first impression to this Court, i.e., whether a zoning ordinance which requires the amortization and discontinuance of a lawful pre-existing nonconforming use is confiscatory and violative of the constitution as a taking of property without just compensation.

On May 4, 1985, after obtaining the necessary permits and certificates to conduct its business on leased premises, appellant, PA Northwestern Distributors, Inc., opened an adult book store in Moon Township, Pennsylvania. Four days later, the Moon Township Board of Supervisors published a public notice of its intention to amend the Moon Township Zoning Ordinance to regulate "adult commercial enterprises." On May 23, 1985, following a public hearing on the matter, the Moon Township Board of Supervisors adopted Ordinance No. 243, effective on May 28, 1985, which ordinance imposes extensive restrictions on the location and operation of "adult commercial enterprises." Section 805 of the ordinance provides as follows:

Amortization. Any commercial enterprise which would constitute a pre-existing use and which would be in conflict with the requirements set forth in this amendment to the Moon Township Zoning Ordinance has 90 days from the date that the ordinance becomes effective to come into compliance with this ordinance. This 90-day grace period is designed to be a period of amortization for those pre-existing businesses which cannot meet the standards set forth in this amendment to the Moon Township Zoning Ordinance.

Appellant's adult book store, by definition, is an adult commercial enterprise under the ordinance, and it does not and cannot meet the place restrictions set forth in the ordinance in that it is not located within an area designated for adult commercial enterprises. The Zoning Officer of Moon Township notified appellant that it was out of compliance with the ordinance. Appellant filed an appeal to the Zoning Hearing Board of the Township of Moon, appellee herein. The appeal was limited to challenging the validity of the amortization provision set forth in the ordinance.

Following a hearing, the Zoning Hearing Board upheld the validity of the amortization provision as applied, and appellant filed an appeal to the Court of Common Pleas of Allegheny County. No further evidence was taken, and appellant's appeal was dismissed. On appeal, Commonwealth Court affirmed, 124 Pa. Commw. 228, 555 A.2d 1368, basing its decision on Sullivan v. Zoning Board of Adjustment, 83 Pa. Commw. 228, 478 A.2d 912 (1984). We granted appellant's petition for allowance of appeal, and we now reverse.

Our scope of review in a zoning case, where the trial court has not taken additional evidence, is limited to determining whether the zoning hearing board committed an error of law or a manifest abuse of discretion.

In the case of *Sullivan, supra*, the Commonwealth Court determined that provisions for the amortization of nonconforming uses are constitutional exercises of the police power so long as they are reasonable. It was the opinion of the Commonwealth Court in that case, that the "distinction between an ordinance restricting future uses and one requiring the termination of present uses within a reasonable period of time is merely one of degree . . ." 83 Pa. Commw. at 244, 478 A.2d at 920. To determine whether the amortization provisions are reasonable, the Commonwealth Court stated:

> Each case in this class must be determined on its own facts; and the answer to the question of whether the provision is reasonable must be decided by observing its impact upon the property under consideration. The true issue is that of whether, considering the nature of the present use, the length of the period for amortization, the present characteristics of and the foreseeable future prospects for development of the vicinage and other relevant facts and circumstances, the beneficial effects upon the community that would result from the discontinuance of the use can be seen to more than offset the losses to the affected landowner.

83 Pa. Commw. at 247, 478 A.2d at 920.

Following this standard, the Zoning Hearing Board herein heard evidence regarding the impact upon the property in question with respect to the nature of the present use, the period for amortization, the characteristics of the vicinage, etc., and determined that the amortization provision was reasonable as applied. In this regard the Zoning Hearing Board stated that the "real and substantial benefits to the Township of elimination of the nonconforming use from this location . . . more than offset the losses to the affected landowner." Opinion of the Board at 13 (May 20, 1987).

If the Commonwealth Court opinion in *Sullivan, supra*, had been a correct statement of the law in this Commonwealth, we would be constrained to find that appellee herein had not committed an error of law or an abuse of discretion. For the following reasons, however, we find that Sullivan is not a correct statement of the law regarding amortization provisions in this Commonwealth.

In this Commonwealth, all property is held in subordination to the right of its reasonable regulation by the government, which regulation is clearly necessary to preserve the health, safety, morals, or general welfare of the people. Moreover, "a presumption of validity attaches to a zoning ordinance which imposes the burden to prove its invalidity upon the one who challenges it." National Land and Investment Co. v. Easttown Township Board of Adjustment, 419 Pa. 504, 522, 215 A.2d 597, 607 (1965). This Court has noted, however, that the presumption of a zoning ordinance's validity must be tempered by the Court's appreciation of the fact that zoning involves governmental restrictions upon a property owner's *constitutionally guaranteed* right to use his or her property, unfettered by governmental restrictions, except where the use violates any law, the use creates a nuisance, or the owner violates any covenant, restriction or easement. *Id.*

Many other jurisdictions have upheld the validity of amortization provisions in zoning ordinances, finding that it is appropriate to balance the property interests of the individual with the health, safety, morals or general welfare of the community at large, and that, where reasonable, amortization provisions succeed in effectuating orderly land use planning and development in a way that the natural attrition of nonconforming uses cannot.

Although this Court has never before considered the validity of an amortization provision in a zoning ordinance, it has long been the law of this Commonwealth that municipalities lack the power to compel a change in the nature of an existing lawful use of property. In addition, municipalities may not prevent the owner of nonconforming property from making those necessary additions to an existing structure as are needed to provide for its natural expansion, so long as such additions would not be detrimental to the public welfare, safety, and health.

A lawful nonconforming use establishes in the property owner a vested property right which cannot be abrogated or destroyed, unless it is a nuisance, it is abandoned, or it is extinguished by eminent domain. This determination is compelled by our constitution which recognizes the "inherent and indefeasible" right of our citizens to possess and protect property, Pa. Const. art. I, § 1, and requires that just compensation be paid for the taking of private property, Pa. Const. art. I, § 10. As we emphasized in *Andress v. Zoning Board of Adjustment*, 410 Pa. 77, 82-84, 188 A.2d 709, 711-12 (1963):

> "The natural or zealous desire of many zoning boards to protect, improve and develop their community, to plan a city or a township or a community that is both practical and beautiful, and to conserve the property values as well as the 'tone' of that community is commendable. But they must remember that property owners have certain rights which are ordained, protected and preserved in our Constitution and which neither zeal nor worthwhile objectives can impinge upon or abolish."

> *   *   *   *   *

> Neither the Executive nor the Legislature, nor any legislative body, nor any zoning or planning commission, nor any other Governmental body has the right—under the guise of the police power, or under the broad power of general welfare, or under the power of Commander-in-Chief of the Armed Forces, or under any other express or implied power—*to take, possess or confiscate private property for public use or to completely prohibit or substantially destroy the lawful use and enjoyment of property, without paying just compensation therefor*: . . .

(citations omitted) (emphasis in original)

Although at times it may be difficult to discern whether zoning legislation is merely regulating as opposed to "taking," this Court has stated that "[a] 'taking' is not limited to an actual physical possession or seizure of the property; if the *effect* of the zoning law or regulation is to deprive a property owner of the lawful use of his property it amounts to a 'taking', for which he must be justly compensated." Cleaver v. Board of Adjustment, 414 Pa. 367, 372, 200 A.2d 408, 412 (1964) (emphasis in original).

The effect of the amortization provision herein is to deprive appellant of the lawful use of its property in that the ordinance forces appellant to cease using its property as an adult book store within 90 days. Appellee argues that appellant is free to relocate to one of the few sites in the

Township of Moon that complies with the place restrictions of the ordinance, or to change its use to sell some other commodity, in an attempt to convince this Court that the ordinance has not effectuated a "taking" of appellant's property without just compensation. The Pennsylvania Constitution, Pa. Const. art. I, § 1, however, protects the right of a property owner to use his or her property in any lawful way that he or she so chooses. If government desires to interfere with the owner's use, where the use is lawful and is not a nuisance nor is it abandoned, it must compensate the owner for the resulting loss. A gradual phasing out of nonconforming uses which occurs when an ordinance only restricts future uses differs in significant measure from an amortization provision which restricts future uses and extinguishes a lawful nonconforming use on a timetable which is not of the property owner's choosing. . . .

Thus, we hold that the amortization and discontinuance of a lawful pre-existing nonconforming use is per se confiscatory and violative of the Pennsylvania Constitution, Pa. Const. art. I, § 1. There are important policy considerations which support this determination. If municipalities were free to amortize nonconforming uses out of existence, future economic development could be seriously compromised. As one commentator has noted:

> The law of zoning should be designed to protect the reasonable expectations of persons who plan to enter business or make improvements on property. The possibility that the municipality could by zoning force removal of installations or cessation of business might serve to deter such investors.

Note, *Nonconforming Uses: A Rationale and an Approach*, 102 U. Pa. L. Rev. 91, 103 (1953). This commentator also notes that forced destruction will often result in economic waste. *Id.* at 104.

It is clear that if we were to permit the amortization of nonconforming uses in this Commonwealth, *any* use could be amortized out of existence without just compensation. Although such a zoning option seems reasonable when the use involves some activity that may be distasteful to some members of the public, *no* use would be exempt from the reach of amortization, and *any* property owner could lose the use of his or her property without compensation. Even a homeowner could find one day that his or her "castle" had become a nonconforming use and would be required to vacate the premises within some arbitrary period of time, *without just compensation*. Such a result is repugnant to a basic protection accorded in this Commonwealth to vested property interests.

Accordingly, we find that the amortization provision, Section 805, of Ordinance No. 243 of the Township of Moon is unconstitutional on its face, and we reverse the order of the Commonwealth Court, which affirmed the order of the Court of Common Pleas of Allegheny County dismissing appellant's appeal from the decision of the Zoning Hearing Board of the Township of Moon.

NIX, Chief Justice, concurring.

While I agree with the result reached by the majority, that Section 805 of Ordinance No. 243 is invalid in this case, I must disagree with the finding that any provision for the amortization of nonconforming uses would be per se confiscatory and unconstitutional. I would uphold the Commonwealth Court's decision relying on Sullivan v. Zoning Board of Adjustment, 83 Pa.Commw. 228, 478 A.2d 912 (1984), and hold that a reasonable amortization provision is valid if it reflects the consideration of certain factors. The instant provision, however, falls short of the reasonableness requirements and therefore must be struck down.

The weight of authority supports the conclusion that a reasonable amortization provision would not be unconstitutional. It has been stated that a blanket rule against amortization provisions should be rejected because such a rule has a debilitating effect on effective zoning, unnecessarily restricts a state's police power, and prevents the operation of a reasonable and flexible method of eliminating nonconforming uses in the public interest. Lachapelle v. Goffstown, 107 N.H. 485,

225 A.2d 624 (1967). The New Hampshire court found acceptable amortization provisions which were reasonable as to time and directed toward some reasonable aspect of land use regulation under properly delegated police power. Other cases have considered several factors in determining the reasonableness of these provisions. Those factors weigh any circumstance bearing upon a balancing of public gain against private loss, including the length of the amortization period in relation to the nature of the nonconforming use, Gurnee v. Miller, 69 Ill. App. 2d 248, 215 N.E.2d 829 (1966); Eutaw Enterprises, Inc. v. Baltimore, 241 Md. 686, 217 A.2d 348 (1966); length of time in relation to the investment, *id.*; and the degree of offensiveness of the nonconforming use in view of the character of the surrounding neighborhood. See City of Los Angeles v. Gage, 127 Cal. App. 2d 442, 274 P.2d 34, 43-44 (1954); Grant v. Baltimore, 212 Md. 301, 129 A.2d 363 (1957); Lachapelle v. Goffstown, *supra*. . . .

I believe that a *per se* prohibition against amortization provisions is too restrictive. A community should have a right to change its character without being locked into pre-existing definitions of what is offensive. As this Court has also noted, "nonconforming uses, inconsistent with a basic purpose of zoning, represent conditions which should be reduced to conformity as speedily as is compatible with the law and the Constitution." Hanna v. Board of Adjustment of Borough of Forest Hills, 408 Pa. 306, 312-13, 183 A.2d 539, 543 (1962). I believe that amortization provisions are an effective method of reconciling interests of the community with those of property owners. Where the provisions are reasonable in consideration of the elements herein discussed, they provide adequate notice to the property owner so that no deprivation of property or use thereof is suffered, yet they simultaneously afford a township the opportunity to alter the character of its neighborhoods when the alteration takes the form of a reasonable land use regulation.

In this case, however, the amortization provision is not a reasonable one because it fails to provide adequate time for elimination of the nonconforming use. The period allowed for the dissolution of appellant's business is ninety days. Certainly ninety days is an insufficient period of time to allow a merchant to close a business. Any contractual obligations appellant has incurred in anticipation of operating the business probably cannot be terminated within such a short period of time without severe hardship on appellant's part. Three months also would not permit appellant to obtain an alternative means of income. Moreover, forcing appellant to liquidate his enterprise within ninety days could prevent him from obtaining a reasonable return on his investment. I therefore agree that the instant provision is confiscatory.

PAPADOKOS, J., joins this concurring opinion.

McDERMOTT, Justice, concurring and dissenting.

I join the result reached by the majority under the facts of this case. Ninety days is too short a period to erase a pre-existing use. I do not agree that pre-existing nonconforming uses are beyond reasonable regulation for health, safety and morals of a community. I respect the constitutional concerns of the majority that property rights must be treated fairly and reasonably and not subject to sudden, simple or easy legislative fiat. Generally, what was done legally before a zoning ordinance must be protected as a property right, which is not, however, to say forever. To amortize means to render land alienable after a debt has been paid. After a given time all debts are extinguishable and a reasonable amortization reflecting the safety, morals and health of a community ought not be rejected as a possibility consistent with a rational use of property.

Notes

1. In Board of Zoning Appeals v. Leisz, 702 N.E.2d 1026, 1027-30, 1032 (Ind. 1998), the Indiana Supreme Court shifted its position, returning to the majority (*Gage*) rule that permits amortization of nonconforming uses. The city of Bloomington passed an ordinance limiting occupancy in

some neighborhoods to three unrelated adults per unit. Under a "grandfathering provision," existing owners who exceeded the new limit were allowed to "preserve their lawful nonconforming use status if they registered it" by a specific deadline. The owners of two properties affected by the ordinance failed to register their nonconformity and, a few years after the deadline, sold the properties to Jack and Barbara Leisz. When the new owners failed to secure a ruling exempting them from the occupancy limitation, they sued, claiming that the ordinance amounted to an unconstitutional taking. Turning to U.S. Supreme Court precedent, the Indiana high court reasoned:

> The Court has identified two discrete categories of regulations that violate the Takings Clause regardless of the legitimate state interest advanced. The first consists of regulations that compel a property owner to suffer a physical invasion, no matter how minute, of his property. The second category concerns regulations that deny "all economically beneficial or productive use of the land." *Lucas* [v. South Carolina Coastal Council, 505 U.S. 1003 (1992)], at 1015.

> A zoning ordinance that provides for the forfeiture of unregistered nonconforming uses does not fall into either of these prohibited categories. The forfeiture involved no physical invasion of the Leiszs' property. It merely limits the use of their rental property to three unrelated adults instead of four, five or more. Second, the ordinance does not deny the Leiszs all economically beneficial or productive use of their land. Rather, it denies them at most 25% to 40% of the rental income that they might otherwise receive.
>
> . . .

The court then noted that the registration requirement had been upheld in other jurisdictions:

> The purpose of the registration requirement, according to the BZA, was to establish an administrative process for making a one-time determination of pre-existing status that protects both the owner and the zoning authority from later lengthy disputes and extensive proof problems related to the validity of a nonconforming use. The landowners make a qualified concession in this regard: "The Leiszs concede that the city may require a grandfather registration form to be filled out by lawful, pre-existing, non-conforming use and that recordkeeping is useful for the BZA, and protects against problems of proof." Brief of Appellee at 11. Thus, the Leiszs do not attack the registration requirement itself, but rather challenge only its forfeiture penalty.

> In upholding a provision similar to Bloomington's, the Court of Civil Appeals of Texas noted that the purpose of this registration ordinance is to provide [the City] with sufficient knowledge of the nature and extent of nonconforming uses claimed within the City so that the City can consider these nonconforming uses in planning and can monitor their abandonment. Without a registration scheme it would be impossible for [the City] to begin to implement the plan for the fair and reasonable return of the property to the character of the surrounding neighborhood. Board of Adjustment of San Antonio v. Nelson, 577 S.W.2d 783, 785 (Tex. Civ. App. 1979), aff'd on other grounds, 584 S.W.2d 701 (Tex. 1979). In discussing a registration requirement in Maryland, the court observed its purpose clearly is to bring about conformance, through the zoning process, of nonconforming uses as speedily as possible. To accomplish this, the County Commissioners needed to know where the applicable nonconforming uses were located; thus, the required certification of the nonconforming uses within a specified time. In addition, the County Commissioners sought to prevent unlawful expansion of such uses; hence the requirement that information concerning the exact nature and extent

of the nonconforming use was required to be furnished. Moreover, the County Commissioners provided a sanction for a landowner's failure to comply with the certification requirement — the discontinuance of the nonconforming use. County Comm'rs of Carroll County v. Uhler, 78 Md. App. 140, 552 A.2d 942, 946 (Md. Ct. Spec. App. 1989) (ordinance required only the registration of used car lots, service garages or junk yards).

There was precedent, however, that supported the landowners' claim that an amortization scheme effected a regulatory taking, precedent that the state court overruled:

The Court of Appeals drew guidance from our opinion in Ailes v. Decatur County Area Planning Comm'n, 448 N.E.2d 1057 (Ind. 1983), in which this Court held certain zoning provisions to be per se violations of the federal constitution. The Court of Appeals inferred from *Ailes* that Indiana's "vigorous[] protect[ion of] vested interests in nonconforming uses" is greater than that of other states. *Leisz*, 686 N.E.2d at 939. The federal constitution does not vary from state to state. Although we are free to find greater restrictions on regulatory takings in our state constitution, this Court in *Ailes* was not interpreting the state constitution. Rather, the Court there, like the Court of Appeals and the *Leiszs*, referred to the taking of property "without due process of law[.]" *Ailes*, 448 N.E.2d at 1060. For the reasons discussed above and because it cited no Indiana constitutional provision or precedent, *Ailes* rested solely on federal constitutional grounds. Accordingly, we now re-examine our holding in *Ailes*, which clearly represents a minority view and is inconsistent with decisions in other jurisdictions interpreting the federal constitution.

Most states allow local zoning authorities to phase out nonconforming uses with amortization provisions that require the owner to discontinue the nonconforming use after a certain period of time. *Leisz*, 686 N.E.2d at 939 (citing Daniel R. Mandelker, Land Use Law § 5.70 (3d ed. 1993)). Under an amortization provision, an owner's property right is absolutely extinguished at some point in time. Our decision in *Ailes* found this to be an unconstitutional "taking of property without due process of law," not specifically a violation of the Takings Clause but inferentially implicating the Fifth Amendment. As noted in *Ailes* and conceded by the Leiszs, however, property rights are not absolute, and many zoning provisions other than amortization are permitted in Indiana. Examples include prohibiting the expansion or increase of a nonconforming use and disallowing reinstatement after abandonment of the nonconforming use.

Because *Ailes* turns on the federal constitution, it is correct only to the extent consistent with U.S. Supreme Court precedent. The Supreme Court has never directly considered the constitutionality of amortization provisions. However, most other courts that have considered the issue have held that amortization provisions are not unconstitutional per se. See Jay M. Zitter, Annotation, Validity of Provisions for Amortization of Nonconforming Uses, 8 A.L.R.5th 391, 412-22 (1992) (listing three federal circuits and twenty-four states as supporting the "view that amortization provisions are valid if they are reasonable," and no federal circuits and only four states adhering to the "view that all amortization provisions are invalid in general"). Although each state is free to find amortization provisions to be in violation of its state constitution, no state court can uphold amortization provisions if they are in violation of the federal constitution.

With the sole exception of this Court's decision in *Ailes*, state courts that have found amortization provisions unconstitutional have done so on the basis of their state constitution. *Id.* at 419; see also Hoffmann v. Kinealy, 389 S.W.2d 745 (Mo. 1965); Akron v. Chapman, 160 Ohio St. 382, 116 N.E.2d 697 (Ohio 1953) (citing both state and federal constitutional provisions); PA Northwestern Distribs., Inc. v.Zoning Hearing Bd., 526 Pa. 186, 584 A.2d 1372 (Pa. 1991). We can only conclude that *Ailes*, in holding that amortization provisions are unconstitutional per se, incorrectly decided an issue of federal constitutional law. No issue has been raised and we express no opinion as to any state constitutional point. . . .

2. A North Carolina appellate case, Graham Court Assocs. v. Town Council of Chapel Hill, 53 N.C. App. 543, 546-47, 281 S.E.2d 418, 420 (Ct. App. 1981), involved the proposed conversion of apartment units to condominium ownership. The court reasoned:

> In the case before us, the court found as facts, and no one argues otherwise, that the Graham Court Apartments property does not comply with the zoning ordinance requirements for multi-family housing and that its continued use as multi-family housing is permitted as a prior nonconforming use under the ordinance providing for the zoning of Chapel Hill. We must decide whether the contemplated change in ownership to condominiums constitutes a change in use which the town can regulate by its zoning ordinance. We answer that it does not. Again, "The test [of nonconforming use] is 'use' and not ownership or tenancy." Arkam Machine & Tool Co. v. Lyndhurst Tp., 73 N.J. Super., 528, 533, 180 A. 2d 348, 350 (App. Div. 1962).

See also Keith v. Saco River Corridor Com., 464 A.2d 150, 154 (Me. 1983):

> Once a nonconforming use or building is shown to exist, neither is affected by the user's title or possessory rights in relation to the owner of the land. Where a nonconformity legally exists, it is a vested right which adheres to the land or building itself and the right is not forfeited by a purchaser who takes with knowledge of the regulations which are inconsistent with the existing use.

3. The Standard State Zoning Enabling Act made no attempt to protect nonconforming uses. That this omission was a calculation rather than an oversight seems clear from Explanatory Note 9, which stated in part:

> While the almost universal practice is to make zoning ordinances nonretroactive, it is recognized that there may arise local conditions of a peculiar character that make it necessary and desirable to deal with some isolated case by means of a retroactive provision affecting that case only. For this reason, it does not seem wise to debar the local legislative body from dealing with such a situation.

4. Consider the following statutory provision from Michigan (Mich. Comp. Laws Serv. §125.3208):

> (3) The legislative body may acquire, by purchase, condemnation, or otherwise, private property or an interest in private property for the removal of nonconforming uses and structures. . . .

> (4) The elimination of the nonconforming uses and structures in a zoning district is declared to be for a public purpose and for a public use. The legislative body may institute proceedings for condemnation of nonconforming uses and structures . . . .

In this connection, it might be well to examine the nature of the legislative weapons that have been employed for the purpose of zoning. The historical choice has been that of the police power. However, there were early attempts to zone entirely by eminent domain. In State ex rel. Twin City

Bldg. & Inv. Co. v. Houghton, 144 Minn. 1, 19, 20, 176 N.W. 159, 162 (1920), the court said in upholding such an enabling law:

> In large cities, where the lots for residences must necessarily be of the minimum size, especially where the man of small means must dwell, it is readily seen that if a home is built on such a lot, and thereafter three-story apartments extending to the lot line are constructed on both sides of the home, it becomes almost unlivable and its value utterly destroyed. Not only that, but the construction of such apartments or other like buildings in a territory of individual homes depreciates very much the values in the whole territory. The loss is not only to the owners, but to the state and municipality, by reason of the diminished taxes resulting from diminished values.
>
> The absence of restrictions of use also gives occasion for extortion. The occurrences have been common in our large cities of unscrupulous and designing persons securing lots in desirable residential districts and then passing the word that an apartment or other objectionable structure is to be erected thereon. In order to protect themselves against heavy loss and bitter annoyance, the adjacent owners, or parties interested in property in the neighborhood, are forced to buy the lots so held at exorbitant price. The well-to-do may in this way be able by financial sacrifice to protect their homes against undesirable invasions. But when this occurs in territory occupied by people of modest homes and moderate means, where all they have is represented by the home, and that, perhaps, not free of mortgage lien, there is nothing to do but to submit to the loss and the injustice. There should be a lawful way to forestall such wrongs. Courts have often resorted to the rule sic utere tuo ut alienum non laedas in administering justice between property owners. Why should not the Legislature also make use of this rule?
>
> Another reason is that giving the people a means to secure for that portion of a city, wherein they establish their homes, fit and harmonious surroundings, promotes contentment, induces further efforts to enhance the appearance and value of the home, fosters civic pride, and thus tends to produce a better type of citizen. It is time that courts recognized the aesthetic as a factor in life. Beauty and fitness enhance values in public and private structures. But it is not sufficient that the building is fit and proper, standing alone, it should also fit in with surrounding structures to some degree. People are beginning to realize this more than before and are calling for city planning, by which the individual homes may be segregated from not only industrial and mercantile districts, but also from the districts devoted to hotels and apartments. The act in question responds to this call and should be deemed to provide for a taking for a public use.

While exercise of the power of eminent domain for the purpose of zoning was thus held valid, it has not achieved any popularity. Under this statute Minneapolis zoned less than 1% of its area, St. Paul only 1.22%, and Duluth less than 0.05.%.[2] As Edward Bassett in, Zoning 27 (1936), put it:

> No effective zoning plan could be accomplished by the exercise of eminent domain. If there were some diminution of the full use of property, the city would need to pay the loss to the private owner. This would mean a laborious and expensive proceeding

---

2. In 1921, another enabling act that based zoning on the police power was passed. MINN. LAWS 1921, ch. 217. Its validity was upheld in State ex rel. Beery v. Houghton, 164 Minn. 146, 204 N.W. 569 (1925). *See also* State ex rel. Sheffield v. City of Minneapolis, 235 Minn. 174, 50 N.W.2d 296 (1951); Naegele Outdoor Adver. Co. v. Minnetonka, 281 Minn. 492, 162 N.W.2d 206 (1968). For other instances imposing restrictions upon use of property by means of eminent domain, see Attorney General v. Williams, 174 Mass. 476, 55 N.E. 77 (1899); Kansas City v. Liebi, 298 Mo. 569, 252 S.W. 404 (1923).

for almost every parcel of land. Since the city could not afford to pay this cost out of public funds, but would need to assess the awards on the property benefited, the cost of the process would be enormous. The restrictions would consist of public easements of a permanent nature. But as every living organism grows and changes, these easements would have to be changed from time to time by successive applications of condemnation. The method would be clumsy and ineffective. Some states in their zoning enabling acts have tried to provide for the employment of eminent domain in whole or part, but the attempts have never been successful.

Are there any reasons for utilizing public purchase as a device to eliminate nonconforming uses in view of this experience? If the legislative determination is to apply eminent domain in solving this planning problem, how would it fare constitutionally, especially in the anti-eminent domain fervor caused by the Supreme Court's controversial holding in Kelo v. City of New London (discussed in Chapter Three)?

5. Sound physical planning may require the removal of some nonconforming structures. The economist may well argue that this will represent a loss not only to the individual owner but to the community as a whole. British planners evolved a theory to confound this argument. Planning, they claimed, does not destroy land values; it merely redistributes them or "shifts" them. If development is prohibited on one piece of land it will rise up triumphant on another. (Some such reasoning was presumably a premise for the *Euclid* decision—that the industrial development prohibited on part of the company's land would materialize elsewhere, perhaps even on property owned by the complaining landowner.) A second prong in this defense of planning is the assumption that the loss in value to the nonconforming owner is offset by increases in value to the surrounding properties.

The theory of "shifting value" appeals to some, because it parallels the findings of the natural sciences. It postulates a law of conservation of land value similar to the physical law of conservation of energy—that matter can be neither created nor destroyed. But what proof is there that development prohibited on one site will nevertheless erupt automatically on another? There is the further consideration that even if planning merely causes a shift in land values, these shifts may jump the boundaries of local planning areas. Thus the elimination of nonconforming uses in one area may bring increased land value—but only in another. And does not the individual landowner deserve individual treatment irrespective of the overall sum of land values? For a practical application of the concept of shifting values, see the groundbreaking work by Donald Hagman, *Zoning by Special Assessment Financed Eminent Domain*, 28 U. Fla. L. Rev. 655 (1976); Windfalls for Wipeouts: Land Value Capture and Compensation (Donald G. Hagman & Dean J. Misczynski eds., 1978).

If, owing to such economic arguments and to the American tradition of nonretroactive regulation, the community decides to compensate for the elimination of nonconforming uses, either by outright payment from the public treasury or by permitting the landowner to amortize his or her capital investment over some period of time, problems still remain. Compensation to the private property owner does not obviate the loss to the community; it merely transfers it from the individual owner to the general taxpayer. Moreover, what is the effect of this elimination of nonconforming uses on those who invest in real estate projects? Having once discovered the caprice of the law, will they not be far more reluctant to risk their capital?

Planners advocate the elimination of nonconforming uses but do not always consider what will occur subsequently. If the building is readily adaptable to a conforming use, there may be no problem. If, however, it has no alternative use within the prescriptions of the zoning law, the result may be to "sterilize" the land. Most nonconforming uses occur in the older and more depressed neighborhoods, and these are precisely the areas least attractive to real estate investors. The landowners may find themselves unable to finance the redevelopment of their land, and the community may find itself with parcels of land that are unused and unproductive of tax revenue. Environmentalists and new urbanists might welcome this scenario, the former because it might reduce urban clutter and provide more green spaces, the latter because it might allow for the assemblage of these parcels for larger-scale, urban reuse projects.

Central to the goal of protecting the nonconforming uses is the idea that the owner has a constitutionally protected vested right to continue to use the property in the same manner, at least for a reasonable time. This raises the question(s) of when and under what conditions a right to use property vests. The following case indicates that even having a building permit in hand will not necessarily do the trick.

PARKVIEW ASSOCIATES v. CITY OF NEW YORK
71 N.Y.2d 274, 525 N.Y.S.2d 176, 519 N.E.2d 1372, *cert. denied*, 488 U.S. 801 (1988)

OPINION OF THE COURT [by Bellacosa, J.] . . . .

Owner-builder Parkview's property, purchased in 1982, is at the southeast corner of Park Avenue and 96th Street, located 90- to 190-feet east of Park Avenue. A portion of the property is within a Special Park Improvement District (P.I.D.) created by enactment of the Board of Estimate of the City of New York in 1973. The enabling and authorizing resolution limits the height of new buildings in that district to 19 stories or 210 feet, whichever is less. The P.I.D. boundary ran uniformly 150-feet east of Park Avenue until, by resolution of the Board of Estimate on March 3, 1983, the metes and bounds description of the P.I.D. was amended, providing in part for a reduction from 150 to 100 feet between East 88 Street to midway between 95th and 96th Streets. The boundary north of this midblock division, pursuant to the metes and bounds, remained at all times 150 feet. Plaintiff's property was thus unaffected by this 1983 change and has always been governed by the 1973 original enactment.

Zoning Map 6b accompanying the March 1983 resolution depicted the amended boundary with a dotted line which fell within a shaded area constituting the existing P.I.D. A numerical designation of "150," included on earlier versions of the map to show the setback, had been removed and a new designation of "100" was inserted adjacent to the dotted line. This left no numerical designation along the northern part of the boundary. The "150" designation signaling the retention of the boundary north of the 95th-96th Street midblock line was reinserted on a version of Map 6b published to reflect a subsequent resolution of September 19, 1985.

Parkview's initial new building application, submitted on June 5, 1985, was rejected for failure to show compliance with the P.I.D. height limitation. Based upon its interpretation of the version of Zoning Map 6b existing in the summer of 1985, Parkview concluded that a 100-foot boundary controlled, and its revised building application, submitted on July 31, 1985, limited the height of the proposed new building to 19 stories between its property line and 100 feet from Park Avenue. The portion of the building setback more than 100 feet from Park Avenue was to rise 31 stories. The application was approved by the Department of Buildings as conforming with all zoning requirements on August 12, 1985 and, after rereview, a building permit was issued on November 21, 1985 by the Borough Superintendent. There is no dispute that at the time the permit was issued the Department erroneously interpreted amended Map 6b as changing the boundary on 96th Street to 100 feet. On July 11, 1986, however, after substantial construction, the Borough Superintendent of the Department of Buildings issued a stop work order for those portions of the building over 19 stories within the full 150 feet of Park Avenue. After review, the Commissioner of Buildings partially revoked the building permit, consistent with the stop work order, on the grounds that the permit, to the extent it authorized a height of 31 stories from 100-feet back instead of 150-feet back, was invalid when issued.

Parkview appealed the Commissioner's decision to the Board of Standards and Appeals (BSA), which denied the appeal and sustained the determination of the Commissioner. In sum, the BSA found that the dotted lines on Zoning Map 6b within the shaded P.I.D., expressly connoting a reduction to 100 from 150 feet of the protected area, excluded the 96th Street frontage of plaintiff from any change; that the original resolution with its metes and bounds description, which was never changed in any event, controlled over the map depicting the boundaries even if the map could be misread; and that the boundary-height limitation applicable to Parkview under the metes and bounds description was and had always been 150-feet east of Park Avenue.

Parkview then turned to the courts, essentially in an article 78 proceeding, seeking to set aside the partial revocation of its building permit. It sought to reinstate the full permit, arguing that the final BSA determination was arbitrary and capricious or affected by error of law because the original permit was properly issued; that its rights pursuant to that permit had vested; that its reliance on the permit caused substantial and irreparable harm requiring that the City be estopped from revoking the permit; and that the partial revocation deprived Parkview of its property without due process or just compensation.

The IAS Judge dismissed the petition holding that the BSA's determination was reasonable and supported by substantial evidence that the building permit was invalid when issued, vesting no rights, because the building plans did not comport with the metes and bounds description for the P.I.D. as contained in the controlling original legislative enactment of the Board of Estimate. The court also held that estoppel was unavailable as a matter of law. Finally, the constitutional taking argument was dismissed as premature because Parkview had failed to apply for a variance which is a prerequisite to that claim. The Appellate Division affirmed, and this appeal ensued by leave of this court.

Parkview argues that its original permit was issued in conformity with a reasonable interpretation of the zoning map, thus making it valid when issued; that the principles of equitable estoppel preclude the partial revocation of the building permit even if the permit was erroneously issued; and that the City's partial revocation of its permit constitutes a taking in violation of due process of law and without just compensation. The City counters that the decision of the BSA has a rational basis because the permit was invalid when issued; that equitable estoppel is not available to estop a municipality from enforcing its zoning laws when the building permit issued by the municipality violated those zoning laws; and that the petition below failed to state a claim for an unconstitutional taking.

There can be little quarrel with the proposition that the New York City Department of Buildings has no discretion to issue a building permit which fails to conform with applicable provisions of law, and that the Commissioner may revoke a permit which "has been issued in error and conditions are such that a permit should not have been issued" (Administrative Code of City of New York § § 27-191, 27-197). Since discrepancies between the map and enabling resolution are controlled by the specifics of the resolution (New York City Zoning Resolution § § 11-22, 12-01), the original permit in this case was invalid inasmuch as it authorized construction within the 150-foot P.I.D. above 19 stories in violation of New York City Zoning Resolution § 92-06 (2 Journal of Proceedings of Board of Estimate of City of NY, at 1708 [Cal No. 6, Apr. 23, 1973], as amended [Cal No. 8, Mar. 3, 1983]). Therefore, the subsequent BSA action in ratifying the decision of the Commissioner partially revoking Parkview's permit had a sound legal basis. Indeed, there was no discretion reposed in these authorities to do otherwise at that point and on the record before them at that time.

Turning to the next stage of our analysis, we have only recently once again said that "[generally], estoppel may not be invoked against a municipal agency to prevent it from discharging its statutory duties" (Scruggs-Leftwich v Rivercross Tenants' Corp., 70 NY2d 849, citing Matter of Daleview Nursing Home v Axelrod, 62 NY2d 30, 33; Matter of Hamptons Hosp. & Med. Center v Moore, 52 NY2d 88, 93; see also, Matter of E.F.S. Ventures Corp. v Foster, 71 NY2d 359 [decided herewith]). Moreover, "[estoppel] is not available against a local government unit for the purpose of ratifying an administrative error" (Morley v Arricale, 66 NY2d 665, 667). In particular, "[a] municipality, it is settled, is not estopped from enforcing its zoning laws either by the issuance of a building permit or by laches" (City of Yonkers v Rentways, Inc., 304 NY 499, 505) and "[the] prior issue to petitioner of a building permit could not 'confer rights in contravention of the zoning laws'" (Matter of B & G Constr. Corp. v Board of Appeals, 309 NY 730, 732, citing City of Buffalo v Roadway Tr. Co., 303 NY 453, 463). Insofar as estoppel is not available to preclude a municipality from enforcing the provisions of its zoning laws and the mistaken or erroneous issuance of a permit does not estop a municipality from correcting errors, even where there are harsh results, the City should not be estopped here from revoking that portion of the building permit which violated the long-standing zoning limits imposed by the applicable P.I.D. resolution. Even if there was municipal error in one map and in the mistaken administrative issuance of the original permit, those factors would be completely outweighed in this case by the doctrine that reasonable diligence would have readily uncovered for a good-faith inquirer the existence of the unequivocal limitations of 150 feet in the original binding metes and bounds description of the enabling legislation, and that this boundary has never been changed by the Board of Estimate. The policy reasons which foreclose estoppel against a governmental entity in all but the rarest cases thus have irrefutable cogency in this case. . . .

Notes

1. As a result of the New York high court's decision, Parkview was left with a partially completed 31-story apartment building, of which 12 floors were "illegal." On the day the opinion was released, Buildings Commissioner Charles Smith ordered the architects to modify the building: "They are required to file engineering documents on how they plan to remove the top 12 stories and how they are going to protect the adjacent buildings while the demolition is going on." Marianne Yen, *Too Tall in Manhattan; Court Orders Developer to Tear Down Building's Top 12 Floors*, Wash. Post, Feb. 10, 1988, at A03. On October 3, the Supreme Court dismissed Parkview's appeal and denied certiorari. 488 U.S. 801 (1988).

A few years later, the building was "cut down to size." A *Chicago Tribune* article reported that Laurence Ginsberg, developer of the too-tall building, began removal of the structure's top 12 floors, using a computer-controlled robot. Genie Rice, leader of Civitas, the neighborhood organization that successfully fought for the partial demolition (with an estimated cost approaching $1 million), was exuberant: "Finally, we're going to see a little more sky. This shows that New Yorkers really care about their zoning." Ginsberg called the removal project "a painful way to correct a mistake on a zoning map." Rick Hampson, *Zoning Hammer Cuts Tower Down to Size*, Chi. Trib., May 2, 1993, at 2R.

2. In Queenside Hills Realty Co. v. Saxl, 328 U.S. 80, 83 (1946), the appellant had operated a lodging house since 1940. It was constructed in compliance with all existing laws, but in 1944 New York amended its Multiple Dwelling Law, and provided that lodging houses "of nonfireproof construction existing prior to the enactment of this subdivision" should comply with new requirements. These included the installation of an automatic wet pipe sprinkler system. The Court held

that "in no case does the owner of property acquire immunity against exercise of the police power because he constructed it in full compliance with the existing laws."

The question of retroactive operation of a zoning ordinance has also been litigated in connection with buildings in process of construction when the ordinance is passed. In these cases the courts usually sustain the revocation of a building permit issued before the enactment of a zoning ordinance, provided there has been no "material" reliance on the permit. The classic case is Brett v. Building Comm'r of Brookline, 250 Mass. 73, 80, 145 N.E. 269, 271-72 (1924):

> Since the petitioners had only barely begun work pursuant to their permits, they had acquired no vested rights against a change in the [zoning] by-law by the exercise of the law-making power. The circumstance, that contracts of the petitioners with third persons, entered into before the passage of the amendment of the by-law, may be affected, does not impair the by-law in its constitutional phases when once it has been determined that in general it is a valid exercise of the police power.

For a more recent case relying on this golden oldie, see Building Comm'r for Ashburnham v. Puccio, 2002 Mass. Super. LEXIS 372, at *1, *4-*5 (2002), in which a landowner was ordered "to cease and desist from any construction activity and prohibiting the defendant from continuing any construction activity without first obtaining a building permit." The court noted:

> The defendant claims to have a constitutional right to sovereignty over his property that takes priority over lawfully appointed governmental officials seeking to enforce the lawful statutes and regulations of the state. The defendant fails or refuses to recognize that the Constitution of the United States and of the Commonwealth of Massachusetts grants to the legislature the police power to regulate matters of public health and safety. Pt. 2, c. 1, § 1, Art. IV of the Constitution of Massachusetts states, in relevant part, as follows: "And further, full power and authority are hereby given and granted to the said general court, from time to time, to make, ordain, and establish, all manner of wholesome and reasonable orders, laws, statutes, and ordinances, directions and instructions, either with penalties or without; so as the same be not repugnant or contrary to this constitution, as they judge to be for the good and welfare of this Commonwealth, and for the government and ordering thereof, and of the subjects of the same . . ." This has been interpreted by our Supreme Judicial Court as follows: "in the exercise of the police power the Legislature may regulate and limit personal rights and rights of property in the interest of the public health, public morals and public safety." Welch v. Swasey, 193 Mass. 364, 372-73, 79 N.E. 745 (1907). In Brett v. Building Commissioner of Brookline, 250 Mass. 73, 145 N.E. 269 (1924), the court, at p. 77, stated:

>> the right to enjoy life and liberty and to acquire, possess and protect property are secured to every one under the Constitution of Massachusetts and under the Constitution of the United States. These guarantees include the right to own land and to use and improve it according to the owner's conceptions of pleasure, comfort or profit, and of the exercise of liberty and the pursuit of happiness . . . These rights are in general subject to the exercise of police power. They are not absolute and unqualified. Liberty may be thought the greatest of all rights. But liberty does not mean unrestricted license to pursue the mandates of one's own will. Liberty is regulated by law to the end that there may be equal enjoyment of its blessings by all. "Liberty implies the absence of arbitrary restraint, not immunity from reasonable regulations and prohibitions imposed in the interests of the community." . . . The right to own and enjoy property is no more sacred than liberty.

> It stands on no firmer foundation than liberty. The police power in its reasonable exercise extends to ownership of land as well as to the enjoyment of liberty . . . The police power is recognized as an attribute of government. It may be put forth in any reasonable way in behalf of the public health, the public morals, the public safety and, when defined with some strictness so as not to include mere expediency, the public welfare.

A few months later, in Building Comm'r for Ashburnham v. Puccio, 2003 Mass. Super. LEXIS 361, at *2-*3, *5, *6, the building commissioner "filed a motion to enforce the contempt judgment, on the grounds that the defendant had not taken any steps to purge himself of the contempt by either applying for the proper municipal permits for construction of the residence on his property nor had he taken any steps to demolish and/or remove the un-permitted structure." After noting that "[t]his court has been more than generous in granting the defendant an opportunity to purge himself of the contempt," Justice Francis R. Fecteau ordered the landowner to remove the unpermitted structures and to pay a $5,000 "compensatory fine" and a "punitive fine" of $11,500.

3. A developer had purchased land in the Nukolii area of the Hawaiian island of Kauai, and had successfully sought amendments to both the county general plan and the comprehensive zoning code to change the zoning designation from "open space/agriculture" to "resort." When the developer began building the resort, the Committee to Save Nukolii circulated a petition calling for repeal of the rezoning and eventually collected enough signatures to place a referendum question on the 1980 general election ballot. The committee finally won voter approval—by a 2 to 1 margin—to repeal the zoning ordinance. In the interim, however, the developer, not having been required by the courts to halt construction, had completed 150 condominium units (priced at $185,000 each) and had begun work on a 350-room hotel. A total of $50 million had been sunk into the project.

Kauai County filed a lawsuit to determine the rights of the parties involved. The circuit court ruled that because the zoning ordinance had not been suspended, the building permits had been validly issued. The developer had acquired "vested rights" by the time of the election, and the county was equitably estopped from prohibiting the developer from completing the project. The Hawaii Supreme Court reversed, in County of Kauai v. Pacific Standard Life Ins. Co., 65 Haw. 318, 653 P.2d 766 (1982), *appeal dismissed sub nom.* Pacific Standard Life Ins. Co. v. Committee to Save Nukolii, 460 U.S. 1077 (1983), ruling that the developer had acquired "vested rights" only if final discretionary action on the project had taken place before the referendum petition was certified. The court then reasoned that because the referendum itself constituted a development approval, the vesting of rights had not occurred. The court restrained further construction and instructed the trial court to order the building permits revoked.

In February 1984, a special election ($50,000 of the cost of which was paid for by the resort developer) was held on Kauai to decide whether to allow completion of the Nukolii project. This time the voters chose to restore resort zoning to the development site, allowing the developer to complete construction of the project. *Voters Back Zoning for Resort on Kauai*, N.Y. Times, Feb. 6, 1984, at A14.

According to Professor David Callies & Julie A. Tappendorf, in *Unconstitutional Land Development Conditions and the Development Agreement Solution: Bargaining for Public Facilities After Nollan and Dolan*, 51 Case W. Res. 663, 670 (2001), the Nukolii controversy "spawned" Hawaii's development agreements statute, passed in 1985. The opening paragraphs of that statute (Haw. Rev. Stat. §46-121) can be found in Chapter Three.

II.   Amendments: Legislating (Or Is It Adjudicating?) Small-Scale Changes

Like any other piece of legislation, a zoning ordinance will have its defenders and detractors. When landowners are dissatisfied with the manner in which their properties have been classified, the most direct route toward relief is a zoning amendment, also known as a rezoning. Because the economic gains to a property owner seeking a change to a more intensive use can be quite substantial, and the externalities experienced by neighbors (such as increased traffic and noise, glaring lights, and aesthetically displeasing scenery) can often be difficult to tolerate, the decision over whether or not to grant a rezoning is often controversial. By the time the issue is resolved, professional planners, planning commissioners, neighborhood associations, local legislators, lawyers, and judges may all play a part in the zoning amendment drama. The set of cases in this section demonstrates that courts have taken very seriously the job of ensuring that the decision to grant the landowners the relief they seek will not disturb a carefully considered plan or be the product of undue influence.

KUEHNE v. TOWN COUNCIL OF EAST HARTFORD
136 Conn. 452, 72 A.2d 474 (1950)

MALTBIE, Chief Justice. The plaintiffs, certain property owners, appealed to the Court of Common Pleas from the granting by the defendant of an application for a change in the zoning of a piece of property owned by Wilfred H. Langlois from an A residence to an A business zone. The trial court dismissed the appeal and the plaintiffs have appealed. . . .

Main Street in East Hartford runs substantially north and south. The petitioner before the town council, Langlois, owned a piece of land on the east side of it which he had been using for growing fruit and vegetables, and he has had upon it a greenhouse and a roadside stand for the sale of products of the land. The premises, ever since zoning was established in East Hartford in 1927, had been in an A residence district. Langlois made an application to the town council to change to an A business district a portion of the tract fronting on Main Street for about 500 feet and extending to a depth of 150 feet. He intended, if the application was granted, to erect upon the tract a building containing six or eight stores, apparently in the nature of retail stores and small business establishments calculated to serve the needs of residents in the vicinity. Starting at a business district to the north and extending for almost three miles to the town boundary on the south, the land along Main Street and extending to a considerable depth on each side of it has been, ever since zoning was established in the town, in an A residence district, with certain exceptions hereinafter described. Seven hundred feet north of the Langlois property is a small business district lying on both sides of Main Street; the land on the east side is used for a fruit and vegetable stand, a milk bar and a garage and gas station; and the land on the west side, with an area a little larger than the Langlois tract in question, is now unoccupied. About 500 feet south of the Langlois property is another small business district in which is located a grill and restaurant, a drugstore, a cleaning and dyeing business and a large grocery and meat market. Formerly the land about the tract in question was used quite largely for agricultural purposes, but within the last few years a large residential community, comprising some one thousand houses, has grown up in the vicinity.

The application to the town council was based upon the claim that residents in the vicinity need the stores and services which could be located in the building Langlois proposed to erect. There was, for example, a petition filed with the council in support of the application signed by fifty-one of those residents which asked it to allow such a change as might be necessary to permit for their benefit a shopping center on the property. None of the signers, however, owned property on Main Street or in the immediate vicinity of the Langlois property. On the other hand, the application was opposed by the owner of property directly opposite the tract in question and by the owners of the two properties fronting on Main. Street immediately south of the Langlois land.

The council voted that the application "be granted for the general welfare and the good of the town in that section." In Bartram v. Zoning Commission, 136 Conn. 89, 68 A.2d 308, we recently had before us an appeal from the granting by a zoning commission of an application to change a lot in Bridgeport even smaller than the tract here in question from a residence to a business zone, and we sustained the action of the commission. We said:

> A limitation upon the powers of zoning authorities which has been in effect ever since zoning statutes were made applicable generally to municipalities in the state is that the regulations they adopt must be made "in accordance with a comprehensive plan." Public Acts, 1925, c. 242, §3, Rev. 1949, §837. . . . Action by a zoning authority which gives to a single lot or a small area privileges which are not extended to other land in the vicinity is in general against sound public policy and obnoxious to the law. It can be justified only when it is done in furtherance of a general plan properly adopted for and designed to serve the best interests of the community as a whole. The vice of spot zoning lies in the fact that it singles out for special treatment a lot or a small area in a way that does not further such a plan. Where, however, in pursuance of it, a zoning commission takes such action, its decision can be assailed only on the ground that it abused the discretion vested in it by law. To permit business in a small area within a residence zone may fall within the scope of such a plan, and to do so, unless it amounts to unreasonable or arbitrary' action, is not unlawful.

It appeared in that case that the change was granted by the commission in pursuance of a policy to encourage decentralization of business in the city and to that end to permit neighborhood stores in outlying districts. It is true that we said in that opinion, 136 Conn. at page 94, 68 A.2d at page 311, that if the commission decided,

> on facts affording a sufficient basis and in the exercise of a proper discretion, that it would serve the best interests of the community as a whole to permit a use of a single lot or small area in a different way than was allowed in surrounding territory, it would not be guilty of spot zoning in any sense obnoxious to the law.

We meant by that statement to emphasize the fact that the controlling test must be, not the benefit to a particular individual or group of individuals, but the good of the community as a whole, and we did not mean in any way to derogate from our previous statement that any such change can only be made if it falls within the requirements of a comprehensive plan for the use and development of property in the municipality or a large part of it.

In the case before us it is obvious that the council looked no further than the benefit which might accrue to Langlois and those who resided in the vicinity of his property, and that they gave no consideration to the larger question as to the effect the change would have upon the general plan of zoning in the community. In fact, the controlling consideration seems to have been that Langlois intended to go ahead at once with his building rather than any consideration of the suitability of the particular lot for business uses, because there is no suggestion in the record that the council considered the fact that only some 700 feet away was a tract of land already zoned for business which, as appears from the zoning map in evidence, was more easily accessible to most of the signers of the petition than was the Langlois land.

In Strain v. Mims, 123 Conn. 275, 287, 193 A. 754, 759, we said "One of the essential purposes of zoning regulations is to stabilize property uses." In this case it is significant that the change was opposed by the owners of three properties so situated as to be most affected by it, while those who supported it were the owner of the tract and residents who did not live in its immediate vicinity. It should also be noted that the petition they signed contained a provision that it should not be construed as supporting permission for the use of the premises as a liquor outlet, but at the hearing before the council the attorney for Langlois in effect conceded that the zoning regulations permitted such a use in an A business district; and if that is so and the change were granted, it is quite possible that the premises would be sooner or later converted to such a use.

The action of the town council in this case was not in furtherance of any general plan of zoning in the community and cannot be sustained. . . .

There is error, the judgment is set aside and the case is remanded to be proceeded with according to law.

Notes

1. For early cases in which Connecticut wrestled with the "in accordance" standard, see Eden v. Zoning Comm'n of Bloomfield, 139 Conn. 59, 89 A.2d 746 (1952) (the neighbors successfully challenged as "spot zoning" the change from residence to business to establish an ice-cream bar with 51 stools); Hills v. Zoning Comm'n of Newington, 139 Conn. 603, 96 A.2d 212 (1953) (rejecting a challenge to the extension of the industrial zone, the court agreed with the zoning commission that the "change was for the general welfare of the community" and observed that the "mere lack of a town plan cannot have the effect of preventing a change of zone"); Kutcher v. Town Planning Comm'n of Manchester, 138 Conn. 705, 88 A.2d 538 (1952) (setting aside the trial court's reversal of the grant of a rezoning to allow a machine shop (at the neighbors' behest), the supreme court upheld the commission's finding that "the change of zone applied for would permit the use of the land for a purpose which was suitable and appropriate and would create a new zone which was in keeping with the orderly development of the comprehensive plan for the zoning of the entire town"; the one dissenter argued that "the defendant commission's action in rezoning the Patten land, instead of being done in furtherance of the fulfilment of a comprehensive master plan, constituted a clear and unwarranted case of spot zoning"). What kind of guidance could Connecticut land use practitioners glean from this decisional array?

2. Is there a way to make the seemingly subjective "in accordance" standard more objective? Under the title, "A Thinking Machine Can Think Like a Judge, 99 Percent of the Time," the *New York Times*, July 15, 1979, reported that "computers are taking degrees in the law." A study for the American Bar Association and the National Science Foundation programmed a computer with more than 1,200 zoning amendment appeals cases recorded by the supreme courts of six states; the study was able to reduce the relevant considerations to 204 variables. An earlier study, Charles M. Haar et al., *Computer Power and Legal Reasoning: A Case Study of Judicial Decision Prediction in Zoning*, 1977 Am. Bar Found. J. 651, 742-44, focused on the state of Connecticut, in which the *Kuehne* case was decided. The researchers offered the following conclusions:

> In the final analysis, the statistical research seems to have managed to identify and, roughly, to quantify crucial issues in the zoning amendment litigation in Connecticut. One of the important questions of this study was whether the articulated rule of decision (found in the court opinions) corresponded to the unarticulated rule of decision (the relationship of the actual facts to the outcome). While verifying many traditional rules, we found important discrepancies. The tentative and confused use of the concept of the "comprehensive plan" remained elusive even when examined by a molecular approach, which did not employ general principles or statements or expound on legal doctrines

but which, using the information gleaned by traditional legal analysis, isolated factors important to outcome and weighted them according to the court's analyses.

How does this "computerized restatement" of the law differ from a traditional legal analysis? Both identify the crucial issues in the zoning amendment litigation in Connecticut. The computer restatement also quantifies the effect of the various factors on the outcome of the decisions and, in so doing, assigns them relative weights. The legal analysis is drawn from the court's explanation of its reasoning process; the computer-aided statistical analysis is drawn from a comparison of the facts of the case with its outcome. There is a large residue of legal analysis in the statistical model, nevertheless, because all the "facts" in the latter analysis (with the exception of the census data) were gleaned from the court's opinions by the conventional legal approach to case analysis, that is, were derived from the court's interpretation of the evidence.

The degree of court deference to the administrative process has been quantified—the decision tree indicates the overwhelming significance given to the decision of the initial trier, the zoning agency. The nature of the plaintiff also is highly significant. Other key factors are size of the subject parcel, capacity of municipal services to support the proposed use, presence of hazardous conditions, and economic impact on adjacent lots. . . .

In the zoning amendment cases, the concept of change "in accordance with a comprehensive plan" lacks the specificity of a workable legal doctrine; like substantive due process, equal protection, and police power, its bounds can be circumscribed only by references to specific factual circumstances where its limits have been tested by the parties and the court has rendered a verdict. The doctrine sets the tone, but it provides no operational guidelines; often it merely sweeps up loose, perhaps troubling, facts after the conclusion has been reached in a case. To get the broom to sweep in the client's direction, however, the lawyer needs to focus on the specific factors given and refined by the computer.

The lawyer must concentrate on preparing his client's case within the constraints of limited time and money. Computer analysis of the cases can help make the decisions of the court more predictable. In preparing his case, the lawyer must try to create a record that establishes that the proposed development either avoids or creates the problems designated as crucial in the Summary Table. The computer analysis has clarified the issues that have sufficient impact to convince the court to overturn the initial decision of the zoning authority. This clear focus can save research and preparation, for the lawyer then knows where to direct his energies and available resources.

In advising his client, the lawyer can use such research as a concrete basis for discussing the risks and costs of litigation and as a more objective standard against which to review the strengths and weaknesses of the case.

The key information from the Summary Table follows:

	Value[1]
Constant[2]	−.57
Variables:	
Zoning authority denies zone change	−.55
Court of common pleas approves zone change	.16
Not a departure from large uniform blocks	.62
Streets inadequate	−.39
Adverse impact of value of adjacent lots	−.35
Physical hazard created	−.30
Area relatively large	.25
Completion of necessary improvements unlikely	−.24
Character of area improving	−.23
Character of area deteriorating	.13
Other municipal services adequate	.10
Retention of control	.07
Proposed use aesthetically compatible	.06[3]
Common zoning technique	.06
Specific, detailed limits in zoning ordinances	.05
More flexible land-use controls	.04
Adequate buffer	.02
Proposed use needed in neighborhood	.02
Existing zoning line a natural boundary	−.02

Using the facts supplied by the courts in *Kuehne* and in the case that follows, consider whether the important factors identified in the Summary Table accurately predict the ultimate outcome of the litigation.

MacDONALD v. BOARD OF COMMISSIONERS
238 Md. 549, 210 A.2d 325 (1965)

OPPENHEIMER, J. Adjacent property owners appeal from an order of the Circuit Court for Prince George's County affirming a zoning action of the Board of County Commissioners for Prince George's County, sitting as a District Council for the Prince George's portion of the Maryland-Washington Regional District (the Council). The Council had approved applications of the Isle of Thye Land Company, one of the appellees (the Land Company), to reclassify three tracts of land all zoned R-R (Rural Residential). Two tracts of approximately nine and three acres

---

1. The sum of all relevant decision variables determines the prediction. A sum close to one predicts approval of the zone change by the court; a net value close to zero implies denial.

2. The constant term is the intercept a of the regression equation $y = a + b_1x_1 + b_2x_2 + \ldots bnxn$. For simplicity, the lawyer can consider it the initial probability of approval when no other information is known; all other variables change the probability from this starting point.

3. From this point in the Summary Table the variables add only marginally to the predictive capability of the model.

respectively were rezoned to C-2 (General Commercial) and the third, of about 29 acres, to R-H (Multiple Family, High Rise Residential).

The three tracts are part of a larger area of 655 acres owned by the Land Company, called Tantallon on the Potomac, located in the southwestern portion of the County on Swan Creek, which empties into the Potomac. The Woodrow Wilson Bridge and the Capital Beltway are four or five miles to the north. Fort Washington National Park, a 341 acre reservation is adjacent to the area on the south and Mount Vernon is across the Potomac River to the west. . . .

The technical staff of the Planning Commission recommended denial of all three applications. Its amended report stated, in part:

> The staff, in its review of this application, concludes that the granting of any zone on this property other than the existing R-R Zone, would be spot zoning. The development which has occurred in the area has been that of single family dwellings on larger than minimum lot size standards, and, the changes which have occurred in this area, the Tantallon community included, are a continuation and solidification of this pattern. . . .

The Planning Board recommended denial of the R-H rezoning for the reasons given by its technical staff. . . .

At the hearing before the Council, the expert witnesses of the Land Company offered voluminous and plausible testimony as to the attractive nature of the plans for the area which it owns. It claimed but offered no evidence to support a mistake in the Master Zoning Map. It relied, instead, upon claimed substantial changes in the area since the adoption of the comprehensive zoning map. The nature of the alleged changes will be considered hereafter. The Chief Engineer of the Planning Commission elaborated upon the reports of the technical staff, and testified that the changes that had occurred in the area of the Land Company's property were oriented towards low density, single family development. Neighboring and adjacent property owners, including the appellants, presented testimony in opposition to the reclassifications, with letters from other protestants, including Secretary of the Interior Udall.

The Council, one of the Commissioners dissenting, approved all three of the Land Company's applications for rezoning. The formal notice of the Council gave no reasons for its decision. The only statement in the nature of reasons is contained in what appears to be a press release on behalf of the Council. This release, apart from some extraneous remarks, contained the following statements:

> Commissioner Brooke, in making his motion, pointed out that the several proposed 20-story apartments would be 3400 feet back from the river, "in a natural valley which would keep them screened from view from the river and the Virginia shore."

> He also noted expanded highway development in the general area and that neither the Board of Education nor the National Capital Planning Commission opposed the planned community. . . .

It was also stated that the Chairman of the Council, who votes only in case of tie, had declared himself in sympathy with the zoning request. Commissioner Gladys Spellman, who dissented, in a separate announcement, said in part:

> The changes which have taken place in the area are not sufficient to warrant rezoning from a low density, single family category. . . . No need has been established for high density apartments in the middle of an area of extremely low density, other than that of remunerative return for the applicant. . . . No proof of error in the original zoning was presented.

The Isle of Thye Land Company plans high rise apartments on approximately 29 acres, and accordingly requests a change to R-H zoning. However, the use of this zone category in a low-density setting is totally at variance with the purpose of R-H zoning as set forth in the text of the classification. . . . We must recognize that the District Council is concerned for the County as a whole and not merely 650 acres of the county. It is certainly not reasonable to assume that because a community is well planned and well-balanced, it may be set down at any point in the County without doing violence to the surrounding areas. Planning must extend beyond the borders of individual communities and encompass the larger areas of the County in order that communities may complement each other rather than inflict harm upon one another.

There was a hearing on the Petition for Review of the Council's order before judge Loveless. In his opinion affirming the order, the Judge pointed out that the Land Company had not contended there had been a mistake in the original zoning, and that the court had no alternative other than to say that no mistake had been shown. Judge Loveless referred to the 14 items relied upon by the Land Company as changes in the area since the original zoning was made and held they were sufficient evidence to justify a reclassification if the Council, in its legislative discretion, so decided. He held, further, that the issues were fairly debatable, and that the Board's action in approving the applications was not arbitrary or capricious. We disagree in respect of the Board's order granting the application to rezone the 29 acres for high-rise apartments.

We have repeatedly held that there is a strong presumption of the correctness of original zoning, and that to sustain a piecemeal change therefrom, there must be strong evidence of mistake in the original zoning or else of a substantial change in conditions. The Land Company contends that here comprehensive rezoning is involved, because of the extent of its entire acreage and the nature of its plans for the development of that acreage. However, as Commissioner Spellman points out in her dissent from the Council's order, it is not the proposed treatment of a particular tract within the broad territory encompassed by the original zoning plan which governs; the impingement of the proposed rezoning upon the general plan is the criterion. We hold that, in this case, it is proposed piecemeal rezoning which is involved and that the strong presumption of the correctness of the original comprehensive zoning prevails.

The majority of the Council, in effect, gave no reasons for its order. The alleged changes of conditions in the immediate area adduced by the Land Company to support their application to rezone the 29 acres for high-rise apartments, in our opinion, do not constitute evidence sufficient to make the facts fairly debatable. A number of these changes have taken place, or are contemplated, within the Tantallon tract itself. The building of a golf course, the dredging of Swan Creek, the reservation of a school site within the tract, and the authorization of public utility services for the Tantallon enterprise are as consistent with increased rural residential development as they are with the building of high-rise apartments. The characterization by the appellants of these alleged changes as "bootstrap" arguments, in our opinion, is appropriate. The report of the technical staff of the Planning Commission states that the development which has occurred within the area, including the Tantallon tract, has been a continuation and solidification of the single family dwelling pattern, with lots larger than the minimum standard, and this statement was not contradicted. The road improvements referred to by the Land Company do not change the character of the neighborhood; as the technical staff pointed out, "[t]he character of the surrounding area is reflected in the road network which consists of generally narrow, winding two-lane pavements designed to serve traffic volumes generated by low density, large lot development." The completion of the Woodrow Wilson Bridge and Anacostia Freeway listed as additional changes presumably were envisaged in the comprehensive zoning plan, adopted by the legislative body only a little less than five years before the Land Company's application. In any event, the Bridge and Freeway are some miles away.

The Planning Board, as well as its technical staff, recommended that the applications for the high-rise apartment rezoning be denied. The majority of the Council refused to accept the Board's recommendations, without substantive evidence to support its actions. In similar circumstances, although on varying facts, we have held that an order of the lower court affirming the Board's action must be reversed.

The Land Company does not contend that denial of the application would preclude the use of its property for any purpose to which it is reasonably adapted. On the contrary, it admitted it would be practical, although from its point of view not as satisfactory, to continue the development of Tantallon without high-rise apartments. The developer's desire to make additional profits is a legitimate motive, but not sufficient to justify a rezoning.

BARNES, J. (dissenting). . . .

[T]he majority's statement that the population boom, together with the new highways and bridges some miles away "presumably were envisaged in the comprehensive plan," does not seem justified to me. There is no evidence that they were so envisaged and the probabilities are strong that they were not. The situation in Prince George's County is too volatile to attribute such prophetic powers to those who prepared the "comprehensive" plan. . . .

The majority states, in effect, that rezoning can only be sustained when there is "strong evidence of mistake" in the original zoning or where there is "a substantial change in conditions" in the neighborhood. This "mistake-change in conditions" rule came into the Maryland law by way of dicta of our predecessors and in a rather oblique way. . . . It was entirely judicially conceived and delivered. It had no legislative assistance. It has had a rapid and, to my mind, unhealthy growth in the Maryland law. The formulae have become talismanic phrases now applied with Draconian severity to the rezoning efforts of the local legislative bodies, with unfortunate results. In my opinion, the time to re-examine the entire doctrine and its premises is long overdue. As it is entirely 'Judge-made," a change in, or broadening of, the doctrine would operate only prospectively and it would no way impair vested rights, inasmuch as it is not a rule of property. Under these circumstances, the doctrine of stare decisis is not a substantial obstacle in effecting a much-needed change. If my Brethren are reluctant to overrule or modify the "mistake-change" doctrine, I suggest with great respect, that the Legislative Council and ultimately the General Assembly give serious thought to a change by appropriate legislation.

Let us examine the syllogisms upon which this "change-or-mistake" rule rests. As I see them they are:

Major premise: The comprehensive zoning plan was a good plan when enacted; the plan is good today, if physical conditions have not changed. Minor premise: Physical conditions have not changed.

Conclusion: The plan is good today.

The "mistake" part of the "change-or-mistake" rule is founded on another such syllogism, equally grim, which goes like this:

Major premise: Today's plan is a good plan, but differs from the original plan; if physical conditions have not changed, the original plan must have been bad.

Minor premise: Physical conditions have not changed.

Conclusion: The original plan must have been bad.

The difficulty lies in the dependence upon the terms "good"—"bad"—"conditions", and the interpretation to be placed on each. Or, to put the matter a different way, the defect may lie in confining the term "conditions" to the connotation of "physical conditions." As a cursory glance at the Index to Legal Periodicals and to other compilations of journal topics will show, the ideas of planning and zoning, for the modern urban complex, have come a long way since that day in 1926 when Euclid, Ohio v. Ambler Realty Company first upheld the idea and practical application of zoning.

The "change-or-mistake" rule derived from the syllogisms above set forth is rendered erroneous by the simple truth: "Ideas change."

In my opinion, the correct rule in considering the validity of rezoning ordinances is whether or not the ordinance is unreasonable, arbitrary or capricious. . . .

There is a strong presumption in favor of the reasonableness of a zoning ordinance, but we have indicated that this presumption of reasonableness does not apply with the same weight or "with as great force" to a rezoning ordinance. . . . In my opinion, the presumption of reasonableness is just as strong in support of the rezoning ordinance as it was in support of the original zoning ordinance. This seems to be the general rule. . . .

If we broadened our perspective and raised our sights in the "change in conditions" portion of the rule to include changes in zoning concepts and philosophy and did not limit it to a change in physical conditions merely, the problem would be largely solved. The people's representatives would then be free to give effect to the new ideas and concepts; they would arise from the present Procrustean bed upon which we have placed them, with renewed vigor, to advance the public interest. The case at bar is an excellent example of the unfortunate effect of the presently restricted rule. . . .

Notes

1. Beall v. Montgomery County Council, 240 Md. 77, 212 A.2d 751, 761 (1965), decided only a few months after *MacDonald* and by the same court, sustained a zoning ordinance creating a similar multiple-family, high-rise planned residential zone. The court distinguished *MacDonald* on the facts: "[T]he factual situation there differed materially from that here presented. In the case at bar, there is an 'island' of land completely surrounding R-60 land. This situation did not exist in *MacDonald*." In Cardon Inv. v. Town of New Market, 466 A.2d 504 (Ct. Spec. App. 1983), the appellate court wrestled with the interstices of the change or mistake rule. The trial court held (and the appellate court agreed) that the town was correct when it asserted that the key date from which alleged changes should be measured was 1977, when a comprehensive rezoning ordinance was adopted in Frederick County, not, as Cardon asserted, 1959, the year "[t]he Board of County Commissioners adopted its first comprehensive zoning ordinance" and the year designated by the 1977 ordinance "for determining any changes or mistakes required to be shown for purposes of rezoning." Because there was no "substantial change in the character of the neighborhood" (as required by Maryland statute) since 1977, the courts' refusal to use 1959 was fatal to Cardon's efforts to sustain the board's approval of a rezoning that would have permitted the company to use the property, located just outside New Market's town limits, as a truck stop. The Maryland Court of Appeals affirmed, 302 Md. 77, 89, 485 A.2d 678, 684 (1984), noting that

> it is clear that the 1977 rezoning is comprehensive. The enacting legislation states that the ordinance is the result of over one year of studies, workshops and public hearings. These hearings and workshops were open to all citizens and were conducted in the smaller regional planning areas of the county. Following that action, approximately fourteen more public hearings were held. Thus the new zoning ordinance was well thought out, carefully considered, and extensively studied. In addition, the common needs of a particular area were presumably addressed by the regional hearings and workshops.

See also Barlow Burke Jr., *The Change-Mistake Rule and Zoning in Maryland*, 25 Am. U. L. Rev. 631 (1976); James W. Gladden Jr., *The Change or Mistake Rule: A Question of Flexibility*, 50 Miss. L.J. 375 (1979).

2. What is the quantum of evidence necessary to show a "change in conditions"? The appellee in Wells v. Pierpont, 253 Md. 554, 253 A.2d 749 (1969), bought his home in 1918; in 1965, "having reached the age of 81," he sold the property to a supermarket concern, conditioned on reclassification from Residence-6 (residence, one- and two-family) to Business-Local. Between 1962, when the property was zoned R-6, and 1965, one road on which the property abutted had been widened and "is . . . a major highway in [the] County"; the neighboring volunteer fire company's building was rebuilt with new kitchen facilities that accommodated 140 people at crab feasts and other social functions; a 22-acre tract one-half mile west of the property had been reclassified from R-6 to Residence-Apartments. The zoning board of appeals granted the reclassification and the trial court affirmed; the court of appeals reversed stating that "Pierpont has failed to sustain his 'onerous burden of proof' that substantial change occurred."

3. Mississippi has followed Maryland's lead in cases such as Fondren North Renaissance v. Mayor of Jackson, 749 So. 2d 974, 977 (Miss. 1999): ("It is well settled law that before a zoning board may reclassify property from one zone to another, there must be proof that either (1) there was a mistake in the original zoning, or (2) that the character of the neighborhood has changed to such an extent as to justify reclassification, and there was a public need for rezoning."). Many more state courts have turned down the invitation to adopt Maryland's approach. See, for example, Palermo Land Co. v. Planning Comm'n of Calcasieu Parish, 561 So. 2d 482, 489-91 (La. 1990); Lum Yip Kee, Ltd. v. Honolulu, 70 Haw. 179, 191 n.14, 767 P.2d 815, 822 n.14 (1989); and Willdel Realty, Inc. v. New Castle County, 281 A.2d 612, 614 (Del. 1971).

4. Virginia applies the change or mistake rule, too, but only in downzoning cases, that is, when the local government imposes a more restrictive zoning change on an unwilling landowner. In Board of Supervisors v. Snell Constr. Corp., 214 Va. 655, 659, 202 S.E. 2d 889, 893 (1974), the court explained:

> With respect to the validity of a piecemeal downzoning ordinance such as that here involved, we are of opinion that when an aggrieved landowner makes a *prima facie* showing that since enactment of the prior ordinance there has been no change in circumstances substantially affecting the public health, safety, or welfare, the burden of going forward with evidence of such mistake, fraud, or changed circumstances shifts to the governing body. If the governing body produces evidence sufficient to make reasonableness fairly debatable, the ordinance must be sustained. If not, the ordinance is unreasonable and void.[1]

In which context—requested or imposed rezonings—does the rule make more sense? Or, should jurisdictions follow New Mexico's lead and consider the "change or mistake criteria" in both contexts, but not "as strict, all-encompassing requirements, without which a zoning change will never be justified," as explained in Albuquerque Commons Partnership v. City Council of City of Albuquerque, 184 P.3d 411, 420 (N.M. 2008)?

---

1. The rule we adopt is similar to the rule applied in Maryland. "[To] sustain a piecemeal change [from the prior zoning], there must be *strong* evidence of mistake in the original zoning, or else of a substantial change in conditions." Board of County Comm'rs for Prince George's County v. Edmonds, 240 Md. 680, 687, 215 A.2d 209, 213 (1965). (Emphasis supplied). The Virginia rule differs from the Maryland rule is two important respects: (1) The Virginia rule is limited in application to piecemeal downzoning such as that here involved; and (2) The Virginia rule does not require the governing body to produce *strong* evidence, but evidence sufficient to render the issue of reasonableness "fairly debatable."

5. Maryland, the setting for *MacDonald* and the "change or mistake" rule, has had something of a reputation for municipal corruption, particularly in the area of land use regulation. National attention centered on Baltimore after Spiro Agnew—the former member of the Baltimore County board of zoning appeals who later served as governor—resigned in October 1973, as President Richard Nixon's vice president after filing a *nolo contendere* plea to federal tax charges growing out of unreported campaign contributions from contractors.

Ed McCahill, in *Stealing: A Primer on Zoning Corruption*, Planning, Dec. 1973, at 6, has reported:

> There were enough tips of icebergs to indicate to the editorial writers at the *Wall Street Journal* that the Agnew mess was a revolution in government: now even those in "planning . . . and other respectable-looking gents in business suits" who steal might get caught. The U.S. Attorney's office in Baltimore concurred. When *Planning* asked how there could be so much kickback money floating around without some zoning corruption, too, a spokesman noted dryly: "Everything in Baltimore County is for sale. We just haven't had time to get into it yet." Planning also called four members of the Baltimore County Planning Department who had been fired last year when they spoke out publicly against the real estate interests who were ripping up the county. Some said they often wondered whether or not their firing had to do with some of the real estate corruption. They all lamented the fact that the department, which has a planning commission noted for its progressiveness, now seemed to have a taint to it. (The man who fired the planners, County Administrative Officer William E. Fornoff, pleaded guilty to an income tax charge early in the Agnew affair.) In a kind of epitaph for Baltimore County, Fornoff told *Planning* in June 1972, "I'm getting out of here in the next two or three years. You've got to be loyal to the administration, but I don't think you should break yourself in half."

Of course, such corruption was not confined to the Old Line State. Consider the sordid facts from newspaper coverage of a New Jersey scandal. *Building in Ft. Lee, One Way or Another*, N.Y. Times, Sept. 15, 1974, at 198, reported that "a Federal grand jury has now charged that the firm . . . was so anxious to get to work that it tried to spend $1.4 million to bribe Ft. Lee public officials" to secure variances. A few months later, Frank J. Prial, in *Witness Tells of Chase to Bribe Ft. Lee Mayor*, N.Y. Times, March 19, 1975, at 101, related witness testimony of two men chasing the mayor through city hall, one of them shouting, "Pay him a million dollars!" The next segment of the sad story appeared in Walter H. Waggoner, *6 Defendants in Fort Lee Bribery Case Draw 5 Years in Prison and Big Fines*, N.Y. Times, June 4, 1975, at 83. Nearly three years later, Waggoner reported that *Terms Cut for 4 in Ft. Lee Bribery*, N.Y. Times, Feb. 4, 1978, at 1. In the interim, a federal appellate court in United States v. Dansker, 537 F.2d 40 (3d Cir. 1976), had ruled in favor of the defendants on two of the three conspiracy counts charged, reversing one and remanding the other.

The dawn of a new century did not cure zoning of its corruption virus, as is evident from reading Tom Bower's article, *Ex-Councilman Prado Gets 4 years in Prison*, San Antonio Express-News, Jan. 4, 2005, at 1B:

> Looking defiant but smiling courteously to court officials, former City Councilman Raul Prado was sentenced Monday to four years in prison for one count of conspiracy to commit bribery . . . .

> Prado and his protege, former City Councilman Enrique "Kike" Martin, entered into plea agreements Aug. 23, within hours of a deadline set by 175th District Judge Mary

Roman, who was about to order a change of venue to hold separate trials for the two in Houston.

"The judge, today, found Prado guilty as charged. He got caught," said Cliff Herberg, chief prosecutor of the white-collar crime division. "He wouldn't have pled guilty if he didn't think that a jury would have found him guilty as charged."

Herberg pointed out that although Prado and Martin each pleaded to a single bribery charge before the state court, the investigation netted 11 defendants and revealed a network that collected at least $55,000 in kickbacks. In exchange for the bribes, the pair exerted influence in contracting and zoning decisions made at City Hall and within the South San Antonio School District and the Alamo Community College District.

It became apparent to some judges and commentators that the "in accordance" and "change or mistake" approaches to checking rezoning abuses, though valiant efforts, were ultimately not effective enough to produce fair and objective decisionmaking, given the reality that money often talks loudly to public officials in the real estate development arena. The result was a re-conceived notion of the nature of the zoning amendment, in an attempt to distinguish small-scale changes from widespread ones.

FASANO v. BOARD OF COMMISSIONERS OF WASHINGTON COUNTY
264 Or. 574, 507 P.2d 23 (1973)

HOWELL, Justice.

The plaintiffs, homeowners in Washington County, unsuccessfully opposed a zone change before the Board of County Commissioners of Washington County. Plaintiffs applied for and received a writ of review of the action of the commissioners allowing the change. The trial court found in favor of plaintiffs, disallowed the zone change, and reversed the commissioners' order. The Court of Appeals affirmed, 489 P.2d 693 (1971), and this court granted review.

The defendants are the Board of County Commissioners and A.G.S. Development Company. A.G.S., the owner of 32 acres which had been zoned R-7 (Single Family Residential), applied for a zone change to P-R (Planned Residential), which allows for the construction of a mobile home park. The change failed to receive a majority vote of the Planning Commission. The Board of County Commissioners approved the change and found, among other matters, that the change allows for "increased densities and different types of housing to meet the needs of urbanization over that allowed by the existing zoning."

The trial court, relying on its interpretation of Roseta v. County of Washington, 254 Or. 161, 458 P.2d 405 (1969), reversed the order of the commissioners because the commissioners had not shown any change in the character of the neighborhood which would justify the rezoning. The Court of Appeals affirmed for the same reason, but added the additional ground that the defendants failed to show that the change was consistent with the comprehensive plan for Washington County.

According to the briefs, the comprehensive plan of development for Washington County was adopted in 1959 and included classifications in the county for residential, neighborhood commercial, retail commercial, general commercial, industrial park and light industry, general and heavy industry, and agricultural areas.

The land in question, which was designated "residential" by the comprehensive plan, was zoned R-7, Single Family Residential.

Subsequent to the time the comprehensive plan was adopted, Washington County established a Planned Residential (P-R) zoning classification in 1963. The P-R classification was adopted by ordinance and provided that a planned residential unit development could be established and should include open space for utilities, access, and recreation; should not be less than 10 acres in size; and should be located in or adjacent to a residential zone. The P-R zone adopted by the 1963 ordinance is of the type known as a "floating zone," so-called because the ordinance creates a zone classification authorized for future use but not placed on the zoning map until its use at a particular location is approved by the governing body. The R-7 classification for the 32 acres, continued until April 1970 when the classification was changed to P-R to permit the defendant A.G.S. to construct the mobile home park on the 32 acres involved. . . .

Any meaningful decision as to the proper scope of judicial review of a zoning decision must start with a characterization of the nature of that decision. The majority of jurisdictions state that a zoning ordinance is a legislative act and is thereby entitled to presumptive validity. . . .

At this juncture we feel we would be ignoring reality to rigidly view all zoning decisions by local governing bodies as legislative acts to be accorded a full presumption of validity and shielded from less than constitutional scrutiny by the theory of separation of powers. Local and small decision groups are simply not the equivalent in all respects of state and national legislatures. There is a growing judicial recognition of this fact of life:

> It is not a part of the legislative function to grant permits, make special exceptions, or decide particular cases. Such activities are not legislative but administrative, quasi judicial, or judicial in character. To place them in the hands of legislative bodies, whose acts as such are not judicially reviewable, is to open the door completely to arbitrary government.

Ward v. Village of Skokie, 26 Ill. 2d 415, 186 N.E.2d 529, 533 (1962) (Klingbiel, J., specially concurring).

The Supreme Court of Washington, in reviewing a rezoning decision, recently stated:

> Whatever descriptive characterization may be otherwise attached to the role or function of the planning commission in zoning procedures, e.g., advisory, recommendatory, investigatory, administrative or legislative, it is manifest . . . that it is a public agency, . . . a principle [sic] and statutory duty of which is to conduct public hearings in specified planning and zoning matters, enter findings of fact—often on the basis of disputed facts—and make recommendations with reasons assigned thereto. Certainly, in its role as a hearing and fact-finding tribunal, the planning commission's function more nearly than not partakes of the nature of an administrative, quasi judicial proceeding. . . .

Chrobuck v. Snohomish County, 78 Wash. 2d 884, 480 P.2d 489, 495-496 (1971).

Ordinances laying down general policies without regard to a specific piece of property are usually an exercise of legislative authority, are subject to limited review, and may only be attacked upon constitutional grounds for an arbitrary abuse of authority. On the other hand, a determination whether the permissible use of a specific piece of property should be changed is usually an exercise of judicial authority and its propriety is subject to an altogether different test. An illustration of an exercise of legislative authority is the passage of the ordinance by the Washington County Commission in 1963 which provided for the formation of a planned residential classification to be located in or adjacent to any residential zone. An exercise of judicial authority is the county commissioners' determination in this particular matter to change the classification of A.G.S. Development Company's specific piece of property. The distinction is stated, as follows, in Comment,

Zoning Amendments—The Product of Judicial or Quasi-Judicial Action, 33 Ohio St. L.J. 130 (1972):

> . . . Basically, this test involves the determination of whether action produces a general rule or policy which is applicable to an open class of individuals, interests, or situations, or whether it entails the application of a general rule or policy to specific individuals, interests, or situations. If the former determination is satisfied, there is legislative action; if the latter determination is satisfied, the action is judicial.

33 Ohio St. L.J. at 137.

> We reject the proposition that judicial review of the county commissioners' determination to change the zoning of the particular property in question is limited to a determination whether the change was arbitrary and capricious.

In order to establish a standard of review, it is necessary to delineate certain basic principles relating to land use regulation.

The basic instrument for county or municipal land use planning is the "comprehensive plan." Haar, In Accordance with a Comprehensive Plan, 68 Harv. L. Rev. 1154 (1955); 1 Yokley, Zoning Law and Practice, §3-2 (1965); 1 Rathkopf, The Law of Zoning and Planning §9-1 (3d ed. 1969). The plan has been described as a general plan to control and direct the use and development of property in a municipality. Nowicki v. Planning and Zoning Board, 148 Conn. 492, 172 A.2d 386, 389 (1961).

In Oregon the county planning commission is required by ORS 215.050 to adopt a comprehensive plan for the use of some or all of the land in the county. Under ORS 215.110 (1), after the comprehensive plan has been adopted, the planning commission recommends to the governing body of the county the ordinances necessary to "carry out" the comprehensive plan. The purpose of the zoning ordinances, both under our statute and the general law of land use regulation, is to "carry out" or implement the comprehensive plan. 1 Anderson, American Law of Zoning, §1.12 (1968). Although we are aware of the analytical distinction between zoning and planning, it is clear that under our statutes the plan adopted by the planning commission and the zoning ordinances enacted by the county governing body are closely related; both are intended to be parts of a single integrated procedure for land use control. The plan embodies policy determinations and guiding principles; the zoning ordinances provide the detailed means of giving effect to those principles.

ORS 215.050 states county planning commissions "shall adopt and may from time to time revise a comprehensive plan." In a hearing of the Senate Committee on Local Government, the proponents of ORS 215.050 described its purpose as follows:

> . . . The intent here is to require a basic document, geared into population, land use, and economic forecasts, which should be the basis of any zoning or other regulations to be adopted by the county. . . .

In addition, ORS 215.055 provides:

> 215.055 Standards for plan. (1) The plan and all legislation and regulations authorized by ORS 215.010 to 215.233 shall be designed to promote the public health, safety and general welfare and shall be based on the following considerations, among others: The various characteristics of the various areas in the county, the suitability of the areas for particular land uses and improvements, the land uses and improvements in the areas, trends in land improvement, density of development, property values, the needs of economic enterprises in the future development of the areas, needed access to particular

sites in the areas, natural resources of the county and prospective needs for development thereof, and the public need for healthful, safe, aesthetic surroundings and conditions.

We believe that the state legislature has conditioned the county's power to zone upon the prerequisite that the zoning attempt to further the general welfare of the community through consciousness, in a prospective sense, of the factors mentioned above. In other words, except as noted later in this opinion, it must be proved that the change is in conformance with the comprehensive plan.

In proving that the change is in conformance with the comprehensive plan in this case, the proof, at a minimum, should show (1) there is a public need for a change of the kind in question, and (2) that need will be best served by changing the classification of the particular piece of property in question as compared with other available property.

In the instant case the trial court and the Court of Appeals interpreted prior decisions of this court as requiring the county commissions to show a change of conditions within the immediate neighborhood in which the change was sought since the enactment of the comprehensive plan, or a mistake in the comprehensive plan as a condition precedent to the zone change. . .

However, *Roseta* [v. County of Washington, which the court discussed above in an omitted portion of its opinion] should not be interpreted as establishing a rule that a physical change of circumstances within the rezoned neighborhood is the only justification for rezoning. The county governing body is directed by ORS 215.055 to consider a number of other factors when enacting zoning ordinances, and the list there does not purport to be exclusive. The important issues, as *Roseta* recognized, are compliance with the statutory directive and consideration of the proposed change in light of the comprehensive plan.

Because the action of the commission in this instance is an exercise of judicial authority, the burden of proof should be placed, as is usual in judicial proceedings, upon the one seeking change. The more drastic the change, the greater will be the burden of showing that it is in conformance with the comprehensive plan as implemented by the ordinance, that there is a public need for the kind of change in question, and that the need is best met by the proposal under consideration. As the degree of change increases, the burden of showing that the potential impact upon the area in question was carefully considered and weighed will also increase. If other areas have previously been designated for the particular type of development, it must be shown why it is necessary to introduce it into an area not previously contemplated and why the property owners there should bear the burden of the departure.

Although we have said in *Roseta* that zoning changes may be justified without a showing of a mistake in the original plan or ordinance, or of changes in the physical characteristics of an affected area, any of these factors which are present in a particular case would, of course, be relevant. Their importance would depend upon the nature of the precise change under consideration.

By treating the exercise of authority by the commission in this case as the exercise of judicial rather than of legislative authority and thus enlarging the scope of review on appeal, and by placing the burden of the above level of proof upon the one seeking change, we may lay the court open to criticism by legal scholars who think it desirable that planning authorities be vested with the ability to adjust more freely to changed conditions. However, having weighed the dangers of making desirable change more difficult against the dangers of the almost irresistible pressures that can be asserted by private economic interests on local government, we believe that the latter dangers are more to be feared.

What we have said above is necessarily general, as the approach we adopt contains no absolute standards or mechanical tests. We believe, however, that it is adequate to provide meaningful guidance for local governments making zoning decisions and for trial courts called upon to review them. With future cases in mind, it is appropriate to add some brief remarks on questions of procedure. Parties at the hearing before the county governing body are entitled to an opportunity to be heard, to an opportunity to present and rebut evidence, to a tribunal which is impartial in the matter—i.e., having had no pre-hearing or ex parte contacts concerning the question at issue—and to a record made and adequate findings executed.

When we apply the standards we have adopted to the present case, we find that the burden was not sustained before the commission. The record now before us is insufficient to ascertain whether there was a justifiable basis for the decision. The only evidence in the record, that of the staff report of the Washington County Planning Department, is too conclusory and superficial to support the zoning change. It merely states:

> The staff finds that the requested use does conform to the residential designation of the Plan of Development. It further finds that the proposed use reflects the urbanization of the County and the necessity to provide increased densities and different types of housing to meet the needs of urbanization over that allowed by the existing zoning. . . .

Such generalizations and conclusions, without any statement of the facts on which they are based, are insufficient to justify a change of use. Moreover, no portions of the comprehensive plan of Washington County are before us, and we feel it would be improper for us to take judicial notice of the plan without at least some reference to its specifics by counsel.

As there has not been an adequate showing that the change was in accord with the plan, or that the factors listed in ORS 215.055 were given proper consideration, the judgment is affirmed.

BRYSON, J., specially concurring.

The basic facts in this case exemplify the prohibitive cost and extended uncertainty to a homeowner when a governmental body decides to change or modify a zoning ordinance or comprehensive plan affecting such owner's real property.

This controversy has proceeded through the following steps:

1. The respondent opposed the zone change before the Washington County Planning Department and Planning Commission.

2. The County Commission, after a hearing, allowed the change.

3. The trial court reversed (disallowed the change).

4. The Court of Appeals affirmed the trial court.

5. We ordered reargument and additional briefs.

6. This court affirmed.

The principal respondent in this case, Fasano, happens to be an attorney at law, and his residence is near the proposed mobile home park of the petitioner A.G.S. No average homeowner or small business enterprise can afford a judicial process such as described above nor can a judicial system cope with or endure such a process in achieving justice. The number of such controversies is ascending.

In this case the majority opinion, in which I concur, adopts some sound rules to enable county and municipal planning commissions and governing bodies, as well as trial courts, to reach finality in decision. However, the procedure is no panacea and it is still burdensome.

It is solely within the domain of the legislative branch of government to devise a new and simplified statutory procedure to expedite finality of decision.

Notes

1. Not surprisingly for a case that challenged nearly one-half century of judicial noninterference, *Fasano* received a mixed reception. Some courts have accepted and cited the Oregon justices' characterization of small-scale rezonings as "quasi judicial." For example, the Colorado high court, in Snyder v. City of Lakewood, 189 Colo. 421, 542 P.2d 371 (1975), upheld a challenge brought by neighboring residential landowners to the grant of a rezoning to a church: "[T]he enactment of a rezoning ordinance pursuant to the statutory criteria, after notice and a public hearing, constituted a quasi judicial function subject to certiorari review. This rule is in accord with the modern trend in zoning law" (citations, including *Fasano*, omitted).

The framers of the Model Land Development Code endorsed the spirit, and much of the substance, of *Fasano*. See, e.g., §2-312(2) and note.

Even a landowner frustrated by the city council's refusal to rezone for a more lucrative use has been able to take advantage of the court's heightened scrutiny. Golden v. City of Overland Park, 224 Kan. 591, 584 P.2d 130 (1978). Does such a holding make sense, given one of the prime motivations for judicial inquiry: the suspicion that the grant of a controversial zoning change is a result of undue economic influence?

Other states have resisted the movement. In State v. City of Rochester, 268 N.W.2d 885 (Minn. 1978), owners of residences surrounding the rezoned property challenged the action, relying on *Fasano*. The court's rejection was explicit:

> We decline to follow the rule applied in those jurisdictions, for we have consistently held that when a municipality adopts or amends a zoning ordinance, it acts in a legislative capacity under its delegated police powers. . . . Our narrow scope of review reflects a policy decision that a legislative body can best determine which zoning classifications best serve the public welfare.

The Michigan Supreme Court, in Sabo v. Monroe Township, 394 Mich. 531, 232 N.W.2d 584 (1975), leapt onto the *Fasano* bandwagon. A year later, in Kirk v. Township of Tyrone, 398 Mich. 427, 247 N.W.2d 848 (1976), a more deferential court reconsidered the leap:

> Upon reflection, it does not seem wise as *Sabo* did to attempt to engraft upon the established legislative scheme of zoning and rezoning, a new system which admittedly requires new legislative action to operate optimally. Should the Legislature choose to revise the approach to zoning amendments in our state, this Court would, of course, view matters differently.

Oregon legislators complemented the work of their co-equal branch by enacting §§227.160-.180 of the Oregon Revised Statutes (Planning and Zoning Hearings and Review).

2. The most important state to follow Oregon's lead, Florida, is a jurisdiction also known for a strong state presence in the planning process and for intense pro-development pressures. The next case introduces the Sunshine State's spin on the legislative-judicial distinction in rezoning cases.

BOARD OF COUNTY COMMISSIONERS v. SNYDER
627 So. 2d 469 (Fla. 1993)

GRIMES, J. . . .

Jack and Gail Snyder owned a one-half acre parcel of property on Merritt Island in the unincorporated area of Brevard County. The property is zoned GU (general use) which allows construction of a single-family residence. The Snyders filed an application to rezone their property to the

RU-2-15 zoning classification which allows the construction of fifteen units per acre. The area is designated for residential use under the 1988 Brevard County Comprehensive Plan Future Land Use Map. Twenty-nine zoning classifications are considered potentially consistent with this land use designation, including both the GU and the RU-2-15 classifications.

After the application for rezoning was filed, the Brevard County Planning and Zoning staff reviewed the application and completed the county's standard "rezoning review worksheet." The worksheet indicated that the proposed multifamily use of the Snyders' property was consistent with all aspects of the comprehensive plan except for the fact that it was located in the one-hundred-year flood plain in which a maximum of only two units per acre was permitted. For this reason, the staff recommended that the request be denied.

At the planning and zoning board meeting, the county planning and zoning director indicated that when the property was developed the land elevation would be raised to the point where the one-hundred-year-flood plain restriction would no longer be applicable. Thus, the director stated that the staff no longer opposed the application. The planning and zoning board voted to approve the Snyders' rezoning request.

When the matter came before the board of county commissioners, Snyder stated that he intended to build only five or six units on the property. However, a number of citizens spoke in opposition to the rezoning request. Their primary concern was the increase in traffic which would be caused by the development. Ultimately, the commission voted to deny the rezoning request without stating a reason for the denial.

The Snyders filed a petition for certiorari in the circuit court. Three circuit judges, sitting en banc, reviewed the petition and denied it by a two-to-one decision. The Snyders then filed a petition for certiorari in the Fifth District Court of Appeal.

The district court of appeal acknowledged that zoning decisions have traditionally been considered legislative in nature. Therefore, courts were required to uphold them if they could be justified as being "fairly debatable." Drawing heavily on Fasano v. Board of County Commissioners, 264 Ore. 574, 507 P.2d 23 (Or. 1973), however, the court concluded that, unlike initial zoning enactments and comprehensive rezonings or rezonings affecting a large portion of the public, a rezoning action which entails the application of a general rule or policy to specific individuals, interests, or activities is quasi-judicial in nature. Under the latter circumstances, the court reasoned that a stricter standard of judicial review of the rezoning decision was required. . . . [T]he [appeals] court found (1) that the Snyders' petition for rezoning was consistent with the comprehensive plan; (2) that there was no assertion or evidence that a more restrictive zoning classification was necessary to protect the health, safety, morals, or welfare of the general public; and (3) that the denial of the requested zoning classification without reasons supported by facts was, as a matter of law, arbitrary and unreasonable. The court granted the petition for certiorari. . . .

Historically, local governments have exercised the zoning power pursuant to a broad delegation of state legislative power subject only to constitutional limitations. Both federal and state courts adopted a highly deferential standard of judicial review early in the history of local zoning. In Village of Euclid v. Ambler Realty Co., 272 U.S. 365 (1926), the United States Supreme Court held that "if the validity of the legislative classification for zoning purposes be fairly debatable, the legislative judgment must be allowed to control." 272 U.S. at 388. This Court expressly adopted the fairly debatable principle in City of Miami Beach v. Ocean & Inland Co., 147 Fla. 480, 3 So. 2d 364 (1941).

Inhibited only by the loose judicial scrutiny afforded by the fairly debatable rule, local zoning systems developed in a markedly inconsistent manner. Many land use experts and practitioners have been critical of the local zoning system. Richard Babcock deplored the effect of "neighborhoodism" and rank political influence on the local decision-making process. Richard F. Babcock, The Zoning Game (1966). Mandelker and Tarlock recently stated that "zoning decisions are too often ad hoc, sloppy and self-serving decisions with well-defined adverse consequences without off-setting benefits." Daniel R. Mandelker and A. Dan Tarlock, *Shifting the Presumption of Constitutionality in Land-Use Law*, 24 Urb. Law. 1, 2 (1992).

Professor Charles Haar, a leading proponent of zoning reform, was an early advocate of requiring that local land use regulation be consistent with a legally binding comprehensive plan which would serve long range goals, counteract local pressures for preferential treatment, and provide courts with a meaningful standard of review. Charles M. Haar, *"In Accordance With A Comprehensive Plan,"* 68 Harv. L. Rev. 1154 (1955). In 1975, the American Law Institute adopted the Model Land Development Code, which provided for procedural and planning reforms at the local level and increased state participation in land use decision-making for developments of regional impact and areas of critical state concern.

Reacting to the increasing calls for reform, numerous states have adopted legislation to change the local land use decision-making process. As one of the leaders of this national reform, Florida adopted the Local Government Comprehensive Planning Act of 1975. Ch. 75-257, Laws of Fla. This law was substantially strengthened in 1985 by the Growth Management Act. Ch. 85-55, Laws of Fla.

Pursuant to the Growth Management Act, each county and municipality is required to prepare a comprehensive plan for approval by the Department of Community Affairs. The adopted local plan must include "principles, guidelines, and standards for the orderly and balanced future economic, social, physical, environmental, and fiscal development" of the local government's jurisdictional area. § 163.3177(1), Fla. Stat. (1991). At the minimum, the local plan must include elements covering future land use; capital improvements generally; sanitary sewer, solid waste, drainage, potable water, and natural ground water aquifer protection specifically; conservation; recreation and open space; housing; traffic circulation; intergovernmental coordination; coastal management (for local government in the coastal zone); and mass transit (for local jurisdictions with 50,000 or more people).

Of special relevance to local rezoning actions, the future land use plan element of the local plan must contain both a future land use map and goals, policies, and measurable objectives to guide future land use decisions. This plan element must designate the "proposed future general distribution, location, and extent of the uses of land" for various purposes. *Id.* § 163.3177(6)(a). It must include standards to be utilized in the control and distribution of densities and intensities of development. In addition, the future land use plan must be based on adequate data and analysis concerning the local jurisdiction, including the projected population, the amount of land needed to accommodate the estimated population, the availability of public services and facilities, and the character of undeveloped land.

The local plan must be implemented through the adoption of land development regulations that are consistent with the plan. In addition, all development, both public and private, and all development orders approved by local governments must be consistent with the adopted local plan. Section 163.3194(3), Florida Statutes (1991), explains consistency as follows:

> (a) A development order or land development regulation shall be consistent with the comprehensive plan if the land uses, densities or intensities, and other aspects of development permitted by such order or regulation are compatible with and further the objectives, policies, land uses, and densities or intensities in the comprehensive plan and if it meets all other criteria enumerated by the local government.

Section 163.3164, Florida Statutes (1991), reads in pertinent part:

(6) "Development order" means any order granting, denying, or granting with conditions an application for a development permit.

(7) "Development permit" includes any building permit, zoning permit, subdivision approval, rezoning, certification, special exception, variance, or any other official action of local government having the effect of permitting the development of land.

Because an order granting or denying rezoning constitutes a development order and development orders must be consistent with the comprehensive plan, it is clear that orders on rezoning applications must be consistent with the comprehensive plan.

The first issue we must decide is whether the Board's action on Snyder's rezoning application was legislative or quasi-judicial. A board's legislative action is subject to attack in circuit court. However, in deference to the policy-making function of a board when acting in a legislative capacity, its actions will be sustained as long as they are fairly debatable. On the other hand, the rulings of a board acting in its quasi-judicial capacity are subject to review by certiorari and will be upheld only if they are supported by substantial competent evidence.

Enactments of original zoning ordinances have always been considered legislative. In Schauer v. City of Miami Beach, this Court held that the passage of an amending zoning ordinance was the exercise of a legislative function. 112 So. 2d at 839. However, the amendment in that case was comprehensive in nature in that it effected a change in the zoning of a large area so as to permit it to be used as locations for multiple family buildings and hotels. . . .

It is the character of the hearing that determines whether or not board action is legislative or quasi-judicial. Generally speaking, legislative action results in the formulation of a general rule of policy, whereas judicial action results in the application of a general rule of policy. In West Flagler Amusement Co. v. State Racing Commission, 122 Fla. 222, 225, 165 So. 64, 65 (1935), we explained:

> A judicial or quasi-judicial act determines the rules of law applicable, and the rights affected by them, in relation to past transactions. On the other hand, a quasi-legislative or administrative order prescribes what the rule or requirement of administratively determined duty shall be with respect to transactions to be executed in the future, in order that same shall be considered lawful. But even so, quasi-legislative and quasi-executive orders, after they have already been entered, may have a quasi-judicial attribute if capable of being arrived at and provided by law to be declared by the administrative agency only after express statutory notice, hearing and consideration of evidence to be adduced as a basis for the making thereof.

Applying this criterion, it is evident that comprehensive rezonings affecting a large portion of the public are legislative in nature. However, we agree with the court below when it said:

> Rezoning actions which have an impact on a limited number of persons or property owners, on identifiable parties and interests, where the decision is contingent on a fact or facts arrived at from distinct alternatives presented at a hearing, and where the decision can be functionally viewed as policy application, rather than policy setting, are in the nature of . . . quasi-judicial action . . . .

Snyder, 595 So. 2d at 78. Therefore, the board's action on Snyder's application was in the nature of a quasi-judicial proceeding and properly reviewable by petition for certiorari.

We also agree with the court below that the review is subject to strict scrutiny. In practical effect, the review by strict scrutiny in zoning cases appears to be the same as that given in the review of other quasi-judicial decisions. See Lee County v. Sunbelt Equities, II, Ltd. Partnership,

619 So. 2d 996 (Fla. 2d DCA 1993) (The term "strict scrutiny" arises from the necessity of strict compliance with comprehensive plan.). This term as used in the review of land use decisions must be distinguished from the type of strict scrutiny review afforded in some constitutional cases. . . .

Upon consideration, we hold that a landowner seeking to rezone property has the burden of proving that the proposal is consistent with the comprehensive plan and complies with all procedural requirements of the zoning ordinance. At this point, the burden shifts to the governmental board to demonstrate that maintaining the existing zoning classification with respect to the property accomplishes a legitimate public purpose. In effect, the landowners' traditional remedies will be subsumed within this rule, and the board will now have the burden of showing that the refusal to rezone the property is not arbitrary, discriminatory, or unreasonable. If the board carries its burden, the application should be denied.

While they may be useful, the board will not be required to make findings of fact. However, in order to sustain the board's action, upon review by certiorari in the circuit court it must be shown that there was competent substantial evidence presented to the board to support its ruling. . . .

Notes

1. Is the "strict scrutiny" approach an improvement over *Fasano* and over the change-mistake rule, or does its easy confusion with constitutional law damn the phrase to misuse and confusion? If the judiciary mandates strict compliance with the comprehensive plan, then why not just ask the local legislature to amend the plan? Martin County v. Yusem, 690 So. 2d 1288, 1289, 1293-94 (1997) answered "no" to the following question: "Can a rezoning decision which has limited impact under *Snyder*, but does require an amendment of the comprehensive land use plan, still be a quasi-judicial decision subject to strict scrutiny review?" The state supreme court explained the "two-stage process for amending a comprehensive plan: transmittal and adoption":

> In the first stage, the local government determines whether to transmit the proposed amendment to the Department [the Florida Department of Community Affairs] for further review. See § 163.3184(3) Fla. Stat. If the local government transmits the proposed amendment, the process moves into the second stage. The Department, after receiving the amendment, provides the local government with its objections, recommendations for modifications, and comments of any other regional agencies. At this point, the local government has three options: (1) adopt the amendment; (2) adopt the amendment with changes; or (3) not adopt the amendment.

> Upon adoption of the amendment by the local government, the Department again reviews the amendment. After this review and an administrative hearing, if an amendment is determined not to be in compliance with the Act, the State Comprehensive Plan, and the Department's minimum criteria rule, then the matter is referred to the Administration Commission. The Administration Commission, composed of the Governor and the Cabinet, is then empowered to levy sanctions against a local government, including directing state agencies not to provide the local government with funding for future projects.

> This integrated review process ensures that the policies and goals of the Act are followed. The strict oversight on the several levels of government to further the goals of the Act is evidence that when a local government is amending its comprehensive plan, it is engaging in a policy decision. This is in contrast to a rezoning proceeding, which is only evaluated on the local level. *See Snyder*.

The court then described the nature of the decision-making process regarding a plan amendment:

> In contrast to the rezonings at issue in *Snyder*, the review of the proposed amendment here required the County to engage in policy reformulation of its comprehensive plan and to determine whether it now desired to retreat from the policies embodied in its future land use map for the orderly development of the County's future growth. The county was required to evaluate the likely impact such amendment would have on the county's provision of local services, capital expenditures, and its overall plan for growth and future development of the surrounding area. The decision whether to allow the proposed amendment to the land use plan to proceed to the DCA for its review and then whether to adopt the amendment involved considerations well beyond the landowner's 54 acres.

Accordingly, the court concluded "that amendments to comprehensive land use plans are legislative decisions. This conclusion is not affected by the fact that the amendments to comprehensive land use plans are being sought as part of a rezoning application in respect to only one piece of property."

2. While Florida's growth management legislation provides a limit of two comprehensive plan amendments per calendar year in Fla. Stat. §163.3187, there are exceptions for emergencies ("any occurrence or threat thereof whether accidental or natural, caused by humankind, in war or peace, which results or may result in substantial injury or harm to the population or substantial damage to or loss of property or public funds"), for "developments of regional impact" (defined in Fla. Stat. §380.06(1) as "any development which, because of its character, magnitude, or location, would have a substantial effect upon the health, safety, or welfare of citizens of more than one county"), and for "small scale developments" of ten or fewer acres subject to a long list of statutory requirements. Not surprisingly, the state courts were asked whether *Snyder*'s strict compliance mandate would apply to a small-scale development amendment to the comprehensive plan. In Coastal Dev. of N. Fla. v. City of Jacksonville Beach, 788 So. 2d 204, 207, 208-09 (2001), the state supreme court followed its approach in *Yusem*, in the process even further cabining the "strict scrutiny" approach. Although the court noted that "[u]nlike regular comprehensive plan amendments, small-scale development amendments only require one reading for adoption by the local government, are not constrained by the two-amendments-per-year rule, and are not subject to mandatory review by the Department [of Community Affairs]," and that they "may not involve a change to the textual goals, policies, or objectives of the comprehensive plan," the justices were persuaded by the following argument:

> [A]mendments to a legislatively adopted statement of general policy are legislative acts. Even if the comprehensive plan amendment consists of an amendment to the comprehensive plan's future land use map [FLUM] which is applicable only to a single tract of land, the amendment should be deemed legislative. The future land use plan map alone does not determine or control the uses which can be made of a particular tract of land. Rather, the comprehensive plan as a whole, including the future land use map and all of the other policies of the plan, consists of legislative policies that must be applied to determine what uses can be made of a specific tract of land.
>
> Thomas G. Pelham, Quasi-Judicial Rezonings: *A Commentary on the Snyder Decision and the Consistency Requirement*, 9 J. Land Use & Envtl. L. 243, 300-301 (1994).

Building on this analysis, the court concluded that there was a distinction between this case and *Snyder* that made a difference:

By its very nature, a proposed amendment to the FLUM, as an element of the comprehensive plan, requires policy reformulation because the amendment seeks a change to the FLUM. However, a proposed zoning change under *Snyder* must be consistent with the FLUM, thus requiring policy application instead of policy reformulation.

3. Disgruntled citizens, frustrated by the ease with which developers have secured comprehensive plan amendments and exploited the loopholes in statutory and decisional law, have organized the Florida Hometown Democracy campaign. Cloaking itself in environmentalist robes, the campaign supports a ballot measure that would add the following language to the state constitution:

Public participation in local government comprehensive land use planning benefits the conservation and protection of Florida's natural resources and scenic beauty, and the long-term quality of life of Floridians. Therefore, before a local government may adopt a new comprehensive land use plan, or amend a comprehensive land use plan, such proposed plan or plan amendment shall be subject to vote of the electors of the local government by referendum, following preparation by the local planning agency, consideration by the governing body as provided by general law, and notice thereof in a local newspaper of general circulation. Notice and referendum will be as provided by general law.

Amendment 4 will be placed on the ballot in November 2010.

4. Professor Carol Rose, in *Planning and Dealing: Piecemeal Land Controls as a Problem of Local Legitimacy*, 71 Cal. L. Rev. 837, 853-57 (1983), has turned to the nation's early history for guidance in deciphering the local "legislative" puzzle posed by zoning and related cases:

One reason that a local representative body is not a legislature is the mere fact of its subordination to a state government. Municipalities, after all, are creatures of the state rather than independent "sovereigns." But this answer is too easy. *Fasano* may have cited administrative law cases, but local governments are not merely administrative bodies that fill in the interstices of statutes passed by state legislatures, or that carry out preestablished state policies. Rather, they exercise wide police powers within their jurisdictions, at least insofar as state legislation is not preemptive. Indeed, many state constitutions guarantee the local powers of home rule against state legislative incursions. Moreover, local governing councils, like larger legislatures, are composed of elected representatives for fixed terms of office. Why, then, even despite subordination to state government, are local governments not "legislative" bodies?

As one pair of administrative law authors has said, the American understanding of governance through separate branches was "developed by Locke and Montesquieu and refined by Madison."[57] Madison's chief refinement has to do precisely with the legislature, and with the qualities that make a legislature's decisions fair and reliable. His celebrated The Federalist No. 10 merits study here, for it suggests why a local elected government should not always be seen as a legislature.

Madison's essay begins with the argument that the chief obstacle to fairness in a legislative body is "faction": the tendency of one interest group to impose its will at the expense of others. The antidote to faction, Madison says, lies in a constituency of sufficient size and variety; The Federalist No. 10 argued that the great advantage of the "extended republic" (i.e., the proposed national government) was that it would contain

---

57. S. Breyer [this is future Supreme Court Justice Stephen Breyer] & R. Stewart, Administrative Law and Regulatory Policy 37 (1979). *See also* D. Walker, Toward a Functioning Federalism 23-43, 227-28 (1981).

such a variety of interests that no one "faction" could tyrannize the others. Where the constituency is large, action is possible only through persuasion and coalitions of interest groups. Through a pattern of shifting alliances and vote trading, every interest can obtain at least partial satisfaction in the legislature of the "extended republic." . . .

A legislative body drawn from too small or too homogeneous a constituency may be dominated by a single, interest or faction. Factional domination may take varying forms. One is sheer corruption, made possible in smaller representative bodies because a limited number of persons have influence which must be bought. Another possibility is domination by a few who are perceived by others as the powerful. The decisions of these few can affect many within the community; others must curry their favor, and even larger interests find difficulty in organizing against their "cabals." Finally, and perhaps most feared by Madison, is the factional domination created by a popular "passion"— sometimes a sudden whim, sometimes a longstanding prejudice—that carries a majority before it. Under any of these various forms of factional domination, all of which are far more likely to occur in a smaller legislature than in a larger one, a dominant group may subject others to sudden destruction or to permanent political disability. . . .

It seems, then, that any model suggesting that local governments are just like larger legislative bodies is unrealistic. It follows that courts should not give local governments' ad hoc land decisions the deference they accord to measures taken by state legislatures. *Fasano*'s plan jurisprudence attempts to solve the problem by agreeing that the local government is not a true legislature; rather, it is more like a court, and its decisions should therefore be made according to judicial standards. The substantive standards for these adjudicative decisions derive from the locality's own plan; the procedures derive from the courts.

5. Here are some proposed solutions to the unrelenting pressure developers seeking zoning changes sometimes exert on public officials, proffered by the National Institute of Law Enforcement and Criminal Justice, in *An Analysis of Zoning Reforms: Minimizing the Incentive for Corruption* vi (1979):

Summary Classification of Problems and Proposed Reforms

Secrecy and Lack of Accountability
> Separate administrative from legislative roles; set up proper procedures. Pass related legislation:
> Sunshine laws
> Financial disclosure law
> Freedom of information law
> Conflict of interest law
> Sunset laws.

Complexity of Procedures
> Establish hearing examiners
> Set up land-use task force
> Define administrative procedures
> Clarify ordinances
> Divide political decision-making from technical decision-making.

Lack of Standards

Establish mandatory planning

Make zoning dependent on plans

Use appropriate technological approaches.

Land Speculation

Remove zoning altogether

Establish windfall and wipeout provisions

Buy and sell zoning

Establish a government land bank.[3]

How realistic are the proposed reforms? Is municipal corruption—the stuff of movies (*Chinatown*, *Against All Odds*, to name but two)—an inevitable byproduct of local democracy? Would private sector exchanges of development rights be any less fraught with intimidation and graft?

6. The question of whether a zoning decision is legislative or quasi-judicial in nature may also determine the outcome of a legal challenge based on alleged conflict of interest. For example, in a pre-*Snyder* case, the Miami Beach City Council voted to change the zoning on an extensive area fronting on the Atlantic Ocean from a private residence or estate district to a multiple-family or hotel district. One of the affirmative votes was cast by a council member holding a personal interest in some of the property affected, which would be increased in value by more than $500,000 as a result of this change in zoning. In City of Miami Beach v. Schauer, 104 So. 2d 129, 131 (Fla. App. 1958), a pre-*Snyder* decision, the court, noting that the city council was acting in legislative capacity, stated: "It is well settled that the motives of the governing body of a municipal corporation, in adopting an ordinance legislative in character, will not be the subject of judicial inquiry." For a contrary view, see Aldom v. Borough of Roseland, 42 N.J. Super. 495, 508, 127 A.2d 190, 197 (1956) ("It is true that review of a purely legislative act of a local governing body is normally beyond the judicial orbit except in the instances stated. However, here the function [a rezoning] was not exclusively legislative; it partook sufficiently of the quasi-judicial to warrant examination by the courts.").

Perhaps there is a statutory solution to this problem. Consider the following sentence from such a statute in Connecticut: "No member of any zoning commission or board and no member of any zoning board of appeals shall participate in the hearing or decision of the board or commission of which he is a member upon any matter in which he is directly or indirectly interested in a personal or financial sense." Conn. Gen. Stat. §8-11. Can a board member participate in a decision affecting the property of her brother-in-law? Her employer? A small client of the board member's larger law firm? A potential employer? A friend with whom the board member sometimes plays golf? Consider these words from Anderson v. Zoning Commission of Norwalk, 157 Conn. 285, 291, 253 A.2d 16, 20 (1968), a case construing the Connecticut statute:

Local governments would . . . be seriously handicapped if any conceivable interest, no matter how remote and speculative, would require the disqualification of a zoning

---

3. Authors' note: The report explained that

[e]very proposed reform has its advantages and drawbacks. It is our conclusion that the best hope for zoning reform which touches the underlying issues involved in zoning corruption lies in the procedural safeguards suggested in the *Fasano* decision and the ALI code. Strict procedures, if followed, will have the additional effect of putting pressure on legislative bodies to provide clearer and more definite standards. Though the other methods of reform offer promise, the institution of procedural reforms directly reaches into the zoning process and appears to be the broadest reform and the one most likely to be accepted by the public at this time. Public scrutiny and public participation is the best protection against corruption, and strict procedures for reviewing and administering zoning appear to offer the best support for these activities.

official. If this were so, it would not only discourage but might even prevent capable men and women from serving as members of the various zoning authorities.

As explained in Raynes v. City of Leavenworth, 118 Wash. 2d 237, 245, 821 P.2d 1204, 1208 (1992), the Supreme Court of Washington developed the "appearance of fairness doctrine" in Smith v. Skagit Cy., 75 Wash. 2d 715, 453 P.2d 832 (1969),

> to ensure fair hearings by legislative bodies. The doctrine requires that public hearings which are adjudicatory in nature meet two requirements: the hearing itself must be procedurally fair, and it must be conducted by impartial decisionmakers. The doctrine provides:
>
>> It is axiomatic that, whenever the law requires a hearing of any sort as a condition precedent to the power to proceed, it means a fair hearing, a hearing not only fair in substance, but fair in appearance as well.

Three years later, in Fleming v. Tacoma, 81 Wash. 2d 292, 299, 502 P.2d 327 (1972), the same court held that the doctrine applied to rezoning hearings by local legislative bodies. In 1982, however, the state legislature limited the doctrine's applicability to land use decisionmaking. Rev. Code Wash. §42.36.010 provides:

> Application of the appearance of fairness doctrine to local land use decisions shall be limited to the quasi-judicial actions of local decision-making bodies as defined in this section. Quasi-judicial actions of local decision-making bodies are those actions of the legislative body, planning commission, hearing examiner, zoning adjuster, board of adjustment, or boards which determine the legal rights, duties, or privileges of specific parties in a hearing or other contested case proceeding. Quasi-judicial actions do not include the legislative actions adopting, amending, or revising comprehensive, community, or neighborhood plans or other land use planning documents or the adoption of area-wide zoning ordinances or the adoption of a zoning amendment that is of area-wide significance.

This provision was supplemented, by Rev. Code Wash. §42.36.030, which specifies that "[n]o legislative action taken by a local legislative body, its members, or local executive officials shall be invalidated by an application of the appearance of fairness doctrine." Against this fluid legal backdrop, the *Raynes* court decided that a city council's decision to pass an amendment authorizing recreational vehicle (RV) parks as conditional uses in the Tourist Commercial district was legislative in nature, and that it survived the arbitrary and capricious standard of review applicable, despite the allegation that the landowner seeking the change and one of the city council members who voted in favor of the amendment were agents for the same real estate company.

MENDOTA GOLF, LLP v. CITY OF MENDOTA HEIGHTS
708 N.W.2d 162 (Minn. 2006)

ANDERSON, Paul H., Justice. . . .

Mendota Golf, LLP, owns a 17.5-acre tract of real property located at the intersection of Dodd Road and Bachelor Avenue in the City of Mendota Heights. Since the early 1960s, the property has been used and operated as a nine-hole par 3 golf course. At present, the character of the neighborhood surrounding the property is residential.

When Mendota Golf acquired the property in January 1995, the city's zoning ordinance designated the property as Residential (R-1 One-Family Residential), while the city's comprehensive plan designated the property as "Golf Course" (GC). At that time, the Metropolitan Land Planning Act (MLPA) provided that a city's zoning designations took priority over conflicting comprehensive plan designations. Minn. Stat. § 473.858, subd. 1 (1994). In R-1 one-family residential districts, "one-family detached dwellings" are a permitted use and golf courses are a conditional use. The comprehensive plan and zoning designations for the property have not changed since 1995. Mendota Golf asserts that it purchased the property with the understanding that if the golf course proved unprofitable, it had the "safety net of developing the Land Parcel at some later point in time."

During the 1995 legislative session, the legislature amended the MLPA by adding a provision directing local government units to reconcile conflicts between comprehensive plans and zoning ordinances. Act of May 17, 1995, ch. 176, § 5, 1995 Minn. Laws 593, 594-95. The amended statute, which became effective on August 1, 1995, provides in relevant part:

> If the comprehensive municipal plan is in conflict with the zoning ordinance, the zoning ordinance shall be brought into conformance with the plan by local government units in conjunction with the review, and, if necessary, amendment of its comprehensive plan required under section 473.864, subdivision 2.[4] After August 1, 1995, a local government unit shall not adopt any fiscal device or official control which is in conflict with its comprehensive plan, including any amendment to the plan, or which permits activity in conflict with metropolitan system plans * * *.

Minn. Stat. § 473.858, subd. 1 (2004) (footnotes added). The amended statute also provides that an official control "shall not be considered to be in conflict with a local government unit's comprehensive plan" if the official control "is adopted to ensure the planned, orderly, and staged development of urbanization or redevelopment areas designated in the comprehensive plan." Id.[5]

Mendota Heights asserts that it "has a long history and commitment to planning which has resulted in unique residential living environments and business centers." The city adopted its first land use plan in 1960, even before the MLPA went into effect and required communities to do such planning. The 1960 plan focused on "high quality residential neighborhoods, open space and parks and well-planned commercial and industrial areas."

In 1979, the city adopted a comprehensive plan that incorporated regional policies and guidelines under the MLPA. The 1979 comprehensive plan placed the subject property in the land use category "(GC) Golf Course" and "guided" the land on all sides of the property as Low-Density Residential. At the time, single-family residential development surrounded the property to the north, south, and west, but the land across Dodd Road to the east was undeveloped.

The city's 1979 comprehensive plan also set forth certain planning goals, which were reaffirmd in 2002. The goals from the 1979 plan that are most relevant to this case are: (1) maintaining the community character and identity; (2) resisting the deterioration of the environment; (3) maintaining the existing residential areas; (4) providing the optimum amount of active and passive open space for the enjoyment of all of the city's residents; (5) encouraging the preservation of open space in the community by private property owners in a manner consistent with the comprehensive plan; (6) encouraging planned usage of existing private recreational facilities in order to avoid duplication and promote maximum enjoyment of all citizens in the city; (7) providing each neighborhood

---

4. This section of the statute provides that local governments shall review and, if necessary, amend their comprehensive plans and fiscal devices and official controls by December 31, 1998, and at least once every 10 years thereafter. Minn. Stat. § 473.864, subd. 2 (2004).

5. The amended statute applies to local government units within the seven-county metropolitan area. Act of May 17, 1995, ch. 176, § 12, 1995 Minn. Laws 593, 598. Mendota Heights is located in Dakota County and is subject to the statute.

in the city with open space; and (8) preserving and enhancing the natural beauty, uniqueness, and attractive appearance of the community.

The city adopted the 2002 comprehensive plan after engaging in a three-year review process during which several public hearings were held. When the city adopted the 2002 comprehensive plan, it reaffirmed that its goals and policies remain consistent with its original vision for development. Included among the 2002 goals and policies is the preservation of green spaces, open spaces, and recreational facilities.

Low-Density Residential (LR) is the most prevalent land use category in the 2002 comprehensive plan. Land designated as LR may be developed with single-family residences at a density of not more than 2.9 units per acre. The corresponding zoning classifications for LR are all One-Family Residential: R-1, R-1B, and R-1C. Other land use categories in the comprehensive plan include Commercial (LB and B), Industrial (I), Mixed Use--Planned Unit Development (MU--PUD), Public (PUB), Open Space (OS), Institutional (INS), and Golf Course (GC).

As part of its process of updating the comprehensive plan, the city "reviewed a number of parcels within the community for consistency between the Zoning Map and Comprehensive Land Use Plan." The city apparently was anticipating the possibility that the character of some of these parcels would change. These parcels were designated as "Infill Sites" in the city's Technical Plan. Mendota Golf's property is one of the parcels designated as an infill site. The Technical Plan indicates that the zoning designation for the property is R-1 and states:

> This site is currently a par-3 golf course and is guided as GC. This designation is proposed to remain. In the event that future redevelopment of this site is contemplated, careful consideration would need to be given to develop the site in a manner consistent with and sensitive to the existing low-density residential neighborhood.

Despite published notice of the city's plans to revise its comprehensive plan, Mendota Golf did not appear before the city to request alternate "guiding" of the property.

Under the 2002 comprehensive plan, all three golf courses in the city, including Mendota Golf's property, are designated as "Golf Course." According to the comprehensive plan:

> The Golf Course land use designation is intended to distinguish the commercial/recreation/open space characteristics associated with golf courses. The corresponding zoning district classifications are R-1, R-1A (One Family Residential) and R-2 (Medium Density Residential District).[6]

---

6. Mendota Golf's property, as well as the city's two other golf courses, are identified in the city's Park Plan as "open space."

Under the city's zoning ordinance, golf courses are a conditional use within these residential districts. The city apparently has not taken any steps to create a special zoning district classification for golf courses that corresponds to the Golf Course land use designation in the comprehensive plan.[7]

In 2003, Mendota Golf decided to sell its property to a developer that planned to dismantle the golf course and build single-family homes. Mendota Golf entered into a purchase agreement with the developer that conditioned the sale of the property on "the buyer's obtaining necessary governmental approvals for proposed residential development." The developer's proposed residential development would eliminate the open space and recreational uses that the property presently provides to the city.

After entering into the purchase agreement, the developer submitted to the city a concept plan for a residential subdivision on the property. According to the minutes of the city council meeting at which the concept plan was considered, the mayor and several council members indicated that they would not support a change in the city's comprehensive plan to allow residential development of the property. The city did not take any formal action on the concept plan.

Mendota Golf subsequently submitted an application to the city requesting that the city amend the comprehensive plan to change the designation of the property from "Golf Course" to "Low Density Residential." In a letter attached to the application, Alan Spaulding, one of Mendota Golf's partners, indicated that Mendota Golf had failed to make the golf course "a profitable venture" and needed to "pursue alternative uses." Spaulding stated that when Mendota Golf purchased the property in 1995, it understood that it had the opportunity to develop the property. However, due to a subsequent change in the MLPA, which Spaulding described as requiring developers to "meet the criteria of both Zoning and Comprehensive Plan" designations, Mendota Golf is "now subject to the confining designation of 'Golf Course' on the Comprehensive Plan." Spaulding explained a "series of financial challenges and setbacks" that Mendota Golf had experienced and emphasized that Mendota Golf has been "a good neighbor" to the community. Spaulding asked the city to give it "more flexibility than the designation of 'Golf Course' allows" and to "restore the rights" Mendota Golf had when it acquired the property.

On June 11, 2003, the city advised Mendota Golf that its application to amend the comprehensive plan was complete. Shortly thereafter, the city's consulting planner prepared a planning report and recommended that "an alternative land use designation for the site is appropriate, subject to qualified review of the information provided by the applicant as to the viability of a golf course operation on the property." On June 24, 2003, the city's planning commission held a public hearing, evaluated Mendota Golf's application, and unanimously (one commissioner abstained) recommended that the city council deny the proposed amendment to the comprehensive plan. The planning commission based its recommendation on a finding that "the golf course is the best use of the property consistent with the surrounding use of the neighborhood."

---

7. When a local governmental unit submits its comprehensive plan to the Metropolitan Council, it must either certify that "no amendments to its plan or fiscal devices or official controls are necessary" or submit the amendments to the Metropolitan Council for information purposes. Minn. Stat. § 473.864, subd. 2 (2004). The implementation program of the city's comprehensive plan indicates that "minor revisions" to the city's zoning ordinance "may be needed to address the development and policy issues identified in the Comprehensive Plan." However, the city's Technical Plan also expresses "concern" regarding the city's obligations under the 1995 amendments to the MLPA:

> Up until passage of the amendments to the Metropolitan Land Planning Act in 1995, zoning took precedence over comprehensive planning when issues of inconsistencies occurred. However, the amended Act now provides that comprehensive plans shall take precedence over zoning when conflicts arise. The change presents challenges due to the fact that comprehensive plans have traditionally served as "guide" plans. Prior to establishing a land use plan and/or modifying existing land use designations, the City must fully understand potential ramifications of these actions. There is currently no case law to provide guidance in this matter. At issue is a lack of understanding of the implications of this law and the mechanisms available to the City to assure that the Mendota Heights Comprehensive Plan is consistent with the Zoning Ordinance.

Mendota Golf's application to amend the comprehensive plan came before the city council on July 1, 2003. The council acknowledged receiving various documents, including staff reports and the letter from Spaulding. According to the minutes of the council meeting, Spaulding told the council that the highest and best use for the property is not as a golf course, "the character of the neighborhood is consistent with single family use of the site," and it is not fair that Mendota Golf has to satisfy the conditions of both the comprehensive plan and the zoning ordinance, unlike other property owners in the city. Spaulding also indicated that the comprehensive guide plan is arbitrary and contradictory to zoning.

A city attorney advised the council that after the legislature amended Minn. Stat. § 473.858 in 1995, a local government cannot adopt any official control that conflicts with the comprehensive plan, and it "is pretty clear that the comprehensive plan controls." The mayor commented that a few years previously the council had updated the city's comprehensive plan and held many public hearings. A councilmember added that the plan updating process was very extensive. When the mayor noted that Mendota Golf chose not to participate in the process even though the law changed, Spaulding responded that Mendota Golf was not aware of the hearings. The mayor then solicited comments from citizens in the audience. Several citizens spoke out against the proposed comprehensive plan amendment, with some speaking on the value of preserving open space and recreational opportunities in the community.

The city council then voted unanimously to adopt Resolution 03-46, denying the proposed comprehensive plan amendment. In the resolution, the council stated that the amendment would have an "adverse impact on the health, safety, and general welfare of the citizens of the community and the surrounding land, and would be adverse to the general purpose and intent of the Zoning Ordinance."

After the city council denied the comprehensive plan amendment, Mendota Golf brought a mandamus action in district court. Mendota Golf asserted that the city's zoning code provision applicable to its property expressly permits single-family residences; the "Golf Course" designation in the comprehensive plan has no direct corresponding zoning classification; and the comprehensive plan designation and the zoning classification for the property are incompatible. Mendota Golf further asserted that the city's "failure and refusal to approve Mendota Golf's application to amend the Comprehensive Plan Land Use designation of the property to 'LR, Low-Density Residential' from 'GC, Golf Course,' at such a time as the Property is and has been zoned 'R-1 One-Family Residential,' constitutes an arbitrary, irrational, capricious, illegal, and unconstitutional act." Mendota Golf requested that the court issue a writ of mandamus commanding the city to approve Mendota Golf's application for an amendment to the city's comprehensive plan.

After a hearing, the district court concluded that the city's denial of Mendota Golf's proposed amendment to the city's comprehensive plan was arbitrary, capricious, and without a rational basis. The court found that: (1) the proposed Low-Density Residential designation corresponds to the existing R-1 zoning of the property; (2) single-family residential use is expressly made a permissible use under the existing R-1 zoning designation; and (3) the city had made no attempts to bring the property's zoning into conformity with the comprehensive plan "which in any way would prohibit the use of the subject property for R-1 zoning." The court then entered judgment in favor of Mendota Golf and against the city and issued a writ of mandamus commanding the city to immediately "approve Petitioner's application for a Comprehensive Plan amendment changing the Land Use Guide Plan designation of the Property from 'GC' Golf Course to 'LR' Low-Density Residential," and to further submit the Comprehensive Plan amendment to the Metropolitan Council for review and approval.

The city appealed, and the court of appeals affirmed the district court. . . .

To determine whether mandamus is available here, we first address whether the city failed to perform a duty clearly imposed by law when it denied Mendota Golf's application for an amendment to the city's comprehensive plan. Mendota Golf's mandamus action is based on the city's duty under Minn. Stat. § 473.858, subd. 1, to reconcile conflicts between the city's comprehensive plan and the zoning ordinance. This subdivision of the MLPA provides:

> If the comprehensive municipal plan is in conflict with the zoning ordinance, the zoning ordinance shall be brought into conformance with the plan by local government units in conjunction with the review and, if necessary, amendment of its comprehensive plan required under section 473.864, subdivision 2.

Minn. Stat. § 473.858, subd. 1 (2004). Mendota Golf asserts that the city's comprehensive plan and its zoning ordinance are "not in conformity" with respect to Mendota Golf's property and that the proposed amendment to the comprehensive plan "would provide the lacking conformity." The city denies that its comprehensive plan is in conflict with its zoning ordinance. . . .

In this case, Mendota Golf's property is located in a one-family residential district that specifically allows "one-family detached dwellings" as a permitted use. In contrast, the comprehensive plan designation allows the property to be used only as a golf course. While the use allowed by the comprehensive plan may be allowed as an exception under the zoning ordinance, the primary use allowed by the zoning ordinance is prohibited by the comprehensive plan. We view this as a conflict. . . .

The writ of mandamus in this case requires the city to reconcile the foregoing conflict by amending the comprehensive plan from its "GC" Golf Course designation to "LR" Low-Density Residential. The city contends that the writ of mandamus "improperly divests the City Council of its constitutionally-based legislative authority to determine local land uses." Therefore, we next consider whether the city had a clear duty to resolve the conflict by amending the comprehensive plan to permit the development of single-family housing on Mendota Golf's property. See Minn. Stat. § 586.01 (providing that a writ of mandamus may be issued "to compel the performance of an act which the law specially enjoins as a duty").

Under Minn. Stat. § 473.858, subd. 1, conflicts between a city's comprehensive plan and its zoning ordinance are to be reconciled either by (1) amending the zoning ordinance to conform to the comprehensive plan, or (2) by amending the comprehensive plan during one of the periodic reviews of the plan. Minn. Stat. § 473.858, subd. 1. The city asserts that the district court's writ of mandamus is problematic because the court directs the city to resolve the conflict in a specific way—by amending the comprehensive plan—even though there are alternative ways that the city could reconcile the conflict. According to the city, specific examples of how the conflict can be resolved include the following:

> The City could bring the zoning ordinance into conformity with the plan, it could bring the plan into conformity with the ordinance, or the City could choose to redesignate the property in a manner different from the property's current designation in either the plan or the ordinance.

Even Mendota Golf acknowledges that there is more than one way to resolve the conflict.

"The Minnesota legislature has delegated to municipalities the power to determine and plan the use of land within their boundaries." VanLandschoot v. City of Mendota Heights, 336 N.W.2d 503, 507 (Minn. 1983); see Minn. Stat. § 462.351 (2004) (stating that the purpose of the Municipal Planning Act is to provide municipalities "with the necessary powers" to conduct and implement municipal planning).[8] A comprehensive plan contains "objectives, policies, standards and programs to guide public and private land use, development, redevelopment and preservation for all lands and waters within the jurisdiction of the local governmental unit. " Minn. Stat. § 473.859, subd. 1 (stating contents of comprehensive plan). Because land use planning and regulation are within a city's legislative prerogative, the city has broad discretion when it makes decisions in that arena. See Honn v. City of Coon Rapids, 313 N.W.2d 409, 414 (Minn. 1981) (stating that "a municipality acts in a legislative capacity" in adopting or amending a zoning ordinance, "regardless of the size of the tract involved").

Here, the presence of alternative ways to reconcile the conflict between the comprehensive plan and the zoning ordinance indicates that the city did not have a clear duty to amend the comprehensive plan to conform to the zoning ordinance. Accordingly, we conclude that the district court exceeded the scope of its authority in this mandamus action by interfering with the exercise of legislative discretion and ordering the city to reconcile the conflict in a specific way—by amending the comprehensive plan.

We also conclude that the district court's writ of mandamus commanding the city to bring its comprehensive plan into conformity with its zoning ordinance is inconsistent with the statutory priority of comprehensive plans over zoning ordinances. Under the MLPA, the comprehensive municipal plan guides land use in cities within the metropolitan area. Minn. Stat. § 473.859, subd. 1 (2004). Zoning ordinances are intended to carry out the policies of a city's comprehensive plan. See Minn. Stat. § 473.851, subd. 9 (2004); Minn. Stat. § 473.859, subd. 4 (2004) (requiring a comprehensive plan to have an "implementation program" that includes "a description of official controls" that may be used to implement the comprehensive plan).

Since 1995, the MLPA has provided that the comprehensive plan constitutes the primary land use control for cities and supersedes all other municipal regulations when these regulations are in conflict with the plan. See Minn. Stat. § 473.858, subd. 1 (providing that "the zoning ordinance shall be brought into conformance with the [comprehensive municipal] plan" if there is a conflict). The MLPA further prohibits cities from adopting any "official control which is in conflict with its comprehensive plan, including any amendment to the plan." Minn. Stat. § 473.858, subd. 1; accord Minn. Stat. § 473.865, subd. 2 (2004). Consequently, there is no statutory support for ordering the city to amend its comprehensive plan to conform to the zoning ordinance. Further, the nature of the order itself—directing the city to bring its comprehensive plan into conformity with its zoning ordinance—appears to violate the MLPA because this approach undermines the supremacy of the comprehensive plan vis-a-vis the zoning ordinance.

We further note that a city's comprehensive plan is part of a regional land use planning process. Because "local governmental units within the metropolitan area are interdependent," the legislature has established "requirements and procedures to accomplish comprehensive local planning with land use controls consistent with planned, orderly, and staged development and the metropolitan system plans." Minn. Stat. § 473.851 (2004); see generally City of Lake Elmo v. Metro. Council, 685 N.W.2d 1, 5-6 (Minn. 2004) (explaining that the Metropolitan Council reviews local comprehensive plans and has broad authority to require modification of plans that are inconsistent with the council's overarching plan). Although the writ of mandamus in this case did require the city to submit the comprehensive plan amendment to the Metropolitan Council for review and approval, the role of the Metropolitan Council in coordinating local land use planning, including "regional recreational open space," through the development of "metropolitan system plans" further suggests

---

8. But see Minn. Stat. § 473.175, subd. 1 (2004) (providing that the Metropolitan Council "may require a local governmental unit to modify any comprehensive plan" if "the plan is more likely than not to have a substantial impact on or contain a substantial departure from metropolitan system plans").

that mandamus is not appropriate to compel the city to amend its comprehensive plan in these circumstances. See Minn. Stat. § 473.852, subd. 8 (2004) (defining "metropolitan system plans"). . . .

When reviewing municipal land use decisions, we typically utilize a rational basis standard of review.[11] Our scope of review is narrow. We uphold a city's land use decision unless the party challenging that decision establishes that the decision is "'unsupported by any rational basis related to promoting the public health, safety, morals, or general welfare.'" [Honn v. City of Coon Rapids, 313 N.W.2d 409,] at 414-15 [(Minn. 1981)] (quoting State by Rochester Ass'n of Neighborhoods v. City of Rochester, 268 N.W.2d 885, 888 (Minn. 1978)). "Even if the city council's decision is debatable, so long as there is a rational basis for what it does, the courts do not interfere." *Id.* at 415. We do not give any special deference to the conclusions of the lower courts, but rather engage in an independent examination of the record and arrive at our own conclusions as to the propriety of the city's decision. . . .

A municipality has legitimate interests in protecting open and recreational space, as well as reaffirming historical land use designations. See Minn. Stat. § 462.357, subd. 1 (including "recreation" among the legitimate objectives of zoning); In re Denial of Eller Media Company's Applications, 664 N.W.2d 1, 10 n.7 (Minn. 2003) (explaining that "governing bodies have the right to meet the desires of their citizens for beauty and space—even in cities"); Sun Oil Co. v. Village of New Hope, 300 Minn. 326, 337-38, 220 N.W.2d 256, 263 (1974) (upholding village's denial of a rezoning petition "based upon a legislative determination to perpetuate its preexisting comprehensive zoning ordinance"). Accordingly, we conclude that legitimate objectives supported the city's denial of Mendota Golf's application for an amendment to the city's comprehensive plan, and Mendota Golf has failed to establish that the city lacked a rational basis for the decision. Indeed, given the statutory priority of municipal comprehensive plans over local zoning ordinances and the role of comprehensive plans in the regional planning process, it would be difficult to conclude that the city abused its discretion by denying the proposed amendment to the comprehensive plan. Therefore, we reverse the district court's decision requiring the city to approve Mendota Golf's application to change the comprehensive plan designation for the property from "Golf Course" to "Low-Density Residential."

The dissent suggests that our decision means that "the owners of the subject property are required, now and in the future, to operate a golf course because it preserves 'open space' and recreational opportunities for residents of the community." Such a suggestion indicates that the dissent has misconstrued our decision by reading it too broadly. It is not our intent, and it is not necessarily the effect of our decision, to prescribe a permanent comprehensive plan designation for the property. Our decision does not foreclose discussion and negotiation between Mendota Golf and the city regarding the use of the property. In fact, in denying the proposed amendment to

---

11. The city proposes that we adopt "the 'change or mistake' doctrine" in reviewing a city's decision to deny a comprehensive plan amendment. Under the city's proposed "change or mistake" standard, the party requesting an amendment to a comprehensive plan must demonstrate either that (1) a mistake was made in the formation of the comprehensive plan or (2) the character of the neighborhood surrounding the land parcel at issue has changed so much that an amendment to the plan is merited. Although the city contends that the change or mistake standard is consistent with case law developed in the context of proposed amendments to zoning ordinance classifications, the change or mistake standard is a legal standard that a local government body may apply in considering a request for a change in a zoning ordinance, not a judicial standard of review. See Sun Oil Co. v. Village of New Hope, 300 Minn. 326, 335, 220 N.W.2d 256, 261-62 (1974) (noting that "there is a presumption that the original zoning was well planned and was intended to be more or less permanent") (quotations omitted); see also *Honn*, 313 N.W.2d at 417 (stating that in legislative zoning decisions, a city considers a "a wide range of value judgments" and the "inquiry focuses on whether the proposed use promotes the public welfare"). Therefore, in reviewing a city's zoning decision, a court may have occasion to assess the city's application of the "change or mistake" standard in determining whether the city had a rational basis for its decision. But the rational basis standard remains the appropriate standard of judicial review because it is most compatible with the broad discretion afforded to cities in zoning matters.

the comprehensive plan, the city expressed a willingness to work with Mendota Golf to explore other options for the property. Our decision also does not foreclose Mendota Golf from asserting a regulatory takings claim if the parties cannot resolve their dispute. Finally, our decision does not foreclose other actions based on the circumstances as they may develop as a part of or following the city's reconciliation of the comprehensive plan and zoning ordinance provisions for the property, which cannot be foreseen at this time. Our decision simply resolves the narrow issue that is properly before the court—whether the city had a rational basis to deny Mendota Golf's proposed amendment to the comprehensive plan. . . .

Reversed and remanded.

ANDERSON, G. Barry, Justice (concurring and dissenting). . . .

I dissent . . .from that portion of the majority opinion that holds that the City of Mendota Heights had a "rational basis" for the city's denial of Mendota Golf's application for an amendment to the city's comprehensive plan. . . .

Notes

1. In the opening years of the 21st century, before the real estate bubble burst, many developers who were eager to find undeveloped or underdeveloped suburban parcels suitable for new residential subdivisions identified golf courses as potential home sites. In many instances, these were newer courses, built in the previous decade as part of the marked increase in the game known as the "Tiger Woods phenomenon." As the pace of conversions accelerated, courts throughout the country have been asked to resolve legal puzzles posed by efforts of course owners to intensify the use of their property to residential or commercial uses (or a combination of the two). In addition to *Mendota Golf*, representative cases include Golf Club of Plantation, Inc. v. City of Plantation, 847 So. 2d 1028 (Fla. Ct. App. 2003) (noting that the city had made clear its policy of banning golf course conversions), In re Realen Valley Forge Greenes Assocs., 576 Pa. 115, 838 A.2d 718 (2003) (successfully challenging the agricultural zoning designation of a golf course as an example of reverse spot zoning), A&F Props., Ltd. Liab. Co. v. Madison County Bd. of Supervisors, 933 So. 2d 296 (Miss. 2006) (enforcing a contract provision to maintain a golf course for 10 years), and Upland Hills Country Club Condo. Ass'n v. Upland Dev. Ltd. Liab. Co., 2006 Cal. App. LEXIS 2122 (unpublished Mar. 14, 2006) (limiting the scope of an easement granting "use and enjoyment over the Golf Course"). In conversion situations, important questions of private and public law converge, as attorneys and judges struggle with difficult issues such as implied servitudes, downzonings, and regulatory takings. In fact, the dissenters in Mendota Golf suspected that by requiring the landowner to maintain the recreational uses of the property and thus to forego the expected profits from creating a residential subdivision, the city might well have effected a regulatory taking. As it turns out, the city amended the comprehensive plan in December 2006, to allow for the development of a smaller subdivision, then decided to allow the voters to decide whether they instead wanted Mendota Heights to purchase (and thereby preserve) the golf course.

2. *Mendota Golf* is an instructive example of the regional approach to land use planning. The court's statutory analysis focused on a key provision of state law mandating comprehensive and coordinated planning. Minnesota lawmakers have recognized that "the local governmental units within the metropolitan area are interdependent" and that "[s]ince problems of urbanization and development transcend local governmental boundaries, there is a need for the adoption of coordinated plans, programs and controls by all local governmental units and school districts in order to protect the health, safety and welfare of the residents of the metropolitan area and to ensure coordinated, orderly and economic development." Minn. Stat. §473.851. The direct impacts of

this statutory scheme on the conflict in *Mendota Golf* are the city's duty to coordinate zoning and the comprehensive plan and its obligation to submit any plan amendments to the Metropolitan Council. This extra layer of regulation and oversight, designed to minimize extra-boundary spillovers and increase the coordination of planning decisionmaking, can also have the added benefit of protecting landowners and neighbors from local government abuses.

3. Environmentalists are often opposed to the construction and expansion of golf courses, based on concerns over poisonous runoff containing pesticides and fertilizers, the destruction of trees and other wildlife habitats, and the normal negative externalities associated with urban and suburban sprawl. The Green Section of the U.S. Golf Association has responded to some of these concerns, as noted on their website: http://www.usga.org/Content.aspx?id=26125. Because golf course conversions threaten some of the few remaining open spaces in heavily urbanized communities, environmentalists have had to reconsider their traditionally negative reaction to fairways, roughs, and greens. In recognition of the potential for golf courses to serve useful ecological functions, Audubon International has created the Cooperative Sanctuary Program: http://acspgolf.audubon-international.org/. More details on the land use law implications of conversions can be found in Steven J. Wernick, *Diamonds in the Rough: Judicial Reaction to Golf Course Conversions*, Zoning & Planning L. Rep., Apr. 2007, at 1; and Powell on Real Property §70D.08 (Michael Allan Wolf gen. ed. 2009).

4. In those jurisdictions with state Environmental Protection Acts (SEPAs) or "little NEPAs"—that is, state versions of the National Environmental Policy Act—there may be an additional regulatory layer when local governments seek to prevent the conversion of golf courses that are already zoned for residential use. In Bonnie Briar Syndicate Inc. v. Town of Mamaroneck, 94 N.Y.2d 96, 721 N.E.2d 971, 699 N.Y.S.2d 721 (1999), the owner of a private golf course unsuccessfully claimed that the town's downzoning of the property from residential to recreational use constituted a regulatory taking. In its opinion, the state high court detailed local government compliance with New York's SEPA:

> In 1986, the Towns of Mamaroneck and Larchmont together adopted a "Local Waterfront Revitalization Program" (LWRP) for a comprehensive examination of land-use policies. The LWRP was primarily concerned with, and sought effectively to protect against, the flooding potential in both the flood plain and coastal areas. The LWRP identified flood damage to the Town's wetlands, fish and other wildlife habitats and streams, cautioning the Town to prepare itself for further adverse effects that would result from future changes in land use.

> The LWRP found that the Town golf clubs were "appropriate uses which, in addition to their ecological, recreational, architectural and scenic value, provide open space and natural water retention. They should remain in their present use if possible." . . .

> Because rezoning these golf course properties required a review pursuant to the State Environmental Quality Review Act (SEQRA), on May 30, 1990, defendant Town Board declared its intention to serve as lead agency for the purpose of conducting the SEQRA review and retained yet another planning firm to assist in the review process. After preparation of a Generic Environmental Impact Statement in 1991, the Board issued a Findings Statement in completion of its SEQRA review in 1994. The Findings Statement described in great detail how the various proposed development and rezoning schemes would impact this environmentally sensitive area.

Specifically, the Findings Statement noted that the area was facing "long-term pressure toward continuing urbanization in an already over-developed landscape," noting that "less than 5% of the Westchester County watershed of the Long Island Sound remains open space." In response to these concerns over dwindling existing open spaces and to ensure their retention, the Board determined that zoning the Winged Foot and Bonnie Briar club properties solely for recreational uses was the best alternative.

In addition, the Findings Statement explained that further residential development would frustrate the Town's goal of preserving recreational opportunities for Town and area residents, noting that 70% of Bonnie Briar's membership resided within a five-mile radius of the property.

Finally, in connection with concerns over flooding, the SEQRA Findings Statement noted that, without even considering further development beyond the Town's control, residential development within the Town could increase the flooding already experienced by many area homeowners. Furthermore, the Board was not adequately persuaded that proposed measures to mitigate the increased flooding associated with residential development would be effective.

Based upon all of the foregoing considerations, the Findings Statement concluded that the "Recreation Zone best achieves the objectives of the Town, State, regional and federal policies that have guided the Town's comprehensive planning process for almost three decades." The Town Board rezoned accordingly, enacting Local Law No. 6.

Professor Daniel Selmi has provided a recent analysis of SEPA activity in *Themes in the Evolution of the State Environmental Policy Acts*, 38 Urb. Law. 949 (2006).

III. Variances and Special Exceptions: From "Safety Valves" to "Steady Leaks"

The framers of the Standard State Zoning Enabling Act (SZEA) were aware that as with nonconforming uses, some landowners would need relief from zoning ordinances as originally promulgated and as amended over time. Section 7 of the SZEA enabled special boards of adjustment

> [t]o authorize upon appeal in specific cases such variance from the terms of the ordinance that will not be contrary to the public interest where owing to specific conditions, a literal enforcement of the ordinance will result in unnecessary hardship and so that the spirit of the ordinance shall be served and substantial justice done.

On the one hand, when used with proper discretion and care, this device would prove invaluable in insulating zoning authorities from many legal challenges brought by landowners who would otherwise assert that they were being treated unfairly and having their property confiscated by arbitrary regulators. On the other hand, local residents appointed as arbiters of their neighbors' landholding status could easily fall into the pattern of being too generous for the community's own good.

Unlike the situation in which a landowner succeeds in securing a zoning amendment, the height, bulk, and use classification for a parcel do not change in the event a variance is granted. Therefore, technically, there is no requirement that the variance be "in accordance with the comprehensive plan." In the many communities in which standards for granting a variance have been too lax, the resulting agglomeration of land uses often runs contrary to the best-laid plans.[4]

The ease with which a landowner can secure a variance from fellow residents on the board of adjustment (or board of zoning appeals), as opposed to a full-fledged zoning amendment from the local legislature, may well explain why several states have abolished the use variance. See, for example, Cal. Gov't Code 65906 ("A variance shall not be granted for a parcel of property which authorizes a use or activity which is not otherwise expressly authorized by the zone regulation governing the parcel of property."). Similar language can be found in, for example, Ariz. Rev. Stat. 9-462.06(H)(1) (2003); Ark. Code Ann. 14-56-416(b)(2)(B)(i)(b); and Minn. Stat. 394.27(7). In other jurisdictions, local governments are given the option of prohibiting use variances. See, for example, 30-A Maine Rev. Stat. § 4353(4) ("Under its home rule authority, a municipality may, in a zoning ordinance, adopt additional limitations on the granting of a variance, including, but not limited to, a provision that a variance may be granted only for a use permitted in a particular zone." The majority of states still permit use variances, and, by statutory or case law, a relaxed standard often applies. See, for example, Kisil v. City of Sandusky, 12 Ohio St. 3d 30, 33, 465 N.E.2d 848, 851 (1984): "The granting of a variance to the appellant should not be judged on the traditional showing of an 'unnecessary hardship' but on the lesser standard of a 'practical difficulty.'"

The following recent decision of Maryland's highest court amply illustrates the practical and theoretical challenges that variance law poses to a court struggling to accommodate a landowner's needs without jeopardizing the overall planning and zoning scheme. You will see that, in order to solve the puzzle of self-created hardships, the court turns to some of the leading treatises in the area. These are authorities that will prove helpful to you as you make the move from student to practitioner. Notice how the law in this area has evolved over the past few decades, in response to localized needs and to federal constitutional law developments as well.

RICHARD ROESER PROFESSIONAL BUILDER, INC. v. ANNE ARUNDEL COUNTY
368 Md. 294, 793 A.2d 545 (2002)

Opinion by Cathell, J. . . .

Petitioner was the contract purchaser of two lots near Annapolis in Anne Arundel County. Only one lot is part of this appeal and part of the lot is located in the Critical Area "buffer" zone adjacent to wetlands. At the time it contracted to purchase the property, petitioner knew that variances from the "Critical Area" and zoning provisions of Anne Arundel County would be required in order for it to be able to build a house of the size it desired. It applied for those variances and, as we have indicated, the Board denied its request.

In relevant part, the Board found:

> "The conditions surrounding the Petitioners' request for a variance have been self-created. The co-petitioner . . . purchased the subject property . . . on February 23, 1999. The wetlands existed on the property at that time. Indeed, it appears from the purchase price of the two lots ($62,000 total) that both seller and buyer were well aware of potential development issues with the land. The buyer apparently elected to purchase the property and now seeks to maximize the investment. Any applicant for a variance, however, must exercise proper diligence in ascertaining the setback requirements prior

---

4. *See* Heady v. Zoning Board of Appeals for Milford, 139 Conn. 463, 467, 94 A.2d 789, 791 (1953):

[U]nless great caution is used and variations are granted only in proper cases, the whole fabric of town- and city-wide planning will be worn through in spots and raveled at the edges until its purpose in protecting property values and securing an orderly development of the community is completely thwarted.

to the acquisition of property. If such diligence is not exercised, any resulting hardship to the property owner is regarded as self-created. *See, Wilson v. Elkton, 35 Md. App. 417, 371 A.2d 443 (1977).*"[3] [Some citations omitted.] . . .

Judge Manck, of the Circuit Court for Anne Arundel County, in correctly rejecting the position of the Board, stated: . . .

"[t]he Court is unconvinced that the hardship was self-created. Hardships of this type are normally those which are created by the owners of the property and not by the property itself. The topography and placement of the property is not a selfinflicted or self-created hardship and there is no evidence of testimony which would lend support to the Board's finding that in some fashion the Petitioner created this hardship. . . .

The Court of Special Appeals, in reversing the Circuit Court, stated, as relevant here:

"In Gleason v. Keswick Improvement Ass'n, Inc., 197 Md. 46, 78 A.2d 164 (1951), the Court of Appeals, citing Charles A. Rathkopf, the Law of Zoning and Planning, § 23, at 262 (2d ed. 1949), stated:

Where a person purchases property with the intention to apply to the board of appeals for a variance from the restrictions imposed by the ordinance he cannot contend that such restrictions cause him such a peculiar hardship that entitles him to the special privileges which he seeks."[4]

Gleason v. Keswick Improvement Association, 197 Md. 46, 78 A.2d 164 (1951), was not an application for an "area" variance. The request was designed to permit commercial use (a grocery store) in a residentially zoned area; accordingly, it concerned "uses," not "area." . . .

In any event, ultimately, we have distinguished, if not overruled, *Gleason*. In Zengerle v. Board of County Commissioners for Frederick County, 262 Md. 1, 276 A.2d 646 (1971), we noted that Frederick County bought the farm for the purpose of building and operating a landfill. It was known to the County at the time it purchased the property that in order to operate a landfill, the County would need to obtain substantial setback variances (area variances). The opinion we adopted distinguished the *Gleason* case, making its ruling, at the least, inapplicable to area variance cases. We referred to the trial judge's opinion, and said: "We shall adopt his opinion as follows . . . ." *Id.* at 3, 276 A.2d at 648. The opinion we adopted as our own distinguished

---

3. It is a relatively common practice throughout the State, and has been so for decades, that buyers contract to buy properties with contingencies that make consummation of the contract conditioned on the granting of variances. So far as we have discovered, in cases involving "area" variances, this Court has never disapproved the practice. Additionally, in such instances in respect to "area" variances, we have never held that such a practice, by itself, constitutes a "self-created" hardship. In *Wilson, infra*, a predecessor in title to the current landowner modified a structure, which put the structure in violation of the existing zoning code. Therefore, the hardship was "self-created" by the applicant's predecessor in title. It was not created by the regulation. Likewise, in *Ad. + Soil, Inc. v. Queen Anne's County*, 307 Md. 307, 513 A.2d 893 (1986), the applicant had built into a setback, and, after the fact, sought a variance of the setback requirements. The issue of the effect of a purchase was not addressed in a variance context in either opinion, and both involved requests for "area" variances, not "use" variances.

   We also note that in this country it is not considered inappropriate to "maximize" investments.

4. The position taken by Anne Arundel County does not indicate what would happen if a property was conveyed by testamentary devise, or by operation of law. This points out another problem with the concept. Such a new owner would, apparently, not be subject to the self-created hardship rule if he or she obtained property by devise after the regulation was enacted. Under the County's theory, the Board would have to determine and distinguish between matters of title, *i.e.*, how an owner acquired title. Such matters are not within a board's areas of expertise. Zoning regulations regulate the land, impact the land—not ownership, and not title. . . .

the *Gleason* case, making its ruling inapplicable to area variance cases. Through the trial judge's opinion, we held:

> "Appellants make the further contention that where one purchases realty intending to apply for a variance from zoning restrictions, he cannot contend that such restrictions cause him the undue hardships that would entitle him to such variance, citing Gleason v. Keswick Improvement Association, 197 Md. 46, 78 A.2d 164. This same rule has been relaxed where there has been an application for area variance such as here, as distinguished from a use variance as in *Keswick*, the Court of Appeals pointing out that a use variance is customarily concerned with unusual hardship where the land cannot yield a reasonable return without a variance whereas an area variance is primarily concerned with practical difficulties.

> "Section 40-145 permits a variance where practical difficulty or unnecessary hardship is present. Since this is an application for an area variance and since there was testimony of practical difficulty in the absence of the grant of a variance, the rule announced in *Keswick* does not apply." . . .

Id. 262 Md. at 21-22, 276 A.2d at 656.

As important, is the fact that Rathkopf, The Law of Zoning and Planning, upon which we spoke in *Gleason*, and in turn the Court of Special Appeals relied on in the case at bar, has abandoned the position upon which the Court of Special Appeals relied. The Supreme Judicial Court of Maine noted the change in its relatively recent case of Twigg v. Town of Kennebunk, 662 A.2d 914, 916 (Me. 1995), saying:

> "The Board ruled there was self-created hardship because 'the applicant knew, prior to his purchase, of the complications and prohibitions attached to this property and its use . . . .' The Board's conclusion that knowledge of zoning restrictions prior to the purchase of property is tantamount to self-created hardship is an error of law. While it was the general rule at one time 'that one who purchases property with actual or constructive knowledge of the restrictions of a zoning ordinance was barred from securing a variance,' the rule has since been 'altogether abandoned or modified into nonexistence' in most jurisdictions. 3 Rathkopf, The Law of Zoning and Planning § 38.06(2) (1988). . . . The modern rule provides that a purchase with knowledge does not preclude the granting of a variance and, at most, is considered a nondeterminative factor in consideration of a variance. Rathkopf at § 38.06." [Some citations omitted.]

Rathkopf, now provides:

> "While this rule may still be applicable in a few jurisdictions, it has been altogether abandoned, or modified into nonexistence, in others. Two basic faults in the old rule have been recognized, and these faults are the reasons behind its demise. First, since hardship can neither be measured by the cost of the property to the owner nor by the difference between the value the land has as restricted and the value it would have if the variance were granted, there is no danger that a knowledgeable purchaser could create evidence of hardship by paying an excessive price for property that is restricted. Second, the old rule failed to acknowledge that if the prior owner would have been entitled to a variance at the time [ ] the zoning ordinance restriction was enacted, the right is not lost to a purchaser simply because he bought with knowledge of the regulation. *In other words, because a purchaser of property acquires no greater right to a variance than his predecessor, he should not be held to acquire less.*

"The 'current trend' in the rule, that purchase with knowledge of restrictions either does not prohibit the granting of a variance, or is at most a nondeterminative factor to consider in the granting of variance, has had proponents at least as early 1957 when the Supreme Court of Rhode Island rejected the notion that purchase with knowledge of restrictions, in itself, constituted self-created hardship. The 'traditional rule,' has been relaxed to leave the decision of whether a purchaser with knowledge of restrictions should receive a variance up to the discretion of the board of appeals.

"It should not be within the discretion of a board of appeals to deny a variance solely because a purchaser bought with knowledge of zoning restrictions. . . .

"The evolution and development of the rule took two slightly different paths. Originally, purchase with knowledge of restriction had its greatest application where a use variance was sought. When the rule was being modified so as to be less harsh, nonuse variances were first to be granted even when there was knowledge."

Arden H. Rathkopf & Daren A. Rathkopf, The Law of Zoning and Planning § 58.22, 141-48 (Edward H. Ziegler, Jr. revision, vol. 3, West 1991) (emphasis added) (footnotes omitted).

Robert M. Anderson, in his American Law of Zoning § 20.44, 566 (Kenneth H. Young revisions, 4th ed., CBC 1996) discusses the application of the rule in New Jersey, saying:

"Although a number of earlier cases . . . repeated a more restrictive rule, the more recent decisions seem clearly to say that the right to a variance is not affected by a sale of land. One decision . . . said the following: 'The hardship criteria of (c) are expressly stated in terms of the objective physical characteristics of the property itself. The hardship thus entailed is not ordinarily mitigated by mere transfer of title to property . . . . *Where an original owner would be entitled to a variance under a specific set of facts, any successor in title is ordinarily also entitled to such a variance, providing that no owner in the chain of title since the adoption of the zoning restriction has done anything to create the condition for which relief by variance is sought.*'

"The Supreme Court of New Jersey has applied the same rule to the granting of variances for 'special reasons.' It said: We wish to make it clear that if a prior owner would be entitled to such relief, that right is not lost to a purchaser simply because he bought with knowledge of the zoning regulation involved. . . ." [Emphasis added.] [Footnotes omitted.]

Anderson then describes, favorably, the position of Delaware courts:

"A Delaware court described the diverse views and elected the more permissive one, explaining: We are inclined to regard the property itself as a permanent entity *and the current ownership merely as a passing phase.* We hesitate to lay down a rule that Darling's property, by his purchase of it, became positively ineligible for a variance. . . ."

". . . Courts which permit relief, but also permit the board of adjustment to consider the fact of self-created hardship, fix their attention on the fact that hardship must relate to the property itself, and they see little relevance in a change of ownership."

Id. at 568-69 (emphasis added) (footnotes omitted). Julian Conrad Juergensmeyer and Thomas E. Roberts, Land Use Planning and Control Law § 5.17, 211 (West 1998), state:

"When one purchases property and then applies for a variance on the grounds of unnecessary hardship, a difference of opinion exists as to whether the variance should be denied on the ground of self-induced hardship. Most courts consider the transfer of title irrelevant, but some cases contain contrary suggestions. . . . *However, since ownership is normally irrelevant to zoning, the transfer of title ought not affect the issue. If the land suffers the requisite hardship, in that the owner can make no reasonable return from its use as zoned, then the board ought to grant a variance. If not, the land becomes permanently zoned in a useless state.*

"The reasons used to deny a variance to one who violates the law and then seeks relief are not applicable to one who purchases with knowledge. In the former, the owner created the hardship; in the latter, the zoning created the hardship, which pre-existed the purchaser's acquisition of title. . . . But it is not an affront to the law to grant relief to one who purchases land where unique circumstances have already zoned the land into a state of uselessness.

". . . A windfall may result, but it is not an unjustifiable one vis-a-vis the public, since the situation assumes that land deserves the variance. It is simply a question of which owner gets the variance, the prior owner or the new owner." [Emphasis added.] [Footnotes omitted.]

Daniel R. Mandelker, Land Use Law § 6.50, 259-60 (4th ed., LEXIS 1997), as to this issue, states:

"A more complicated problem is presented when self-created hardship is claimed because the land owner purchased a lot with knowledge of the zoning restrictions. The rule that hardship is self-created in this situation stems from early New York cases and is followed in some states. . . .

"The present status of the New York rule is in doubt. The New York courts adopted the rule in use variance cases in which there were other reasons for denying the variance. In the area variance cases they hold that self-created hardship based on purchase with knowledge of existing zoning is only one factor to consider.

"The cases that reject the rule that purchase with knowledge of existing zoning [is] self-created hardship are correct. The rule is fair in cases where a prior owner created a hardship through some action relating to the land. Purchase should not relieve a subsequent owner of this infirmity. To hold that mere purchase with knowledge of existing zoning is self-created hardship improperly makes the purchase of land a basis for denying a variance." [Footnotes omitted.]

Several jurisdictions have held similarly to both our cases distinguishing *Gleason* in respect to area variances, and the Maine court's overruling of the prior position taken by Rathkopf, and Rathkopf's disavowal of his previous position. . . .

Even in those jurisdictions that still, to a degree, adhere to the older Rathkopf standard, more often than not the standard has been greatly relaxed where area, as opposed to use, variances are at issue. The Court of Special Appeals in a case in which it reversed the granting of a variance, described the differences between "area" variances and "use" variances, as:

"'[A]rea variance' (a variance from area, height, density, setback, or sideline restrictions, such as a variance from the distance required between buildings) and not a 'use variance' (a variance which permits a use other than that permitted in the particular district by the ordinance, such as a variance for an office or commercial use in a zone restricted to residential uses)."

Anderson v. Board of Appeals, 22 Md. App. 28, 37-38, 322 A.2d 220, 225-26 (1974).[6]

Subsequent to Zengerle v. Board of County Commissioners for Frederick County, 262 Md. 1, 276 A.2d 646 (1971), we reiterated its holding in McLean v. Soley, 270 Md. 208, 215, 310 A.2d 783, 787 (1973), where we also distinguished between area and use variances, saying:

> "It is also contended by McLean that Soley is precluded from asserting 'practical difficulty' because he was charged with knowledge of the sideyard requirements when he purchased this property. We see no merit in this argument. We noted in Zengerle v. Bd. of Co. Comm'rs, 262 Md.1, 21, 276 A.2d 646 (1971), citing *Loyola, supra*, that this 'rule' is more strictly applied in 'use variance' cases than in cases of 'area variances,' such as the one at bar." . . .

The types of hardships that are normally considered to be self-created in cases of this type do not arise from purchase, but from those actions of the landowner, himself or herself, that create the hardship, rather than the hardship impact, if any, of the zoning ordinance on the property. Our courts have spoken to these types of actions on several occasions. Relatively recently in Ad + Soil, Inc. v. County Commissioners of Queen Anne's County, 307 Md. 307, 316, 513 A.2d 893, 897-98 (1986), the Board found that "'The only extraordinary circumstances which would seem to exist in this case are self inflicted and a result of [Ad + Soil's] construction of the facilities on the site without conforming to the Ordinance's required setbacks.'" (Alteration in original.) We concurred that such a "hardship" was self-imposed.

In Salisbury Board of Zoning Appeals v. Bounds, 240 Md. 547, 214 A.2d 810 (1965), an earlier, but seminal case, a property owner had constructed a building without a valid building permit (although he thought a valid permit existed). The building was in violation of the zoning code. After it was discovered, the property owner, much as *Ad + Soil* would do twenty-one years later, sought a variance to legalize what he had already done. The Board declined to grant the variance on the grounds that it was Bounds' responsibility to obtain a valid permit, and thus the resulting hardship resulted from his failures. The trial court reversed the Board's denial of the variance, and we held that in doing so the trial court erred. We cited to Rathkopf's The Law of Zoning and Planning in reversing the trial court:

> "'§ 1. Hardship Caused by Affirmative Acts of Commission.
>
> 'Where property, due to unique circumstances applicable to it, cannot reasonably be adopted [sic] to use in conformity with the restrictions of the zoning ordinance, hardship arises which is capable of being relieved through the grant of a variance. . . . If the

---

6. E.C. Yokley, Zoning Law and Practice § 21-6, 321 (vol. 3, 4th ed., Michie 1979), describes the difference between "use" and "area" variances as:

> "A use variance is one that permits a use other than that prescribed by the zoning ordinance in a particular district. An area variance has no relationship to a change of use. It is primarily a grant to erect, alter, or use a structure for a permitted use in a manner other than that prescribed by the restrictions of a zoning ordinance."

Anderson's American Law of Zoning, *supra*, at § 20.48, 578, distinguishes the two, as:

> "A use variance authorizes a use of land which otherwise is proscribed by the zoning regulations. An area variance authorizes deviation from restrictions upon the construction and placement of buildings and structures which are employed to house or otherwise serve permitted uses. . . . More specifically, area variances include those relating to setback, yard, lot-area, lot-coverage, floor-area, frontage, height, and similar restrictions." [Footnote omitted.]

peculiar circumstances which render the property incapable of being used in accordance with the restrictions contained in the ordinance have been themselves caused or created by the property owner *or his predecessor in title*, the essential basis of a variance, i.e., that the hardship be caused *solely* through the manner of operation of the ordinance upon the particular property, is lacking. In such case, a variance will not be granted . . . .

. . .

'There is a uniform application of the rule in those cases in which there has been an act on the part of the property owner or his predecessor which has physically so affected the property as to create a unique circumstance or which in itself created either a practical difficulty or hardship in conforming to the restrictions of the ordinance.'"

Id. at 554-55, 214 A.2d at 814 (some emphasis added). We then held that the *Bounds* case "fits squarely within the above general rule." *Id.* at 555, 214 A.2d at 814. As can be seen, the self-created hardship in *Bounds* was the actual structural modification of a building by the current owner that put the building into violation of the ordinance. In other words, it was the owner's act of commission that created the claimed hardship. . . .

In Evans v. Shore Communications, 112 Md. App. 284, 309, 685 A.2d 454, 466 (1996), the Court of Special Appeals agreed with the "Board" that "the needs of SCI's customers have nothing to do with the peculiarity of the property in question. Thus, any hardship claimed by SCI—the second prong of the test—is self-inflicted, and thus not a ground for a variance." The hardship complained of in the Court of Special Appeals' case of Cromwell v. Ward, 102 Md. App. 691, 651 A.2d 424 (1995), was also self-created. The current property owner erected a structure that exceeded the height limitation on structures in Baltimore County. The court held that the activity of the owner had been self-imposed. Similarly, in Wilson v. Mayor and Commissioners of the Town of Elkton, 35 Md. App. 417, 371 A.2d 443 (1977), the Court of Special Appeals found a self-created hardship where an owner, albeit a predecessor owner, had illegally transformed a two-unit non-conforming apartment building into a three-unit non-conforming apartment building, and her successor owner was attempting to obtain a variance from set-back requirements to permit an exterior fire escape, necessitated by the change in the number of units, to be built in a required side yard. That court noted: "The finding of the Board of Appeals that the circumstances requiring the variance are not the result of actions on the applicant's part must be read to mean the applicant, or his predecessor. When so read, the finding is directly contrary to the evidence, and must be rejected." *Id.* at 428, 371 A.2d at 449.

This typical type of self-created hardship (an act of commission by the owner) is also the law in other jurisdictions. Martin v. Board of Adjustment, 464 So. 2d 123 (Ala. Civ. App. 1985) (illegally building a carport in a setback, pursuant to a permit application that stated the carport would not be in the setback deemed self-imposed); Board of Zoning Appeals v. Kempf, 656 N.E.2d 1201 (Ind. App. 1995) (the paving over of a required green space deemed to be selfcreated); CDK Restaurant, Inc. v. Krucklin, 118 A.D.2d 851, 500 N.Y.S.2d 339 (1986) (the illegal enclosure around a walkway was deemed self-inflicted); Midgett v. Schermerhorn, 24 A.D.2d 572, 262 N.Y.S.2d 269 (1965) (disregard of conditions imposed on prior grant of a variance held to be self-imposed); Pittsburgh v. Zoning Board of Adjustment, 522 Pa. 44, 559 A.2d 896 (1989) (reliance on city permits that had been obtained on false information in permit applications held to be self-created hardship); In re Cumberland Farms, 151 Vt. 59, 557 A.2d 486 (1989) (failure to procure permits self-created); In re Fecteau, 149 Vt. 319, 543 A.2d 693 (1988) (reliance on his surveyor's measurements held to be self-created). . . .

As we failed to discern, or at least to discuss, in *Gleason*, zoning constitutes restrictions on land, not on title. Both the Maryland Declaration of Rights and the Fifth Amendment of the United States Constitution guarantee rights to property owners. Property owners start out with the unrestricted right to use their land as they see fit. Under the common-law, those rights are limited only by a restriction as to uses that create traditional nuisances. Lucas v. South Carolina Coastal Council, 505 U.S. 1003 (1992). Our cases, however, and the cases of the Supreme Court of the United States, *see* Euclid v. Ambler Realty Co., 272 U.S. 365 (1926), and its progeny, have held that reasonable regulation is constitutional. That said, it must, nonetheless, be recognized that regulation of land, including zoning regulations, are limitations on the full exercise of a property owner's constitutional rights as well as his or her rights under the common-law.

In Aspen Hill Venture v. Montgomery County Council, 265 Md. 303, 313-14, 289 A.2d 303, 308 (1972), we quoted from our earlier case of Landay v. Board of Zoning Appeals, 173 Md. 460, 466, 196 A. 293, 296 (1938):

> "In such a situation we must not forget the underlying principle that, 'Such ordinances [zoning ordinances] are in derogation of the common law right to so use private property as to realize its highest utility, and while they should be liberally construed to accomplish their plain purpose and intent, they should not be extended by implication to cases not clearly within the scope of the purpose and intent manifest in their language.'" [Alteration in original.]

In that respect, reasonable zoning limitations are always directed to the property, itself, and its uses and structures, not to the completely separate matter of title to property, which is another whole field of law. In zoning, it is the property that is regulated, not the title.

In Maryland, when title is transferred, it takes with it all the encumbrances and burdens that attach to title; but it also takes with it all the benefits and rights inherent in ownership. If a predecessor in title was subject to a claim that he had created his own hardship, that burden, for variance purposes, passes with the title. But, at the same time, if the prior owner has not selfcreated a hardship, a self-created hardship is not immaculately conceived merely because the new owner obtains title. . . .

Notes

1. The oft-stated requirement that the problems faced by the landowner who is seeking a variance must be attributable to "unique circumstances" has also posed interpretative problems for courts, as illustrated by Professor Osborne M. Reynolds Jr., in *The "Unique Circumstances" Rule in Zoning Variances—An Aid in Achieving Greater Prudence and Less Leniency*, 31 Urb. Law. 127, 127-30, 148 (1999):

> Variances are the principal administrative device for granting relief to individual property owners from the unnecessary harshness of zoning laws. Their grant or denial is generally determined by a quasi-judicial body known as a board of adjustment or board of zoning appeals. Such boards, and their power to allow the special originated in New York City's 1916 zoning ordinance and are now found in almost every locality that engages in zoning. A variance permits a property owner to depart from the literal requirements of the zoning law as it applies to his or her land. The basic requirement for the grant of such a variance is usually said to be a showing of "unnecessary hardship" if the law is literally applied, and the commonly accepted components of such hardship are: (1) that the property cannot earn a reasonable return if used as zoned, (2) that this

problem arises from unique circumstances peculiar to the property, not from general conditions in the neighborhood, and (3) that the use allowed by the variance will not alter the essential character of the neighborhood.[6]

It has frequently been emphasized by courts and commentators that the power to award variances should be exercised sparingly and that a variance should be awarded only if it will not substantially disturb the comprehensive plan of the community but will alleviate hardships that are unnecessary to the general purpose of the plan. It has even been suggested that a variance that disturbs the community's comprehensive planning might be invalid as a form of "spot zoning": zoning that unreasonably singles out a particular piece of property for unmerited special treatment. . . .

Use variances are considered highly dangerous because they jeopardize achievement of one of zoning's chief purposes—the separation of incompatible land uses. Studies have shown that in many communities the great majority of requested variances, including use variances, are granted, despite clear indications in the authorizing legislation that such deviations are to be allowed only in cases of extreme need and that zoning is intended to achieve, wherever possible, the elimination of all uses not allowed by the legislation. . . .

The unique circumstances rule has been shown to be a well-established prerequisite for the award of a variance. It has been applied correctly by many boards and courts over the years, but it has also been blatantly ignored by others. Its use will obviously not solve all of the problems connected with variances, such as those relating to unsatisfactory procedures of boards and inadequate education of board members. But its strict and consistent application could help alleviate the wholesale and improvident granting of variances that has resulted in a crazy-quilt pattern of ad hoc zoning—the antithesis of zoning according to a comprehensive plan—that now characterizes some communities. Boards of adjustment and courts should keep in mind the basic purpose of variances: to provide a particularized waiver in exceptional situations where the unique circumstances of a lot call for relief. Variances should be awarded prudently, not liberally; strictly, not leniently. Where the general zoning law, through changed circumstances or otherwise, has become inappropriate for the neighborhood, the appeal should be to the legislative body for amendment. . . . The unique circumstances rule, if properly considered and applied, can often provide a negative answer to the question, "Is zoning increasingly becoming the rule of man rather than the rule of law?"

2. Ronald M. Shapiro, *The Zoning Variance Power*, 29 Md. L. Rev. 1 (1969), an article that contrasts the theory of the variance power with its practice, states that "the board of appeals variance procedure, conceived as the 'safety valve' of the zoning ordinance, has ruptured into a steady leak." See also Jonathan E. Cohen, in his student comment, *A Constitutional Safety Valve; The Variance in Zoning and Land Use-Based Environmental Controls*, 22 B.C. Envtl. Aff. L. Rev. 307, 364 (1995), notes that the variance serves an anti-regulatory taking function as well:

Modern land-use regulation has developed techniques to provide needed flexibility so as to properly protect and preserve vital natural resources without unduly and unnecessarily imposing burdens. Yet it is equally clear that a regulation can go too far. It is against the background of such a possibility that the zoning variance and much of the caselaw

---

6. The leading case is Otto v. Steinhilber, 282 N.Y. 71, 76, 24 N.E.2d 851, 853 (1939). . . .

of zoning developed. Environmental controls serve fundamentally different, and often broader, purposes than traditional zoning regulations. In most circumstances, courts can apply zoning variance caselaw where variances from land-use based environmental controls are at issue. To the extent that the application does not undermine the intent and purpose of the regulation, importation of other aspects of the caselaw is not only useful, but appropriate.

3. That the reports, year after year, contain numerous cases dealing with variances is itself an indication that all is not well in the administration of zoning. Especially in the formative decades of zoning, commentators have been keeping track of the variance phenomenon. For example, out of the 248 appellate cases reported in 1953 that could be classified as zoning-type cases, 48 dealt with variances. Charles M. Haar, *Emerging Legal Issues in Zoning*, in Planning 138 (1954). In Cincinnati, during the period 1926-1937, out of 1,940 applications, 1,493 variances were granted; in Philadelphia from 1933 to 1937, 4,000 variances were granted out of 4,800 requests. ASPO, *Zoning Changes and Variances*, Bull. No. 43, at 3, 5 (April 1938); *Administration of Zoning Variances in 20 Cities*, 30 Pub. Mgmt. 70 (1948). From 1949 to 1963, only 29 variance decisions were appealed to the Massachusetts Supreme Court. In Baltimore, only 15 of 464 zoning variance cases were appealed to the city court. Ronald M. Shapiro, *The Zoning Variance Power*, 29 Md. L. Rev. 1 (1969). Jesse Dukeminier & Clyde L. Stapleton, *The Zoning Board of Adjustment: A Case Study in Misrule*, 50 Ky. L.J. 273, 320 (1962), observed that the 70% of variance petitions granted by the Lexington Board "seems generally in line with the percentage granted by boards elsewhere." More recent observations confirm this pattern of acceptance, such as those found in Note, *Zoning Variance Administration in Vermont*, 8 Vt. L. Rev. 371, 388, 391, 393 (1983) (Brattleboro: 57 of 88 area variances granted; Montpelier: 51 of 71 granted; East Montpelier: 44 of 59 granted); and David P. Bryden, *The Impact of Variances: A Study of Statewide Zoning*, 61 Minn. L. Rev. 769 (1977). Those students looking for a down-and-dirty seminar project should consider a study of local variance practices.

4. In Emmi v. Zoning Board of Appeals, 63 N.Y.2d 853, 855, 472 N.E.2d 39, 482 N.Y.S.2d 263 (1984), the court noted that §267 of the Town Law allows any "aggrieved person" to bring an appeal before the Zoning Board of Appeals. This included a commercial tenant seeking variances, apparently without the consent of its landlord:

> In this case, where the evidence before the Board showed that Mobil was the tenant, had paid the property taxes, and had made prior applications to the Board on its own, and on one occasion with the support of the owner, it cannot be said that the Board acted unreasonably in considering and granting its application for the zoning variances.

5. In Edwards v. Steele, 170 Cal. App. 3d 676, 216 Cal. Rptr. 283 (Ct. Ct. App. 1985), one particularly persistent property owner not only won a variance after bringing his case before the state supreme court, but also later convinced an appellate court to uphold $125,000 in damages from the Zoning Administrator for the official's refusal to grant the variance after the city's board of permit appeals decided in the landowner's favor. Associate Justice Edward Scott was not persuaded by the administrator's assertion of governmental immunity.

6. The Board of Adjustment or Board of Zoning Appeals, the body that typically makes zoning decisions, usually has responsibility as well for determining whether or not to grant a special use permit, also known as a conditional use permit. For this and other reasons, courts, lawyers, and commentators often confuse these two devices. For a valuable explanation of the difference, see Bucholz v. Board of Adjustment of Bremer County, 199 N.W.2d 73, 74-75 (Iowa 1972):

This zoning dispute arises over the application of the Board of Supervisors of Bremer County for a special use permit to establish and operate a sanitary landfill.

The defendant board of adjustment granted the request and plaintiffs, who own land in close proximity to the proposed landfill, brought certiorari . . . , asserting the action of the defendant was illegal and void. . . .

[W]e should settle one matter about which the parties have been in disagreement. Plaintiffs argue that the board of supervisors sought a variance. The defendant insists the application requested a special use permit. The matter assumes importance because the procedural requirements depend on which it is. We have discussed the difference between variances and special uses several times recently. A variance authorizes a party upon a showing of undue hardship to use his property in a manner forbidden by the zoning ordinance. A special use permit, on the other hand, allows property to be put to a purpose which the zoning ordinance *conditionally* allows.

In the present case the board of supervisors asks permission to operate a landfill in an A-agricultural district. Section 15 of the Bremer County Zoning Ordinance, which is hereafter set out, makes provision for such use if the conditions there specified are fulfilled. We are dealing, therefore, with a special use request, not a variance, and we give no further attention to plaintiffs' insistence to the contrary.

The following two cases illustrate that the decision to grant or deny a special use permit can involve local decisionmakers in important and sensitive public policy matters. Notice that unlike in a variance situation, the zoning ordinance itself describes what uses may be allowed using the special use permit procedure. Does Euclidean deference make sense in these settings? Should a distinction be made between "routine" special use cases and those involving particularly vulnerable populations?

CITY OF CLEBURNE v. CLEBURNE LIVING CENTER
473 U.S. 432 (1985)

Justice WHITE delivered the opinion of the Court. . . .

In July, 1980, respondent Jan Hannah purchased a building at 201 Featherston Street in the city of Cleburne, Texas, with the intention of leasing it to Cleburne Living Centers, Inc. (CLC) for the operation of a group home for the mentally retarded. It was anticipated that the home would house 13 retarded men and women, who would be under the constant supervision of CLC staff members. The house had four bedrooms and two baths, with a half bath to be added. CLC planned to comply with all applicable state and federal regulations.

The city informed CLC that a special use permit would be required for the operation of a group home at the site, and CLC accordingly submitted a permit application. In response to a subsequent inquiry from CLC, the city explained that under the zoning regulations applicable to the site, a special use permit, renewable annually, was required for the construction of "[h]ospitals for the insane or feeble-minded, or alcoholic [sic] or drug addicts, or penal or correctional institutions.[3] The city had determined that the proposed group home should be classified as a "hospital for the feebleminded." After holding a public hearing on CLC's application, the City Council voted 3 to 1 to deny a special use permit.

CLC then filed suit in Federal District Court against the city and a number of its officials, alleging, inter alia, that the zoning ordinance was invalid on its face and as applied because it discriminated against the mentally retarded in violation of the equal protection rights of CLC and its potential residents. The District Court found that "[i]f the potential residents of the Featherston Street home were not mentally retarded, but the home was the same in all other respects, its use would be permitted under the city's zoning ordinance," and that the city counsel's decision "was motivated primarily by the fact that the residents of the home would be persons who are mentally retarded." App. 93, 94. Even so, the District Court held the ordinance and its application constitutional. Concluding that no fundamental right was implicated and that mental retardation was neither a suspect nor a quasi-suspect classification, the court employed the minimum level of judicial scrutiny applicable to equal protection claims. The court deemed the ordinance, as written and applied, to be rationally related to the City's legitimate interests in "the legal responsibility of CLC and its residents, . . . the safety and fears of residents in the adjoining neighborhood, and the number of people to be housed in the home. *Id.*, at 103.

The Court of Appeals for the Fifth Circuit reversed, determining that mental retardation was a quasi-suspect classifcation and that it should assess the validity of the ordinance under intermediate-level scrutiny. 726 F.2d 191 (1984). . . .

Doubtless, there have been and there will continue to be instances of discrimination aganst the retarded that are in fact invidious, and that are properly subject to judicial correction under constitutional norms. But the appropriate method of reaching such instances is not to create a

---

3. The site of the home is an area zoned "R-3," an "Apartment House District." App. 51. Section 8 of the Cleburne zoning ordinance, in pertinent part, allows the following uses in an R-3 district:

1. Any use permitted in District R-2.

2. Apartment houses, or multiple dwellings.

3. Boarding and lodging houses.

4. Fraternity or sorority houses and dormitories.

5. Apartment hotels.

6. Hospitals, sanitariums, nursing homes or homes for convalescents or aged, *other than for the* insane or *feebleminded* or alcoholics or drug addicts.

7. Private clubs or fraternal orders, except those whose chief activity is carried on as a business.

8. Philanthropic or eleemosynary institutions, other than penal institutions.

9. Accessory uses customarily incident to any of the above uses.

. . .

Id., at 60-61 (emphasis added).

Section 16 of the ordinance specifies the uses for which a special use permit is required. These include "[h]ospitals for the insane or feebleminded, or alcoholic [sic] or drug addicts, or penal or correctional institutions." Id., at 63. Section 16 provides that a permit for such a use may be issued by "the Governing Body, after public hearing, and after recommendation of the Planning Commission." All special use permits are limited to one year, and each applicant is required "to obtain the signatures of the property owners within two hundred (200) feet of the property to be used." Ibid.

new quasi-suspect classification and subject all governmental action based on that classification to more searching evaluation. Rather, we should look to the likelihood that governmental action premised on a particular classification is valid as a general matter, not merely to the specifics of the case before us. Because mental retardation is a characteristic that the government may legitimately take into account in a wide range of decisions, and because both State and Federal Governments have recently committed themselves to assisting the retarded, we will not presume that any given legislative action, even one that disadvantages retarded individuals, is rooted in considerations that the Constitution will not tolerate.

Our refusal to recognize the retarded as a quasi-suspect class does not leave them entirely unprotected from invidious discrimination. To withstand equal protection review, legislation that distinguishes between the mentally retarded and others must be rationally related to a legitimate governmental purpose. This standard, we believe, affords government the latitude necessary both to pursue policies designed to assist the retarded in realizing their full potential, and to freely and efficiently engage in activities that burden the retarded in what is essentially an incidental manner. The State may not rely on a classification whose relationship to an asserted goal is so attenuated as to render the distinction arbitrary or irrational. Furthermore, some objectives — such as "a bare . . . desire to harm a politically unpopular group," id., at 534 — are not legitimate state interests. Beyond that, the mentally retarded, like others, have and retain their substantive constitutional rights in addition to the right to be treated equally by the law.

The constitutional issue is clearly posed. The city does not require a special use permit in an R-3 zone for apartment houses, multiple dwellings, boarding and lodging houses, fraternity or sorority houses, dormitories, apartment hotels, hospitals, sanitariums, nursing homes for convalescents or the aged (other than for the insane or feebleminded or alcoholics or drug addicts), private clubs or fraternal orders, and other specified uses. It does, however, insist on a special permit for the Featherston home, and it does so, as the District Court found, because it would be a facility for the mentally retarded. May the city require the permit for this facility when other care and multiple-dwelling facilities are freely permitted?

It is true, as already pointed out, that the mentally retarded as a group are indeed different from others not sharing their misfortune, and in this respect they may be different from those who would occupy other facilities that would be permitted in an R-3 zone without a special permit. But this difference is largely irrelevant unless the Featherston home and those who would occupy it would threaten legitimate interests of the city in a way that other permitted uses such as boarding houses and hospitals would not. Because in our view the record does not reveal any rational basis for believing that the Featherston home would pose any special threat to the city's legitimate interests, we affirm the judgment below insofar as it holds the ordinance invalid as applied in this case. . . .

The short of it is that requiring the permit in this case appears to us to rest on an irrational prejudice against the mentally retarded, including those who would occupy the Featherston facility and who would live under the closely supervised and highly regulated conditions expressly provided for by state and federal law.

The judgment of the Court of Appeals is affirmed insofar as it invalidates the zoning ordinance as applied to the Featherston home. The judgment is otherwise vacated, and the case is remanded.

Notes

1. The Supreme Court rejected the U.S. Court of Appeals for the Fifth Circuit panel's conclusion that mental retardation was a quasi-suspect classification triggering intermediate (somewhat heightened) scrutiny. The appellate court had argued

that although mental retardates are not a suspect class, they do share enough of the characteristics of a suspect class to warrant heightened scrutiny. Discrimination against the mentally retarded is likely to reflect deep-seated prejudice. They have been subjected to a history of unfair and often grotesque mistreatment. Until the 1970s, they were universally denied admittance into public schools in the United States. In addition, the Eugenic Society of America fought during the first half of this century to have retarded persons eradicated entirely through euthanasia and compulsory sterilization. Euthanasia was rejected; but thirty-two states have had statutes providing for the sterilization of retarded individuals.

Mental retardates have been segregated in remote, stigmatizing institutions and when permitted in society, they have often been subjected to ridicule. Once-technical terms for various degrees of retardation—e.g. "idiots," "imbeciles," "morons—have become popular terms of derision.

In addition, mentally retarded persons have lacked political power. The trial court found that they "historically have been subjected to exclusion from the political process. . . ." Indeed, as of 1979, most states disqualified mentally retarded individuals from voting. Furthermore, political organizations for the mentally retarded have emerged only recently and still possess relatively little power. . . .

Finally, the mentally retarded deserve special consideration because their condition is immutable. Dr. Phillip Roos explained at trial that mental retardation is "irreversible." "There may be some amelioration, but to date it is not a curable condition."

The combination of these factors—historical prejudice, political powerlessness, and immutability—calls for heightened scrutiny of classifications discriminating against the mentally retarded. We are not prepared to say that they are a full-fledged suspect class, however. . . .Therefore, we hold that mentally retarded persons are only a "quasi-suspect" class and that laws discriminating against the mentally retarded should be given intermediate scrutiny.

If the Supreme Court had adopted the Fifth Circuit's three-factor test ("historical prejudice, political powerlessness, and immutability"), can you think of other groups whose shared characteristics would have qualified as "quasi-suspect," therefore making it easier to challenge discriminatory land use regulations and other state actions? How about senior citizens; or gays, lesbians, bisexuals, and transsexuals? Can you see how the Court dodged a potent bullet by relying on the rational basis test instead?

2. As indicated by *Cleburne* and the case that follows, in some localities the local legislative body has responsibility for granting or denying special use permits. There is not unanimity on the issue of the nature of the decisionmaking process, as illustrated by the opinion of the Illinois Supreme Court in City of Chicago Heights v. Living Word Outreach Full Gospel Church & Ministries, Inc., 196 Ill. 2d 1, 13-16, 25, 749 N.E.2d 916, 924-26, 931 (2001):

It is widely held that when a zoning ordinance, such as the one in the case at bar, reserves the power to grant or deny an application for a special use permit in a legislative body, that body acts in an administrative capacity rather than a legislative capacity when it rules on a permit application. See, e.g., K. Young, Anderson's American Law of Zoning § 21.10, at 718-19 (4th ed. 1996) ("When permit issuing authority is retained by the legislature, the granting or denial of special permits by that body is regarded by most courts as an administrative rather than a legislative function."); 83 Am. Jur. 2d Zoning & Planning § 980, at 819 (1992) ("The granting or denial of special permits by the legislature is regarded by most courts as an administrative rather than a legislative function."). When a legislative body acts administratively in ruling on a permit application, its decision is subject to general principles of administrative review: "As the legislature is acting in an administrative capacity, it must follow the zoning regulations, and its actions are reviewable, and subject to judicial reversal if they are without support in the record or are otherwise arbitrary or unreasonable." K. Young, Anderson's American Law of Zoning § 21.10, at 720 (4th ed. 1996). In particular, the decision to grant or deny the permit application may be reviewed to determine whether the decision was made in compliance with any criteria listed in the zoning ordinance. K. Young, Anderson's American Law of Zoning § 21.10, at 725 (4th ed. 1996).

Although the clear weight of authority in the United States holds that a legislative body acts administratively when it rules on applications for special use permits, there is authority in this state which holds that the granting or denial of a permit application is a legislative act. For example, a line of cases from this court holds, with respect to the legislative bodies of counties, that the decision to grant or deny an application for a special use permit is a legislative act. See, e.g., Kotrich v. County of Du Page, 19 Ill. 2d 181, 166 N.E.2d 601 (1960) (county board of supervisors acted in a legislative capacity in granting a special use permit). When a legislative body acts in a legislative capacity in ruling on a permit application, its decision is not subject to principles of administrative review. Instead, the legislative body's decision is reviewed for arbitrariness as a matter of substantive due process under the six-part test set forth in La Salle National Bank v. County of Cook, 12 Ill. 2d 40, 145 N.E.2d 65 (1957). In this context, the landholder's compliance with any special use criteria listed in the zoning ordinance is merely a factor to consider, not the dispositive consideration, in determining whether the granting or denial of the permit application was arbitrary and unreasonable. . . .

We note that there is considerable force to the view that the decision of a legislative body to grant or deny an application for a special use permit, whether made by a county or municipality, should be viewed as an administrative act. The decisions from this court which have held to the contrary have been criticized. See, e.g., O. Browder, R. Cunningham, G. Nelson, W. Stoebuck & D. Whitman, Note on "Special Exceptions," "Special Uses," or "Conditional Uses," in Basic Property Law 1184, 1186 (5th ed. 1989) (*Kotrich*'s statement that " 'since the board of supervisors is a legislative body, precise standards to govern its determination are not required' will not bear analysis. The decision to grant or deny a 'special use' permit is clearly 'administrative' or 'quasi-judicial' rather than 'legislative,' whether the decision is made by a purely 'administrative' agency such as the zoning board of adjustment or a local governing body which may exercise both 'legislative' and 'administrative' powers"). Further, our appellate court has suggested that, in light of amendments made to the Illinois Municipal Code governing special uses, the General Assembly has indicated a desire to treat the application process for a special use permit as an administrative function, at least with respect to municipalities.

However, we need not decide, in this case, whether the city council's decision to deny Living Word's application for a special use permit was an administrative or legislative act. As discussed below, the result of this case is the same, regardless of how the city council's action is characterized. . . .

The City has emphasized that the council's decision to deny Living Word's application for a special use permit was based on a desire to exclude all noncommercial uses from the West Lincoln Highway corridor and not on any objection or ill-will directed to Living Word in particular. Further, as the City has made clear on appeal, the city council does not intend to apply this policy of excluding noncommercial uses from the West Lincoln Highway corridor on an *ad hoc* basis, but will, instead, consistently deny all noncommercial applications for special use permits. It is clear, therefore, that to uphold the rationale offered by the council for denying Living Word's application for a special use permit would result in the effective amendment of the City's zoning ordinance. Adopting the council's reasoning would completely remove churches from the list of special uses set forth in the City's zoning ordinance. Other noncommercial uses which are listed as special uses under the zoning ordinance, such as public parks and public libraries, would also be eliminated. A new zoning district, one exclusively commercial in character, would thus be created in the West Lincoln Highway corridor. Under the present circumstances, this *de facto* amendment of the City's zoning ordinance cannot be allowed. . . .

[T]he city council's reliance on the comprehensive plan does not change this result. As it is not law, the comprehensive plan cannot override the procedural prerequisites to amending the City's zoning ordinance. Moreover, we note that the comprehensive plan itself recognizes that it is not controlling legal authority and that the zoning ordinance must be amended if the goals of the comprehensive plan are to be met. The comprehensive plan points out that "the City's current zoning regulations were originally adopted in 1954. Although the ordinance has been incrementally amended and updated over the last 40 years, it has not received any comprehensive review or amendment." . . .

3. In a 2008 special exception case, the Court of Appeals of Maryland issued a far-reaching opinion touching on the sensitive relationship of local zoning to state planning mandates, the legal import of the comprehensive plan. The "zoning" facts in Trail v. Terrapin Run, Ltd. Liab. Co., 403 Md. 523, 525, 527, 528-29, 548-49, 569, 573-74, 575, 943 A.2d 1192, 1193, 1194, 1195-96, 1207, 1219, 1221-22 (2008), were fairly straightforward:

The site at issue is located in the A and C zones in Allegany County. In those zones planned unit developments, such as that in the case at bar, are permitted as special exceptions to the provisions of the zoning code. The site had been expressly designated for urban development as far back as 1995 and that designation continued through the 2002 version of the County Comprehensive Plan. The site was not included under the County's master plans as a "sensitive area." There is nothing we have found in the record of this case indicating that the Maryland Department of State Planning prior to this action ever objected to the inclusion of this site as suitable for urban development in the County's Master Plans.

Prior to the application at issue here, the Allegany Planning Commission had visited the site and determined that the proposed development then contemplated, that later was the subject of the application and of the grant of the special exception at issue, was consistent with the Comprehensive Plan.

In August 2005, Terrapin Run, LLC ("respondent") applied to the Board of Appeals of Allegany County (the "Board") for a special exception provided for in the local zoning code to establish a planned residential development (the "development"). The development was to be located on 935 acres of land, primarily zoned as District "A" (Agricultural, Forestry and Mining), with a portion of the tract located in District "C" (Conservation). The 935-acre tract of land abuts Route 40 and Shipley Road on the east side, and Green Ridge Road on the west. Green Ridge State Forest is located to the east of the tract, and there are also forested lands south of the tract. The development would consist of 4,300 residential units, an equestrian center, a community building and a 125,000 square foot shopping center. Additionally, the development would require a sewage treatment plant, to be located along Route 40. The Board noted that the project would take twenty years to complete and during that time, 150 to 200 separate permits and approvals would be required for its completion.

As relevant to the case at bar, after eight sessions in which the Board heard from 11 experts (nine for the applicants and two for the protestants), and received more than 80 exhibits, the Board, in a lengthy finding of facts, found that the proposed development would be in harmony with the Allegany County Comprehensive Plan, 2002 Update (the "Plan"). The Board opined that the Plan was advisory in nature, rather than regulatory, and that strict conformance with the plan was not required. . . .

The request for a special exception was eventually approved by the Board using the traditional "in harmony with" standard. Petitioners objected to the "in harmony" standard set forth by the Board of Appeals, and appealed to the Circuit Court for Allegany County. They contended that the Board erred as a matter of law in granting a special exception where there was no finding that the proposed use "conformed" to the Plan.[5] . . .

The semantic battle between "harmony" (or "consistency") and "conformance" made its way to a trial and appellate court before reaching the state's highest tribunal. The majority (in a 4-3 decision) began by setting the political context for the conflict before the court:

With the inclusion of certain of the amici (via their briefs),[6] this case, in one sense is a continuation of legislative battles that began in the early 1990s, where representatives of the environmental protection and professional land planning interests attempted to establish that the State, or State planners, should exercise greater control than theretofore enjoyed over most aspects of land use decision-making that then reposed in the local jurisdictions.

The court spent pages parsing statutory language, detailing legislative history for several bills and statutes, and consulting case law and dictionary entries for guidance. The majority rejected the petitioners' (and their allies') attempt to interpret "conformance" in a more demanding fashion than "the phrase 'in harmony with'" which has long been the standard utilized in Maryland land use administrative practice:

We fail to see any sufficient indication or support in the abbreviated legislative history surrounding the passage of the 1970 recodification legislation, in the general permissive character of Article 66B (that does not require zoning in the first instance), or in

---

5. Authors' note: The petitioners' argument is based on the definition of "special exception," found in MD. CODE ANN. art. 66B, §1.00(k) (emphasis added): "'Special exception' means a grant of a specific use that would not be appropriate generally or without restriction and shall be based upon a finding that certain conditions governing special exceptions as detailed in the zoning ordinance exist, that the use *conforms* to the plan and is compatible with the existing neighborhood."

6. Authors' note: Amici curiae included the Maryland Department of Planning, the Chesapeake Bay Foundation, and the American Planning Association.

the dictionary definitions prevalent at the time, that the Legislature was attempting to change the longstanding court recognized standard of "in harmony with" to some type of mandatory imposition of absolutism in the consideration by local governments of the relationship between "special exceptions" (and other land use devices) and local master or comprehensive plans or other local land use ordinances or regulatory devices. There is no sufficient evidence that the General Assembly was attempting to change long accepted legal standards in "special exception" practice. . . .

Neither have we been directed to any holding of this Court since 1970, and we know of none, where we have held that the use of the word "conform" in the 1970 statute created an absolute requirement in Article 66B that in order for special exceptions to be granted they must be in full and complete compliance with every aspect of the various types of land use plans and ordinances adopted by the respective local governments. Our cases prior to the 1970 statute, immediately after the 1970 statute, and since, even after the subsequent statutes in 1992 and 2000, have consistently applied the "in harmony with" standard. . . .

In our extensive review of the statutes we have found no indication that any of the statutes actually enacted by the Legislature were intended to diminish the local control of land use issues, albeit many additional considerations were imposed upon local governments in their planning processes. . . .

More specifically, neither have we found a single indication that when the word "conform" first found its way into the definition of "special exception" that it was intended to modify or restrict the use of the traditional "in harmony with" standard that had previously prevailed. Nor have we found a single instance since 1970 that offers any evidence that the Legislature has thereafter desired to have the word "conform" be defined as a requirement that local governments must absolutely meet every local guide, every local or State vision, or every local desire mentioned in their respective master plans, comprehensive plans or the like. . . .

Could the State find ways to impose absolutely mandatory requirements on local governments in the exercise of local controls? As we have noted—probably. But, the Legislature has been asked time and again to do so, and time and again it has intentionally declined to do so when offered the opportunity. In light of that history, the use of the word "conform," standing alone, in the 1970 definition does not create such a mandatory requirement.

In *The Comprehensive Plan and the Specific Ordinance: Judges as Connoisseurs of Meaning*, Planning & Envtl. L., July 2008, at 7, Professor Haar has noted:

The synonym approach of both opinions in *Terrapin Run* is interesting, but of not much practical use in the setting of standards for administrative agencies or, ultimately, for the courts, nor for the lawyers and their clients who live within these folds.

In May 2009, state lawmakers reacted to the *Trail Run* decision by passing the Smart and Sustainable Growth Act of 2009, in which the legislature expressed "concern[ ] that a broader interpretation of the decision could undermine the importance of making land use decisions that are consistent with the comprehensive plan," noted that "[t]he people of Maryland are best served if land use decisions are consistent with locally adopted comprehensive plans," and explained "that comprehensive plans should be followed as closely as possible while not being elevated to the status of an ordinance and that deviations from the plan should be rare."

AMES v. TOWN OF PAINTER
239 Va. 343, 389 S.E.2d 702 (1990)

Charles B. Ames and his wife, Jean, farmed approximately 190 acres in Accomack and Northampton Counties, raising primarily cucumbers and potatoes, relatively labor-intensive crops. Before 1988, they had relied mainly upon local labor, which they often found to be unavailable when needed during the harvest season. Because other agricultural operations in the area had been more successful when using migrant labor, the Ameses intended to employ migrant workers on contract during the 1988 and subsequent seasons.

The Ameses owned a 52-acre tract on U.S. Route 13, in Accomack County, adjacent to the southern boundary of the Town of Painter, four-tenths of a mile from the center of town. The tract contained an old, frame, two-story, six-room tenant house which had been occupied by six migrant workers and their children during the 1987 growing season. The Ameses developed a plan for the conversion of the tenant house into a migrant labor camp to accommodate 20 occupants, and, in March 1988, applied to the Board of Zoning Appeals of Accomack County (the Board) for a special use permit.

The Ameses' land was zoned "Agricultural District A." The Accomack County Zoning Ordinance did not permit the requested use in that district as a matter of right, but provided, in § 3-2-15, that such a use could be authorized by a special use permit granted by the Board. The language appearing on the application for a special use permit required that the application be signed by the owners of all lands within 500 feet of the boundary lines of the affected property, indicating their approval or disapproval of the requested use. Fourteen neighboring owners signed the application, four expressing approval and ten expressing disapproval. In addition, 226 citizens living in the immediate area filed a petition stating their "strong opposition" to the proposal.

The Board conducted a hearing on May 26, 1988, at which the Ameses and a number of other witnesses testified. At the conclusion of the hearing, a member of the Board, citing the requirements of the zoning ordinance, moved that the application be denied. The member stated his view that the proposed use would not be harmonious with the community and that it would have a harmful effect upon the property rights and values of neighboring owners. The motion failed for lack of a second. Another member then made the following motion:

> Mr. Chairman, I realize that this is a situation which every-one has talked about this morning, this labor has to be and also it is an effect on the community, and I am some-what familiar with what goes on in labor camps, and it is true, the larger the labor camp, the more problems you have. This is unfortunately, is near a residential area. I am willing to make a motion if it can be accepted to permit a camp there of at least ten people. Six last year and no one even knew they lived in the community, and if this gentleman can get by with ten I would make this recommendation or a motion that we approve it for ten people to be housed there.

That motion carried by a vote of four to one. Except for those two motions, there was no discussion or debate among the board members. The Board expressed no findings or conclusions. A special use permit was issued for a migrant-labor camp, limited to 10-person occupancy.

The Town of Painter, its mayor and vice-mayor, and the 226 objecting petitioners, brought the case to the circuit court by petition for certiorari. The court heard the matter ore tenus on December 19, 1988, reviewing the record made before the Board and hearing the testimony of Mr. Ames and other witnesses. At the conclusion of the hearing, the court ruled that the Board had failed to follow the guidelines of the zoning ordinance, reversed the Board, and dismissed the Ameses' application. We granted the Ameses an appeal.

Pursuant to enabling legislation, Accomack County has adopted a zoning ordinance which delegates authority to the Board to grant special use permits under certain conditions prescribed by the ordinance. Section 10-2-5 provides, in pertinent part:

> Before issuance of a Special Use Permit the Board of Zoning Appeals shall consider the general character of the surrounding neighborhood in order to facilitate the preservation and creation of an attractive and harmonious community. The Board of Zoning Appeals shall also consider the environmental effect on scenic, historic and waterfront areas including the property rights and values of adjoining and nearby property owners.

On appeal, the Ameses contend that the trial court failed to accord the Board's decision the presumption of correctness to which it is entitled, and impermissibly substituted the court's judgment for that of the Board. The Town argues that the Board's decision could not be sustained because it failed to comport with the standards prescribed by the zoning ordinance.

In County Board of Arlington v. Bratic, 237 Va. 221, 377 S.E.2d 368 (1989), we recently restated the principles of law governing the standards of judicial review which govern use-permit cases, which are the same as those governing judicial review of zoning enactments. A board of zoning appeals, acting under a delegated power to grant or refuse special exceptions and special use permits, acts in a legislative capacity. Therefore, its action is presumed to be reasonable. The presumption is rebuttable, but it stands until surmounted by evidence of unreasonableness. The litigant attacking the legislative act has the burden of producing probative evidence of unreasonableness. If he produces such probative evidence, the legislative act cannot be sustained unless the governing body (or in cases of this kind, the Board of Zoning Appeals) meets the challenge with some evidence of reasonableness. The governing body is not required to go forward with evidence sufficient to persuade the fact-finder of reasonableness by a preponderance of the evidence. It must only produce evidence sufficient to make the question "fairly debatable," for the legislative act to be sustained. "An issue may be said to be fairly debatable when, measured by both quantitative and qualitative tests, the evidence offered in support of the opposing views would lead objective and reasonable persons to reach different conclusions." Bratic, at 227, 377 S.E.2d at 371 (quoting Loudoun Co. v. Lerner, 221 Va. 30, 34, 267 S.E.2d 100, 102 (1980) (citation omitted)).

In a different but analogous context, we have consistently held that a board of zoning appeals, exercising its administrative functions in considering a zoning variance, must make certain findings of fact required by statute. If it does not do so, "the parties cannot properly litigate, the circuit court cannot properly adjudicate, and this Court cannot properly review the issues on appeal." Packer v. Hornsby, 221 Va. 117, 121, 267 S.E.2d 140, 142 (1980). Those prerequisite findings are, in variance cases, crucial to the exercise of the power of judicial review which the General Assembly has vested in the courts.

Although no findings of fact are required by statute when a board of zoning appeals acts in a legislative capacity to consider a special use permit, the observations we made in Packer v. Hornsby are instructive nonetheless. Code § 15.1-497 vests in the circuit court a power of judicial review of "any decision of the board of zoning appeals" by writ of certiorari. The issuance of such a writ on petition of "any person or persons jointly or severally aggrieved," id., is not discretionary, but is a matter of right. Bd. Sup. of Fairfax County v. Bd. Zoning Appeals, 225 Va. 235, 238, 302 S.E.2d 19, 21 (1983). Whether the board of zoning appeals has exercised an administrative function in considering a variance, or a legislative function in considering an application for a special use permit, it is equally essential to the exercise of judicial review that a sufficient record be made to enable the reviewing court to make an objective determination whether the issue is "fairly debatable."

Judicial review of legislative acts must be approached with particular circumspection because of the principle of separation of powers, embedded in the Constitution. That principle precludes judicial inquiry into the motives of legislative bodies elected by the people. Where the courts are called upon to review the acts of officials, agencies, and boards exercising delegated legislative powers, the inquiry must ordinarily be whether the official, agency, or board has acted arbitrarily or capriciously, or rather, whether it has acted in accordance with the policies and standards specified in the legislative delegation of power. That inquiry becomes necessary because delegations of legislative power are valid only if they establish specific policies and fix definite standards to guide the official, agency, or board in the exercise of the power. Delegations of legislative power which lack such policies and standards are unconstitutional and void.

The Accomack County Zoning Ordinance avoids that difficulty because it contains standards for the guidance of the Board in the exercise of its delegated legislative power to consider an application for a special use permit. Those standards are contained in the two sentences of § 10-2-5 quoted above. It is, therefore, essential to the exercise of the circuit court's statutory duty of judicial review, that the record be such as to enable the court to determine whether the Board adhered to those standards.

The record made before the Board consisted of the statements of Mr. and Mrs. Ames, the applicants, which related entirely to their need for migrant labor, the testimony of witnesses opposing the application, and the arguments of counsel. The witnesses opposing the application expressed concern relating to adverse environmental effects, increased criminal activity, particularly drug distribution which was being experienced in nearby migrant labor camps, and adverse effects upon property values.

The supplemental record made before the circuit court was similar. Several witnesses testified to the anticipated harm the proposed special use would cause to the Town, the neighboring properties, and the residents of the affected area. The only testimony in support of the application was given by Mr. Ames, whose statements again related primarily to his need for migrant labor. As a result, the record is devoid of any evidence to support a finding that the proposed special use would "facilitate the preservation and creation of an attractive and harmonious community," as required by § 10-2-5. The record is similarly devoid of any evidence to support a finding that "the environmental effect on scenic, historic and waterfront areas including the property rights and values of adjoining and nearby property owners," *id.*, would be anything other than harmful.

How may the power of judicial review be exercised where the record is silent with respect to the Board's adherence to a legislatively-prescribed standard? The zoning ordinance merely requires that the Board, in making its decision, take into consideration the attractiveness and character of the surrounding neighborhood, the harmony of the proposed use with the neighborhood, the environmental effects of the proposed use, and any effect upon "property rights and values of adjoining and nearby property owners." Some or all of the members of the Board, in reaching their individual decisions, may have considered those factors in good faith, but with the exception of the statements of the member who moved a denial of the application on those grounds, there is no basis in the record for an objective conclusion by the reviewing court that the legislative standards had been given any consideration.

We hold that the "fairly debatable" standard cannot be established by a silent record. Unless the Board makes appropriate findings, supported by the record, or states appropriate conclusions supported by the record, or unless the record itself, taken as a whole, suffices to render the issue fairly debatable, probative evidence of unreasonableness adduced by a litigant attacking the Board's action will be deemed unrefuted. Because that was the situation here, the judgment will be *Affirmed.*

Notes

1. The Iowa Supreme Court, in Holland v. City Council of Decorah, 662 N.W.2d 681, 681-82, 688 (Iowa 2003), determined that according to state law the city council did not have the authority to bypass the board of adjustment in determining whether to grant Wal-Mart a special exception to the city's floodplain ordinance:

> This is an appeal in a certiorari case brought by landowners along the Upper Iowa River in Decorah to block the filling of a portion of the floodplain for the purpose of building a Wal-Mart Super Center. The defendants are Wal-Mart and the City Council of Decorah, to which we will collectively refer as Wal-Mart. The district court annulled the writ of certiorari, allowing the project to go forward, and the plaintiffs appealed. The court of appeals reversed, concluding the city council had exceeded its statutory authority in permitting the fill. . . .

> In reliance on City Ordinance section 17.120.020, Wal-Mart applied to the Decorah City Council for a permit to place fill on the floodplain. That ordinance provides this with respect to floodplains in the city:

>> Principal permitted uses. Only the uses of structures or land listed in this section shall be permitted in the F-1 floodplain district:

>> A. Agriculture, truck gardening, and nurseries, and the usual accessory buildings, but not including livestock feedlots or poultry farms or similar uses; provided, that no permanent dwelling units shall be erected thereon;

>> B. Forests and forestry preserves, wildlife areas;

>> C. Publicly owned parks, nature areas, playgrounds, golf courses and similar non-commercial recreational uses;

>> D. Any use erected or maintained by a public agency, public and private parking lots;

>> E. Public utility structures, subject to approval of the board of adjustment, except those utilities and structures constructed by the city.

>> F. *Dumping of approved materials for landfill purposes, subject to prior approval of the city council and appropriate state agencies.*

> (Emphasis added.) The last use, "F," is relied on by Wal-Mart, and the interpretation of that provision lies at the heart of this appeal.

> In July 1999, before Wal-Mart applied to the city council, it wrote to the Decorah City Administrator to say Wal-Mart would be applying to the board of adjustment for a special exception to the floodplain ordinance. However, the application was never filed. On August 15, 2000, Wal-Mart's representatives appeared before the city council, which, by a four-to-three vote, approved Wal-Mart's request to fill the property. The fill request was presented and granted as part of a plan to build a Wal-Mart Super Center on

the site. However, the council's vote only approved the fill; it did not change the zoning of the area or approve a site plan. . . .

If Wal-Mart's interpretation of ordinance section 17.120.020(F) is correct, the ordinance would violate Iowa Code section 414.3, which requires ordinances to comply with the city's comprehensive plan. Under Wal-Mart's interpretation, the ordinance grants broad authority to the council to alter the character of the floodplain without any consideration of the city's comprehensive plan. By assuming, through the ordinance, the authority to decide this issue, the council has violated Iowa Code sections 414.7 and 414.12, concerning the jurisdiction of the board of adjustment. To the extent the council has claimed authority to grant the fill permit in this case, it has diminished the jurisdiction of the board of adjustment.

2. Who sits on the board of adjustment and what is the extent of their knowledge concerning the (often-confusing) state of the law? Consider the results of Contemporary Studies Project, *Rural Land Use Regulation in Iowa: An Empirical Analysis of County Board of Adjustment Practices*, 68 Iowa L. Rev. 1083, 1146-47 (1983), a comprehensive study of rural boards in Iowa:

Obviously, the requirement that a majority of the board be comprised of residents of unincorporated areas makes likely that farmers will be chosen to serve on the board. Over one-half of the board members responding to the Project questionnaire were people engaged in farming or spouses of farmers. Also, most board of adjustment members are longtime residents of their counties. Only two percent have lived in their counties for less than ten years, while over eighty percent have resided in their counties for more than thirty years.

A clear majority of county board of adjustment members have high school degrees; only six and one-half percent have less than a high school education. Board members rarely possess any formal education related to land use planning, however. Although one-third of all county board of adjustment members in Iowa have some education beyond high school, only four percent have a formal education related to land use planning.

3. One survey of zoning boards of appeals for large cities, in *Zoning News*, June 1985, at 2-3, included the following information: the annual zoning caseload for these boards ranged from a low of 49 in Norfolk, Virginia (a state in which use variances are not allowed) to nearly 800 in Boston. While the board members served with no pay in Phoenix and Birmingham, the chair of the New York City Board of Standards and Appeals, who was expected to hold no other employment, was paid $71,000 per year, the vice chair was paid over $64,000, and the other members were paid over $58,000. While in Norfolk members were appointed by the circuit court, in Boston, one member and three alternates were appointed by the mayor, one by the board of architects or engineers, one by the board of realtors, one by the building trades union, and one by the central labor union. In Atlanta, at least two members of the five-person board had to be selected from the fields of law, planning, or engineering. In several cities, including Cincinnati, Los Angeles, Portland, and San Diego, other officials (such as a zoning administrator, planning director, director of building inspections, or a hearing officer) were responsible for the duties handled in other cities by board members.

Chapter Five

The Regulatory Takings Battleground: Environmental Regulation of Land Versus Private-Property Rights

I.   A New Activism? Judicial Reactions to Regulatory Overreaching (and a Suggested Response)

For more than eight decades, zoning and land use planning have been located squarely within the "comfort zone" of local government.[1] Indeed, as noted in Chapter Three, it has been an unshaken principle of American constitutional jurisprudence since the Supreme Court handed down its decision in *Euclid* in 1926 that local governments are entitled to generous deference when exercising their traditional police powers, including zoning and planning.

As the nation entered the second half of the 20th century, its local governments began to experiment with the incorporation of environmental policies and practices into their zoning and planning schemes, a practice that by century's end brought local officials into direct conflict with the ideology shared by many Justices on the Rehnquist Court. Beginning in the late 1960s and early 1970s, environmental issues began to capture the attention of elected officials (driven by constituent concerns and demands) on the federal level. By the time Ronald Reagan took office in 1981 with his "government is the problem"[2] philosophy, the *U.S. Code* and the *Code of Federal Regulations* contained reams of pages devoted to regulation of air pollution[3]; water pollution[4]; waste treatment, transport, and disposal[5]; toxic chemicals[6]; pesticides and other poisons[7]; ocean dumping[8]; safe drinking water[9]; protection of endangered and threatened species[10]; management of the coastal zone[11]; federal public land management[12]; and releases of hazardous substances.[13] All of this statutory and regulatory activity was not confined to the federal level, however, as activists

---

1. Much of the discussion in this introduction derives from Michael Allan Wolf, *Earning Deference: Reflections on the Merger of Environmental and Land Use Law, in* New Ground: The Advent of Local Environmental Law 347 (John R. Nolon ed. 2003).
2. President Ronald Reagan, Inaugural Address (Jan. 20, 1981), 1981 Pub. Papers 1 (Jan. 20, 1981).
3. *See* Clean Air Act, 42 U.S.C. §§7401-7671q.
4. *See* Federal Water Pollution Control Act, 33 U.S.C. §§1251-1387.
5. *See* Resource Conservation and Recovery Act of 1976, 42 U.S.C. §§6901-6992k.
6. *See* Toxic Substances Control Act, 15 U.S.C. §§2601-2692.
7. *See* Federal Insecticide, Fungicide, and Rodenticide Act, 7 U.S.C. §§136-136y.
8. *See* Marine Protection, Research, and Sanctuaries Act of 1972, 33 U.S.C. §§1401-1445.
9. *See* Safe Drinking Water Act, 42 U.S.C. §§300f to 300j-26.
10. *See* Endangered Species Act, 16 U.S.C. §§1531-1544.
11. *See* Coastal Zone Management Act, 16 U.S.C. §§1451-1465.
12. *See* Federal Land Policy and Management Act, 43 U.S.C. §§1701-1785.
13. *See* Comprehensive Environmental Response, Compensation, and Liability Act of 1980, 42 U.S.C. §§9601-9675.

in states and localities successfully urged lawmakers to implement legal controls over activities that endangered our fragile ecological balance.

By the close of the 20th century, this nonfederal experimentation was in serious jeopardy. This is because one legacy of the Reagan years proved to be a significant barrier to the growth and even continued vitality of state and local environmental activity: President Reagan and his successor, President George H.W. Bush, remade the federal judiciary, particularly the Court. One key and controversial contribution to American jurisprudence made by the new conservative majority on the Court was the reinvigoration of the Takings Clause, a move that has posed serious problems for a wide range of environmental regulations promulgated and enforced by local and state officials.[14] State and local floodplain controls, wetlands restrictions, coal mining regulations, beach access easements, bicycle paths, coastal development bans, endangered species protections, and open-space ordinances have all been subjected to regulatory takings analysis, and some of these regulations have fallen as a result of increased and heightened judicial scrutiny.

A study of the leading regulatory takings cases included in this chapter reveals the Court's tension between nonfederal environmental regulation and private-property rights protection. For several years following the Court's invocation of Justice Holmes' opinion in *Pennsylvania Coal*, discussed at the end of Chapter Three, the Court avoided deciding the substantive question of whether, in fact, a regulation that went "too far" effected a taking that required compensation from the government.[15] In 1987, the new Chief Justice, William H. Rehnquist, writing for the Court in First English Evangelical Lutheran Church of Glendale v. County of Los Angeles, 482 U.S. 304, 321 (1987), answered that question affirmatively, assuming for the purpose of the appeal that the challenged restriction (local floodplain controls) deprived the landowner "of all use of [his] property."

A few weeks later, in Nollan v. California Coastal Comm'n, 483 U.S. 825, 834 (1987), a five-member majority expanded the reach of the regulatory takings doctrine beyond deprivation of value to allow for the invalidation of regulations that do not "substantially" (as opposed to "rationally" or "reasonably") advance a "legitimate state interest." A state coastal commission's exaction of a beach access easement use in exchange for permitting beachfront construction was thereby voided because of lack of a substantial connection between ends and means.

The regulatory takings steamroller picked up momentum five years later when, in Lucas v. South Carolina Coastal Council, 505 U.S. 1003, 1027 (1992), the Court held that "where the State seeks to sustain regulation that deprives land of all economically beneficial use, [the State] may resist compensation only if the logically antecedent inquiry into the nature of the owner's estate shows that the proscribed use interests were not part of his title to begin with." Two years after *Lucas*, regulators received an even more significant jolt from the Justices. The majority in Dolan v. City of Tigard, 512 U.S. 374, 391 (1994), built on *Nollan*'s activist foundation and obligated a local government to carry the significant burden of demonstrating that the bicycle path and floodplain easements it had exacted from a plumbing supply business were roughly proportional to the impact of a planned expansion of its building. This was a far cry from Euclidean deference, occasioned (and justified) most likely by the majority's concern about the motives and abilities of local regulators to craft and impose fair environmental protection measures.

Subsequent cases brought additional bad news to state and local environmental regulators and their supporters. Five years after *Dolan*, in City of Monterey v. Del Monte Dunes at Monterey, Ltd., 526 U.S. 687, 697-98 (1999), the Court considered a case involving a frustrated landown-

---

14. *See* Charles M. Haar & Michael Allan Wolf, Euclid *Lives: The Survival of Progressive Jurisprudence*, 115 Harv. L. Rev. 2158 (2002).

15. *See, e.g.*, MacDonald, Sommer & Frates v. Yolo County, 477 U.S. 340, 348 (1986) (in which the Court could not decide whether a regulatory taking had occurred because the local regulator had not yet made "a final and authoritative determination of the type and intensity of development legally permitted on the subject property").

er's efforts to secure site plan approval for a beachfront residential development (county officials imposed open-space requirements and were concerned about the impact on the critical habitat of an endangered butterfly). This time, there was no need to expand the substantive reach of regulatory takings; instead, the Court permitted the extremely puzzling questions of "economically viable use" and "substantially advancing a legitimate public purpose" to be submitted to a jury. Then, in Palazzolo v. Rhode Island, 533 U.S. 606, 616, 626-30 (2001), we learned that even landowners who maintained a "token interest" could claim a *Lucas*-type total deprivation. Moreover, we were told that, even if those landowners acquired their ownership interest in the property with notice of existing restrictions, they were not necessarily foreclosed from bringing a regulatory takings lawsuit challenging those very regulations. At risk in *Palazzolo* were state controls over filling coastal wetlands.

This litany of decisions demonstrates quite clearly the hazards of implementing and enforcing state and local environmental controls affecting the use of land. Although not all nonfederal regulation has been struck down in recent years,[16] a majority of the Rehnquist Court viewed such restrictions as the Achilles' heel of property regulation generally, and the result was the dramatic expansion of the judiciary's power to strike down a wide and increasing array of regulatory work product by elected and administrative officials.

Given the eagerness with which some disgruntled landowners pursue regulatory takings challenges to environmentally flavored land use restrictions, often with the assistance of public interest lawyers from groups such as the Institute for Justice and the Pacific Legal Foundation,[17] local governments should be especially careful when creating and implementing new land use controls that threaten to reduce the existing and potential value of real property. One strategy that local officials should consider pursuing, a strategy borrowed from a key federal environmental law statute, is to "stop and think" before regulating.

A few decades ago, environmental law was revolutionized by a seemingly simple statute that appeared to require very little of federal agencies—the National Environmental Policy Act (NEPA) of 1969.[18] In the hands of activist judges, led by the legendary J. Skelley Wright, NEPA quickly shed its "paper tiger" image.[19] By the mid-1970s, NEPA was widely understood to mandate federal agencies to "stop and think" carefully and expansively about the implications of "major Federal actions significantly affecting the quality of the human environment,"[20] and, perhaps, to engage in time- and resource-consuming studies of those wide-ranging implications. As a result, the environmental impact statement process triggered by NEPA, and by state versions in several jurisdictions, has become a focal point for active public participation and, at times, lawsuits orchestrated by federal, state, and local nongovernmental organizations.

The process of making and enforcing local environmental law could benefit from the adoption of four NEPA elements. First, at the proposal stage for a new environmental regulation device or program, local regulators could do an initial analysis concerning whether the implementation of that device or program would "significantly affect the market value of private property within the

---

16. *See, e.g.*, Tahoe-Sierra Preservation Council v. Tahoe Reg'l Planning Agency, 535 U.S. 302 (2002) (holding that development moratoria totaling 30 months did not effect a per se regulatory taking).

17. In fact, the Pacific Legal Foundation filed amicus or party briefs in all of the major cases included in this chapter. The Institute for Justice filed amicus briefs, carrying Professor Richard Epstein's name, in *Tahoe-Sierra, Palazzolo, Del Monte Dunes, Dolan*, and *Lucas*.

18. NEPA §§2-209, 42 U.S.C. §§4321-4370d.

19. Calvert Cliffs' Coordinating Comm. v. Atomic Energy Comm'n, 449 F.2d 1109, 1114 (D.C. Cir. 1971) (Judge J. Skelly Wright, writing for the court, noted that "Congress did not intend the Act to be a paper tiger").

20. NEPA §102(2)(C), 42 U.S.C. §4332(2)(C).

jurisdiction."[21] While it is hard to imagine any land use or environmental regulation that does not have some negative effect on property values, the impact of some measures can be quite dramatic. The first stage would identify those "high-impact" devices or programs that are most likely to raise serious property rights concerns.

Should the answer to the first inquiry be "yes," local officials would then "consult with and obtain the comments of any federal, local, or state agency or governmental unit that has special expertise with respect to the type of proposed regulation."[22] In this second, consultative step, local officials would receive the counsel of those who have access to information regarding (1) actual experiences with the operation of the proposed or closely related devices or programs, and (2) ways to mitigate the negative impact on property values while maintaining the essential environmental character of the proposed tool.

During the next step, local officials would, in a document made available for public comment, explain the proposed measure and any feedback received during the consultative step, and "objectively evaluate reasonable alternatives to the proposed device or program in a document that is made available for public comment."[23] Local governments, like all lawmakers, often govern least effectively when they quickly respond to perceived emergencies. Moreover, as noted in Chapter Four, local land use regulation has always been associated with suspicions of graft and corruption that, regrettably, are sometimes warranted. A common concern voiced by judges in modern regulatory takings cases is that one or a few landowners may be unfairly singled out to bear heavy burdens for the benefit of the wider community. Requiring local environmental regulators to report to the public their plans, findings, and evaluations of reasonable alternatives would be an effective step toward reducing the perception and reality of corruption, favoritism, and bias. By inviting public comments, government officials will be able to consider arguments and alternatives offered by private property owners and their advocates, and by interest groups favoring real estate development, in a nonconfrontational setting removed from the pressures and expenses of litigation.

The fourth step before implementation of the device or program would be the production of a document that responds to the public comments received as a result of the third step. In this final stage, local government officials will have the opportunity to make some private parties stakeholders in the final product that emerges from the regulatory process. Should landowners challenge the implemented program or device in court on regulatory takings grounds, the judge might very well look askance at plaintiffs who failed to participate in this "stop and think" process, or who allege that the local government acted hastily or arbitrarily.

The regulatory takings cases included in this chapter are organized thematically and chronologically, enabling the reader to understand how the Justices built on (and at times seemingly departed from) precedent (*Penn Central*), dictum (*Agins*), or an influential dissent (*San Diego Gas*) in an attempt to bring coherence to the muddled, Holmesean idea that regulation that goes "too far" somehow amounts to a violation of the Takings Clause. Understanding the arguments in this set of cases is tough going at times, as the Court has often found itself torn between the need to protect private rights and the obligation to allow its co-equal branches to protect the general welfare. A rhetorical shift in the former direction—the authorization of a monetary remedy (*First English*) or a jury trial (*Del Monte Dunes*), the recognition of a new per se takings rule (*Lucas*), the subtle elevation of judicial scrutiny (*Nollan*), or the shift in burden (*Dolan*)—might well have a chilling effect on a wide range of innovative environmental and land use programs, while the adop-

---

21. *Cf. id.* ("major Federal actions significantly affecting the quality of the human environment").

22. *Cf. id.* ("responsible Federal official shall consult with and obtain the comments of any Federal agency which has jurisdiction by law or special expertise with respect to any environmental impact involved").

23. *Cf.* 42 C.F.R. §1502.14(a) ("rigorously explore and objectively evaluate all reasonable alternatives").

tion of a more deferential position—the decision not to narrow the takings denominator (*Keystone*) and the refusal to expand the scope of the "total takings" test (*Palazzolo* and *Tahoe-Sierra*)—might leave landowners defenseless against costly, even confiscatory, regulations. After you complete your examination of over 20 years of jurisprudential exploration, consider whether the Court and its audience are any closer to a coherent understanding of when a regulatory taking occurs than Justice Holmes and his brethren were many decades ago.

II.   Open Space Mandates

Cal. Gov. Code §65561

The Legislature finds and declares as follows:

(a) That the preservation of open-space land, as defined in this article, is necessary not only for the maintenance of the economy of the state, but also for the assurance of the continued availability of land for the production of food and fiber, for the enjoyment of scenic beauty, for recreation and for the use of natural resources.

(b) That discouraging premature and unnecessary conversion of open-space land to urban uses is a matter of public interest and will be of benefit to urban dwellers because it will discourage noncontiguous development patterns which unnecessarily increase the costs of community services to community residents.

(c) That the anticipated increase in the population of the state demands that cities, counties, and the state at the earliest possible date make definite plans for the preservation of valuable open-space land and take positive action to carry out such plans by the adoption and strict administration of laws, ordinances, rules and regulations as authorized by this chapter or by other appropriate methods.

(d) That in order to assure that the interests of all its people are met in the orderly growth and development of the state and the preservation and conservation of its resources, it is necessary to provide for the development by the state, regional agencies, counties and cities, including charter cities, of statewide coordinated plans for the conservation and preservation of open-space lands.

(e) That for these reasons this article is necessary for the promotion of the general welfare and for the protection of the public interest in open-space land.

AGINS v. CITY OF TIBURON
447 U.S. 255 (1980)

MR. JUSTICE POWELL delivered the opinion of the Court. . . .

After the appellants acquired five acres of unimproved land in the city of Tiburon, Cal., for residential development, the city was required by state law to prepare a general plan governing both land use and the development of open-space land. Cal. Govt. Code Ann. §§ 65302 (a) and (e) (West Supp. 1979); see § 65563. In response, the city adopted two ordinances that modified existing zoning requirements. Tiburon, Cal., Ordinances Nos. 123 N. S. and 124 N. S. (June 28, 1973). The zoning ordinances placed the appellants' property in "RPD-1," a Residential Planned Development and Open Space Zone. RPD-1 property may be devoted to one-family dwellings, accessory buildings, and open-space uses. Density restrictions permit the appellants to build between one and five single-family residences on their 5-acre tract. The appellants never have sought approval for development of their land under the zoning ordinances.[1]

The appellants filed a two-part complaint against the city in State Superior Court. The first cause of action sought $ 2 million in damages for inverse condemnation.[2] The second cause of action requested a declaration that the zoning ordinances were facially unconstitutional. The gravamen of both claims was the appellants' assertion that the city had taken their property without just compensation in violation of the Fifth and Fourteenth Amendments. The complaint alleged that land in Tiburon has greater value than any other suburban property in the State of California. App. 3. The ridgelands that appellants own "possess magnificent views of San Francisco Bay and the scenic surrounding areas [and] have the highest market values of all lands" in Tiburon. *Id.*, at 4. Rezoning of the land "forever prevented [its] development for residential use. . . ." *Id.*, at 5. Therefore, the appellants contended, the city had "completely destroyed the value of [appellants'] property for any purpose or use whatsoever. . . ." *Id.*, at 7.

The city demurred, claiming that the complaint failed to state a cause of action. The Superior Court sustained the demurrer, and the California Supreme Court affirmed. 24 Cal. 3d 266, 598 P. 2d 25 (1979). The State Supreme Court first considered the inverse condemnation claim. It held that a landowner who challenges the constitutionality of a zoning ordinance may not "sue in inverse condemnation and thereby transmute an excessive use of the police power into a lawful taking for which compensation in eminent domain must be paid." *Id.*, at 273, 598 P. 2d, at 28. The sole remedies for such a taking, the court concluded, are mandamus and declaratory judgment. Turning therefore to the appellants' claim for declaratory relief, the California Supreme Court held that the zoning ordinances had not deprived the appellants of their property without compensation in violation of the Fifth Amendment.

We noted probable jurisdiction. We now affirm the holding that the zoning ordinances on their face do not take the appellants' property without just compensation.[6]

The Fifth Amendment guarantees that private property shall not "be taken for public use, without just compensation." The appellants' complaint framed the question as whether a zoning ordinance that prohibits all development of their land effects a taking under the Fifth and Fourteenth Amendments. The California Supreme Court rejected the appellants' characterization of the issue by holding, as a matter of state law, that the terms of the challenged ordinances allow the appellants to construct between one and five residences on their property. The court did not consider whether the zoning ordinances would be unconstitutional if applied to prevent appellants from building five homes. Because the appellants have not submitted a plan for development of their property as the ordinances permit, there is as yet no concrete controversy regarding the appli-

---

1. Shortly after it enacted the ordinances, the city began eminent domain proceedings against the appellants' land. The following year, however, the city abandoned those proceedings, and its complaint was dismissed. The appellants were reimbursed for costs incurred in connection with the action.

2. Inverse condemnation should be distinguished from eminent domain. Eminent domain refers to a legal proceeding in which a government asserts its authority to condemn property. United States v. Clarke, 445 U.S. 253, 255-258 (1980). Inverse condemnation is "a shorthand description of the manner in which a landowner recovers just compensation for a taking of his property when condemnation proceedings have not been instituted." *Id.*, at 257.

6. The appellants also contend that the state courts erred by sustaining the demurrer despite their uncontroverted allegations that the zoning ordinances would "forever [prevent] . . . development for residential use," id., at 5, and "completely [destroy] the value of [appellant's] property for any purpose or use whatsoever . . . ," id., at 7. The California Supreme Court compared the express terms of the zoning ordinances with the factual allegations of the complaint. The terms of the ordinances permit construction of one to five residences on the appellants' 5-acre tract. The court therefore rejected the contention that the ordinances prevented all use of the land. . . .

cation of the specific zoning provisions. Thus, the only question properly before us is whether the mere enactment of the zoning ordinances constitutes a taking.

The application of a general zoning law to particular property effects a taking if the ordinance does not substantially advance legitimate state interests, see Nectow v. Cambridge, 277 U.S. 183, 188 (1928), or denies an owner economically viable use of his land, see Penn Central Transp. Co. v. New York City, 438 U.S. 104, 138, n. 36 (1978). The determination that governmental action constitutes a taking is, in essence, a determination that the public at large, rather than a single owner, must bear the burden of an exercise of state power in the public interest. Although no precise rule determines when property has been taken, see Kaiser Aetna v. United States, 444 U.S. 164 (1979), the question necessarily requires a weighing of private and public interests. The seminal decision in Euclid v. Ambler Co., 272 U.S. 365 (1926), is illustrative. In that case, the landowner challenged the constitutionality of a municipal ordinance that restricted commercial development of his property. Despite alleged diminution in value of the owner's land, the Court held that the zoning laws were facially constitutional. They bore a substantial relationship to the public welfare, and their enactment inflicted no irreparable injury upon the landowner. Id., at 395-397.

In this case, the zoning ordinances substantially advance legitimate governmental goals. The State of California has determined that the development of local open-space plans will discourage the "premature and unnecessary conversion of open-space land to urban uses." Cal. Govt. Code Ann. § 65561 (b) (West. Supp. 1979).[7] The specific zoning regulations at issue are exercises of the city's police power to protect the residents of Tiburon from the ill effects of urbanization.[8] Such governmental purposes long have been recognized as legitimate. See Penn Central Transp. Co. v. New York City, supra, at 129; Village of Belle Terre v. Boraas, 416 U.S. 1, 9 (1974); Euclid v. Ambler Co., supra, at 394-395.

The ordinances place appellants' land in a zone limited to single-family dwellings, accessory buildings, and open-space uses. Construction is not permitted until the builder submits a plan compatible with "adjoining patterns of development and open space." Tiburon, Cal., Ordinance No. 123 N. S. § 2 (F). In passing upon a plan, the city also will consider how well the proposed development would preserve the surrounding environment and whether the density of new construction will be offset by adjoining open spaces. The zoning ordinances benefit the appellants as well as the public by serving the city's interest in assuring careful and orderly development of residential property with provision for open-space areas. There is no indication that the appellants' 5-acre tract is the only property affected by the ordinances. Appellants therefore will share with other owners the benefits and burdens of the city's exercise of its police power. In assessing the fairness of the zoning ordinances, these benefits must be considered along with any diminution in market value that the appellants might suffer.

Although the ordinances limit development, they neither prevent the best use of appellants' land, see United States v. Causby, 328 U.S. 256, 262, and n. 7 (1946), nor extinguish a fundamental attribute of ownership, see Kaiser Aetna v. United States, supra, at 179-180. The appellants have alleged that they wish to develop the land for residential purposes, that the land is the most expensive suburban property in the State, and that the best possible use of the land is residential. The California Supreme Court has decided, as a matter of state law, that appellants may be permitted

---

7. The State also recognizes that the preservation of open space is necessary "for the assurance of the continued availability of land for the production of food and fiber, for the enjoyment of scenic beauty, for recreation and for the use of natural resources." Cal. Govt. Code Ann. § 65561 (a) (West. Supp. 1979); see Tiburon, Cal., Ordinance No. 124 N. S. §§ 1 (f) and (h).

8. The City Council of Tiburon found that "[it] is in the public interest to avoid unnecessary conversion of open space land to strictly urban uses, thereby protecting against the resultant adverse impacts, such as air, noise and water pollution, traffic congestion, destruction of scenic beauty, disturbance of the ecology and environment, hazards related to geology, fire and flood, and other demonstrated consequences of urban sprawl." Id., §1 (c).

to build as many as five houses on their five acres of prime residential property. At this juncture, the appellants are free to pursue their reasonable investment expectations by submitting a development plan to local officials. Thus, it cannot be said that the impact of general land-use regulations has denied appellants the "justice and fairness" guaranteed by the Fifth and Fourteenth Amendments.

The State Supreme Court determined that the appellants could not recover damages for inverse condemnation even if the zoning ordinances constituted a taking. The court stated that only mandamus and declaratory judgment are remedies available to such a landowner. Because no taking has occurred, we need not consider whether a State may limit the remedies available to a person whose land has been taken without just compensation.

The judgment of the Supreme Court of California is
Affirmed.

Notes

1. Open-space zoning is one of many approaches state and local governments have taken to preserve undeveloped parcels in urbanizing areas and of farmland outside of rapidly expanding metropolises. Other strategies include purchase or condemnation of fee interests or of conservation easements, cluster zoning, land-banking, incentive zoning, transferable development rights, urban growth boundaries, and exactions in exchange for rezoning or development permission. Professor John R. Nolon has provided a very valuable introduction in *In Praise of Parochialism: The Advent of Local Environmental Law*, 26 Harv. Envtl. L. Rev. 365, 365 (2002):

> [T]here has been a remarkable and unnoticed trend among local governments to adopt laws that protect natural resources. These local environmental laws take on a number of forms. They include local comprehensive plans expressing environmental values, zoning districts created to protect watershed areas, environmental standards contained in subdivision and site plan regulations, and stand-alone environmental laws adopted to protect particular natural resources such as ridgelines, wetlands, floodplains, stream banks, existing vegetative cover, and forests. The purposes of these laws are to preserve natural resources from the adverse impacts of land development and to control nonpoint source pollution. In inventing these controls, local governments have creatively used a variety of traditional and modern powers that their state legislatures have delegated to them.

2. The *Agins* Court sought to distinguish "inverse condemnation" from instances in which government officials purposefully bring eminent domain proceedings to acquire private property. Twenty-five years later, in Lingle v. Chevron U.S.A., Inc., 544 U.S. 528, 532, 539, 540, 542, 545 (2005), the Court attempted to reconcile the two kinds of takings, noting that in its regulatory takings jurisprudence, the Court "aims to identify regulatory actions that are functionally equivalent to the classic taking in which government directly appropriates private property or ousts the owner from his domain. Accordingly, each of these tests focuses directly upon the severity of the burden that government imposes upon private property rights."

The *Lingle* Court retracted dictum from *Agins* that as you will see in subsequent cases, appeared in several subsequent regulatory takings decisions. *Lingle* was ultimately an unsuccessful attempt to demonstrate that the state of Hawaii had taken personal (nor real) property, as Justice Sandra Day O'Connor explained:

> In the case before us, the lower courts applied *Agins*' "substantially advances" formula to strike down a Hawaii statute that limits the rent that oil companies may charge to dealers who lease service stations owned by the companies. The lower courts held that

the rent cap effects an uncompensated taking of private property in violation of the Fifth and Fourteenth Amendments because it does not substantially advance Hawaii's asserted interest in controlling retail gasoline prices. This case requires us to decide whether the "substantially advances" formula announced in *Agins* is an appropriate test for determining whether a regulation effects a Fifth Amendment taking. We conclude that it is not. . . .

Although a number of our takings precedents have recited the "substantially advances" formula minted in *Agins*, this is our first opportunity to consider its validity as a free-standing takings test. We conclude that this formula prescribes an inquiry in the nature of a due process, not a takings, test, and that it has no proper place in our takings jurisprudence. . . .

Although *Agins*' reliance on due process precedents is understandable, the language the Court selected was regrettably imprecise. The "substantially advances" formula suggests a means-ends test: It asks, in essence, whether a regulation of private property is effective in achieving some legitimate public purpose. An inquiry of this nature has some logic in the context of a due process challenge, for a regulation that fails to serve any legitimate governmental objective may be so arbitrary or irrational that it runs afoul of the Due Process Clause. But such a test is not a valid method of discerning whether private property has been "taken" for purposes of the Fifth Amendment.

In stark contrast to . . . regulatory takings tests . . . , the "substantially advances" inquiry reveals nothing about the *magnitude or character of the burden* a particular regulation imposes upon private property rights. Nor does it provide any information about how any regulatory burden is *distributed* among property owners. In consequence, this test does not help to identify those regulations whose effects are functionally comparable to government appropriation or invasion of private property; it is tethered neither to the text of the Takings Clause nor to the basic justification for allowing regulatory actions to be challenged under the Clause. . . .

[T]he "substantially advances" formula is not only doctrinally untenable as a takings test—its application as such would also present serious practical difficulties. The *Agins* formula can be read to demand heightened means-ends review of virtually any regulation of private property. If so interpreted, it would require courts to scrutinize the efficacy of a vast array of state and federal regulations—a task for which courts are not well suited. Moreover, it would empower—and might often require—courts to substitute their predictive judgments for those of elected legislatures and expert agencies.

Justice O'Connor then proceeded to explain how the Court's rejection of the "substantially advances" dictum "does not require us to disturb any of our prior holdings." You can form your own conclusions as to whether the Court was back-tracking from its takings activism, based on your independent interpretations of the key post-*Agins* decisions, many of which followed the lead of Justice William Brennan's dissent in a second California open-space zoning case.

3. You might find it surprising that one of the most vigilant protectors of private property rights expressed discomfort with Justice Lewis Powell's "substantially advances" formula. Professor Richard Lazarus, in his fascinating study, *The Measure of a Justice: Justice Scalia and the Faltering of the Property Rights Movement Within the Supreme Court*, 57 Hastings L.J. 759, 775 (2006), learned the following from studying Justice Harry Blackmun's Court papers:

The other prong of the *Agins* test—whether the regulation "substantially advances legitimate state interests"— . . . strongly expanded constitutional protection of property rights, even while the *Agins* Court was seemingly just quickly dismissing a takings claim that lacked all merit. As now revealed by the Blackmun Papers, then-Justice Rehnquist is the one member of the Court who took explicit notice of the potential shift implicated by the test and specifically questioned Powell about it in formal written correspondence between their chambers. Rehnquist expressed some disquiet—"somewhat uneasy"— about the lack of latitude that the substantially advance test appeared to give local government and proposed to Powell substitute language that would "allow[] the states somewhat more latitude." Rehnquist indicated that if Powell declined, he would "simply write a short separate concurrence." Powell did in fact decline, but Rehnquist nevertheless joined Powell's majority opinion for the Court without any separate writing.

It would not be the last time that a conservative jurist found it difficult to protect individual rights without encroaching on state sovereignty.

Cal. Gov. Code §65563

On or before December 31, 1973, every city and county shall prepare, adopt and submit to the Secretary of the Resources Agency a local open-space plan for the comprehensive and long-range preservation and conservation of open-space land within its jurisdiction. . . .

SAN DIEGO GAS & ELECTRIC CO. v. CITY OF SAN DIEGO
450 U.S. 621 (1981)

JUSTICE BLACKMUN delivered the opinion of the Court.

Appellant San Diego Gas & Electric Company, a California corporation, asks this Court to rule that a State must provide a monetary remedy to a landowner whose property allegedly has been "taken" by a regulatory ordinance claimed to violate the Just Compensation Clause of the Fifth Amendment. This question was left open last Term in Agins v. City of Tiburon, 447 U.S. 255, 263 (1980). Because we conclude that we lack jurisdiction in this case, we again must leave the issue undecided.

Appellant owns a 412-acre parcel of land in Sorrento Valley, an area in the northwest part of the city of San Diego, Cal. It assembled and acquired the acreage in 1966, at a cost of about $1,770,000, as a possible site for a nuclear power plant to be constructed in the 1980's. Approximately 214 acres of the parcel lie within or near an estuary known as the Los Penasquitos Lagoon. These acres are low-lying land which serves as a drainage basin for three river systems. About a third of the land is subject to tidal action from the nearby Pacific Ocean. The 214 acres are unimproved, except for sewer and utility lines.

When appellant acquired the 214 acres, most of the land was zoned either for industrial use or in an agricultural "holding" category. The city's master plan, adopted in 1967, designated nearly all the area for industrial use.

Several events that occurred in 1973 gave rise to this litigation. First, the San Diego City Council rezoned parts of the property. It changed 39 acres from industrial to agricultural, and increased the minimum lot size in some of the agricultural areas from 1 acre to 10 acres. The

Council recommended, however, that 50 acres of the agricultural land be considered for industrial development upon the submission of specific development plans.

Second, the city, pursuant to Cal. Gov't Code Ann. § 65563 (West Supp. 1981), established an open-space plan. This statute required each California city and county to adopt a plan "for the comprehensive and long-range preservation and conservation of open-space land within its jurisdiction." The plan adopted by the city of San Diego placed appellant's property among the city's open-space areas, which it defined as "any urban land or water surface that is essentially open or natural in character, and which has appreciable utility for park and recreation purposes, conservation of land, water or other natural resources or historic or scenic purposes." App. 159. The plan acknowledged appellant's intention to construct a nuclear power plant on the property, stating that such a plant would not necessarily be incompatible with the open-space designation. The plan proposed, however, that the city acquire the property to preserve it as parkland.

Third, the City Council proposed a bond issue in order to obtain funds to acquire open-space lands. The Council identified appellant's land as among those properties to be acquired with the proceeds of the bond issue. The proposition, however, failed to win the voters' approval. The open-space plan has remained in effect, but the city has made no attempt to acquire appellant's property.

On August 15, 1974, appellant instituted this action in the Superior Court for the County of San Diego against the city and a number of its officials. It alleged that the city had taken its property without just compensation, in violation of the Constitutions of the United States and California. Appellant's theory was that the city had deprived it of the entire beneficial use of the property through the rezoning and the adoption of the open-space plan. It alleged that the city followed a policy of refusing to approve any development that was inconsistent with the plan, and that the only beneficial use of the property was as an industrial park, a use that would be inconsistent with the open-space designation.[6] . . .

Appellant sought damages of $6,150,000 in inverse condemnation, as well as mandamus and declaratory relief. Prior to trial, the court dismissed the mandamus claim, holding that "mandamus is not the proper remedy to challenge the validity of a legislative act." Clerk's Tr. 42. After a nonjury trial on the issue of liability, the court granted judgment for appellant . . . . A subsequent jury trial on the question of damages resulted in a judgment for appellant for over $3 million.

On appeal, the California Court of Appeal, Fourth District, affirmed. It held that neither a change in zoning nor the adoption of an open-space plan automatically entitled a property owner to compensation for any resulting diminution in the value of the property. In this case, however, the record revealed that the city followed the policy of enacting and enforcing zoning ordinances that were consistent with its open-space plan. The Court of Appeal also found that the evidence supported the conclusion that industrial use was the only feasible use for the property and that the city would have denied any application for industrial development because it would be incompatible with the open-space designation. Appellant's failure to present a plan for developing the property therefore did not preclude an award of damages in its favor. The Court of Appeal, with one judge dissenting, denied the city's petition for rehearing.

The Supreme Court of California, however, on July 13, 1978, granted the city's petition for a hearing. This action automatically vacated the Court of Appeal's decision, depriving it of all effect. Before the hearing, the Supreme Court in June 1979 retransferred the case to the Court of Appeal for reconsideration in light of the intervening decision in Agins v. City of Tiburon, 24 Cal. 3d 266, 598 P. 2d 25 (1979), aff'd, 447 U.S. 255 (1980). The California court in Agins held that an owner

6. Appellant abandoned its plan to construct a nuclear power plant after the discovery of an off-shore fault that rendered the project unfeasible. Its witnesses acknowledged that only about 150 acres were usable as an industrial park, and that 1.25 million cubic yards of fill would be needed to undertake such a development.

who is deprived of substantially all beneficial use of his land by a zoning regulation is not entitled to an award of damages in an inverse condemnation proceeding. Rather, his exclusive remedy is invalidation of the regulation in an action for mandamus or declaratory relief. *Agins* also held that the plaintiffs in that case were not entitled to such relief because the zoning ordinance at issue permitted the building of up to five residences on their property. Therefore, the court held, it did not deprive those plaintiffs of substantially all reasonable use of their land.

When the present case was retransferred, the Court of Appeal, in an unpublished opinion, reversed the judgment of the Superior Court. It relied upon the California decision in *Agins* and held that appellant could not recover compensation through inverse condemnation. It, however, did not invalidate either the zoning ordinance or the open-space plan. Instead, it held that factual disputes precluded such relief on the present state of the record:

> "[Appellant] complains it has been denied all use of its land which is zoned for agriculture and manufacturing but lies within the open space area of the general plan. It has not made application to use or improve the property nor has it asked [the] City what development might be permitted. Even assuming no use is acceptable to the City, [appellant's] complaint deals with the alleged overzealous use of the police power by [the] City. Its remedy is mandamus or declaratory relief, not inverse condemnation. [Appellant] did in its complaint seek these remedies asserting that [the] City had arbitrarily exercised its police power by enacting an unconstitutional zoning law and general plan element or by applying the zoning and general plan unconstitutionally. However, on the present record these are disputed fact issues not covered by the trial court in its findings and conclusions. They can be dealt with anew should [appellant] elect to retry the case." App. 66.

The Supreme Court of California denied further review. Appellant appealed to this Court, arguing that the Fifth and Fourteenth Amendments require that compensation be paid whenever private property is taken for public use. Appellant takes issue with the California Supreme Court's holding in *Agins* that its remedy is limited to invalidation of the ordinance in a proceeding for mandamus or declaratory relief. We postponed consideration of our jurisdiction until the hearing on the merits. We now conclude that the appeal must be dismissed because of the absence of a final judgment. . . .

The Court of Appeal has decided that monetary compensation is not an appropriate remedy for any taking of appellant's property that may have occurred, but it has not decided whether any other remedy is available because it has not decided whether any taking in fact has occurred. Thus, however we might rule with respect to the Court of Appeal's decision that appellant is not entitled to a monetary remedy—and we are frank to say that the federal constitutional aspects of that issue are not to be cast aside lightly—further proceedings are necessary to resolve the federal question whether there has been a taking at all. The court's decision, therefore, is not final, and we are without jurisdiction to review it. . . .

JUSTICE REHNQUIST, concurring.

If I were satisfied that this appeal was from a "final judgment or decree" of the California Court of Appeal, as that term is used in 28 U. S. C. § 1257, I would have little difficulty in agreeing with much of what is said in the dissenting opinion of JUSTICE BRENNAN. . . .

JUSTICE BRENNAN, with whom JUSTICE STEWART, JUSTICE MARSHALL, and JUSTICE POWELL join, dissenting. . . .

Title 28 U. S. C. § 1257 limits this Court's jurisdiction to review judgments of state courts to "[final] judgments or decrees rendered by the highest court of a State in which a decision could be had." The Court today dismisses this appeal on the ground that the Court of Appeal of California,

Fourth District, failed to decide the federal question whether a "taking" of appellant's property had occurred, and therefore had not entered a final judgment or decree on that question appealable under § 1257. Because the Court's conclusion fundamentally mischaracterizes the holding and judgment of the Court of Appeal, I respectfully dissent from the Court's dismissal and reach the merits of appellant's claim. . . .

The principle applied in all these [regulatory takings] cases has its source in Justice Holmes' opinion for the Court in Pennsylvania Coal Co. v. Mahon, 260 U.S. 393, 415 (1922), in which he stated: "The general rule at least is, that while property may be regulated to a certain extent, if regulation goes too far it will be recognized as a taking." The determination of a "taking" is "a question of degree—and therefore cannot be disposed of by general propositions." Id., at 416.[15] While acknowledging that "[government] hardly could go on if to some extent values incident to property could not be diminished without paying for every such change in the general law," id., at 413, the Court rejected the proposition that police power restrictions could never be recognized as a Fifth Amendment "taking."[16] Indeed, the Court concluded that the Pennsylvania statute forbidding the mining of coal that would cause the subsidence of any house effected a "taking." Id., at 414-416. . . .

The typical "taking" occurs when a government entity formally condemns a landowner's property and obtains the fee simple pursuant to its sovereign power of eminent domain. See, e. g., Berman v. Parker, 348 U.S. 26, 33 (1954). However, a "taking" may also occur without a formal condemnation proceeding or transfer of fee simple. . . .

In service of this principle, the Court frequently has found "takings" outside the context of formal condemnation proceedings or transfer of fee simple, in cases where government action benefiting the public resulted in destruction of the use and enjoyment of private property. E. g., Kaiser Aetna v. United States, 444 U.S., at 178-180 (navigational servitude allowing public right of access); United States v. Dickinson, 331 U.S. 745, 750-751 (1947) (property flooded because of Government dam project); United States v. Causby, 328 U.S. 256, 261-262 (1946) (frequent low altitude flights of Army and Navy aircraft over property); Pennsylvania Coal Co. v. Mahon, 260 U.S., at 414-416 (state regulation forbidding mining of coal).

Police power regulations such as zoning ordinances and other land-use restrictions can destroy the use and enjoyment of property in order to promote the public good just as effectively as formal condemnation or physical invasion of property. From the property owner's point of view, it may matter little whether his land is condemned or flooded, or whether it is restricted by regulation to

---

15. More recent Supreme Court cases have emphasized this aspect of "taking" analysis, commenting that the Court has been unable to develop any "set formula to determine where regulation ends and taking begins," Goldblatt v. Town of Hempstead, 369 U.S. 590, 594 (1962), and that "[it] calls as much for the exercise of judgment as for the application of logic," Andrus v. Allard, 444 U.S. 51, 65 (1979). See Penn Central Transp. Co. v. New York City, 438 U.S., at 124 ("ad hoc, factual inquiries"); United States v. Central Eureka Mining Co., 357 U.S. 155, 168 (1958) ("question properly turning upon the particular circumstances of each case").

One distinguished commentator has characterized the attempt to differentiate "regulation" from "taking" as "the most haunting jurisprudential problem in the field of contemporary land-use law . . . one that may be the lawyer's equivalent of the physicist's hunt for the quark." C. Haar, Land-Use Planning 766 (3d ed. 1976). See generally id., at 766-777; Berger, A Policy Analysis of the Taking Problem, 49 N. Y. U. L. Rev. 165 (1974); Michelman, Property, Utility, and Fairness: Comments on the Ethical Foundations of "Just Compensation" Law, 80 Harv. L. Rev. 1165 (1967); Sax, Takings and the Police Power, 74 Yale L. J. 36 (1964). Another has described a 30-year series of Court opinions resulting from this case-by-case approach as a "crazy-quilt pattern." Dunham, Griggs v. Allegheny County in Perspective: Thirty Years of Supreme Court Expropriation Law, 1962 S. Ct. Rev. 63.

16. Justice Brandeis, in dissent, argued the absolute position that a "restriction imposed to protect the public health, safety or morals from dangers threatened is not a taking." 260 U.S., at 417. In partial reliance on Justice Brandeis' dissent, one report urges that the Court overrule the Pennsylvania Coal case and hold that "a regulation of the use of land, if reasonably related to a valid public purpose, can never constitute a taking." F. Bosselman, D. Callies, & J. Banta, The Taking Issue 238-255 (1973).

use in its natural state, if the effect in both cases is to deprive him of all beneficial use of it. From the government's point of view, the benefits flowing to the public from preservation of open space through regulation may be equally great as from creating a wildlife refuge through formal condemnation or increasing electricity production through a dam project that floods private property. Appellees implicitly posit the distinction that the government *intends* to take property through condemnation or physical invasion whereas it does not through police power regulations. But "the Constitution measures a taking of property not by what a State says, or by what it intends, but by what it does." Hughes v. Washington, 389 U.S. 290, 298 (1967) (STEWART, J., concurring) (emphasis in original); see Davis v. Newton Coal Co., 267 U.S. 292, 301 (1925). It is only logical, then, that government action other than acquisition of title, occupancy, or physical invasion can be a "taking," and therefore a *de facto* exercise of the power of eminent domain, where the effects completely deprive the owner of all or most of his interest in the property.

Having determined that property may be "taken for public use" by police power regulation within the meaning of the Just Compensation Clause of the Fifth Amendment, the question remains whether a government entity may constitutionally deny payment of just compensation to the property owner and limit his remedy to mere invalidation of the regulation instead. Appellant argues that it is entitled to the full fair market value of the property. Appellees argue that invalidation of the regulation is sufficient without payment of monetary compensation. In my view, once a court establishes that there was a regulatory "taking," the Constitution demands that the government entity pay just compensation for the period commencing on the date the regulation first effected the "taking," and ending on the date the government entity chooses to rescind or otherwise amend[19] the regulation. This interpretation, I believe, is supported by the express words and purpose of the Just Compensation Clause, as well as by cases of this Court construing it.

The language of the Fifth Amendment prohibits the "[taking]" of private property for "public use" without payment of "just compensation." As soon as private property has been taken, whether through formal condemnation proceedings, occupancy, physical invasion, or regulation, the landowner has *already* suffered a constitutional violation, and "'the self-executing character of the constitutional provision with respect to compensation,'" United States v. Clarke, 445 U.S. 253, 257 (1980), quoting 6 J. Sackman, Nichols' Law of Eminent Domain § 25.41 (rev. 3d ed. 1980), is triggered. This Court has consistently recognized that the just compensation requirement in the Fifth Amendment is not precatory: once there is a "taking," compensation must be awarded. . . . Invalidation hardly prevents enactment of subsequent unconstitutional regulations by the government entity.[22]

Moreover, mere invalidation would fall far short of fulfilling the fundamental purpose of the Just Compensation Clause. That guarantee was designed to bar the government from forcing some

---

19. Under this rule, a government entity is entitled to amend the offending regulation so that it no longer effects a "taking." It may also choose formally to condemn the property.

22. At the 1974 annual conference of the National Institute of Municipal Law Officers in California, a California City Attorney gave fellow City Attorneys the following advice:

"*IF ALL ELSE FAILS, MERELY AMEND THE REGULATION AND START OVER AGAIN.*

"If legal preventive maintenance does not work, and you still receive a claim attacking the land use regulation, or if you try the case and lose, don't worry about it. All is not lost. One of the extra 'goodies' contained in the recent [California] Supreme Court case of Selby v. City of San Buenaventura, 10 C. 3d 110, appears to allow the City to change the regulation in question, even after trial and judgment, make it more reasonable, more restrictive, or whatever, and everybody starts over again.

. . . .

"See how easy it is to be a City Attorney. Sometimes you can lose the battle and still win the war. Good luck."
Longtin, Avoiding and Defending Constitutional Attacks on Land Use Regulations (Including Inverse Condemnation), in 38B NIMLO Municipal Law Review 192-193 (1975) (emphasis in original).

individuals to bear burdens which, in all fairness, should be borne by the public as a whole. Armstrong v. United States, 364 U.S. 40, 49 (1960). When one person is asked to assume more than a fair share of the public burden, the payment of just compensation operates to redistribute that economic cost from the individual to the public at large. Because police power regulations must be substantially related to the advancement of the public health, safety, morals, or general welfare, see Village of Euclid v. Ambler Realty Co., 272 U.S. 365, 395 (1926), it is axiomatic that the public receives a benefit while the offending regulation is in effect.[23] If the regulation denies the private property owner the use and enjoyment of his land and is found to effect a "taking," it is only fair that the public bear the cost of benefits received during the interim period between application of the regulation and the government entity's rescission of it. The payment of just compensation serves to place the landowner in the same position monetarily as he would have occupied if his property had not been taken.

The fact that a regulatory "taking" may be temporary, by virtue of the government's power to rescind or amend the regulation, does not make it any less of a constitutional "taking." Nothing in the Just Compensation Clause suggests that "takings" must be permanent and irrevocable. Nor does the temporary reversible quality of a regulatory "taking" render compensation for the time of the "taking" any less obligatory. This Court more than once has recognized that temporary reversible "takings" should be analyzed according to the same constitutional framework applied to permanent irreversible "takings." . . .

The constitutional rule I propose requires that, once a court finds that a police power regulation has effected a "taking," the government entity must pay just compensation for the period commencing on the date the regulation first effected the "taking," and ending on the date the government entity chooses to rescind or otherwise amend the regulation. . . .

Notes

1. Should the fact that the city had attempted to acquire the property (an attempt that was thwarted by the voters) have been relevant to the Court's decision regarding the constitutionality of the open-space designation? Are zoning schemes, the acquisition of land from a willing seller, and the condemnation of land from an unwilling owner just three equally legitimate ways for local governments to realize the same goal of the preservation of open spaces? If so, then why would any local government resort to the latter two options, which involve much higher costs than the first?

2. After the Court rendered its (non)decision in *San Diego Gas*, there was some question as to whether there was a five-member majority that endorsed the notion that regulatory takings required compensation under the Fifth Amendment (as incorporated through the Fourteenth Amendment). Here is how one appellate court, in In re Aircrash in Bali, 684 F.2d 1301, 1311 n.7 (9th Cir. 1982), did the math:

> Justice Rehnquist agreed with the majority that the *San Diego* case was not appealable for lack of a final judgment, but observed that "I would have little difficulty in agreeing with much of what is said in the dissenting opinion" on the merits. Thus, we take it to be the view of the majority of the Supreme Court that "the general rule at least is, that while property may be regulated to a certain extent, if regulation goes too far it will be

---

23. A different case may arise where a police power regulation is not enacted in furtherance of the public health, safety, morals, or general welfare so that there may be no "public use." Although the government entity may not be forced to pay just compensation under the Fifth Amendment, the landowner may nevertheless have a damages cause of action under 42 U. S. C. § 1983 for a Fourteenth Amendment due process violation.

recognized as a taking.'"" Pennsylvania Coal Co. v. Mahon, 260 U.S. 393, 415 (1922) (quoted in San Diego Gas & Electric, 101 S. Ct. at 1302 (Brennan, J., dissenting)).[24]

Unless the disconcerting dance around the issues was to continue, the Court seemed to have three options: (1) decide that regulation, perhaps even temporary decisionmaking, may under certain circumstances amount to a Fifth Amendment taking that requires compensation; (2) decide that as a police power function regulation can never amount to a "taking" in the eminent domain sense of the word, but might, under due process analysis, be invalidated; or (3) decide not to decide the issue, until the Justices had the chance to observe the significant amount of state[2255] and lower federal court experimentation with the first two options.

The High Court's next two attempts were equally frustrating to those awaiting a firm answer. In MacDonald, Sommer & Frates v. Yolo County, 477 U.S. 340, 344, 350-51 (1986), appellant's tentative subdivision map was rejected by the Yolo County Planning Commission, owing to concerns over public access, sewer service, police protection, and water service. Appellant's actions for declaratory judgment and monetary relief alleged that "'none of the beneficial uses' allowed even for agricultural land would be suitable."

The Court was not ready to hear the takings claim, however:

[A] court cannot determine whether a municipality has failed to provide "just compensation" until it knows what, if any, compensation the responsible administrative body intends to provide. . . .

Our cases uniformly reflect an insistence on knowing the nature and extent of permitted development before adjudicating the constitutionality of the regulations that purport to limit it. . . .

Here, in comparison to the situations of the property owners in the three preceding cases, appellant has submitted one subdivision proposal and has received the Board's response thereto. . . . In *Agins, San Diego Gas & Electric,* and *Williamson Planning Comm'n,* we declined to reach the question whether the Constitution requires a monetary remedy to redress some regulatory takings because the records in those cases left us uncertain whether the property at issue had in fact been taken. Likewise, in this case, the holdings of both courts below leave open the possibility that some development

---

24. Authors' note: *See also* Nika Corp. v. Kansas City, 582 F. Supp. 343, 363 n.8 (W.D. Mo. 1983) ("At least some members of the Court—perhaps even a majority—felt that if a 'taking' was in fact involved, injunctive relief alone would be inadequate.").

25. *See, e.g.,* Corrigan v. City of Scottsdale, 149 Ariz. 538, 540-42, 720 P.2d 513, 515-17 (1986):

We believe that once a taking is found, the Arizona Constitution mandates the payment of money as damages for any injury suffered. We agree with the simple logic expressed by Justice Brennan in his San Diego Gas & Electric v. City of San Diego dissent . . . .

We are not alone in holding that a landowner may recover damages for a temporary taking by zoning. In a case where the plaintiff-landowner's Waterway Development Permit application was denied because the city "sought to impose a servitude upon the property to preserve 'the natural and traditional character of the land and waterway,'" the Texas Supreme Court stated, "[t]here was no suggestion that government may take or hold another's property without paying for it, just because the land is pretty. Our conclusion is that the City of Austin was liable in damages to the plaintiffs." City of Austin v. Teague, 570 S.W.2d 389, 394 (Tex.1978).

In New Jersey, it has been flatly held that '[t]emporary takings are compensable.' Sheerr v. Township of Evesham, 184 N.J. Super. 11, 445 A.2d 46, 73 (1982). . . .

More significantly, in a case very similar to the one before us the New Hampshire Supreme Court not only allowed damages for a temporary taking but also reasonable attorneys fees and double costs. Burrows v. City of Keene, 121 N.H. at 601-602, 432 A.2d at 22. In *Burrows,* the city not only failed to approve the plaintiff's subdivision plans but further, as in this case, zoned 109 acres of the plaintiff's land into a conservation area.

will be permitted, and thus again leave us in doubt regarding the antecedent question whether appellant's property has been taken.

Not until the end of the 1986-1987 Term would the Court provide the answer to the compensation question.

III. Mining Controls

52 Pa. Stat. §1406.2

This act shall be deemed to be an exercise of the police powers of the Commonwealth for the protection of the health, safety and general welfare of the people of the Commonwealth, by providing for the conservation of surface land areas which may be affected in the mining of bituminous coal by methods other than "open pit" or "strip" mining, to aid in the protection of the safety of the public, to enhance the value of such lands for taxation, to aid in the preservation of surface water drainage and public and private water supplies, to provide for the restoration or replacement of water supplies affected by underground mining, to provide for the restoration or replacement of or compensation for surface structures damaged by underground mining and generally to improve the use and enjoyment of such lands and to maintain primary jurisdiction over surface coal mining in Pennsylvania.

KEYSTONE BITUMINOUS COAL ASS'N v. DeBENEDICTIS
480 U.S. 470 (1987)

JUSTICE STEVENS, delivered the opinion of the Court.

In Pennsylvania Coal Co. v. Mahon, 260 U.S. 393 (1922), the Court reviewed the constitutionality of a Pennsylvania statute that admittedly destroyed "previously existing rights of property and contract." *Id.*, at 413. . . .

Now, 65 years later, we address a different set of "particular facts," involving the Pennsylvania Legislature's 1966 conclusion that the Commonwealth's existing mine subsidence legislation had failed to protect the public interest in safety, land conservation, preservation of affected municipalities' tax bases, and land development in the Commonwealth. Based on detailed findings, the legislature enacted the Bituminous Mine Subsidence and Land Conservation Act (Subsidence Act or Act), Pa. Stat. Ann., Tit. 52, § 1406.1 et seq. (Purdon Supp. 1986). Petitioners contend, relying heavily on our decision in *Pennsylvania Coal*, that §§ 4 and 6 of the Subsidence Act and certain implementing regulations violate the Takings Clause, and that § 6 of the Act violates the Contracts Clause of the Federal Constitution. . . .

Coal mine subsidence is the lowering of strata overlying a coal mine, including the land surface, caused by the extraction of underground coal. This lowering of the strata can have devastating effects. It often causes substantial damage to foundations, walls, other structural members, and the integrity of houses and buildings. Subsidence frequently causes sinkholes or troughs in land which make the land difficult or impossible to develop. Its effect on farming has been well documented— many subsided areas cannot be plowed or properly prepared. Subsidence can also cause the loss of groundwater and surface ponds. In short, it presents the type of environmental concern that has been the focus of so much federal, state, and local regulation in recent decades.[3]

---

3. Indeed, in 1977, Congress passed the Federal Surface Mining Control and Reclamation Act, 91 Stat. 445, 30 U.S.C. § 1201 *et seq.*, which includes regulation of subsidence caused by underground coal mining. See 30 U.S.C. § 1266.

Despite what their name may suggest, neither of the "full extraction" mining methods currently used in western Pennsylvania enables miners to extract all subsurface coal; considerable amounts need to be left in the ground to provide access, support, and ventilation to the mines. Additionally, mining companies have long been required by various Pennsylvania laws and regulations, the legitimacy of which is not challenged here, to leave coal in certain areas for public safety reasons. Since 1966, Pennsylvania has placed an additional set of restrictions on the amount of coal that may be extracted; these restrictions are designed to diminish subsidence and subsidence damage in the vicinity of certain structures and areas.

Pennsylvania's Subsidence Act authorizes the Pennsylvania Department of Environmental Resources (DER) to implement and enforce a comprehensive program to prevent or minimize subsidence and to regulate its consequences. Section 4 of the Subsidence Act, Pa. Stat. Ann., Tit. 52, § 1406.4 (Purdon Supp. 1986), prohibits mining that causes subsidence damage to three categories of structures that were in place on April 17, 1966: public buildings and noncommercial buildings generally used by the public; dwellings used for human habitation; and cemeteries. Since 1966 the DER has applied a formula that generally requires 50% of the coal beneath structures protected by § 4 to be kept in place as a means of providing surface support. 7 Section 6 of the Subsidence Act, Pa. Stat. Ann., Tit. 52, § 1406.6 (Purdon Supp. 1986), authorizes the DER to revoke a mining permit if the removal of coal causes damage to a structure or area protected by § 4 and the operator has not within six months either repaired the damage, satisfied any claim arising therefrom, or deposited a sum equal to the reasonable cost of repair with the DER as security.

In 1982, petitioners filed a civil rights action in the United States District Court for the Western District of Pennsylvania seeking to enjoin officials of the DER from enforcing the Subsidence Act and its implementing regulations. Petitioners are an association of coal mine operators, and four corporations that are engaged, either directly or through affiliates, in underground mining of bituminous coal in western Pennsylvania. The members of the association and the corporate petitioners own, lease, or otherwise control substantial coal reserves beneath the surface of property affected by the Subsidence Act. The defendants in the action, respondents here, are the Secretary of the DER, the Chief of the DER's Division of Mine Subsidence, and the Chief of the DER's Section on Mine Subsidence Regulation.

The complaint alleges that Pennsylvania recognizes three separate estates in land: The mineral estate; the surface estate; and the "support estate." Beginning well over 100 years ago, landowners began severing title to underground coal and the right of surface support while retaining or conveying away ownership of the surface estate. It is stipulated that approximately 90% of the coal that is or will be mined by petitioners in western Pennsylvania was severed from the surface in the period between 1890 and 1920. When acquiring or retaining the mineral estate, petitioners or their predecessors typically acquired or retained certain additional rights that would enable them to extract and remove the coal. Thus, they acquired the right to deposit wastes, to provide for drainage and ventilation, and to erect facilities such as tipples, roads, or railroads, on the surface. Additionally, they typically acquired a waiver of any claims for damages that might result from the removal of the coal.

In the portions of the complaint that are relevant to us, petitioners alleged that both § 4 of the Subsidence Act, as implemented by the 50% rule, and § 6 of the Subsidence Act, constitute a taking of their private property without compensation in violation of the Fifth and Fourteenth Amendments. They also alleged that § 6 impairs their contractual agreements in violation of Article I, § 10, of the Constitution. The parties entered into a stipulation of facts pertaining to petitioners' facial challenge, and filed cross-motions for summary judgment on the facial challenge. The District Court granted respondents' motion.

In rejecting petitioners' Takings Clause claim, the District Court first distinguished *Pennsylvania Coal*, primarily on the ground that the Subsidence Act served valid public purposes that the Court had found lacking in the earlier case. The District Court found that the restriction on the use of petitioners' property was an exercise of the Commonwealth's police power, justified by Pennsylvania's interest in the health, safety, and general welfare of the public. In answer to petitioners' argument that the Subsidence Act effectuated a taking because a separate, recognized interest in realty—the support estate—had been entirely destroyed, the District Court concluded that under Pennsylvania law the support estate consists of a bundle of rights, including some that were not affected by the Act. That the right to cause damage to the surface may constitute the most valuable "strand" in the bundle of rights possessed by the owner of a support estate was not considered controlling under our decision in Andrus v. Allard, 444 U.S. 51 (1979). . . .

The Court of Appeals affirmed, agreeing that *Pennsylvania Coal* does not control because the Subsidence Act is a legitimate means of "[protecting] the environment of the Commonwealth, its economic future, and its well-being." 771 F.2d 707, 715 (1985). The Court of Appeals' analysis of the Subsidence Act's effect on petitioners' property differed somewhat from the District Court's, however. In rejecting the argument that the support estate had been entirely destroyed, the Court of Appeals did not rely on the fact that the support estate itself constitutes a bundle of many rights, but rather considered the support estate as just one segment of a larger bundle of rights that invariably includes either the surface estate or the mineral estate. . . .

Petitioners assert that disposition of their takings claim calls for no more than a straightforward application of the Court's decision in *Pennsylvania Coal Co. v. Mahon*. Although there are some obvious similarities between the cases, we agree with the Court of Appeals and the District Court that the similarities are far less significant than the differences, and that Pennsylvania Coal does not control this case. . . .

The holdings and assumptions of the Court in *Pennsylvania Coal* provide obvious and necessary reasons for distinguishing *Pennsylvania Coal* from the case before us today. The two factors that the Court considered relevant, have become integral parts of our takings analysis. We have held that land use regulation can effect a taking if it "does not substantially advance legitimate state interests, . . . or denies an owner economically viable use of his land." Agins v. Tiburon, 447 U.S. 255, 260 (1980) (citations omitted); see also Penn Central Transportation Co. v. New York City, 438 U.S. 104, 124 (1978). Application of these tests to petitioners' challenge demonstrates that they have not satisfied their burden of showing that the Subsidence Act constitutes a taking. First, unlike the Kohler Act, the character of the governmental action involved here leans heavily against finding a taking; the Commonwealth of Pennsylvania has acted to arrest what it perceives to be a significant threat to the common welfare. Second, there is no record in this case to support a finding, similar to the one the Court made in *Pennsylvania Coal*, that the Subsidence Act makes it impossible for petitioners to profitably engage in their business, or that there has been undue interference with their investment-backed expectations.

The Public Purpose

Unlike the Kohler Act, which was passed upon in Pennsylvania Coal, the Subsidence Act does not merely involve a balancing of the private economic interests of coal companies against the private interests of the surface owners. The Pennsylvania Legislature specifically found that important public interests are served by enforcing a policy that is designed to minimize subsidence in certain areas. . . . The District Court and the Court of Appeals were both convinced that the legislative purposes set forth in the statute were genuine, substantial, and legitimate, and we have no reason to conclude otherwise.

None of the indicia of a statute enacted solely for the benefit of private parties identified in Justice Holmes' opinion are present here. First, Justice Holmes explained that the Kohler Act was a "private benefit" statute since it "ordinarily does not apply to land when the surface is owned by the owner of the coal." 260 U.S., at 414. The Subsidence Act, by contrast, has no such exception. The current surface owner may only waive the protection of the Act if the DER consents. See 25 Pa. Code § 89.145(b) (1983). Moreover, the Court was forced to reject the Commonwealth's safety justification for the Kohler Act because it found that the Commonwealth's interest in safety could as easily have been accomplished through a notice requirement to landowners. The Subsidence Act, by contrast, is designed to accomplish a number of widely varying interests, with reference to which petitioners have not suggested alternative methods through which the Commonwealth could proceed. . . .

Thus, the Subsidence Act differs from the Kohler Act in critical and dispositive respects. With regard to the Kohler Act, the Court believed that the Commonwealth had acted only to ensure against damage to some private landowners' homes. Justice Holmes stated that if the private individuals needed support for their structures, they should not have "[taken] the risk of acquiring only surface rights." 260 U.S., at 416. Here, by contrast, the Commonwealth is acting to protect the public interest in health, the environment, and the fiscal integrity of the area. That private individuals erred in taking a risk cannot estop the Commonwealth from exercising its police power to abate activity akin to a public nuisance. The Subsidence Act is a prime example that "circumstances may so change in time . . . as to clothe with such a [public] interest what at other times . . . would be a matter of purely private concern." Block v. Hirsh, 256 U.S. 135, 155 (1921).

In *Pennsylvania Coal* the Court recognized that the nature of the State's interest in the regulation is a critical factor in determining whether a taking has occurred, and thus whether compensation is required. The Court distinguished the case before it from a case it had decided eight years earlier, Plymouth Coal Co. v. Pennsylvania, 232 U.S. 531 (1914). There, "it was held competent for the legislature to require a pillar of coal to be left along the line of adjoining property." Pennsylvania Coal, 260 U.S., at 415. Justice Holmes explained that unlike the Kohler Act, the statute challenged in Plymouth Coal dealt with "a requirement for the safety of employees invited into the mine, and secured an average reciprocity of advantage that has been recognized as a justification of various laws." 260 U.S., at 415.

Many cases before and since *Pennsylvania Coal* have recognized that the nature of the State's action is critical in takings analysis. In Mugler v. Kansas, 123 U.S. 623 (1887), for example, a Kansas distiller who had built a brewery while it was legal to do so challenged a Kansas constitutional amendment which prohibited the manufacture and sale of intoxicating liquors. Although the Court recognized that the "buildings and machinery constituting these breweries are of little value" because of the Amendment, *id.*, at 657, Justice Harlan explained that a

> "prohibition simply upon the use of property for purposes that are declared, by valid legislation, to be injurious to the health, morals, or safety of the community, cannot, in any just sense, be deemed a taking or appropriation of property . . . .
>
> The power which the States have of prohibiting such use by individuals of their property as will be prejudicial to the health, the morals, or the safety of the public, is not—and, consistently with the existence and safety of organized society cannot be—burdened with the condition that the State must compensate such individual owners for pecuniary losses they may sustain, by reason of their not being permitted, by a noxious use of their property, to inflict injury upon the community." *Id.*, at 668-669.

We reject petitioners' implicit assertion that *Pennsylvania Coal* overruled these cases which focused so heavily on the nature of the State's interest in the regulation. . . .

The Court's hesitance to find a taking when the State merely restrains uses of property that are tantamount to public nuisances is consistent with the notion of "reciprocity of advantage" that Justice Holmes referred to in *Pennsylvania Coal*. Under our system of government, one of the State's primary ways of preserving the public weal is restricting the uses individuals can make of their property. While each of us is burdened somewhat by such restrictions, we, in turn, benefit greatly from the restrictions that are placed on others. . . .

In *Agins v. Tiburon*, we explained that the "determination that governmental action constitutes a taking, is, in essence, a determination that the public at large, rather than a single owner, must bear the burden of an exercise of state power in the public interest," and we recognized that this question "necessarily requires a weighing of private and public interests." 447 U.S., at 260-261. As the cases discussed above demonstrate, the public interest in preventing activities similar to public nuisances is a substantial one, which in many instances has not required compensation. The Subsidence Act, unlike the Kohler Act, plainly seeks to further such an interest. Nonetheless, we need not rest our decision on this factor alone, because petitioners have also failed to make a showing of diminution of value sufficient to satisfy the test set forth in *Pennsylvania Coal* and our other regulatory takings cases.

Diminution of Value and Investment-Backed Expectations

The second factor that distinguishes this case from *Pennsylvania Coal* is the finding in that case that the Kohler Act made mining of "certain coal" commercially impracticable. In this case, by contrast, petitioners have not shown any deprivation significant enough to satisfy the heavy burden placed upon one alleging a regulatory taking. For this reason, their takings claim must fail. . . .

The posture of the case is critical because we have recognized an important distinction between a claim that the mere enactment of a statute constitutes a taking and a claim that the particular impact of government action on a specific piece of property requires the payment of just compensation. . . . Petitioners thus face an uphill battle in making a facial attack on the Act as a taking.

The hill is made especially steep because petitioners have not claimed, at this stage, that the Act makes it commercially impracticable for them to continue mining their bituminous coal interests in western Pennsylvania. Indeed, petitioners have not even pointed to a single mine that can no longer be mined for profit. The only evidence available on the effect that the Subsidence Act has had on petitioners' mining operations comes from petitioners' answers to respondents' interrogatories. Petitioners described the effect that the Subsidence Act had from 1966-1982 on 13 mines that the various companies operate, and claimed that they have been required to leave a bit less than 27 million tons of coal in place to support § 4 areas. The total coal in those 13 mines amounts to over 1.46 billion tons. Thus § 4 requires them to leave less than 2% of their coal in place. But, as we have indicated, nowhere near all of the underground coal is extractable even aside from the Subsidence Act. The categories of coal that must be left for § 4 purposes and other purposes are not necessarily distinct sets, and there is no information in the record as to how much coal is actually left in the ground solely because of § 4. We do know, however, that petitioners have never claimed that their mining operations, or even any specific mines, have been unprofitable since the Subsidence Act was passed. Nor is there evidence that mining in any specific location affected by the 50% rule has been unprofitable.

Instead, petitioners have sought to narrowly define certain segments of their property and assert that, when so defined, the Subsidence Act denies them economically viable use. They advance two alternative ways of carving their property in order to reach this conclusion. First, they focus on the specific tons of coal that they must leave in the ground under the Subsidence Act, and argue that the Commonwealth has effectively appropriated this coal since it has no other useful purpose if not mined. Second, they contend that the Commonwealth has taken their separate legal interest in property—"support estate."

Because our test for regulatory taking requires us to compare the value that has been taken from the property with the value that remains in the property, one of the critical questions in determining how to define the unit of property "whose value is to furnish the denominator of the fraction." Michelman, Property, Utility, and Fairness: Comments on the Ethical Foundations of "Just Compensation" Law, 80 Harv. L. Rev. 1165, 1192 (1967). In *Penn Central* the Court explained:

> "'Taking' jurisprudence does not divide a single parcel into discrete segments and attempt to determine whether rights in a particular segment have been entirely abrogated. In deciding whether a particular governmental action has effected a taking, this Court focuses rather both on the character of the action and on the nature of the interference with rights *in the parcel as a whole*—here the city tax block designated as the 'landmark site.'" 438 U.S., at 130-131.

Similarly, in Andrus v. Allard, 444 U.S. 51 (1979), we held that "where an owner possesses a full 'bundle' of property rights, the destruction of one 'strand' of the bundle is not a taking because the aggregate must be viewed in its entirety." *Id.*, at 65-66. Although these verbal formulizations do not solve all of the definitional issues that may arise in defining the relevant mass of property, they do provide sufficient guidance to compel us to reject petitioners' arguments.

The Coal in Place

The parties have stipulated that enforcement of the DER's 50% rule will require petitioners to leave approximately 27 million tons of coal in place. Because they own that coal but cannot mine it, they contend that Pennsylvania has appropriated it for the public purposes described in the Subsidence Act.

This argument fails for the reason explained in *Penn Central* and *Andrus*. The 27 million tons of coal do not constitute a separate segment of property for takings law purposes. Many zoning ordinances place limits on the property owner's right to make profitable use of some segments of his property. A requirement that a building occupy no more than a specified percentage of the lot on which it is located could be characterized as a taking of the vacant area as readily as the requirement that coal pillars be left in place. Similarly, under petitioners' theory one could always argue that a setback ordinance requiring that no structure be built within a certain distance from the property line constitutes a taking because the footage represents a distinct segment of property for takings law purposes. Cf. Gorieb v. Fox, 274 U.S. 603 (1927) (upholding validity of setback ordinance) (Sutherland, J.). There is no basis for treating the less than 2% of petitioners' coal as a separate parcel of property. . . .

When the coal that must remain beneath the ground is viewed in the context of any reasonable unit of petitioners' coal mining operations and financial-backed expectations, it is plain that petitioners have not come close to satisfying their burden of proving that they have been denied the economically viable use of that property. The record indicates that only about 75% of petitioners' underground coal can be profitably mined in any event, and there is no showing that petitioners' reasonable "investment-backed expectations" have been materially affected by the additional duty to retain the small percentage that must be used to support the structures protected by § 4. 27.

The Support Estate

Pennsylvania property law is apparently unique in regarding the support estate as a separate interest in land that can be conveyed apart from either the mineral estate or the surface estate. Petitioners therefore argue that even if comparable legislation in another State would not constitute a taking, the Subsidence Act has that consequence because it entirely destroys the value of their unique support estate. It is clear, however, that our takings jurisprudence forecloses reliance on such legalistic distinctions within a bundle of property rights. For example, in *Penn Central*, the Court rejected the argument that the "air rights" above the terminal constituted a separate segment of property for Takings Clause purposes. Likewise, in *Andrus v. Allard*, we viewed the right to sell property as just one element of the owner's property interest. In neither case did the result turn on whether state law allowed the separate sale of the segment of property.

The Court of Appeals, which is more familiar with Pennsylvania law than we are, concluded that as a practical matter the support estate is always owned by either the owner of the surface or the owner of the minerals. . . .

Thus, in practical terms, the support estate has value only insofar as it protects or enhances the value of the estate with which it is associated. Its value is merely a part of the entire bundle of rights possessed by the owner of either the coal or the surface. Because petitioners retain the right to mine virtually all of the coal in their mineral estates, the burden the Act places on the support estate does not constitute a taking. Petitioners may continue to mine coal profitably even if they may not destroy or damage surface structures at will in the process.

But even if we were to accept petitioners' invitation to view the support estate as a distinct segment of property for "takings" purposes, they have not satisfied their heavy burden of sustaining a facial challenge to the Act. Petitioners have acquired or retained the support estate for a great deal of land, only part of which is protected under the Subsidence Act, which, of course, deals with subsidence in the immediate vicinity of certain structures, bodies of water, and cemeteries. The record is devoid of any evidence on what percentage of the purchased support estates, either in the aggregate or with respect to any individual estate, has been affected by the Act. Under these circumstances, petitioners' facial attack under the Takings Clause must surely fail.

In addition to their challenge under the Takings Clause, petitioners assert that § 6 of the Subsidence Act violates the Contracts Clause by not allowing them to hold the surface owners to their contractual waiver of liability for surface damage. Here too, we agree with the Court of Appeals and the District Court that the Commonwealth's strong public interests in the legislation are more than adequate to justify the impact of the statute on petitioners' contractual agreements. . . .

The judgment of the Court of Appeals is

Affirmed.

CHIEF JUSTICE REHNQUIST, with whom JUSTICE POWELL, JUSTICE O'CONNOR, and JUSTICE SCALIA join, dissenting.

More than 50 years ago, this Court determined the constitutionality of Pennsylvania's Kohler Act as it affected the property interests of coal mine operators. Pennsylvania Coal Co. v. Mahon, 260 U.S. 393 (1922). The Bituminous Mine Subsidence and Land Conservation Act approved today effects an interference with such interests in a strikingly similar manner. The Court finds at least two reasons why this case is different. First, we are told, "the character of the governmental action involved here leans heavily against finding a taking." Second, the Court concludes that the Subsidence Act neither "makes it impossible for petitioners to profitably engage in their business," nor involves "undue interference with [petitioners'] investment-backed expectations." *Ibid.* Neither of these conclusions persuades me that this case is different, and I believe that the Subsidence Act works a taking of petitioners' property interests. I therefore dissent. . . .

The Court's conclusion that the restriction on particular coal does not work a taking is primarily the result of its view that the 27 million tons of coal in the ground "do not constitute a separate segment of property for takings law purposes." This conclusion cannot be based on the view that the interests are too insignificant to warrant protection by the Fifth Amendment, for it is beyond cavil that government appropriation of "relatively small amounts of private property for its own use" requires just compensation. Instead, the Court's refusal to recognize the coal in the ground as a separate segment of property for takings purposes is based on the fact that the alleged taking is "regulatory," rather than a physical intrusion. On the facts of this case, I cannot see how the label placed on the government's action is relevant to consideration of its impact on property rights. . . .

In this case, enforcement of the Subsidence Act and its regulations will require petitioners to leave approximately 27 million tons of coal in place. There is no question that this coal is an identifiable and separable property interest. Unlike many property interests, the "bundle" of rights in this coal is sparse. "'For practical purposes, the right to coal consists in the right to mine it.'" *Pennsylvania Coal*, 260 U.S., at 414, quoting Commonwealth ex rel. Keater v. Clearview Coal Co., 256 Pa. at 331, 100 A. at 820. From the relevant perspective—that of the property owners—this interest has been destroyed every bit as much as if the government had proceeded to mine the coal for its own use. The regulation, then, does not merely inhibit one strand in the bundle, but instead destroys completely any interest in a segment of property. In these circumstances, I think it unnecessary to consider whether petitioners may operate individual mines or their overall mining operations profitably, for they have been denied all use of 27 million tons of coal. I would hold that § 4 of the Subsidence Act works a taking of these property interests.

Petitioners also claim that the Subsidence Act effects a taking of their support estate. Under Pennsylvania law, the support estate, the surface estate, and the mineral estate are "three distinct estates in land which can be held in fee simple separate and distinct from each other . . . ." Captline v. County of Allegheny, 74 Pa. Commw. 85, 91, 459 A. 2d 1298, 1301 (1983), *cert. denied*, 466 U. S. 904 (1984). In refusing to consider the effect of the Subsidence Act on this property interest alone, the Court dismisses this feature of Pennsylvania property law as simply a "legalistic [distinction] within a bundle of property rights." "Its value," the Court informs us, "is merely a part of the entire bundle of rights possessed by the owner of either the coal or the surface." This view of the support estate allows the Court to conclude that its destruction is merely the destruction of one "strand" in petitioners' bundle of property rights, not significant enough in the overall bundle to work a taking. . . .

I see no reason for refusing to evaluate the impact of the Subsidence Act on the support estate alone, for Pennsylvania has clearly defined it as a separate estate in property. The Court suggests that the practical significance of this estate is limited, because its value "is merely part of the bundle of rights possessed by the owner of either the coal or the surface." Though this may accurately describe the usual state of affairs, I do not understand the Court to mean that one holding the support estate alone would find it worthless, for surely the owners of the mineral or surface estates would be willing buyers of this interest. Nor does the Court suggest that the owner of both the mineral and support estates finds his separate interest in support to be without value. In these circumstances, where the estate defined by state law is both severable and of value in its own right, it is appropriate to consider the effect of regulation on that particular property interest. . . .

In sum, I would hold that Pennsylvania's Bituminous Mine Subsidence and Land Conservation Act effects a taking of petitioners' property without providing just compensation. Specifically, the Act works to extinguish petitioners' interest in at least 27 million tons of coal by requiring that coal to be left in the ground, and destroys their purchased support estates by returning to them financial liability for subsidence. I respectfully dissent from the Court's decision to the contrary.

Notes

1. Judges on the U.S. Court of Federal Claims, and on the court to which appeals from that tribunal are taken—the U.S. Court of Appeals for the Federal Circuit—have seen more than their fair share of regulatory takings challenges brought by mining companies. Indeed, these two courts, which were established so that certain monetary claims could be brought against the federal government, have been a hotbed of regulatory takings activities, often with positive results for property owners.[26] In Whitney Benefits, Inc. v. United States, 926 F.2d 1169, 1170, 1176-77 (Fed. Cir. 1991), for example, the appellate panel affirmed a $60-million-dollar judgment (plus interest), noting that "the Claims Court correctly concluded, based on not-clearly-erroneous findings, that on enactment SMCRA's [the federal Surface Mining and Control Reclamation Act of 1977, 30 U.S.C. §§1201 et seq.] prohibition of surface mining of alluvial valley floors (AVF's) constituted a taking of the Whitney coal property." The statute, at 30 U.S.C. §1265(b)(10)(F) ("Environmental protection performance standards"), notes "the essential hydrologic functions of alluvial valley floors in the arid and semiarid areas of the country." Not surprisingly, the government sought to rely on *Keystone*, without much success:

> Relying primarily on Keystone Bituminous Coal Ass'n. v. DeBenedictis, 480 U.S. 470, (1987), the government argues that SMCRA's AVF prohibition effected no taking because it was aimed at a public purpose entitled to "deference." Nothing in *Keystone*, however, supports the notion that public purpose alone permits total destruction of property rights without compensation. The government simply ignores *Keystone*'s analysis: a regulation effects a taking if it *either* (1) "does not substantially advance legitimate state interests," or (2) "denies an owner economically viable use of his land."

> Under the second prong of the analysis in *Keystone*, SMCRA denied Benefits all use of their property and completely destroyed its value. Thus Benefits is in the position occupied by the citizens in *Mahon*, who were denied all economically viable use of their coal, and in a fundamentally different position from that of the citizens in *Keystone*, who were not. In *Keystone*, the Subsidence Act simply required a small portion (1.8%) of the involved coal to be left in the ground. That was critical to the Court, which noted ". . . petitioners have not claimed, at this stage, that the Act makes it commercially impracticable for them to continue mining their bituminous coal interests in western Pennsylvania. *Indeed, petitioners have not even pointed to a single mine that can no longer be mined for profit.*" 480 U.S. at 495-96 (emphasis added). As the record here makes plain, Whitney coal is such a mine.

> Thus, in the present case, as in *Keystone*, the surface-related purpose of the statute is valid, but not controlling. The Court in *Keystone* went on separately to analyze the impact of the regulation on the properties before it, and found evidence of value destruction wanting. Here the Claims Court also thoroughly analyzed the impact of SMCRA,

---

26. For evaluations of these courts' regulatory takings track records, see, for example, Roger J. Marzulla & Nancie G. Marzulla, *Regulatory Takings in the United States Claims Court: Adjusting the Burdens that in Fairness and Equity Ought to Be Borne by Society as a Whole*, 40 Cath. U. L. Rev. 549 (1991); George W. Miller & Jonathan L. Abram, *A Survey of Recent Takings Cases in the Court of Federal Claims and the Court of Appeals for the Federal Circuit*, 42 Cath. U. L. Rev. 863 (1993); Courtney C. Tedrowe, Note, *Conceptual Severance and Takings in the Federal Circuit*, 85 Cornell L. Rev. 586 (2000); Thomas Hanley, Comment, *A Developer's Dream: The United States Claims Court's New Analysis of Section 404 Takings Challenges*, 19 B.C. Envtl. Aff. L. Rev. 317 (1991); Patrick Kennedy, Comment, *The United States Claims Court: A Safe "Harbor" From Government Regulation of Privately Owned Wetlands*, 9 Pace Envtl. L. Rev. 723 (1992); and Timothy G. Warner, Note, *Recent Decisions by the United States Claims Court and the Need for Greater Supreme Court Direction in Wetlands Takings Cases*, 43 Syracuse L. Rev. 901 (1992).

and correctly found compelling the evidence of value destruction. The evidence having shown the total destruction of all economically viable use, the conclusion is inescapable that SMCRA constituted a taking of the Whitney coal property. That the government may certainly do, but when it does so in the circumstances of this case it is required by the Constitution to pay just compensation.

Mining companies were also successful in United Nuclear Corp. v. United States, 912 F.2d 1432, 1433 (Fed. Cir. 1990) (finding that the Secretary of the Interior's "refusal to approve the mining plan constituted a taking of [United's] leases" to conduct uranium mining on Navajo reservation land), in Yuba Nat. Resources, Inc. v. United States, 821 F.2d 638, 639 (Fed. Cir. 1987) (finding a temporary (not permanent) regulatory taking had occurred when the government prohibited Yuba from mining "during a period in which the United States contended that it owned the mineral rights"). Despite these mining company victories in the Federal Circuit, however, in most of the mining regulatory takings cases that reached that appeals court the federal government prevailed. This was the case in, for example, Appolo Fuels, Inc. v. United States, 381 F.3d 1338, 1341 (Fed. Cir. 2004) (rejecting Appolo's assertions "that a permanent taking occurred when the Office of Surface Mining Reclamation and Enforcement ('OSM') designated the lands subject to its leases as unsuitable for mining pursuant" or, in the alternative, that the company was entitled to "compensation for a temporary taking allegedly resulting from extraordinary delay in OSM's decisionmaking process"); Wyatt v. United States, 271 F.3d 1090, 1100 (Fed. Cir. 2001) (reversing the trial court and finding that "[t]here was no extraordinary government delay sufficient to constitute a taking"); and Rith Energy v. United States, 247 F.3d 1355, 1358 (Fed. Cir. 2001) (affirming the grant of summary judgment in the government's favor, rejecting the company's assertion that OSM's suspension of a coal mining permit amounted to a taking; the agency had "concluded that a portion of the property on which Rith was mining contained high levels of potentially toxic materials that could pollute the groundwater in the area through a process known as 'acid mine drainage'").

2. The *Keystone* majority's adherence to the *Penn Central* "parcel as a whole" test is an outright rejection of what Professor Margaret Jane Radin, in *The Liberal Conception of Property: Cross-Currents in the Jurisprudence of Takings*, 88 Colum. L. Rev. 1667, 1676 (1988), labeled "conceptual severance," a strategy that

> consists of delineating a property interest consisting of just what the government action has removed from the owner, and then asserting that that particular whole thing has been permanently taken. Thus, this strategy hypothetically or conceptually "severs" from the whole bundle of rights just those strands that are interfered with by the regulation, and then hypothetically or conceptually construes those strands in the aggregate as a separate whole thing. . . .

> In *Penn Central*, . . . Rehnquist in dissent explicitly relied on the conceptual severance strategy. He argued that depriving Penn Central of the right to develop an office building over Grand Central Terminal was a complete taking—of its air rights. The whole thing taken, in other words, was a particular negative servitude precluding building into the air space above the existing building.

Notice how Chief Justice Rehnquist's *Keystone* dissent, focusing on the separate support estate, was a second unsuccessful attempt to shrink the takings denominator.

Professor Frank I. Michelman raised the "denominator" problem more than 20 years before *Keystone*, in *Property, Utility, and Fairness: Comments on the Ethical Foundations of "Just Compensation" Law*, 80 Harv. L. Rev. 1165, 1192 (1967):

> Is the supposedly critical factor the size of the private loss absolutely, or rather the size of that loss compared with some other quantity? And if, as seems clear, a comparison of magnitudes is intended—a comparison in which, were it fractionally expressed, the loss in value of the affected property would compose the numerator—what value supplies the denominator? Is it the preexisting value of the affected property, or is it the whole preexisting wealth or income of the complainant?

In a more recent exploration of this tricky concept, Professor Danaya Wright, in *A New Time for Denominators: Toward a Dynamic Theory of Property in the Regulatory Takings Relevant Parcel Analysis*, 34 Envtl. L. 175, 193, 200, 206, 214 (2004), has noted that courts and commentators tend to analyze the denominator in four ways: "physically (both horizontally and vertically), functionally, and temporally." Horizontal severance, for example, seeks "to determine the size of the relevant parcel when a landowner owns one hundred acres, only ten of which are affected by a regulation. Is the denominator one hundred acres or ten acres?" The vertical variety was present in Pennsylvania Coal v. Mahon, in which "[t]he vertical separation of the fee into mineral, support, and surface estates was deemed, by Justice Holmes, to be an acceptable way to think about the consequences of the legislation." Functional severance involves property owners who "have tried to narrowly identify the property right that is affected in a way that implies a 100% taking," while the temporal version concerns "the taking of a temporal slice of the property pie over time. An obvious example of temporal severance is the division of ownership over time with the use of future interests," such as the "fee simple determinable followed by a possibility of reverter" or the "life estate followed by a remainder."

IV. Floodplain Regulation

Los Angeles County Ordinance No. 11.855

The Board of Supervisors of the County of Los Angeles does ordain as follows:

Section 1. A person shall not construct, reconstruct, place or enlarge any building or structure, any portion of which is, or will be, located within the outer boundary lines of the interim flood protection area located in Mill Creek Canyon, vicinity of Hidden Springs . . . .

Section 4. Studies are now under way by the Department of Regional Planning in connection with the County Engineer and the Los Angeles County Flood Control District, to develop permanent flood protection areas for Mill Creek and other specific areas as part of a comprehensive flood plain management project. Mapping and evaluation of flood data has progressed to the point where an interim flood protection area in Mill Creek can be designated. Development is now occurring which will encroach within the limits of the permanent flood protection area and which will be incompatible with the anticipated uses to be permitted within the permanent flood protection area. If this ordinance does not take immediate effect, said uses will be established prior to the contemplated ordinance amendment, and once established may continue after such amendment has been made . . . .

By reason of the foregoing facts this ordinance is urgently required for the immediate preservation of the public health and safety, and the same shall take effect immediately upon passage thereof.

FIRST ENGLISH EVANGELICAL LUTHERAN CHURCH OF GLENDALE v. COUNTY OF LOS ANGELES
482 U.S. 304 (1987)

CHIEF JUSTICE REHNQUIST delivered the opinion of the Court. . . .

In this case the California Court of Appeal held that a landowner who claims that his property has been "taken" by a land-use regulation may not recover damages for the time before it is finally determined that the regulation constitutes a "taking" of his property. We disagree, and conclude that in these circumstances the Fifth and Fourteenth Amendments to the United States Constitution would require compensation for that period.

In 1957, appellant First English Evangelical Lutheran Church purchased a 21-acre parcel of land in a canyon along the banks of the Middle Fork of Mill Creek in the Angeles National Forest. The Middle Fork is the natural drainage channel for a watershed area owned by the National Forest Service. Twelve of the acres owned by the church are flat land, and contained a dining hall, two bunkhouses, a caretaker's lodge, an outdoor chapel, and a footbridge across the creek. The church operated on the site a campground, known as "Lutherglen," as a retreat center and a recreational area for handicapped children.

In July 1977, a forest fire denuded the hills upstream from Lutherglen, destroying approximately 3,860 acres of the watershed area and creating a serious flood hazard. Such flooding occurred on February 9 and 10, 1978, when a storm dropped 11 inches of rain in the watershed. The runoff from the storm overflowed the banks of the Mill Creek, flooding Lutherglen and destroying its buildings.

In response to the flooding of the canyon, appellee County of Los Angeles adopted Interim Ordinance No. 11,855 in January 1979. The ordinance provided that "[a] person shall not construct, reconstruct, place or enlarge any building or structure, any portion of which is, or will be, located within the outer boundary lines of the interim flood protection area located in Mill Creek Canyon . . . ." App. to Juris. Statement A31. The ordinance was effective immediately because the county determined that it was "required for the immediate preservation of the public health and safety . . . ." *Id.*, at A32. The interim flood protection area described by the ordinance included the flat areas on either side of Mill Creek on which Lutherglen had stood.

The church filed a complaint in the Superior Court of California a little more than a month after the ordinance was adopted. As subsequently amended, the complaint alleged two claims against the county and the Los Angeles County Flood Control District. The first alleged that the defendants were liable under Cal. Govt. Code Ann. § 835 (West 1980) for dangerous conditions on their upstream properties that contributed to the flooding of Lutherglen. As a part of this claim, appellant also alleged that "Ordinance No. 11,855 denies [appellant] all use of Lutherglen." App. 12, 49. The second claim sought to recover from the Flood Control District in inverse condemnation and in tort for engaging in cloud seeding during the storm that flooded Lutherglen. Appellant sought damages under each count for loss of use of Lutherglen. The defendants moved to strike the portions of the complaint alleging that the county's ordinance denied all use of Lutherglen, on the view that the California Supreme Court's decision in Agins v. Tiburon, 24 Cal. 3d 266, 598 P. 2d 25 (1979), aff'd on other grounds, 447 U.S. 255 (1980), rendered the allegation "entirely immaterial and irrelevant[, with] no bearing upon any conceivable cause of action herein." App. 22.

In *Agins v. Tiburon, supra,* the California Supreme Court decided that a landowner may not maintain an inverse condemnation suit in the courts of that State based upon a "regulatory" taking. 24 Cal. 3d, at 275-277, 598 P. 2d, at 29-31. In the court's view, maintenance of such a suit would allow a landowner to force the legislature to exercise its power of eminent domain. Under this decision, then, compensation is not required until the challenged regulation or ordinance has been held excessive in an action for declaratory relief or a writ of mandamus and the government has nevertheless decided to continue the regulation in effect. Based on this decision, the trial court in the present case granted the motion to strike the allegation that the church had been denied all use of Lutherglen. It explained that "a careful rereading of the Agins case persuades the Court that when an ordinance, even a non-zoning ordinance, deprives a person of the total use of his lands, his challenge to the ordinance is by way of declaratory relief or possibly mandamus." App. 26. Because the appellant alleged a regulatory taking and sought only damages, the allegation that the ordinance denied all use of Lutherglen was deemed irrelevant.

On appeal, the California Court of Appeal read the complaint as one seeking "damages for the uncompensated taking of all use of Lutherglen by County Ordinance No. 11,855 . . . ." App. to Juris. Statement A13-A14. It too relied on the California Supreme Court's decision in *Agins* in rejecting the cause of action, declining appellant's invitation to reevaluate *Agins* in light of this Court's opinions in San Diego Gas & Electric Co. v. San Diego, 450 U.S. 621 (1981). The court found itself obligated to follow *Agins* "because the United States Supreme Court has not yet ruled on the question of whether a state may constitutionally limit the remedy for a taking to nonmonetary relief . . . ." App. to Juris. Statement A16. It accordingly affirmed the trial court's decision to strike the allegations concerning appellee's ordinance. The California Supreme Court denied review.

This appeal followed, and we noted probable jurisdiction. Appellant asks us to hold that the California Supreme Court erred in *Agins v. Tiburon* in determining that the Fifth Amendment, as made applicable to the States through the Fourteenth Amendment, does not require compensation as a remedy for "temporary" regulatory takings—those regulatory takings which are ultimately invalidated by the courts. Four times this decade, we have considered similar claims and have found ourselves for one reason or another unable to consider the merits of the *Agins* rule. See MacDonald, Sommer & Frates v. Yolo County, 477 U.S. 340 (1986); Williamson County Regional Planning Comm'n v. Hamilton Bank, 473 U.S. 172 (1985); *San Diego Gas & Electric Co., supra; Agins v. Tiburon, supra.* For the reasons explained below, however, we find the constitutional claim properly presented in this case, and hold that on these facts the California courts have decided the compensation question inconsistently with the requirements of the Fifth Amendment.

Concerns with finality left us unable to reach the remedial question in the earlier cases where we have been asked to consider the rule of *Agins.* See *MacDonald, Sommer & Frates, supra,* at 351 (summarizing cases). In each of these cases, we concluded either that regulations considered to be in issue by the state court did not effect a taking, *Agins v. Tiburon,* 447 U.S., at 263, or that the factual disputes yet to be resolved by state authorities might still lead to the conclusion that no taking had occurred. *MacDonald, Sommer & Frates, supra,* at 351-353; *Williamson County, supra,* at 188-194; *San Diego Gas & Electric Co., supra,* at 631-632. Consideration of the remedial question in those circumstances, we concluded, would be premature.

The posture of the present case is quite different. Appellant's complaint alleged that "Ordinance No. 11,855 denies [it] all use of Lutherglen," and sought damages for this deprivation. App. 12, 49. In affirming the decision to strike this allegation, the Court of Appeal assumed that the complaint sought "damages for the uncompensated *taking* of all use of Lutherglen by County Ordinance No. 11,855." App. to Juris. Statement A13-A14 (emphasis added). It relied on the California Supreme Court's *Agins* decision for the conclusion that "the remedy for a *taking* [is limited] to nonmonetary relief . . . ." App. to Juris. Statement A16 (emphasis added). The disposition of the case on these grounds isolates the remedial question for our consideration. The rejection of appellant's allegations did not rest on the view that they were false. Nor did the court rely on the theory that regulatory measures such as Ordinance No. 11,855 may never constitute a taking in the constitutional sense. Instead, the claims were deemed irrelevant solely because of the California Supreme Court's decision in *Agins* that damages are unavailable to redress a "temporary" regulatory taking. The California Court of Appeal has thus held that, regardless of the correctness of appellant's claim that the challenged ordinance denies it "all use of Lutherglen," appellant may not recover damages until the ordinance is finally declared unconstitutional, and then only for any period after that declaration for which the county seeks to enforce it. The constitutional question pretermitted in our earlier cases is therefore squarely presented here.

We reject appellee's suggestion that, regardless of the state court's treatment of the question, we must independently evaluate the adequacy of the complaint and resolve the takings claim on the merits before we can reach the remedial question. However "cryptic"—to use appellee's description—the allegations with respect to the taking were, the California courts deemed them sufficient to present the issue. We accordingly have no occasion to decide whether the ordinance at issue actually denied appellant all use of its property or whether the county might avoid the conclusion that a compensable taking had occurred by establishing that the denial of all use was insulated as a part of the State's authority to enact safety regulations. See, *e. g.*, Goldblatt v. Hempstead, 369 U.S. 590 (1962); Hadacheck v. Sebastian, 239 U.S. 394 (1915); Mugler v. Kansas, 123 U.S. 623 (1887). These questions, of course, remain open for decision on the remand we direct today. We now turn to the question whether the Just Compensation Clause requires the government to pay for "temporary" regulatory takings.

Consideration of the compensation question must begin with direct reference to the language of the Fifth Amendment, which provides in relevant part that "private property [shall not] be taken for public use, without just compensation." As its language indicates, and as the Court has frequently noted, this provision does not prohibit the taking of private property, but instead places a condition on the exercise of that power. This basic understanding of the Amendment makes clear that it is designed not to limit the governmental interference with property rights *per se*, but rather to secure *compensation* in the event of otherwise proper interference amounting to a taking. Thus, government action that works a taking of property rights necessarily implicates the "constitutional obligation to pay just compensation." Armstrong v. United States, 364 U.S. 40, 49 (1960).

We have recognized that a landowner is entitled to bring an action in inverse condemnation as a result of "'the self-executing character of the constitutional provision with respect to compensation . . . .'" United States v. Clarke, 445 U.S. 253, 257 (1980), quoting 6 P. Nichols, Eminent Domain § 25.41 (3d rev. ed. 1972). As noted in JUSTICE BRENNAN's dissent in *San Diego Gas & Electric Co.*, 450 U.S., at 654-655, it has been established at least since Jacobs v. United States, 290 U.S. 13 (1933), that claims for just compensation are grounded in the Constitution itself . . . .

It has also been established doctrine at least since Justice Holmes' opinion for the Court in Pennsylvania Coal Co. v. Mahon, 260 U.S. 393 (1922), that "the general rule at least is, that while property may be regulated to a certain extent, if regulation goes too far it will be recognized as a taking." *Id.*, at 415. While the typical taking occurs when the government acts to condemn property in the exercise of its power of eminent domain, the entire doctrine of inverse condemnation is predicated on the proposition that a taking may occur without such formal proceedings. . . .

While the California Supreme Court may not have actually disavowed this general rule in *Agins*, we believe that it has truncated the rule by disallowing damages that occurred prior to the ultimate invalidation of the challenged regulation. . . .

We, of course, are not unmindful of these considerations, but they must be evaluated in the light of the command of the Just Compensation Clause of the Fifth Amendment. The Court has recognized in more than one case that the government may elect to abandon its intrusion or discontinue regulations. Similarly, a governmental body may acquiesce in a judicial declaration that one of its ordinances has effected an unconstitutional taking of property; the landowner has no right under the Just Compensation Clause to insist that a "temporary" taking be deemed a permanent taking. But we have not resolved whether abandonment by the government requires payment of compensation for the period of time during which regulations deny a landowner all use of his land.

In considering this question, we find substantial guidance in cases where the government has only temporarily exercised its right to use private property. In United States v. Dow, [357 U.S. 17,] at 26 [(1958)], though rejecting a claim that the Government may not abandon condemnation proceedings, the Court observed that abandonment "results in an alteration in the property interest taken—from [one of] full ownership to one of temporary use and occupation. . . . In such cases compensation would be measured by the principles normally governing the taking of a right to use property temporarily. See Kimball Laundry Co. v. United States, 338 U.S. 1 [1949]; United States v. Petty Motor Co., 327 U.S. 372 [1946]; United States v. General Motors Corp., 323 U.S. 373 [1945]." Each of the cases cited by the *Dow* Court involved appropriation of private property by the United States for use during World War II. Though the takings were in fact "temporary," there was no question that compensation would be required for the Government's interference with the use of the property; the Court was concerned in each case with determining the proper measure of the monetary relief to which the property holders were entitled.

These cases reflect the fact that "temporary" takings which, as here, deny a landowner all use of his property, are not different in kind from permanent takings, for which the Constitution clearly requires compensation. Cf. *San Diego Gas & Electric Co.*, 450 U.S., at 657 (BRENNAN, J., dissenting) ("Nothing in the Just Compensation Clause suggests that 'takings' must be permanent and irrevocable"). It is axiomatic that the Fifth Amendment's just compensation provision is "designed to bar Government from forcing some people alone to bear public burdens which, in all fairness and justice, should be borne by the public as a whole." Armstrong v. United States, 364 U.S., at 49. In the present case the interim ordinance was adopted by the County of Los Angeles in January 1979, and became effective immediately. Appellant filed suit within a month after the effective date of the ordinance and yet when the California Supreme Court denied a hearing in the case on October 17, 1985, the merits of appellant's claim had yet to be determined. The United States has been required to pay compensation for leasehold interests of shorter duration than this. The value of a leasehold interest in property for a period of years may be substantial, and the burden on the property owner in extinguishing such an interest for a period of years may be great indeed. Where this burden results from governmental action that amounted to a taking, the Just Compensation Clause of the Fifth Amendment requires that the government pay the landowner for the value of the use of the land during this period. Invalidation of the ordinance or its successor ordinance after this period of time, though converting the taking into a "temporary" one, is not a sufficient remedy to meet the demands of the Just Compensation Clause. . . .

We also point out that the allegation of the complaint which we treat as true for purposes of our decision was that the ordinance in question denied appellant all use of its property. We limit our holding to the facts presented, and of course do not deal with the quite different questions that would arise in the case of normal delays in obtaining building permits, changes in zoning ordinances, variances, and the like which are not before us. We realize that even our present holding will undoubtedly lessen to some extent the freedom and flexibility of land-use planners and governing bodies of municipal corporations when enacting land-use regulations. But such consequences necessarily flow from any decision upholding a claim of constitutional right; many of the provisions of the Constitution are designed to limit the flexibility and freedom of governmental authorities, and the Just Compensation Clause of the Fifth Amendment is one of them. As Justice Holmes aptly noted more than 50 years ago, "a strong public desire to improve the public condition is not enough to warrant achieving the desire by a shorter cut than the constitutional way of paying for the change." Pennsylvania Coal Co. v. Mahon, 260 U.S., at 416.

Here we must assume that the Los Angeles County ordinance has denied appellant all use of its property for a considerable period of years, and we hold that invalidation of the ordinance without payment of fair value for the use of the property during this period of time would be a constitutionally insufficient remedy. The judgment of the California Court of Appeal is therefore reversed, and the case is remanded for further proceedings not inconsistent with this opinion.

It is so ordered.

JUSTICE STEVENS, with whom JUSTICE BLACKMUN and JUSTICE O'CONNOR join as to Parts I and III, dissenting.

One thing is certain. The Court's decision today will generate a great deal of litigation. Most of it, I believe, will be unproductive. But the mere duty to defend the actions that today's decision will spawn will undoubtedly have a significant adverse impact on the land-use regulatory process. The Court has reached out to address an issue not actually presented in this case, and has then answered that self-imposed question in a superficial and, I believe, dangerous way.

Four flaws in the Court's analysis merit special comment. First, the Court unnecessarily and imprudently assumes that appellant's complaint alleges an unconstitutional taking of Lutherglen. Second, the Court distorts our precedents in the area of regulatory takings when it concludes that all ordinances which would constitute takings if allowed to remain in effect permanently, necessarily also constitute takings if they are in effect for only a limited period of time. Third, the Court incorrectly assumes that the California Supreme Court has already decided that it will never allow a state court to grant monetary relief for a temporary regulatory taking, and then uses that conclusion to reverse a judgment which is correct under the Court's own theories. Finally, the Court errs in concluding that it is the Takings Clause, rather than the Due Process Clause, which is the primary constraint on the use of unfair and dilatory procedures in the land-use area. . . .

Notes

1. It is one thing to win a regulatory takings dispute *in theory*. It is a much more difficult challenge for a property owner to prevail after the facts are in. The Supreme Court did not pretend to have the last word in the dispute between the church and the county. Upon remand, at 210 Cal. App. 3d 1353, 1356, 1367, 1372-73, 258 Cal. Rptr. 893, 894, 902, 906 (1989), the state court, noting that "the Supreme Court expressly reserved the question whether respondent's regulatory action in this case amounted to an unconstitutional taking," found that the takings assertion failed for two reasons:

> (1) The interim ordinance in question substantially advanced the preeminent state interest in public safety and did not deny appellant all use of its property. (2) The interim ordinance only imposed a reasonable moratorium for a reasonable period of time while the respondent conducted a study and determined what uses, if any, were compatible with public safety.

While the Justices "assume[d] that the Los Angeles County ordinance has denied appellant all use of its property for a considerable period of years," after examining the facts in more detail, the state court concluded that the ordinance *does not* deny First English "all use" of this property. It does not even prevent occupancy and use of any structures which may have survived the flood. It only prohibits the reconstruction of structures which were demolished or damaged by the raging waters and the construction of new structures. In no sense does it prohibit uses of this campground property which can be carried out without the reconstruction of demolished buildings or the erection of new ones. First English's complaint stated solely a facial challenge to the interim ordinance and *as far as this ordinance itself was concerned*, many camping activities could continue on this property. Meals could be cooked, games played, lessons given, tents pitched. (If Lutherglen had been a factory or a coal mine, these sorts of uses would have meant little to the landowner. But Lutherglen is a camping facility. So uses of value to that purpose remained available during the time the interim ordinance was in effect.)

Moreover, the court found a second "independent and sufficient ground" for its decision in favor of the local government:

> [T]he interim ordinance did not constitute a "temporary unconstitutional taking" even were we to assume its restrictions were too broad if permanently imposed on First English. This interim ordinance was by design a temporary measure—in effect a total moratorium on any construction on First English's property—while the County conducted a study to determine what uses and what structures, if any, could be permitted on this property consistent with considerations of safety. We do not read the United States Supreme Court's decision . . . as converting moratoriums and other interim land-use restrictions into unconstitutional "temporary takings" requiring compensation unless, perhaps, if these interim measures are unreasonable in purpose, duration or scope. On its face, ordinance No. 11,855 is reasonable in all these dimensions.

Because the ordinance did not effect a taking, ultimately the landowner was not entitled to compensation.

2. The *First English* Court found historical support for its temporary takings holding in three cases involving the computation of just compensation for the federal government's condemnation, for a limited period, of leasehold or fee interests during World War II: United States v. General Motors Corp., 323 U.S. 373, 374, 377-78 (1945), Kimball Laundry Co. v. United States, 338 U.S. 1 (1949), and United States v. Petty Motor Co., 327 U.S. 372 (1946). The specific question addressed by the *General Motors* Court was "the ascertainment of the just compensation required by the Fifth Amendment of the Constitution, where, in the exercise of the power of eminent domain, temporary occupancy of a portion of a leased building is taken from a tenant who holds under a long term lease." Included in Justice Owen Roberts' opinion was this memorable discussion of the "modern" view of property imbedded in the words of the Takings Clause:

> The critical terms are "property," "taken" and "just compensation." It is conceivable that the first was used in its vulgar and untechnical sense of the physical thing with respect to which the citizen exercises rights recognized by law. On the other hand, it may have been employed in a more accurate sense to denote the group of rights inhering in the citizen's relation to the physical thing, as the right to possess, use and dispose of it. In point of fact, the construction given the phrase has been the latter. When the sovereign exercises the power of eminent domain it substitutes itself in relation to the physical thing in question in place of him who formerly bore the relation to that thing, which we denominate ownership. In other words, it deals with what lawyers term the

individual's "interest" in the thing in question. That interest may comprise the group of rights for which the shorthand term is "a fee simple" or it may be the interest known as an "estate or tenancy for years," as in the present instance. The constitutional provision is addressed to every sort of interest the citizen may possess.

Decades later, in cases such as *First English* and the decision that follows, the Court would take very seriously the notion that owners could suffer a compensable taking for the loss of their rights, even if they consistently maintained title and physical possession of their property.

3. A few weeks after issuing the *Keystone* decision, the Court considered another mining case—California Coastal Comm'n v. Granite Rock Co., 480 U.S. 572, 576, 589-90 (1987). As noted in Chapter One, Justice Sandra Day O'Connor's opinion in *Granite Rock* tackled the difficult task of distinguishing between the "core activit[ies]" of environmental regulation and land use planning. One (ultimately unsuccessful) argument made by Granite Rock, which mined white limestone on federal lands, was that the federal Coastal Zone Management Act (CZMA) of 1972 preempted a requirement under the California Coastal Act that "any person undertaking any development, including mining, in the State's coastal zone must secure a permit from the California Coastal Commission." The mining company asserted

> that the exclusion of "lands the use of which is by law subject solely to the discretion of or which is held in trust by the Federal Government, its officers or agents" [quoting 16 U. S. C. §1453(1)] excludes all federally owned land from the CZMA definition of a State's coastal zone, and demonstrates a congressional intent to pre-empt any possible Coastal Commission permit requirement as applied to the mining of Granite Rock's unpatented claim in the national forest land.

After reviewing the CZMA legislative history, the Court disagreed: "Because Congress specifically disclaimed any intention to pre-empt pre-existing state authority in the CZMA, we conclude that even if all federal lands are excluded from the CZMA definition of 'coastal zone,' the CZMA does not automatically pre-empt all state regulation of activities on federal lands." Three months later, a majority of the Justices would find that the same California Coastal Commission had violated the federal Constitution when it sought to exact too much from residential landowners who were seeking development permission.

V.   Coastal Zone Management

Cal. Pub. Resources Code §30600 (original version)

(a) In addition to obtaining any other permit required by law from any local government or from any state, regional, or local agency, on or after January 1, 1977, any person wishing to perform or undertake any development in the coastal zone, other than a facility subject to the provisions of Section 25500, shall obtain a coastal development permit.

Cal. Pub. Resources Code §30212

(a) Public access from the nearest public roadway to the shoreline and along the coast shall be provided in new development projects except where (1) it is inconsistent with public safety, military security needs, or the protection of fragile coastal resources, (2) adequate access exists nearby, or (3) agriculture would be adversely affected. . . .

NOLLAN v. CALIFORNIA COASTAL COMMISSION
483 U.S. 825 (1987)

JUSTICE SCALIA delivered the opinion of the Court. . . .

The Nollans own a beachfront lot in Ventura County, California. A quarter-mile north of their property is Faria County Park, an oceanside public park with a public beach and recreation area. Another public beach area, known locally as "the Cove," lies 1,800 feet south of their lot. A concrete seawall approximately eight feet high separates the beach portion of the Nollans' property from the rest of the lot. The historic mean high tide line determines the lot's oceanside boundary.

The Nollans originally leased their property with an option to buy. The building on the lot was a small bungalow, totaling 504 square feet, which for a time they rented to summer vacationers. After years of rental use, however, the building had fallen into disrepair, and could no longer be rented out.

The Nollans' option to purchase was conditioned on their promise to demolish the bungalow and replace it. In order to do so, under Cal. Pub. Res. Code Ann. §§ 30106, 30212, and 30600 (West 1986), they were required to obtain a coastal development permit from the California Coastal Commission. On February 25, 1982, they submitted a permit application to the Commission in which they proposed to demolish the existing structure and replace it with a three-bedroom house in keeping with the rest of the neighborhood.

The Nollans were informed that their application had been placed on the administrative calendar, and that the Commission staff had recommended that the permit be granted subject to the condition that they allow the public an easement to pass across a portion of their property bounded by the mean high tide line on one side, and their seawall on the other side. This would make it easier for the public to get to Faria County Park and the Cove. The Nollans protested imposition of the condition, but the Commission overruled their objections and granted the permit subject to their recordation of a deed restriction granting the easement.

On June 3, 1982, the Nollans filed a petition for writ of administrative mandamus asking the Ventura County Superior Court to invalidate the access condition. They argued that the condition could not be imposed absent evidence that their proposed development would have a direct adverse impact on public access to the beach. The court agreed, and remanded the case to the Commission for a full evidentiary hearing on that issue.

On remand, the Commission held a public hearing, after which it made further factual findings and reaffirmed its imposition of the condition. It found that the new house would increase blockage of the view of the ocean, thus contributing to the development of "a 'wall' of residential structures" that would prevent the public "psychologically . . . from realizing a stretch of coastline exists nearby that they have every right to visit." *Id.*, at 58. The new house would also increase private use of the shorefront. These effects of construction of the house, along with other area development, would cumulatively "burden the public's ability to traverse to and along the shorefront." *Id.*, at 65-66. Therefore the Commission could properly require the Nollans to offset that burden by providing additional lateral access to the public beaches in the form of an easement across their property. The Commission also noted that it had similarly conditioned 43 out of 60 coastal development permits along the same tract of land, and that of the 17 not so conditioned, 14 had been approved when the Commission did not have administrative regulations in place allowing imposition of the condition, and the remaining 3 had not involved shorefront property.

The Nollans filed a supplemental petition for a writ of administrative mandamus with the Superior Court, in which they argued that imposition of the access condition violated the Takings Clause of the Fifth Amendment, as incorporated against the States by the Fourteenth Amendment. The Superior Court ruled in their favor on statutory grounds, finding, in part to avoid "issues of constitutionality," that the California Coastal Act of 1976, Cal. Pub. Res. Code Ann. § 30000 et seq. (West 1986), authorized the Commission to impose public access conditions on coastal development permits for the replacement of an existing single-family home with a new one only where the proposed development would have an adverse impact on public access to the sea. In the court's view, the administrative record did not provide an adequate factual basis for concluding that replacement of the bungalow with the house would create a direct or cumulative burden on public access to the sea. Accordingly, the Superior Court granted the writ of mandamus and directed that the permit condition be struck.

The Commission appealed to the California Court of Appeal. While that appeal was pending, the Nollans satisfied the condition on their option to purchase by tearing down the bungalow and building the new house, and bought the property. They did not notify the Commission that they were taking that action.

The Court of Appeal reversed the Superior Court. 177 Cal. App. 3d 719, 223 Cal. Rptr. 28 (1986). It disagreed with the Superior Court's interpretation of the Coastal Act, finding that it required that a coastal permit for the construction of a new house whose floor area, height or bulk was more than 10% larger than that of the house it was replacing be conditioned on a grant of access. It also ruled that that requirement did not violate the Constitution under the reasoning of an earlier case of the Court of Appeal, Grupe v. California Coastal Comm'n, 166 Cal. App. 3d 148, 212 Cal. Rptr. 578 (1985). In that case, the court had found that so long as a project contributed to the need for public access, even if the project standing alone had not created the need for access, and even if there was only an indirect relationship between the access exacted and the need to which the project contributed, imposition of an access condition on a development permit was sufficiently related to burdens created by the project to be constitutional. The Court of Appeal ruled that the record established that that was the situation with respect to the Nollans' house. It ruled that the Nollans' taking claim also failed because, although the condition diminished the value of the Nollans' lot, it did not deprive them of all reasonable use of their property. Since, in the Court of Appeal's view, there was no statutory or constitutional obstacle to imposition of the access condition, the Superior Court erred in granting the writ of mandamus. The Nollans appealed to this Court, raising only the constitutional question.

Had California simply required the Nollans to make an easement across their beachfront available to the public on a permanent basis in order to increase public access to the beach, rather than conditioning their permit to rebuild their house on their agreeing to do so, we have no doubt there would have been a taking. To say that the appropriation of a public easement across a landowner's premises does not constitute the taking of a property interest but rather (as JUSTICE BRENNAN contends) "a mere restriction on its use," is to use words in a manner that deprives them of all their ordinary meaning. Indeed, one of the principal uses of the eminent domain power is to assure that the government be able to require conveyance of just such interests, so long as it pays for them. Perhaps because the point is so obvious, we have never been confronted with a controversy that required us to rule upon it, but our cases' analysis of the effect of other governmental action leads to the same conclusion. We have repeatedly held that, as to property reserved by its owner for private use, "the right to exclude [others is] 'one of the most essential sticks in the bundle of rights that are commonly characterized as property.'" Loretto v. Teleprompter Manhattan CATV Corp., 458 U.S. 419, 433 (1982), quoting Kaiser Aetna v. United States, 444 U.S. 164, 176 (1979). In *Loretto* we observed that where governmental action results in "[a] permanent physical occupation" of the property, by the government itself or by others, see 458 U.S., at 432-433, n. 9, "our cases uniformly have found a taking to the extent of the occupation, without regard to whether the action achieves an important public benefit or has only minimal economic impact on the owner," *id.*, at 434-435. We think a "permanent physical occupation" has occurred, for purposes of that rule, where individuals are given a permanent and continuous right to pass to and fro, so that the real property may continuously be traversed, even though no particular individual is permitted to station himself permanently upon the premises. . . .

Given, then, that requiring uncompensated conveyance of the easement outright would violate the Fourteenth Amendment, the question becomes whether requiring it to be conveyed as a condition for issuing a land-use permit alters the outcome. We have long recognized that land-use regulation does not effect a taking if it "substantially advance[s] legitimate state interests" and does not "den[y] an owner economically viable use of his land," Agins v. Tiburon, 447 U.S. 255, 260 (1980). See also Penn Central Transportation Co. v. New York City, 438 U.S. 104, 127 (1978) ("[A] use restriction may constitute a 'taking' if not reasonably necessary to the effectuation of a substantial government purpose"). Our cases have not elaborated on the standards for determining what constitutes a "legitimate state interest" or what type of connection between the regulation and the state interest satisfies the requirement that the former "substantially advance" the latter.[3] They have made clear, however, that a broad range of governmental purposes and regulations satisfies these requirements. See Agins v. Tiburon, *supra*, at 260-262 (scenic zoning); Penn Central Transportation Co. v. New York City, *supra* (landmark preservation); Euclid v. Ambler Realty Co., 272 U.S. 365 (1926) (residential zoning); Laitos & Westfall, Government Interference with Private Interests in Public Resources, 11 Harv. Envtl. L. Rev. 1, 66 (1987). The Commission argues that among these permissible purposes are protecting the public's ability to see the beach, assisting the public in overcoming the "psychological barrier" to using the beach created by a developed shorefront, and preventing congestion on the public beaches. We assume, without deciding, that this is so—in which case the Commission unquestionably would be able to deny the Nollans their permit outright if their new house (alone, or by reason of the cumulative impact produced in conjunction with other construction)[4] would substantially impede these purposes, unless the denial would interfere so drastically with the Nollans' use of their property as to constitute a taking.

The Commission argues that a permit condition that serves the same legitimate police-power purpose as a refusal to issue the permit should not be found to be a taking if the refusal to issue the permit would not constitute a taking. We agree. Thus, if the Commission attached to the permit some condition that would have protected the public's ability to see the beach notwithstanding

---

3. Contrary to JUSTICE BRENNAN's claim, our opinions do not establish that these standards are the same as those applied to due process or equal protection claims. To the contrary, our verbal formulations in the takings field have generally been quite different. We have required that the regulation "substantially advance" the "legitimate state interest" sought to be achieved, Agins v. Tiburon, 447 U.S. 255, 260 (1980), not that "the State 'could rationally have decided' that the measure adopted might achieve the State's objective." [Justice Brennan's dissent], at 843, quoting Minnesota v. Clover Leaf Creamery Co., 449 U.S. 456, 466 (1981). JUSTICE BRENNAN relies principally on an equal protection case, Minnesota v. Clover Leaf Creamery Co., and two substantive due process cases, Williamson v. Lee Optical of Oklahoma, Inc., 348 U.S. 483, 487-488 (1955), and Day-Brite Lighting, Inc. v. Missouri, 342 U.S. 421, 423 (1952), in support of the standards he would adopt. But there is no reason to believe (and the language of our cases gives some reason to disbelieve) that so long as the regulation of property is at issue the standards for takings challenges, due process challenges, and equal protection challenges are identical; any more than there is any reason to believe that so long as the regulation of speech is at issue the standards for due process challenges, equal protection challenges, and First Amendment challenges are identical. Goldblatt v. Hempstead, 369 U.S. 590 (1962), does appear to assume that the inquiries are the same, but that assumption is inconsistent with the formulations of our later cases.

4. If the Nollans were being singled out to bear the burden of California's attempt to remedy these problems, although they had not contributed to it more than other coastal landowners, the State's action, even if otherwise valid, might violate either the incorporated Takings Clause or the Equal Protection Clause. One of the principal purposes of the Takings Clause is "to bar Government from forcing some people alone to bear public burdens which, in all fairness and justice, should be borne by the public as a whole." Armstrong v. United States, 364 U.S. 40, 49 (1960); see also San Diego Gas & Electric Co. v. San Diego, 450 U.S. 621, 656 (1981) (BRENNAN, J., dissenting); Penn Central Transportation Co. v. New York City, 438 U.S. 104, 123 (1978). But that is not the basis of the Nollans' challenge here.

construction of the new house—for example, a height limitation, a width restriction, or a ban on fences—so long as the Commission could have exercised its police power (as we have assumed it could) to forbid construction of the house altogether, imposition of the condition would also be constitutional. Moreover (and here we come closer to the facts of the present case), the condition would be constitutional even if it consisted of the requirement that the Nollans provide a viewing spot on their property for passersby with whose sighting of the ocean their new house would interfere. Although such a requirement, constituting a permanent grant of continuous access to the property, would have to be considered a taking if it were not attached to a development permit, the Commission's assumed power to forbid construction of the house in order to protect the public's view of the beach must surely include the power to condition construction upon some concession by the owner, even a concession of property rights, that serves the same end. If a prohibition designed to accomplish that purpose would be a legitimate exercise of the police power rather than a taking, it would be strange to conclude that providing the owner an alternative to that prohibition which accomplishes the same purpose is not.

The evident constitutional propriety disappears, however, if the condition substituted for the prohibition utterly fails to further the end advanced as the justification for the prohibition. When that essential nexus is eliminated, the situation becomes the same as if California law forbade shouting fire in a crowded theater, but granted dispensations to those willing to contribute $100 to the state treasury. While a ban on shouting fire can be a core exercise of the State's police power to protect the public safety, and can thus meet even our stringent standards for regulation of speech, adding the unrelated condition alters the purpose to one which, while it may be legitimate, is inadequate to sustain the ban. Therefore, even though, in a sense, requiring a $100 tax contribution in order to shout fire is a lesser restriction on speech than an outright ban, it would not pass constitutional muster. Similarly here, the lack of nexus between the condition and the original purpose of the building restriction converts that purpose to something other than what it was. The purpose then becomes, quite simply, the obtaining of an easement to serve some valid governmental purpose, but without payment of compensation. Whatever may be the outer limits of "legitimate state interests" in the takings and land-use context, this is not one of them. In short, unless the permit condition serves the same governmental purpose as the development ban, the building restriction is not a valid regulation of land use but "an out-and-out plan of extortion." J. E. D. Associates, Inc. v. Atkinson, 121 N. H. 581, 584, 432 A. 2d 12, 14-15 (1981); see Brief for United States as Amicus Curiae 22, and n. 20.[5]

The Commission claims that it concedes as much, and that we may sustain the condition at issue here by finding that it is reasonably related to the public need or burden that the Nollans' new house creates or to which it contributes. We can accept, for purposes of discussion, the Commission's proposed test as to how close a "fit" between the condition and the burden is required, because we find that this case does not meet even the most untailored standards. The Commission's principal contention to the contrary essentially turns on a play on the word "access." The Nollans' new house, the Commission found, will interfere with "visual access" to the beach. That in turn (along with other shorefront development) will interfere with the desire of people who drive past the Nollans' house to use the beach, thus creating a "psychological barrier" to "access." The Nollans' new house will also, by a process not altogether clear from the Commission's opinion but presumably potent enough to more than offset the effects of the psychological barrier, increase

5. One would expect that a regime in which this kind of leveraging of the police power is allowed would produce stringent land-use regulation which the State then waives to accomplish other purposes, leading to lesser realization of the land-use goals purportedly sought to be served than would result from more lenient (but nontradeable) development restrictions. Thus, the importance of the purpose underlying the prohibition not only does not justify the imposition of unrelated conditions for eliminating the prohibition, but positively militates against the practice.

the use of the public beaches, thus creating the need for more "access." These burdens on "access" would be alleviated by a requirement that the Nollans provide "lateral access" to the beach.

Rewriting the argument to eliminate the play on words makes clear that there is nothing to it. It is quite impossible to understand how a requirement that people already on the public beaches be able to walk across the Nollans' property reduces any obstacles to viewing the beach created by the new house. It is also impossible to understand how it lowers any "psychological barrier" to using the public beaches, or how it helps to remedy any additional congestion on them caused by construction of the Nollans' new house. We therefore find that the Commission's imposition of the permit condition cannot be treated as an exercise of its land-use power for any of these purposes. Our conclusion on this point is consistent with the approach taken by every other court that has considered the question, with the exception of the California state courts.

JUSTICE BRENNAN argues that imposition of the access requirement is not irrational. In his version of the Commission's argument, the reason for the requirement is that in its absence, a person looking toward the beach from the road will see a street of residential structures including the Nollans' new home and conclude that there is no public beach nearby. If, however, that person sees people passing and repassing along the dry sand behind the Nollans' home, he will realize that there is a public beach somewhere in the vicinity. The Commission's action, however, was based on the opposite factual finding that the wall of houses completely blocked the view of the beach and that a person looking from the road would not be able to see it at all.

Even if the Commission had made the finding that JUSTICE BRENNAN proposes, however, it is not certain that it would suffice. We do not share JUSTICE BRENNAN's confidence that the Commission "should have little difficulty in the future in utilizing its expertise to demonstrate a specific connection between provisions for access and burdens on access," that will avoid the effect of today's decision. We view the Fifth Amendment's Property Clause to be more than a pleading requirement, and compliance with it to be more than an exercise in cleverness and imagination. As indicated earlier, our cases describe the condition for abridgment of property rights through the police power as a "*substantial* advanc[ing]" of a legitimate state interest. We are inclined to be particularly careful about the adjective where the actual conveyance of property is made a condition to the lifting of a land-use restriction, since in that context there is heightened risk that the purpose is avoidance of the compensation requirement, rather than the stated police-power objective.

We are left, then, with the Commission's justification for the access requirement unrelated to land-use regulation:

> "Finally, the Commission notes that there are several existing provisions of pass and repass lateral access benefits already given by past Faria Beach Tract applicants as a result of prior coastal permit decisions. The access required as a condition of this permit is part of a comprehensive program to provide continuous public access along Faria Beach as the lots undergo development or redevelopment." App. 68.

That is simply an expression of the Commission's belief that the public interest will be served by a continuous strip of publicly accessible beach along the coast. The Commission may well be right that it is a good idea, but that does not establish that the Nollans (and other coastal residents) alone can be compelled to contribute to its realization. Rather, California is free to advance its "comprehensive program," if it wishes, by using its power of eminent domain for this "public purpose," see U.S. Const., Amdt. 5; but if it wants an easement across the Nollans' property, it must pay for it.

Reversed.

JUSTICE BRENNAN, with whom JUSTICE MARSHALL joins, dissenting. . . .

Appellants in this case sought to construct a new dwelling on their beach lot that would both diminish visual access to the beach and move private development closer to the public tidelands. The Commission reasonably concluded that such "buildout," both individually and cumulatively, threatens public access to the shore. It sought to offset this encroachment by obtaining assurance that the public may walk along the shoreline in order to gain access to the ocean. The Court finds this an illegitimate exercise of the police power, because it maintains that there is no reasonable relationship between the effect of the development and the condition imposed.

The first problem with this conclusion is that the Court imposes a standard of precision for the exercise of a State's police power that has been discredited for the better part of this century. Furthermore, even under the Court's cramped standard, the permit condition imposed in this case directly responds to the specific type of burden on access created by appellants' development. Finally, a review of those factors deemed most significant in takings analysis makes clear that the Commission's action implicates none of the concerns underlying the Takings Clause. The Court has thus struck down the Commission's reasonable effort to respond to intensified development along the California coast, on behalf of landowners who can make no claim that their reasonable expectations have been disrupted. The Court has, in short, given appellants a windfall at the expense of the public. . . .

There can be no dispute that the police power of the States encompasses the authority to impose conditions on private development. It is also by now commonplace that this Court's review of the rationality of a State's exercise of its police power demands only that the State *"could rationally have decided"* that the measure adopted might achieve the State's objective. Minnesota v. Clover Leaf Creamery Co., 449 U.S. 456, 466 (1981) (emphasis in original).[1] In this case, California has employed its police power in order to condition development upon preservation of public access to the ocean and tidelands. The Coastal Commission, if it had so chosen, could have denied the Nollans' request for a development permit, since the property would have remained economically viable without the requested new development. Instead, the State sought to accommodate the Nollans' desire for new development, on the condition that the development not diminish the overall amount of public access to the coastline. Appellants' proposed development would reduce

---

1. See also Williamson v. Lee Optical of Oklahoma, Inc., 348 U.S. 483, 487-488 (1955) ("The law need not be in every respect logically consistent with its aims to be constitutional. It is enough that there is an evil at hand for correction, and that it might be thought that the particular legislative measure was a rational way to correct it"); Day-Brite Lighting, Inc. v. Missouri, 342 U.S. 421, 423 (1952) ("Our recent decisions make it plain that we do not sit as a super-legislature to weigh the wisdom of legislation nor to decide whether the policy which it expresses offends the public welfare. . . . State legislatures have constitutional authority to experiment with new techniques; they are entitled to their own standard of the public welfare").

Notwithstanding the suggestion otherwise, our standard for reviewing the threshold question whether an exercise of the police power is legitimate is a uniform one. As we stated over 25 years ago in addressing a takings challenge to government regulation:

"The term 'police power' connotes the time-tested conceptional limit of public encroachment upon private interests. Except for the substitution of the familiar standard of 'reasonableness,' this Court has generally refrained from announcing any specific criteria. The classic statement of the rule in Lawton v. Steele, 152 U.S. 133, 137 (1894), is still valid today: . . . "It must appear, first, that the interests of the public . . . require [government] interference; and, second, that the means are reasonably necessary for the accomplishment of the purpose, and not unduly oppressive upon individuals.' Even this rule is not applied with strict precision, for this Court has often said that 'debatable questions as to reasonableness are not for the courts but for the legislature . . . .' E. g., Sproles v. Binford, 286 U.S. 374, 388 (1932)." Goldblatt v. Hempstead, 369 U.S. 590, 594-595 (1962). . . .

Of course, government action may be a valid exercise of the police power and still violate specific provisions of the Constitution. JUSTICE SCALIA is certainly correct in observing that challenges founded upon these provisions are reviewed under different standards. Our consideration of factors such as those identified in *Penn Central*, for instance, provides an analytical framework for protecting the values underlying the Takings Clause, and other distinctive approaches are utilized to give effect to other constitutional provisions. This is far different, however, from the use of different standards of review to address the threshold issue of the rationality of government action.

public access by restricting visual access to the beach, by contributing to an increased need for community facilities, and by moving private development closer to public beach property. The Commission sought to offset this diminution in access, and thereby preserve the overall balance of access, by requesting a deed restriction that would ensure "lateral" access: the right of the public to pass and repass along the dry sand parallel to the shoreline in order to reach the tidelands and the ocean. In the expert opinion of the Coastal Commission, development conditioned on such a restriction would fairly attend to both public and private interests. . . .

The Commission is charged by both the State Constitution and legislature to preserve overall public access to the California coastline. Furthermore, by virtue of its participation in the Coastal Zone Management Act (CZMA) program, the State must "exercise effectively [its] responsibilities in the coastal zone through the development and implementation of management programs to achieve wise use of the land and water resources of the coastal zone," 16 U. S. C. § 1452(2), so as to provide for, *inter alia*, "public access to the coas[t] for recreation purposes." § 1452(2)(D). The Commission has sought to discharge its responsibilities in a flexible manner. It has sought to balance private and public interests and to accept tradeoffs: to permit development that reduces access in some ways as long as other means of access are enhanced. In this case, it has determined that the Nollans' burden on access would be offset by a deed restriction that formalizes the public's right to pass along the shore. In its informed judgment, such a tradeoff would preserve the net amount of public access to the coastline. The Court's insistence on a precise fit between the forms of burden and condition on each individual parcel along the California coast would penalize the Commission for its flexibility, hampering the ability to fulfill its public trust mandate. . . .

Examination of the economic impact of the Commission's action reinforces the conclusion that no taking has occurred. Allowing appellants to intensify development along the coast in exchange for ensuring public access to the ocean is a classic instance of government action that produces a "reciprocity of advantage." Pennsylvania Coal, 260 U.S., at 415. Appellants have been allowed to replace a one-story, 521-square-foot beach home with a two-story, 1,674-square-foot residence and an attached two-car garage, resulting in development covering 2,464 square feet of the lot. Such development obviously significantly increases the value of appellants' property; appellants make no contention that this increase is offset by any diminution in value resulting from the deed restriction, much less that the restriction made the property less valuable than it would have been without the new construction. Furthermore, appellants gain an additional benefit from the Commission's permit condition program. They are able to walk along the beach beyond the confines of their own property only because the Commission has required deed restrictions as a condition of approving other new beach developments. Thus, appellants benefit both as private landowners and as members of the public from the fact that new development permit requests are conditioned on preservation of public access. . . .

JUSTICE BLACKMUN, dissenting. . . .

I disagree with the Court's rigid interpretation of the necessary correlation between a burden created by development and a condition imposed pursuant to the State's police power to mitigate that burden. The land-use problems this country faces require creative solutions. These are not advanced by an "eye for an eye" mentality. The close nexus between benefits and burdens that the Court now imposes on permit conditions creates an anomaly in the ordinary requirement that a State's exercise of its police power need be no more than rationally based. See, *e. g.*, Minnesota v. Clover Leaf Creamery Co., 449 U.S. 456, 466 (1981). In my view, the easement exacted from appellants and the problems their development created are adequately related to the governmental interest in providing public access to the beach. Coastal development by its very nature makes public access to the shore generally more difficult. Appellants' structure is part of that general development and, in particular, it diminishes the public's visual access to the ocean and decreases the public's sense that it may have physical access to the beach. These losses in access can be counteracted, at least in part, by the condition on appellants' construction permitting public passage that ensures access along the beach.

Traditional takings analysis compels the conclusion that there is no taking here. The governmental action is a valid exercise of the police power, and, so far as the record reveals, has a nonexistent economic effect on the value of appellants' property. No investment-backed expectations were diminished. It is significant that the Nollans had notice of the easement before they purchased the property and that public use of the beach had been permitted for decades.

For these reasons, I respectfully dissent.

JUSTICE STEVENS, with whom JUSTICE BLACKMUN joins, dissenting. . . .

In his dissent in San Diego Gas & Electric Co. v. San Diego, 450 U.S. 621 (1981), JUSTICE BRENNAN proposed a brand new constitutional rule. He argued that a mistake such as the one that a majority of the Court believes that the California Coastal Commission made in this case should automatically give rise to pecuniary liability for a "temporary taking." *Id.*, at 653-661. Notwithstanding the unprecedented chilling effect that such a rule will obviously have on public officials charged with the responsibility for drafting and implementing regulations designed to protect the environment and the public welfare, six Members of the Court recently endorsed JUSTICE BRENNAN's novel proposal. *See First English Evangelical Lutheran Church..*

I write today to identify the severe tension between that dramatic development in the law and the view expressed by JUSTICE BRENNAN's dissent in this case that the public interest is served by encouraging state agencies to exercise considerable flexibility in responding to private desires for development in a way that threatens the preservation of public resources. I like the hat that JUSTICE BRENNAN has donned today better than the one he wore in *San Diego*, and I am persuaded that he has the better of the legal arguments here. Even if his position prevailed in this case, however, it would be of little solace to land-use planners who would still be left guessing about how the Court will react to the next case, and the one after that. As this case demonstrates, the rule of liability created by the Court in *First English* is a shortsighted one. Like JUSTICE BRENNAN, I hope that "a broader vision ultimately prevails."

I respectfully dissent.

Notes

1. Professor Linda Malone, in *The Coastal Zone Management Act and the Takings Clause in the 1990's: Making the Case for Federal Land Use to Preserve Coastal Areas*, 62 U. Colo. L. Rev. 711, 714 (1991), has explained that the CZMA's purpose

> is to preserve the unique values of coastal lands and waters by encouraging states to devise land and water use plans for coastal protection. The Act provides funds to states that develop programs for management of land and water uses consistent with the Act's standards. The Secretary of Commerce must approve state programs upon finding that they satisfy the requirements of sections 305 and 306 of the CZMA. After approval, the Secretary may award grants to the state for the costs of administration of the approved state management program. In addition to grants states obtain for having an approved program, states also benefit from the requirement that federal agencies, permittees, and licensees must show that their proposed developments, including oil and gas activities on the outer continental shelf, are consistent with the state's management program.

It is perhaps ironic that regulatory activity in support of legislation often referred to as an example of "creative federalism" fell victim to the activism of conservative Justices.

2. The Court made clear that the Nollans were not entitled to the development permit; therefore, an unconditional denial of their request would not have been viewed as an illegal confiscation of their property rights, especially because there was no evidence that the Nollans could not make a reasonable use of their property. *Nollan* thus added a new twist to the takings puzzle, as the "Takings" Clause was used successfully to protect landowners who, in actuality, were financially better off than before they sought development permission. This is because the loss attributed to the grant of the public easement would be more than offset by the increased value attributable to the improvements that the Nollans would make on the rest of the property. The problem arose when the commission said "yes, but" to the Nollans' request, enabling Justice Antonin Scalia and the other members of the majority to invoke the doctrine of unconstitutional conditions. ("The evident constitutional propriety disappears, however, if the condition substituted for the prohibition utterly fails to further the end advanced as the justification for the prohibition.") In other words, the *Nollan* majority concluded that the commission's unquestionably greater power to say "no" to landowners did not necessarily include the lesser power to say "yes, subject to the following conditions."

3. Exactions of land in fee, of easements, and of cash payments to offset the costs of public amenities are quite common when developers seek permission (typically from local planning commissions) to build residential subdivisions. Indeed, when the property is already zoned for the desired use (as opposed to instances when the envisioned residential neighborhood is currently zoned for agricultural uses only), the subdivision stage may be the local government's last opportunity to ensure that the impacts caused by more intensive use of land are partially (or even fully) borne by the party seeking approval. Those often very costly impacts are commonly felt in areas such as public schools, transportation, parks and recreation, water and sewage, and police and fire protection. The open-ended nature of the *Nollan* opinion, and its potentially far-reaching implications, threatened a wide range of exaction practices.

In Commercial Builders of N. Cal. v. Sacramento, 941 F.2d 872, 873, 874-75 (9th Cir. 1991), for example, a divided panel found that Sacramento, California's Housing Trust Fund Ordinance, which became law on March 7, 1989, did not effect a regulatory taking. The court provided the following description of the city's "linkage" program:

> The Ordinance lists several city-wide findings, including the finding that nonresidential development is "a major factor in attracting new employees to the region" and that the influx of new employees "creates a need for additional housing in the City." Pursuant to these findings, the Ordinance imposes a fee in connection with the issuance of permits for nonresidential development of the type that will generate jobs. The fees, calculated using the Keyser-Marston formula, are to be paid into a fund to assist in the financing of low-income housing. The city projects that the fund will raise about $3.6 million annually, nine percent of the projected annual cost of $42 million for the needed housing. Additional money will come from other sources, such as debt funding and general revenues.

While conceding that the city had "a legitimate interest in expanding low-income housing," Commercial Builders asserted that the ordinance "constitutes an impermissible means to advance that interest, because it places a burden of paying for low-income housing on nonresidential development without a sufficient showing that nonresidential development contributes to the need for low-income housing in proportion to that burden." Commercial Builders relied on *Nollan* for the proposition that "the Supreme Court has now articulated a more stringent standard under which courts must analyze the imposition of conditions upon development."

The panel then reviewed cases from other courts:

> Other circuits that have considered the constitutionality of ordinances that placed burdens on land use after *Nollan*. None have interpreted that case as changing the level of scrutiny to be applied to regulations that do not constitute a physical encroachment on land. *See, e.g.,* St. Bartholomew's Church v. City of New York, 914 F.2d 348, 357 n.6 (2d Cir. 1990), *cert. denied sub nom.* Committee to Oppose Sale of St. Bartholomew's Church v. Rector, 499 U.S. 905 (1991); Adolph v. Federal Emergency Management Agency, 854 F.2d 732, 737 (5th Cir. 1988); Naegele Outdoor Advertising, Inc. v. City of Durham, 844 F.2d 172, 178 (4th Cir. 1988). . . .

In the coming years, state and lower federal courts would produce conflicting opinions regarding (1) the applicability of *Nollan* to exactions of fees as opposed to real property, and (2) the exact nature of judicial scrutiny demanded by *Nollan*. Before these issues were resolved, however, the Court would further complicate the area of inquiry by pushing the regulatory takings envelope even farther.

4. In the 1990s, the conservative and moderate bloc of Justices that made up the majority in the controversial regulatory takings case that follows poured old wine (the common law of nuisance) into new bottles (eminent domain via state and local regulation, as opposed to the traditional mode of government condemnation). In the process, the Court once again made private and public nuisance doctrines the subject of serious judicial and academic attention. As you read the various opinions in *Lucas*, consider whether the property rights protectors on the Court were employing nuisance law to place a stranglehold on new environmental protections at the state and local level. Or have police power measures always been inherently and closely bound to the protection of private property from unreasonable interference and the protection of society from harmful activities?

S.C. Code Ann. §48039-290 (original version)

(A) No new construction or reconstruction is allowed seaward of the baseline except:

(1) wooden walkways no larger in width than six feet;

(2) small wooden decks no larger than one hundred forty-four square feet;

(3) fishing piers which are open to the public . . . ;

(4) golf courses;

(5) normal landscaping;

(6) structures specifically permitted by special permit . . .;

(7) pools may be reconstructed if they are landward of an existing, functional erosion control structure or device . . .

A permit must be obtained from the department for items (2) through (7).

LUCAS v. SOUTH CAROLINA COASTAL COUNCIL
505 U.S. 1003 (1992)

Justice SCALIA delivered the opinion of the Court.

In 1986, petitioner David H. Lucas paid $975,000 for two residential lots on the Isle of Palms in Charleston County, South Carolina, on which he intended to build single-family homes. In 1988, however, the South Carolina Legislature enacted the Beachfront Management Act, S.C.Code Ann. § 48-39-250 et seq. (Supp.1990), which had the direct effect of barring petitioner from erecting any permanent habitable structures on his two parcels. See § 48-39-290(A). A state trial court found that this prohibition rendered Lucas's parcels "valueless." App. to Pet. for Cert. 37. This case requires us to decide whether the Act's dramatic effect on the economic value of Lucas's lots accomplished a taking of private property under the Fifth and Fourteenth Amendments requiring the payment of "just compensation." U.S. Const., Amdt. 5.

South Carolina's expressed interest in intensively managing development activities in the so-called "coastal zone" dates from 1977 when, in the aftermath of Congress's passage of the federal Coastal Zone Management Act of 1972, 86 Stat. 1280, as amended, 16 U.S.C. § 1451 et seq., the legislature enacted a Coastal Zone Management Act of its own. See S.C.Code Ann. § 48- 39-10 et seq. (1987). In its original form, the South Carolina Act required owners of coastal zone land that qualified as a "critical area" (defined in the legislation to include beaches and immediately adjacent sand dunes, § 48-39-10(J)) to obtain a permit from the newly created South Carolina Coastal Council (Council) (respondent here) prior to committing the land to a "use other than the use the critical area was devoted to on [September 28, 1977]." § 48-39-130(A).

In the late 1970's, Lucas and others began extensive residential development of the Isle of Palms, a barrier island situated eastward of the city of Charleston. Toward the close of the development cycle for one residential subdivision known as "Beachwood East," Lucas in 1986 purchased the two lots at issue in this litigation for his own account. No portion of the lots, which were located approximately 300 feet from the beach, qualified as a "critical area" under the 1977 Act; accordingly, at the time Lucas acquired these parcels, he was not legally obliged to obtain a permit from the Council in advance of any development activity. His intention with respect to the lots was to do what the owners of the immediately adjacent parcels had already done: erect single-family residences. He commissioned architectural drawings for this purpose.

The Beachfront Management Act brought Lucas's plans to an abrupt end. Under that 1988 legislation, the Council was directed to establish a "baseline" connecting the landward-most "point[s] of erosion . . . during the past forty years" in the region of the Isle of Palms that includes Lucas's lots. S.C.Code Ann. § 48-39-280(A)(2) (Supp.1988). In action not challenged here, the Council fixed this baseline landward of Lucas's parcels. That was significant, for under the Act construction of occupiable improvements[2] was flatly prohibited seaward of a line drawn 20 feet landward of, and parallel to, the baseline. § 48-39- 290(A). The Act provided no exceptions.

Lucas promptly filed suit in the South Carolina Court of Common Pleas, contending that the Beachfront Management Act's construction bar effected a taking of his property without just compensation. Lucas did not take issue with the validity of the Act as a lawful exercise of South Carolina's police power, but contended that the Act's complete extinguishment of his property's value entitled him to compensation regardless of whether the legislature had acted in furtherance of legitimate police power objectives. Following a bench trial, the court agreed. Among its factual determinations was the finding that "at the time Lucas purchased the two lots, both were zoned for

---

2. The Act did allow the construction of certain nonhabitable improvements, e.g., "wooden walkways no larger in width than six feet," and "small wooden decks no larger than one hundred forty-four square feet." §§ 48-39-290(A)(1) and (2).

single-family residential construction and . . . there were no restrictions imposed upon such use of the property by either the State of South Carolina, the County of Charleston, or the Town of the Isle of Palms." App. to Pet. for Cert. 36. The trial court further found that the Beachfront Management Act decreed a permanent ban on construction insofar as Lucas's lots were concerned, and that this prohibition "deprive[d] Lucas of any reasonable economic use of the lots, . . . eliminated the unrestricted right of use, and render[ed] them valueless." Id., at 37. The court thus concluded that Lucas's properties had been "taken" by operation of the Act, and it ordered respondent to pay "just compensation" in the amount of $1,232,387.50. Id., at 40.

The Supreme Court of South Carolina reversed. It found dispositive what it described as Lucas's concession "that the Beachfront Management Act [was] properly and validly designed to preserve . . . South Carolina's beaches." 304 S.C. 376, 379, 404 S.E.2d 895, 896 (1991). Failing an attack on the validity of the statute as such, the court believed itself bound to accept the "uncontested . . . findings" of the South Carolina Legislature that new construction in the coastal zone--such as petitioner intended--threatened this public resource. Id., at 383, 404 S.E.2d, at 898. The court ruled that when a regulation respecting the use of property is designed "to prevent serious public harm," id., at 383, 404 S.E.2d, at 899 (citing, *inter alia*, Mugler v. Kansas, 123 U.S. 623 (1887)), no compensation is owing under the Takings Clause regardless of the regulation's effect on the property's value.

Two justices dissented. They acknowledged that our *Mugler* line of cases recognizes governmental power to prohibit "noxious" uses of property—*i.e.*, uses of property akin to "public nuisances"—without having to pay compensation. But they would not have characterized the Beachfront Management Act's "primary purpose [as] the prevention of a nuisance." 304 S.C., at 395, 404 S.E.2d, at 906 (Harwell, J., dissenting). To the dissenters, the chief purposes of the legislation, among them the promotion of tourism and the creation of a "habitat for indigenous flora and fauna," could not fairly be compared to nuisance abatement. *Id.*, at 396, 404 S.E.2d, at 906. As a consequence, they would have affirmed the trial court's conclusion that the Act's obliteration of the value of petitioner's lots accomplished a taking. We granted certiorari. . . .

Prior to Justice Holmes's exposition in Pennsylvania Coal Co. v. Mahon, 260 U.S. 393 (1922), it was generally thought that the Takings Clause reached only a "direct appropriation" of property, Legal Tender Cases, 12 Wall. 457, 551 (1871), or the functional equivalent of a "practical ouster of [the owner's] possession," Transportation Co. v. Chicago, 99 U.S. 635, 642 (1879). Justice Holmes recognized in *Mahon*, however, that if the protection against physical appropriations of private property was to be meaningfully enforced, the government's power to redefine the range of interests included in the ownership of property was necessarily constrained by constitutional limits. If, instead, the uses of private property were subject to unbridled, uncompensated qualification under the police power, "the natural tendency of human nature [would be] to extend the qualification more and more until at last private property disappear[ed]." *Id.*, at 415. These considerations gave birth in that case to the oft-cited maxim that, "while property may be regulated to a certain extent, if regulation goes too far it will be recognized as a taking." *Ibid.*

Nevertheless, our decision in *Mahon* offered little insight into when, and under what circumstances, a given regulation would be seen as going "too far" for purposes of the Fifth Amendment. In 70-odd years of succeeding "regulatory takings" jurisprudence, we have generally eschewed any "'set formula'" for determining how far is too far, preferring to "engag[e] in . . . essentially ad hoc, factual inquiries." Penn Central Transportation Co. v. New York City, 438 U.S. 104, 124 (1978) (quoting Goldblatt v. Hempstead, 369 U.S. 590, 594 (1962)). See Epstein, Takings: Descent and Resurrection, 1987 S.Ct. Rev. 1, 4. We have, however, described at least two discrete categories of regulatory action as compensable without case-specific inquiry into the public interest advanced in support of the restraint. The first encompasses regulations that compel the property owner to suffer a physical "invasion" of his property. In general (at least with regard to permanent invasions), no matter how minute the intrusion, and no matter how weighty the public purpose behind it, we have required compensation. For example, in Loretto v. Teleprompter Manhattan CATV Corp., 458 U.S. 419 (1982), we determined that New York's law requiring landlords to allow television cable companies to emplace cable facilities in their apartment buildings constituted a taking, even though the facilities occupied at most only 1 1/2 cubic feet of the landlords' property.

The second situation in which we have found categorical treatment appropriate is where regulation denies all economically beneficial or productive use of land. As we have said on numerous occasions, the Fifth Amendment is violated when land-use regulation "does not substantially advance legitimate state interests *or denies an owner economically viable use of his land.*" Agins [v. City of Tiburon], 447 U.S. [255], at 260 (1980) (citations omitted) (emphasis added).[7]

We have never set forth the justification for this rule. Perhaps it is simply, as Justice Brennan suggested, that total deprivation of beneficial use is, from the landowner's point of view, the equivalent of a physical appropriation. See San Diego Gas & Electric Co. v. San Diego, 450 U.S., at 652 (dissenting opinion). "[F]or what is the land but the profits thereof[?]" 1 E. Coke, Institutes, ch. 1, § 1 (1st Am. ed. 1812). Surely, at least, in the extraordinary circumstance when no productive or economically beneficial use of land is permitted, it is less realistic to indulge our usual assumption that the legislature is simply "adjusting the benefits and burdens of economic life," Penn Central Transportation Co., 438 U.S., at 124, in a manner that secures an "average reciprocity of advantage" to everyone concerned, Pennsylvania Coal Co. v. Mahon, 260 U.S., at 415. And the functional basis for permitting the government, by regulation, to affect property values without compensation—that "Government hardly could go on if to some extent values incident to property could not be diminished without paying for every such change in the general law," *id.*, at 413— does not apply to the relatively rare situations where the government has deprived a landowner of all economically beneficial uses. . . .

---

7. Regrettably, the rhetorical force of our "deprivation of all economically feasible use" rule is greater than its precision, since the rule does not make clear the "property interest" against which the loss of value is to be measured. When, for example, a regulation requires a developer to leave 90% of a rural tract in its natural state, it is unclear whether we would analyze the situation as one in which the owner has been deprived of all economically beneficial use of the burdened portion of the tract, or as one in which the owner has suffered a mere diminution in value of the tract as a whole. (For an extreme— and, we think, unsupportable—view of the relevant calculus, see Penn Central Transportation Co. v. New York City, 42 N.Y.2d 324, 333-334, 397 N.Y.S.2d 914, 920, 366 N.E.2d 1271, 1276-77 (1977), *aff'd*, 438 U.S. 10 (1978), where the state court examined the diminution in a particular parcel's value produced by a municipal ordinance in light of total value of the takings claimant's other holdings in the vicinity.) Unsurprisingly, this uncertainty regarding the composition of the denominator in our "deprivation" fraction has produced inconsistent pronouncements by the Court. Compare Pennsylvania Coal Co. v. Mahon, 260 U.S. 393, 414 (1922) (law restricting subsurface extraction of coal held to effect a taking), with Keystone Bituminous Coal Assn. v. DeBenedictis, 480 U.S. 470, 497-502 (1987) (nearly identical law held not to effect a taking); see also *id.*, at 515-20 (REHNQUIST, C.J., dissenting); Rose, Mahon Reconstructed: Why the Takings Issue is Still a Muddle, 57 S. Cal. L. Rev. 561, 566-69 (1984). The answer to this difficult question may lie in how the owner's reasonable expectations have been shaped by the State's law of property—*i.e.*, whether and to what degree the State's law has accorded legal recognition and protection to the particular interest in land with respect to which the takings claimant alleges a diminution in (or elimination of) value. In any event, we avoid this difficulty in the present case, since the "interest in land" that Lucas has pleaded (a fee simple interest) is an estate with a rich tradition of protection at common law, and since the South Carolina Court of Common Pleas found that the Beachfront Management Act left each of Lucas's beachfront lots without economic value.

We think, in short, that there are good reasons for our frequently expressed belief that when the owner of real property has been called upon to sacrifice all economically beneficial uses in the name of the common good, that is, to leave his property economically idle, he has suffered a taking.[8]

The trial court found Lucas's two beachfront lots to have been rendered valueless by respondent's enforcement of the coastal-zone construction ban. Under Lucas's theory of the case, which rested upon our "no economically viable use" statements, that finding entitled him to compensation. Lucas believed it unnecessary to take issue with either the purposes behind the Beachfront Management Act, or the means chosen by the South Carolina Legislature to effectuate those purposes. The South Carolina Supreme Court, however, thought otherwise. In its view, the Beachfront Management Act was no ordinary enactment, but involved an exercise of South Carolina's "police powers" to mitigate the harm to the public interest that petitioner's use of his land might occasion. 304 S.C., at 384, 404 S.E.2d, at 899. By neglecting to dispute the findings enumerated in the

---

8. Justice STEVENS criticizes the "deprivation of all economically beneficial use" rule as "wholly arbitrary," in that "[the] landowner whose property is diminished in value 95% recovers nothing," while the landowner who suffers a complete elimination of value "recovers the land's full value." This analysis errs in its assumption that the landowner whose deprivation is one step short of complete is not entitled to compensation. Such an owner might not be able to claim the benefit of our categorical formulation, but, as we have acknowledged time and again, "[t]he economic impact of the regulation on the claimant and . . . the extent to which the regulation has interfered with distinct investment-backed expectations" are keenly relevant to takings analysis generally. Penn Central Transportation Co. v. New York City, 438 U.S. 104, 124 (1978). It is true that in at least *some* cases the landowner with 95% loss will get nothing, while the landowner with total loss will recover in full. But that occasional result is no more strange than the gross disparity between the landowner whose premises are taken for a highway (who recovers in full) and the landowner whose property is reduced to 5% of its former value by the highway (who recovers nothing). Takings law is full of these "all-or-nothing" situations.

    Justice STEVENS similarly misinterprets our focus on "developmental" uses of property (the uses proscribed by the Beachfront Management Act) as betraying an "assumption that the only uses of property cognizable under the Constitution are developmental uses." We make no such assumption. Though our prior takings cases evince an abiding concern for the productive use of, and economic investment in, land, there are plainly a number of noneconomic interests in land whose impairment will invite exceedingly close scrutiny under the Takings Clause. See, e.g., Loretto v. Teleprompter Manhattan CATV Corp., 458 U.S. 419, 436 (1982) (interest in excluding strangers from one's land).

Act[10] or otherwise to challenge the legislature's purposes, petitioner "concede[d] that the beach/ dune area of South Carolina's shores is an extremely valuable public resource; that the erection of new construction, *inter alia*, contributes to the erosion and destruction of this public resource; and that discouraging new construction in close proximity to the beach/dune area is necessary to prevent a great public harm." *Id.*, at 382-383, 404 S.E.2d, at 898. In the court's view, these concessions brought petitioner's challenge within a long line of this Court's cases sustaining against Due Process and Takings Clause challenges the State's use of its "police powers" to enjoin a property owner from activities akin to public nuisances. See Mugler v. Kansas, 123 U.S. 623 (1887) (law prohibiting manufacture of alcoholic beverages); Hadacheck v. Sebastian, 239 U.S. 394 (1915) (law barring operation of brick mill in residential area); Miller v. Schoene, 276 U.S. 272 (1928) (order to destroy diseased cedar trees to prevent infection of nearby orchards); Goldblatt v. Hempstead, 369 U.S. 590 (1962) (law effectively preventing continued operation of quarry in residential area).

It is correct that many of our prior opinions have suggested that "harmful or noxious uses" of property may be proscribed by government regulation without the requirement of compensation. For a number of reasons, however, we think the South Carolina Supreme Court was too quick to conclude that that principle decides the present case. The "harmful or noxious uses" principle was the Court's early attempt to describe in theoretical terms why government may, consistent with the Takings Clause, affect property values by regulation without incurring an obligation to compensate—a reality we nowadays acknowledge explicitly with respect to the full scope of the State's police power. We made this very point in *Penn Central Transportation Co.*, where, in the

---

10. The legislature's express findings include the following: "The General Assembly finds that:

"(1) The beach/dune system along the coast of South Carolina is extremely important to the people of this State and serves the following functions:

"(a) protects life and property by serving as a storm barrier which dissipates wave energy and contributes to shoreline stability in an economical and effective manner;

"(b) provides the basis for a tourism industry that generates approximately two-thirds of South Carolina's annual tourism industry revenue which constitutes a significant portion of the state's economy. The tourists who come to the South Carolina coast to enjoy the ocean and dry sand beach contribute significantly to state and local tax revenues;

"(c) provides habitat for numerous species of plants and animals, several of which are threatened or endangered. Waters adjacent to the beach/dune system also provide habitat for many other marine species;

"(d) provides a natural health environment for the citizens of South Carolina to spend leisure time which serves their physical and mental well-being.

"(2) Beach/dune system vegetation is unique and extremely important to the vitality and preservation of the system.

"(3) Many miles of South Carolina's beaches have been identified as critically eroding.

"(4) [D]evelopment unwisely has been sited too close to the [beach/dune] system. This type of development has jeopardized the stability of the beach/dune system, accelerated erosion, and endangered adjacent property. It is in both the public and private interests to protect the system from this unwise development.

"(5) The use of armoring in the form of hard erosion control devices such as seawalls, bulkheads, and rip-rap to protect erosion-threatened structures adjacent to the beach has not proven effective. These armoring devices have given a false sense of security to beachfront property owners. In reality, these hard structures, in many instances, have increased the vulnerability of beachfront property to damage from wind and waves while contributing to the deterioration and loss of the dry sand beach which is so important to the tourism industry.

"(6) Erosion is a natural process which becomes a significant problem for man only when structures are erected in close proximity to the beach/dune system. It is in both the public and private interests to afford the beach/ dune system space to accrete and erode in its natural cycle. This space can be provided only by discouraging new construction in close proximity to the beach/dune system and encouraging those who have erected structures too close to the system to retreat from it.

. . . . .

"(8) It is in the state's best interest to protect and to promote increased public access to South Carolina's beaches for out-of-state tourists and South Carolina residents alike." S.C. Code Ann. §48-39-250 (Supp.1991).

course of sustaining New York City's landmarks preservation program against a takings challenge, we rejected the petitioner's suggestion that *Mugler* and the cases following it were premised on, and thus limited by, some objective conception of "noxiousness" . . . . "Harmful or noxious use" analysis was, in other words, simply the progenitor of our more contemporary statements that "land-use regulation does not effect a taking if it 'substantially advance[s] legitimate state interests'. . . ." *Nollan, supra*, 483 U.S., at 834 (quoting Agins v. Tiburon, 447 U.S., at 260); see also Penn Central Transportation Co., *supra*, 438 U.S., at 127; Euclid v. Ambler Realty Co., 272 U.S. 365, 387-388 (1926).

The transition from our early focus on control of "noxious" uses to our contemporary understanding of the broad realm within which government may regulate without compensation was an easy one, since the distinction between "harm-preventing" and "benefit-conferring" regulation is often in the eye of the beholder. It is quite possible, for example, to describe in *either* fashion the ecological, economic, and esthetic concerns that inspired the South Carolina Legislature in the present case. One could say that imposing a servitude on Lucas's land is necessary in order to prevent his use of it from "harming" South Carolina's ecological resources; or, instead, in order to achieve the "benefits" of an ecological preserve.[11] Whether one or the other of the competing characterizations will come to one's lips in a particular case depends primarily upon one's evaluation of the worth of competing uses of real estate. A given restraint will be seen as mitigating "harm" to the adjacent parcels or securing a "benefit" for them, depending upon the observer's evaluation of the relative importance of the use that the restraint favors. Whether Lucas's construction of single-family residences on his parcels should be described as bringing "harm" to South Carolina's adjacent ecological resources thus depends principally upon whether the describer believes that the State's use interest in nurturing those resources is so important that any competing adjacent use must yield.

When it is understood that "prevention of harmful use" was merely our early formulation of the police power justification necessary to sustain (without compensation) *any* regulatory diminution in value; and that the distinction between regulation that "prevents harmful use" and that which "confers benefits" is difficult, if not impossible, to discern on an objective, value-free basis; it becomes self-evident that noxious-use logic cannot serve as a touchstone to distinguish regulatory "takings"—which require compensation—from regulatory deprivations that do not require compensation. *A fortiori* the legislature's recitation of a noxious-use justification cannot be the basis for departing from our categorical rule that total regulatory takings must be compensated. If it were, departure would virtually always be allowed. The South Carolina Supreme Court's approach would essentially nullify *Mahon's* affirmation of limits to the noncompensable exercise of the police power. Our cases provide no support for this: None of them that employed the logic of "harmful use" prevention to sustain a regulation involved an allegation that the regulation wholly eliminated the value of the claimant's land

Where the State seeks to sustain regulation that deprives land of all economically beneficial use, we think it may resist compensation only if the logically antecedent inquiry into the nature of the owner's estate shows that the proscribed use interests were not part of his title to begin with.

---

11. In the present case, in fact, some of the "[South Carolina] legislature's 'findings' " to which the South Carolina Supreme Court purported to defer in characterizing the purpose of the Act as "harm-preventing," 304 S.C. 376, 385, 404 S.E.2d 895, 900 (1991), seem to us phrased in "benefit-conferring" language instead. For example, they describe the importance of a construction ban in enhancing "South Carolina's annual tourism industry revenue," S.C. Code Ann. § 48-39- 250(1)(b) (Supp.1991), in "provid[ing] habitat for numerous species of plants and animals, several of which are threatened or endangered," § 48-39-250(1)(c), and in "provid[ing] a natural healthy environment for the citizens of South Carolina to spend leisure time which serves their physical and mental well-being," § 48-39-250(1)(d). It would be pointless to make the outcome of this case hang upon this terminology, since the same interests could readily be described in "harm-preventing" fashion. . . .

This accords, we think, with our "takings" jurisprudence, which has traditionally been guided by the understandings of our citizens regarding the content of, and the State's power over, the "bundle of rights" that they acquire when they obtain title to property. It seems to us that the property owner necessarily expects the uses of his property to be restricted, from time to time, by various measures newly enacted by the State in legitimate exercise of its police powers; "[a]s long recognized, some values are enjoyed under an implied limitation and must yield to the police power." Pennsylvania Coal Co. v. Mahon, 260 U.S., at 413. And in the case of personal property, by reason of the State's traditionally high degree of control over commercial dealings, he ought to be aware of the possibility that new regulation might even render his property economically worthless (at least if the property's only economically productive use is sale or manufacture for sale). In the case of land, however, we think the notion pressed by the Council that title is somehow held subject to the "implied limitation" that the State may subsequently eliminate all economically valuable use is inconsistent with the historical compact recorded in the Takings Clause that has become part of our constitutional culture.

Where "permanent physical occupation" of land is concerned, we have refused to allow the government to decree it anew (without compensation), no matter how weighty the asserted "public interests" involved, Loretto v. Teleprompter Manhattan CATV Corp., 458 U.S., at 426—though we assuredly *would* permit the government to assert a permanent easement that was a pre-existing limitation upon the landowner's title. We believe similar treatment must be accorded confiscatory regulations, *i.e.*, regulations that prohibit all economically beneficial use of land: Any limitation so severe cannot be newly legislated or decreed (without compensation), but must inhere in the title itself, in the restrictions that background principles of the State's law of property and nuisance already place upon land ownership. A law or decree with such an effect must, in other words, do no more than duplicate the result that could have been achieved in the courts--by adjacent landowners (or other uniquely affected persons) under the State's law of private nuisance, or by the State under its complementary power to abate nuisances that affect the public generally, or otherwise.[16]

On this analysis, the owner of a lake-bed, for example, would not be entitled to compensation when he is denied the requisite permit to engage in a landfilling operation that would have the effect of flooding others' land. Nor the corporate owner of a nuclear generating plant, when it is directed to remove all improvements from its land upon discovery that the plant sits astride an earthquake fault. Such regulatory action may well have the effect of eliminating the land's only economically productive use, but it does not proscribe a productive use that was previously permissible under relevant property and nuisance principles. The use of these properties for what are now expressly prohibited purposes was *always* unlawful, and (subject to other constitutional limitations) it was open to the State at any point to make the implication of those background principles of nuisance and property law explicit. See Michelman, Property, Utility, and Fairness, Comments on the Ethical Foundations of "Just Compensation" Law, 80 Harv.L.Rev. 1165, 1239-1241 (1967). In light of our traditional resort to "existing rules or understandings that stem from an independent source such as state law" to define the range of interests that qualify for protection as "property" under the Fifth and Fourteenth Amendments, Board of Regents of State Colleges v. Roth, 408 U.S. 564, 577 (1972), this recognition that the Takings Clause does not require compensation when an owner is barred from putting land to a use that is proscribed by those "existing rules or understandings" is surely unexceptional. When, however, a regulation that declares "off-limits"

---

16. The principal "otherwise" that we have in mind is litigation absolving the State (or private parties) of liability for the destruction of "real and personal property, in cases of actual necessity, to prevent the spreading of a fire" or to forestall other grave threats to the lives and property of others. Bowditch v. Boston, 101 U.S. 16, 18-19 (1880); see United States v. Pacific R., Co., 120 U.S. 227, 238-39 (1887).

all economically productive or beneficial uses of land goes beyond what the relevant background principles would dictate, compensation must be paid to sustain it.

The "total taking" inquiry we require today will ordinarily entail (as the application of state nuisance law ordinarily entails) analysis of, among other things, the degree of harm to public lands and resources, or adjacent private property, posed by the claimant's proposed activities, see, *e.g.*, Restatement (Second) of Torts §§ 826, 827, the social value of the claimant's activities and their suitability to the locality in question, see, *e.g.*, *id.*, §§ 828(a) and (b), 831, and the relative ease with which the alleged harm can be avoided through measures taken by the claimant and the government (or adjacent private landowners) alike, see, *e.g.*, *id.*, §§ 827(e), 828(c), 830. The fact that a particular use has long been engaged in by similarly situated owners ordinarily imports a lack of any common-law prohibition (though changed circumstances or new knowledge may make what was previously permissible no longer so, see *id.*, § 827, Comment g. So also does the fact that other landowners, similarly situated, are permitted to continue the use denied to the claimant.

It seems unlikely that common-law principles would have prevented the erection of any habitable or productive improvements on petitioner's land; they rarely support prohibition of the "essential use" of land, Curtin v. Benson, 222 U.S. 78, 86 (1911). The question, however, is one of state law to be dealt with on remand. We emphasize that to win its case South Carolina must do more than proffer the legislature's declaration that the uses Lucas desires are inconsistent with the public interest, or the conclusory assertion that they violate a common-law maxim such as *sic utere tuo ut alienum non laedas*. As we have said, a "State, by *ipse dixit*, may not transform private property into public property without compensation. . . ." Webb's Fabulous Pharmacies, Inc. v. Beckwith, 449 U.S. 155, 164 (1980). Instead, as it would be required to do if it sought to restrain Lucas in a common-law action for public nuisance, South Carolina must identify background principles of nuisance and property law that prohibit the uses he now intends in the circumstances in which the property is presently found. Only on this showing can the State fairly claim that, in proscribing all such beneficial uses, the Beachfront Management Act is taking nothing. . . .

Justice KENNEDY, concurring in the judgment. . . .

In my view, reasonable expectations must be understood in light of the whole of our legal tradition. The common law of nuisance is too narrow a confine for the exercise of regulatory power in a complex and interdependent society. The State should not be prevented from enacting new regulatory initiatives in response to changing conditions, and courts must consider all reasonable expectations whatever their source. The Takings Clause does not require a static body of state property law; it protects private expectations to ensure private investment. I agree with the Court that nuisance prevention accords with the most common expectations of property owners who face regulation, but I do not believe this can be the sole source of state authority to impose severe restrictions. Coastal property may present such unique concerns for a fragile land system that the State can go further in regulating its development and use than the common law of nuisance might otherwise permit. . . .

Justice BLACKMUN, dissenting.

Today the Court launches a missile to kill a mouse. . . .

My fear is that the Court's new policies will spread beyond the narrow confines of the present case. For that reason, I, like the Court, will give far greater attention to this case than its narrow scope suggests--not because I can intercept the Court's missile, or save the targeted mouse, but because I hope perhaps to limit the collateral damage. . . .

The Court does not reject the South Carolina Supreme Court's decision simply on the basis of its disbelief and distrust of the legislature's findings. It also takes the opportunity to create a new scheme for regulations that eliminate all economic value. From now on, there is a categorical rule finding these regulations to be a taking unless the use they prohibit is a background common-law nuisance or property principle. . . .

Ultimately even the Court cannot embrace the full implications of its *per se* rule: It eventually agrees that there cannot be a categorical rule for a taking based on economic value that wholly disregards the public need asserted. Instead, the Court decides that it will permit a State to regulate all economic value only if the State prohibits uses that would not be permitted under "background principles of nuisance and property law."[15]

Until today, the Court explicitly had rejected the contention that the government's power to act without paying compensation turns on whether the prohibited activity is a common-law nuisance. The brewery closed in *Mugler* itself was not a common-law nuisance, and the Court specifically stated that it was the role of the legislature to determine what measures would be appropriate for the protection of public health and safety. . . .

Even more perplexing, however, is the Court's reliance on common-law principles of nuisance in its quest for a value-free takings jurisprudence. In determining what is a nuisance at common law, state courts make exactly the decision that the Court finds so troubling when made by the South Carolina General Assembly today: They determine whether the use is harmful. Common-law public and private nuisance law is simply a determination whether a particular use causes harm. See Prosser, Private Action for Public Nuisance, 52 Va.L.Rev. 997 (1966) ("*Nuisance* is a French word which means nothing more than harm"). There is nothing magical in the reasoning of judges long dead. They determined a harm in the same way as state judges and legislatures do today. If judges in the 18th and 19th centuries can distinguish a harm from a benefit, why not judges in the 20th century, and if judges can, why not legislators? There simply is no reason to believe that new interpretations of the hoary common-law nuisance doctrine will be particularly "objective" or "value free."[19] Once one abandons the level of generality of *sic utere tuo ut alienum non laedas*, one searches in vain, I think, for anything resembling a principle in the common law of nuisance.

Finally, the Court justifies its new rule that the legislature may not deprive a property owner of the only economically valuable use of his land, even if the legislature finds it to be a harmful use, because such action is not part of the "'long recognized'" "understandings of our citizens." These "understandings" permit such regulation only if the use is a nuisance under the common law. Any other course is "inconsistent with the historical compact recorded in the Takings Clause." It is not clear from the Court's opinion where our "historical compact" or "citizens' understanding" comes from, but it does not appear to be history. . . .

Nothing in the discussions in Congress concerning the Takings Clause indicates that the Clause was limited by the common-law nuisance doctrine. Common-law courts themselves rejected such an understanding. . . .

---

15. Although it refers to state nuisance and property law, the Court apparently does not mean just any state nuisance and property law. Public nuisance was first a common-law creation, see Newark, The Boundaries of Nuisance, 65 L. Q. Rev. 480, 482 (1949) (attributing development of nuisance to 1535), but by the 1800's in both the United States and England, legislatures had the power to define what is a public nuisance, and particular uses often have been selectively targeted. See Prosser, Private Action for Public Nuisance, 52 Va. L. Rev. 997, 999-1000 (1966); J. Stephen, A General View of the Criminal Law of England 105-107 (2d ed. 1890). The Court's references to "common-law" background principles, however, indicate that legislative determinations do not constitute "state nuisance and property law" for the Court.

19. "There is perhaps no more impenetrable jungle in the entire law than that which surrounds the word 'nuisance.' It has meant all things to all people, and has been applied indiscriminately to everything from an alarming advertisement to a cockroach baked in a pie." W. Keeton, D. Dobbs, R. Keeton & D. Owen, Prosser and Keeton on The Law of Torts 616 (5th ed. 1984) (footnotes omitted). It is an area of law that "straddles the legal universe, virtually defies synthesis, and generates case law to suit every taste." W. Rodgers, Environmental Law § 2.4, p. 48 (1986) (footnotes omitted). The Court itself has noted that "nuisance concepts" are "often vague and indeterminate." Milwaukee v. Illinois, 451 U.S. 304, 317 (1981).

In short, I find no clear and accepted "historical compact" or "understanding of our citizens" justifying the Court's new takings doctrine. Instead, the Court seems to treat history as a grab bag of principles, to be adopted where they support the Court's theory, and ignored where they do not. If the Court decided that the early common law provides the background principles for interpreting the Takings Clause, then regulation, as opposed to physical confiscation, would not be compensable. If the Court decided that the law of a later period provides the background principles, then regulation might be compensable, but the Court would have to confront the fact that legislatures regularly determined which uses were prohibited, independent of the common law, and independent of whether the uses were lawful when the owner purchased. What makes the Court's analysis unworkable is its attempt to package the law of two incompatible eras and peddle it as historical fact.[26]

The Court makes sweeping and, in my view, misguided and unsupported changes in our takings doctrine. While it limits these changes to the most narrow subset of government regulation—those that eliminate all economic value from land—these changes go far beyond what is necessary to secure petitioner Lucas' private benefit. One hopes they do not go beyond the narrow confines the Court assigns them to today.

I dissent.

Justice STEVENS, dissenting.

Today the Court restricts one judge-made rule and expands another. In my opinion it errs on both counts. Proper application of the doctrine of judicial restraint would avoid the premature adjudication of an important constitutional question. Proper respect for our precedents would avoid an illogical expansion of the concept of "regulatory takings." . . .

Like many bright-line rules, the categorical rule established in this case is only "categorical" for a page or two in the U.S. Reports. No sooner does the Court state that "total regulatory takings must be compensated," than it quickly establishes an exception to that rule.

The exception provides that a regulation that renders property valueless is not a taking if it prohibits uses of property that were not "previously permissible under relevant property and nuisance principles." The Court thus rejects the basic holding in Mugler v. Kansas, 123 U.S. 623 (1887). There we held that a state-wide statute that prohibited the owner of a brewery from making alcoholic beverages did not effect a taking, even though the use of the property had been perfectly lawful and caused no public harm before the statute was enacted. We squarely rejected the rule the Court adopts today:

> It is true, that, when the defendants . . . erected their breweries, the laws of the State did not forbid the manufacture of intoxicating liquors. But the State did not thereby give any assurance, or come under an obligation, that its legislation upon that subject would remain unchanged. [T]he supervision of the public health and the public morals is a governmental power, "continuing in its nature," and "to be dealt with as the special exigencies of the moment may require;" . . . "for this purpose, the largest legislative discretion is allowed, and the discretion cannot be parted with any more than the power itself." *Id.*, at 669.

---

26. The Court asserts that all early American experience, prior to and after passage of the Bill of Rights, and any case law prior to 1897 are "entirely irrelevant" in determining what is "the historical compact recorded in the Takings Clause." Nor apparently are we to find this compact in the early federal takings cases, which clearly permitted prohibition of harmful uses despite the alleged loss of all value, whether or not the prohibition was a common-law nuisance, and whether or not the prohibition occurred subsequent to the purchase. I cannot imagine where the Court finds its "historical compact," if not in history.

Under our reasoning in *Mugler*, a State's decision to prohibit or to regulate certain uses of property is not a compensable taking just because the particular uses were previously lawful. Under the Court's opinion today, however, if a State should decide to prohibit the manufacture of asbestos, cigarettes, or concealable firearms, for example, it must be prepared to pay for the adverse economic consequences of its decision. One must wonder if government will be able to "go on" effectively if it must risk compensation "for every such change in the general law." *Mahon*, 260 U.S., at 413.

The Court's holding today effectively freezes the State's common law, denying the legislature much of its traditional power to revise the law governing the rights and uses of property. Until today, I had thought that we had long abandoned this approach to constitutional law. More than a century ago we recognized that "the great office of statutes is to remedy defects in the common law as they are developed, and to adapt it to the changes of time and circumstances." Munn v. Illinois, 94 U.S. 113, 134 (1877). As Justice Marshall observed about a position similar to that adopted by the Court today:

> "If accepted, that claim would represent a return to the era of Lochner v. New York, 198 U.S. 45 (1905), when common-law rights were also found immune from revision by State or Federal Government. Such an approach would freeze the common law as it has been constructed by the courts, perhaps at its 19th-century state of development. It would allow no room for change in response to changes in circumstance. The Due Process Clause does not require such a result." PruneYard Shopping Center v. Robins, 447 U.S. 74, 93 (1980) (concurring opinion).

Arresting the development of the common law is not only a departure from our prior decisions; it is also profoundly unwise. The human condition is one of constant learning and evolution-- both moral and practical. Legislatures implement that new learning; in doing so they must often revise the definition of property and the rights of property owners. Thus, when the Nation came to understand that slavery was morally wrong and mandated the emancipation of all slaves, it, in effect, redefined "property." On a lesser scale, our ongoing self-education produces similar changes in the rights of property owners: New appreciation of the significance of endangered species, see, *e.g.*, Andrus v. Allard, 444 U.S. 51 (1979); the importance of wetlands, see, *e.g.*, 16 U.S.C. § 3801 *et seq.*; and the vulnerability of coastal lands, see, *e.g.*, 16 U.S.C. § 1451 *et seq.*, shapes our evolving understandings of property rights.

Of course, some legislative redefinitions of property will effect a taking and must be compensated—but it certainly cannot be the case that every movement away from common law does so. There is no reason, and less sense, in such an absolute rule. We live in a world in which changes in the economy and the environment occur with increasing frequency and importance. If it was wise a century ago to allow government "'the largest legislative discretion' 'to deal with the special exigencies of the moment,'" *Mugler*, 123 U.S., at 669, it is imperative to do so today. The rule that should govern a decision in a case of this kind should focus on the future, not the past. . . .

Statement of Justice SOUTER.

I would dismiss the writ of certiorari in this case as having been granted improvidently. After briefing and argument it is abundantly clear that an unreviewable assumption on which this case comes to us is both questionable as a conclusion of Fifth Amendment law and sufficient to frustrate the Court's ability to render certain the legal premises on which its holding rests. . . .

The nature of nuisance law . . . indicates that application of a regulation defensible on grounds of nuisance prevention or abatement will quite probably not amount to a complete deprivation in fact. The nuisance enquiry focuses on conduct, not on the character of the property on which that conduct is performed, see 4 Restatement (Second) of Torts § 821B (1979) (public nuisance); *id.*, § 822 (private nuisance), and the remedies for such conduct usually leave the property owner with other reasonable uses of his property, see W. Keeton, D. Dobbs, R. Keeton, & D. Owen, Prosser and Keeton on Law of Torts § 90 (5th ed. 1984) (public nuisances usually remedied by criminal prosecution or abatement), *id.*, § 89 (private nuisances usually remedied by damages, injunction, or abatement); see also, *e.g.*, Mugler v. Kansas, 123 U.S. 623, 668-669 (1887) (prohibition on use of property to manufacture intoxicating beverages "does not disturb the owner in the control or use of his property for lawful purposes, nor restrict his right to dispose of it, but is only a declaration by the State that its use . . . for certain forbidden purposes, is prejudicial to the public interests"); Hadacheck v. Sebastian, 239 U.S. 394, 412 (1915) (prohibition on operation of brickyard did not prohibit extraction of clay from which bricks were produced). Indeed, it is difficult to imagine property that can be used only to create a nuisance, such that its sole economic value must presuppose the right to occupy it for such seriously noxious activity. . . .

Notes

1. On remand, in Lucas v. South Carolina Coastal Council, 309 S.C. 424, 424 S.E.2d 484, 486 (1992), the Supreme Court of South Carolina

> reviewed the record and heard arguments from the parties regarding whether Coastal Council possesses the ability under the common law to prohibit Lucas from constructing a habitable structure on his land. Coastal Council has not persuaded us that any common law basis exists by which it could restrain Lucas's desired use of his land; nor has our research uncovered any such common law principle.

The case was then returned to the circuit court for a determination of damages. Settlement negotiations resulted in a payment of $1.575 million to Lucas. He then transferred title to the Coastal Council, which then sold the two parcels along with special permits that allowed two homes to be built on the disputed land. The details can be found in Professor Vicki Been's *Lucas v. The Green Machine: Using the Takings Clause to Promote More Efficient Regulation?*, in Property Stories 221, 239 (Gerald Korngold & Andrew P. Morriss eds., 2004). Professor Carol Rose, in *The Story of Lucas: Environmental Land Use Regulation Between Developers and the Deep Blue Sea*, in Environmental Law Stories 237, 271 (Richard J. Lazarus & Oliver A. Houck eds., 2005), has noted that "the coast is a notorious consumer of public subsidies. These include not just such general programs as roads and sewers, but also the highly specific programs like flood insurance and emergency assistance, programs through which the Isle of Palms itself has repeatedly fed itself at the public trough." On the one hand, does the especially strong "public" component of the value of Lucas' "private" property mean that he should be entitled to less protection than the average landowner? On the other hand, could current owners successfully argue that government restriction on or elimination of flood insurance or other beachfront (over)development programs effect a regulatory taking?

2. For the landowner's colorful account of his struggle to vindicate his private-property rights, see David Lucas, Lucas vs. The Green Machine: Landmark Supreme Court Property Rights Decision by Man Who Won It Against All Odds, and His Continuing Fight to Protect YOUR Property Rights! 282-83 (1995). Here is how Lucas sized up the forces in opposition:

> You must remember that The Green Machine is a multi-billion dollar industry. The Green Machine has become just another special interest group, with high paid, high profile and powerful lobbyists trying to promote its agenda at the expense of the American taxpayer and property owner. This struggle over property rights is no longer simply over what's best for the environment or even over "saving the environment." As usual in

this world, it is about money and power and no longer solely about the protection of the environment.

3. A recent study by Michael C. Blumm & Lucus Ritchie, *Lucas's Unlikely Legacy: The Rise of Background Principles as Categorical Takings Defenses*, 29 Harv. Envtl. L. Rev. 321, 322 (2005), has found that the legacy of *Lucas* is probably not what was intended by its authors:

> The Supreme Court's decision in Lucas v. South Carolina Coastal Council is one of the most celebrated cases of the Rehnquist Court's property jurisprudence. Justice Scalia's opinion for a 6-3 Court declared that a regulation depriving a landowner of all economic value was a categorical constitutional taking of private property for public use requiring government compensation regardless of the public purpose served by the regulation. This new categorical rule was welcomed by private property advocates[3] but denounced by defenders of government regulations.[4]

> But now, over a dozen years later, the legacy of the *Lucas* decision seems neither as revolutionary as its advocates hoped, nor as dire as its detractors feared. In fact, the *Lucas* legacy represents one of the starkest recent examples of the law of unintended consequences. For rather than heralding in a new era of landowner compensation or government deregulation, *Lucas* instead spawned a surprising rise of categorical defenses to takings claims in which governments can defeat compensation suits without case-specific inquiries into the economic effects and public purposes of regulations. *Lucas* accomplished this by establishing the prerequisite that a claimant must first demonstrate that its property interest was unrestrained by prior restrictions. The decision suggested that those restrictions had to be imposed by common law courts interpreting state nuisance and property law, but *Lucas* has not been interpreted by either the lower courts or the Supreme Court so narrowly.

Among the post-*Lucas* cases cited by Blumm and Ritchie are Department of Health v. The Mill, 887 P.2d 993, 1002 (Colo. 1994), *cert. denied*, 515 U.S. 1159 (1995) ("Under these principles of Colorado nuisance law, the right to make any use of the property that would create a hazard to public health by spreading radioactive contamination was excluded from The Mill's title at the onset."); and Aztec Minerals Corp. v. Romer, 940 P.2d 1025, 1031-32 (Colo. Ct. App. 1996) ("A landowner cannot reasonably expect to put property to a use that constitutes a nuisance, even if that is the only economically viable use for the property. More specifically, a landowner has no right to pollute a stream or use property in a manner that could result in the spread of radioactive contamination.").

4. The Blackmun Papers reveal the following, according to Professor Richard J. Lazarus, in *The Measure of a Justice: Justice Scalia and the Faltering of the Property Rights Movement Within the Supreme Court*, 57 Hastings L.J. 759, 775 (2006):

---

3. *See, e.g.*, James L. Huffman, Lucas: *A Small Step in the Right Direction*, 23 ENVTL. L. 901, 901-02 (1993) (commenting that *Lucas* "has promise from the point of view of those interested in maintaining a coherent system of property rights, not to mention those interested in complying with the Constitution"); Richard A. Epstein, Lucas v. South Carolina Coastal Council: *A Tangled Web of Expectations*, 45 STAN. L. REV. 1369, 1369 (1993) (arguing that *Lucas* "represents something of a high water mark in takings jurisprudence" because a six justice majority of the Court "allowed that some restrictions on land use might . . . be caught by the Takings Clause").

4. Michael C. Blumm, *Property Myths, Judicial Activism, and the* Lucas *Case*, 23 ENVTL. L. 907, 916 (1993) (*Lucas* is a "flawed decision because it assumes that property rights amount to development rights"); *see, e.g.*, Joseph L. Sax, *Property Rights and the Economy of Nature: Understanding* Lucas v. South Carolina Coastal Council, 45 STAN. L. REV. 1433, 1455 (1993) (arguing that the *Lucas* Court's "outdated view of property. . . is not satisfactory in an age of ecological awareness").

At conference, the vote in favor of the landowner was not nearly as close or as divided as suggested by the final Court opinion. The conference vote had seven Justices in the majority and only two (Blackmun and Stevens) in dissent. In addition to the four members of the Court who ended up joining Scalia's final opinion for the Court, Justices Kennedy and Souter also voted for the landowner, without much qualification. . . .

Although the case was argued on March 2, Justice Scalia did not circulate his draft opinion until early June, three months later, leaving relatively little time for further internal deliberations before the Court adjourned at the end of that same month. The Blackmun Papers contain little formal correspondence between chambers but the correspondence that does exist, along with the conference notes, suggest why and how Justice Scalia may have lost his seven-Justice majority. Justice Scalia's per se approach pushed Justice Kennedy away, as it did Justice Souter, both of whom would have likely joined an opinion that pursued something more akin to the *Penn Central* balancing approach mentioned by the Chief Justice during conference. Scalia's inclusion, on the other hand, of the extended discussion of background principles and nuisance law seems likely to have been in response to Justice O'Connor, who mentioned the need for a nuisance exception at conference. . . .

In sum, there was a cost to Justice Scalia's decision to craft the majority opinion in a more aggressive way. He lost the votes of two of the newer (and more junior) Justices on the Court, both of whom had expressed a willingness to join a majority opinion in favor of the landowner. The opinion instead relied on the vote, never fully explained by any of the papers, of Justice White, the oldest member of the Court by far and, accordingly, the most likely to leave the Court soon thereafter. In fact, Justice White resigned from the Court one year later, which immediately raised legitimate questions concerning the continuing vitality of *Lucas.*

5. *Lucas* was one of three land use regulation cases that the Court agreed to hear during the 1991-1992 Term. In Yee v. City of Escondido, 503 U.S. 519, 523, 527, 539 (1992), the Justices rejected the contention of a group of mobile home park owners "that a local rent control ordinance, when viewed against the backdrop of California's Mobilehome Residency Law, amounts to a physical occupation of their property, entitling them to compensation." This was not an *actual* physical occupation by cable television equipment, as in Loretto v. Teleprompter Manhattan CATV Corp., 458 U.S. 419 (1982) or even by a flood caused by the government, as in Pumpelly v. Green Bay Co., 80 U.S. 166 (1872). Instead, the park owners seemed to be alleging something in the nature of *constructive* physical possession: they alleged that "the rent control ordinance has transferred a discrete interest in land—the right to occupy the land indefinitely at a submarket rent—from the park owner to the mobile home owner. Petitioners contend that what has been transferred from park owner to mobile home owner is no less than a right of physical occupation of the park owner's land." Justice O'Connor explained that "[t]he government effects a physical taking only where it *requires* the landowner to submit to the physical occupation of his land" and concluded that, "[b]ecause the Escondido rent control ordinance does not compel a landowner to suffer the physical occupation of his property, it does not effect a *per se* taking under *Loretto.*"

During the same Term, the Court agreed to hear arguments in a third land use case—PFZ Props. v. Rodriguez, 503 U.S. 257 (1992) (per curiam)—in order to consider the following question: "Whether an arbitrary, capricious or illegal denial of a construction permit to a developer by officials acting under color of state law can state a substantive due process claim under 42 U.S.C. § 1983." PFZ's tale of woe began in 1976 when a planning board adopted a resolution approving a hotel and residential development project in Puerto Rico. In the ensuing 15 years, the developer found itself litigating in Puerto Rico and federal courts, waiting for the approval of its construction drawings, and being denied a construction permit. The federal district court had dismissed PFZ's procedural due process, equal protection, and substantive due process claims.

The Supreme Court's decision to consider only the last claim posed a strategic problem for PFZ: without a procedural due process claim in reserve, PFZ's attorneys devoted a good deal of their argument to articulating and defending a landowner's constitutionally protected "Right to Devote Private Property to a Legitimate Use." During an especially convoluted oral argument by petitioner PFZ's counsel, Justice O'Connor observed: "It sounds like you're trying to make a takings claim dressed up as a due process claim." The respondent's attorney stated in the summary of her argument that

> if we don't have a fundamental interest and if he [PFZ] doesn't have a liberty interest which has been qualifying for protection under the due process clause, then I don't know what he has unless it is a claim that there has been a wrongful adjudication of his claim, which sounds to me like procedural due process.

Perhaps the Court agreed, because only 12 days after the oral argument the Justices dismissed the certiorari writ as "improvidently granted." As it turns out, PFZ would come closer than any subsequent land use litigant to achieving a substantive due process victory in the High Court.

VI. Alternative Transportation Methods

Oregon's Statewide Planning Goals & Guidelines
GOAL 12: TRANSPORTATION
OAR 660-015-0000(12)

To provide and encourage a safe, convenient and economic transportation system.

A transportation plan shall (1) consider all modes of transportation including mass transit, air, water, pipeline, rail, highway, bicycle and pedestrian; (2) be based upon an inventory of local, regional and state transportation needs; (3) consider the differences in social consequences that would result from utilizing differing combinations of transportation modes; (4) avoid principal reliance upon any one mode of transportation; (5) minimize adverse social, economic and environmental impacts and costs; (6) conserve energy; (7) meet the needs of the transportation disadvantaged by improving transportation services; (8) facilitate the flow of goods and services so as to strengthen the local and regional economy; and (9) conform with local and regional comprehensive land use plans. Each plan shall include a provision for transportation as a key facility.

Tigard (Oregon) Community Development Code 18.120.180.A.8 (previous version)

Where landfill and/or development is allowed within and adjacent to the 100-year floodplain, the City shall require the dedication of sufficient open land area for greenway adjoining and within the floodplain. This area shall include portions at a suitable elevation for the construction of a pedestrian/ bicycle pathway within the floodplain in accordance with the adopted pedestrian/bicycle plan.

DOLAN v. CITY OF TIGARD
512 U.S. 374 (1994)

CHIEF JUSTICE REHNQUIST delivered the opinion of the Court.

Petitioner challenges the decision of the Oregon Supreme Court which held that the city of Tigard could condition the approval of her building permit on the dedication of a portion of her property for flood control and traffic improvements. 317 Ore. 110, 854 P.2d 437 (1993). We granted certiorari to resolve a question left open by our decision in Nollan v. California Coastal Comm'n, 483 U.S. 825, 97 L. Ed. 2d 677, 107 S. Ct. 3141 (1987), of what is the required degree of connection between the exactions imposed by the city and the projected impacts of the proposed development.

The State of Oregon enacted a comprehensive land use management program in 1973. Ore. Rev. Stat. §§ 197.005-197.860 (1991). The program required all Oregon cities and counties to adopt new comprehensive land use plans that were consistent with the statewide planning goals. §§ 197.175(1), 197.250. The plans are implemented by land use regulations which are part of an integrated hierarchy of legally binding goals, plans, and regulations. §§ 197.175, 197.175(2)(b). Pursuant to the State's requirements, the city of Tigard, a community of some 30,000 residents on the southwest edge of Portland, developed a comprehensive plan and codified it in its Community Development Code (CDC). The CDC requires property owners in the area zoned Central Business District to comply with a 15% open space and landscaping requirement, which limits total site coverage, including all structures and paved parking, to 85% of the parcel. After the completion of a transportation study that identified congestion in the Central Business District as a particular problem, the city adopted a plan for a pedestrian/bicycle pathway intended to encourage alternatives to automobile transportation for short trips. The CDC requires that new development facilitate this plan by dedicating land for pedestrian pathways where provided for in the pedestrian/bicycle pathway plan.[1]

The city also adopted a Master Drainage Plan (Drainage Plan). The Drainage Plan noted that flooding occurred in several areas along Fanno Creek, including areas near petitioner's property. The Drainage Plan also established that the increase in impervious surfaces associated with continued urbanization would exacerbate these flooding problems. To combat these risks, the Drainage Plan suggested a series of improvements to the Fanno Creek Basin, including channel excavation in the area next to petitioner's property. Other recommendations included ensuring that the floodplain remains free of structures and that it be preserved as greenways to minimize flood damage to structures. The Drainage Plan concluded that the cost of these improvements should be shared based on both direct and indirect benefits, with property owners along the water-ways paying more due to the direct benefit that they would receive. CDC Chapters 18.84 and 18.86 and CDC § 18.164.100 and the Tigard Park Plan carry out these recommendations.

Petitioner Florence Dolan owns a plumbing and electric supply store located on Main Street in the Central Business District of the city. The store covers approximately 9,700 square feet on the eastern side of a 1.67-acre parcel, which includes a gravel parking lot. Fanno Creek flows through the southwestern corner of the lot and along its western boundary. The year-round flow of the creek renders the area within the creek's 100-year floodplain virtually unusable for commercial

---

1. CDC § 18.86.040.A.1.b provides: "The development shall facilitate pedestrian/bicycle circulation if the site is located on a street with designated bikepaths or adjacent to a designated greenway/open space/park. Specific items to be addressed [include]: (i) Provision of efficient, convenient and continuous pedestrian and bicycle transit circulation systems, linking developments by requiring dedication and construction of pedestrian and bikepaths identified in the comprehensive plan. If direct connections cannot be made, require that funds in the amount of the construction cost be deposited into an account for the purpose of constructing paths." App. to Brief for Respondent B-33 to B-34.

development. The city's comprehensive plan includes the Fanno Creek floodplain as part of the city's greenway system.

Petitioner applied to the city for a permit to redevelop the site. Her proposed plans called for nearly doubling the size of the store to 17,600 square feet and paving a 39-space parking lot. The existing store, located on the opposite side of the parcel, would be razed in sections as construction progressed on the new building. In the second phase of the project, petitioner proposed to build an additional structure on the northeast side of the site for complementary businesses and to provide more parking. The proposed expansion and intensified use are consistent with the city's zoning scheme in the Central Business District.

The City Planning Commission (Commission) granted petitioner's permit application subject to conditions imposed by the city's CDC. The CDC establishes the following standard for site development review approval:

> "Where landfill and/or development is allowed within and adjacent to the 100-year floodplain, the City shall require the dedication of sufficient open land area for green-way adjoining and within the floodplain. This area shall include portions at a suitable elevation for the construction of a pedestrian/bicycle pathway within the floodplain in accordance with the adopted pedestrian/bicycle plan." CDC § 18.120.180.A.8, App. to Brief for Respondent B-45 to B-46.

Thus, the Commission required that petitioner dedicate the portion of her property lying within the 100-year floodplain for improvement of a storm drainage system along Fanno Creek and that she dedicate an additional 15-foot strip of land adjacent to the floodplain as a pedestrian/bicycle pathway. The dedication required by that condition encompasses approximately 7,000 square feet, or roughly 10% of the property. In accordance with city practice, petitioner could rely on the dedicated property to meet the 15% open space and landscaping requirement mandated by the city's zoning scheme. The city would bear the cost of maintaining a landscaped buffer between the dedicated area and the new store.

Petitioner requested variances from the CDC standards. Variances are granted only where it can be shown that, owing to special circumstances related to a specific piece of the land, the literal interpretation of the applicable zoning provisions would cause "an undue or unnecessary hardship" unless the variance is granted. Rather than posing alternative mitigating measures to offset the expected impacts of her proposed development, as allowed under the CDC, petitioner simply argued that her proposed development would not conflict with the policies of the comprehensive plan. The Commission denied the request.

The Commission made a series of findings concerning the relationship between the dedicated conditions and the projected impacts of petitioner's project. First, the Commission noted that "it is reasonable to assume that customers and employees of the future uses of this site could utilize a pedestrian/bicycle pathway adjacent to this development for their transportation and recreational needs." City of Tigard Planning Commission Final Order No. 91-09 PC, App. to Pet. for Cert. G-24. The Commission noted that the site plan has provided for bicycle parking in a rack in front of the proposed building and "it is reasonable to expect that some of the users of the bicycle parking provided for by the site plan will use the pathway adjacent to Fanno Creek if it is constructed." *Ibid.* In addition, the Commission found that creation of a convenient, safe pedestrian/bicycle pathway system as an alternative means of transportation "could offset some of the traffic demand on [nearby] streets and lessen the increase in traffic congestion." *Ibid.*

The Commission went on to note that the required floodplain dedication would be reasonably related to petitioner's request to intensify the use of the site given the increase in the impervious surface. The Commission stated that the "anticipated increased storm water flow from the subject property to an already strained creek and drainage basin can only add to the public need to manage the stream channel and floodplain for drainage purposes." *Id.*, at G-37 Based on this anticipated increased storm water flow, the Commission concluded that "the requirement of dedication of the floodplain area on the site is related to the applicant's plan to intensify development on the site." *Ibid.* The Tigard City Council approved the Commission's final order, subject to one minor modification; the city council reassigned the responsibility for surveying and marking the floodplain area from petitioner to the city's engineering department.

Petitioner appealed to the Land Use Board of Appeals (LUBA) on the ground that the city's dedication requirements were not related to the proposed development, and, therefore, those requirements constituted an uncompensated taking of her property under the Fifth Amendment. In evaluating the federal taking claim, LUBA assumed that the city's findings about the impacts of the proposed development were supported by substantial evidence. Dolan v. Tigard, LUBA 91-161 (Jan. 7, 1992), reprinted at App. to Pet. for Cert. D-15, n. 9. Given the undisputed fact that the proposed larger building and paved parking area would increase the amount of impervious surfaces and the runoff into Fanno Creek, LUBA concluded that "there is a 'reasonable relationship' between the proposed development and the requirement to dedicate land along Fanno Creek for a greenway." *Id.*, at D-16. With respect to the pedestrian/bicycle pathway, LUBA noted the Commission's finding that a significantly larger retail sales building and parking lot would attract larger numbers of customers and employees and their vehicles. It again found a "reasonable relationship" between alleviating the impacts of increased traffic from the development and facilitating the provision of a pedestrian/bicycle pathway as an alternative means of transportation. *Ibid.*

The Oregon Court of Appeals affirmed, rejecting petitioner's contention that in Nollan v. California Coastal Comm'n, 483 U.S. 825 (1987), we had abandoned the "reasonable relationship" test in favor of a stricter "essential nexus" test. 113 Ore. App. 162, 832 P.2d 853 (1992). The Oregon Supreme Court affirmed. 317 Ore. 110, 854 P.2d 437 (1993). The court also disagreed with petitioner's contention that the *Nollan* Court abandoned the "reasonably related" test. 317 Ore. at 118, 854 P.2d at 442. Instead, the court read *Nollan* to mean that an "exaction is reasonably related to an impact if the exaction serves the same purpose that a denial of the permit would serve." 317 Ore. at 120, 854 P.2d at 443. The court decided that both the pedestrian/bicycle pathway condition and the storm drainage dedication had an essential nexus to the development of the proposed site. Therefore, the court found the conditions to be reasonably related to the impact of the expansion of petitioner's business. We granted certiorari, because of an alleged conflict between the Oregon Supreme Court's decision and our decision in *Nollan.*

The Takings Clause of the Fifth Amendment of the United States Constitution, made applicable to the States through the Fourteenth Amendment, Chicago, B. & Q. R. Co. v. Chicago, 166 U.S. 226, 239 (1897), provides: "Nor shall private property be taken for public use, without just compensation."[5] One of the principal purposes of the Takings Clause is "to bar Government from forcing some people alone to bear public burdens which, in all fairness and justice, should be borne by the public as a whole." Armstrong v. United States, 364 U.S. 40, 49, 4 L. Ed. 2d 1554, 80 S. Ct.

---

5. JUSTICE STEVENS' dissent suggests that this case is actually grounded in "substantive" due process, rather than in the view that the Takings Clause of the Fifth Amendment was made applicable to the States by the Fourteenth Amendment. But there is no doubt that later cases have held that the Fourteenth Amendment does make the Takings Clause of the Fifth Amendment applicable to the States, see Penn Central Transp. Co. v. New York City, 438 U.S. 104, 122 (1978); Nollan v. California Coastal Comm'n, 483 U.S. 825, 827 (1987). Nor is there any doubt that these cases have relied upon Chicago, B. & Q. R. Co. v. Chicago, 166 U.S. 226 (1897), to reach that result. See, *e. g., Penn Central, supra*, at 122 ("The issue presented . . . [is] whether the restrictions imposed by New York City's law upon appellants' exploitation of the Terminal site effect a 'taking' of appellants' property for a public use within the meaning of the Fifth Amendment, which of course is made applicable to the States through the Fourteenth Amendment, see Chicago, B. & Q. R. Co. v. Chicago, 166 U.S. 226, 239 (1897)").

1563 (1960). Without question, had the city simply required petitioner to dedicate a strip of land along Fanno Creek for public use, rather than conditioning the grant of her permit to redevelop her property on such a dedication, a taking would have occurred. *Nollan, supra*, at 831. Such public access would deprive petitioner of the right to exclude others, "one of the most essential sticks in the bundle of rights that are commonly characterized as property." Kaiser Aetna v. United States, 444 U.S. 164, 176 (1979).

On the other side of the ledger, the authority of state and local governments to engage in land use planning has been sustained against constitutional challenge as long ago as our decision in Village of Euclid v. Ambler Realty Co., 272 U.S. 365 (1926). "Government hardly could go on if to some extent values incident to property could not be diminished without paying for every such change in the general law." Pennsylvania Coal Co. v. Mahon, 260 U.S. 393, 413 (1922). A land use regulation does not effect a taking if it "substantially advances legitimate state interests" and does not "deny an owner economically viable use of his land." Agins v. City of Tiburon, 447 U.S. 255, 260 (1980).[6]

The sort of land use regulations discussed in the cases just cited, however, differ in two relevant particulars from the present case. First, they involved essentially legislative determinations classifying entire areas of the city, whereas here the city made an adjudicative decision to condition petitioner's application for a building permit on an individual parcel. Second, the conditions imposed were not simply a limitation on the use petitioner might make of her own parcel, but a requirement that she deed portions of the property to the city. In *Nollan, supra*, we held that governmental authority to exact such a condition was circumscribed by the Fifth and Fourteenth Amendments. Under the well-settled doctrine of "unconstitutional conditions," the government may not require a person to give up a constitutional right—here the right to receive just compensation when property is taken for a public use—in exchange for a discretionary benefit conferred by the government where the benefit sought has little or no relationship to the property.

Petitioner contends that the city has forced her to choose between the building permit and her right under the Fifth Amendment to just compensation for the public easements. Petitioner does not quarrel with the city's authority to exact some forms of dedication as a condition for the grant of a building permit, but challenges the showing made by the city to justify these exactions. She argues that the city has identified "no special benefits" conferred on her, and has not identified any "special quantifiable burdens" created by her new store that would justify the particular dedications required from her which are not required from the public at large.

In evaluating petitioner's claim, we must first determine whether the "essential nexus" exists between the "legitimate state interest" and the permit condition exacted by the city. *Nollan*, 483 U.S. at 837. If we find that a nexus exists, we must then decide the required degree of connection between the exactions and the projected impact of the proposed development. We were not required to reach this question in *Nollan*, because we concluded that the connection did not meet even the loosest standard. Here, however, we must decide this question. . . .

We addressed the essential nexus question in *Nollan*. . . .

We agreed that the Coastal Commission's concern with protecting visual access to the ocean constituted a legitimate Public interest. . . . The absence of a nexus left the Coastal Commission in the position of simply trying to obtain an easement through gimmickry, which converted a valid regulation of land use into "'an out-and-out plan of extortion.'" *Ibid.*, quoting J. E. D. Associates, Inc. v. Atkinson, 121 N.H. 581, 584, 432 A.2d 12, 14-15 (1981).

---

6. There can be no argument that the permit conditions would deprive petitioner of "economically beneficial use" of her property as she currently operates a retail store on the lot. Petitioner assuredly is able to derive some economic use from her property.

No such gimmicks are associated with the permit conditions imposed by the city in this case. Undoubtedly, the prevention of flooding along Fanno Creek and the reduction of traffic congestion in the Central Business District qualify as the type of legitimate public purposes we have upheld. It seems equally obvious that a nexus exists between preventing flooding along Fanno Creek and limiting development within the creek's 100-year floodplain. Petitioner proposes to double the size of her retail store and to pave her now-gravel parking lot, thereby expanding the impervious surface on the property and increasing the amount of storm water runoff into Fanno Creek.

The same may be said for the city's attempt to reduce traffic congestion by providing for alternative means of transportation. In theory, a pedestrian/bicycle pathway provides a useful alternative means of transportation for workers and shoppers: "Pedestrians and bicyclists occupying dedicated spaces for walking and/or bicycling . . . remove potential vehicles from streets, resulting in an overall improvement in total transportation system flow." A. Nelson, Public Provision of Pedestrian and Bicycle Access Ways: Public Policy Rationale and the Nature of Private Benefits 11, Center for Planning Development, Georgia Institute of Technology, Working Paper Series (Jan. 1994). See also Intermodal Surface Transportation Efficiency Act of 1991, Pub. L. 102-240, 105 Stat. 1914 (recognizing pedestrian and bicycle facilities as necessary components of any strategy to reduce traffic congestion).

The second part of our analysis requires us to determine whether the degree of the exactions demanded by the city's permit conditions bears the required relationship to the projected impact of petitioner's proposed development. *Nollan, supra*, at 834, quoting Penn Central Transp. Co. v. New York City, 438 U.S. 104, 127, 57 L. Ed. 2d 631, 98 S. Ct. 2646 (1978) ("'[A] use restriction may constitute a "taking" if not reasonably necessary to the effectuation of a substantial government purpose'"). Here the Oregon Supreme Court deferred to what it termed the "city's unchallenged factual findings" supporting the dedication conditions and found them to be reasonably related to the impact of the expansion of petitioner's business. 317 Ore. at 120-121, 854 P.2d at 443.

The city required that petitioner dedicate "to the City as Greenway all portions of the site that fall within the existing 100-year floodplain [of Fanno Creek] . . . and all property 15 feet above [the floodplain] boundary." *Id.*, at 113, n. 3, 854 P.2d at 439, n. 3. In addition, the city demanded that the retail store be designed so as not to intrude into the greenway area. The city relies on the Commission's rather tentative findings that increased storm water flow from petitioner's property "can only add to the public need to manage the [floodplain] for drainage purposes" to support its conclusion that the "requirement of dedication of the floodplain area on the site is related to the applicant's plan to intensify development on the site." City of Tigard Planning Commission Final Order No. 91-09 PC, App. to Pet. for Cert. G-37.

The city made the following specific findings relevant to the pedestrian/bicycle pathway:

> "In addition, the proposed expanded use of this site is anticipated to generate additional vehicular traffic thereby increasing congestion on nearby collector and arterial streets. Creation of a convenient, safe pedestrian/bicycle pathway system as an alternative means of transportation could offset some of the traffic demand on these nearby streets and lessen the increase in traffic congestion." *Id.*, at G-24.

The question for us is whether these findings are constitutionally sufficient to justify the conditions imposed by the city on petitioner's building permit. Since state courts have been dealing with this question a good deal longer than we have, we turn to representative decisions made by them.

In some States, very generalized statements as to the necessary connection between the required dedication and the proposed development seem to suffice. See, *e. g.*, Billings Properties, Inc. v. Yellowstone County, 144 Mont. 25, 394 P.2d 182 (1964); Jenad, Inc. v. Scarsdale, 18 N.Y.2d 78, 218

N.E.2d 673, 271 N.Y.S.2d 955 (1966). We think this standard is too lax to adequately protect petitioner's right to just compensation if her property is taken for a public purpose.

Other state courts require a very exacting correspondence, described as the "specific and uniquely attributable" test. The Supreme Court of Illinois first developed this test in Pioneer Trust & Savings Bank v. Mount Prospect, 22 Ill. 2d 375, 380, 176 N.E.2d 799, 802 (1961). Under this standard, if the local government cannot demonstrate that its exaction is directly proportional to the specifically created need, the exaction becomes "a veiled exercise of the power of eminent domain and a confiscation of private property behind the defense of police regulations." Id., at 381, 176 N.E.2d at 802. We do not think the Federal Constitution requires such exacting scrutiny, given the nature of the interests involved.

A number of state courts have taken an intermediate position, requiring the municipality to show a "reasonable relationship" between the required dedication and the impact of the proposed development. Typical is the Supreme Court of Nebraska's opinion in Simpson v. North Platte, 206 Neb. 240, 245, 292 N.W.2d 297, 301 (1980), where that court stated:

> "The distinction, therefore, which must be made between an appropriate exercise of the police power and an improper exercise of eminent domain is whether the require-ment has some reasonable relationship or nexus to the use to which the property is being made or is merely being used as an excuse for taking property simply because at that particular moment the landowner is asking the city for some license or permit."

Thus, the court held that a city may not require a property owner to dedicate private property for some future public use as a condition of obtaining a building permit when such future use is not "occasioned by the construction sought to be permitted." Id., at 248, 292 N.W.2d at 302.

Some form of the reasonable relationship test has been adopted in many other jurisdictions. See, e. g., Jordan v. Menomonee Falls, 28 Wis. 2d 608, 137 N.W.2d 442 (1965); Collis v. Bloomington, 310 Minn. 5, 246 N.W.2d 19 (1976) (requiring a showing of a reasonable relationship between the planned subdivision and the municipality's need for land); College Station v. Turtle Rock Corp., 680 S.W.2d 802, 807 (Tex. 1984); Call v. West Jordan, 606 P.2d 217, 220 (Utah 1979) (affirming use of the reasonable relation test). Despite any semantical differences, general agreement exists among the courts "that the dedication should have some reasonable relationship to the needs created by the [development]." Ibid.

We think the "reasonable relationship" test adopted by a majority of the state courts is closer to the federal constitutional norm than either of those previously discussed. But we do not adopt it as such, partly because the term "reasonable relationship" seems confusingly similar to the term "rational basis" which describes the minimal level of scrutiny under the Equal Protection Clause of the Fourteenth Amendment. We think a term such as "rough proportionality" best encapsulates what we hold to be the requirement of the Fifth Amendment. No precise mathematical calculation is required, but the city must make some sort of individualized determination that the required dedication is related both in nature and extent to the impact of the proposed development.[8]

---

8. JUSTICE STEVENS' dissent takes us to task for placing the burden on the city to justify the required dedication. He is correct in arguing that in evaluating most generally applicable zoning regulations, the burden properly rests on the party challenging the regulation to prove that it constitutes an arbitrary regulation of property rights. See, e. g., Village of Euclid v. Ambler Realty Co., 272 U.S. 365 (1926). Here, by contrast, the city made an adjudicative decision to condition petitioner's application for a building permit on an individual parcel. In this situation, the burden properly rests on the city. See *Nollan*, 483 U.S. at 836. This conclusion is not, as he suggests, undermined by our decision in Moore v. East Cleveland, 431 U.S. 494 (1977), in which we struck down a housing ordinance that limited occupancy of a dwelling unit to members of a single family as violating the Due Process Clause of the Fourteenth Amendment. The ordinance at issue in Moore intruded on choices concerning family living arrangements, an area in which the usual deference to the legislature was found to be inappropriate. Id., at 499.

JUSTICE STEVENS' dissent relies upon a law review article for the proposition that the city's conditional demands for part of petitioner's property are "a species of business regulation that heretofore warranted a strong presumption of constitutional validity." But simply denominating a governmental measure as a "business regulation" does not immunize it from constitutional challenge on the ground that it violates a provision of the Bill of Rights. . . . We turn now to analysis of whether the findings relied upon by the city here, first with respect to the floodplain easement, and second with respect to the pedestrian/bicycle path, satisfied these requirements.

It is axiomatic that increasing the amount of impervious surface will increase the quantity and rate of storm water flow from petitioner's property. Therefore, keeping the floodplain open and free from development would likely confine the pressures on Fanno Creek created by petitioner's development. In fact, because petitioner's property lies within the Central Business District, the CDC already required that petitioner leave 15% of it as open space and the undeveloped floodplain would have nearly satisfied that requirement. But the city demanded more—it not only wanted petitioner not to build in the floodplain, but it also wanted petitioner's property along Fanno Creek for its greenway system. The city has never said why a public greenway, as opposed to a private one, was required in the interest of flood control.

The difference to petitioner, of course, is the loss of her ability to exclude others. As we have noted, this right to exclude others is "one of the most essential sticks in the bundle of rights that are commonly characterized as property." *Kaiser Aetna*, 444 U.S. at 176. It is difficult to see why recreational visitors trampling along petitioner's floodplain easement are sufficiently related to the city's legitimate interest in reducing flooding problems along Fanno Creek, and the city has not attempted to make any individualized determination to support this part of its request.

The city contends that the recreational easement along the greenway is only ancillary to the city's chief purpose in controlling flood hazards. It further asserts that unlike the residential property at issue in *Nollan*, petitioner's property is commercial in character and, therefore, her right to exclude others is compromised. The city maintains that "there is nothing to suggest that preventing [petitioner] from prohibiting [the easements] will unreasonably impair the value of [her] property as a [retail store]." PruneYard Shopping Center v. Robins, 447 U.S. 74, 83 (1980).

Admittedly, petitioner wants to build a bigger store to attract members of the public to her property. She also wants, however, to be able to control the time and manner in which they enter. The recreational easement on the greenway is different in character from the exercise of state-protected rights of free expression and petition that we permitted in *PruneYard*. In *PruneYard*, we held that a major private shopping center that attracted more than 25,000 daily patrons had to provide access to persons exercising their state constitutional rights to distribute pamphlets and ask passers-by to sign their petitions. We based our decision, in part, on the fact that the shopping center "may restrict expressive activity by adopting time, place, and manner regulations that will minimize any interference with its commercial functions." *Id.*, at 83. By contrast, the city wants to impose a permanent recreational easement upon petitioner's property that borders Fanno Creek. Petitioner would lose all rights to regulate the time in which the public entered onto the greenway, regardless of any interference it might pose with her retail store. Her right to exclude would not be regulated, it would be eviscerated.

If petitioner's proposed development had somehow encroached on existing greenway space in the city, it would have been reasonable to require petitioner to provide some alternative greenway space for the public either on her property or elsewhere. But that is not the case here. We conclude that the findings upon which the city relies do not show the required reasonable relationship between the floodplain easement and the petitioner's proposed new building.

With respect to the pedestrian/bicycle pathway, we have no doubt that the city was correct in finding that the larger retail sales facility proposed by petitioner will increase traffic on the streets of the Central Business District. The city estimates that the proposed development would generate roughly 435 additional trips per day.[9] Dedications for streets, sidewalks, and other public ways are generally reasonable exactions to avoid excessive congestion from a proposed property use. But on the record before us, the city has not met its burden of demonstrating that the additional number of vehicle and bicycle trips generated by petitioner's development reasonably relate to the city's requirement for a dedication of the pedestrian/bicycle pathway easement. The city simply found that the creation of the pathway "could offset some of the traffic demand . . . and lessen the increase in traffic congestion."

As Justice Peterson of the Supreme Court of Oregon explained in his dissenting opinion, however, "the findings of fact that the bicycle pathway system 'could offset some of the traffic demand' is a far cry from a finding that the bicycle pathway system will, or is likely to, offset some of the traffic demand." 317 Ore. at 127, 854 P.2d at 447 (emphasis in original). No precise mathematical calculation is required, but the city must make some effort to quantify its findings in support of the dedication for the pedestrian/bicycle pathway beyond the conclusory statement that it could offset some of the traffic demand generated.

Cities have long engaged in the commendable task of land use planning, made necessary by increasing urbanization, particularly in metropolitan areas such as Portland. The city's goals of reducing flooding hazards and traffic congestion, and providing for public greenways, are laudable, but there are outer limits to how this may be done. "A strong public desire to improve the public condition [will not] warrant achieving the desire by a shorter cut than the constitutional way of paying for the change." *Pennsylvania Coal*, 260 U.S. at 416.

The judgment of the Supreme Court of Oregon is reversed, and the case is remanded for further proceedings not inconsistent with this opinion.

It is so ordered.

JUSTICE STEVENS, with whom JUSTICE BLACKMUN and JUSTICE GINSBURG join, dissenting. . . .

The Court is correct in concluding that the city may not attach arbitrary conditions to a building permit or to a variance even when it can rightfully deny the application out-right. I also agree that state court decisions dealing with ordinances that govern municipal development plans provide useful guidance in a case of this kind. Yet the Court's description of the doctrinal underpinnings of its decision, the phrasing of its fledgling test of "rough proportionality," and the application of that test to this case run contrary to the traditional treatment of these cases and break considerable and unpropitious new ground. . . .

The Court's narrow focus on one strand in the property owner's bundle of rights is particularly misguided in a case involving the development of commercial property. As Professor Johnston has noted:

> "The subdivider is a manufacturer, processer, and marketer of a product; land is but one of his raw materials. In subdivision control disputes, the developer is not defending hearth and home against the king's intrusion, but simply attempting to maximize his profits from the sale of a finished product. As applied to him, subdivision control exactions are actually business regulations." Johnston, *Constitutionality of Subdivision Control Exactions: The Quest for A Rationale*, 52 Cornell L. Q. 871, 923 (1967).

---

9. The city uses a weekday average trip rate of 53.21 trips per 1,000 square feet. Additional Trips Generated = 53.21 X (17,600 - 9,720).

The exactions associated with the development of a retail business are likewise a species of business regulation that heretofore warranted a strong presumption of constitutional validity. . . .

The Court has made a serious error by abandoning the traditional presumption of constitutionality and imposing a novel burden of proof on a city implementing an admittedly valid comprehensive land use plan. Even more consequential than its incorrect disposition of this case, however, is the Court's resurrection of a species of substantive due process analysis that it firmly rejected decades ago.

The Court begins its constitutional analysis by citing Chicago, B. & Q. R. Co. v. Chicago, 166 U.S. 226, 239 (1897), for the proposition that the Takings Clause of the Fifth Amendment is "applicable to the States through the Fourteenth Amendment." That opinion, however, contains no mention of either the Takings Clause or the Fifth Amendment;[7] it held that the protection afforded by the Due Process Clause of the Fourteenth Amendment extends to matters of substance as well as procedure,[8] and that the substance of "the due process of law enjoined by the Fourteenth Amendment requires compensation to be made or adequately secured to the owner of private property taken for public use under the authority of a State." 166 U.S. at 235, 236-241. It applied the same kind of substantive due process analysis more frequently identified with a better known case that accorded similar substantive protection to a baker's liberty interest in working 60 hours a week and 10 hours a day. See Lochner v. New York, 198 U.S. 45, 49 L. Ed. 937, 25 S. Ct. 539 (1905).[9]

Later cases have interpreted the Fourteenth Amendment's substantive protection against uncompensated deprivations of private property by the States as though it incorporated the text of the Fifth Amendment's Takings Clause. See, e. g., Keystone Bituminous Coal Assn. v. DeBenedictis, 480 U.S. 470, 481, n. 10 (1987). There was nothing problematic about that interpretation in cases enforcing the Fourteenth Amendment against state action that involved the actual physical invasion of private property. Justice Holmes charted a significant new course, however, when he opined that a state law making it "commercially impracticable to mine certain coal" had "very nearly the same effect for constitutional purposes as appropriating or destroying it." Pennsylvania Coal Co. v. Mahon, 260 U.S. 393, 414 (1922). The so-called "regulatory takings" doctrine that the Holmes dictum kindled has an obvious kinship with the line of substantive due process cases that Lochner exemplified. Besides having similar ancestry, both doctrines are potentially open-ended sources of judicial power to invalidate state economic regulations that Members of this Court view as unwise or unfair. . . .

The Court has decided to apply its heightened scrutiny to a single strand—the power to exclude—in the bundle of rights that enables a commercial enterprise to flourish in an urban environment. That intangible interest is undoubtedly worthy of constitutional protection—much like the grandmother's interest in deciding which of her relatives may share her home in Moore v. East Cleveland, 431 U.S. 494 (1977). Both interests are protected from arbitrary state action by the Due Process Clause of the Fourteenth Amendment. It is, however, a curious irony that Members of

---

7. An earlier case deemed it "well settled" that the Takings Clause "is a limitation on the power of the Federal government, and not on the States." Pumpelly v. Green Bay Co., 80 U.S. 166 (1872)

8. The Court held that a State "may not, by any of its agencies, disregard the prohibitions of the Fourteenth Amendment. Its judicial authorities may keep within the letter of the statute prescribing forms of procedure in the courts and give the parties interested the fullest opportunity to be heard, and yet it might be that its final action would be inconsistent with that amendment. In determining what is due process of law regard must be had to substance, not to form." Chicago, B. & Q. R. Co. v. Chicago, 166 U.S. 226, 234-235 (1897).

9. The Lochner Court refused to presume that there was a reasonable connection between the regulation and the state interest in protecting the public health. 198 U.S. at 60-61. A similar refusal to identify a sufficient nexus between an enlarged building with a newly paved parking lot and the state interests in minimizing the risks of flooding and traffic congestion proves fatal to the city's permit conditions in this case under the Court's novel approach

the majority in this case would impose an almost insurmountable burden of proof on the property owner in the *Moore* case while saddling the city with a heightened burden in this case.

In its application of what is essentially the doctrine of substantive due process, the Court confuses the past with the present. On November 13, 1922, the village of Euclid, Ohio, adopted a zoning ordinance that effectively confiscated 75 percent of the value of property owned by the Ambler Realty Company. Despite its recognition that such an ordinance "would have been rejected as arbitrary and oppressive" at an earlier date, the Court (over the dissent of Justices Van Devanter, McReynolds, and Butler) upheld the ordinance. Today's majority should heed the words of Justice Sutherland:

> "Such regulations are sustained, under the complex conditions of our day, for reasons analogous to those which justify traffic regulations, which, before the advent of automobiles and rapid transit street railways, would have been condemned as fatally arbitrary and unreasonable. And in this there is no inconsistency, for while the meaning of constitutional guaranties never varies, the scope of their application must expand or contract to meet the new and different conditions which are constantly coming within the field of their operation. In a changing world, it is impossible that it should be otherwise." Village of Euclid v. Ambler Realty Co., 272 U.S. 365, 387 (1926).

In our changing world one thing is certain: uncertainty will characterize predictions about the impact of new urban developments on the risks of floods, earthquakes, traffic congestion, or environmental harms. When there is doubt concerning the magnitude of those impacts, the public interest in averting them must outweigh the private interest of the commercial entrepreneur. If the government can demonstrate that the conditions it has imposed in a land use permit are rational, impartial and conducive to fulfilling the aims of a valid land use plan, a strong presumption of validity should attach to those conditions. The burden of demonstrating that those conditions have unreasonably impaired the economic value of the proposed improvement belongs squarely on the shoulders of the party challenging the state action's constitutionality. That allocation of burdens has served us well in the past. The Court has stumbled badly today by reversing it.

I respectfully dissent.

JUSTICE SOUTER, dissenting. . . .

I cannot agree that the application of *Nollan* is a sound one here, since it appears that the Court has placed the burden of producing evidence of relationship on the city, despite the usual rule in cases involving the police power that the government is presumed to have acted constitutionally. Having thus assigned the burden, the Court concludes that the city loses based on one word ("could" instead of "would"), and despite the fact that this record shows the connection the Court looks for. Dolan has put forward no evidence that the burden of granting a dedication for the bicycle path is unrelated in kind to the anticipated increase in traffic congestion, nor, if there exists a requirement that the relationship be related in degree, has Dolan shown that the exaction fails any such test. The city, by contrast, calculated the increased traffic flow that would result from Dolan's proposed development to be 435 trips per day, and its Comprehensive Plan, applied here, relied on studies showing the link between alternative modes of transportation, including bicycle paths, and reduced street traffic congestion. See, *e. g.*, App. to Brief for Respondent A-5, quoting City of Tigard's Comprehensive Plan ("'Bicycle and pedestrian pathway systems will result in some reduction of automobile trips within the community'"). *Nollan*, therefore, is satisfied, and on that assumption the city's conditions should not be held to fail a further rough proportionality test or any other that might be devised to give meaning to the constitutional limits. . . .

Notes

1. When, as noted above, the Court in Lingle v. Chevron U.S.A., Inc., 544 U.S. 528, 541, 546-48 (2005), rejected the "substantially advances" formula from *Agins*, Justice O'Connor was compelled to explain how *Nollan* and *Dolan* survived this delicate jurisprudential excision:

> [W]e the Court drew upon the language of *Agins* in these cases, it did not apply the "substantially advances" test that is the subject of today's decision. Both *Nollan* and *Dolan* involved Fifth Amendment takings challenges to adjudicative land-use exactions—specifically, government demands that a landowner dedicate an easement allowing public access to her property as a condition of obtaining a development permit. . . .
>
> Although *Nollan* and *Dolan* quoted *Agins'* language, the rule those decisions established is entirely distinct from the "substantially advances" test we address today. Whereas the "substantially advances" inquiry before us now is unconcerned with the degree or type of burden a regulation places upon property, *Nollan* and *Dolan* both involved dedications of property so onerous that, outside the exactions context, they would be deemed *per se* physical takings. In neither case did the Court question whether the exaction would substantially advance some legitimate state interest. Rather, the issue was whether the exactions substantially advanced the same interests that land-use authorities asserted would allow them to deny the permit altogether. As the Court explained in *Dolan*, these cases involve a special application of the "doctrine of 'unconstitutional conditions,'" which provides that "the government may not require a person to give up a constitutional right—here the right to receive just compensation when property is taken for a public use—in exchange for a discretionary benefit conferred by the government where the benefit has little or no relationship to the property." That is worlds apart from a rule that says a regulation affecting property constitutes a taking on its face solely because it does not substantially advance a legitimate government interest. In short, *Nollan* and *Dolan* cannot be characterized as applying the "substantially advances" test we address today, and our decision should not be read to disturb these precedents.

Are you convinced by this attempt to keep *Nollan* and *Dolan* alive despite the *Lingle* Court's conclusion that the "substantially advances" language quoted in both cases "prescribes an inquiry in the nature of a due process, not a takings, test, and that it has no proper place in our takings jurisprudence"?

2. The following excerpt from the oral argument in *Dolan* illustrates the difficulty the city's counsel had in explaining the purpose of the widespread use of bicycle paths throughout the country:

> MR. RAMIS: Another property might reconstruct the sidewalk. Another property might contribute to the synchronization of street lights in order to provide more capacity on the streets.
>
> The problem the City was facing in this case was not bringing people to the property on bikes. The problem was that this expansion—major expansion, over—close to double the size, would add hundreds of additional car trips to—to streets that were already so congested that fire vehicles—
>
> QUESTION: And the solution to that was a bike path?
>
> MR. RAMIS: The solution was to offset those car trips by an alternative system of transportation.

QUESTION: People are going to go to the hardware store on their bike?

MR. RAMIS: No, Your Honor. That's not the basis of our decision.

QUESTION: That isn't even contended by the City, is it? So, there is no relationship between the increased traffic volume and the bike path?

MR. RAMIS: Your Honor, the relationship is that this project is a retail project that puts additional cars on the road. The bike path is mitigation device that takes trips off the road. They don't have to be the same people.

QUESTION: I see, people who would otherwise be driving their cars for recreation will instead ride bicycles for recreation; is that the—

MR. RAMIS: No, Your Honor.

QUESTION: Is that the notion?

MR. RAMIS: No, Your Honor. The—the concept is that the City is trying to encourage people to go to other places to do their shopping by means of bicycle rather than car. If they can achieve that, then we will free up spaces on the streets for those people who are coming in the car to this business.

This is not a radical notion or a particularly innovative notion. It is an idea that Congress has legislated.[27] Dollars that—

QUESTION: There are a lot of bike paths around Washington, and I've never seen people carrying shopping bags on their bikes.

3. It is not unusual to find provisions for off-street parking of bicycles in local zoning ordinances. Section 6.37.1 of the Cambridge, Massachusetts, ordinance, for example, provides that "[f]or multifamily residences there shall be one bicycles space or locker for each two dwelling units or portion thereof," while § 6.49 contains details on the design of bicycle parking spaces (size, location, separation, and the like).

In some zoning ordinances, particularly those that endorse the notion of transit-oriented development (TOD), there is a direct relationship between automobile parking requirements and bike parking. See, for example, §330-07 of the Zoning Code of Sacramento County, California:

A proponent of an office, commercial or industrial project may provide alternative facilities or programs which serve to reduce parking demand in return for a reduction in vehicle parking requirements. Vehicle parking requirements may be reduced in accordance with the following provisions:

(a) Shower/Locker Facilities. Developments with one hundred (100) or more employees may reduce their parking requirement by providing shower and clothing locker facilities for bicycle commuting employees. Maximum reduction: two percent (2%) of required parking.

(b) Secure Bicycle Parking. Developments which provide additional secure bicycle parking facilities over-and-above the minimum requirement may reduce their parking

---

27. Authors' note: *See, e.g.*, 23 U.S.C. §217(a) ("a State may obligate [federal] funds apportioned to it . . . for construction of pedestrian walkways and bicycle transportation facilities [defined in §217(j) as "a new or improved lane, path, or shoulder for use by bicyclists and a traffic control device, shelter, or parking facility for bicycles"] and for carrying out nonconstruction projects related to safe bicycle use").

requirement by one (1) vehicle space for every three (3) additional bicycle spaces provided. Maximum reduction: two percent (2%) of required parking. . . .

As the search for strategies designed to address global warning becomes more intense, we anticipate that other communities will explore the adoption of these and other alternative transportation strategies.

VII. Endangered Species Protection

Monterey, California City Council Resolution No. 86-96 (adopted June 17, 1986)

WHEREAS, the City Council held a duly noticed public hearing on May 6, 1986, continued to June 3, 1986, at which time testimony was received regarding the application for a Tentative Subdivision Map for Monterey Bay Dunes Project, 2301 Del Monte Avenue, Monterey, a 190-unit planned unit development;

NOW, THEREFORE, BE IT RESOLVED THAT THE COUNCIL OF THE CITY OF MONTEREY FINDS:

1. The site is not physically suitable for the type and density of development proposed, in that sand relocation and grading necessary for construction of the project results in significant environmental impacts that are not mitigable nor adequately addressed given the current size of the project.

2. The site is further not physically suitable for the type and density of development proposed in that significant impacts upon the native flora and fauna habitat will result which are not adequately mitigated in this proposal.

3. The site is further not physically suitable for the project proposed in that the design of the subdivision does not provide adequate access to and from the property over lands owned or controlled by the developer, and as proposed the project fails to provide adequate easements or other legally acceptable means of insuring access to this project in the future.

4. The design of the subdivision, as noted in 2 and 3 above, is likely to cause substantial environmental damage and substantially injure the habitat of the endangered Smith's Blue Butterfly.

5. The project as submitted is not in conformance with the General Plan, in that it fails to protect important native flora and fauna . . . .

6. The project will have a significant effect on the environment, and no demonstration of overriding considerations has been made which would support approval of this project.

CITY OF MONTEREY v. DEL MONTE DUNES
526 U.S. 687 (1999)

JUSTICE KENNEDY delivered the opinion of the Court, except as to Part IV-A-2 [which is not included in this edited version].

This case began with attempts by the respondent, Del Monte Dunes, and its predecessor in inteest to develop a parcel of land within the jurisdiction of the petitioner, the city of Monterey. The city, in a series of repeated rejections, denied proposals to develop the property, each time imposing more rigorous demands on the developers. Del Monte Dunes brought suit in the United States District Court for the Northern District of California, under Rev. Stat. § 1979, 42 U.S.C. § 1983. After protracted litigation, the case was submitted to the jury on Del Monte Dunes' theory that the city effected a regulatory taking or otherwise injured the property by unlawful acts, without paying compensation or providing an adequate postdeprivation remedy for the loss. The jury found for Del Monte Dunes, and the Court of Appeals affirmed.

The petitioner contends that the regulatory takings claim should not have been decided by the jury and that the Court of Appeals adopted an erroneous standard for regulatory takings liability. We need not decide all of the questions presented by the petitioner, nor need we examine each of the points given by the Court of Appeals in its decision to affirm. The controlling question is whether, given the city's apparent concession that the instructions were a correct statement of the law, the matter was properly submitted to the jury. We conclude that it was, and that the judgment of the Court of Appeals should be affirmed.

The property which respondent and its predecessor in interest (landowners) sought to develop was a 37.6 acre ocean-front parcel located in the city of Monterey, at or near the city's boundary to the north, where Highway 1 enters. With the exception of the ocean and a state park located to the northeast, the parcel was virtually surrounded by a railroad right-of-way and properties devoted to industrial, commercial, and multifamily residential uses. The parcel itself was zoned for multifamily residential use under the city's general zoning ordinance.

The parcel had not been untouched by its urban and industrial proximities. A sewer line housed in 15-foot man-made dunes covered with jute matting and surrounded by snow fencing traversed the property. Trash, dumped in violation of the law, had accumulated on the premises. The parcel had been used for many years by an oil company as a terminal and tank farm where large quantities of oil were delivered, stored, and reshipped. When the company stopped using the site, it had removed its oil tanks but left behind tank pads, an industrial complex, pieces of pipe, broken concrete, and oil-soaked sand. The company had introduced nonnative ice plant to prevent erosion and to control soil conditions around the oil tanks. Ice plant secretes a substance that forces out other plants and is not compatible with the parcel's natural flora. By the time the landowners sought to develop the property, ice plant had spread to some 25 percent of the parcel, and, absent human intervention, would continue to advance, endangering and perhaps eliminating the parcel's remaining natural vegetation.

The natural flora the ice plant encroached upon included buckwheat, the natural habitat of the endangered Smith's Blue Butterfly. The butterfly lives for one week, travels a maximum of 200 feet, and must land on a mature, flowering buckwheat plant to survive. Searches for the butterfly from 1981 through 1985 yielded but a single larva, discovered in 1984. No other specimens had been found on the property, and the parcel was quite isolated from other possible habitats of the butterfly.

In 1981 the landowners submitted an application to develop the property in conformance with the city's zoning and general plan requirements. Although the zoning requirements permitted the development of up to 29 housing units per acre, or more than 1,000 units for the entire parcel, the landowners' proposal was limited to 344 residential units. In 1982 the city's planning commission denied the application but stated that a proposal for 264 units would receive favorable consideration. In keeping with the suggestion, the landowners submitted a revised proposal for 264 units. In late 1983, however, the planning commission again denied the application. The commission once more requested a reduction in the scale of the development, this time saying a plan for 224 units would be received with favor. The landowners returned to the drawing board and prepared a proposal for 224 units, which, its previous statements notwithstanding, the planning commission denied in 1984. The landowners appealed to the city council, which overruled the planning commission's denial and referred the project back to the commission, with instructions to consider a proposal for 190 units.

The landowners once again reduced the scope of their development proposal to comply with the city's request, and submitted four specific, detailed site plans, each for a total of 190 units for the whole parcel. Even so, the planning commission rejected the landowners' proposal later in 1984. Once more the landowners appealed to the city council. The council again overruled the commission, finding the proposal conceptually satisfactory and in conformance with the city's previous decisions regarding, inter alia, density, number of units, location on the property, and access. The council then approved one of the site plans, subject to various specific conditions, and granted an 18-month conditional use permit for the proposed development.

The landowners spent most of the next year revising their proposal and taking other steps to fulfill the city's conditions. Their final plan, submitted in 1985, devoted 17.9 of the 37.6 acres to public open space (including a public beach and areas for the restoration and preservation of the buckwheat habitat), 7.9 acres to open, landscaped areas, and 6.7 acres to public and private streets (including public parking and access to the beach). Only 5.1 acres were allocated to buildings and patios. The plan was designed, in accordance with the city's demands, to provide the public with a beach, a buffer zone between the development and the adjoining state park, and view corridors so the buildings would not be visible to motorists on the nearby highway; the proposal also called for restoring and preserving as much of the sand dune structure and buckwheat habitat as possible consistent with development and the city's requirements.

After detailed review of the proposed buildings, roads, and parking facilities, the city's architectural review committee approved the plan. Following hearings before the planning commission, the commission's professional staff found the final plan addressed and substantially satisfied the city's conditions. It proposed the planning commission make specific findings to this effect and recommended the plan be approved.

In January 1986, less than two months before the landowners' conditional use permit was to expire, the planning commission rejected the recommendation of its staff and denied the development plan. The landowners appealed to the city council, also requesting a 12-month extension of their permit to allow them time to attempt to comply with any additional requirements the council might impose. The permit was extended until a hearing could be held before the city council in June 1986. After the hearing, the city council denied the final plan, not only declining to specify measures the landowners could take to satisfy the concerns raised by the council but also refusing to extend the conditional use permit to allow time to address those concerns. The council's decision, moreover, came at a time when a sewer moratorium issued by another agency would have prevented or at least delayed development based on a new plan.

The council did not base its decision on the landowners' failure to meet any of the specific conditions earlier prescribed by the city. Rather, the council made general findings that the landowners had not provided adequate access for the development (even though the landowners had twice changed the specific access plans to comply with the city's demands and maintained they could satisfy the city's new objections if granted an extension), that the plan's layout would damage the environment (even though the location of the development on the property was necessitated by the city's demands for a public beach, view corridors, and a buffer zone next to the state park), and that the plan would disrupt the habitat of the Smith's Blue Butterfly (even though the plan would remove the encroaching ice plant and preserve or restore buckwheat habitat on almost half of the property, and even though only one larva had ever been found on the property).

After five years, five formal decisions, and 19 different site plans, respondent Del Monte Dunes decided the city would not permit development of the property under any circumstances. Del

Monte Dunes commenced suit against the city in the United States District Court for the Northern District of California under 42 U.S.C. § 1983, alleging, *inter alia*, that denial of the final development proposal was a violation of the Due Process and Equal Protection provisions of the Fourteenth Amendment and an uncompensated, and so unconstitutional, regulatory taking.

The District Court dismissed the claims as unripe under Williamson County Regional Planning Comm'n v. Hamilton Bank of Johnson City, 473 U.S. 172 (1985), on the grounds that Del Monte Dunes had neither obtained a definitive decision as to the development the city would allow nor sought just compensation in state court. The Court of Appeals reversed. 920 F.2d 1496 (CA9 1990). After reviewing at some length the history of attempts to develop the property, the court found that to require additional proposals would implicate the concerns about repetitive and unfair procedures expressed in MacDonald, Sommer & Frates v. Yolo County, 477 U.S. 340, 350, n. 7 (1986), and that the city's decision was sufficiently final to render Del Monte Dunes' claim ripe for review. 920 F.2d at 1501-1506. The court also found that because the State of California had not provided a compensatory remedy for temporary regulatory takings when the city issued its final denial, see First English Evangelical Lutheran Church of Glendale v. County of Los Angeles, 482 U.S. 304 (1987), Del Monte Dunes was not required to pursue relief in state court as a precondition to federal relief. See 920 F.2d at 1506-1507.

On remand, the District Court determined, over the city's objections, to submit Del Monte Dunes' takings and equal protection claims to a jury but to reserve the substantive due process claim for decision by the court. Del Monte Dunes argued to the jury that, although the city had a right to regulate its property, the combined effect of the city's various demands—that the development be invisible from the highway, that a buffer be provided between the development and the state park, and that the public be provided with a beach—was to force development into the "bowl" area of the parcel. As a result, Del Monte Dunes argued, the city's subsequent decision that the bowl contained sensitive buckwheat habitat which could not be disturbed blocked the development of any portion of the property. While conceding the legitimacy of the city's stated regulatory purposes, Del Monte Dunes emphasized the tortuous and protracted history of attempts to develop the property, as well as the shifting and sometimes inconsistent positions taken by the city throughout the process, and argued that it had been treated in an unfair and irrational manner. Del Monte Dunes also submitted evidence designed to undermine the validity of the asserted factual premises for the city's denial of the final proposal and to suggest that the city had considered buying, or inducing the State to buy, the property for public use as early as 1979, reserving some money for this purpose but delaying or abandoning its plans for financial reasons. The State of California's purchase of the property during the pendency of the litigation may have bolstered the credibility of Del Monte Dunes' position.

At the close of argument, the District Court instructed the jury it should find for Del Monte Dunes if it found either that Del Monte Dunes had been denied all economically viable use of its property or that "the city's decision to reject the plaintiff's 190 unit development proposal did not substantially advance a legitimate public purpose." App. 303. With respect to the first inquiry, the jury was instructed, in relevant part, as follows:

> "For the purpose of a taking claim, you will find that the plaintiff has been denied all economically viable use of its property, if, as the result of the city's regulatory decision there remains no permissible or beneficial use for that property. In proving whether the plaintiff has been denied all economically viable use of its property, it is not enough that the plaintiff show that after the challenged action by the city the property diminished in value or that it would suffer a serious economic loss as the result of the city's actions."
> *Ibid.*

With respect to the second inquiry, the jury received the following instruction:

> "Public bodies, such as the city, have the authority to take actions which substantially advance legitimate public interests and legitimate public interests can include protecting the environment, preserving open space agriculture, protecting the health and safety of its citizens, and regulating the quality of the community by looking at development. So one of your jobs as jurors is to decide if the city's decision here substantially advanced any such legitimate public purpose.

> "The regulatory actions of the city or any agency substantially advance a legitimate public purpose if the action bears a reasonable relationship to that objective.

> "Now, if the preponderance of the evidence establishes that there was no reasonable relationship between the city's denial of the . . . proposal and legitimate public purpose, you should find in favor of the plaintiff. If you find that there existed a reasonable relationship between the city's decision and a legitimate public purpose, you should find in favor of the city. As long as the regulatory action by the city substantially advances their legitimate public purpose, . . . its underlying motives and reasons are not to be inquired into." *Id.* at 304.

The essence of these instructions was proposed by the city.

The jury delivered a general verdict for Del Monte Dunes on its takings claim, a separate verdict for Del Monte Dunes on its equal protection claim, and a damages award of $1.45 million. After the jury's verdict, the District Court ruled for the city on the substantive due process claim, stating that its ruling was not inconsistent with the jury's verdict on the equal protection or the takings claim. The court later denied the city's motions for a new trial or for judgment as a matter of law.

The Court of Appeals affirmed. 95 F.3d 1422 (CA9 1996). The court first ruled that the District Court did not err in allowing Del Monte Dunes' regulatory takings claim to be tried to a jury, 95 F.3d at 1428, because Del Monte Dunes had a right to a jury trial under § 1983, 95 F.3d at 1426-1427, and whether Del Monte Dunes had been denied all economically viable use of the property and whether the city's denial of the final proposal substantially advanced legitimate public interests were, on the facts of this case, questions suitable for the jury, 95 F.3d at 1430. The court ruled that sufficient evidence had been presented to the jury from which it reasonably could have decided each of these questions in Del Monte Dunes' favor. 95 F.3d at 1430-1434. Because upholding the verdict on the regulatory takings claim was sufficient to support the award of damages, the court did not address the equal protection claim. 95 F.3d at 1426.

The questions presented in the city's petition for certiorari were (1) whether issues of liability were properly submitted to the jury on Del Monte Dunes' regulatory takings claim, (2) whether the Court of Appeals impermissibly based its decision on a standard that allowed the jury to reweigh the reasonableness of the city's land-use decision, and (3) whether the Court of Appeals erred in assuming that the rough-proportionality standard of Dolan v. City of Tigard, 512 U.S. 374 (1994), applied to this case. We granted certiorari, and now address these questions in reverse order.

In the course of holding a reasonable jury could have found the city's denial of the final proposal not substantially related to legitimate public interests, the Court of Appeals stated: "even if the City had a legitimate interest in denying Del Monte's development application, its action must be 'roughly proportional' to furthering that interest . . . . That is, the City's denial must be related 'both in nature and extent to the impact of the proposed development.'" 95 F.3d at 1430, quoting *Dolan, supra*, at 391.

Although in a general sense concerns for proportionality animate the Takings Clause, see Armstrong v. United States, 364 U.S. 40, 49 (1960) ("The Fifth Amendment's guarantee . . . was designed to bar the Government from forcing some people alone to bear public burdens which, in all fairness and justice, should be borne by the public as a whole"), we have not extended the rough-proportionality test of *Dolan* beyond the special context of exactions—land-use decisions conditioning approval of development on the dedication of property to public use. See Dolan, *supra*, at 385; Nollan v. California Coastal Comm'n, 483 U.S. 825, 841 (1987). The rule applied in *Dolan* considers whether dedications demanded as conditions of development are proportional to the development's anticipated impacts. It was not designed to address, and is not readily applicable to, the much different questions arising where, as here, the landowner's challenge is based not on excessive exactions but on denial of development. We believe, accordingly, that the rough-proportionality test of *Dolan* is inapposite to a case such as this one.

The instructions given to the jury, however, did not mention proportionality, let alone require it to find for Del Monte Dunes unless the city's actions were roughly proportional to its asserted interests. The Court of Appeals' discussion of rough proportionality, we conclude, was unnecessary to its decision to sustain the jury's verdict. Although the court stated that "significant evidence supports Del Monte's claim that the City's actions were disproportional to both the nature and extent of the impact of the proposed development," 95 F.3d at 1432, it did so only after holding that

> "Del Monte provided evidence sufficient to rebut each of these reasons [for denying the final proposal]. Taken together, Del Monte argued that the City's reasons for denying their application were invalid and that it unfairly intended to forestall any reasonable development of the Dunes. In light of the evidence proffered by Del Monte, the City has incorrectly argued that no rational juror could conclude that the City's denial of Del Monte's application lacked a sufficient nexus with its stated objectives." 95 F.3d at 1431-1432.

Given this holding, it was unnecessary for the Court of Appeals to discuss rough proportionality. That it did so is irrelevant to our disposition of the case.

The city challenges the Court of Appeals' holding that the jury could have found the city's denial of the final development plan not reasonably related to legitimate public interests. Although somewhat obscure, the city's argument is not cast as a challenge to the sufficiency of the evidence; rather, the city maintains that the Court of Appeals adopted a legal standard for regulatory takings liability that allows juries to second-guess public land-use policy.

As the city itself proposed the essence of the instructions given to the jury, it cannot now contend that the instructions did not provide an accurate statement of the law. In any event, although this Court has provided neither a definitive statement of the elements of a claim for a temporary regulatory taking nor a thorough explanation of the nature or applicability of the requirement that a regulation substantially advance legitimate public interests outside the context of required dedications or exactions, cf., *e.g.*, Nollan, 483 U.S. at 834-835, n. 3, we note that the trial court's instructions are consistent with our previous general discussions of regulatory takings liability. The city did not challenge below the applicability or continued viability of the general test for regulatory takings liability recited by these authorities and upon which the jury instructions appear to have been modeled. Given the posture of the case before us, we decline the suggestions of *amici* to revisit these precedents.

To the extent the city contends the judgment sustained by the Court of Appeals was based upon a jury determination of the reasonableness of its general zoning laws or land-use policies, its argument can be squared neither with the instructions given to the jury nor the theory on which the case was tried. The instructions did not ask the jury whether the city's zoning ordinances or policies were unreasonable but only whether "the City's decision to reject the plaintiff's 190 unit development proposal did not substantially advance a legitimate public purpose," App. 303, that is, whether "there was no reasonable relationship between the city's denial of the . . . proposal and legitimate public purpose." *Id.* at 304. Furthermore, Del Monte Dunes' lawyers were explicit in conceding that "this case is not about the right of a city, in this case the city of Monterey, to regulate land." 10 Tr. 1286 (Feb. 9, 1994). See also *id.* at 1287 (proposals were made "keeping in mind various regulations and requirements, heights, setbacks, and densities and all that. That's not what this case is about"); *id.* at 1287-1288 ("They have the right to set height limits. They have the right to talk about where they want access. That's not what this case is about. We all accept that in today's society, cities and counties can tell a land owner what to do to some reasonable extent with their property"). Though not presented for review, Del Monte Dunes' equal protection argument that it had received treatment inconsistent with zoning decisions made in favor of owners of similar properties, and the jury's verdict for Del Monte Dunes on this claim, confirm the understanding of the jury and Del Monte Dunes that the complaint was not about general laws or ordinances but about a particular zoning decision.

The instructions regarding the city's decision also did not allow the jury to consider the reasonableness, *per se*, of the customized, ad hoc conditions imposed on the property's development, and Del Monte Dunes did not suggest otherwise. On the contrary, Del Monte Dunes disclaimed this theory of the case in express terms: "Del Monte Dunes partnership did not file this lawsuit because they were complaining about giving the public the beach, keeping it [the development] out of the view shed, devoting and [giving] to the State all this habitat area. One-third [of the] property is going to be given away for the public use forever. That's not what we filed the lawsuit about." *Id.* at 1288; see also *id.* at 1288-1289 (conceding that the city may "ask an owner to give away a third of the property without getting a dime in compensation for it and providing parking lots for the public and habitats for the butterfly, and boardwalks").

Rather, the jury was instructed to consider whether the city's denial of the final proposal was reasonably related to a legitimate public purpose. Even with regard to this issue, however, the jury was not given free rein to second-guess the city's land-use policies. Rather, the jury was instructed, in unmistakable terms, that the various purposes asserted by the city were legitimate public interests.

The jury, furthermore, was not asked to evaluate the city's decision in isolation but rather in context, and, in particular, in light of the tortuous and protracted history of attempts to develop the property. Although Del Monte Dunes was allowed to introduce evidence challenging the asserted factual bases for the city's decision, it also highlighted the shifting nature of the city's demands and the inconsistency of its decision with the recommendation of its professional staff, as well as with its previous decisions. Del Monte Dunes also introduced evidence of the city's long-standing interest in acquiring the property for public use.

In short, the question submitted to the jury on this issue was confined to whether, in light of all the history and the context of the case, the city's particular decision to deny Del Monte Dunes' final development proposal was reasonably related to the city's proffered justifications. This question was couched, moreover, in an instruction that had been proposed in essence by the city, and as to which the city made no objection.

Thus, despite the protests of the city and its *amici*, it is clear that the Court of Appeals did not adopt a rule of takings law allowing wholesale interference by judge or jury with municipal land-use policies, laws, or routine regulatory decisions. To the extent the city argues that, as a matter of law, its land-use decisions are immune from judicial scrutiny under all circumstances, its position is contrary to settled regulatory takings principles. We reject this claim of error.

We next address whether it was proper for the District Court to submit the question of liability on Del Monte Dunes' regulatory takings claim to the jury. . . . As the Court of Appeals recognized, the answer depends on whether Del Monte Dunes had a statutory or constitutional right to a jury trial, and, if it did, the nature and extent of the right. Del Monte Dunes asserts the right to a jury trial is conferred by § 1983 and by the Seventh Amendment. . . .

The Seventh Amendment provides that "in Suits at common law, where the value in controversy shall exceed twenty dollars, the right of trial by jury shall be preserved . . . ." Consistent with the textual mandate that the jury right be preserved, our interpretation of the Amendment has been guided by historical analysis comprising two principal inquiries. "We ask, first, whether we are dealing with a cause of action that either was tried at law at the time of the founding or is at least analogous to one that was." Markman v. Westview Instruments, Inc., 517 U.S. 370, 376 (1996). "If the action in question belongs in the law category, we then ask whether the particular trial decision must fall to the jury in order to preserve the substance of the common-law right as it existed in 1791." *Ibid.* . . .

Del Monte Dunes brought this suit pursuant to § 1983 to vindicate its constitutional rights. We hold that a § 1983 suit seeking legal relief is an action at law within the meaning of the Seventh Amendment. JUSTICE SCALIA's concurring opinion presents a comprehensive and convincing analysis of the historical and constitutional reasons for this conclusion. We agree with his analysis and conclusion.

It is undisputed that when the Seventh Amendment was adopted there was no action equivalent to § 1983, framed in specific terms for vindicating constitutional rights. It is settled law, however, that the Seventh Amendment jury guarantee extends to statutory claims unknown to the common law, so long as the claims can be said to "sound basically in tort," and seek legal relief.

As JUSTICE SCALIA explains, there can be no doubt that claims brought pursuant to § 1983 sound in tort. Just as common-law tort actions provide redress for interference with protected personal or property interests, § 1983 provides relief for invasions of rights protected under federal law. Recognizing the essential character of the statute, "'we have repeatedly noted that 42 U.S.C. § 1983 creates a species of tort liability,'" Heck v. Humphrey, 512 U.S. 477, 483 (1994) (quoting Memphis Community School Dist. v. Stachura, 477 U.S. 299, 305 (1986)), and have interpreted the statute in light of the "background of tort liability," Monroe v. Pape, 365 U.S. 167, 187 (1961) (overruled on other grounds, Monell v. New York City Dept. of Social Servs., 436 U.S. 658 (1978)). Our settled understanding of § 1983 and the Seventh Amendment thus compel the conclusion that a suit for legal relief brought under the statute is an action at law.

Here Del Monte Dunes sought legal relief. It was entitled to proceed in federal court under § 1983 because, at the time of the city's actions, the State of California did not provide a compensatory remedy for temporary regulatory takings. The constitutional injury alleged, therefore, is not that property was taken but that it was taken without just compensation. Had the city paid for the property or had an adequate postdeprivation remedy been available, Del Monte Dunes would have suffered no constitutional injury from the taking alone. See *Williamson*, 473 U.S. at 194-195. Because its statutory action did not accrue until it was denied just compensation, in a strict sense Del Monte Dunes sought not just compensation *per se* but rather damages for the unconstitutional denial of such compensation. Damages for a constitutional violation are a legal remedy.

Even when viewed as a simple suit for just compensation, we believe Del Monte Dunes' action sought essentially legal relief. . . .

Having decided Del Monte Dunes' § 1983 suit was an action at law, we must determine whether the particular issues of liability were proper for determination by the jury. See Markman v. Westview Instruments, Inc., 517 U.S. 370 (1996). In actions at law, issues that are proper for the jury must be submitted to it "to preserve the right to a jury's resolution of the ultimate dispute," as guaranteed by the Seventh Amendment. 517 U.S. at 377. We determine whether issues are proper for the jury, when possible, "by using the historical method, much as we do in characterizing the suits and actions within which [the issues] arise." *Id.* at 378. We look to history to determine whether the particular issues, or analogous ones, were decided by judge or by jury in suits at common law at the time the Seventh Amendment was adopted. Where history does not provide a clear answer, we look to precedent and functional considerations.

Just as no exact analogue of Del Monte Dunes' § 1983 suit can be identified at common law, so also can we find no precise analogue for the specific test of liability submitted to the jury in this case. We do know that in suits sounding in tort for money damages, questions of liability were decided by the jury, rather than the judge, in most cases. This allocation preserved the jury's role in resolving what was often the heart of the dispute between plaintiff and defendant. Although these general observations provide some guidance on the proper allocation between judge and jury of the liability issues in this case, they do not establish a definitive answer.

We look next to our existing precedents. Although this Court has decided many regulatory takings cases, none of our decisions has addressed the proper allocation of liability determinations between judge and jury in explicit terms. This is not surprising. Most of our regulatory takings decisions have reviewed suits against the United States, suits decided by state courts, or suits seeking only injunctive relief. It is settled law that the Seventh Amendment does not apply in these contexts. . . .

In actions at law predominantly factual issues are in most cases allocated to the jury. . . .

Almost from the inception of our regulatory takings doctrine, we have held that whether a regulation of property goes so far that "there must be an exercise of eminent domain and compensation to sustain the act . . . depends upon the particular facts." Pennsylvania Coal Co. v. Mahon, 260 U.S. 393, 413 (1922); accord *Keystone Bituminous Coal*, 480 U.S. at 473-474. Consistent with this understanding, we have described determinations of liability in regulatory takings cases as "'essentially ad hoc, factual inquiries,'" *Lucas, supra*, at 1015 (quoting Penn Central Transp. Co. v. New York City, 438 U.S. 104, 124 (1978)), requiring "complex factual assessments of the purposes and economic effects of government actions," *Yee*, 503 U.S. at 523.

In accordance with these pronouncements, we hold that the issue whether a landowner has been deprived of all economically viable use of his property is a predominantly factual question. . . . [I]n actions at law otherwise within the purview of the Seventh Amendment, this question is for the jury.

The jury's role in determining whether a land-use decision substantially advances legitimate public interests within the meaning of our regulatory takings doctrine presents a more difficult question. Although our cases make clear that this inquiry involves an essential factual component, it no doubt has a legal aspect as well, and is probably best understood as a mixed question of fact and law.

In this case, the narrow question submitted to the jury was whether, when viewed in light of the context and protracted history of the development application process, the city's decision to reject a particular development plan bore a reasonable relationship to its proffered justifications. As the Court of Appeals recognized, this question was "essentially fact-bound [in] nature." 95 F.3d at 1430 (internal quotation marks omitted) (alteration by Court of Appeals). Under these circumstances, we hold that it was proper to submit this narrow, factbound question to the jury.

We note the limitations of our Seventh Amendment holding. We do not address the jury's role in an ordinary inverse condemnation suit. The action here was brought under § 1983, a context in which the jury's role in vindicating constitutional rights has long been recognized by the federal courts. A federal court, moreover, cannot entertain a takings claim under § 1983 unless or until the complaining landowner has been denied an adequate postdeprivation remedy. Even the State of California, where this suit arose, now provides a facially adequate procedure for obtaining just compensation for temporary takings such as this one. Our decision is also circumscribed in its conceptual reach. The posture of the case does not present an appropriate occasion to define with precision the elements of a temporary regulatory takings claim; although the city objected to submitting issues of liability to the jury at all, it approved the instructions that were submitted to the jury and therefore has no basis to challenge them.

For these reasons, we do not attempt a precise demarcation of the respective provinces of judge and jury in determining whether a zoning decision substantially advances legitimate governmental interests. The city and its *amici* suggest that sustaining the judgment here will undermine the uniformity of the law and eviscerate state and local zoning authority by subjecting all land-use decisions to plenary, and potentially inconsistent, jury review. Our decision raises no such specter. Del Monte Dunes did not bring a broad challenge to the constitutionality of the city's general land-use ordinances or policies, and our holding does not extend to a challenge of that sort. In such a context, the determination whether the statutory purposes were legitimate, or whether the purposes, though legitimate, were furthered by the law or general policy, might well fall within the province of the judge. Nor was the gravamen of Del Monte Dunes' complaint even that the city's general regulations were unreasonable as applied to Del Monte Dunes' property; we do not address the proper trial allocation of the various questions that might arise in that context. Rather, to the extent Del Monte Dunes' challenge was premised on unreasonable governmental action, the theory argued and tried to the jury was that the city's denial of the final development permit was inconsistent not only with the city's general ordinances and policies but even with the shifting ad hoc restrictions previously imposed by the city. Del Monte Dunes' argument, in short, was not that the city had followed its zoning ordinances and policies but rather that it had not done so. As is often true in § 1983 actions, the disputed questions were whether the government had denied a constitutional right in acting outside the bounds of its authority, and, if so, the extent of any resulting damages. These were questions for the jury.

For the reasons stated, the judgment of the Court of Appeals is affirmed.

It is so ordered.

JUSTICE SCALIA, concurring in part and concurring in the judgment. . . .

In my view, all § 1983 actions must be treated alike insofar as the Seventh Amendment right to jury trial is concerned; that right exists when monetary damages are sought; and the issues submitted to the jury in the present case were properly sent there. . . .

JUSTICE SOUTER, with whom JUSTICE O'CONNOR, JUSTICE GINSBURG, and JUSTICE BREYER join, concurring in part and dissenting in part. . . .

Respondents had no right to a jury trial either by statute or under the Constitution; the District Court thus erred in submitting their claim to a jury. In holding to the contrary, that such a right does exist under the Seventh Amendment, the Court misconceives a taking claim under § 1983 and draws a false analogy between such a claim and a tort action. I respectfully dissent from the erroneous Parts III and IV of the Court's opinion.

I see eye to eye with the Court on some of the preliminary issues. I agree in rejecting extension of "rough proportionality" as a standard for reviewing land-use regulations generally and so join Parts I and II of the majority opinion. . . . The Court soundly concedes that at the adoption of the Seventh Amendment there was no action like the modern inverse condemnation suit for obtaining just compensation when the government took property without invoking formal condemnation procedures. Like the Court, I am accordingly remitted to a search for any analogy that may exist and a consideration of any implication going to the substance of the jury right that the results of that enquiry may raise. But this common launching ground is where our agreement ends.

The city's proposed analogy of inverse condemnation proceedings to direct ones is intuitively sensible, given their common Fifth Amendment constitutional source and link to the sovereign's power of eminent domain.

The intuition is borne out by closer analysis of the respective proceedings. The ultimate issue is identical in both direct and inverse condemnation actions: a determination of "the fair market value of the property [taken] on the date it is appropriated," as the measure of compensation required by the Fifth Amendment. Kirby Forest Industries, Inc. v. United States, 467 U.S. 1, 10 (1984). . . .

The strength of the analogy is fatal to respondents' claim to a jury trial as a matter of right. Reaffirming what was already a well-established principle, the Court explained over a century ago that "the estimate of the just compensation for property taken for the public use, under the right of eminent domain, is not required to be made by a jury," Bauman v. Ross, 167 U.S. 548, 593 (1897) (citing, *inter alia*, Custiss v. Georgetown & Alexandria Turnpike Co., 10 U.S. 233 (1810); United States v. Jones, 109 U.S. 513 (1883); and Shoemaker v. United States, 147 U.S. 282, 300, 301 (1893)),[1] and we have since then thought it "long . . . settled that there is no constitutional right to a jury in eminent domain proceedings." United States v. Reynolds, 397 U.S. 14, 18 (1970). . . . [A]t the time of the framing the notion of regulatory taking or inverse condemnation was yet to be derived, the closest analogue to the then-unborn claim was that of direct condemnation, and the right to compensation for such direct takings carried with it no right to a jury trial, just as the jury right is foreign to it in the modern era. On accepted Seventh Amendment analysis, then, there is no reason to find a jury right either by direct analogy or for the sake of preserving the substance of any jury practice known to the law at the crucial time. Indeed, the analogy with direct condemnation actions is so strong that there is every reason to conclude that inverse condemnation should implicate no jury right. . . .

Notes

1. State and federal endangered species protections have faced not only regulatory takings lawsuits, but other constitutional challenges as well. See, for example, National Ass'n of Home Builders v. Babbitt, 130 F.3d 1041, 1043, 1057-58, 1060-61 (D.C. Cir. 1997):

> The National Association of Home Builders of the United States, the Building Industry Legal Defense Fund, the County of San Bernardino, and the City of Colton, California brought this action in the United States District Court for the District of Columbia to challenge an application of section 9(a)(1) of the Endangered Species Act ("ESA"), 16 U.S.C. § 1538(a)(1), which makes it unlawful for any person to "take"— *i.e.*, "to harass, harm, pursue, hunt, shoot, wound, kill, trap, capture, or collect, or attempt to engage in any such conduct," 16 U.S.C. § 1532(19)—any endangered species. The plaintiffs sought a declaration that the application of section 9 of the ESA to the Delhi Sands Flower-Loving Fly ("the Fly"), which is located only in California, exceeds Congress'

---

1. In *Bauman*, the Court upheld a statute (providing for condemnation of land for streets) that contemplated a form of jury "differing from an ordinary jury in consisting of less than twelve persons, and in not being required to act with unanimity," and stated that the just compensation determination "may be entrusted by Congress to commissioners appointed by a court or by the executive, or to an inquest consisting of more or fewer men than an ordinary jury." 167 U.S. at 593. The Court relied upon prior cases that had assumed the absence of a constitutional right to a jury determination of just compensation.

Commerce Clause power and an injunction against application of the section to the plaintiff's construction activities in areas containing Fly habitat.

This dispute arose when the Fish and Wildlife Service ("FWS") placed the Fly, an insect that is native to the San Bernardino area of California, on the endangered species list. The listing of the Fly, the habitat of which is located entirely within an eight mile radius in southwestern San Bernardino County and northwestern Riverside County, California, forced San Bernardino County to alter plans to construct a new hospital on a recently purchased site that the FWS had determined contained Fly habitat. The FWS and San Bernardino County agreed on a plan that would allow the County to build the hospital and a power plant in the area designated as Fly habitat in return for modification of the construction plans and purchase and set aside of nearby land as Fly habitat. In November 1995, FWS issued a permit to allow construction of the power plant. During the same month, however, the County notified the FWS that it planned to redesign a nearby intersection to improve emergency vehicle access to the hospital. The FWS informed the County that expansion of the intersection as planned would likely lead to a "taking" of the Fly in violation of ESA section 9(a). After brief unsuccessful negotiations between the County and FWS, the County filed suit in district court challenging the application of section 9(a)(1) to the Fly.

Two members of the three-judge panel of the U.S. Court of Appeals for the District of Columbia (D.C.) Circuit found that the "take" provision of the Endangered Species Act (ESA) (§9(a)(1)) fell within Congress' Commerce Clause power. Judge Karen L. Henderson concurred with Judge Patricia Wald's conclusion, but on different grounds, explaining:

Judge Wald first asserts that section 9(a)(1) is a proper regulation of the "channels of commerce." In support she cites decisions upholding regulation of commercially marketable goods, such as machine guns and lumber, and public accommodations. In each case, the object of regulation was necessarily connected to movement of persons or things interstate and could therefore be characterized as regulation of the channels of commerce. Not so with an endangered species, as the facts here graphically demonstrate. The Delhi Sands Flower-loving Flies the Department of the Interior seeks to protect are (along with many other species no doubt) entirely intrastate creatures. They do not move among states either on their own or through human agency. As a result, like the Gun-Free School Zones Act in [United States v.] *Lopez*, the statutory protection of the flies "is not a regulation of the use of the channels of interstate commerce." 514 U.S. 549 at 559 [(1995)].

Judge Wald also justifies the protection of endangered species on the ground that the loss of biodiversity "substantially affects" interstate commerce because of the resulting loss of potential medical or economic benefit. Yet her opinion acknowledges that it is "impossible to calculate the exact impact" of the economic loss of an endangered species. As far as I can tell, it is equally impossible to ascertain that there will be any such impact at all. It may well be that no species endangered now or in the future will have any of the economic value proposed. Given that possibility, I do not see how we can say that the protection of an endangered species has any effect on interstate commerce (much less a substantial one) by virtue of an uncertain potential medical or economic value. Nevertheless, I believe that the loss of biodiversity itself has a substantial effect on our ecosystem and likewise on interstate commerce. In addition, I would uphold section

9(a)(1) as applied here because the Department's protection of the flies regulates and substantially affects commercial development activity which is plainly interstate.

Dissenting Judge Frank Sentelle painted this stark picture of the effect that the ESA had on the proposed project:

> In 1982, the County began considering construction of a $470 million "state-of-the-art," "earthquake-proof" hospital complex. The day before ground breaking was scheduled to occur in 1993, the U.S. Fish and Wildlife Service ("Service") of the Department of the Interior ("Interior") added the fly to the endangered species list and notified the County that construction of the hospital, on County land using County funds, would harm a colony of six to eight flies and would therefore violate federal law. To prevent being prosecuted by the Service, County officials were forced to move the hospital complex 250 feet northward and to set aside 8 acres of land for the fly, delaying construction for a year and costing County taxpayers around $3.5 million. The Service also imposed a variety of other stringent requirements, including preservation of a flight corridor for the insect which today prevents improvements to a traffic intersection necessary to allow emergency access and avoid "virtual gridlock" when the hospital opens. At one point, the Service threatened to require shutting down the eight-lane San Bernardino Freeway (US 10, one of the most heavily traveled in southern California) for two months every year (I am not making this up). It did later drop this demand. The Service has also impeded several localities from complying with County-mandated weed-control programs which are an integral part of preventing brush fires in the area. Construction planning and projects, including an electrical substation and housing developments, have also been threatened, impeded, or prohibited because of the fly. Local land-use planning, including the authority to balance environmental concerns with development in a way to best serve citizens' interests, has been disrupted; the financial health of the local governments has been impacted; a local enterprise zone has been threatened; and private land development has been impeded.

Judge Sentelle's skepticism about the need for and constitutional validity of federal protections for the fly was palpable (and entertaining):

> Unfortunately for the County and its citizens, however, the Secretary of the Interior has determined that the word "take" includes within its definition "harm" and, therefore, activities which alter the habitat of an endangered species are covered by the statute prohibiting the taking of that species since the habitat modification might harm it. Even more unfortunately for the County and the citizens, the Supreme Court has agreed with that expansive definition of "take." Babbitt v. Sweet Home Chapter of Communities for a Great Oregon, 515 U.S. 687 (1995). Therefore, we may take it as a given that the statute forbidding the taking of endangered species can be used, provided it passes constitutional muster, to prevent counties and their citizens from building hospitals or from driving to those hospitals by routes in which the bugs smashed upon their windshields might turn out to include the Delhi Sands Flower-Loving Fly or some other species of rare insect. That leaves the question for today as: by what constitutional justification does the federal government purport to regulate local activities that might disturb a local fly?

Not surprisingly, he concluded that "attempts to regulate the killing of a fly under the Commerce Clause fail because there is certainly no interstate commerce in the Delhi Sands Flower-Loving

Fly." For more on the issue that divided this court, see Bradford C. Mank, *Can Congress Regulate Intrastate Endangered Species Under the Commerce Clause*, 69 Brooklyn L. Rev. 923 (2004).

2. Landowners have generally been unsuccessful in making *regulatory* takings challenges based on habitat protection under the ESA. In Tulare Lake Basin v. United States, 49 Fed. Cl. 313, 314, 319 (Fed. Cl. 2001), a group of water users successfully demonstrated that the government had effected a *physical* taking, however. They convinced the trial court "that their contractually-conferred right to the use of water was taken from them when the federal government imposed water use restrictions under the Endangered Species Act":

> Unlike other species of property where use restrictions may limit some, but not all of the incidents of ownership, the denial of a right to the use of water accomplishes a complete extinction of all value. Thus, by limiting plaintiffs' ability to use an amount of water to which they would otherwise be entitled, the government has essentially substituted itself as the beneficiary of the contract rights with regard to that water and totally displaced the contract holder. . . .To the extent, then, that the federal government, by preventing plaintiffs from using the water to which they would otherwise have been entitled, have rendered the usufructuary right to that water valueless, they have thus effected a physical taking.

The very stiff challenge for other property owners is to convince judges (and, perhaps, juries) that they have suffered the same (or an analogous) physical invasion at the hands of federal (or state) endangered species regulators as the *Tulare Lake* plaintiffs.

3. The disagreement among the Justices in *Del Monte Dunes* over whether regulatory takings are more tort- or eminent-domain-like derives from a fundamental problem with the very idea that a regulation can amount to a violation of the Takings Clause. Some forms of inverse condemnation—floods and other physical harms caused by government actors—can easily be placed in the "tort box." Indeed, the reason why courts in "physical takings" cases such as Pumpelly v. Green Bay Co., 80 U.S. 166 (1872) (the flooding of the plaintiff's property was caused by dam construction) invoked the protections afforded by state takings clauses may well have been the fact that sovereign immunity shielded the government from damages actions sounding in common-law tort. More recently, however, the Court has emphasized that what the two *per se* situations discussed in *Lucas* and the (admittedly small) set of fact patterns that violates the *Penn Central* balancing test have in common are their similarity to the affirmative exercise of eminent domain. As explained in Lingle v. Chevron U.S.A. Inc., 544 U.S. 528, 539 (2005): "Each aims to identify regulatory actions that are functionally equivalent to the classic taking in which government directly appropriates private property or ousts the owner from his domain. Accordingly, each of these tests focuses directly upon the severity of the burden that government imposes upon private property rights." The dissenters in *Del Monte Dunes* can justifiably ask whether it makes sense to treat regulatory takings as the "functional equivalent" of condemnation for one purpose (determining if the property has been "taken") but not for another (determining if a jury is appropriate).

VIII. Wetlands Restrictions

Rhode Island Coastal Resources Management Program §210.3

A. Definitions

1. Coastal wetlands include salt marshes and freshwater or brackish wetlands contiguous to salt marshes or physiographical features. Areas of open water within coastal wetlands

are considered a part of the wetland. In addition, coastal wetlands also include freshwater and/or brackish wetlands that are directly associated with non-tidal coastal ponds and freshwater or brackish wetlands that occur on a barrier beach or are separated from tidal waters by a barrier beach. . . .

B. Findings

1. Coastal wetlands are important for a variety of reasons. They provide food and shelter for large populations of juvenile fish and are nurseries for several species of fish. The mud flats and creeks associated with many coastal wetlands are rich in shellfish, particularly soft-shelled clams. Coastal wetlands also provide important habitat for shore birds and waterfowl, and many are among the most scenic features of the Rhode Island shore. Coastal wetlands are effective in slowing erosion along protected shores. . . .

4. Land uses and activities abutting coastal wetlands may have a strong impact upon the wetland itself. Nearby drainage patterns which affect sedimentation processes and the salinity of waters may easily be altered, with detrimental effects. Wildlife must be protected from harassment. Bulkheading and filling along the inland perimeter of a marsh prevents inland migration of wetland vegetation as sea level rises. . . .

PALAZZOLO v. RHODE ISLAND
533 U.S. 606 (2001)

JUSTICE KENNEDY delivered the opinion of the Court. . . .

The town of Westerly is on an edge of the Rhode Island coastline. The town's western border is the Pawcatuck River, which at that point is the boundary between Rhode Island and Connecticut. . . .

Westerly today has about 20,000 year-round residents, and thousands of summer visitors come to enjoy its beaches and coastal advantages.

One of the more popular attractions is Misquamicut State Beach, a lengthy expanse of coastline facing Block Island Sound and beyond to the Atlantic Ocean. The primary point of access to the beach is Atlantic Avenue, a well-traveled 3-mile stretch of road running along the coastline within the town's limits. At its western end, Atlantic Avenue is something of a commercial strip, with restaurants, hotels, arcades, and other typical seashore businesses. The pattern of development becomes more residential as the road winds eastward onto a narrow spine of land bordered to the south by the beach and the ocean, and to the north by Winnapaug Pond, an intertidal inlet often used by residents for boating, fishing, and shellfishing.

In 1959 petitioner, a lifelong Westerly resident, decided to invest in three undeveloped, adjoining parcels along this eastern stretch of Atlantic Avenue. To the north, the property faces, and borders upon, Winnapaug Pond; the south of the property faces Atlantic Avenue and the beachfront homes abutting it on the other side, and beyond that the dunes and the beach. To purchase and hold the property, petitioner and associates formed Shore Gardens, Inc. (SGI). After SGI purchased the property petitioner bought out his associates and became the sole shareholder. In the first decade of SGI's ownership of the property the corporation submitted a plat to the town subdividing the property into 80 lots; and it engaged in various transactions that left it with 74 lots, which together encompassed about 20 acres. During the same period SGI also made initial attempts to develop the property and submitted intermittent applications to state agencies to fill substantial portions of the parcel. Most of the property was then, as it is now, salt marsh subject to tidal flooding. The wet ground and permeable soil would require considerable fill—as much as six feet in some places—before significant structures could be built. SGI's proposal, submitted in

1962 to the Rhode Island Division of Harbors and Rivers (DHR), sought to dredge from Winnapaug Pond and fill the entire property. The application was denied for lack of essential information. A second, similar proposal followed a year later. A third application, submitted in 1966 while the second application was pending, proposed more limited filling of the land for use as a private beach club. These latter two applications were referred to the Rhode Island Department of Natural Resources, which indicated initial assent. The agency later withdrew approval, however, citing adverse environmental impacts. SGI did not contest the ruling.

No further attempts to develop the property were made for over a decade. Two intervening events, however, become important to the issues presented. First, in 1971, Rhode Island enacted legislation creating the Council, an agency charged with the duty of protecting the State's coastal properties. 1971 R. I. Pub. Laws ch. 279, § 1 et seq. Regulations promulgated by the Council designated salt marshes like those on SGI's property as protected "coastal wetlands," Rhode Island Coastal Resources Management Program (CRMP) § 210.3 (as amended, June 28, 1983), on which development is limited to a great extent. Second, in 1978 SGI's corporate charter was revoked for failure to pay corporate income taxes; and title to the property passed, by operation of state law, to petitioner as the corporation's sole shareholder.

In 1983 petitioner, now the owner, renewed the efforts to develop the property. An application to the Council, resembling the 1962 submission, requested permission to construct a wooden bulkhead along the shore of Winnapaug Pond and to fill the entire marsh land area. The Council rejected the application, noting it was "vague and inadequate for a project of this size and nature." App. 16. The agency also found that "the proposed activities will have significant impacts upon the waters and wetlands of Winnapaug Pond," and concluded that "the proposed alteration . . . will conflict with the Coastal Resources Management Plan presently in effect." *Id.* at 17. Petitioner did not appeal the agency's determination.

Petitioner went back to the drawing board, this time hiring counsel and preparing a more specific and limited proposal for use of the property. The new application, submitted to the Council in 1985, echoed the 1966 request to build a private beach club. The details do not tend to inspire the reader with an idyllic coastal image, for the proposal was to fill 11 acres of the property with gravel to accommodate "50 cars with boat trailers, a dumpster, port-a-johns, picnic tables, barbecue pits of concrete, and other trash receptacles." *Id.* at 25.

The application fared no better with the Council than previous ones. Under the agency's regulations, a landowner wishing to fill salt marsh on Winnapaug Pond needed a "special exception" from the Council. CRMP § 130. In a short opinion the Council said the beach club proposal conflicted with the regulatory standard for a special exception. To secure a special exception the proposed activity must serve "a compelling public purpose which provides benefits to the public as a whole as opposed to individual or private interests." CRMP § 130A(1). This time petitioner appealed the decision to the Rhode Island courts, challenging the Council's conclusion as contrary to principles of state administrative law. The Council's decision was affirmed.

Petitioner filed an inverse condemnation action in Rhode Island Superior Court, asserting that the State's wetlands regulations, as applied by the Council to his parcel, had taken the property without compensation in violation of the Fifth and Fourteenth Amendments. The suit alleged the Council's action deprived him of "all economically beneficial use" of his property, ibid. resulting in a total taking requiring compensation under Lucas v. South Carolina Coastal Council, 505 U.S. 1003 (1992). He sought damages in the amount of $3,150,000, a figure derived from an appraiser's estimate as to the value of a 74-lot residential subdivision. The State countered with a host of defenses. After a bench trial, a justice of the Superior Court ruled against petitioner, accepting some of the State's theories.

The Rhode Island Supreme Court affirmed. 746 A.2d 707 (2000).Like the Superior Court, the State Supreme Court recited multiple grounds for rejecting petitioner's suit. The court held, first, that petitioner's takings claim was not ripe; second, that petitioner had no right to challenge regulations predating 1978, when he succeeded to legal ownership of the property from SGI; and third, that the claim of deprivation of all economically beneficial use was contradicted by undisputed evidence that he had $200,000 in development value remaining on an upland parcel of the property. In addition to holding petitioner could not assert a takings claim based on the denial of all economic use the court concluded he could not recover under the more general test of Penn Central Transp. Co. v. New York City, 438 U.S. 104 (1978). On this claim, too, the date of acquisition of the parcel was found determinative, and the court held he could have had "no reasonable investment-backed expectations that were affected by this regulation" because it predated his ownership, 746 A.2d at 717; see also *Penn Central, supra*, at 124.

We disagree with the Supreme Court of Rhode Island as to the first two of these conclusions; and, we hold, the court was correct to conclude that the owner is not deprived of all economic use of his property because the value of upland portions is substantial. We remand for further consideration of the claim under the principles set forth in *Penn Central*. . . .

At the outset, . . . we face the two threshold considerations invoked by the state court to bar the claim: ripeness, and acquisition which postdates the regulation. . . .

[After finding that the case was ripe for review, the majority proceeded to the second threshold issue.]

When the Council promulgated its wetlands regulations, the disputed parcel was owned not by petitioner but by the corporation of which he was sole shareholder. When title was transferred to petitioner by operation of law, the wetlands regulations were in force. The state court held the postregulation acquisition of title was fatal to the claim for deprivation of all economic use and to the *Penn Central* claim. While the first holding was couched in terms of background principles of state property law, see *Lucas*, 505 U.S. at 1015, and the second in terms of petitioner's reasonable investment-backed expectations, see *Penn Central*, 438 U.S. at 124, the two holdings together amount to a single, sweeping, rule: A purchaser or a successive title holder like petitioner is deemed to have notice of an earlier-enacted restriction and is barred from claiming that it effects a taking.

The theory underlying the argument that post-enactment purchasers cannot challenge a regulation under the Takings Clause seems to run on these lines: Property rights are created by the State. So, the argument goes, by prospective legislation the State can shape and define property rights and reasonable investment-backed expectations, and subsequent owners cannot claim any injury from lost value. After all, they purchased or took title with notice of the limitation.

The State may not put so potent a Hobbesian stick into the Lockean bundle. The right to improve property, of course, is subject to the reasonable exercise of state authority, including the enforcement of valid zoning and land-use restrictions. See *Pennsylvania Coal Co.*, 260 U.S. at 413 ("Government hardly could go on if to some extent values incident to property could not be diminished without paying for every such change in the general law"). The Takings Clause, however, in certain circumstances allows a landowner to assert that a particular exercise of the State's regulatory power is so unreasonable or onerous as to compel compensation. Just as a prospective enactment, such as a new zoning ordinance, can limit the value of land without effecting a taking because it can be understood as reasonable by all concerned, other enactments are unreasonable and do not become less so through passage of time or title. Were we to accept the State's rule, the postenactment transfer of title would absolve the State of its obligation to defend any action restricting land use, no matter how extreme or unreasonable. A State would be allowed, in effect, to put an expiration date on the Takings Clause. This ought not to be the rule. Future generations, too, have a right to challenge unreasonable limitations on the use and value of land.

Nor does the justification of notice take into account the effect on owners at the time of enactment, who are prejudiced as well. Should an owner attempt to challenge a new regulation, but not survive the process of ripening his or her claim (which, as this case demonstrates, will often take years), under the proposed rule the right to compensation may not by asserted by an heir or successor, and so may not be asserted at all. The State's rule would work a critical alteration to the nature of property, as the newly regulated landowner is stripped of the ability to transfer the interest which was possessed prior to the regulation. The State may not by this means secure a windfall for itself. The proposed rule is, furthermore, capricious in effect. The young owner contrasted with the older owner, the owner with the resources to hold contrasted with the owner with the need to sell, would be in different positions. The Takings Clause is not so quixotic. A blanket rule that purchasers with notice have no compensation right when a claim becomes ripe is too blunt an instrument to accord with the duty to compensate for what is taken.

Direct condemnation, by invocation of the State's power of eminent domain, presents different considerations than cases alleging a taking based on a burdensome regulation. In a direct condemnation action, or when a State has physically invaded the property without filing suit, the fact and extent of the taking are known. In such an instance, it is a general rule of the law of eminent domain that any award goes to the owner at the time of the taking, and that the right to compensation is not passed to a subsequent purchaser. See Danforth v. United States, 308 U.S. 271, 284 (1939); 2 Sackman, Eminent Domain, at § 5.01[5][d][i] ("It is well settled that when there is a taking of property by eminent domain in compliance with the law, it is the owner of the property at the time of the taking who is entitled to compensation"). A challenge to the application of a land-use regulation, by contrast, does not mature until ripeness requirements have been satisfied, under principles we have discussed; until this point an inverse condemnation claim alleging a regulatory taking cannot be maintained. It would be illogical, and unfair, to bar a regulatory takings claim because of the post-enactment transfer of ownership where the steps necessary to make the claim ripe were not taken, or could not have been taken, by a previous owner.

There is controlling precedent for our conclusion. Nollan v. California Coastal Comm'n, 483 U.S. 825 (1987), presented the question whether it was consistent with the Takings Clause for a state regulatory agency to require oceanfront landowners to provide lateral beach access to the public as the condition for a development permit. The principal dissenting opinion observed it was a policy of the California Coastal Commission to require the condition, and that the Nollans, who purchased their home after the policy went into effect, were "on notice that new developments would be approved only if provisions were made for lateral beach access." Id. at 860 (Brennan, J., dissenting). A majority of the Court rejected the proposition. "So long as the Commission could not have deprived the prior owners of the easement without compensating them," the Court reasoned, "the prior owners must be understood to have transferred their full property rights in conveying the lot." Id. at 834, n. 2.

It is argued that Nollan's holding was limited by the later decision in Lucas v. South Carolina Coastal Council, 505 U.S. 1003 (1992). In Lucas the Court observed that a landowner's ability to recover for a government deprivation of all economically beneficial use of property is not absolute but instead is confined by limitations on the use of land which "inhere in the title itself." Id. at 1029. This is so, the Court reasoned, because the landowner is constrained by those "restrictions that background principles of the State's law of property and nuisance already place upon land ownership." Id. at 1029. It is asserted here that Lucas stands for the proposition that any new regulation, once enacted, becomes a background principle of property law which cannot be challenged by those who acquire title after the enactment.

We have no occasion to consider the precise circumstances when a legislative enactment can be deemed a background principle of state law or whether those circumstances are present here. It suffices to say that a regulation that otherwise would be unconstitutional absent compensation is not transformed into a background principle of the State's law by mere virtue of the passage of title. This relative standard would be incompatible with our description of the concept in *Lucas*, which is explained in terms of those common, shared understandings of permissible limitations derived from a State's legal tradition. A regulation or common-law rule cannot be a background principle for some owners but not for others. The determination whether an existing, general law can limit all economic use of property must turn on objective factors, such as the nature of the land use proscribed. See *Lucas, supra*, at 1030 ("The 'total taking' inquiry we require today will ordinarily entail . . . analysis of, among other things, the degree of harm to public lands and resources, or adjacent private property, posed by the claimant's proposed activities"). A law does not become a background principle for subsequent owners by enactment itself. *Lucas* did not overrule our holding in *Nollan*, which, as we have noted, is based on essential Takings Clause principles.

For reasons we discuss next, the state court will not find it necessary to explore these matters on remand in connection with the claim that all economic use was deprived; it must address, however, the merits of petitioner's claim under *Penn Central*. That claim is not barred by the mere fact that title was acquired after the effective date of the state-imposed restriction.

As the case is ripe, and as the date of transfer of title does not bar petitioner's takings claim, we have before us the alternative ground relied upon by the Rhode Island Supreme Court in ruling upon the merits of the takings claims. It held that all economically beneficial use was not deprived because the uplands portion of the property can still be improved. On this point, we agree with the court's decision. Petitioner accepts the Council's contention and the state trial court's finding that his parcel retains $200,000 in development value under the State's wetlands regulations. He asserts, nonetheless, that he has suffered a total taking and contends the Council cannot sidestep the holding in Lucas "by the simple expedient of leaving a landowner a few crumbs of value." Brief for Petitioner 37.

Assuming a taking is otherwise established, a State may not evade the duty to compensate on the premise that the landowner is left with a token interest. This is not the situation of the landowner in this case, however. A regulation permitting a landowner to build a substantial residence on an 18-acre parcel does not leave the property "economically idle." *Lucas, supra*, at 1019.

In his brief submitted to us petitioner attempts to revive this part of his claim by reframing it. He argues, for the first time, that the upland parcel is distinct from the wetlands portions, so he should be permitted to assert a deprivation limited to the latter. This contention asks us to examine the difficult, persisting question of what is the proper denominator in the takings fraction. See Michelman, Property, Utility, and Fairness: Comments on the Ethical Foundations of "Just Compensation Law," 80 Harv. L. Rev. 1165, 1192 (1967). Some of our cases indicate that the extent of deprivation effected by a regulatory action is measured against the value of the parcel as a whole, see, *e.g.*, Keystone Bituminous Coal Assn. v. DeBenedictis, 480 U.S. 470, 497 (1987); but we have at times expressed discomfort with the logic of this rule, see *Lucas, supra*, at 1016-1017, n. 7, a sentiment echoed by some commentators, see, *e.g.*, Epstein, Takings: Descent and Resurrection, 1987 Sup. Ct. Rev. 1, 16-17 (1987); Fee, Unearthing the Denominator in Regulatory Takings Claims, 61 U. Chi. L. Rev. 1535 (1994). Whatever the merits of these criticisms, we will not explore the point here. Petitioner did not press the argument in the state courts, and the issue was not presented in the petition for certiorari. The case comes to us on the premise that petitioner's entire parcel serves as the basis for his takings claim, and, so framed, the total deprivation argument fails. . . .

The [state supreme] court did not err in finding that petitioner failed to establish a deprivation of all economic value, for it is undisputed that the parcel retains significant worth for construction of a residence. The claims under the *Penn Central* analysis were not examined, and for this purpose the case should be remanded.

The judgment of the Rhode Island Supreme Court is affirmed in part and reversed in part, and the case is remanded for further proceedings not inconsistent with this opinion.

It is so ordered.

JUSTICE O'CONNOR, concurring. . . .

The more difficult question is what role the temporal relationship between regulatory enactment and title acquisition plays in a proper *Penn Central* analysis. Today's holding does not mean that the timing of the regulation's enactment relative to the acquisition of title is immaterial to the *Penn Central* analysis. Indeed, it would be just as much error to expunge this consideration from the takings inquiry as it would be to accord it exclusive significance. Our polestar instead remains the principles set forth in *Penn Central* itself and our other cases that govern partial regulatory takings. Under these cases, interference with investment-backed expectations is one of a number of factors that a court must examine. Further, the regulatory regime in place at the time the claimant acquires the property at issue helps to shape the reasonableness of those expectations. . . .

The Rhode Island Supreme Court concluded that, because the wetlands regulations predated petitioner's acquisition of the property at issue, petitioner lacked reasonable investment-backed expectations and hence lacked a viable takings claim. 746 A.2d 707, 717 (2000). The court erred in elevating what it believed to be "[petitioner's] lack of reasonable investment-backed expectations" to "dispositive" status. *Ibid.* Investment-backed expectations, though important, are not talismanic under *Penn Central.* Evaluation of the degree of interference with investment-backed expectations instead is one factor that points toward the answer to the question whether the application of a particular regulation to particular property "goes too far." Pennsylvania Coal Co. v. Mahon, 260 U.S. 393, 415 (1922).

Further, the state of regulatory affairs at the time of acquisition is not the only factor that may determine the extent of investment-backed expectations. For example, the nature and extent of permitted development under the regulatory regime vis-a-vis the development sought by the claimant may also shape legitimate expectations without vesting any kind of development right in the property owner. We also have never held that a takings claim is defeated simply on account of the lack of a personal financial investment by a postenactment acquirer of property, such as a donee, heir, or devisee. Courts instead must attend to those circumstances which are probative of what fairness requires in a given case.

If investment-backed expectations are given exclusive significance in the *Penn Central* analysis and existing regulations dictate the reasonableness of those expectations in every instance, then the State wields far too much power to redefine property rights upon passage of title. On the other hand, if existing regulations do nothing to inform the analysis, then some property owners may reap windfalls and an important indicium of fairness is lost.* As I understand it, our decision today does not remove the regulatory backdrop against which an owner takes title to property from the purview of the *Penn Central* inquiry. It simply restores balance to that inquiry. Courts properly consider the effect of existing regulations under the rubric of investment-backed expectations in determining whether a compensable taking has occurred. As before, the salience of these facts cannot be reduced to any "set formula." *Penn Central*, 438 U.S. at 124 (internal quotation marks omitted). The temptation to adopt what amount to *per se* rules in either direction must be resisted. The Takings Clause requires careful examination and weighing of all the relevant circumstances in this context. The court below therefore must consider on remand the array of relevant factors under Penn Central before deciding whether any compensation is due.

JUSTICE SCALIA, concurring.

The principle that underlies [Justice O'Connor's] separate concurrence is that it may in some (unspecified) circumstances be "unfai[r]," and produce unacceptable "windfalls," to allow a subsequent purchaser to nullify an unconstitutional partial taking (though, inexplicably, not an unconstitutional total taking) by the government. The polar horrible, presumably, is the situation in which a sharp real estate developer, realizing (or indeed, simply gambling on) the unconstitutional excessiveness of a development restriction that a naive landowner assumes to be valid, purchases property at what it would be worth subject to the restriction, and then develops it to its full value (or resells it at its full value) after getting the unconstitutional restriction invalidated.

This can, I suppose, be called a windfall—though it is not much different from the windfalls that occur every day at stock exchanges or antique auctions, where the knowledgeable (or the venturesome) profit at the expense of the ignorant (or the risk averse). There is something to be said (though in my view not much) for pursuing abstract "fairness" by requiring part or all of that windfall to be returned to the naive original owner, who presumably is the "rightful" owner of it. But there is nothing to be said for giving it instead to the government—which not only did not lose something it owned, but is both the cause of the miscarriage of "fairness" and the only one of the three parties involved in the miscarriage (government, naive original owner, and sharp real estate developer) which acted unlawfully—indeed unconstitutionally. JUSTICE O'CONNOR would eliminate the windfall by giving the malefactor the benefit of its malefaction. It is rather like eliminating the windfall that accrued to a purchaser who bought property at a bargain rate from a thief clothed with the indicia of title, by making him turn over the "unjust" profit to the thief.**

In my view, the fact that a restriction existed at the time the purchaser took title (other than a restriction forming part of the "background principles of the State's law of property and nuisance," Lucas v. South Carolina Coastal Council, 505 U.S. 1003, 1029 (1992)) should have no bearing upon the determination of whether the restriction is so substantial as to constitute a taking. The

---

* JUSTICE SCALIA's inapt "government-as-thief" simile is symptomatic of the larger failing of his opinion, which is that he appears to conflate two questions. The first question is whether the enactment or application of a regulation constitutes a valid exercise of the police power. The second question is whether the State must compensate a property owner for a diminution in value effected by the State's exercise of its police power. We have held that "the 'public use' requirement [of the Takings Clause] is . . . coterminous with the scope of a sovereign's police powers." Hawaii Housing Authority v. Midkiff, 467 U.S. 229, 240 (1984). The relative timing of regulatory enactment and title acquisition, of course, does not affect the analysis of whether a State has acted within the scope of these powers in the first place. That issue appears to be the one on which JUSTICE SCALIA focuses, but it is not the matter at hand. The relevant question instead is the second question described above. It is to this inquiry that "investment-backed expectations" and the state of regulatory affairs upon acquisition of title are relevant under Penn Central. JUSTICE SCALIA's approach therefore would seem to require a revision of the Penn Central analysis that this Court has not undertaken.

** Contrary to JUSTICE O'CONNOR's assertion, my contention of governmental wrongdoing does not assume that the government exceeded its police powers by ignoring the "public use" requirement of the Takings Clause, see Hawaii Housing Authority v. Midkiff, 467 U.S. 229, 240 (1984). It is wrong for the government to take property, even for public use, without tendering just compensation.

"investment-backed expectations" that the law will take into account do not include the assumed validity of a restriction that in fact deprives property of so much of its value as to be unconstitutional. Which is to say that a *Penn Central* taking, no less than a total taking, is not absolved by the transfer of title.

JUSTICE GINSBURG, with whom JUSTICE SOUTER and JUSTICE BREYER join, dissenting. . . .

[A]s I see this case, we still do not know "the nature and extent of permitted development" under the regulation in question. I would therefore affirm the Rhode Island Supreme Court's judgment [on ripeness grounds].

JUSTICE BREYER, dissenting.

I agree with JUSTICE GINSBURG that Palazzolo's takings claim is not ripe for adjudication, and I join her opinion in full. Ordinarily I would go no further. But because the Court holds the takings claim to be ripe and goes on to address some important issues of substantive takings law, I add that, given this Court's precedents, I would agree with JUSTICE O'CONNOR that the simple fact that a piece of property has changed hands (for example, by inheritance) does not always and *automatically* bar a takings claim. Here, for example, without in any way suggesting that Palazzolo has any valid takings claim, I believe his postregulatory acquisition of the property (through automatic operation of law) by itself should not prove dispositive. . . .

Several *amici* have warned that to allow complete regulatory takings claims, see Lucas v. South Carolina Coastal Council, 505 U.S. 1003 (1992), to survive changes in land ownership could allow property owners to manufacture such claims by strategically transferring property until only a nonusable portion remains. But I do not see how a constitutional provision concerned with "'fairness and justice,'" *Penn Central, supra,* at 123-124 (quoting Armstrong v. United States, 364 U.S. 40, 49 (1960)), could reward any such strategic behavior.

JUSTICE STEVENS, concurring in part and dissenting in part.

In an admirable effort to frame its inquiries in broadly significant terms, the majority offers six pages of commentary on the issue of whether an owner of property can challenge regulations adopted prior to her acquisition of that property without ever discussing the particular facts or legal claims at issue in this case. While I agree with some of what the Court has to say on this issue, an examination of the issue in the context of the facts of this case convinces me that the Court has over-simplified a complex calculus and conflated two separate questions. . . .

Though the majority leaves open the possibility that the scope of today's holding may prove limited, the extension of the right to compensation to individuals other than the direct victim of an illegal taking admits of no obvious limiting principle. If the existence of valid land-use regulations does not limit the title that the first postenactment purchaser of the property inherits, then there is no reason why such regulations should limit the rights of the second, the third, or the thirtieth purchaser. Perhaps my concern is unwarranted, but today's decision does raise the spectre of a tremendous—and tremendously capricious—one-time transfer of wealth from society at large to those individuals who happen to hold title to large tracts of land at the moment this legal question is permanently resolved. . . .

Notes

1. Upon remand from the Supreme Court of Rhode Island, a state superior court justice heard further evidence in the case and decided in 2005 that Palazzolo had not suffered a *Penn Central* regulatory taking.[28] Before reaching that conclusion, the lower court found that "[b]ecause clear

---

28. The decision was filed on July 5, 2005. *See* http://www.courts.ri.gov/superior/pdf/88-0297.pdf.

and convincing evidence demonstrates that Palazzolo's development would constitute a public nuisance, he has no right to develop the site as he has proposed." (at 12) Moreover, the state asserted "that because the Public Trust Doctrine and trial evidence proving that one-half of the site is below mean high water, Plaintiff could not have expected to develop his subdivision absent the consent of the state." (at 14) The superior court justice quoted the following passage from Shively v. Bowlby, 152 U.S. 1, 57 (1894), an early Supreme Court that "established beyond question a nationwide Public Trust Doctrine which is to be applied based upon *state* law":

> Lands under tide waters are incapable of cultivation or improvement in the manner of lands above high water mark. They are of great value to the public for the purposes of commerce, navigation and fishery. Their improvement by individuals, when permitted, is incidental or subordinate to the public use and right. Therefore the title and the control of them are vested in the sovereign for the benefit of the whole people.
>
> . . .
>
> The title and rights of riparian or littoral proprietors in the soil below high water mark, therefore, are governed by the laws of the several States, subject to the rights granted to the United States by the Constitution.

Applying the doctrine as it is understood in Rhode Island, the lower court found that

> neither Plaintiff nor SGI has ever had the right to fill or develop that portion of the site which is below mean high water. Thus, as against the State, Palazzolo has gained title and the corresponding property rights to only on-half of the parcel in question. Although the Public Trust Doctrine cannot be a total ban to recovery as to this takings claim, it substantially impacts Plaintiff's title to the parcel in question and has a direct relationship to Plaintiff's reasonable investment-backed expectations . . . . (at 16-17)

On the question of those expectations, the justice observed:

> The modest investment made by Plaintiff, the transfer of prime lots almost coincidentally with Palazzolo's initial investment, his personal assessment of the value of the remaining lots, the obvious engineering difficulty in developing the site, existing state regulation over dredging and filling of tidal waters, the Public Trust Doctrine, a well publicized and growing nationwide movement toward the preservation of ecologically valuable sites during the last half of the twentieth century, and Urso's [the former co-owner] removal of himself as an owner suggests that Palazzolo's <u>reasonable</u> investment-backed expectations were modest.
>
> . . .
>
> [D]espite wishful thinking on Palazzolo's part, he paid a modest sum to invest in a proposed subdivision that he must have known from the outset was problematic at best. Under the facts and circumstances unique to this case, Palazzolo could have had little or no reasonable expectation to develop the parcel as he has now proposed. Constitutional law does not require the state to guarantee a bad investment.

On March 31, 2008, the Coastal Resources Management Council granted the 87-year-old Palazzolo a permit to build a three-bedroom house. Peter B. Lord, in *After Nearly 50 Years, He's Ready to Build*, Providence J.-Bull., June 25, 2008, at 1, reported that "[b]ecause the lot is just above sea level, and . . . subject to storm flooding and wash-over, the permit specifies that no loam be brought in for a lawn." Furthermore, "[t]he permit also specifies that no fertilizers or pesticides be used on the property." While Palazzolo stated that he was building the house for his children, he indicated his willingness to sell if he received a "good offer."

2. The Supreme Court has considered the nature, extent, and validity of wetlands regulations on a number of occasions—before and since *Palazzolo*. In United States v. Riverside Bayview Homes, 474 U.S. 121, 123-24, 139 (1985), the Court addressed the question of "whether the Clean Water Act (CWA), 33 U. S. C. §1251 et seq., together with certain regulations promulgated under its authority by the U.S. Army Corps of Engineers (the Corps), authorizes the Corps to require land-owners to obtain permits from the Corps before discharging fill material into wetlands adjacent to navigable bodies of water and their tributaries." Justice Byron White, writing for a unani-mous Court, explained the federal regulations that amplified (and perhaps expanded) the CWA's coverage:

> Under §§ 301 and 502 of the Act, 33 U. S. C. §§ 1311 and 1362, any discharge of dredged or fill materials into "navigable waters"—defined as the "waters of the United States"—is forbidden unless authorized by a permit issued by the Corps of Engineers pursuant to § 404, 33 U. S. C. § 1344. After initially construing the Act to cover only waters navigable in fact, in 1975 the Corps issued interim final regulations redefining "the waters of the United States" to include not only actually navigable waters but also tributaries of such waters, interstate waters and their tributaries, and nonnavigable intra-state waters whose use or misuse could affect interstate commerce. 40 Fed. Reg. 31320 (1975). More importantly for present purposes, the Corps construed the Act to cover all "freshwater wetlands" that were adjacent to other covered waters.

Not unlike many property owners over the last several decades, Riverside Bayview viewed federal wetlands regulations as a barrier to their plans for a housing development in Michigan, near the shores of Lake St. Clair, especially when the Corps filed suit to enjoin the developer from continuing to place fill materials on the property. The High Court sided with the regulators, as the Justices were "persuaded that the language, policies, and history of the Clean Water Act compel a finding that the Corps has acted reasonably in interpreting the Act to require permits for the discharge of fill material into wetlands adjacent to the 'waters of the United States.'"

Fifteen years later, Solid Waste Agency of N. Cook County (SWANCC) v. U.S. Army Corps of Eng'rs, 531 U.S. 159, 162, 171-72 (2001), brought better news to landowners, as a five-member majority, in an opinion by Chief Justice Rehnquist, held that §404 of the CWA did not "confer federal authority over an abandoned sand and gravel pit in northern Illinois which provides habitat for migratory birds." SWANCC, "a consortium of 23 suburban Chicago cities and villages that united in an effort to locate and develop a disposal site for baled nonhazardous solid waste," pre-vailed over the Corps, "declin[ing] respondents' invitation to take what they see as the next ineluc-table step after *Riverside Bayview Homes*: holding that isolated ponds, some only seasonal, wholly located within two Illinois counties, fall under §404(a)'s definition of "navigable waters" because they serve as habitat for migratory birds."

In part because the Corps and the U.S. Environmental Protection Agency (EPA) failed in an effort to revise wetlands regulations after *SWANCC*, wetlands law became even murkier when, in Rapanos v. United States, 547 U.S. 715, 729-30, 738, 739, 742, 787-88, 779-80, 792 (2006), the Justices presented five different opinions (none for a majority) in two consolidated cases from Michigan. The first case involved a landowner (Rapanos) who, by attempting to make his property more attractive to potential developers, was found by the federal district court to have unlawfully filled wetlands on three separate parcels without securing permits under §404 of the CWA. The Sixth Circuit affirmed the lower court decision, "holding that there was federal jurisdiction over the wetlands at all three sites as 'there were hydrological connections between all three sites and corresponding adjacent tributaries of navigable waters.'" In the second case, the Carabells, who were denied a permit that would have allowed them to deposit fill material as part of their condominium construction project, unsuccessfully challenged the exercise of federal authority over their site. The Sixth Circuit affirmed the lower court's judgment in favor of the government, "holding that the Carabell wetland was 'adjacent' to navigable waters."

To Justice Scalia and the three other Justices who joined his plurality opinion, the central question posed by these fact patterns boiled down to "whether four Michigan wetlands, which lie near ditches or man-made drains that eventually empty into traditional navigable waters, constitute 'waters of the United States' within the meaning of the Act." Not surprisingly, the plurality was not convinced that the Corps' reach extended this far. What was unusual was Justice Scalia's seeming endorsement of state and local controls:

> Regulation of land use, as through the issuance of the development permits sought by petitioners in both of these cases, is a quintessential state and local power. The extensive federal jurisdiction urged by the Government would authorize the Corps to function as a de facto regulator of immense stretches of intrastate land—an authority the agency has shown its willingness to exercise with the scope of discretion that would befit a local zoning board. We ordinarily expect a "clear and manifest" statement from Congress to authorize an unprecedented intrusion into traditional state authority. The phrase "the waters of the United States" hardly qualifies.

Quoting a dictionary definition, the plurality defined this key phrase as "those relatively permanent, standing or continuously flowing bodies of water 'forming geographic features' that are described in ordinary parlance as 'streams[,] . . . oceans, rivers, [and] lakes,'" and "*only* those wetlands with a continuous surface connection to bodies that are 'waters of the United States' in their own right."

The four dissenters, in an opinion written by Justice Stevens, had a different perspective on the issue facing the Court: "The broader question is whether regulations that have protected the quality of our waters for decades, that were implicitly approved by Congress, and that have been repeatedly enforced in case after case, must now be revised in light of the creative criticisms voiced by the plurality and Justice Kennedy [who concurred with the majority on different grounds] today." To this group of Justices, the Court's 1985 decision "in *Riverside Bayview* squarely controls these cases. There, we evaluated the validity of the very same regulations at issue today. These regulations interpret 'waters of the United States' to cover all traditionally navigable waters; tributaries of these waters; and wetlands adjacent to traditionally navigable waters or their tributaries."

Justice Anthony Kennedy cast the swing vote, aligning with the majority in its decision to vacate and remand the cases, but offered his own explanation of which wetlands qualified for protection:

> [T]he Corps' jurisdiction over wetlands depends upon the existence of a significant nexus between the wetlands in question and navigable waters in the traditional sense. . . . With respect to wetlands, the rationale for Clean Water Act regulation is, as the Corps has recognized, that wetlands can perform critical functions related to the integrity of other waters—functions such as pollutant trapping, flood control, and runoff storage. Accordingly, wetlands possess the requisite nexus, and thus come within the statutory phrase "navigable waters," if the wetlands, either alone or in combination with similarly situated lands in the region, significantly affect the chemical, physical, and biological integrity of other covered waters more readily understood as "navigable." When, in con-

trast, wetlands' effects on water quality are speculative or insubstantial, they fall outside the zone fairly encompassed by the statutory term "navigable waters."

It would be up to the two federal agencies to try somehow to interpret and follow this cacophony of judicial voices.

On June 5, 2007, the Corps and EPA issued a joint agency guidance regarding "Coordination on Jurisdictional Determinations (JDs) under Clean Water Act (CWA) Section 404 in Light of the *SWANCC* and *Rapanos* Supreme Court Decisions."[29] Despite this good-faith effort, as long as dry land is worth more to developers than wetlands, landowners and their counsel will continue to butt heads with government officials and lawyers over the issue of whether filling and other development activities come within federal and state regulatory jurisdiction.

IX. Watershed Protection

Tahoe Regional Planning Compact (Public Law 96-551, December 19, 1980)

(a) It is found and declared that:

(1) The waters of Lake Tahoe and other resources of the region are threatened with deterioration or degeneration, which endangers the natural beauty and economic productivity of the region.

(2) The public and private interests and investments in the region are substantial.

(3) The region exhibits unique environmental and ecological values which are irreplaceable.

(4) By virtue of the special conditions and circumstances of the region's natural ecology, developmental pattern, population distributions and human needs, the region is experiencing problems of resource use and deficiencies of environmental control.

(5) Increasing urbanization is threatening the ecological values of the region and threatening the public opportunities for use of the public lands.

(6) Maintenance of the social and economic health of the region depends on maintaining the significant scenic, recreational, educational, scientific, natural public health values provided by the Lake Tahoe Basin.

(7) There is a public interest in protecting, preserving and enhancing these values for the residents of the region and for visitors to the region.

(8) Responsibilities for providing recreational and scientific opportunities, preserving scenic and natural areas, and safeguarding the public who live, work and play in or visit the region are divided among local governments, regional agencies, the States of California and Nevada, and the Federal Government.

(9) In recognition of the public investment and multistate and national significance of the recreational values, the Federal Government has an interest in the acquisition of recreational property and the management of resources in the region to preserve environmental and recreational values, and the Federal Government should assist the States in fulfilling their responsibilities.

---

29. Available at http://www.epa.gov/owow/wetlands/pdf/RapanosMOA6507.pdf.

(10) In order to preserve the scenic beauty and outdoor recreational opportunities of the region, there is a need to insure an equilibrium between the region's natural endowment and its manmade environment.

(b) In order to enhance the efficiency and governmental effectiveness of the region, it is imperative that there be established a Tahoe Regional Planning Agency with the powers conferred by this compact including the power to establish environmental threshold carrying capacities and to adopt and enforce a regional plan and implementing ordinances which will achieve and maintain such capacities while providing opportunities for orderly growth and development consistent with such capacities.

(c) The Tahoe Regional Planning Agency shall interpret and administer its plans, ordinances, rules and regulations in accordance with the provisions of this compact.

TAHOE-SIERRA PRESERVATION COUNCIL, INC. v. TAHOE REGIONAL PLANNING AGENCY
535 U.S. 302 (2002)

JUSTICE STEVENS delivered the opinion of the Court.

The question presented is whether a moratorium on development imposed during the process of devising a comprehensive land-use plan constitutes a per se taking of property requiring compensation under the Takings Clause of the United States Constitution. This case actually involves two moratoria ordered by respondent Tahoe Regional Planning Agency (TRPA) to maintain the status quo while studying the impact of development on Lake Tahoe and designing a strategy for environmentally sound growth. The first, Ordinance 81-5, was effective from August 24, 1981, until August 26, 1983, whereas the second more restrictive Resolution 83-21 was in effect from August 27, 1983, until April 25, 1984. As a result of these two directives, virtually all development on a substantial portion of the property subject to TRPA's jurisdiction was prohibited for a period of 32 months. Although the question we decide relates only to that 32-month period, a brief description of the events leading up to the moratoria and a comment on the two permanent plans that TRPA adopted thereafter will clarify the narrow scope of our holding.

The relevant facts are undisputed. The Court of Appeals, while reversing the District Court on a question of law, accepted all of its findings of fact, and no party challenges those findings. All agree that Lake Tahoe is "uniquely beautiful," [Tahoe-Sierra Pres. Council, Inc. v. Tahoe Reg'l Planning Agency,] 34 F. Supp. 2d 1226, 1230 (Nev. 1999), that President Clinton was right to call it a "'national treasure that must be protected and preserved,'" *ibid.*, and that Mark Twain aptly described the clarity of its waters as "'not *merely* transparent, but dazzlingly, brilliantly so,'" *ibid.* (emphasis added) (quoting M. Twain, Roughing It 174-175 (1872)).

Lake Tahoe's exceptional clarity is attributed to the absence of algae that obscures the waters of most other lakes. Historically, the lack of nitrogen and phosphorous, which nourish the growth of algae, has ensured the transparency of its waters. Unfortunately, the lake's pristine state has deteriorated rapidly over the past 40 years; increased land development in the Lake Tahoe Basin (Basin) has threatened the "'noble sheet of blue water'" beloved by Twain and countless others. 34 F. Supp. 2d at 1230. As the District Court found, "dramatic decreases in clarity first began to be noted in the 1950's/early 1960's, shortly after development at the lake began in earnest." *Id.* at 1231. The lake's unsurpassed beauty, it seems, is the wellspring of its undoing.

The upsurge of development in the area has caused "increased nutrient loading of the lake largely because of the increase in impervious coverage of land in the Basin resulting from that development." *Ibid.*

> "Impervious coverage—such as asphalt, concrete, buildings, and even packed dirt—prevents precipitation from being absorbed by the soil. Instead, the water is gathered and concentrated by such coverage. Larger amounts of water flowing off a driveway or a roof have more erosive force than scattered raindrops falling over a dispersed area—especially one covered with indigenous vegetation, which softens the impact of the raindrops themselves." *Ibid.*

Given this trend, the District Court predicted that "unless the process is stopped, the lake will lose its clarity and its trademark blue color, becoming green and opaque for eternity."

Those areas in the Basin that have steeper slopes produce more runoff; therefore, they are usually considered "high hazard" lands. Moreover, certain areas near streams or wetlands known as "Stream Environment Zones" (SEZs) are especially vulnerable to the impact of development because, in their natural state, they act as filters for much of the debris that runoff carries. Because "the most obvious response to this problem . . . is to restrict development around the lake—especially in SEZ lands, as well as in areas already naturally prone to runoff," *id.* at 1232, conservation efforts have focused on controlling growth in these high hazard areas.

In the 1960's, when the problems associated with the burgeoning development began to receive significant attention, jurisdiction over the Basin, which occupies 501 square miles, was shared by the States of California and Nevada, five counties, several municipalities, and the Forest Service of the Federal Government. In 1968, the legislatures of the two States adopted the Tahoe Regional Planning Compact, see 1968 Cal. Stats., ch. 998, p. 1900, § 1; 1968 Nev. Stats. 4, which Congress approved in 1969, Pub. L. 91-148, 83 Stat. 360. The compact set goals for the protection and preservation of the lake and created TRPA as the agency assigned "to coordinate and regulate development in the Basin and to conserve its natural resources." Lake Country Estates, Inc. v. Tahoe Regional Planning Agency, 440 U.S. 391, 394 (1979).

Pursuant to the compact, in 1972 TRPA adopted a Land Use Ordinance that divided the land in the Basin into seven "land capability districts," based largely on steepness but also taking into consideration other factors affecting runoff. Each district was assigned a "land coverage coefficient—a recommended limit on the percentage of such land that could be covered by impervious surface." Those limits ranged from 1% for districts 1 and 2 to 30% for districts 6 and 7. Land in districts 1, 2, and 3 is characterized as "high hazard" or "sensitive," while land in districts 4, 5, 6, and 7 is "low hazard" or "non-sensitive." The SEZ lands, though often treated as a separate category, were actually a subcategory of district 1. 34 F. Supp. 2d at 1232.

Unfortunately, the 1972 ordinance allowed numerous exceptions and did not significantly limit the construction of new residential housing. California became so dissatisfied with TRPA that it withdrew its financial support and unilaterally imposed stricter regulations on the part of the Basin located in California. Eventually the two States, with the approval of Congress and the President, adopted an extensive amendment to the compact that became effective on December 19, 1980. Pub. L. 96-551, 94 Stat. 3233; Cal. Govt Code Ann. § 66801 (West Supp. 2002); Nev. Rev. Stat. § 277.200 (1980).

The 1980 Tahoe Regional Planning Compact (Compact) redefined the structure, functions, and voting procedures of TRPA, and directed it to develop regional "environmental threshold carrying capacities"—a term that embraced "standards for air quality, water quality, soil conservation, vegetation preservation and noise." 94 Stat. 3235, 3239. The Compact provided that TRPA "shall adopt" those standards within 18 months, and that "within 1 year after" their adoption (i.e., by

June 19, 1983), it "shall" adopt an amended regional plan that achieves and maintains those carrying capacities. *Id.* at 3240. The Compact also contained a finding by the Legislatures of California and Nevada "that in order to make effective the regional plan as revised by [TRPA], it is necessary to halt temporarily works of development in the region which might otherwise absorb the entire capability of the region for further development or direct it out of harmony with the ultimate plan." *Id.* at 3243. Accordingly, for the period prior to the adoption of the final plan ("or until May 1, 1983, whichever is earlier"), the Compact itself prohibited the development of new subdivisions, condominiums, and apartment buildings, and also prohibited each city and county in the Basin from granting any more permits in 1981, 1982, or 1983 than had been granted in 1978.

During this period TRPA was also working on the development of a regional water quality plan to comply with the Clean Water Act, 33 U.S.C. § 1288 (1994 ed.). Despite the fact that TRPA performed these obligations in "good faith and to the best of its ability," 34 F. Supp. 2d at 1233, after a few months it concluded that it could not meet the deadlines in the Compact. On June 25, 1981, it therefore enacted Ordinance 81-5 imposing the first of the two moratoria on development that petitioners challenge in this proceeding. The ordinance provided that it would become effective on August 24, 1981, and remain in effect pending the adoption of the permanent plan required by the Compact.

The District Court made a detailed analysis of the ordinance, noting that it might even prohibit hiking or picnicking on SEZ lands, but construed it as essentially banning any construction or other activity that involved the removal of vegetation or the creation of land coverage on all SEZ lands, as well as on class 1, 2, and 3 lands in California. Some permits could be obtained for such construction in Nevada if certain findings were made. It is undisputed, however, that Ordinance 81-5 prohibited the construction of any new residences on SEZ lands in either State and on class 1, 2, and 3 lands in California.

Given the complexity of the task of defining "environmental threshold carrying capacities" and the division of opinion within TRPA's governing board, the District Court found that it was "unsurprising" that TRPA failed to adopt those thresholds until August 26, 1982, roughly two months after the Compact deadline. Under a liberal reading of the Compact, TRPA then had until August 26, 1983, to adopt a new regional plan. 94 Stat. 3240. "Unfortunately, but again not surprisingly, no regional plan was in place as of that date." 34 F. Supp. 2d at 1235. TRPA therefore adopted Resolution 83-21, "which completely suspended all project reviews and approvals, including the acceptance of new proposals," and which remained in effect until a new regional plan was adopted on April 26, 1984. Thus, Resolution 83-21 imposed an 8-month moratorium prohibiting all construction on high hazard lands in either State. In combination, Ordinance 81-5 and Resolution 83-21 effectively prohibited all construction on sensitive lands in California and on all SEZ lands in the entire Basin for 32 months, and on sensitive lands in Nevada (other than SEZ lands) for eight months. It is these two moratoria that are at issue in this case.

On the same day that the 1984 plan was adopted, the State of California filed an action seeking to enjoin its implementation on the ground that it failed to establish land-use controls sufficiently stringent to protect the Basin. The District Court entered an injunction that was upheld by the Court of Appeals and remained in effect until a completely revised plan was adopted in 1987. Both the 1984 injunction and the 1987 plan contained provisions that prohibited new construction on sensitive lands in the Basin. As the case comes to us, however, we have no occasion to consider the validity of those provisions.

Approximately two months after the adoption of the 1984 Plan, petitioners filed parallel actions against TRPA and other defendants in federal courts in Nevada and California that were ultimately consolidated for trial in the District of Nevada. The petitioners include the Tahoe Sierra

Preservation Council, a nonprofit membership corporation representing about 2,000 owners of both improved and unimproved parcels of real estate in the Lake Tahoe Basin, and a class of some 400 individual owners of vacant lots located either on SEZ lands or in other parts of districts 1, 2, or 3. Those individuals purchased their properties prior to the effective date of the 1980 Compact, App. 34, primarily for the purpose of constructing "at a time of their choosing" a single-family home "to serve as a permanent, retirement or vacation residence," *id.* at 36. When they made those purchases, they did so with the understanding that such construction was authorized provided that "they complied with all reasonable requirements for building." *Ibid.*[5]

Petitioners' complaints gave rise to protracted litigation that has produced four opinions by the Court of Appeals for the Ninth Circuit and several published District Court opinions. For present purposes, however, we need only describe those courts' disposition of the claim that three actions taken by TRPA—Ordinance 81-5, Resolution 83-21, and the 1984 regional plan—constituted takings of petitioners' property without just compensation.[7] Indeed, the challenge to the 1984 plan is not before us because both the District Court and the Court of Appeals held that it was the federal injunction against implementing that plan, rather than the plan itself, that caused the post-1984 injuries that petitioners allegedly suffered, and those rulings are not encompassed within our limited grant of certiorari. Thus, we limit our discussion to the lower courts' disposition of the claims based on the 2-year moratorium (Ordinance 81-5) and the ensuing 8-month moratorium (Resolution 83-21). . . .

Emphasizing the temporary nature of the regulations, the testimony that the "average holding time of a lot in the Tahoe area between lot purchase and home construction is twenty-five years," and the failure of petitioners to offer specific evidence of harm, the District Court concluded that "consideration of the *Penn Central* factors clearly leads to the conclusion that there was no taking." 34 F. Supp. 2d at 1240. In the absence of evidence regarding any of the individual plaintiffs, the court evaluated the "average" purchasers' intent and found that such purchasers "did not have reasonable, investment-backed expectations that they would be able to build single-family homes on their land within the six-year period involved in this lawsuit."

The District Court had more difficulty with the "total taking" issue. Although it was satisfied that petitioners' property did retain some value during the moratoria, it found that they had been temporarily deprived of "all economically viable use of their land." *Id.* at 1245. The court concluded that those actions therefore constituted "categorical" takings under our decision in Lucas v. South Carolina Coastal Council, 505 U.S. 1003 (1992). It rejected TRPA's response that Ordinance 81-5 and Resolution 83-21 were "reasonable temporary planning moratoria" that should be excluded from Lucas' categorical approach. The court thought it "fairly clear" that such interim actions would not have been viewed as takings prior to our decisions in *Lucas* and First English Evangelical Lutheran Church of Glendale v. County of Los Angeles, 482 U.S. 304 (1987), because "zoning boards, cities, counties and other agencies used them all the time to 'maintain the status quo pending study and governmental decision making.'" 34 F. Supp. 2d at 1248-1249 (quoting Williams v. Central, 907 P.2d 701, 706 (Colo. App. 1995)). After expressing uncertainty as to whether those cases required a holding that moratoria on development automatically effect takings, the court concluded that TRPA's actions did so, partly because neither the ordinance nor

5. As explained above, the petitioners who purchased land after the 1972 compact did so amidst a heavily regulated zoning scheme. Their property was already classified as part of land capability districts 1, 2, and 3, or SEZ land. And each land classification was subject to regulations as to the degree of artificial disturbance the land could safely sustain.

7. In 1991, petitioners amended their complaint to allege that the adoption of the 1987 plan also constituted an unconstitutional taking. Ultimately both the District Court and the Court of Appeals held that this claim was barred by California's 1-year statute of limitations and Nevada's 2-year statute of limitations. See 216 F.3d at 785-789. Although the validity of the 1987 plan is not before us, we note that other litigants have challenged certain applications of that plan. See Suitum v. Tahoe Regional Planning Agency, 520 U.S. 725 (1997).

the resolution, even though intended to be temporary from the beginning, contained an express termination date. 34 F. Supp. 2d at 1250-1251. Accordingly, it ordered TRPA to pay damages to most petitioners for the 32-month period from August 24, 1981, to April 25, 1984, and to those owning class 1, 2, or 3 property in Nevada for the 8-month period from August 27, 1983, to April 25, 1984.

Both parties appealed. TRPA successfully challenged the District Court's takings determination, and petitioners unsuccessfully challenged the dismissal of their claims based on the 1984 and 1987 plans. Petitioners did not, however, challenge the District Court's findings or conclusions concerning its application of *Penn Central*. With respect to the two moratoria, the Ninth Circuit noted that petitioners had expressly disavowed an argument "that the regulations constitute a taking under the ad hoc balancing approach described in Penn Central" and that they did not "dispute that the restrictions imposed on their properties are appropriate means of securing the purpose set forth in the Compact." Accordingly, the only question before the court was "whether the rule set forth in *Lucas* applies—that is, whether a categorical taking occurred because Ordinance 81-5 and Resolution 83-21 denied the plaintiffs' 'all economically beneficial or productive use of land.'" 216 F.3d 764, 773 (2000). Moreover, because petitioners brought only a facial challenge, the narrow inquiry before the Court of Appeals was whether the mere enactment of the regulations constituted a taking.

Contrary to the District Court, the Court of Appeals held that because the regulations had only a temporary impact on petitioners' fee interest in the properties, no categorical taking had occurred. It reasoned:

> "Property interests may have many different dimensions. For example, the dimensions of a property interest may include a physical dimension (which describes the size and shape of the property in question), a functional dimension (which describes the extent to which an owner may use or dispose of the property in question), and a temporal dimension (which describes the duration of the property interest). At base, the plaintiffs' argument is that we should conceptually sever each plaintiff's fee interest into discrete segments in at least one of these dimensions—the temporal one—and treat each of those segments as separate and distinct property interests for purposes of takings analysis. Under this theory, they argue that there was a categorical taking of one of those temporal segments." 216 F.3d at 774.

Putting to one side "cases of physical invasion or occupation," *ibid.*, the court read our cases involving regulatory taking claims to focus on the impact of a regulation on the parcel as a whole. In its view a "planning regulation that prevents the development of a parcel for a temporary period of time is conceptually no different than a land-use restriction that permanently denies all use on a discrete portion of property, or that permanently restricts a type of use across all of the parcel." 216 F.3d at 776. In each situation, a regulation that affects only a portion of the parcel—whether limited by time, use, or space—does not deprive the owner of all economically beneficial use.

The Court of Appeals distinguished *Lucas* as applying to the "'relatively rare'" case in which a regulation denies all productive use of an entire parcel, whereas the moratoria involve only a "temporal 'slice'" of the fee interest and a form of regulation that is widespread and well established. 216 F.3d at 773-774. It also rejected petitioners' argument that our decision in *First English* was controlling. According to the Court of Appeals, *First English* concerned the question whether compensation is an appropriate remedy for a temporary taking and not whether or when such a taking has occurred. Faced squarely with the question whether a taking had occurred, the court held that *Penn Central* was the appropriate framework for analysis. Petitioners, however, had failed to challenge the District Court's conclusion that they could not make out a taking claim under the *Penn Central* factors.

Over the dissent of five judges, the Ninth Circuit denied a petition for rehearing en banc. 228 F.3d 998 (2000). In the dissenters' opinion, the panel's holding was not faithful to this Court's decisions in *First English* and *Lucas*, nor to Justice Holmes admonition in Pennsylvania Coal Co. v. Mahon, 260 U.S. 393, 416 (1922), that "'a strong public desire to improve the public condition is not enough to warrant achieving the desire by a shorter cut than the constitutional way of paying for the change.'" 228 F.3d at 1003. Because of the importance of the case, we granted certiorari limited to the question stated at the beginning of this opinion. We now affirm.

Petitioners make only a facial attack on Ordinance 81-5 and Resolution 83-21. They contend that the mere enactment of a temporary regulation that, while in effect, denies a property owner all viable economic use of her property gives rise to an unqualified constitutional obligation to compensate her for the value of its use during that period. Hence, they "face an uphill battle," Keystone Bituminous Coal Ass'n v. DeBenedictis, 480 U.S. 470, 495 (1987), that is made especially steep by their desire for a categorical rule requiring compensation whenever the government imposes such a moratorium on development. Under their proposed rule, there is no need to evaluate the land-owners' investment-backed expectations, the actual impact of the regulation on any individual, the importance of the public interest served by the regulation, or the reasons for imposing the temporary restriction. For petitioners, it is enough that a regulation imposes a temporary deprivation—no matter how brief—of all economically viable use to trigger a *per se* rule that a taking has occurred. Petitioners assert that our opinions in *First English* and *Lucas* have already endorsed their view, and that it is a logical application of the principle that the Takings Clause was "designed to bar Government from forcing some people alone to bear burdens which, in all fairness and justice, should be borne by the public as a whole." Armstrong v. United States, 364 U.S. 40, 49 (1960).

We shall first explain why our cases do not support their proposed categorical rule—indeed, fairly read, they implicitly reject it. Next, we shall explain why the *Armstrong* principle requires rejection of that rule as well as the less extreme position advanced by petitioners at oral argument. In our view the answer to the abstract question whether a temporary moratorium effects a taking is neither "yes, always" nor "no, never"; the answer depends upon the particular circumstances of the case. Resisting "the temptation to adopt what amount to *per se* rules in either direction," Palazzolo v. Rhode Island, 533 U.S. 606, 636 (2001) (O'CONNOR, J., concurring), we conclude that the circumstances in this case are best analyzed within the *Penn Central* framework.

The text of the Fifth Amendment itself provides a basis for drawing a distinction between physical takings and regulatory takings. Its plain language requires the payment of compensation whenever the government acquires private property for a public purpose, whether the acquisition is the result of a condemnation proceeding or a physical appropriation. But the Constitution contains no comparable reference to regulations that prohibit a property owner from making certain uses of her private property. Our jurisprudence involving condemnations and physical takings is as old as the Republic and, for the most part, involves the straightforward application of *per se* rules. Our regulatory takings jurisprudence, in contrast, is of more recent vintage and is characterized by "essentially ad hoc, factual inquiries," *Penn Central*, 438 U.S. at 124, designed to allow "careful examination and weighing of all the relevant circumstances." *Palazzolo*, 533 U.S. at 636 (O'CONNOR, J., concurring).

When the government physically takes possession of an interest in property for some public purpose, it has a categorical duty to compensate the former owner, regardless of whether the interest that is taken constitutes an entire parcel or merely a part thereof. Thus, compensation is mandated when a leasehold is taken and the government occupies the property for its own purposes, even though that use is temporary. United States v. General Motors Corp., 323 U.S. 373 (1945), United States v. Petty Motor Co., 327 U.S. 372 (1946). Similarly, when the government appropriates part of a rooftop in order to provide cable TV access for apartment tenants, Loretto v. Teleprompter Manhattan CATV Corp., 458 U.S. 419 (1982); or when its planes use private airspace to approach a government airport, United States v. Causby, 328 U.S. 256 (1946), it is required to pay for that share no matter how small. But a government regulation that merely prohibits landlords from evicting tenants unwilling to pay a higher rent, Block v. Hirsh, 256 U.S. 135 (1921); that bans certain private uses of a portion of an owner's property, Village of Euclid v. Ambler Realty Co., 272 U.S. 365 (1926); Keystone Bituminous Coal Ass'n v. DeBenedictis, 480 U.S. 470 (1987); or that forbids the private use of certain airspace, Penn Central Transp. Co. v. New York City, 438 U.S. 104 (1978), does not constitute a categorical taking. "The first category of cases requires courts to apply a clear rule; the second necessarily entails complex factual assessments of the purposes and economic effects of government actions." Yee v. Escondido, 503 U.S. 519, 523 (1992).

This longstanding distinction between acquisitions of property for public use, on the one hand, and regulations prohibiting private uses, on the other, makes it inappropriate to treat cases involving physical takings as controlling precedents for the evaluation of a claim that there has been a "regulatory taking," and vice versa. For the same reason that we do not ask whether a physical appropriation advances a substantial government interest or whether it deprives the owner of all economically valuable use, we do not apply our precedent from the physical takings context to regulatory takings claims. Land-use regulations are ubiquitous and most of them impact property values in some tangential way—often in completely unanticipated ways. Treating them all as *per se* takings would transform government regulation into a luxury few governments could afford. By contrast, physical appropriations are relatively rare, easily identified, and usually represent a greater affront to individual property rights. . . .

Perhaps recognizing this fundamental distinction, petitioners wisely do not place all their emphasis on analogies to physical takings cases. Instead, they rely principally on our decision in Lucas v. South Carolina Coastal Council, 505 U.S. 1003 (1992)—a regulatory takings case that, nevertheless, applied a categorical rule—to argue that the *Penn Central* framework is inapplicable here. A brief review of some of the cases that led to our decision in *Lucas*, however, will help to explain why the holding in that case does not answer the question presented here.

As we noted in *Lucas*, it was Justice Holmes' opinion in Pennsylvania Coal Co. v. Mahon, 260 U.S. 393 (1922), that gave birth to our regulatory takings jurisprudence. In subsequent opinions we have repeatedly and consistently endorsed Holmes' observation that "if regulation goes too far it will be recognized as a taking." *Id.* at 415. . . .

In the decades following that decision, we have "generally eschewed" any set formula for determining how far is too far, choosing instead to engage in "'essentially ad hoc, factual inquiries.'" *Lucas*, 505 U.S. at 1015 (quoting *Penn Central*, 438 U.S. at 124). Indeed, we still resist the temptation to adopt per se rules in our cases involving partial regulatory takings, preferring to examine "a number of factors" rather than a simple "mathematically precise" formula. Justice Brennan's opinion for the Court in *Penn Central* did, however, make it clear that even though multiple factors are relevant in the analysis of regulatory takings claims, in such cases we must focus on "the parcel as a whole" . . . .

While the foregoing cases considered whether particular regulations had "gone too far" and were therefore invalid, none of them addressed the separate remedial question of how compensation is measured once a regulatory taking is established. In his dissenting opinion in San Diego Gas & Elec. Co. v. San Diego, 450 U.S. 621, 636 (1981), Justice Brennan identified that question and explained how he would answer it:

"The constitutional rule I propose requires that, once a court finds that a police power regulation has effected a 'taking,' the government entity must pay just compensation for the period commencing on the date the regulation first effected the 'taking,' and ending on the date the government entity chooses to rescind or otherwise amend the regulation." *Id.* at 658.

Justice Brennan's proposed rule was subsequently endorsed by the Court in *First English*, 482 U.S. at 315, 318, 321. *First English* was certainly a significant decision, and nothing that we say today qualifies its holding. Nonetheless, it is important to recognize that we did not address in that case the quite different and logically prior question whether the temporary regulation at issue had in fact constituted a taking.

In *First English*, the Court unambiguously and repeatedly characterized the issue to be decided as a "compensation question" or a "remedial question." *Id.* at 311 ("The disposition of the case on these grounds isolates the remedial question for our consideration."). And the Court's statement of its holding was equally unambiguous: "We merely hold that where the government's activities have already worked a taking of all use of property, no subsequent action by the government can relieve it of the duty to provide compensation for the period during which the taking was effective." *Id.* at 321 (emphasis added). In fact, *First English* expressly disavowed any ruling on the merits of the takings issue because the California courts had decided the remedial question on the assumption that a taking had been alleged. After our remand, the California courts concluded that there had not been a taking, First English Evangelical Church of Glendale v. County of Los Angeles, 210 Cal. App. 3d 1353, 258 Cal. Rptr. 893 (1989), and we declined review of that decision, 493 U.S. 1056 (1990).

To the extent that the Court in *First English* referenced the antecedent takings question, we identified two reasons why a regulation temporarily denying an owner all use of her property might not constitute a taking. First, we recognized that "the county might avoid the conclusion that a compensable taking had occurred by establishing that the denial of all use was insulated as a part of the State's authority to enact safety regulations." 482 U.S. at 313. Second, we limited our holding "to the facts presented" and recognized "the quite different questions that would arise in the case of normal delays in obtaining building permits, changes in zoning ordinances, variances, and the like which [were] not before us." *Id.* at 321. Thus, our decision in *First English* surely did not approve, and implicitly rejected, the categorical submission that petitioners are now advocating.

Similarly, our decision in *Lucas* is not dispositive of the question presented. Although *Lucas* endorsed and applied a categorical rule, it was not the one that petitioners propose. . . .   The categorical rule that we applied in *Lucas* states that compensation is required when a regulation deprives an owner of "all economically beneficial uses" of his land. Under that rule, a statute that "wholly eliminated the value" of Lucas' fee simple title clearly qualified as a taking. But our holding was limited to "the extraordinary circumstance when no productive or economically beneficial use of land is permitted." The emphasis on the word "no" in the text of the opinion was, in effect, reiterated in a footnote explaining that the categorical rule would not apply if the diminution in value were 95% instead of 100%. Anything less than a "complete elimination of value," or a "total loss," the Court acknowledged, would require the kind of analysis applied in *Penn Central. Lucas*, 505 U.S. at 1019-1020, n. 8.

Certainly, our holding that the permanent "obliteration of the value" of a fee simple estate constitutes a categorical taking does not answer the question whether a regulation prohibiting any economic use of land for a 32-month period has the same legal effect. Petitioners seek to bring this case under the rule announced in *Lucas* by arguing that we can effectively sever a 32-month segment from the remainder of each landowner's fee simple estate, and then ask whether that segment has been taken in its entirety by the moratoria. Of course, defining the property interest taken in terms of the very regulation being challenged is circular. With property so divided, every delay would become a total ban; the moratorium and the normal permit process alike would constitute categorical takings. Petitioners' "conceptual severance" argument is unavailing because it ignores *Penn Central*'s admonition that in regulatory takings cases we must focus on "the parcel as a whole." 438 U.S. at 130-131. We have consistently rejected such an approach to the "denominator" question. See *Keystone*, 480 U.S. at 497. Thus, the District Court erred when it disaggregated petitioners' property into temporal segments corresponding to the regulations at issue and then analyzed whether petitioners were deprived of all economically viable use during each period. The starting point for the court's analysis should have been to ask whether there was a total taking of the entire parcel; if not, then *Penn Central* was the proper framework.

An interest in real property is defined by the metes and bounds that describe its geographic dimensions and the term of years that describes the temporal aspect of the owner's interest. Both dimensions must be considered if the interest is to be viewed in its entirety. Hence, a permanent deprivation of the owner's use of the entire area is a taking of "the parcel as a whole," whereas a temporary restriction that merely causes a diminution in value is not. Logically, a fee simple estate cannot be rendered valueless by a temporary prohibition on economic use, because the property will recover value as soon as the prohibition is lifted.

Neither *Lucas*, nor *First English*, nor any of our other regulatory takings cases compels us to accept petitioners' categorical submission. In fact, these cases make clear that the categorical rule in *Lucas* was carved out for the "extraordinary case" in which a regulation permanently deprives property of all value; the default rule remains that, in the regulatory taking context, we require a more fact specific inquiry. Nevertheless, we will consider whether the interest in protecting individual property owners from bearing public burdens "which, in all fairness and justice, should be borne by the public as a whole," Armstrong v. United States, 364 U.S. at 49, justifies creating a new rule for these circumstances.

Considerations of "fairness and justice" arguably could support the conclusion that TRPA's moratoria were takings of petitioners' property based on any of seven different theories. First, even though we have not previously done so, we might now announce a categorical rule that, in the interest of fairness and justice, compensation is required whenever government temporarily deprives an owner of all economically viable use of her property. Second, we could craft a narrower rule that would cover all temporary land-use restrictions except those "normal delays in obtaining building permits, changes in zoning ordinances, variances, and the like" which were put to one side in our opinion in *First English*, 482 U.S. at 321.Third, we could adopt a rule like the one suggested by an amicus supporting petitioners that would "allow a short fixed period for deliberations to take place without compensation—say maximum one year—after which the just compensation requirements" would "kick in."[28] Fourth, with the benefit of hindsight, we might characterize the successive actions of TRPA as a "series of rolling moratoria" that were the functional equivalent of a permanent taking. Fifth, were it not for the findings of the District Court that TRPA acted diligently and in good faith, we might have concluded that the agency was stalling in order to avoid promulgating the environmental threshold carrying capacities and regional plan mandated by the 1980 Compact. Sixth, apart from the District Court's finding that TRPA's actions represented a proportional response to a serious risk of harm to the lake, petitioners might have argued that the moratoria did not substantially advance a legitimate state interest. Finally, if petitioners had

---

28. Brief for the Institute for Justice as *Amicus Curiae* 30. Although *amicus* describes the 1-year cut off proposal as the "better approach by far," *ibid.* its primary argument is that *Penn Central* should be overruled, *id.* at 20 ("All partial takings by way of land use restriction should be subject to the same prima facie rules for compensation as a physical occupation for a limited period of time.").

challenged the application of the moratoria to their individual parcels, instead of making a facial challenge, some of them might have prevailed under a *Penn Central* analysis.

As the case comes to us, however, none of the last four theories is available. The "rolling moratoria" theory was presented in the petition for certiorari, but our order granting review did not encompass that issue; the case was tried in the District Court and reviewed in the Court of Appeals on the theory that each of the two moratoria was a separate taking, one for a 2-year period and the other for an 8-month period. And, as we have already noted, recovery on either a bad faith theory or a theory that the state interests were insubstantial is foreclosed by the District Court's unchallenged findings of fact. Recovery under a *Penn Central* analysis is also foreclosed both because petitioners expressly disavowed that theory, and because they did not appeal from the District Court's conclusion that the evidence would not support it. Nonetheless, each of the three *per se* theories is fairly encompassed within the question that we decided to answer.

With respect to these theories, the ultimate constitutional question is whether the concepts of "fairness and justice" that underlie the Takings Clause will be better served by one of these categorical rules or by a *Penn Central* inquiry into all of the relevant circumstances in particular cases. From that perspective, the extreme categorical rule that any deprivation of all economic use, no matter how brief, constitutes a compensable taking surely cannot be sustained. Petitioners' broad submission would apply to numerous "normal delays in obtaining building permits, changes in zoning ordinances, variances, and the like," 482 U.S. at 321, as well as to orders temporarily prohibiting access to crime scenes, businesses that violate health codes, fire-damaged buildings, or other areas that we cannot now foresee. Such a rule would undoubtedly require changes in numerous practices that have long been considered permissible exercises of the police power. As Justice Holmes warned in *Mahon*, "government hardly could go on if to some extent values incident to property could not be diminished without paying for every such change in the general law." 260 U.S. at 413. A rule that required compensation for every delay in the use of property would render routine government processes prohibitively expensive or encourage hasty decisionmaking. Such an important change in the law should be the product of legislative rulemaking rather than adjudication.

More importantly, for reasons set out at some length by JUSTICE O'CONNOR in her concurring opinion in Palazzolo v. Rhode Island, 533 U.S. at 636 (2001), we are persuaded that the better approach to claims that a regulation has effected a temporary taking "requires careful examination and weighing of all the relevant circumstances." . . .

In rejecting petitioners' *per se* rule, we do not hold that the temporary nature of a land-use restriction precludes finding that it effects a taking; we simply recognize that it should not be given exclusive significance one way or the other.

A narrower rule that excluded the normal delays associated with processing permits, or that covered only delays of more than a year, would certainly have a less severe impact on prevailing practices, but it would still impose serious financial constraints on the planning process. Unlike the "extraordinary circumstance" in which the government deprives a property owner of all economic use, *Lucas*, 505 U.S. at 1017, moratoria like Ordinance 81-5 and Resolution 83-21 are used widely among land-use planners to preserve the status quo while formulating a more permanent development strategy.[32] In fact, the consensus in the planning community appears to be that moratoria, or "interim development controls" as they are often called, are an essential tool of successful development. Yet even the weak version of petitioners' categorical rule would treat these interim measures as takings regardless of the good faith of the planners, the reasonable expectations of the landowners, or the actual impact of the moratorium on property values. . . .

Indeed, the interest in protecting the decisional process is even stronger when an agency is developing a regional plan than when it is considering a permit for a single parcel. In the proceedings involving the Lake Tahoe Basin, for example, the moratoria enabled TRPA to obtain the benefit of comments and criticisms from interested parties, such as the petitioners, during its deliberations. Since a categorical rule tied to the length of deliberations would likely create added pressure on decisionmakers to reach a quick resolution of land-use questions, it would only serve to disadvantage those landowners and interest groups who are not as organized or familiar with the planning process. Moreover, with a temporary ban on development there is a lesser risk that individual landowners will be "singled out" to bear a special burden that should be shared by the public as a whole. At least with a moratorium there is a clear "reciprocity of advantage," *Mahon*, 260 U.S. at 415, because it protects the interests of all affected landowners against immediate construction that might be inconsistent with the provisions of the plan that is ultimately adopted. "While each of us is burdened somewhat by such restrictions, we, in turn, benefit greatly from the restrictions that are placed on others." *Keystone*, 480 U.S. at 491. In fact, there is reason to believe property values often will continue to increase despite a moratorium. Such an increase makes sense in this context because property values throughout the Basin can be expected to reflect the added assurance that Lake Tahoe will remain in its pristine state. Since in some cases a 1-year moratorium may not impose a burden at all, we should not adopt a rule that assumes moratoria always force individuals to bear a special burden that should be shared by the public as a whole.

It may well be true that any moratorium that lasts for more than one year should be viewed with special skepticism. But given the fact that the District Court found that the 32 months required by TRPA to formulate the 1984 Regional Plan was not unreasonable, we could not possibly conclude that every delay of over one year is constitutionally unacceptable. Formulating a

---

32. *See, e.g.*, Santa Fe Village Venture v. City of Albuquerque, 914 F. Supp. 478, 483 (N. M. 1995)(30-month moratorium on development of lands within the Petroglyph National Monument was not a taking); Williams v. City of Central, 907 P.2d 701, 703-706 (Colo. App. 1995)(10-month moratorium on development in gaming district while studying city's ability to absorb growth was not a compensable taking); Woodbury Place Partners v. Woodbury, 492 N.W.2d 258 (Minn. App. 1993) (moratorium pending review of plan for land adjacent to interstate highway was not a taking even though it deprived property owner of all economically viable use of its property for two years); Zilber v. Moraga, 692 F. Supp. 1195 (ND Cal. 1988) (18-month development moratorium during completion of a comprehensive scheme for open space did not require compensation). See also Wayman, Leaders Consider Options for Town Growth, Charlotte Observer, Feb. 3, 2002, p. 15M (describing 10-month building moratorium imposed "to give town leaders time to plan for development"); Wallman, City May Put Reins on Beach Projects, Sun-Sentinel, May 16, 2000, p. 1B (2-year building moratorium on beachfront property in Fort Lauderdale pending new height, width, and dispersal regulations); Foderaro, In Suburbs, They're Cracking Down on the Joneses, N. Y. Times, Mar. 19, 2001, p. A1 (describing moratorium imposed in Eastchester, New York during a review of the town's zoning code to address the problem of oversized homes); Dawson, Commissioners recommend Aboite construction ban be lifted, Fort Wayne News Sentinel, May 4, 2001, p. 1A (3-year moratorium to allow improvements in the water and sewage treatment systems).

general rule of this kind is a suitable task for state legislatures.[37] In our view, the duration of the restriction is one of the important factors that a court must consider in the appraisal of a regulatory takings claim, but with respect to that factor as with respect to other factors, the "temptation to adopt what amount to per se rules in either direction must be resisted." *Palazzolo*, 533 U.S. at 636 (O'CONNOR, J., concurring). There may be moratoria that last longer than one year which interfere with reasonable investment-backed expectations, but as the District Court's opinion illustrates, petitioners' proposed rule is simply "too blunt an instrument," for identifying those cases. *Id.* at 628. We conclude, therefore, that the interest in "fairness and justice" will be best served by relying on the familiar *Penn Central* approach when deciding cases like this, rather than by attempting to craft a new categorical rule.

Accordingly, the judgment of the Court of Appeals is affirmed.

It is so ordered.

CHIEF JUSTICE REHNQUIST, with whom JUSTICE SCALIA and JUSTICE THOMAS join, dissenting.

For over half a decade petitioners were prohibited from building homes, or any other structures, on their land. Because the Takings Clause requires the government to pay compensation when it deprives owners of all economically viable use of their land, see Lucas v. South Carolina Coastal Council, 505 U.S. 1003, (1992), and because a ban on all development lasting almost six years does not resemble any traditional land-use planning device, I dissent. . . .

Lake Tahoe is a national treasure and I do not doubt that respondent's efforts at preventing further degradation of the lake were made in good faith in furtherance of the public interest. But, as is the case with most governmental action that furthers the public interest, the Constitution requires that the costs and burdens be borne by the public at large, not by a few targeted citizens. . . .

JUSTICE THOMAS, with whom JUSTICE SCALIA joins, dissenting.

I join the CHIEF JUSTICE'S dissent. I write separately to address the majority's conclusion that the temporary moratorium at issue here was not a taking because it was not a "taking of 'the parcel as a whole.'" While this questionable rule has been applied to various alleged regulatory takings, it was, in my view, rejected in the context of temporal deprivations of property by First English Evangelical Lutheran Church of Glendale v. County of Los Angeles, 482 U.S. 304, 318 (1987), which held that temporary and permanent takings "are not different in kind" when a landowner is deprived of all beneficial use of his land. I had thought that *First English* put to rest the notion that the "relevant denominator" is land's infinite life. Consequently, a regulation effecting a total deprivation of the use of a so-called "temporal slice" of property is compensable under the Takings Clause unless background principles of state property law prevent it from being deemed a taking; "total deprivation of use is, from the landowner's point of view, the equivalent of a physical appropriation." Lucas v. South Carolina Coastal Council, 505 U.S. 1003, 1017 (1992). . . .

I would hold that regulations prohibiting all productive uses of property are subject to *Lucas'* per se rule, regardless of whether the property so burdened retains theoretical useful life and value

---

37. Several States already have statutes authorizing interim zoning ordinances with specific time limits. See Cal. Govt. Code Ann. § 65858 (West Supp. 2002) (authorizing interim ordinance of up to two years); Colo. Rev. Stat. § 30-28-121 (2001) (six months); Ky. Rev. Stat. Ann. § 100.201 (2001) (one year); Mich. Comp. Laws Ann. § 125.215 (2001) (three years); Minn. Stat. § 394.34 (2000) (two years); N. H. Rev. Stat. § 674:23 (2001) (one year); Ore. Rev. Stat. Ann. § 197.520 (1997) (10 months); S. D. Codified Laws § 11-2-10 (2001) (two years); Utah Code Ann. § 17-27-404 (1995) (18 months); Wash. Rev. Code § 35.63.200 (2001) Wis. Stat. § 62.23(7)(d) (2001) (two years). Other States, although without specific statutory authority, have recognized that reasonable interim zoning ordinances may be enacted. See, e.g., S. E. W. Friel v. Triangle Oil Co., 76 Md. App. 96, 543 A.2d 863 (1988); New Jersey Shore Builders Assn. v. Dover Twp. Comm., 191 N.J. Super. 627, 468 A.2d 742 (1983); SCA Chemical Waste Servs., Inc. v. Konigsberg, 636 S.W.2d 430 (Tenn. 1982); Sturges v. Chilmark, 380 Mass. 246, 402 N.E.2d 1346 (1980); Lebanon v. Woods, 153 Conn. 182, 215 A.2d 112 (1965).

if, and when, the "temporary" moratorium is lifted. To my mind, such potential future value bears on the amount of compensation due and has nothing to do with the question whether there was a taking in the first place. It is regrettable that the Court has charted a markedly different path today.

Notes

1. The attorney for the prevailing party in *Tahoe-Sierra* was none other than John G. Roberts Jr., a successful appellate attorney who a few years later would be named Chief Justice of the United States. As reported in "Judging Roberts," an article that appeared in the August 1, 2005, edition of *Newsweek*: "Roberts took on all kinds of cases, without regard to politics. . . . Before the Supreme Court, he represented environmentalists trying to preserve Lake Tahoe—not because he was pro-Green, says a liberal friend, Georgetown Law professor Richard Lazarus, who was working the case, but because Lazarus had a scheduling conflict . . . ." Note also that the Solicitor General, Theodore B. Olson, participated in the oral argument and filed an amicus brief in support of the Tahoe Regional Planning Agency (TRPA), arguing that "[a] temporary development moratorium, reasonably designed to preserve the status quo pending completion of a comprehensive land-use plan, does not effect a per se taking of property." Of course, Olson's most famous victory before the Supreme Court came two years before in Bush v. Gore, 531 U.S. 98 (2000).

2. The oral arguments in *Tahoe-Sierra* suggested that even comprehensive zoning would be at risk should the Court follow the regulatory takings doctrine to its "logical" conclusion. Consider, for example, the following exchange between the Justices and counsel for the landowners:

> QUESTION [O'Connor]: . . . Now, what about your basic zoning law? I'm going to, as a city, limit the use of this property to one house per acre. You can't have unlimited apartments or commercial property owner. Now, for the enactment of that, is there a taking immediately?

> MR. BERGER: No, Your Honor.

> QUESTION [O'Connor]: Well, you're permanently deprived of the use of it for commercial purposes.

> MR. BERGER: Yes, Your Honor, but you are not totally deprived of the use of it.

> QUESTION [Kennedy]: But can we get back to the basic question that Justice Scalia asked, and Justice O'Connor asked it as well. I want your answer. Why is it that a delay for purposes of ordinary zoning, which, let's assume, prohibits you from any use of the property, is not a taking?

> MR. BERGER: Because you are there in a process working toward the actual development of the process, of the property, pardon me, in contrast to being in a situation like these people are, where there is no process for development. There is instead the desire—

> QUESTION [Kennedy]: Let's assume that the Tahoe Regional Planning Agency thought, in good faith, that there would be some development allowed, but they needed a year to think about it. . . . We know something very valuable is going to be built, but you say it's a taking, and I don't understand the difference between that and the regular zoning procedure.

> MR. BERGER: The difference is that in the second situation there is a conscious and total prohibition on use, and that's the purpose of the regulation, is to prohibit the use.

In the former situation, where you're applying for a permit, the purpose of the regulation is not to prohibit use but, in fact, to enable use.

3. *Tahoe-Sierra* is one of three cases involving the regional planning effort to protect the Lake Tahoe Basin to reach the High Court. In Lake Country Estates, Inc. v. Tahoe Reg'l Planning Agency, 440 U.S. 391, 394, 400, 402, 406 (1979), landowners filed a federal lawsuit in 1973, "alleging that TRPA, the individual members of its governing body, and its executive officer had adopted a land-use ordinance and general plan, and engaged in other conduct, that destroyed the economic value of petitioners' property." The majority, in an opinion by Justice Stevens, first found that the facts in the case "adequately characterize the alleged actions of the respondents [TRPA] as 'under color of state law' within the meaning of" 42 U.S.C. §1983. The Court also reversed the finding of the U.S. Court of Appeals for the Ninth Circuit panel that TRPA, which was created by two states, was protected by Eleventh Amendment sovereign immunity. Justice Stevens considered the special nature of the regional regulatory approach in this case:

> The regulation of land use is traditionally a function performed by local governments. Concern with the proper performance of that function in the bistate area was a primary motivation for the creation of TRPA itself, and gave rise to the specific controversy at issue in this litigation. Moreover, while TRPA, like cities, towns, and counties, was originally created by the States, its authority to make rules within its jurisdiction is not subject to veto at the state level. Indeed, that TRPA is not in fact an arm of the State subject to its control is perhaps most forcefully demonstrated by the fact that California has resorted to litigation in an unsuccessful attempt to impose its will on TRPA.

However, the Court noted that so long as the individual respondents were acting in their legislative capacity, they enjoyed absolute immunity from federal damages claims. Because the Court was "unable to determine from the record the extent to which petitioners seek to impose liability upon the individual respondents for the performance of their legislative duties," the case was remanded. The district court dismissed the case in Jacobson v. Tahoe Reg'l Planning Agency, 474 F. Supp. 901 (D. Nev. 1979), *aff'd*, 661 F.2d 940 (1981).

The third case, Suitum v. Tahoe Reg'l Planning Agency, 520 U.S. 725, 728, 729, 731, 733, 739, 744, 747-48 (1997), was a ripeness case that is more interesting for the issue that the Court chose not to address. The TRPA "determined that [Bernadine] Suitum's property [near the Nevada shore of Lake Tahoe] is ineligible for development but entitled to receive certain allegedly valuable 'Transferable Development Rights' (TDRs)." Suitum brought a regulatory taking action under §1983, "alleging that in denying her the right to construct a house on her lot, the agency's restrictions deprived her of 'all reasonable and economically viable use' of her property, and so amounted to a taking of her property without just compensation in violation of the Fifth and Fourteenth Amendments."

In 1980, Congress had mandated tighter controls in the Lake Tahoe Basin. Accordingly, in 1987, the TRPA employed a novel strategy, adopting

> a new Regional Plan providing for an "Individual Parcel Evaluation System" (IPES) to rate the suitability of vacant residential parcels for building and other modification. Whereas any property must attain a minimum IPES score to qualify for construction, an undeveloped parcel in certain areas carrying run-off into the watershed (known as "Stream Environment Zones" (SEZs)) receives an IPES score of zero. With limited exceptions . . . , the agency permits no "additional land coverage or other permanent land disturbance" on such a parcel.

To soften the economic blow of the 1987 plan, TRPA offered transferable development rights (TDRs) to owners of restricted parcels. The TDRs could then be sold to owners of other parcels in the region that were eligible for construction. One kind of TDR, known as the Residential Allocation, was awarded by local jurisdictions in random drawings held each year.

Suitum acquired her undeveloped parcel in 1972, but was unable to build on her property after 1987, as it was located in an SEZ with a zero IPES score. She did secure a Residential Allocation in a local drawing, but never attempted to transfer the TDRs that she held and to which she would be entitled. She brought the lawsuit instead.

The federal district and appellate courts decided that Suitum's claim was not ripe, the latter ruling that in an absence of an application to transfer the TDRs, "there would be no way to 'know the regulations' full economic impact or the degree of their interference with [Suitum's] reasonable investment-backed expectations[,]' and without action on a transfer application there would be no 'final decision from [the agency] regarding the application of the regulations to the property at issue.'" The Supreme Court disagreed, holding that "that Suitum has received a 'final decision' consistent with *Williamson County*'s ripeness requirement." Justice David Souter's majority opinion was referring to the holding in Williamson County Reg'l Planning Comm'n v. Hamilton Bank, 473 U.S. 172 (1985), which is discussed in Chapter Six:

> It is undisputed that the agency "has finally determined that petitioner's land lies entirely within an SEZ," Brief for Respondent 21, and that it may therefore permit "no additional land coverage or other permanent land disturbance" on the parcel, TRPA Code § 20.4. Because the agency has no discretion to exercise over Suitum's right to use her land, no occasion exists for applying *Williamson County*'s requirement that a landowner take steps to obtain a final decision about the use that will be permitted on a particular parcel.

Justice Souter's next sentence identified a more interesting, substantive issue that the majority avoided: "The parties, of course, contest the relevance of the TDRs to the issue of whether a taking has occurred, but resolution of that legal issue will require no further agency action of the sort demanded by *Williamson County*."

Justice Scalia, joined by Justices Sandra Day O'Connor and Clarence Thomas, concurred in part and concurred in the judgment. To these three Justices, the value of the TDRs that were offered to Suitum and others was relevant not to the question of *compensation* for a regulatory taking, but instead to the question of whether a taking had *occurred* in the first place. Justice Scalia explained:

> In essence, the TDR permits the landowner whose right to use and develop his property has been restricted or extinguished to extract money from others. Just as a cash payment from the government would not relate to whether the regulation "goes too far" (*i.e.*, restricts use of the land so severely as to constitute a taking), but rather to whether there has been adequate compensation for the taking; and just as a chit or coupon from the government, redeemable by and hence marketable to third parties, would relate not to the question of taking but to the question of compensation; so also the marketable TDR, a peculiar type of chit which enables a third party not to get cash from the government but to use his land in ways the government would otherwise not permit, relates not to taking but to compensation. It has no bearing upon whether there has been a "final decision" concerning the extent to which the plaintiff's land use has been constrained.

> Putting TDRs on the taking rather than the just-compensation side of the equation (as the Ninth Circuit did below) is a clever, albeit transparent, device that seeks to take advantage of a peculiarity of our takings-clause jurisprudence: Whereas once there *is* a taking, the Constitution requires just (*i.e.*, full) compensation, a regulatory taking gener-

ally does not *occur* so long as the land retains substantial (albeit not its full) value. If money that the government-regulator gives to the landowner can be counted on the question of whether there *is* a taking (causing the courts to say that the land retains substantial value, and has thus not been taken), rather than on the question of whether the compensation for the taking is adequate, the government can get away with paying much less. That is all that is going on here. It would be too obvious, of course, for the government simply to say "although your land is regulated, our land-use scheme entitles you to a government payment of $1,000." That is patently compensation and not retention of land-value. It would be a little better to say "under our land-use scheme, TDRs are attached to every parcel, and if the parcel is regulated its TDR can be cashed in with the government for $1,000." But that still looks too much like compensation. The cleverness of the scheme before us here is that it causes the payment to come, not from the government but from third parties—whom the government reimburses for their outlay by granting them (as the TDRs promise) a variance from otherwise applicable land-use restrictions.

In other words, if the simple act of designating a parcel in an SEZ reduces the value of that parcel from $100 to $0 (or to a token value such as $1), doesn't the designation effect a taking that requires just compensation of $100 (or $99) be paid to the owner? Or, can the finding that a taking has occurred be avoided altogether by coupling the designation with a TDR scheme that transfers something more than token value (say $20) to the parcel owner?

4. Professor Tony Arnold asks, *Is Wet Growth Smarter Than Smart Growth?: The Fragmentation and Integration of Land Use and Water*, in 35 Environmental Law Reporter 10152 (Mar. 2005). He has defined "wet growth" as the "integration of concerns about water quality and the availability of water supply into the density, form, pattern, and location of land development," presenting an illustrative list of local experimentation:

Cities and counties are using land use regulatory powers to restrict land use and development on lands that have the greatest impact on waters because of location and hydrologic processes: riparian lands, coastal lands, aquifer recharge zones, wetlands, and critical watershed drainage lands. For example, some Pennsylvania localities like Kennett Township, Lycoming County, Montgomery County, and West Brandywine Township have created riparian buffer zones covering lands bordering streams and rivers and limited land development and use in those zones. Likewise, the Massachusetts Watershed Protection Act and Massachusetts River Protection Act prohibit certain kinds of land uses in setbacks along the banks of rivers and streams. Austin, Texas, has a comprehensive watershed ordinance that restricts development densities according to various watershed categories and prohibits or limits development in setbacks near creeks or streams. Wisconsin's Shoreland Management Program is a state statutory and regulatory program that mandates local land use regulation of shorefront lands along lakes, ponds, rivers, and streams, subject to state review and approval. These regulations create a mandatory setback from shores for all building and regulate the types of shoreland use and development according to the classification of the water body according to its ecological and physical features. One of the most interesting exercises of land use powers to prohibit development in watersheds is New York City's state-granted authority to regulate land use in seven upstate counties containing watersheds from which New York City obtains its drinking water; New York City regulates waste-water treatment plants, subsurface sewage treatment systems, and impervious cover in these watersheds.

Zoning codes increasingly contain aquifer recharge overlay zones to limit development on critical lands from which waters recharge groundwater aquifers. For example,
the Cape Cod Commission created a "Model Aquifer Protection Bylaw" for Cape Cod
towns to adopt. This suggested addition to local zoning rules contains the creation of an
aquifer protection overlay district in the town's zoning, the prohibition of certain uses,
e.g., gas stations, hazardous waste sites, automotive salvage yards, road salt stockpiles,
landfills, airports, dry cleaning establishments, certain manufacturing facilities, in the
district, the designation of certain uses allowable only by special permit and criteria for
review of special permit applications, and performance standards for nitrogen management and stormwater management within the district. San Antonio, Texas, also established the Edwards Aquifer Recharge Zone, an overlay zone limiting development on
lands through which water percolates into the Edwards Aquifer, which is the primary
source of the region's drinking water and supports habitat for endangered species. This
overlay zone prohibits virtually all development in certain preservation areas and buffer
zones, restricts the type of development and amount of impervious cover on other lands
in the recharge zone, imposes additional land use approval procedures to evaluate the
water-related impacts of the proposed development (done by the San Antonio Water
System), and mandates best management practices (BMPs), including detention, sedimentation, and filtration for water quality control, vegetation buffer zones, water conservation, integrated pest management programs, and plans for construction sequencing
and erosion control.

As the debate in *Tahoe-Sierra* suggests, like the bi-state regulatory regime instituted to protect the
Lake Tahoe watershed, local governments that threaten the bottom line of developers or who put
construction plans on hold while officials are studying the best "wet growth" approach to take, are
vulnerable to costly and time-consuming regulatory takings challenges. Even if government attorneys are confident that they will ultimately prevail (especially if the court uses the *Penn Central*
test), even a local official who is strongly committed to environmental protection and the preservation of sensitive water resources will be chilled by a lawsuit that threatens millions of dollars in
damages and that could run up hundreds of thousands of dollars in attorneys fees.

X. On and Beyond the Horizon: Global Warming and Rising Seas

In what promises to be a movement that will envelope smart growth's already ambitious anti-sprawl
strategy, a growing number of activists and government officials have begun to act locally to attack
global warming and all that frightening phrase encompasses. In an effort to reduce greenhouse
gases and shrink carbon footprints, local governments, often with state support, have, for example,
begun to offer incentives to owners who use "green building" techniques to construct and renovate
commercial, industrial, and residential structures; to encourage compact development and urban
infilling; to remove impediments to the use of alternative energy sources such as solar and wind
even in residential neighborhoods; and to implement tree preservation and planting programs.

The following case is a fitting close for this chapter for two reasons. First, the Supreme Judicial
Court of Massachusetts skillfully works its way through the minefield of regulatory takings jurisprudence that began with Holmes' "too far" puzzle. For the student who needs help "putting it all
together" *Gove* is a godsend.

Second, local regulators in this Cape Cod town are already contending with the rising waters
and receding coastline that scientists predict will become much more familiar in the not-too-
distant future. If other courts follow *Gove*'s lead, the payment of compensation to disgruntled

landowners who are told they may not maximize the profits on their coastal investment (at least in the short run) will not be part of the already colossal costs all levels of government will face in combating relentlessly surging waters. If, however, activist judges read the precedents differently (or expand *Lucas-Nollan-Dolan* in new decisions), the price tag for this race against time and nature might well break the bank.

GOVE v. ZONING BOARD OF APPEALS
444 Mass. 754, 831 N.E.2d 865 (2005)

MARSHALL, C.J. Roberta Gove owns "lot 93," an undeveloped parcel of land within a "coastal conservancy district" (conservancy district) in Chatham. In 1998, Ann and Donald J. Grenier agreed to buy lot 93 from Gove, contingent on regulatory approval for the construction of a single-family house on the property. Because Chatham prohibits construction of new residences in the conservancy district, the zoning board of appeals of Chatham (board) denied the Greniers a building permit. Gove and the Greniers sought relief in the Superior Court on statutory and constitutional grounds, contending that the prohibition against residential construction on lot 93 did not substantially further a legitimate State interest and that the board had effected a taking of lot 93, without compensation, in violation of the Fifth and Fourteenth Amendments to the United States Constitution and art. 10 of the Massachusetts Declaration of Rights. After a two-day bench trial, a judge in the Superior Court ruled in favor of the defendants on all counts. The Appeals Court affirmed. . . .

1. Background. Lot 93 is located in the Little Beach section of Chatham, nearly all of which was acquired by Gove's parents (the Horne family) in 1926. In time, members of the Horne family developed a motel, marina, rental "cottage colonies," and a number of single-family houses in Little Beach. The family also sold several lots for development. In 1975, that portion of Little Beach still owned by the Horne family was divided, by the terms of the will of Gove's mother, among Gove and her three brothers. Gove received several lots outright and sixteen other lots in fractional ownership, to be shared with her brothers. Gove also obtained title to at least two cottages. Gove continues to own one cottage in Little Beach; she sold a second in 1996.

Little Beach is part of a narrow, low-lying peninsula, bounded by Chatham Harbor and Stage Harbor, at the extreme southeastern corner of Cape Cod. In recent years, a "breach" has formed in the barrier island that long separated Chatham Harbor from the open ocean. The breach, which is widening, lies directly across the harbor from Little Beach, and a land surveyor familiar with the area testified that Little Beach is now "wide open to the Atlantic Ocean" and prone to northeasterly storm tides. Chatham is known for its vulnerability to storms, and, according to an expert retained by Gove and the Greniers, in recent years Chatham has "as a direct result of the breach" experienced a "significant erosion problem," including "houses falling into the sea." The same expert testified that, since the appearance of the breach, "there had been a significant rise in the mean high water [near lot 93] along Chatham Harbor." The record indicates that virtually no development has occurred in Little Beach since 1980.

Even before the breach developed, Little Beach was prone to inundation by seawater. Gove testified that the area was flooded by hurricanes in 1938, 1944, and 1954, and by a significant off-shore ocean storm in 1991. None of these storms struck Chatham directly, but in the 1944 hurricane, Stage Harbor experienced a storm surge some nine feet above sea level. The 1954 hurricane damaged buildings and flooded roads in Little Beach. The 1991 storm flooded the area around lot 93 to a depth of between seven and nine feet above sea level, placing most, if not all, of the parcel underwater. The 1944, 1954, and 1991 storms, while significant, were less severe than the hypothetical "hundred year storm"[6] used for planning purposes, which is projected to flood the area to a depth of ten feet. According to another expert called by Gove and the Greniers, during storms, roads in Little Beach can become so flooded as to be impassable even to emergency vehicles, and access to the area requires "other emergency response methods," such as "helicopters or boats." The same expert conceded that, in an "extreme" event, the area could be flooded for four days, and that, in "more severe events" than a hundred year storm, storm surge flooding in Little Beach would exceed ten feet.

Lot 93 itself consists of approximately 1.8 acres. The lot is within approximately 500 feet of both Stage Harbor and Chatham Harbor and, according to one expert, is susceptible to coastal flooding "from both the front side and the backside of [the] property." The lot is bisected by a tidal creek, which is prone to flooding as well. The highest point on the property is 8.7 feet above sea level, and much of the property is less than four feet above sea level and technically a "wetland." According to a 1998 map issued by the Federal Emergency Management Agency, lot 93 lies entirely within flood hazard "Zone A," an area defined by its vulnerability to "significant flooding" in "hundred year storms." Lot 93 also lies immediately outside "Zone V" where, during a hundred year storm, significant flooding with wave action can be expected.

Gove inherited lot 93 in 1975, when residential development was permitted on the parcel. In 1985, however, the town placed all of the land within the hundred year coastal flood plain, including lot 93, into the conservancy district. The stated purposes of the conservancy district include maintaining the ground water supply, protecting coastal areas, protecting public health and safety, reducing the risk to people and property from "extreme high tides and the rising sea level," and conserving natural resources. The town zoning officer testified that the conservancy district serves to mitigate the "total public safety problem" of coastal flooding, and was specifically intended to protect both residents and public safety personnel.

The bylaw governing the conservancy district bars without exception the construction of new residential dwellings. The bylaw does allow specified nonresidential uses, either as of right or by special permit.[7] The zoning officer testified that the nonresidential uses are less likely to create a danger in the event of a flood than are residential structures, in part because structures "ancillary" to homes "tend to break off" in storms and "do a lot of collateral damage to other structures and property," whereas such damage is less likely when nonresidential structures, normally more firmly anchored to the ground, are built.

In the years before the zoning regulations were amended to restrict development in the hundred year flood zone, Gove attempted to sell lot 93. She listed the lot and another she owned with a local broker but "had no offers" on the properties, and she withdrew them from the market. Gove further testified that, whatever its value before the breach developed, lot 93's worth had "plummeted" as a result of the breach and the property "had no value . . . whatsoever" in the early 1990's. By the late 1990's, property in the area had gained value, she said, but the land, she clarified, was still most attractive to those who "have lived in the area" and were unswayed by frequent media reports of storm damage in Chatham.

In 1998, the Greniers contracted to purchase lot 93 from Gove for $192,000, contingent on their ability to obtain permits for a home and a septic system on the site. The Greniers proposed to

---

6. "A hundred year storm" is, as the term suggests, a statistical approximation of the most severe storm likely to occur in one century.

7. Uses allowed as of right include fishing and harvesting activities, shellfishing, outdoor recreation, the installation of floats, maintenance of roadways, installation of utilities, agricultural activities, dredging for navigational purposes, and construction and maintenance of public boat launches and public beaches. By special permit, additional uses are allowed, including the construction of "catwalks, piers, ramps, stairs, unpaved trails, boathouses, boat shelters, [and] roadside stands"; structures for marinas and boatyards; driveways and roadways; and private boat launching ramps.

develop a house on lot 93 on land between 5.3 and 7.0 feet in elevation. They proposed to construct the home raised on pilings, so that the level of the first floor would be above the level of a hundred year flood.

A zoning officer denied the Greniers a permit to build a house on the property. The board upheld the decision of the zoning officer. Gove and the Greniers then filed one suit against the selectmen and board and another against the conservation commission of Chatham. . . .

After a two-day trial during which both parties presented expert testimony, the Superior Court judge found "it is undisputed that [lot 93] lies in the flood plain and that its potential flooding would adversely affect the surrounding area." He found insufficient evidence to support Gove's takings claim, and concluded that she and the Greniers had failed to carry their burden of demonstrating that the board's decision was "legally untenable," "an abuse of discretion, or was arbitrary or capricious."

2. Discussion. At trial, Gove attempted to prove that the board had effected a taking of lot 93 by subjecting the property to land use regulation in a manner that failed substantially to advance legitimate State interests. Lopes v. Peabody, 417 Mass. 299, 303-304, 629 N.E.2d 1312 (1994) (*Lopes*). See Nectow v. Cambridge, 277 U.S. 183 (1928) (invalidating irrational application of zoning ordinance). Gove also contended that the town had deprived her of any beneficial use of lot 93, see Lucas v. South Carolina Coastal Council, 505 U.S. 1003 (1992) (*Lucas*), and disrupted her reasonable expectation of developing the property. See Penn Cent. Transp. Co. v. New York City, 438 U.S. 104 (1978) (*Penn Central*). We discuss Gove's theories in turn.

a. Legitimate State interests. Relying on *Lopes*, Gove argues first that the zoning regulations, as applied to lot 93, failed substantially to advance legitimate State interests. *Lopes* followed the Supreme Court's holding in Agins v. Tiburon, 447 U.S. 255, 260 (1980) (*Agins*), that "the application of a general zoning law to particular property effects a taking if the ordinance does not substantially advance legitimate State interests." This term, however, the United States Supreme Court reconsidered the validity of the *Agins* "substantially advances State interests" standard "as a freestanding takings test," and concluded that "this formula prescribes an inquiry in the nature of a due process, not a takings test, and that it has no proper place in our takings jurisprudence." Lingle v. Chevron U.S.A. Inc., [544 U.S. 528, 540] (2005) (Lingle).[11] In practical effect, *Lingle* renders a zoning ordinance valid under the United States Constitution unless its application bears no "reasonable relation to the State's legitimate purpose." Exxon Corp. v. Governor of Maryland, 437 U.S. 117, 125 (1978). This highly deferential test neither involves "heightened scrutiny," nor allows a court to question the "wisdom" of an ordinance. Exxon Corp. v. Governor of Maryland, *supra* at 124. See Ferguson v. Skrupa, 372 U.S. 726, 730-732 (1963); Nectow v. Cambridge, *supra* at 188; Euclid v. Ambler Realty Co., 272 U.S. 365, 395 (1926). To the extent that *Lopes* conflicts with *Lingle*, our earlier decision is, of course, overruled.[12]

---

11. As the *Lingle* Court explained: "The Takings Clause presupposes that the government has acted in pursuit of a valid public purpose. . . . Conversely, if a government action is found to be impermissible -- for instance because it fails to meet the 'public use' requirement or is so arbitrary as to violate due process -- that is the end of the inquiry. No amount of compensation can authorize such action" (citations omitted). Lingle v. Chevron U.S.A. Inc., [544 U.S. 528, 543] (2005).

12. We decided that case solely on Federal constitutional grounds. Lopes v. Peabody, 417 Mass. 299, 300 n.2, 629 N.E.2d 1312 (1994).

In this case, the evidence clearly establishes a reasonable relationship between the prohibition against residential development on lot 93 and legitimate State interests.[13] Gove offered no testimony meaningfully questioning the conservancy district's reasonable relationship to the protection of rescue workers and residents, the effectiveness of the town's resources to respond to natural disasters, and the preservation of neighboring property.[14] Having addressed Gove's due process concerns, we turn now to consider her takings claim.

b. Takings. While the takings clause is directed primarily at "direct government appropriation or physical invasion of private property," the Supreme Court has "recognized that government regulation of private property may, in some instances, be so onerous that its effect is tantamount to a direct appropriation or ouster—and that such 'regulatory takings' may be compensable under the Fifth Amendment." *Lingle, supra* at [537]. Not every regulation affecting the value of real property constitutes a taking, for "Government hardly could go on if to some extent values incident to property could not be diminished without paying for every such change." *Lingle, supra,* quoting Pennsylvania Coal Co. v. Mahon, 260 U.S. 393, 413 (1922). A regulation "goes too far" and becomes a "taking" in any case "where government requires an owner to suffer a permanent physical invasion of her property" or where it "completely deprives an owner of '*all* economically beneficial use' of her property" (emphasis in original). *Lingle, supra,* quoting *Lucas, supra* at 1019. "Outside these two relatively narrow categories . . . regulatory takings challenges are governed by the standards set forth in [*Penn Central*]." *Lingle, supra.*

Gove does not claim that the conservancy district regulations effected a physical occupation of her property, so we discuss, first, why Gove has not shown a "total" regulatory taking under *Lucas, supra* at 1026. We then address why she has not shown that she is entitled to compensation under Penn Central, *supra.*

i. "Total" regulatory takings. In *Lucas, supra* at 1019, the Supreme Court concluded that a land use regulation that denies a plaintiff "*all* economically beneficial use of her property," constitutes a taking "except to the extent that 'background principles of nuisance and property law' independently restrict the owner's intended use of the property" (emphasis in original). *Lingle, supra* at 2081, citing *Lucas, supra* at 1026-1032. The plaintiff in Lucas had paid $975,000 for two residential lots at a time when he was "not legally obliged to obtain a permit . . . in advance of any development activity." *Id.* at 1006, 1008. Two years later, the State enacted laws that, a State court found, rendered the two parcels "valueless," *id.* at 1007, leading the Supreme Court to conclude that a total regulatory taking could be established. *Id.* at 1031-1032.

In Palazzolo v. Rhode Island, 533 U.S. 606, 630-631 (2001) (*Palazzolo*), the Supreme Court further explained that, to prove a total regulatory taking, a plaintiff must demonstrate that the challenged regulation leaves "the property 'economically idle'" and that she retains no more than "a token interest." *Id.* at 631, quoting *Lucas, supra* at 1019. The plaintiff in *Palazzolo* was unable to prove a total taking by showing that an eighteen-acre property appraised for $3,150,000 had been

---

13. In addition to evidence of potential danger to rescue workers, an expert for Gove and the Greniers testified that in an especially severe storm, the proposed house "could certainly be picked up off its foundation and floated" away, potentially damaging neighboring homes. There was other evidence on which the judge could base a finding that a house on lot 93 would pose a danger to surrounding structures, including that the stairs required to reach the raised home, "tend to break off" in storms and "do a lot of collateral damage to other structures and property."

14. Gove points to the testimony of her expert engineer that "nothing man can do (e.g., constructing houses on pilings in a Zone A or building mounded septic systems) will alter the storm water characteristics of an ocean storm." We need not determine whether this evidence meaningfully implicates the "rational relationship" test, because the validity of the regulations as applied to lot 93 is established easily on other grounds. That the Greniers' proposed residential development would have been in compliance with wetlands and State health regulations also does not lessen the legitimacy of the challenged zoning regulation, which serves different purposes.

limited, by regulation, to use as a single residence with "$200,000 in development value." *Id*. at 616, 631.

Here, the facts are no more indicative of a total taking than those considered by the Supreme Court in *Palazzolo*. Even if we limit our analysis to lot 93, Gove has failed to prove that the challenged regulation left her property "economically idle."[15] Her own expert testified that the property was worth $23,000, a value that itself suggests more than a "token interest" in the property. Moreover, the expert's $23,000 valuation did not take into account uses allowed in the conservancy district, either as of right or by special permit, which she admitted could make the property "an income producing proposition." The judge's finding that lot 93 retained significant value despite the challenged regulation invalidates Gove's theory: she cannot prove a total taking by proving only that one potential use of her property—i.e., as the site of a house— is prohibited. *Lucas, supra* at 1019, requires that the challenged regulation "denies all economically beneficial use" of land. See *Lingle, supra* at [539] (in *Lucas* context "the complete elimination of a property's value is the determinative factor").[17] We now turn to the *Penn Central* inquiry.

> *ii. The* Penn Central *inquiry.* Recent Supreme Court opinions have emphasized that almost all regulatory takings cases involve the "essentially ad hoc factual inquiries" described in *Penn Central, supra* at 124. See *Lingle, supra*; Tahoe-Sierra Preservation Council, Inc. v. Tahoe Regional Planning Agency, [535 U.S. 302,] at 321-326, 335-336 (2002) (temporary moratoria on development); *Palazzolo, supra.*

The *Penn Central* framework eschews any "set formula" or "mathematically precise variables" for evaluating whether a regulatory taking has occurred, emphasizing instead "important guideposts" and "careful examination . . . of all the relevant circumstances." *Palazzolo, supra* at 633, 634, 636 (O'Connor, J., concurring). The relevant "guideposts" include: the actual "economic impact of the regulation" on the plaintiff; the extent to which the regulation "has interfered with" a landowner's "distinct investment-backed expectations"; and the "character of the governmental action." *Lingle, supra* at [538-39], quoting *Penn Central, supra* at 124. In the end, "the *Penn Central* inquiry turns in large part, albeit not exclusively, upon the magnitude of a regulation's economic impact and the degree to which it interferes with legitimate property interests." *Lingle, supra* at [540].

Considering all of the evidence at trial, we agree with the judge that Gove failed to show that the conservancy district regulations had a substantial "economic impact" on her or deprived her of "distinct investment-backed expectations" in lot 93. As an initial matter, Gove's failure to introduce a thorough assessment of lot 93's current value left the judge no basis to conclude that she suffered any economic loss at all. But even if we assume that residential development is the most valuable potential use of lot 93, Gove did not prove that the prohibition against a house on lot 93 caused her a loss outside the range of normal fluctuation in the value of coastal property.

Lot 93 is a highly marginal parcel of land, exposed to the ravages of nature, that for good reason remained undeveloped for several decades even as more habitable properties in the vicinity were put to various productive uses. Lot 93 is now even more vulnerable than ever to coastal flooding. Nevertheless, recent appreciation in coastal property (belatedly, and for the time being)

---

15. There may be good reason to view the impact of the conservancy district regulations on lot 93, in the context of Gove's entire holding in Little Beach, and perhaps even the entire parcel purchased by her parents in 1926. Because we conclude that the facts as applicable solely to lot 93 do not warrant a conclusion that there has been a taking, we need not address the so-called "denominator problem," and we leave the vexing questions there involved for another day, as did the Supreme Court in Palazzolo v. Rhode Island, 533 U.S. 606, 631-632 (2001) (*Palazzolo*).

17. Because Gove has failed to prove that the challenged regulation left lot 93 "economically idle," and because she retains far more than a token interest in her property, *Palazzolo, supra* at 631, quoting *Lucas, supra* at 1019, we need not consider whether the house the Greniers had proposed to construct on lot 93 otherwise would have been prohibited by "background principles of nuisance and property law." *Lingle, supra* at [538], quoting *Lucas, supra* at 1026-1032.

has given the parcel some development value. Absent the coastal conservancy district regulations, lot 93 might well be worth more. But this is a new—and insofar as it relates to residential development, wholly speculative—value that has arisen after the regulations became effective. Before the enactment of the regulations, Gove had no reasonable expectation of selling the property for residential development, a fact she recognized by removing the property from the market for want of an offer. Nor did Gove have any reasonable expectations of a better outcome as late as the early 1990's, when lot 93 had, by Gove's own estimation, "no value whatsoever." Gove could not have developed reasonable expectations of selling lot 93 for residential development after the early 1990's, by which time the regulations had barred any such development for several years. The takings clause was never intended to compensate property owners for property rights they never had. See *Lucas, supra* at 1030 (outside "total" regulatory takings context, "the Takings Clause does not require compensation when an owner is barred from putting land to a use that is proscribed by . . . 'existing rules or understandings'"); Boston Chamber of Commerce v. Boston, 217 U.S. 189, 195 (1910) (Holmes, J.) ("the question is what has the owner lost"). Gove's argument is not furthered by the Greniers' tentative offer to pay $192,000 for the parcel contingent on receiving approval to build a single-family house, a proposition that all parties reasonably should have known was highly dubious at best, particularly since the regulations did not permit such variances. It is similarly fallacious for Gove to claim that the regulations diminished the value of her property from $346,000 (the appraiser's estimate of the value of lot 93 at the time of the trial if it were suitable for a three-bedroom home) to $23,000 (the appraiser's estimate of the land's "unbuildable" worth).

This is not a case where a bona fide purchaser for value invested reasonably in land fit for development, only to see a novel regulation destroy the value of her investment. Gove did not purchase lot 93; she inherited the property as part of the devise from her mother in which she received other real property of significant value. By this we do not suggest that Gove's takings claim is defeated simply on account of her lack of a personal financial investment. See *Palazzolo, supra* at 634-635 (O'Connor, J., concurring) ("We . . . have never held that a takings claim is defeated simply on account of the lack of a personal financial investment by a . . . donee, heir, or devisee"). Rather, Gove's failure to show any substantial "personal financial investment" in lot 93 emphasizes her inability to demonstrate that she ever had any reasonable expectation of selling that particular lot for residential development, or that she has suffered any substantial loss as a result of the regulations. In these circumstances "justice and fairness" do not require that Gove be compensated. *Penn Central, supra* at 124, quoting Goldblatt v. Hempstead, 369 U.S. 590, 594 (1962). To the contrary, it seems clear that any compensation would constitute a "windfall" for Gove.

We add that "the character of the governmental action" here, *Lingle, supra* at [539], quoting *Penn Central, supra* at 124, is the type of limited protection against harmful private land use that routinely has withstood allegations of regulatory takings. It is not at all clear that Gove has "legitimate property interests" in building a house on lot 93. The judge found that "it is undisputed that [lot 93] lies in the flood plain and that its potential flooding would adversely affect the surrounding areas" if the property were developed with a house. Reasonable government action mitigating such harm, at the very least when it does not involve a "total" regulatory taking or a physical invasion, typically does not require compensation. See Agins v. Tiburon, 447 U.S. 255, 261 (1980) (regulation reducing "ill effects of urbanization"); *Penn Central, supra* at 138 (regulation restricting alteration of historic landmarks); Goldblatt v. Hempstead, *supra* (regulation restricting extent of excavation below ground water level); Miller v. Schoene, 276 U.S. 272 (1928) (statute requiring landowner to destroy disease-harboring trees).

Judgment affirmed.

Notes

1. Can the state legitimately destroy the property rights of one individual to save the property of others? In the last case cited in *Gove*, Miller v. Schoene, 276 U.S. 272, 279-80 (1928), the state of Virginia opted to favor apple orchards over cedar trees. As Justice Harlan Fiske Stone explained in his unanimous opinion:

> [C]edar rust is an infectious plant disease in the form of a fungoid organism which is destructive of the fruit and foliage of the apple, but without effect on the value of the cedar. Its life cycle has two phases which are passed alternately as a growth on red cedar and on apple trees. It is communicated by spores from one to the other over a radius of at least two miles. It appears not to be communicable between trees of the same species but only from one species to the other, and other plants seem not to be appreciably affected by it. The only practicable method of controlling the disease and protecting apple trees from its ravages is the destruction of all red cedar trees, subject to the infection, located within two miles of apple orchards.
>
> The red cedar, aside from its ornamental use, has occasional use and value as lumber. It is indigenous to Virginia, is not cultivated or dealt in commercially on any substantial scale, and its value throughout the state is shown to be small as compared with that of the apple orchards of the state. Apple growing is one of the principal agricultural pursuits in Virginia. The apple is used there and exported in large quantities. Many millions of dollars are invested in the orchards, which furnish employment for a large portion of the population, and have induced the development of attendant railroad and cold storage facilities.

The Court found that a state statute condemning and destroying the infected red cedar trees located within two miles of an apple orchard did not violate the Due Process Clause:

> When forced to such a choice the state does not exceed its constitutional powers by deciding upon the destruction of one class of property in order to save another which, in the judgment of the legislature, is of greater value to the public. It will not do to say that the case is merely one of a conflict of two private interests and that the misfortune of apple growers may not be shifted to cedar owners by ordering the destruction of their property; for it is obvious that there may be, and that here there is, a preponderant public concern in the preservation of the one interest over the other. And where the public interest is involved preferment of that interest over the property interest of the individual, to the extent even of its destruction, is one of the distinguishing characteristics of every exercise of the police power which affects property.

2. For the problems the Florida courts encountered when evaluating state efforts to stop the spread of citrus canker during various outbreaks of the disease, see State Plant Bd. v. Roberts, 71 Fla. 663, 72 So. 175 (1916) (finding that the board did not exceed its authority in promulgating a rule reading in part: "Every grove, nursery or separate plant, situated in the State of Florida which is, has been or shall become affected with citrus canker is hereby declared to be the center of an infected and dangerous zone, which zone shall extend for a mile in every direction from said center."); Florida Dep't of Agric. & Consumer Servs. v. Mid-Florida Growers, Inc., 521 So. 2d 101, 105 (Fla. 1988) (holding that "full and just compensation is required when the state, pursuant to its police power, destroys healthy trees"); Florida Dep't of Agric. & Consumer Servs. v. Polk, 568 So. 2d 35, 43 (Fla. 1990) ("affirm[ing] the trial court's determination that the destruction of the

trees actually exhibiting physical symptoms of the bacterial disease and those within 125 feet of those trees did not constitute a taking, but that Polk is entitled to compensation for the remainder of the destroyed nursery stock"); Haire v. Florida Dep't of Agric. & Consumer Servs., 870 So. 2d 774, 777 (Fla. 2004) (declaring the state Citrus Canker Law constitutional and holding that the state "is acting within permissible constitutional boundaries by destroying privately owned citrus trees that are within 1900 feet of a tree infected with citrus canker, even though the destroyed trees show no outward signs of infection and appear healthy"); and Patchen v. Florida Dep't of Agric. & Consumer Servs., 906 So. 2d 1005, 1005-06 (Fla. 2005) (holding that *Polk* did not apply "to the Department's destruction of uninfected, healthy *noncommercial, residential* citrus trees within 1900 feet of trees infected with citrus canker").

3. As you probably noticed, *Nollan, Lucas,* and several other regulatory takings cases decided by the Supreme Court over the past few decades involved parcels located quite close to major water bodies. Today, coastal jurisdictions are not just contending with the tension between environmental protection and intense development pressure; these localities are beginning to plan now for the devastating prospects of rising sea levels. Consider which of the following strategies for addressing this deadly serious aspect of global warming would be most and least likely to survive judicial scrutiny:

> (1) banning the construction of permanent structures on undeveloped parcels within a certain number of feet from the retreating shoreline;

> (2) dramatically increasing setback requirements for new, permanent structures;

> (3) amortizing the use of existing structures based the best current estimates of potential erosion and breaches;

> (4) creating special assessment districts in which only certain landowners will pay for beach renourishment, seawalls, and other costly measures; and

> (5) making transferable development rights available to landowners whose structures are threatened and partially offsetting the costs of moving smaller structures to the new location.

4. Motivated by concerns over global warming and other environmental issues, a growing number of municipalities are seeking to incorporate green building practices into their zoning and land use regulations. See, for example, Town of Normal, Illinois, Municipal Code, §15.17-14 (Environmentally Sensitive Design):

> *Preamble.* The Town of Normal is committed to encouraging the use of environmentally sensitive design techniques in the B-2 District in order to improve community and environmental health. In order to meet the goal of increased environmental sustainability, the Town hereby adopts the U.S. Green Building Council's LEED [Leadership in Energy and Environmental Design] Rating System, Version 2.0 for new construction in the B-2 District. The LEED standards aim to improve environmental and economic performance of commercial buildings using established and/or advanced industry principles, practices, materials and standards. These standards may change from time to time, so the Town reserves the right to adopt future versions of the LEED standards. . . . The LEED system establishes several levels of environmental "achievement," from a "Certified" rating (26-32 points) up to a "Platinum" rating (52+ points). The ratings are attained by earning LEED points in the categories of Sustainable Sites, Water Efficiency, Energy & Atmosphere, Materials & Resources, Indoor Environmental Quality, and Innovation & Design Process.

Requirements. While the LEED system will generally serve as guidance for developers, the Town mandates that all new construction with more than 7,500 square feet at the ground level in the B-2 District at least achieve enough LEED points to attain LEED "Certified" status. This requirement does not apply to stand-alone parking decks nor to portions of a building that are a parking deck.

For more examples of state and local programs encouraging and requiring green building practices, see Powell on Real Property §78B.03 (Michael Allan Wolf gen. ed. 2009).

5. In 2008, New Hampshire lawmakers sought to prevent local governments from using their police power to squeeze out "small wind energy systems." N.H. Rev. Stat. Ann. §674:63 provides:

Ordinances or regulations adopted by municipalities to regulate the installation and operation of small wind energy systems shall not unreasonably limit such installations or unreasonably hinder the performance of such installations. Unreasonable limits or hindrances to performance shall include the following:

I. Prohibiting small wind energy systems in all districts within the municipality.

II. Restricting tower height or system height through application of a generic ordinance or regulation on height that does not specifically address allowable tower height or system height of a small wind energy system.

III. Requiring a setback from property boundaries for a tower greater than 150 percent of the system height. In a municipality that does not adopt specific setback requirements for small wind energy systems, any small wind energy system shall be set back from the nearest property boundary a distance at least equal to 150 percent of the system height; provided, however, that this requirement may be modified by the zoning board of adjustment upon application in an individual case if the applicant establishes the conditions for a variance under this chapter.

IV. Setting a noise level limit lower than 55 decibels, as measured at the site property line, or not allowing for limit overages during short-term events such as utility outages and severe wind storms.

V. Setting electrical or structural design criteria that exceed applicable state, federal, or international building or electrical codes or laws.

Can you identify other traditional land use restrictions that might stand in the way of "greening" a municipality? You should be able to see that this New Hampshire law protects the private-property rights of the owner of a wind energy system, thus obviating the need for a regulatory takings challenge to otherwise onerous regulations. If a municipality complies with this new state law, and neighboring landowners complain that the increased noise generated by a wind energy system and the system's aesthetic appearance significantly reduce the value of their property, does that amount to a regulatory taking?

Chapter Six

The Centrality of Exclusion: Legal Impediments to Keeping "Undesirable" People and Uses Out of the Community

Exclusion is the essence of Euclidean zoning. Structures and lots are classified according to the height, area, and use deemed appropriate for the specific location. The *Euclid* majority had no trouble with the village's segregation of residential and industrial uses, a course of separation consistent with and abetted by the then-current state of nuisance law. Exclusion of apartment houses and hotels posed the "serious question" left unresolved in "numerous and conflicting" state court decisions. In the name of health, safety, morals, and general welfare—the legitimate goals of the police power—and with the blessings of "commissions and experts," Justice George Sutherland and his colleagues refused to find that setting apart single-family housing, in theory, necessarily violated Fourteenth Amendment due process and equal protection strictures.

In many ways Euclidean zoning is a quintessential Progressive concept. Several of the key components are present: (1) the reliance on experts to craft and enforce a regulatory scheme[1]; (2) the belief that a pleasant environment would foster healthy, responsible citizens[2]; (3) the trust in decentralized control; and (4) the dream that the city, in the words of one prominent reformer, could be the "hope of democracy."[3] But there was another sentiment shared by many active in the Progressive movement that underlay zoning and that contributed to its approval and popularity in the conservative climate of the 1920s: a decidedly negative view of the immigrants, particularly southern and eastern Europeans, who from the 1880s to the mid-1920s poured into America's cities in "alarming" numbers.[4]

The less-than-holy alliance between zoning as a particular land use planning tool and anti-immigration sentiment dates back to the birthplace of American height, area, and use zoning—New York City. As demonstrated by Seymour Toll in his insightful Zoned American 110 (1969), one of the driving forces behind passage of New York's 1916 ordinance was a coalition of Fifth Avenue retailers. The garment industry that had worked its way up the avenue over the previous

---

1. *See* RICHARD HOFSTADTER, THE AGE OF REFORM 155 (1955):

    Reform brought with it the brain trust. In Wisconsin even before the turn of the century there was an intimate union between the La Follette regime and the state university at Madison that foreshadowed all later brain trusts. National recognition of the importance of the academic scholar came in 1918 under Woodrow Wilson, himself an ex-professor, when the President took with him as counselors to Paris that grand conclave of expert advisers from several fields of knowledge which was known to contemporaries as The Inquiry.

2. *See, e.g.*, ARTHUR A. EKIRCH JR., PROGRESSIVISM IN AMERICA 77-78 (1974).

3. FREDERICK HOWE, THE CITY: THE HOPE OF DEMOCRACY (1909).

4. *See, e.g.*, GEORGE E. MOWRY, THE ERA OF THEODORE ROOSEVELT AND THE BIRTH OF MODERN AMERICA, 1900-1912, at 91-94 (1958); BARBARA SOLOMON, ANCESTORS AND IMMIGRANTS: A CHANGING NEW ENGLAND TRADITION (1956). Of course, there were many reformers who were dedicated to "Americanizing" the nation's newcomers, and others who, "[l]ike the rest of their generation . . . felt little enmity toward the immigrants but little identification with them either." JOHN HIGHAM, STRANGERS IN THE LAND: PATTERNS OF AMERICAN NATIVISM 1860-1925, at 118 (2d ed. 1977).

few decades, with its mass of eastern European workers, posed a serious threat to the future of high-class retailing:

> What was coming up the avenue in hot pursuit was the garment industry. It sought the same thing as the carriage trade merchant—gain—but its route was lower Fifth Avenue, its great weapon was the tall loft building, its generals were real estate speculators, and its troops were lower East Side immigrants.

That the Justices who participated in the *Euclid* case (at least those who studied the lower court opinion) were aware of the socioeconomic ramifications of their holding is undeniable. As the members of the Court reviewed Judge David Westenhaver's opinion in Ambler Realty Co. v. Village of Euclid, 297 F. 307, 313, 316 (N.D. Ohio 1924), they should have pondered this direct allusion to the exclusionary purpose and potential of land use controls:

> The purpose to be accomplished [by Euclid's zoning ordinance] is really to regulate the mode of living of persons who may hereafter inhabit [the village]. In the last analysis, the result to be accomplished is to classify the population and segregate them according to their income or situation in life. The true reason why some persons live in a mansion and others in a shack, why some live in a single-family dwelling and others in a double-family dwelling, why some live in a two-family dwelling and others in an apartment, or why some live in a well-kept apartment and others in a tenement, is primarily economic.

Indeed, Judge Westenhaver provided his reader with an important clue as to zoning's exclusionary potential:

> [I]t is equally apparent that the next step in the exercise of this police power would be to apply similar restrictions for the purpose of segregating in like manner various groups of newly arrived immigrants. The blighting of property values and the congesting of population, whenever the colored or certain foreign races invade a residential section, are so well known as to be within the judicial cognizance.

In 1926, despite this warning, the Supreme Court allowed the bold experiment in urban and suburban planning to continue.

The careful student of the Court's opinion in *Euclid* should not be surprised at the most recent developments described in the following section—efforts (primarily by courts, with the occasional legislative encouragement) to sanction the abusive use of ostensibly neutral zoning and planning tools to exclude the poor, minorities, and other "undesirable" groups and uses. For the potential use of governmental property restrictions to exclude those "not like us"—not unlike private restrictions before Shelley v. Kraemer, 334 U.S. 1 (1948)—is one of the seeds of *Euclid*.

I.   Excluding People I: The *Mount Laurel* Experiment

Nearly five decades after the Supreme Court approved the work of Euclid's planners, the New Jersey Supreme Court dropped a bombshell on the law and planning community. In their 1975 opinion in Southern Burlington County NAACP v. Township of Mount Laurel, the justices recognized and attacked the link between land use restrictions and socioeconomic segregation, a tie that was particularly distasteful because of the state's "crisis"—a "desperate need for housing, especially of decent living accommodations economically suitable for low and moderate income families." To commentators who had perceived this connection two decades before—for example, Charles M. Haar, *Zoning for Minimum Standards: The* Wayne Township *Case*, 66 Harv. L. Rev. 1051 (1953), and Norman Williams Jr., *Planning Law and Democratic Living*, 20 Law & Contemp. Probs. 316

(1955)—*Mount Laurel* was an appropriate, if somewhat delayed, judicial response. To a number of critics, particularly local and state legislators and skeptical judges from other jurisdictions, those who sat on New Jersey's high court were mistaken arbiters at best, socialist usurpers at worst.

During the more than three succeeding decades, the legacy of *Mount Laurel* has been impressive: some corrective legislation, replication and modification in a number of state courts, oceans of ink in planning and law journals, and stubborn resistance leading to a second (more restrictive and demanding) supreme court decision in the Garden State. Even if one opposed the court's activism and social tampering, it was now evident that zoning and socioeconomic exclusion were intertwined.

SOUTHERN BURLINGTON COUNTY NAACP v. TOWNSHIP OF MOUNT LAUREL
67 N.J. 151, 336 A.2d 713, *appeal dismissed & cert. denied*, 423 U.S. 808 (1975)
[MOUNT LAUREL I]

The opinion of the Court was delivered by HALL, J. . . .

Plaintiffs represent the minority group poor (black and Hispanic) seeking such [affordable] quarters. But they are not the only category of persons barred from so many municipalities by reason of restrictive land use regulations. We have reference to young and elderly couples, single persons and large, growing families not in the poverty class, but who still cannot afford the only kinds of housing realistically permitted in most places—relatively high-priced, single-family detached dwellings on sizeable lots and, in some municipalities, expensive apartments. We will, therefore, consider the case from the wider viewpoint that the effect of Mount Laurel's land use regulation has been to prevent various categories of persons from living in the township because of the limited extent of their income and resources. In this connection, we accept the representation of the municipality's counsel at oral argument that the regulatory scheme was not adopted with any desire or intent to exclude prospective residents on the obviously illegal bases of race, origin or believed social incompatibility.

As already intimated, the issue here is not confined to Mount Laurel. The same question arises with respect to any number of other municipalities of sizeable land area outside the central cities and older built-up suburbs of our North and South Jersey metropolitan areas (and surrounding some of the smaller cities outside those areas as well) which, like Mount Laurel, have substantially shed rural characteristics and have undergone great population increase since World War II, or are now in the process of doing so, but still are not completely developed and remain in the path of inevitable future residential, commercial and industrial demand and growth. Most such municipalities, with but relatively insignificant variation in details, present generally comparable physical situations, courses of municipal policies, practices, enactments and results and human, governmental and legal problems arising therefrom. It is in the context of communities now of this type or which become so in the future, rather than with central cities or older builtup suburbs or areas still rural and likely to continue to be for some time yet, that we deal with the question raised. . . .

Mount Laurel is a flat, sprawling township, 22 square miles, or about 14,000 acres, in area, on the west central edge of Burlington County. It is roughly triangular in shape, with its base, approximately eight miles long, extending in a northeasterly-southwesterly direction roughly parallel with and a few miles east of the Delaware River. Part of its southerly side abuts Cherry Hill in Camden County. That section of the township is about seven miles from the boundary line of the city of Camden and not more than 10 miles from the Benjamin Franklin Bridge crossing the river to Philadelphia.

In 1950, the township had a population of 2817, only about 600 more people than it had in 1940. It was then, as it had been for decades, primarily a rural agricultural area with no sizeable settlements or commercial or industrial enterprises. The populace generally lived in individual houses scattered along country roads. There were several pockets of poverty, with deteriorating or dilapidated housing (apparently 300 or so units of which remain today in equally poor condition). After 1950, as in so many other municipalities similarly situated, residential development and some commerce and industry began to come in. By 1960 the population had almost doubled to 5249 and by 1970 had more than doubled again to 11,221. These new residents were, of course, "outsiders" from the nearby central cities and older suburbs or from more distant places drawn here by reason of employment in the region. The township is now definitely a part of the outer ring of the South Jersey metropolitan area, which area we define as those portions of Camden, Burlington and Gloucester Counties within a semicircle having a radius of 20 miles or so from the heart of Camden city. And 65% of the township is still vacant land or in agricultural use.

The growth of the township has been spurred by the construction or improvement of main highways through or near it. The New Jersey Turnpike, and now route I-295, a freeway paralleling the turnpike, traverse the municipality near its base, with the main Camden-Philadelphia turnpike interchange at the corner nearest Camden. State route 73 runs at right angles to the turnpike at the interchange and route 38 slices through the northeasterly section. Routes 70 and U.S. 130 are not far away. This highway network gives the township a most strategic location from the standpoint of transport of goods and people by truck and private car. There is no other means of transportation.

The location and nature of development has been, as usual, controlled by the local zoning enactments. The general ordinance presently in force, which was declared invalid by the trial court, was adopted in 1964. We understand that earlier enactments provided, however, basically the same scheme but were less restrictive as to residential development. The growth pattern dictated by the ordinance is typical.

Under the present ordinance, 29.2% of all the land in the township, or 4,121 acres, is zoned for industry. . . . At the time of trial no more than 100 acres, mostly in the southwesterly corner along route 73 adjacent to the turnpike and I-295 interchanges, were actually occupied by industrial uses. They had been constructed in recent years, mostly in several industrial parks, and involved tax ratables of about 16 million dollars. The rest of the land so zoned has remained undeveloped. If it were fully utilized, the testimony was that about 43,500 industrial jobs would be created, but it appeared clear that, as happens in the case of so many municipalities, much more land has been so zoned than the reasonable potential for industrial movement or expansion warrants. At the same time, however, the land cannot be used for residential development under the general ordinance.

The amount of land zoned for retail business use under the general ordinance is relatively small—169 acres, or 1.2% of the total. . . .

The balance of the land area, almost 10,000 acres, has been developed until recently in the conventional form of major subdivisions. The general ordinance provides for four residential zones, designated R-1, R-1D, R-2 and R-3. All permit only single-family, detached dwellings, one house per lot—the usual form of grid development. Attached townhouses, apartments (except on farms for agricultural workers) and mobile homes are not allowed anywhere in the township under the general ordinance. This dwelling development, resulting in the previously mentioned quadrupling of the population, has been largely confined to the R-1 and R-2 districts in two sections—the northeasterly and southwesterly corners adjacent to the turnpike and other major highways. The result has been quite intensive development of these sections, but at a low density. The dwellings are substantial; the average value in 1971 was $32,500 and is undoubtedly much higher today.

The general ordinance requirements, while not as restrictive as those in many similar municipalities, nonetheless realistically allow only homes within the financial reach of persons of at least middle income. The R-1 zone requires a minimum lot area of 9,375 square feet, minimum lot width of 75 feet at the building line, and a minimum dwelling floor area of 1,100 square feet if a one-story building and 1,300 square feet if one and one-half stories or higher. Originally this zone comprised about 2,500 acres. Most of the subdivisions have been constructed within it so that only a few hundred acres remain (the testimony was at variance as to the exact amount). The R-2 zone, comprising a single district of 141 acres in the northeasterly corner, has been completely developed. While it only required a minimum floor area of 900 square feet for a one-story dwelling, the minimum lot size was 11,000 square feet; otherwise the requisites were the same as in the R-1 zone.

The general ordinance places the remainder of the township, outside of the industrial and commercial zones and the R-1D district (to be mentioned shortly), in the R-3 zone. This zone comprises over 7,000 acres—slightly more than half of the total municipal area—practically all of which is located in the central part of the township extending southeasterly to the apex of the triangle. The testimony was that about 4,600 acres of it then remained available for housing development. Ordinance requirements are substantially higher, however, in that the minimum lot size is increased to about one-half acre (20,000 square feet). (We understand that sewer and water utilities have not generally been installed, but, of course, they can be.) Lot width at the building line must be 100 feet. Minimum dwelling floor area is as in the R-1 zone. Presently this section is primarily in agricultural use; it contains as well most of the municipality's substandard housing. . . .

The legal question before us . . . is whether a developing municipality like Mount Laurel may validly, by a system of land use regulation, make it physically and economically impossible to provide low and moderate income housing in the municipality for the various categories of persons who need and want it and thereby, as Mount Laurel has, exclude such people from living within its confines because of the limited extent of their income and resources. Necessarily implicated are the broader questions of the right of such municipalities to limit the kinds of available housing and of any obligation to make possible a variety and choice of types of living accommodations.

We conclude that every such municipality must, by its land use regulations, presumptively make realistically possible an appropriate variety and choice of housing. More specifically, presumptively it cannot foreclose the opportunity of the classes of people mentioned for low and moderate income housing and in its regulations must affirmatively afford that opportunity, at least to the extent of the municipality's fair share of the present and prospective regional need therefor. These obligations must be met unless the particular municipality can sustain the heavy burden of demonstrating peculiar circumstances which dictate that it should not be required so to do.

We reach this conclusion under state law and so do not find it necessary to consider federal constitutional grounds urged by plaintiffs. We begin with some fundamental principles as applied to the scene before us. . . . It is required that, affirmatively, a zoning regulation, like any police power enactment, must promote public health, safety, morals or the general welfare. (The last term seems broad enough to encompass the others.) Conversely, a zoning enactment which is contrary to the general welfare is invalid. . . .

This court . . . has plainly warned, even in cases decided some years ago sanctioning a broad measure of restrictive municipal decisions, of the inevitability of change in judicial approach and view as mandated by change in the world around us.

The warning implicates the matter of whose general welfare must be served or not violated in the field of land use regulation. Frequently the decisions in this state . . . have spoken only in terms of the interest of the enacting municipality, so that it has been thought, at least in some quarters, that such was the only welfare requiring consideration. It is, of course, true that many cases have dealt only with regulations having little, if any, outside impact where the local decision is ordinarily entitled to prevail. However, it is fundamental and not to be forgotten that the zoning power is a police power of the state and the local authority is acting only as a delegate of that power and is restricted in the same manner as is the state. So, when regulation does have a substantial external impact, the welfare of the state's citizens beyond the borders of the particular municipality cannot be disregarded and must be recognized and served. . . .

It is plain beyond dispute that proper provision for adequate housing of all categories of people is certainly an absolute essential in promotion of the general welfare required in all local land use regulation. Further, the universal and constant need for such housing is so important and of such broad public interest that the general welfare which developing municipalities like Mount Laurel must consider extends beyond their boundaries and cannot be parochially confined to the claimed good of the particular municipality. It has to follow that, broadly speaking, the presumptive obligation arises for each such municipality affirmatively to plan and provide, by its land use regulations, the reasonable opportunity for an appropriate variety and choice of housing, including, of course, low and moderate cost housing, to meet the needs, desires and resources of all categories of people who may desire to live within its boundaries. Negatively, it may not adopt regulations or policies which thwart or preclude the opportunity.

It is also entirely clear, as we pointed out earlier, that most developing municipalities, including Mount Laurel, have not met their affirmative or negative obligations, primarily for local fiscal reasons. . . .

In sum, we are satisfied beyond any doubt that, by reason of the basic importance of appropriate housing and the long-standing pressing need for it, especially in the low and moderate cost category, and of the exclusionary zoning practices of so many municipalities, conditions have changed, and consistent with the warning in *Pierro*, judicial attitudes must be altered from that espoused in that and other cases cited earlier, to require, as we have just said, a broader view of the general welfare and the presumptive obligation on the part of developing municipalities at least to afford the opportunity by land use regulations for appropriate housing for all.

We have spoken of this obligation of such municipalities as "presumptive." The term has two aspects, procedural and substantive. Procedurally, we think the basic importance of appropriate housing for all dictates that, when it is shown that a developing municipality in its land use regulations has not made realistically possible a variety and choice of housing, including adequate provision to afford the opportunity for low and moderate income housing or has expressly prescribed requirements or restrictions which preclude or substantially hinder it, a facial showing of violation of substantive due process or equal protection under the state constitution has been made out and the burden, and it is a heavy one, shifts to the municipality to establish a valid basis for its action or non-action. . . . The substantive aspect of "presumptive" relates to the specifics, on the one hand, of what municipal land use regulation provisions, or the absence thereof, will evidence invalidity and shift the burden of proof and, on the other hand, of what bases and considerations will carry the municipality's burden and sustain what it has done or failed to do. Both kinds of specifics may well vary between municipalities according to peculiar circumstances. . . .

Without further elaboration at this point, our opinion is that Mount Laurel's zoning ordinance is presumptively contrary to the general welfare and outside the intended scope of the zoning power in the particulars mentioned. A facial showing of invalidity is thus established, shifting to the municipality the burden of establishing valid superseding reasons for its action and non-action. We now examine the reasons it advances.

The township's principal reason in support of its zoning plan and ordinance housing provisions, advanced especially strongly at oral argument, is the fiscal one previously adverted to, i.e., that by reason of New Jersey's tax structure which substantially finances municipal governmental and educational costs from taxes on local real property, every municipality may, by the exercise of the zoning power, allow only such uses and to such extent as will be beneficial to the local tax rate. In other words, the position is that any municipality may zone extensively to seek and encourage the "good" tax ratables of industry and commerce and limit the permissible types of housing to those having the fewest school children or to those providing sufficient value to attain or approach paying their own way taxwise.

We have previously held that a developing municipality may properly zone for and seek industrial ratables to create a better economic balance for the community vis-a-vis educational and governmental costs engendered by residential development, provided that such was ". . . done reasonably as part of and in furtherance of a legitimate comprehensive plan for the zoning of the entire municipality." Gruber v. Mayor and Township Committee of Raritan Township, 39 NJ. 1, 911 (1962). We adhere to that view today. But we were not there concerned with, and did not pass upon, the validity of municipal exclusion by zoning of types of housing and kinds of people for the same local financial end. We have no hesitancy in now saying, and do so emphatically, that, considering the basic importance of the opportunity for appropriate housing for all classes of our citizenry, no municipality may exclude or limit categories of housing for that reason or purpose. While we fully recognize the increasingly heavy burden of local taxes for municipal governmental and school costs on homeowners, relief from the consequences of this tax system will have to be furnished by other branches of government. It cannot legitimately be accomplished by restricting types of housing through the zoning process in developing municipalities.

The propriety of zoning ordinance limitations on housing for ecological or environmental reasons seems also to be suggested by Mount Laurel in support of the one-half acre minimum lot size in that very considerable portion of the township still available for residential development. It is said that the area is without sewer or water utilities and that the soil is such that this plot size is required for safe individual lot sewage disposal and water supply. The short answer is that, this being flat land and readily amenable to such utility installations, the township could require them as improvements by developers or install them under the special assessment or other appropriate statutory procedure. The present environmental situation of the area is, therefore, no sufficient excuse in itself for limiting housing therein to single-family dwellings on large lots. Cf. National Land and Investment Co. v. Kohn, 419 Pa. 504, 215 A.2d 597 (1965). This is not to say that land use regulations should not take due account of ecological or environmental factors or problems. Quite the contrary. Their importance, at least being recognized, should always be considered. Generally only a relatively small portion of a developing municipality will be involved, for, to have a valid effect, the danger and impact must be substantial and very real (the construction of every building or the improvement of every plot has some environmental impact) — not simply a makeweight to support exclusionary housing measures or preclude growth — and the regulation adopted must be only that reasonably necessary for public protection of a vital interest. Otherwise difficult additional problems relating to a "taking" of a property owner's land may arise. . . .

By way of summary, what we have said comes down to this. As a developing municipality, Mount Laurel must, by its land use regulations, make realistically possible the opportunity for an appropriate variety and choice of housing for all categories of people who may desire to live there, of course including those of low and moderate income. It must permit multi-family housing, without bedroom or similar restrictions, as well as small dwellings on very small lots, low cost housing of other types and, in general, high density zoning, without artificial and unjustifiable minimum requirements as to lot size, building size and the like, to meet the full panoply of these needs. Certainly when a municipality zones for industry and commerce for local tax benefit purposes, it without question must zone to permit adequate housing within the means of the employees involved in such uses. (If planned unit developments are authorized, one would assume that each must include a reasonable amount of low and moderate income housing in its residential "mix," unless opportunity for such housing has already been realistically provided for elsewhere in the municipality.) The amount of land removed from residential use by allocation to industrial and commercial purposes must be reasonably related to the present and future potential for such purposes. In other words, such municipalities must zone primarily for the living welfare of people and not for the benefit of the local tax rate.[20]

We have earlier stated that a developing municipality's obligation to afford the opportunity for decent and adequate low and moderate income housing extends at least to ". . . that municipality's fair share of the present and prospective regional need therefor." Some comment on that conclusion is in order at this point. Frequently it might be sounder to have more of such housing, like some specialized land uses, in one municipality in a region than in another, because of greater availability of suitable land, location of employment, accessibility of public transportation or some other significant reason. But, under present New Jersey legislation, zoning must be on an individual municipal basis, rather than regionally. So long as that situation persists under the present tax structure, or in the absence of some kind of binding agreement among all the municipalities of a region, we feel that every municipality therein must bear its fair share of the regional burden. (In this respect our holding is broader than that of the trial court, which was limited to Mount Laurel-related low and moderate income housing needs.)

The composition of the applicable "region" will necessarily vary from situation to situation and probably no hard and fast rule will serve to furnish the answer in every case. Confinement to or within a certain county appears not to be realistic, but restriction within the boundaries of the state seems practical and advisable. (This is not to say that a developing municipality can ignore a demand for housing within its boundaries on the part of people who commute to work in another state.) Here we have already defined the region at present as "those portions of Camden, Burlington and Gloucester Counties within a semicircle having a radius of 20 miles or so from the heart of Camden City." The concept of "fair share" is coming into more general use and, through the expertise of the municipal planning adviser, the county planning boards and the state planning agency, a reasonable figure for Mount Laurel can be determined, which can then be translated to the allocation of sufficient land therefor on the zoning map. . . .

There is no reason why developing municipalities like Mount Laurel, required by this opinion to afford the opportunity for all types of housing to meet the needs of various categories of people, may not become and remain attractive, viable communities providing good living and adequate services for all their residents in the kind of atmosphere which a democracy and free institutions demand. They can have industrial sections, commercial sections and sections for every kind of housing from low cost and multi-family to lots of more than an acre with very expensive homes. Proper planning and governmental cooperation can prevent over-intensive and too sudden development, insure against future suburban sprawl and slums and assure the preservation of open space and local beauty. We do not intend that developing municipalities shall be overwhelmed by voracious land speculators and developers if they use the powers which they have intelligently and in the broad public interest. Under our holdings today, they can be better communities for all than they previously have been. . . .

We are of the view that the trial court's judgment should be modified in certain respects. We see no reason why the entire zoning ordinance should be nullified. Therefore we declare it to be

---

20. This case does not properly present the question of whether a developing municipality may time its growth and, if so, how. *See, e.g.*, Golden v. Planning Board of the Town of Ramapo, 30 N.Y.2d 359, 285 N.E.2d 291 (1972), appeal dismissed, 409 U.S. 1003 (1972); Construction Industry Association of Sonoma County v. City of Petaluma, 375 F. Supp. 574 (N.D. Cal. 1974), appeal pending (citation of these cases is not intended to indicate either agreement or disagreement with their conclusions). [Authors' note: These cases are discussed in Chapter Seven.] We now say only that, assuming some type of timed growth is permissible, it cannot be utilized as an exclusionary device or to stop all further development and must include early provision for low and moderate income housing.

invalid only to the extent and in the particulars set forth in this opinion. The township is granted 90 days from the date hereof, or such additional time as the trial court may find it reasonable and necessary to allow, to adopt amendments to correct the deficiencies herein specified. It is the local function and responsibility, in the first instance at least, rather than the court's, to decide on the details of the same within the guidelines we have laid down. If plaintiffs desire to attach such amendments, they may do so by supplemental complaint filed in this cause within 30 days of the final adoption of the amendments.

We are not at all sure what the trial judge had in mind as ultimate action with reference to the approval of a plan for affirmative public action concerning the satisfaction of indicated housing needs and the entry of a final order requiring implementation thereof. Courts do not build housing nor do municipalities. That function is performed by private builders, various kinds of associations, or, for public housing, by special agencies created for that purpose at various levels of government. The municipal function is initially to provide the opportunity through appropriate land use regulations and we have spelled out what Mount Laurel must do in that regard. It is not appropriate at this time, particularly in view of the advanced view of zoning law as applied to housing laid down by this opinion, to deal with the matter of the further extent of judicial power in the field or to exercise any such power. . . . The municipality should first have full opportunity to itself act without judicial supervision. We trust it will do so in the spirit we have suggested, both by appropriate zoning ordinance amendments and whatever additional action encouraging the fulfillment of its fair share of the regional need for low and moderate income housing may be indicated as necessary and advisable. (We have in mind that there is at least a moral obligation in a municipality to establish a local housing agency pursuant to state law to provide housing for its resident poor now living in dilapidated, unhealthy quarters.) The portion of the trial court's judgment ordering the preparation and submission of the aforesaid study, report and plan to it for further action is therefore vacated as at least premature. Should Mount Laurel not perform as we expect, further judicial action may be sought by supplemental pleading in this cause.

The judgment of the Law Division is modified as set forth herein. . . .

PASHMAN, J. (concurring).

With this decision, the Court begins to cope with the dark side of municipal land use regulation—the use of zoning power to advance the parochial interests of the municipality at the expense of the surrounding region and to establish and perpetuate social and economic segregation. . . .

It is not the business of this Court or any member of it to instruct the municipalities of the State of New Jersey on the good life. Nevertheless, I cannot help but note that many suburban communities have accepted at face value the traditional canard whispered by the "blockbuster": "When low income families move into your neighborhood, it will cease being a decent place to live." But as there is no difference between the love of low income mothers and fathers and those of high income for their children, so there is no difference between the desire for a decent community felt by one group and that felt by the other. Many low income families have learned from necessity the desirability of community involvement and improvement. At least as well as persons with higher incomes, they have learned that one cannot simply leave the fate of the community in the hands of the government, that things do not run themselves, but simply run down.

Equally important, many suburban communities have failed to learn the lesson of cultural pluralism. . . .

The people of New Jersey should welcome the result reached by the Court in this case, not merely because it is required by our laws, but, more fundamentally, because the result is right and true to the highest American ideals.

Notes

1. Not surprisingly, the popular, expert, and judicial reactions to the *Mount Laurel I* decision were swift and at times furious. Before Volume 336 of the *Atlantic Reporter 2d* was shelved, one symposium had already been assembled. A review of the titles from Land Use L. & Zoning Dig., June 1975, provides a good introduction to the immediate (and in some cases lasting) concerns of several astute observers of land use planning and law:

> Delogu, *On the Choice of Remedies*, at 6; Babcock, *On the Choice of Forum*, at 7; Franklin, *The Commandments from* Mount Laurel: *New Route to the Unpromised Land*, at 9; Fessler, Mt. Laurel: *A Note to* Petaluma, at 10; Kushner, *Land Use Litigation and Low-Income Housing: Mandating Regional Fair Share Plans*, at 12; Slade, Mt. Laurel: *A View from the Bridge*, at 15; Rose, Mt. Laurel: *Is It Based on Wishful Thinking?*, at 18; Keene, *What's the Next Step After* Mt. Laurel?, at 22; Anderson, Mt. Laurel: *A Move in the Right Direction*, at 25; Scott, *Beyond 'Sic Utere. . ." to the Regional General Welfare*, at 27; Rahenkamp, *Fair Share Housing for Managed Growth*, at 30; Williams, Mt. Laurel: *A Major Transition in American Planning Law*, at 33.

These and numerous other early attempts to interpret the procedural and substantive contributions of Justice Hall and his fellow justices—as well as the political, economic, and jurisprudential ramifications—were replicated, augmented, and reargued in a wide range of fora.[5]

2. The anti-exclusionary trend spread rapidly in state courts. A number of other jurisdictions have adopted portions of the *Mount Laurel I* doctrine, often with variations reflecting local concerns and limitations. The New York Court of Appeals declared, in Berenson v. Town of New Castle, 38 N.Y.2d 102, 110, 341 N.E.2d 236, 242 (1975), that a valid zoning ordinance must provide adequately for regional needs. The court put forth a two-part test:

> The first branch of the test . . . is simply whether the board has provided a properly balanced and well ordered plan for the community. . . .

> Secondly, in enacting a zoning ordinance, consideration must be given to regional needs and requirements. . . . There must be a balancing of the local desire to maintain the *status quo* within the community and the greater public interest that regional needs be met.

---

5. *See* Oakwood at Madison, Inc. v. Township of Madison, 72 N.J. 481, 371 A.2d 1192, 1198-199 n.3 (1977):

    Mount Laurel has been the subject of extensive discussion in the literature. See Ackerman, *The* Mount Laurel *Decision: Expanding the Boundaries of Zoning Reform*, 1976 U. Ill. Law Forum 1; Payne, *Delegation Doctrine in the Reform of Local Government Law: The Case of Exclusionary Zoning*, 29 Rutgers L. Rev. 803, 805-19, 859, 866 (1976); Williams, American Land Planning Law (1975) Addendum Ch. 66; Rose, *The* Mount Laurel *Decision: Is It Based on Wishful Thinking?*, 4 Real Estate L.J. 61 (1975); Mytelka and Mytelka, *Exclusionary Zoning: A Consideration of Remedies*, 7 Seton Hall L. Rev. 1, 3-4 (1975); Kushner, *Land Use Litigation and Low Income Housing: Mandating Regional Fair Share Plans*, 9 Clearinghouse Rev. 10 (1975) (terming *Mount Laurel* the "Magna Carta of suburban low and moderate income housing"); Rohan, *Property Planning and the Search for a Comprehensive Housing Policy—The View From* Mount Laurel, 49 St. Johns L. Rev. 653 (1975); Williams and Doughty, *Studies on Legal Realism:* Mount Laurel, Belle Terre *and* Berman, 29 Rutgers L. Rev. 73 (1975) (calling *Mount Laurel* a "major turnaround on a major current problem"); Mallach, *Do Law Suits Build Housing? The Implications of Exclusionary Zoning Litigation*, 6 Rutgers-Camden L.J. 653 (1975); Rose, *Exclusionary Zoning and Managed Growth: Some Unresolved Issues*, 6 Rutgers-Camden L.J. 689 (1975); 6 Powell, Real Property, §872.1[2][g] (1975); Rose and Levin, *What is a "Developing Municipality" Within the Meaning of the* Mount Laurel *Decision?*, 4 Real Estate L.J. 359 (1976). See also Berger, Land Ownership and Use 790-799 (2d ed. 1975). For a journalistic appraisal, see *U.S. Journal: Mount Laurel, N.J.—Some Thoughts on Where Lines Are Drawn*, New Yorker, Feb. 2, 1976, at 69. *See also* Note, *The Inadequacy of Judicial Remedies in Cases of Exclusionary Zoning*, 74 Mich. L. Rev. 760 (1976).

In Associated Home Builders v. City of Livermore, 18 Cal. 3d 582, 607, 557 P.2d 473, 487, 135 Cal. Rptr. 41, 55 (1976), the court refused to apply the *Mount Laurel I* standard of review, as urged by the plaintiff, and "reaffirm[ed] the established constitutional principle that a local land use ordinance falls within the authority of the police power if it is reasonably related to the public welfare." Still, the court held open one strategy for overcoming this burden:

> When we inquire whether an ordinance reasonably relates to the public welfare, inquiry should begin by asking whose welfare must the ordinance serve. . . .
>
> If [the challenged ordinance's] impact is limited to the city boundaries, the inquiry may be limited accordingly; if, as alleged here, the ordinance may strongly influence the supply and distribution of housing for an entire metropolitan region, judicial inquiry must consider the welfare of that region.

This time the California justices cited their New Jersey counterparts approvingly for the notion of regional obligation.

3. The Pennsylvania Supreme Court, with its own approach toward striking down exclusionary ordinances, explicitly adopted the "fair share" doctrine in Surrick v. Zoning Hearing Bd. of Upper Providence Twp., 476 Pa. 182, 382 A.2d 105, 110-11 (1977), setting forth an "analytical matrix" to be applied to the facts of exclusionary zoning cases:

> The initial inquiry must focus upon whether the community in question is a logical area for development and population growth. . . .
>
> Having determined that a particular community is in the path of urban-suburban growth, the present level of development within the particular community must be examined. Population density data and the percentage of total undeveloped land and the percentage available for the development of multi-family dwellings are factors highly relevant to this inquiry.
>
> Assuming that a community is situated in the path of population expansion and is not already highly developed, this Court has, in the past, determined whether the challenged zoning scheme effected an exclusionary result or, alternatively, whether there was evidence of a "primary purpose" or exclusionary intent to zone out the natural growth of population. . . .
>
> In analyzing the effect of a zoning ordinance, the extent of the exclusion, if any, must be considered. Is there *total* exclusion of multi-family dwellings, which we disapproved in *Girsh Appeal* [437 Pa. 237, 263 A.2d 395 (1970)], or is the exclusion *partial*? If the zoning exclusion is partial, obviously the question of the ordinance's validity is more difficult to answer. In resolving this issue, once again the percentage of community land available under the zoning ordinance for multi-family dwellings becomes relevant. This percentage must be considered in light of current population growth pressure, within the community as well as the region, and in light of the total amount of undeveloped land in the community. Where the amount of land zoned as being available for multi-family dwellings is disproportionately small in relation to these latter factors, the ordinance will be held to be exclusionary.

In three post-*Surrick* cases, however, a sharply divided supreme court struggled with the implications and scope of its fair share mandate. In In re Appeal of M.A. Kravitz Co., 501 Pa. 200, 460 A.2d 1075 (1983), the plurality found that the Board of Supervisors for the Wrightstown Township—given the absence of major employers within the township, the lack of major highway links with Trenton and Philadelphia, and expert testimony that the "area has experienced little growth in the past and is designated as an area slated for little growth in the future"—had legitimately denied a zoning amendment to allow plaintiff to create a townhouse development on its 96-acre parcel. Justice William D. Hutchinson, one of three dissenters, was disturbed by the township's "total exclusion of townhouses."

Two days later the court decided In re Appeal of Elocin, Inc., 501 Pa. 348, 353, 461 A.2d 771, 773 (1983). In another plurality opinion, Justice Stephen Zappala wrote:

> We do not agree that a municipality must necessarily provide for every conceivable use. Where a municipality provides for a reasonable share of multi-family dwellings [semi-detached homes, two-family homes, and apartment homes with up to four units] as Springfield has done [12 percent of its housing units], it need not provide for every conceivable subcategory of such dwellings.

Thus, the rejection of Elocin's proposal "to construct 567 mid- or high-rise apartment units and 305 townhouse units" was not unconstitutional.

Two years after this apparent shift from the activism of the 1970s, in Fernley v. Board of Supervisors of Schuylkill Twp., 509 Pa. 413, 417-18, 425, 502 A.2d 585, 587, 591 (1985), a four-member majority decided an issue that lay unresolved since Surrick:

> We are now confronted with the question of whether a fair share analysis must be employed to assess the exclusionary impact of zoning regulations which totally prohibit a basic type of housing. We hold that the fair share analysis is inapplicable to this Schuylkill Township ordinance which absolutely prohibits apartment buildings.

The balancing test appropriate for de facto exclusion was found inappropriate for municipalities engaged in de jure bans, even if the municipality could demonstrate that it projected little or no growth in the future. Predictably, there were dissents, objecting to the reformulation of the court's strategy and to the extreme remedy ordered by the majority: "[R]emand . . . to the Court of Common Pleas for approval of appellants' proposed development [245 acres with garden apartments, townhouses, and quadraplexes] unless the appellee can show that appellants' plan is incompatible with the site or reasonable, pre-existing health and safety codes and regulations."

Some of the Pennsylvania decisional shifts, as in the New Jersey line of cases, can be attributed to changes in court membership. How well have these courts balanced the desire to fine-tune doctrines with the need for predictability and continuity? What are the benefits of trial and appellate judges working out the nuances of reform on a case-by-case basis, as opposed to the wholesale change ushered in by comprehensive legislation? How do the efforts of the courts in these two key jurisdictions to correct the injustices they perceived, to draw meaningful distinctions (de facto versus de jure, developing versus developed, and the like), and to craft effective remedies, compare with the efforts of the Supreme Court in Brown v. Board of Education (I and II), 347 U.S. 483 (1954), 349 U.S. 294 (1955), and their controversial, often-complicated progeny?

4. There are important environmental aspects to Mount Laurel. First, the New Jersey high court, while noting generally that "ecological or environmental factors or problems" "should always be considered," was suspicious of the defendant municipality's "present environmental situation," which was deemed "no sufficient excuse in itself for limiting housing therein to single-family dwellings on large lots." Second, Mount Laurel I demonstrates the apparent incompatibility of two goals traditionally associated with "liberals"—the provision of adequate, affordable, suburban housing for lower income city denizens (particularly minorities) and the protection of the natural environment outside of highly populated urban areas. The reuse of underutilized urban areas, even contami-

nated former industrial sites known as "brownfields," is a popular solution among Smart Growth advocates,[66] although there are some serious concerns.[77] Third, an interesting wrinkle was added by the Supreme Court of Washington in Save a Valuable Environment v. City of Bothell, 89 Wash. 2d 862, 871, 576 P.2d 401, 406 (1978), a challenge mounted by a nonprofit group against the rezoning of farmland for a major regional shopping center. The court noted that California, New Jersey, and New York "have imposed a duty to serve regional welfare when considering adequate housing. . . . We find such a duty to exist when the interest at stake is the quality of the environment."

5. The good faith that Judge Wood perceived in Mount Laurel's efforts to comply with the 1975 mandate did not bring the desired results. On October 20-22, and December 15, 1980, the New Jersey Supreme Court—frustrated by the refusal or inability of local officials throughout the state to allow for the provision of low-cost housing—once again heard oral argument, this time with an eye toward framing an effective remedy to realize the ambitious fair share goals of Mount Laurel I. Twenty-five more months would pass before the court announced its dramatic opinion, running nearly 250 pages. By January 1983, as national attention once again turned to the South Jersey flatlands, not much had changed, as reported in Robert Hanley, After 7 Years, Town Remains Under Fire for Its Zoning Code, N.Y. Times, Jan. 22, 1983, at 31:

> Despite the order's potential for broad social and economic change, Mount Laurel's landscape remains dominated by horse farms, orchards, farms, woods and back-country roads, even though it is a 15-minute drive east of Philadelphia. None of the 515 new housing units that the Planning Board in 1976 thought would satisfy the court's dictate were ever built. . . .

> Mount Laurel's response to the 1975 holding—the action that drew the court's wrath in the ruling Thursday—was to rezone three widely scattered plots for low-income housing. Together, the three parcels contain 33 of the 14,176 predominantly rural acres in the town. . . .

> The 33 acres set aside years ago remain as they did then. One plot of 13 acres is a field on the fringe of an apple orchard. . . .

> Another plot has 13 acres of idle land at the rear of the Moorestown Shopping Mall. Another Philadelphia company, the Binswanger Management Corporation, which plans and manages office buildings, owns it. Binswanger has never proposed construction of housing on the site. . . . although Binswanger attempted to win approval for an industrial park on adjacent land it owns. . . .

---

6. See, e.g., http://www.nj.gov/dca/divisions/osg/commissions/:

> The New Jersey Brownfields Redevelopment Task Force assists municipalities and counties in using brownfield redevelopment to help implement Smart Growth strategies in their plans and initiating an inventory of marketable brownfield sites for prospective developers with the support of the Brownfields Redevelopment InterAgency Team.

7. See Michael Allan Wolf, Dangerous Crossing: State Brownfields Recycling and Federal Enterprise Zoning, 9 FORDHAM ENVTL. L.J. 495, 496 (1998):

> [O]n the one hand, in the nation's depressed city centers there are hundreds of thousands of abandoned buildings—vestiges of America's industrial heyday—that can house the engines of the post-industrial economy of the new century (especially in the service and technology sectors) and in turn provide living-wage jobs for some of the nation's neediest residents. On the other hand, the redevelopment and reuse of many of these structures and the parcels upon which they sit pose a real health threat to some of our most vulnerable and politically powerless communities.

The third designated low-income housing plot, with seven acres, has for years been a farm for Christmas trees owned by Alfred DiPietro, an engineer for RCA, who lives in Guam. His nephews run the farm.

Mr. Godfrey, the owner of the country store and a friend of Mr. DiPietro, said, "Until he gets a fortune for the land, he'll never sell it for any housing."

Could the court fashion affirmative remedies and create incentives strong enough to overcome such recalcitrance? How sincere is the court in its repeated entreaties for legislative assistance (even preemption)? Had the inflation and high interest rates of the hiatus between opinions I and II, coupled with housing program budget cuts out of Washington, D.C., eliminated any real hope for large-scale real estate development for low- and moderate-income buyers and renters? Could the court avoid complicating even further the process by which municipalities calculated their regional obligations? Despite their repeated protests, were not the justices indeed trying to "build houses"?

SOUTHERN BURLINGTON COUNTY NAACP v. TOWNSHIP OF MOUNT LAUREL
92 N.J. 158, 456 A.2d 390 (1983)
[MOUNT LAUREL II]

The opinion of the Court was delivered by WILENTZ, C. J.

This is the return, eight years later, of Southern Burlington County N.A.A.C.P. v. Township of Mount Laurel, 67 N .J. 151, 336 A.2d 713 (1975) (*Mount Laurel I*). We set forth in that case, for the first time, the doctrine requiring that municipalities' land use regulations provide a realistic opportunity for low and moderate income housing. The doctrine has become famous. The *Mount Laurel* case itself threatens to become infamous. After all this time, ten years after the trial court's initial order invalidating its zoning ordinance, Mount Laurel remains afflicted with a blatantly exclusionary ordinance. Papered over with studies, rationalized by hired experts, the ordinance at its core is true to nothing but Mount Laurel's determination to exclude the poor. Mount Laurel is not alone; we believe that there is widespread noncompliance with the constitutional mandate of our original opinion in this case.

To the best of our ability, we shall not allow it to continue. This Court is more firmly committed to the original *Mount Laurel* doctrine than ever, and we are determined, within appropriate judicial bounds, to make it work. The obligation is to provide a realistic opportunity for housing, not litigation. We have learned from experience, however, that unless a strong judicial hand is used, *Mount Laurel* will not result in housing, but in paper, process, witnesses, trials and appeals. We intend by this decision to strengthen it, clarify it, and make it easier for public officials, including judges, to apply it.

This case is accompanied by five others, heard together and decided in this opinion.[1] All involve questions arising from the *Mount Laurel* doctrine. They demonstrate the need to put some steel into that doctrine. The deficiencies in its application range from uncertainty and inconsistency at

---

1. Because these cases raised many similar issues concerning the *Mount Laurel* doctrine, they were argued together and have been disposed of in this single opinion.

We would prefer that our opinion took less time and less space. The subject is complex, highly controversial, and obviously of great importance. We have not one, but six cases before us that raise practically all of the major questions involved in the *Mount Laurel* doctrine; furthermore we have dealt with other questions that, strictly speaking, might not be necessary for resolving these cases, since we thought it important to settle them as well. Unfortunately, as the history of the *Mount Laurel* doctrine proves, the clear resolution of issues of this kind requires extensive time and extensive discussion. . . .

the trial level to inflexible review criteria at the appellate level. The waste of judicial energy involved at every level is substantial and is matched only by the often needless expenditure of talent on the part of lawyers and experts. The length and complexity of trials is often outrageous, and the expense of litigation is so high that a real question develops whether the municipality can afford to defend or the plaintiffs can afford to sue. . . .

These six cases not only afford the opportunity for, but demonstrate the necessity of reexamining the *Mount Laurel* doctrine. We do so here. The doctrine is right but its administration has been ineffective. . . .

[W]hile we have always preferred legislative to judicial action in this field, we shall continue— until the Legislature acts—to do our best to uphold the constitutional obligation that underlies the *Mount Laurel* doctrine. That is our duty. We may not build houses, but we do enforce the Constitution.[7]

We note that there has been some legislative initiative in this field. We look forward to more. The new Municipal Land Use Law explicitly recognizes the obligation of municipalities to zone with regional consequences in mind, N J.S.A. 40:55D-28(d); it also recognizes the work of the Division of State and Regional Planning in the Department of Community Affairs (DCA), in creating the State Development Guide Plan (1980) (SDGP), which plays an important part in our decisions today. Our deference to these legislative and executive initiatives can be regarded as a clear signal of our readiness to defer further to more substantial actions.

The judicial role, however, which could decrease as a result of legislative and executive action, necessarily will expand to the extent that we remain virtually alone in this field. In the absence of adequate legislative and executive help, we must give meaning to the constitutional doctrine in the cases before us through our own devices, even if they are relatively less suitable. That is the basic explanation of our decisions today. . . .

The following is a summary of the more significant rulings of these cases:

(1) Every municipality's land use regulations should provide a realistic opportunity for decent housing for at least some part of its resident poor who now occupy dilapidated housing. The zoning power is no more abused by keeping out the region's poor than by forcing out the resident poor. In other words, each municipality must provide a realistic opportunity for decent housing for its indigenous poor except where they represent a disproportionately large segment of the population as compared with the rest of the region. This is the case in many of our urban areas.

(2) The existence of a municipal obligation to provide a realistic opportunity for a fair share of the region's present and prospective low and moderate income housing need will no longer be determined by whether or not a municipality is "developing." The obligation extends, instead, to every municipality, any portion of which is designated by the State, through the SDGP as a

---

7. In New Jersey, it has traditionally been the judiciary, and not the Legislature, that has remedied substantive abuses of the zoning power by municipalities. A review of zoning litigation and legislation since the enactment of the zoning enabling statute in the 1920's shows that the Legislature has confined itself largely to regulating the procedural aspects of zoning. The judiciary has at the same time invalidated or modified zoning ordinances that violated constitutional rights or failed to serve the general welfare. . . . Although the complexity and political sensitivity of the issue now before us make it especially appropriate for legislative resolution, we have no choice, absent that resolution, but to exercise our traditional constitutional duty to end an abuse of the zoning power.

"growth area."[8] This obligation, imposed as a remedial measure, does not extend to those areas where the SDGP discourages growth—namely, open spaces, rural areas, prime farmland, conservation areas, limited growth areas, parts of the Pinelands and certain Coastal Zone areas. The SDGP represents the conscious determination of the State, through the executive and legislative branches, on how best to plan its future. It appropriately serves as a judicial remedial tool. The obligation to encourage lower income housing, therefore, will hereafter depend on rational long-range land use planning (incorporated into the SDGP) rather than upon the sheer economic forces that have dictated whether a municipality is "developing." Moreover, the fact that a municipality is fully developed does not eliminate this obligation although, obviously, it may affect the extent of the obligation and the timing of its satisfaction. The remedial obligation of municipalities that consist of both "growth areas" and other areas may be reduced, based on many factors, as compared to a municipality completely within a "growth area."

There shall be a heavy burden on any party seeking to vary the foregoing remedial consequences of the SDGP designations.

(3) *Mount Laurel* litigation will ordinarily include proof of the municipality's fair share of low and moderate income housing in terms of the number of units needed immediately, as well as the number needed for a reasonable period of time in the future. "Numberless" resolution of the issue based upon a conclusion that the ordinance provides a realistic opportunity for some low and moderate income housing will be insufficient. Plaintiffs, however, will still be able to prove a prima facie case, without proving the precise fair share of the municipality, by proving that the zoning ordinance is substantially affected by restrictive devices, that proof creating a presumption that the ordinance is invalid.

The municipal obligation to provide a realistic opportunity for low and moderate income housing is not satisfied by a good faith attempt. The housing opportunity provided must, in fact, be the substantial equivalent of the fair share.

(4) Any future *Mount Laurel* litigation shall be assigned only to those judges selected by the Chief Justice with the approval of the Supreme Court. The initial group shall consist of three judges, the number to be increased or decreased hereafter by the Chief Justice with the Court's approval. The Chief Justice shall define the area of the State for which each of the three judges is responsible: any *Mount Laurel* case challenging the land use ordinance of a municipality included in that area shall be assigned to that judge.

Since the same judge will hear and decide all *Mount Laurel* cases within a particular area and only three judges will do so in the entire state, we believe that over a period of time a consistent pattern of regions will emerge. Consistency is more likely as well in determinations of regional housing needs and allocations of fair share to municipalities within the region. Along with this consistency will come the predictability needed to give full effect to the *Mount Laurel* doctrine. While determinations of region and regional housing need will not be conclusive as to any munici-

---

8. Authors' note: Not all concerned were as comfortable with the suitability of the State Development Guide Plan (SDGP) for the purposes the court had in mind:

   George Sternlieb, Director of the Center for Urban Policy Research at Rutgers University, has called the entire document "poorly done. The administration of Governor Kean, openly opposed to the mandate because of what the Governor has called "overly aggressive judicial action," has refused to endorse it on the ground the plan is not sufficient as a statewide zoning map.

   "It's a good plan for the purpose for which it was written—to help with new infrastructure projects," said W. Cary Edwards, the Governor's chief counsel. "It simply is not a very accurate tool for the purposes the court wants it used."

   Anthony De Palma, *N.J. Housing Woes Are All Over the Map*, N.Y. Times, Apr. 17, 1983.

pality not a party to the litigation, they shall be given presumptive validity in subsequent litigation involving any municipality included in a previously determined region. . . .

(5) The municipal obligation to provide a realistic opportunity for the construction of its fair share of low and moderate income housing may require more than the elimination of unnecessary cost-producing requirements and restrictions. Affirmative governmental devices should be used to make that opportunity realistic, including lower-income density bonuses and mandatory set-asides. Furthermore the municipality should cooperate with the developer's attempts to obtain federal subsidies. For instance, where federal subsidies depend on the municipality providing certain municipal tax treatment allowed by state statutes for lower income housing, the municipality should make a good faith effort to provide it. Mobile homes may not be prohibited, unless there is solid proof that sound planning in a particular municipality requires such prohibition.

(6) The lower income regional housing need is comprised of both low and moderate income housing. A municipality's fair share should include both in such proportion as reflects consideration of all relevant factors, including the proportion of low and moderate income housing that make up the regional need.

(7) Providing a realistic opportunity for the construction of least-cost housing will satisfy a municipality's *Mount Laurel* obligation if, and only if, it cannot otherwise be satisfied. In other words, it is only after all alternatives have been explored, all affirmative devices considered, including, where appropriate, a reasonable period of time to determine whether low and moderate income housing is produced, only when everything has been considered and tried in order to produce a realistic opportunity for low and moderate income housing that least-cost housing will provide an adequate substitute. Least-cost housing means what it says, namely, housing that can be produced at the lowest possible price consistent with minimal standards of health and safety.

(8) Builder's remedies will be afforded to plaintiffs in *Mount Laurel* litigation where appropriate, on a case-by-case basis. Where the plaintiff has acted in good faith, attempted to obtain relief without litigation, and thereafter vindicates the constitutional obligation in *Mount Laurel*-type litigation, ordinarily a builder's remedy will be granted, provided that the proposed project includes an appropriate portion of low and moderate income housing, and provided further that it is located and designed in accordance with sound zoning and planning concepts, including its environmental impact.

(9) The judiciary should manage *Mount Laurel* litigation to dispose of a case in all of its aspects with one trial and one appeal, unless substantial considerations indicate some other course. This means that in most cases after a determination of invalidity, and prior to final judgment and possible appeal, the municipality will be required to rezone, preserving its contention that the trial court's adjudication was incorrect. If an appeal is taken, all facets of the litigation will be considered by the appellate court including both the correctness of the lower court's determination of invalidity, the scope of remedies imposed on the municipality, and the validity of the ordinance adopted after the judgment of invalidity. The grant or denial of a stay will depend upon the circumstances of each case. The trial court will appoint a master to assist in formulating and implementing a proper remedy whenever that course seems desirable.

(10) The *Mount Laurel* obligation to meet the prospective lower income housing need of the region is, by definition, one that is met year after year in the future, throughout the years of the particular projection used in calculating prospective need. In this sense the affirmative obligation to provide a realistic opportunity to construct a fair share of lower income housing is met by a "phase-in" over those years; it need not be provided immediately. Nevertheless, there may be circumstances in which the obligation requires zoning that will provide an immediate opportunity—for instance, zoning to meet the region's present lower income housing need. In some cases,

the provision of such a realistic opportunity might result in the immediate construction of lower income housing in such quantity as would radically transform the municipality overnight. Trial courts shall have the discretion, under those circumstances, to moderate the impact of such housing by allowing even the present need to be phased in over a period of years. Such power, however, should be exercised sparingly. The same power may be exercised in the satisfaction of prospective need, equally sparingly, and with special care to assure that such further postponement will not significantly dilute the *Mount Laurel* obligation. . . .

There are two basic types of affirmative measures that a municipality can use to make the opportunity for lower income housing realistic: (1) encouraging or requiring the use of available state or federal housing subsidies, and (2) providing incentives for or requiring private developers to set aside a portion of their developments for lower income housing. Which, if either, of these devices will be necessary in any particular municipality to assure compliance with the constitutional mandate will be initially up to the municipality itself. Where necessary, the trial court overseeing compliance may require their use. We note again that least-cost housing will not ordinarily satisfy a municipality's fair share obligation to provide low and moderate income housing unless and until it has attempted the inclusionary devices outlined below or otherwise has proven the futility of the attempt. . . .

There are several inclusionary zoning techniques that municipalities must use if they cannot otherwise assure the construction of their fair share of lower income housing. Although we will discuss some of them here, we in no way intend our list to be exhaustive; municipalities and trial courts are encouraged to create other devices and methods for meeting fair share obligations.

The most commonly used inclusionary zoning techniques are incentive zoning and mandatory set-asides. The former involves offering economic incentives to a developer through the relaxation of various restrictions of an ordinance (typically density limits) in exchange for the construction of certain amounts of low and moderate income units. The latter, a mandatory set-aside, is basically a requirement that developers include a minimum amount of lower income housing in their projects.

In addition to the mechanisms we have just described, municipalities and trial courts must consider such other affirmative devices as zoning substantial areas for mobile homes and for other types of low cost housing and establishing maximum square footage zones, i.e., zones where developers cannot build units with more than a certain footage or build anything other than lower income housing or housing that includes a specified portion of lower income housing. In some cases, a realistic opportunity to provide the municipality's fair share may require over-zoning, i.e., zoning to allow for more than the fair share if it is likely, as it usually is, that not all of the property made available for lower income housing will actually result in such housing.

Although several of the defendants concede that simply removing restrictions and exactions is unlikely to result in the construction of lower income housing, they maintain that requiring the municipality to use affirmative measures is beyond the scope of the courts' authority. We disagree. . . .

The specific contentions are that inclusionary measures amount to a taking without just compensation and an impermissible socio-economic use of the zoning power, one not substantially related to the use of land. Reliance is placed to some extent on Board of Supervisors v. DeGroff Enterprises, Inc., 214 Va. 235, 198 S.E. 2d 600 (1973), to that effect. We disagree with that decision. . . . We hold that where the *Mount Laurel* obligation cannot be satisfied by removal of restrictive barriers, inclusionary devices such as density bonuses and mandatory set-asides keyed to the construction of lower income housing, are constitutional and within the zoning power of a municipality. . . .

The contention that generally these devices are beyond the municipal power because they are "socio-economic" is particularly inappropriate. The very basis for the constitutional obligation underlying *Mount Laurel* is a belief, fundamental, that excluding a class of citizens from housing on an economic basis (one that substantially corresponds to a socio-economic basis) distinctly disserves the general welfare. That premise is essential to the conclusion that such zoning ordinances are an abuse of the zoning power and are therefore unconstitutional.

It is nonsense to single out inclusionary zoning (providing a realistic opportunity for the construction of lower income housing) and label it "socio-economic" if that is meant to imply that other aspects of zoning are not. Detached single family residential zones, high-rise multi-family zones of any kind, factory zones, "clean" research and development zones, recreational, open space, conservation, and agricultural zones, regional shopping mall zones, indeed practically any significant kind of zoning now used, has a substantial socio-economic impact and, in some cases, a socio-economic motivation. It would be ironic if inclusionary zoning to encourage the construction of lower income housing were ruled beyond the power of a municipality because it is "socio-economic" when its need has arisen from the socio-economic zoning of the past that excluded it. . . .

Townships such as Mount Laurel that now ban mobile homes do so in reliance upon Vickers v. Gloucester, 37 N.J. 232, 181 A.2d 129 (1962), in which this Court upheld such bans. Vickers, however, explicitly recognized that changed circumstances could require a different result. *Id.* at 250, 181 A.2d 129. We find that such changed circumstances now exist. As Judge Wood found in *Mount Laurel II*, mobile homes have since 1962 become "structurally sound [and] attractive in appearance." 161 N.J. Super. at 357, 391 A.2d 935. Further, since 1974, the safety and soundness of mobile homes have been regulated by the National Mobile Home Construction and Safety Standards Act, 42 U.S.C. 5401 (1974). *Vickers*, therefore, is overruled; absolute bans of mobile homes are no longer permissible on the grounds stated in that case. . . .

We hold that where a developer succeeds in *Mount Laurel* litigation and proposes a project providing a substantial amount of lower income housing, a builder's remedy should be granted unless the municipality establishes that because of environmental or other substantial planning concerns, the plaintiff's proposed project is clearly contrary to sound land use planning. We emphasize that the builder's remedy should not be denied solely because the municipality prefers some other location for lower income housing, even if it is in fact a better site. Nor is it essential that considerable funds be invested or that the litigation be intensive. . . .

Trial courts should guard the public interest carefully to be sure that plaintiff-developers do not abuse the *Mount Laurel* doctrine. Where builder's remedies are awarded, the remedy should be carefully conditioned to assure that in fact the plaintiff-developer constructs a substantial amount of lower income housing. Various devices can be used for that purpose, including prohibiting construction of more than a certain percentage of the non-lower income housing until a certain amount of the lower income housing is completed. . . .

The scope of remedies authorized by this opinion is similar to those used in a rapidly growing area of the law commonly referred to as "institutional litigation" or "public law litigation."[43] . . . What we said in *Mount Laurel* in reference to remedy eight years ago was that such remedies were "not appropriate at this time, particularly in view of the advanced view of zoning law as applied to housing laid down by this opinion . . . ." 67 N.J. at 192, 336 A.2d 713. That view is no longer "advanced," at least not in this state. It is eight years old. . . .

The provision of decent housing for the poor is not a function of this Court. Our only role is to see to it that zoning does not prevent it, but rather provides a realistic opportunity for its construction as required by New Jersey's Constitution. The actual construction of that housing will continue to depend, in a much larger degree, on the economy, on private enterprise, and on the actions of the other branches of government at the national, state and local level. We intend here only to make sure that if the poor remain locked into urban slums, it will not be because we failed to enforce the Constitution.

Notes

1. Once again the New Jersey court's bold move inspired reactions pro and con. The January 30, 1983, editorial in the *New York Times—Zoning People In, Not Out* (at 4-18)—was supportive, but tempered with caution:

> Will the opinion prevail? The answer isn't clear. Aware of the radical implications, the court called for gradual implementation. The troubles of the housing market and shrinking funds for subsidies may frustrate this ruling even more than legal battles frustrated the first. Over time, however, some change seems inevitable—and highly desirable.

This time the "instant symposium," entitled Mount Laurel II: *A Case of National Significance*, Land Use L. & Zoning Dig., March 1983, featured the following contributions: Paul Davidoff & Phil Tegeler, Mount Laurel II: *Well Worth the Wait*; Washburn, *Some Unresolved Issues in* Mount Laurel II; Daniel Mandelker, *Fair Share and Set-Aside Issues*; Charles Siemon, *Remedies Under* Mount Laurel II; Rose, *How Will New Jersey Municipalities Comply?* See also the symposium in 14 Seton Hall L. Rev. 829 (1984).

2. One of the more challenging legacies of *Mount Laurel II* was the proliferation of complicated quantitative studies and complex formulas that were devised, criticized, and reformulated to respond to the court's demands. For example, the tables entitled "Mount Laurel Cost for Moderate Income Housing and Mount Laurel Cost for Low Income Housing" were prepared by one group of planning and development consultants (Abeles Schwartz Associates) to counter the data used by a developer as the basis for a decision not to complete its acquisition of property in Princeton,

---

43. These cases have involved school desegregation, prison overcrowding, reapportionment and, significantly, housing. In them the courts, and they are usually federal courts, have found that the scope of a particular constitutional obligation, and the resistance to its vindication, are such as to require much more active judicial involvement in the remedial stage of litigation than is conventional if the constitutional obligation is to be satisfied. Federal district courts have retained particular school desegregation disputes for many years, fashioning remedies year after year as the circumstances seem to require; in some, they have actually taken over school districts, administered prisons, hospitals, and other institutions, ordered housing authorities to build housing in certain areas, in some cases even outside of the municipality involved. The authorities, both case and comment, are unanimous in their conclusion that exclusionary zoning cases fall within this category, that they are "institutional litigation" or "public law litigation" for the purpose of determining what kinds of procedures, including remedies, are appropriate. . . .

New Jersey, for a large-scale project. According to Abeles, the developer had overestimated the total subsidy required for a projected 2000 units by $1.7 million dollars.

The private sector did not have a monopoly on statistical analysis by any means, however. For example, in AMG Realty Co. v. Warren Twp., 207 N.J. Super. 388, 411, 504 A.2d 692, 703-04 (Super. Ct. App. Div. 1984), Judge Eugene Serpentelli calculated that for 1980-1990, "[u]sing the 11-county present need region, Warren's fair share of the reallocation pool of 35,014 is 162," "Warren's present need percentage of the present regional need is 1.126%," "Warren's fair share of the prospective regional need of 49,004 is 732 units," and "Warren's prospective need percentage of the prospective regional need is 1.208%." For an insider's view of the development, intricacies, and drawbacks of the "Urban League formula" used by the special *Mount Laurel II* courts, see John M. Payne, *Rethinking Fair Share: The Judicial Enforcement of Affordable Housing Policies*, 16 Real Est. L.J. 20, 22-29 (1987).

3. Though not to the level of its predecessor, *Mount Laurel II* has provoked some judicial responses in other jurisdictions. In Asian Americans for Equality v. Koch, 129 Misc. 2d 67, 80, 82-83, 84, 492 N.Y.S.2d 837, 846, 848, 849 (1985), plaintiffs were challenging a 1981 New York City zoning amendment, creating the Special Manhattan Bridge District,

> as part of a plan of gentrification to specifically exclude minority and low-income people from New York City, and Chinatown in particular. . . . Here, the plaintiffs do not wish to relocate to the suburbs (the normal situation in exclusionary zoning cases) but rather state that they are compelled by their jobs, cultures and family ties to remain in the inner city region of Chinatown. While the zoning amendment here is not exclusionary as classically defined, if as alleged, it will result in displacement of Chinatown's low-income residents, then, its effect is the same. Accordingly, the proper scope of inquiry for analysis is that line of cases involving exclusionary zoning. . . .
>
> While New York courts have previously been hesitant to adopt the *Mount Laurel* doctrine because it places a heavier burden on municipalities, upon consideration of the important constitutional considerations at stake, it is my opinion that it is now appropriate to adopt the *Mount Laurel* doctrine as the law of New York. Moreover, at the time *Berenson* was decided by the Court of Appeals, *Mount Laurel II* had not yet been decided. The *Mount Laurel II* decision not only expands upon the reasoning initially set forth in *Mount Laurel I*, but also discusses its application within the urban setting.

Because the plaintiffs contended that the city failed "to affirmatively provide a reasonable opportunity for the construction of low-income housing," despite the availability of density bonuses to developers who include lower-income units, the court found that a "*Mount Laurel* doctrine" cause of action had been stated.

On appeal, 128 A.D.2d 99, 115, 514 N.Y.S.2d 939, 950 (App. Div. 1987),, a divided court emphatically rejected the lower court's reliance on New Jersey law: "Not by the widest stretch of the imagination could the fact pattern in *Mount Laurel* be applicable to New York City's record for providing low and moderate income housing." See also Suffolk Housing Servs. v. Town of Brookhaven, 109 A.D.2d 323, 491 N.Y.S.2d 396, 402 (App. Div. 1985), *aff'd*, 70 N.Y.2d 122, 517 N.Y.S.2d 924 (1987) ("present acceptance of the legal theories advanced by the plaintiffs [adopting New Jersey law] would require us to work a change of historic proportions in the development of New York zoning law, a step we respectfully decline to take").

4. Many localities, in an effort to increase the supply of affordable housing, have experimented with inclusionary zoning techniques over the past few decades, with mixed success. Economics Profs.

Benjamin Powell & Edward Stringham, in *"The Economics of Inclusionary Zoning Reclaimed": How Effective Are Price Controls?*, 33 Fla. St. U. L. Rev. 471, 472-77 (2005), offered a review of the national landscape and a critique of competing studies:

> To deal with high housing costs, many local governments are investigating and implementing a price-control program called inclusionary zoning. Nearly every economist agrees that rent control reduces the quantity and quality of housing, and places such as Massachusetts and California have statewide mandates that prohibit new rent control ordinances, so planners have devised a more complicated alternative to rent control. Inclusionary zoning, also known as an affordable housing mandate, places a price control on a percentage of new development, requiring builders to sell or rent those homes which are deemed affordable to very low-, low-, or moderate-income households. The units must retain price controls for a specified period of time; in California the amount is typically fifty-five years or more.
>
> Although the program is legally and economically distinct from rent control, law-and-economics scholars who have analyzed the issue have argued that price controls on a percentage of new housing will have many of the same negative effects as rent control. In one classic article, *The Irony of "Inclusionary" Zoning*, Yale Law Professor Robert Ellickson argues that inclusionary zoning actually decreases development and makes housing less affordable; thus, it should be called exclusionary rather than inclusionary.[12] The widely accepted view within the law-and-economics literature has been that price controls through inclusionary zoning will have negative, unintended consequences on the housing market.
>
> In recent years, however, a few noneconomists have written law review articles that attempt to defend inclusionary zoning on economic grounds. Andrew Dietderich's *An Egalitarian's Market: The Economics of Inclusionary Zoning Reclaimed*, Laura Padilla's *Reflections on Inclusionary Housing and a Renewed Look at Its Viability*, and Barbara Kautz's *In Defense of Inclusionary Zoning: Successfully Creating Affordable Housing* all attempt to show that inclusionary zoning makes sense from an economic point of view.[14] Rather than dismissing inclusionary zoning as a policy that discourages production, these authors argue that economics tells us that governments should embrace inclusionary zoning as a way of encouraging more affordable housing. These articles have had considerable impact in the academic literature and in the policy world as well—at least thirty-five California jurisdictions have adopted an inclusionary ordinance since the first of these articles was published in 1995.
>
> Despite the increasing popularity of their view, we believe that they fail to prove their case. . . .
>
> Inclusionary zoning typically refers to a program that imposes price controls on a percentage of new development. The ordinances vary, but they typically require a certain

---

12. Robert C. Ellickson, *The Irony of "Inclusionary" Zoning*, 54 S. Cal. L. Rev. 1167, 1170 (1981). The New Jersey Supreme Court disagreed with Ellickson because it felt incentives offered to developers may be enough to offset the burden of inclusionary zoning. *See* Holmdel Home Builders Ass'n v. Township of Holmdel, 583 A.2d 277, 294 (N.J. 1990).

14. Andrew G. Dietderich, *An Egalitarian's Market: The Economics of Inclusionary Zoning Reclaimed*, 24 Fordham Urb. L.J. 23 (1996); Laura M. Padilla, *Reflections on Inclusionary Housing and a Renewed Look at Its Viability*, 23 Hofstra L. Rev. 539 (1995); Barbara Ehrlich Kautz, Comment, *In Defense of Inclusionary Zoning: Successfully Creating Affordable Housing*, 36 U.S.F. L. Rev. 971 (2002).

percentage of new units be "affordable" to certain low-income families. In California, most ordinances target very low, low, or moderate incomes: "very low" is usually classified as up to 50% of the county median income, "low" as 51-80% of the median, and "moderate" as 81-120% of the median. Depending on the ordinance, builders must sell or lease 5-25% of the new homes at below-market rates. When the units are for sale in most California cities, the below-market rate is often hundreds of thousands of dollars below the market rate. If the units are for lease, the present discounted value of the revenue stream from that property is equivalently decreased, so the economics behind the price control are the same.

Most often, the below-market units must be of similar size and quality as the market-rate units and must be spread throughout the project in order to create integration and avoid "ghettoization." Some jurisdictions allow off-site construction or allow developers to pay a fee in lieu of building a below-market unit, but the intent of inclusionary zoning is to have the below-market units "included" among the market-rate units. Most ordinances are mandatory, meaning builders must participate in order to get permission to build, but a few ordinances are "voluntary" in that they offer incentives in exchange for a builder selling at price-controlled rates. Jurisdictions may also offer compensating incentives, such as density bonuses, fast-track permitting, or fee waivers, but as evidenced by builders' unwillingness to participate in voluntary ordinances, the value of these incentives is oftentimes small.

Inclusionary zoning has become most prevalent over the past fifteen years, but it was first implemented in the 1970s in California and the New York and Washington, D.C., metropolitan areas. In 1971, Fairfax County, Virginia, enacted inclusionary zoning by applying price controls to 15% of large dwellings if a developer built fifty or more units. The Virginia Supreme Court ruled that the law was a taking because landowners were not compensated for the new regulation; thus, Fairfax had to make it a voluntary ordinance. In 1973, Montgomery County, Maryland, passed its "moderately priced dwelling unit" ordinance, requiring 12.5-15% of units (in developments of more than fifty units) be affordable to families with 50-80% of the median income. The ordinance in Montgomery County is still in effect today. Since Palo Alto first enacted inclusionary zoning ordinances in 1973, over one hundred California jurisdictions have followed suit. Today, affordable housing mandates are found in parts of Colorado, Connecticut, Delaware, Florida, Illinois, Massachusetts, New Jersey, New Mexico, New York, Oregon, and Washington.[32] "A 1991 survey found that nine percent of U.S. cities with populations over 100,000 had inclusionary zoning ordinances and the number appears to be growing."[33]

With over one hundred ordinances and over thirty years of experience, California has the most familiarity with inclusionary zoning. California is often held up as a success story because so many cities have adopted these ordinances. Yet many advocates measure success based on the number of ordinances rather than the number of units actually built. Just as economic theory predicts that price controls do not encourage production,

---

32. Benjamin Powell & Edward Stringham, *"Affordable" Housing Laws Make Homes More Expensive*, Econ. Educ. Bull., Dec. 2003, at 1 (referring to Edward G. Goetz, *Promoting Low Income Housing Through Innovations in Land Use Regulations*, 13 J. Urb. Aff. 337, 342 tbl.2, 344 (1991)), *available at* http://www.sjsu.edu/stringham/docs/Powell.Stringham.2003.Econ.Ed.Bulletin.pdf.

33. *Id.* at 1-2.

when one looks at the data one notices surprisingly few below-market units built. . . . The affordable housing mandates in California and elsewhere hardly put a dent in the regional need for affordable housing.

5. Exclusionary zoning dodged a constitutional bullet in Home Builders Ass'n v. City of Napa, 90 Cal. App. 4th 188, 192, 196, 197, 108 Cal. Rptr. 2d 60 62, 65, 66 (Ct. App. 2001), *cert. denied*, 535 U.S. 954 (2002). The city passed an ordinance that applied to all residential and nonresidential development:

> The primary mandate imposed by the ordinance on residential developers is a requirement that 10 percent of all newly constructed units must be "affordable" as that term is defined. The ordinance offers developers two alternatives. First, developers of single-family units may, at their option, satisfy the so called inclusionary requirement through an "alternative equivalent proposal" such as a dedication of land, or the construction of affordable units on another site. Developers of multifamily units may also satisfy the 10 percent requirement through an "alternative equivalent proposal" if the city council, in its sole discretion, determines that the proposed alternative results in affordable housing opportunities equal to or greater than those created by the basic inclusionary requirement.
>
> As a second alternative, a residential developer may choose to satisfy the inclusionary requirement by paying an in-lieu fee. Developers of single-family units may choose this option by right, while developers of multi-family units are permitted this option if the city council, again in its sole discretion, approves. All fees generated through this option are deposited into a housing trust fund, and may only be used to increase and improve the supply of affordable housing in City.
>
> Developments that include affordable housing are eligible for a variety of benefits including expedited processing, fee deferrals, loans or grants, and density bonuses that allow more intensive development than otherwise would be allowed. In addition, the ordinance permits a developer to appeal for a reduction, adjustment, or *complete waiver* of obligations under the ordinance "based upon the absence of any reasonable relationship or nexus between the impact of the development and . . . the inclusionary requirement."

The appeals court, noting the waiver provision, turned down the association's assertion that the ordinance on its face effected an unconstitutional taking. Moreover, the court rejected "HBA's principal constitutional claim . . . that City's ordinance is invalid under Nollan v. California Coastal Comm'n and Dolan v. City of Tigard," two cases that are included in Chapter Five. The court reasoned,

> Here, we are not called upon to determine the validity of a particular land use bargain between a governmental agency and a person who wants to develop his or her land. Instead we are faced with a facial challenge to economic legislation that is generally applicable to *all* development in City. We conclude the heightened standard of review described in *Nollan* and *Dolan* is inapplicable under these facts.

6. Following the line of predecessors occupying his position, Gov. Thomas H. Kean (R-N.J.) was less than pleased with what he perceived as intrusions by a co-equal branch, as reported in Henry A. Hill, *Proposed Legislation in Response to* Mount Laurel II, 13 Real Est. L.J. 170, 170-71 (1984):

Kean, in his Annual Message to the New Jersey State Legislature, delivered on January 10, 1984, acknowledged the tremendous impact this decision has had on housing development in the state and invited the legislature to come up with a more efficient and less disruptive way of satisfying the constitutional mandate. Among other things, the governor said the following about that decision:

> The decision by our State Supreme Court in the case known as *Mount Laurel II* has caused a significant change in the law with respect to the obligation of various municipalities to provide a "fair share" of low and moderate income housing. Because of the novel and far-reaching implications of the Supreme Court's decision in this case, my Administration has been carefully monitoring efforts of municipalities, builders, land use planners and other groups and individuals affected by the decision. . . .
>
> I will be glad to cooperate with you in the design of legislation that would encourage municipalities to assume this responsibility voluntarily rather than leave to the judiciary the task of redesigning zoning ordinances throughout the State of New Jersey.

7. On March 7, 1985, the state legislature passed the Fair Housing Act (S. 2046, S. 2334); the governor, displeased with some components of the legislation, exercised a conditional veto. The lawmakers then responded with an amended proposal, and the bill was signed into law on July 3, 1985. The Act, codified at N.J. Stat. §§52:27D-301 to -329, includes these legislative findings:

a. The New Jersey Supreme Court, through its rulings in South Burlington County NAACP v. Mount Laurel, 67 N.J. 151 (1975) and South Burlington County NAACP v. Mount Laurel, 92 N.J. 158 (1983), has determined that every municipality in a growth area has a constitutional obligation to provide through its land use regulations a realistic opportunity for a fair share of its region's present and prospective needs for housing for low and moderate income families.

b. In the second Mount Laurel ruling, the Supreme Court stated that the determination of the methods for satisfying this constitutional obligation "is better left to the Legislature," that the court has "always preferred legislative to judicial action in their field," and that the judicial role in upholding the Mount Laurel doctrine "could decrease as a result of legislative and executive action."

c. The interest of all citizens, including low and moderate income families in need of affordable housing, would be best served by a comprehensive planning and implementation response to this constitutional obligation.

d. There are a number of essential ingredients to a comprehensive planning and implementation response, including the establishment of reasonable fair share housing guidelines and standards, the initial determination of fair share by officials at the municipal level and the preparation of a municipal housing element, State review of the local fair share study and housing element, and continuous State funding for low and moderate income housing to replace the federal housing subsidy programs which have been almost completely eliminated.

e. The State can maximize the number of low and moderate income units provided in New Jersey by allowing its municipalities to adopt appropriate phasing schedules for meeting their fair share, so long as the municipalities permit a timely achievement of an appropriate fair share of the regional need for low and moderate income housing as required by the Mt. Laurel I and II opinions.

f. The State can also maximize the number of low and moderate income units by rehabilitating existing, but substandard, housing in the State, and, in order to achieve this end, it is appropriate to permit the transfer of a limited portion of the fair share obligations among municipalities in a housing region, so long as the transfer occurs on the basis of sound, comprehensive planning, with regard to an adequate housing financing plan, and in relation to the access of low and moderate income households to employment opportunities.

g. Since the urban areas are vitally important to the State, construction, conversion and rehabilitation of housing in our urban centers should be encouraged. However, the provision of housing in urban areas must be balanced with the need to provide housing throughout the State for the free mobility of citizens.

h. The Supreme Court of New Jersey in its Mount Laurel decisions demands that municipal land use regulations affirmatively afford a reasonable opportunity for a variety and choice of housing including low and moderate cost housing, to meet the needs of people desiring to live there. While provision for the actual construction of that housing by municipalities is not required, they are encouraged but not mandated to expend their own resources to help provide low and moderate income housing.

8. On November 15, 1985, Stephen Townsend, Clerk of the Supreme Court of New Jersey, notified counsel in 12 pending cases that the court had granted leave to appeal, and included a one and one-half-page list of "Issues to Be Addressed," questions raised by the long-awaited legislative (and executive) contribution to the exclusionary zoning debate. Oral arguments followed on January 6 and 7 and the decision was announced February 20, 1986. As you read *Mount Laurel III*, not only the court's summary of the Fair Housing Act but also the justices' determination of the validity and efficacy of the new regime, consider whether the judiciary should feel vindicated or corrected. Is the survival of the fair share doctrine, given the legislature's modification of remedies and the authorization of contribution agreement transfers, victory enough? In repeatedly reminding its audience that the legislative branch had an important role to play, was the court protesting too much?

HILLS DEVELOPMENT CO. v. TOWNSHIP OF BERNARDS
103 N.J. 1, 510 A.2d 621 (1986)
[MOUNT LAUREL III]

The opinion of the Court was delivered by WILENTZ, C.J.

In this appeal we are called upon to determine the constitutionality and effect of the "Fair Housing Act (L. 1985, c. 222), the Legislature's response to the *Mount Laurel* cases. The Act creates an administrative agency (the Council on Affordable Housing) with power to define housing regions within the state and the regional need for low and moderate income housing, along with the power to promulgate criteria and guidelines to enable municipalities within each region to determine their fair share of that regional need. The Council is further empowered, on application, to decide whether proposed ordinances and related measures of a particular municipality will, if enacted, satisfy its *Mount Laurel* obligation, i.e., will they create a realistic opportunity for the construction of that municipality's fair share of the regional need for low and moderate income housing. The agency's determination that the municipality's *Mount Laurel* obligation has been satisfied will ordinarily amount to a final resolution of that issue; it can be set aside in court only by "clear and convincing evidence" to the contrary. The Act includes appropriations and other financial means designed to help achieve the construction of low and moderate income housing.

In order to assure that the extent and satisfaction of a municipality's *Mount Laurel* obligation are decided and managed by the Council through this administrative procedure, rather than by the courts, the Act provides for the transfer of pending and future *Mount Laurel* litigation to the agency. Transfer is required in all cases except, as to cases commenced more than 60 days before the effective date of the Act (July 2, 1985), when it would result in "manifest injustice to any party to the litigation." §16.

The statutory scheme set forth in the Act is intended to satisfy the constitutional obligation enunciated by this Court in the *Mount Laurel* cases. . . .

The Council will determine the total need for lower income housing, the regional portion of that need, and the standards for allocating to each municipality its fair share. The Council is charged by law with that responsibility, imparting to it the legitimacy and presumed expertise that derives from selection by the Governor and confirmation by the Senate, in accordance with the will of the Legislature. Instead of varying and potentially inconsistent definitions of total need, regions, regional need, and fair share that can result from the case-by-case determinations of courts involved in isolated litigation, an overall plan for the entire state is envisioned, with definitions and standards that will have the kind of consistency that can result only when full responsibility and power are given to a single entity. . . .

There are other significant provisions of the Act. One allows municipalities to share *Mount Laurel* obligations by entering into regional contribution agreements. This device requires either Council or court approval to be effective. Under this provision, one municipality can transfer to another, if that other agrees, a portion, under 50%, of its fair share obligation, the receiving municipality adding that to its own. The Act contemplates that the first municipality will contribute funds to the other, presumably to make the housing construction possible and to eliminate any financial burden resulting from the added fair share. The provisions seem intended to allow suburban municipalities to transfer a portion of their obligation to urban areas (see §2g, evincing a legislative intent to encourage construction, conversion, or rehabilitation of housing in urban areas), thereby aiding in the construction of decent lower income housing in the area where most lower income households are found, provided, however, that such areas are "within convenient access to employment opportunities," and conform to "sound comprehensive regional planning." § 12c. . . .

The main challenges to the Act's constitutionality are based on a measurement of the Act against the *Mount Laurel* constitutional obligation. It is also asserted that this legislation impermissibly interferes with the Court's exclusive power over prerogative writ actions. We hold that the Act, as interpreted herein, is constitutional.

A major claim is that the Act is unconstitutional because it will result in delay in the satisfaction of the *Mount Laurel* obligation. That claim is based on a totally false premise, namely, that there is some constitutional timetable implicit in that obligation. . . .

The next claim is that the builder's remedy moratorium is unconstitutional since that remedy is part of the constitutional obligation. This claim suffers from two deficiencies. First, the moratorium on builder's remedies imposed by section 28 is extremely limited; our courts have, in analogous contexts, upheld the power to enact a reasonable moratorium. Second, and more significant, the builder's remedy itself has never been made part of the constitutional obligation. In *Mount Laurel II* we noted that the concept of a "developing municipality," whereby only municipalities so characterized had a *Mount Laurel* obligation, was not of constitutional dimension. It was simply a method for achieving the "constitutionally mandated goal" of providing a realistic opportunity for lower income housing needed by the citizens of this state. . . .

By virtue of the Act, the three branches of government in New Jersey are now committed to a common goal: the provision of a realistic opportunity for the construction of needed lower income housing. It is a most difficult goal to achieve. It is pursued within an even larger context, for the implications of the State Development and Redevelopment Plan legislation indicate significant movement by the State in the direction of regional planning. . . .

No one should assume that our exercise of comity today signals a weakening of our resolve to enforce the constitutional rights of New Jersey's lower income citizens. The constitutional obligation has not changed; the judiciary's ultimate duty to enforce it has not changed; our determination to perform that duty has not changed. What has changed is that we are no longer alone in this field. The other branches of government have fashioned a comprehensive statewide response to the *Mount Laurel* obligation. This kind of response, one that would permit us to withdraw from this field, is what this Court has always wanted and sought. It is potentially far better for the State and for its lower income citizens.

Notes

1. The following year, Robert Hanley, in *Housing the Poor in Suburbia: A Vision Lags in Jersey*, N.Y. Times, June, 1, 1987, at B1, reported that

> Warren's housing obligation . . . has been more than halved, to 367 homes, by the state's Council on Affordable Housing. In addition, the township is negotiating to pay the city of New Brunswick to assume the obligation for construction of 166 of those homes.

> Warren is attempting to comply with the Mount Laurel doctrine. But nearly 80 percent of the state's municipalities have ignored the housing council, which the Kean administration and the Legislature created in 1985 to enforce the law.

> By law, the nine-member council has virtually no enforcement powers. Its emphasis is on using the Mount Laurel doctrine to rebuild inner-city housing, a Kean administration tactic that some suggest is overly ambitious, underfinanced and a reversal of Mount Laurel's spirit.

2. Is the transfer of fair-share obligations allowed by the New Jersey Fair Housing Act via regional contribution agreements (RCAs) a good-faith effort to rebuild decayed urban neighborhoods or the legislative embodiment of the not in my backyard (NIMBY) syndrome? There is no question that RCAs were a political and legal hot potato, according to Professor Charles Haar, in Suburbs Under Siege: Race, Space, and Audacious Judges 113-14 (1996):

> The RCA first had to survive the charge of perpetrating racial stratification in metropolitan areas. In the 1991 case of In re Township of Warren [247 N.J. Super. 146, 588 A.2d 1227 (1991)], for example, Judge Skillman rejected the public advocate's challenge to an RCA on the ground that it would shift Mount Laurel housing to a municipality already burdened with a disproportionate share of the region's lower-income households. The legislature, he emphasized, "must be presumed to have been aware that such agreements ordinarily would be entered into between suburban municipalities with small minority populations and urban municipalities with substantial minority populations." Warren's Mount Laurel obligation had been originally calculated at 946 units. Under

COAH's formula, its responsibility was reduced to 367 affordable units; of these, half were sent under the RCA to New Brunswick, with Warren agreeing to pay out $4.3 million for the privilege.

Although the RCA provision undermined the suburban remedy aspect of the affordable housing requirement, in its favor it may be said that many regard the provision as the political glue that holds the FHA together. After all, at the time of the statutes's enactment, there was a legislative stampede to undercut the Mount Laurel Doctrine. In the same Panglossian vein, without a mechanism like the RCA, one has to wonder whether the legislature would have enacted any statute that supported the production of low- and moderate-income housing in suburban areas. So perceived, RCAs appear as a safety valve to a doctrine of integration so potentially disruptive of perceived local prerogatives that the entire ship of low-income housing production could sink without such a concession. RCAs allow a move in the right direction after all, just at a slower, more politically realistic pace. Indeed, although arguments can be advanced to the contrary, the RCA ended up as the jewel in the crown of the legislative counterreformation. . . .

Exemplary of a key divergence between legislative and judicial aspirations for Mount Laurel reform, the RCA shifted the rationale of the Mount Laurel doctrine away from the broad goal of ending geographic segregation surrounding inner-city minorities and toward the raw provision of low-income housing. RCAs evoke a disheartening picture of the haves continuing to distance themselves from the have-nots. Suburbanites who would fight to the death to exclude people of low income from within their towns' borders and to maintain the value of their houses—their major (often sole) capital asset—are amenable, it turns out, to paying a form of ransom, through taxes, that preserves local control of new entrants while allowing lower-income housing to be built elsewhere. . . .

RCAs, then, are likely to contribute to the most troublesome inadequacy of the Mount Laurel Doctrine, the problem that has dogged reform from the start: too few of the intended beneficiaries—African-Americans and other minorities from the inner city—enjoy the benefits of the new housing.

3. One state supreme court justice—Stewart G. Pollock—almost paid the political piper for his vote in *Mount Laurel II*. Although John H. Dorsey approved the justice's renomination after his first term (he could have blocked it, as the senator from Pollock's home county), Dorsey "said he would publicly oppose judge Pollock's confirmation because of the judge's concurrence in the landmark Mount Laurel decisions attacking exclusionary zoning," according to Joseph F. Sullivan, *Senator Agrees Not to Block Renomination of Jersey Judge*, N.Y. Times, June 18, 1987, at B4. Justice Pollock retired in 1999, a few years before he reached the mandatory retirement age of 70.

4. The debate over the requirements of the New Jersey Supreme Court's *Mount Laurel* cases continued in the new century. See, for example, the court's opinion in Toll Bros., Inc. v. Township of West Windsor, 173 N.J. 502, 509-10, 803 A.2d 53, 57 (2002):

This is a second round *Mount Laurel* exclusionary zoning case brought by Toll Brothers, Inc. (Toll Brothers) against the Township of West Windsor, the Township Committee of the Township of West Windsor, and the Planning Board of the Township of West Windsor (collectively "West Windsor" or the "Township"). Toll Brothers, the owner of a 293 acre tract of land located in West Windsor, alleged below that the Township had engaged in exclusionary zoning in violation of the New Jersey Constitution and the Fair Housing Act of New Jersey (FHA), and sought a builder's remedy from the trial court.

Toll Bros., Inc. v. Township of West Windsor, 303 N.J. Super. 518, 526-27, 697 A.2d 201 (Law Div. 1996) (*West Windsor*). Following a bench trial, the court concluded that West Windsor was "not in compliance with the *Mount Laurel* mandate, and thus . . . [had] violated . . . the New Jersey Constitution and the New Jersey Fair Housing Act." *Id.* at 574, 697 A.2d 201. Based on that finding, the trial court held that Toll Brothers was entitled to a builder's remedy, the specifics of which were to be addressed at a later date. . . .

West Windsor chose not to submit to COAH's jurisdiction when its period of repose expired after the first round of *Mount Laurel* litigation. West Windsor chose again not to pass a resolution of participation after Toll Brothers filed this second round litigation in 1993. The matter therefore remained in the Superior Court and was adjudicated there. When a municipality like West Windsor does not avail itself of the COAH processes and protections, that municipality remains vulnerable to a *Mount Laurel* challenge.

If municipalities believe, as the League of Municipalities contends, that the builder's remedy has become a developer's weapon, it is the municipalities that possess the shield of COAH-afforded protection to ward off builder's remedy litigation. Until practically all municipalities with a significant *Mount Laurel* obligation use the COAH process, however, the builder's remedy remains a necessary mechanism for the enforcement of constitutional values. Experience demonstrates that absent adequate enforcement, the *Mount Laurel* doctrine can deliver little more than a vague and hollow promise that a reasonable opportunity for the development of affordable housing will be provided. This case demonstrates that unfortunate fact.

5. Judicial frustration with COAH's failure to meet the goals of *Mount Laurel* and the FHA is palpable in a more recent opinion from an appellate division panel in In re Adoption of N.J.A.C. 5:94 & 5:95 by New Jersey COAH, 390 N.J. Super. 1, 10, 73-74, 914 A.2d 348, 352, 392 (Super Ct. App. Div. 2007). The court found wanting the agency's third-round rules "that calculate affordable housing needs from 1999 to 2014 and establish criteria for satisfaction of the need between 2004 and 2014." One of many aspects of the rules challenged by the New Jersey Builders Association concerned the absence of incentives to encourage the construction of affordable units. The court was sympathetic to the industry's complaint:

We conclude that the *Mount Laurel* doctrine, as articulated in *Mount Laurel II* and *Toll Bros.* and as codified by the FHA, requires municipalities to provide incentives to developers to construct affordable housing. Land use ordinances requiring all developers to provide some affordable housing conflict with the essence of the *Mount Laurel* doctrine, which requires that municipal land use ordinances create a realistic opportunity. N.J.A.C. 5:94-4.4 discourages development, even in growth areas where development is supposed to occur because it makes development both more expensive and less predictable. The rules allow municipalities in growth areas to discourage development of any kind, and therefore the development of any affordable housing, by zoning selected areas for uncompensated inclusionary development, or by negotiating fees unguided by any standards.

History has shown that many municipalities believe that it is in their best financial interest to exclude low- and moderate-income households, especially households with children. Permitting municipalities to demand that developers build affordable housing without any additional incentives provides municipalities with an effective tool to exclude the poor by combining an affordable housing requirement with large-lot zoning and excessive demands for compensating fees in lieu of providing such housing. Under N.J.A.C. 5:94-4.4, municipalities need not consider the economic feasibility of complying with the ordinance. Yet, this is counter to the very definition of realistic opportunity adopted by COAH. . . . A regulatory regime that relies on developers to incur the uncompensated expense of providing affordable housing is unlikely to result in municipal zoning ordinances that make it realistically probable that the statewide need for affordable housing can be met.

Throughout this opinion, we have referred to the considerable discretion reposed in the agency to discharge its constitutional mission. We have also noted the Court's skepticism that affordable housing units will be produced by private sources without incentives. This record is lacking in any experiential or theoretical support for the agency conclusion that affordable housing units will be constructed during the 2004-2014 period in the numbers that are required to satisfy the constitutional imperative of providing affordable housing in this State.

Furthermore, the rules' impact is not limited to developers. Households with incomes only slightly higher than those who qualify as low- or moderate-income will also be affected. Developers who go uncompensated for providing housing for the poor must charge more for market-rate housing, which will inevitably drive up the cost of housing that would otherwise be affordable to the near poor. . . . Because the rules place no limit on a municipality's right to compel uncompensated exactions from developers of middle-income housing, they unnecessarily drive up the already high cost of housing for the near poor. As such, the rules frustrate, rather than further, a realistic opportunity for the production of affordable housing. . . .

The Supreme Court of New Jersey denied a petition for certification.192 N.J. 71, 926 A.2d 856 (2007). Only time will tell whether, in the face of continued friction among judges, legislators, agency officials, builders, and municipalities, the Garden State will come closer to realizing the original vision of the state high court in the 1970s than it would have absent judicial activism.

6. Perhaps, as noted by Professor Haar in *Suburbs Under Siege*, at 196-97, the key to understanding the resistance to *Mount Laurel* mandates lies in the recognition that

[w]ith its fairness-inspired requirement for land-use policies, Mount Laurel can be said, in a more symbolic way, to be a forerunner of the environmental justice movement. Justice Hall's discussion anticipated the quest for environmental justice that has slowly pressed itself on the national consciousness. Surprisingly, only recently has it become apparent that the burden of pollution caused by industry, waste dumps, incinerators, and other high-risk activities falls disproportionately on the neighborhoods of the poor and minorities. As one response, President Clinton [in Executive Order No. 12,898,] Feb. 11, 1994] required federal agencies to monitor whether their regulations affect minorities unequally and to determine the extent to which "environmental racism" is a national problem. With similar fairness concerns in mind, New Jersey chose in Mount Laurel II to address more traditional environmental concerns arising from subdivisions—focusing on water quality, soil erosion, or impacts on features of natural beauty—for reasons of balance, not simply as pretexts for keeping land scarce and away form the unwanted. This approach allowed for an assessment of both the environmental justice concerns that

might arise because of inner-city concentrations of poverty and the potential damage to environmental resources caused by unplanned development in the suburbs.

II.   Excluding People II: Running the Federal Gauntlet

Although the U.S. Supreme Court declined to hear a number of state exclusionary zoning cases—including *Mount Laurel I*—it seemed but a matter of time before the Justices would hold forth on whether the Constitution's Equal Protection and Due Process Clause protections, so greatly expanded in the area of personal liberties during the years of the Warren Court, would extend to reach persons shut out from the modern American dream of life in suburbia. In two cases from the mid-1970s an answer did come from the Court; but for observers anxious for duplication of the New Jersey and Pennsylvania judicial experimentation on the federal level, the answer was disappointing. Two formidable barriers—a restrictive formulation of standing and the need to demonstrate discriminatory intent—were placed before many potential litigants eager to air Constitution-grounded complaints in federal court. Nevertheless, there remained some hope for injunctive, even monetary relief, at least according to some lower federal judges who turned to two federal civil rights statutes—one enacted following the Civil War, the other a product of the struggles for racial justice that took place nearly 100 years later.

WARTH v. SELDIN
422 U.S. 490 (1975)

Mr. Justice POWELL delivered the opinion of the Court.

Petitioners, various organizations and individuals resident in the Rochester, N. Y., metropolitan area, brought this action in the District Court for the Western District of New York against the town of Penfield, an incorporated municipality adjacent to Rochester, and against members of Penfield's Zoning, Planning, and Town Boards. Petitioners claimed that the town's zoning ordinance, by its terms and as enforced by the defendant board members, respondents here, effectively excluded persons of low and moderate income from living in the town, in contravention of petitioners' First, Ninth, and Fourteenth Amendment rights and in violation of 42 U. S. C. §§ 1981, 1982, 1983. The District Court dismissed the complaint and denied a motion to add petitioner Housing Council in the Monroe County Area, Inc., as party-plaintiff and also a motion by petitioner Rochester Home Builders Association, Inc., for leave to intervene as party-plaintiff. The Court of Appeals for the Second Circuit affirmed, holding that none of the plaintiffs, and neither Housing Council nor Home Builders Association, had standing to prosecute the action. . . .

Petitioners further alleged certain harm to themselves. The Rochester property owners and taxpayers Vinkey, Reichert, Warth, Harris, and Ortiz claimed that because of Penfield's exclusionary practices, the city of Rochester had been forced to impose higher tax rates on them and others similarly situated than would otherwise have been necessary. The low- and moderate-income, minority plaintiffs—Ortiz, Broadnax, Reyes, and Sinkler—claimed that Penfield's zoning practices had prevented them from acquiring, by lease or purchase, residential property in the town, and thus had forced them and their families to reside in less attractive environments. To relieve these various harms, petitioners asked the District Court to declare the Penfield ordinance unconstitutional, to enjoin the defendants from enforcing the ordinance, to order the defendants to enact and administer a new ordinance designed to alleviate the effects of their past actions, and to award $750,000 in actual and exemplary damages. . . .

In its constitutional dimension, standing imports justiciability: whether the plaintiff has made out a "case or controversy" between himself and the defendant within the meaning of Art. III. This is the threshold question in every federal case, determining the power of the court to entertain the suit. As an aspect of justiciability, the standing question is whether the plaintiff has "alleged such a personal stake in the outcome of the controversy" as to warrant his invocation of federal-court jurisdiction and to justify exercise of the court's remedial powers on his behalf. . . .

[W]e turn first to the claims of petitioners Ortiz, Reyes, Sinkler, and Broadnax, each of whom asserts standing as a person of low or moderate income and, coincidentally, as a member of a minority racial or ethnic group. We must assume, taking the allegations of the complaint as true, that Penfield's zoning ordinance and the pattern of enforcement by respondent officials have had the purpose and effect of excluding persons of low and moderate income, many of whom are members of racial or ethnic minority groups. We also assume, for purposes here, that such intentional exclusionary practices, if proved in a proper case, would be adjudged violative of the constitutional and statutory rights of the persons excluded.

But the fact that these petitioners share attributes common to persons who may have been excluded from residence in the town is an insufficient predicate for the conclusion that petitioners themselves have been excluded, or that the respondents' assertedly illegal actions have violated their rights. Petitioners must allege and show that they personally have been injured, not that injury has been suffered by other, unidentified members of the class to which they belong and which they purport to represent. . . .

In their complaint, petitioners Ortiz, Reyes, Sinkler, and Broadnax alleged in conclusory terms that they are among the persons excluded by respondents' actions. None of them has ever resided in Penfield; each claims at least implicitly that he desires, or has desired, to do so. Each asserts, moreover, that he made some effort, at some time, to locate housing in Penfield that was at once within his means and adequate for his family's needs. Each claims that his efforts proved fruitless. We may assume, as petitioners allege, that respondents' actions have contributed, perhaps substantially, to the cost of housing in Penfield. But there remains the question whether petitioners' inability to locate suitable housing in Penfield reasonably can be said to have resulted, in any concretely demonstrable way, from respondents' alleged constitutional and statutory infractions. Petitioners must allege facts from which it reasonably could be inferred that, absent the respondents' restrictive zoning practices, there is a substantial probability that they would have been able to purchase or lease in Penfield and that, if the court affords the relief requested, the asserted inability of petitioners will be removed.

We find the record devoid of the necessary allegations. As the Court of Appeals noted, none of these petitioners has a present interest in any Penfield property; none is himself subject to the ordinance's strictures; and none has ever been denied a variance or permit by respondent officials. Instead, petitioners claim that respondents' enforcement of the ordinance against third parties—developers, builders, and the like—has had the consequence of precluding the construction of housing suitable to their needs at prices they might be able to afford. . . .

Here, by their own admission, realization of petitioners' desire to live in Penfield always had depended on the efforts and willingness of third parties to build low- and moderate-cost housing. The record specifically refers to only two such efforts: that of Penfield Better Homes Corp., in late 1969, to obtain the rezoning of certain land in Penfield to allow the construction of subsidized cooperative townhouses that could be purchased by persons of moderate income; and a similar effort by O'Brien Homes, Inc., in late 1971. But the record is devoid of any indication that these projects, or other like projects, would have satisfied petitioners' needs at prices they could afford, or that, were the court to remove the obstructions attributable to respondents, such relief would benefit petitioners. Indeed, petitioners' descriptions of their individual financial situations and housing needs suggest precisely the contrary—that their inability to reside in Penfield is the consequence of the economics of the area housing market, rather than of respondents' assertedly illegal acts. In short, the facts alleged fail to support an actionable causal relationship between Penfield's zoning practices and petitioners asserted injury. . .

We hold only that a plaintiff who seeks to challenge exclusionary zoning practices must allege specific, concrete facts demonstrating that the challenged practices harm him, and that he personally would benefit in a tangible way from the court's intervention.[18] . . .

[The Court also rejected the standing assertions of the "taxpayer-petitioners" and of the association plaintiffs.]

Mr. Justice BRENNAN, with whom Mr. Justice WHITE and Mr. Justice MARSHALL join, dissenting. . . .

The Court today, in an opinion that purports to be a "standing" opinion but that actually, I believe, has overtones of outmoded notions of pleading and of justiciability, refuses to find that any of the variously situated plaintiffs can clear numerous hurdles, some constructed here for the first time, necessary to establish "standing." While the Court gives lip service to the principle, oft repeated in recent years, that "standing in no way depends on the merits of the plaintiff's contention that particular conduct is illegal," in fact the opinion, which tosses out of court almost every conceivable kind of plaintiff who could be injured by the activity claimed to be unconstitutional, can be explained only by an indefensible hostility to the claim on the merits. . . .

Notes

1. More than 30 years later, *Warth* poses a serious challenge for litigants bringing federal challenges to exclusionary zoning practices. For example, in Taliaferro v. Darby Twp. Zoning Bd., 458 F.3d 181, 185, 186, 190-91 (3d Cir. 2006), the challenge concerned "the propriety of the Darby Township Zoning Hearing Board's ("Board") decision to grant a variance, which permitted the construction of a storage facility in a residential zone, and the attendant State court decisions issued in the course of appeal." Two of the plaintiffs, Lee Taliaferro and Samuel Alexander, were "members of the African-American community in Darby Township and neighboring property owners to the land in question." The court did find that "[t]o the extent Taliaferro and Alexander have alleged injuries to their property values and neighborhood arising from the approval of the variance, . . . they have alleged a constitutionally cognizable injury." However, after reviewing the standing requirements found in *Warth*, the court noted:

> In this case, accepting as true the material allegations of the Amended Complaint, Appellants have failed to allege an injury in fact that is concrete, particularized, or actual in order to confer standing upon them in regard to a denial of equal treatment as a result of the Appellees' alleged conspiracy to block the construction of residential housing on the Property. Such a claim is generalized, and does not allege any actual injury to the Appellants. Thus, to the extent Taliaferro and Alexander have alleged that Appellees made land use decisions in order to limit the effect of the African-American vote in Darby Township, they have not asserted an actual injury that would confer constitutional standing upon them. That is, Appellants have not demonstrated that they, as individuals, have suffered a concrete loss as the result of Appellees' actions, even if

---

18. This is not to say that the plaintiff who challenges a zoning ordinance or zoning practices must have a present contractual interest in a particular project. A particularized personal interest may be shown in various ways, which we need not undertake to identify in the abstract. But usually the initial focus should be on a particular project. We also note that zoning laws and their provisions, long considered essential to effective urban planning, are peculiarly within the province of state and local legislative authorities. They are, of course, subject to judicial review in a proper case. But citizens dissatisfied with provisions of such laws need not overlook the availability of the normal democratic process.

Appellees had acted to ensure that the Property would not be used for low-to-moderate income residential housing.

2. Part of *Warth*'s legacy has been the Supreme Court's narrow view of standing in a wide range of environmental law cases. Most significantly, the majority in Lujan v. Defenders of Wildlife, 504 U.S. 555, 560-61 (1992), placed special emphasis on *Warth*, in the process of articulating and applying the three elements comprising "the irreducible constitutional minimum of standing":

> First, the plaintiff must have suffered an "injury in fact"—an invasion of a legally protected interest which is (a) concrete and particularized, and (b) "actual or imminent, not 'conjectural' or 'hypothetical.'" Second, there must be a causal connection between the injury and the conduct complained of—the injury has to be "fairly . . . trace[able] to the challenged action of the defendant, and not . . . the result [of] the independent action of some third party not before the court." Third, it must be "likely," as opposed to merely "speculative," that the injury will be "redressed by a favorable decision."

3. *Warth* is not an absolute bar to recovery, however. Only two terms after deciding *Warth*, the Supreme Court did allow a lawsuit brought by a nonprofit entity and an individual to survive standing scrutiny. The group was the Metropolitan Housing Development Corporation (MHDC), a developer of low- and moderate-income housing in the metropolitan Chicago area. The individual, one Ransom, was a black resident of Evanston, Illinois, who testified that if the Court would allow the MHDC's challenged project to proceed he would be able to live in the same town that housed the Honeywell factory where Ransom worked. The town was Arlington Heights, and the opinion that follows introduced the second barrier to exclusionary zoning litigation based on constitutional, particularly Fourteenth Amendment, grounds.

VILLAGE OF ARLINGTON HEIGHTS v. METROPOLITAN HOUSING DEVELOPMENT CORP.
429 U.S. 252 (1977)

Mr. Justice POWELL delivered the opinion of the Court.

In 1971 respondent Metropolitan Housing Development Corporation (MHDC) applied to petitioner, the Village of Arlington Heights, Ill., for the rezoning of a 15-acre parcel from single-family to multiple-family classification. Using federal financial assistance, MHDC planned to build 190 clustered townhouse units for low- and moderate-income tenants. The Village denied the rezoning request. MHDC, joined by other plaintiffs who are also respondents here, brought suit in the United States District Court for the Northern District of Illinois. They alleged that the denial was racially discriminatory and that it violated, inter alia, the Fourteenth Amendment and the Fair Housing Act of 1968, 42 U.S.C. §3601 et seq. . . .

Arlington Heights is a suburb of Chicago, located about 26 miles northwest of the downtown Loop area. Most of the land in Arlington Heights is zoned for detached single-family homes, and this is in fact the prevailing land use. The Village experienced substantial growth during the 1960's, but, like other communities in northwest Cook County, its population of racial minority groups remained quite low. According to the 1970 census, only 27 of the Village's 64,000 residents were black.

The Clerics of St. Viator, a religious order (Order), own an 80-acre parcel just east of the center of Arlington Heights. Part of the site is occupied by the Viatorian high school, and part by the Order's three-story novitiate building, which houses dormitories and a Montessori school. Much of the site, however, remains vacant. Since 1959, when the Village first adopted a zoning ordinance, all the land surrounding the Viatorian property has been zoned R-3, a single-family specification with relatively small minimum lot size requirements. On three sides of the Viatorian land there are single-family homes just across a street; to the east the Viatorian property directly adjoins the back yards of other single-family homes.

The Order decided in 1970 to devote some of its land to low- and moderate-income housing. Investigation revealed that the most expeditious way to build such housing was to work through a nonprofit developer experienced in the use of federal housing subsidies under §236 of the National Housing Act, 12 U.S.C. §1715z-1.[2]

MHDC is such a developer. It was organized in 1968 by several prominent Chicago citizens for the purpose of building low- and moderate-income housing throughout the Chicago area. In 1970 MHDC was in the process of building one §236 development near Arlington Heights and already had provided some federally assisted housing on a smaller scale in other parts of the Chicago area.

After some negotiation, MHDC and the Order entered into a 99-year lease and an accompanying agreement of sale covering a 15-acre site in the southeast corner of the Viatorian property. MHDC became the lessee immediately but the sale agreement was contingent upon MHDC's securing zoning clearances from the Village and §236 housing assistance from the Federal Government. If MHDC proved unsuccessful in securing either, both the lease and the contract of sale would lapse. The agreement established a bargain purchase price of $300,000, low enough to comply with federal limitations governing land acquisition costs for §236 housing.

MHDC engaged an architect and proceeded with the project, to be known as Lincoln Green. The plans called for 20 two-story buildings with a total of 190 units, each unit having its own private entrance from the outside. One hundred of the units would have a single bedroom, thought likely to attract elderly citizens. The remainder would have two, three or four bedrooms. A large portion of the site would remain open, with shrubs and trees to screen the homes abutting the property to the east.

The planned development did not conform to the Village's zoning ordinance and could not be built unless Arlington Heights rezoned the parcel to R-5, its multiple-family housing classification. Accordingly, MHDC filed with the Village Plan Commission a petition for rezoning, accompanied by supporting materials describing the development and specifying that it would be subsidized under §236. The materials made clear that one requirement under §236 is an affirmative marketing plan designed to assure that a subsidized development is racially integrated. MHDC also submitted studies demonstrating the need for housing of this type and analyzing the probable impact of the development. To prepare for the hearings before the Plan Commission and to assure compliance with the Village building code, fire regulations, and related requirements, MHDC consulted with the Village staff for preliminary review of the development. The parties have stipulated that every change recommended during such consultations was incorporated into the plans.

---

2. Section 236 provides for "interest reduction payments" to owners of rental housing projects which meet the Act's requirements, if the savings are passed on to the tenants in accordance with a rather complex formula. Qualifying owners effectively pay one percent interest on money borrowed to construct, rehabilitate or purchase their properties.

New commitments under §236 were suspended in 1973 by executive decision, and they have not been revived. Projects which formerly could claim §236 assistance, however, will now generally be eligible for aid under §8 of the United States Housing Act of 1937. . . . Under the §8 program, the Department of Housing and Urban Development contracts to pay the owner of the housing units a sum which will make up the difference between a fair market rent for the area and the amount contributed by the low-income tenant. The eligible tenant family pays between 15 and 25 percent of its gross income for rent. Respondents indicated at oral argument that, despite the demise of the §236 program, construction of the MHDC project could proceed under §8 if zoning clearance is now granted.

During the Spring of 1971, the Plan Commission considered the proposal at a series of three public meetings, which drew large crowds. Although many of those attending were quite vocal and demonstrative in opposition to Lincoln Green, a number of individuals and representatives of community groups spoke in support of rezoning. Some of the comments, both from opponents and supporters, addressed what was referred to as the "social issue" — the desirability or undesirability of introducing at this location in Arlington Heights low- and moderate-income housing, housing that would probably be racially integrated.

Many of the opponents, however, focused on the zoning aspects of the petition, stressing two arguments. First, the area always had been zoned single-family, and the neighboring citizens had built or purchased there in reliance on that classification. Rezoning threatened to cause a measurable drop in property value for neighboring sites. Second, the Village's apartment policy, adopted by the Village Board in 1962 and amended in 1970, called for R-5 zoning primarily to serve as a buffer between single-family development and land uses thought incompatible, such as commercial or manufacturing districts. Lincoln Green did not meet this requirement, as it adjoined no commercial or manufacturing district.

At the close of the third meeting, the Plan Commission adopted a motion to recommend to the Village's Board of Trustees that it deny the request. The motion stated: "While the need for low and moderate income housing may exist in Arlington Heights or its environs, the Plan Commission would be derelict in recommending it at the proposed location." Two members voted against the motion and submitted a minority report, stressing that in their view the change to accommodate Lincoln Green represented "good zoning." The Village Board met on September 28, 1971, to consider MHDC's request and the recommendation of the Plan Commission. After a public hearing, the Board denied the rezoning by a 6-1 vote.

The following June MHDC and three Negro individuals filed this lawsuit against the Village, seeking declaratory and injunctive relief. A second nonprofit corporation and an individual of Mexican-American descent intervened as plaintiffs. The trial resulted in a judgment for petitioners. Assuming that MHDC had standing to bring the suit, the District Court held that the petitioners were not motivated by racial discrimination or intent to discriminate against low income groups when they denied rezoning, but rather by a desire "to protect property values and the integrity of the Village's zoning plan." The District Court concluded also that the denial would not have a racially discriminatory effect.

A divided Court of Appeals reversed. . . .
[It] ruled that the denial of the Lincoln Green proposal had racially discriminatory effects and could be tolerated only if it served compelling interests. Neither the buffer policy nor the desire to protect property values met this exacting standard. The court therefore concluded that the denial violated the Equal Protection Clause of the Fourteenth Amendment. . . .

Clearly MHDC has met the constitutional requirements [for standing], and it therefore has standing to assert its own rights. Foremost among them is MHDC's right to be free of arbitrary or irrational zoning actions. See Euclid v. Ambler Realty Co., 272 U.S. 365 (1926); Nectow v. Cambridge, 277 U.S. 183 (1928); Village of Belle Terre v. Boraas, 416 U.S. 1 (1974). But the heart of this litigation has never been the claim that the Village's decision fails the generous *Euclid* test, recently reaffirmed in *Belle Terre*. Instead it has been the claim that the Village's refusal to rezone discriminates against racial minorities in violation of the Fourteenth Amendment. . . .

Our decision last Term in Washington v. Davis, 426 U.S. 229 (1976), made it clear that official action will not be held unconstitutional solely because it results in a racially, disproportionate impact. "Disproportionate impact is not irrelevant, but it is not the sole touchstone of an invidious racial discrimination." *Id.*, at 242. Proof of racially discriminatory intent or purpose is required to show a violation of the Equal Protection Clause. Although some contrary indications may be drawn from some of our cases, the holding in *Davis* reaffirmed a principle well established in a variety of contexts.

Davis does not require a plaintiff to prove that the challenged action rested solely on racially discriminatory purposes. Rarely can it be said that a legislative or administrative body operating under a broad mandate made a decision motivated solely by a single concern, or even that a particular purpose was the "dominant" or "primary" one. In fact, it is because legislators and administrators are properly concerned with balancing numerous competing considerations that courts refrain from reviewing the merits of their decisions, absent a showing of arbitrariness or irrationality. But racial discrimination is not just another competing consideration. When there is a proof that a discriminatory purpose has been a motivating factor in the decision, this judicial deference is no longer justified.

Determining whether invidious discriminatory purpose was a motivating factor demands a sensitive inquiry into such circumstantial and direct evidence of intent as may be available. The impact of the official action — whether it "bears more heavily on one race than another," Washington v. Davis, *supra*, at 242 — may provide an important starting point. Sometimes a clear pattern, unexplainable on grounds other than race, emerges from the effect of the state action even when the governing legislation appears neutral on its face. . . .

The historical background of the decision is one evidentiary source, particularly if it reveals a series of official actions taken for invidious purposes. The specific sequence of events leading up to the challenged decision also may shed some light on the decisionmaker's purposes. For example, if the property involved here always had been zoned R-5 but suddenly was changed to R-3 when the town learned of MHDC's plans to erect integrated housing, we would have a far different case. Departures from the normal procedural sequence also might afford evidence that improper purposes are playing a role. Substantive departures too may be relevant, particularly if the factors usually considered important by the decision-maker strongly favor a decision contrary to the one reached.

The legislative or administrative history may be highly relevant, especially where there are contemporary statements by members of the decisionmaking body, minutes of its meetings, or reports. In some extraordinary instances the members might be called to the stand at trial to testify concerning the purpose of the official action, although even then such testimony frequently will be barred by privilege. . . .

[T]he Court of Appeals focused primarily on respondents' claim that the Village's buffer policy had not been consistently applied and was being evoked with a strictness here that could only demonstrate some other underlying motive. The court concluded that the buffer policy, though not always applied with perfect consistency, had on several occasions formed the basis for the Board's decision to deny other rezoning proposals. "The evidence does not necessitate a finding that Arlington Heights administered this policy in a discriminatory manner." The Court of Appeals therefore approved the District Court's findings concerning the Village's purposes in denying rezoning to MHDC. . . .

The impact of the Village's decision does arguably bear more heavily on racial minorities. Minorities comprise 18 percent of the Chicago area population, and 40 percent of the income groups said to be eligible for Lincoln Green. But there is little about the sequence of events leading up to the decision that would spark suspicion. The area around the Viatorian property has been zoned R-3 since 1959, the year when Arlington Heights first adopted a zoning map. Single-family homes surround the 80-acre site, and the Village is undeniably committed to single-family homes as its dominant residential land use. The rezoning request progressed according to the usual procedures. The Plan Commission even scheduled two additional hearings, at least in part to accommodate MHDC and permit it to supplement its presentation with answers to questions generated at the first hearing.

The statements by the Plan Commission and Village Board members, as reflected in the official minutes, focused almost exclusively on the zoning aspects of the MHDC petition, and the zoning factors on which they relied are not novel criteria in the Village's rezoning decisions. There is no reason to doubt that there has been reliance by some neighboring property owners on the maintenance of single-family zoning in the vicinity. The Village originally adopted its buffer policy long before MHDC entered the picture and has applied the policy too consistently for us to infer discriminatory purpose from its application in this case. Finally, MHDC called one member of the Village Board to the stand at trial. Nothing in her testimony supports an inference of invidious purpose.

In sum, the evidence does not warrant overturning the concurrent findings of both courts below. Respondents simply failed to carry their burden of proving that discriminatory purpose was a motivating factor in the Village's decision.[21] This conclusion ends the constitutional inquiry. The Court of Appeals' further finding that the Village's decision carried a discriminatory "ultimate effect" is without independent constitutional significance.

Respondents' complaint also alleged that the refusal to rezone violated the Fair Housing Act of 1968, 42 U.S.C. §3601 et seq. They continue to urge here that a zoning decision made by a public body may, and that petitioners' action did, violate §3604 or §3617. The Court of Appeals, however, proceeding in a somewhat unorthodox fashion, did not decide the statutory question. We remand the case for further consideration of respondents' statutory claims.

Reversed and remanded.

Notes

1. Professor Robert Ellickson, in *Suburban Growth Controls: An Economic and Legal Analysis*, 86 Yale L.J. 385, 511 (1977), commented: "The few judicial opinions worthy of unreserved praise are those—like the Supreme Court's decision in *Arlington Heights* and that of the U.S. Court of Appeals for the Ninth Circuit in the *Petaluma* case [included in Chapter Seven]—in which federal courts have declined to federalize essentially intrastate controversies." Do you agree, or do you believe that government might have intentionally played a role in excluding minorities for Chicago's (and other major cities') suburbs and exurbs? Historian Thomas J. Sugrue's meticulously researched *Sweet Land of Liberty: The Forgotten Struggle for Civil Rights in the North* (2008) is an impassioned exploration of the roles played by public and private actors in institutionalizing segregated housing and other forms of discrimination throughout the 20th century.

2. Is there another approach for plaintiffs? Consider the court's holding after remand in Metropolitan Hous. Dev. Corp. v. Village of Arlington Heights, 558 F.2d 1283, 1290 (7th Cir. 1977):

> We therefore hold that at least under some circumstances a violation of section 3604(a) [of the Fair Housing Act] can be established by a showing of discriminatory effect without a showing of discriminatory intent. A number of courts have agreed. . . .

---

21. Proof that the decision by the Village was motivated in part by a racially discriminatory purpose would not necessarily have required invalidation of the challenged decision. Such proof would, however, have shifted to the Village the burden of establishing that the same decision would have resulted even had the impermissible purpose not been considered. If this were established, the complaining party in a case of this kind no longer fairly could attribute the injury complained of to improper consideration of a discriminatory purpose. In such circumstances, there would be no justification for judicial interference with the challenged decision. But in this case respondents failed to make the required threshold showing.

Plaintiffs contend that once a racially discriminatory effect is shown a violation of section 3604(a) is necessarily established. We decline to extend the reach of the Fair Housing Act this far. Although we agree that a showing of discriminatory intent is not required under section 3604(a), we refuse to conclude that every action which produces discriminatory effects is illegal. Such a per se rule would go beyond the intent of Congress and would lead courts into untenable results in specific cases. Rather, the courts must use their discretion in deciding whether, given the particular circumstances of each case, relief should be granted under the statute.

We turn now to determining under what circumstances conduct that produces a discriminatory impact but which was taken without discriminatory intent will violate section 3604(a). Four critical factors are discernible from previous cases. They are: (1) how strong is the plaintiff's showing of discriminatory effect; (2) is there some evidence of discriminatory intent, though not enough to satisfy the constitutional standard of Washington v. Davis; (3) what is the defendant's interest in taking the action complained of; and (4) does the plaintiff seek to compel the defendant to affirmatively provide housing for members of minority groups or merely to restrain the defendant from interfering with individual property owners who wish to provide such housing.

Should the remedy differ if the violation is statutory rather than constitutional? For subsequent developments in the *Arlington Heights* case, see 616 F.2d 1006, 1009 (7th Cir. 1980) (affirming the trial court's grant of a consent decree ending the dispute between MHDC and the village). The consent decree identified an alternative parcel located in unincorporated Cook County, between Arlington Heights and the Village of Mount Prospect. The plan was for Arlington Heights to annex the parcel, upon which MHDC would build nearly 200 rental and townhouse units. The appeals court rejected four objections raised by Mount Prospect as intervenor:

(1) the district court did not have jurisdiction or authority to enter the consent decree; (2) the decision of Arlington Heights to approve the consent decree abridged Mount Prospect's right to procedural due process; (3) Arlington Heights' approval was procedurally and substantively unlawful; and (4) the district court's decree "improperly intruded judicial authority into the legislative process."

In dissent, Judge Wilbur Pell was concerned with the manner in which the new plan was suddenly sprung on an unsuspecting neighboring community.

3. Running parallel to the federal exclusionary cases such as *Arlington Heights* was the saga of public housing in Chicagoland—the decades-long *Gautreaux* litigation. From the vantage point of Gautreaux v. Chicago Hous. Auth., 491 F.3d 649, 651-53 (7th Cir. 2007), in which the court affirmed the award of attorneys fees to the plaintiffs who were deemed "prevailing parties," here is the U.S. Court of Appeals for the Seventh Circuit panel's account of the intricate history of this legendary case:

More than four decades ago, Dorothy Gautreaux and other African-American tenants who lived in public housing projects, along with applicants for public housing, sued the CHA [Chicago Housing Authority], claiming that its policies with respect to the selection of sites for public housing and for assignment of tenants were racially discriminatory. The plaintiffs prevailed [in 1969], and the district court entered a remedial decree that was designed to ban racially discriminatory site selection and tenant assignment policies and to undo the harm that had already occurred. Central to the remedial decree was the requirement that for every unit built in an area where the population was more than 30% non-white ("Limited Areas"), the CHA had to construct three housing units in an area where the population was less than 30% non-white ("General Area"). The ratio was later modified to one-to-one. The *Gautreaux II* remedial order also limited new construction of public apartments that had more than three floors and required changes to tenant assignment practices. The order did not, however, require the construction of any new housing.

The CHA reacted to *Gautreaux II* by instituting a virtual moratorium on the construction of new housing that lasted 18 years. At the plaintiffs' behest, in 1987 the district court appointed Daniel Levin and the Habitat Company as a receiver for the development of all new non-elderly housing for the CHA. This indeed prompted some change: the receiver built a number of small-scale public housing units, which were scattered throughout the General Area. In the 1990s, in part because of the availability of federal funds through the HOPE VI program (an acronym for "Homeownership and Opportunity for People Everywhere"), *see* 42 U.S.C. § 1437l, repealed by Pub. L. 105-276, Title V, § 522(a), Oct. 21, 1998, 112 Stat. 2564, the CHA developed plans to overhaul its public housing stock.

This culminated in 2000 with the CHA's announcement of the Plan for Transformation. The CHA's web page explains that this new plan, which is "the largest, most ambitious redevelopment effort of public housing in the United States, with the goal of rehabilitating or redeveloping the entire stock of public housing in Chicago," will reach "far beyond the physical structure of public housing. It aims to build and strengthen communities by integrating public housing and its leaseholders into the larger social, economic and physical fabric of Chicago." See http://www.thecha.org/pages/the_plan_for_transformation/22.php.

In deciding where to locate new construction that will benefit from HOPE VI funds and be subject to the Plan, the CHA has used the locations of the old high-rise projects almost exclusively. These were the same locations that were branded as racially isolated in *Gautreaux I*. They fell within the Limited Areas, in which new construction was restricted by *Gautreaux II*. In addition, some of the developments contemplated by the plan are mid-rise buildings in which public housing units are located above the third floor. To avoid the *Gautreaux II* restrictions when spending federal dollars, the CHA asked the district court in 1998 "to 'clarify' the judgment order and read it as not governing the use of HOPE VI funds." The court declined to do so; instead, it concluded that "any construction of public housing in Cook County must conform to the judgment order's locational requirements." Other construction under the Plan similarly has continued to operate within the restrictions of *Gautreaux II*'s remedial order.

The result of the continued application of the remedial order to this new construction was, as Terry Peterson attested, that "[t]he *Gautreaux* case presented a major obstacle to the Plan for Transformation. . . . [U]nless the 1969 judgment order was modified, [the CHA] could not proceed with the Plan." What the CHA has had to do, in essence, is to negotiate new building plans with plaintiffs, whenever the Plan would require something inconsistent with *Gautreaux II*. The plaintiffs have been cooperative. Beginning with the redevelopment of the Henry Horner housing project on the City's near west side in 1995, the plaintiffs repeatedly have joined the CHA in requests for waivers from the district court of various restrictions in its remedial decree, so that construction of replacement public housing units can go forward.

On the 40th anniversary of the federal Fair Housing Act, two sociologists who are leading scholars in this field, James E. Rosenbaum & Stefanie DeLuca, in *What Kinds of Neighborhoods Change Lives? The Chicago* Gautreaux *Housing Program and Recent Mobility Programs*, 41 Ind. L. Rev. 653, 662 (2008), offered these insightful observations concerning research on the success of the *Gautreaux* program:

> Many policy reforms have tried to improve individuals' education or employability while they remain in the same poor schools or labor markets, but these reforms have often failed. Such policies may be fighting an uphill battle as long as families remain in the same social contexts and opportunity structures. In contrast, Gautreaux findings suggest that housing policy is one possible lever to assist poor families, moving them into much better neighborhoods with much better schools and labor markets. The initial gains in neighborhood quality that many of the Gautreaux families achieved persisted for at least one to two decades. The Gautreaux findings suggest that it is possible for low-income black families to make permanent escapes from neighborhoods with concentrated racial segregation, crime, and poverty and that these moves are associated with large significant gains in education, employment, and racially integrated friendships, particularly for children. However, as the MTO [Moving to Opportunity] findings suggest, there is much that we still need to learn about what kinds of moves are required to make major changes in outcomes, and, like MTO, strong research designs will be needed to remove alternative interpretations.

We can only speculate, somewhat wistfully, whether meaningful improvements in the lives of public housing residents would have resulted much earlier had public officials and their legal counsel taken a more cooperative posture.

4. United States v. City of Parma, 661 F.2d 562 (6th Cir. 1981), *reh'g denied*, 669 F.2d 1100, *cert. denied*, 456 U.S. 1012 (1982), suggests that an egregious pattern of discrimination could warrant extreme relief under the aegis of the Fair Housing Act. In order to become acquainted with the rich history of segregation in this Cleveland suburb, one need only consult the opinion of Judge Frank J. Battisti in United States v. City of Parma, 494 F. Supp. 1049, 1057, 1059, 1062, 1065-66 (N.D. Ohio 1980). Contrary to Judge Battisti's assertion that "[t]he black ghetto on the east side of Cleveland was created and has been maintained by a series of systematic and pervasive practices of private and public discrimination," the city offered two explanations for the metropolitan area's "dual housing market." First:

> Parma insists that the extreme racial segregation . . . actually is caused by the free associational preferences of whites and blacks. Under this theory, ethnicity rather than race is considered to be the principal motivating factor influencing decisions on residential location. . . . Parma would have this Court believe that blacks prefer the life of the ghetto with its attendant filth, degradation, and crime to the life of suburbia because they do not wish to live in white or integrated neighborhoods.

The court rejected the city's second argument as well: "Parma's other explanation for racial segregation is economics. However, a review of census data for the Cleveland Metropolitan area reveals that economics has little to do with racial segregation." Finally, Judge Battisti offered this evidence of racism:

> A city's reputation can be created and affected by the publicly-expressed attitudes of its leadership. Racial statements made by Parma's elected officials contributed to the perpetuation and intensification of this image of exclusion based on race. It takes little

education or sensitivity to perceive the attitude reflected by City Council President Kuczma when he stated "I do not want Negroes in the City of Parma." His remarks were made at a public meeting and were publicized widely in the press and television. They served to reinforce Parma's reputation as a place that "did not want blacks to live there. . . ." Also publicized and contributing to the exclusionary image was Parma Mayor John Petruska's assurance that the "entire east side of Cleveland" would not be moving into Parma. The statement was made at a public meeting on a federally subsidized low-income housing proposal, and followed a discussion which touched on racial concerns. The suggestion that the remark was referring to general housing conditions as opposed to blacks is not credible.

Mayor Petruska's remarks were not limited to public meetings in Parma. His nationally televised statement that Parma was integrated when it had three black families was widely known and is still remembered for the racial attitude it expressed. As former [Cleveland] Mayor Carl Stokes noted afterwards:

> It was something that is tragic in its fact, in its being a fact, and yet a person literally saying out loud something that so unconsciously by itself reflects the actuality of the racial exclusion . . . There is nothing surprising to black Clevelanders about racism in Parma.

There is unavoidable irony in such statements uttered by eastern-European surnamed suburbanites, many descendants of earlier immigrants "trapped" within the city limits of Cleveland, who were using land use controls to exclude another set of "outsiders."

According to the appellate panel, the trial's court's broad remedy imposed a veritable straitjacket on the city:

The general provision permanently enjoined the City, its officers, etc. from:

1. Engaging in any conduct having the purpose or effect of perpetuating or promoting racial residential segregation or of denying or abridging the right of any person to equal housing opportunity on account of race, color, religion, sex or national origin;

2. Discriminating against any person or group of persons on account of race, color, religion, sex or national origin in connection with the planning, development, construction, acquisition, financing, operation or approval of any low-income or public housing units;

3. Interfering with any person in the exercise of his right to secure equal housing opportunity for himself or for others; and

4. Taking any action which in any way denies or makes unavailable housing to persons on the basis of race, color, religion, sex or national origin.

The defendant was additionally ordered to: (1) establish a mandatory fair housing educational program for all city officials and employees involved in carrying out the terms of the remedial order; (2) enact a resolution welcoming persons of all races, creeds and colors to reside in Parma and setting forth its policy of nondiscrimination in housing; (3) undertake a comprehensive program of newspaper advertising to promote Parma as an equal housing opportunity community and to make copies of the liability opinions and remedial order available, free of charge; (4) take "whatever action is necessary in order to allow the construction of public housing in the City,"; (5) adopt a plan for use of an existing "Section 8" housing program; (6) take required steps for submitting an acceptable application for CDBG funds; (7) "make all efforts necessary to ensure that at least 133 units of low and moderate-income housing are provided annually in Parma. This number is a threshold beyond which Parma must strive to go in providing new housing opportunities in the City. This is so because, in addition to addressing its current needs, Parma must address those low-income housing needs which have been in existence since at least 1968 but which have been ignored by Parma for racial reasons. This Court can require no less in carrying out its obligations in this action." . . .

The court of appeals, affirming Judge Battisti's finding of a "pattern or practice" of discrimination, only slightly modified the remedy, implementing a "numberless" approach and reversing the lower court's appointment of a special master.

The Supreme Court skirted the issue of intent versus effects under the Fair Housing Act in Huntington Branch, NAACP v. Town of Huntington, 488 U.S. 15 (1988). In a per curiam opinion by six Justices, the Supreme Court found: "Since appellants conceded the applicability of the disparate-impact test for evaluating the zoning ordinance . . . , we do not reach the question whether that test is the appropriate one." In the absence of guidance from the Justices, there are opinions from nearly every circuit adopting the "disparate impact" approach.[9]

5. One of the boldest Fair Housing Act violations involved the registered voters of a 1,700-acre area in unincorporated St. Louis County, Missouri. Disturbed by the prospect of a federally financed, multi-family housing development in their neighborhood, these citizens (with the approval of the St. Louis County Council) incorporated a new city, Black Jack, and a mere three months later passed an ordinance prohibiting the construction of multi-family dwellings. In United States v. City of Black Jack, 508 F.2d 1179 (8th Cir. 1974), cert. denied, 422 U.S. 1042 (1975), the court of appeals agreed with the trial court that as the plaintiff had made out a prima facie case by demonstrating racially discriminatory effect, the burden was on the city to proffer a compelling state interest furthered by the ordinance. Both courts rejected the city's justifications—traffic control, school crowding, and the devaluation of nearby single-family homes—and the appellate court remanded the case to the district court with instructions to enjoin permanently the enforcement of the multi-family dwelling ban. In subsequent related actions, reported in Land Use L. & Zoning Dig., April 1982, at 3, the city agreed to pay the frustrated developer damages of $450,000, and entered into a consent decree with a group of potential tenants by which the city demonstrated its commitment to "equal access to housing."

In 1988, Congress enacted Pub L. No. 100-430, the Fair Housing Amendments Act of 1988, extending coverage to families with children under 18 and to the mentally and physically handicapped, and strengthening the private enforcement sections of the 1968 Act.

---

9. See 2922 Sherman Ave. Tenants' Ass'n v. District of Columbia, 444 F.3d 673, 679 (D.C. Cir. 2006):

The Supreme Court has yet to consider the availability of disparate impact claims under the FHA. Significantly, however, the FHA's language prohibiting discrimination—"because of . . . race . . . or national origin"—is identical to Title VII's, and since Griggs [v. Duke Power Co., 401 U.S. 424 (1971)], everyone of the eleven circuits to have considered the issue has held that the FHA similarly prohibits not only intentional housing discrimination, but also housing actions having a disparate impact. See John F. Stanton, The Fair Housing Act and Insurance: An Update and the Question of Disability Discrimination, 31 Hofstra L. Rev. 141, 174 n. 180 (2002) (listing cases). The tenants urge us to take the same approach here. Expressing no view on the issue, the District "assumes arguendo that a violation of the FHA may be found based on evidence of disparate effect alone." Given that only one side of the issue has been briefed, however, instead of simply adopting the approach of our respected sister circuits, we think it more appropriate to assume without deciding that the tenants may bring a disparate impact claim under the FHA.

6. Many states have followed Congress' lead in passing fair housing legislation. In North Carolina Human Relations Council v. Weaver Realty Co., 79 N.C. App. 710, 340 S.E.2d 766, 769, 770 (Ct. App.1986), the North Carolina Court of Appeals, in interpreting the state Fair Housing Act, N.C. Gen. Stat. §41A-4, chose not to adopt the "'adverse' or 'disparate impact' theory through which a plaintiff may show a violation of the federal Fair Housing Act." In addition, the court

> refuse[d] to adopt the peculiar standard of causation adopted by federal courts. . . . We see no reason not to adopt the traditional proximate cause standard which the courts of our State have ample experience in applying. Thus race, color, religion, sex or national origin must be more than a mere factor in a defendant's decision not to engage in a real estate transaction.

Even given this heavier burden, the council "raised a genuine issue of material fact as to whether defendants discriminated against plaintiff in the leasing of an apartment because plaintiff is black."

For a different approach to the issue, see Canady v. Prescott Canyon Estates Homeowners Ass'n, 204 Ariz. 91, 60 P.3d 231, 233 (Ct. App. 2002) ("Because the provisions of Arizona's Fair Housing Act involved in this appeal are virtually identical to those provisions of the federal Act, federal case authority is persuasive in interpreting Arizona's statute."); and Sisemore v. Master Financial, Inc., 151 Cal. App. 4th 1386, 1418, 60 Cal. Rptr. 3d 719, 745 (Ct. App. 2007) ("As a threshold matter, we consider whether a FEHA [California Fair Housing and Employment Act] housing discrimination claim may be founded on a disparate impact theory. We conclude that this theory is recognized both under the California statute (§12955.8, subd. (b)) and under federal decisional authority applicable to FEHA.").

While federal law, with its standing and proof requirements often taketh away, it can also giveth—quite generously in the form of damages and attorneys fees. The vehicle for recovery is 42 U.S.C. §1983, a constitutional tort provision protecting individuals from civil rights violations caused by other persons (including political subdivisions) that can be traced back to the Reconstruction era. For example, in Buckeye Community Hope Found. v. City of Cuyahoga Falls, 263 F.3d 627, 632 (6th Cir. 2001), the court explained that "[t]he plaintiffs alleged violations of the Fair Housing Act, 42 U.S.C. §§ 3601 et seq., 42 U.S.C. §§ 1981 and 1982, the Due Process Clause of the Fourteenth Amendment via 42 U.S.C. § 1983, and the Equal Protection Clause of the Fourteenth Amendment via 42 U.S.C. § 1983." While the plaintiffs prevailed at the circuit court level, the following Supreme Court decision illustrates how difficult it can be for a developer of affordable housing, especially one without a vested property right who has not been the target of invidious discrimination, to recover under due process and equal protection theories. The case also illustrates the popularity of plebiscites—the use of referenda and initiatives—to give local voters the chance to vote up or down on land use decisions.

CITY OF CUYAHOGA FALLS v. BUCKEYE COMMUNITY HOPE FOUNDATION
538 U.S. 188 (2003)

JUSTICE O'CONNOR delivered the opinion of the Court. . . .

In June 1995, respondents Buckeye Community Hope Foundation, a nonprofit corporation dedicated to developing affordable housing through the use of low-income tax credits, and others (hereinafter Buckeye or respondents), purchased land zoned for apartments in Cuyahoga Falls, Ohio. In February 1996, Buckeye submitted a site plan for Pleasant Meadows, a multifamily, low-income housing complex, to the city planning commission. Residents of Cuyahoga Falls immediately expressed opposition to the proposal. See Buckeye Cmty. Hope Found. v. City of Cuyahoga Falls, 263 F.3d 627, 630 (CA6 2001). After respondents agreed to various conditions, including that it build an earthen wall surrounded by a fence on one side of the complex, the commission unanimously approved the site plan and submitted it to the city council for final authorization.

As the final approval process unfolded, public opposition to the plan resurfaced and eventually coalesced into a referendum petition drive. See Cuyahoga Falls City Charter, Art. 9, § 2 (hereinafter City Charter), App. 14 (giving voters "the power to approve or reject at the polls any ordinance or resolution passed by the Council" within 30 days of the ordinance's passage). At city council meetings and independent gatherings, some of which the mayor attended to express his personal opposition to the site plan, citizens of Cuyahoga Falls voiced various concerns: that the development would cause crime and drug activity to escalate, that families with children would move in, and that the complex would attract a population similar to the one on Prange Drive, the City's only African-American neighborhood. Nevertheless, because the plan met all municipal zoning requirements, the city council approved the project on April 1, 1996, through City Ordinance No. 48-1996.

On April 29, a group of citizens filed a formal petition with the City requesting that the ordinance be repealed or submitted to a popular vote. Pursuant to the City Charter, which provides that an ordinance challenged by a petition "shall [not] go into effect until approved by a majority" of voters, the filing stayed the implementation of the site plan. Art. 9, § 2, App. 15. On April 30, respondents sought an injunction against the petition in state court, arguing that the Ohio Constitution does not authorize popular referendums on administrative matters. On May 31, the Court of Common Pleas denied the injunction. A month later, respondents nonetheless requested building permits from the City in order to begin construction. On June 26, the city engineer rejected the request after being advised by the city law director that the permits "could not be issued because the site plan ordinance 'does not take effect' due to the petitions." 263 F.3d at 633.

In November 1996, the voters of Cuyahoga Falls passed the referendum, thus repealing ordinance No. 48-1996. In a joint stipulation, however, the parties agreed that the results of the election would not be certified until the litigation over the referendum was resolved. In July 1998, the Ohio Supreme Court, having initially concluded that the referendum was proper, reversed itself and declared the referendum unconstitutional. Buckeye Community Hope Foundation v. Cuyahoga Falls, 82 Ohio St. 3d 539, 697 N.E.2d 181 (holding that the Ohio State Constitution authorizes referendums only in relation to legislative acts, not administrative acts, such as the site-plan ordinance). The City subsequently issued the building permits, and Buckeye commenced construction of Pleasant Meadows.

In July 1996, with the state-court litigation still pending, respondents filed suit in federal court against the City and several city officials, seeking an injunction ordering the City to issue the building permits, as well as declaratory and monetary relief. Buckeye alleged that "in allowing a site plan approval ordinance to be submitted to the electors of Cuyahoga Falls through a referendum and in rejecting [its] application for building permits," the City and its officials violated the Equal Protection and Due Process Clauses of the Fourteenth Amendment, as well as the Fair Housing Act, 42 U.S.C. § 3601. In June 1997, the District Court dismissed the case against the mayor in his individual capacity but denied the City's motion for summary judgment on the equal protection and due process claims, concluding that genuine issues of material fact existed as to both claims. After the Ohio Supreme Court declared the referendum invalid in 1998, thus reducing respondents' action to a claim for damages for the delay in construction, the City and its officials again moved for summary judgment. On November 19, 1999, the District Court granted the motion on all counts.

The Court of Appeals for the Sixth Circuit reversed. As to respondents' equal protection claim, the court concluded that they had produced sufficient evidence to go to trial on the allegation that the City, by allowing the referendum petition to stay the implementation of the site plan, gave effect to the racial bias reflected in the public's opposition to the project. The court then held that even if respondents failed to prove intentional discrimination, they stated a valid claim under the Fair Housing Act on the theory that the City's actions had a disparate impact based on race and family status. Finally, the court concluded that a genuine issue of material fact existed as to whether the City, by denying respondents the benefit of the lawfully approved site plan, engaged in arbitrary and irrational government conduct in violation of substantive due process. . . .

Respondents allege that by submitting the petition to the voters and refusing to issue building permits while the petition was pending, the City and its officials violated the Equal Protection Clause. Petitioners claim that the Sixth Circuit went astray by ascribing the motivations of a handful of citizens supportive of the referendum to the City. We agree with petitioners that respondents have failed to present sufficient evidence of an equal protection violation to survive summary judgment.

We have made clear that "proof of racially discriminatory intent or purpose is required" to show a violation of the Equal Protection Clause. Arlington Heights v. Metropolitan Housing Development Corp., 429 U.S. 252, 265 (1977) (citing Washington v. Davis, 426 U.S. 229 (1976)). In deciding the equal protection question, the Sixth Circuit erred in relying on cases in which we have subjected enacted, discretionary measures to equal protection scrutiny and treated decision-makers' statements as evidence of such intent. Because respondents claim injury from the referendum petitioning *process* and not from the referendum itself—which never went into effect—these cases are inapposite. Ultimately, neither of the official acts respondents challenge reflects the intent required to support equal protection liability.

First, in submitting the referendum petition to the voters, the City acted pursuant to the requirements of its charter, which sets out a facially neutral petitioning procedure. By placing the referendum on the ballot, the City did not enact the referendum and therefore cannot be said to have given effect to voters' allegedly discriminatory motives for supporting the petition. Similarly, the city engineer, in refusing to issue the building permits while the referendum was still pending, performed a nondiscretionary, ministerial act. He acted in response to the city law director's instruction that the building permits "could not . . . issue" because the City Charter prohibited a challenged site-plan ordinance from going into effect until "approved by a majority of those voting thereon," *ibid*. See 263 F.3d at 633. Respondents point to no evidence suggesting that these official acts were themselves motivated by racial animus. Respondents do not, for example, offer evidence that the City followed the obligations set forth in its charter *because of* the referendum's discriminatory purpose, or that city officials would have selectively refused to follow standard charter procedures in a different case.

Instead, to establish discriminatory intent, respondents and the Sixth Circuit both rely heavily on evidence of allegedly discriminatory voter sentiment. But statements made by private individuals in the course of a citizen-driven petition drive, while sometimes relevant to equal protection analysis, do not, in and of themselves, constitute state action for the purposes of the Fourteenth Amendment. Cf. Blum v. Yaretsky, 457 U.S. 991, 1002-1003 (1982) ("'The principle has become firmly embedded in our constitutional law that the action inhibited by the first section of the Fourteenth Amendment is only such action as may fairly be said to be that of the States'") (quoting Shelley v. Kraemer, 334 U.S. 1, 13 (1948)). Moreover, respondents put forth no evidence that the "private motives [that] triggered" the referendum drive "can fairly be attributable to the State." *Blum* v. *Yaretsky, supra*, at 1004.

In fact, by adhering to charter procedures, city officials enabled public debate on the referendum to take place, thus advancing significant First Amendment interests. In assessing the referendum as a "basic instrument of democratic government," Eastlake v. Forest City Enterprises, Inc., 426 U.S. 668, 679 (1976), we have observed that "provisions for referendums demonstrate devotion to democracy, not to bias, discrimination, or prejudice," James v. Valtierra, 402 U.S. 137, 141 (1971). And our well established First Amendment admonition that "government may not prohibit the expression of an idea simply because society finds the idea itself offensive or disagreeable," Texas v. Johnson, 491 U.S. 397, 414 (1989), dovetails with the notion that all citizens, regardless of the content of their ideas, have the right to petition their government. Again, statements made by decisionmakers or referendum sponsors during deliberation over a referendum may constitute relevant evidence of discriminatory intent in a challenge to an ultimately enacted initiative. But respondents do not challenge an enacted referendum. . . .

In evaluating respondents' substantive due process claim, the Sixth Circuit found, as a threshold matter, that respondents had a legitimate claim of entitlement to the building permits, and therefore a property interest in those permits, in light of the city council's approval of the site plan. The court then held that respondents had presented sufficient evidence to survive summary judgment on their claim that the City engaged in arbitrary conduct by denying respondents the benefit of the plan. Both in their complaint and before this Court, respondents contend that the City violated substantive due process, not only for the reason articulated by the Sixth Circuit, but also on the grounds that the City's submission of an administrative land-use determination to the charter's referendum procedures constituted *per se* arbitrary conduct. We find no merit in either claim.

We need not decide whether respondents possessed a property interest in the building permits, because the city engineer's refusal to issue the permits while the petition was pending in no sense constituted egregious or arbitrary government conduct. See County of Sacramento v. Lewis, 523 U.S. 833, 846 (1998) (noting that in our evaluations of "abusive executive action," we have held that "only the most egregious official conduct can be said to be 'arbitrary in the constitutional sense'"). In light of the charter's provision that "no such ordinance [challenged by a petition] shall go into effect until approved by a majority of those voting thereon," Art. 9, § 2, App. 15, the law director's instruction to the engineer to not issue the permits represented an eminently rational directive. Indeed, the site plan, by law, could not be implemented until the voters passed on the referendum.

Respondents' second theory of liability has no basis in our precedent. As a matter of federal constitutional law, we have rejected the distinction that respondents ask us to draw, and that the Ohio Supreme Court drew as a matter of state law, between legislative and administrative referendums. In Eastlake v. Forest City Enterprises, Inc., 426 U.S., at 672, 675, we made clear that because all power stems from the people, "[a] referendum cannot . . . be characterized as a delegation of power," unlawful unless accompanied by "discernible standards." The people retain the power to govern through referendum "'with respect to any matter, legislative or administrative, within the realm of local affairs.'" *Id.*, at 674, n. 9. Though the "substantive result" of a referendum may be invalid if it is "arbitrary and capricious," Eastlake v. Forest City Enterprises, *supra*, at 676, respondents do not challenge the referendum itself. The subjection of the site-plan ordinance to the City's referendum process, regardless of whether that ordinance reflected an administrative or legislative decision, did not constitute *per se* arbitrary government conduct in violation of due process.

For the reasons detailed above, we reverse the Sixth Circuit's judgment with regard to respondents' equal protection and substantive due process claims. The Sixth Circuit also held that respondents' disparate impact claim under the Fair Housing Act could proceed to trial, but respondents have now abandoned the claim. We therefore vacate the Sixth Circuit's disparate impact holding and remand with instructions to dismiss, with prejudice, the relevant portion of the complaint.

The judgment of the United States Court of Appeals for the Sixth Circuit is, accordingly, reversed in part, and vacated in part, and the case is remanded for further proceedings consistent with this opinion.

It is so ordered.

JUSTICE SCALIA, with whom JUSTICE THOMAS joins, concurring. . . .

I write separately to observe that, *even if* there had been arbitrary government conduct, that would not have established the substantive-due-process violation that respondents claim.

It would be absurd to think that all "arbitrary and capricious" government action violates substantive due process—even, for example, the arbitrary and capricious cancellation of a public employee's parking privileges. The judicially created substantive component of the Due Process Clause protects, we have said, certain "fundamental liberty interests" from deprivation by the government, unless the infringement is narrowly tailored to serve a compelling state interest. Freedom from delay in receiving a building permit is not among these "fundamental liberty interests." To the contrary, the Takings Clause allows government *confiscation* of private property so long as it is taken for a public use and just compensation is paid; mere *regulation* of land use need not be "narrowly tailored" to effectuate a "compelling state interest." Those who claim "arbitrary" deprivations of nonfundamental liberty interests must look to the Equal Protection Clause, and Graham v. Connor, 490 U.S. 386, 395(1989), precludes the use of "'substantive due process'"analysis when a more specific constitutional provision governs.

As for respondents' assertion that referendums may not be used to decide whether low income housing may be built on their land: that is not a substantive-due-process claim, but rather a challenge to the *procedures* by which respondents were deprived of their alleged liberty interest in building on their land. There is nothing procedurally defective about conditioning the right to build low-income housing on the outcome of a popular referendum, and the delay in issuing the permit was prescribed by a duly enacted provision of the Cuyahoga Falls City Charter (Art. 9, § 2), which surely constitutes "due process of law." . . .

Notes

1. The operative language from 42 U.S.C. §1983 reads as follows:

> Every person who, under color of any statute, ordinance, regulation, custom, or usage, of any State or Territory or the District of Columbia, subjects, or causes to be subjected, any citizen of the United States or other person within the jurisdiction thereof to the deprivation of any rights, privileges, or immunities secured by the Constitution and laws, shall be liable to the party injured in an action at law, suit in equity, or other proper proceeding for redress . . . .

The two "essential elements" of the cause of action under this constitutional torts statute are quite straightforward: "(1) whether the conduct complained of was committed by a person acting under color of state law; and (2) whether this conduct deprived a person of rights, privileges, or immunities secured by the Constitution or laws of the United States." Parratt v. Taylor, 451 U.S. 527, 535 (1981).

While recovery under §1983 can be substantial, those plaintiffs challenging improper land use practices have to meet certain threshold requirements, which fall into three general categories: (1) the types of defendants and conduct covered; (2) the availability of absolute or qualified immunity; and (3) the appropriateness of punitive damages. Full exploration of these concepts fall far outside the scope of this text. However, all land use professionals should be aware that cities, counties, and other local governments are treated as "persons" under the statute, as established in Monell v. Department of Social Servs., 436 U.S. 658 (1978); that the function being performed by the local officials can determine the availability of either absolute immunity (for legislative and quasi-judicial acts) or qualified immunity (see Harlow v. Fitzgerald, 457 U.S. 800, 818 (1982) ("government officials performing discretionary functions, generally are shielded from liability for civil damages insofar as their conduct does not violate clearly established statutory or constitutional rights of which a reasonable person would have known")); and that punitive damages are available against individuals (see Smith v. Wade, 462 U.S. 30, 56 (1983) ("when the defendant's conduct is shown to be motivated by evil motive or intent, or when it involves reckless or callous indifference to the federally protected rights of others")), but not against governmental units, as explained in City of Newport v. Fact Concerts, Inc., 453 U.S. 247, 271 (1981).

2. As *Cuyahoga Falls* suggests, the requirement for a property owner to demonstrate "egregious or arbitrary government conduct" in order to prevail under a due process deprivation theory is just as difficult to overcome as the "racially discriminatory intent or purpose" hurdle in equal protection cases. Compounding this difficulty is the issue that the Supreme Court chose not to address: "[W]hether respondents possessed a property interest in the building permits." As the U.S. Court of Appeals for the Sixth Circuit panel had noted in Buckeye Community Hope Found. v. City of Cuyahoga Falls, 263 F.3d 627, 641 (6th Cir. 2001), before the case reached the High Court: "In order 'to establish a violation of substantive due process, a plaintiff must first establish the existence of a constitutionally protected property or liberty interest.' Silver v. Franklin Township Bd. of Zoning Appeals, 966 F.2d 1031, 1036 (6th Cir. 1992)."

There is not universal agreement among the lower federal courts as to which "property interests" are protected by the Due Process Clause. Professor Stephen Eagle, a due process (please excuse the pun) "hawk," has explained, in *Property Tests, Due Process Tests, and Regulatory Takings Jurisprudence*, 2007 B.Y.U. L. Rev. 899, 954-55, 957 (2007):

> Valid due process challenges to governmental action must be related to some form of property interest. In Board of Regents of State Colleges v. Roth, [408 U.S. 564, 569 (1972),] the Supreme Court held that a due process challenge to a governmental action must be predicated upon a "deprivation of interests encompassed by the Fourteenth Amendment's protection of liberty and property." The U.S. Courts of Appeals have adopted varying standards for determining what constitutes the requisite property interest in land use cases.

> The Third Circuit held, in DeBlasio v. Zoning Board of Adjustment, that an ownership interest in the land qualifies.[337] Other courts have utilized a structural "entitlement" analysis, focusing on the degree of discretion permitted the regulator. The Supreme Court's decision in Board of Regents v. Roth plays a pivotal role in this analysis, focusing on reasonable claims of entitlement as well as ownership. Thus, the Second Circuit, in RRI Realty Corp. v. Village of Southampton, [870 F.2d 911, 917 (2d Cir. 1989)] noted that its post-*Roth* cases "have been significantly influenced by the *Roth* 'entitlement' analysis." The court noted that it had earlier "focused initially on whether the landowner had 'a legitimate claim of entitlement' to the license he sought and formulated the test

---

337. 53 F.3d 592, 601 (3d Cir. 1995). *DeBlasio* subsequently was overruled because it applied the less "demanding 'improper motive' test" instead of the "shocks the conscience" standard required by [County of Sacramento v.] *Lewis*, [523 U.S. 833 (1998)]. United Artists Theatre Circuit, Inc. v. [Township of] Warrington, 316 F.3d 392, 400 (3d Cir. 2003).

for this inquiry to be that 'absent the alleged denial of due process, there is either a certainty or a very strong likelihood that the application would have been granted.'" Other circuits have adopted similar formulations.[342]

In George Washington University v. District of Columbia, the District of Columbia Circuit analyzed the standards for entitlement, and termed entitlement analysis "a 'new property' inquiry."[343] The court concluded that the University had a protectable property interest in use of land under the "new property" standard.

Can you see how difficult it is for disgruntled property owners in run-of-the-mill rezoning or special use permit disputes to demonstrate that they have been deprived of an entitlement, when the government officials who caused their frustration claim merely to be exercising discretion? Professor Eagle would proffer this alternative to an "egregious or arbitrary government conduct" or "shocks the conscience" standard:

Unlike the life or death consequences of the police chase in County of Sacramento v. Lewis, property rights cases typically involve determinations that are reviewable by supervisors and local officials at their leisure, and with the assistance of the municipal attorney. As such, the final rendition of decisions based on arbitrary or capricious behavior may be seen as premeditated ratification of such misconduct.

Meaningful substantive due process review would not necessarily require that burdens be placed upon the regulator in the nature of heightened or strict scrutiny. All that meaningful substantive due process review would require is basic ends-means analysis and some showing of proportionality. The bar would be low, but unlike the situation with deferential rational basis review, the locality would have to meet it.

3. Should a court make it even harder to bring a §1983 action by requiring the exhaustion of all administrative remedies before hearing the case? In Williamson County Reg'l Planning Comm'n v. Hamilton Bank, 473 U.S. 172, 192-94 (1985), a regulatory taking challenge, the Supreme Court provided this answer:

Respondent asserts that it should not be required to seek variances from the regulations because its suit is predicated upon 42 U.S.C. § 1983, and there is no requirement that a plaintiff exhaust administrative remedies before bringing a § 1983 action. Patsy v. Florida Board of Regents, 457 U.S. 496 (1982). The question whether administrative remedies must be exhausted is conceptually distinct, however, from the question whether an administrative action must be final before it is judicially reviewable. While the policies underlying the two concepts often overlap, the finality requirement is concerned with whether the initial decisionmaker has arrived at a definitive position on the issue that inflicts an actual, concrete injury; the exhaustion requirement generally refers to administrative and judicial procedures by which an injured party may seek review of an adverse decision and obtain a remedy if the decision is found to be unlawful or otherwise inappropriate. Patsy concerned the latter, not the former.

Twenty years later, in his concurring opinion for four Justices, in San Remo Hotel, Ltd. Partnership v. City & County of San Francisco, 545 U.S. 323, 348-49, 352-52 (2005) (Rehnquist, C.J.,

---

342. Bituminous Materials, Inc. v. Rice County 126 F.3d 1068, 1070 (8th Cir. 1997); Gardner v. City of Baltimore Mayor & City Council, 969 F.2d 63, 68 (4th Cir. 1992); Jacobs, Visconsi & Jacobs, Co. v. City of Lawrence, 927 F.2d 1111 (10th Cir. 1991).

343. 318 F.3d 203, 206-07 (D.C. Cir. 2003) (citing Charles Reich, The New Property, 73 Yale L.J. 733 (1964)).

concurring),[10] Chief Justice William H. Rehnquist explained that *Hamilton Bank* packed a powerful one-two ripeness combination that knocked out many §1983 takings challenges:

> In *Williamson County*, the respondent land developer filed a § 1983 suit in federal court alleging a regulatory takings claim after a regional planning commission disapproved respondent's plat proposals, but before respondent appealed that decision to the zoning board of appeals. Rather than reaching the merits, we found the claim was brought prematurely. We first held that the claim was "not ripe until the government entity charged with implementing the regulations [had] reached a final decision regarding the application of the regulations to the property at issue." [473 U.S.], at 186. Because respondent failed to seek variances from the planning commission or the zoning board of appeals, we decided that respondent had failed to meet the final-decision requirement. We then noted a "second reason the taking claim [was] not yet ripe": "respondent did not seek compensation through the procedures the State [had] provided for doing so." *Id.*, at 194. Until the claimant had received a final denial of compensation through all available state procedures, such as by an inverse condemnation action, we said he could not "claim a violation of the Just Compensation Clause." *Id.*, at 195-196.

The ripeness analysis presented in *Williamson County* had thereby added serious procedural complications to the area of regulatory takings, an area already plagued by substantive confusion (as we saw in Chapter Five). After having second thoughts, Chief Justice Rehnquist expressed discomfort with the labyrinthine legacy of *Williamson County*:

> It is not clear to me that *Williamson County* was correct in demanding that, once a government entity has reached a final decision with respect to a claimant's property, the claimant must seek compensation in state court before bringing a federal takings claim in federal court. The Court in *Williamson County* purported to interpret the Fifth Amendment in divining this state-litigation requirement. More recently, we have referred to it as merely a prudential requirement. Suitum v. Tahoe Regional Planning Agency, 520 U.S. 725, 733-734 (1997). It is not obvious that either constitutional or prudential principles require claimants to utilize all state compensation procedures before they can bring a federal takings claim. *Cf.* Patsy v. Board of Regents of Fla., 457 U.S. 496, 516 (1982) (holding that plaintiffs suing under § 1983 are not required to have exhausted state administrative remedies). . . .

---

10. In *San Remo*, 545 U.S. at 326-27 (2005), the Court declined the invitation to

craft an exception to the full faith and credit statute, 28 U.S.C. § 1738, for claims brought under the Takings Clause of the Fifth Amendment.

Petitioners, who own and operate a hotel in San Francisco, California (hereinafter City), initiated this litigation in response to the application of a city ordinance that required them to pay a $567,000 "conversion fee" in 1996. After the California courts rejected petitioners' various state-law takings claims, they advanced in the Federal District Court a series of federal takings claims that depended on issues identical to those that had previously been resolved in the state-court action. In order to avoid the bar of issue preclusion, petitioners asked the District Court to exempt from § 1738's reach claims brought under the Takings Clause of the Fifth Amendment.

Petitioners' argument is predicated on Williamson County Regional Planning Comm'n v. Hamilton Bank of Johnson City, 473 U.S. 172 (1985), which held that takings claims are not ripe until a State fails "to provide adequate compensation for the taking." *Id.*, at 195. Unless courts disregard § 1738 in takings cases, petitioners argue, plaintiffs will be forced to litigate their claims in state court without any realistic possibility of ever obtaining review in a federal forum. The Ninth Circuit's rejection of this argument conflicted with the Second Circuit's decision in Santini v. Connecticut Hazardous Waste Management Serv., 342 F.3d 118 (2003). We granted certiorari to resolve the conflict, 543 U.S. 1032 (2004), and now affirm the judgment of the Ninth Circuit.

Williamson County's state-litigation rule has created some real anomalies, justifying our revisiting the issue. For example, our holding today ensures that litigants who go to state court to seek compensation will likely be unable later to assert their federal takings claims in federal court. . . . As the Court recognizes, *Williamson County* all but guarantees that claimants will be unable to utilize the federal courts to enforce the Fifth Amendment's just compensation guarantee. The basic principle that state courts are competent to enforce federal rights and to adjudicate federal takings claims is sound, and would apply to any number of federal claims. But that principle does not explain why federal takings claims in particular should be singled out to be confined to state court, in the absence of any asserted justification or congressional directive. . . .

I joined the opinion of the Court in *Williamson County*. But further reflection and experience lead me to think that the justifications for its state-litigation requirement are suspect, while its impact on takings plaintiffs is dramatic. Here, no court below has addressed the correctness of *Williamson County*, neither party has asked us to reconsider it, and resolving the issue could not benefit petitioners. In an appropriate case, I believe the Court should reconsider whether plaintiffs asserting a Fifth Amendment takings claim based on the final decision of a state or local government entity must first seek compensation in state courts.

III. Excluding Profane and Sacred Uses (and Those in Between)

While many zoning ordinances have the *effect* of excluding those deemed outsiders, the segregation and elimination of uses is the clearly articulated *purpose* of Euclidean (and post-Euclidean) regulatory schemes. In Chapter Three, we studied the ways in which state courts primarily judged the classification and distribution of uses against evolving common and constitutional law standards. While courts did intervene in cases of confiscatory regulation, the predominant posture was decidedly deferential, signaling a judicial decision not to enshrine the right to own and use private property as constitutionally "fundamental." In this section, we see how courts respond when aggrieved landowners claim that widely recognized fundamental, individual, constitutional rights are being burdened by government officials.

The contrast presented in Section I of this chapter—between activist courts in a states such as New Jersey and the relative passivity of their federal counterparts—should be apparent, despite some recent movement in the area of federal civil rights legislation. Notwithstanding the *Warth–Arlington Heights* pattern of hesitation sketched above, in the area of use exclusion the Burger Court began to subject the legislative and regulatory decisions of local officials to scrutiny that was more serious than the search for rationality employed in traditional police power cases. Stated otherwise, the revolutionary discovery (critics would say invention) of fundamental rights that began during the years of the Warren Court did not leave the area of land use litigation unaffected.

For those of you who have never taken a course in First Amendment law, you are about to encounter unfamiliar legal jargon (is this "time, place, and manner," "content-neutral," or "prior restraint"?), confusing doctrinal matrices (has the "*Lemon*" test soured yet?), and a shifting legislative playing field (in which the Religious Freedom Act (RFRA) morphs into the Religious Land Use and Institutionalized Persons Act (RLUIPA)). You will soon see why local governments and developers often turn to constitutional law experts when negotiations break down and litigation rears its ugly head.

YOUNG v. AMERICAN MINI THEATRES, INC.
427 U.S. 50 (1976)

Mr. Justice STEVENS delivered the opinion of the Court.[*] . . .

Effective November 2, 1972, Detroit adopted the ordinances challenged in this litigation. Instead of concentrating "adult" theaters in limited zones, these ordinances require that such theaters be dispersed. Specifically, an adult theater may not be located within 1,000 feet of any two other "regulated uses" or within 500 feet of a residential area. The term "regulated uses" includes 10 different kinds of establishments in addition to adult theaters.[3] . . .

The 1972 ordinances were amendments to an "Anti-Skid Row Ordinance" which had been adopted 10 years earlier. At that time the Detroit Common Council made a finding that some uses of property are especially injurious to a neighborhood when they are concentrated in limited areas.[6] The decision to add adult motion picture theaters and adult book stores to the list of businesses which, apart from a special waiver, could not be located within 1,000 feet of two other "regulated uses," was, in part, a response to the significant growth in the number of such establishments. In the opinion of urban planners and real estate experts who supported the ordinances, the location of several such businesses in the same neighborhood tends to attract an undesirable quantity and quality of transients, adversely affects property values, causes an increase in crime, especially prostitution, and encourages residents and businesses to move elsewhere.

Respondents are the operators of two adult motion picture theaters. One, the Nortown, was an established theater which began to exhibit adult films in March 1973. The other, the Pussy Cat, was a corner gas station which was converted into a "mini theater," but denied a certificate of occupancy because of its plan to exhibit adult films. Both theaters were located within 1,000 feet of two other regulated uses and the Pussy Cat was less than 500 feet from a residential area. The respondents brought two separate actions against appropriate city officials, seeking a declaratory judgment that the ordinances were unconstitutional and an injunction against their enforcement. Federal jurisdiction was properly invoked and the two cases were consolidated for decision. . . .

Petitioners acknowledge that the ordinances prohibit theaters which are not licensed as "adult motion picture theaters" from exhibiting films which are protected by the First Amendment. Respondents argue that the ordinances are therefore invalid as prior restraints on free speech. . . .

Putting to one side for the moment the fact that adult motion picture theaters must satisfy a locational restriction not applicable to other theaters, we are also persuaded that the 1,000-foot restriction does not, in itself, create an impermissible restraint on protected communication. The city's interest in planning and regulating the use of property for commercial purposes is clearly adequate to support that kind of restriction applicable to all theaters within the city limits. In

---

[*]. Part III of this opinion is joined by only THE CHIEF JUSTICE, MR. JUSTICE WHITE, and MR. JUSTICE REHNQUIST.

3. In addition to adult motion picture theaters and "mini" theaters, which contain less than 50 seats, the regulated uses include adult bookstores; cabarets (group "D"); establishments for the sale of beer or intoxicating liquor for consumption on the premises; hotels or motels; pawnshops; pool or billiard halls; public lodging houses; secondhand stores; shoeshine parlors; and taxi dance halls.

6. Section 66.000 of the Official Zoning Ordinance (1972) recited:

In the development and execution of this Ordinance, it is recognized that there are some uses which, because of their very nature, are recognized as having serious objectionable operational characteristics, particularly when several of them are concentrated under certain circumstances thereby having a deleterious effect upon the adjacent areas. Special regulation of these uses is necessary to insure that these adverse effects will not contribute to the blighting or downgrading of the surrounding neighborhood. These special regulations are itemized in this section. The primary control or regulation is for the purpose of preventing a concentration of these uses in any one area (i. e. not more than two such uses within one thousand feet of each other which would create such adverse effects).

short, apart from the fact that the ordinances treat adult theaters differently from other theaters and the fact that the classification is predicated on the content of material shown in the respective theaters, the regulation of the place where such films may be exhibited does not offend the First Amendment.[18] . . .

III . . .

Whether political oratory or philosophical discussion moves us to applaud or to despise what is said, every schoolchild can understand why our duty to defend the right to speak remains the same. But few of us would march our sons and daughters off to war to preserve the citizen's right to see "Specified Sexual Activities" exhibited in the theaters of our choice. Even though the First Amendment protects communication in this area from total suppression, we hold that the State may legitimately use the content of these materials as the basis for placing them in a different classification from other motion pictures.

The remaining question is whether the line drawn by these ordinances is justified by the city's interest in preserving the character of its neighborhoods. On this question we agree with the views expressed by District Judges Kennedy and Gubow. The record discloses a factual basis for the Common Council's conclusion that this kind of restriction will have the desired effect. It is not our function to appraise the wisdom of its decision to require adult theaters to be separated rather than concentrated in the same areas. In either event, the city's interest in attempting to preserve the quality of urban life is one that must be accorded high respect. Moreover, the city must be allowed a reasonable opportunity to experiment with solutions to admittedly serious problems.

Since what is ultimately at stake is nothing more than a limitation on the place where adult films may be exhibited, even though the determination of whether a particular film fits that characterization turns on the nature of its content, we conclude that the city's interest in the present and future character of its neighborhoods adequately supports its classification of motion pictures. We hold that the zoning ordinances requiring that adult motion picture theaters not be located within 1,000 feet of two other regulated uses does not violate the Equal Protection Clause of the Fourteenth Amendment. . . .

Mr. Justice POWELL.

Although I agree with much of what is said in the Court's opinion, and concur in Parts I and II, my approach to the resolution of this case is sufficiently different to prompt me to write separately.[1] I view the case as presenting an example of innovative land-use regulation, implicating First Amendment concerns only incidentally and to a limited extent.

Mr. Justice STEWART, with whom Mr. Justice BRENNAN, Mr. Justice MARSHALL, and Mr. Justice BLACKMUN join, dissenting. . . .

This case does not involve a simple zoning ordinance, or a content-neutral time, place, and manner restriction, or a regulation of obscene expression or other speech that is entitled to less than the full protection of the First Amendment. The kind of expression at issue here is no doubt objection-

---

18. Reasonable regulations of the time, place, and manner of protected speech, where those regulations are necessary to further significant governmental interests, are permitted by the First Amendment. See, e.g., Kovacs v. Cooper, 336 U.S. 77 (limitation on use of sound trucks); Cox v. Louisiana, 379 U.S. 559 (ban on demonstrations in or near a courthouse with the intent to obstruct justice); Grayned v. City of Rockford, 408 U.S. 104 (ban on willful making, on grounds adjacent to a school, of any noise which disturbs the good order of the school session).

1. I do not think we need reach, nor am I inclined to agree with, the holding in Part III (and supporting discussion) that nonobscene, erotic materials may be treated differently under First Amendment principles from other forms of protected expression. I do not consider the conclusions in Part I of the opinion to depend on distinctions between protected speech.

able to some, but that fact does not diminish its protected status any more than did the particular content of the "offensive" expression in Erznoznik v. City of Jacksonville, 422 U. S. 205. . . .

What this case does involve is the constitutional permissibility of selective interference with protected speech whose content is thought to produce distasteful effects. It is elementary that a prime function of the First Amendment is to guard against just such interference. By refusing to invalidate Detroit's ordinance the Court rides roughshod over cardinal principles of First Amendment law, which require that time, place, and manner regulations that affect protected expression be content neutral except in the limited context of a captive or juvenile audience. In place of these principles the Court invokes a concept wholly alien to the First Amendment. Since "few of us would march our sons and daughters off to war to preserve the citizen's right to see 'Specified Sexual Activities' exhibited in the theaters of our choice," the Court implies that these films are not entitled to the full protection of the Constitution. . . . For if the guarantees of the First Amendment were reserved for expression that more than a "few of us" would take up arms to defend, then the right of free expression would be defined and circumscribed by current popular opinion. The guarantees of the Bill of Rights were designed to protect against precisely such majoritarian limitations on individual liberty. . . .

Notes

1. During oral argument, the Court was interested in the reasons Detroit chose to scatter adult uses throughout the city, abandoning the cluster approach used in Baltimore's Block and Boston's Combat Zone:

> QUESTION: I take it, or have you suggested, that one of the purposes of these restrictions is to maintain property values, like zoning sometimes is aimed at that.

> MRS. REILLY: It is very definitely directed to preserve property values, yes, your Honor. . . .

> QUESTION: It's an environmental problem which has an incidental impact on property values, is that not a fair way to say it?

> MRS. REILLY: Yes, your Honor.

> QUESTION: They didn't set out in the first place to try to hold up property values; they set out to try to, as you describe it in your briefs, they set out to try to preserve a decent environment in the city and one of the consequences of that is it will also help the property values.

Based on this and other information, the plurality was convinced that despite the dissent's concerns about interference with protected speech, there was a "factual basis" for the city's regulation.

2. How thoroughly must local officials investigate the need for, and ramifications of, what has been called "erogenous zoning"? In City of Renton v. Playtime Theatres, 475 U.S. 41, 51-52 (1986); the majority approved the Seattle suburb's (population 32,000) plan "that prohibits adult motion picture theaters from locating within 1,000 feet of any residential zone, single- or multiple-family dwelling, church, park, or school." The effect of the ordinance was to leave 520 acres available for such restricted uses. According to the majority: "The appropriate inquiry in this case, then, is whether the Renton ordinance is designed to serve a substantial governmental interest and allows for reasonable alternative avenues of communication." The court of appeals, and dissenting Justices William Brennan and Thurgood Marshall, were skeptical concerning the availability and suitability of the alternative sites.

The Court relied primarily on *Young* in upholding the ordinance, despite the fact that Renton did not engage in its own study before settling on the plan, instead utilizing studies prepared by the city of Seattle. (The Supreme Court of Washington had approved that city's cluster or "Combat Zone" approach in Northend Cinema v. City of Seattle, 90 Wash. 2d 709, 585 P.2d 1153 (1978)):

> The First Amendment does not require a city, before enacting such an ordinance, to conduct new studies or produce evidence independent of that already generated by other cities, so long as whatever evidence the city relies upon is reasonably believed to be relevant to the problem the city addresses. That was the case here. Nor is our holding affected by the fact that Seattle ultimately chose a different method than that chosen by Renton, since Seattle's choice of a different remedy to combat the secondary effects of adult theaters does not call into, question either Seattle's identification of those secondary effects or the relevance of Seattle's experience to Renton.

Has the Court invited any municipality (regardless of size or location) merely to review studies prepared by Detroit or Seattle (or the summaries provided by the Supreme Court) before embarking on its own plan for restricting less desirable uses?

3. How far can a city take this scattering approach before the court will step in? Although many such ordinances, inspired by Detroit's victory in *Young*, have been approved, there is a limit to the exclusionary effect they may produce. In Executive Arts Studio, Inc. v. City of Grand Rapids, 391 F.3d 783, 797 (6th Cir. 2004), the court noted that

> it is undisputed that Executive Arts is currently foreclosed from opening its [adult book] store in all but around a half dozen possible sites in a City with over 2,500 parcels of commercially useable real estate. This is wholly inadequate to provide for reasonable alternative avenues of communication. See *Renton*, 475 U.S. at 53 ("the ordinance leaves some 520 acres, or more than five percent of the entire land area of Renton, open to use as [] adult sites"); CLR Corp., 702 F.2d at 639 (unconstitutional zoning ordinance only permitted two to four restricted uses in a 2500 foot frontage area for a city of 70,000); Dia v. City of Toledo, 937 F. Supp. 673, 678 (N.D. Ohio 1996) ("Courts have generally found the number to be inadequate if fewer than a dozen sites, or under 1% of the city acreage, is potentially available").

Similarly, in Alexander v. City of Minneapolis, 698 F.2d 936 (8th Cir. 1983), the city's Zoning Supervisor testified that 5 out of 30 existing adult uses would be allowed to remain under Minneapolis's 500-foot radius ordinance. The appellate court, citing an exception in *Young* for regulations "greatly restricting access," affirmed the district court's holding that the ordinance violated the First and Fourteenth Amendments. See also Christy v. City of Ann Arbor, 824 F.2d 489 (6th Cir. 1987), in which the plaintiff asserted that under the challenged ordinance only .23 of 1% of the city was available for the location of an adult bookstore.

4. The availability of pornography on the Internet poses a serious challenge for local officials who seek to "zone out" all adult uses. In Voyeur Dorm, L.C. v. City of Tampa, 265 F.3d 1232, 1235-36 (11th Cir. 2001), the federal appeals court found that the city incorrectly applied "to the alleged activities occurring at 2312 West Farwell Drive" a code section that included the following definition of "adult entertainment establishment": "any premises . . . on which is offered to members of the public or any person, for a consideration, entertainment featuring or in any way including specified sexual activities, . . . or entertainment featuring the displaying or depicting of specified anatomical areas . . . ." Voyeur Dorm was the operator of an Internet website "portraying the lives of the residents of 2312 West Farwell Drive" 24 hours a day.

The appeals court avoided the need to determine whether the ordinance was unconstitutional, as the judges agreed with the business owner that the code provision "applies to locations or premises wherein adult entertainment is actually offered to the public." Such was not the case with Voyeur Dorm:

> The City Code cannot be applied to a location that does not, itself, offer adult entertainment to the public. As a practical matter, zoning restrictions are indelibly anchored in particular geographic locations. Residential areas are often cordoned off from business districts in order to promote a State's interest. *See e.g., City of Renton*, 475 U.S. at 50 ("A city's interest in attempting to preserve the quality of urban life is one that must be accorded high respect."). It does not follow, then, that a zoning ordinance designed to restrict facilities that offer adult entertainment can be applied to a particular location that does not, at that location, offer adult entertainment. Moreover, the case law relied upon by Tampa and the district court concerns adult entertainment in which customers physically attend the premises wherein the entertainment is performed. Here, the audience or consumers of the adult entertainment do not go to 2312 West Farwell Drive or congregate anywhere else in Tampa to enjoy the entertainment. Indeed, the public offering occurs over the Internet in "virtual space." While the district court read section 27-523 in a literal sense, finding no requirement that the paying public be on the premises, we hold that section 27-523 does not apply to a residence at which there is no public offering of adult entertainment. Accordingly, because the district court misapplied section 27-523 to the residence of 2312 West Farwell Drive, we reverse the district court's order granting summary judgment to Tampa.

5. States and localities have begun to draw circles around residences occupied by sex offenders, in an effort to protect children from predators and other violators. Steven J. Wernick, in Note, *In Accordance With a Public Outcry: Zoning Out Sex Offenders Through Residence Restrictions in Florida*, 58 Fla. L. Rev. 1147 (2006), provided an overview of a growing national movement:

> Twenty different states and a spate of local governments have turned to residential buffer zones as a possible method of preventing sex crimes against children. Expanding upon registration laws aimed at keeping tabs on previously convicted sex offenders, state lawmakers have enacted residence restrictions prohibiting sex offenders from living near schools and other child-centered facilities. Not satisfied with existing state legislation, numerous municipalities have passed or are considering laws imposing even harsher restrictions. In the spirit of the Not in My Backyard (NIMBY) movement, these laws often appear to be an attempt by towns, cities, counties, and other local governments to expel sex offenders altogether.

> Proponents of residence restrictions argue that there is no cure for sex offenders and that sex offenders have a high rate of recidivism that makes them a potential threat forever. Opponents counter that recent studies show no causal link between proximity of sex offenders to children and the propensity of recidivism. Despite evidence that residence restrictions may be missing the mark when it comes to preventing sex crimes involving child victims, courts are typically reluctant to interfere with state legislatures on how best to protect the health and safety of their citizens. . . .

In Doe v. Miller, 405 F.3d 700 (8th Cir. 2005), the appellate panel held that the following statute (Iowa Code §692A.2A, enacted in 2002) was not unconstitutional on its face:

> Residency restrictions—child care facilities and schools.

1. For purposes of this section, "person" means a person who has committed a criminal offense against a minor, or an aggravated offense, sexually violent offense, or other relevant offense that involved a minor.

2. A person shall not reside within two thousand feet of the real property comprising a public or nonpublic elementary or secondary school or a child care facility.

3. A person who resides within two thousand feet of the real property comprising a public or nonpublic elementary or secondary school, or a child care facility, commits an aggravated misdemeanor.

4. A person residing within two thousand feet of the real property comprising a public or nonpublic elementary or secondary school or a child care facility does not commit a violation of this section if any of the following apply:

> a. The person is required to serve a sentence at a jail, prison, juvenile facility, or other correctional institution or facility.

> b. The person is subject to an order of commitment under chapter 229A.

> c. The person has established a residence prior to July 1, 2002, or a school or child care facility is newly located on or after July 1, 2002.

> d. The person is a minor or a ward under a guardianship.

The court reversed the trial court, which had

> declared that § 692A.2A was unconstitutional on several grounds, to wit: that it was an unconstitutional ex post facto law with respect to offenders who committed an offense prior to July 1, 2002; that it violated the plaintiffs' rights to avoid self-incrimination because, coupled with registration requirements elsewhere in Chapter 692A, it required offenders to report their addresses even if those addresses were not in compliance with § 692A.2A; that it violated procedural due process rights of the plaintiffs; and that it violated the plaintiffs' rights under the doctrine of substantive due process, because it infringed fundamental rights to travel and to "privately choose how they want to conduct their family affairs," and was not narrowly tailored to serve a compelling state interest. Although the district court believed the law was punitive, the court rejected the plaintiffs' final argument that the law imposed cruel and unusual punishment in violation of the Eighth Amendment

Several federal and state courts have followed the U.S. Court of Appeals for the Eighth Circuit's lead in approving similar state and local residency restrictions. See Powell on Real Property §79D.07 [2][h] (Michael Allan Wolf gen. ed. 2009).

6. One New Jersey community employed a "total ban" strategy to eliminate live adult entertainment. The strategy was struck down as a violation of the First Amendment in Schad v. Borough of Mt. Ephraim, 452 U.S. 61, 62, 65, 68, 71-74, 75-76 (1981), a case in which the successful appellants, who owned an adult bookstore, "introduced an additional coin-operated mechanism permitting the customer to watch a live dancer, usually nude, performing behind a glass panel." This put the store owners in direct conflict with the municipality's zoning ordinance, which prohibited all live entertainment. The result was a finding of guilt and the imposition of fines, which the appellants failed to overturn in state trial and appellate courts. Before the Supreme Court, the appellants' "principal claim is that the imposition of criminal penalties under an ordinance prohibiting

all live entertainment, including nonobscene, nude dancing, violated their rights of free expression guaranteed by the First and Fourteenth Amendments of the United States Constitution."

Justice John Paul Stevens wrote the majority opinion in which he noted that, "when a zoning law infringes upon a protected liberty it must be narrowly drawn and must further a sufficiently substantial government interest." He then distinguished Mt. Ephraim's situation from Detroit's:

> As an initial matter, this case is not controlled by Young v. American Mini Theatres, Inc., the decision relied upon by the Camden County Court. Although the Court there stated that a zoning ordinance is not invalid merely because it regulates activity protected under the First Amendment, it emphasized that the challenged restriction on the location of adult movie theaters imposed a minimal burden on protected speech. . . .

> In this case, however, Mount Ephraim has not adequately justified its substantial restriction of protected activity. None of the justifications asserted in this Court was articulated by the state courts and none of them withstands scrutiny. First, the Borough contends that permitting live entertainment would conflict with its plan to create a commercial area that caters only to the "immediate needs" of its residents and that would enable them to purchase at local stores the few items they occasionally forgot to buy outside the Borough. No evidence was introduced below to support this assertion, and it is difficult to reconcile this characterization of the Borough's commercial zones with the provisions of the ordinance. Section 99-15A expressly states that the purpose of creating commercial zones was to provide areas for "local and *regional* commercial operations." (Emphasis added.) The range of permitted uses goes far beyond providing for the "immediate needs" of the residents. Motels, hardware stores, lumber stores, banks, offices, and car showrooms are permitted in commercial zones. The list of permitted "retail stores" is nonexclusive, and it includes such services as beauty salons, barbershops, cleaners, and restaurants. Virtually the only item or service that may not be sold in a commercial zone is entertainment, or at least live entertainment. The Borough's first justification is patently insufficient.

> Second, Mount Ephraim contends that it may selectively exclude commercial live entertainment from the broad range of commercial uses permitted in the Borough for reasons normally associated with zoning in commercial districts, that is, to avoid the problems that may be associated with live entertainment, such as parking, trash, police protection, and medical facilities. The Borough has presented no evidence, and it is not immediately apparent as a matter of experience, that live entertainment poses problems of this nature more significant than those associated with various permitted uses; nor does it appear that the Borough's zoning authority has arrived at a defensible conclusion that unusual problems are presented by live entertainment. . . .

> [N]o evidence has been presented to establish that live entertainment is incompatible with the uses presently permitted by the Borough. Mount Ephraim asserts that it could have chosen to eliminate all commercial uses within its boundaries. Yet we must assess the exclusion of live entertainment in light of the commercial uses Mount Ephraim allows, not in light of what the Borough might have done.[18]

---

18. Thus, our decision today does not establish that every unit of local government entrusted with zoning responsibilities must provide a commercial zone in which live entertainment is permitted.

To be reasonable, time, place, and manner restrictions not only must serve significant state interests but also must leave open adequate alternative channels of communication. . . .

Subsequent efforts to shield live nude dancing from more targeted land use restrictions have proved much less successful. See, for example, City of Erie v. Pap's A.M., 529 U.S. 277, 296 (2000) (plurality):

We conclude that Erie's asserted interest in combating the negative secondary effects associated with adult entertainment establishments like Kandyland is unrelated to the suppression of the erotic message conveyed by nude dancing. The ordinance prohibiting public nudity is therefore valid if it satisfies the four-factor test from [United States v.] O'Brien [, 381 U.S. 367 (1968),] for evaluating restrictions on symbolic speech.

Applying that standard here, we conclude that Erie's ordinance is justified under O'Brien.

7. In 1983, the city of Los Angeles closed a loophole in its regulations governing "adult entertainment" businesses, amending the municipal code to prohibit the co-location of more than one such business in the same "building, structure or portion thereon." The preexisting regulation (enacted in 1977) had outlawed the "establishment, substantial enlargement, or transfer of ownership of [adult businesses] within 1000 feet of another such enterprise or within 500 feet of any religious institution, school, or public park." Two adult businesses housed in the same building (a bookstore and a video arcade) challenged the ordinance, alleging that it violated their First Amendment free speech rights. The federal district court and the Ninth Circuit on appeal agreed that the ordinance as amended was unconstitutional, although the basis for their holdings differed somewhat. The trial court deemed the prohibition a "content-based regulation" and concluded that the regulation could not withstand strict scrutiny, while the appellate court noted that even if the regulation were "content-neutral," it would not pass muster under the Supreme Court's approach to adult use zoning that was set forth in Renton.

In City of Los Angeles v. Alameda Books, 535 U.S. 425 (2002), the Supreme Court reversed the Ninth Circuit, ruling in favor of the city. Four Justices, in a plurality opinion written by Justice Sandra Day O'Connor, held that the Ninth Circuit's Renton analysis was flawed, as the appeals court had wrongly concluded that the city had improperly relied on a 1977 report by the Los Angeles Planning Department regarding the secondary effects of adult businesses (chiefly increased crime rates). Citing Renton, the plurality noted that for such a time, place, and manner regulation, "a municipality may rely on any evidence that is 'reasonably believed to be relevant' for demonstrating a connection between speech and a substantial, independent government interest." Having done so with the 1977 study, the city had met its constitutional obligation.

The fifth vote in favor of the city came from Justice Anthony Kennedy who, in a concurring opinion, expressed his discomfort with applying the "content-neutral" label to these kinds of ordinances. Even so, applying "intermediate," not "strict" scrutiny, Justice Kennedy concluded that the ordinance was not an invalid restriction of free speech protections. The four dissenters, led by Justice David Souter, were dissatisfied with the city's failure to demonstrate a sufficient rationale for its "content-correlated zoning restrictions."

While Alameda Books did not reverse directions in the adult use regulation area, there are signs that the Justices may have reached their limit in the amount of deference they grant local governments in this sensitive area. Now that five members of the Court have expressed discomfort with the "content-neutral" label for these kinds of controls on the use of property, localities should be careful not to stray too far from the scheme approved in Renton.

8. For a case testing the limits of good taste, see Pensack v. City and County of Denver, 630 F. Supp. 177, 177-78 (D. Colo. 1986):

> The plaintiff, Laurie Pensack, is the sole proprietor of a bakery business which she operates under the name Le Bakery Sensual . . . in Aurora, Colorado. Le Bakery is different from other bakeries in that it specializes in "theme" cakes made to meet customers' requests. . . . Le Bakery's advertising emphasizes that it is an "outlet for erotic edible and custom baked goods beyond your wildest dreams!" . . .
>
> On March 12, 1984, the Zoning Administrator of the City and County of Denver issued a cease and desist order to Le Bakery, contending that the retail bakery use which had been approved had been converted "into an adult bookstore and a sexually-oriented commercial enterprise" in violation of that provision of the Denver Zoning Ordinance which requires that certain uses in a B-4 zone must be located more than 500 feet from any residential district, and that not more than two such uses may be located within 1,000 feet of each other. The uses subject to that separation requirement include adult amusement or entertainment centers, adult bookstores, sexually-oriented commercial enterprises; and adult theaters.

The trial court held that despite defendants' *Young* argument, the ordinance as applied violated the baker's first amendment rights.

CITY OF LADUE v. GILLEO
512 U.S. 43 (1994)

Justice STEVENS delivered the opinion of the Court.

An ordinance of the City of Ladue prohibits homeowners from displaying any signs on their property except "residence identification" signs, "for sale" signs, and signs warning of safety hazards. The ordinance permits commercial establishments, churches, and nonprofit organizations to erect certain signs that are not allowed at residences. The question presented is whether the ordinance violates a Ladue resident's right to free speech.

Respondent Margaret P. Gilleo owns one of the 57 single-family homes in the Willow Hill subdivision of Ladue. On December 8, 1990, she placed on her front lawn a 24- by 36-inch sign printed with the words, "Say No to War in the Persian Gulf, Call Congress Now." After that sign disappeared, Gilleo put up another but it was knocked to the ground. When Gilleo reported these incidents to the police, they advised her that such signs were prohibited in Ladue. The city council denied her petition for a variance. Gilleo then filed this action under 42 U.S.C. § 1983 against the City, the mayor, and members of the city council, alleging that Ladue's sign ordinance violated her First Amendment right of free speech.

The District Court issued a preliminary injunction against enforcement of the ordinance. 774 F. Supp. 1559 (ED Mo. 1991). Gilleo then placed an 8.5- by 11-inch sign in the second story window of her home stating, "For Peace in the Gulf." The Ladue City Council responded to the injunction by repealing its ordinance and enacting a replacement.[4] Like its predecessor, the new

---

4. The new ordinance eliminates the provision allowing for variances and contains a grandfather clause exempting signs already lawfully in place.

ordinance contains a general prohibition of "signs" and defines that term broadly.[5] The ordinance prohibits all signs except those that fall within 1 of 10 exemptions. Thus, "residential identification signs" no larger than one square foot are allowed, as are signs advertising "that the property is for sale, lease or exchange" and identifying the owner or agent. Also exempted are signs "for churches, religious institutions, and schools," "commercial signs in commercially zoned or industrial zoned districts," and on-site signs advertising "gasoline filling stations." Unlike its predecessor, the new ordinance contains a lengthy "Declaration of Findings, Policies, Interests, and Purposes," part of which recites that the

> "proliferation of an unlimited number of signs in private, residential, commercial, industrial, and public areas of the City of Ladue would create ugliness, visual blight and clutter, tarnish the natural beauty of the landscape as well as the residential and commercial architecture, impair property values, substantially impinge upon the privacy and special ambience of the community, and may cause safety and traffic hazards to motorists, pedestrians, and children."

Gilleo amended her complaint to challenge the new ordinance, which explicitly prohibits window signs like hers. The District Court held the ordinance unconstitutional, 774 F. Supp. 1559 (ED Mo. 1991), and the Court of Appeals affirmed, 986 F.2d 1180 (CA8 1993). Relying on the plurality opinion in Metromedia, Inc. v. San Diego, 453 U.S. 490, the Court of Appeals held the ordinance invalid as a "content based" regulation because the City treated commercial speech more favorably than noncommercial speech and favored some kinds of noncommercial speech over others. 986 F.2d at 1182. Acknowledging that "Ladue's interests in enacting its ordinance are substantial," the Court of Appeals nevertheless concluded that those interests were "not sufficiently 'compelling' to support a content-based restriction." 986 F.2d at 1183-1184 (citing Simon & Schuster, Inc. v. Members of N. Y. State Crime Victims Bd., 502 U.S. 105, 118, 116 L. Ed. 2d 476, 112 S. Ct. 501 (1991)). . . .

While signs are a form of expression protected by the Free Speech Clause, they pose distinctive problems that are subject to municipalities' police powers. Unlike oral speech, signs take up space and may obstruct views, distract motorists, displace alternative uses for land, and pose other problems that legitimately call for regulation. It is common ground that governments may regulate the physical characteristics of signs—just as they can, within reasonable bounds and absent censorial purpose, regulate audible expression in its capacity as noise. However, because regulation of a medium inevitably affects communication itself, it is not surprising that we have had occasion to review the constitutionality of municipal ordinances prohibiting the display of certain outdoor signs.

In Linmark Associates, Inc. v. Willingboro, 431 U.S. 85, we addressed an ordinance that sought to maintain stable, integrated neighborhoods by prohibiting homeowners from placing "For Sale" or "Sold" signs on their property. Although we recognized the importance of Willingboro's objective, we held that the First Amendment prevented the township from "achieving its

---

5. Section 35-2 of the ordinance declares that "No sign shall be erected [or] maintained" in the City except in conformity with the ordinance; § 35-3 authorizes the City to remove nonconforming signs. Section 35-1 defines "sign" as:

"A name, word, letter, writing, identification, description, or illustration which is erected, placed upon, affixed to, painted or represented upon a building or structure, or any part thereof, or in any manner upon a parcel of land or lot, and which publicizes an object, product, place, activity, opinion, person, institution, organization or place of business, or which is used to advertise or promote the interests of any person. The word 'sign' shall also include 'banners', 'pennants', 'insignia', 'bulletin boards', 'ground signs', 'billboard', 'poster billboards', 'illuminated signs', 'projecting signs', 'temporary signs', 'marquees', 'roof signs', 'yard signs', 'electric signs', 'wall signs', and 'window signs', wherever placed out of doors in view of the general public or wherever placed indoors as a window sign."

goal by restricting the free flow of truthful information." 431 U.S. at 95. In some respects *Linmark* is the mirror image of this case. For instead of prohibiting "For Sale" signs without banning any other signs, Ladue has exempted such signs from an otherwise virtually complete ban. Moreover, whereas in *Linmark* we noted that the ordinance was not concerned with the promotion of esthetic values unrelated to the content of the prohibited speech, here Ladue relies squarely on that content-neutral justification for its ordinance.

In *Metromedia*, we reviewed an ordinance imposing substantial prohibitions on outdoor advertising displays within the city of San Diego in the interest of traffic safety and esthetics. The ordinance generally banned all except those advertising "on-site" activities.[7] The Court concluded that the city's interest in traffic safety and its esthetic interest in preventing "visual clutter" could justify a prohibition of offsite commercial billboards even though similar on-site signs were allowed. 453 U.S. at 511-512.[8] Nevertheless, the Court's judgment in *Metromedia*, supported by two different lines of reasoning, invalidated the San Diego ordinance in its entirety. According to Justice White's plurality opinion, the ordinance impermissibly discriminated on the basis of content by permitting on-site commercial speech while broadly prohibiting noncommercial messages. 453 U.S. at 514-515. On the other hand, Justice Brennan, joined by JUSTICE BLACKMUN, concluded that "the practical effect of the San Diego ordinance [was] to eliminate the billboard as an effective medium of communication" for noncommercial messages, and that the city had failed to make the strong showing needed to justify such "content-neutral prohibitions of particular media of communication." 453 U.S. at 525-527. The three dissenters also viewed San Diego's ordinance as tantamount to a blanket prohibition of billboards, but would have upheld it because they did not perceive "even a hint of bias or censorship in the city's actions" nor "any reason to believe that the overall communications market in San Diego is inadequate." 453 U.S. at 552-553 (Stevens, J., dissenting in part). See also 453 U.S. at 563, 566 (Burger, C. J., dissenting); 453 U.S. at 569-570 (Rehnquist, J., dissenting).

In Members of City Council of Los Angeles v. Taxpayers for Vincent, 466 U.S. 789 (1984), we upheld a Los Angeles ordinance that prohibited the posting of signs on public property. Noting the conclusion shared by seven Justices in *Metromedia* that San Diego's "interest in avoiding visual clutter" was sufficient to justify a prohibition of commercial billboards, 466 U.S. at 806-807, in *Vincent* we upheld the Los Angeles ordinance, which was justified on the same grounds. We rejected the argument that the validity of the city's esthetic interest had been compromised by failing to extend the ban to private property, reasoning that the "private citizen's interest in controlling the use of his own property justifies the disparate treatment." *Id.*, at 811. We also rejected as "misplaced" respondents' reliance on public forum principles, for they had "failed to demonstrate the existence of a traditional right of access respecting such items as utility poles . . . comparable to that recognized for public streets and parks." *Id.*, at 814.

These decisions identify two analytically distinct grounds for challenging the constitutionality of a municipal ordinance regulating the display of signs. One is that the measure in effect

---

7. The San Diego ordinance defined "on-site signs" as "those 'designating the name of the owner or occupant of the premises upon which such signs are placed, or identifying such premises; or signs advertising goods manufactured or produced or services rendered on the premises upon which such signs are placed.'" Metromedia, Inc. v. San Diego, 453 U.S. at 494. The plurality read the "on-site" exemption of the San Diego ordinance as inapplicable to noncommercial messages. See 453 U.S. at 513. Cf. 453 U.S. at 535-536 (Brennan, J., concurring in judgment). The ordinance also exempted 12 categories of displays, including religious signs; for sale signs; signs on public and commercial vehicles; and "'temporary political campaign signs.'" 453 U.S. at 495, n.3.

8. Five Members of the Court joined Part IV of Justice White's opinion, which approved of the city's decision to prohibit off-site commercial billboards while permitting on-site billboards. None of the three dissenters disagreed with Part IV. See 453 U.S. at 541 (Stevens, J., dissenting in part) (joining Part IV); 453 U.S. at 564-565 (Burger, C. J., dissenting); 453 U.S. at 570 (Rehnquist, J., dissenting).

restricts too little speech because its exemptions discriminate on the basis of the signs' messages. See *Metromedia*, 453 U.S. at 512-517 (opinion of White, J.). Alternatively, such provisions are subject to attack on the ground that they simply prohibit too much protected speech. See 453 U.S. at 525-534 (Brennan, J., concurring in judgment). The City of Ladue contends, first, that the Court of Appeals' reliance on the former rationale was misplaced because the City's regulatory purposes are content neutral, and, second, that those purposes justify the comprehensiveness of the sign prohibition. A comment on the former contention will help explain why we ultimately base our decision on a rejection of the latter.

While surprising at first glance, the notion that a regulation of speech may be impermissibly *underinclusive* is firmly grounded in basic First Amendment principles. Thus, an exemption from an otherwise permissible regulation of speech may represent a governmental "attempt to give one side of a debatable public question an advantage in expressing its views to the people." First Nat. Bank of Boston v. Bellotti, 435 U.S. 765, 785-786 (1978). Alternatively, through the combined operation of a general speech restriction and its exemptions, the government might seek to select the "permissible subjects for public debate" and thereby to "control . . . the search for political truth." Consolidated Edison Co. of N. Y. v. Public Serv. Comm'n of N. Y., 447 U.S. 530, 538 (1980).

The City argues that its sign ordinance implicates neither of these concerns, and that the Court of Appeals therefore erred in demanding a "compelling" justification for the exemptions. The mix of prohibitions and exemptions in the ordinance, Ladue maintains, reflects legitimate differences among the side effects of various kinds of signs. These differences are only adventitiously connected with content, and supply a sufficient justification, unrelated to the City's approval or disapproval of specific messages, for carving out the specified categories from the general ban. Thus, according to the Declaration of Findings, Policies, Interests, and Purposes supporting the ordinance, the permitted signs, unlike the prohibited signs, are unlikely to contribute to the dangers of "unlimited proliferation" associated with categories of signs that are not inherently limited in number. Because only a few residents will need to display "for sale" or "for rent" signs at any given time, permitting one such sign per marketed house does not threaten visual clutter. Because the City has only a few businesses, churches, and schools, the same rationale explains the exemption for on-site commercial and organizational signs. Moreover, some of the exempted categories (*e.g.*, danger signs) respond to unique public needs to permit certain kinds of speech. Even if we assume the validity of these arguments, the exemptions in Ladue's ordinance nevertheless shed light on the separate question whether the ordinance prohibits too much speech.

Exemptions from an otherwise legitimate regulation of a medium of speech may be noteworthy for a reason quite apart from the risks of viewpoint and content discrimination: They may diminish the credibility of the government's rationale for restricting speech in the first place. In this case, at the very least, the exemptions from Ladue's ordinance demonstrate that Ladue has concluded that the interest in allowing certain messages to be conveyed by means of residential signs outweighs the City's esthetic interest in eliminating outdoor signs. Ladue has not imposed a flat ban on signs because it has determined that at least some of them are too vital to be banned.

Under the Court of Appeals' content discrimination rationale, the City might theoretically remove the defects in its ordinance by simply repealing all of the exemptions. If, however, the ordinance is also vulnerable because it prohibits too much speech, that solution would not save it. Moreover, if the prohibitions in Ladue's ordinance are impermissible, resting our decision on its exemptions would afford scant relief for respondent Gilleo. She is primarily concerned not with the scope of the exemptions available in other locations, such as commercial areas and on church property; she asserts a constitutional right to display an antiwar sign at her own home. Therefore, we first ask whether Ladue may properly *prohibit* Gilleo from displaying her sign, and then, only if necessary, consider the separate question whether it was improper for the City simultaneously to *permit* certain other signs. In examining the propriety of Ladue's neartotal prohibition of residential signs, we will assume, *arguendo*, the validity of the City's submission that the various exemptions are free of impermissible content or viewpoint discrimination.

In *Linmark* we held that the city's interest in maintaining a stable, racially integrated neighborhood was not sufficient to support a prohibition of residential "For Sale" signs. We recognized that even such a narrow sign prohibition would have a deleterious effect on residents' ability to convey important information because alternatives were "far from satisfactory." 431 U.S. at 93. Ladue's sign ordinance is supported principally by the City's interest in minimizing the visual clutter associated with signs, an interest that is concededly valid but certainly no more compelling than the interests at stake in *Linmark*. Moreover, whereas the ordinance in *Linmark* applied only to a form of commercial speech, Ladue's ordinance covers even such absolutely pivotal speech as a sign protesting an imminent governmental decision to go to war.

The impact on free communication of Ladue's broad sign prohibition, moreover, is manifestly greater than in *Linmark*. Gilleo and other residents of Ladue are forbidden to display virtually any "sign" on their property. The ordinance defines that term sweepingly. A prohibition is not always invalid merely because it applies to a sizeable category of speech; the sign ban we upheld in *Vincent*, for example, was quite broad. But in *Vincent* we specifically noted that the category of speech in question—signs placed on public property—was not a "uniquely valuable or important mode of communication," and that there was no evidence that "appellees' ability to communicate effectively is threatened by ever-increasing restrictions on expression." 466 U.S. at 812.

Here, in contrast, Ladue has almost completely foreclosed a venerable means of communication that is both unique and important. It has totally foreclosed that medium to political, religious, or personal messages. Signs that react to a local happening or express a view on a controversial issue both reflect and animate change in the life of a community. Often placed on lawns or in windows, residential signs play an important part in political campaigns, during which they are displayed to signal the resident's support for particular candidates, parties, or causes. They may not afford the same opportunities for conveying complex ideas as do other media, but residential signs have long been an important and distinct medium of expression.

Our prior decisions have voiced particular concern with laws that foreclose an entire medium of expression. . . . Although prohibitions foreclosing entire media may be completely free of content or viewpoint discrimination, the danger they pose to the freedom of speech is readily apparent—by eliminating a common means of speaking, such measures can suppress too much speech.

Ladue contends, however, that its ordinance is a mere regulation of the "time, place, or manner" of speech because residents remain free to convey their desired messages by other means, such as hand-held signs, "letters, handbills, flyers, telephone calls, newspaper advertisements, bumper stickers, speeches, and neighborhood or community meetings." Brief for Petitioners 41. However, even regulations that do not foreclose an entire medium of expression, but merely shift the time, place, or manner of its use, must "leave open ample alternative channels for communication." Clark v. Community for Creative Non-Violence, 468 U.S. 288, 293 (1984). In this case, we are not persuaded that adequate substitutes exist for the important medium of speech that Ladue has closed off.

Displaying a sign from one's own residence often carries a message quite distinct from placing the same sign someplace else, or conveying the same text or picture by other means. Precisely because of their location, such signs provide information about the identity of the "speaker." As an early and eminent student of rhetoric observed, the identity of the speaker is an important component of many attempts to persuade.[14] A sign advocating "Peace in the Gulf" in the front lawn of a retired general or decorated war veteran may provoke a different reaction than the same sign in a 10-year-old child's bedroom window or the same message on a bumper sticker of a passing automobile. An espousal of socialism may carry different implications when displayed on the grounds of a stately mansion than when pasted on a factory wall or an ambulatory sandwich board.

Residential signs are an unusually cheap and convenient form of communication. Especially for persons of modest means or limited mobility, a yard or window sign may have no practical substitute. Even for the affluent, the added costs in money or time of taking out a newspaper advertisement, handing out leaflets on the street, or standing in front of one's house with a hand-held sign may make the difference between participating and not participating in some public debate. Furthermore, a person who puts up a sign at her residence often intends to reach neighbors, an audience that could not be reached nearly as well by other means.

A special respect for individual liberty in the home has long been part of our culture and our law; that principle has special resonance when the government seeks to constrain a person's ability to speak there. Most Americans would be understandably dismayed, given that tradition, to learn that it was illegal to display from their window an 8- by 11-inch sign expressing their political views. Whereas the government's need to mediate among various competing uses, including expressive ones, for public streets and facilities is constant and unavoidable, its need to regulate temperate speech from the home is surely much less pressing.

Our decision that Ladue's ban on almost all residential signs violates the First Amendment by no means leaves the City powerless to address the ills that may be associated with residential signs.[17] It bears mentioning that individual residents themselves have strong incentives to keep their own property values up and to prevent "visual clutter" in their own yards and neighborhoods—incentives markedly different from those of persons who erect signs on others' land, in others' neighborhoods, or on public property. Residents' self-interest diminishes the danger of the "unlimited" proliferation of residential signs that concerns the City of Ladue. We are confident that more temperate measures could in large part satisfy Ladue's stated regulatory needs without harm to the First Amendment rights of its citizens. As currently framed, however, the ordinance abridges those rights.

Accordingly, the judgment of the Court of Appeals is
Affirmed.

Notes

1. The *Ladue* Court sought to make sense out of a cacophony of voices that spoke in previous Supreme Court decisions, chiefly Metromedia, Inc. v. San Diego, 453 U.S. 490, 510, 530-31 (1981), and Members of the City Council of Los Angeles v. Taxpayers for Vincent, 466 U.S. 789, 816-17, 818 (1984). *Metromedia* presents a confusing array of opinions regarding the constitutionality of a city ordinance that severely restricted outdoor advertising displays. Justice Byron White, writing for a plurality that viewed the ordinance as encompassing invalid time, place, and manner restrictions, sympathetically addressed the city's aesthetic justification for the ban:

---

14. *See* Aristotle 2, Rhetoric, Book 1, ch. 2, in 8 Great Books of the Western World, Encyclopedia Brittanica 595 (M. Adler ed., 2d ed. 1990) ("We believe good men more fully and more readily than others: this is true generally whatever the question is, and absolutely true where exact certainty is impossible and opinions are divided.").

17. Nor do we hold that every kind of sign must be permitted in residential areas. Different considerations might well apply, for example, in the case of signs (whether political or otherwise) displayed by residents for a fee, or in the case of off-site commercial advertisements on residential property. We also are not confronted here with mere regulations short of a ban.

It is not speculative to recognize that billboards by their very nature, wherever located and however constructed, can be perceived as an "esthetic harm." San Diego, like many States and other municipalities, has chosen to minimize the presence of such structures.[16] Such esthetic judgments are necessarily subjective, defying objective evaluation, and for that reason must be carefully scrutinized to determine if they are only a public rationalization of an impermissible purpose. But there is no claim in this case that San Diego has as an ulterior motive the suppression of speech, and the judgment involved here is not so unusual as to raise suspicions in itself.

Though concurring in the judgment, Justice Brennan analogized what he perceived as a total billboard ban to *Schad*'s prohibition of live entertainment:

I think that the city has failed to show that its asserted interest in aesthetics is sufficiently substantial in the commercial and industrial areas of San Diego. I do not doubt that "[i] t is within the power of the [city] to determine that the community should be beautiful," Berman v. Parker, 348 U.S. 26, 33, (1954), but that power may not be exercised in contravention of the First Amendment. This Court noted in *Schad* that "[t]he [city] has presented no evidence, and it is not immediately apparent as a matter of experience, that live entertainment poses problems . . . more significant than those associated with various permitted uses; nor does it appear that the [city] has arrived at a defensible conclusion that unusual problems are presented by live entertainment." 452 U.S., at 73. Substitute the word "billboards" for the words "live entertainment," and that sentence would equally apply to this case.

It is no doubt true that the appearance of certain areas of the city would be enhanced by the elimination of billboards, but "it is not immediately apparent as a matter of experience" that their elimination in all other areas as well would have more than a negligible impact on aesthetics. . . .

A billboard is not *necessarily* inconsistent with oil storage tanks, blighted areas, or strip development. Of course, it is not for a court to impose its own notion of beauty on San Diego. But before deferring to a city's judgment, a court must be convinced that the city is seriously and comprehensively addressing aesthetic concerns with respect to its environment. Here, San Diego has failed to demonstrate a comprehensive coordinated effort in its commercial and industrial areas to address other obvious contributors to an unattractive environment.

Three years later, in *Vincent*, the city proffered aesthetic, economic, and safety interests in support of its prohibition of the posting of signs on public property, including those carrying political messages. The majority, this time in an opinion written by Justice Stevens, accepted

the City's position that it may decide that the esthetic interest in avoiding "visual clutter" justifies a removal of signs creating or increasing that clutter. . . .

As is true of billboards, the esthetic interests that are implicated by temporary signs are presumptively at work in all parts of the city, including those where appellees posted

---

16. The federal Highway Beautification Act of 1965, Pub. L. 89-285, 79 Stat. 1028, as amended, 23 U.S.C. § 131 (1976 ed. and Supp.III), requires that States eliminate billboards from areas adjacent to certain highways constructed with federal funds. The Federal Government, also prohibits billboards on federal lands. 43 CFR § 2921.0-6(a) (1980). Three States have enacted statewide bans on billboards. Maine, Me. Rev. Stat. Ann., Tit. 23, § 1901 et seq. (1980); Hawaii, Haw. Rev. Stat. § 264-71 et seq., § 445-111 et seq. (1976); Vermont, Vt. Stat. Ann., Tit. 10, § 488 et seq. (1973).

their signs, and there is no basis in the record in this case upon which to rebut that presumption. These interests are both psychological and economic.

In dissent, Justice Brennan, joined by Justices Marshall and Harry Blackmun, stated that "the Court's lenient approach towards the restriction of speech for reasons of aesthetics threatens seriously to undermine the protections of the First Amendment." He continued: "In my view, the City of Los Angeles has not shown that its interest in eliminating 'visual clutter' justifies its restriction of appellees' ability to communicate with the local electorate."

Has the Court trapped itself within the overly complex analytical matrix it has devised to evaluate governmental impact on various forms of speech—some (such as political) more protected than others (such as commercial)? Does *Ladue* exacerbate or ameliorate this jurisprudential quagmire?

2. The Supreme Court of Georgia, in Fulton County v. Galberaith, 282 Ga. 314, 314, 316-19, 647 S.E.2d 24, 24, 27-28 (2007), accepted the plea of billboard owners that the county's "prohibition against off-premise signs in commercially-zoned areas was an unconstitutional violation of free speech." Turning to Supreme Court precedent, the state high court reasoned:

> [T]he Fulton County ordinance sweeps far more broadly than the ordinance at issue in *Metromedia*. . . . [T]he Fulton County ordinance defines a "billboard" much more broadly, so as to include any "sign which advertises services, merchandise, entertainment or information," and "sign," in turn, is defined as:
>
>> Any name, identification, description, display, illustration, writing, emblem, pictorial representation or device which is affixed to or represented directly or indirectly upon a building, structure or land in view of the general public, and which directs attention to a product, place, activity, person, institution or business.
>
> Fulton County Code §§ 3.3.2, 3.3.19. Thus, the definition of "sign" at issue here is more extensive than the definition of "billboard" considered in *Metromedia*, and the initial reach of the Fulton County ban goes well beyond commercial speech. . . .
>
> Accordingly, unlike the ordinance in *Metromedia*, the Fulton County ordinance evidences a hostility to signs in general and to commercial signs in particular. It commences with what is, in effect, a declaration that all signs are presumptively illegal throughout the county. Fulton County Code §§ 33.3, 33.4. This proscription is not limited to commercial signs or signs on public property or traditional billboards. The outright ban is then followed by a list of 18 specific examples of prohibited signs, described according to their physical characteristics, location or content. Fulton County Code § 33.3 (a)-(r). The ordinance does contain a "savings clause" which purports to authorize any noncommercial message at the locations where on-premises commercial messages are allowed, if that noncommercial message does not direct attention to a business operated for profit or to a commodity or service for sale. However, by broadly excluding messages that merely direct attention to a business operated for profit, this so-called "savings clause" may actually prevent the presentation of noncommercial speech in places where commercial speech is allowed.. The ordinance also lists various types of signs, both commercial and noncommercial, that the County will allow landowners to place on their own property or the property of others if they first obtain a permit, pay a fee and comply with detailed restrictions applicable to each category. It then enumerates various types of signs that are categorically excluded from the outright ban and the fee and permitting requirements. Fulton County Code § 33.4.12(b). . . .

(1) Banning all signs, including all commercial signs, and then deciding on a case-by-case basis which ones will be permitted is the antithesis of the narrow tailoring that is required under the First Amendment, even in the context of commercial speech. Because the regulatory approach taken by Fulton County provides insufficient protection for protected speech, both commercial and otherwise, we conclude that the broad sweep and basic structure of the Fulton County ordinance, whereby all signs are presumed to be illegal and are then permitted only on a case-by-case determination, does not comport with the First Amendment. See City of Ladue v. Gilleo, 512 U. S. 43 (1994).

3. Speech is not the only fundamental individual right that can trump police power regulations. In Planned Parenthood v. City of Manchester, 2001 U.S. Dist. LEXIS 6379, at *3-*4, *11, *13 (D.N.H.) a federal district court granted a preliminary injunction to Planned Parenthood of Northern New England and a building owner, when a New Hampshire city and its Zoning Board of Adjustment revoked a building permit that had been granted to the owner, who had obtained a variance to use a former automobile parts store for "medical offices." Several months after Planned Parenthood leased the building, the group

> publicly announced its intent to occupy the building and provide medical services to the residents of greater Manchester, including family planning and, at some future date, abortion services. That announcement provoked some public opposition to Planned Parenthood's use of the building, and various people sought relief from the Zoning Board of Adjustment. By a divided vote, the ZBA revoked the building permit on January 3, 2001, after hearing from interested parties and members of the public. Plaintiffs then filed this suit seeking to remedy what they see as an unconstitutional deprivation of federal rights under color of state law.

The court was not swayed by the city's argument "that the board members probably meant (and implicitly 'found') that the *nature* of the 'medical practice' to be carried out at the site was misrepresented and, consequently, the variance was procured by misrepresentation, or even fraud . . . ." Instead, the court found that

> the conclusion is nearly inescapable that plaintiffs are likely to prove at trial that the actual factor motivating the ZBA to revoke the Owner's building permit was not any legitimate zoning, or unlitigated "intensity of use" concern, or any inconsistency between the planned construction and the permissible use, but, rather, was its antipathy for the abortion and contraception services PPNNE will provide, or, its acquiescence in the expression of public antipathy for such constitutionally protected activity. In either event, revocation of the permit based upon such considerations operates to deprive the Owner and PPNNE (and its patients) of their constitutionally protected freedoms. See Deerfield Medical Center, 661 F.2d at 336; P.L.S. Partners, Women's Medical Center of Rhode Island, Inc. v. City of Cranston, 696 F. Supp. 788, 796-97 (D.R.I. 1988) (citing cases); see also generally Family Planning Clinic, Inc. v. City of Cleveland, 594 F. Supp. 1410 (N.D. Ohio 1984) (zoning ordinance disallowing clinic operated primarily for abortions in residence-office district unconstitutionally interfered with woman's right to seek and obtain abortion and did not survive constitutional scrutiny); West Side Women's Services, Inc. v. City of Cleveland, 573 F. Supp. 504 (N.D. Ohio 1983) (permitting medical offices, but not abortion clinics, to operate in business district is not sustainable). Such decisions, taken under color of state law, are clearly unlawful and actionable.

The Massachusetts Supreme Judicial Court, relying on a woman's fundamental privacy rights as articulated in Roe v. Wade, 410 U.S. 113 (1973), invalidated a local bylaw amendment that classified an "abortion clinic" as a "prohibited use" throughout the town of Southborough. Framingham Clinic, Inc. v. Board of Selectmen, 373 Mass. 279, 367 N.E.2d 606, 611-12 (1977):

> The Southborough regulation . . . is a serious abridgment of constitutional rights. The desires of members of the community to disfavor an "abortion clinic —desires which, reflexively, may cause these persons to see an economic detriment to themselves in the existence of the clinic—cannot extenuate such a violation. The report of the Southborough planning board about public sentiment was thus an irrelevancy, and a dangerous one, for that way would lie the extinction of many liberties which are, indeed, constitutionally guaranteed against invasion by a majority. . . .
>
> Neither could Southborough justify its own exclusionary rule by saying that a woman might overcome it by going elsewhere in the Commonwealth. . . . The picture of one community attempting to throw off on others would not be a happy one.

The clinic's troubles with the town continued, leading to a subsequent decision by the state's high court: Framingham Clinic, Inc. v. Zoning Board of Appeals, 382 Mass. 283, 415 N.E.2d 840 (1981) (the plaintiffs were entitled to the building permit, despite the building commissioner's "view that an abortion could not 'promote life'").

LARKIN v. GRENDEL'S DEN, INC.
459 U.S. 116 (1982)

Chief Justice BURGER delivered the opinion of the Court. . . .

Appellee operates a restaurant located in the Harvard Square area of Cambridge, Mass. The Holy Cross Armenian Catholic Parish is located adjacent to the restaurant; the back walls of the two buildings are 10 feet apart. In 1977, appellee applied to the Cambridge License Commission for approval of an alcoholic beverages license for the restaurant.

Section 16C of Chapter 138 of the Massachusetts General Laws provides: "Premises . . . located within a radius of five hundred feet of a church or school shall not be licensed for the sale of alcoholic beverages if the governing body of such church or school files written objection thereto."[1]

Holy Cross Church objected to appellee's application, expressing concern over "having so many licenses *so* near" (emphasis in original).[2] The License Commission voted to deny the application, citing only the objection of Holy Cross Church and noting that the church "is within 10 feet of the proposed location."

On appeal, the Massachusetts Alcoholic Beverages Control Commission upheld the License Commission's action. The Beverages Control Commission found that "the church's objection under Section 16C was the only basis on which the [license] was denied."

---

1. Section 16C defines "church" as "a church or synagogue building dedicated to divine worship and in regular use for that purpose, but not a chapel occupying a minor portion of a building primarily devoted to other uses." "School" is defined as "an elementary or secondary school, public or private, giving not less than the minimum instruction and training required by [state law] to children of compulsory school age." Mass. Gen. Laws. Ann., ch. 138, §16C (1974).

   Section 16C originally was enacted in 1954 as an absolute ban on liquor licenses within 500 feet of a church or school, 1954 Mass. Acts, ch. 569, §1. A 1968 amendment modified the absolute prohibition, permitting licenses within the 500-foot radius "if the governing body of such church assents in writing," 1968 Mass. Acts, ch. 435. In 1970, the statute was amended to its present form, 1970 Mass. Acts, ch. 192.

2. In 1979, there were 26 liquor licensees in Harvard Square and within a 500-foot radius of Holy Cross Church; 25 of these were in existence at the time Holy Cross Church objected to appellee's application.

Appellee then sued the License Commission and the Beverages Control Commission in United States District Court. Relief was sought on the grounds that § 16C, on its face and as applied, violated the Equal Protection and Due Process Clauses of the Fourteenth Amendment, the Establishment Clause of the First Amendment, and the Sherman Act.

Appellants contend that the State may, without impinging on the Establishment Clause of the First Amendment, enforce what it describes as a "zoning" law in order to shield schools and places of divine worship from the presence nearby of liquor-dispensing establishments. It is also contended that a zone of protection around churches and schools is essential to protect diverse centers of spiritual, educational, and cultural enrichment. It is to that end that the State has vested in the governing bodies of all schools, public or private, and all churches, the power to prevent the issuance of liquor licenses for any premises within 500 feet of their institutions.

Plainly schools and churches have a valid interest in being insulated from certain kinds of commercial establishments, including those dispensing liquor. Zoning laws have long been employed to this end, and there can be little doubt about the power of a state to regulate the environment in the vicinity of schools, churches, hospitals, and the like by exercise of reasonable zoning laws. . . .

The zoning function is traditionally a governmental task requiring the "balancing [of] numerous competing considerations," and courts should properly "refrain from reviewing the merits of [such] decisions, absent a showing of arbitrariness or irrationality."Arlington Heights v. Metropolitan Housing Dev. Corp., 429 U.S. 252, 265 (1977). Given the broad powers of states under the Twenty-first Amendment, judicial deference to the legislative exercise of zoning powers by a city council or other legislative zoning body is especially appropriate in the area of liquor regulation.

However, § 16C is not simply a legislative exercise of zoning power. As the Massachusetts Supreme Judicial Court concluded, § 16C delegates to private, nongovernmental entities power to veto certain liquor license applications, Arno v. Alcoholic Beverages Control Comm'n, 377 Mass., at 89, 384 N.E.2d, at 1227. This is a power ordinarily vested in agencies of government. . . . We need not decide whether, or upon what conditions, such power may ever be delegated to nongovernmental entities; here, of two classes of institutions to which the legislature has delegated this important decisionmaking power, one is secular, but one is religious. Under these circumstances, the deference normally due a legislative zoning judgment is not merited. . . .

This Court has consistently held that a statute must satisfy three criteria to pass muster under the Establishment Clause:

> "First, the statute must have a secular legislative purpose; second, its principal or primary effect must be one that neither advances nor inhibits religion . . . ; finally, the statute must not foster "an excessive government entanglement with religion." Lemon v. Kurtzman, [403 U.S. 602] at 612-613 [(1971)], quoting Waltz v. Tax Comm'n, [397 U.S.] at 674.

Independent of the first of those criteria, the statute, by delegating a governmental power to religious institutions, inescapably implicates the Establishment Clause.

The purpose of §16C, as described by the District Court, is to "protec[t] spiritual, cultural, and educational centers from the 'hurlyburly' associated with liquor outlets." 495 F. Supp., at 766. There can be little doubt that this embraces valid secular legislative purposes. However, these valid secular objectives can be readily accomplished by other means—either through an absolute legislative ban on liquor outlets within reasonable prescribed distances from churches, schools, hospitals, and like institutions,[7] or by ensuring a hearing for the views of affected institutions at licensing proceedings where, without question, such views would be entitled to substantial weight.[8] . . .

The churches' power under the statute is standardless, calling for no reasons, findings, or reasoned conclusions. That power may therefore be used by churches to promote goals beyond insulating the church from undesirable neighbors; it could be employed for explicitly religious goals, for example, favoring liquor licenses for members of that congregation or adherents of that faith. . . . In addition, the mere appearance of a joint exercise of legislative authority by Church and State provides a significant symbolic benefit to religion in the minds of some by reason of the power conferred. It does not strain our prior holdings to say that the statute can be seen as having a "primary" and "principal" effect of advancing religion.

Turning to the third phase of the inquiry called for by Lemon v. Kurtzman, we see that we have not previously had occasion to consider the entanglement implications of a statute vesting significant governmental authority in churches. This statute enmeshes churches in the exercise of substantial governmental powers contrary to our consistent interpretation of the Establishment Clause; . . .

[T]he core rationale underlying the Establishment Clause is preventing "a fusion of governmental and religious functions," Abington School District v. Schempp, 374 U.S. 203, 222 (1963).[10] The Framers did not set up a system of government in which important, discretionary governmental powers would be delegated to or shared with religious institutions.

Section 16C substitutes the unilateral and absolute power of a church for the reasoned decisionmaking of a public legislative body acting on evidence and guided by standards, on issues with significant economic and political implications. The challenged statute thus enmeshes churches in the processes of government and creates the danger of "[p]olitical fragmentation and divisiveness on religious lines," Lemon v. Kurtzman, *supra*, at 623. Ordinary human experience and a long line of cases teach that few entanglements could be more offensive to the spirit of the Constitution.

The judgment of the Court of Appeals is affirmed.

So ordered.

Justice REHNQUIST, dissenting.

Dissenting opinions in previous cases have commented that "great" cases, like "hard" cases, make bad law. Northern Securities Co. v. United States, 193 U.S. 197, 400-401 (1904) (Holmes, J., dissenting); Nixon v. Administrator of General Services, 433 U.S. 425, 505 (1977) (Burger, C. J., dissenting). Today's opinion suggests that a third class of cases—silly cases—also make bad law. The Court wrenches from the decision of the Massachusetts Supreme Judicial Court the word "veto," and rests its conclusions on this single term. The aim of this effort is to prove that a quite sensible Massachusetts liquor zoning law is apparently some sort of sinister religious attack on secular government reminiscent of St. Bartholemew's Night. Being unpersuaded, I dissent. . . .

Notes

1. Note how in its brief each party framed the question that the case presented to the Court:

---

7. . . . Section 16C, as originally enacted, consisted of an absolute ban on liquor licenses within 500 feet of a church or school; and 27 States continue to prohibit liquor outlets within a prescribed distance of various categories of protected institutions, with certain exceptions and variations. . . . The Court does not express an opinion as to the constitutionality of any statute other than that of Massachusetts.

8. Eleven States have statutes or regulations directing the licensing authority to consider the proximity of the proposed liquor outlet to schools or other institutions in deciding whether to grant a liquor license. . . . .

10. At the time of the Revolution, Americans feared not only a denial of religious freedom, but also the danger of political oppression through a union of civil and ecclesiastical control. B. Bailyn, Ideological Origins of the American Revolution 98-99, n. 3 (1967). See McDaniel v. Paty, 435 U.S. 618, 622-623 (1978). In 18th-century England, such a union of civil and ecclesiastical power was reflected in legal arrangements granting church officials substantial control over various occupations, including the liquor trade. See, e.g., 26 Geo. 2, ch. 31, §2 (1753) (church officials given authority to grant certificate of character, a prerequisite for an alehouse license); S. Webb & B. Webb, The History of Liquor Licensing in England, Principally from 1700 to 1830, pp. 8, n. 1, 62-67, 102-103 (1903).

Appellants: Whether a state may, within the limits imposed by the Establishment Clause of the First Amendment, accommodate the diverse interests of its citizens through a zoning statute which shields objecting schools and churches from the disturbances associated with the distribution and consumption of liquor within their immediate vicinity.

Appellee: May a state delegate to each "church or synagogue . . . dedicated to divine worship" an unfettered governmental power to decide which restaurants, liquor stores, and bars may be licensed to serve or sell alcoholic beverages within a 500-foot radius of the religious body's premises?

Which question(s) did the Justices deem worthy of their consideration and resolution?

2. Did Harvard Law Professor Lawrence Tribe, counsel for Grendel's Den, go overboard in his use of historical sources and history-based arguments? Apparently so, according to a three-judge panel of the U.S. Court of Appeals for the First Circuit. In Grendel's Den v. Larkin, 749 F.2d 945, 948, 951-52, 953, 954, 960 (lst Cir. 1984), an appeal of the district court's assessment of attorneys fees and costs under 42 U.S.C. §1988, Judge Frank Coffin wrote:

> When we look at the First Amendment portion of plaintiff's brief, we note that, seven of the fourteen pages are devoted to a historical analysis, largely in four footnotes, summarizing anti-"establishment" attitudes of seventeenth and eighteenth century Americans, and of lessons to be learned from sixteenth, and seventeenth century England. While this analysis may be fresh and interesting, it was only briefly reflected in a footnote in the Supreme Court's opinion.

There are other interpretations. For example, one wonders, given Chief Justice Warren Burger's strong record of supporting local decisionmaking generally, and his specific approval of popular participation in zoning matters in City of Eastlake v. Forest City Enterprises, 426 U.S. 668, 672 (1976),[11] whether Professor Tribe's argument could have carried the day without this evidence of original intent.

The court was also concerned about the "failure to keep accurate and contemporaneous time records," and even criticized counsel for being too enthusiastic: "[T]he early economy of effort and careful focus upon only what was necessary was lost in the heat and excitement of litigating an interesting First Amendment case." Based on these and other findings (even counsel's lodging at the Watergate Hotel was judged too extravagant), the court reduced Professor Tribe's fees from $176,137.50 to $81,987.50.

Who foots the bill for such high-priced services? While the district court split the fees and costs down the middle between the Cambridge License Commission and the Massachusetts Alcoholic Beverage Control Commission, the court of appeals reduced the city agency's share to 25%. As the fight over fees raged on, Grendel's Den, over the objection of the Holy Cross Church, was

---

11. In that case, Chief Justice Burger, relying on historical sources, reasoned:

> The conclusion that Eastlake's procedure violates federal constitutional guarantees rests upon the proposition that a zoning referendum involves a delegation of legislative power. A referendum cannot, however, be characterized as a delegation of power. Under our constitutional assumptions, all power derives from the people, who can delegate it to representative instruments which they create. See, e.g., The Federalist, No. 39 (J. Madison). In establishing legislative bodies, the people can reserve to themselves power to deal directly with matters which might otherwise be assigned to the legislature.
>
> The reservation of such power is the basis for the town meeting, a tradition which continues to this day in some States as both a practical and symbolic part of our democratic processes. The referendum, similarly, is a means for direct political participation, allowing the people the final decision, amounting to a veto power, over enactments of representative bodies. The practice is designed to "give citizens a voice on questions of public policy." James v. Valtierra, [402 U.S. 137], at 141 [(1971)].

issued a license and began serving alcoholic beverages on April Fool's Day, 1983. You can find the restaurant's current (and ample) beer, wine, cocktail, and other beverage menus here: http://www. grendelsden.com/.

3. In Ehlers-Renzi v. Connelly School of the Holy Child, Inc., 224 F.3d 283, 285, 288-89, 291, 292-93 (4th Cir. 2000), homeowners who lived across the street from a Catholic school that was permitted to engage in the construction of improvements and additions without securing a "special exception" challenged the constitutionality of the county zoning ordinance that "exempts from the special exception requirement parochial schools located on land owned or leased by a church or religious organization." The county offered some "plausible secular purposes" that the appellate court found met the first prong of the *Lemon* test:

> It notes that by exempting parochial schools from the special exception procedure, Montgomery County avoids the interference with such schools' religious missions that otherwise might result from subjecting the schools to the scrutiny and procedures that the Zoning Ordinance otherwise would require. Connelly School also notes that by "stepping out of the way of religion," the County avoids the creation of a forum in which anti-religious animus underlying opposition to a special exception petition might be expressed.

Circuit Judge Murnaghan disagreed with the other two panel members, arguing that

> [a]pplication of the County's special exception procedures to the Connelly School would not significantly interfere with the school's ability to define and carry out its mission. There is no danger that Montgomery County will become involved in regulating the school's program of religious education by simply enforcing the generally applicable zoning rules and special exception procedures at issue in this case.

In Boyajian v. Gatzunis, 212 F.3d 1, 3, 12 (2000), a case involving the construction of a Mormon temple in Belmont, Massachusetts, a divided First Circuit panel turned down an Establishment Clause challenge to the municipality's

> by-law allowing religious uses by right in the residential zone where the Church's property is located is in accordance with Mass. Gen. Laws ch. 40A, § 3, known as the "Dover Amendment." That law provides, in part, that a zoning regulation may not restrict the use of land for religious or educational purposes when the property is owned by the Commonwealth, a religious organization, or a nonprofit educational corporation, except that "reasonable regulations" are permitted concerning such characteristics as the bulk and height of structures, open space, and parking.

In dissent, Judge Juan Torruella was troubled by the state law:

> [T]he Dover Amendment does not embody the "benevolent neutrality" deigned by the Supreme Court to be the proper balance between the competing mandates of the Religion Clauses. A "neutral" statute, in any ordinary sense of that word, would permit (and require) religious uses and religious users to operate on an even playing field with other uses and users, without special hindrances and without special advantage. The Dover Amendment, in contrast, eschews neutrality to place religion in an exalted position, exempt from the ordinary land-use decision making process. . . .
>
> The Dover Amendment insulates religion, HAM radio operators, solar energy users, et cetera, from these typical zoning concerns for one simple reason, which the majority

recognizes—the state considers these uses "beneficial." Although the state may generally be free to protect a use or activity solely on the basis that the state likes it, the Establishment Clause prohibits such bare favoritism where the beneficiary is religion.

4. Local government officials (and their attorneys) who want to accommodate religious uses without unduly favoring them often find themselves forced to navigate the Scylla of the Establishment Clause and the Charybdis of the Free Exercise Clause. Stated otherwise, on the one hand localities are accused of unduly burdening religious beliefs and practices when they don't do enough to accommodate, and, on the other hand, accused of improperly intermingling church and state when they do too much to accommodate. As the next case demonstrates, Congress has only made the predicament worse for land use regulators.

WESTCHESTER DAY SCHOOL v. VILLAGE OF MAMARONECK
504 F.3d 338 (2d Cir. 2007)

CARDAMONE, Circuit Judge: . . .

Westchester Day School is located in the Orienta Point neighborhood of the Village of Mamaroneck, Westchester County, New York. Its facilities are situated on 25.75 acres of largely undeveloped land (property) owned by Westchester Religious Institute. Westchester Religious Institute allows the school and other entities to use the property. . . .

The Mamaroneck Village Code permits private schools to operate in "R-20 Districts" if the Zoning Board of Appeals of the Village of Mamaroneck (ZBA or zoning board) grants them a special permit. The property is in an R-20 district and WDS operates subject to obtaining such a permit which must be renewed every three years. Most recently the day school's permit was unanimously renewed on November 2, 2000, before the dispute giving rise to this litigation began. Several other schools are located in the vicinity of Orienta Point, including the Liberty Montessori School and Mamaroneck High School. Numerous large properties border the school property, including the Orienta Beach Club, the Beach Point Club, the Hampshire Country Club, and several boat yards.

As a Jewish private school, Westchester Day School provides its students with a dual curriculum in Judaic and general studies. Even general studies classes are taught so that religious and Judaic concepts are reinforced. In the nursery and kindergarten classes no distinction exists between Judaic and general studies; the dual curriculum is wholly integrated. In grades first through eighth, students spend roughly half their day on general subjects such as mathematics and social studies and half on Judaic studies that include the Bible, the Talmud, and Jewish history. . . .

By 1998 WDS believed its current facilities inadequate to satisfy the school's needs. The district court's extensive findings reveal the day school's existing facilities are deficient and that its effectiveness in providing the education Orthodox Judaism mandates has been significantly hindered as a consequence. The school's enrollment has declined since 2001, a trend the district court attributed in part to the zoning board's actions. As a result of the deficiencies in its current facilities the school engaged professional architects, land planners, engineers, and an environmental consulting firm to determine what new facilities were required. Based on these professionals' recommendations, WDS decided to renovate Wolfson Hall and the Castle and to construct a new building, Gordon Hall, specifically designed to serve the existing student population. The renovations would add 12 new classrooms; a learning center; small-group instructional rooms; a multi-purpose room; therapy, counseling, art and music rooms; and computer and science labs. All of them were to be used from time to time for religious education and practice.

In October 2001 the day school submitted to the zoning board an application for modification of its special permit to enable it to proceed with this $12 million expansion project. On February 7, 2002 the ZBA voted unanimously to issue a "negative declaration," which constituted a finding that the project would have no significant adverse environmental impact and thus that consideration of the project could proceed. After the issuance of the negative declaration, a small but vocal group in the Mamaroneck community opposed the project. As a result of this public opposition, on August 1, 2002 the ZBA voted 3-2 to rescind the negative declaration. The effect of the rescission was to require WDS to prepare and submit a full Environmental Impact Statement.

Instead, the school commenced the instant litigation on August 7, 2002 contending the rescission of the negative declaration violated RLUIPA [the federal Religious Land Use and Institutionalized Persons Act] and was void under state law. The suit named as defendants the Village of Mamaroneck, its ZBA, and the members of the zoning board in their official capacities (collectively, the Village or defendant).

On December 4, 2002 the district court granted WDS's motion for partial summary judgment and held that the negative declaration had not been properly rescinded, and therefore remained in full force and effect. The Village did not appeal this ruling. Instead, the ZBA proceeded to conduct additional public hearings to consider the merits of the application. The ZBA had the opportunity to approve the application subject to conditions intended to mitigate adverse effects on public health, safety, and welfare that might arise from the project. Rather, on May 13, 2003 the ZBA voted 3-2 to deny WDS's application in its entirety.

The stated reasons for the rejection included the effect the project would have on traffic and concerns with respect to parking and the intensity of use. Many of these grounds were conceived after the ZBA closed its hearing process, giving the school no opportunity to respond. The district court found the stated reasons for denying the application were not supported by evidence in the public record before the ZBA, and were based on several factual errors. It surmised that the application was in fact denied because the ZBA gave undue deference to the public opposition of the small but influential group of neighbors who were against the school's expansion plans. It also noted that the denial of the application would result in long delay of WDS's efforts to remedy the gross inadequacies of its facilities, and substantially increase construction costs.

On May 29, 2003 the school filed an amended complaint challenging the denial of its application. It asserted claims under RLUIPA, 42 U.S.C. § 1983, and the All Writs Act. Neither party demanded a jury trial. WDS moved for partial summary judgment, and on September 5, 2003 the district court granted that motion, holding that the Village had violated RLUIPA. When the Village appealed, we vacated the district court's order and remanded the case for further proceedings. After remand, the Village, for the first time, demanded a jury trial, which the district court denied. The Village moved for summary judgment, which the trial court denied as to WDS's RLUIPA and All Writs Act claims, but granted as to the school's claim under 42 U.S.C. § 1983.

A seven-day bench trial began on November 14, 2005 and resulted in the March 2006 judgment. The district court ordered the Village to issue WDS's special permit immediately, but reserved decision on damages and attorneys' fees pending appellate review. From this ruling the Village appeals. . . .

RLUIPA prohibits the government from imposing or implementing a land use regulation in a manner that

> imposes a substantial burden on the religious exercise of a person, including a religious assembly or institution, unless the government demonstrates that imposition of the burden on that person, assembly, or institution (A) is in furtherance of a compelling gov-

ernmental interest; and (B) is the least restrictive means of furthering that compelling governmental interest.

42 U.S.C. § 2000cc(a)(1). This provision applies only when the substantial burden imposed (1) is in a program that receives Federal financial assistance; (2) affects commerce with foreign nations, among the several states, or with Indian tribes; or (3) "is imposed in the implementation of a land use regulation or system of land use regulations, under which a government makes, or has in place formal or informal procedures or practices that permit the government to make, individualized assessments of the proposed uses for the property involved." 42 U.S.C. § 2000cc(a)(2).

Religious exercise under RLUIPA is defined as "any exercise of religion, whether or not compelled by, or central to, a system of religious belief." § 2000cc-5(7)(A). Further, using, building, or converting real property for religious exercise purposes is considered to be religious exercise under the statute. § 2000cc-5(7)(B). To remove any remaining doubt regarding how broadly Congress aimed to define religious exercise, RLUIPA goes on to state that the Act's aim of protecting religious exercise is to be construed broadly and "to the maximum extent permitted by the terms of this chapter and the Constitution." § 2000cc-3(g).

Commenting at an earlier stage in this litigation on how to apply this standard, we expressed doubt as to whether RLUIPA immunized all conceivable improvements proposed by religious schools. That is to say, to get immunity from land use regulation, religious schools need to demonstrate more than that the proposed improvement would enhance the overall experience of its students. For example, if a religious school wishes to build a gymnasium to be used exclusively for sporting activities, that kind of expansion would not constitute religious exercise. Or, had the ZBA denied the Westchester Religious Institute's 1986 request for a special permit to construct a headmaster's residence on a portion of the property, such a denial would not have implicated religious exercise. Nor would the school's religious exercise have been burdened by the denial of a permit to build more office space. Accordingly, we suggested the district court consider whether the proposed facilities were for a religious purpose rather than simply whether the school was religiously-affiliated.

On remand, the district court conducted the proper inquiry. It made careful factual findings that each room the school planned to build would be used at least in part for religious education and practice, finding that Gordon Hall and the other facilities renovated as part of the project, in whole and in all of their constituent parts, would be used for "religious education and practice." In light of these findings, amply supported in the record, the expansion project is a "building [and] conversion of real property for the purpose of religious exercise" and thus is religious exercise under § 2000cc-5(7)(B).

Hence, we need not now demarcate the exact line at which a school expansion project comes to implicate RLUIPA. That line exists somewhere between this case, where every classroom being constructed will be used at some time for religious education, and a case like the building of a headmaster's residence, where religious education will not occur in the proposed expansion.

Since substantial burden is a term of art in the Supreme Court's free exercise jurisprudence, we assume that Congress, by using it, planned to incorporate the cluster of ideas associated with the Court's use of it. Further, RLUIPA's legislative history indicates that Congress intended the term substantial burden to be interpreted "by reference to Supreme Court jurisprudence." 146 Cong. Rec. S7774, S7776 (2000).

Supreme Court precedents teach that a substantial burden on religious exercise exists when an individual is required to "choose between following the precepts of her religion and forfeiting benefits, on the one hand, and abandoning one of the precepts of her religion . . . on the other hand." Sherbert v. Verner, 374 U.S. 398, 404 (1963). A number of courts use this standard as the starting point for determining what is a substantial burden under RLUIPA. In the context in which this standard is typically applied—for example, a state's denial of unemployment compensation to a Jehovah's Witness who quit his job because his religious beliefs prevented him from participating in the production of war materials, see Thomas v. Review Bd. of Ind. Employment Sec. Div., 450 U.S. 707, 709 (1981)—it is not a difficult standard to apply. By denying benefits to Jehovah's Witnesses who follow their beliefs, the state puts undue pressure on the adherents to alter their behavior and to violate their beliefs in order to obtain government benefits, thereby imposing a substantial burden on religious exercise.

But in the context of land use, a religious institution is not ordinarily faced with the same dilemma of choosing between religious precepts and government benefits. When a municipality denies a religious institution the right to expand its facilities, it is more difficult to speak of substantial pressure to change religious behavior, because in light of the denial the renovation simply cannot proceed. Accordingly, when there has been a denial of a religious institution's building application, courts appropriately speak of government action that directly coerces the religious institution to change its behavior, rather than government action that forces the religious entity to choose between religious precepts and government benefits. Here, WDS contends that the denial of its application in effect coerced the day school to continue teaching in inadequate facilities, thereby impeding its religious exercise.

Yet, when the denial of a religious institution's application to build is not absolute, such would not necessarily place substantial pressure on the institution to alter its behavior, since it could just as easily file a second application that remedies the problems in the first. As a consequence, as we said when this case was earlier before us, "rejection of a submitted plan, while leaving open the possibility of approval of a resubmission with modifications designed to address the cited problems, is less likely to constitute a 'substantial burden' than definitive rejection of the same plan, ruling out the possibility of approval of a modified proposal." *Westchester Day Sch.*, 386 F.3d at 188. Of course, a conditional denial may represent a substantial burden if the condition itself is a burden on free exercise, the required modifications are economically unfeasible, or where a zoning board's stated willingness to consider a modified plan is disingenuous. However, in most cases, whether the denial of the application was absolute is important; if there is a reasonable opportunity for the institution to submit a modified application, the denial does not place substantial pressure on it to change its behavior and thus does not constitute a substantial burden on the free exercise of religion.

We recognize further that where the denial of an institution's application to build will have minimal impact on the institution's religious exercise, it does not constitute a substantial burden, even when the denial is definitive. There must exist a close nexus between the coerced or impeded conduct and the institution's religious exercise for such conduct to be a substantial burden on that religious exercise. Imagine, for example, a situation where a school could easily rearrange existing classrooms to meet its religious needs in the face of a rejected application to renovate. In such case, the denial would not substantially threaten the institution's religious exercise, and there would be no substantial burden, even though the school was refused the opportunity to expand its facilities.

Note, however, that a burden need not be found insuperable to be held substantial. See Saints Constantine and Helen Greek Orthodox Church, Inc. v. City of New Berlin, 396 F.3d 895, 901 (7th Cir. 2005). When the school has no ready alternatives, or where the alternatives require substantial "delay, uncertainty, and expense," a complete denial of the school's application might be indicative of a substantial burden. *See id.* . . .

[C]ourts confronting free exercise challenges to zoning restrictions rarely find the substantial burden test satisfied even when the resulting effect is to completely prohibit a religious congregation from building a church on its own land. See Christian Gospel Church, Inc. v. City and County of S.F., 896 F.2d 1221, 1224 (9th Cir. 1990); Messiah Baptist Church v. County of Jefferson, 859 F.2d 820, 824-25 (10th Cir. 1988); Grosz v. City of Miami Beach, 721 F.2d 729, 739-40 (11th Cir. 1983); Lakewood, Ohio Congregation of Jehovah's Witnesses, Inc. v. City of Lakewood, 699 F.2d 303, 304 (6th Cir. 1983); cf. Islamic Ctr. of Miss., Inc. v. City of Starkville, 840 F.2d 293, 302-03 (5th Cir. 1988) (finding substantial burden where city intentionally discriminated against Muslims and ordinance "leaves no practical alternatives for establishing a mosque in the city limits").

A number of our sister circuits have applied this same reasoning in construing RLUIPA's substantial burden requirement. For example, the Seventh Circuit has held that land use conditions do not constitute a substantial burden under RLUIPA where they are "neutral and traceable to municipal land planning goals" and where there is no evidence that government actions were taken "because [plaintiff] is a religious institution." Vision Church v. Vill. of Long Grove, 468 F.3d 975, 998-99 (7th Cir. 2006). Similarly, the Ninth Circuit has held that no substantial burden was imposed, even where an ordinance "rendered [plaintiff] unable to provide education and/or worship" on its property, because the plaintiff was not "precluded from using other sites within the city" and because "there [is no] evidence that the City would not impose the same requirements on any other entity." San Jose Christian Coll. [v. City of Morgan Hill], 360 F.3d [1024,] at 1035 [(9th Cir. 2004)]. The Eleventh Circuit has also ruled that "reasonable 'run of the mill' zoning considerations do not constitute substantial burdens." Midrash Sephardi, [Inc. v. Town of Surfside,] 366 F.3d [1214,] at 1227-28 & n.11 [(11th Cir. 2004)].

The same reasoning that precludes a religious organization from demonstrating substantial burden in the neutral application of legitimate land use restrictions may, in fact, support a substantial burden claim where land use restrictions are imposed on the religious institution arbitrarily, capriciously, or unlawfully. The arbitrary application of laws to religious organizations may reflect bias or discrimination against religion. . . . Where the arbitrary, capricious, or unlawful nature of a defendant's challenged action suggests that a religious institution received less than even-handed treatment, the application of RLUIPA's substantial burden provision usefully "backstops the explicit prohibition of religious discrimination in the later section of the Act." Saints Constantine and Helen, 396 F.3d at 900.

Accordingly, we deem it relevant to the evaluation of WDS's particular substantial burden claim that the district court expressly found that the zoning board's denial of the school's application was "arbitrary and capricious under New York law because the purported justifications set forth in the Resolution do not bear the necessary substantial relation to public health, safety or welfare," and the zoning board's findings are not supported by substantial evidence. Westchester Day Sch., 417 F. Supp. 2d at 564. Although the Village disputes this finding, we conclude that it is amply supported by both the law and the record evidence. . . .

[T]he record convincingly demonstrates that the zoning decision in this case was characterized not simply by the occasional errors that can attend the task of government but by an arbitrary blindness to the facts. As the district court correctly concluded, such a zoning ruling fails to comply with New York law.

While the arbitrary and unlawful nature of the ZBA denial of WDS's application supports WDS's claim that it has sustained a substantial burden, two other factors drawn from our earlier discussion must be considered in reaching such a burden determination: (1) whether there are quick, reliable, and financially feasible alternatives WDS may utilize to meet its religious needs absent its obtaining the construction permit; and (2) whether the denial was conditional. These two considerations matter for the same reason: when an institution has a ready alternative—be it an entirely different plan to meet the same needs or the opportunity to try again in line with a zoning board's recommendations—its religious exercise has not been substantially burdened. The plaintiff has the burden of persuasion with respect to both factors. See § 2000cc-2 (putting burden on plaintiff to prove that government's action substantially burdened plaintiff's exercise of religion).

Here, the school could not have met its needs simply by reallocating space within its existing buildings. . . .

In examining the second factor—whether the Village's denial of the school's application was conditional or absolute—we look at several matters: (a) whether the ZBA classified the denial as complete, (b) whether any required modification would itself constitute a burden on religious exercise; (c) whether cure of the problems noted by the ZBA would impose so great an economic burden as to make amendment unworkable; and (d) whether the ZBA's stated willingness to consider a modified proposal was disingenuous.

For any of the following reasons, we believe the denial of WDS's application was absolute. First, we observe that the ZBA could have approved the application subject to conditions intended to mitigate adverse effects on public health, safety, and welfare. Yet the ZBA chose instead to deny the application in its entirety. It is evident that in the eyes of the ZBA's members, the denial was final since all of them discarded their notes after voting on the application. Second, were WDS to prepare a modified proposal, it would have to begin the application process anew. This would have imposed so great an economic burden as to make the option unworkable. Third, the district court determined that ZBA members were not credible when they testified they would give reasonable consideration to another application by WDS. When the board's expressed willingness to consider a modified proposal is insincere, we do not require an institution to file a modified proposal before determining that its religious exercise has been substantially burdened.

Consequently, we are persuaded that WDS has satisfied its burden in proving that there was no viable alternative to achieve its objectives, and we conclude that WDS's religious exercise was substantially burdened by the ZBA's arbitrary and unlawful denial of its application.

Under RLUIPA, once a religious institution has demonstrated that its religious exercise has been substantially burdened, the burden of proof shifts to the municipality to prove it acted in furtherance of a compelling governmental interest and that its action is the least restrictive means of furthering that interest. § 2000cc-2(b). Compelling state interests are "interests of the highest order." Church of the Lukumi Babalu Aye, Inc. v. City of Hialeah, 508 U.S. 520, 546 (1993). The Village claims that it has a compelling interest in enforcing zoning regulations and ensuring residents' safety through traffic regulations. However, it must show a compelling interest in imposing the burden on religious exercise in the particular case at hand, not a compelling interest in general.

The district court's findings reveal the ZBA's stated reasons for denying the application were not substantiated by evidence in the record before it. The court stated the application was denied not because of a compelling governmental interest that would adversely impact public health, safety, or welfare, but was denied because of undue deference to the opposition of a small group of neighbors.

Further, even were we to determine that there was a compelling state interest involved, the Village did not use the least restrictive means available to achieve that interest. The ZBA had the opportunity to approve the application subject to conditions, but refused to consider doing so.

III Constitutionality of RLUIPA

Given our conclusion that the ZBA violated RLUIPA by denying WDS's application, the question remains whether RLUIPA was constitutionally applied. The Village challenges RLUIPA on the grounds that it exceeds Congress' Fourteenth Amendment (§ 5) and Commerce Clause powers and that the Act is unconstitutional under the Tenth Amendment and the Establishment Clause.

RLUIPA states that it only applies when (1) "the substantial burden is imposed in a program or activity that receives Federal financial assistance . . . ," (2) "the substantial burden affects, or removal of that substantial burden would affect, commerce with foreign nations, among the several States, or with Indian tribes . . . ," or (3) "the substantial burden is imposed in the implementation of a land use regulation or system of land use regulations, under which a government makes, or has in place formal or informal procedures or practices that permit the government to make, individualized assessments of the proposed uses for the property involved." § 2000cc(a)(2).

By limiting RLUIPA's scope to cases that present one of these jurisdictional nexuses, Congress alternatively grounded RLUIPA, depending on the facts of a particular case, in the Spending Clause, the Commerce Clause, and § 5 of the Fourteenth Amendment. There is no claim here that the ZBA receives federal financial assistance, but WDS does assert both that the substantial burden on its religious exercise affects interstate commerce and that it is imposed through formal procedures that permit the government to make individualized assessments of the proposed uses for the property involved. Thus, we must examine whether RLUIPA is constitutionally applied under Congress' Commerce Clause power or whether it is constitutionally applied under Congress' power to create causes of action vindicating Fourteenth Amendment rights.

The Constitution grants Congress the power "[t]o regulate Commerce . . . among the several States." U.S. Const. art. I, § 8, cl. 3. As noted above, Congress made explicit reference to this grant by limiting the application of RLUIPA to cases in which, inter alia, "the substantial burden affects, or removal of that substantial burden would affect, commerce . . . among the several States." § 2000cc(a)(2)(B).

As the Supreme Court has made plain, the satisfaction of such a jurisdictional element—common in both civil and criminal cases—is sufficient to validate the exercise of congressional power because an interstate commerce nexus must be demonstrated in each case for the statute in question to operate. See United States v. Morrison, 529 U.S. 598, 611-12 (2000) ("Such a jurisdictional element may establish that the enactment is in pursuance of Congress' regulation of interstate commerce."); United States v. Lopez, 514 U.S. 549, 561 (1995) (noting that statute in question "contains no jurisdictional element which would ensure, through case-by-case inquiry, that the [activity] in question affects interstate commerce"). Following suit, this Court has consistently upheld statutes under the Commerce Clause on the basis of jurisdictional elements. Consistent with this precedent, we now hold that, where the relevant jurisdictional element is satisfied, RLUIPA constitutes a valid exercise of congressional power under the Commerce Clause.

In this case, the district court found the jurisdictional element satisfied by evidence that the construction of Gordon Hall, a 44,000 square-foot building with an estimated cost of $9 million, will affect interstate commerce. We identify no error in this conclusion. As we have recognized, the evidence need only demonstrate a minimal effect on commerce to satisfy the jurisdictional element. Further, we have expressly noted that commercial building construction is activity affecting interstate commerce.

In light of our determination that RLUIPA's application in the present case is constitutional under the Commerce Clause, there is no need to consider or decide whether its application could be grounded alternatively in § 5 of the Fourteenth Amendment. . . .

In determining whether a particular law violates the Establishment Clause, which provides in the First Amendment that "Congress shall make no law respecting an establishment of religion," U.S. Const. amend. I, we examine the government conduct at issue under the three-prong analysis articulated by the Supreme Court in Lemon v. Kurtzman, 403 U.S. 602 (1971). Under Lemon, government action that interacts with religion must: (1) have a secular purpose, (2) have a principal effect that neither advances nor inhibits religion, and (3) not bring about an excessive government entanglement with religion. Id. at 612-13. RLUIPA's land use provisions plainly have a secular purpose, that is, the same secular purpose that RLUIPA's institutionalized persons provisions have: to lift government-created burdens on private religious exercise. See Cutter v. Wilkinson, 544 U.S. 709, 720 (2005). As the Supreme Court explained in *Cutter*, such purpose is "compatible with the Establishment Clause." *Id.*

Similarly, the principal or primary effect of RLUIPA's land use provisions neither advances nor inhibits religion. As the Supreme Court has explained, a law produces forbidden effects under *Lemon* if "the government itself has advanced religion through its own activities and influence." Corp. of Presiding Bishop of Church of Jesus Christ of Latter-day Saints v. Amos, 483 U.S. 327, 337 (1987). Under RLUIPA, the government itself does not advance religion; all RLUIPA does is permit religious practitioners the free exercise of their religious beliefs without being burdened unnecessarily by the government.

Finally, RLUIPA's land use provisions do not foster an excessive government entanglement with religion. Although the Village contends that RLUIPA fails every part of the *Lemon* test, it makes no argument that the land use provisions foster intolerable levels of interaction between church and state or the continuing involvement of one in the affairs of the other. Further, entanglement becomes excessive only when it advances or inhibits religion. RLUIPA cannot be said to advance religion simply by requiring that states not discriminate against or among religious institutions.

Accordingly, we find that RLUIPA's land use provisions do not violate the Establishment Clause. . . .

Accordingly, for the foregoing reasons, the judgment of the district court is affirmed.

Notes

1. The road to RLUIPA was long and winding. In Employment Div. v. Smith, 494 U.S. 872 (1990), a five-member majority refused to apply the "balancing test" established in Sherbert v. Verner, 374 U.S. 398 (1963), to a "neutral, generally applicable law" (which in *Smith* was a law regulating controlled substances). As a result of the Court's move away from *Sherbert*'s requirement of a "compelling state interest," religious individuals and groups felt especially vulnerable to a wide range of government regulation, particularly in the area of land use. Because zoning and other regulations and restrictions on land use are typically deemed neutral, generally applicable laws under *Smith*, religious bodies that own land would, in the absence of a change in federal law, be treated the same as their secular neighbors. Accordingly, local government zoning authorities would be entitled to the same generous deference they have been accorded since *Euclid*.

Congress responded to the widespread clamor after *Smith* by passing the Religious Freedom Restoration Act (RFRA) of 1993, codified at 42 U.S.C. §§2000bb to 2000bb-4. The legislation sailed through with strong bi-partisan support in both chambers and in the Clinton White House. RFRA was a direct attempt to restore the "compelling governmental interest" and "least restrictive means" tests to a wide range of governmental activity that burdened the free exercise of religion.

This first legislative response proved fruitless at least as far as state and local government regulation was concerned, however, when the Supreme Court struck down the nonfederal aspects of RFRA in City of Boerne v. Flores, 521 U.S. 507, 519, 536, 537 (U.S. 1997). In this RFRA-based challenge brought by the Catholic Archbishop of San Antonio, Texas, because of the denial of a building permit for enlarging a church in an historic district, the majority found that Congress had overstepped its enforcement powers under §5 of the Fourteenth Amendment. Justice Kennedy wrote: "Legislation which alters the meaning of the Free Exercise Clause cannot be said to be enforcing the Clause. Congress does not enforce a constitutional right by changing what the right is. It has been given the power "to enforce," not the power to determine what constitutes a constitutional violation." Concluding that "RFRA contradicts vital principles necessary to maintain separation of powers and the federal balance," the Court reversed the lower court's opinion that the Act was constitutional. In a short concurrence, Justice Stevens opined that the Act also amounted to an unconstitutional violation of the Establishment Clause, noting: "This governmental preference for religion, as opposed to irreligion, is forbidden by the First Amendment."

Refusing to be outflanked by the High Court, Congress went back to the drawing board, producing RLUIPA, codified at 42 U.S.C. §2000cc to 42 U.S.C. §2000cc-5, a statute with a more limited scope (as suggested by its title) that articulated alternative constitutional foundations for restoring the "compelling governmental interest" and "least restrictive means" tests.

2. Stripped of its federal statutory and constitutional elements, the opinion in *Westchester Day School* looks suspiciously like judicial review of an unfair or arbitrary decision to deny a special use permit request that is unsupported by the record. Consider, for example, the following statement that could easily be found in any state-court zoning decision involving the denial of a zoning change: "[T]he record convincingly demonstrates that the zoning decision in this case was characterized not simply by the occasional errors that can attend the task of government but by an arbitrary blindness to the facts." Indeed, in the very next sentence, the panel reports: "As the district court correctly concluded, such a zoning ruling fails to comply with New York law."

One very curious aspect of this decision is that the court seems to suggest that the religious landowner might have to demonstrate that a zoning decision is already suspect under state law for it to amount to a "substantial burden" that would trigger relief under RLUIPA. If that is the case, then perhaps RLUIPA is nothing more than a federal supplement to state land use and zoning law—a federal hammer (with attorneys fees thrown in) that is designed to prevent local land use regulators from acting in an "arbitrary or capricious" manner.

In this way, *Westchester Day School* is essentially a first cousin of the Supreme Court's decision in City of Cleburne v. Cleburne Living Center (discussed in Chapter Four), in which the Justices, even using minimal scrutiny (the rational basis test) found that the decision of city officials to require that the operator of a group home for the mentally retarded secure a special use permit in a residential zone "rest[ed] on an irrational prejudice" and therefore violated the Equal Protection Clause.

The zoning officials of the Village of Mamaroneck, by heeding "the public opposition of the small but influential group of neighbors," rather than sound planning principles, may have fallen into the *Cleburne* irrationality trap. The passage of time (during which we will see decisions in many more RLUIPA cases) will tell whether the substantial burden requirement of the statute is merely a proxy for the traditional arbitrary and capricious test that has governed zoning law for more than eight decades.[12]

3. The Supreme Court, in Cutter v. Wilkinson, 544 U.S. 709, 719-20 (2005), found that RLUIPA did not violate the Establishment Clause, at least in the institutionalized person context:

> The Religion Clauses of the First Amendment provide: "Congress shall make no law respecting an establishment of religion, or prohibiting the free exercise thereof." The first of the two Clauses, commonly called the Establishment Clause, commands a separation of church and state. The second, the Free Exercise Clause, requires government respect for, and noninterference with, the religious beliefs and practices of our Nation's

---

12. Much of the discussion in this and the previous note is found in Michael Allan Wolf, *LexisNexis Expert Commentary on* Westchester Day School v. Village of Mamaroneck (linked to Lexis version of the decision and also available at 2-7 LexisNexis Real Estate Rep. 39 (2007)).

people. While the two Clauses express complementary values, they often exert conflicting pressures.

Our decisions recognize that "there is room for play in the joints" between the Clauses, some space for legislative action neither compelled by the Free Exercise Clause nor prohibited by the Establishment Clause. In accord with the majority of Courts of Appeals that have ruled on the question, we hold that § 3 of RLUIPA fits within the corridor between the Religion Clauses: On its face, the Act qualifies as a permissible legislative accommodation of religion that is not barred by the Establishment Clause.

While many federal district and circuit courts have applied and evaluated the constitutionality of RLUIPA in the land use context, as illustrated by many of the cases cited by the court in *Westchester Day School*, litigants have not yet reached the Supreme Court with such a challenge. The Becket Fund for Religious Liberty, which filed an amicus brief in *Westchester Day School*, maintains valuable, up-to-date information on RLUIPA disputes at http://www.rluipa.com.

Chapter Seven
The Holy Grail: Managing Growth While Maintaining Affordability and Protecting Natural Resources

I.   Parochialism or Sprawl Control?: The Challenge of Growth Management

You may recall that Justice George Sutherland's majority opinion in *Euclid v. Ambler* contained this strong (and enduring) endorsement of local control of land use:

> It is said that the Village of Euclid is a mere suburb of the City of Cleveland. . . . But the village, though physically a suburb of Cleveland, is politically a separate municipality, with powers of its own and authority to govern itself as it sees fit within the limits of the organic law of its creation and the State and Federal Constitutions.

In many ways, the Court's 1926 decision cleared the way for similarly situated communities to limit population and to ward off the evils of urbanization despite the fact that the municipality in question stood in the way of residential development for central city residents hoping to escape the physical confinement and other problems of inner-city life.

The use of public and private land use controls was closely connected to the growth of politically distinct suburbs. In the words of one suburban Chicago critic of annexation: "Under local government we can absolutely control every objectionable thing that may try to enter our limits but once annexed we are at the mercy of city hall."[1] Boston's experience, as presented by Sam Bass Warner Jr., in his influential study, Streetcar Suburbs: The Process of Growth in Boston (1870-1900), at 164-65 (2d ed. 1978), was not atypical:

> It was already apparent in the 1880's that to join Boston was to assume all the burdens and conflicts of a modern industrial metropolis. To remain apart was to escape, at least for a time, some of these problems. In the face of this choice the metropolitan middle class abandoned their central city. . . .

> Beyond Boston the special suburban form of popularly managed local government continued to flourish. In suburbs of substantial income and limited class structure, high standards of education and public service were often achieved: Each town, however, now managed its affairs as best it could surrounded by forces largely beyond its control.

Zoning out, or segregating, the city's most distasteful uses could help ensure that the escape to the suburbs would not mean replicating the problems left behind.

Because of zoning's contribution to the continued isolation of middle-class communities, courts and legislatures in some states beginning in the late 20th century began to mandate regional

---

1.   KENNETH T. JACKSON, CRABGRASS FRONTIER: THE SUBURBANIZATION OF THE UNITED STATES 151 (1985) (quoting a Mar. 9, 1907, editorial from the *Morgan Park Post*).

responsibility for suburban areas, while in other areas planning and zoning controls were, at least in part, recaptured by state officials. These shifts in the nature and operation of zoning law are not necessarily timely reactions to 21st-century socioeconomic and governance realities. They can also be appreciated as the inevitable, if sorely delayed, responses to the negative externalities of the suburban (and eventually exurban) movement that was given credence and support by the Court in *Euclid v. Ambler*. Chief among these externalities are duplicative and costly municipal services, resegregation of public school systems, the despoiling of undeveloped forest, farmland, wetlands, and other critical habitats, located far from the city center, and unsightly and energy-wasting sprawl.

In the late 1990s, the national debate over the nature and implications of urban and suburban sprawl began to attract page-one media coverage (and its Internet equivalent—the on-line poll) and the attention of national policymakers and candidates for America's highest political offices. Legislative and administrative policies and numerous policy studies have endorsed the strategy of harnessing growth and redirecting development away from the prime farmland, precious open space, and environmentally sensitive settings that often define those regions that lie beyond the more populous cities and older suburbs. In fact, environmental concerns often appear to be the chief impetus for a broad-based attack on the visual clutter, low-density construction, and automobile-dependent development on the metropolitan fringes.

While sprawling cities have been a part of civilization for hundreds, even thousands, of years, the "crisis" that attracted the current flurry of regulatory and political attention has its roots in the dramatic expansion of single-family home ownership in the second half of the 20th century—a phenomenon that had been viewed as one of the major accomplishments of the post-World War II years. While many critics place a large part of the blame for modern American sprawl on lawmakers and bureaucrats inside the D.C. beltway, the extent of federal responsibility is still a matter of dispute, as evidenced by the title of a 1999 Government Accountability Office (GAO) report—Community Development: Extent of Federal Influence on "Urban Sprawl" Is Unclear.

For decades, courts, legislatures, and legal and planning commentators have wrestled with the negative social, economic, and environmental externalities of unbridled growth. For example, in Mansfield and Swett, Inc. v. Town of West Orange, 198 A. 225, 229 (N.J. Sup. Ct. 1938), the state court observed (in the gendered vernacular of that time):

> We are surrounded with the problems of planless growth. The baneful consequences of haphazard development are everywhere apparent. There are evils affecting the health, safety and prosperity of our citizens that are well-nigh insurmountable because of the prohibitive corrective cost. To challenge the power to give proper direction to community growth and development . . . is to deny the vitality of a principle that has brought men together in organized society for their mutual advantage.

Even the best-laid schemes for long-term regulation of land use will be frustrated by the whims and caprices of the market. This is especially true for residential development. The *Mansfield and Swett* court was not alone in its deep fear for the future of the American metropolitan landscape, as indicated by the cases and notes that follow.

Over the last few years, a growing number of commentators—chiefly environmentalists who are concerned about the loss of precious "greenfields" to make way for "edge cities," and New Urbanist architects and planners frustrated and bored by cul-de-sac-obsessed suburban developers and their customers—have placed much of the blame for sprawl on the federal government. The former mayor of Albuquerque, David Rusk, in his oft-cited study, Cities Without Suburbs (1993), places much of the blame for the emergence of a suburban nation (and the decline of the central city) on a range of federal policies including Federal Housing Administration and Veterans Administration mortgage support for single-family homes, federal aid for the construction of roads and highways (much more than for public transit), and billions of dollars in foregone tax revenue attributable to the mortgage interest deduction.

Unfortunately for those who seek to rally the anti-sprawl forces against one enemy, this morality play is far more complex. The GAO study mentioned above noted that "[s]ome experts believe—and anecdotal evidence exists to support their belief--that the federal government currently influences 'urban sprawl' through spending for specific programs, taxation, and regulation, among other things, but few studies document the extent of the federal influence." Given the absence of hard data on housing and other subjects, the researchers could only conclude that "the level of the federal influence is difficult to determine."[2]

How seriously should we take dire warnings that are unaccompanied by alternative programs for accommodating natural population growth and for fostering upward social mobility? What role can the lawyer play in minimizing the harms identified by these critics? Does (or should) the lawyer's obligation to counsel a developer-client include the duty to propose alternative construction plans or locations? What role can lawyer-legislators play in crafting effective laws that reward urban infilling (targeting undeveloped or underdeveloped sites within or close to the city center that the market has bypassed) and punish leap-frogging (skipping over undeveloped stretches of land to build suburban and exurban, low-density developments)? Can traditional neighborhood codes (TNDs) and other New Urbanist-style approaches be smoothly incorporated into existing Euclidean schemes, or does it make more sense to move to alternatives such as "form-based" or "smart" codes?[3]

II. Two Enduring Templates

While localities have been using zoning and other land use tools to slow the pace of multi-family residential development since the 1920s, the "growth management" movement took off in the 1970s with the implementation (and judicial approval) of two key strategies: tying private development of new housing to the availability of adequate public facilities (also known as concurrency) and enacting residential building quotas (also known as tempo or time controls). There are many rationales for adopting these and other devices; while some of these reasons are stated outright—protecting natural resources and conserving open space, passing the costs of growth onto developers (and in turn the new homeowners), and preserving the small-town character of communities at the exurban fringe—others, particularly the desire to exclude potential residents of affordable units, remain unspoken.

As it turns out, we now know that by 1975 the legitimacy of these two basic approaches had been settled by two highly influential cases—one from New York's highest state court, the other a federal case from California decided by the Ninth Circuit. As in the *Mount Laurel* line of cases addressed in Chapter Six, those parties challenging growth "controls" often emphasize their exclusionary purpose and effect, despite the claims of public officials that local governments are merely

---

2. U.S. GAO, Community Development: Extent of Federal Influence on "Urban Sprawl" Is Unclear 2-3 (1999).

3. *See* Daniel K. Slone et al., A Legal Guide to Urban and Sustainable Development for Planners, Developers, and Architects 90 (2008):

> Traditional neighborhood development codes (TND codes) plug into existing Euclidean zoning codes as a new district. *Form-based codes* substitute a focus on the form of a building for the Euclidean focus on use and have been advanced by urbanists as the best way to deliver urbanism and appropriate design. Finally, the *SmartCode*, a particular version of form-based code tied to the transect, has been developed as a model unified code to address subdivision, zoning and comprehensive planning issues.

> For a graphic illustration of the transect, running from the T1 Natural Zone, through intermediate Rural, Suburban, General Urban, Urban Center, and Urban Core Zones, see http://www.dpz.com/pdf/07-Transect%20Charts.pdf.

pursuing fiscally responsible and environmentally sound planning policies. In this group of decisions, however, judges from the beginning have tended to defer to government decisionmakers, and this early approval has encouraged the spread of "*Ramapo*" and "*Petaluma*" type plans far from their points of origin.

GOLDEN v. PLANNING BOARD OF TOWN OF RAMAPO
30 N.Y.2d 359, 285 N.E.2d 291, 334 N.Y.S.2d 138, *appeal dismissed*, 409 U.S. 1003 (1972)

SCILEPPI, Judge. . . . .

Experiencing the pressures of an increase in population and the ancillary problem of providing municipal facilities and services,[1] the Town of Ramapo, as early as 1964, made application for grant under section 801 of the Housing Act of 1964 (78 U.S. Stat. 769) to develop a master plan. The plan's preparation included a four-volume study of the existing land uses, public facilities, transportation, industry and commerce, housing needs and projected population trends. The proposals appearing in the studies were subsequently adopted pursuant to section 272-a of the Town Law, Consol. Laws, c. 62, in July, 1966 and implemented by way of a master plan. The master plan was followed by the adoption of a comprehensive zoning ordinance. Additional sewage district and drainage studies were undertaken which culminated in the adoption of a capital budget, providing for the development of the improvements specified in the master plan within the next six years. Pursuant to section 271 of the Town Law, authorizing comprehensive planning, and as a supplement to the capital budget, the Town Board adopted a capital program which provides for the location and sequence of additional capital improvements for the 12 years following the life of the capital budget. The two plans, covering a period of 18 years, detail the capital improvements projected for maximum development and conform to the specifications set forth in the master plan, the official map and drainage plan.

Based upon these criteria, the Town subsequently adopted the subject amendments for the alleged purpose of eliminating premature subdivision and urban sprawl. Residential development is to proceed according to the provision of adequate municipal facilities and services, with the assurance that any concomitant restraint upon property use is to be of a "temporary" nature and that other private uses, including the construction of individual housing, are authorized.

---

1. The Town's allegations that present facilities are inadequate to service increasing demands go uncontested. We must assume, therefore, that the proposed improvements, both as to their nature and extent, reflect legitimate community needs and are not veiled efforts at exclusion (see National Land & Inv. Co. v. Easttown Twp. Bd. of Adj., 419 Pa. 504, 215 A.2d 597). In the period 1940-1968 population in the unincorporated areas of the Town increased 285.9%. Between the years of 1950-1960 the increase, again in unincorporated areas, was 130.8%; from 1960-1966 some 78.5%; and from the years 1966-1969 20.4%. In terms of real numbers, population figures compare at 58,626 as of 1966 with the largest increment of growth since the decennial census occurring in the undeveloped areas. Projected figures, assuming current land use and zoning trends, approximate a total Town population of 120,000 by 1985. Growth is expected to be heaviest in the currently undeveloped western and northern tiers of the town, predominantly in the form of subdivision development with some apartment construction. A growth rate of some 1,000 residential units per annum has been experienced in the unincorporated areas of the Town.

The amendments did not rezone or reclassify any land into different residential or use districts,[2] but, for the purposes of implementing the proposals appearing in the comprehensive plan, consist, in the main, of additions to the definitional sections of the ordinance, section 46-3, and the adoption of a new class of "Special Permit Uses," designated "Residential Development Use." "Residential Development Use" is defined as "The erection or construction of dwellings on any vacant plots, lots or parcels of land" (§46-3, as amd.); and, any person who acts so as to come within that definition, "shall be deemed to be engaged in residential development which shall be a separate use classification under this ordinance and subject to the requirement of obtaining a special permit from the Town Board" (§46-3, as amd.).

The standards for the issuance of special permits are framed in terms of the availability to the proposed subdivision plat of five essential facilities or services: specifically (1) public sanitary sewers or approved substitutes; (2) drainage facilities; (3) improved public parks or recreation facilities, including public schools; (4) State, county or town roads — major, secondary or collector; and, (5) firehouses. No special permit shall issue unless the proposed residential development has accumulated 15 development points, to be computed on a sliding scale of values assigned to the specified improvements under the statute. Subdivision is thus a function of immediate availability to the proposed plat of certain municipal improvements; the avowed purpose of the amendments being to phase residential development to the Town's ability to provide the above facilities or services.

Certain savings and remedial provisions are designed to relieve of potentially unreasonable restrictions. Thus, the board may issue special permits vesting a present right to proceed with residential development in such year as the development meets the required point minimum, but in no event later than the final year of the 18-year capital plan. The approved special use permit is fully assignable, and improvements scheduled for completion within one year from the date of an application are to be credited as though existing on the date of the application. A prospective developer may advance the date of subdivision approval by agreeing to provide those improvements which will bring the proposed plat within the number of development points required by the amendments. And applications are authorized to the "Development Easement Acquisition Commission" for a reduction of the assessed valuation. Finally, upon application to the Town Board, the development point requirements may be varied should the board determine that such a variance or modification is consistent with the on-going development plan.

The undisputed effect of these integrated efforts in land use planning and development is to provide an over-all program of orderly growth and adequate facilities through a sequential development policy commensurate with progressing availability and capacity of public facilities. While its goals are clear and its purposes undisputably laudatory, serious questions are raised as to the manner in which these ends are to be effected, not the least of which relates to their legal viability under present zoning enabling legislation, particularly sections 261 and 263 of the Town Law. The owners of the subject premises argue, and the Appellate Division has sustained the proposition,

---

2. As of July, 1966, the only available figures, six residential zoning districts with varying lot size and density requirements accounted for in excess of nine tenths of the Town's unincorporated land area. Of these the RR classification (80,000 square feet minimum lot area) plus R-35 zone (35,000 square feet minimum lot area) comprise over one half of all zoned areas. The subject sites are presently zoned RR-50 (50,000 square feet minimum lot area). The reasonableness of these minimum lot requirements are not presently controverted, though we are referred to no compelling need in their behalf. Under present zoning regulations, the population of the unincorporated areas could be increased by about 14,600 families (3.5 people) when all suitable vacant land is occupied. Housing values as of 1960 in the unincorporated areas range from a modest $15,000 (approx. 30%) to higher than $25,000 (25%), with the undeveloped western tier of Town showing the highest percentage of values in excess of $25,000 (41%). Significantly, for the same year only about one half of one percent of all housing units were occupied by nonwhite families. Efforts at adjusting this disparity are reflected in the creation of a public housing authority and the authority's proposal to construct biracial low-income family housing.

that the primary purpose of the amending ordinance is to control or regulate population growth within the Town and as such is not within the authorized objectives of the zoning enabling legislation. We disagree.

In enacting the challenged amendments, the Town Board has sought to control subdivision in all residential districts, pending the provision (public or private) at some future date of various services and facilities. A reading of the relevant statutory provisions reveals that there is no specific authorization for the "sequential" and "timing" controls adopted here. That, of course, cannot be said to end the matter, for the additional inquiry remains as to whether the challenged amendments find their basis within the perimeters of the devices authorized and purposes sanctioned under current enabling legislation. Our concern is, as it should be, with the effects of the statutory scheme taken as a whole and its role in the propagation of a viable policy of land use and planning. . . .

In the end, zoning properly effects, and only in the manner prescribed, those purposes detailed under section 263 of the Town Law. It may not be invoked to further the general police powers of a municipality.[5]

Even so, considering the activities enumerated by section 261 of the Town Law, and relating those powers to the authorized purposes detailed in section 263, the challenged amendments are proper zoning techniques, exercised for legitimate zoning purposes. The power to restrict and regulate conferred under section 261 includes within its grant, by way of necessary implication, the authority to direct the growth of population for the purposes indicated, within the confines of the township. It is the matrix of land use restrictions, common to each of the enumerated powers and sanctioned goals, a necessary concomitant to the municipalities' recognized authority to determine the lines along which local development shall proceed, though it may divert it from its natural course (Euclid v. Ambler Co., 272 U.S. 365, 389-390).

Of course, zoning historically has assumed the development of individual plats and has proven characteristically ineffective in treating with the problems attending subdivision and development of larger parcels, involving as it invariably does, the provision of adequate public services and facilities. To this end, subdivision control (Town Law, §§ 276, 277) purports to guide community development in the directions outlined here, while at the same time encouraging the provision of adequate facilities for the housing, distribution, comfort and convenience of local residents. It reflects in essence, a legislative judgment that the development of unimproved areas be accompanied by provision of essential facilities. And though it may not, in a definitional or conceptual sense be identified with the power to zone, it is designed to complement other land use restrictions, which, taken together, seek to implement a broader, comprehensive plan for community development (see Haar, The Master Plan: An Impermanent Constitution, 20 Law & Contemp. Probs. 353). . . .

Experience, over the last quarter century, however, with greater technological integration and drastic shifts in population distribution has pointed up serious defects and community autonomy in land use controls has come under increasing attack by legal commentators, and students of urban problems alike, because of its pronounced insularism and its correlative role in producing distortions in metropolitan growth patterns, and perhaps more importantly, in crippling efforts toward regional and State-wide problem solving, be it pollution, decent housing, or public transportation.

Recognition of communal and regional interdependence, in turn, has resulted in proposals for schemes of regional and State-wide planning, in the hope that decisions would then correspond roughly to their level of impact. Yet, as salutary as such proposals may be, the power to zone under

---

5. This distinction, though often unarticulated, is elemental and we have in the past held the exercise of the zoning power *ultra vires* and void where the end sought to be accomplished was not peculiar to the locality's basic land use scheme, but rather related to some general problem, incidental to the community at large.

current law is vested in local municipalities, and we are constrained to resolve the issues accordingly. What does become more apparent in treating with the problem, however, is that though the issues are framed in terms of the developer's due process rights, those rights cannot, realistically speaking, be viewed separately and apart from the rights of others "'in search of a [more] comfortable place to live.'"

There is, then, something inherently suspect in a scheme which, apart from its professed purposes, effects a restriction upon the free mobility of a people until sometime in the future when projected facilities are available to meet increased demands. Although zoning must include schemes designed to allow municipalities to more effectively contend with the increased demands of evolving and growing communities, under its guise, townships have been wont to try their hand at an array of exclusionary devices in the hope of avoiding the very burden which, growth must inevitably bring. Though the conflict engendered by such tactics is certainly real, and its implications vast, accumulated evidence, scientific and social, points circumspectly at the hazards of undirected growth and the naive, somewhat nostalgic imperative that egalitarianism is a function of growth.

Of course, these problems cannot be solved by Ramapo or any single municipality, but depend upon the accommodation of widely disparate interests for their ultimate resolution. To that end, State-wide or regional control of planning would insure that interests broader than that of the municipality underlie various land use policies. Nevertheless, that should not be the only context in which growth devices such as these, aimed at population assimilation, not exclusion, will be sustained; especially where, as here, we would have no alternative but to strike the provision down in the wistful hope that the efforts of the State Office of Planning Coordination and the American Law Institute will soon bear fruit.

Hence, unless we are to ignore the plain meaning of the statutory delegation, this much is clear: phased growth is well within the ambit of existing enabling legislation. And, of course, it is no answer to point to emergent problems to buttress the conclusion that such innovative schemes are beyond the perimeters of statutory authorization. These considerations, admittedly real, to the extent which they are relevant, bear solely upon the continued viability of "localism" in land use regulation; obviously, they can neither add nor detract from the initial grant of authority, obsolescent though it may be. The answer which Ramapo has posed can by no means be termed definitive; it is, however, a first practical step toward controlled growth achieved without forsaking broader social purposes. . . .

It is the nature of all land use and development regulations to circumscribe the course of growth within a particular town or district and to that extent such restrictions invariably impede the forces of natural growth. Where those restrictions upon the beneficial use and enjoyment of land are necessary to promote the ultimate good of the community and are within the bounds of reason, they have been sustained. "Zoning [, however,] is a means by which a governmental body can plan for the future—it may not be used as a means to deny the future" (National Land & Inv. Co. v. Easttown Twp. Bd. of Adj., 419 Pa. 504, 528, 215 A.2d 597, 610). Its exercise assumes that development shall not stop at the community's threshold, but only that whatever growth there may be shall proceed along a predetermined course (Euclid v. Ambler Co., 272 U.S. 365, 387). It is inextricably bound to the dynamics of community life and its function is to guide, not to isolate or facilitate efforts at avoiding the ordinary incidents of growth. What segregates permissible from impermissible restrictions, depends in the final analysis upon the purpose of the restrictions and their impact in terms of both the community and general public interest. The line of delineation between the two is not a constant, but will be found to vary with prevailing circumstances and conditions.

What we will not countenance, then, under any guise, [are] community efforts at immunization or exclusion. But, far from being exclusionary, the present amendments merely seek, by the implementation of sequential development and timed growth, to provide a balanced cohesive community dedicated to the efficient utilization of land. The restrictions conform to the community's considered land use policies as expressed in its comprehensive plan and represent a bona fide effort to maximize population density consistent with orderly growth. True other alternatives, such as requiring off-site improvements as a prerequisite to subdivision, may be available, but the choice as how best to proceed, in view of the difficulties attending such exactions cannot be faulted.

Perhaps even more importantly, timed growth, unlike the minimum lot requirements recently struck down by the Pennsylvania Supreme Court as exclusionary, does not impose permanent restrictions upon land use. Its obvious purpose is to prevent premature subdivision absent essential municipal facilities and to insure continuous development commensurate with the Town's obligation to provide such facilities. They seek, not to freeze population at present levels but to maximize growth by the efficient use of land, and in so doing testify to this community's continuing role in population assimilation. In sum, Ramapo asks not that it be left alone, but only that it be allowed to prevent the kind of deterioration that has transformed well-ordered and thriving residential communities into blighted ghettos with attendant hazards to health, security and social stability— a danger not without substantial basis in fact.

We only require that communities confront the challenge of population growth with open doors. Where in grappling with that problem, the community undertakes, by imposing temporary restrictions upon development, to provide required municipal services in a rational manner, courts are rightfully reluctant to strike down such schemes. The timing controls challenged here parallel recent proposals put forth by various study groups and have their genesis in certain of the pronouncements of this and the courts of sister States. While these controls are typically proposed as an adjunct of regional planning, the preeminent protection against their abuse resides in the mandatory ongoing planning and development requirement, present here, which attends their implementation and use.

We may assume, therefore, that the present amendments are the product of foresighted planning calculated to promote the welfare of the township. The Town has imposed temporary restrictions upon land use in residential areas while committing itself to a program of development. It has utilized its comprehensive plan to implement its timing controls and has coupled with these restrictions provisions for low and moderate income housing on a large scale. Considered as a whole, it represents both in its inception and implementation a reasonable attempt to provide for the sequential, orderly development of land in conjunction with the needs of the community, as well as individual parcels of land, while simultaneously obviating the blighted aftermath which the initial failure to provide needed facilities so often brings.

The proposed amendments have the effect of restricting development for onwards to 18 years in certain areas. Whether the subject parcels will be so restricted for the full term is not clear, for it is equally probable that the proposed facilities will be brought into these areas well before that time. Assuming, however, that the restrictions will remain outstanding for the life of the program, they still fall short of a confiscation within the meaning of the Constitution. . . . .

In sum, where it is clear that the existing physical and financial resources of the community are inadequate to furnish the essential services and facilities which a substantial increase in population requires, there is a rational basis for "phased growth" and hence, the challenged ordinance is not violative of the Federal and State Constitutions. Accordingly, the order appealed from should be reversed and the actions remitted to Special Term for entry of a judgment declaring section 46-13.1 of the Town Ordinance constitutional.

BREITEL, Judge (dissenting).

The limited powers of district zoning and subdivision regulation delegated to a municipality do not include the power to impose a moratorium on land development. Such conclusion is dictated by settled doctrine that a municipality has only those powers, and especially land use powers, delegated or necessarily implied.

But there is more involved in these cases than the arrogation of undelegated powers. Raised are vital constitutional issues, and, most important, policy issues trenching on grave domestic problems of our time, without the benefit of a legislative determination which would reflect the interests of the entire State. The policy issues relate to needed housing, planned land development under government control, and the exclusion in effect or by motive, of walled-in urban populations of the middle class and the poor. . . . .

A glance at history suggests that Ramapo's plan to have public services installed in advance of development is unrealistic. Richard Babcock, the distinguished practitioner in land development law, some years ago addressed himself to the natural desire of communities to stay development while they caught up with the inexorable thrust of population growth and movement. He observed eloquently that this country was built and is still being built by people who moved about, innovated, pioneered, and created industry and employment, and thereby provided both the need and the means for the public services and facilities that followed (Babcock, The Zoning Game, at pp. 149-150). Thus, the movement has not been in the other direction, first the provision of public and utility services and then the building of homes, farms, and businesses. . . .

As said earlier, when the problem arose outside the State the judicial response has been the same, frustrating communities, intent on walling themselves from the mainstream of development, namely, that the effort was invalid under existing enabling acts or unconstitutional. The response may not be charged to judicial conservatism or self-restraint. In short, it has not been illiberal. It has indeed reflected the larger understanding that American society is at a critical crossroads in the accommodation of urbanization and suburban living, with effects that are no longer confined, bad as they are, to ethnic exclusion or "snob" zoning. Ramapo would preserve its nature, delightful as that may be, but the supervening question is whether it alone may decide this or whether it must be decided by the larger community represented by the Legislature. Legally, politically, economically, and sociologically, the base for determination must be larger than that provided by the town fathers.

Accordingly, I dissent and vote to affirm the orders in both cases.

Notes

1. Ramapo is about 35 miles from midtown Manhattan. It became more accessible because of the construction of the New York State Thruway, the Tappan Zee Bridge, and the extension of the Garden State Parkway to the Thruway. Statistics from the 1970 census showed that Ramapo Township, including the incorporated villages, had 71,739 white residents and 4,563 black residents; of the black residents, 4,147 lived in the incorporated village of Spring Valley. Of all vacant land set aside for residential use, fully 65% was limited to what may fairly be described as "large lot" zoning, the minimum required lot areas ranging from 25,000 to 80,000 square feet. The lawsuit arose in connection with the proposed development of 50,000-square-foot lots. There was no district in the town of Ramapo that was set aside for multi-family housing. Multi-family housing was limited to the incorporated areas, such as Suffern and Spring Valley, which already contained most of such housing.

To what extent do you think the court was influenced by the town's fight (including litigation against some town residents) to build "biracial low-income family housing"? See footnote 2 in the opinion. This housing consisted of approximately 200 units, 75% of which were designed for and occupied by the elderly, all of whom were white. About 50 units were occupied by low-income families, 5 or 10 of whom were black. Robert Freilich, in Ramapo Township: *Comments of Attorney Who Drafted the Ordinance*, 24 Zoning Dig. 72, 73-74 (1972), wrote that this was "not an exclusionary zoning case":

> The confusion of many attorneys in the battle against exclusionary zoning is unfortunate. There is a tendency to view all zoning as intrinsically evil simply because some communities utilize these tools in an exclusionary manner. This problem has been around for a long time. Should we go back to no zoning at all, to unlimited urban sprawl and development chaos in suburban areas merely because some of the tools are essentially neutral? They can be used correctly or incorrectly, depending upon the motivation of the regulators. Our efforts must be to eliminate the abuses, while simultaneously developing stronger efforts to preserve the quality of our communities and of the environment. We must assure economic and racial equality in planning, not without planning.

Do you agree? If it is not exclusionary, why do the planning devices control only housing, not industrial and commercial development? Should the court have compared Ramapo's resulting tax effort with that of other communities in the region? If so, what standard should it have applied and why?

2. How did the original "Ramapo Plan" actually work in the limited time period in which it was in effect? Under the ordinance, development, as a matter of right, required the accumulation of 15 points (for example, five points for public sewers, one point for a park or recreation area within one mile). How can a long-range capital budget plan take into account changing circumstances suggesting revised local priorities, inflation, unpredictable construction costs, delays in related state or county projects, and delays or moratoria on state and federal aid affecting projects essential to the plan? Ramapo encountered some difficulty completing its capital budget programs. Two severe hurricanes, Doria in August 1971 and Agnes in June 1972, caused serious flood damage. The town was forced to appropriate $1.5 million to mop up. Much of the work scheduled for those years in the 1971 capital budget was deferred and, as a consequence, no formal capital budgets were adopted for 1972 and 1973. The adopted 1974 capital budget differed significantly from the 1971 budget; the major emphasis in the later budget was directed toward road improvements believed necessary because of state road projects, including a new state Thruway interchange, moving more traffic onto roads in the town.

Prior to institution of the plan, the town grew at an average of about 620 dwelling units per year. In the first five years of the plan (through June 1974), Ramapo granted special permits for development meeting the 15-point test on 71 applications involving 1,084 acres and 991 lots. It granted variances for development not passing the point test on 146 applications involving 488 acres and 648 lots, and denied variances on 12 applications involving 100 acres and 113 lots. The total approved special permits and variances involved 1,639 lots and 1,714 dwelling units over the five-year period, or approval for an average of 367 dwelling units per year. Generally, approved development was located near prior development. The approvals were not spread evenly over the years; the first year had a particularly high number of variances, while activity in the last year declined along with the nationwide slump in the home-building industry. And it should be clear that the granting of a special permit or variance does not mean actual construction.

3. In Charles v. Diamond, 41 N.Y.2d 318, 324-25, 360 N.E.2d 1265, 1300-01 (1977), the court held that a municipality cannot use its own delay, otherwise unjustified, in providing public services as the basis for refusing approval to new development: "Temporary restraints necessary to promote the over-all public interest are permissible. Permanent interference with the reasonable

use of private property for the purposes for which it is suited is not." Immediately after citing the eighteen-year period upheld in *Ramapo*, the court said:

> However, the crucial factor, perhaps even the decisive one, is whether the ultimate economic cost of the benefits is being shared by the members of the community at large, or, rather, is being hidden from the public by the placement of the entire burden upon particular property owners. . . . .
>
> Petitioner has alleged sufficient facts to create a triable issue as to whether the village sewer ordinance is being applied to his property unconstitutionally. Ultimate constitutionality hinges upon several important and diverse, yet not exclusive, factors. At the trial, it will be relevant to establish the exact nature of the village sewage disposal problem. Only when the problem has been specifically identified can it be determined what steps are necessary to correct the difficulty and at what cost, in terms both of expense and time. (Cf. Berenson v. Town of New Castle, 38 N.Y.2d 102, 378 N.Y.S.2d 672, 341 N.E.2d 236.) . . .
>
> Although reasonable excuse may justify delay, the village must be committed firmly to the construction and installation of the necessary improvements. (See Matter of Golden v. Planning Bd. of Town of Ramapo, 30 N.Y.2d 359, 382, 334 N.Y.S.2d 138, 155, 285 N.E.2d 291, 304.) Absent the constraints imposed by law or contract, governmental officials may conduct affairs of government at their own pace. However, where the municipality has affirmatively barred substantially all use of private property pending remedial municipal improvements, unreasonable and dilatory tactics, targeted really to frustrate all private use of property, are not justified. The municipality may not, by withholding the improvements that the municipality has made the necessary prerequisites for development, achieve the result of barring development, a goal that would perhaps be otherwise unreachable. Development may not be zoned out of a community by the indirection of needless municipal delay in providing the essentials for construction.

4. According to *Reconsidering Innovative Land Use Controls*, Land Use L. & Zoning Dig., May 1983, at 3: "On March 14, 1983, the town board of Ramapo, New York, drastically revised its famous growth control program by dropping its point system allocation for subdivision approval." The *Wall Street Journal* reported, in an article dated August 31, 1983: "Ramapo's problem now is too little growth. Fred Rella, township supervisor, says, 'We want more growth, but growth that's compatible with our country-like atmosphere.'" In light of these developments, should the judges who approved the scheme feel foolish for their assumption that the now-abandoned plan was "the product of foresighted planning calculated to promote the welfare of the community"?

For a more recent update on Ramapo's planning woes, see Julienne Marshall, *Whatever Happened to Ramapo?*, Planning, December, 2003, at 4. Marshall has described the town as "[s]prawling, ethnically and racially diverse, and teeming with villages, . . . a mixture of parkland, suburban tracts, high-density enclaves, and bustling shopping centers, in different degrees of decay and renewal." The fiscal woes of the early 1970s meant the end of the capital improvements program and translated into grants of variances to developers. During the decade and a half that the Ramapo plan was in effect, no new villages were incorporated, but between 1982 and 1991 the number of these small communities rose from 6 to 12, often because of dissatisfaction with the town government's inability to enforce zoning controls. The resulting "Balkanization" of the town has led to many problems faced by typical sprawling localities that never experimented with a Ramapo-like plan.

5. Perhaps *Ramapo's* most important impact has been felt hundreds of miles south of the New York state border in the form of Florida's "concurrency" approach to growth management. A key figure in drafting and implementing the Sunshine State's ambitious legislation, Thomas W. Pelham, in *From the Ramapo Plan to Florida's Statewide Concurrency System:* Ramapo's *Influence on Infrastructure Planning*, 35 Urb. Law. 113, 132-33 (2003), has explained:

> The enduring legacy of *Ramapo* is manifest in Florida's statewide concurrency system for managing growth. The Florida system utilizes the planning principles of the Ramapo Plan. However, learning from the *Ramapo* experience and heeding the criticisms discussed in the case and other forums, the drafters of the Florida growth management legislation included provisions to address the concerns raised about the purposes and effects of such growth management systems. As a result, the Florida concurrency system is the nation's most comprehensive and innovative attempt to integrate capital improvements programming into the local comprehensive planning process. Just as implementation of the Ramapo Plan fell short of its goals, the Florida concurrency system has not always lived up to the expectations of its creators and proponents. Nevertheless, the Florida system represents a significant achievement in comprehensive planning that has benefited the state and its citizenry. . . .

Here is the relevant statutory language from Fla. Stat. § 163.3177(10(h):

> It is the intent of the Legislature that public facilities and services needed to support development shall be available concurrent with the impacts of such development in accordance with s. 163.3180.[4] In meeting this intent, public facility and service availability shall be deemed sufficient if the public facilities and services for a development are phased, or the development is phased, so that the public facilities and those related services which are deemed necessary by the local government to operate the facilities necessitated by that development are available concurrent with the impacts of the development. The public facilities and services, unless already available, are to be consistent with the capital improvements element of the local comprehensive plan as required by paragraph (3)(a) [the required "capital improvements" in the local comprehensive plan] or guaranteed in an enforceable development agreement. . . .

Interpreting and applying these statutory provisions can be a daunting task for judges. See, for example, D.R. Horton, Inc. v. Peyton, 959 So. 2d 390, 391-93 (Fla. Ct. App. 2007), involving the judicial review of mayor's veto of a resolution passed by the Jacksonville City Council that would have allowed a landowner to proceed with its plans to build a multi-use development. After city officials "denied Horton's application for a concurrency certificate on the ground that the existing roads in the area of the development would be unable to handle the increased traffic resulting from the development, as determined by a traffic study," the landowner took advantage of a legislative provision by "submit[ting] a 'fair share assessment' application to enter into a contract with the City by which Horton would pay for the cost of the infrastructure improvements made necessary by the proposed development." The costs that the council approved exceeded $4.8 million, but the veto was motivated by the mayor's "conclu[sion] that the proposed list of improvements is inad-

---

4. Authors' note: This provision contains many of the details regarding concurrency, including the following:

(1) (a) Sanitary sewer, solid waste, drainage, potable water, parks and recreation, schools, and transportation facilities, including mass transit, where applicable, are the only public facilities and services subject to the concurrency requirement on a statewide basis. Additional public facilities and services may not be made subject to concurrency on a statewide basis without appropriate study and approval by the Legislature; however, any local government may extend the concurrency requirement so that it applies to additional public facilities within its jurisdiction.

equate to address the traffic impacts which would be created by the proposed development." The appellate court affirmed the trial court's summary judgment favoring the mayor.

CONSTRUCTION INDUSTRY ASSOCIATION v. CITY OF PETALUMA
522 F.2d 897 (9th Cir.), *cert. denied*, 424 U.S. 934 (1975)

CHOY, Circuit Judge.

The City of Petaluma (the City) appeals from a district court decision voiding as unconstitutional certain aspects of its five-year housing and zoning plan. We reverse.

The City is located in southern Sonoma County, about 40 miles north of San Francisco. In the 1950's and 1960's, Petaluma was a relatively self-sufficient town. It experienced a steady population growth from 10,315 in 1950 to 24,870 in 1970. Eventually, the City was drawn into the Bay Area metropolitan housing market as people working in San Francisco and San Rafael became willing to commute longer distances to secure relatively inexpensive housing available there. By November 1972, according to unofficial figures, Petaluma's population was at 30,500, a dramatic increase of almost 25 percent in little over two years.

The increase in the City's population, not surprisingly, is reflected in the increase in the number of its housing units. From 1964 to 1971, the following number of residential housing units were completed:

1964	270
1965	440
1966	321
1967	234
1968	379
1969	358
1970	591
1971	891

In 1970 and 1971, the years of the most rapid growth, demand for housing in the City was even greater than above indicated. Taking 1970 and 1971 together, builders won approval of a total of 2000 permits although only 1482 were actually completed by the end of 1971.

Alarmed by the accelerated rate of growth in 1970 and 1971, the demand for even more housing, and the sprawl of the City eastward, the City adopted a temporary freeze on development in early 1971. The construction and zoning change moratorium was intended to give the City Council and the City planners an opportunity to study the housing and zoning situation and to develop short and long range plans. The Council made specific findings with respect to housing patterns and availability in Petaluma, including the following: That from 1960-1970 housing had been in almost unvarying 6000 square-foot lots laid out in regular grid patterns; that there was a density of approximately 4.5 housing units per acre in the single-family home areas; that during 1960-1970, 88 percent of housing permits issued were for single-family detached homes; that in 1970, 83 percent of Petaluma's housing was single-family dwellings; that the bulk of recent development (largely single-family homes) occurred in the eastern portion of the City, causing a large deficiency in moderately priced multi-family and apartment units on the east side.

To correct the imbalance between single-family and multi-family dwellings, curb the sprawl of the City on the east, and retard the accelerating growth of the City, the Council in 1972 adopted several resolutions, which collectively are called the "Petaluma Plan" (the Plan).

The Plan, on its face limited to a five-year period (1972-1977), fixes a housing development growth rate not to .exceed 500 dwelling units per year. Each dwelling unit represents approximately three people. The 500-unit figure is somewhat misleading, however, because it applies only to housing units (hereinafter referred to as "development-units") that are part of projects involving five units or more. Thus, the 500-unit figure does not reflect any housing and population growth due to construction of single-family homes or even four-unit apartment buildings not part of any larger project.

The Plan also positions a 200 foot wide "greenbelt" around the City, to serve as a boundary for urban expansion for at least five years, and with respect to the east and north sides of the City, for perhaps ten to fifteen years. One of the most innovative features of the Plan is the Residential Development Control System which provides procedures and criteria for the award of the annual 500 development-unit permits. At the heart of the allocation procedure is an intricate point system, whereby a builder accumulates points for conformity by his projects with the City's general plan and environmental design plans, for good architectural design, and for providing low and moderate income dwelling units and various recreational facilities. The Plan further directs that allocations of building permits are to be divided as evenly as feasible between the west and east sections of the City and between single-family dwellings and multiple residential units (including rental units), that the sections of the City closest to the center are to be developed first in order to cause "infilling" of vacant area, and that 8 to 12 percent of the housing units approved be for low and moderate income persons.

In a provision of the Plan, intended to maintain the close-in rural space outside and surrounding Petaluma, the City solicited Sonoma County to establish stringent subdivision and appropriate acreage parcel controls for the areas outside the urban extension line of the City and to limit severely further residential infilling.

The purpose of the Plan is much disputed in this case. According to general statements in the Plan itself, the Plan was devised to ensure that "development in the next five years, will take place in a reasonable, orderly, attractive manner, rather than in a completely haphazard and unattractive manner." The controversial 500-unit limitation on residential development-units was adopted by the City "[i]n order to protect its small town character and surrounding open space. The other features of the Plan were designed to encourage an east-west balance in development, to provide for variety in densities and building types and wide ranges in prices and rents, to ensure infilling of close-in vacant areas, and to prevent the sprawl of the city to the east and north. The Construction Industry Association of Sonoma County (the Association) argues and the district court found, however, that the Plan was primarily enacted "to limit Petaluma's demographic and market growth rate in housing and in the immigration of new residents." . . .

According to undisputed expert testimony at trial, if the Plan (limiting housing starts to approximately 6 percent of existing housing stock each year) were to be adopted by municipalities throughout the region, the impact on the housing market would be substantial. For the decade 1970 to 1980, the shortfall in needed housing in the region would be about 105,000 units (or 25 percent of the units needed). Further, the aggregate effect of a proliferation of the Plan throughout the San Francisco region would be a decline in regional housing stock quality, a loss of the mobility of current and prospective residents and a deterioration in the quality and choice of housing available to income earners with real incomes of $14,000 per year or less. If, however, the Plan were considered by itself and with respect to Petaluma only, there is no evidence to suggest that there would be a deterioration in the quality and choice of housing available there to persons in the lower and middle income brackets. Actually, the Plan increases the availability of multi-family units (owner-occupied and rental units) and low-income units which were rarely constructed in the pre-Plan days. . . . .

The City also challenges the standing of the Association and the Landowners to maintain the suit. The standing requirement raises the threshold question in every federal case whether plaintiff has made out a "case or controversy" between himself and the defendant within the meaning of Article III of the Constitution. In order to satisfy the constitutional requirement that courts decide only cases or controversies and to ensure the requisite concreteness of facts and adverseness of parties, plaintiff must show that he has a "personal stake in the outcome of the controversy," or that he has suffered "some threatened or actual injury resulting from the putatively illegal action." Further, the plaintiff must satisfy the additional court-imposed standing requirement that the "interest sought to be protected by the complainant is arguably within the zone of interests to be protected or regulated by the statute or constitutional guarantee in question." A corollary to the "zone of interest" requirement is the well-recognized general rule that "even when the plaintiff has alleged injury sufficient to meet the 'case or controversy' requirement, . . . the plaintiff generally must assert his own legal rights and interests, and cannot rest his claim to relief on the legal rights or interests of third parties." Warth v. Seldin, 422 U.S. 490, 499 (1975).

Appellees easily satisfy the "injury in fact" standing requirement. The Association alleges it has suffered in its own right monetary damages due to lost revenues. Sonoma County builders contribute dues to the Association in a sum proportionate to the amount of business the builders do in the area. Thus, in a very real sense a restriction on building in Petaluma causes economic injury to the Association.

The two Landowners also have already suffered or are threatened with a direct injury. It is their position that the Petaluma Plan operated, of itself, to adversely affect the value and marketability of their land for residential uses, and such an allegation is sufficient to show that they have a personal stake in the outcome of the controversy.

Although appellees have suffered or are threatened with direct personal injury, the "zone of interest" requirement poses a huge stumbling block to their attempt to show standing. The primary federal claim upon which this suit is based—the right to travel or migrate—is a claim asserted not on the appellees' own behalf, but on behalf of a group of unknown third parties allegedly excluded from living in Petaluma. Although individual builders, the Association, and the Landowners are admittedly adversely affected by the Petaluma Plan, their economic interests are undisputedly outside the zone of interest to be protected by any purported constitutional right to travel. Accordingly, appellees' right to travel claim "falls squarely within the prudential standing rule that normally bars litigants from asserting the rights or legal interests of others in order to obtain relief from injury to themselves." Warth v. Seldin, 422 U.S. at 509. . . . .

Although we conclude that appellees lack standing to assert the rights of third parties, they nonetheless have standing to maintain claims based on violations of rights personal to them. Accordingly, appellees have standing to challenge the Petaluma Plan on the grounds asserted in their complaint that the Plan is arbitrary and thus violative of their due process rights guaranteed by the Fourteenth Amendment and that the Plan poses an unreasonable burden on interstate commerce. . . .

Appellees claim that the Plan is arbitrary and unreasonable and, thus, violative of the due process clause of the Fourteenth Amendment. According to appellees, the Plan is nothing more than an exclusionary zoning device, designed solely to insulate Petaluma from the urban complex in which it finds itself. The Association and the Landowners reject, as falling outside the scope of any legitimate governmental interest, the City's avowed purposes in implementing the Plan—the preservation of Petaluma's small town character and the avoidance of the social and environmental problems caused by an uncontrolled growth rate.

In attacking the validity of the Plan, appellees rely heavily on the district court's finding that the express purpose and the actual effect of the Plan is to exclude substantial numbers of people who would otherwise elect to move to the City. The existence of an exclusionary purpose and effect reflects, however, only one side of the zoning regulation. Practically all zoning restrictions have as a purpose and effect the *exclusion* of some activity or type of structure or a certain density of inhabitants. And in reviewing the reasonableness of a zoning ordinance, our inquiry does not terminate with a finding that it is for an exclusionary purpose. We must determine further whether the *exclusion* bears any rational relationship to a *legitimate state interest*. If it does not, then the zoning regulation is invalid. If, on the other hand, a legitimate state interest is furthered by the zoning regulation, we must defer to the legislative act. Being neither a super legislature nor a zoning board of appeal, a federal court is without authority to weigh and reappraise the factors considered or ignored by the legislative body in passing the challenged zoning regulation.[12] The reasonableness, not the wisdom, of the Petaluma Plan is at issue in this suit.

It is well settled that zoning regulations "must find their justification in some aspect of the police power, asserted for the public welfare." Village of Euclid v. Ambler Realty Co., 272 U.S. 365, 387 (1926). The concept of the public welfare, however, is not limited to the regulation of noxious activities or dangerous structures. As the Court stated in Berman v. Parker, 348 U.S. 26, 33 (1954):

> The concept of the public welfare is broad and inclusive. The values it represents are spiritual as well as physical, aesthetic as well as monetary. It is within the power of the legislature to determine that the community should be beautiful as well as healthy, spacious as well as clean, well-balanced as well as carefully patrolled.

(citations omitted). Accord, Village of Belle Terre v. Boraas, 416 U.S. 1, 6, 9 (1974).

In determining whether the City's interest in preserving its small town character and in avoiding uncontrolled and rapid growth falls within the broad concept of "public welfare", we are considerably assisted by two recent cases. *Belle Terre* and Ybarra v. City of Town of Los Altos Hills, 503 F.2d 250 (9th Cir. 1974), each of which upheld as not unreasonable a zoning regulation much more restrictive than the Petaluma Plan, are dispositive of the due process issue in this case. . . .

Following the *Belle Terre* decision, this court in *Los Altos Hills* had an opportunity to review a zoning ordinance providing that a housing lot shall contain not less than one acre and that no lot shall be occupied by more than one primary dwelling unit. The ordinance as a practical matter prevented poor people from living in Los Altos Hills and restricted the density, and thus the population, of the town. This court, nonetheless, found that the ordinance was rationally related to a legitimate governmental interest—the preservation of the town's rural environment—and, thus, did not violate the equal protection clause of the Fourteenth Amendment.

Both the Belle Terre ordinance and the Los Altos Hills regulation had the purpose and effect of permanently restricting growth; nonetheless, the court in each case upheld the particular law before it on the ground that the regulation served a legitimate governmental interest falling within the concept of the public welfare: the preservation of quiet family neighborhoods (*Belle Terre*) and the preservation of a rural environment (*Los Altos Hills*). Even less restrictive or exclusionary than the above zoning ordinances is the Petaluma Plan which, unlike those ordinances, does not freeze the population at present or near-present levels. Further, unlike the Los Altos Hills ordinance and the various zoning regulations struck down by state courts in recent years, the Petaluma Plan does

---

12. Appellees' brief is unnecessarily oversize (125 pages) mainly because it is rife with quotations from writers on regional planning, economic regulation and sociological policies and themes. These types of considerations are more appropriate for legislative bodies than for courts.

not have the undesirable effect of walling out any particular income class nor any racial minority group. . . .

Although we assume that some persons desirous of living in Petaluma will be excluded under the housing permit limitation and that, thus, the Plan may frustrate some legitimate regional housing needs, the Plan is not arbitrary or unreasonable. We agree with appellees that unlike the situation in the past most municipalities today are neither isolated nor wholly independent from neighboring municipalities and that, consequently, unilateral land use decisions by one local entity affect the needs and resources of an entire region. It does not necessarily follow, however, that the due process rights of builders and landowners are violated merely because a local entity exercises in its own self-interest the police power lawfully delegated to it by the state. If the present system of delegated zoning power does not effectively serve the state interest in furthering the general welfare of the region or entire state, it is the state legislature's and not the federal courts' role to intervene and adjust the system. As stated *supra*, the federal court is not a super zoning board and should not be called on to mark the point at which legitimate local interests in promoting the welfare of the community are outweighed by legitimate regional interests. . . . .

We conclude therefore that under *Belle Terre* and *Los Altos Hills* the concept of the public welfare is sufficiently broad to uphold Petaluma's desire to preserve its small town character, its open spaces and low density of population, and to grow at an orderly and deliberate pace.

The district court found that housing in Petaluma and the surrounding areas is produced substantially through goods and services in interstate commerce and that curtailment of residential growth in Petaluma will cause serious dislocation to commerce. Our ruling today, however, that the Petaluma Plan represents a reasonable and legitimate exercise of the police power obviates the necessity of remanding the case for consideration of appellees' claim that the Plan unreasonably burdens interstate commerce.

It is well settled that a state regulation validly based on the police power does not impermissibly burden interstate commerce where the regulation neither discriminates against interstate commerce nor operates to disrupt its required uniformity. . . .

Consequently, since the local regulation here is rationally related to the social and environmental welfare of the community and does not discriminate against interstate commerce or operate to disrupt its required uniformity, appellees' claim that the plan unreasonably burdens commerce must fail.

Notes

1. According to William C. McGivern (then the Petaluma Director of Planning), in *Putting a Limit on Growth*, 38 Planning 263 (1972), the criteria used to review development proposals in Petaluma fell into two categories: (1) "public facilities and services"; and (2) "quality of design and contribution of public welfare and amenity." Within the first category were items (each on a zero to five-point scale) such as water, sanitary sewer, drainage systems capacity, fire protection, school population, and traffic. The second category included items such as architectural design quality for buildings and landscaping, open space, enhancement of bicycle paths and equestrian trails, and meeting the city's annual affordable housing goal of 8-12% of units.

Details on modifications of the original plan can be found in Warren Salmons, *Petaluma's Experiment in Growth Management*, Urban Land, Sept. 1986, at 7, in which the author (a subsequent planning director for the city) reported:

> In spite of Petaluma's 500-unit limit, and its later 5 percent limit, its average population growth has actually been around 2 percent, and its housing unit production has

remained around 2.5 percent. There has not been the demand for as many units as are now available through the system.

Census figures indicate that Petaluma's population grew from 43,184 in 1990, to 54,548 in 2000, and 54,496 in 2007.

2. In order to conclude that the Petaluma plan violates the right to travel, must the court find that there is an identifiable class of persons whose rights have been violated? What is the classification in Petaluma? If the right extends to intrastate travel, do all zoning ordinances violate the right to travel? If the right is limited to interstate travel, could California pass a Petaluma-type plan for the entire state? Can California delegate to every community in the state the power to pass a Petaluma-type plan? Would such a delegation violate the right to travel from state to state?

3. In 1972, the voters of Boca Raton, Florida, passed the following charter amendment:

> The total number of dwelling units within the existing boundaries of the City is hereby limited to forty thousand (40,000). No building permit shall be issued for the construction of a dwelling unit within the City which would permit the total number of dwelling units within the City to exceed forty thousand (40,000).

In accordance with this cap, densities were cut in half for multi-family zoning classifications. The changes were successfully challenged by landowners in two separate actions. See City of Boca Raton v. Boca Villas Corp., 371 So. 2d 154, 156 (Fla. Ct. App. 1979) (affirming the trial court's holding that "the cap lacks any rational relationship to a permissible objection"); City of Boca Raton v. Arvida Corp., 371 So. 2d 160 (Fla. Ct. App. 1979). Can you distinguish these holdings from the supportive decision in Sustainable Growth Initiative Comm. v. Jumpers, Ltd. Liab. Co., 128 P.3d 452 (Nev. 2007) ("In 2002, the voters of Douglas County passed the Sustainable Growth Initiative (SGI), which limited the number of new dwelling units in the county to 280 per annum.").

4. Another response to growth has been enactment of a temporary regulation to prevent further development pending further planning and the adoption of permanent controls. Judicial review has focused on legislative authorization to impose such restrictions and on the reasonableness of the regulations. Reasonable limitations as to time and area are important, and there should be a variance procedure for those suffering unnecessary hardship. As you know from Chapter Five, the Supreme Court weighed in on this subject in Tahoe-Sierra Pres. Council v. Tahoe Reg'l Planning Agency, 535 U.S. 302 (2002). Footnote 32 of that opinion contains a helpful list of state court decisions.

III. Shifting the Costs of Growth: Impact Fees

Beginning in the 1970s, America's local government officials have had to contend with the stark economic and political reality of dramatically reduced federal and state subsidies and an angry electorate that often viscerally reacts against attempts to hike local taxes. The judicial skepticism toward one solution—fixing exactions upon those seeking development permission—is best represented by the *Nollan* and *Dolan* opinions included in Chapter Five. These decisions and their lower court progeny have given pause to municipalities of all sizes and in all regions of the country that have resorted not only to exactions of real property interests, but also to impact fees, cash proffers, and other pay-as-you-go devices that are designed to make up revenue gaps.

Professor Ronald Rosenberg, in *The Changing Culture of American Land Use Regulation: Paying for Growth With Impact Fees*, 59 S.M.U. L. Rev. 177, 179-80 (2006) has explained the squeeze experienced by local government officials:

Most growing communities are under tremendous fiscal pressure to fund community services expected by residents and often required by state and federal government. Public debate in many communities often focuses upon the question of how to supply needed public improvements without increasing the general taxes on existing residents. This local funding problem has been exacerbated over the last twenty years by at least two factors: 1) significant reductions in intergovernmental funding transfers from both state and federal government and 2) the imposition of voter-mandated limitations on the ability of the locality to generate tax revenues from community-wide taxation sources.[13] In this atmosphere of fiscal conservatism, even the local funding of public services for existing residents becomes a controversial and disputed public issue. Not surprisingly, there is often little support for using scarce local tax revenues to pay for the capital needs caused by the influx of future community residents. Often the public discourse repeats the mantra that new growth "should pay its own way." . . .

We should not be surprised that municipalities would use impact fees as a direct and potentially effective method for recouping the costs (current and anticipated) of public amenities such as water, sewer, roads, education, and recreation—significant expenses that are necessitated in whole or in large part by new development. Neither should we be surprised that many critics have cautioned that impact fees, like exactions and environmental regulations, have made it much more difficult for homebuilders to build affordable housing.[5] As indicated by the case that follows, from a leading impact fee jurisdiction, the Takings Clause is not the only legal impediment that local officials must overcome before implementing an impact fee program.

ST. JOHNS COUNTY v. NORTHEAST FLORIDA BUILDERS ASS'N
583 So. 2d 635 (Fla. 1991)

GRIMES, J. . . .

In 1986, St. Johns County initiated a comprehensive study of whether to impose impact fees to finance additional infrastructure required to serve new growth and development. At the request of the St. Johns County School Board, the county included educational facilities impact fees within the scope of the study. In August of 1987, the county's consultant, Dr. James Nicholas, submitted a methodology report setting forth what action the county could take to maintain an acceptable level of service for public facilities. The report calculated the cost of educational facilities needed to provide sufficient school capacity to serve the estimated new growth and development and suggested a method of allocating that cost to each unit of new residential development. As a consequence, on October 20, 1987, the county enacted the St. Johns County Educational Facilities Impact Fee Ordinance.

The ordinance specifies that no new building permits will be issued except upon the payment of an impact fee. The fees are to be placed in a trust fund to be spent by the school board solely to

---

13. The most famous example of this kind of property tax revolt was the 1978 California statewide initiative known as Proposition 13, which served to amend the California Constitution to impose strict limits on the rate at which real property was to be taxed and upon the rate at which realty assessments were to be increased from year to year. Nordlinger v. Hahn, 505 U.S. 1, 1 (1992). The United States Supreme Court sustained this method of preferential tax assessment against a Fourteenth Amendment Equal Protection challenge finding at least two constitutionally satisfying justifications for the system in *Nordlinger v. Hahn. Id.* at 15.

5. For a provocative set of essays on the subject, see Growth Management and Affordable Housing: Do They Conflict? (Anthony Downs ed. 2004). An interesting one-state study is Jerry Anthony, The Effects of Florida's Growth Management Act on Housing Affordability, 69 J. Am. Plan. Assn. 282, 288 (2003) (indicating "that growth management reduced housing affordability in a statistically significant manner").

"acquire, construct, expand and equip the educational sites and educational capital facilities necessitated by new development." St. Johns County, Fla., Ordinance 87-60, § 10(B) (Oct. 20, 1987). Any funds not expended within six years, together with interest, will be returned to the current landowner upon application. The ordinance also provides credits to feepayers for land dedications and construction of educational facilities. The ordinance recites that it is applicable in both unincorporated and incorporated areas of the county, except that it is not effective within the boundaries of any municipality until the municipality enters into an interlocal agreement with the county to collect the impact fees.

The Northeast Florida Builders Association together with a private developer (builders) filed suit against the county and its county administrator (county) seeking a declaratory judgment that the ordinance was unconstitutional. The opposing sides each filed a motion for summary judgment. The trial court entered summary judgment for the builders, declaring the ordinance to be unconstitutional on a variety of grounds. In a split decision, the district court of appeal affirmed, holding that the ordinance violated the constitutional mandate for a uniform system of free public schools.

This Court upheld the imposition of impact fees to pay for the expansion of water and sewer facilities in Contractors & Builders Association v. City of Dunedin, 329 So. 2d 314 (Fla. 1976). We stated:

> Raising expansion capital by setting connection charges, which do not exceed a pro rata share of reasonably anticipated costs of expansion, is permissible where expansion is reasonably required, if use of the money collected is limited to meeting the costs of expansion.

Id. at 320. In essence, we approved the imposition of impact fees that meet the requirements of the dual rational nexus test adopted by other courts in evaluating impact fees. See Juergensmeyer & Blake, Impact Fees: An Answer to Local Governments' Capital Funding Dilemma, 9 Fla. St. U.L. Rev. 415 (1981). This test was explained in Hollywood, Inc. v. Broward County, 431 So. 2d 606, 611-12 (Fla. 4th DCA), review denied, 440 So. 2d 352 (Fla. 1983), as follows:

> In order to satisfy these requirements, the local government must demonstrate a reasonable connection, or rational nexus, between the need for additional capital facilities and the growth in population generated by the subdivision. In addition, the government must show a reasonable connection, or rational nexus, between the expenditures of the funds collected and the benefits accruing to the subdivision. In order to satisfy this latter requirement, the ordinance must specifically earmark the funds collected for use in acquiring capital facilities to benefit the new residents.

The use of impact fees has become an accepted method of paying for public improvements that must be constructed to serve new growth. See Home Builders & Contractors Ass'n v. Board of County Comm'rs, 446 So. 2d 140 (Fla. 4th DCA 1983) (road impact fees upheld), review denied, 451 So. 2d 848 (Fla.), appeal dismissed, 469 U.S. 976 (1984); Hollywood, Inc. v. Broward County, 431 So. 2d at 606 (park impact fees upheld). However, the propriety of imposing impact fees to finance new schools is an issue of first impression in Florida.

Turning to the first prong of the dual rational nexus test, we must decide whether St. Johns County demonstrated that there is a reasonable connection between the need for additional schools and the growth in population that will accompany new development. In the ordinance, the county commissioners made a legislative finding that the county "must expand its educational facilities in order to maintain current levels of service if new development is to be accommodated without decreasing current levels of service." St. Johns County, Fla., Ordinance 87-60, § 1(C) (Oct. 20, 1987). No one quarrels with this proposition. However, an impact fee to be used to fund new schools is different from one required to build water and sewer facilities or even roads. Many of the new residents who will bear the burden of the fee will not have children who will benefit from the new schools. Thus, Dr. Nicholas determined that on average there are 0.44 public school children per single-family home in St. Johns County. Applying the singlefamily home ratio to a per-student cost calculation, he concluded that it required $2,899 per new single-family home to build the school space anticipated to be needed to serve the children who would live in the new homes. Finding that existing taxes and revenue sources would produce $2,451 per single-family home, Dr. Nicholas concluded that for each new single-family home there was an average net cost of $448 for building new schools that would not be covered by existing revenue mechanisms. He made similar calculations based upon his determination of the number of public school children residing in multiple family units of construction.

The builders argue that because many of the new residences will have no impact on the public school system, the impact fee is nothing more than a tax insofar as those residences are concerned. We reject this contention as too simplistic. The same argument could be made with respect to many other facilities that governmental entities are expected to provide. Not all of the new residents will use the parks or call for fire protection, yet the county will have to provide additional facilities so as to be in a position to serve each dwelling unit. During the useful life of the new dwelling units, school-age children will come and go. It may be that some of the units will never house children. However, the county has determined that for every one hundred units that are built, forty-four new students will require an education at a public school. The St. Johns County impact fee is designed to provide the capacity to serve the educational needs of all one hundred dwelling units. We conclude that the ordinance meets the first prong of the rational nexus test.

The question of whether the ordinance meets the requirements of the second prong of the test is more troublesome. As indicated, we see no requirement that every new unit of development benefit from the impact fee in the sense that there must be a child residing in that unit who will attend public school. It is enough that new public schools are available to serve that unit of development. Thus, if this were a countywide impact fee designed to fund construction of new schools as needed throughout the county, we could easily conclude that the second prong of the test had been met.

However, the St. Johns County impact fee is not effective within the boundaries of a municipality unless the municipality enters into an interlocal agreement with the county to collect the fee. The ordinance provides that the funds shall be spent solely for school construction necessitated by new development. However, there is nothing to keep impact fees from being spent to build schools to accommodate new development within a municipality that has not entered into the interlocal agreement. Therefore, as in the ordinance first considered in *Contractors & Builders Association v. City of Dunedin*, there is no restriction on the use of the funds to ensure that they will be spent to benefit those who have paid the fees.[4] As a consequence, we hold that no impact fee may be collected under the ordinance until such time as substantially all of the population of St. Johns County is subject to the ordinance. . . .

We quash the decision below and uphold the validity of the ordinance upon the severance of section 7(B) therefrom. However, no impact fee may be collected under the ordinance until the second prong of the dual rational nexus test has been met.

It is so ordered.

---

4. In Home Builders & Contractors Association v. Board of County Commissioners, 446 So. 2d 140 (Fla. 4th DCA 1983), an impact fee to build roads imposed by the county was upheld over the objection that many of the municipalities in the county had declined to join in the collection of the fees. However, because the impact fees in that case were designed to be spent only on roads serving the developments that paid the fees, we assume that the nonparticipating municipalities did not benefit from the funds that were collected.

Notes

1. In Volusia County v. Aberdeen at Ormond Beach, 760 So. 2d 126, 135-36 (Fla. 2000), a mobile home park providing housing to persons who were at least 55 years old successfully challenged the constitutionality of public school impact fees that the county assessed on new homes in the park. The court, quoting *St. Johns County*, found that the county flunked the "dual nexus" test:

> [O]ur repeated citations to the special-benefit standard and our interpretation of *St. Johns County* demonstrate that we did not abandon the subdivision-based standard. Indeed, imposing a countywide standard would eviscerate the substantial nexus requirement. This nexus is significant because of the distinction between taxes and fees. As this Court noted in *Collier County*, "There is no requirement that taxes provide any specific benefit to the property; instead, they may be levied throughout the particular taxing unit for the general benefit of residents and property." *Collier County* [v. State], 733 So. 2d [1012,] at 1016 [(Fl. 1999)] (quoting *City of Boca Raton v. State*, 595 So. 2d 25, 29 (Fla. 1992)). Fees, by contrast, must confer a special benefit on feepayers "in a manner not shared by those not paying the fee." 733 So. 2d at 1019. We likewise noted in State v. City of Port Orange, 650 So. 2d 1, 3 (Fla. 1994), that "the power of a municipality to tax should not be broadened by semantics which would be the effect of labeling what the City is here collecting a fee rather than a tax." Thus, a liberal reading of the dual rational nexus test would obliterate the distinction between an unconstitutional tax and a valid fee.

> Volusia County also contends that St. Johns County's refusal to exempt households with no minor children from paying public school impact fees demonstrates that a countywide standard is required. This contention, however, is less persuasive when considered in context. The rationale underlying this Court's statement was that "during the useful life of the new dwelling units, school-age children will come and go." *St. Johns County*, 583 So. 2d at 638. We were concerned with exempting some units because of the potential in the future that students would be residing in the developments. We did, however, distinguish restricted housing, noting that "we would not find objectionable a provision that exempted from the payment of an impact fee permits to build adult facilities in which, because of land use restrictions, minors could not reside." *Id.* at 640 n.6. This statement negates the contention that a countywide standard must be utilized. Thus, the logical conclusion is that where there is no potential for student-generating housing to exist within the subdivision, the subdivision may be exempt from paying public school impact fees. In short, the foregoing analysis demonstrates that the specific-need/special-benefit standard is a more favorable construction of the dual rational nexus test. . . .

> Volusia County is also unable to satisfy the "benefits" prong of the dual rational nexus test. Because no children can live at Aberdeen, impact fees collected at Aberdeen will not be spent for Aberdeen's benefit, but for the benefit of children living in other developments. Volusia County contends that Aberdeen benefits from the construction of new schools because they also serve as emergency shelters and sites for adult education classes. However, the connection between the expenditure of impact fee funds for the construction of new schools and the tangential benefit of having places of refuge in natural disasters is too attenuated to demonstrate a substantial nexus. Put another way, the schools are built primarily for the educational benefit of school-age children and,

to the extent that Aberdeen derives any incidental benefit from their construction, it is insufficient to satisfy the dual rational nexus test.

In sum, Aberdeen neither contributes to the need for additional schools nor benefits from their construction. Accordingly, the imposition of impact fees as applied to Aberdeen does not satisfy the dual rational nexus test.

2. Compare the "dual nexus" test employed by Florida courts in impact fee cases to the approach taken by the U. S. Supreme Court in adjudging the validity of exactions of real property interests in exchange for development permission in Dolan v. City of Tigard, 512 U.S. 374 (1994) (included in Chapter Six). Local governments in the 21st century have many potential tools at their disposal in order to discourage unwanted development (such as oversized McMansions) or to encourage desirable development (such as affordable housing). Consider whether each of the following tools justifies significant, moderate, or highly deferential judicial oversight: Euclidean zoning; local environmental controls; condemnation (eminent domain); local taxes; exactions of real property interests; impact fees; timed growth measures; and building moratoria.

IV.   Drawing the Line With Urban Growth Boundaries

Planners and other visionaries dating back at least as far as the biblical Levite cities discussed in Chapter One have long pondered the advantages of surrounding urban settlements with permanent greenbelts of agricultural land or other low-intensity uses. Perhaps the most famous and influential advocate was Ebenezer Howard, the author of *Garden Cities of To-Morrow* (1902).[6] American variations have included Radburn, New Jersey (a planned community located within Fair Lawn, New Jersey, and known as the "Town for the Motor Age" when it was founded in 1929), and Greenbelt, Maryland (one of three New Deal-era new towns).[7] In decades following World War II, a few ambitious developers experimented with the idea of creating new towns outside central cities, the most prominent examples being Reston, Virginia, Park Fores, Illinois, and James Rouse's Columbia, Maryland.

In 1968, President Lyndon Baines Johnson signed the New Communities Act of 1968, following years of give and take with members of Congress and powerful interest groups such as homebuilders, mortgage bankers, and big-city mayors. The program directed loan guarantees and grants to 13 communities, including Soul City, North Carolina, proposed by civil rights leader Floyd McKissick, and Flower Mound, Texas, originally backed by Ray Nasher (the Dallas-based real estate developer and renowned art collector) and Edward Marcus (from the Neiman-Marcus department store chain). Ultimately, only one community—The Woodlands, outside of Houston—could be deemed a success. Professor Roger Biles, in *New Towns for the Great Society: A Case Study in Politics and Planning*, 13 Planning Perspectives 113, 127-28 (1998), has proffered this explanation for the failure of the program:

> Like many other Great Society programmes that foundered in the less congenial environment of the Nixon era, the new towns suffered when the Republican White House suffocated the programme in bureaucracy and refused to provide the financial support authorized by Congress—a precarious situation exacerbated by a stagnating national economy that undermined the real estate market and made any speculative building

---

6. For illustrations of Howard's "Three Magnets" (town, country, and town-country) and the "Garden-City," see http://www.library.cornell.edu/Reps/DOCS/howard.htm.

7. For links between New Urbanist communities and their early 20th-century precursors, see Chang-Moo Lee & Kun Hyuck Ahn, *Is Kentlands Better Than Radburn: The American Garden City and New Urbanist Paradigms*, 69 J. Am. Plan. Ass'n 50 (2003).

ventures hazardous. Simply put, the new towns perished in floods of red tape and red ink.

Not surprisingly, during the post-Great Society milieu in which government was viewed more as a problem than a solution to society's ills, government financial support for new communities has been a political non-starter.

Today, the greenbelt idea (or urban growth boundary (UGB)) is the major legacy of these experimental programs. One method for establishing a greenbelt is to purchase (or accept from donors) fee and less-than-fee interests from owners in the target area. One of the most well-known examples can be found in Boulder, Colorado. In 1986, Boulder voters passed a city charter provision mandating the acquisition of open space for the following purposes:

(a) Preservation or restoration of natural areas characterized by or including terrain, geologic formations, flora, or fauna that are unusual, spectacular, historically important, scientifically valuable, or unique, or that represent outstanding or rare examples of native species;

(b) Preservation of water resources in their natural or traditional state, scenic areas or vistas, wildlife habitats, or fragile ecosystems;

(c) Preservation of land for passive recreational use, such as hiking, photography or nature studies, and, if specifically designated, bicycling, horseback riding, or fishing;

(d) Preservation of agricultural uses and land suitable for agricultural production;

(e) Utilization of land for shaping the development of the city, limiting urban sprawl, and disciplining growth;

(f) Utilization of non-urban land for spatial definition of urban areas;

(g) Utilization of land to prevent encroachment on floodplains; and

(h) Preservation of land for its aesthetic or passive recreational value and its contribution to the quality of life of the community.[8]

The city's website reports that more than 45,000 acres in and around Boulder are publicly owned and managed.[9]

A growing number of American states and localities seeking to manage growth have turned to a modern variation on this theme—the UGB effected through land use controls. As the following case from Oregon[10] (the leading UGB state) indicates, while it is a difficult task to draw the original line, special challenges arise when officials decide that demographic, social, or other factors require a redrawing. If, on the one hand, the line is erased and redrawn too frequently, then owners of agricultural and underdeveloped parcels will continue to believe that land speculators with enough skill in persuading land use regulators will one day offer them a windfall for their acreage, thus replicating one of the evils the UGB was designed to eliminate.

---

8. Authors' note: Charter of the City of Boulder, Colorado, art. XII, §176.

9. The website also contains a revealing set of animated maps tracing the history of open space acquisition: http://www. ci.boulder.co.us/images/departments/openspace/images_gis/osmp-4.gif.

10. For an introduction to Oregon's UGB program, with links to relevant maps of metropolitan Portland, see http://www. metro-region.org/index.cfm/go/by.web/id/277.

HILDENBRAND v. CITY OF ADAIR VILLAGE
217 Or. App. 623, 177 P.3d 40 (Ct. App. 2008)

SERCOMBE, J.

Petitioners seek judicial review of an opinion and order of the Land Use Board of Appeals (board) that remands city and county ordinances adopted to expand an urban growth boundary. Petitioners claim that the board erred in not requiring additional justification from the local governments for the urban growth boundary expansion. . . .

Respondent JT Smith, Inc., applied to the City of Adair Village and Benton County for comprehensive plan amendments to expand the city's urban growth boundary and to enact plan designations and zoning changes to accommodate the development of high-density residential housing and a school athletic field. The proposed urban growth boundary expansion area is agricultural land that is located south of the city. The city and county approved the application, expanding the urban growth boundary by 142 acres, changing the plan designation of the property from agricultural to high-density residential and open space designations, and amending the zoning for the property from an exclusive farm use zone to zoning districts for urban residential and open space uses. Petitioners appealed the approval ordinances to the board, which reviewed them in a consolidated proceeding. The ordinances included findings adopted to show compliance with state statutes and administrative rules regulating urban growth boundary changes.

Before the board, petitioners argued that the approval findings were insufficient to justify the urban growth boundary amendment in several respects, three of which are relevant to our review. First, petitioners contend that the local governments erred by "failing to demonstrate the need for housing, recreational, and schools lands, as required by Goal 14, prior to expansion of an urban growth boundary." In particular, petitioners asserted that the findings failed to comply with the requirements of Goal 14 to limit urban growth boundary expansions if there is underdeveloped or vacant land already inside the boundary that can be developed for the desired land uses.[1] Second, petitioners contended that the city and county added too much land to the expansion based on incorrect assumptions about the expected growth in city population and by understating the density of the residential development allowed in the expansion area. Third, petitioners complained about the location of the expansion area, contending that ORS 197.298 foreclosed including agricultural land within the boundary because suitable nonagricultural land was available as an alternative.

The board found that the city's and county's findings improperly discounted the availability of vacant or underdeveloped land for the desired land uses within the existing boundary, contrary to Goal 14 and its implementing rules, and remanded the ordinances to the local governments for further proceedings. But the board rejected petitioners' remaining claims of error. Petitioners seek review of the board's rulings approving the local governments' findings as to the quantity of land to be added to the urban growth boundary area and the location of the expansion.

We review the board's order to determine whether it is "unlawful in substance or procedure." ORS 197.850(9)(a). Petitioners' first assignment of error on review is that the board erred in approving the local governments' calculation of the quantity of land to be added by an urban growth

---

1. Statewide planning goals, adopted by the Land Conservation and Development Commission under ORS 197.040(2), apply to the adoption or amendment of city or county land use comprehensive plans, including an amendment to adopt or alter an urban growth boundary. ORS 197.175(2)(a) (obligation to adopt and amend comprehensive plans "in compliance with goals approved by the commission"). Goal 14 (Urbanization), OAR 660-015-0000(14), requires that the establishment or change of an urban growth boundary be based on a demonstrated need for additional land. Goal 14 further provides that "[p]rior to expanding an urban growth boundary, local governments shall demonstrate that needs cannot reasonably be accommodated on land already inside the urban growth boundary."

boundary change. The city and county approved a 142-acre expansion to the boundary, designating 118 acres for high-density residential uses and 24 acres for open space uses. The adopted findings forecast a population increase of 1,909 persons during the relevant planning period, a likely household size of 2.75 persons, and a resulting need for 694 additional housing units. The city and county assumed that the average lot size for each housing unit would be 6,000 square feet and, based on that assumption, projected a need to expand the urban growth boundary by 118 acres to accommodate those housing and auxiliary uses. The 694 additional housing units will nearly triple the housing stock in the city from the number of existing dwelling units.

Before the board, petitioners challenged the evidentiary foundation of the finding that land designated and zoned for high-density residential uses would develop at a density of 6,000 square foot lots. Petitioners asserted:

> "[B]ecause the land proposed to be added to the UGB would be designated for high-density residential development, no evidence supports an 'average lot size' of 6000 square feet. Minimum lot sizes in the R-3 zone range from 1200 square feet for row houses up to 7600 square feet for duplexes (which would provide two housing units); single family homes may be constructed on lots between a minimum of 3800 square feet and a *maximum* of 6000 square feet." (Emphasis in original.)

The board rejected petitioners' challenge to the adopted findings on the likely lot size:

> "[Respondent] answers that the assumptions used by the city and county are based on policies set forth in the City of Adair Village Comprehensive Plan (Plan). * * * Section 9.800 of the Plan expresses a policy of providing 'new minimum lot sizes that result in an overall average lot size of 6,000 square feet.' Those Plan policies were adopted by the city in February, 2006. It is appropriate for the city and county to rely on assumptions included in the city's acknowledged comprehensive plan policies in computing the acreage for the proposed UGB expansion. See 1000 Friends of Oregon v. City of Dundee, 203 Ore. App. 207, 216, 124 P.3d 1249 (2005) (an acknowledged comprehensive plan and information integrated into that plan must serve as the basis for land use decisions)."

On review, petitioners complain that the board "seems to have missed the petitioners' point." Petitioners argue that the density of residential development in the expansion area will be controlled by the likely R-3 high-density residential zoning, which sets a maximum 6,000 square foot lot allowance, and not a plan policy espousing a goal of an average lot size for the entire city. In fact, because existing lots in the city are larger than 6,000 square feet, petitioners suggest that new lots in the city must be smaller in order to comply with the plan requirement of an average citywide lot size of 6,000 square feet. Thus, petitioners conclude that the board order is "unlawful in substance" because it affirmed a critical finding for the calculation of the size of the boundary change that was not supported by substantial evidence in the local government record. . . .

We conclude that the board improperly relied on a plan policy about citywide average lot sizes to justify the likely lot size that would be developed in a smaller part of the city. Plan policies or inventories can serve to justify subsequent and related plan amendments because comprehensive plans must be internally consistent under Goal 2.[2] Thus, in D.S. Parklane Development, Inc. v. Metro, 165 Ore. App. 1, 994 P.2d 1205 (2000), we determined that, in amending its adopted plan pertaining to its urban growth boundary, Metro erred in relying on a draft analysis instead

---

2. Goal 2 (Land Use Planning), OAR 660-015-0000(2), requires the incorporation of information into a comprehensive plan that is used to make the policy choices in the plan. That "required information shall be contained in the plan document or in supporting documents." The plans, together with their supporting documents, "shall be the basis for specific implementation measures."

of a study incorporated into the plan on the same topic. Respondent here contends that the urban growth boundary plan amendment in this case must be similarly reconciled to the plan policy on average lot sizes.

Respondent quotes the plan policy in its brief before the board as providing that, "[i]n order to provide for the efficient utilization of residential lands[,] the City will provide for new minimum lot sizes that result in an overall average lot size of 6,000 square feet." The adopted findings reference that policy in the discussion of the need to counterbalance the historical low-density residential development of the city by adding high-density residential land to the urban growth boundary:

> "To rectify this imbalance in densities and type the City Council amended its Development Code in 2006 after three years of review to allow for higher densities, multiple family units, and mixed use developments. The new Development Code language provides for a new R-3 zone with lots as small as 1,200 square feet. The Council also adopted new comprehensive plan policies providing for an average lot size of 6,000 square feet. These new zones will provide for a broader mix of housing type, style and cost based on the smaller lots size and allowances for multi-family housing. To assure that development occurs at densities sufficient to accommodate the housing needs without another expansion the City's Code also provides for maximum lot size in the R-3 zone."

The city council did not expressly interpret the meaning of the plan policy in the adopted findings. There is no occasion for board deference to any local government interpretation of its plan under ORS 197.829(1). That statute requires the board to defer to a local government plan interpretation unless the interpretation is inconsistent with the express language, purpose, or underlying policy of the plan provision. To whatever extent the city council implicitly interpreted the policy in the adopted findings, that interpretation is "inadequate for review" under ORS 197.829(2) and does not aid the board's conclusion.

In the absence of any city council interpretation of its plan policy to assist the board, we determine its meaning from the text and context of the policy. By its plain terms and in this context, the average lot size policy directs the content of future zoning legislation (to "provide for new minimum lot sizes"). At the very most, the policy regulates the "overall lot size" within the city. On its face, however, it does not prescribe a 6,000 square foot lot density for any particular development or part of the city.

Assuming that the plan policy on "new minimum lot sizes that will result in an overall average lot size of 6,000 square feet" applies to plan amendments (and not just to zoning legislation on minimum lot sizes), the policy arguably requires that development allowed by an urban growth boundary amendment not result in an average city lot size that is less compliant with the 6,000 square foot standard. The policy does not dictate that the average size of the lots in all new development must be 6,000 square feet. It requires that lot sizes in new development be arrayed in a way that brings the citywide average lot size closer to the 6,000 square foot standard. If the rest of the city had developed with 10,000 square foot lots, then lots smaller than 6,000 square feet would need to be added to reach an average lot size of 6,000 square feet. But that calculation was not made by the city and county. The adopted findings do not determine what residential density will be required in the expansion area in order to meet the purported plan standard. The plan policy provides no guidance for any assumed residential density without that context.

Instead, Goal 14 requires that:

> "Establishment and change of urban growth boundaries shall be based on the following:
>
> "(1) Demonstrated need to accommodate long range urban population, consistent with a 20-year population forecast with affected local governments; and

"(2) Demonstrated need for housing, employment opportunities, livability or uses such as public facilities, streets and roads, schools, parks or open space, or any combination of the need categories in this subsection (2)."

Goal 14 requires that the quantity of land added to an urban growth boundary be justified by a calculated or "demonstrated" need to add land for housing or other urban uses. How much land is needed to site 694 dwelling units is a function of how densely the land is developed, which depends, in part, on the residential density permitted by the plan designation and likely zoning. The city plans to use the urbanizing area for high-density residential uses and proposes to zone it accordingly. The necessary justification under Goal 14 of the quantity of land to be added to the urban growth boundary requires a projection of likely development under the densities allowed by the city's high-density residential zoning, the R-3 zoning district, rather than the local governments' assumption that all development will occur under the lowest density permitted by that zoning. That unsupported assumption does not constitute substantial evidence of a "demonstrated need" under Goal 14, and the board's conclusion to the contrary is unlawful in substance.

Petitioners' second assignment of error challenges the board's rulings on their assertion that the local governments insufficiently justified the location of the urban growth boundary expansion. The expansion area is land south of the city that is planned and zoned for agricultural uses. The city chose not to expand the boundary to the west to include the "Tampico Road" exception area, an area that is not designated for agricultural uses. Petitioners argued to the board that the city and county erred in adding agricultural lands to the boundary when nonagricultural land was available to be added, because ORS 197.298 expresses a preference for adding nonagricultural land.

ORS 197.298(1) sets out policies on the priority of land to be added to an urban growth boundary that apply "[i]n addition to any requirements established by rule addressing urbanization." The first priority is land designated as urban reserve land; the second priority is "an exception area," *i.e.*, land determined to be unsuitable for agricultural or forestry uses under criteria set out in Goal 2 and ORS 197.732, or "nonresource land"; the third priority is land designated as marginal land under ORS 197.247; and, if the land under the preceding priorities is "inadequate to accommodate the amount of land needed," the fourth priority is "land designated in an acknowledged comprehensive plan for agricultural or forestry, or both." ORS 197.298(1).

ORS 197.298(3) relaxes the prioritization requirements in certain circumstances. It provides:

"Land of lower priority under subsection (1) of this section may be included in an urban growth boundary if land of higher priority is found to be inadequate to accommodate the amount of land estimated in subsection (1) of this section for one or more of the following reasons:

"(a) Specific types of identified land needs cannot be reasonably accommodated on higher priority lands;

"(b) Future urban services could not reasonably be provided to the higher priority lands due to topographical or other physical constraints; or

"(c) Maximum efficiency of land uses within a proposed urban growth boundary requires inclusion of lower priority lands in order to include or to provide services to higher priority lands."

The rationale adopted by the city and county for expanding the urban growth boundary to include fourth priority lands under ORS 197.298(1) was that extension of sewer and water services to the exception area would be cost prohibitive because of the need for expensive borings under the state highway; a more efficient transportation system could be engineered on land east of the highway; and the exception area was not configured to accommodate a stated plan objective of "compact community development" and plan growth management policies favoring a "'village center" and a transportation system disassociated from the highway. After summarizing the adopted findings, the board determined:

> "ORS 197.298(3) allows the city to include resource land within the [Urban Growth Boundary (UGB)] over existing exception areas if urban services cannot reasonably be provided due to physical constraints. Highway 99W physically separates the existing UGB from the Tampico Road exception area, and the evidence in the record indicates that due to the high cost of extending urban services across the highway, those services cannot be reasonably provided to that area. Coupled with the findings that inclusion of the Tampico Road exception area within the UGB would be contrary to adopted Plan policies, we think the findings are sufficient under ORS 197.298(3) to justify the inclusion of lower-priority resource land in the UGB rather than the higher priority Tampico Road exception area."

On review, petitioners categorically contend that the board erred in allowing the addition of any lower-priority land to the urban growth area without proof that the quantity of all types of higher-priority lands was inadequate. That contention is inconsistent with the plain language of ORS 197.298(3) that sets out qualitative considerations for including lower-priority land. We rejected the same contention in City of West Linn v. LCDC, 201 Ore. App. 419, 119 P.3d 285 (2005). In that case, we concluded that whether there is "inadequate" land to serve a need depends on not only the constraints identified by ORS 197.298(3), but also the criteria for locating an urban growth boundary expansion under Goal 14. The "statutory reference to 'inadequate' land addresses suitability, not just quantity, of higher priority land." 201 Ore. App. at 440. Thus, the ranking of land under ORS 197.298(1) is a function of its prior classification as urban reserve land, exception land, marginal land, or resource land, as well as the application of the qualitative factors under Goal 14 and ORS 197.298(3).

Petitioners argue that the local governments' determinations that the Tampico Road area is inadequate to meet city needs were insufficient under ORS 197.298(3) . . . .

Petitioners' . . . contention is that the findings on plan policies about community form, growth management, and transportation needs are irrelevant to the urban growth boundary expansion decision under ORS 197.298(3), and that the local governments and the board erred in relying on that part of the justification. Petitioners' contention is incorrect. The findings are relevant to the boundary location factors in Goal 14. Goal 14 requires that the location of an urban growth boundary change be determined by "evaluating alternative boundary locations consistent with ORS 197.298" and with consideration of the following factors:

"(1) Efficient accommodation of identified land needs;

"(2) Orderly and economic provision of public facilities and services;

"(3) Comparative environmental, energy, economic and social consequences; and

"(4) Compatibility of the proposed urban uses with nearby agricultural and forest activities occurring on farm and forest land outside the UGB."

Those factors allow comparison of needed transportation improvements in the alternative expnsion areas as part of the consideration of the "[o]rderly and economic provision of public facilities and services." It is likewise proper to consider the effects of an expansion on compact growth and community form in assessing the "[c]omparative * * * social consequences" of the alternative expansion areas.

Furthermore, we determined in *City of West Linn* that a higher priority of land under ORS 197.298(1) may be "inadequate" because of "the locational considerations that must be taken into account under Goal 14." 201 Ore. App. at 440.[3] For the foregoing reasons, the board did not err in upholding an urban growth boundary expansion decision justified on the qualitative factors in ORS 197.298(3), as well as those in Goal 14.

Thus, the order under review is reversed and remanded as "unlawful in substance" because the board failed to require a justification of the quantity of land needed for high-density residential use that is necessary for the urban growth boundary change to pass muster under Goal 14. The board did not err in upholding a justification of the location of the boundary change based on both ORS 197.298 and Goal 14.

Reversed and remanded.

Notes

1. In Washington, another western state with a strong state growth management statute, certain counties are required to designate "urban growth area or areas within which urban growth shall be encouraged and outside of which growth can occur only if it is not urban in nature." Wash. Rev. Code §36.70A.110 also provides:

> (2) Based upon the growth management population projection made for the county by the office of financial management, the county and each city within the county shall include areas and densities sufficient to permit the urban growth that is projected to occur in the county or city for the succeeding twenty-year period, except for those urban growth areas contained totally within a national historical reserve. . . .

> (3) Urban growth should be located first in areas already characterized by urban growth that have adequate existing public facility and service capacities to serve such development, second in areas already characterized by urban growth that will be served adequately by a combination of both existing public facilities and services and any additional needed public facilities and services that are provided by either public or private sources, and third in the remaining portions of the urban growth areas. . . .

In Thurston County v. Western Wash. Growth Mgmt. Hearings Bd., 164 Wash. 2d 329, 336, 353, 190 P.3d 38 (2008), the state supreme court provided this summary of the statutory scheme:

> The legislature enacted the GMA [Growth Management Act] in 1990 to address concerns related to "uncoordinated and unplanned growth" in the State and "a lack of common goals expressing the public's interest in the conservation and the wise use of our lands." RCW 36.70A.010. The GMA provides a "framework" of goals and requirements to guide local governments who have "the ultimate burden and responsibility for planning." RCW 36.70A.3201. Great deference is accorded to a local government's decisions that are "consistent with the requirements and goals" of the GMA. *Id.* The GMA's

---

3. After we decided City of West Linn, Goal 14 was amended to explicitly state that the location of an urban growth boundary expansion is to be determined by applying both the Goal 14 locational factors and ORS 197.298 ("location of * * * changes to the boundary shall be determined by evaluating alternative boundary locations consistent with ORS 197.298 and with consideration of" the Goal 14 factors). The Land Conservation and Development Commission adopted OAR 660-024-0060 on October 5, 2006. The effective date of that rule is after the date of the local government decision under review here. However, the rule recognizes the coincident application of the Goal 14 locational factors and ORS 197.298(1) in evaluating urban growth boundary changes.

goals include encouraging development in urban areas and reducing rural sprawl. RCW 36.70A.020(1), (2).

The GMA requires counties to develop a "'comprehensive plan,'" which sets out the "generalized coordinated land use policy statement" of the county's governing body. Former RCW 36.70A.030(4) (1997). Among other things, the comprehensive plan must designate a UGA "within which urban growth shall be encouraged and outside of which growth can occur only if it is not urban in nature." RCW 36.70A.110(1). The plan also must include a rural element that provides for a variety of rural densities. The GMA recognizes regional differences and allows counties to consider local circumstances when designating rural densities so long as the local government creates a written record explaining how the rural element harmonizes the GMA requirements and goals.

One of the issues decided by the court in *Thurston County* was "[w]hether a UGA violates RCW 36.70A.110 when the supply of developable residential land in the UGA exceeds the projected demand for such land in 25 years by 38 percent."

Once a petitioner challenges the size of a county's UGA, the county may explain whether the difference between the supply and demand is due to a land market supply factor or other circumstances. If the county asserts a land market supply factor was used in designating the UGA boundaries, the petitioner may argue the factor employed was clearly erroneous and unreasonable based on the facts in the record. No brightline rule regarding the reasonableness of a land market supply factor may be used by the GMHBs [growth management hearing boards]. Depending on local circumstances, 15 percent may be reasonable in one county, while 40 percent may be reasonable in another. A GMHB may not reject a UGA simply because the land market supply factor used is greater than 25 percent, nor may they subject higher percentages to greater scrutiny. Instead, in determining whether a market supply factor is reasonable, a board must recognize counties have great discretion in making choices about accommodating growth and the land market supply factor may be based on local circumstances. RCW 36.70A.110(2). A board shall not find a county's use of a land market supply factor unreasonable unless it is shown to be clearly erroneous in light of the entire record. RCW 36.70A.320(2).

See also Tenn. Code Ann. §6-58-106(a)(1): "The urban growth boundaries of a municipality shall: (A) Identify territory that is reasonably compact yet sufficiently large to accommodate residential and nonresidential growth projected to occur during the next twenty (20) years . . . ."

2. Not all states have been enthusiastic about urban growth boundaries and other modern growth management tools. In November, 1998, Arizona voters adopted the following restrictions (codified in Ariz .Rev .Stat. §9-461.13):

A. There shall not be a state mandate that a city, charter city, town or county:

1. Adopt by ordinance or otherwise any "growth management" plan, however denominated, containing any provisions relating to such issues as mandatory development fees, mandatory air and water quality controls and street and highway environmental impacts, and requiring that, before adoption, the growth management plan, amendments and exceptions be automatically referred to the voters for approval.

2. Establish or recognize, formally or informally, urban growth boundaries, however denominated, that effectively prevent new urban development and extension of public services outside those boundaries. . . .

V. Moratoria

In his decidedly pro-planning opinion for the majority in Tahoe-Sierra Pres. Council v. Tahoe Reg'l Planning Agency, 535 U.S. 302, 337-38 (2002) (included in Chapter Five), Justice John Paul Stevens noted that "the consensus in the planning community appears to be that moratoria, or 'interim development controls' as they are often called, are an essential tool of successful development." By its very nature, careful planning requires pauses between idea and reality, but courts are often called upon to distinguish good-faith, reasonable moratoria from confiscatory slow-downs motivated by the desire to frustrate some or even all new land development. Today, the suburban landscape in many states is marked by the remnants of "premature" subdivisions. Some of these unfinished neighborhoods date back to the boom times of the first half of the 20th century; others are stark symbols of the 21st century's first recession, an economic downturn that can be traced directly to a real estate bubble that was perilously overinflated by an unregulated home finance market.

Local governments have successfully employed temporary moratoria to ensure that development does not outpace the availability of public amenities; to allow the community to catch its breath after unanticipated growth spurts; and to take the necessary time to develop strategies in response to new information regarding critical habitats for protected species, floodplain locations, beach erosion, and other threats to natural resources. Indeed, we can anticipate even more reliance on the moratorium tool as local and state governments, particularly but not only in coastal areas, develop strategies for confronting the impacts of global warming. As *Tahoe-Sierra* and the following decision illustrate, judges are often put in the difficult position of informing landowners that the public good (such as the preservation of natural resources and the protection of health and safety from natural and artificial harms) often supersedes the desire to maximize an investment in real estate.

WILD RICE RIVER ESTATES, INC. v. CITY OF FARGO
705 N.W.2d 850 (N.D. 2005)

VandeWalle, Chief Justice. . . .

Wild Rice is the owner and developer of a rural residential subdivision along the banks of the Wild Rice River located about three miles south of Fargo. Wild Rice was owned by Anton Rutten, who acquired the farmland in 1947. Rutten anticipated that the property would one day become a part of Fargo, and he hoped to develop a subdivision on the property when the city grew. The subdivision was platted in 1993 with 38 lots, and 16 of those lots are located on an oxbow of the river. Wild Rice was incorporated in 1994 for the purpose of developing the subdivision. Because of county and township regulations, Wild Rice was required to construct at its expense a connection to the local sanitary sewer system operated by Southeast Cass Water Resource District. Fargo and Wild Rice entered into a 10-year agreement for the city to treat the sewage collected from the development, and Wild Rice installed sewer and water services for 14 of the lots. At the time of the platting, the required flood elevation for lots in Wild Rice was one foot above base floor elevation. Wild Rice sold the first lot in the development in 1994 for $24,000 and Rutten purchased a lot in 1996 or 1997. In the meantime, Wild Rice invested approximately $500,000 to develop and promote the subdivision.

The Red River Valley, including the Wild Rice River, has a long and significant history of flooding. A bridge that once connected a road to the oxbow of the Wild Rice River where lots are currently located was removed in 1989 because of flood damage. During the April 1997 flood, all undeveloped lots in Wild Rice were under water. The homes then existing at the subdivision were not under water, but the partially constructed Rutten home was damaged by water and "muck."

After the 1997 flood, Fargo began working with the Federal Emergency Management Agency ("FEMA") to plan for future floods, and on August 1, 1997, Fargo brought the Wild Rice subdivision into its extraterritorial jurisdiction. On June 15, 1998, FEMA developed a preliminary flood insurance rate-map for the area and several Wild Rice lots were located within the preliminary floodway. The Wild Rice River did not have a mapped floodway before this time, and city officials believed the FEMA designation for the river would be formalized in about 18 months. On August 10, 1998, the Fargo City Commission decided that a "moratorium be placed on the issuance of all building permits for new construction in the floodway within the City of Fargo and its four-mile extraterritorial zone effective August 10, 1998 for a period until the Fargo City Ordinances have been passed and FEMA has made a final determination on their flood plain map." Although several of Wild Rice's lots were affected by the moratorium, others were not affected. During the approximately 21-month period the moratorium was in effect, Fargo city officials participated in many meetings with local, state and federal officials concerning flood plan mitigation issues.

In May 1999, Anton Rutten's daughter, Bonnie Rutten, applied for a building permit to construct a home on one of the lots in Wild Rice, but the permit was denied because the lot was located within the area identified by FEMA in the preliminary designated floodway covered by the moratorium. During the moratorium, some buyers showed interest in purchasing Wild Rice lots and several people contacted Wild Rice for information. One potential buyer signed two purchase agreements and another signed a lot-hold agreement, but no lots were sold. Wild Rice repeatedly attempted to persuade Fargo to lift the moratorium and issue permits for construction, but the city refused.

Wild Rice brought this inverse condemnation and tortious interference action on March 30, 2000, and Fargo filed its answer on April 21, 2000. On April 27, 2000, the Fargo city engineer wrote to the city commissioners and recommended that the building permit moratorium be lifted and the city adopt FEMA's June 15, 1998 preliminary flood insurance rate-map panel as the governing panel for all flood-prone areas. Following a public hearing, the city commission voted to lift the moratorium on May 1, 2000.

After the moratorium was lifted, Wild Rice sold five lots. The party who signed a purchase agreement during the moratorium purchased a lot in May 2000 for $32,900. Lots were also purchased in March 2002 for $39,000, in November 2002 for $39,000, in July 2003 for $55,900, and in April 2004 for $59,900. Other sales were pending at the time of these proceedings.

Following a bench trial, the trial court ruled in favor of Fargo, concluding there had been no "taking" of Wild Rice's property and no malicious interference with third-party contract rights. The court also denied Wild Rice's post-trial motions.

Wild Rice does not challenge the trial court's dismissal of its claim for malicious interference with third-party contract rights, but asserts the court erred in dismissing its claim for inverse condemnation because Fargo's 21-month moratorium constituted a "taking" of its property. . . .

In Lingle v. Chevron U.S.A. Inc., 544 U.S. 528 (2005), the United States Supreme Court recently disavowed the "stand-alone" regulatory takings test announced in Agins v. City of Tiburon, 447 U.S. 255, 260 (1980), that "'the application of a general zoning law to particular property effects a taking if the ordinance does not substantially advance legitimate state interests.'" In doing so, the Court summarized the remaining valid rules that govern its takings clause jurisprudence. . . .

The United States Supreme Court has addressed whether a moratorium on land development imposed during a government agency's process of devising a comprehensive land-use plan constitutes a per se taking of property requiring compensation under the takings clause of the Fifth Amendment. The Court's decision in Tahoe-Sierra, 535 U.S. 302, 306, involved two moratoria that prohibited virtually all development on property for a 32-month period in an effort to maintain the status quo while the government agency studied the impact of development on Lake Tahoe and designed a strategy for environmentally sound growth. The Court rejected the argument that a temporary deprivation of all economically viable use compels a finding that a categorical taking has occurred under *Lucas*. . . .

The Supreme Court in *Tahoe-Sierra* also rejected a proposed per se rule that any moratorium lasting more than one year is constitutionally unacceptable. The Court acknowledged "it may well be true that any moratorium that lasts for more than one year should be viewed with special skepticism" and "the duration of the restriction is one of the important factors that a court must consider in the appraisal of a regulatory takings claim," but concluded "the interest in 'fairness and justice' will be best served by relying on the familiar Penn Central approach when deciding cases like this, rather than by attempting to craft a new categorical rule." *Tahoe-Sierra*, 535 U.S. at 341-42.

Under N.D. Const. art. I, § 16, "private property shall not be taken or damaged for public use without just compensation." This Court has said our state constitutional provision is broader in some respects than its federal counterpart because the state provision "'was intended to secure to owners, not only the possession of property, but also those rights which render possession valuable.'" Grand Forks-Traill Water Users, Inc. v. Hjelle, 413 N.W.2d 344, 346 (N.D. 1987) (quoting Donaldson v. City of Bismarck, 3 N.W.2d 808 Syll. P1 (1942)). Nevertheless, this Court has looked to both state and federal precedents in construing takings claims under the state constitution, and our cases on inverse condemnation under the state constitution bear some similarities to the federal analysis. . . .

We conclude that the moratorium did not constitute a per se categorical taking of Wild Rice's property under the federal and state constitutions.

Wild Rice argues the moratorium constituted a taking under the Supreme Court's *Penn Central* analysis. Under *Penn Central*, 438 U.S. at 124, the particularly significant factors a court must consider are: 1) the "economic impact of the regulation on the claimant"; 2) "the extent to which the regulation has interfered with distinct investment-backed expectations"; and 3) "the character of the governmental action."

Wild Rice contends the evidence supports a conclusion that a taking has occurred. There was evidence of economic impact on the claimant, according to Wild Rice, because of the nearly $500,000 it invested in the property between 1992 and 1999, most of which was mandated by governmental entities that required a public sewer system and road infrastructure for the development. Wild Rice also relies on the pending sales of lots that did not take place because potential purchasers were unable to obtain building permits. Wild Rice argues the moratorium interfered with its investment-backed expectations because of its inability to sell residential lots after investing $500,000 in the property. Wild Rice argues the governmental action in this case is characterized by bad faith, because the city conducted no reviews or studies to create new ordinances applicable to its property during the moratorium period and lifted the moratorium only after impacted landowners brought inverse condemnation actions. Wild Rice claims the moratorium was used by the city simply "to prevent construction on Wild Rice's previously platted real property during an unsuccessful attempt to secure Federal funding to purchase Wild Rice's real property at a lower price (a price without need for compensation for new construction)."

However, in concluding Wild Rice had not established a taking under the *Penn Central* factors, the trial court reasoned:

12. [Wild Rice] retained economically viable use of its property during the moratorium. *Cf.* Palazzolo v. Rhode Island, 533 U.S. 606, 632 (2001) (holding that reduction in developer's property from $3,150,000 to $200,000, due to a state coastal committee's refusal to allow development in costal area, did not amount to a deprivation of all economic value and therefore did not amount to a total takings claim).

13. There is a huge disconnect between the fact of the history of [Wild Rice] development and its claim for compensation. Pre-moratorium sales were at the rate of 1/2 lot per year (the average lots sales for 1994 until July 1998). Rounding up 21 to 24 months, the loss was one (1) lost/delayed lot sale. At trial, loss on one of the riverside lots would be approximately $30,000 according to the Wild Rice River Estates brokers. A mere delay equals the sum of delayed investment opportunity ("interest") would be more in the nature of $3,000, a far cry from the one million dollars plus claimed by [Wild Rice]. Furthermore, "mere fluctuations in value during the process of governmental decision-making, absent extraordinary delay, are incidents of ownership. They cannot be considered a taking in the constitutional sense." *Tahoe-Sierra*, 535 U.S. at 332.
. . . .

15. The moratorium did not single out Plaintiff's property. Rather, it applied to other developments as well and the City has not paid compensation to other developers similarly affected. *Cf.* Tahoe-Sierra, 535 U.S. at 340 (stating that the need to protect planners' decisional process is stronger when developing a regional plan as opposed to considering a permit for a single parcel).

16. The moratorium was not an appropriation of [Wild Rice's] property for public use, but rather a temporary moratorium until local, State and Federal officials could adequately review a flood plain management for the area so devastated by the 1997 flood.
. . . .

18. Fargo city officials acted in good faith and with proper diligence concerning the moratorium as part of an overall effort to maintain the status quo until flood planning efforts and development could be re-evaluated after the devastating 1997 flood.

19. Fargo city officials were justified in waiting for FEMA's final adoption of a floodway for the Wild Rice River and other rivers in the Red River Valley.

20. The moratorium protected prospective buyers who might build on a river lot, not knowing, for example, that a home previously located on or next to the lot was damaged or destroyed by the 1997 flood.

21. Given the devastation and cost in damages caused by the flood, the City's moratorium was a reasonable, appropriate land-use regulation, issued in an effort to maintain the status quo of development in flood-prone areas until Fargo city officials and local, state and federal agencies had an opportunity to properly review and prepare an appropriate flood management plan for flood-prone areas within the City of Fargo's extraterritorial jurisdiction.

22. The City's moratorium bears a reasonable relationship to a legitimate governmental purpose; it is not arbitrary or capricious and does not amount to an unconstitutional taking of property requiring payment of just compensation.

The trial court's factual findings are supported by the record. Although Wild Rice had originally projected sales of four lots per year, Wild Rice had difficulty selling any lots from the very beginning of its existence. Only one lot was sold to an outside party between 1994 and 1998 before the moratorium became effective, notwithstanding the assistance of a realtor experienced in river developments and a two-year tax exemption offer. Lots in Wild Rice were prone to flooding and all but two of the Wild Rice lots were covered by water during the 1997 flood. Additional flooding occurred in 2001. After the moratorium was lifted, prospective buyers expressed concerns about water and flood issues. As the trial court found, "many factors" besides the moratorium "affected [Wild Rice's] investment over the years." The evidence suggests Wild Rice's investment-backed expectations were unreasonable.

Moreover, courts have said the focus of the economic impact criterion is the change in fair market value of the subject property caused by the regulatory imposition measured by comparing the market value of the property immediately before the governmental action with the market value of the same property immediately after the action is terminated. Here, Wild Rice sold more lots at higher prices after the moratorium was lifted than it did before the moratorium became effective. The most recent lot sale reflected in the record was for $59,900, more than double the $24,000 Wild Rice received for a lot in 1994. Under these circumstances, it is far less likely that a compensable taking has occurred.

An extraordinary delay in governmental decisionmaking coupled with bad faith on the part of the governmental body may result in a compensable taking of property. Fargo claimed it issued the moratorium in an effort to maintain the status quo until the city, along with other governmental bodies, could determine whether it was safe to build in flood prone areas. The moratorium applied to all land located within the preliminary designated floodway, not only to property owned by Wild Rice. According to Fargo, the city believed it was appropriate to wait for FEMA's final adoption of a floodway before building should continue. Although Wild Rice argues the city was simply keeping the value of its property deflated while waiting to secure federal funding to purchase the property, the trial court found that "city officials acted in good faith and with proper diligence concerning the moratorium." We apply the clearly erroneous standard to trial court determinations of good or bad faith. In light of the evidence, the trial court's finding that the city acted in good faith is not clearly erroneous nor can we say the 21-month length of the moratorium was extraordinary under these circumstances.

Wild Rice has failed to establish that the city's temporary moratorium resulted in an unconstitutional taking of Wild Rice's property under the *Penn Central* analysis. Wild Rice has not advanced a principled theory for modifying the *Penn Central* analysis for state constitutional purposes. We conclude no unconstitutional taking of Wild Rice's property has occurred under the federal and state constitutions. . . .

We conclude Fargo's 21-month moratorium on building permits did not constitute a taking of Wild Rice's property under the federal and state constitutions. We have considered Wild Rice's other arguments and deem them to be either without merit or unnecessary to resolve in view of our disposition of this case. The judgment and the order denying Wild Rice's post-trial motions are affirmed.

Notes

1. In some states, legislation defines the scope and purpose of land use moratoria. Still, courts are not left out of the lawmaking equation, for they are often called upon to interpret statutory terms. For example, a Maine statute—30-A Me. Rev. Stat. §4356—provides that moratoria "on the processing or issuance of development permits or licenses must" only be used

> A. To prevent a shortage or an overburden of public facilities that would otherwise occur during the effective period of the moratorium or that is reasonably foreseeable as a result of any proposed or anticipated development; or

> B. Because the application of existing comprehensive plans, land use ordinances or regulations or other applicable laws, if any, is inadequate to prevent serious public harm from residential, commercial or industrial development in the affected geographic area.

Moreover, such moratoria "must be of a definite term of not more than 180 days," unless the municipality chooses to extend for additional periods if "[t]he problem giving rise to the need for the moratorium still exists," and "[r]easonable progress is being made to alleviate the problem giving rise to the need for the moratorium."

Another statutory provision—30-A Me. Rev. Stat. §4301—defines "moratorium" as "a land use ordinance or other regulation approved by a municipal legislative body that . . . temporarily defers all development, or a type of development, by withholding any permit, authorization or approval necessary for the specified type or types of development." In Home Builders Ass'n of Me. v. Town of Eliot, 750 A.2d 566, 569, 570-71 (2000), the Supreme Judicial Court of Maine was called upon "to determine whether the provisions of the Town's Growth Management Ordinance, placing limits on growth and building permits, constitute a moratorium within the meaning of 30-A Me. Rev. Stat. §4301(11)."

The court explained:

> We must answer two questions: (A) whether section 4301(11) can apply to the Town's ordinance even though the ordinance is permanent, in other words, whether the language of section 4301(11) is directed only at "temporary" ordinances; and (B) whether the Town's ordinance, which places limits on but does not prevent *all* development, is a "moratorium" within the meaning of 4301(11). We conclude that, although the application of section 4301(11) is not limited to ordinances that are temporary in duration, the Growth Management Ordinance enacted by the Town in this case does not constitute a moratorium within the meaning of that statute.

The court was not persuaded by the town's creative reading of the statute, noting that the provision's "plain language . . . includes within its definition of 'moratorium' *any* ordinance that temporarily defers development, whether the ordinance *itself* is a temporary or a permanent ordinance." Nevertheless, the town's Growth Management Ordinance did not constitute a "moratorium" under the state statute for a different reason: the local law "does not prevent all development, but rather allows up to forty-eight new housing starts each year."

2. Do coastal communities have an implied power to impose development moratoria? The answer is "no" in the state of Washington, despite that state's strong commitment to growth management. In Biggers v. City of Bainbridge Island, 162 Wash. 2d 683, 685, 169 P.3d 14, 17 (2007), the state supreme court examined

the Bainbridge Island City (City) Council's adoption of rolling moratoria, which imposed a multi-year freeze on private property development in shoreline areas. The City denied the processing of permit applications for more than three years. There is no state statutory authority for the City's moratoria or for these multiple extensions. Clearly, this usurpation of state power by the local government disregards article XVII, section 1 of the Washington Constitution, which expressly provides that shorelines are owned by the State, subject only to state regulation. The City is not authorized to adopt moratoria on shoreline development arising out of its police powers under article XI, section 11 of the Washington Constitution, which limits local government to regulation "not in conflict with general laws."

The target of the moratoria was "the construction of shoreline structures designed to protect the land of shoreline property owners. These structures are, by definition, improper subjects for city-issued moratoria because inaction leaves all shoreline property defenseless against erosion." The court reasoned that "[d]espite the clear violation of property owners' rights, the City embraced the moratoria as a means to refuse consideration of any permit applications, thereby deferring difficult development decisions." The local moratoria thus conflicted with state statutory and constitutional law.

3. Sometimes growth management measures may conflict. A New Hampshire statute—N.H. Rev. Stat. Ann. §74:21(V)(h)–provides: "The adoption of a growth management limitation or moratorium by a municipality shall not affect any development with respect to which an impact fee has been paid or assessed as part of the approval for that development." In Monahan-Fortin Props. v. Town of Hudson, 148 N.H. 769, 770, 813 A.2d 523, 524 (2002), the state's high court reversed a lower court's ruling that prevented the town "from applying its growth management ordinance to the plaintiff's condominium project on the basis that the project was also subject to the town's impact fee ordinance." The site plan for the proposed project, "a 101-unit elderly housing condominium project known as Riverwalk," was submitted (but not approved) shortly before the town announced a new growth management ordinance.

The supreme court found no need to define the word "assessed" as it appears in the statute, reasoning that

> it is sufficient to state both that a preliminary estimate of an impact fee by a municipality does not constitute an assessment within the meaning of the statute, and that a municipality does not assess fees implicitly by merely receiving an application wherein fees are represented. While the town acknowledges that it had preliminarily calculated the amount of the impact fees that were to be charged to the Riverwalk project, they were never finally determined due, in part, to the planning board's rejection of the Riverwalk site plan.

VI. (Anti-)Big Box Zoning: Problems With Targeting Certain Types of Development

Every generation has its own prototypical Not in My Backyard (NIMBY) use. Like locally undesirable or unwanted land uses (LULUs) and not on planet earth (NOPE), NIMBYs are often the focus of targeted public land use restrictions. In the early years of zoning, residential owners needed filling stations for gasoline and automobile service, but not too close by. In the post-World War II boom, strip shopping centers provided many of the essential for suburban residents, but preferably at a comfortable distance. Beginning in the late 1970s, as the nation awoke to the problems posed by hazardous waste sites, landfills and waste treatment facilities were deemed necessary but locally undesirable. By the late 20th century, big-box stores that offered deep discounts, such as Wal-Mart, Target, and Home Depot, had become consumer magnets, despite widespread concerns about (1) harmful runoff across acres of newly paved parking lots and gigantic roof surfaces, (2) traffic tie-ups starting on the urban fringes and spreading for miles in all directions, and (3) the impact on erstwhile competitors—local "mom and pop" businesses and established retailers in the now-distressed central business districts.

While these retail behemoths, easily exceeding 100,000 square feet in area, may appear to be *sui generis*, in reality they are merely the latest in a long phase of an evolution that began with the supermarkets and general stores that replaced the local butcher, baker, green grocer, and similar establishments in which Americans shopped before World War II. Similarly, the national chains such as Sears, Montgomery Wards, and regional department stores that replaced hardware, dry goods, clothing, and appliance stores have themselves been eclipsed by Wal-Mart and its competitors. As with enclosed shopping malls in the closing decades of the 20th century, many local government officials have not only been unable or unwilling to stop these new displacements, they have encouraged big-box commerce by offering generous tax and financing incentives and by relaxing land use controls. As the following cases illustrate, the inevitable backlash has come in the form of reactive zoning measures and ballot-box efforts to stem the mega-retailing tide.

GRISWOLD v. CITY OF HOMER
186 P.3d 558 (Alaska 2008)

EASTAUGH , Justice. . . .

When Fred Meyer, Inc. publicly announced plans in late 2002 to build a 95,000-square-foot store in Homer, the city began an extensive review of its existing zoning code to determine whether it needed to alter floor area limits for retail and wholesale stores. For two years, beginning in March 2003, the question was considered by a special task force, by the Homer Advisory Planning Commission, and by the Homer City Council in more than a dozen hearings. After analyzing issues including traffic impact, the ideal rate of development, landscaping, maintaining the local character of Homer, and protecting groundwater, the planning commission made a series of recommendations to the city council regarding the appropriate floor area for retail and wholesale stores.

While those hearings were still being conducted, Homer voters in March 2004 filed with the city clerk an initiative petition that proposed a "footprint area" of 66,000 square feet for retail and wholesale business buildings in the Central Business District, General Commercial 1 District, and General Commercial 2 District. On April 12, 2004, the city council passed Ordinance 04-11(A), which set building floor area limits of 35,000 square feet in the Central Business District, 20,000 to 45,000 square feet in the General Commercial 1 District, and 45,000 square feet in the General Commercial 2 District. On the same day, in response to the initiative petition, the city council scheduled an election on the initiative for June 15, 2004. The voters approved the initiative at the June 15 election; the initiative became effective on June 21, 2004 as Ordinance 04-18.

Stating that a change in the zoning code sections was "required to properly convey the will of the voters," and that an ordinance was "necessary to implement the will of the voters," in February 2005 the city council enacted Ordinance 05-02, adopting a maximum floor area of 66,000 square feet for retail and wholesale business buildings in the three affected zoning districts. Ordinance 05-02 amended Ordinance 04-11(A) to reflect the text of the initiative. Ordinance 05-02 also effectively defined "footprint area" as "floor area," meaning "the total area occupied by a building, taken on a horizontal plane at the main grade level, exclusive of steps and any accessory buildings."

Frank Griswold challenged the initiative in the superior court, claiming among other things that the initiative process could not be used to amend the zoning code. The city prevailed on summary judgment. . . . .

Griswold argues that the zoning initiative is invalid for several reasons. He contends, among other things, that the zoning authority delegated to the City of Homer requires it to pass only zoning ordinances that are consistent with the city's comprehensive plan. The city, citing Citizens Coalition for Tort Reform v. McAlpine,[4] responds that the voters' constitutional right to enact initiatives should be broadly construed to permit the voters to amend zoning laws. The city contends that because the city council has the power to enact zoning ordinances, the voters must have the same power.

The power to initiate cannot exceed the power to legislate.[5] To decide whether Homer voters could invoke the initiative process to amend the City of Homer zoning code we must determine the extent of the city council's zoning power and the explicit and implicit limitations on that power. The city's zoning power flows from two sources: Alaska statutes providing for planning, platting, and land use regulation by local governments, and Kenai Peninsula Borough ordinances delegating zoning powers to cities within the borough. . . .

The relevant state statutes are clear. A borough or a city, having the power possessed by the City of Homer, cannot pass or amend a zoning ordinance without involving its planning commission in reviewing that ordinance. This review includes considering whether a proposed ordinance is consistent with the comprehensive plan. A borough assembly or city council may eventually choose not to follow the recommendations of the planning commission, but the statutes preclude bypassing the planning commission altogether.

Likewise, KPBC 21.01.020(B) gives the city council power to establish a planning commission to hear all requests for amendments to zoning codes. This provision can be read as giving the planning commission the primary authority for initial consideration of zoning amendments. At the very least, this provision confirms the commission's role in considering proposed amendments to an existing zoning code that was itself adopted "[i]n accordance with a comprehensive plan . . . and in order to implement the plan . . . ."

It is for this reason that zoning by initiative is invalid. The Homer City Council does not have the power to pass piecemeal zoning amendments without at least giving the Homer Advisory Planning Commission opportunity to review the proposals and make recommendations. Therefore, voters, who have no obligation to consider the views of the planning commission or be informed by its expertise, cannot use the initiative process to eliminate the planning commission's role in "areawide" land use planning and regulation, and thus potentially undermine the comprehensive plan for "systematic and organized" local development.

The city contends that we must determine "[w]hether the Constitution and statutes preempt the use of the initiative for zoning ordinances." But, because the initiative was local, and not statewide, the power to initiate here was directly derived from AS 29.26.100, not article XI, section 1 of the Alaska Constitution. And we conclude that zoning by initiative exceeds the scope of the legislative power granted by the legislature to the city council.

The city also contends that initiatives are not "governed by all the procedures ordinarily applicable to the enactment of city council ordinances." The city seems to argue that because notice and a hearing are required for a city council ordinance but not an initiative, it is acceptable for initia-

---

4. Citizens Coal. for Tort Reform v. McAlpine, 810 P.2d 162 (Alaska 1991) (stating that people's constitutional right to initiate is broad and should be liberally construed).

5. Municipality of Anchorage v. Frohne, 568 P.2d 3, 8 (Alaska 1977) (citations omitted) ("[T]he subject of the initiative must constitute such legislation as the legislative body to which it is directed has the power to enact.").

tives to bypass certain procedural requirements. But as seen above, the participation of the city's planning commission in the zoning process required by the legislature and the borough is more than just a mere procedural requirement.

The facts in this case illustrate how the initiative process limits or even eliminates the intended role of a planning commission. The planning commission spent many months considering appropriate floor area limits for business buildings in the affected zoning districts. The city council charged the commission with "develop[ing] standards for addressing large retail and wholesale development" and "recommend[ing] a size cap for large retail and wholesale development." To that end, the commission, city council, and a task force conducted more than a dozen hearings. The commission reviewed recommendations from the Large Structure Impact Task Force and the Chamber of Commerce Legislative Committee; researched necessary improvements to lighting, landscaping, stormwater drainage, and parking; and developed standards for traffic and economic impact analyses. The commission explicitly applied the standards found in the Homer Comprehensive Plan in its decision-making process. And before the initiative election, the city council considered the planning commission's recommendations and amended the zoning code, adopting different floor area limitations for the subject zoning districts. The voters then approved the initiative and adopted a single, and greater, limitation for all three districts before the commission completed its findings.

Given the public hearings that were being conducted and the opportunity for public debate, it is logical to ask whether the voters had, in effect, the same access as the council to the recommendations of the planning commission, and thus whether the initiative process did not actually bypass the planning commission. The council was required to consider the commission's recommendations, even if it ultimately rejected them. The council acts as a collegial and public body; it is a matter of public record whether it addresses the commission's recommendations and attempts to reconcile proposed amendments with the comprehensive plan and state and borough ordinances. That is not at all the process an initiative election follows. Just as the council cannot choose to completely ignore the recommendations in adopting a zoning amendment, the voters cannot pass an initiative in which the commission's recommendations play no formal, or perhaps even informal, role at all.

The commission does more than simply give notice of hearings and allow the public to be heard on the subject of zoning ordinances. If a zoning amendment is proposed, the commission's role is to analyze the impact of the proposed changes in light of the city's development goals as stated in the comprehensive plan, and to suggest other changes that should accompany the proposed zoning amendment. Even if a city council chooses to disregard the recommendations of the city planning commission, its decision has been informed by the planning commission's consideration of the potential social and regulatory costs and benefits of the proposed amendment. The city's planning commission's role is not merely "procedural," but is substantive. Homer voters therefore could not bypass the commission by using the initiative power.

The city argues that if an initiative fails to comply with the comprehensive plan, a court could review it post-enactment. Because the dispute here turns not on consistency with the comprehensive plan, but on the involvement of the planning commission in the amendment process, we are unconvinced by this argument.

The city argues that the ultimate issue here is "whether the Alaska Constitution or statutes do or do not delegate the power to enact zoning regulations exclusively to the city council." The city argues the people's power to enact zoning measure by initiative is precluded if the constitution and statutes delegate the power to zone exclusively to the city council. The city implies that for Griswold to prevail we must find that the city council exclusively has the power to zone. We disagree, and instead conclude that Griswold prevails because zoning by initiative eliminates the planning commission's role both specified and implied in state statutes and borough ordinances.[30] Even if the power to zone was exclusively and ultimately delegated to the city council, the initiative process prevents the planning commission from exercising the review and recommendation power clearly delegated to it. . . .

We REVERSE the superior court's grant of summary judgment and REMAND for entry of judgment for Griswold.

CARPENETI , Justice, dissenting.

Because the initiative power gives voters the ability to legislate without being subject to the restrictions applicable to other legislative bodies, I cannot agree that the procedural requirements applicable to the Homer City Council apply to a voter initiative that involves a zoning ordinance. Therefore, I respectfully dissent. . . .

[T]he court's decision conflicts with well-reasoned holdings from other states that have addressed zoning by initiative. California has definitively resolved the issue before us today in favor of allowing zoning by initiative. As the California Supreme Court succinctly explained, "[p]rocedural requirements which govern [City] Council action . . . generally do not apply to initiatives, any more than the provisions of the initiative law govern the enactment of ordinances in council."[20] The Nevada Supreme Court similarly concluded that voters could enact zoning laws through the initiative process without following the procedures applicable to the city council attempting to enact the same ordinance.[21] In both cases special procedures applied to the enactment of zoning laws by the local government bodies, but the courts nevertheless recognized that subjecting voter initiatives to those procedures would impermissibly restrict the voters' initiative powers.

In sum, the initiative process is unique. When exercising the initiative power, municipal voters do not simply step into the shoes of the legislative body they are bypassing, as the court today assumes. Instead, voters in an initiative election are participating in a process that is separate from the regular means used for legislating. Because the initiative process is intended to be separate from the procedures that the Homer City Council must follow when passing a zoning ordinance, the initiative ordinance in this case should not be subject to review by the Homer Advisory Planning Commission. I would hold that the initiated ordinance does not violate any of the subject matter restrictions imposed by article XI, section 7 of the Alaska Constitution (and made applicable to municipal elections through AS 29.26.100 and to elections in Homer through HCC 4.60.010), and I therefore would affirm the superior court's grant of summary judgment to the City of Homer.

---

30. Both parties cite cases from other jurisdictions that either reject or approve zoning by initiative. *See, e.g.*, Kaiser Hawaii Kai Dev. Co. v. City & County of Honolulu, 70 Haw. 480, 777 P.2d 244, 247 (Haw. 1989) (holding that "[z]oning by initiative is inconsistent with the goal of long range comprehensive planning" and was not intended by legislature); *see also* Garvin v. Ninth Judicial Dist. Court, 118 Nev. 749, 59 P.3d 1180, 1190 (Nev. 2002) (holding that "[if] a city council can enact zoning legislation, the county and city voters can do the same by initiative"). The only cited case that deals with the scope of the delegated power is Transamerica Title Ins. Co. v. City of Tucson, 157 Ariz. 346, 757 P.2d 1055, 1059 (Ariz. 1988) ("The power to zone is part of the police power and may be delegated by the State, but the subordinate governmental unit has no greater power than that which is delegated."). *Transamerica* supports the views we express in this case. In *Transamerica* the Arizona Supreme Court adhered to a prior holding "that 'zoning law is exempted from the initiative process,' in order to prevent private citizens from usurping the governing body's delegated power and from circumventing the notice and hearing requirements of the zoning statute." *Id.* at 1058. The Arizona court noted that its holding in the case on which it relied was "in harmony with the law in the vast majority of other jurisdictions, which prohibits zoning by initiative." *Id.* at 1059.

20. Assoc. Home Builders, Inc. v. City of Livermore, 18 Cal. 3d 582, 135 Cal. Rptr. 41, 557 P.2d 473, 479 (Cal. 1976) (citation omitted); accord DeVita v. County of Napa, 9 Cal. 4th 763, 38 Cal. Rptr. 2d 699, 889 P.2d 1019, 1037-38 (Cal. 1995) (allowing initiative to amend Napa's general plan despite failure to comply with procedures county planning agency must follow to enact amendment).

21. Garvin v. Dist. Court, 118 Nev. 749, 59 P.3d 1180, 1190 (Nev. 2002).

Notes

1. Even when regulations limiting square footage are properly enacted, they may not accomplish their goals. When Dunkirk, Maryland, imposed a 75,000-square-foot limitation, Wal-Mart went to the drawing board and proposed two stores to sit side by side, a 74,998-square-foot store and a neighboring garden center measuring 22,689 square feet. In the face of negative national attention and local opposition, the company changed its mind and submitted plans for one store that fit within the limitation. The county planning commission approved the new plans by a 5-2 vote, as reported in Amit R. Paley, *Wal-Mart in Dunkirk Is Approved, Ending Fight*, Wash. Post, July 24, 2005, at 1B.

2. In 2006, the city of Turlock, California, successfully defended an ordinance that excluded "discount superstores" from the municipality. The ordinance, which defined "discount superstore" as "a discount store that exceeds 100,000 square feet of gross floor area and devotes at least 5 percent of the total sales floor area to the sale of nontaxable merchandise, often in the form of a full-service grocery department," was proposed and enacted after Wal-Mart officials had initiated plans to build a local Supercenter meeting that carefully tailored definition.

    In Wal-Mart Stores, Inc. v. City of Turlock, 138 Cal. App. 4th 273, 285, 294, 299, 303, 41 Cal. Rptr. 3d 420, 426, 434, 437, 441 (2006), the state appeals court affirmed the trial court's dismissal of the company's claims that the city had "unconstitutionally exceeded its police powers and failed to comply with the [California Environmental Quality Act (CEQA)]." Much like its federal analogue—the National Environmental Policy Act (NEPA)—as stated in Cal. Pub. Resources Code §21001, the state CEQA was enacted to ensure that "governmental agencies at all levels . . . consider qualitative factors as well as economic and technical factors and long-term benefits and costs, in addition to short-term benefits and costs and to consider alternatives to proposed actions affecting the environment." The court explained that under CEQA,

> [d]uring a preliminary review, the public agency considers whether the proposed activity is a discretionary project and, if so, whether an exemption from CEQA applies. When the preliminary review results in a determination that the proposed activity is a discretionary project that is not exempt, CEQA requires the public agency to proceed with an initial study. In contrast, when the preliminary review results in a determination that the proposed activity is not a project or is exempt, the public agency's CEQA inquiry ends and it may file a notice of exemption.

Despite the company's arguments that the enacting of the ordinance would effect negative consequences within and outside the city, the court noted that

> a physical change in the environment will be peculiar to the Ordinance if that physical change belongs exclusively or especially to the Ordinance or if it is characteristic of only the Ordinance. In general, these definitions illustrate how difficult it will be for a zoning amendment or other land use regulation that does not have a physical component to have a sufficiently close connection to a physical change to allow the physical change to be regarded as 'peculiar to' the zoning amendment or other land use regulation.

For this and other reasons, the court determined that the city was not required to perform "further environmental review."

    On the question of local authority, the court concluded that "the police power empowers cities to control and organize development within their boundaries as a means of serving the general welfare. City legitimately chose to organize the development within its boundaries using neighbor-hood shopping centers dispersed throughout the city."

The federal district court, in Wal-Mart Stores, Inc. v. City of Turlock, 483 F. Supp. 2d 987 (E.D. Cal. 2006), was equally dismissive of the company's three constitutional challenges, which were deemed to be facial, not as-applied, in nature: (1) violation of equal protection; (2) discrimina-tion against interstate commerce; and (3) void for vagueness. Adding insult to injury, in Wal-Mart Stores, Inc. v. City of Turlock, 483 F. Supp. 2d 1023, 1041 (E.D. Cal. 2007) the city was awarded more than $8,000 in attorneys fees for defending the vagueness claim, which the court labeled "frivolous from the outset of the litigation."

3. The Internet abounds with anti-Big Box sites, including http://www.sprawl-busters.com ("An International Clearinghouse on Big Box Anti-Sprawl Information") and numerous sites devoted to local fights, such as http://www.stopwalmartventura.com, which includes links to other like-minded citizen activists (http://www.stopwalmartventura.com/Other_Site_Fights.php).

ISLAND SILVER & SPICE, INC. v. ISLAMORADA
542 F.3d 844 (11th Cir. 2008)

RESTANI , Judge: . . .

In January 2002, Islamorada enacted Ordinance 02-02, which prohibited "formula restaurant[s]" and restricted "formula retail" establishments to limited street level frontage and total square footage. (See Ordinance 02-02 §§ 6.4.3-4(a-b), available at R.E. Tab 2 at 22 ("Ordi-nance 02-02" or "the ordinance").) The ordinance defines formula retail as:

> [a] type of retail sales activity of retail sales establishment . . . that is required by con-tractual or other arrangement to maintain any of the following: standardized array of services or merchandise, trademark, logo, service mark, symbol, decor, architecture, lay-out, uniform, or similar standardized feature.

(Id. at § 6.4.1(e).)

Island Silver owns and operates an independent retail store in Islamorada. See Island Silver & Spice, Inc. v. Islamorada, 475 F. Supp. 2d 1281, 1282 (S.D. Fla. 2007) ("Island Silver"). In June 2002, Island Silver entered into a contract to sell its property to a developer seeking to estab-lish a Walgreens drug store in the same footprint of Island Silver's existing mixed-retail store. After unsuccessfully protesting the ordinance's restrictions on formula retail stores through the local administrative process, the developer withdrew from the purchase. Island Silver brought a complaint against Islamorada in district court, seeking damages, injunctive relief, and a writ of mandamus on the grounds that the ordinance's formula retail provisions violated its rights to Due Process, Commercial Speech, Equal Protection, Privileges and Immunities, the Commerce Clause, and the terms of the Florida Constitution.

On February 28, 2007, the district court granted injunctive and monetary relief in favor of Island Silver and invalidated the ordinance's formula retail provisions. The district court found that the provisions violated the Dormant Commerce Clause because they had a discriminatory impact on interstate commerce unsupported by a legitimate state purpose and the putative local benefits were outweighed by the burden imposed on interstate commerce. Islamorada appeals. . . .

The Dormant Commerce Clause prohibits "regulatory measures designed to benefit in-state economic interests by burdening out-of-state competitors." New Energy Co. of Ind. v. Limbach, 486 U.S. 269, 273 (1988). To determine whether a regulation violates the Dormant Commerce Clause, we apply one of two levels of analysis. See Brown-Forman Distillers Corp. v. N.Y. State

Liquor Auth., 476 U.S. 573, 578-79 (1986). If a regulation "directly regulates or discriminates against interstate commerce," or has the effect of favoring "in-state economic interests," the regulation must be shown to "advance[ ] a legitimate local purpose that cannot be adequately served by reasonable nondiscriminatory alternatives." Bainbridge v. Turner, 311 F.3d 1104, 1109 (11th Cir. 2002) (quotations and citations omitted). If a regulation has "only indirect effects on interstate commerce," we "examine[ ] whether the State's interest is legitimate and whether the burden on interstate commerce clearly exceeds the local benefits." *Brown-Forman*, 476 U.S. at 579 (citing Pike v. Bruce Church, Inc., 397 U.S. 137, 142 (1970)).

The district court correctly determined that the formula retail provision does not facially discriminate against interstate commerce. *See Island Silver*, 475 F. Supp. 2d at 1290 (stating that "the ordinance is facially neutral"). With respect to the provision's effects, however, the parties stipulated that the ordinance "effectively prevents the establishment of new formula retail stores," and "[a] facility limited to no more than 2,000 square feet or 50' of frontage [as required by the ordinance] can not accommodate the minimum requirements of nationally and regionally branded formula retail stores." Although the fact that the burden of a regulation falls onto a subset of out-of-state retailers "does not, by itself, establish a claim of discrimination against interstate commerce," Exxon Corp. v. Governor of Maryland, 437 U.S. 117, 126 (1978), the ordinance's effective elimination of all new interstate chain retailers has the "practical effect of . . . discriminating against" interstate commerce, Hunt v. Washington Apple Advertising Commission, 432 U.S. 333, 350(1977). The formula retail provision is therefore subject to elevated scrutiny.[2]

Under the elevated scrutiny test, a regulation must be supported by "a legitimate local purpose that cannot be adequately served by reasonable nondiscriminatory alternatives."[3] *Bainbridge*, 311 F.3d at 1109 (quotations and citation omitted). The burden is on Islamorada to justify the ordinance's discriminatory effects. *Hunt*, 432 U.S. at 353 ("When discrimination against commerce . . . is demonstrated, the burden falls on the State to justify it both in terms of the local benefits flowing from the statute and the unavailability of nondiscriminatory alternatives adequate to preserve the local interests at stake.").

The ordinance's stated local purposes include the preservation of "unique and natural" "small town" community characteristics, encouragement of "small scale uses, water-oriented uses, [and] a nationally significant natural environment," and avoidance of increased "traffic congestion . . . [and] litter, garbage and rubbish offsite." (Ordinance 02-02 at Preamble.) The parties stipulated, however, that "Islamorada has a number of [pre-existing] 'formula retail' businesses," Islamorada "has no Historic District, and there are no historic buildings in the vicinity of [Island Silver's] property," and "[t]he Ordinance is not necessary for preservation of the historic characteristics of any buildings in the Village." In addition, because the ordinance "does not address small formula retail stores, which are permitted under the ordinance, but would presumably affect the Village's small town character as well," or large non-chain businesses, the district court found that "[r]estricting formula retail stores, while allowing other large [and] non-unique structures, does not preserve a small town character." *Island Silver*, 475 F. Supp. 2d at 1292. The district court properly determined that, although "[i]n general, preserving a small town community is a legitimate purpose . . . , in this instance, [Islamorada] has not demonstrated that it has any small town character to preserve." *Id.* at 1291.

---

2. The district court applied both the elevated scrutiny and balancing tests, finding that "[the] ordinance fails both tests: it is discriminatory in impact . . . without an adequate legislative purpose, and the burden it imposes is clearly excessive in relation to its putative local benefits." *Island Silver*, 475 F. Supp. 2d at 1290. We agree that on this record it fails both.

3. Regulations that facially discriminate or have a discriminatory effect on interstate commerce rarely pass the elevated scrutiny test. See *Brown-Forman*, 476 U.S. at 579 (stating that such regulations are "virtually per se invalid").

With respect to the stated purpose of encouraging small-scale and natural uses, the parties also stipulated that Islamorada's existing "zoning allows the use of the property as a retail pharmacy . . . and other retail uses," and that Island Silver operated as "a street level business comprising over twelve thousand square feet of floor area," which "greatly exceeds the [ordinance's] dimensional limitations" for formula retail businesses. The district court correctly found that Islamorada "[did] not explain why the ordinance singles out retail stores and restaurants with standardized features," *Island Silver*, 475 F. Supp. 2d at 1292, and that the record did not indicate that Islamorada is "uniquely relaxed or natural," or that there is "a pre-dominance of natural conditions and characteristics over human intrusions," *id.* at 1291.

Similarly, the stated purposes of reducing traffic and garbage are undermined by the parties' stipulations that Islamorada has existing "land development regulations, other than the Ordinance, that govern and control traffic generation of retail uses," and "that limit the dimensions, location, and use of buildings and signs." The district court therefore properly concluded that Islamorada failed to provide a legitimate local purpose to justify the ordinance's discriminatory effects, and that even if such purpose had been shown, "the ordinance does not serve this interest." *Island Silver*, 475 F. Supp. 2d at 1292.

Islamorada's failure to indicate a legitimate local purpose to justify the ordinance's discriminatory effects is sufficient to support the district court's determination that the formula retail provision is invalid under the Dormant Commerce Clause. *See id.* ("Because the ordinance clearly fails the first two prongs of the [elevated scrutiny] test, the Court does not need to reach the merits of the third prong of the test. Whether [Islamorada] can show that no adequate, non-discriminatory methods were available is therefore immaterial."). It should be noted, however, that Islamorada does not assert that the stated purposes of the ordinance cannot be furthered by reasonable nondiscriminatory alternatives, such as Islamorada's existing land development regulations. Even under the balancing approach advocated by Islamorada, the stipulated facts indicate that the formula retail provision's disproportionate burden on interstate commerce, such as the effective exclusion of interstate formula retailers, clearly outweighs any legitimate local benefits.

Accordingly, the district court did not err in concluding that the ordinance's formula retail provision violated the Dormant Commerce Clause.

We therefore AFFIRM the judgment of the district court.

Notes

1. In a companion case, Cachia v. Islamorada, 542 F.3d 839, 841, 843-44 (11th Cir. 2008), the same appellate panel reversed the district court's dismissal of a dormant Commerce Clause challenge to the town's prohibition of "formula restaurants," defined as

> [a]n eating place that is one of a chain or group of three (3) or more existing establishments and which satisfies at least two of the following three descriptions: (1) has the same or similar name, tradename, or trademark as others in the chain or group; (2) offers any of the following characteristics in a style which is distinctive to and standardized among the chain or group: i. exterior design or architecture; ii. uniforms, except that a personal identification or simply logo will not render the clothing a uniform; or iii. has a standardized menu; or (3) is a fast food restaurant.

The case was remanded to enable the trial court to consider

> 1) whether the ordinance's stated interests constitute a legitimate local purpose; 2) whether the prohibition of formula restaurants adequately serves such purpose; or 3) whether

Islamorada could demonstrate the unavailability of nondiscriminatory alternatives, such as zoning ordinances or building codes, to fulfill the same needs.

2. The Roberts Court is sharply divided as to the legitimacy and extent of the reach of the dormant Commerce Clause. United Haulers Ass'n v. Oneida-Herkimer Solid Waste Mgmt. Auth., 550 U.S. 330 (2007), was a case involving the legitimacy of two New York counties' "flow control ordinances" that required all solid waste generated locally to be transported to the authority's processing sites. The authority also collected "tipping fees" to pay for the costs incurred in operating and maintaining the facilities. Writing for a majority of five Justices, Chief Justice John Roberts established that this dispute came under the so-called dormant aspect of the Commerce Clause and distinguished the Court's prior holding in C&A Carbone, Inc. v. Clarkstown, 511 U.S. 383 (1994), which invalidated a town's flow control ordinance that benefited a private contractor whom the town allowed to charge an above-market tipping fee.

The *United Haulers* Court concluded that *Carbone* did not "decide the public-private question" presented by the requirement that the solid waste be delivered to a public authority. The facts of the two cases were different, the Chief Justice asserted, and "[b]ecause the question is now squarely presented on the facts of the case before us, we decide that such flow control ordinances do not discriminate against interstate commerce for purposes of the dormant Commerce Clause." The majority found "[c]ompelling reasons [to] justify treating these laws differently from laws favoring particular private businesses over their competitors," such as the fact that "government is vested with the responsibility of protecting the health, safety, and welfare of its citizens." Moreover, "treating public and private entities the same under the dormant Commerce Clause would lead to unprecedented and unbounded interference by the courts with state and local government." The majority endorsed county control over the traditionally local governmental function of waste disposal, especially when "the most palpable harm imposed by the ordinances—more expensive trash removal—is likely to fall upon the very people who voted for the laws."

The final part of Chief Justice Roberts' opinion only carried four votes, but this plurality section included this intriguing dictum:

> There is a common thread to these arguments [by the Association]: They are invitations to rigorously scrutinize economic legislation passed under the auspices of the police power. There was a time when this Court presumed to make such binding judgments for society, under the guise of interpreting the Due Process Clause. See Lochner v. New York, 198 U.S. 45 (1905). We should not seek to reclaim that ground for judicial supremacy under the banner of the dormant Commerce Clause.

Justice Antonin Scalia was pleased with the Chief Justice's decision not to contort the written text of the Commerce Clause any further ("I write separately to reaffirm my view that 'the so-called "negative" Commerce Clause is an unjustified judicial invention, not to be expanded beyond its existing domain."). Justice Clarence Thomas, also concurring in the judgment only, expressed even greater disdain for the Dormant (or "negative") Commerce Clause, asserting that the concept "has no basis in the Constitution and has proved unworkable in practice." Following a strong argument based on constitutional text, history, and precedent, Justice Thomas then turned to the Chief Justice's condemnation of the *Lochner* decision. He, too, went on record in opposition to the practice of reading words and phrases into the substance of the Due Process Clause:

> The Court's negative Commerce Clause jurisprudence, created from whole cloth, is just as illegitimate as the "right" it vindicated in *Lochner*. Yet today's decision does not repudiate that doctrinal error. Rather, it further propagates the error by narrowing the nega-

tive Commerce Clause for policy reasons—reasons that later majorities of this Court may find to be entirely illegitimate.

Three Justices dissented, convinced that "the provisions challenged in this case are essentially identical to the ordinance invalidated in *Carbone*."

3. In 2003, the city of Hanford, California, enacted an ordinance designed "to protect the economic viability of Hanford's downtown commercial district—a prominent feature of which is a large number of regionally well-regarded retail furniture stores." The owners of a "stand-alone" store that sold home furnishings and mattresses, located in another part of the city (the Planned Commercial (PC) district), challenged the new regulation as it would prevent the store from expanding its merchandise to include bedroom furniture. In Hernandez v. City of Hanford, 41 Cal. 4th 279, 283, 291, 295-97, 159 P.3d 33, 35, 40, 44-45, 59 Cal. Rptr. 3d 442, 444, 450, 454-56 (2007), the Supreme Court of California reversed the lower court's finding that the ordinance's "'disparate treatment of these similarly situated retailers based on square footage is not rationally related to the purpose behind the ordinance and is unconstitutional as a violation of equal protection.'" The state high court also rejected the store's claim "that the city exceeded its authority under the police power by enacting a zoning ordinance that regulates or restricts economic competition":

> Our court has not previously had occasion to address the question whether a municipality, in order to protect or preserve the economic viability of its downtown business district or neighborhood shopping areas, may enact a zoning ordinance that regulates or controls competition by placing limits on potentially competing commercial activities or development in other areas of the municipality. More than a half-century ago, however, this court explained that "[i]t is well settled that a municipality may divide land into districts and prescribe regulations governing the uses permitted therein, and that zoning ordinances, when reasonable in object and not arbitrary in operation, constitute a justifiable exercise of police power." (Lockard v. City of Los Angeles (1949) 33 Cal.2d 453, 460 [202 P.2d 38]) . . . [E]ven when the regulation of economic competition reasonably can be viewed as a direct and intended effect of a zoning ordinance or action, so long as the primary purpose of the ordinance or action—that is, its principal and ultimate objective—is not the impermissible private anticompetitive goal of protecting or disadvantaging a particular favored or disfavored business or individual, but instead is the advancement of a legitimate public purpose—such as the preservation of a municipality's downtown business district for the benefit of the municipality as a whole—the ordinance reasonably relates to the general welfare of the municipality and constitutes a legitimate exercise of the municipality's police power. . . .

> In the present case, it is clear that the zoning ordinance's general prohibition on the sale of furniture in the PC district— although concededly intended, at least in part, to regulate competition—was adopted to promote the legitimate public purpose of preserving the economic viability of the Hanford downtown business district, rather than to serve any impermissible private anticompetitive purpose. Furthermore, . . . here the zoning ordinance's restrictions are aimed at regulating "where, within the city" a particular type of business generally may be located, a very traditional zoning objective. Under these circumstances, we agree with the lower court's conclusion that the zoning ordinance cannot be found invalid as an improper limitation on competition.

VII. The Backlash: State Takings Legislation as a Check on Growth Management Abuses (Real and Perceived)

Property owners and their advocates did not sit idly by while state lawmakers expanded growth controls in the closing decades of the 20th century. When court challenges failed to invalidate the Ramapo, Petaluma, and copycat plans across the country, in several states the battle for stiffer protection of property rights by bolstering takings law was waged more successfully in legislative chambers and voting booths. The idea is relatively simple—pass legislative or constitutional changes that will make it more difficult procedurally or costly (in the form of compensation) to pass and enforce regulations that significantly (but not totally) reduce the value of property. Takings legislation has consistently failed in Congress, despite the best efforts of conservative lawmakers in the early 1990s to put a price tag on wetlands and endangered species protections. In contrast, a few states have mandated compensation for regulations whose impact does not rise to the level of a Fifth Amendment violation. Because two of those states—Florida and Oregon—have a very strong growth management track record, it is easy to conceive of these takings measures as a backlash against land use controls designed to slow the pace of development, particularly in environmentally sensitive areas. The Bert J. Harris Jr., Private Property Rights Protection Act of 1995 has been in effect in the Sunshine State for more than a decade, while Oregon's Measure 37, which in 2004 made it onto the ballot after a hard-fought struggle, three years later was watered down by Measure 49.

In their careful study, The Track Record on Takings Legislation: Lessons From Democracy's Laboratories 2-3 (Georgetown Envtl. L. & Pol'y Inst. 2008), John D. Echeverria and Thekla Hansen-Young arrived at "five overarching conclusions":

> The Takings Agenda Undermines Community Protections;
> Special Interests Benefit the Most From the Takings Agenda;
> The Takings Agenda Generates Land Use Conflicts;
> The Takings Agenda Confers Special Windfalls; and
> The Takings Agenda Undermines Local Democracy.

The two cases that follow demonstrate that, despite apparently widespread concern about confiscatory land use measures, the gap between envisioning and achieving a deregulatory agenda remains quite wide.

PALM BEACH POLO, INC. v. VILLAGE OF WELLINGTON
918 So. 2d 988 (Fla. Ct. App. 2006)

WARNER, J. . . .

The Village of Wellington filed a declaratory action and also requested injunctive relief against appellant Palm Beach Polo, Inc. in connection with the 1972 Wellington Planned Unit Development. Pursuant to the PUD, Wellington sought to have Polo restore, enhance, and preserve an area known as Big Blue Reserve. Polo counterclaimed for inverse condemnation and violation of the Bert J. Harris, Jr., Private Property Rights Protection Act, claiming that the "Conservation" designation of Big Blue in Wellington's Code, as well as Wellington's insistence that Polo "preserve" and "restore" the area, constituted an "as applied" taking. . . .

Big Blue Reserve or Forest is an undeveloped tract of land, approximately ninety-two acres in size, in the Village of Wellington. It contains wetlands and many old-growth cypress trees, some more than 300 years old. Big Blue is the focus of this appeal.

In 1971 most of the Village of Wellington was owned by AlphaBeta, Inc. and Breakwater Housing Corp. Desiring to develop Wellington, they entered into a Planned Unit Development with Palm Beach County. The result became the Wellington PUD.

Planned Unit Development is a zoning device used to permit flexibility in design and use of property. See Frankland v. City of Lake Oswego, 267 Ore. 452, 517 P.2d 1042 (Or. 1973). It is an agreement between the land owner and the zoning authority, and the terms of development are negotiated between the parties in accordance with the conditions set forth in the governing ordinances. A PUD plan, in compliance with zoning regulations, is submitted to the county for approval.

In 1972, the Zoning Resolution for Palm Beach County provided that, with respect to the Wellington PUD, "The intent and purpose of this section is to provide an alternative means of land development and to provide design latitude for the site planner." That year, the county approved the Wellington PUD submitted by AlphaBeta and Breakwater. It covered the development plan for 7400 acres. At the hearing approving the plan, several conditions were placed upon the approval. These included:

> Developer proposes an overall average of 2 dwelling units per acre with public open space of over 25%. Development expected to take at least until year 2000;

> Will enhance and preserve big blue areas and pine tree forests. Will develop a ring of water around it for protection. Will increase water level 1 foot (back to its original condition) and animal life can be restored to its original condition.

> Will preserve natural vegetation.

> A planned community of open spaces, bicycle paths, golf course and recreation areas, with restoration and preservation of big blue pristine forest areas.

The notes of the commission meeting reflect that as a reason for approval, the property, as zoned, could be developed with single-family dwellings with a density of four units per acre. However, the developer committed to an overall density of two units per acre, which was made one of the conditions of the plan. Big Blue was given an OS-R designation, meaning Open Space-Reserve, in an Agricultural/Residential zoning district.

A year later, in connection with an application for a binding letter of interpretation, the developer submitted an informational package to the State Department of Administration. In that package the developer stated the following regarding Big Blue:

> This 120-acre pristine forest containing some yet unnamed fern specimens, has been explored recently by a team of hardy souls who have ventured into this area to determine how best this untouched area can be preserved in its natural state.

> There have been claims of ferns 15 feet and higher as well as cypress trees reaching 85 to 100 feet in height flourishing in this wilderness area, along with abundant animal life. There is a definite contrast between the deafing [sic] quietness within the forest and the pure shrill sounds of literally dozens of species of birds.

> You can now walk into the Big Blue, very carefully, with proper guides; no vehicles will be allowed on the path. The Big Blue is a "must" evidencing an appreciation of the conservation, preservation and environmental attitude that is typical of the Wellington project.

In addition, the application by the Acme Improvement District for surface water management for the Wellington area noted that the environmental considerations upon most of the Wellington PUD property were not significant because it was abandoned agricultural land, except for Big Blue. In its application the District noted that Big Blue "will be preserved in its existing state . . . ."

In 1987 the surface water permit plan was modified with a particular emphasis on the Big Blue. This was done based upon application of the Landmark Land Company of Florida, Inc. The South Florida Water Management analysis refers to the proposed modification as completing the berm around Big Blue. The review stated, "The restoration of the Big Blue is dependent upon the perimeter berm being completed and constant inundation being maintained. . . . Constant inundation will kill most of the Brazillian Pepper [exotic vegetation present] and prevent further invasion."

The county adopted its Comprehensive Plan in 1988. The next year, the developer asked for another modification of the Wellington PUD. In the ordinance approving the modification, the county made it conditional upon the amending of the tabular data of the plan to reflect the "acreage of the OS-R natural reserve known as Big Blue reserve."

Landmark experienced financial difficulties and went into bankruptcy. In 1993, Palm Beach Polo's sister company purchased Landmark's interest in Wellington, including the Big Blue Reserve at a bankruptcy auction. Prior to the purchase, it received and reviewed a five volume Due Diligence Report regarding the entire property. Prepared by the bankruptcy trustee, the report conceded that it had not exhausted all information available about the property, but it included the Wellington Master Plan which designated the Big Blue Reserve as OS-R. The Surface Water Management Permits were also referenced in the report. However, no one on behalf of Polo contacted Palm Beach County Planning and Zoning Department or the county records to check the local land use regulations and other resolutions or permits. The sister company purchased the property essentially "as is." It then transferred the property to Polo in November 1993.

Prior to trial, Wellington and Polo submitted a joint pretrial stipulation, in which they stated:

> As of 1993, the zoning designation of the land in the Wellington PUD as a whole, which included Big Blue, was and is AR-SE (PUD), which stands for Agricultural/Residential subject to a Special Exception for a Planned Unit Development. The Wellington PUD Master Plan in 1993, and still today, designated Big Blue as "OS-R," which means Open Space-Recreation. Big Blue has remained undeveloped until today.

Wellington became incorporated after the purchase by Polo. In 1999, it adopted its own comprehensive plan which essentially followed the Palm Beach County Comprehensive Plan. The 1999 Wellington plan included a "conservation" designation for Big Blue. According to its officials, this was merely a restatement of the property's longstanding OS-R designation under the PUD. It imposed no duties that were not in existence prior to its designation as conservation.

Polo protested the conservation designation in the plan, making a claim under the Bert J. Harris Act, and Wellington responded with a letter reciting its position that no change would be made to the comprehensive plan designation for Big Blue. Polo then invited the council members to visit the site. At a subsequent meeting, the Polo president offered to give Wellington fifty acres of the site, but based on the council members' responses at the meeting, he believed that the proposed plan had no chance of approval.

Wellington then filed its own suit for declaratory judgment seeking to enforce the requirements of the 1972 PUD regarding Big Blue for flooding of the property and removal of exotic vegetation. Polo answered, contending that it had no legal obligation to preserve Big Blue. It asserted that the preservation boundaries were not legally described and that the restorative measures were too general in the original 1972 PUD to be enforced, nor were they properly implemented prior to Polo's acquisition in 1993. It counterclaimed for inverse condemnation, contending that the requirements for preserving Big Blue constituted an unlawful taking and a violation of the Bert J. Harris Act.

After a lengthy trial with voluminous exhibits, the court found in favor of Wellington. . . . As relief, the court required Polo to comply with the PUD Master Plan's restrictions by preserving Big Blue and protecting it from alteration and development activities, to enhance it by removing exotic vegetation, and to preserve and enhance it by increasing the property's water levels by one foot above existing levels. Polo appeals this judgment.

We dispose first of Polo's claim that it is entitled to compensation under the Bert J. Harris Act, section 70.001, Florida Statutes. That statute creates a cause of action where a law, regulation, or ordinance, as applied inordinately burdens, restricts, or limits use of property without amounting to a taking. Section 70.001(2) provides:

> When a specific action of a governmental entity has inordinately burdened an existing use of real property or a vested right to a specific use of real property, the property owner of that real property is entitled to relief, which may include compensation for the actual loss to the fair market value . . . .

Section 70.001(3)(e) provides, in part:

> The terms "inordinate burden" or "inordinately burdened" mean that an action of one or more governmental entities has directly restricted or limited the use of real property such that the property owner is permanently unable to attain the reasonable, invest-ment-backed expectation for the existing use of the real property or a vested right to a specific use of the real property with respect to the real property as a whole, or that the property owner is left with existing or vested uses that are unreasonable such that the property owner bears permanently a disproportionate share of a burden imposed for the good of the public, which in fairness should be borne by the public at large.

The statute defines "existing use" in section 70.001(3)(b) as follows:

> The term "existing use" means an actual, present use or activity on the real property, including periods of inactivity which are normally associated with, or are incidental to, the nature or type of use or activity or such reasonably foreseeable, nonspeculative land uses which are suitable for the subject real property and compatible with adjacent land uses and which have created an existing fair market value in the property greater than the fair market value of the actual, present use or activity on the real property.

We think it is fairly obvious from the abundant history of Big Blue that there was no "reasonable, investment-backed expectation" for an existing use of Big Blue at all. From 1972 forward it was designated as a natural reserve and extraordinary efforts were made to preserve this important pristine forest. As part of the PUD, any development density available to the acreage in Big Blue was transferred to other property in the Wellington PUD. At the time Polo purchased the Wellington property, Big Blue was designated as a nature reserve. Wellington's redesignation of it as a "conservation area" in its comprehensive plan changed nothing regarding the property. Polo failed to establish that at any time it was entitled to build on the property. In sum, Polo's claim that a violation of the Bert J. Harris Act occurred is frivolous. . . .

The trial court was correct in deferring to the agency's interpretation of its zoning code. The entire history of Big Blue and its regulation by the county and then the Village of Wellington shows that the meanings of the terms were well understood by all parties. Not only were they understood generally, but substantial evidence shows that specific requirements were also understood. The

South Florida Water Management District Surface Water Management Permits are quite specific in the berming of Big Blue to inundate the property and also to remove exotic vegetation. . . .

[I]n this case, the original developers of the PUD property, AlphaBeta, Inc. and Breakwater Housing Co., included in their 1972 PUD application the specific conditions regarding Big Blue that were ultimately adopted and incorporated into the 1972 PUD plan. Stribling testified that in working up the PUD application he had several meetings with the Palm Beach County Planning and Zoning Board in which there was an exchange of information and ideas. Breakwater's and AlphaBeta's intentions were to preserve Big Blue and restore it to its original state. In return, the county permitted them to have great flexibility in their development plans, and the trial court found that the owner received compensating development rights for the preservation of Big Blue. It would be contrary to the original agreements to allow Polo to now avoid the obligations that its predecessors in title consented to, and which it had actual knowledge of through the extensive history in the public documents regarding the Wellington PUD.

Finally, we need not spend further time or effort in analyzing a takings claim. Although the Big Blue property will be flooded and thus unusable for development, that is precisely the condition of the property that Polo's predecessors agreed to in exchange for developing other property with higher densities. In City of Riviera Beach v. Shillingburg, 659 So. 2d 1174 (Fla. 4th DCA 1995), a regulatory takings case, this court explained that the denial of use of some of a landowner's property does not itself constitute an unlawful taking, because the property must be considered in its entirety. In determining if a portion of the land should be considered as a whole or treated separately, the factors to be considered are whether the land is contiguous and whether there is unity of ownership. Whether there is a taking of Big Blue property requires a consideration of what occurred when the PUD was originally developed on the 7400 acres of Wellington in 1972. It was at that time that the owners bargained for development of vast sections at higher densities in return for preservation of Big Blue. This was an agreed restriction, compensated by the transfer of development rights to other property. No taking has occurred.

The trial court's judgment was thorough and correct. We affirm it in its entirety.

Notes

1. According to a vocal critic of the Bert Harris Act, Professor Roy Hunt, in *Property Rights and Wrongs: Historic Preservation and Florida's 1995 Private Property Rights Protection Act*, 48 Fla. L. Rev. 709, 715 (1996), the legislation was an ungainly creature of compromise:

On May 19, 1995 the Associated Press distributed a photograph of a smiling Governor [Lawton] Chiles, seated under a stand of live oaks in a sunny pasture near Lakeland, signing into law a measure passed unanimously by the House and with only one dissenting vote by the Senate. The measure he was signing is the Bert J. Harris, Jr., Private Property Rights Protection Act.

Why was our governor smiling? In his own words, he was smiling because "we can be proud of this legislation. . . . It safeguards our environmental and growth-management protections while also offering private property owners a means to seek compensation for devalued land." Other media characterizations were less charitable. The Miami Herald's Carl Hiaasen, for example, said the

"so-called 'property rights bill' passed by the Legislature is really the Land Speculator's Relief Act. . . . The law will make it harder for homeowners to shape and preserve their neighborhoods. . . . In truth, the new law wasn't written to prevent ordinary citizens from being screwed. It was written to intimidate government from doing its job." . . .

Why was our Governor smiling? He was smiling because politics is the art of compromise, and he deemed this bill the best compromise possible in view of the property rights steamroller that began rolling in Florida in 1993.

2. The Bert Harris Act has so far withstood state and federal constitutional challenges. In Brevard County v. Stack, 932 So. 2d 1258, 1261, 1262 (Fla. Ct. App. 2006), the appellate court denied the county's arguments that the act (1) "authorizes local governments to contract away their inherent sovereign police powers, and requires them to buy-back their ability to exercise those powers, both of which violate the due process clause; (2) "constitutes an illegal gift of public funds"; (3) "violates the separation of powers doctrine, and alters and enlarges the judiciary's interpretation of a taking under the Florida Constitution"; and (4) "delegates legislative power to the courts because the Act contains no standards, conditions or criteria to guide the judiciary in interpreting it." Another appellate court, in Royal World Metro., Inc. v. City of Miami Beach, 863 So. 2d 320, 321, 322 (Fla. Ct. App. 2003) rejected a more "creative" theory—that the landowner "could not maintain the action in light of Section 13 of the Act which provides: 'This section does not affect the sovereign immunity of government.'" The court concluded "that a fair reading of [the legislation] evinces a sufficiently clear legislative intent to waive sovereign immunity as to a private property owner whose property rights are inordinately burdened, restricted, or limited by government actions where the governmental regulation does not rise to the level of a taking under the Florida and United States Constitutions."

3. The drafters of the Bert Harris Act did more than just codify the notions of investment-backed expectations and unfair burdens found in *Penn Central* (see Chapter Five) and Armstrong v. United States, 364 U.S. 40 (1960). For example, the act, which targets inordinate burdens on a "vested right" and on an "existing use," includes within the definition of the latter term "such reasonably foreseeable, nonspeculative land uses which are suitable for the subject real property and compatible with adjacent land uses and which have created an existing fair market value in the property greater than the fair market value of the actual, present use or activity on the real property" (Fla. Stat. Ann. §70.001(3)(b)). On the one hand, this language seems to invite lawsuits by landowners whose neighbors have benefited from generous rezoning and variance decisions. On the other hand, the existence of this provision could have a chilling effect on spot zoning and other pro-development departures from the comprehensive plan.

4. Some state takings measures include a quantitative threshold. Texas lawmakers, for example, included a provision (Tex. Gov't Code §2007.002(5)(B) in the Private Real Property Rights Preservation Act (1995)) that defines a "taking" as a "governmental action" that either requires compensation under the Texas or United States Constitution or:

(i) affects an owner's private real property that is the subject of the governmental action, in whole or in part or temporarily or permanently, in a manner that restricts or limits the owner's right to the property that would otherwise exist in the absence of the governmental action; and

(ii) is the producing cause of a reduction of at least 25 percent in the market value of the affected private real property, determined by comparing the market value of the property as if the governmental action is not in effect and the market value of the property determined as if the governmental action is in effect.

John D. Echeverria & Thekla Hansen-Young, in The Track Record on Takings Legislation: Lessons From Democracy's Laboratories 22 (Georgetown Envtl. L. & Pol'y Inst. 2008), have observed that "[t]he legislation is both complex and relatively limited in scope, which probably explains why property owners have rarely invoked the Act and why legal claims based on the Act have seldom if ever succeeded."

COREY v. DEPARTMENT OF LAND CONSERVATION & DEVELOPMENT
344 Or. 457, 184 P.3d 1109 (2008)

GILLETTE , J.

This proceeding arises out of a land use case. In that case, the Department of Land Conservation and Development (DLCD) sought review of the Court of Appeals decision in Corey v. DLCD, 210 Ore. App. 542, 152 P.3d 933, *adh'd to*, 212 Ore. App. 536, 159 P.3d 327 (2007), a case decided under Ballot Measure 37 (2004) (Measure 37).[11] We allowed DLCD's petition for review.

---

11. Authors' note: Measure 37 read, in pertinent part:

The following provisions are added to and made a part of ORS chapter 197:

(1) If a public entity enacts or enforces a new land use regulation or enforces a land use regulation enacted prior to the effective date of this amendment that restricts the use of private real property or any interest therein and has the effect of reducing the fair market value of the property, or any interest therein, then the owner of the property shall be paid just compensation.

(2) Just compensation shall be equal to the reduction in the fair market value of the affected property interest resulting from enactment or enforcement of the land use regulation as of the date the owner makes written demand for compensation under this act.

(3) Subsection (1) of this act shall not apply to land use regulations:

(A) Restricting or prohibiting activities commonly and historically recognized as public nuisances under common law. This subsection shall be construed narrowly in favor of a finding of compensation under this act;

(B) Restricting or prohibiting activities for the protection of public health and safety, such as fire and building codes, health and sanitation regulations, solid or hazardous waste regulations, and pollution control regulations;

(C) To the extent the land use regulation is required to comply with federal law;

(D) Restricting or prohibiting the use of a property for the purpose of selling pornography or performing nude dancing. Nothing in this subsection, however, is intended to affect or alter rights provided by the Oregon or United States Constitutions; or

(E) Enacted prior to the date of acquisition of the property by the owner or a family member of the owner who owned the subject property prior to acquisition or inheritance by the owner, whichever occurred first. . . .

(8) [I]n lieu of payment of just compensation under this act, the governing body responsible for enacting the land use regulation may modify, remove, or not to apply the land use regulation or land use regulations to allow the owner to use the property for a use permitted at the time the owner acquired the property. . . .

However, DLCD now believes that the recent passage of Ballot Measure 49 (2007)[12] rendered Corey moot. It therefore asks this court to dismiss its petition and to vacate the decision of the Court of Appeals. Plaintiffs, who are landowner parties in Corey, deny that that decision is moot. As we discuss below, we agree with DLCD that Corey is moot, and we dismiss DLCD's petition for review on that ground. However, we deny DLCD's request that we vacate the decision of the Court of Appeals.

Measure 37 was adopted through the initiative process in the 2004 general election and was codified at ORS 197.352 (2005), amended by Ballot Measure 49, Oregon Laws 2007, chapter 424, section 4, and renumbered as ORS 195.305. It requires public entities that enact and enforce land use regulations to pay a landowner whose property is affected by any such regulations "just compensation," which the statute generally defines as an amount equal to the "reduction in the fair market value of the affected property interest" resulting from enforcement of any land use regulation enacted after the date of acquisition of the property by the landowner or a family member of the landowner. ORS 197.352(1) - (3) (2005). The provision authorizes affected landowners to make a "written demand for compensation" to the regulating entity, ORS 197.352(5), and states that the compensation "shall be due" when and if the land use regulations at issue continue to be enforced 180 days after the landowner makes his or her written demand, ORS 197.352(4) (2005).

Plaintiffs in this case are Virginia Corey and Bergis Road, LLC, a limited liability corporation that is wholly owned and controlled by Corey's sister, Bernita Johnston. Plaintiffs own interests in a 23-acre parcel of land in rural Clackamas County. Early in 2005, they filed a written demand under Ballot Measure 37, seeking compensation from DLCD for reduction in the fair market value of that land caused by application of, among other things, Statewide Planning Goals 3 (Agricultural Lands) and 14 (Urbanization). In the demand, plaintiffs asserted that Corey and Johnston had inherited their interests in the land from their mother in 1978. They further asserted that their demand for compensation properly extended to all regulations enacted after 1973—the year that Corey's and Johnston's mother first acquired the property.[1]

DLCD issued a final order resolving plaintiffs' demand in July 2005. In the order, DLCD chose to waive enforcement of certain of the land use regulations to which plaintiffs objected,

---

12. Authors' note: The Explanatory Statement that the state legislature drafted for inclusion with Measure 49 read in pertinent part:

> Ballot measure 37 (2004) requires governments to pay landowners or forgo enforcement when certain land use regulations reduce their property values. This measure modifies Measure 37 to give landowners who have filed Measure 37 claims the right to build homes as compensation for land use regulations imposed after they acquired their properties.
>
> Claimants may build up to three homes if allowed when they acquired their properties
>
> Claimants may build up to 10 homes if allowed when they acquired their properties and they have suffered reductions in property values that justify the additional home sites.
>
> This measure protects farmlands, forestlands and lands with groundwater shortages in two ways.
>
> First, subdivisions are not allowed on high-value farmlands, forestlands and groundwater-restricted lands. Claimants may not build more than three homes on such lands.
>
> Second, claimants may not use this measure to override current zoning laws that prohibit commercial and industrial developments, such as strip malls and mines, on land reserved for homes, farms, forests and other uses.
>
> . . .
>
> This measure modifies Measure 37 for compensation claims that arise from land use regulations in the future. It authorizes such claims based on regulations that limit residential uses of property or farm and forest practices, requires documentation of reduced values and provides for proportionate compensation when such reductions in value occur. Property owners will have five years to file claims over regulations enacted after January 1, 2007. . . .

1.   Under ORS 197.352(3)(E) (2005), compensation is not due for any diminution in the value of the property resulting from a land use regulation "[e]nacted prior to the date of acquisition of the property *by the owner or a family member of the owner who owned the subject property prior to acquisition or inheritance by the owner, whichever occurred first.*" (Emphasis added.)

rather than to compensate plaintiffs for the effects of those regulations on the value of their property.[2] However, the waiver that DLCD granted did not extend to all of the regulations that plaintiffs had targeted in their claim: For plaintiff Corey, DLCD waived land use regulations and statutes enacted after December 11, 1978, which it found to be the date when Corey inherited her interest in the property from her mother; and for plaintiff Bergis Road LLC, DLCD waived regulations and statutes enacted after August 12, 2004, when that entity acquired its interest in the property from Virginia Johnston. In announcing those waiver dates, DLCD implicitly rejected plaintiffs' contention that, because Bernita Johnston is the sole creator, member, and manager of Bergis Road LLC, her transfer of her interest in the property to that entity should be ignored for purposes of Measure 37.

Plaintiffs sought judicial review of DLCD's final order in the Court of Appeals. . . . [I]n the November 2007 general election, the voters adopted Ballot Measure 49 (2007) (Measure 49), which amended Measure 37 and added provisions that altered the claims and remedies available to landowners whose property values are adversely affected by land use regulations. Of particular relevance here, Measure 49 directly addresses Measure 37 claims filed before the end of the 2007 legislative session. Section 5 of Measure 49 provides:

> "A claimant that filed a claim under ORS 197.352[, *i.e.*, Measure 37,] on or before the date of adjournment sine die of the 2007 regular session of the Seventy-fourth Legislative Assembly is entitled to just compensation as provided in:
>
>> "(1) Sections 6 or 7 of this 2007 Act, at the claimant's election, if the property described in the claim is located entirely outside any urban growth boundary and entirely outside the boundaries of any city;
>>
>> "(2) Section 9 of this 2007 Act if the property described in the claim is located, in whole or in part, within an urban growth boundary; or
>>
>> "(3) A waiver issued before the effective date of this 2007 Act to the extent that the claimant's use of the property complies with the waiver and the claimant has a common law vested right on the effective date of this 2007 Act to complete and continue the use described in the waiver."

Sections 6 and 7, referenced in subsection 5(1), generally provide that claimants whose claims relate to land outside any urban growth boundary are limited to three home site approvals, unless their land is not high value farm or forest land, in which case they may be eligible for up to ten home site approvals, if certain requirements are met. Section 9, referenced in subsection 5(2), sets out a different remedy for claims relating to land within an urban growth boundary.

Soon after Measure 49 was adopted, DLCD filed a "Notice of Potential Mootness" in this court respecting the impending review of *Corey*. Later, DLCD filed the present motion to "vacate and remand," arguing that Measure 49 has rendered the controversy in *Corey* moot. In the motion, DLCD relies on the provisions quoted and summarized above and on section 8 of Measure 49, which provides procedures and deadlines for refiling Measure 37 claims under Measure 49. In essence, DLCD argues that Measure 49 extinguishes all claims and orders under Measure 37 and directs Measure 37 claimants—successful or not—to proceed instead under section 6 or 7 of Measure 49, if their property lies outside an urban growth boundary, and under section 9, if their property lies inside an urban growth boundary. Consequently (in DLCD's view), any controversy

---

2. Under ORS 197.352(8) (2005), public entities may choose to waive (i.e. "modify, remove, or not [] apply") a land use regulation "in lieu of payment of just compensation."

regarding the correctness of an order issued under Measure 37—including the proper forum for reviewing the order—is moot.

If it becomes clear in the course of a judicial proceeding that resolving the merits of a claim will have no practical effect on the rights of the parties, this court will dismiss the claim as moot. Our task, then, is to determine whether resolution of the jurisdictional question that DLCD brought to us can have any practical effect on the rights of the parties.

We already have summarized DLCD's position—that Measure 49 has rendered the waiver order at the center of the jurisdictional dispute wholly ineffective and, thus, any further judicial consideration of the order, including the question of the proper forum for review, is inherently meaningless. As we shall explain, we generally agree with DLCD's analysis.

An examination of the text and context of Measure 49 conveys a clear intent to extinguish an replace the benefits and procedures that Measure 37 granted to landowners. As noted, section 5 of Measure 49, set out above, provides that claimants who filed "claim[s]" under ORS 197.352 before Measure 49 became effective (*i.e.*, Measure 37 claimants), are entitled to "just compensation" as provided in designated provisions of Measure 49. Subsection 2(2) of Measure 49 defines "claim" to include any "written demand for compensation filed under * * * ORS 197.352," including those filed under the version of the statute that was "in effect immediately before the effective date of [Measure 49]." That definition establishes that Measure 49 pertains to all Measure 37 claims, successful or not, and regardless of where they are in the Measure 37 process. Subsection 2(13) then defines "just compensation" purely in terms of Measure 49 remedies, *i.e.*, "[r]elief under sections 5 to 11 of this 2007 Act for land use regulations enacted on or before January 1, 2007," and "[r]elief under sections 12 to 14 of this 2007 Act for land use regulations enacted after January 1, 2007." At the same time, section 4 of Measure 49 extensively amends ORS 197.352 (2005) (Measure 37) in a way that wholly supercedes [*sic*] the provisions of Measure 37 pertaining to monetary compensation for and waivers from the burdens of certain land use regulations under that earlier measure.

A statement of legislative policy at section 3 of Measure 49 confirms that the legislature intended to create new forms of relief in place of the ones available under Measure 37: "The purpose of sections 4 to 22 of this 2007 Act and the amendments to Ballot Measure 37 (2004) *is to modify Ballot Measure 37 (2004)* to ensure that Oregon law provides *just compensation for unfair burdens while retaining Oregon's protections for farm and forest uses and the state's water resources.*" (Emphases added.)

Plaintiffs argue that, whatever the theoretical merits of DLCD's arguments, subsection 5(3) of Measure 49 applies to their claim (subsection 5(3) provides that Measure 37 claimants are entitled to "just compensation" *as provided in a waiver issued before Measure 49 became effective*). Plaintiffs acknowledge that subsection 5(3) of Measure 49 speaks of a "common law vested right" in the waiver. But that is no obstacle, in their view, because, once DLCD concluded that post-acquisition land use regulations had reduced the fair market value of their property and granted relief in the form of a waiver, they had a constitutionally protected "property right" in that waiver that cannot be taken away without just compensation—*i.e.*, a vested right. In a related vein, plaintiffs argue that the waiver that DLCD granted under Measure 37 is the equivalent of rights obtained under a judgment granting a monetary award, and is vested in the sense that it cannot be diminished by legislative action.

However, in so arguing, plaintiffs fail to confront the entire wording of subsection 5(3). The "vested right" that that subsection requires is a "common law vested right * * * to complete and continue the use described in the waiver." It is clear from text and context alone that that phrase is referring to broadly applicable legal precedents describing a property owner's rights when land use laws are enacted that make a partially finished project unlawful. See, e.g., Clackamas Co. v.

Holmes, 265 Ore. 193, 197, 508 P.2d 190 (1973) (describing "vested rights" in those terms). But plaintiffs have made no claims that they have partially completed any "use described in the waiver" that they received.

To the extent that plaintiffs wish to assert that the scope of subsection 5(3) is any broader, then Measure 49 provides plaintiffs with an opportunity to assert that claim, and a forum in which they may assert it. The same is true of any other objections that plaintiffs have to the effects of Measure 49. In short, this is a Measure 37 case, and we confine our substantive discussion to that legislation.

In the end, we hold only that plaintiffs' contention that Measure 49 does not affect the rights of persons who already have obtained Measure 37 waivers is incorrect. In fact, Measure 49 by its terms deprives Measure 37 waivers—and all orders disposing of Measure 37 claims—of any continuing viability, with a single exception that does not apply to plaintiffs' claim. Thus, after December 6, 2007 (the effective date of Measure 49), the final order at issue in the present case had no legal effect. It follows that resolution of the issue that the Court of Appeals decided in *Corey* and as to which we allowed review—whether the Court of Appeals or the circuit court has jurisdiction to review DLCD's final order respecting plaintiffs' Measure 37 claim—can have no practical effect upon the parties: If the order at issue has no continuing legal effect, then neither party can gain anything from review in either forum. The case is moot.

Plaintiffs suggest that, in any event, the case is justiciable under ORS 14.175, which provides:

> "In any action in which a party alleges that an act, policy or practice of a public body, as defined in ORS 174.109, or of any officer, employee or agent of a public body, as defined in ORS 174.109, is unconstitutional or is otherwise contrary to law, the party may continue to prosecute the action and the court may issue a judgment on the validity of the challenged act, policy or practice *even though the specific act, policy or practice giving rise to the action no longer has a practical effect on the party*, if the court determines that:

> "(1) The party had standing to commence the action;

> "(2) The act challenged by the party is capable of repetition, or the policy or practice challenged by the party continues in effect; and

> "(3) The challenged policy or practice, or similar acts, are likely to evade judicial review in the future."

(Emphasis added.) Plaintiffs suggest that that provision applies because the "Legislative Assembly's practice of changing constitutionally protected rights will necessarily evade review if a claimant * * * cannot try to protect those rights." However, ORS 14.175 does not present a basis for review in this case, because, as we already have observed, plaintiffs can pursue their claim pursuant to the procedure set out in Measure 49, including any assertion that Measure 49 acts on them in an unconstitutional way. . . .

The decision of the Court of Appeals in *Corey* was a decision under Measure 37. The fact that such a decision remains on the books does not require DLCD to treat it as binding precedent in future proceedings, because any such future proceedings will be under Measure 49. Therefore, no inequity will result from denying DLCD's request for vacatur.

The petition for review is dismissed as moot. The motion to vacate and remand is denied.

Notes

1. The ballot measure has been a favorite tactic of private property rights advocates, although, as *Corey* demonstrates, what the people give they can take away just as easily. Proponents of initiatives designed to implement legislative or constitutional changes face two significant hurdles—securing enough signatures to get the proposed change on the ballot and ensuring that the title, language, description, and subject matter of the initiative pass judicial muster. In League of Oregon Cities v. State, 334 Or. 645, 649, 654, 56 P.3d 892, 896, 899, (2002), the Supreme Court of Oregon affirmed the trial court's determination that Measure 7 (an earlier incarnation of Measure 37) "was adopted in violation of the 'separate-vote' requirement of Article XVII, section 1, of the Oregon Constitution," which reads, in pertinent part: "When two or more amendments shall be submitted in the manner aforesaid to the voters of this state at the same election, they shall be so submitted that each amendment shall be voted on separately."

One major difference between Measure 7 and Measure 37 was that the former included the following provision: "Nothing in this 2000 Amendment shall require compensation due to a government regulation prohibiting the use of a property for the purpose of selling pornography, performing nude dancing, selling alcoholic beverages or other controlled substances, or operating a casino or gaming parlor." The supreme court provided the following chronology, illustrating the complicated path from petition to ballot:

> (1) Measure 7 began as Initiative Petition 46 (2000); (2) the petition originally was filed with the Secretary of State on March 10, 1999; (3) the Attorney General certified the ballot title on April 9, 1999; (4) the Secretary of State approved the proposed initiative for circulation on May 28, 1999; and (5) the Secretary of State certified the ballot measure (as Measure 7) on July 26, 2000.

Unfortunately for the ballot measure's sponsors, the state high court would

> conclude that the change that Measure 7 makes to Article I, section 18 [of the Oregon Constitution], that is, an expanded just-compensation requirement for restrictive regulations that reduce the value of private real property, is not closely related to the change that it makes to Article I, section 8, that is, creating an exception to the historical requirement that laws cannot [ ] treat those engaged in expressive activity 'more restrictively' than others not engaged in expressive activity.

After proponents of regulatory takings changes went back to the drawing board and submitted Measure 37, they were much more successful in defending their revised work product. In Macpherson v. Department of Admin. Servs., 340 Or. 117, 122, 141, 130 P.3d 308, 311-12, 322 (2006), the state supreme court disagreed with the trial court, which had found the ballot measure invalid on the grounds that it

> (1) impermissibly intruded on the legislature's plenary power; (2) violated the equal privileges and immunities guarantee of the Oregon Constitution; (3) impermissibly suspended the laws in violation of the Oregon Constitution; (4) violated the separation of powers principles of the Oregon Constitution; and (5) violated the Due Process Clause of the Fourteenth Amendment to the United States Constitution.

The justices took efforts to point out that theirs was not necessarily a judgment concerning the wisdom of the constitutional change: "Whether Measure 37 as a policy choice is wise or foolish, farsighted or blind, is beyond this court's purview."

2. The widespread uproar after *Kelo* (discussed in Chapter Three) provided an unprecedented opportunity for proponents of takings law changes to take their case to the people. In the elections held in November 2006, voters in Arizona, California, Idaho, North Dakota, Oregon, Nevada, and Washington considered eminent domain reform ballot measures originating in citizen petitions. These initiatives were successful in Arizona (statutory change), North Dakota (constitutional change), Oregon (statutory change), and Nevada (constitutional change). However, Nevada law required a second positive statewide vote before the new constitutional language went into effect, and the voters provided that positive vote in November 2008.

The Arizona measure not only narrowed the definition of "public use," but it also included a regulatory takings provision that puts at risk land use regulations that reduce property values. Ariz. Rev. Stat. §12-1134(A) provides that subject to certain exceptions,

> [i]f the existing rights to use, divide, sell or possess private real property are reduced by the enactment or applicability of any land use law enacted after the date the property is transferred to the owner and such action reduces the fair market value of the property the owner is entitled to just compensation from this state or the political subdivision of the state that enacted the land use law.

Voters in California, Idaho, and Washington struck down ballot measures that would have enacted this same one-two takings punch. The successful initiatives in North Dakota and Oregon, which narrowed the definition of "public use," did not include the regulatory takings language. In Nevadans for the Protection of Property Rights, Inc. v. Heller, 141 P.3d 1235, 1238 (Nev. 2006), the court removed the following language from the ballot measure called the Nevada Property Owners' Bill of Rights:

> Government actions which result in substantial economic loss to private property shall require the payment of just compensation. Examples of such substantial economic loss include, but are not limited to, the down zoning of private property, the elimination of any access to private property, and limiting the use of private air space.

The court ruled that this provision did not "pertain to eminent domain," which was the "primary subject" of the ballot measure.

And so, a century after officials and experts in New York began the extensive study process that led to the adoption of the nation's first "real" zoning ordinance, courts, legislators (federal, state, and local), and the American people continue to wrestle with what was and remains the essential question posed by the regulation of land—historically, financially, physically, psychologically, and ecologically our most important form of property: When should the private right yield to the public good?

Index